Dear Reader

D1943146

With the aim of giving a maximum amount of information in a limited number of pages Michelin has adopted a system of symbols which is today known the world over.

Failing this system the present publication would run to six volumes.

Judge for yourselves by comparing the descriptive text below with the equivalent extract from the Guide in symbol form.

Cheval Blanc (Durand) M, 28 31 42, lake, « garden » – wc. AE
closed December and Wednesday – **M** 80/145 **st** – 22 – **32 rm** 145/210
Spec. Ris de veau à la crème, Poularde bressanne, tarte flambée. **Wines.** Viré, Morgon.

A comfortable hotel where you will enjoy a pleasant stay and be tempted to prolong your visit.
The excellence of the cuisine, which is personally supervised by the proprietor Mr Durand, is worth a detour.
The hotel in its quiet secluded setting away from the built-up-area offers every modern amenity.
To reserve phone 28 31 42.

The hotel affords a fine view of the lake ; in good weather it is possible to eat out of doors. The hotel is enhanced by an attractive garden.

Bedrooms with private bathroom with toilet or private shower without toilet. Telephone in room.

Parking facilities, under cover, are available to all guests with this Guide.

The hotel accepts payment by American Express credit cards.

The establishment is closed throughout December and every Wednesday.

Prices : st = service is included in all prices. There should be no supplementary charge for service, taxes or VAT on your bill.

The set meal prices range from 80 F for the lowest to 145 F for the highest.

The cost of continental breakfast served in the bedroom is 22 F.

32 bedroomed hotel. The charges vary from 145 F for a single to 210 F for the best twin bedded room.

Included for the gourmet are some culinary specialities, recommended by the hotelier : Ris de veau à la crème, Poularde bressanne, tarte flambée. In addition to the best quality wines you will find many of the local wines worth sampling : Viré, Morgon.

This demonstration clearly shows that each entry contains a great deal of information. The symbols are easily learnt and to know them will enable you to understand the Guide and to choose those establishments that you require.

CONTENTS

In addition to those situated in the main cities, restaurants renowned for their exceptional cuisine will be found in the towns printed in italics.

NEW YORK

GMT – 5

DIRECT DAILY FLIGHTS
Total time of journey
(in hours)

Amsterdam	9 1/4
Barcelona	9 1/4
Berlin	12 3/4
Bruxelles	10 3/4
Dublin	10
Düsseldorf	9 1/4
Frankfurt	9 3/4
Genève	9 1/2
Glasgow	10
Hamburg	11
København	9 3/4
Lisboa	8 3/4
London	9 1/2
Luxembourg	11 1/2
Madrid	9 1/4
Milano	9 3/4
München	11 3/4
Oslo	9 1/2
Paris	9 3/4
Roma	10 1/2
Stockholm	11 1/2
Zürich	9 3/4

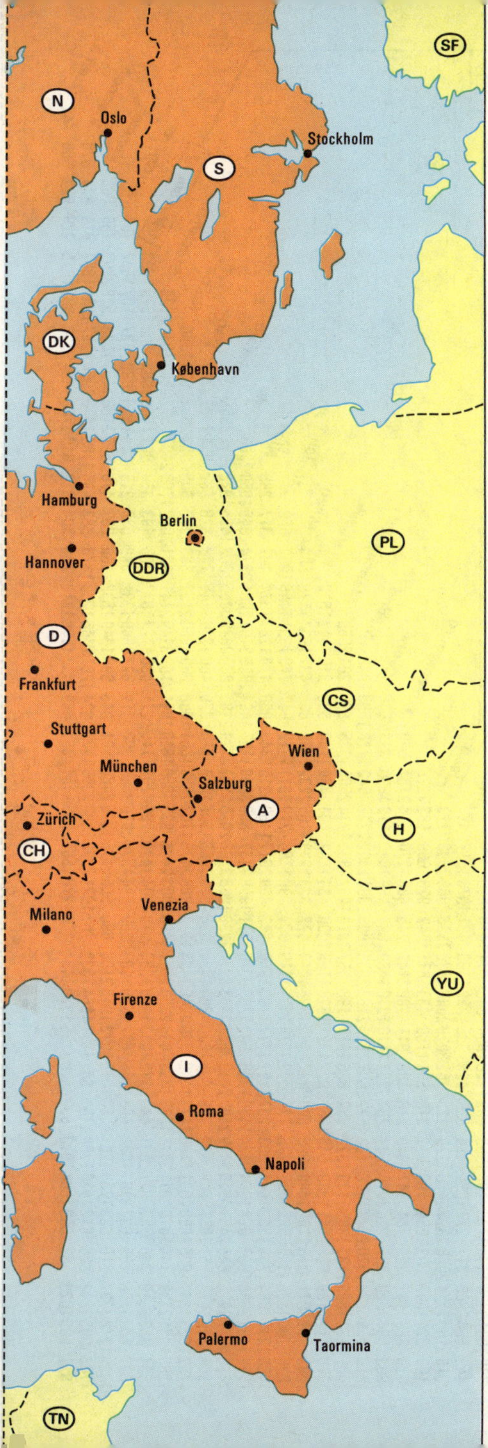

AIRPORTS

Amsterdam *Schiphol*
Antwerpen *Deurne*
Barcelona
Basel *Bâle/Mulhouse*
Berlin *Tegel*
Birmingham *International*
Bordeaux *Mérignac*
Bruxelles-Brussel *National*
Dublin
Düsseldorf *Lohausen*
Edinburgh *Turnhouse*
Firenze
Frankfurt *Rhein-Main*
Genève *Cointrin*
Glasgow
Hamburg *Fuhlsbüttel*
Hannover *Langenhagen*
København *Kastrup*
Köln *Köln/Bonn*
Leeds *Leeds/Bradford*
Lisboa
Liverpool
London *Heathrow, Gatwick*
Luxembourg *Findel*
Lyon *Satolas*
Madrid *Barajas*
Málaga
Manchester
Marseille *Marignane*
Milano *Forlanini di Linate*
München *Riem*
Napoli *Capodichino*
Nice *Nice Côte-d'Azur*
Oslo *Fornebu*
Palermo *Punta-Raisi*
Paris *Charles-de-Gaulle, Orly*
Roma *Leonardo da Vinci*
Rotterdam *Zestienhoven*
Salzburg
Sevilla *San Pablo*
Stockholm *Arlanda*
Strasbourg *Entzheim*
Stuttgart *Echterdingen*
Torino *Citta di Torino*
Valencia *Manises*
Venezia *Marco Polo*
Wien *Schwechat*
Zürich *Kloten*

DISTANCES BY ROAD

(in kilometres)

	Amsterdam	Antwerp	Barcelona	Basle	Berlin	Birmingham	Bordeaux	Brussels	Cologne	Copenhagen	Dublin	Edinburg	Frankfort	Geneva	Glasgow	Hamburg	Lisbon	London	Luxembourg	Lyons	Madrid	Manchester	Marseilles	Milan	Münich	Nice	Oslo	Palermo	Paris	Rome	Stockholm	Strasbourg	Stuttgart	Venice	Vienna
Antwerp	158																																		
Barcelona	1592	1433																																	
Basle	745	599	1007																																
Berlin	671	725	1855	864																															
Birmingham	374	531	1703	1003	1255																														
Bordeaux	1081	922	631	828	1634	1192																													
Brussels	204	48	1396	552	783	522	885																												
Cologne	263	206	1336	489	576	755	1063	212																											
Copenhagen	739	851	2105	1114	385	1381	1781	897	723																										
Dublin	608	769	1941	1241	1493	246	1432	760	993	1620																									
Edinburg	743	936	2109	1409	1661	484	1598	928	1161	1787	416																								
Frankfort	443	395	1320	329	553	943	1158	401	187	788	1164	1349																							
Geneva	904	752	748	259	1123	1127	695	705	748	1373	1365	1533	588																						
Glasgow	779	1004	2176	1476	1728	483	1665	995	1228	1854	343	74	1416	1600																					
Hamburg	442	554	1808	817	297	1084	1484	600	426	305	1323	1490	491	1076	1557																				
Lisbon	2319	2160	1274	2066	2873	2430	1229	2123	2302	3020	2668	2836	2396	2009	2903	2723																			
London	196	324	1502	802	1054	196	992	315	554	1180	433	671	742	926	669	883	2229																		
Luxembourg	419	266	1147	333	764	747	946	219	189	911	980	1147	245	486	1220	614	2184	540																	
Lyons	963	804	629	387	1226	1074	547	767	707	1476	1313	1480	691	159	1547	1179	1890	873	518																
Madrid	1818	1659	626	1620	2372	1929	728	1622	1801	2519	2167	2335	1895	1361	2402	2222	648	1728	1683	1242															
Manchester	501	660	1833	1133	1385	138	1322	652	885	1511	196	357	1073	1257	355	1214	2560	325	871	1204	2059														
Marseilles	1278	1119	499	693	1541	1389	648	1082	1022	1791	1628	1795	1006	434	1862	1494	1760	1188	833	315	1112	1519													
Milan	1093	947	971	348	1162	1440	995	900	837	1462	1678	1846	677	323	1913	1165	2232	1239	681	437	1584	1570	504												
Münich	829	765	1338	396	585	1313	1273	771	573	1076	1551	1719	393	590	1786	779	2511	1112	517	749	1951	1443	1052	559											
Nice	1408	1274	654	736	1339	1544	803	1237	1152	1777	1783	1950	992	489	2017	1480	1915	1343	988	470	1267	1674	187	317	865										
Oslo	1322	1434	2688	1697	968	1964	2364	1480	1306	583	2203	2370	1371	1956	2437	888	3603	1763	1494	2059	3102	2094	2374	2045	1659	2360									
Palermo	2675	2447	2270	1848	2431	2925	2419	2400	2419	2922	3163	3331	2239	1808	3398	2625	3531	2724	2181	1888	2883	3055	1803	1495	1828	1616	3505								
Paris	504	345	1090	551	1057	615	579	308	486	1204	854	1021	586	513	1088	907	1817	414	375	460	1316	745	776	826	832	931	1787	2311							
Rome	1752	1524	1347	925	1508	2002	1496	1477	1496	1999	2240	2408	1316	885	2475	1702	2608	1801	1258	965	1960	2132	880	572	905	693	2582	929	1388						
Stockholm	1369	1481	2735	1744	1015	2011	2411	1527	1353	630	2250	2417	1418	2003	2484	935	3650	1810	1541	2106	3149	2141	2421	2092	1706	2407	522	3552	1834	2629					
Strasbourg	634	487	1110	145	753	947	921	440	378	1003	1186	1353	218	404	1420	706	2298	746	221	480	1723	1077	796	493	359	951	1586	1993	488	1070	1633				
Stuttgart	621	553	1256	265	632	1101	1068	559	365	967	1339	1507	205	524	1574	670	2306	900	312	627	1869	1231	942	530	219	845	1550	2030	627	1107	1597	154			
Venice	1326	1213	1227	610	1082	1702	1257	1162	1070	1573	1940	2108	890	585	2175	1276	2488	1501	943	699	1840	1832	760	267	479	573	2156	1451	1088	528	2203	755	668		
Vienna	1143	1095	1843	826	642	1626	1799	1101	887	1257	1864	2032	707	1021	2099	960	2966	1425	924	1287	2456	1756	1376	883	435	1189	1840	2054	1227	1131	1887	814	674	620	
Zurich	827	683	1026	85	850	1088	913	636	570	1185	1326	1494	410	278	1561	888	2151	887	449	437	1639	1218	713	304	312	619	1768	1804	636	881	1815	229	222	566	742

Lisbon – Strasbourg: 2298

AIR LINKS (in hours)

3 1/2 not daily

	Amsterdam	Antwerp	Barcelona	Basle	Berlin	Birmingham	Bordeaux	Brussels	Cologne	Copenhagen	Dublin	Edinburgh	Frankfort	Geneva	Glasgow	Hamburg	Lisbon	London	Luxembourg	Lyons	Madrid	Manchester	Marseilles	Milan	Munich	Nice	Oslo	Palermo	Paris	Rome	Stockholm	Strasbourg	Stuttgart	Venice	Vienna
Antwerp	2 1/4																																		
Barcelona	3 3/4	6																																	
Basle	3 1/4	4 3/4	4 1/2																																
Berlin	3	6	5 3/4	4 1/2																															
Birmingham	2 3/4	5 1/4	8	5 1/4	5 1/4																														
Bordeaux	2 3/4			4 1/4	8 1/2	5 3/4																													
Brussels	2 1/2		3 3/4	3	4 1/4	3 1/4	5 1/2																												
Cologne			5 1/4	4	2 3/4	4 1/4	7 1/4																												
Copenhagen	3	4 3/4	4 1/2	4 3/4	4	4 1/2	6	3 1/4	4 1/4																										
Dublin	3 1/4	4 3/4	6 1/2	5	5 1/2	2 1/2	5 3/4	3 1/4	5 1/2	4																									
Edinburgh	3 3/4	5 1/2	6 1/4	4 1/4	6	2 3/4	5 1/2	4 3/4	5 1/4	5 1/2	2 3/4																								
Frankfort	2 3/4	4 1/4	3 3/4	2 3/4	2 3/4	3 1/4	6 1/4	2 3/4	2 1/2	3 1/4	3 3/4	5 3/4																							
Geneva	3	4 1/2	3	2 1/4	4 1/2	5	3	3	4 1/2	3 3/4	4	5 1/2	3																						
Glasgow	3 1/4	5 1/4	6 3/4	5 1/2	6 3/4	2 3/4	6	4 3/4	5 1/2	3 1/2	2 1/2	2 1/4	5 1/2	5 1/2																					
Hamburg	2 3/4	4 1/2	5 1/2	4 1/2	2 1/2	5	5 3/4	3	2 3/4	2 1/2	5 1/2	6 1/4	2 3/4	4 3/4	6																				
Lisbon	4 1/2	6 1/4	3 1/4	5 1/2	7 1/2	7		4 1/2	7 1/2	5 1/2	6 3/4	7 1/4	4 3/4	3 1/4	7	6 1/4																			
London	2 3/4	3 1/4	4 1/4	3 1/2	7	3	3 3/4	3 1/4	3 1/2	4	3 1/4	3 1/2	3 1/2	3 1/2	3 1/2	3 3/4	4 3/4																		
Luxembourg	2 1/2		6 3/4	3 3/4	4 3/4	6	6 1/4	2 1/4	4 1/2	4 3/4	5 1/2		2 1/2	4	5 1/2	4 3/4	6 3/4	3 1/4																	
Lyons	3 1/2	5 1/2	3	3	4	4 3/4	3	3 1/4	5	4	6	6	3 1/4		6	5 1/2	4 1/4	4																	
Madrid	3	5 3/4	2 3/4	6	6 1/4	6 1/4	3	4	5 1/2	4 3/4	4	6	4 1/4	3 1/2	6 1/4	6	2 3/4	4 1/4	6	4 3/4															
Manchester	3	4 1/2	6	5 1/2	5 1/2	2 1/2	5 3/4	3	5 1/2	3 3/4	2 3/4	3	3 3/4	4	2	5	4 3/4	3 1/4	5 3/4	6	4 1/4														
Marseilles	4 1/2		2 3/4	4 1/4	7 1/4	4 3/4	2 3/4	3 1/2	6 1/2	5 1/4	6 1/4	6 1/4	4 1/2	2 1/2	6 1/2	6 1/2	4	4	6	2 3/4	3 1/4	5 3/4													
Milan	3	5 1/4	3 1/4	3 1/2	5	4 3/4	5 1/4	3 1/4	4 1/4	3 3/4	5 1/4	6 1/4	3	2 1/2	5 1/2	4 3/4	5 1/4	4	4 3/4	3	3 3/4	4	3												
Munich	3 1/4	5	3 3/4	2 3/4	3	5	6	3	2 3/4	3 1/4	4 1/4	6 1/4	2 3/4	3 1/2	6	3	6 1/2	4	4 1/4	5 1/4	5 1/2	5 1/2	8	2 3/4											
Nice	3 1/4	4 3/4	2 3/4	4 1/4	6 1/4	5 3/4	3	3	5 1/4	4	5 1/2	6 1/2	3 1/4	2 1/2	6	5 1/2	4	4	4	2 3/4	3 1/4	4	2 1/4	2 3/4	3										
Oslo	3	6	6 1/4	6 1/4	4 1/2	4 3/4	7 1/4	4 3/4	6 3/4	3 1/2	6	7 1/2	3 1/2	5 1/4	4 1/4	2 3/4	7 1/4	3	6	5 3/4	6 1/2	5 1/4	7	5 1/4	5	5 3/4									
Palermo	3		7			8 1/2		6 1/2	9 3/4	9 1/2	10		5 1/4	6 3/4	10 3/4			7	6	7 3/4	7 1/2	9 3/4	8	3 1/2	6 1/2	5 1/2	11								
Paris	2	4 1/2	3 1/2	2 3/4	4 3/4	3	3	2 3/4	3	3 3/4	3 3/4	5	3 1/4	3	3 3/4	3 1/2	4 1/2	3 1/2	2 3/4	3	3 3/4	3 1/4	3	3 1/4	3 1/2	3 1/4	4	6 3/4							
Rome	3	6	3 1/2	4 3/4	5 1/4	6 1/4	8 1/4	4	5 3/4	4 1/2	4 1/4	6 3/4	3 3/4	3 1/2	7 1/4	5 3/4	4 3/4	4 3/4	3 3/4	5	4 1/4	5	3 1/2	3	3 1/2	2 3/4	6 1/2	3 1/4	4 1/4						
Stockholm	4	5 3/4	7 3/4	6 1/4	5	5 1/4	6 3/4	5 1/4	6 1/2	3 1/4	7	7 1/4	4	6	7	3 1/2	9 1/4	5	6 3/4	6 1/2	7	6	7 3/4	6	5 3/4	6	2 3/4		4 3/4	7					
Strasbourg	2 1/2		6 3/4	4 1/2		5 1/2	4 1/2	2 1/2		5 3/4	6 1/2	5 3/4		2 3/4	6 1/2		6 1/2	4 1/2		3 1/4	7	4 3/4	3 3/4	2 3/4		2 3/4	6 3/4		3	4 3/4	8 1/2				
Stuttgart	3 3/4	4 1/2	3 3/4	4	3	5	8	3 3/4	2 1/2	3 1/4	5 1/2	6 3/4	2 1/2	3 3/4	6	3	4 3/4	3 3/4	4 1/4	5	4 1/4	5	6 1/4	2 3/4	2 1/2	2 3/4	5		3 1/4	5 1/2	5 1/2				
Venice	5 1/2		5 3/4		5	5 3/4		4 3/4	5 1/4	5 3/4	6 1/4		3	4 3/4	6	5	7	4 1/4	5	5	5 1/4	6 1/2	4 3/4	2 1/2	3	3 1/4	6	4 3/4	3 1/2	3	6 1/2		5		
Vienna	3 1/2	5	4	4	5	4 3/4	6	3 1/2	4 1/2	3 1/4	5 3/4	6 1/4	3	3 1/4	6	4 3/4	6 1/2	4 1/2	4 3/4	5 1/2	4 3/4	5 3/4	6	3	2 3/4	3 1/4	5	6	3 3/4	3 1/2	4 1/4		3	3 1/4	
Zurich	3	5 1/4	3 1/4	2	3 1/4	4 1/4	6	3	2 3/4	3 1/2	5 3/4	5 1/2	2 3/4	2 1/2	5 1/4	3	4 1/2	3 3/4	2 1/2	3 1/4	3 3/4	3 3/4	5	2 1/2	2 1/2	2 3/4	5	5 1/2	3 1/4	3 1/2	4 1/2	2 1/2	2 1/2	3 3/4	3

Hamburg – Oslo: 2 3/4

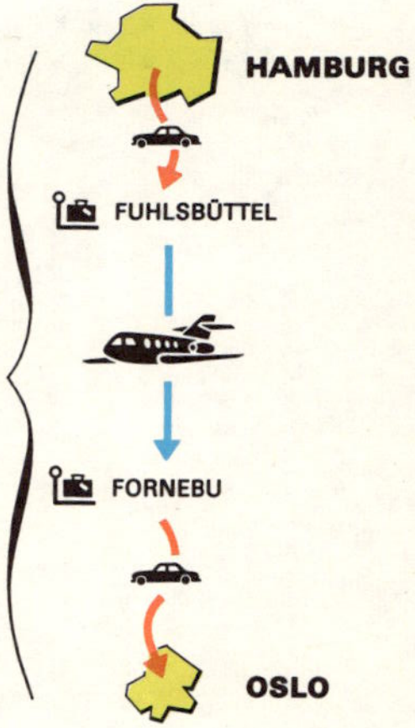

This revised edition from
Michelin Tyre Company's Tourism Department
offers you a selection of
hotels and restaurants in the main European cities.
The latter have been chosen for
their business or tourist interest.

In addition the guide indicates establishments,
located in other towns,
renowned for the excellence of their cuisine.

We hope that the guide will help you
with your choice of a hotel or restaurant
and prove useful for your sightseeing.
Have an enjoyable stay.

Signs and symbols

HOTELS AND RESTAURANTS

CLASS, STANDARD OF COMFORT

Luxury in the traditional style
Top class comfort
Very comfortable
Good average
Quite comfortable
In its class, hotel with modern amenities

AMENITY

Pleasant hotels
Pleasant restaurants
Particularly attractive feature — « Park »
Very quiet or quiet secluded hotel
Quiet hotel
Exceptional view – Panoramic view — sea,
Interesting or extensive view

CUISINE

Exceptional cuisine in the country, worth a special journey
Excellent cooking : worth a detour
An especially good restaurant in its class
Other recommended carefully prepared meals — M

HOTEL FACILITIES

	Lift (elevator) – Television in room
	Air conditioning
wc	Private bathroom with toilet, private bathroom without toilet
wc	Private shower with toilet, private shower without toilet
	Telephone in room : direct dialling for outside calls
	Telephone in room : outside calls connected by operator
	Hotel tennis court(s) – Outdoor or indoor swimming pool
	Sauna – Garden – Beach with bathing facilities
	Meals served in garden or on terrace
	Free garage – Charge made for garage – Car park
	Bedrooms accessible to the physically handicapped
	Equipped conference hall
	Dogs are not allowed
without rest.	The hotel has no restaurant

PRICES

These prices are given in the currency of the country in question. Valid for 1986 the rates shown should only vary if the cost of living changes to any great extent.

	Meals
M 65/110	Set meal prices
M a la carte 80/160	" a la carte " meals
	Hotels
30 rm 110/240	Lowest price for a comfortable single and highest price for the best double room
	Breakfast
22	Price of breakfast
17 Bb	Breakfast with choice from buffet
	Service and taxes
s. t.	Service only included. V.A.T. only included.

In Austria, Benelux, Denmark, Germany, Italy, Norway, Sweden and Switzerland, prices shown are inclusive, that is to say service and V.A.T. included.

SIGHTS

Worth a journey	★★★
Worth a detour	★★
Interesting	★

TOWN PLANS

Main conventional signs

Tourist Information Centre ....

Hotel, restaurant – Reference letter on the town plan ....

Place of interest and its main entrance } Reference letter on the town plan ..
Interesting church or chapel ....

Shopping street – Public car park ....

Tram ....

Underground station ....

One-way street ....

Church or chapel – Poste restante, telegraph – Telephone ....

Public buildings located by letters :

Police (in large towns police headquarters) – Theatre – Museum ....

Coach station – Airport – Hospital – Covered market ....

Ruins – Monument, statue – Fountain ....

Garden, park, wood – Cemetery, Jewish cemetery ....

Outdoor or indoor swimming pool – Racecourse – Golf course ....

Cable-car – Funicular ....

Sports ground, stadium – View – Panorama..........

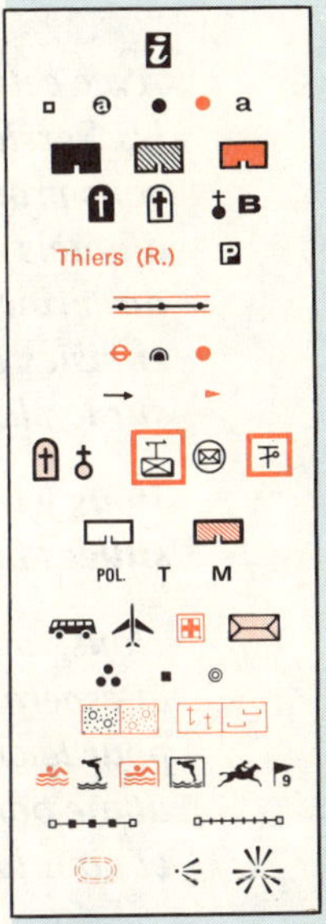

Names shown on the street plans are in the language of the country to conform to local signposting.

Avec cette nouvelle édition,
les Services de Tourisme du Pneu Michelin
vous proposent une sélection
d'hôtels et restaurants
des principales villes d'Europe,
choisies en raison de leur vocation internationale
sur le plan des affaires et du tourisme.

Vous y trouverez également les grandes tables
situées hors de ces grandes villes.

Nous vous souhaitons d'agréables séjours
et espérons que ce guide vous aidera utilement
pour le choix d'un hôtel,
d'une bonne table
et pour la visite des principales curiosités.

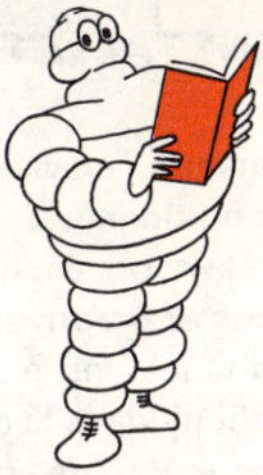

Signes et symboles

HOTELS ET RESTAURANTS

CLASSE ET CONFORT

Grand luxe et tradition
Grand confort
Très confortable
Bon confort
Assez confortable
Dans sa catégorie, hôtel d'équipement moderne

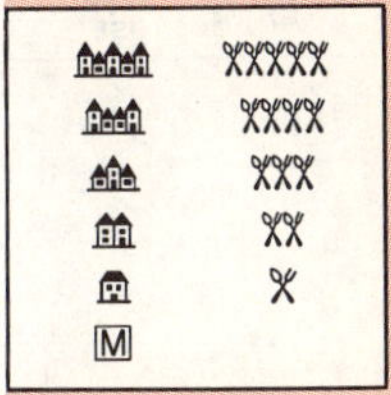

L'AGRÉMENT

Hôtels agréables
Restaurants agréables
Élément particulièrement agréable
Hôtel très tranquille, ou isolé et tranquille
Hôtel tranquille
Vue exceptionnelle, panorama
Vue intéressante ou étendue

LA TABLE

Une des meilleures tables du pays, vaut le voyage
Table excellente, mérite un détour
Une très bonne table dans sa catégorie
Autre table soignée

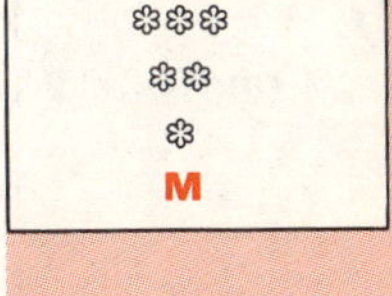

L'INSTALLATION

	Ascenseur, Télévision dans la chambre
	Air conditionné
wc	Bain et wc privés, bain sans wc
wc	Douche et wc privés, douche privée sans wc
	Téléphone dans la chambre direct avec l'extérieur
	Téléphone dans la chambre relié par standard
	Tennis — Piscine : de plein air ou couverte
	Sauna — Jardin — Plage aménagée
	Repas servis au jardin ou en terrasse
	Garage gratuit — Garage payant — Parc à voitures
	Chambres accessibles aux handicapés physiques
	L'hôtel reçoit les séminaires
	Accès interdit aux chiens
without rest.	L'hôtel n'a pas de restaurant

LES PRIX

Les prix sont indiqués dans la monnaie du pays. Établis pour l'année 1986, ils ne doivent être modifiés que si le coût de la vie subit des variations importantes.

Au restaurant

M 65/110	Prix des repas à prix fixes
M a la carte 80/160	Prix des repas à la carte

A l'hôtel

30 rm 110/240	Prix minimum pour une chambre d'une personne et maximum pour la plus belle chambre occupée par deux personnes

Petit déjeuner

22 17	Prix du petit déjeuner.
Bb	Petit déjeuner buffet

Service et taxes

s. **t.**	Service compris T.V.A. comprise

En Allemagne, Autriche, Benelux, Danemark, Italie, Norvège, Suède et Suisse, les prix indiqués sont nets.

LES CURIOSITÉS

Vaut le voyage	★★★
Mérite un détour	★★
Intéressante	★

LES PLANS

Principaux signes conventionnels

Information touristique ...

Hôtel, restaurant – Lettre les repérant sur le plan ...

Monument intéressant et entrée principale
Église ou chapelle intéressante ...
} Lettre les repérant sur le plan ...

Rue commerçante – Parc de stationnement public ...

Tramway ...

Station de métro ...

Sens unique ...

Église ou chapelle – Poste restante, télégraphe – Téléphone ...

Édifices publics repérés par des lettres :

Police (dans les grandes villes commissariat central) – Théâtre – Musée ...

Gare routière – Aéroport – Hôpital – Marché couvert ...

Ruines – Monument, statue – Fontaine ...

Jardin, parc, bois – Cimetière, cimetière israélite ...

Piscine de plein air, couverte – Hippodrome – Golf ...

Téléphérique – Funiculaire ...

Stade – Vue – Panorama ...

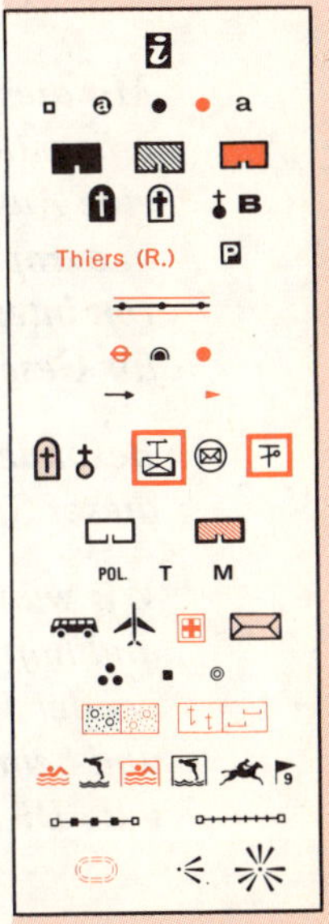

Les indications portées sur les plans sont dans la langue du pays, en conformité avec la dénomination locale.

*Mit dieser Neuauflage
präsentieren Ihnen die Michelin-Touristikabteilungen
eine Auswahl von Hotels und Restaurants
in europäischen Hauptstädten
von internationaler Bedeutung
für Geschäftsreisende und Touristen.*

*Besonders gute Restaurants in der näheren Umgebung
dieser Städte wurden ebenfalls aufgenommen.*

*Wir wünschen einen angenehmen Aufenthalt
und hoffen, daß Ihnen dieser Führer
bei der Wahl eines Hotels, eines Restaurants
und beim Besuch der Hauptsehenswürdigkeiten
gute Dienste leisten wird.*

Zeichen und Symbole

HOTELS UND RESTAURANTS

KLASSENEINTEILUNG UND KOMFORT

Großer Luxus und Tradition
Großer Komfort
Sehr komfortabel
Mit gutem Komfort
Mit ausreichendem Komfort
Moderne Einrichtung

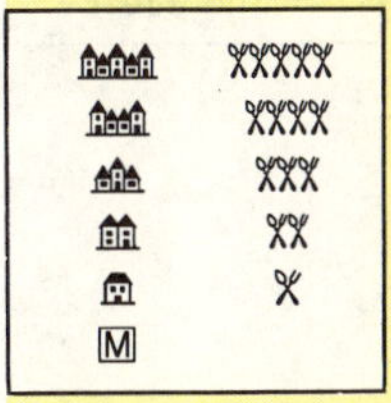

ANNEHMLICHKEITEN

Angenehme Hotels
Angenehme Restaurants
Besondere Annehmlichkeit
Sehr ruhiges oder abgelegenes und ruhiges Hotel
Ruhiges Hotel
Reizvolle Aussicht, Rundblick
Interessante oder weite Sicht

KÜCHE

Eine der besten Küchen des Landes : eine Reise wert
Eine hervorragende Küche : verdient einen Umweg
Eine sehr gute Küche : verdient Ihre besondere Beachtung
Andere sorgfältig zubereitete Mahlzeiten

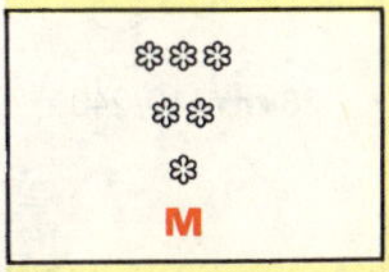

EINRICHTUNG

TV	Fahrstuhl – Fernsehen im Zimmer
	Klimaanlage
wc	Privatbad mit wc, Privatbad ohne wc
wc	Privatdusche mit wc, Privatdusche ohne wc
	Zimmertelefon mit direkter Außenverbindung
	Zimmertelefon mit Außenverbindung über Telefonzentrale
	Tennis – Freibad – Hallenbad
	Sauna – Garten – Strandbad
	Garten-, Terrassenrestaurant
P	Garage kostenlos – Garage wird berechnet – Parkplatz
	Für Körperbehinderte leicht zugängliche Zimmer
	Konferenzraum
	Das Mitführen von Hunden ist unerwünscht
without rest	Hotel ohne Restaurant

DIE PREISE

Die Preise sind in der jeweiligen Landeswährung angegeben. Sie gelten für das Jahr 1986 und können nur geändert werden, wenn die Lebenshaltungskosten starke Veränderungen erfahren.

Im Restaurant

M 65/110	Feste Menupreise
M a la carte 80/160	Mahlzeiten "a la carte"

Im Hotel

30 rm 110/240	Mindestpreis für ein Einzelzimmer und Höchstpreis für das schönste Doppelzimmer für zwei Personen

Frühstück

22 17	Preis des Frühstücks
Bb	Frühstücksbuffet

Bedienungsgeld und Gebühren

s. t.	Bedienung inbegriffen – MWSt inbegriffen.

In Benelux, Dänemark, Deutschland, Italien, Norwegen, Österreich, Schweden und Schweiz sind die angegebenen Preise Inklusivpreise.

SEHENSWÜRDIGKEITEN

Eine Reise wert	★★★
Verdient einen Umweg	★★
Sehenswert	★

STADTPLÄNE

Erklärung der wichtigsten Zeichen

Informationsstelle

Hotel, Restaurant – Referenzbuchstabe auf dem Plan

Sehenswertes Gebäude mit Haupteingang }
Sehenswerte Kirche oder Kapelle } Referenzbuchstabe auf dem Plan

Einkaufsstraße – Öffentlicher Parkplatz, Parkhaus

Straßenbahn

U-Bahnstation

Einbahnstraße

Kirche oder Kapelle – Postlagernde Sendungen, Telegraph – Telefon

Öffentliche Gebäude, durch Buchstaben gekennzeichnet :

Polizei (in größeren Städten Polizeipräsidium) – Theater – Museum

Autobusbahnhof – Flughafen – Krankenhaus – Markthalle

Ruine – Denkmal, Statue – Brunnen

Garten, Park, Wald – Friedhof, Jüd. Friedhof

Freibad – Hallenbad – Pferderennbahn – Golfplatz und Lochzahl

Seilschwebebahn – Standseilbahn

Sportplatz – Aussicht – Rundblick

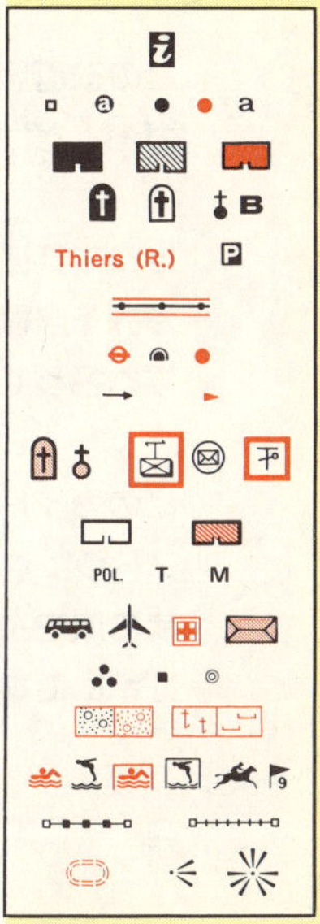

Die Angaben auf den Stadtplänen erfolgen, übereinstimmend mit der örtlichen Beschilderung, in der Landessprache.

3

この改訂版ガイドブックはミシュラン・タイヤ社観光部がおとどけするものです。

ビジネスに、観光に、国際的な拠点ヨーロッパ主要都市が誇る自慢のホテルとレストランを、そして郊外にたたずむ名うてのレストランをあわせて、御紹介いたします。

このガイドブックが、より快適なホテル、味わい深いレストランやあこがれの地と出逢うきっかけとなり、皆さまの旅をより素晴らしいものにするお手伝いができれば幸いです。

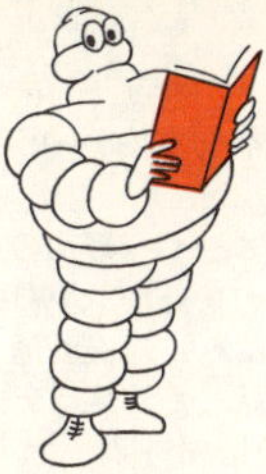

記号と シンボルマーク

ホテルとレストラン

等級と快適さ

豪華で伝統的様式
トップクラス
たいへん快適
快適
かなり快適
等級内での近代的設備のホテル

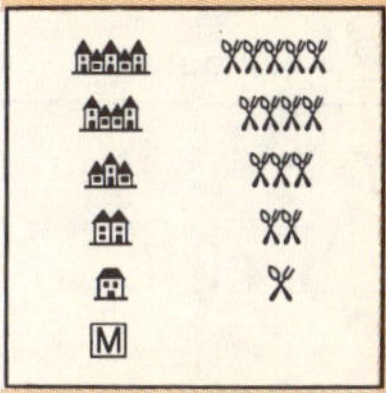

居心地

居心地よいホテル
居心地よいレストラン
特に魅力的な特徴
大変静かなホテル又は人里離れた静かなホテル
静かなホテル
見晴らしがよい展望（例：海）、パノラマ
素晴らしい風景

料理

最上の料理、出かける価値あり
素晴らしい料理、寄り道の価値あり
等級内では大変おいしい料理
その他の心のこもった料理

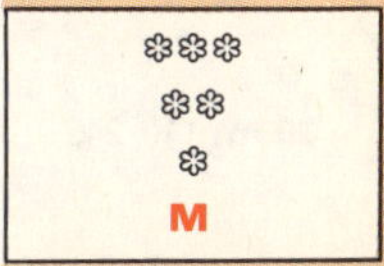

設備

TV	エレベーター、室内テレビ
	空調設備
wc	専用のバスとトイレ。専用のバスのみでトイレなし
wc	専用のシャワーとトイレ。専用のシャワーのみでトイレなし
	室内に電話あり、外線直通
	室内に電話あり、外線は交換台経由
	テニスコート。屋外プール。屋内プール。
	サウナ。くつろげる庭。整備された海水浴場
	食事が庭またはテラスでできる
P	無料駐車場。有料駐車場。駐車場
	体の不自由な方のための設備あり
	会議又は研修会の出来るホテル
	犬の連れ込みおことわり
without rest.	レストランの無いホテル

料金

料金は1986年のその国の貨幣単位で示してありますが、物価の変動などで変わる場合もあります。

M 65/110 **M** a la carte 80/160	**レストラン** 定食、ア・ラ・カルトそれぞれの最低料金と最高料金。
30 rm 110/240	**ホテル** 一人部屋の最低料金と二人部屋の最高料金。
22 17 Bb	**朝食** 朝食代 朝食はビュッフェ形式
s. t.	**サービス料と税金** サービス料込み。付加価値税込み。

オーストリア、ベネルクス、デンマーク、ドイツ、イタリア、ノルウェー、スウェーデン、スイスに関しては正価料金。

名　所

出かける価値あり………………………………………… ★★★
立ち寄る価値あり………………………………………… ★★
興味深い……………………………………………………… ★

地　図

主な記号

ツーリストインフォメーション…………………………
ホテル・レストラン――地図上での目印番号…………………
興味深い歴史的建造物と、その中央入口／興味深い教会または聖堂 ｝地図上での目印番号……………
商店街――公共駐車場……………………………………
路面電車………………………………………………………
地下鉄駅………………………………………………………
一方通行路……………………………………………………
教会または聖堂――局留郵便、電報――電話………………
公共建造物、記号は下記の通り………………………………
警察（大都市では、中央警察署）――劇場――美術館、博物館……
長距離バス発着所――空港――病院――屋内市場……………
遺跡――歴史的建造物、像――泉………………………………
庭園、公園、森林――墓地――ユダヤ教の墓地…………………
屋外プール、屋内プール――競馬場――ゴルフ場………………
ロープウェイ――ケーブルカー…………………………………
スタジアム――風景――パノラマ…………………………………

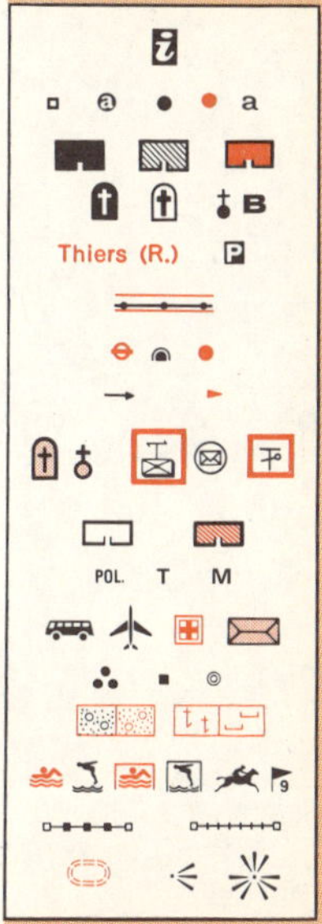

地図上の名称は、地方の標識に合わせてその国の言葉で表記されています。

Austria
Österreich

Vienna
Salzburg

PRACTICAL INFORMATION

LOCAL CURRENCY

Austrian Schilling ; 100 S = 5.77 US $ (Jan. 86)

TOURIST INFORMATION

In Vienna : Österreich-Information, Margaretenstr. 1, ✆ (0222) 57 57 14
Niederösterreich-Information, Paulanergasse 11, ✆ (0222) 57 67 18

In Salzburg : Landesverkehrsamt, Mozartplatz 5, ✆ (0662) 4 15 61

AIRLINES

AUSTRIAN AIRLINES : 1107 Wien, Kärntner Ring 18, ✆ (0222) 65 57 57

AIR FRANCE : 1010 Wien, Kärntnerstr. 49, ✆ (0222) 52 66 52

BRITISH AIRWAYS : 1010 Wien, Kärntner Ring 10, ✆ (0222) 65 76 90

DEUTSCHE LUFTHANSA : 1015 Wien, Opernring 1, ✆ (0222) 57 56 49

PAN AM : 1010 Wien, Kärntner Ring 5, ✆ (0222) 52 66 46

FOREIGN EXCHANGE

Hotels, restaurants and shops do not always accept foreign currencies and it is wise, therefore, to change money and cheques at the banks and exchange offices which are found in the larger stations, airports and at the frontier.

SHOPPING and BANK HOURS

Shops are open from 9am to 6pm, but often close for a lunch break. They are closed Saturday afternoon, Sunday and Bank Holidays (except the shops in railway stations).

Branch offices of banks are open from Monday to Friday between 8am and 12.30pm (in Salzburg 12am) and from 1.30pm to 3pm (in Salzburg 2pm to 4.30pm), Thursday to 5.30pm (only in Vienna).

In the index of street names those printed in red are where the principal shops are found.

BREAKDOWN SERVICE

ÖAMTC : See addresses in the text of Vienna and Salzburg

ARBÖ : in Vienna : Mariahilfer Str. 180, ✆ (0222) 85 35 35
in Salzburg : Münchner Bundesstr. 9, ✆ (0662) 3 36 01

In Austria the ÖAMTC and the ARBÖ make a special point of assisting foreign motorists. They have motor patrols covering main roads.

TIPPING

Service is generally included in hotel and restaurant bills. But in Austria, it is usual to give more than the expected tip in hotels, restaurants and cafés. Taxi-drivers, porters, barbers and theatre attendants also expect tips.

SPEED LIMITS

The speed limit in built up areas (indicated by place name signs at the beginning and end of such areas) is 50 km/h - 31 mph ; on motorways 130 km/h - 80 mph and on all other roads 100 km/h - 62 mph.

SEAT BELTS

The wearing of seat belts in Austria is compulsory for drivers and front seat passengers.

VIENNA

SIGHTS

HOFBURG★★★ BV

Imperial Palace of the Habsburgs (Kaiserpalast der Habsburger) : Swiss Court – Castle Chapel – Amalienhof – Stallburg – Leopold Wing – Ballhausplatz – Imperial Chancellery – Spanish Riding School – Neue Burg – Josefsplatz – Michaelerplatz – In der Burg – Capuchins Crypt – Church of the Augustinians. Art Collections : Imperial Treasury★★★ – Imperial Apartments★★ – Austrian National Library (Great Hall★) – Collection of Court Porcelain and Silver★★ – Collection of Arms and Armour★★ – Collection of Old Musical Instruments★ – Albertina (Dürer Collection★) – Museum of Ephesian Sculpture (Reliefs of Ephesus★★).

BUILDINGS AND MONUMENTS

St Stephen's Cathedral★★ (Stephansdom) CV – Schönbrunn★★ (Apartments★★★, Park★★, Coach Room★) S – Upper and Lower Belvedere★★ (Oberes und Unteres Belvedere) (Terraced Gardens and Art Collections★) DX and S – Opera★ (Staatsoper)★ CV – Church of St Charles★ (Karlskirche) CX – Church of St Michael (Michaeler Kirche) BCV – Church of the Monorities (Minoritenkirche) BV – Church of the Teutonic Order (Deutschordenskirche) (Altarpiece★, Treasure★) CV – Church of the Jesuits (Jesuitenkirche) CV **B** – Church of Our Lady of the River Bank (Maria am Gestade) CU – Church of the Faithful Virgin (Maria Treu) S **F** – Mozart Memorial (Mozart-Gedenkstätte) CV **D** – Dreimäderlhaus BU **K**.

STREETS, PLACES, PARKS

Kärntner Straße CVX – Graben (Colum of the Pest) CV – Am Hof (Colum to the Virgin) BV – Herrengasse★ BV – Maria-Theresien-Platz BV – Prater★ (Giant Whell, ⋞★) S – Oberlaapark★ S – Heldenplatz BV – Burggarten BV – Volksgarten BV – Rathausplatz BV.

IMPORTANT MUSEUMS (Hofburg and Belvedere see above)

Museum of Fine Arts★★★ (Kunsthistorisches Museum) BV – Historical Museum of the City of Vienna★★ (Historisches Museum der Stadt Wien) CX **M1** – Austrian Folklore Museum★★ (Österreichisches Museum für Volkskunde) S **M2** – Gallery of Painting and Fine Arts★ (Gemäldegalerie der Akademie der Bildenden Künste) BX **M3** – Natural History Museum★ (Naturhistorisches Museum) BV **M4** – Birthplace of Schubert (Schubert-Museum) R **M5** – Austrian Museum of Applied Arts★ (Österreichisches Museum für angewandte Kunst) DV **M6**.

EXCURSIONS

Danube Tower★★ (Donauturm) R – Leopoldsberg⋞★★ R – Kahlenberg⋞★ R – Klosterneuburg Abbey (Stift Klosterneuburg) (Altarpiece by Nicolas of Verdun★) R – Grinzing R – Baden★ S – Vienna Woods★ (Wienerwald) S.

VIENNA (WIEN) Austria **987** ⑩, **426** ⑫ – pop. 1 527 000 – alt. 156 m. – ☎ 0222.

✈ Wien-Schwechat by ②, ✆ 7 77 00 – 🚗 ✆ 56 50 29 89.

Exhibition Centre, Messeplatz 1, ✆ 9 31 52 40.

ℹ Tourist-Information, Opernpassage (Basement), ✆ 43 16 08 – ÖAMTC, Schubertring, ✆ 72 99

Budapest 208 ③ – München 435 ⑥ – Praha 292 ① – Salzburg 292 ⑥ – Zagreb 362 ⑤.

City districts (Stadtbezirke) 1-9 :

Imperial (converted 19 C palace), Kärntner Ring 16, ✉ A-1015, ✆ 65 17 65, Telex 112630 – |‡| ▤ 🏊. AE ⊙ E VISA. ✻ rest CX a
M a la carte 270/570 (booking essential) – **Imperial Café M** a la carte 195/340 – **162 rm** 1820/4320.

Sacher, Philharmonikerstr. 4, ✉ A-1015, ✆ 52 55 75/5 14 56, Telex 112520, « Antique furniture, restaurant Sacherstöckl » – |‡| ▤ TV. ✻ rest CV x
M a la carte 265/620 – **124 rm** 1100/3000.

Bristol, Kärntner Ring 1, ✉ A-1015, ✆ 52 95 52/5 15 16, Telex 112474 – |‡| ▤ rest TV 🏊 (with ▤). AE ⊙ E VISA. ✻ rest CX m
M a la carte 230/540 (see also **Korso rest. below**) – **152 rm** 2200/3640.

✿ **Hotel im Palais Schwarzenberg** ⛰, Schwarzenbergplatz 9, ✉ A-1030, ✆ 78 45 15, Telex 136124, « Converted 1727 baroque palace, park », ≘ – |‡| TV P 🏊. AE ⊙ E VISA
M a la carte 330/710 (booking essential) – **38 rm** 2700/4500 CX
Spec. Zwiebeltörtchen "Vulgaris", Zanderstrudel mit Krebsmousse in Rotweinsauce, Masthuhn und Kalbshirn im Netz mit Entenlebersauce.

Marriott-Hotel M, Parkring 12a, ✉ A-1015, ✆ 53 36 11, Telex 112249, ≘, ▣ – |‡| ▤ TV ♿ P 🏊. ✻ rest CV d
Restaurants : – **Symphonika** – **Parkring-Restaurant** – **304 rm** Bb.

✿ **Hilton International-Rôtisserie Prinz Eugen**, Landstraßer Hauptstr. 2 (near Stadtpark), ✉ A-1030, ✆ 75 26 52, Telex 136799, ≘ – |‡| ▤ TV ♿ 🏊. AE ⊙ E VISA. ✻ rest DV e
M *(closed Saturday lunch)* a la carte 335/710 (booking essential) – **Café am Park M** a la carte 240/460 – **620 rm** 1750/3100
Spec. Delice vom Beluga Malossol Kaviar im Lachsrosenbouquet, Das Beste vom Kalb mit Kräutermousseline, Waldbeeren in Blätterkrokant.

Intercontinental, Johannesgasse 28, ✉ A-1037, ✆ 75 05, Telex 131235, ≘ – |‡| ▤ TV ♿ 🏊. AE ⊙ E VISA. ✻ rest DX p
Restaurants : – **Rôtisserie M** a la carte 250/650 – **Brasserie M** a la carte 200/415 – **500 rm** 1960/4450.

Hotel de France, Schottenring 3, ✉ A-1010, ✆ 34 35 40, Telex 114360, ≘ – |‡| ▤ rest TV 🏊. AE ⊙ E VISA BU b
M a la carte 255/530 – **186 rm** 1095/2580 Bb.

SAS-Palais-Hotel M (modern hotel in a historical building), Parkring/Weihburggasse 32, ✉ A-1010, ✆ 5 32 63 10/51 51 70, Telex 136127, ≘ – |‡| ▤ TV 🏊. AE ⊙ E VISA. ✻
M a la carte 265/580 – **165 rm** 1500/2800 Bb. CV z

König von Ungarn, Schulerstr. 10, ✉ A-1010, ✆ 52 65 20, Telex 116240 – |‡| TV 🏊. ✻ rest CV n
32 rm.

Biedermeier, Landstraßer Hauptstr. 28 (at Sünnhof), ✉ A-1030, ✆ 75 55 75, Telex 11 10 39 – |‡| TV 🚗 🏊. AE ⊙ E VISA. ✻ rest S w
M a la carte 250/495 – **200 rm** 1500/1800.

Ambassador, Neuer Markt 5, ✉ A-1010, ✆ 52 75 11, Telex 111906 – |‡|. AE ⊙ VISA
M a la carte 285/615 – **107 rm** 1250/2400. CV s

Europa, Neuer Markt 3, ✉ A-1015, ✆ 52 15 94/5 15 94, Telex 112292 – |‡| ▤ TV 🏊. AE ⊙ E VISA. ✻ rest CV a
M a la carte 220/490 – **102 rm** 1140/1770 Bb.

Stefanie, Taborstr. 12, ✉ A-1020, ✆ 24 24 12, Telex 134589 – |‡| TV 🛁wc 🚿wc ☎ 🚗 🏊. AE ⊙ E VISA DU d
M a la carte 170/435 – **140 rm** 1080/1640 Bb.

Ibis, Mariahilfer Gürtel 22, ✉ A-1060, ✆ 56 56 26, Telex 133833 – |‡| ▤ TV 🛁wc 🚿wc ☎ ♿ P 🏊 S d
M a la carte 125/280 – **341 rm** 780/1270 Bb.

Amadeus without rest, Wildpretmarkt 5, ✉ A-1010, ✆ 63 87 38 – |‡| TV 🛁wc 🚿wc ☎. AE ⊙ CV y
closed 22 December - 6 January – **30 rm** 890/1540.

Capricorno without rest, Schwedenplatz 3, ✉ A-1010, ✆ 63 31 04, Telex 115266 – |‡| TV 🛁wc 🚿wc ☎ 🚗 P. AE VISA DV f
46 rm 890/1480.

K u. K Palais Hotel without rest (modern hotel in a former palace), Rudolfsplatz 11, ✉ A-1010, ✆ 63 13 53, Telex 134049 – |‡| TV 🛁wc 🚿wc ☎. AE ⊙ E VISA CU h
66 rm 1190/1590 Bb.

Hungaria, Rennweg 51, ✉ A-1030, ✆ 73 25 21, Telex 13 17 97 – |‡| 🛁wc 🚿wc ☎ 🚗. AE ⊙ E VISA. ✻ rest S h
M a la carte 180/330 ♁ – **168 rm** 850/1400.

ETAP Hotel Belvedere, Am Heumarkt 35, ✉ A-1030, ✆ 75 25 36, Telex 111822 – |‡| TV 🛁wc ☎ 🚗 🏊. AE ⊙ E VISA CX e
M a la carte 135/300 ♁ – **211 rm** 990/1380 Bb.

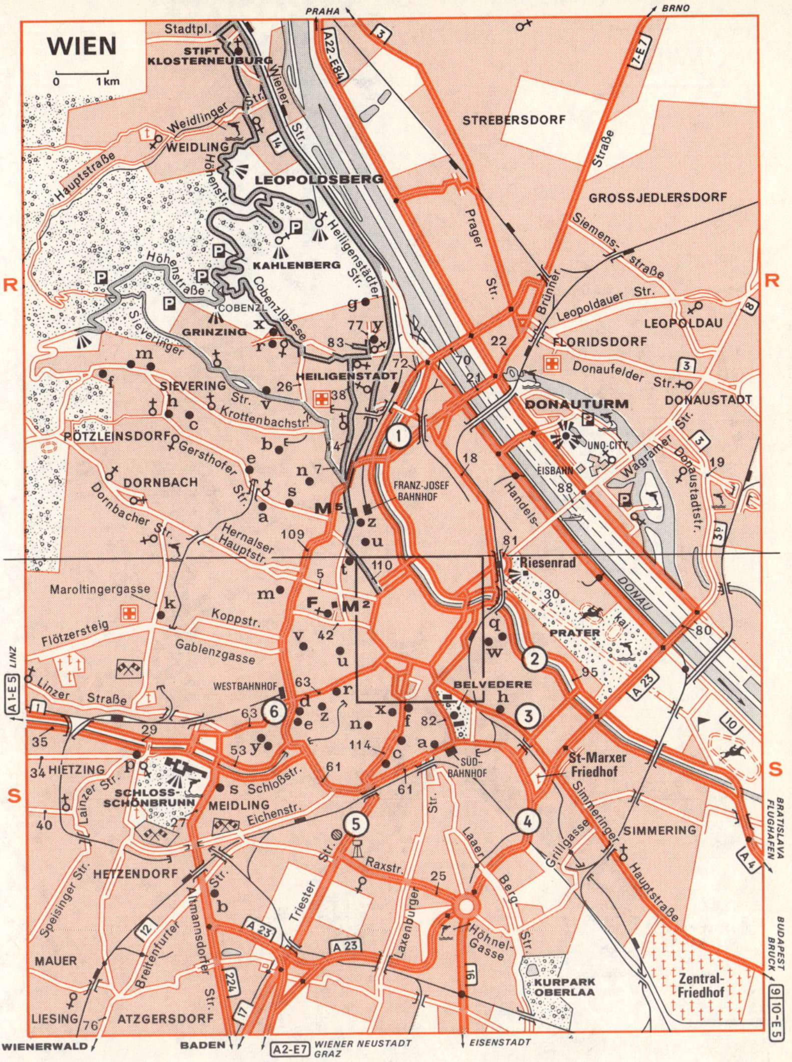

Alser Straße	S	5	Hauptallee	S	30	Perchtoldsdorfer Str.	S	76
Billrothstraße	R	7	Hietzinger Hauptstr.	S	34	Pfarrplatz	R	77
Döblinger Hauptstraße	R	14	Hietzinger Kai	S	35	Praterbrücke	S	80
Dresdner Straße	R	18	Hohe Warte	R	38	Praterstern	RS	81
Erzherzog-Karl-Str.	R	19	Jagdschloßgasse	S	40	Prinz Eugen-Straße	S	82
Floridsdorferbrücke	R	21	Josefstädter Straße	S	42	Probusgasse	R	83
Floridsdorfer Hauptstr.	R	22	Linke Wienzeile	S	53	Reichsbrücke	R	88
Grenzackerstraße	S	25	Margaretengürtel	S	61	Schüttelstraße	S	95
Grinzinger Allee	R	26	Mariahilfer Straße	S	63	Währinger Gürtel	R	109
Grünbergstraße	S	27	Nordbrücke	R	70	Währinger Straße	R	110
Hadikgasse	S	29	Nußdorfer Lände	R	72	Wiedner Hauptstraße	S	114

Do not lose your way in Europe, use the Michelin **Main Road** maps, scale : 1 inch : 16 miles.

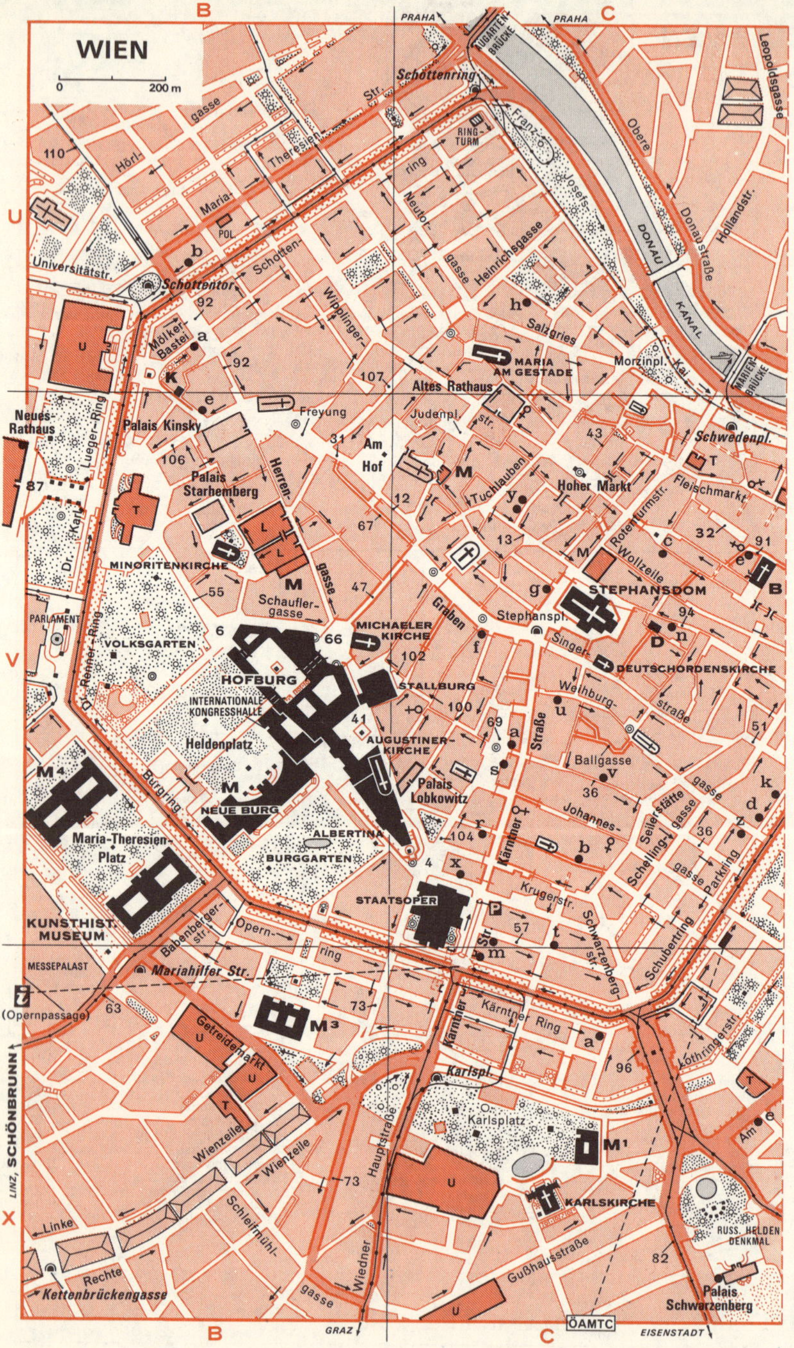

WIEN
0
200 m
B
C
U
V
X
PRAHA
PRAHA
AUGARTEN-BRÜCKE
Schottenring
RING-TURM
Leopoldsgasse
Obere
Donaustraße
Hollandstr.
DONAU
KANAL
Franz-Josefs-Kai
Neutorgasse
Heinrichsgasse
Salzgries
Morzinpl.
MARIEN-BRÜCKE
Hörl-gasse
Maria-Theresien-Str.
Schotten-ring
Schottentor
Universitätsstr.
Mölker-Bastei
Wipplinger-
Maria am Gestade
Altes Rathaus
Judenpl.
Freyung
Palais Kinsky
Neues-Rathaus
Dr. Karl-Lueger-Ring
Am Hof
Palais Starhemberg
Herrengasse
Schwedenpl.
Fleischmarkt
Hoher Markt
Tuchlauben
Rotenturmstr.
Wollzeile
MINORITENKIRCHE
Schauflergasse
STEPHANSDOM
Stephanspl.
Singer-
DEUTSCHORDENSKIRCHE
Graben
MICHAELER KIRCHE
STALLBURG
PARLAMENT
VOLKSGARTEN
Dr. Renner-Ring
HOFBURG
INTERNATIONALE KONGRESSHALLE
Heldenplatz
AUGUSTINER-KIRCHE
Palais Lobkowitz
Weihburg-straße
Ballgasse
Johannes-gasse
Seilerstätte
Schelling-gasse
Parkring
Kärntner Straße
NEUE BURG
Burgring
Maria-Theresien-Platz
KUNSTHIST. MUSEUM
ALBERTINA
BURGGARTEN
STAATSOPER
Krugerstr.
Schwarzenbergstr.
Schubertring
Babenbergerstr.
Opernring
MESSEPALAST
Mariahilfer Str.
(Opernpassage)
Kärntner Ring
Lothringerstr.
Getreidemarkt
Karlspl.
Karlsplatz
Am
Hauptstraße
KARLSKIRCHE
RUSS. HELDEN DENKMAL
Wienzeile
Wienzeile
Schleifmühlgasse
Linke
Rechte
Kettenbrückengasse
Wiedner
Gußhausstraße
Palais Schwarzenberg
LINZ, SCHÖNBRUNN
GRAZ
ÖAMTC
EISENSTADT

STREET INDEX TO WIEN TOWN PLANS

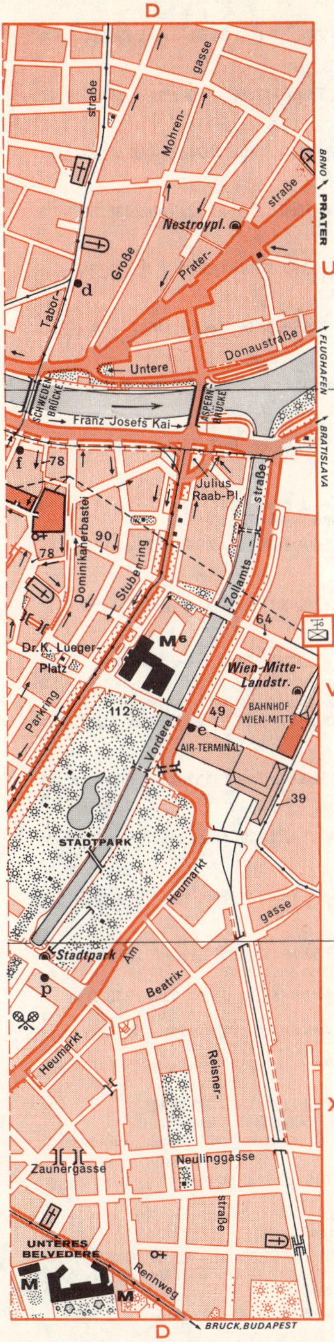

🏨 **Dorkahof** without rest, Breite Gasse 9, ✉ A-1070, ☏ 9 31 34 50, Telex 136614 – 🛁wc 🚿wc ☎. AE ⓓ E VISA — S u
closed 23 to 26 December – **55 rm** 900/1380 Bb.

🏨 **Astoria**, Führichgasse 1, ✉ A-1015, ☏ 52 65 85, Telex 112856 – 🛁wc 🚿wc ☎. AE ⓓ E VISA — CV r
M 255/440 – **108 rm** 1140/2200 Bb.

🏨 **Prinz Eugen**, Wiedner Gürtel 14, ✉ A-1040, ☏ 65 17 41, Telex 132483 – 🛁wc 🚿wc ☎. AE ⓓ E VISA — S a
M a la carte 182/365 – **106 rm** 1000/2050.

🏨 **Strudlhof** without rest, Pasteurgasse 1, ✉ A-1090, ☏ 31 25 22, Telex 135256 – 📺 🛁wc ☎ 🅿. AE ⓓ E VISA — R u
48 rm 890/1300.

🏨 **President**, Wallgasse 23, ✉ A-1060, ☏ 57 36 36/5 99 90, Telex 112523 – 📺 🛁wc ☎ 🅿. AE ⓓ E VISA — S e
M a la carte 135/310 – **77 rm** 1040/1540.

🏨 **Kummer**, Mariahilfer Str. 71 A, ✉ A-1061, ☏ 57 36 95/5 88 95, Telex 111417 – 🛁wc 🚿wc ☎. AE ⓓ E VISA. rest — S r
M a la carte 195/400 – **110 rm** 1100/1810.

🏨 **Erzherzog Rainer**, Wiedner Hauptstr. 27, ✉ A-1041, ☏ 65 46 46, Telex 132329 – rest 📺 🛁wc 🚿wc ☎. AE ⓓ E VISA — S f
M a la carte 200/430 – **84 rm** 825/1660.

🏨 Attaché without rest, Wiedner Hauptstr. 71, ✉ A-1040, ☏ 65 18 18, Telex 111146 – 📺 🛁wc 🚿wc ☎ — S c
23 rm.

🏨 Graben, Dorotheergasse 3, ✉ A-1010, ☏ 52 15 31 – 🛁wc 🚿wc ☎ — CV f
Restaurants : – **Altenberg** – **Trattoria Santo Stefano** – **46 rm** Bb.

🏨 **Mailberger Hof** without rest, Annagasse 7, ✉ A-1010, ☏ 52 06 41, Telex 133828 – 📺 🛁wc ☎. AE ⓓ VISA — CV b
40 rm 1050/1840.

🏨 **Am Parkring**, Parkring 12, ✉ A-1015, ☏ 52 65 24, Telex 113420, ≤ – 📺 🛁wc ☎ 🅿. AE ⓓ E VISA. — CV k
M a la carte 155/340 – **64 rm** 980/1640 Bb.

🏨 **Am Stephansplatz**, Stephansplatz 9, ✉ A-1010, ☏ 63 56 05, Telex 114334 – 📺 🛁wc 🚿wc ☎. AE ⓓ E VISA — CV g
M a la carte 190/320 – **62 rm** 1040/1540 Bb.

🏨 **Alpha** without rest, Boltzmanngasse 8, ✉ A-1090, ☏ 31 16 46, Telex 115749 – 🛁wc 🚿wc ☎ 🅿. AE ⓓ E VISA — R u
70 rm 975/1360.

🏨 **Alba**, Margaretenstr. 53, ✉ A-1050, ☏ 57 55 85/5 88 50, Telex 113264 – rm 📺 🛁wc 🚿wc ☎ 🅿. AE ⓓ E VISA — S n
M a la carte 155/290 – **46 rm** 1090/1540 Bb.

🏨 Atlanta without rest, Währinger Str. 33, ✉ A-1090, ☏ 42 12 39, Telex 115002 – 🛁wc 🚿wc ☎ — RS t
69 rm.

🏨 Albatros, Liechtensteinstr. 89, ✉ A-1090, ☏ 34 35 08, Telex 114300, – 📺 🛁wc ☎ 🅿 — R z
70 rm Bb.

XXXX ✿ **Korso**, Mahlerstr. 2 (at Bristol-H.), ✉ A-1015, ☏ 52 16 42 – . AE ⓓ E VISA. — CV m
closed Saturday lunch – **M** a la carte 230/580 (booking essential).

XXX ✿ **Steirereck**, Rasumofskygasse 2 / Ecke Weißgerberlände, ✉ A-1030, ☏ 73 31 68 – AE — S q
closed Saturday, Sunday, Bank Holidays and 22 December - 1 January – **M** a la carte 271/500(booking essential) (wine list with more than 440 wines)
Spec. Parfait von der Blutwurst, Gefüllter Kaninchenrücken in weißer Thymiansauce, Variation von böhmischen und altösterreichischen Mehlspeisen.

XXX ✿ **Hauswirth**, Otto-Bauer-Gasse 20, ✉ A-1060, ☏ 57 12 61 – AE ⓓ E VISA — S z
closed Sunday and Bank Holidays – **M** a la carte 275/505(booking essential)
Spec. Donauwaller in Oberskrensauce, Überbackener Rinderrücken mit kleinem Gemüseteller, Desser-Variation in Marzipan und Blätterteig.

XXX **Zu den drei Husaren**, Weihburggasse 4, ✉ A-1010, ☏ 52 11 92/5 12 10 92 – AE ⓓ E VISA — CV u
closed mid July - mid August and Sunday from December to March and June to August – **M** (dinner only) a la carte 390/680 (booking essential).

XXX **Kervansaray** (Turkish rest.), Mahlerstr. 9, ✉ A-1010, ☏ 52 88 43 – . AE ⓓ E VISA. — CVX t
closed Sunday – **M** a la carte 250/540 (booking essential) – **Hummer Bar** *(dinner only, mainly Seafood)* **M** a la carte 275/550 (booking essential).

XXX **Belvedere Stöckl**, Prinz-Eugen-Str. 25, ✉ A-1030, ☏ 78 41 98, « Garden » – E VISA — S
M a la carte 275/590.

XX ✿ **Mattes**, Schönlaterngasse 8, ✉ A-1010, ✆ 52 62 75 – AE ◑ E VISA. ✗ CV e
closed Sunday, Bank Holidays, August and 24 December - 1 January – **M** (dinner only) a la carte 270/625 (booking essential)
Spec. Flußkrebse auf Kohlrabi gratiniert, Lammrücken im Wirsingmantel, Mohnsoufflé mit Weinschaum.

XX **Kupferdachl**, Schottengasse 7, ✉ A-1010, ✆ 63 93 81 – AE ◑ E VISA BU a
closed Saturday lunch, Sunday and 26 July - 17 August – **M** a la carte 225/430 (booking essential).

XX **Schubertstüberln**, Schreyvogelgasse 4, ✉ A-1010, ✆ 63 71 87 – AE ◑ E VISA BV e
closed Sunday and 23 December - 6 January – **M** a la carte 235/425 ꕯ.

XX Steinerne Eule, Halbgasse 30, ✉ A-1070, ✆ 93 22 50, 🏕 S v

XX **Steirer Stüberl**, Wiedner Hauptstr. 111, ✉ A-1050, ✆ 55 43 49 – ◑ E VISA S c
closed Sunday – **M** a la carte 190/355 ꕯ.

XX Zum Kuckuck, Himmelpfortgasse 15, ✉ A-1010, ✆ 52 84 70/5 12 84 70 CV v
(booking essential).

XX **Salut** (French rest.), Wildpretmarkt 3, ✉ A-1010, ✆ 63 13 22 – AE ◑ VISA CV y
closed Sunday and Bank Holidays – **M** a la carte 290/450.

XX **Wiener Rathauskeller** (vaults with murals turn of the century), Rathausplatz 1, ✉ A-1010, ✆ 42 12 19 – *closed Sunday* – **M** a la carte 170/350 ꕯ. BV

X **Do und Co** (Bistro in a delicatessen store), Akademiestr. 3, ✉ A-1010, ✆ 52 64 74 – AE ◑ E VISA. ✗ CV t
closed from 6,30 p.m. and Sunday – **M** a la carte 205/330 (booking essential).

X **Wein-Comptoir**, Bäckerstr. 6, ✉ A-1010, ✆ 52 17 60 – AE ◑ E VISA CV c
closed Saturday, Sunday, Bank Holidays and 4 to 24 August – **M** a la carte 140/400 (booking essential) ꕯ.

X Goldener Hecht, Waaggasse 5, ✉ A-1040, ✆ 57 06 95, 🏕 S x

City districts (Stadtbezirke) 12-15 :

🏨 **Parkhotel Schönbrunn** (former imperial guest-house), Hietzinger Hauptstr. 10, ✉ A-1131, ✆ 82 26 76, Telex 132513, Massage, ≘s, 🏊 (duty), 🌳 – 🛗 📺 🛁wc 🚿wc ☎ 🏋. AE ◑ E VISA. ✗ rest S p
M a la carte 255/440 – **487 rm** 980/2470.

🏨 **Novotel Wien-West**, Wientalstraße (Auhof motorway station), ✉ A-1140, ✆ 97 25 42, Telex 135584, 🏊, 🌳 – 🛗 📺 🛁wc ☎ ♿ 🅿 🏋. AE ◑ E VISA by A 1 S
M a la carte 155/435 – **115 rm** 900/1440 Bb.

🏨 **Garten Hotel Altmannsdorf**, Hoffingergasse 26, ✉ A-1120, ✆ 84 75 27, Telex 135327, 🏕, Park, ≘s – 🛗 📺 🛁wc 🚿wc ☎ 🚗 🅿 🏋. AE ◑ E VISA S b
closed 21 to 28 December – **M** a la carte 180/430 – **41 rm** 820/1200 Bb.

🏨 **Reither**, Graumanngasse 16, ✉ A-1150, ✆ 83 54 46, Telex 136430, ≘s, 🏊 – 🛗 📺 🛁wc ☎ 🚗. AE ◑ E VISA. ✗ rest S y
M *(dinner only, closed Saturday and Sunday)* a la carte 165/315 – **50 rm** 820/1160 Bb.

🏨 **Arabella - Hotel Jagdschloß** without rest, Jagdschloßgasse 79, ✉ A-1130, ✆ 84 35 08, 🏊, 🌳 – 🛗 🛁wc 🚿wc ☎ by Jagdschloßgasse S
40 rm 640/980.

🏨 **Kaiserpark-Schönbrunn**, Grünbergstr. 9, ✉ A-1120, ✆ 83 86 10, Telex 134754 – 🛗 📺 🛁wc 🚿wc ☎. AE ◑ E VISA S s
closed 24 December - 15 January – **M** *(dinner only)* a la carte 165/300 – **46 rm** 950/1700 Bb.

🏨 **Ekazent** without rest, Hietzinger Hauptstr. 22, ✉ A-1130, ✆ 82 74 01, Telex 134352 – 🛗 🛁wc ☎. AE ◑ E VISA – **45 rm** 750/1100. S p

XX **Altwienerhof** with rm (wine list with 400 wines), Herklotzgasse 6, ✉ A-1150, ✆ 83 71 45, 🏕, « Winter garden » – 🛗 🛁wc 🚿wc ☎. AE S y
closed 1 to 21 January – **M** *(closed Sunday)* a la carte 217/465 (booking essential) – **24 rm** 480/1400 Bb.

X Schenke Steinmetz (Heurigen rest.), Firmiangasse 23, ✉ A-1130, ✆ 82 22 16 (booking essential). by Hietzinger Hauptstraße S

City districts (Stadtbezirke) 16-19 :

🏨 **Modul** Ⓜ, Peter-Jordan-Str. 78, ✉ A-1190, ✆ 47 15 84, Telex 116736 – 🛗 ▤ 📺 ♿ 🚗 🅿 🏋. AE ◑ E VISA R b
M a la carte 235/470 – **42 rm** 1030/2130 Bb.

🏨 **Maté**, Ottakringer Str. 34, ✉ A-1170, ✆ 43 61 33, Telex 115485, ≘s, 🏊 – 🛗 ▤ rest 📺 🛁wc 🚿wc ☎ 🅿. AE ◑ E VISA S m
M a la carte 165/320 – **125 rm** 820/1380 Bb.

🏨 **Clima Villenhotel** 🐌, Nussberggasse 2c, ✉ A-1190, ✆ 37 15 16, Telex 115670, « Rest. Bockkeller, vaulted cellar with Tyrolian farmhouse furniture », ≘s, 🏊, 🏊, 🌳 – 🛗 📺 🛁wc ☎ 🚗 🅿 🏋. AE ◑ E VISA R g
M *(dinner only, closed Sunday)* a la carte 160/300 ꕯ – **33 rm** 1300/1700 Bb – 8 apartments.

🏨 **Cottage** without rest, Hasenauerstr. 12, ✉ A-1190, ✆ 31 25 71, Telex 134146 – 🛗 📺 🛁wc 🚿wc ☎ 🏋. AE ◑ E VISA R n
closed 22 to 28 December – **23 rm** 900/1400 Bb.

Hadrigan, Maroltinger Gasse 68, ✉ A-1160, ✆ 92 54 26, Telex 135951 – |≑| ⇔wc ⋔wc ☎ – **47 rm** S k

Gartenhotel Glanzing without rest, Glanzinggasse 23, ✉ A-1190, ✆ 47 42 72 – |≑| TV ⇔wc ☎ . VISA R c
21 rm 450/1100.

Schild without rest, Neustift am Walde 97, ✉ A-1190, ✆ 44 21 91, – |≑| ⇔wc ⋔wc ☎ P – **34 rm.** R f

Sailer, Gersthofer Str. 14, ✉ A-1180, ✆ 47 21 21, , « Kellerstuben » – AE ◐ E VISA
closed Saturday from July to August, Sunday and Bank Holidays – **M** a la carte 190/390 (booking essential). R e

Bürgerhof, Gentzgasse 127, ✉ A-1180, ✆ 47 34 41 – AE ◐ E VISA R a
M a la carte 148/315.

Zauberlehrling, Lazaristengasse 2, ✉ A-1180, ✆ 34 51 35 – AE ◐ VISA R s
closed Sunday, Bank Holidays, 19 July - 17 August and 24 December - 1 January – **M** *(dinner only)* a la carte 215/390.

Römischer Kaiser, Neustift am Walde 2, ✉ A-1190, ✆ 44 11 04, Terraced garden with ≤ Vienna R h

Eckel, Sieveringer Str. 46, ✉ A-1190, ✆ 32 32 18, – AE ◐ R v
closed Sunday, Monday and 10 to 18 August – **M** a la carte 156/385 .

Heurigen and Buschen-Schänken (wine gardens) – (mostly self-service, hot and cold dishes from buffet, prices according to weight of chosen meals, Buschen-Schänken sell their own wines only) :

Oppolzer, Himmelstr. 22, ✉ A-1190, ✆ 32 24 16, « Garden » R r
(booking essential).

Altes Preßhaus, Cobenzlgasse 15, ✉ A-1190, ✆ 32 23 93, , « Old vaulted wine cellar » – AE ◐ E VISA R x
closed until 4 p.m and 5 January - 28 February – **M** a la carte 125/230 (and buffet) .

Fuhrgassl Huber (Wine-garden with Viennese Schrammelmusik), Neustift am Walde 68, ✉ A-1190, ✆ 44 14 05, « Court-terrace » R m

Grinzinger Hauermandl, Cobenzlgasse 20, ✉ A-1190, ✆ 32 30 27, – AE ◐ E VISA. R x
closed until 5.30 p.m. and Sunday – **M** a la carte 146/300 .

Wolff (Buschenschank), Rathstr. 44, ✉ A-1190, ✆ 44 23 35, « Terraced Garden »
closed Monday to Saturday until 2.30 p.m., Sunday until 11.30 a.m. – **M** a la carte 130/300 (buffet) . R m

Grinzinger Weinbottich, Cobenzlgasse 28, ✉ A-1190, ✆ 32 42 37, « Shady garden » – AE ◐ E VISA R x
closed until 5.30 p.m. and Monday – **M** a la carte 141/260 .

Mayer (Buschenschank with Viennese Schrammelmusik), Pfarrplatz 2, ✉ A-1190, ✆ 37 12 87, « Shady garden » – AE VISA R y
closed until 4 p.m.and 20 December - 10 January – **M** a la carte 120/300 (buffet) .

at Perchtoldsdorf ⑤ : 10 km :

Killermann (Heurigen-Lokal), Sonnbergstr. 22, ✉ A-2380 Perchtoldsdorf, ✆ (0222) 86 81 81, –
closed until 6 p.m., Sunday, Monday, 25 to 31 March, 12 August - 1 September and 23 December - 12 January – **M** *(self-service)* a la carte 120/250 (buffet, booking essential).

at Vösendorf S : 11 km by A 2 or B 17 S :

Park-Hotel, Parkallee 2 (recreation centre El Dorado), ✉ A-2334 Vösendorf, ✆ (0222) 13 48 55, , Massage, , , , , (indoor) – |≑| ▤ TV ♿ P . rest
195 rm Bb.

Novotel Wien-Süd, Shopping City Süd, ✉ A-2334 Vösendorf, ✆ (0222) 69 26 01, Telex 134793, – |≑| ▤ rest TV ⇔wc ☎ ♿ P . AE ◐ E VISA
M a la carte 140/335 – **102 rm** 950/1280 Bb.

at Schwechat ③ : 13 km by B 9 :

Jesuitenmühle, Werkbachgasse 30, ✉ A-2320 Schwechat, ✆ (0222) 77 76 14, Telex 135020, – |≑| TV ⇔wc ⋔wc ☎ P . AE
M *(dinner only)* a la carte 150/235 – **62 rm** 590/790 Bb.

Reinisch, Mannswörther Str. 76 (Mannswörth), ✉ A-2323 Schwechat, ✆ (0222) 77 82 18, – ⋔wc ☎ P. VISA
M *(closed Sunday and Bank Holidays)* a la carte 100/210 – **36 rm** 430/700.

at Vienna-Schwechat airport ② : 20 km :

Novotel Wien Airport , ✉ A-1300 Schwechat, ✆ (0222) 77 66 66, Telex 111566, , – |≑| ▤ rest TV ⇔wc ☎ ♿ P (with ▤). AE ◐ E VISA
M a la carte 150/270 – **127 rm** 950/1280 Bb.

at Groß-Enzersdorf E : 16 km, by Erzherzog-Karl-Str. R :

Am Sachsengang, Schloßhofer Str. 60 (B 3), ✉ A-2301 Groß-Enzersdorf, ✆ (02249) 29 01, Telex 13 62 36, « Terrace », Massage, ≘s, 🏊, 🌳 – ⇔wc ☎ ♿ **P** 🏛. AE ⓓ E VISA
closed 22 to 25 December – **M** a la carte 220/350 – **54 rm** 690/970 Bb.

at Baden ⑤ : 28 km by B 17 or A 2 – Spa – ✆ 02252 :

Sauerhof zu Rauhenstein, Weilburgstr. 11, ✉ A-2500 Baden, ✆ 4 12 51, Telex 14334, 🏞, Massage, ⛹, ≘s, 🏊, 🌳, 🎾 – |♦| 📺 ♿ **P** 🏛. AE ⓓ E
M a la carte 220/445 – **87 rm** 900/1500 Bb.

Parkhotel, Kaiser-Franz-Ring 5, ✉ A-2500 Baden, ✆ 4 43 86, Telex 14461, 🏞, Massage, ⛹, ≘s, 🏊, 🌳 – |♦| ⇔wc ☎ 🚗 **P**. ⚘ rest
90 rm Bb.

Gutenbrunn 🔇, Pelzgasse 22, ✉ A-2500 Baden, ✆ 4 81 71, Telex 14304, 🏞, direct entrance to the spa-centre – |♦| ⇔wc ☎ **P** 🏛. AE ⓓ E VISA
M a la carte 180/400 – **80 rm** 870/1350 Bb.

Krainerhütte, Helenental (W : 6 km), ✉ A-2500 Baden, ✆ 4 45 11, Telex 14303, 🏞, ≘s, 🏊, 🌳, 🎾 – |♦| ⇔wc ⋔wc ☎ **P** 🏛. AE ⓓ E
M a la carte 197/460 – **67 rm** 800/1440 Bb.

at motorway A 1 W : 30 km :

Motor-Hotel Grossram, ✉ A-3033 Großram, ✆ (02773) 66 51, Telex 15692 – |♦| 📺 ⇔wc ☎ ♿ **P** 🏛. AE ⓓ E VISA
M a la carte 145/350 – **42 rm** 580/765.

If you find you cannot take up a hotel booking you have made, please let the hotel know immediately.

SALZBURG 5020. Austria 987 ㊳, 426 ⑲ ⑳ – pop. 140 000 – alt. 425 m – ✆ 0662.

See : Site (Stadtbild)★★ Y **K** – Hohensalzburg★★ : ≤★★ (from the Künberg Bastion) Z – St. Peter's Churchyard (Petersfriedhof)★★ Z – St. Peter's Church (Stiftskirche St. Peter)★★ Z – Residenz★★ Z – Natural History Museum (Haus der Natur)★★ Y **M2** – Franciscan's Church (Franziskanerkirche)★ Z **A** – Getreidegasse★ Y – Mirabell Gardens (Mirabellgarten)★ V – Hettwer Bastei★ : ≤★ Y – Castle and the Museum (Burg und Museum)★ : ☼★★ (from Reck-tower)Z **M3** – Mozart's Birthplace (Mozarts Geburtshaus) Y **D**.

Envir. : Road to the Gaisberg (Gaisbergstraße)★★ (≤★) by ① – Untersberg★ by ② : 10 km (with 🚡) – Mondsee★ ① : 28 km (by motorway A 1).

🚗 ✆ 71 54 14 22.

Exhibition Centre (Messegelände), Linke Glanzeile 65, ✆ 3 45 66.

ℹ Tourist Information (Stadtverkehrsbüro), Auerspergstr. 7, ✆ 7 15 11.

ÖAMTC, Alpenstr. 102, ✆ 2 05 01.

Wien 292 ① – Innsbruck 177 ③ – München 140 ③.

Plans on following pages

Salzburg Sheraton Hotel Ⓜ, Auerspergstr. 4, ✆ 79 32 10, Telex 632518, entrace to the spa facilities – |♦| ▤ 📺 ♿ 🏛. AE ⓓ E VISA. ⚘ rest V **s**
Restaurants : – **Mirabell M** a la carte 240/490 – **Bistro M** a la carte 100/350 – **165 rm** 1650/2950 Bb.

Bristol, Marktplatz 4, ✆ 7 35 57, Telex 633337, « Tastefully furnished, collection of pictures » – |♦| ▤ rest 📺. AE ⓓ E VISA Y **a**
closed November - 21 December – **M** a la carte 235/600 – **80 rm** 1230/3450.

Österreichischer Hof, Schwarzstr. 5, ✆ 7 25 41, Telex 633590, « Salzach-side setting, terrace with ≤ old town and castle » – |♦| 📺 🚗 🏛 (with ▤). AE ⓓ E VISA Y **b**
Restaurants : – **Roter Salon M** a la carte 190/490 – **Salzach Grill M** a la carte 115/370 – **120 rm** 980/2530.

Goldener Hirsch, Getreidegasse 37, ✆ 84 14 11, Telex 632967, « 15 C Patrician house, tastefully furnished » – |♦| ▤ rest. AE ⓓ E VISA Y **e**
M a la carte 240/520 – **57 rm** 1500/3700.

Pitter, Rainerstr. 6, ✆ 7 85 71, Telex 633532, 🏞 – |♦| 📺 ⇔wc ⋔wc ☎ 🏛. AE ⓓ E VISA. ⚘ rest V **n**
M a la carte 110/310 – **220 rm** 570/1500.

Europa, Rainerstr. 31, ✆ 7 32 93, Telex 633424, rest. on the 14th floor with ≤ Salzburg and environs – |♦| ▤ rest ⇔wc ⋔wc ☎ **P** 🏛 (with ▤). AE ⓓ E VISA V **b**
M a la carte 140/380 – **104 rm** 820/1570 Bb.

Winkler, Franz-Josef-Str. 7, ✆ 7 35 13, Telex 633961 – |♦| ⇔wc ☎. AE ⓓ E VISA V **f**
M a la carte 150/460 – **103 rm** 810/1800 Bb.

Kasererhof, Alpenstr. 6, ✆ 2 12 65, Telex 633477, 🏞, 🌳 – |♦| 📺 ⇔wc ⋔wc ☎ **P**. AE E VISA by ②
closed February – **M** *(closed Saturday and Sunday)* a la carte 190/400 – **51 rm** 1160/2115 Bb.

SALZBURG

Auerspergstraße .... V 3
Bürglsteinstraße .... X 5
Dreifaltigkeitsgasse .. X 6
Erzabt-Klotz-Str. ..... X 9
Kaiserschützenstr. ... V 14
Nonntaler Hauptstr. .. X 20
Späthgasse .... X 27

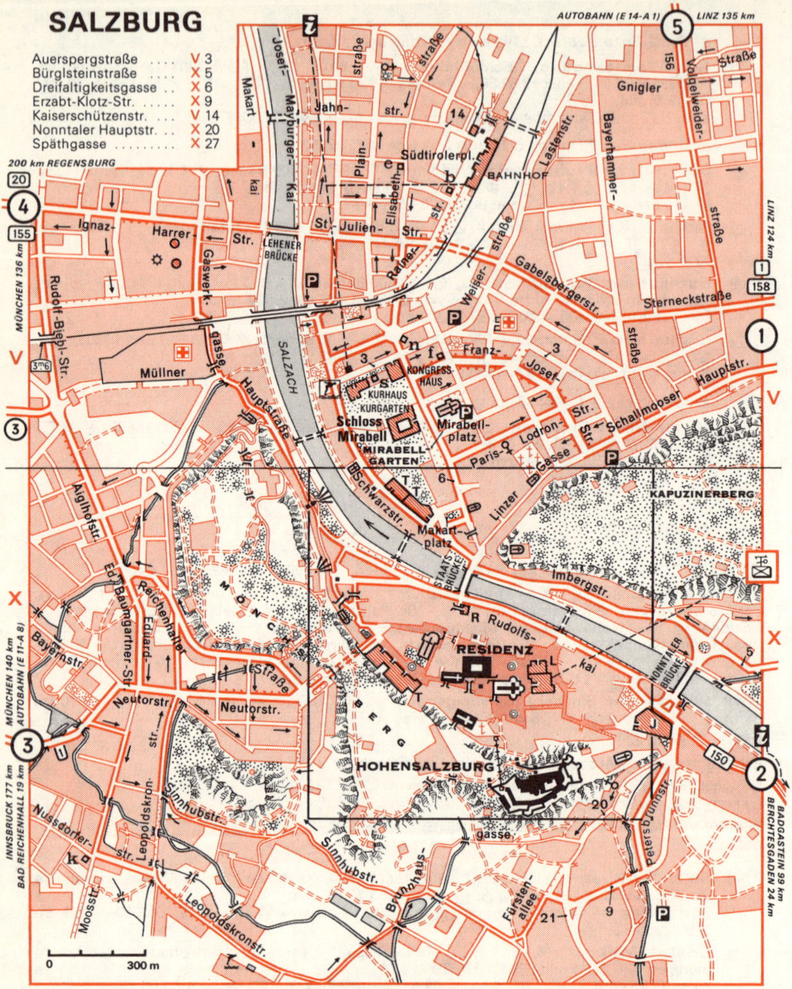

🏨 **Fuggerhof** without rest, Eberhard-Fugger-Str. 9, ✆ 2 04 79, Telex 632533, <, 🏊, 🌳 – 🛁wc 🚿wc ☎ 🚗 🅟 — by Bürglsteinstr. X
closed 23 December - 7 January – **20 rm** 600/1600.

🏨 **Hohenstaufen** without rest, Elisabethstr. 19, ✆ 72 19 30 – 🛗 🛁wc 🚿wc ☎ 🚗. AE ⓓ E VISA — V e
28 rm 620/1290.

🏨 **Schaffenrath**, Alpenstr. 115, ✆ 2 31 53, Telex 633207 – 🛗 TV 🛁wc 🚿wc ☎ 🅟 🏃. AE ⓓ E VISA — by ②
M a la carte 110/270 – **50 rm** 550/1250.

🏨 Elefant 🐘, Sigmund-Haffner-Gasse 4, ✆ 4 33 97, Telex 632725 – 🛗 🛁wc 🚿wc ☎
36 rm. — Y f

🏨 **Weiße Taube** without rest, Kaigasse 9, ✆ 84 24 04, Telex 633065 – 🛗 🛁wc 🚿wc ☎. AE ⓓ E VISA. 🐕 — Z r
30 rm 380/1220.

🏨 **Nußdorfer Hof** without rest, Moosstr. 36, ✆ 45 22 40, Telex 632515, 🏊, 🏊 (heated), 🌳, 🎾 – 🛗 🛁wc 🚿wc ☎ 🚗 🅟. AE E VISA — X k
closed February – **35 rm** 540/1040.

XX **Café Winkler**, Mönchsberg 32 (access by lift, 15 A.S.), ☎ 4 12 15/84 12 15, < Salzburg, « Modern café-rest. on the Mönchsberg, terraces » – . AE ⓓ E VISA Y
closed Monday from September to July – **M** a la carte 220/450.

XX **K u. K Restaurant am Waagplatz**, Waagplatz 2, ☎ 4 21 56, , « Medieval dinner with period performance in the Freysauff-Keller (by arrangement) » – AE ⓓ E VISA
closed 3 to 23 February – **M** a la carte 125/365 (booking essential) . Z **h**

XX **Zum Mohren**, Judengasse 9, ☎ 4 23 87/84 23 87 Y **g**
closed Sunday, Bank Holidays and November – **M** a la carte 130/310 (booking essential).

X **Purzelbaum** (Rest. in Bistro-style), Zugallistr. 7, ☎ 2 78 43 – Ⓟ. AE ⓓ E VISA.
closed Sunday from September to May – **M** a la carte 120/430. Z **e**

***at Salzburg-Aigen* 5026** by Bürglsteinstr. X :

Doktorwirt, Glaser Str. 9, ☎ 2 29 73, Telex 632938, beer-garden, , (heated), – wc wc ☎ Ⓟ. AE E VISA
closed November - 8 December – **M** *(closed Monday)* a la carte 100/230 – **39 rm** 380/850.

***at Salzburg-Flughafen* 5035** by ③ :

Flughafen-Hotel, Innsbrucker Bundesstr. 105, ☎ 85 02 12, Telex 633671 – wc ☎ Ⓟ . AE ⓓ E VISA
M a la carte 155/380 – **14 rm** 405/980.

at Salzburg-Liefering by ④ :

Brandstätter, Münchner Bundesstr. 69, ☎ 3 45 35, beer-garden, , – wc wc ☎ Ⓟ . AE
closed 23 December - 13 January – **M** a la carte 165/410 – **36 rm** 550/1000 Bb.

at Salzburg-Maria Plain **5028** by Plainstr. V :

Maria Plain (17 C inn), Plainbergweg 33, 5 07 01, Telex 632801, « Garden with < » – wc
closed 8 January - 14 February – **M** *(closed Tuesday dinner and Wednesday from October to April)* a la carte 90/240 – **40 rm** 385/960.

at Salzburg-Parsch by Bürglsteinstr. X :

Fondachhof, Gaisbergstr. 46, 2 09 06, Telex 632519, <, « 18 C Manor house in a park », (heated), – VISA
15 March - October – (rest. for residents only) – **30 rm** 800/2400.

Cottage, Joseph-Messner-Str. 12, 2 45 71, Telex 632011, Massage, – wc E VISA
M a la carte 170/340 – **115 rm** 900/1840 Bb.

Haus Ingeborg, Sonnleitenweg 9, 2 17 49, Telex 631141, < town and Hohensalzburg, – wc
season only – (rest. for residents only) – **11 rm**.

on the Heuberg NE : 3 km by ① – alt. 565 m :

Schöne Aussiht, 65023 Salzburg, (0662) 7 82 26, « Garden with < Salzburg and Alps », (heated), – wc wc
March - October – **M** a la carte 130/350 – **30 rm** 540/950 Bb.

on the Gaisberg by ① :

Kobenzl, Judenbergalpe (E : 9 km alt. 750 m), 5020 Salzburg, (0662) 2 17 76, Telex 633833, « Beautiful panoramic-location with < Salzburg and Alps », Massage, – rest
end March - mid November – **M** a la carte 215/505 – **35 rm** 900/3200 Bb.

Berghotel Zistel-Alm, (E : 12 km alt. 1 001 m), 5026 Salzburg-Aigen, (0662) 2 01 04, < Alps, summer-toboggan-slide – wc wc E VISA
closed November - 15 December – **M** a la carte 95/280 – **24 rm** 210/790 – 6 apartments 1200.

at Anif **5081** by ② : 7 km :

Romantik-Hotel Schloßwirt (17 C inn with Biedermeier furniture), (06246) 21 75, Telex 631169, « Garden », – wc wc E VISA
closed February – **M** a la carte 180/370 – **32 rm** 490/1090 Bb.

Friesacher, (06246) 20 75, Telex 632943, « Garden », – wc wc
M *(closed Wednesday from October to June)* a la carte 100/350 – **70 rm** 450/840.

at Hof **5322** by ① : 20 km :

Schloß Fuschl (former 15C hunting seat with 3 annexes), (06229) 25 30, <, Massage, – E VISA. rest
M a la carte 310/560 (booking essential) – **70 rm** 1000/3800.

Jagdhof am Fuschlsee, (06229) 3 72, <, « Hunting museum », – wc wc E VISA
M a la carte 120/330 – **40 rm** 450/900.

at Mondsee **5310** ① : 28 km (by motorway A 1) :

Weißes Kreuz, Herzog-Odilo-Str. 25, (06232) 22 54, « Garden » – wc wc
closed 10 November - 10 December – **M** *(closed Wednesday from September to June)* a la carte 230/490 (booking essential) – **10 rm** 400/1200.

XXX **Plomberg-Eschlböck** with rm, NE : 5 km, (06232) 29 12, <, – wc E VISA
M *(closed Monday November - mid March)* a la carte 270/550 (booking essential) – **11 rm** 480/840.

Benelux

Belgium

Brussels
Antwerp
Bruges

Luxembourg

Netherlands

Amsterdam
The Hague
Rotterdam

PRACTICAL INFORMATION

LOCAL CURRENCY

Belgian Franc : 100 F = 1.98 US $ (Jan. 86) can also be used in Luxembourg
Dutch Florin : 100 Fl. = 36.02 US $ (Jan. 86)

TOURIST INFORMATION

In Belgium : The B.B.B. Tourist House, rue du Marché-aux-Herbes 61, Brussels, open from 9am to 6pm (Sundays 1 to 5pm) in winter, and 9am to 8pm (weekends 9am to 7pm) in Summer.
In the Netherlands : Offices in Amsterdam open daily from 9am to 11.30pm ; in Den Haag (Scheveningen) weekdays from 9am to 9pm, Sundays 9am to 6pm, and in Rotterdam weekdays 9am to 6pm, Sundays 10am to 6pm.

FOREIGN EXCHANGE

In Belgium, banks close at 3.30pm and weekends ; **in the Netherlands,** banks close at 5.00pm and weekends, Schiphol Airport exchange offices open daily from 6.30am to 11.30pm.

TRANSPORT

Taxis : may be hailed in the street, found day and night at taxi ranks or called by telephone.
Bus, tramway : practical for long and short distances and good for sightseeing.

POSTAL SERVICES

Post offices open Monday to Friday from 9am to 5pm in Benelux.

SHOPPING

Shops and boutiques are generally open from 8am to 7pm in Belgium and Luxembourg, and from 9am to 6pm in the Netherlands. The main shopping areas are :
in Brussels : Rue Neuve, Porte de Namur, Avenue Louise - Second-hand goods and antiques : Brussels antique market on Saturday from 9am to 3pm, and Sunday from 9am to 1pm (around place du Grand-Sablon) - Flower market (Grand-Place) on Sunday morning.
in Antwerp : Bird Market : Sunday 8.30am to 1pm - Antwerp diamond quarter.
in Bruges : Calashes on the Market Place for shopping and town sightseeing.
in Amsterdam : Kalverstraat, Leidsestraat, Nieuwendijk, P.C. Hoofstraat and Utrechtsestraat. Second-hand goods and antiques. Amsterdam Flea Market (near Waterlooplein).
in Den Haag : Hoogstraat, Korte Poten, Paleispromenade, De Passage and Spuistraat.
in Rotterdam : Binnenweg, Hoogstraat, Karel Doormanstraat, Lijnbaan and Stadhuisplein.

BREAKDOWN SERVICE

RACB : rue d'Arlon 53, Brussels ✆ (02) 230 08 68 and **TCB** : rue de la Loi 44, Brussels ✆ (02) 233 22 11 operate a 24 hour breakdown service. In the Netherlands, **ANWB**-Wegenwacht also offer 24 hour assistance.

TIPPING

In Benelux, prices include service and taxes. You may choose to leave a tip if you wish but there is no obligation to do so.

SPEED LIMITS

In Belgium and Luxembourg, the maximum speed limits are 120 km/h-74 mph on motorways and dual carriageways, 90 km/h-56 mph on all other roads and 60 km/h-37 mph in built-up areas. In the Netherlands, 100 km/h-62 mph on motorways and "autowegen", 80 km/h-50 mph on other roads and 50 km/h-31 mph in built-up areas.

SEAT BELTS

In each country, the wearing of seat belts is compulsory.

BRUSSELS

SIGHTS

See : Market Square★★★ (Grand-Place) LZ – Manneken Pis★★ KZ – Rue des Bouchers LZ – St. Michael's Cathedral★★ FU – Place du Grand Sablon★ and the Church of Notre-Dame du Sablon★ FV **D** – Anderlecht : Erasmus's House★.

Museums : Old Masters Gallery★★★ (Musée d'Art ancien : Brueghel) FV – Royal museum of Art and History★★★ (antiques, Belgian decorative art) – Musical Instruments★★ FV **M18**.

Env. Forest of Soignes★★ – Tervuren : Royal Museum of Central Africa★ ⑥ : 13 km – Beersel : Castle★ S : 11 km – Gaasbeek : estate and castle★ SW : 12 km by rue de Lennick – Meise : Bouchout Estate★(Domaine de Bouchout) : Plant Palace★★ by ① : 13 km – Grimbergen : Confessional★ in the church of St. Servais (St. Servaaskerk) by ① : 18 km – Vilvoorde : Choir stalls★ of Our Lady's Church (O.L. Vrouwkerk).

BRUSSELS **(Bruxelles - Brussel) 1000** Brabant 213 ⑱ and 409 ⑬ – Pop. 982 434 agglomeration – ☎ 02.

Château de Ravenstein at Tervuren by ⑥ : 13 km ✆ 7675801.

National NE : 12 km ✆ 7518080 – **Air Terminal :** Air Terminus, r. du Cardinal-Mercier 35 LZ ✆ 5119060.

✆ 2186050 ext. 4106.

r. du Marché-aux-Herbes 61 ✆ 5138940 – Tourist Association of the Province, r. Marché-aux-Herbes 61 ✆ 5130750.

Paris 308 ⑨ – Amsterdam 204 ① – Düsseldorf 222 ⑤ – Lille 116 ⑫ – Luxembourg 219 ⑦.

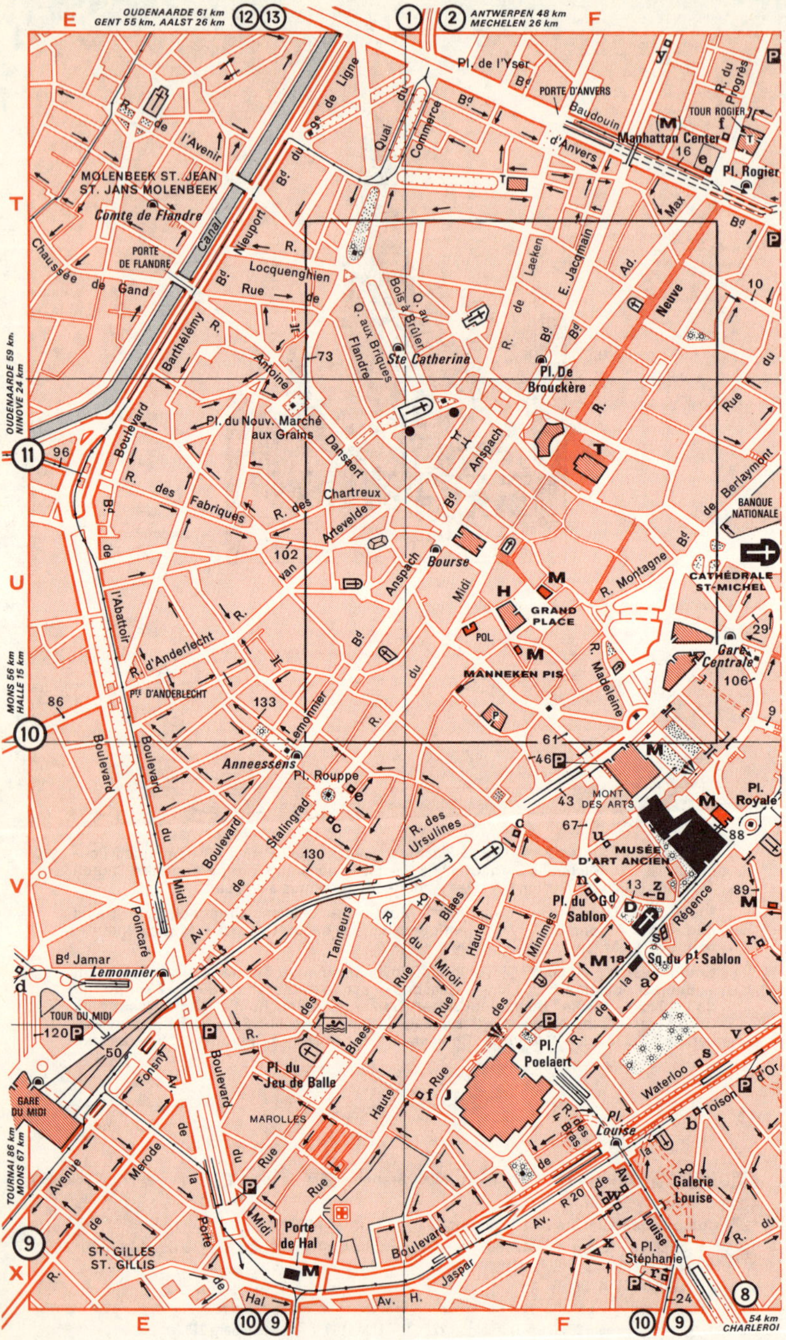
OUDENAARDE 61 km
GENT 55 km. AALST 26 km
ANTWERPEN 48 km
MECHELEN 26 km
E
F
T
U
V
X
Pl. de l'Yser
PORTE D'ANVERS
Bd Baudouin
d'Anvers
TOUR ROGIER
Manhattan Center
Pl. Rogier
R. du Progrès
Max
MOLENBEEK ST. JEAN
ST. JANS MOLENBEEK
Comte de Flandre
PORTE DE FLANDRE
Chaussée de Gand
Canal
l'Avenir
Bd de Nieuport
Locquenghien
Rue de
Quai du Commerce
Bd du 9e de Ligne
Q. aux Briques
Q. au Bois à Brûler
Flandre
Ste Catherine
R. de Laeken
Bd E. Jacqmain
Bd Ad.
Neuve
Pl. De Brouckère
Barthélemy
Antoine
OUDENAARDE 59 km
NINOVE 24 km
Pl. du Nouv. Marché aux Grains
Dansaert
Chartreux
Artevelde
Anspach
Bourse
Bd Anspach
Boulevard
R. des Fabriques
R. des
van
Bd de Berlaymont
BANQUE NATIONALE
CATHÉDRALE ST-MICHEL
R. Montagne
GRAND PLACE
POL
MANNEKEN PIS
R. Madeleine
Gare Centrale
Bd de l'Abattoir
R. d'Anderlecht
Pte D'ANDERLECHT
MONS 56 km
HALLE 15 km
Lemonnier
Anneessens
Pl. Rouppe
R. du Midi
R. des Ursulines
MONT DES ARTS
MUSÉE D'ART ANCIEN
Pl. Royale
Pl. du Gd Sablon
Sq. du Pt Sablon
Régence
Boulevard du Midi
Boulevard de Stalingrad
Av. de
Poincaré
Bd Jamar
Lemonnier
TOUR DU MIDI
GARE DU MIDI
R. des Tanneurs
R. du Miroir
Rue Haute
Rue Blaes
Minimes
R. des
R. de la
Pl. Poelaert
Waterloo
Toison d'Or
Pl. Louise
R. des 4 Bras
Galerie Louise
Pl. du Jeu de Balle
MAROLLES
Fonsny
Av. de la Porte de Hal
Av. Merode
Avenue de
Bd du Midi
Porte de Hal
Boulevard
Jaspar
Av. H.
Hal
Av. Louise
Pl. Stéphanie
R. du
ST. GILLES
ST. GILLIS
TOURNAI 86 km
MONS 67 km
54 km
CHARLEROI

BRUXELLES BRUSSEL CENTRE

Baron-Horta (R.)	FU	9
Blanchisserie (R. de la)	FT	10
Bodenbroek (R.)	FV	13
Boulevard (Av. du)	FT	16
Charleroi (Chaussée de)	FX	24
Colonies (R. des)	FGU	29
Empereur (Bd de l')	FV	43
Ernest-Solvay (R.)	GX	45
Escalier (R. de l')	FV	46
Esplanade (R. de l')	GV	47
Europe (Bd de l')	EX	50
Hôpital (R. de l')	FUV	61
Joseph-Lebeau (R.)	FV	67
Léon-Lepage (R.)	ET	73
Mons (Chée de)	EU	86
Musée (R. du)	FV	88
Namur (R. de)	FGV	89

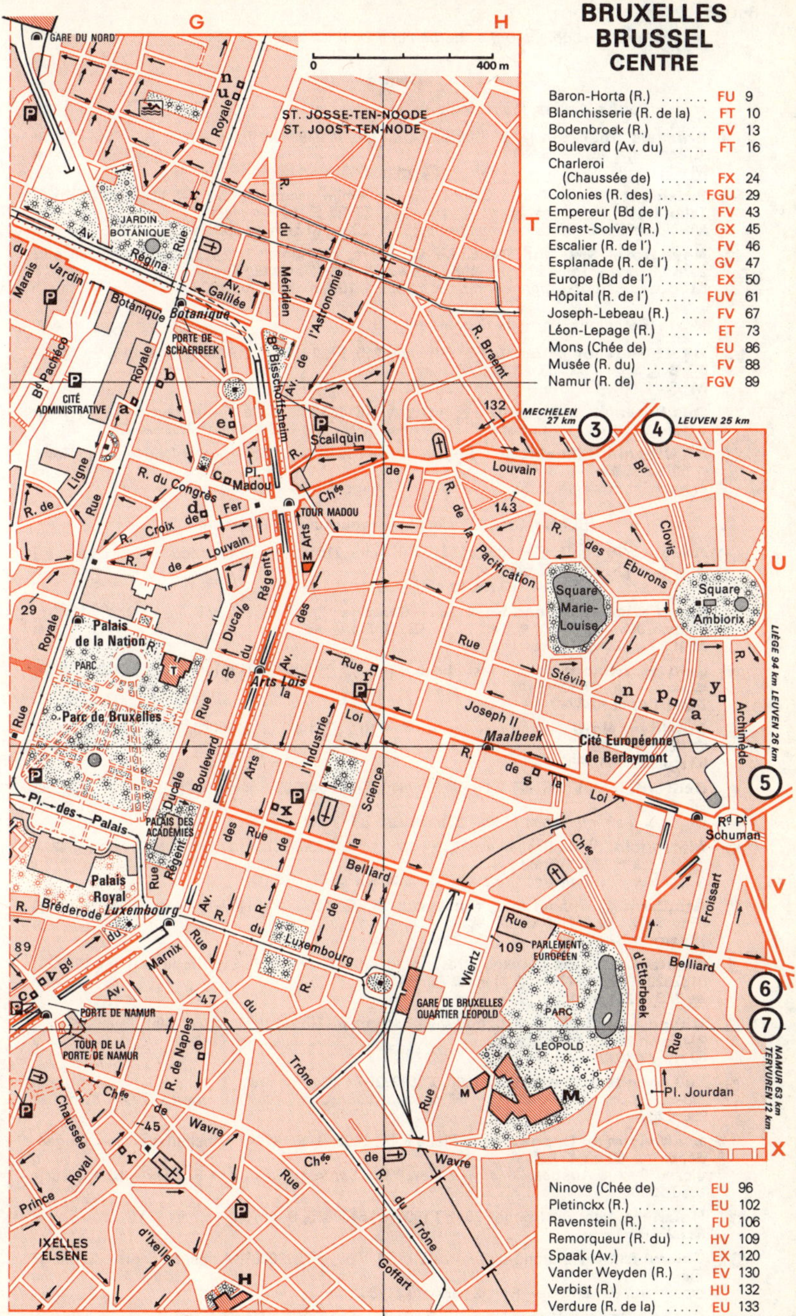

Ninove (Chée de)	EU	96
Pletinckx (R.)	EU	102
Ravenstein (R.)	FU	106
Remorqueur (R. du)	HV	109
Spaak (Av.)	EX	120
Vander Weyden (R.)	EV	130
Verbist (R.)	HU	132
Verdure (R. de la)	EU	133
Willems (R.)	HU	143

Room prices are subject to the addition of a local tax of 6%

Centre

North (Porte d'Anvers, Place Rogier) FT :

Brussels-Sheraton [M], pl. Rogier 3, ✉ 1210, ☎ 2193400, Telex 26887, – . AE E VISA — FT **e**
M a la carte 630/1255 – 340 – **483 rm** and **43** apartments 4400/4900.

President World Trade Center [M], bd Emile Jacqmain 180, ✉ 1210, ☎ 2172020, Telex 21066 – rest – . AE E VISA. rest — FT **y**
M *(closed Saturday lunch and Sunday)* 950/1200 – **312 rm** 3900/4800.

New Hotel Siru and Rest. Le Couvert, pl. Rogier 1, ✉ 1210, ☎ 2177580 and 2178308 (rest.), Telex 21722 – wc wc . AE E VISA. — FT **f**
M *(closed Saturday dinner and Sunday)* 995 – **100 rm** 2425/3190.

North (Botanique, Porte de Schaerbeek) GHT :

Hyatt Regency Brussels [M], r. Royale 250, ✉ 1210, ☎ 2194640, Telex 61871 – – . AE VISA. rest — GT **r**
M 935/1300 – 375 – **315 rm** 6310/7810.

Den Botaniek, r. Royale 328, ✉ 1210, ☎ 2184838, , « Garden-terrace » — GT **n**
closed Saturday, Sunday and 25 December-3 January – **M** a la carte 1220/2000.

De Ultieme Hallucinatie r. Royale 316, ✉ 1210, ☎ 2170614, « Art Nouveau Interior » – AE E VISA. — GT **u**
closed Saturday lunch, Sunday and 1 to 17 August – **M** 950/1650.

Town Centre (Bourse, Grand'Place, Pl. de Brouckère, Ste-Catherine)

Amigo, r. Amigo 1, ✉ 1000, ☎ 5115910, Telex 21618, « Tasteful decor » – rest – . AE E VISA. rest — KZ **h**
M a la carte 720/1200 – **183 rm** 4200/4900.

Royal Windsor H. and Rest. les 4 Saisons [M], r. Duquesnoy 5, ✉ 1000, ☎ 5114215, Telex 62905 – – . AE E VISA. — LZ **k**
M 1090 – **300 rm** 5840/6850.

Jolly H. Atlanta without rest., bd A.-Max 7, ✉ 1000, ☎ 2170120, Telex 21475 – – . AE E VISA — LY **a**
242 rm 3570/5290.

Président Nord without rest., bd A.-Max 107, ✉ 1000, ☎ 2190060, Telex 61417 – . AE E VISA — LY **b**
63 rm 2460/2880.

Bedford, r. Midi 135, ✉ 1000, ☎ 5127840, Telex 24059 – rest – . AE E VISA. — KZ **r**
M *(closed after 8.30 p.m.)* 700 – **275 rm** 2725/3700.

Métropole, pl. de Brouckère 31, ✉ 1000, ☎ 2172300, Telex 21234 – rest – . AE E VISA. rest — LY **r**
M *(closed Saturday and Sunday)* 850 – **320 rm** 2500/4700.

Arenberg [M] without rest., r. d'Assaut 15, ✉ 1000, ☎ 5110770, Telex 25660 – wc wc . AE E VISA. — LZ **p**
155 rm 3400.

Sainte-Catherine [M] without rest., r. Joseph Plateau 2 (Pl. Ste-Catherine), ✉ 1000, ☎ 5137620, Telex 22476 – wc . VISA — KY **s**
160 – **234 rm** 1650/1920.

Queen Anne without rest., bd Émile-Jacqmain 110, ✉ 1000, ☎ 2171600, Telex 22676 – wc . AE E VISA — LY **y**
60 rm 1910.

La Légende, r. Etuve 33, ✉ 1000, ☎ 5128290 – wc — KZ **p**
closed 12 December-January – **M** *(closed Wednesday)* a la carte approx. 700 – **31 rm** 990/1260.

Maison du Cygne, Grand'Place 9, ✉ 1000, ☎ 5118244, « Ancient mansion, elegant decor » – AE E VISA. — LZ **q**
closed 9 to 18 August, Christmas, New Year, Saturday lunch and Sunday – **M** a la carte 1350/2380.

Huîtrière, quai aux Briques 20, ✉ 1000, ☎ 5120866, Seafood – AE E VISA — KY **v**
M 925/1350.

Cheval Marin, Marché-aux-Porcs 25, ✉ 1000, ☎ 5130287, Ancient decor – AE E VISA — KY **u**
closed Sunday dinner – **M** a la carte 930/1480.

Café de Paris, r. Vierge Noire 12, ✉ 1000, ☎ 5123940 – AE E VISA — KY **x**
closed Saturday lunch, Sunday and 20 July-17 August – **M** 1275/1675.

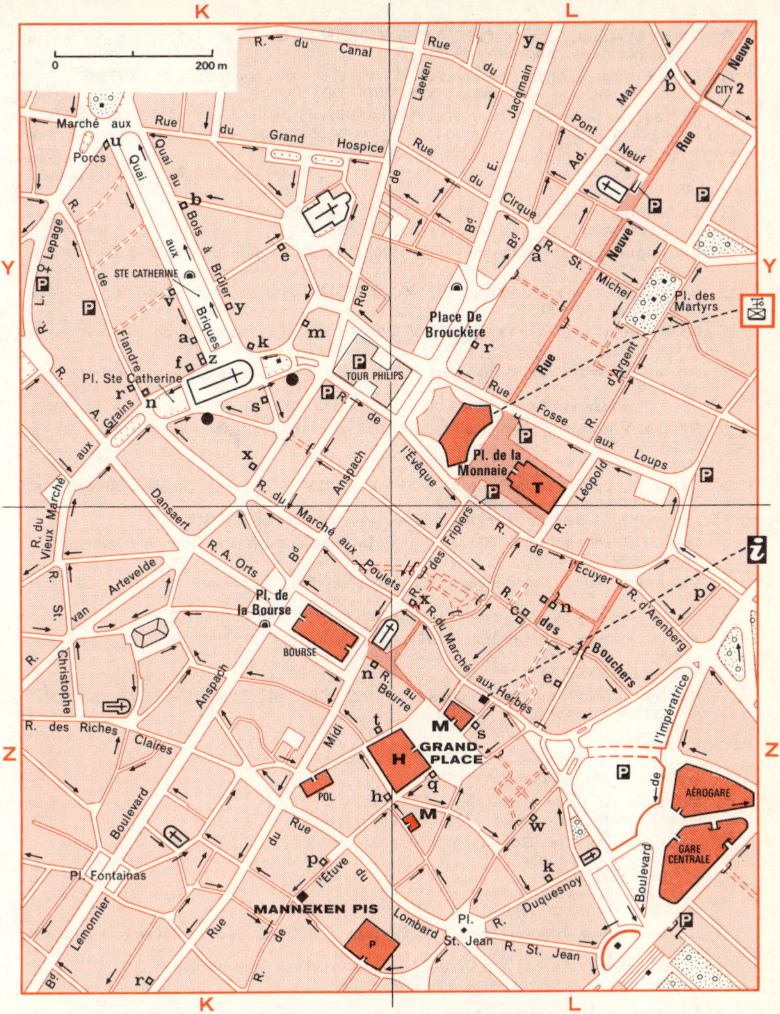

XX **Filet de Boeuf,** r. Harengs 8, ✉ 1000, ☎ 5119559, « Old Brussels decor » – AE ⓓ E VISA – *closed Saturday and Sunday* – **M** a la carte 1250/1700 LZ **s**

XX ✿ **Sirène d'Or** (Van Duuren), pl. Ste-Catherine 1 a, ✉ 1000, ☎ 5135198 – AE ⓓ VISA
closed Sunday, Monday, July, 24, 25, 31 December and 1 January – **M** a la carte 1300/2000
Spec. Fricassée de sole et ris de veau aux jets de houblon (March-April), Bouillabaisse, Turbot au plat, poivrade de bigorneaux. KY **n**

XX ✿ **La Belle Maraîchère** (Devreker), pl. Ste-Catherine 11, ✉ 1000, ☎ 5129759 – AE ⓓ E VISA KY **f**
closed Wednesday and Thursday – **M** a la carte 1150/1700
Spec. Soupe de poissons, Fricassée de homard aux petits légumes, Turbot grillé.

XX **Bon Vieux Temps,** 1st floor, r. Marché-aux-Herbes 12, ✉ 1000, ☎ 2181546, « Ancient Brussels residence » – AE ⓓ E LZ **x**
closed Saturday lunch, Sunday and 15 July-15 August – **M** 675/1095.

XX **Tête d'Or,** r. Tête d'Or 9, ✉ 1000, ☎ 5110201, « Old Brussels decor » – AE ⓓ E VISA
closed Saturday, Sunday and 18 July-17 August – **M** a la carte 1250/1950. KZ **t**

XX **Éperon d'Or,** r. Éperonniers 8, ✉ 1000, ☎ 5125239 – AE ⓓ E VISA LZ **w**
closed Saturday, Sunday and 21 July-14 August – **M** 500/1000.

XX **Serge et Anne,** r. Peuplier 23, ✉ 1000, ℘ 2181662 – AE ⓓ KY e
closed Wednesday and July – **M** 950/1200.

XX **Chez François,** quai aux Briques 2, ✉ 1000, ℘ 5116089, Seafood – AE ⓓ E VISA
closed Monday and June – **M** a la carte 1070/1890. KY z

XX **Rôtiss. Au Cochon d'Or,** quai au Bois-à-Brûler 15, ✉ 1000, ℘ 2180771 – AE ⓓ E VISA
closed Sunday dinner, Monday and 15 August-14 September – **M** 600/975. KY y

XX **L'Ami Michel,** pl. du Samedi 17, ✉ 1000, ℘ 2175377 – AE E KY m
closed Saturday lunch, Sunday, Monday and 21 July-14 August – **M** a la carte approx. 1400.

XX **Le Chablis,** r.Flandre 6, ✉ 1000, ℘ 5124631 – AE ⓓ E VISA KY r
closed Saturday lunch and Sunday – **M** 675/1590.

XX **Les Algues,** pl. Ste-Catherine 15, ✉ 1000, ℘ 2179012, Seafood – AE ⓓ E VISA KY k
M a la carte 1100/1500.

XX **Crustacés,** quai aux Briques 8, ✉ 1000, ℘ 5131493, Seafood – AE ⓓ E VISA KY a
M a la carte 850/1530.

XX **La Marée,** r. au Beurre 19, ✉ 1000, ℘ 5119444, Seafood – AE ⓓ E VISA KZ n
M 695/1500.

X **Armes de Bruxelles,** r. Bouchers 13, ✉ 1000, ℘ 5115598, Brussels atmosphere – AE ⓓ E VISA LZ c
closed Monday and 1 to 15 June – **M** a la carte 700/1380.

X **Rôtiss. Vincent,** r. Dominicains 8, ✉ 1000, ℘ 5112302, Brussels atmosphere – AE ⓓ E VISA LZ n
closed August – **M** a la carte 640/1260.

X **Passage,** Galerie de la Reine 30, ✉ 1000, ℘ 5123731, Pub rest., Brussels atmosphere, Open until midnight – AE ⓓ E VISA LZ e
closed Wednesday and Thursday in June-July – **M** a la carte 620/1150.

X **Léon,** r. Bouchers 18, ✉ 1000, ℘ 5111415, Brussels atmosphere, Open until midnight
M a la carte 600/1130. LZ c

X **Ogenblik,** Galerie des Princes 1, ✉ 1000, ℘ 5116151, Open until midnight – AE ⓓ E VISA LZ n
closed Sunday – **M** *(dinner only on Bank Holidays)* a la carte 1150/1760.

X **Marie-Joseph,** quai au Bois-à-Brûler 47, ✉ 1000, ℘ 2180596, Seafood, Open until midnight – AE ⓓ VISA KY b
M a la carte 1060/1560.

X **Rugbyman Nr 1,** quai aux Briques 4, ✉ 1000, ℘ 5125640, Shellfish – ▤. AE ⓓ E VISA
M a la carte 1100/1950. KY z

Centre South

Quartier Place Rouppe, Lemonnier EV :

🏨 **Windsor** without rest., pl. Rouppe 13, ✉ 1000, ℘ 5112014 – |‡| EV e
closed Christmas-New Year – **24 rm** ☕ 1300/1705.

XXX ✿✿✿ **Comme Chez Soi** (Wynants), pl. Rouppe 23, ✉ 1000, ℘ 5122921 – ▤. AE ⓓ
closed Sunday, Monday, 22 June-28 July and Christmas-New Year – **M** (booking essential) a la carte 1700/2250 EV c
Spec. Les mousses Wynants, Suprême de bar à la vapeur, Perdreau roti à la feuille de vigne (Sept.-Oct.), Noisettes de chevreuil à la royale au cassis (Oct.-Nov.).

XXX ✿ **Da Gesuino** (Todde), r. Fiennes 3, ✉ 1070, ℘ 5215163, Elegant, Italian rest. – AE ⓓ E EV d
closed Saturday, Sunday and 18 July-17 August – **M** a la carte 1090/1890
Spec. Assagi di Pasta, Sole Florentino, Agneau de lait (Dec.-May).

Quartier Sablon et Place Royale FV :

XXX ✿✿ **L'Écailler du Palais Royal,** r. Bodenbroek 18, ✉ 1000, ℘ 5128751, Seafood – AE ⓓ E VISA FV z
closed Sunday, Bank Holidays and 28 July-29 August – **M** (booking essential) a la carte 1500/2100
Spec. Banc d'huîtres et coquillages (Sept.-April), Raviolis de homard au curry léger, Turbot à l'anis vert et aubergine.

XXX **Les Gourmands,** pl. Grand Sablon 39a (village gourmand), ✉ 1000, ℘ 5136749 – ▤. AE ⓓ E VISA FV n
closed Saturday lunch and Monday – **M** a la carte 1600/2210.

XXX **Debussy,** pl. Petit Sablon 2, ✉ 1000, ℘ 5128041 – AE ⓓ E VISA FV s
closed Saturday lunch, Sunday, Bank Holidays, 5 July-5 August and 22 to 28 December – **M** a la carte 1180/2120.

XXX **En Provence,** pl. Petit-Sablon 1, ✉ 1000, ℘ 5111208, Rustic – ▤. AE ⓓ E VISA. ✻
closed 13 July-11 August – **M** a la carte 1400/2050. FV s

XX **Au Duc d'Arenberg,** pl. Petit-Sablon 9, ✉ 1000, ℘ 5111475, Rustic Pub-rest., Open until midnight – AE ⓓ VISA FV a
closed Sunday – **M** a la carte 1490/2500.

X ❀ **Trente rue de la Paille** (Martiny), r. Paille 30, ✉ 1000, ✆ 5120715 – AE ◑ E VISA
closed Saturday lunch, Sunday, Bank Holidays, July and 21 December-1 January – **M** a la carte 1130/1660 FV **u**
Spec. Bâtonnets de lotte fumés à la minute, aux pleurottes et beurre blanc ciboulette, Ris de veau poêlé sauce au vinaigre de champagne, Panaché de fondants noir et blanc.

X **Les Années Folles,** r. Haute 17, ✉ 1000, ✆ 5135858 – AE ◑ E VISA FV **c**
closed Saturday lunch and Sunday – **M** 1100/1400.

X **Au Vieux Saint-Martin,** Grand Sablon 38, ✉ 1000, ✆ 5126476, Pub-rest., Open until midnight FV **n**
M a la carte 670/1130.

X **J. et B.,** r. Baudet 5, ✉ 1000, ✆ 5120484, Open until 11 p.m. – AE ◑ E VISA FV **r**
closed Saturday lunch, Sunday and 20 July-4 August – **M** 675/995.

Quartier Porte Louise, Palais Justice, Place Stéphanie FX :

Hilton International Brussels M, bd Waterloo 38, ✉ 1000, ✆ 5138877, Telex 22744, « Rest. Plein Ciel on 27th floor with ≤ of town » – |‡| ☰ TV ☎ ♿ ⇔ – 🏛. AE ◑ E VISA. ✻ rest FX **s**
M (**Maison du Boeuf**) a la carte 1190/2300 – ☕ 450 – **369 rm** 5800/7000.

Ramada-Brussels M, chaussée de Charleroi 38, ✉ 1060, ✆ 5393000, Telex 25539 – |‡| ☰ TV ☎ – 🏛. AE ◑ E VISA
M *(closed Sunday)* a la carte 1330/1800 – ☕ 390 – **201 rm** 3440/4200.

Ascot without rest., pl. Loix 1, ✉ 1060, ✆ 5388835, Telex 25010 – |‡| ☎. AE ◑ E VISA
58 rm ☕ 1720/2150.

Delta M without rest., chaussée de Charleroi 17, ✉ 1060, ✆ 5390160, Telex 63225 – |‡| TV ⛀wc ⛆wc ☎ ⇔ – 🏛. AE ◑ E VISA FX **r**
253 rm ☕ 2800/3500.

Diplomat M without rest., r. Jean-Stas 32, ✉ 1060, ✆ 5374250, Telex 61012 – |‡| TV ⛀wc ☎. AE ◑ E VISA FX **x**
68 rm ☕ 2800/3500.

La Cascade without rest., r. Source 14, ✉ 1060, ✆ 5388830, Telex 26637 – |‡| TV ⛀wc ☎ ⇔ – 🏛. AE ◑ E VISA. ✻
42 rm ☕ 2150/2670.

XXXXX ❀❀ **Carlton,** bd Waterloo 28, ✉ 1000, ✆ 5137831, « Luxurious decor, fountain, visible wine cellar » – ☰. AE ◑ E VISA FX **v**
closed Saturday lunch, Sunday and mid July-mid August – **M** 1775/2775
Spec. Hure marinée à la rogue, Saumon au sang, Canard Louise Passard.

XX **La Closerie,** r. Jourdan 15, ✉ 1060, ✆ 5381448 – AE ◑ E VISA. ✻ FX **w**
closed Saturday and Sunday – **M** a la carte 1180/1480.

XX **Al Piccolo Mondo,** r. Jourdan 19, ✉ 1060, ✆ 5388794, Italian rest., Open until 1 a.m. – AE ◑ E VISA FX **w**
M a la carte 1020/1540.

XX **Meo Patacca,** r. Jourdan 20, ✉ 1060, ✆ 5381546, Italian rest. – AE ◑ E VISA FX **w**
closed Sunday – **M** a la carte 840/1400.

X ❀ **Au Beurre Blanc,** r. Faucon 2a, ✉ 1000, ✆ 5130111 – AE ◑ E FX **f**
closed 15 to 30 August, Christmas-New Year, Saturday lunch and Sunday – **M** a la carte 750/1500.

Quartier Porte de Namur, Luxembourg, Palais des Académies GV :

Chambord without rest., r. Namur 8, ✉ 1000, ✆ 5134119, Telex 20373 – |‡| TV ⛀wc ☎. AE ◑ E VISA. ✻ GV **v**
69 rm ☕ 2525/3500.

XXX **Bernard,** 1st floor, r. Namur 93, ✉ 1000, ✆ 5128821, Seafood – AE ◑ GV **c**
closed Sunday, Monday dinner and July – **M** a la carte 1090/2100.

XX **Marie-José "Chez Callens"** with rm, r. Commerce 73, ✉ 1040, ✆ 5120843 – |‡| ⛀wc ⛆wc ☎. AE ◑ E VISA. ✻ rest GV **x**
M *(closed Saturday dinner and Sunday)* a la carte 710/1630 – **17 rm** ☕ 1400/1600.

Quartier Porte de Namur (côté Tour), Quartier St. Boniface GX :

XX **Charles-Joseph,** r. E. Solvay 9, ✉ 1050, ✆ 5134390 – AE ◑ E VISA GX **r**
closed Saturday lunch, Sunday and 19 July-17 August – **M** 850/1750.

XX **Old Mario,** r. Alsace Lorraine 44, ✉ 1050, ✆ 5116161, Italian rest. – Ⓟ. AE ◑ E VISA
closed Saturday and Sunday – **M** a la carte approx. 1400. GX **e**

Centre East

Quartier St. Josse, Square Marie-Louise, Square Ambiorix, Cité Européenne HU :

Archimède M without rest., r. Archimède 22, ✉ 1040, ✆ 2310909, Telex 20420 – |‡| TV ☎. AE ◑ E VISA. ✻ HU **y**
56 rm ☕ 3400/4000.

Euro-Flat without rest., bd Charlemagne 50, ✉ 1040, ☎ 2300010, Telex 21120, – ☰ ▣ ⌂wc ☎. AE ◑ E VISA HU p
closed August – **134 rm** ☐ 4050/7000.

Charlemagne without rest., bd Charlemagne 25, ✉ 1040, ☎ 2302135, Telex 22772 – ☰ ⌂wc ☎ – ♙. AE ◑ E VISA. ✻ HU a
60 rm ☐ 1845/2145.

XX **Gigotin,** r. Stevin 102, ✉ 1040, ☎ 2303091, ☂ – AE ◑ E HU n
closed Saturday, Sunday, Bank Holidays and last 2 weeks August – **M** a la carte 770/1330.

Rue de la Loi, Quartier Schuman, Quartier Léopold HV :

Brussels Europa H., Ⓜ, r. de la Loi 107, ✉ 1040, ☎ 2301333, Telex 25121 – ☰ ▤ ▣ ☎ Ⓟ – ♙ – **240 rm.** HV s

Quartier Cité Administrative, Madou, Parc de Bruxelles GU :

Astoria and Rest. Palais Royal, r. Royale 103, ✉ 1000, ☎ 2176290, Telex 25040 – ☰ ▣ ☎ – ♙. AE ◑ E VISA. ✻ rest GTU b
M *(closed Saturday and Sunday dinner)* 1220 – ☐ 420 – **125 rm** 2890/3890 – ½ p 3160.

Président Centre Ⓜ without rest., r. Royale 160, ✉ 1000, ☎ 2190065, Telex 26784 – ☰ ▤ ▣ ☎. AE ◑ E VISA GU a
73 rm ☐ 2660/2880.

City Garden Ⓜ without rest., with suites, r. Joseph II 59, ✉ 1040, ☎ 2300945, Telex 63570 – ☰ ▣ ☎ ⇔. AE ◑ E VISA. ✻ GU r
☐ 185 – **96 rm** 2325/2600.

Congrès and Rest. Le Carrousel, r. Congrès 42, ✉ 1000, ☎ 2171890 – ☰ ⌂wc ⋒ ☎. AE ◑ E VISA GU c
M *(closed week-ends in August)* – **38 rm** ☐ 960/1290 – P 1500/1840.

Résidence Sabina without rest., r. Nord 78, ✉ 1000, ☎ 2182637 – ⋒ ☎ GU e
22 rm ☐ 700/1200.

XXX **Astrid "Chez Pierrot",** r. de la Presse 21, ✉ 1000, ☎ 2173831, Classic – AE ◑ E VISA
closed Sunday, Easter and 15 July-14 August – **M** a la carte 1000/1400. GU d

Suburbs

North

Quartier Basilique (Koekelberg, Ganshoren, Jette) :

XXX ✿✿ **Dupont,** av. Vital-Riethuisen 46, ✉ 1080, ☎ 4275450, Classic-elegant – AE ◑ E VISA
closed Monday, Tuesday and mid July-mid August – **M** a la carte 1330/2250
Spec. Blanc de loup de mer au gingembre et passe-pierre (May-Sept.), Noix de St-Jacques grillés, beurre nantais (end Sept.-April), Selle de chevreuil au thym frais (Oct.-10 Dec.).

XXX ✿✿ **Bruneau,** av. Broustin 73, ✉ 1080, ☎ 4276978, Classic-elegant – AE ◑ E VISA
closed holiday Thursdays, Tuesday dinner, Wednesday, mid June-mid July and Christmas-New Year – **M** a la carte 1940/2520
Spec. Filet de bar de ligne tartiné au caviar d'Iran, Pot-au-feu de foie d'oie aux truffes à l'essence de homard, Filet de bœuf blanc-bleu-belge à la façon des moutardiers.

XXX Park Side, av. Panthéon 4, ✉ 1080, ☎ 4242482, Classic-elegant.

XXX **Au Chaudron d'Or,** Drève du Château 71, ✉ 1080, ☎ 4283737, « Converted farmhouse » – Ⓟ. AE ◑ E VISA
closed Sunday dinner, Monday and September – **M** 795/1195.

XXX ✿ **Le Sermon** (Kobs), av. Jacques-Sermon 91, ✉ 1090, ☎ 4268935 – AE E VISA
closed Sunday, Monday and 24 June-28 July – **M** a la carte 1160/1700
Spec. Moules au champagne (Sept.-March), Sole Sermon, Caneton aux pommes confites et poivre vert.

XX **Pannenhuis,** r. Léopold-1er 317, ✉ 1090, ☎ 4258373, « Converted 17C inn » – AE ◑ E VISA
M a la carte 1360/1830.

XX **Cambrils,** av. Charles-Quint 365, ✉ 1080, ☎ 4669582, ☂ – ▤. E
closed Sunday, Monday dinner and July – **M** 600/950.

XX **Le Barolo,** av. de Laeken 57, ✉ 1090, ☎ 4254576, ☂ – AE ◑ E VISA
closed Tuesday dinner, Wednesday and August – **M** a la carte 990/1380.

Quartier Centenaire and Atomium (Laeken, Wemmel, Strombeek-Bever) :

XXX **De Kam,** chaussée de Bruxelles 7, ✉ 1810, ☎ 4600374, Rustic – Ⓟ. AE ◑ E VISA
closed Sunday dinner, Monday, Tuesday dinner, Wednesday dinner and August – **M** 1050/1700.

XXX ✿✿ **Eddie Van Maele,** chaussée Romaine 964, ✉ 1810, ☎ 4785445, « Flower terrace and garden » – AE ◑. ✻
closed Saturday lunch, Sunday, Monday, July and 23 December-14 January – **M** (booking essential) a la carte 2040/2820
Spec. Roulade de turbot et langoustines (May-Sept.), Pâtisseries et glaces maison.

XXX **Centenaire,** av. J.-Sobieski 84, ✉ 1020, ☎ 4786623 – AE ◑ E VISA
closed Sunday dinner, Monday, July and 21 to 31 December – **M** 995/1650.

XX **Val Joli,** r. Leestbeek 16, ✉ 1820, ☎ 4783443, «Garden-terrace» – Ⓟ. AE VISA
closed Monday, Tuesday and 1 to 20 October – **M** 700/1300.

XX **Aub. Arbre Ballon,** chaussée de Bruxelles 416, ✉ 1810, ☎ 4789759 – Ⓟ. AE ⓓ E VISA
closed Monday and last 3 weeks July – **M** 695/1095.

XX **Castel,** av. Houba-de-Strooper 96, ✉ 1020, ☎ 4784392 – AE ⓓ E VISA
closed Tuesday dinner except Bank Holidays – **M** 650/925.

XX ✿ **Les Baguettes Impériales** (Ma), av. J. Sobieski 70, ✉ 1020, ☎ 4796732, Vietnamese rest. – AE.
closed Sunday dinner, Tuesday and 30 July-29 August – **M** a la carte 950/1280
Spec. Langoustines géantes à l'ancienne, Canette de Barbarie des Baguettes Impériales.

XX **Figaro,** r. Émile-Wauters 137, ✉ 1020, ☎ 4786529
closed Sunday dinner, Monday and July – **M** a la carte approx. 1000.

X **Adrienne Atomium,** Parc Expositions, ✉ 1020, ☎ 4783000, ≤, Hors d'œuvre – AE ⓓ E VISA
closed Sunday, Bank Holidays and 3 weeks July – **M** (lunch only except Friday and Saturday) 650.

West

Anderlecht :

XX **La Réserve,** chaussée de Ninove 675, ✉ 1080, ☎ 5222653 – AE ⓓ E VISA.
closed Saturday lunch, Tuesday and 16 July-5 August – **M** a la carte 940/1800.

Molenbeek St-Jean (Sint-Jans Molenbeek) :

XXX ✿ **Béarnais** (Dela Rue), bd Mettewie 318, ✉ 1080, ☎ 5231151, Classic – ▤. AE ⓓ E VISA
closed Sunday and Monday dinner – **M** a la carte 1600/2200
Spec. Côtelette de homard, Loup de mer grillé au fenouil, Biche Grand Veneur (Oct.-10 Dec.).

Berchem Ste Agathe (Sint-Agatha Berchem) :

XX **Saule,** chaussée de Gand 1110, ✉ 1080, ☎ 4656682 – AE ⓓ E VISA
closed Sunday dinner, Monday and July – **M** a la carte 900/1390.

South

Bois de la Cambre :

Lloyd George without rest., av. Lloyd George 12, ✉ 1050, ☎ 6483072 – wc. AE ⓓ E VISA
14 rm 950/1850.

XXXX ✿✿ **Villa Lorraine,** av. Vivier-d'Oie 75, ✉ 1180, ☎ 3743163, Classic-elegant – Ⓟ. AE ⓓ E VISA
closed Sunday and 6 to 29 July – **M** (booking essential) a la carte 1850/3450
Spec. Filets de sole au fumet de homard, Noisettes de chevreuil aux champignons des bois et genièvre (Oct.-10 Dec.), Parfait aux figues confites et marrons glacés.

Quartier "Ma Campagne" (Ixelles, St-Gilles) :

Forum Ⓜ without rest., av. Haut-Pont 2, ✉ 1060, ☎ 3430100, Telex 62311 – wc – **78 rm** 2560.

XXX **Chouan,** av. Brugmann 100, ✉ 1060, ☎ 3440999, Seafood – ▤. AE ⓓ VISA
closed Sunday in May-June, Saturday lunch and July-24 August – **M** a la carte 1180/2100.

XX **Fruit de ma Passion,** r. Jean-Baptiste Meunier 53a, ✉ 1180, ☎ 3473294 – AE ⓓ E VISA
closed Saturday, Sunday and last 3 weeks July – **M** a la carte 940/1370.

XX **L'Auvergne,** r. Aqueduc 61, ✉ 1050, ☎ 5373125, Rustic interior – AE ⓓ E
closed Sunday dinner, Monday, 20 July-19 August and 23 to 31 December – **M** 685.

Quartier Avenue Louise et Bascule (Ixelles) :

Mayfair without rest., quick-lunch, av. Louise 381, ✉ 1050, ☎ 6499800, Telex 24821 – –. AE ⓓ E
100 rm 3840/4825.

Arcade Stéphanie Ⓜ, av. Louise 91, ✉ 1050, ☎ 5390240, Telex 25558, – . AE ⓓ E VISA.
M 695 – **142 rm** 3750/4320.

Brussels without rest., av. Louise 315, ✉ 1050, ☎ 6402415, Telex 25075 – . AE ⓓ E VISA.
40 rm 3050/3450.

L'Agenda Ⓜ without rest., r. Florence 6, ✉ 1050, ☎ 5390031, Telex 63947 – . AE E VISA
240 – **38 rm** 2100/2350.

Alfa Louise without rest., r. Blanche 4, ✉ 1050, ☎ 5379210, Telex 62434 – wc . AE ⓓ E VISA
65 rm 2900.

XXX ✿✿ **Cravache d'Or,** pl. A.-Leemans 10, ✉ 1050, ✆ 5383746 – ▤. AE ◑ E VISA
closed Saturday lunch – **M** a la carte 1960/2720
Spec. Eventail de foie de canard confit sur gelée de homard, Loup de mer fumé à la minute, Rouget de roche à la pimprenelle et julienne d'artichauts violets.

XX **Fontaine de Perles,** av. Louise 124, ✉ 1050, ✆ 6480770, ☂, Chinese rest. – AE ◑ E VISA
closed Saturday lunch – **M** a la carte 600/1260.

XX **Tagawa,** av. Louise 279, ✉ 1050, ✆ 6405095, Japanese rest. – ▤. AE ◑ E. ✻
closed Sunday and Bank Holidays – **M** 600/2380.

XX **Comme Ça,** r. Châtelain 61, ✉ 1050, ✆ 6496290, ☂ – AE
closed Sunday, Monday dinner, Bank Holidays and July – **M** 650/890.

XX **Armagnac,** chaussée de Waterloo 591, ✉ 1060, ✆ 3459279 – AE ◑ E VISA
closed Sunday, Monday dinner and 21 July-19 August – **M** 750/850.

X **Arche de Noé,** r. Beau-Site 27, ✉ 1050, ✆ 6475383 – AE ◑ E VISA
closed Sunday – **M** a la carte 790/1670.

X **La Thailande,** av. Legrand 29, ✉ 1050, ✆ 6402462, Thaï rest. – ✻
closed Sunday – **M** a la carte approx. 800.

Forest (Vorst) :

XX ✿ **De Reu,** chaussée de Bruxelles 226, ✉ 1190, ✆ 3435460 – AE E
closed Tuesday, 5 August-1 September and 2 February-1 March – **M** (booking essential) a la carte 1130/2250
Spec. Foie d'oie frais au naturel, Agneau sarladaise, Fraises Romanoff.

Quartier Boondael (Ixelles) :

XXXX ✿✿ **L'Oasis** (Beyls), Place Marie-José 9, ✉ 1050, ✆ 6484545, « Elegant » – ▤ Ⓟ. AE ◑ E VISA. ✻
closed Sunday, Monday, 3 weeks in August and Christmas – **M** a la carte 2100/2900
Spec. Epinards farcis aux huîtres et au caviar, Turbot au four en croûte de mie de pain au basilic, Agneau de Pauillac en casserole au thym.

XXX **Aub. de Boendael,** square du Vieux-Tilleul 12, ✉ 1050, ✆ 6727055, Grill, « Rustic » – AE ◑ E VISA
closed Saturday, Sunday, Bank Holidays, 26 July-18 August and 24 December-5 January – **M** a la carte 1200/2000.

XX **Le Chalet Rose,** av. Bois de la Cambre 49, ✉ 1050, ✆ 6727864, ☂, « Ancient interior, terrace » – Ⓟ. AE ◑ E VISA
closed Saturday lunch, Sunday and Bank Holidays – **M** a la carte 1480/2170.

Uccle (Ukkel) :

🏨 **County House,** Square des Héros 2, ✉ 1180, ✆ 3754420, Telex 22392 – |♦| 📺 ⇔wc ☎ 🚗 Ⓟ – 🏛. ◑ E VISA. ✻ rest
M 650/1200 – **96 rm** ☕ 1975/3150 – P 3275.

XXX ✿ **Kolmer,** Drève de Carloo 18, ✉ 1180, ✆ 3755653, ☂, « Elegant, Garden-terrace » – Ⓟ. AE ◑ E VISA
closed Sunday, Monday, February and September – **M** a la carte 1650/2200
Spec. Tartare de saumon, Paupiettes de sole et langoustines aux poireaux.

XXX **Prince d'Orange,** av. Prince-d'Orange 1, ✉ 1180, ✆ 3744871, ☂, Classic – Ⓟ. AE ◑ E VISA
closed Monday except Bank Holidays – **M** 775/1175.

XX ✿ **Villa d'Este,** r. Etoile 142, ✉ 1180, ✆ 3778646, ☂ – Ⓟ. ◑ VISA
closed Sunday dinner, Monday, July-4 August and 23 December-5 January – **M** a la carte 1220/1930.

XX **Les Délices de la Mer,** chaussée de Waterloo 1020, ✉ 1180, ✆ 3755467, ☂, Seafood – Ⓟ. AE ◑ E VISA
closed Sunday and Easter – **M** 1250/1750.

XX **L'Éléphant Bleu,** chaussée de Waterloo 1120, ✉ 1180, ✆ 3744962, Thaï rest. – ▤. AE ◑ E VISA
closed Wednesday – **M** a la carte 810/1160.

XX **Dikenek,** chaussée de Waterloo 830, ✉ 1180, ✆ 3748346, ☂, Rustic tavern – ▤. AE ◑ E VISA
closed 1 to 13 April, 26 August-1 September, Wednesday dinner from September to July and Saturday lunch – **M** a la carte 1350/1880.

XX **Les Pélerins,** av. de Fré 190, ✉ 1180, ✆ 3742046 – Ⓟ. AE ◑ E VISA
closed Saturday, Sunday and Bank Holidays – **M** a la carte 950/1270.

XX **Le Calvados,** av. de Fré 182, ✉ 1180, ✆ 3747098 – AE ◑ E VISA
closed Sunday – **M** a la carte 1290/2130.

XX **Ventre-Saint-Gris,** r. Basse 10, ✉ 1180, ✆ 3752755 – AE ◑ E VISA
M 790/1175.

XX **L'Ascoli,** chaussée de Waterloo 940, ✉ 1180, ✆ 3755775, ☂, Italian rest. – Ⓟ. AE ◑ E VISA
closed Sunday, Monday and 30 July-August – **M** a la carte 990/1530.

XX **Pavillon Impérial,** chaussée de Waterloo 1296, ✉ 1180, ✆ 3746751, Chinese rest. – ▤. AE ⓓ. ✻
closed Wednesday – **M** a la carte 600/1010.

XX **Pierrot au Surcouf,** r. Doyenné 89, ✉ 1180, ✆ 3457538 – AE ⓓ E VISA
closed Sunday dinner, Monday and 15 July-19 August – **M** 690/1395.

X **Willy et Marianne,** chaussée d'Alsemberg 705, ✉ 1180, ✆ 3436009 – AE ⓓ E VISA
closed Tuesday dinner, Wednesday and 15 to 31 July – **M** a la carte 960/1340.

X **De Hoef,** r. Edith-Cavell 218, ✉ 1180, ✆ 3743417, 余, 17C inn – AE ⓓ E VISA
closed 10 to 31 July – **M** 565.

East

Quartier Cinquantenaire (Etterbeek) :

Chelton Concorde Ⓜ without rest., r. Véronèse 48, ✉ 1040, ✆ 7364095, Telex 64253 – |‡| TV – 🏊. AE E VISA
220 – **41 rm** 2940.

XX **Fontaine de Jade,** av. Tervuren 5, ✉ 1040, ✆ 7363210, Chinese rest. – ▤. AE ⓓ VISA
closed Tuesday – **M** a la carte 700/1700.

XX **St-Laurent,** bd Louis Schmidt 30, ✉ 1040, ✆ 7360398 – AE ⓓ E VISA
closed Monday and 18 August-4 September – **M** a la carte 800/1370.

XX **Casse-Dalle,** av. Celtes 37, ✉ 1040, ✆ 7336625 – AE
closed Sunday and Christmas-New Year – **M** a la carte 970/1420.

Quartier Place Eugène-Flagey (Ixelles) :

XX **Piano à Bretelles,** r. A.-Dewitte 40, ✉ 1050, ✆ 6476105 – AE
closed Saturday lunch, Sunday and August – **M** a la carte 770/1290.

Quartier Place Meiser (Schaerbeek) :

Lambermont Ⓜ without rest., bd Lambermont 322, ✉ 1030, ✆ 2425595, Telex 62220 – |‡| TV ☎. AE ⓓ E VISA
42 rm 1950/2400.

Plasky without rest., av. Eugène-Plasky 212, ✉ 1040, ✆ 7337518 – |‡| wc ⋔ ☎. AE ⓓ E VISA
115 – **30 rm** 880/1545.

XXX **Le Meiser,** bd Gén.-Wahis 55, ✉ 1030, ✆ 7353769, Classic – AE ⓓ E VISA
closed Saturday and Sunday – **M** a la carte 1120/1800.

XX **L'Armor,** av. Milcamps 126, ✉ 1040, ✆ 7331981 – AE ⓓ E VISA. ✻
closed Saturday lunch, Sunday and 14 July-1 August – **M** 750/1400.

X **Au Cadre Noir,** av. Milcamps 158, ✉ 1040, ✆ 7341445 – AE ⓓ E VISA
closed Saturday lunch, Sunday dinner, Monday and 1 to 21 July – **M** a la carte 845/1400.

X **Anak Timoer,** av. Rogier 357, ✉ 1030, ✆ 7338987, Indonesian and Chinese rest. – AE ⓓ E VISA
closed Sunday dinner, Wednesday and July-14 August – **M** a la carte 640/1120.

Auderghem (Oudergem) :

XX **L'Abbaye de Rouge Cloître,** Rouge Cloître 8, ✉ 1160, ✆ 6724525, ←, 余, « Garden setting » – Ⓟ. AE ⓓ E VISA
closed 26 to 31 December, February, Sunday dinner and Monday – **M** 1235.

X ✲ **La Grignotière** (Chanson), chaussée de Wavre 2045, ✉ 1160, ✆ 6728185 – AE ⓓ VISA
closed Sunday, Monday and first 2 weeks August – **M** 850
Spec. Foie gras de canard, Langoustines à la vapeur de fenouil, Ris et rognon de veau gratinés Dauphinois.

Evere :

Belson Ⓜ without rest., chaussée de Louvain 805, ✉ 1140, ✆ 7350000, Telex 64921 – |‡| TV ☎. AE ⓓ E VISA
90 rm 3150/3650.

Woluwé-St-Lambert (Sint-Lambrechts-Woluwé) :

Armorial without rest., bd Brand-Whitlock 101, ✉ 1200, ✆ 7345636 – TV wc ⋔ ☎. AE ⓓ E VISA – **15 rm** 700/1800.

Léopold III without rest., square Jos.-Charlotte 11, ✉ 1200, ✆ 7628288 – ☎
15 rm 795/1550.

Résidence Lambeau without rest., av. Lambeau 150, ✉ 1200, ✆ 7338414 – TV ☎
12 rm 990/1650.

XXX ✲ **Mon Manège à Toi,** r. Neerveld 1, ✉ 1200, ✆ 7700238, « Villa with flower garden » – Ⓟ. AE ⓓ E VISA
closed 7 to 31 July, 24 to 31 December, Saturday, Sunday and Bank Holidays – **M** a la carte 1450/2250
Spec. Coquilles St. Jacques au witloof (Oct.-February), Poêlée de langoustines au basilic (April-Sept.), Sole braisée au citron et coulis d'artichauts.

XXX **Coq en Pâte,** r. Tomberg 259, ✉ 1200, ✆ 7621971 – AE ⓓ E VISA
closed Monday and 20 July-19 August – **M** a la carte 970/1270.

XX **Sugito,** 1st floor, bd Brand-Whitlock 107, ✉ 1200, ✆ 7335045, Indonesian rest. – AE ⓓ E VISA
closed Monday – **M** a la carte approx. 900.

XX **Lindekemale,** av. J.F. Debecker 6, ✉ 1200, ✆ 7708489, 🏠 – Ⓟ. AE ⓓ E VISA
closed Saturday, Sunday, 29 March-12 April and 9 to 17 August – **M** a la carte 1130/1600.

XX **Le Relais de la Woluwe,** pl. Verheyleweghen 2, ✉ 1200, ✆ 7626636 – AE ⓓ E VISA
closed Saturday lunch and Sunday – **M** a la carte 1010/1330.

XX **Le Grand Veneur,** r. Tomberg 253, ✉ 1200, ✆ 7706122, Rustic – AE ⓓ E VISA
closed Tuesday and July – **M** 1180/1480.

XX **Le Chaplin,** av. Prince Héritier 22, ✉ 1200, ✆ 7713415, 🏠 – AE ⓓ E VISA
closed Sunday dinner, Monday and September – **M** a la carte approx. 1100.

Woluwé-St-Pierre (Sint-Pieters Woluwé) :

XXX **Des 3 Couleurs,** av. Tervuren 453, ✉ 1150, ✆ 7703321
closed 1 to 14 April, September, Saturday lunch, Sunday dinner and Monday – **M** a la carte 1140/1520.

XX **La Madonette,** r. Eglise 92, ✉ 1150, ✆ 7310298, 🏠 – AE ⓓ E VISA
closed Monday, 20 May-9 June and 20 September-9 October – **M** a la carte 880/1270.

XX **La Salade Folle,** av. Jules Dujardin 9, ✉ 1150, ✆ 7701961, Grill – AE ⓓ VISA
closed Sunday dinner, Monday, last 2 weeks February and 20 August-4 September – **M** a la carte 700/1370.

Watermael-Boitsfort (Watermael-Bosvoorde) :

🏠 **Aub. du Souverain** without rest., av. Fauconnerie 1, ✉ 1170, ✆ 6721601 – TV ⋔. AE VISA
10 rm ☕ 1300.

XXX **Trois Tilleuls** ⑂ with rm, Berensheide 8, ✉ 1170, ✆ 6723014, 🏠 – TV ⌂wc ⋔ ☎. AE ⓓ E VISA. ✻ rm
M *(closed Sunday)* a la carte 1140/1950 – **8 rm** ⌂ 1745/3085.

XX **Samambaia,** r. Philippe Dewolfs 7, ✉ 1170, ✆ 6728720, 🏠, Brazilian rest., « Tasteful decor » – AE ⓓ E
closed Sunday, Monday and 22 July-20 August – **M** a la carte 920/1120.

XX **Le Canard Sauvage,** chaussée de la Hulpe 194, ✉ 1170, ✆ 6730975 – AE ⓓ E VISA
closed Saturday, Easter and August – **M** a la carte 1080/1580.

Brussels environs

at Diegem : C Machelen – pop. 11 300 – ✉ 1920 Diegem – ☎ 02 :

🏨 **Holiday Inn** M, Holidaystraat 7, near Brussels-Zaventem motorway, ✆ 7205865, Telex 24285, 🏊, ✂ – ⇕ TV ☎ ♿ Ⓟ – 🏛. AE ⓓ E VISA. ✻ rest
M a la carte 1160/1450 – ⌂ 400 – **288 rm** 4300/5600.

🏨 **Sofitel** M, Bessenveldstraat 15, Brussels-Zaventem motorway Diegem exit, ✆ 7206050, Telex 26595, 🏊 – ▤ TV ☎ Ⓟ – 🏛. AE ⓓ E VISA
M a la carte 1150/1520 – ⌂ 380 – **125 rm** 3770/4120.

🏨 **Novotel** M, Olmenstraat (near Brussels-Zaventem motorway), ✆ 7205830, Telex 26751, 🏊 heated, 🏠 – ⇕ ▤ TV ⌂wc ☎ Ⓟ – 🏛. AE ⓓ E VISA
M a la carte 690/1340 – ⌂ 275 – **158 rm** 2830/3100.

XX **Diegemhof,** Calenbergstraat 51, ✆ 7201134, 🏠 – AE ⓓ E VISA. ✻
closed Saturday, Sunday and August – **M** a la carte 990/1340.

at Essene C Hekelgem, by ⑫ : 18 km, by E 40 outway Ternat – pop. 11 165 – ✉ 1705 Essene – ☎ 053 :

XXXX ✿ **Host. Bellemolen** ⑂ with rm, Stationstraat 11, SW : 1,5 km, ✆ 666238, ≤, « Tastefully converted 12C mill », 🏠 – ▤ ⌂wc Ⓟ – 🏛. AE ⓓ E. ✻
closed 7 to 31 July, 22 December-1 January, Sunday dinner and Monday – **M** a la carte 1430/2100 – **6 rm** ⌂ 1850/2500
Spec. Turbot aux écrevisses, Coquilles St-Jacques meunière chiconettes, Ris de veau aux fleurs vertes et blanches.

at Groenendaal : – ✉ 1990 Hoeilaart – ☎ 02 :

XXXX ✿✿✿ **Romeyer,** chaussée de Groenendaal 109, ✆ 6570581, « Stately home, ≤ garden and private lake » – Ⓟ. AE ⓓ E VISA
closed Sunday dinner, Monday except Bank Holidays, February and August – **M** a la carte 1850/2530
Spec. Sole fourrée aux crevettes grises, sauce homardine, Homard sauté au coulis de tomate et corail, Aile de volaille aux clous de girofle, pommes soufflées.

XXX ✿ **Aloyse Kloos,** chaussée de la Hulpe 2, ✆ 6573737, 🏠, Classic-elegant – Ⓟ. AE ⓓ E VISA
closed 24 February-21 March, 18 August-12 September, Sunday dinner and Monday – **M** a la carte 1120/1640
Spec. Jambon de nos fumoirs, Ecrevisses à la luxembourgeoise (June-April), Champignons des bois.

at Groot-Bijgaarden (Grand-Bigard) C Dilbeek, by ⑫ : 7 km – pop. 36 003 – ✉ 1720 Groot-Bijgaarden – ☎ 02 :

XXXX ✿✿ **De Bijgaarden,** I. Van Beverenstraat 20 (near castle), ✆ 4664485, ≤ – AE ⓓ E VISA
closed 31 March-7 April, 18 August-8 September, Saturday lunch and Sunday – **M** a la carte 1730/2750
Spec. Langoustines en ravioli julienne de truffes, Selle d'agneau cloutée aux truffes, Turbot rôti au four, sabayon à la graine de moutarde.

XXX ✿ **Michel** (Coppens), Schepen Gossetlaan 31, ✆ 4666591 – Ⓟ. AE ⓓ
closed Sunday, Monday and August – **M** 1200/1850
Spec. Huîtres au champagne et witloof, Homard rôti à la crème d'estragon, Ris de veau aux navets et poireaux.

at Jezus-Eik by ⑦ : 12 km – ✉ 1900 Overijse – ☎ 02 :

XXXX ✿✿ **Barbizon** (Deluc), Welriekendedreef 95, ✆ 6570462 – Ⓟ. AE ⓓ E VISA
closed Tuesday, Wednesday, mid July-early August and February – **M** (booking essential) a la carte 1620/2370
Spec. Homard en chemise beurre Barbizon, Huîtres chaudes en habit vert (Sept.-March), Chariot de gourmandises.

ANTWERP (ANTWERPEN) 2000 212 ⑮ and 409 ④ – pop. 488 425 – ☎ 03.

See : Old Antwerp★★★ : Cathedral★★★ and Market Square★ (Grote Markt) FY – Rubens' House★★ (Rubenshuis) GZ – Butchers' House★ (Vleeshuis) : museum FY D – Rubens' burial chapel★ in the St. James' church (St-Jacobskerk) GY – The port★★★ (Haven) ⛴ FY – Zoo★★ (Dierentuin) EU.

Museums : Royal Art Gallery★★★ (Koninklijk Museum voor Schone Kunsten) CV – Plantin-Moretus★★★ (ancient printing-office) FZ – Mayer Van den Bergh★★ (Brueghel) GZ – Maritime Steen★ (Nationaal Scheepvaartmuseum Steen) FY M¹.

⛳18 ⛳9 Kapellen by ② : 22 km, Georges Capiaulei 2 ✆ 6668456 – ⛳18 Uilenbaan 15 at Wommelgem by ⑥ ✆3530292.

ℹ Gildekamersstraat 7 ✆ 2320103 and 2322284 – Inquiry Office, Koningin Astridplein ✆ 2330570 – Tourist association of the province, Karel Oomsstraat 11, ✉ 2018, ✆ 2162810.

Brussels 48 ⑩ – Amsterdam 158 ④ – Luxembourg 266 ⑨ – Rotterdam 103 ④.

Plans on following pages

Room prices are subject to the addition of a local tax of 6%

Town Centre

Plaza M without rest., Charlottalei 43, ✉ 2018, ✆ 2189240, Telex 31531 – 🛗 TV ☎. AE ⓓ E VISA — EV v
250 – **79 rm** 2870/3820.

De Keyser M, De Keyserlei 66, ✉ 2018, ✆ 2340135, Telex 34219 – 🛗 ▤ rest TV ☎ – 🏛. AE ⓓ E VISA. ✽ rest — EU b
M a la carte 1220/1720 – **117 rm** 3230/4670.

Switel Eurotel, Copernicuslaan 2, ✉ 2018, ✆ 2316780, Telex 33965, 🏊, ✂ – 🛗 ▤ rest TV ☎ 🚗 – 🏛. AE ⓓ E VISA — EV k
M a la carte 900/1400 – 595 – **350 rm** 2400/4000.

Empire M without rest., Appelmansstraat 31, ✉ 2018, ✆ 2314755, Telex 33909 – 🛗 TV. AE ⓓ E VISA — DU s
70 rm 3020/3570.

Alfa Congress M, Plantin en Moretuslei 136, ✉ 2018, ✆ 2353000, Telex 31959 – 🛗 TV ⛀wc ☎ 🚗 Ⓟ – 🏛. AE ⓓ E VISA — EV s
closed 25 December-1 January – **M** *(closed Saturday and Sunday)* a la carte 730/1170 – **61 rm** 2000/2350.

Antwerp Tower Hotel M without rest. with 11 apartments in annex, Van Ertbornstraat 10, ✉ 2018, ✆ 2340120, Telex 34478 – 🛗 TV ⛀wc ☎ – 🏛. AE ⓓ E VISA. ✽ — DU b
40 rm 2250/3100.

XXX ✿ **Vateli,** Kipdorpvest 50, ✆ 2331781, Classic – ▤ Ⓟ. AE ⓓ E VISA — DU g
closed Sunday, Monday, Bank Holidays and July – **M** a la carte 1600/2300
Spec. Caneton à la rouennaise, Saumon mariné, Escalope de ris de veau au céleri.

XXX **De Lepeleer,** Lange St-Annastr. 8, ✆ 2342225, « Rustic interior » – Ⓟ. AE ⓓ E VISA
closed 8 to 22 August, 22 December-1 January, Saturday lunch, Sunday and Bank Holidays – **M** a la carte 1640/1980. — DU n

XXX **Liang's Garden,** Markgravelei 141, ✉ 2018, ✆ 2372222, Chinese rest. – AE ⓓ VISA. ✽
closed Monday, Wednesday and 4 to 21 August – **M** a la carte 1170/1600.

XXX **Relais Estérel,** Tolstraat 70, ✆ 2373261, Open until 1 a.m. – ▤. AE E VISA. ✽ — CV n
closed Thursday, 29 June-3 August and 9 to 20 February – **M** (dinner only) a la carte 1520/2460.

XX **De Poterne,** Desguinlei 186, ✉ 2018, ✆ 2382824 – AE ⓓ
closed Sunday, 15 July-14 August and Christmas-New Year – **M** a la carte 1200/1820.

XX **Sawadee,** 1st floor, Britselei 16, ✆ 2330859, Thai rest., « Ancient mansion » – AE ⓓ E VISA — DV b
closed Tuesday – **M** a la carte approx. 1000.

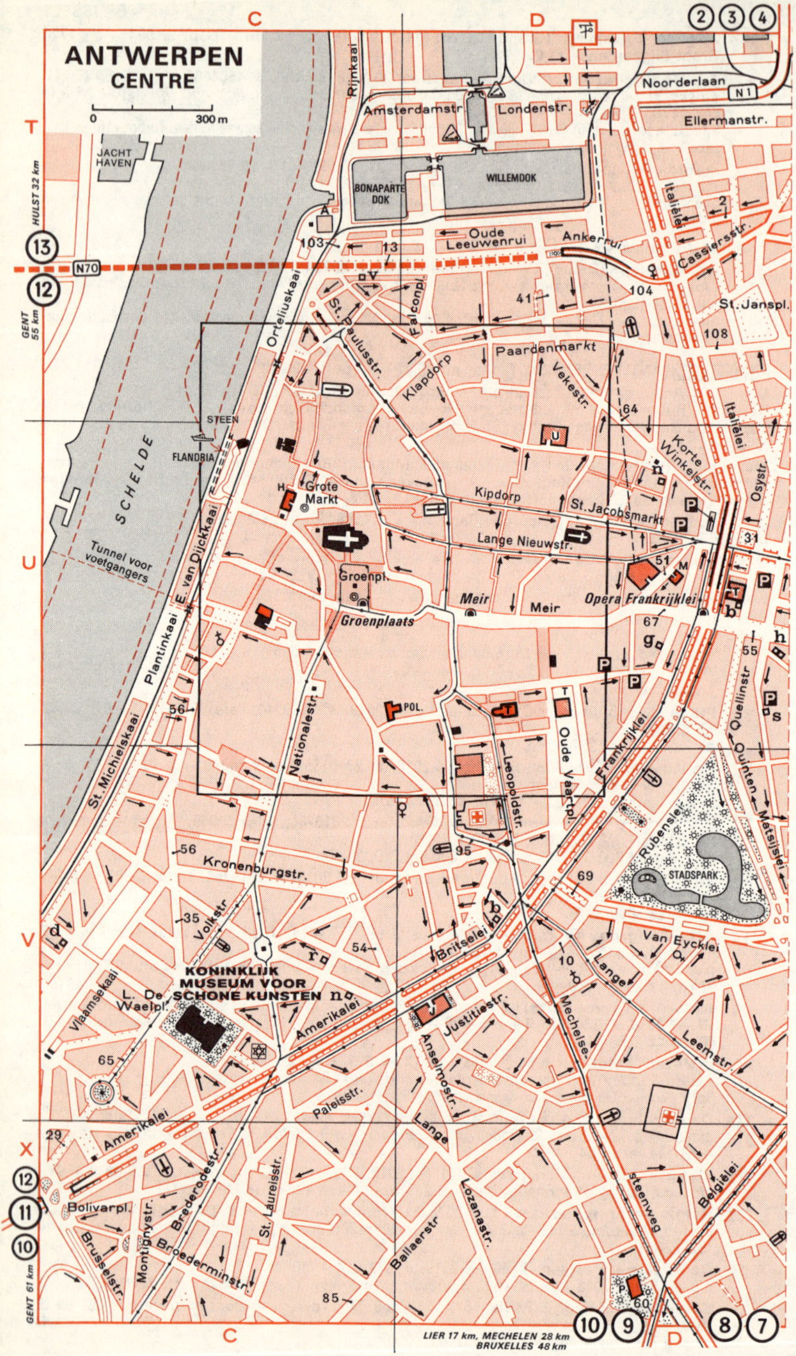
ANTWERPEN
CENTRE
0
300 m
SCHELDE
Tunnel voor voetgangers
JACHT HAVEN
BONAPARTE DOK
WILLEMDOK
Amsterdamstr.
Londenstr.
Noorderlaan
Ellermanstr.
Rijnkaai
Oude Leeuwenrui
Ankerrui
Italiëlei
Cassiersstr.
St. Janspl.
Orteliuskaai
St. Paulusstr.
Falconpl.
Paardenmarkt
Klapdorp
Vekestr.
Korte Winkelstr.
Osystr.
STEEN
FLANDRIA
Grote Markt
Kipdorp
St. Jacobsmarkt
Lange Nieuwstr.
Groenpl.
Groenplaats
Meir
Opera
Frankrijklei
E. van Dijckkaai
Plantinkaai
St. Michielskaai
Nationalestr.
POL.
Oude Vaartpl.
Leopoldstr.
Quellinstr.
Quinten Matsijslei
Rubenslei
STADSPARK
Kronenburgstr.
Volkstr.
Britselei
Van Eycklei
Lange
Mechelse
KONINKLIJK MUSEUM VOOR SCHONE KUNSTEN
L. De Waelpl.
Vlaamsekaai
Amerikalei
Justitiestr.
Anselmostr.
Leemstr.
Paleisstr.
Lange
Bolivarpl.
Brusselstr.
Montignystr.
Brederodestr.
Broederminstr.
St. Laureisstr.
Ballaerstr.
Lozanastr.
steenweg
Belgiëlei
HULST 32 km
GENT 55 km
GENT 61 km
N70
N1
LIER 17 km, MECHELEN 28 km
BRUXELLES 48 km

STREET INDEX TO ANTWERPEN TOWN PLANS

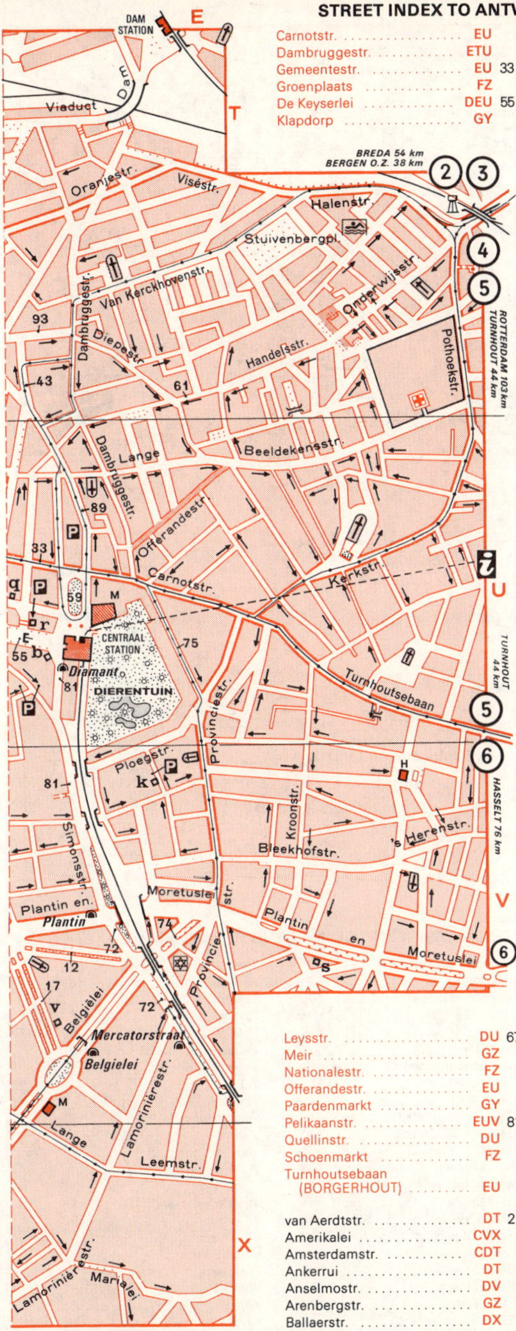

Continued on next page

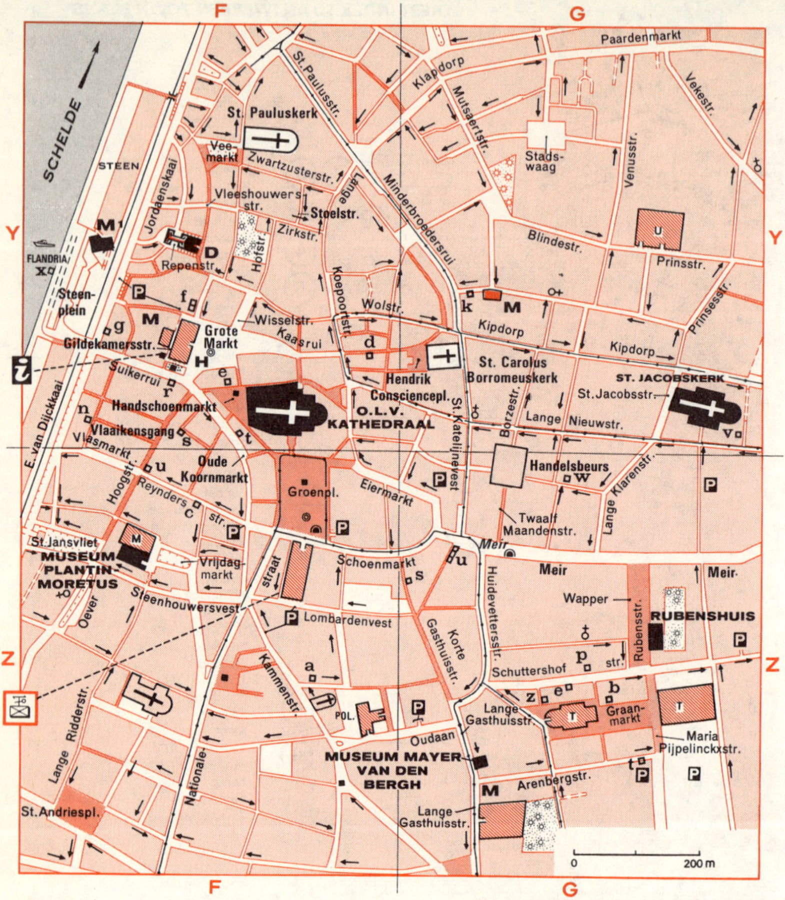

STREET INDEX TO ANTWERPEN TOWN PLANS (Concluded)

XX **Epicurus,** Verbondstraat 44, ✆ 2373699 – 🐕 CV r
closed Saturday lunch, Sunday, Monday and 3 to 25 August – **M** 1250/1700.

XX **Panaché,** Statiestr. 17, ✉ 2018, ✆ 2326905, Open until 1.30 a.m. – ▤. AE ① VISA
closed 30 July-26 August – **M** a la carte 660/1100. EU q

XX La Moule Parquée, Wapenstraat 18, ✆ 2384908, Seafood – ▤ CV d

XX **Gourmet sans Chiqué,** Vestingstraat 3, ✉ 2018, ✆ 2329002, Alsacian atmosphere – ① E VISA DU h
closed Friday, Saturday lunch, 20 January-1 February and 1 to 25 August – **M** 600/1000.

X **Solmar,** Breidelstraat 23, ✉ 2018, ✆ 2325053, Portugese rest., Open until 11.30 p.m. – ▤. AE ① E VISA. 🐕 EU r
closed Tuesday and February – **M** a la carte 750/1170.

X **Rimini,** Vestingstraat 5, ✉ 2018, ✆ 2314290, Italian rest. DU h
closed Wednesday and August – **M** a la carte 790/1330.

Old Antwerp

🏨 **Alfa Theater** Ⓜ without rest., Arenbergstraat 30, ✆ 2311720, Telex 33910 – |‡| TV ☎ – 🅿. AE ① E VISA. 🐕 GZ t
83 rm ⊐ 2230/2950.

XXXX ✿✿ **La Pérouse,** Steenplein (pontoon), ✆ 2323528, ←, « Anchored vessel » – ▤ Ⓟ. AE ① E. 🐕 FY x
2 October-end May except Sunday, Monday, Bank Holidays, 25 December-6 January and Good Friday – **M** (booking essential) a la carte 1650/2040
Spec. Raviolis de St.Jacques aux girolles et aux mousserons, Côteléttes de homard et de barbue au lait d'amandes, Pot-au-feu à la flamande.

XXX ✿✿ **Sir Anthony Van Dijck** (Paesbrugghe), Oude Koornmarkt 16 (Vlaeykensgang), ✆ 2316170, « Situated in a 16C lane, tasteful ancient interior » – AE ① E. 🐕 FY s
closed Saturday, Sunday, 29 March-5 April, 1 to 24 August and 22 to 31 December – **M** a la carte 1420/1970
Spec. Salade d'huîtres au saumon et au witloof (Oct.-March), Selle d'agneau en croûte, Rognon de veau à la bière de Rodenbach.

XXX **La Rade,** 1st floor, Van Dijckkaai 8, ✆ 2334963, « 18C mansion » – AE ① E VISA FY g
closed Saturday lunch and Sunday – **M** 1250.

XXX ✿ **'t Fornuis,** Reyndersstraat 24, ✆ 2336270, « Rustic » – AE ①. 🐕 FZ c
closed Saturday, Sunday, last 3 weeks August and Christmas-New Year – **M** a la carte 1650/2400.

XXX **St. Jacob in Galicië,** Braderijstraat 14, ✆ 2318043, « 16C and 17C interior » – AE ① E VISA FY f
closed Saturday, Sunday and 13 July-4 August – **M** a la carte 1600/2170.

XXX **Den Gulden Greffoen,** Hoogstraat 37, ✆ 2315046, « In a 13C restored house » – ▤. AE ① E VISA. 🐕 FZ u
closed Saturday, Sunday, Bank Holidays, first 3 weeks August and 25 to 30 December – **M** a la carte 1700/2050.

XX **Petrus,** Kelderstraat 1, ✆ 2252734 – AE ① E VISA GZ z
closed Monday, Saturday lunch and July – **M** a la carte 1440/1780.

XX **Criterium,** Schuttershofstraat 39, ✆ 2328346, Elegant interior – AE ① E VISA. 🐕
closed Saturday lunch, Sunday, Bank Holidays, 28 July-17 August and 24 December-1 January – **M** a la carte 1300/2100. GZ p

XX **Laurent,** Korte Klarenstraat 5, ✆ 2329547 – AE ① E VISA. 🐕 GZ w
closed 30 March-7 April and 24 August-8 September – **M** a la carte 1250/1990.

XX **Cigogne d'Alsace,** Wiegstraat 9, ✆ 2339716 – AE ① E VISA. 🐕 GZ u
closed Saturday lunch, Sunday, Bank Holidays and 20 December-1 January – **M** a la carte approx. 2000.

XX **De Kerselaar,** Grote Pieter Potstraat 22, ✆ 2335969 – AE ① E VISA. 🐕 FY n
closed Saturday lunch, Sunday, Monday lunch, 27 March-2 April and 7 to 28 July – **M** a la carte approx. 1200.

XX **V.I.P. Diners,** Lange Nieuwstraat 95, ✆ 2331317 – AE ① E VISA GY v
closed Saturday lunch, Sunday, Bank Holidays, 30 March-13 April and 20 July-2 August – **M** 1050/1580.

XX **Manoir,** Everdijstraat 13, ✆ 2327697, « Old panelling » – AE ① E VISA FZ a
closed Wednesday and 1 to 20 July – **M** a la carte 1100/1900.

XX **Koperen Ketel,** Wiegstraat 5, ✆ 2331274 – AE ① E VISA GZ u
closed Saturday lunch, Sunday and Bank Holidays – **M** a la carte 880/1340.

XX **De Zeven Schaken,** Braderijstraat 24 (Grote Markt), ✆ 2337003, « Rustic » – AE ① E VISA – *closed Sunday and 1 to 21 August* – **M** 875/1500 FY f

XX **Preud'homme,** Suikerrui 28, ✆ 2334200 – AE ① E VISA. 🐕 FY r
closed Tuesday and February – **M** a la carte 1300/1620.

XX **Zagreb,** Brouwersvliet 30, ✆ 2310173, Yugoslavian rest. – AE ① E VISA. 🐕 CT v
closed Saturday, Sunday and 15 July-14 August – **M** (lunch only) a la carte 1000/1530.

XX **Meirbrug,** 1st floor, Wiegstraat 1, ✆ 2336700 – AE ⓓ E VISA. ✻ GZ **u**
closed Sunday – **M** a la carte 830/1700.

XX **De Twee Atheners,** Keizerstraat 2, ✆ 2320851, Greek rest., Open until 2 a.m. – ▤. ⓓ
closed Wednesday except Bank Holidays and September – **M** a la carte 650/950. GY **k**

X **Henri,** Graanmarkt 3, ✆ 2329258 – AE ⓓ E VISA. ✻ GZ **b**
closed Saturday lunch, Sunday and September – **M** a la carte 820/1420.

X **Fourchette,** Schuttershofstraat 28, ✆ 2313335 – AE ⓓ E VISA GZ **e**
closed Saturday lunch, Sunday, Monday and 14 July-3 August – **M** a la carte 1050/1320.

X **Bistro 15,** Schrijnwerkerstraat 15, ✆ 2337826 – AE ⓓ E GZ **s**
closed Sunday and 12 August-1 September – **M** (lunch only Monday to Friday, Saturday dinner only) a la carte 1030/1150.

X **Rooden-Hoed,** Oude Koornmarkt 25, ✆ 2332844, Mussels in season – ▤. AE. ✻
closed 10 to 16 February, 19 June-15 July and Wednesday – **M** a la carte 940/1400. FY **t**

X **A l'Ombre de la Cathédrale,** Handschoenmarkt 17, ✆ 2324014 – AE ⓓ E VISA FY **e**
closed Tuesday – **M** a la carte 760/1250.

X **Peerdestal,** Wijngaardstraat 8, ✆ 2319503 – AE ⓓ E VISA FY **d**
M a la carte 600/1420.

Left Bank (Linker Oever)

XX **Lido,** Hanegraefstraat 8, ✉ 2050, ✆ 2193590, Chinese rest. – ▤. AE ⓓ E
closed Tuesday and Wednesday – **M** a la carte approx. 700.

Suburbs

North – ✉ 2030 :

Novotel Ⓜ, Luithagen-Haven 6, ✆ 5420320, Telex 32488, heated pool, garden – lift ▤ rest TV bathwc ☎ ♿ Ⓟ – conference. AE ⓓ E VISA – 275 – **119 rm** 2000/2730.

XXX **Terminal,** Leopolddok 214, ✆ 5412680, < harbour – Ⓟ
closed Saturday, Sunday and August – **M** (lunch only) a la carte 1090/1750.

South – ✉ 2020 :

Crest H. Ⓜ, G. Legrellelaan 10, ✆ 2372900, Telex 33843 – lift ▤ TV ☎ – conference. AE ⓓ E VISA. ✻ rest – **M** 600/2550 – **306 rm** 3380/3950.

at Berchem – pop. 45 128 – ✉ 2600 Berchem – ⓞ 03 :

X **Ten Carvery,** Rooiplein 6, ✆ 2304733, Grill, « Converted ancient farm » – ✻
M 625.

X **Euterpia,** Generaal Capiaumontstraat 2, ✆ 2368356, terrace
closed Monday and Tuesday – **M** (dinner only) a la carte 1100/1550.

at Borgerhout – pop. 43 556 – ✉ 2200 Borgerhout – ⓞ 03 :

Holiday Inn Ⓜ, Luitenant Lippenslaan 66, ✆ 2359191, Telex 34479, indoor pool – lift ▤ TV ☎ ♿ Ⓟ – conference. AE ⓓ E VISA
M a la carte 900/1500 – **176 rm** 2725/3500.

at Deurne – pop. 76 744 – ✉ 2100 Deurne – ⓞ 03 :

XXX **Den Uyl,** Bosuil 1, ✆ 3243404, « Converted farm » – Ⓟ. AE ⓓ E VISA. ✻
closed Saturday lunch, Sunday and July – **M** a la carte 1280/1800.

XX **Périgord,** Turnhoutsebaan 273, ✆ 3255200 – AE ⓓ E VISA. ✻
closed Tuesday dinner, Wednesday, Saturday lunch and July – **M** 1075/1475.

at Mortsel – pop. 26 534 – ✉ 2510 Mortsel – ⓞ 03 :

Bristol International without rest., Edegemstraat 1, ✆ 4498049 – lift showerwc ☎. AE ⓓ E VISA – *closed 19 December-4 January* – **26 rm** 890/1300.

Environs

at Aartselaar : by ⑩ : 10 km – pop. 12 749 – ✉ 2630 Aartselaar – ⓞ 03 :

XXX ✿ **Lindenbos,** Boomsesteenweg 139, ✆ 8880965, « Converted castle with park » – Ⓟ. AE ⓓ. ✻
closed Monday and August – **M** 1200/1850
Spec. Fantaisie des deux saumons au parfum d'aneth, Fricassée de homard et d'écrevisses au beurre de corail et riz sauvage, Filet de boeuf poêlé et mignonnette de foie de canard grillée au coulis de Pomerol.

at Brasschaat : by ② and ③ : 11 km – pop. 32 845 – ✉ 2130 Brasschaat – ⓞ 03 :

XXX **Het Villasdal,** Kapelsesteenweg 480, ✆ 6645821 – Ⓟ. AE ⓓ
closed Monday and 14 July-11 August – **M** a la carte 1550/1700.

XXX **Halewijn,** Donksesteenweg 212 (Ekeren-Donk), ✆ 6450490, terrace – ▤. AE ⓓ E
closed Monday – **M** a la carte 1120/1900.

at Ekeren : by ② : 11 km – pop. 30 271 – ✉ 2070 Ekeren – ⓞ 03 :

XX **Hof de Bist,** Veltwijcklaan 258, ✆ 6646130 – Ⓟ. AE ⓓ E
closed Sunday and Monday – **M** a la carte approx. 1500.

at Kapellen : by ② : 15,5 km – pop. 22 477 – ✉ 2080 Kapellen – ☎ 03 :

XXX ✿ **De Bellefleur** (Buytaert), Antwerpsesteenweg 253, ✆ 6646719 – Ⓟ. AE ⓓ
closed Saturday, Sunday and July – **M** (booking essential) a la carte 1600/2340
Spec. Homard tiède aux haricots de mer (April-August), Filet d'agneau farci, Blanc de coucou de Malines au vieux Madère.

XX **De Graal,** Kapellenboslei 11 (N : 5 km by N 122 direction Kalmthout), ✆ 6665510, « Terrace and garden » – AE ⓓ E. ✻
closed Saturday lunch and Tuesday – **M** a la carte 1330/1830.

XX **De Pauw,** Antwerpsesteenweg 48, ✆ 6642282 – E VISA
closed Tuesday dinner and Wednesday dinner – **M** a la carte 1200/1820.

X **Cappelleke,** Dorpstraat 70, ✆ 6646728 – AE
closed Tuesday, Wednesday and 16 August-4 September – **M** 895.

at Kontich : by ⑨ : 12 km – pop. 18 003 – ✉ 2550 Kontich – ☎ 03 :

XXX **Alexander's,** Mechelsesteenweg 318, ✆ 4572631 – Ⓟ. AE ⓓ E VISA. ✻
closed Sunday dinner, Monday and July – **M** 1295.

at Merksem : 10 km – ✉ 2060 Merksem – ☎ 03 :

XXX **Maritime,** Bredabaan 978, ✆ 6462223, 佘, « Elegant interior » – Ⓟ. AE ⓓ VISA
closed 1 to 10 January, 27 July-10 August and Sunday – **M** a la carte 1250/1700.

at Schoten : 10 km – pop. 30 774 – ✉ 2120 Schoten – ☎ 03 :

XXX **Kleine Barreel,** Bredabaan 1147, ✆ 6458584 – ▤ Ⓟ. AE ⓓ VISA
M a la carte 1200/1850.

XXX **Uilenspiegel,** Brechtsebaan 277, ✆ 6516145, 佘, « Terrace and garden » – Ⓟ. AE ⓓ E VISA – *closed Saturday lunch and Monday* – **M** 975/1750.

XX **Witte Raaf,** Horstebaan 97, ✆ 6588664, 佘 – Ⓟ. AE ⓓ E VISA
closed Sunday except June to September, Wednesday dinner, Saturday lunch and Easter – **M** a la carte 1210/1960.

XX **Peerdsbos,** Bredabaan 1293, ✆ 6457469 – Ⓟ. AE ⓓ. ✻
closed 8 to 20 June, 10 to 22 September, Monday and Tuesday – **M** a la carte 750/1300.

XX **Ten Weyngaert,** Winkelstapstraat 151, ✆ 6455516, Grill, « Converted 17C farm » – ▤ Ⓟ. AE ⓓ E VISA. ✻
M 985/1055.

at Wijnegem : 10 km – pop. 8 186 – ✉ 2110 Wijnegem – ☎ 03 :

XXX **Ter Vennen,** Merksemsebaan 278, ✆ 3538140, « Converted farm, elegant interior » – Ⓟ. AE ⓓ E VISA
closed Monday, Easter and 1 to 15 September – **M** 875.

BRUGES (BRUGGE) **8000** West-Vlaanderen **213** ③ and **409** ② – pop. 118 146 agglomeration – ☎ 050.

See : Trips on the canals★★★ (Boottocht) CY – Procession of the Holy Blood★★★ – Belfry and Halles★★★ (Belfort en Hallen) CY – Market square★★ (Markt) CY – Market-town★★ (Burg) CY – Beguinage★★ (Begijnhof) CZ – Basilica of the Holy Blood★ – Church of Our Lady★ : tower★★, statue of the Madonna★★, tombstone of Mary of Burgundy★★ CZ **S** – Rosery quay (Rozenhoedkaai) ≤★★ CY – Dijver ≤★★ CZ – St. Boniface bridge (Bonifaciusbrug) : site★★ CZ – Chimney of the "Brugse Vrijë" in the Court of Justice (Gerechtshof) CY **B**.

Museums : Groeninge★★★ CZ – Memling (St. John's Hospital)★★★ CZ – Gruuthuse★ CZ **M¹** – Arents House★ (Arentshuis) CZ **M⁴**.

Envir. : Zedelgem : baptismal font★ in the St.Lawrence's church by ⑥ : 10,5 km.

🅸 Markt 7 ✆ 330711 – Tourist association of the province, Vlamingstraat 55 ✆ 337344.

Brussels 96 ③ – Ghent 44 ③ – Lille 72 ⑪ – Ostend 28 ⑤.

Plans on following pages

🏨 **Orangerie** without rest., Karthuizerinnestraat 10, ✆ 341649, Telex 82443, « Ancient mansion with tasteful decor » – 🛗 TV ☎ – 🏋. AE ⓓ E VISA — CY **y**
18 rm ☕ 3375/5200.

🏨 **Portinari** Ⓜ ⛽ without rest., 't Zand 15, ✆ 341034, Telex 82400 – 🛗 TV ☎ ♿ Ⓟ – 🏋. AE ⓓ E VISA — CZ **x**
32 rm ☕ 2500/3400.

🏨 **Karos** without rest., Hoefijzerlaan 37, ✆ 341448, Telex 82377 – 🛗 ☎ ♿ 🚗. AE ⓓ E VISA
closed 5 January-6 February – **20 rm** ☕ 2780/5130. — BY **r**

🏨 **Park H.** Ⓜ without rest., Vrijdagmarkt 5, ✆ 333364, Telex 81686 – 🛗 TV ☎ – 🏋. AE ⓓ E VISA — CZ **g**
61 rm ☕ 2570/3140.

🏨 **Die Swaene** ⛽ without rest., Steenhouwersdijk 1, ✆ 342798, Telex 82446, ≤ – 🛗 TV 🛁wc ☎. AE E VISA — CY **g**
17 rm ☕ 2450/3400.

🏨 **Erasmus** Ⓜ without rest., Wollestraat 35, ✆ 335781, ≤ – 🛗 TV 🛁wc ☎. AE E VISA. ✻ — CY **a**
10 rm ☕ 2650/4150.

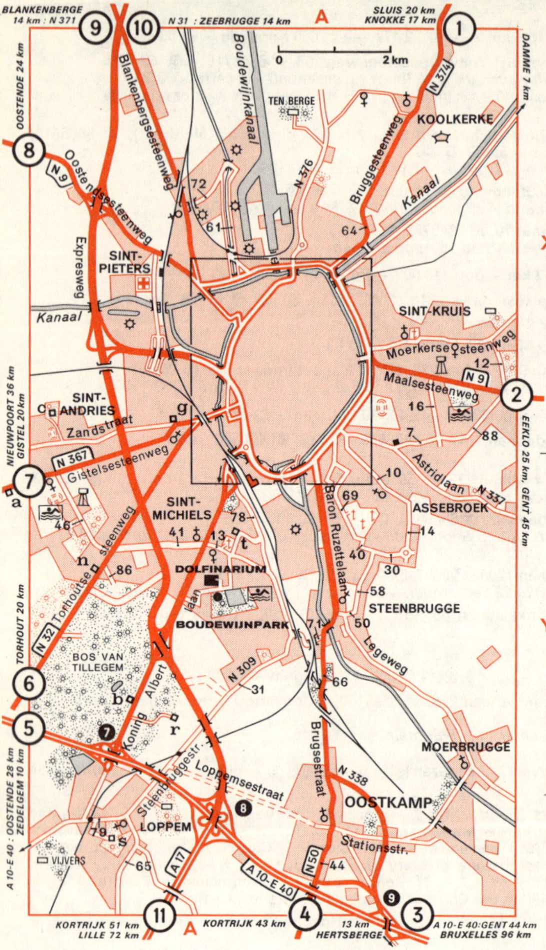

BLANKENBERGE 14 km : N 371
9
10
N 31 : ZEEBRUGGE 14 km
A
SLUIS 20 km
KNOKKE 17 km
1
DAMME 7 km
0
2 km
OOSTENDE 24 km
Blankenbergsesteenweg
Boudewijnkanaal
TEN BERGE
N 374
KOOLKERKE
Bruggesteenweg
N 376
8
N 9
Oostendsesteenweg
72
61
64
Kanaal
Expresweg
SINT-PIETERS
SINT-KRUIS
Kanaal
Moerkerse steenweg
12
N 9
Maalsesteenweg
2
16
88
7
NIEUWPOORT 36 km
GISTEL 20 km
SINT-ANDRIES
c
g
Zandstraat
N 367
Gistelsesteenweg
7
a
46
10
Astridlaan
N 337
EEKLO 25 km, GENT 45 km
SINT-MICHIELS
78
69
ASSEBROEK
41
13
t
14
40
30
Baron Ruzettelaan
n
86
Torhoutse steenweg
DOLFINARIUM
58
STEENBRUGGE
TORHOUT 20 km
N 32
laan
BOUDEWIJNPARK
71
50
Legeweg
BOS VAN TILLEGEM
N 309
31
66
6
b
Albert
r
Koning
5
Steenbruggestr.
Loppemsestraat
MOERBRUGGE
N 338
Brugsestraat
OOSTKAMP
79
s
LOPPEM
A 17
Stationsstr.
44
N 50
A 10-E 40
A 10 - E 40 : OOSTENDE 28 km
ZEDELGEM 10 km
VIJVERS
65
11
4
3
KORTRIJK 51 km
LILLE 72 km
A
KORTRIJK 43 km
13 km
HERTSBERGE
A 10-E 40: GENT 44 km
BRUXELLES 96 km

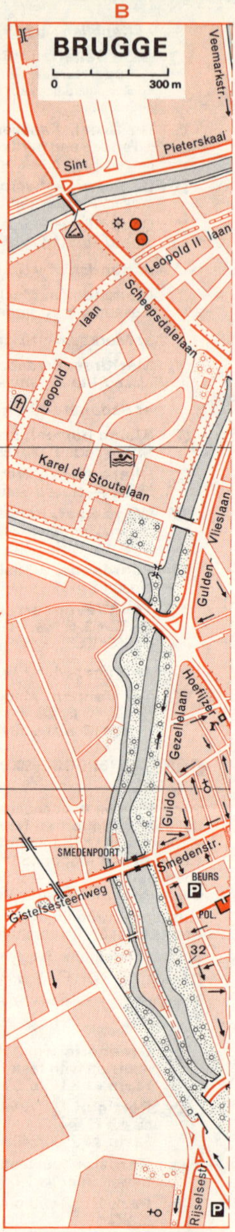

B
BRUGGE
0
300 m
Veemarktstr.
Sint
Pieterskaai
X
Leopold II laan
Scheepsdalelaan
Leopold I laan
Karel de Stoutelaan
Vlieslaan
Y
Gulden-
Hoefijzer
r
Gezellelaan
Guido
SMEDENPOORT
Smedenstr.
BEURS
P
POL.
Gistelsesteenweg
32
Z
Rijselsestr.
P
B

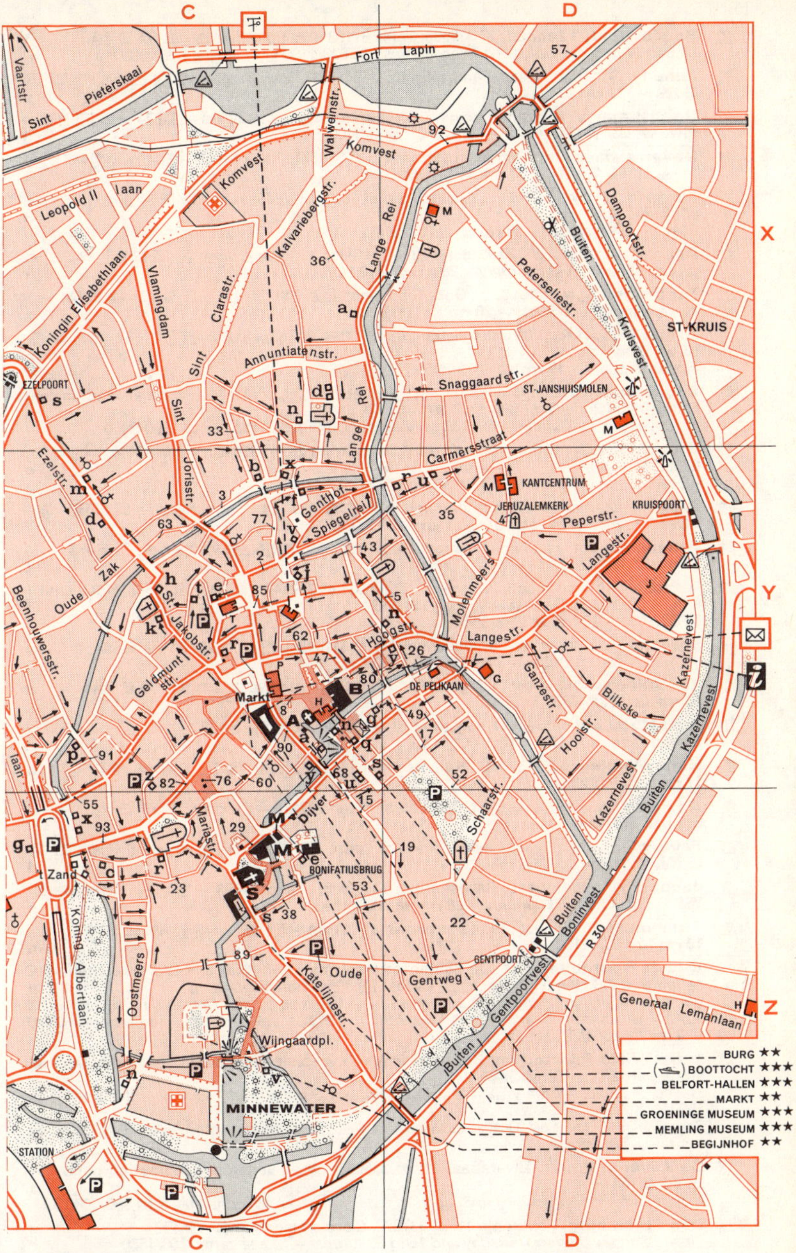

Roelandtsstr. .... A 66	Simon Stevinpl .... CY 76	Vogelzangdreef .... A 86
Rozenhoedkaai .... CY 68	Spanjaardstr. .... CY 77	Vossensteertstr. .... A 88
St. Katarinastr. .... A 69	Spoorwegstr. .... A 78	Walplein .... CZ 89
St. Michielsestr. .... A 71	Stationsstr. .... A 79	Wulfhagestr. .... CY 91
St. Pieterskerklaan .... A 72	Steenhouwersdijk .... CY 80	Wulpenstr. .... DX 92

Boudewijn I, 't Zand 21, 336999, Telex 81163 – wc. AE E VISA — CZ t
closed 14 to 30 January – **M** *(closed Tuesday)* 600/1100 – **11 rm** 1550/3000.

Pand H. without rest., Pandreitje 16, 334434, Telex 81282 – wc. AE E VISA – **17 rm** 2050/2700. — CY u

De Biskajer without rest., Biskajersplein 4, 341506, Telex 81874 – wc wc. AE E VISA. – **17 rm** 2700/3400. — CY j

Navarra without rest., St-Jacobsstraat 41, 340561, Telex 81035 – wc wc – . AE E VISA – **64 rm** 1100/2900. — CY k

Europ H. without rest., Augustijnenrei 18, 337975, Telex 82490 – wc wc. E VISA. — CY b
March-17 November – **28 rm** 1895/2810.

Adornes without rest., St-Annarei 26, – wc. AE E VISA. — DX r
closed 13 January-9 February – **20 rm** 1700/2900.

Ter Brughe without rest., Oost-Gisthelhof 2, 340324 – wc. AE E VISA — CY x
closed January-February – **20 rm** 2050/2500.

Azalea without rest., Wulfhagestraat 43, 331478, Telex 81282 – wc wc. AE E VISA — CY p
closed January – **15 rm** 1975/3050.

Bourgoensch Hof without rest., Wollestraat 39, 331645, canals and ancient Flemish houses – wc wc. — CY a
15 November to March week-ends only except Christmas – **12 rm** 1850/3950.

Groeninghe without rest., Korte Vuldersstraat 29, 336495, Telex 82446 – wc. AE E VISA — CZ c
closed January – **8 rm** 1600/1900.

Bryghia without rest., Oosterlingenplein 4, 338059 – wc wc. AE E VISA. — CY f
closed 2 January-14 February – **18 rm** 2070/2370.

Aragon without rest., Naaldenstraat 24, 333533 – wc wc. AE E VISA — CY t
16 rm 1800/2800.

't Putje with apartments in annex, 't Zand 31, 332847, , Buffet lunch, open until 1 a.m. – wc wc – . AE VISA — CZ t
M 600/850 – **10 rm** 2100/2950.

Egmond without rest., Minnewater 15, 341445 – wc. AE E VISA — CZ v
15 March-14 November – **8 rm** 2150/2800.

Ter Duinen without rest., Langerei 52, 330437 – wc. AE E VISA — CX a
10 rm 1240/1780.

Post Hotel without rest., Hoogstraat 18, 337889 – wc. VISA — DY y
closed January – **22 rm** 1600/1900.

Hans Memling without rest., Kuipersstraat 18, 332096 – wc. VISA — CY e
17 rm 1760/2060.

De Pauw without rest., St-Gilliskerkhof 8, 337118 – wc. AE E VISA — CX d
8 rm 870/1500.

Fevery without rest., Collaert Mansionstraat 3, 331269 – wc wc. AE E VISA – **11 rm** 1115/1530. — CX d

Jacobs without rest., Baliestraat 1, 339831, Telex 81693 – wc wc. AE VISA – *closed 6 to 31 January* – **28 rm** 1050/1640 — CX n

Anselmus without rest., Ridderstraat 15, 341374 – wc wc. AE E VISA — DY n
10 rm 1600/2100.

Duc de Bourgogne with rm, Huidenvettersplaats 12, 332038, « Old style interior, canals and old Flemish houses » – rest wc. AE E VISA — CY n
closed January, July and Sunday dinner, Monday except Bank Holidays from October to April – **M** *(closed Tuesday lunch from April to October and Monday)* a la carte 1470/2020 – **9 rm** 2050/3950.

De Witte Poorte (Van Boven), Jan Van Eyckplein 6, 330883, « Former vaulted store, garden » – AE VISA — CY v
closed 9 to 20 February, last 2 weeks August, Sunday and Monday – **M** a la carte 1500/2300
Spec. Terrine de foie d'oie, Queues de langoustines aux petits légumes et beurre blanc, Médaillon de homard aux filets de sole.

De Zilveren Pauw, Zilverstraat 41, 335566, , « Belle-époque interior, patio » – AE E VISA — CY z
closed 13 to 27 February, 16 to 31 July, Tuesday dinner and Wednesday – **M** 980/2000.

Den Braamberg, Pandreitje 11, 337370, Classic-elegant – AE VISA — CY u
closed Sunday dinner, Thursday and 15 to 30 August – **M** a la carte 1100/1500.

De Karmeliet (Van Hecke), Jeruzalemstraat 1, 338259 – AE E VISA — DY u
closed Sunday dinner, Monday, 24 August-9 September and 1 week February – **M** a la carte 1720/2000
Spec. Lapereau et cervelle de veau cuit en torchon, Pithivier de poularde aux truffes et salsifis (January-March), Choix de pâtisseries.

XX **'t Pandreitje,** Pandreitje 6, ✆ 331190, « Elegant interior » – AE ⓓ E VISA. ✻ CDY s
closed 1 to 16 June, 14 to 30 December, Sunday and Monday – **M** a la carte 1400/2100.

XX ✿ **De Snippe** (Huysentruyt), Achiel van Ackerplein 2, ✆ 337070 – AE ⓓ E VISA CY m
closed 3 weeks February, 1 week July, Sunday and Monday lunch – **M** (booking essential) 1750
Spec. Médaillon de homard et cervelle de veau au vinaigre d'échalotes, Civet de pigeonneau truffé en papillote, Queues de langoustines à la ciboulette.

XX **Kardinaalshof,** Sint-Salvatorkerkhof 14, ✆ 341691, Seafood – AE E VISA CZ r
closed Sunday dinner, Tuesday, last 2 weeks January and last 2 weeks June – **M** a la carte 1150/1570.

XX **Den Gouden Harynck,** Groeninge 25, ✆ 337637 – AE ⓓ E VISA CZ e
closed 27 July-11 August – **M** a la carte 1570/2000.

XX **'t Bourgoensche Cruyce** with rm, Wollestraat 41, ✆ 337926, ≤ canals and old Flemish houses – TV wc. AE VISA. ✻ CY a
closed February, first week November, Tuesday from May to October and Sunday, Monday lunch from October to May – **M** a la carte 1400/1780 – **6 rm** 1150/1765.

XX **Criterium,** 't Zand 12, ✆ 331984, – AE ⓓ E VISA CZ x
closed 1 to 7 July, 22 to 31 October and Tuesday dinner, Wednesday except July-August – **M** 795/1250.

XX **'t Lammetje,** Braambergstraat 3, ✆ 332495 – AE ⓓ E VISA. ✻ CY q
closed Monday, 28 August-4 September and 10 to 28 February – **M** a la carte 1240/1610.

X **Eglantier,** Ezelstraat 120, ✆ 332946 – VISA CX s
closed Sunday dinner and Monday – **M** a la carte 900/1450.

X **'t Presidentje,** Ezelstraat 21, ✆ 339521 – AE ⓓ E VISA CY d
closed Wednesday dinner, Sunday and 16 June-5 July – **M** a la carte 800/1300.

X **'t Kluizeke,** Sint Jacobstraat 58, ✆ 341224 – AE ⓓ VISA. ✻ CY h
closed Wednesday and February – **M** 990.

X **De Watermolen,** Oostmeers 130, ✆ 332448, , « Terrace » – E VISA CZ n
closed Monday dinner, Tuesday dinner, Thursday dinner from October to May, Wednesday, 2 weeks October and 2 weeks February – **M** 600/850.

X **Postiljon,** Katelijnestraat 3, ✆ 335616 – AE ⓓ E VISA CZ s
closed Sunday dinner, Tuesday and 20 November-9 December – **M** a la carte 680/1340.

X **Malpertuus,** Eiermarkt 9, ✆ 333038 – AE ⓓ E VISA CY r
closed Wednesday and July – **M** 420/770.

South – ✉ 8200 – ☎ 050 :

Novotel M, Chartreuseweg 20, ✆ 382851, Telex 81507, , , – rest TV wc ☎ P – AE ⓓ E VISA A r
M a la carte 640/1150 – 265 – **101 rm** 2150/2950.

XXXX ✿✿ **Weinebrugge** (Galens), Koning Albertlaan 242, ✆ 384440 – P. AE A b
closed Sunday dinner from December to March, Wednesday, Thursday and January – **M** (week-end booking essential) a la carte 1730/2550.

XXX **Casserole** (Hotel. school), Groene Poortdreef 17, ✆ 383888, « Country atmosphere » – P. AE VISA A t
closed 30 June-16 August – **M** (lunch only except Friday and Saturday) a la carte 1200/1950.

South-West – ✉ 8200 – ☎ 050 :

Pannenhuis M, Zandstraat 2, ✆ 311907, Telex 82345, ≤, , « Garden-terrace » – TV ☎ P – AE ⓓ E VISA. ✻ rest A g
closed 15 to 31 January – **M** *(closed 15 to 31 January, 1 to 15 July, Tuesday dinner except July-August and Wednesday)* a la carte 1200/1700 – **20 rm** 1250/3100 – ½ p 1950/2200.

XXX ✿ **Ter Heyde** (Hanbuckers) with rm, Torhoutsesteenweg 620 (by ⑥ : 8 km on N 32), ✆ 383858, ≤, « Stately home in extensive grounds » – TV wc P. ⓓ E VISA. ✻ rm
closed Wednesday dinner, Thursday and 15 December-22 January – **M** 1850 – **5 rm** 2000/3100.

XX **Vossenburg** with rm, Zandstraat 272 (Coude Ceuken), ✆ 317026, « Converted castle in a park » – wc P. ✻ rm A c
closed 15 to 30 November – **M** *(closed Tuesday and Sunday dinner)* 600/795 – **8 rm** 915/1280.

X **De Boekeneute,** Torhoutsesteenweg 380, ✆ 382632, – P. AE ⓓ E VISA A n
closed Sunday dinner, Monday and 16 to 31 August – **M** 850/1600.

à Jabbeke par ⑦ : 11 km par N 367 – pop. 11 186 – ✉ 8220 Jabbeke – ☎ 050:

XXX **Haeneveld,** Krauwerstraat 1 (SE : 2 km by N 367), ✆ 812700, ≤, , « In an old farm, garden-terrace » – P. AE E VISA
closed 14 to 24 July, 22 December-3 January, Sunday dinner and Monday – **M** 1000/1600.

at Loppem C Zedelgem, South : 5 km – pop. 19 494 – ✉ 8021 Loppem – ☎ 050 :

XX **Bakkershof,** Parklaan 16, ✆ 824987 – P. AE ⓓ A s
closed Tuesday dinner from October to April and Wednesday – **M** a la carte 900/1830.

at Oostkamp by ④ bridge E40 then 2nd street on the left – pop. 20 081 – ✉ 8020 Oostkamp – ☎ 050 :

XX **De Kampveldhoeve,** Kampveldstraat 16, ☎ 824258, ←, « Country atmosphere » – Ⓟ
closed Tuesday – **M** 700/1295.

at Ruddervoorde Ⓒ Oostkamp, by ④ : 12 km – pop. 20 081 – ✉ 8040 Ruddervoorde – ☎ 050 :

XXX **Leegendael** with rm, Kortrijkstraat 486 (N 50), ☎ 277699, ←, Ancient residence in a country atmosphere – wc Ⓟ. AE E VISA
closed Monday, Sunday dinner and 3 to 24 February – **M** 1200/1650 – **7 rm** 1750/2550.

at Sint-Kruis by ② : 6 km – ✉ 8310 Sint-Kruis – ☎ 050 :

Lodewijk van Male, Maalsesteenweg 488, ☎ 355763, « Extensive park with lake » – wc wc Ⓟ. rm
M *(closed Monday)* 600/895 – **14 rm** 1140/1620.

XX **Jonkman,** Maalsesteenweg 438, ☎ 360767, ←, – AE E VISA
closed Sunday, Monday and 1 to 15 September – **M** 850/1500.

at Varsenare by ⑦ : 6,5 km – ✉ 8202 Varsenare – ☎ 050 :

XX **Stuivenberg,** Gistelsteenweg 27, ☎ 318402, – Ⓟ. AE E VISA A a
closed Sunday dinner and Monday – **M** a la carte 1130/1500.

at Waardamme Ⓒ Oostkamp, by ④ : 11 km – pop. 20 081 – ✉ 8041 Waardamme – ☎ 050 :

XXX **Ter Talinge,** Rooiveldstraat 46, ☎ 279061, « Country atmosphere, terrace » – Ⓟ. AE VISA
closed Wednesday dinner and Thursday – **M** a la carte 920/1300.

at Zedelgem by ⑥ : 10,5 km – pop. 19 494 – ✉ 8210 Zedelgem – ☎ 050 :

Zuidwege Ⓜ without rest., Torhoutsesteenweg 126, ☎ 201339 – wc wc Ⓟ. AE E VISA
closed Tuesday dinner – **17 rm** 800/2300.

Bonne Auberge, Torhoutsesteenweg 201, ☎ 209525, Telex 81227 – wc Ⓟ – . AE E VISA
M *(closed Sunday except Bank Holidays and December-January)* a la carte 740/1400 – **27 rm** 1315/2530 – P 2100.

XX **Ter Leepe,** Torhoutsesteenweg 168, ☎ 200197 – Ⓟ. AE VISA
closed 20 July-3 August, 18 to 30 January, Sunday and Wednesday dinner – **M** 725/1295.

Oostende 8400 West-Vlaanderen 213 ② and 409 ① – pop. 69 039 – ☎ 059 – 27 km.

XXXX ❀❀ **Au Vigneron and Oostendse Compagnie** (Daue) with rm, Koningstraat 79 ☎ 704816 – wc Ⓟ. AE E VISA
closed Sunday dinner, Monday, October and 1 to 15 March – **M** (Saturday and Sunday booking essential) a la carte 1630/2250
Spec. Trois services de homard, Turbot Edouard Nignon, Sole à la ciboulette.

Knokke 8300 West-Vlaanderen 212 ⑪ and 409 ② – pop. 29 730 – ☎ 050 – 17 km.

XXX ❀❀ **Aquilon** (De Spae), 1st floor, Lippenslaan 306, ☎ 601274, « Classic-elegant » – AE E.
closed 15 November-January, Sunday dinner, Monday and Tuesday from 15 September to Easter, Tuesday dinner from Easter to 15 September and Wednesday – **M** (Saturday and Sunday booking essential) a la carte 1700/2550
Spec. Feuilleté aux asperges et langoustines, Foie d'oie au naturel, Turbotin à la marinière en papillote.

Oostkerke 8350 West-Vlaanderen 213 ③ and 409 ② – ☎ 050 – 7 km.

XX ❀❀ **Bruegel** (Fonteyne), Damse Vaart Zuid 26, ☎ 500346, ←, « Rustic interior » – Ⓟ. AE E
closed Tuesday, Wednesday and 24 December-5 March – **M** (Saturday and Sunday booking essential) a la carte 1800/2500
Spec. Terrine d'anguilles, Gratinée de crevettes grises à la flamande, Homard puce au witloof (Sept.-July).

Waregem 8790 West-Vlaanderen 213 ⑮ and 409 ⑪ – pop. 33 575 – ☎ 056 – 47 km.

South : 2 km, near motorway :

XXX ❀❀ **'t Oud Konijntje** (Desmedt), Bosstraat 53, ☎ 601937, , « Elegant inn - garden setting » – Ⓟ. AE E VISA
closed Thursday dinner, Friday, Sunday dinner, 22 July-12 August and 23 December-3 January – **M** a la carte 1200/2200
Spec. Langouste Alexandre, Petite raie à la vapeur aux choux verts, Riz de veau en croûte.

LUXEMBOURG

SIGHTS

See : Site★★ – Old Luxembourg★★ – "Promenade de la Corniche" ≤★★ and the rocks of the city ≤★★ DY – The Bock cliff ≤★★, Bock Casemates★★ DY – Place de la Constitution ≤★★ DY – Grand-Ducal Palace★ DY K – Our Lady's Cathedral (Notre Dame)★ DY L – Grand-Duchess Charlotte Bridge★ DY – State Museum★★ DY

LUXEMBOURG 8 ⑧ and 409 ㉖ – pop. 78 912.

18 Höhenhof, near Airport ✆ 34090.

Findel by ③ : 6 km ✆ 47981 and 47983 – **Air terminal :** pl. de la Gare ✆ 481820.

pl. d'Armes. ✉ 2011. ✆ 22809.

Amsterdam 419 ⑧ – Bonn 190 ③ – Brussels 219 ⑧.

Plan on next page

Luxembourg-Centre :

Le Royal M, bd Royal 12, ✉ 2449, ✆ 41616, Telex 2979, – AE E VISA. rest CY e
M *(closed Saturday dinner and 4 to 24 August)* a la carte 1210/1860 – **170 rm** 4300/6200.

Cravat, bd Roosevelt 29, ✉ 2450, ✆ 21975, Telex 2846 – TV ☎ – AE E VISA. rest DY a
M 600/950 – **59 rm** 3100/3900.

Rix H. without rest., bd Royal 20, ✉ 2449, ✆ 27545, Telex 1234 – TV wc wc ☎ – . CY b
closed 20 December-4 January – **19 rm** 1350/2950.

XXX ✿✿ **St-Michel** (Guillou), 1st floor, r. Eau 32, ✉ 1449, ✆ 23215, Seafood, « Rustic interior » – AE E VISA DY e
closed 1 to 30 August, 25 December-5 January, Saturday and Sunday – **M** (booking essential) a la carte 1580/2540
Spec. Raviolis de langoustines, Mosaïque de saumon, langoustines et anguilles au Loerum, Emincé de veau au jus de truffes. **Wines** Pinot gris, Riesling.

XXX **Le Vert Galant,** 1st floor, r. Aldringen 23 (r. Poste), ✉ 1118, ✆ 470822 – . AE E VISA – *closed Saturday lunch and Sunday* – **M** a la carte 1350/1770 CY r

XXX **Alsacien,** r. du Curé 24, ✉ 1368, ✆ 28250 – AE VISA. DY r
closed Saturday, Sunday, Bank Holidays and August – **M** a la carte 1220/1615.

XXX **Astoria,** av. du X-Septembre 14, ✉ 2550, ✆ 446223 – AE E VISA CY y
closed Saturday – **M** (lunch only) a la carte 1390/1790.

XXX **Gourmet,** r. Chimay 8, ✉ 1333, ✆ 25561 – AE DY h
closed Sunday dinner, Monday, 23 January-14 February and 22 July-14 August – **M** a la carte 975/1535.

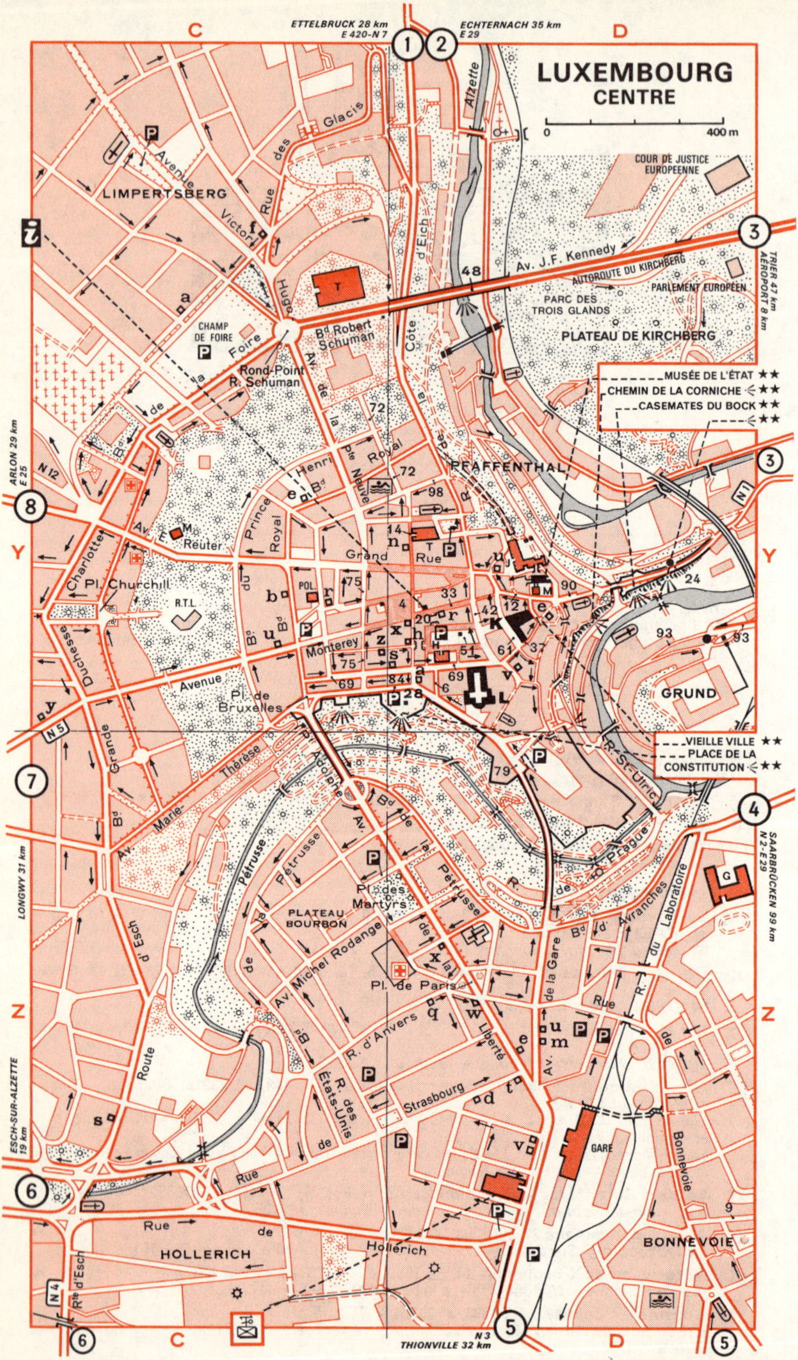
LUXEMBOURG
CENTRE
0
400 m
ETTELBRUCK 28 km
E 420-N 7
ECHTERNACH 35 km
E 29
TRIER 47 km
AÉROPORT 8 km
ARLON 29 km
E 25
LONGWY 31 km
ESCH-SUR-ALZETTE 19 km
SAARBRÜCKEN 99 km
N 2-E 29
N 3
THIONVILLE 32 km
COUR DE JUSTICE EUROPÉENNE
PARLEMENT EUROPÉEN
PARC DES TROIS GLANDS
PLATEAU DE KIRCHBERG
Av. J.F. Kennedy
AUTOROUTE DU KIRCHBERG
MUSÉE DE L'ÉTAT ★★
CHEMIN DE LA CORNICHE ★★
CASEMATES DU BOCK ★★
VIEILLE VILLE ★★
PLACE DE LA CONSTITUTION ★★
LIMPERTSBERG
CHAMP DE FOIRE
Rond-Point R. Schuman
Bd Robert Schuman
Rue des Glacis
Avenue Victor Hugo
Côte d'Eich
Alzette
PFAFFENTHAL
GRUND
Av. de la Pte Neuve
Bd Royal
Bd Prince Henri
Grand Rue
Pl. Churchill
R.T.L.
Av. E. Reuter
Bd Charlotte
Bd Grande Duchesse
Avenue Monterey
Pl. de Bruxelles
Av. Marie-Thérèse
Pétrusse
Bd de la Pétrusse
Av. de la Liberté
Pl. des Martyrs
PLATEAU BOURBON
Av. Michel Rodange
Pl. de Paris
R. d'Anvers
Bd de la Pétrusse
Rue de Strasbourg
R. des États-Unis
Route d'Esch
R. St-Ulric
Bd d'Avranches
R. du Laboratoire
Av. de la Gare
Rue de Bonnevoie
GARE
BONNEVOIE
HOLLERICH
Rue de Hollerich
Rte d'Esch
N 4
N 5
N 12
N 1
C
D
Y
Z

STREET INDEX TO LUXEMBOURG TOWN PLAN

Capucins (R. des) .... DY 14
Chimay (R.) .... DY 20
Curé (R. du) .... DY 33
Fossé (R. du) .... DY 42
Gare (Av. de la) .... DZ
Grand-Rue .... CDY
Liberté (Av. de la) .... DZ
Philippe-II (R.) .... CY 75
Porte-Neuve (Av.) .... CY
Strasbourg (R. de) .... CDZ

Adolphe (Pont) .... CYZ
Anvers (R. d') .... CDZ
Armes (Pl. d') .... DY 4
Athénée (R. de l') .... DY 6
Avranches (Bd d') .... DZ
Bonnevoie (R. de) .... DZ
Boucherie (R. de la) .... DY 12
Bruxelles (Pl. de) .... CY
Clausen (Montée de) .... DY 24
Constitution (Pl. de la) .... DY 28
Eau (R. de l') .... DY 37
Emile-Reuter (Av.) .... CY
Esch (Rte d') .... CZ
États-Unis (R. des) .... CZ
Foire (Bd de la) .... CY
Franklin-Roosevelt (Bd) .... CDY 45
Glacis (R. des) .... CY
Grande-Duchesse-Charlotte (Bd) .... CYZ
Grande-Duchesse-Charlotte (Pont) .... DY 48
Guillaume (Pl.) .... DY 51
Hollerich (R. de) .... CDZ
John-F.-Kennedy (Av.) .... DY
Laboratoire (R. du) .... DZ
Marché-aux-Herbes (R. du) .... DY 61
Marie-Thérèse (Av.) .... CY
Martyrs (Pl. des) .... CDZ
Michel-Rodange (Av.) .... CZ
Monterey (Av.) .... CY
Notre-Dame (R.) .... CDY 69
Paris (Pl. de) .... DZ
Pescatore (Av.) .... CY 72
Pétrusse (Bd de la) .... CDZ
Prague (R. de) .... DZ
Prince-Henri (Bd du) .... CY
Robert-Schuman (Rd-Pt) .... CY
Robert-Schuman (R.) .... CY
Royal (Bd) .... CY
St-Ulric (R.) .... DZ
Sigefroi (R.) .... DY 90
Trèves (R. de) .... DY 93
Victor-Hugo (Av.) .... CY
Wily-Goergen (R.) .... DY 98

XX **Theatre Musculus,** r. Beaumont 3, ✉ 1219, ✆ 40534, 😊, Luxemburg rustic – AE VISA. 🐕 — DY **n**
closed Sunday dinner, Monday and 10 August-9 September – **M** a la carte 1200/1750.

XX **Caesar,** av. Monterey 18, ✉ 2163, ✆ 470925, Tavern restaurant, « Tasteful decor » – AE ⓓ E VISA — CY **u**
closed Sunday lunch – **M** a la carte 800/1300.

XX **L'Obernai,** r. Palais de Justice 1, ✉ 1841, ✆ 22212 – VISA — DY **u**
closed Saturday lunch, Sunday and 25 August-14 September – **M** a la carte 1035/1710.

X **Roma,** r. Louvigny 5, ✉ 1946, ✆ 23692, Italian rest. – AE VISA — CY **z**
closed Sunday dinner, Monday, 10 August-10 September and 24 December-2 January – **M** a la carte 740/1090.

X **Gëlle Fra,** r. Notre-Dame 10, ✉ 2240, ✆ 471794, Tavern restaurant – AE E VISA — DY **s**
closed Wednesday dinner, Thursday, 20 July-19 August and 24 December-3 January – **M** 600/980.

Luxembourg-Station :

🏨 **Kons,** pl. Gare 24, ✉ 1616, ✆ 486021, Telex 2306 – 🛗 TV ☎ – 🏛. AE ⓓ E VISA. 🐕 rest — DZ **v**
M *(closed Sunday)* 600 – **141 rm** ☕ 2140/3380.

🏨 **Arcotel** Ⓜ without rest., av. Gare 43, ✉ 1611, ✆ 494001, Telex 3776 – 🛗 TV ☎. AE ⓓ E VISA. 🐕 — DZ **u**
30 rm ☕ 2300/2600.

🏨 **Nobilis and Rest. Calao** Ⓜ, av. Gare 47, ✉ 1611, ✆ 494971, Telex 3212 – 🛗 ▤ TV ☎ 🚗 – 🏛. AE ⓓ E VISA — DZ **m**
M 600/795 – ☕ 313 – **43 rm** 2500/2600.

🏨 **Central-Molitor,** av. Liberté 28, ✉ 1930, ✆ 489911, Telex 2613 – 🛗 TV ☎. AE ⓓ E VISA. 🐕 rest — DZ **x**
M *(closed Friday and mid December-mid January)* 615/860 – **36 rm** ☕ 1990/2630.

🏨 **President,** pl. Gare 32, ✉ 1616, ✆ 486161, Telex 1510 – 🛗 TV ☎. AE ⓓ E VISA — DZ **v**
M *(closed Sunday)* (dinner only) 630 – **40 rm** ☕ 2500/3900.

🏨 **Ardennes** Ⓜ without rest., av. Liberté 59, ✉ 1931, ✆ 488141 – 🛗 TV 🛁wc ☎ — DZ **e**
21 rm ☕ 2100/2400.

🏨 **Bristol** without rest., r. Strasbourg 11, ✉ 2561, ✆ 485829, Telex 2328 – 🛗 TV 🚿wc ☎. AE ⓓ E VISA. 🐕 — DZ **d**
29 rm ☕ 1900/2400.

🏨 **City** without rest., r. Strasbourg 1, ✉ 2561, ✆ 484608 – 🛗 🚿wc ☎. AE ⓓ E VISA — DZ **t**
closed 21 December-9 January – ☕ 180 – **30 rm** 850/2100.

XXX **Cordial,** 1st floor, pl. Paris 1, ✉ 2314, ✆ 488538, « Elegant interior » – VISA. 🐕 — DZ **w**
closed Friday, Saturday lunch, 15 July-14 August and 8 to 15 February – **M** a la carte 1370/2100.

XX **Arlecchino,** rte d'Esch 100, ✉ 1470, ✆ 446456, Italian rest. – Ⓟ. E VISA — CZ **s**
closed Saturday lunch, Sunday and 24 December-1 January – **M** a la carte 1080/1520.

XX **Italia** with rm, r. Anvers 15, ✉ 1130, ✆ 486626, Telex 3644, 😊, Italian rest. – TV 🛁wc 🚿wc ☎. AE ⓓ E VISA — DZ **q**
M a la carte 820/1280 – **20 rm** ☕ 1700/2200.

Upland of Kirchberg – ✉ Luxembourg :

🏨 **Holiday Inn and Rest. Les Trois Glands** Ⓜ, Kirchberg, ✉ 2015, ✆ 437761, Telex 2751, 🏊 – 🛗 ▤ TV ☎ ♿ Ⓟ – 🏛. AE ⓓ E VISA. 🐕 rest
M *(closed Saturday lunch)* (Open until midnight) a la carte 950/1480 – **260 rm** ☕ 3300/5000.

North, at Limpertsberg – ✉ Luxembourg :

Europe without rest., av. du Bois 1, ✉ 1251, ✆ 470444, Telex 3707 – wc ☎. AE E VISA CY **f**
50 rm 1850/2300.

XX **Osteria del Teatro,** Allée Scheffer 21, ✉ 2520, ✆ 28811, Italian rest. – AE E VISA
closed Sunday – **M** a la carte 770/1180. CY **a**

North-East – ✉ Luxembourg :

XXX **Le Grimpereau,** r. Cents 140, ✉ 1319, ✆ 436787, « Converted villa, garden setting » – P. AE VISA
closed Saturday lunch, Sunday, Bank Holidays and last 2 weeks July – **M** a la carte 1520/1930.

at Dommeldange – ✉ Dommeldange :

Inter-Continental M, r. Jean Engling, ✉ 1466, ✆ 43781, Telex 3754, ←, – TV ☎ P – . AE E VISA. rest
M a la carte 1300/1890 – 500 – **344 rm** 3900/6900.

Novotel M, rte d'Echternach, ✉ 1453, ✆ 435643, Telex 1418, – TV ☎ P – . AE E VISA
M a la carte 710/1620 – **238 rm** 2500/3200.

XXX ✻ **Host. Grünewald** with rm, rte d'Echternach 10, ✉ 1453, ✆ 431882, « Tasteful decor » – rest wc wc ☎ P. AE E VISA.
closed 6 to 21 January – **M** *(closed Saturday lunch and Sunday)* (booking essential week-ends) a la carte 1350/1820 – **28 rm** 1950/2900
Spec. Mousse de jambon, Homard fin bec, Turbot aux graines de moutarde. **Wines** Pinot gris, Riesling.

at Hesperange – pop. 9 090 – ✉ Hespérange :

XXX ✻ **L'Agath** (Steichen) with rm, rte de Thionville 274, ✉ 5884, ✆ 488687, , « Classic-elegant », – TV wc wc ☎ P. AE E VISA
closed Sunday and mid July-mid August – **M** *(closed Saturday lunch, Sunday and Monday lunch)* a la carte 1780/2270 – **7 rm** 1500/3200
Spec. Chartreuse de foie gras, Turbot aux petits choux de langoustines. **Wines** Pinot gris.

at the skating-rink of Kockelscheuer – ✉ Luxembourg :

XXX ✻ **Patin d'Or** (Berring), r. Bettembourg 40, ✉ 1899, ✆ 26499 – P. AE E VISA
closed Saturday lunch, Sunday dinner, Monday, 25 August-7 September and 22 December-11 January – **M** a la carte 1330/2050
Spec. Pot-au-feu de foie d'oie en chartreuse (Sept.-March), Cul de lapereau farci au romarin, nouilles fraîches, Dodines de soles et épinards en feuillantine. **Wines** Pinot gris, Riesling.

Airport by ③ : 8 km – ✉ Luxembourg :

Aérogolf-Sheraton, M, rte de Trèves, ✉ 1019, ✆ 34571, Telex 2662, ← – TV ☎ P – – **148 rm**.

Diekirch 8 ③ and 409 ㉖ – pop. 5 585 – 35 km :

XXX ✻✻ **Hiertz** with rm, r. Clairefontaine 1, ✉ 9220, ✆ 803562, « Tasteful decoration, terrace and flower garden » – wc. AE E VISA
closed Monday dinner, Tuesday, end August-beginning September and 23 December-14 January – **M** (booking essential) a la carte 1350/1870 – **7 rm** 1400/1900
Spec. Salade d'épinards au foie gras, Grande assiette du pêcheur, Nougatine glacée. **Wines** Riesling.

Echternach 8 ④ and 409 ㉗ – pop. 4 159 – 35 km :

at Geyershof SW : 7 km by E 42 C Consthum – pop. 278 – ✉ Echternach :

XXX ✻✻ **La Bergerie** (Phal), ✉ 6251, ✆ 79464, ←, , « Converted farm, country atmosphere » – P. AE E VISA
closed Monday lunch except Bank Holidays, Sunday dinner and February – **M** a la carte 1350/2130
Spec. Poêlée de langoustines aux herbes, Filet d'agneau en croûte, Gigotin de poulette aux pois gourmands. **Wines** Riesling, Pinot gris.

AMSTERDAM

SIGHTS

See : Old Amsterdam★★★ : the canals★★★ (Grachten) : Singel, Herengracht, Reguliersgracht, Keizersgracht, boattrip★ (Rondvaart) – Beguine Convent★★ (Begijnhof) LY – Dam : New Church★ (Nieuwe Kerk) LXY – Flower market★ (Bloemenmarkt) LY – Rembrandt Square (Rembrandtsplein) MY – Small Bridge (Magere Brug) MZ.

Museums : Rijksmuseum★★★ KZ – Rijksmuseum Vincent van Gogh★★★ – Municipal★★ (Stedelijk Museum) : Modern Art – History of Amsterdam★★ (Amsterdams Historisch Museum) LY – Madame Tussaud★ : wax museum LY **M1** – Museum Amstelkring Ons'Lieve Heer op Solder : ancient secret chapel★ MX **M4** – Rembrandt's House★ (Rembrandthuis) : (graphic arts of the master) MY **M5** – Maritime Museum of the Netherlands★ (Nederlands Scheepvaart Museum) – The Tropics Museum★ (Tropenmuseum) – Allard Pierson★ : archaeological collections.

AMSTERDAM Noord-Holland 211 ③ and 408 ⑩ ㉗ ㉘ – Pop. 676 439 – ☎ 0 20.

18 Zwarte Laantje 4 at Duivendrecht ☎ (0 20) 943650.
9 Sportpark Overamstel, Jan Vroegopsingel ☎ (0 20) 651863.

at Schiphol SW : 9,5 km ☎ (0 20) 5110432 (information) and (0 20) 747747 (reservations) – **Air Terminal :** Central Station ☎ (0 20) 495575.

(Departure from 's-Hertogenbosch) ☎ (0 20) 238383 and (0 20) 141959 (Schiphol).

Stationsplein (Koffiehuis), ✉ 1012 AB ☎ 266444 – Tourist Association of the Province, Rokin 9-15, ✉ 1012 KK, ☎ 221016, Telex 12324.

Bruxelles 204 ③ – Düsseldorf 227 ③ – Den Haag 60 ④ – Luxembourg 419 ③ – Rotterdam 76 ④.

AMSTERDAM
CENTRE

van Baerlestr.	JZ	5
Damstr.	LMY	32
Constant Huygensstr. (1e)	JZ	28
Heiligeweg	LY	69
Hekelveld	MX	71
Kattengat	LX	102
Langebrugsteeg	LY	107
Martelaarsgracht	MX	116
Muntpl.	LY	127
Nieuwe Hoogstr.	MY	132
Oudebrugsteeg	MX	140
Oude Doelenstr.	MY	142
Oude Hoogstr.	MY	144
Oude Turfmarkt	LY	146
Reguliersbreestr.	LY	156
Stromarkt	LX	174
Thorbeckepl	MZ	177

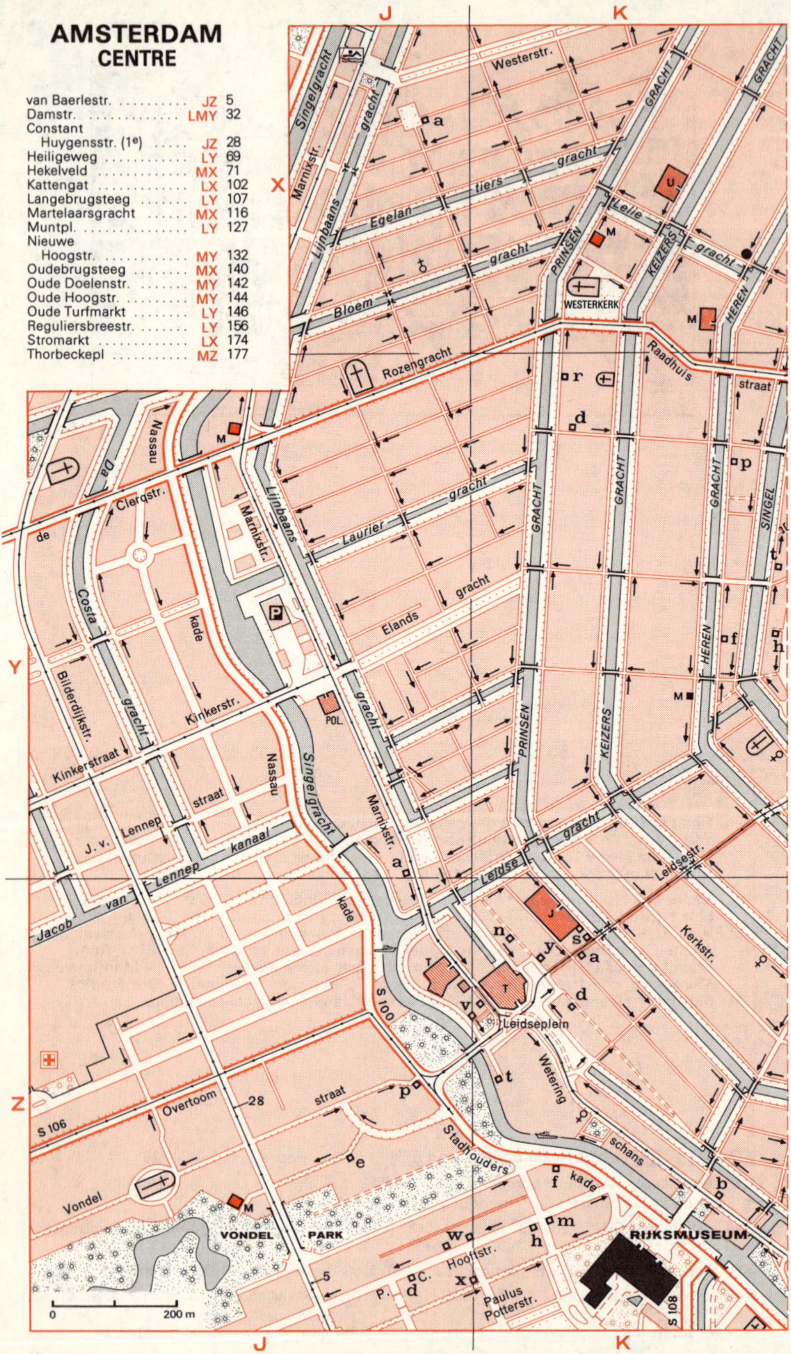

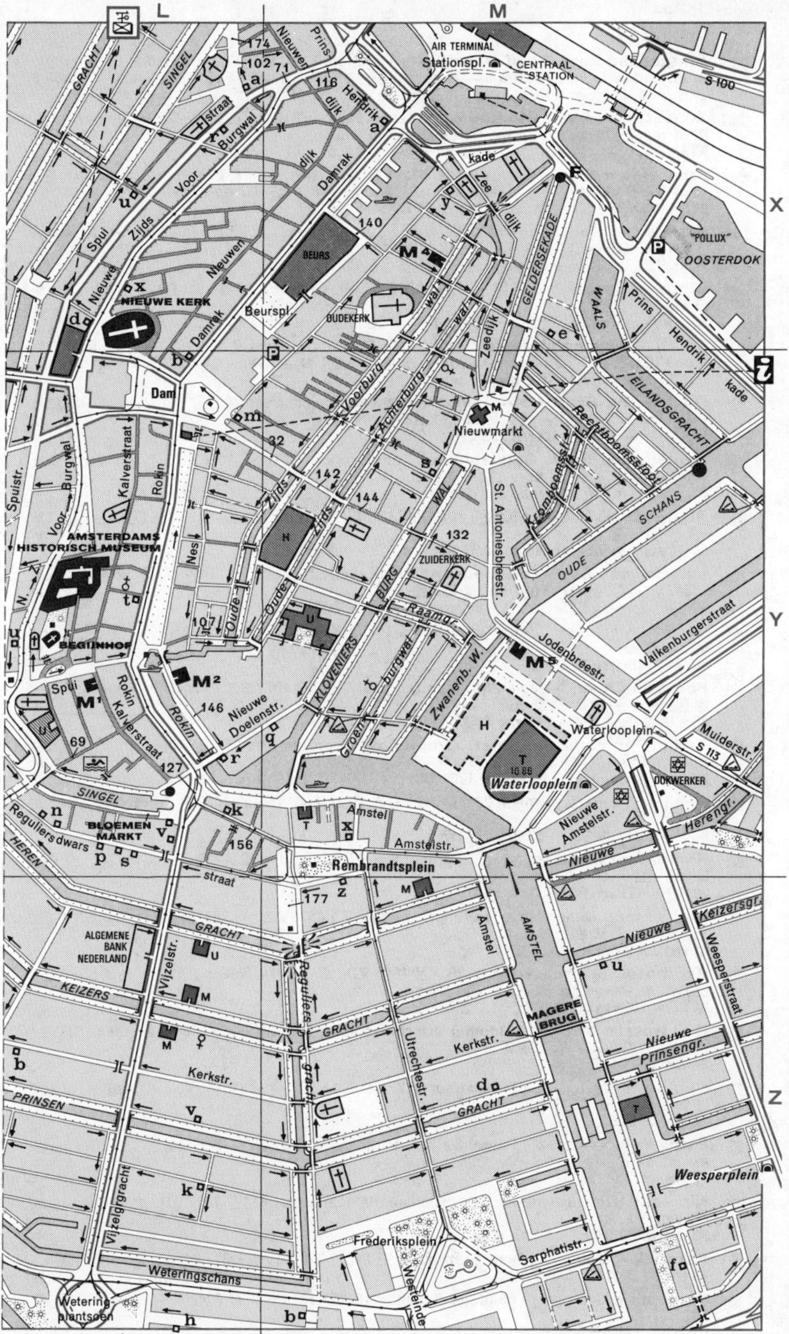
L
M
X
Y
Z
AIR TERMINAL
Stationspl.
CENTRAAL STATION
S 100
"POLLUX"
OOSTERDOK
SINGEL
GRACHT
Nieuwen
Prins
Hendrik
dijk
Burgwal
Voor
Zijds
Spui
Nieuwe
Damrak
BEURS
Beurspl.
NIEUWE KERK
OUDEKERK
kade
Zee
dijk
GELDERSEKADE
WAALS
EILANDSGRACHT
Dam
Nieuwmarkt
Voorburg
Achterburg
Zeedijk
Rechtboomssloot
Kromboomssl.
St. Antoniesbreestr.
SCHANS
OUDE
Spuistr.
Kalverstraat
Rokin
AMSTERDAMS HISTORISCH MUSEUM
Nes
ZUIDERKERK
KLOVENIERS
BURG
WAL
Raamgr.
Jodenbreestr.
Valkenburgerstraat
BEGIJNHOF
Oude
Nieuwe Doelenstr.
Groen
burgwal
Zwanenb. W.
Waterlooplein
Muiderstr.
S 113
DOKWERKER
Nieuwe Amstelstr.
Herengr.
Reguliersdwars
BLOEMEN MARKT
HEREN
straat
Amstel
Amstelstr.
Rembrandtsplein
Nieuwe
Keizersgr.
ALGEMENE BANK NEDERLAND
Vijzelstr.
Reguliers
AMSTEL
Weesperstraat
KEIZERS
MAGERE BRUG
Kerkstr.
Utrechtestr.
Prinsengr.
PRINSEN
gracht
Vijzelgracht
Weesperplein
Frederiksplein
Sarphatistr.
Weteringschans
Wetering-plantsoen
Westeinde

Centre

Amstel and Rest. La Rive, Professor Tulpplein 1, 1018 GX, 226060, Telex 11004, « Shaded terrace Amstel » – rest – . rest MZ f
closed 25, 26, and 31 December – **M** (dinner only) 65/115 – 24 – **111 rm** 395/500.

Sonesta and Rest. Rib Room M, Kattengat 1, 1012 SZ, 212223, Telex 17149 – rest – . rest LX a
M *(closed Saturday lunch)* a la carte 75/97 – 29 – **425 rm** 395/500.

Amsterdam Marriott and Rest. Port O'Amsterdam M, Stadhouderskade 21, 1054 ES, 835151, Telex 15087 – – . rest JZ p
M a la carte 58/95 – 28 – **395 rm** 430/470.

Europe and Rest. Excelsior M, Nieuwe Doelenstraat 2, 1012 CP, 234836, Telex 12081, – – . LY r
M 75/150 – 25 – **79 rm** 325/475.

Victoria, Damrak 1, 1012 LG, 234255, Telex 16625 – rest – . MX a
M *(closed Sunday)* 35/63 – **160 rm** 310/338.

Gd H. Krasnapolsky and Rest. Le Reflet d'Or, Dam 9, 1012 JS, 5549111, Telex 12262, with Japanse rest. Edo – rest – . rest
M a la carte 55/75 – **370 rm** 295/390. LY m

Doelen and Rest. Café Savarin, Nieuwe Doelenstraat 24, 1012 CP, 220722, Telex 14399 – – . MY q
M 40/70 – 22 – **85 rm** 235/325 – P 322.

Pulitzer and Rest. Goudsbloem, Prinsengracht 323, 1016 GZ, 228333, Telex 16508 – rest – . rest KY r
M *(closed lunch Saturday and Sunday)* a la carte 75/98 – 24 – **194 rm** 300.

American, Leidsekade 97, 1017 PN, 245322, Telex 12545, – – . rest JKZ v
M (Café Américain) a la carte 37/61 – 26 – **185 rm** 230/360.

Caransa and Rest. Four Seasons, Rembrandtsplein 19, 1017 CT, 229455, Telex 13342 – – . MY x
M a la carte 48/80 – 20 – **66 rm** 250/325 – P 368.

Carlton without rest., Vijzelstraat 2, 1017 HK, 222266, Telex 11670 – – . LY v
24 – **156 rm** 197/275.

Port van Cleve, Nieuwe Zijds Voorburgwal 178, 1012 SJ, 244860, Telex 13129 – – . LX d
M a la carte 48/74 – **110 rm** 139/257 – P 183/202.

Arthur Frommer and Rest. Oranjehof, Noorderstraat 46, 1017 TV, 220328, Telex 14047 – . . LZ k
M (dinner only) 30 – **90 rm** 175/200.

Schiller, Rembrandtsplein 26, 1017 CV, 231660, Telex 14058 – – . MZ z
M a la carte 49/90 – 22 – **97 rm** 235/400 – P 275/310.

Rembrandt without rest., Herengracht 255, 1016 BJ, 221727, Telex 15424 – . KY p
20 – **111 rm** 240/350.

Ambassade without rest., Herengracht 341, 1016 AZ, 262333, Telex 10158 – wc . KY f
41 rm 150/170.

Parkhotel, Stadhouderskade 25, 1071 ZD, 717474, Telex 11412 – rest wc – . rm KZ f
M 35 – **186 rm** 230/335 – P 295.

Owl Hotel without rest., Roemer Visscherstraat 1, 1054 EV, 189484, Telex 13360 – wc wc . JZ e
34 rm 99/145.

Choura without rest., Marnixstraat 372, 1016 XX, 237524, Telex 15362 – wc wc . JY a
22 rm 89/208.

Estheréa without rest., Singel 305, 1012 WJ, 245146, Telex 14019 – wc . . KY t
72 rm 109/180.

Nicolaas Witsen without rest., Nicolaas Witsenstraat 6, 1017 ZH, 266546 – wc wc MZ b
32 rm 60/140.

Asterisk without rest., Den Texstraat 16, 1017 ZA, 262396 – wc wc.
19 rm 63/150. LZ h

Parklane without rest., Plantage Parklaan 16, 1018 ST, 224804 – wc.
9 rm 85/125.

Roode Leeuw, Damrak 93, ✉ 1012 LP, ✆ 240396 – wc – AE VISA LXY **b**
M a la carte 33/44 – **85 rm** 77/158.

Fantasia without rest., Nieuwe Keizersgracht 16, ✉ 1018 DR, ✆ 238259 – wc. MZ **u**
closed 3 November-22 December – **19 rm** 50/95.

Linda without rest., Stadhouderskade 131, ✉ 1074 AW, ✆ 625668 – .
17 rm 90/135.

XXXX **Dikker en Thijs and Alexander H.** with rm, Prinsengracht 444, angle Leidsestraat, ✉ 1017 KE, ✆ 267721, Telex 13161 – wc wc . AE E VISA. KZ **s**
M *(closed Sunday)* (dinner only, open until midnight) 67/95 – 17 – **25 rm** 150/210.

XXX **Swarte Schaep,** 1st floor, Korte Leidsedwarsstraat 24, ✉ 1017 RC, ✆ 223021, « 17C interior » – . AE E VISA KZ **d**
closed 5, 25, 26, 31 December and 1 January – **M** 80/93.

XXX **Martinn,** 12th floor, De Ruyterkade 7, ✉ 1013 AA, ✆ 256277, ← – . AE E
closed Saturday, Sunday and 24 December-1 January – **M** 50/80.

XXX Sea Palace, Oosterdokskade 8, ✉ 1011 LH, ✆ 264777, ←, Floating Chinese rest. – .

XXX **Bali,** 1st floor, Leidsestraat 89, ✉ 1017 NZ, ✆ 227878, Indonesian rest. – . AE E VISA KZ **a**
closed 5, 24, 31 December and 1 January – **M** 30/50.

XX **Prinsenkelder,** Prinsengracht 438, ✉ 1017 KE, ✆ 267721 – AE E VISA. KZ **s**
closed Saturday and Sunday lunch – **M** 55/75.

XX **Les Quatre Canetons,** Prinsengracht 1111, ✉ 1017 JJ, ✆ 246307 – AE E VISA MZ **d**
closed Saturday lunch, Sunday, Easter, Whitsuntide and New Year – **M** 58/90.

XX **L'Entrée,** 1st floor, Reguliersdwarsstraat 42, ✉ 1017 BM, ✆ 258788, Open until midnight – AE E VISA. LY **s**
closed Sunday and 24 to 26 December – **M** a la carte 50/103.

XX **Dynasty,** Reguliersdwarsstraat 30, ✉ 1017 BM, ✆ 268400, , Oriental rest. – . AE E VISA. LY **p**
closed Tuesday and mid December-mid January – **M** (dinner only) a la carte 46/64.

XX **Pêcheur,** Reguliersdwarsstraat 32, ✉ 1017 BM, ✆ 243121, , Seafood – AE E VISA. LY **s**
closed Saturday lunch, Sunday lunch, 5, 24 and 31 December – **M** a la carte 48/97.

XX **Oesterbar,** Leidseplein 10, ✉ 1017 PT, ✆ 232988, Seafood – . AE KZ **y**
M a la carte 43/89.

XX **Indonesia,** 1st floor, Singel 550, ✉ 1017 AZ, ✆ 232035, Indonesian rest. – . AE E VISA LY **v**
M 30/40.

XX **Treasure,** Nieuwe Zijds Voorburgwal 115, ✉ 1012 RH, ✆ 234061, Chinese rest. – AE E VISA. LX **x**
M a la carte 30/55.

XX **Le Rêve,** Kerkstraat 148, ✉ 1017 GR, ✆ 241394 – AE E VISA LZ **b**
closed 4 to 20 August, 27 December-14 January and Tuesday lunch – **M** (dinner only) a la carte 49/69.

XX **Da Canova,** Warmoesstraat 9, ✉ 1012 HT, ✆ 266725, Italian rest. – AE E MX **y**
closed Sunday and Monday – **M** (dinner only) a la carte 51/66.

XX **Camargue,** Reguliersdwarsstraat 7, ✉ 1017 BJ, ✆ 239352 – . AE E VISA. LY **n**
closed New Year – **M** a la carte 53/80.

XX **Tai-Pan,** Marnixstraat 406, ✉ 1017 PL, ✆ 254389, Chinese rest. – . AE E VISA JKZ **v**
closed Sunday and Monday – **M** (dinner only) a la carte 32/79.

XX **Lotus,** Binnen Bantammerstraat 5, ✉ 1011 CH, ✆ 242614, Chinese rest. – . AE E VISA MX **e**
closed Saturday – **M** *(dinner only)* a la carte 38/50.

XX **Sancerre,** Reestraat 28, ✉ 1016 DN, ✆ 278794 – AE E VISA. KY **d**
closed Easter, Whitsuntide, Christmas and New Year – **M** 47/80.

XX **Vijff Vlieghen,** Spuistraat 294, ✉ 1012 VX, ✆ 248369, « Old Dutch atmosphere » – AE E VISA KY **h**
closed 5, 25, 26 and 31 December – **M** (dinner only) 60/80.

XX **Kopenhagen,** Rokin 84, ✉ 1012 KX, ✆ 249376, Danish rest. – . AE E VISA LY **t**
closed Sunday – **M** 30/55.

XX **Gravenmolen,** 1st floor, Lijnbaansteeg 5, ✉ 1012 TE, ✆ 246531 – . AE E VISA LX **u**
closed Sunday – **M** a la carte 56/71.

XX **Les Trois Neufs,** Prinsengracht 999, ✉ 1017 KM, ✆ 229044, Open until midnight – AE E VISA LZ **v**
closed Saturday lunch, Sunday lunch, Monday and mid July-mid August – **M** a la carte 44/78.

XX **Adrian,** Reguliersdwarsstraat 21, ✉ 1017 BJ, ✆ 239582, Open until midnight – ▤. AE ⓓ E VISA LY **n**
M 38/93.

XX **Dorrius,** Nieuwe Zijds Voorburgwal 336, ✉ 1012 RX, ✆ 235245, Dutch rest. – AE ⓓ E VISA LY **u**
M a la carte 54/64.

XX **Lido,** Leidsekade 105, ✉ 1017 PP, ✆ 263300, 余 – ▤. AE ⓓ E VISA KZ **t**
closed Sunday and Monday – **M** (dinner only from September to March) a la carte 45/75.

XX **Opatija,** Weteringschans 93, ✉ 1017 RZ, ✆ 225184, Balkan rest. – ✻ KZ **b**
closed Monday – **M** (dinner only) 30/43.

XX **Djawa,** 1st floor, Korte Leidsedwarsstraat 18, ✉ 1017 RC, ✆ 246016, Indonesian rest. – ▤. AE ⓓ E VISA. ✻ KZ **n**
closed 31 December – **M** (dinner only) 30/55.

X **Valentijn,** Kloveniersburgwal 6, ✉ 1012 CT, ✆ 242028 – ▤. AE ⓓ E VISA. ✻ MY **s**
closed Monday, Tuesday and 9 to 30 June – **M** 50/95.

X **Bacchus,** Spuistraat 3 e, ✉ 1012 SP, ✆ 230051 – ▤. AE ⓓ E VISA LX **r**
M (dinner only) a la carte 56/86.

X **Cartouche,** Anjeliersstraat 177, ✉ 1015 NG, ✆ 227438 – AE ⓓ E VISA. ✻ JX **a**
closed Monday – **M** (dinner only) a la carte 71/80.

X **Ardjuna,** 1st floor, Reguliersbreestraat 21, ✉ 1017 CL, ✆ 220204, Indonesian rest. – AE ⓓ E VISA LY **k**
M 30.

South and West Quarters

Amsterdam Hilton M with Japanese rest. **Kei, Apollolaan 138,** ✉ 1077 BG, ✆ 780780, Telex 11025 – |♦| ▤ rest TV ☎ ♿ P – 🏛. AE ⓓ E VISA. ✻
M 40/65 – ☕ 25 – **274 rm** 370/450.

✿ **Garden Hotel and Rest. De Kersentuin** M, Dijsselhofplantsoen 7, ✉ 1077 BJ, ✆ 642121, Telex 15453 – |♦| ▤ TV ☎ P – 🏛. AE ⓓ E VISA
M *(closed Saturday lunch, Sunday, 1 January, 31 March, 8 and 19 May)* 80/125 – **97 rm** ☕ 235/350
Spec. Rouleau de lapereau et d'anguille fumée aux escargots, Cabillaud à la mousse de poissons, Pintade en demi-deuil à l'anchois.

Okura and Rest. Ciel Bleu M with Japanese rest. **Yamazato, Ferdinand Bolstraat 175,** ✉ 1072 LH, ✆ 787111, Telex 16182, « Rest. on the 23rd floor with ≤ town » – |♦| ▤ TV ☎ 🚗 P – 🏛. AE ⓓ E VISA. ✻
M (Ciel Bleu) (dinner only, open until midnight) a la carte 87/128 – ☕ 26 – **403 rm** 320/400.

Apollohotel, Apollolaan 2, ✉ 1077 BA, ✆ 735922, Telex 14084, « Terrace with ≤ canal » – |♦| TV ☎ ♿ P – 🏛. AE ⓓ E VISA. ✻ rest
M a la carte 64/97 – ☕ 25 – **217 rm** 270/370.

Crest H. Amsterdam M, De Boelelaan 2, ✉ 1083 HJ, ✆ 462300, Telex 13647 – |♦| ▤ TV ☎ P – 🏛. AE ⓓ E VISA. ✻ rm
M a la carte 58/89 – ☕ 20 – **260 rm** 250/300.

Novotel Amsterdam M, Europaboulevard 10, ✉ 1083 AD, ✆ 5411123, Telex 13375 – |♦| ▤ rest TV ☎ P – 🏛. AE ⓓ E VISA. ✻
M 45/65 – **600 rm** ☕ 225/275 – P 288.

Jan Luyken without rest., Jan Luykenstraat 58, ✉ 1071 CS, ✆ 764111, Telex 16254 – |♦| TV ☎. AE ⓓ E VISA JZ **x**
63 rm ☕ 173/205.

Memphis, De Lairessestraat 87, ✉ 1071 NX, ✆ 733141, Telex 12450 – |♦| TV. AE ⓓ E VISA. ✻
81 rm ☕ 204/297.

Beethoven M, Beethovenstraat 43, ✉ 1077 HN, ✆ 644816, Telex 18504 – |♦| ▤ rest TV 🛁wc 🚿wc ☎. AE ⓓ E VISA. ✻ rest
M a la carte 47/70 – **58 rm** ☕ 178/230.

Delphi without rest., Apollolaan 105, ✉ 1077 AN, ✆ 795152, Telex 16659 – |♦| TV 🛁wc 🚿wc ☎. AE ⓓ E VISA
46 rm ☕ 123/190.

Apollofirst, Apollolaan 123, ✉ 1077 AP, ✆ 730333, Telex 13446 – |♦| TV 🛁wc 🚿wc ☎. AE ⓓ E VISA
M *(closed Sunday)* (dinner only) a la carte 45/97 – **35 rm** ☕ 155/240 – ½ p 178.

Atlas H., Van Eeghenstraat 64, ✉ 1071 GK, ✆ 766336, Telex 17081 – |♦| TV 🛁wc ☎. AE ⓓ E VISA
M 35/55 – **24 rm** ☕ 140/180.

Casa 400, James Wattstraat 75, ✉ 1097 DL, ✆ 651171, Telex 14677 – |♦| 🚿wc ☎ – 🏛. AE VISA
June-September – **M** 31 – **387 rm** ☕ 150/160.

Zandbergen without rest., Willemsparkweg 205, ✉ 1071 HB, ✆ 769321, Telex 33756 – TV wc wc ☎. AE ⓓ E VISA
17 rm ☕ 128/150.

Wilhelmina without rest., Koninginneweg 169, ✉ 1075 CN, ✆ 625467 – wc
☕ 10 – **15 rm** 49/98.

Toro without rest., Koningslaan 64, ✉ 1075 AG, ✆ 737223 – wc. AE ⓓ E VISA
12 rm ☕ 65/140.

Belfort, Surinameplein 53, ✉ 1058 GN, ✆ 174333 – TV wc. AE E VISA
M a la carte 30/54 – **20 rm** ☕ 94/150.

XXX **Parkrest. Rosarium,** Europa boulevard, Amstelpark 1, ✉ 1083 HZ, ✆ 444085, « Flowered park » – . AE ⓓ E VISA
closed Sunday – **M** 50/125.

XX **Petit Culinair,** P.C. Hooftstraat 87, ✉ 1071 BP, ✆ 6214747 – . AE ⓓ E VISA JZ **d**
closed 7 to 25 July and 22 December-5 January – **M** 58/98.

XX **Henri Smits,** Beethovenstraat 55, ✉ 1077 HN, ✆ 791715 – . AE ⓓ E VISA
closed Sunday lunch, 25 and 26 December – **M** 33/55.

XX **In den Nederhoven,** Nederhoven 13, ✉ 1083 AM, ✆ 425619 – AE ⓓ E VISA
closed Saturday lunch and Sunday lunch – **M** a la carte 52/87.

XX ✿ **Trechter** (de Wit), Hobbemakade 63, ✉ 1071 XL, ✆ 711263 – AE ⓓ E.
closed Sunday, Monday, 8 to 30 July and 25 December-6 January – **M** (dinner only) a la carte approx. 70
Spec. Consommé de homard, Solette fumée à l'instant, Côte de porc fumée et rôtie aux poireaux.

XX **Castheele,** Kastelenstraat 172, ✉ 1082 EJ, ✆ 447267 – AE ⓓ E.
closed Sunday, Bank Holidays, last week July and first 2 weeks August – **M** a la carte 51/62.

XX **Fong Lie,** P.C. Hooftstraat 80, ✉ 1071 CB, ✆ 716404, Chinese rest. – . AE ⓓ JZ **w**
closed Monday, Bank Holidays, 7 July-1 August and 29 December-1 January – **M** a la carte 42/80.

XX **Bistro Lapin,** 1st floor, Scheldeplein 3, ✉ 1078 GR, ✆ 642211 – . ⓓ VISA.
closed Monday – **M** (dinner only) 30/69.

XX **Keijzer,** Van Baerlestraat 96, ✉ 1071 BB, ✆ 711441 – AE ⓓ E.
closed Sunday, Easter and Whitsuntide – **M** a la carte 53/68.

XX **Miranda Paviljoen,** Amsteldijk 223, ✉ 1079 LK, ✆ 445768 – P. AE ⓓ E VISA
closed New Year – **M** 30/45.

XX **Hamilcar,** Overtoom 306, ✉ 1054 JC, ✆ 837981, Tunisian rest. – AE ⓓ E VISA
closed Monday – **M** (dinner only) a la carte 30/50.

X **L'Entrecôte,** P.C. Hooftstraat 70, ✉ 1071 CB, ✆ 737776, 1920 Style, Grill rest. JZ **w**
closed Sunday, Monday, Bank Holidays and July – **M** a la carte approx. 40.

X **Rembrandt,** P.C. Hooftstraat 31, ✉ 1071 BM, ✆ 629011 – . AE ⓓ E VISA KZ **h**
closed Monday and 23 December-3 January – **M** 33/65.

X **Beddington's,** Roelof Hartstraat 6, ✉ 1071 VH, ✆ 765201 – AE ⓓ E VISA.
closed Saturday, Sunday, last week December and first week January – **M** a la carte 59/69.

X **Sama Sebo,** P.C. Hooftstraat 27, ✉ 1071 BL, ✆ 628146, Indonesian rest. – . AE ⓓ E
closed Sunday, Bank Holidays and 15 July-4 August – **M** 30/48. KZ **m**

Environs

at Schiphol – ☏ 0 20 :

Airport, arrival ✆ 175657.

Hilton International Schiphol and Rest. Dutch Oven M, Herbergierstraat 1, ✉ 1118 ZK (near airport), ✆ 5115911, Telex 15186, – TV ☎ P – . AE ⓓ E. rest
M a la carte 59/99 – ☕ 20 – **204 rm** 330/390.

XXX **Aviorama** with Indonesian rest. **Ken Dedes**, 3rd Floor, Schipholweg 1, airport, ✉ 1118 AA, ✆ 152150, ← – . AE ⓓ E VISA.
M a la carte 38/65.

near The Hague motorway A 4 :

Euromotel Amsterdam M, Oude Haagseweg 20, ✉ 1066 BW, ✆ 179005, Telex 15524 – TV P – . AE ⓓ E VISA
M 30/85 – **157 rm** ☕ 115/145 – P 160/200.

XX **De Boekanier,** Oude Haagseweg 49, ✉ 1066 BV, ✆ 173525 – P. AE ⓓ E VISA
closed Saturday, Sunday, 19 July-10 August and 23 December-1 January – **M** 70/120.

on The Hague motorway A 4 **by ④ : 15 km** – ☏ 0 2503 :

Schiphol, M, Kruisweg 495, Hoofddorp, ✉ 2132 NA, ✆ 15851, Telex 74546 – TV ☎ P –
168 rm.

Amstelveen Noord-Holland 211 ③ and 408 ⑩㉗ – pop. 68 894 – ✆ 0 20 – 11 km.

XXXX ✿ **Molen De Dikkert,** Amsterdamseweg 104a, ✉ 1182 HG, ✆ 411378, « 17C converted mill » – P. AE ① E VISA
closed Saturday lunch, Sunday, 26 July-17 August and 29 December-4 January – **M** 75/135
Spec. Terrine de foie gras de canard, Saumon en marbré de crustacés au beurre de caviar, Râble de lièvre aux pruneaux farcis de foie gras (15 Oct.-Dec.).

XXX ✿ **Rôtiss. Ile de France,** Pieter Lastmanweg 9, ✉ 1181 XG, ✆ 453509 – ▤. ✈
closed Saturday lunch, Sunday, Monday and 28 December-12 January – **M** a la carte 72/97
Spec. Huîtres au champagne (Sept.- April), Champignons farcis de saumon fumé, Turbot sauté.

Bosch en Duin Utrecht 211 ⑭ – ✆ 0 30 – 50 km.

XXX ✿✿ **Hoefslag,** Vossenlaan 28, ✉ 3735 KN, ✆ 784395, ← – P. AE ① E VISA
closed Sunday and Monday – **M** a la carte 90/128
Spec. Ravioli géant farci de crustacés en consommé, Bar marinière, Canard sauvage à la sauge (July-December).

The HAGUE (Den HAAG or 's-GRAVENHAGE) Zuid-Holland 211 ⑪ and 408 ⑨ – pop. 445 213 – ✆ 0 70.

See: Scheveningen★★ – Binnenhof★ : The Knights' Room★ (Ridderzaal) JV **A** – Hofvijver (Court pool) ←★ JV – Lange Voorhout★ JV – Panorama Mesdag★ HV **B** – Madurodam★.

Museums: Mauritshuis★★★ JV – Municipal★★ (Gemeentemuseum) – Bredius★ HX **M¹** – Mesdag★ HU **M²**.

18 Gr. Haesebroekseweg 22 at Wassenaar N : 4 km ✆ (0 1751) 79607.

✈ Amsterdam-Schiphol NE : 37 km ✆ (0 70) 824141, (0 20) 5110432 (information) and (0 20) 747747 (reservations) – Rotterdam-Zestienhoven SE : 17 km ✆ (0 10) 157633 (information) and (0 10) 372745, 155430 (reservations).

🚗 (departs from 's-Hertogenbosch) ✆ (0 70) 824141.

ℹ (Centraal station) Kon. Julianaplein, ✉ 2595 AA, ✆ 546200.

Amsterdam 60 – Brussels 177 – Rotterdam 26 – Delft 13

Plan opposite

Promenade and Rest. Cigogne M, van Stolkweg 1, ✉ 2585 JL, ✆ 525161, Telex 31162, « Elegant decoration, collection of modern paintings » – ⧉ ▤ rest TV ☎ P – 🏛. AE ① E VISA
M a la carte 42/90 – ☕ 23 – **101 rm** 220/250.

Sofitel M, Koningin Julianaplein 35, ✉ 2595 AA, ✆ 814901, Telex 34001 – ⧉ ▤ TV ☎ ♿ 🚗 – 🏛. AE ① E VISA. ✈ rest
M a la carte 45/95 – ☕ 25 – **143 rm** 235/360.

Des Indes and Le Restaurant, Lange Voorhout 54, ✉ 2514 EG, ✆ 469553, Telex 31196 – ⧉ ▤ rest TV ☎ P – 🏛. AE ① E VISA JV **s**
M 49/88 – ☕ 30 – **77 rm** 335/435 – P 458.

Bel Air, Johan de Wittlaan 30, ✉ 2517 JR, ✆ 502021, Telex 31444, 🏊 – ⧉ ▤ ☎ ♿ P – 🏛. AE ① E VISA
M a la carte 60/93 – ☕ 18 – **350 rm** 145/180 – P 155/225.

Parkhotel-De Zalm without rest. (annex 🏠), Molenstraat 53, ✉ 2513 BJ, ✆ 624371, Telex 33005 – ⧉ ☎ – 🏛. AE ① E VISA HV **a**
130 rm ☕ 61/191.

XXXX **Royal,** Lange Voorhout 44, ✉ 2514 EG, ✆ 600772 – AE ①. ✈ JV **t**
M 43/50.

XXX ✿ **Saur,** 1st floor, Lange Voorhout 51, ✉ 2514 EC, ✆ 463344, Seafood – ▤. AE ① E VISA. ✈ JV **h**
closed Saturday lunch, Sunday and Bank Holidays – **M** a la carte 80/135
Spec. Turbot en papillote, Homard nonante-huit, Sole Lafayette.

XXX **Raden Ajoe,** Lange Poten 31, ✉ 2511 CM, ✆ 644592, Indonesian rest. – ▤. AE ① E VISA JV **a**
M a la carte approx. 50.

XX **Gemeste Schaap,** Raamstraat 9, ✉ 2512 BX, ✆ 639572, Old Dutch interior – AE ① E VISA HX **y**
closed Thursday – **M** (dinner only) a la carte 47/67.

XX **Aubergerie,** Nieuwe Schoolstraat 19, ✉ 2514 HT, ✆ 648070 – AE ① VISA JV **b**
closed Tuesday – **M** (dinner only) 55/75.

XX **Hof van Brederode,** Grote Halstraat 3, ✉ 2513 AX, ✆ 646455, « Converted cellar of a 16C townhall » – AE ① E VISA HV **s**
closed Sunday – **M** 30.

XX **Da Roberto,** Noordeinde 196, ✉ 2514 GS, ✆ 464977, Italian rest. – AE ① E VISA
closed Saturday lunch, Sunday lunch and Tuesday – **M** a la carte 60/80. HV **k**

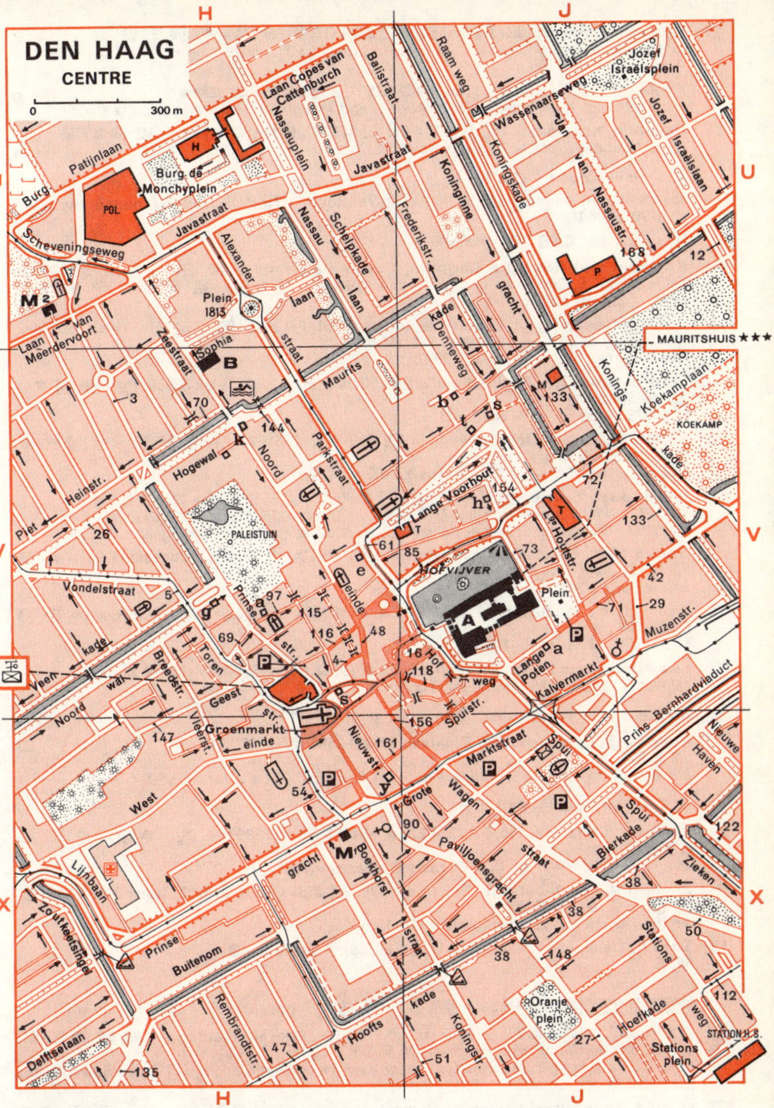

Anna Paulownastr.	HV	3
Annastr.	HV	4
Boslaan	JU	12
Buitenhof	JV	16
Elandstr.	HV	26
Fannius Scholtenstr.	JX	27
Fluwelen Burgwal	JV	29
Groenewegje	JX	38
Herengracht	JV	42
Hoogstr.	HV	48
Huijgensstr.	JX	50
Jacob Catsstr.	JX	51
Jan Hendrikstr.	HX	54
Kneuterdijk	HV	61
Korte Molenstr.	HV	69
Kortenaerkade	HV	70
Korte Poten	JV	71
Korte Voorhout	JV	72
Korte Vijverberg	JV	73
Lange Vijverberg	JV	85
Lutherse Burgwal	JX	90
Molenstr.	HV	97
Oranjelaan	JX	112
Paleispromenade	HV	115
Papestr.	HV	116
de Passage	JV	118
Pletterijkade	JX	123
Prinsessegracht	JV	133
Ruijsdaelstr.	HX	135
Scheveningseveer	HV	144
Slijkeinde	HX	147
Spinozastr.	JX	148
Tournooiveld	JV	154
Venestr.	JX	156
Vlamingstr.	HX	161
Zuid-Hollandlaan	JU	168

XX **La Grande Bouffe,** Maziestraat 10, ✉ 2514 GT, ℘ 654274 – AE ⓓ E VISA HV **k**
closed Saturday lunch, Sunday, Monday lunch, 23 July-19 August and 26 December-4 January – **M** 57/85.

XX **Table du Roi,** Prinsestraat 130, ✉ 2513 CH, ℘ 461908 – ▤. AE ⓓ HV **g**
closed Monday, Tuesday, 3 weeks August and 1 week January – **M** a la carte 45/75.

XX **Garoeda,** Kneuterdijk 18a, ✉ 2514 EN, ℘ 465319, Indonesian rest. – AE ⓓ E VISA HV **e**
closed Sunday lunch – **M** a la carte 40/65.

at Scheveningen – ☎ 0 70 :

Shipping connections with Great Yarmouth : Norfolk Line, Kranenburgweg 211 ℘ (0 70) 514601.

Zwolsestraat 30, ✉ 2587 VJ, ℘ 546200.

Kurhaus and Rest. La Coquille, Gevers Deijnootplein 30, ✉ 2586 CK, ℘ 520052, Telex 33295, ≤, Casino on ground-floor – |‡| ▤ rest TV ☎ ♿ – 🏛. AE ⓓ E VISA. ✂ rest
M 88 – **252 rm** ⊏ 245/360.

Carlton Beach H. Ⓜ, Gevers Deijnootweg 201, ✉ 2586 HZ, ℘ 541414, Telex 33687, ≤, ☂ – |‡| TV ☎ Ⓟ – 🏛. AE ⓓ E VISA. ✂ rest
M a la carte 47/60 – **95 rm** ☕ 125/220.

Europa Crest H., Zwolsestraat 2, ✉ 2587 VJ, ℘ 512651, Telex 33138, ▣ – |‡| TV ☎ – 🏛. AE ⓓ E VISA
M 44/73 – ☕ 16 – **174 rm** 189/314.

Badhotel, Gevers Deijnootweg 15, ✉ 2586 BB, ℘ 512221, Telex 31592 – |‡| TV ⛀wc ⛆wc ☎. AE ⓓ E VISA
M a la carte 40/66 – ⊏ 23 – **96 rm** 95/150 – P 139/179.

XXX ✿ **Seinpost** (Savelberg), Zeekant 60, ✉ 2586 AD, ℘ 555250, ≤ – AE ⓓ E
closed Saturday lunch, Sunday, Monday and 20 July-10 August – **M** 90/115
Spec. Homard au four au Sauternes, Huîtres chaudes au safran et au caviar (Sept.-April).

XXX **Raden Mas,** Gevers Deijnootplein 125, ✉ 2586 CX, ℘ 545432, Indonesian rest. – ▤. AE ⓓ E VISA. ✂
M a la carte 50/64.

XX **Bali** with rm, Badhuisweg 1, ✉ 2587 CA, ℘ 502434, Indonesian rest. – ⛀wc ☏. AE ⓓ E VISA. ✂ rm
M 30/55 – **34 rm** ☕ 38/100.

XX **Les Pieds dans l'Eau,** Dr. Lelykade 33, ✉ 2583 CL, ℘ 550040 – AE ⓓ E. ✂
closed Thursday – **M** (dinner only) 55/75.

on the way to Wassenaar : 3 km :

XXX **Boerderij De Hoogwerf,** Zijdelaan 20, ✉ 2594 BV, ℘ 475514, ☂, « 17C farm » – AE ⓓ E VISA. ✂
closed Sunday and Bank Holidays except Christmas – **M** a la carte 65/90.

at Kijkduin : 4 km – ☎ 0 70 :

Atlantic, Deltaplein 200, ✉ 2554 EJ, ℘ 254025, Telex 33399, ≤, ▣ – |‡| Ⓟ – 🏛. AE ⓓ E VISA. ✂ rest
M a la carte 34/73 – ☕ 15 – **60 rm** and **58 apartments** 150/200.

Zeehaghe Ⓜ without rest., Deltaplein 675, ✉ 2554 GK, ℘ 256262, Telex 31407, ≤ – |‡| TV Ⓟ – 🏛. AE ⓓ E VISA
☕ 15 – **42 rm** and 28 **apartments** 170/190.

XX **Turpin,** Deltaplein 524, ✉ 2554 GJ, ℘ 687881 – AE ⓓ E VISA
M 38.

Leidschendam Zuid-Holland **211** ⑫ and **408** ⑩ – pop. 30 597 – ☎ 0 70 – 50 km.

XXX ✿ **Chagall,** Weigelia 20, ✉ 2262 AB, ℘ 276910, « Lake side setting » – ▤. AE ⓓ E VISA
closed Sunday lunch and Monday – **M** 70/95
Spec. Terrine de foie gras de canard aux raisins, Cassolette de homard au gratin à l'orange, Selle d'agneau aux herbes.

XXX ✿ **Villa Rozenrust,** Veursestraatweg 104, ✉ 2265 CG, ℘ 277460, ☂ – Ⓟ. AE ⓓ E VISA
closed Saturday lunch, Sunday and 21 July-2 August – **M** a la carte 64/85
Spec. Soufflé de turbot et de saumon aux épinards, Pâtes fraîches à la Nonna Lina, Homard au four.

Pleasant hotels and restaurants are shown in the Guide by a red sign.
Please send us the names of any where you have enjoyed your stay.
Your Michelin Guide will be even better.

🏨🏨🏨🏨🏨 ... 🏨

XXXXX ... X

ROTTERDAM Zuid-Holland 211 ⑫ and 408 ㉔㉕ – pop. 555 349 – 0 10.

See : The harbour*** KZ – Lijnbaan* (Shopping center) JKY – St. Laurence Church (Grote-of St. Laurenskerk) : interior* KY D – Euromast* (tower) (**, <*) JZ.

Museums : Boymans van Beuningen*** JZ – History Museum* "De Dubbele Palmboom".

Kralingseweg 200 (0 10) 527646.

Zestienhoven (0 10) 157633 (information) and (0 10) 155430, 322745 (reservations).

(departs from 's-Hertogenbosch) (0 10) 117100.

Europoort to Kingston-upon-Hull : Shipping connections North Sea Ferries (Cie Noordzee Veerdiensten) (0 1819) 62077.

Stadhuisplein 19, 3012 AR, 136000, Telex 21228 and Central Station 136006.

Amsterdam 76 – The Hague 26 – Antwerp 103 – Brussels 149 – Utrecht 57.

Plan on next page

In May 1986 the telephone numbers of Rotterdam will take 4 before the existing number

Hilton International Rotterdam, Weena 10, 3012 CM, 144044, Telex 22666 – rest – . AE E. rest JKY **a**
M a la carte 60/89 – 23 – **259 rm** 255/395.

Parkhotel, Westersingel 70, 3015 LB, 363611, Telex 22020 – – . AE E. JZ **a**
M a la carte 36/81 – **157 rm** 120/241.

Atlanta, Aert van Nesstraat 4, 3012 CA, 110420, Telex 21595 – – . AE E VISA KY **e**
M a la carte 60/93 – 18 – **167 rm** 160/180 – P 225.

Central and Rest. Alexander, Kruiskade 12, 3012 EH, 140744, Telex 24040 – – . AE E VISA KY **u**
M a la carte 42/66 – **64 rm** 117/203 – P 175/225.

Rijnhotel and Rest. Falstaff, Schouwburgplein 1, 3012 CK, 333800, Telex 21640 – – . AE E VISA. JY **e**
M a la carte 38/55 – **140 rm** 113/230 – P 188/285.

Scandia, Willemsplein 1, 3016 DN, 134790, Telex 21662, < – wc wc . AE E VISA. KZ **r**
M a la carte 42/105 – 18 – **52 rm** 48/210.

Pax without rest., Schiekade 658, 3032 AK, 663344 – wc wc. AE E VISA JY **m**
44 rm 52/118.

Emma without rest, Nieuwe Binnenweg 6, 3015 BA, 365533, Telex 25320 – wc . AE E VISA JZ **w**
26 rm 120/150.

Savoy, Hoogstraat 81, 3011 PJ, 139280, Telex 21525 – wc wc . AE E VISA KY **n**
M *(closed week-ends)* (dinner only) a la carte 30/74 – 18 – **94 rm** 90/140.

Van Walsum, Mathenesserlaan 199, 3014 HC, 363275 – wc wc . AE E VISA. rest JZ **e**
M *(closed after 8 p.m.)* (dinner only) 30/35 – **28 rm** 60/120 – P 85/95.

Baan without rest., Rochussenstraat 345, 3023 DH, 770555 – wc.
closed 15 December-4 January – **14 rm** 55/90.

Bienvenue without rest., Spoorsingel 24, 3033 GL, 669394 – wc. AE E VISA JY **d**
10 rm 50/90.

Breitner without rest., Breitnerstraat 23, 3015 XA, 360262 – wc . AE E VISA JZ **d**
22 rm 40/100.

Geervliet without rest., 's-Gravendijkwal 14, 3014 EA, 366109 – wc JZ **b**
closed 10 December-1 January – **15 rm** 42/84.

Heemraad without rest., Heemraadssingel 90, 3021 DE, 775461 – wc. E VISA
8 – **10 rm** 60/80.

Holland without rest., Provenierssingel 7, 3033 ED, 653100 – AE E VISA JY **n**
24 rm 68/85.

XXX ✿ **Coq d'Or,** 1st floor, Van Vollenhovenstraat 25, 3016 BG, 366405, , (quick bar lunch) – . AE E VISA KZ **a**
closed Saturday, Sunday, Bank Holidays and 24 December-1 January – **M** a la carte 75/100
Spec. Blanc de turbotin à la moëlle et filaments de poireaux, Magret de canard au miel.

XXX **La Vilette,** Westblaak 160, 3012 KM, 148692 – . AE E VISA JZ **t**
closed Saturday lunch, Sunday and Bank Holidays – **M** a la carte 75/100.

XXX **Old Dutch,** Rochussenstraat 20, 3015 EK, 360344, , « Old Dutch interior » – . AE E VISA JZ **r**
closed Saturday, Sunday and Bank Holidays – **M** 78/115.

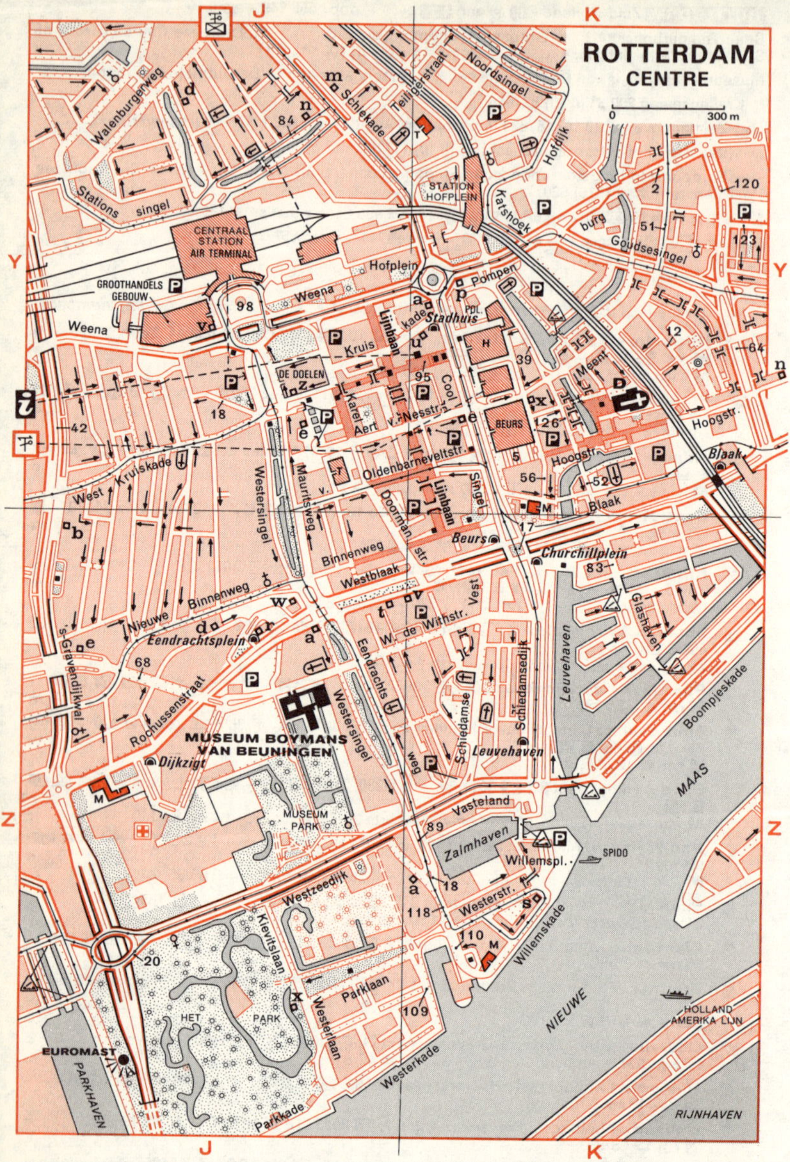

Beurspl.	KY	5
Binnenweg	JZ	
Hoogstr.	KY	
Karel Doormanstr.	JY	
Korte Hoogstr.	KY	56
Lijnbaan	KYZ	
Stadhuispl.	KY	95
Admiraal de Ruyterweg	KY	2
Botersloot	KY	12
Churchillpl.	KY	17
Diergaardesingel	JY	18
Droogleever Fortuynpl.	JZ	20
Haagsever	KY	39
Henegouwerlaan	JY	42
Jonker Fransstr.	KY	51
Keizerstr.	KY	52
Mariniersweg	KY	64
Mathenesserlaan	JZ	68
Posthoornstr.	KZ	83
Provenierssingel	JY	84
Scheepstimmermanslaan	KZ	89
Stationspl.	JY	98
Veerhaven	KZ	109
Veerkade	KZ	110
van Vollenhovenstr.	KZ	118
Vondelweg	KY	120
Warande	KY	123
Westewagenstr.	KY	126

XXX **Euromast** (Rest. **La Rôtisserie mid-height of a tower of 180 m - Entrance : 7,5 Fl**), Parkhaven 20, ✉ 3016 GM, ✆ 364811, ✳ city and port – ▤ Ⓟ. AE ⓓ E VISA. ✻ JZ
closed Monday dinner from 15 October to 15 March – **M** a la carte 54/98.

XXX **Archipel,** Westblaak 82, ✉ 3012 KM, ✆ 116533, Indonesian rest. – ▤. AE ⓓ E VISA. ✻ JKZ **v**
M 30/42.

XX **Beefeater,** Stationsplein 45, ✉ 3013 AK, ✆ 119551, English Pub rest., Open until midnight – ▤. AE ⓓ E VISA JY **v**
M a la carte 40/70.

XX **Chez François,** Stationsplein 45, ✉ 3013 AK, ✆ 119551, Pub rest., Open until midnight – ▤. AE ⓓ E VISA JY **v**
M a la carte 40/70.

XX **Don Quijote,** Stationsplein 45, ✉ 3013 AK, ✆ 119551, Spanish rest., Open until midnight – ▤. AE ⓓ E VISA JY **v**
closed Monday dinner – **M** a la carte 40/70.

XX **New Yorker,** Stationsplein 45, ✉ 3013 AK, ✆ 119551, Counter rest., Open until midnight – ▤. AE ⓓ E VISA JY **v**
M a la carte 40/70.

XX **Tokaj,** Stationsplein 45, ✉ 3013 AK, ✆ 119551, Hungarian rest., Open until midnight – ▤. AE ⓓ E VISA JY **v**
M a la carte 40/70.

XX **Viking,** Stationsplein 45, ✉ 3013 AK, ✆ 119551, Scandinavian rest., Open until midnight – ▤. AE ⓓ E VISA JY **v**
M a la carte 40/70.

XX **Festival,** Schouwburgplein 53, ✉ 3012 CL, ✆ 333888 – AE ⓓ E JY **z**
closed Saturday and Sunday – **M** a la carte 56/88.

XX **Indonesia,** 1st floor, Rodezand 34, ✉ 3011 AN, ✆ 148588, Indonesian rest. – ▤. AE ⓓ E VISA KY **x**
M 30/40.

XX **Marie Antoinette,** Pompenburg 652 (Hofplein), ✉ 3011 AX, ✆ 333595 – AE ⓓ E VISA. ✻ KY **p**
closed Saturday lunch and Sunday lunch – **M** a la carte 53/88.

XX **Aub. Marie Louise,** Bergweg 64, ✉ 3036 BC, ✆ 671919 – Ⓟ. AE ⓓ E VISA. ✻
M a la carte 62/102.

XX **Statenhof,** Bentinckplein 1, ✉ 3039 KL, ✆ 661508 – E
closed Saturday lunch and Sunday lunch – **M** 40/85.

XX **Chalet Suisse,** Kievitslaan 31, ✉ 3016 CG, ✆ 365062, « Parkside cottage » – ▤. AE ⓓ E VISA JZ **x**
closed 25 and 26 December – **M** a la carte 45/60 JZ **x**

at Rotterdam-East :

XXX **In den Rustwat,** Honingerdijk 96, ✉ 3062 NX, ✆ 134110, « 16C converted house » – ▤ Ⓟ. AE ⓓ E
closed Saturday, Sunday and 14 to 28 July – **M** a la carte 59/77.

at Rotterdam-South :

🏨 **Zuiderparkhotel,** Dordtsestraatweg 285, ✉ 3083 AJ, ✆ 850055, Telex 28755 – 🛗 TV ☎ Ⓟ – 🏛. AE ⓓ E VISA
M a la carte 47/60 – **77 rm** 🛏 110/150.

at Hillegersberg – ⓞ 0 10 :

XXX **Beau Rivage,** Weissenbruchlaan 149, ✉ 3054 LM, ✆ 184040, ☂, « Elegant interior, lake side setting terrace » – AE ⓓ E VISA
closed Saturday lunch, Sunday and Bank Holidays – **M** 60/75.

at Ommoord NE : 7 km – ⓞ 0 10 :

XXX **Keizershof,** Martin Luther Kingweg 7, ✉ 3069 EW, ✆ 551333, « Renovated Saxon farm » – Ⓟ. AE ⓓ E
M 60.

Denmark
Danmark

Copenhagen

PRACTICAL INFORMATION

LOCAL CURRENCY

Danish Kroner : 100 D.Kr = 11.13 US $ (Jan. 86)

TOURIST INFORMATION

The telephone number and address of the Tourist Information office is given in the text under ℹ.

FOREIGN EXCHANGE

Banks are open between 9.30am and 4.00pm (6.00pm on Thursdays) on weekdays except Saturdays. The main banks in the centre of Copenhagen, the Central Station and the Airport have exchange facilities outside these hours.

SHOPPING IN COPENHAGEN

Strøget (Department stores, exclusive shops, boutiques).

Kompagnistraede (Antiques).

See also in the index of street names, those printed in red are where the principal shops are found.

CAR HIRE

The international car hire companies have branches in Copenhagen - Your hotel porter will be able to give details and help you with your arrangements.

TIPPING

In Denmark, all hotels and restaurants include a service charge. As for the taxis, there is no extra charge to the amount shown on the meter.

SPEED LIMITS

The maximum permitted speed in cities is 50 km/h - 31mph, outside cities 80 km/h - 50mph and 100 km/h - 62mph on motorways.

SEAT BELTS

The wearing of seat belts is compulsory for drivers and front seat passengers.

COPENHAGEN

SIGHTS

See : Tivoli★★★ : May 1 to September 15 BZ – Harbour and Canal Tour★★★ (Kanaltur) : May to September 15 (Gammel Strand and Nyhavn) – Little Mermaid★★★ (Den Lille Havfrue) DX – Strøget★★ BCYZ – Nyhavn★★ DY – Amalienborg★★ : Changing of the Guard at noon DY – Rosenborg Castle★★ (Rosenborg Slot) CX Christiansborg Palace★★ (Christiansborg Slot) CZ – Old Stock Exchange★★ (Børsen) CZ – Round Tower★★ (Rundetårn) CY **D** Gråbrødretorv★ CY **28** – Gammel Strand★ CZ **26** – Marble Church★ (Marmorkirke) DY **E** – Royal Chapel and Naval Church★ (Holmen's Kirke) CZ **B** – King's Square★ (Kongens Nytorv) DY – Charlottenborg Palace★ (Charlottenborg Slot) DY **F** – Citadel★ (Kastellet) DX – Christianshavn★ DZ – Botanical Garden★ (Botanisk Have) BX – Frederiksberg Garden★ (Frederiksberg Have) AZ – Town Hall (Radhus) : World Clock★ (Jen Olsen's Verdensur) BZ **H**. Breweries – Porcelain Factories – Danish Design Centre (" Den Permanente ") AZ.

Museums : Ny Carlsberg Glyptotek★★★ (Glyptoteket) BZ – National Museum★★ (Nationalmuseet) CZ – Royal Museum of Fine Arts★★ (Statens Museum for Kunst) CX – Thorvaldsen Museum★ CZ **M1** – Royal Arsenal Museum★ (Tøjhusmuseet) CZ **M2** – Royal Theatre Museum★ (Teaterhistoriskmuseum) CZ **M3** – Copenhagen City Museum★ (By Museum) AZ **M4**.

Outskirts : Open Air Museum★★ (Frilandsmuseet) NW : 12 km BX – Ordrupgaard Museum★ (Ordrupgaardsamlingen) N : 10 km CX – Dragør★ SW : 13 km DZ.

COPENHAGEN **(KØBENHAVN)** Danmark 920 L 3 – pop. 622 000 – ☏ 01.

Dansk Golf Union 56 ✆ (01) 13.12.21.

Copenhagen/Kastrup SW : 10 km ✆ (01) 54.17.01 – Air Terminal : main railway station.

Motorail for Southern Europe : ✆ (01) 14.17.01.

Further information from the D S B, main railway station or tourist information centre (see below).

Danmarks Turistråd, H.C. Andersens Bould. 22 A - 1553 København.V ✆ (01) 11.13.25

Berlin 385 – Hamburg 305 – Oslo 583 – Stockholm 630.

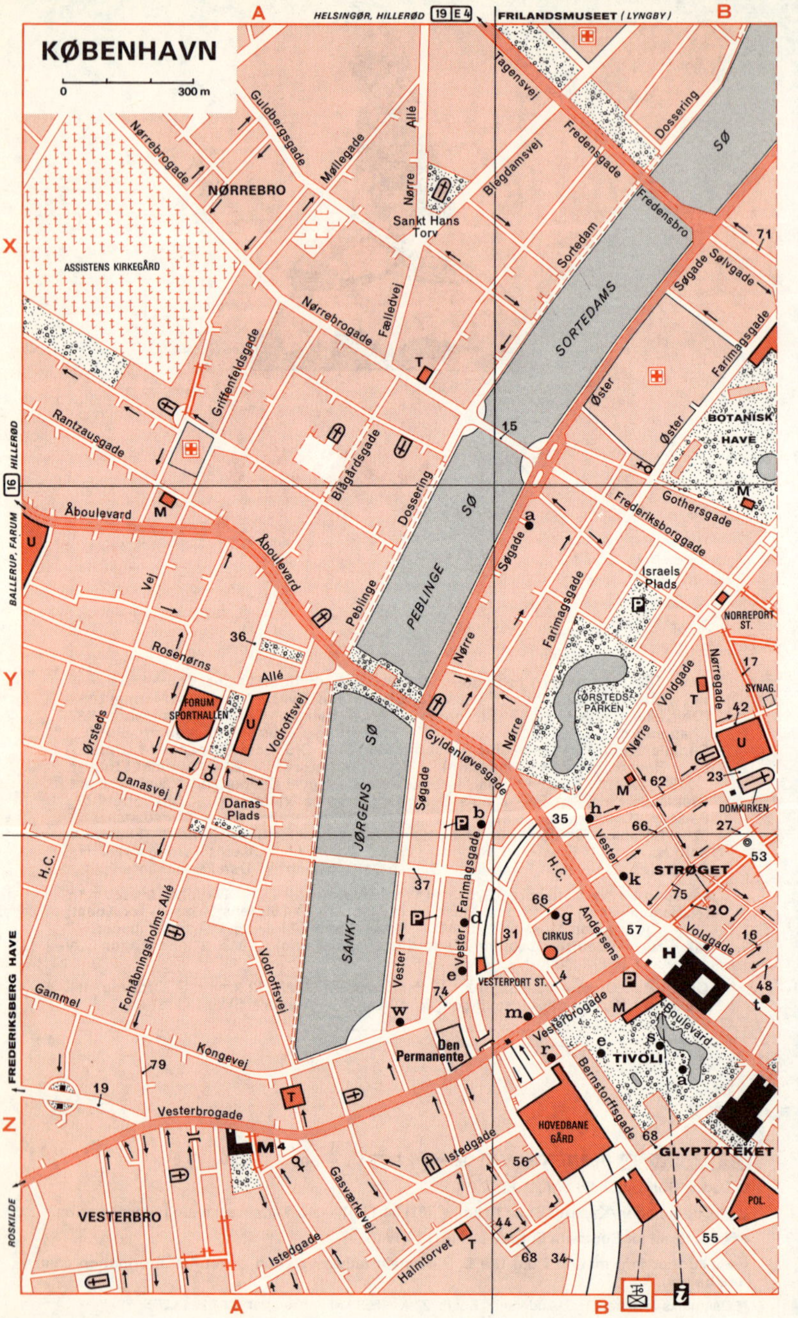
KØBENHAVN
0
300 m
A
B
X
Y
Z
HELSINGØR, HILLERØD
19
E 4
FRILANDSMUSEET (LYNGBY)
16
HILLERØD
BALLERUP, FARUM
FREDERIKSBERG HAVE
ROSKILDE
NØRREBRO
ASSISTENS KIRKEGÅRD
Nørrebrogade
Guldbergsgade
Møllegade
Nørre Allé
Sankt Hans Torv
Tagensvej
Blegdamsvej
Fredensgade
Dossering
SØ
Fredensbro
Sortedam
SORTEDAMS
Søgade
Sølvgade
Farimagsgade
Fælledvej
Griffenfeldsgade
Rantzausgade
Blågårdsgade
Dossering
15
Øster
BOTANISK HAVE
Gothersgade
Frederiksborggade
Åboulevard
Peblinge
PEBLINGE
SØ
Søgade
Israels Plads
NØRREPORT ST.
Nørregade
17
SYNAG.
Vej
Rosenørns
Allé
36
Nørre
Voldgade
ØRSTEDS-PARKEN
FORUM SPORTHALLEN
Vodroffsvej
42
Ørsteds
Danasvej
Danas Plads
Gyldenløvesgade
23
DOMKIRKEN
62
35
66
27
53
JØRGENS
SANKT
Søgade
Farimagsgade
37
H.C.
Vester
STRØGET
75
20
H.C.
Andersens
66
CIRKUS
57
Voldgade
16
48
31
Vester
Vester
4
VESTERPORT ST.
Forhåbningsholms Allé
Vodroffsvej
74
Den Permanente
Vesterbrogade
TIVOLI
Boulevard
Bernstorffsgade
Gammel
Kongevej
79
19
Vesterbrogade
HOVEDBANE GÅRD
68
GLYPTOTEKET
Istedgade
56
Gasværksvej
M⁴
VESTERBRO
Istedgade
Halmtorvet
44
68
34
POL.
55
a
b
d
e
g
h
k
m
r
s
t
w
H
M
T
U
P

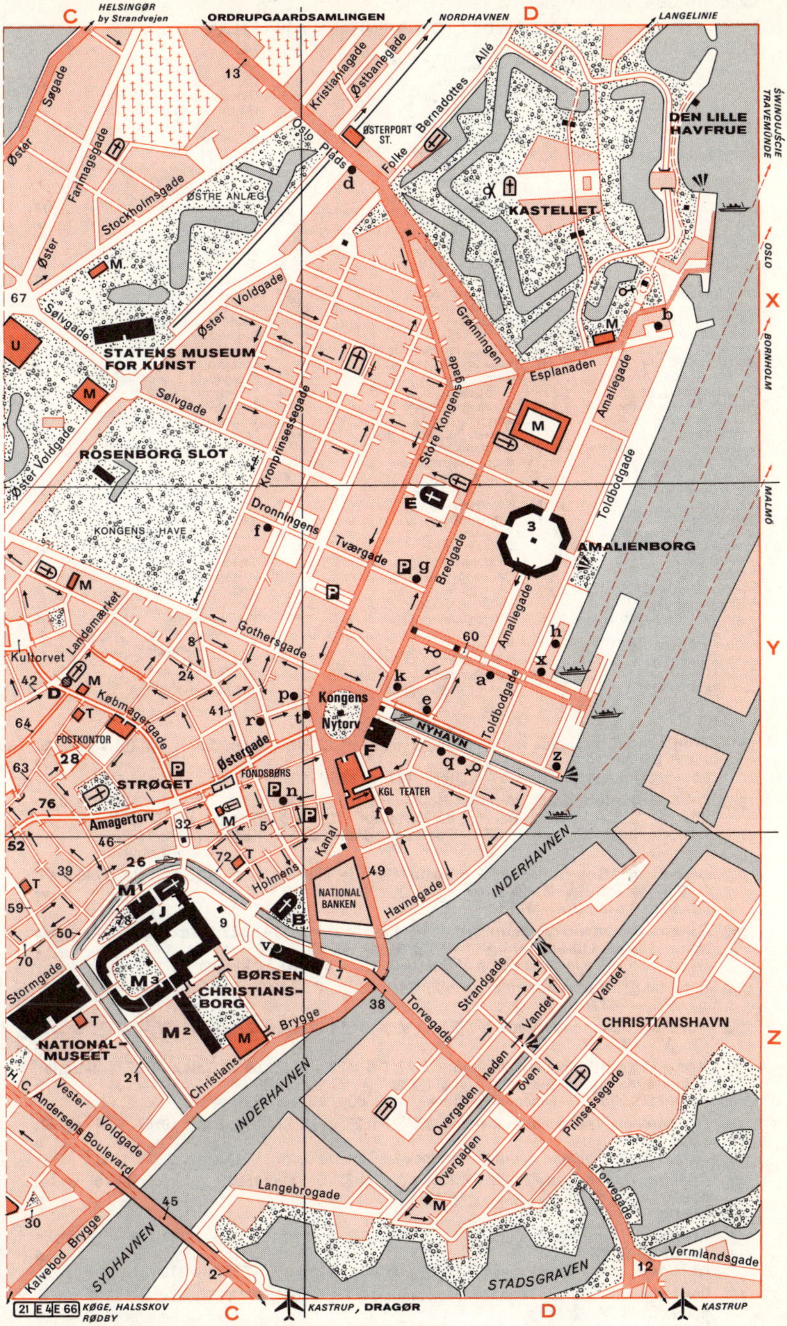
HELSINGØR by Strandvejen
ORDRUPGAARDSAMLINGEN
NORDHAVNEN
LANGELINIE
DEN LILLE HAVFRUE
KASTELLET
ØSTERPORT ST.
ØSTRE ANLÆG
STATENS MUSEUM FOR KUNST
ROSENBORG SLOT
KONGENS HAVE
AMALIENBORG
Kongens Nytorv
NYHAVN
KGL TEATER
STRØGET
POSTKONTOR
FONDSBØRS
Amagertorv
NATIONAL BANKEN
BØRSEN
CHRISTIANSBORG
NATIONAL-MUSEET
CHRISTIANSHAVN
INDERHAVNEN
SYDHAVNEN
STADSGRAVEN
Kultorvet
Esplanaden
Bredgade
Store Kongensgade
Kronprinsessegade
Dronningens Tværgade
Gothersgade
Købmagergade
Østergade
Holmens Kanal
Havnegade
Amaliegade
Toldbodgade
Grønningen
Folke Bernadottes Allé
Oslo Plads
Kristianiagade
Østbanegade
Sølvgade
Øster Voldgade
Øster Søgade
Farimagsgade
Stockholmsgade
Landemærket
Stormgade
Christians Brygge
Vester Voldgade
H. C. Andersens Boulevard
Kalvebod Brygge
Langebrogade
Torvegade
Strandgade
Overgaden neden Vandet
Overgaden oven Vandet
Prinsessegade
Vermlandsgade
ŚWINOUJŚCIE TRAVEMÜNDE
OSLO
BORNHOLM
MALMÖ
KØGE, HALSSKOV RØDBY
KASTRUP, DRAGØR
KASTRUP
C
D
X
Y
Z
21 E 4 E 66

STREET INDEX TO KØBENHAVN TOWN PLAN

Street	Grid	No.
Amagertorv (Strøget)	CY	
Bredgade	DY	
Frederiksberggade (Strøget)	BZ	20
Købmagergade	CY	
Nygade (Strøget)	CYZ	52
Nørre Voldgade	BY	
Store Kongensgade	DX	
Vesterbrogade	ABZ	
Vimmelskaftet (Strøget)	CY	76
Østergade (Strøget)	CY	
Amager Boulevard	CZ	2
Amaliegade	DXY	
Amalienborg Plads	DY	3
Axeltorv	BZ	4
Bernstorffsgade	BZ	
Blegdamsvej	BX	
Blågårdsgade	AX	
Bremerholm	CY	5
Børsgade	DZ	7
Christan IX's Gade	CY	8
Christiansborg Slotsplads	CZ	9
Christians Brygge	CZ	
Christmas Møllers Plads	DZ	12
Dag Hammarskjölds Allé	CX	13
Danas Plads	AY	
Danasvej	AY	
Dronningens Tvaergade	CDY	
Dronning Louises Bro	BX	15
Esplanaden	DX	
Farvergade	BZ	16
Fiolstraede	BY	17
Folke Bernadottes Allé	DX	
Forhåbningsholms Allé	AZ	
Fredensbro	BX	
Fredensgade	BX	
Frederiksberg Allé	AZ	19
Frederiksborggade	BY	
Frederiksholms Kanal	CZ	21
Frue Plads	BY	23
Faelledvej	AX	
Gammel Kongevej	AZ	
Gammel Mønt	CY	24
Gammel Strand	CZ	26
Gammeltorv	BYZ	27
Gasvaerksvej	AZ	
Gothersgade	BCY	
Griffenfeldsgade	AX	
Grønningen	DX	
Gråbrødretorv	CY	28
Guldbergsgade	AX	
Gyldenløvesgade	AY	
Halmtorvet	AZ	
Hambrosgade	CZ	30
Hammerichsgade	BZ	31
Havnegade	DZ	
H.C.Andersens Boulevard	BCZ	
H.C.Ørsteds Vej	AY	
Holmens Kanal	CDZ	
Højbro Plads	CY	32
Ingerslevsgade	BZ	34
Israels Plads	BY	
Istedgade	AZ	
Jarmers Plads	BY	35
Julius Thomsens Gade	AY	36
Kalvebod Brygge	CZ	
Kampmannsgade	AZ	37
Knippelsbro	DZ	38
Kompagnistraede	CZ	39
Kongens Nytorv	DY	
Kristen Bernikows Gade	CY	41
Kristianiagade	DX	
Kronprinsessegade	CXY	
Krystalgade	BCY	42
Kultorvet	CY	
Kvaegtorvsgade	ABZ	44
Landemaerket	CY	
Langebro	CZ	45
Langebrogade	CDZ	
Laederstraede	CYZ	46
Løngangstraede	BZ	48
Møllegade	AX	
Niels Juels Gade	DZ	49
Nybrogade	CZ	50
Nyhavn	DY	
Nytorv	BZ	53
Nørre Allé	AX	
Nørrebrogade	AX	
Nørre Farimagsgade	BY	
Nørregade	BY	
Nørre Søgade	ABY	
Oslo Plads	DX	
Overgaden neden Vandet	DZ	
Overgaden oven Vandet	DZ	
Peblinge Dossering	AY	
Politorvet	BZ	55
Prinsessegade	DZ	
Rantzausgade	AX	
Reventlowsgade	BZ	56
Rosenørns Allé	AY	
Rådhuspladsen	BZ	57
Rådhusstraede	CZ	59
Sankt Annae Plads	DY	60
Sankt Hans Torv	AX	
Sankt Peders Straede	BY	62
Skindergade	CY	63
Sortedam Dossering	BX	
Stockholmsgade	CX	
Store Kannikestraede	CY	64
Stormgade	CZ	
Strandgade	DZ	
Studiestraede	BYZ	66
Sølvgade	BCX	
Sølvtorvet	CX	67
Tagensvej	BX	
Tietgensgade	BZ	68
Toldbodgade	DXY	
Torvegade	DZ	
Vandkunsten	CZ	70
Webersgade	BX	71
Ved Stranden	CZ	72
Ved Vesterport	AZ	74
Vermlandsgade	DZ	
Vester Farimagsgade	AZ	
Vestergade	BZ	75
Vester Søgade	AYZ	
Vester Voldgade	BCZ	
Vindebrogade	CZ	78
Vodroffsvej	AYZ	
Vaernedamsvej	AZ	79
Østbanegade	DX	
Øster Farimagsgade	BCX	
Øster Søgade	BCX	
Øster Voldgade	CX	
Åboulevard	AY	

Angleterre, Kongens Nytorv 34, ✉ 1050 K, ✆ 12 00 95, Telex 15877 – AE E VISA. CDY **t**
M a la carte approx 275/375 – ☐ 80 – **139 rm** 875/1750.

SAS Scandinavia M, Amager Boulevard 70, ✉ 2300 S, ✆ 11 23 24, Telex 31330, <, city, « Panoramic restaurant on 25th floor », – AE E VISA
M buffet lunch 110/dinner 165/375 and a la carte – ☐ 175 – **543 rm** 1125/1475.
by Amager Boulevard CZ

Sheraton - Copenhagen M, 6 Vester Ségade, ✉ 1601 V, ✆ 14 35 35, Telex 27450, – AE E VISA AZ **w**
M 210 and a la carte – **471 rm** ☐ 950/1550.

Plaza - Sheraton M, Bernstorffsgade 4, ✉ 1577 V, ✆ 14 92 62, Telex 15330, « Antiques and paintings, Library bar » – AE E VISA BZ **r**
M 250/395 and a la carte **Baron of Beef** – ☐ 80 – **96 rm** 930/1485.

Impérial M, Vester Farimagsgade 9, ✉ 1606 V, ✆ 12 80 00, Telex 15556 – **163 rm.** AZ **e**

Royal M, Hammerichsgade 1, ✉ 1611 V, ✆ 14 14 12, Telex 27155, <, – **275 rm.** BZ **m**

Kong Frederik, Vester Voldgade 23-27, ✉ 1552 V, ✆ 12 59 02, Telex 19702, « Victorian pub and restaurant, antiques » – AE E VISA. BZ **k**
closed Christmas – **M Queen's** 165/407 – ☐ 80 – **127 rm** 695/1445.

Richmond, Vester Farimagsgade 33, ✉ 1625 V, ✆ 12 33 66, Telex 19767 – AE E VISA AY **b**
closed 22 December-1 January – **M** (see **La Cocotte** below) – **132 rm** ☐ 740/1100.

Admiral, Toldbodgade 24-28, ✉ 1253 K, ✆ 11 82 82, Telex 15941, <, « Former 18C warehouse » – DY **h**
366 rm.

Mercur, Vester Farimagsgade 17, ✉ 1625 V, ✆ 12 57 11, Telex 19767, – wc AE E VISA AZ **d**
M *(closed Bank Holiday lunch, Sunday and April)* a la carte 107/231 – **110 rm** ☐ 740/1100.

Codan M without rest., Sankt Annae Plads 21, ✉ 1250 K, ✆ 13 34 00, Telex 15815, – wc DY **x**
134 rm.

71 Nyhavn, Nyhavn 71, ✉ 1051 K, ✆ 11 85 85, Telex 27558, ←, « Former warehouse » – wc wc. AE E VISA DY z
M (buffet lunch) 165 a la carte 132/302 – **82 rm** 768/1318.

Opera, Tordenskjoldsgade 15, 1055 K, ✆ 12 15 19, Telex 15812 – wc wc. AE E VISA DY f
M *(closed Sunday and Bank Holidays)* 98/190 and a la carte – **66 rm** 668/1048.

Ascot without rest., Studiestraede 57, ✉ 1554 V, ✆ 12 60 00, Telex 15730 – wc wc. AE E VISA BZ g
58 rm 490/775.

Neptun without rest., Sankt Annae Plads 18, ✉ 1250 K, ✆ 13 89 00, Telex 19554 – wc. AE E VISA DY a
60 rm 480/730.

Kong Arthur without rest., Nérre Ségade 11, ✉ 1370 K, ✆ 11 12 12, Telex 16512, – wc wc. AE E VISA BY a
closed 16 December-5 January – **53 rm** 570/795.

Park without rest., Jarmers Plads 3, ✉ 1551 V, ✆ 13 30 00, Telex 15692 – wc wc. AE E VISA. BY h
50 – **66 rm** 265/760.

Danmark without rest., Vester Voldgade 89, 1552 V, ✆ 11 48 06 – wc wc. AE E VISA. BZ t
49 rm 420/620.

XXX ✿ **Kong Hans,** Vingardsstraede 6, ✉ 1070 K, ✆ 11 68 68, « Ancient vaulted cellar » – AE E VISA CY n
closed Sunday, mid July-mid August and Bank Holidays – **M** (dinner only) a la carte 360/535
Spec. Saumon du Roi Jean fumé à la maison, Salade de caille confit aux truffes, Filet de boeuf en pâte salée.

XXX Bourgogne, Dronningens Tvaergade 2, ✉ 1302 K, ✆ 14 80 66 DY g

XXX **La Cocotte,** (at Richmond H.), Vester Farimagsgade 33, ✉ 1625 V, ✆ 14 04 07 AY b
closed Sunday, 1 week at Christmas and Bank Holidays – **M** a la carte 175/355.

XX ✿ **Les Etoiles,** Dronningens Tvaergade 43, ✉ 1302 K, ✆ 15 05 54 – AE E VISA CY f
closed Sunday, July and Bank Holidays – **M** (dinner only) a la carte 250/375
Spec. Menu poisson de la Baltique.

XX ✿ **Saison,** (at østerport H.), Oslo Plads 5, ✉ 2100 ø, ✆ 11 22 66, Telex 15888 – AE E VISA DX d
closed Saturday lunch, Sunday, Monday, July, 23 December-2 January and Bank Holidays – **M** a la carte 160/340
Spec. Menu aux poissons, Menu végétarien, Gibier pendant la saison de chasse.

XX **Leonore Christine,** Nyhavn 9, ✉ 1051 K, ✆ 13 50 40 – E VISA DY e
closed Saturday lunch, Sunday, Christmas and Bank Holidays – **M** a la carte 172/335.

XX **Den Sorte Ravn,** Nyhavn 14-16, ✉ 1051 K, ✆ 13 12 33 – AE E VISA DY q
M a la carte 95/295.

XX **Els,** Store Strandstraede 3, ✉ 1255 K, ✆ 14 13 41, « 19C wall paintings » – . AE E VISA DY k
closed Christmas and New Year – **M** 164/218 and a la carte.

X **L'Alsace,** Ny Ostergade 9, ✉ 1101 K, ✆ 14 57 43 – AE E VISA CY r
M a la carte 140/285.

X **Egoisten,** Hovedvagtsgade 2, ✉ 1103 K, ✆ 12 79 71 – AE E VISA CY p
closed Saturday, Sunday, 1 week at Christmas and Bank Holidays – **M** a la carte 265/340.

X **Lumskebugten,** Esplanaden 21, ✉ 1263 K, ✆ 15 60 29 – E VISA DX b
closed Sunday – **M** a la carte 170/325.

X Børskaelderen, Børsen, Børsgade 2, ✉ 1217 K, ✆ 12 14 40 CZ v

X **Gilleleje,** Nyhavn 10, ✉ 1051 K, ✆ 12 58 58, « Old sailors inn » – AE E VISA DY q
closed Sunday and July – **M** a la carte 108/307.

in Tivoli :

XXX **Divan 2,** Tivoli Gardens, Vesterbrogade 3, ✉ 1620 V, ✆ 12 51 51, « Floral decoration and terrace » – AE E VISA BZ a
May-14 September – **M** a la carte 198/408.

XXX **Belle Terrasse,** Tivoli Gardens, Vesterbrogade 3, ✉ 1620 V, ✆ 12 11 36, « Floral decoration and terrace » – AE E VISA BZ s
May-14 September – **M** a la carte 98/369.

XXX **La Crevette,** Tivoli Gardens, Vesterbrogade 3, 1620 V, ✆ 14 68 47, Seafood, « Floral decoration and terrace » – AE E VISA BZ e
May-14 September – **M** a la carte 225/410.

at Søllerød N : 19 km by exit Tagensvej – BX – and A 43 – ✉ 2840 Holte – 02 Holte :

XXX **Søllerød Kro,** Søllerødvej 35, ✆ 80 25 05, « 17C thatched inn » – Ⓟ. AE E VISA
closed 24 December – **M** a la carte 170/310.

France

Paris and Environs
Bordeaux
Cannes
Lyons
Marseilles
Monaco (Principality of)
Nice
Strasbourg
Valley of the Loire

FRANCE

PRACTICAL INFORMATION

LOCAL CURRENCY

French Franc : 100 F = 13.21 US $ (Jan. 86)

TOURIST INFORMATION IN PARIS

Paris "Welcome" Office (Office de Tourisme de Paris - Accueil de France) : 127 Champs-Élysées, 8th, ✆ 47 23 61 72, Telex 611984

American Express 11 Rue Scribe, 9th, ✆ 42 66 09 99

AIRLINES

T.W.A. : 101 Champs Élysées, 8th, ✆ 47 20 62 11
PAN AM : 1 Rue Scribe, 9th, ✆ 42 66 45 45
BRITISH AIRWAYS : 91 Champs Élysées, 8th, ✆ 47 78 14 14
AIR FRANCE : 119 Champs Élysées, 8th, ✆ 45 35 61 61
AIR INTER : 12 Rue de Castiglione, 1st, ✆ 45 39 25 25
U.T.A. : 3 Boulevard Malesherbes, 8th, ✆ 48 38 80 80

FOREIGN EXCHANGE OFFICES

Banks : close at 5pm and at weekends

Orly Airport : daily 6.30am to 11.30pm

Charles de Gaulle Airport : daily 6am to 11.30pm

TRANSPORT IN PARIS

Taxis : may be hailed in the street when showing the illuminated sign-available day and night at taxi ranks or called by telephone

Bus-Métro (subway) : for full details see the Michelin Plan de Paris no 11. The metro is quickest but the bus is good for sightseeing and practical for short distances.

POSTAL SERVICES

Local post offices : open Mondays to Fridays 8am to 7pm ; Saturdays 8am to noon

General Post Office, 52 rue du Louvre, 1st : open 24 hours

SHOPPING IN PARIS

Department stores : Boulevard Haussmann, Rue de Rivoli and Rue de Sèvres

Exclusive shops and boutiques : Faubourg St-Honoré, Rue de la Paix and Rue Royale

Second-hand goods and antiques : Flea Market (Porte Clignancourt) ; Swiss Village (Avenue de la Motte Picquet), Louvre des Antiquaires (Place du Palais Royal), Flea Market - type shops around the "Halles" (the old Paris Central Market)

TIPPING

Service is generally included in hotel and restaurants bills. But you may choose to leave more than the expected tip to the staff. Taxi-drivers, porters, barbers and theatre or cinema attendants also expect a small gratuity.

BREAKDOWN SERVICE

Certain garages in central and outer Paris operate a 24 hour breakdown service. If you breakdown the police are usually able to help by indicating the nearest one.

SPEED LIMITS

The maximum permitted speed in built up areas is 60 km/h - 37 mph ; on motorways the speed limit is 130 km/h - 80 mph and 110 km/h - 68 mph on dual carriageways. On all other roads 90 km/h - 56 mph.

SEAT BELTS

The wearing of seat belts is compulsory for drivers and front seat passengers.

PARIS

and environs

PARIS 75 Maps : 10, 11, 12 and 14 G. Paris.

Population : Paris 2 166 449 ; Ile-de-France region : 10 034 108.
Altitude : Observatory : 60 m ; Place Concorde : 34 m
Air Terminals : Esplanade des Invalides, 7th, ☎ 43 23 97 10 – Palais des Congrès, Porte Maillot, 17th, ☎ 42 99 20 18
Airports : see Orly and Charles de Gaulle (Roissy)
Railways, motorail, sleepers : apply to the appropriate railway station (S.N.C.F.)

ARRONDISSEMENTS

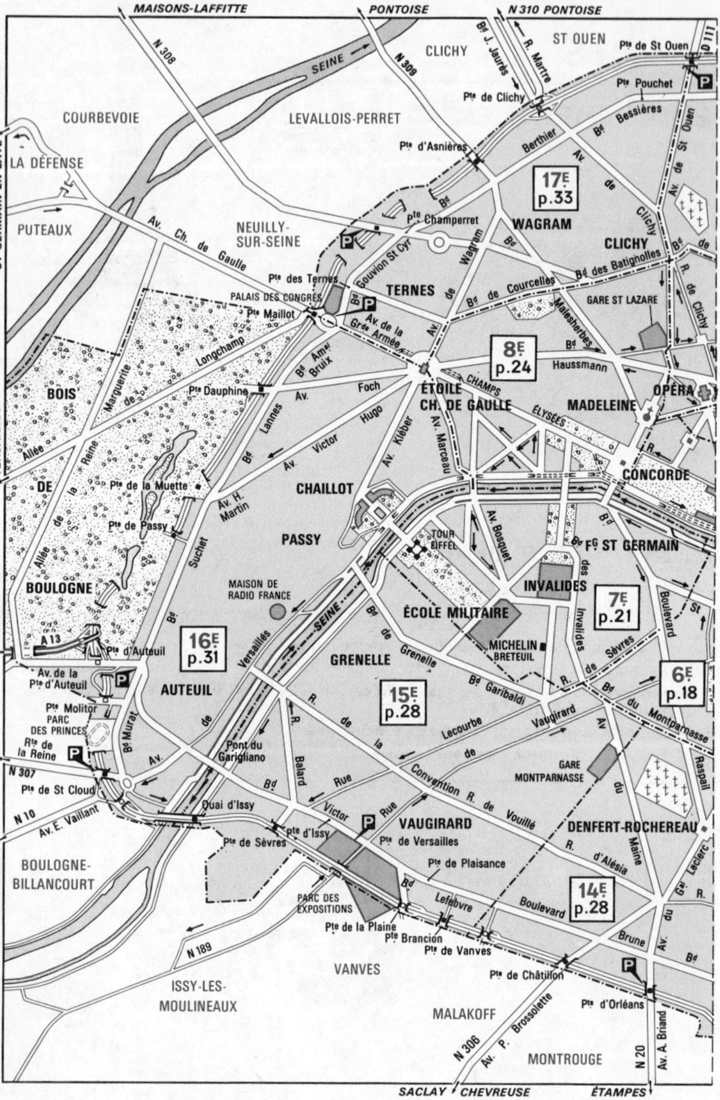

P Car park — Arrondissement boundary

One-way street

Ring road (interchange: ▪ complete, ▫ partial)

AND DISTRICTS

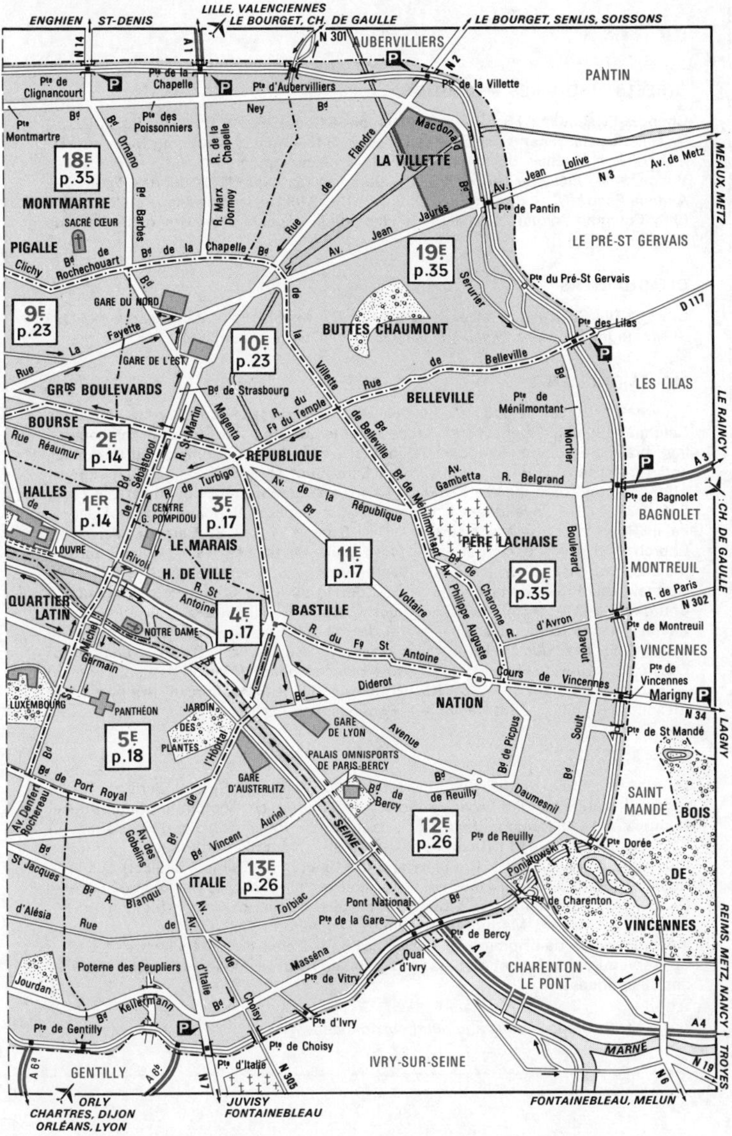

To find your way in the capital, use the **Michelin street plans of Paris**

10 sheet map, **12** sheet map with street index,

11 atlas with street index and practical information,

14 atlas with street index.

SIGHTS

STREETS – SQUARES – GARDENS

Champs-Élysées*** F 8, F 9, G 10 – Place de la Concorde*** G 11 (Obelisk of Luxor) – Tuileries Gardens** (Jardin des Tuileries) H 12 – Rue du Faubourg St-Honoré** G 11, G 12 – Avenue de l'Opéra** G 13 – Place Vendôme** G 12 – Place des Vosges** – Place du Tertre** D 14 – Botanical Gardens** (Jardin des Plantes) – Avenue Foch* F 7 – Rue de Rivoli* G 12 – Rue Mouffetard* – Place de la Bastille (July Column : Colonne de Juillet) – Place de la République – Grands Boulevards F 13, F 14.

OLD QUARTERS

Cité*** (Ile St-Louis, The Quays) J 14, J 15 – Le Marais*** – Montmartre*** D 14 – Montagne Ste Geneviève** (Latin Quarter : Quartier Latin) K 14.

MAIN MONUMENTS

Louvre*** (Royal Palace : Palais des Rois de France ; Cour Carrée, Perrault's Colonnade, Embankment Façade : façade sur le quai, the "two arms" of the Louvre : les "bras" du Louvre, Carrousel Triumphal Arch : Arc de Triomphe du Carrousel, and The Parterres.) H 13 – Notre Dame Cathedral*** K 15 – Sainte Chapelle*** J 14 – Arc de Triomphe*** F 8 (Place Charles de Gaulle) – Eiffel Tower*** (Tour Eiffel) J 7 – The Invalides*** (Dôme Church : église, Napoléon's tomb) J 10 – Palais Royal** H 13 – Madeleine** G 11 – Opera** F 12 – St. Germain l'Auxerrois Church** H 14 – Conciergerie** J 14 – Ecole Militaire** K 9 – Luxembourg** (Palace, gardens : palais, jardins) – Panthéon** – St. Séverin Church** K 14 – St. Germain des Prés Church** J 13 – St. Etienne du Mont Church** – St. Sulpice Church** K 13 – Hôtel de Lamoignon**, Hôtel Guénégaud** (museum of the Chase : musée de la chasse) – Hôtel de Rohan** – Soubise Palace** – The Sacré Cœur Basilica** D 14 – Maine Montparnasse Tower** (Tour) – Institute of France* (Institut de France) J 13 – Radio France House* (Maison de Radio France) – Palais des Congrès* – St. Roch Church* G 13 – Alexandre III Bridge* (Pont Alexandre III) H 10 – Pont Neuf J 14 – Pont des Arts J 13.

MAIN MUSEUMS

Louvre*** (Stele of the Vultures : stèle des Vautours, Seated Scribe : Scribe accroupi, Vénus de Milo, Winged Victory of Samothrace : Victoire de Samothrace, Nymphs of Jean Goujon, Mona Lisa : La Joconde, Regent diamond : le Régent...) H 13 – Jeu de Paume*** (Impressionists) G 11 – Decorative Arts** H 13 – Hôtel de Cluny and its museum** (The Lady and the Unicorn : la Dame à la Licorne) K 14 – Rodin** (hôtel de Biron) J 10 – Hôtel Carnavalet** – Georges Pompidou Centre** (Modern Art Museum) H 15 – Chaillot Palace (Museum of French Monuments**, Museum of Man**, Maritime Museum** : Palais de Chaillot, musées des Monuments Français, de l'Homme, de la Marine) H 7 – Palais de la Découverte** G 10 – Conservatoire des Arts et Métiers** (National Technical Museum : musée National des Techniques).

K 14, G 10 : *Reference letters and numbers on the town plan.*

LISTE ALPHABÉTIQUE DES HOTELS ET RESTAURANTS

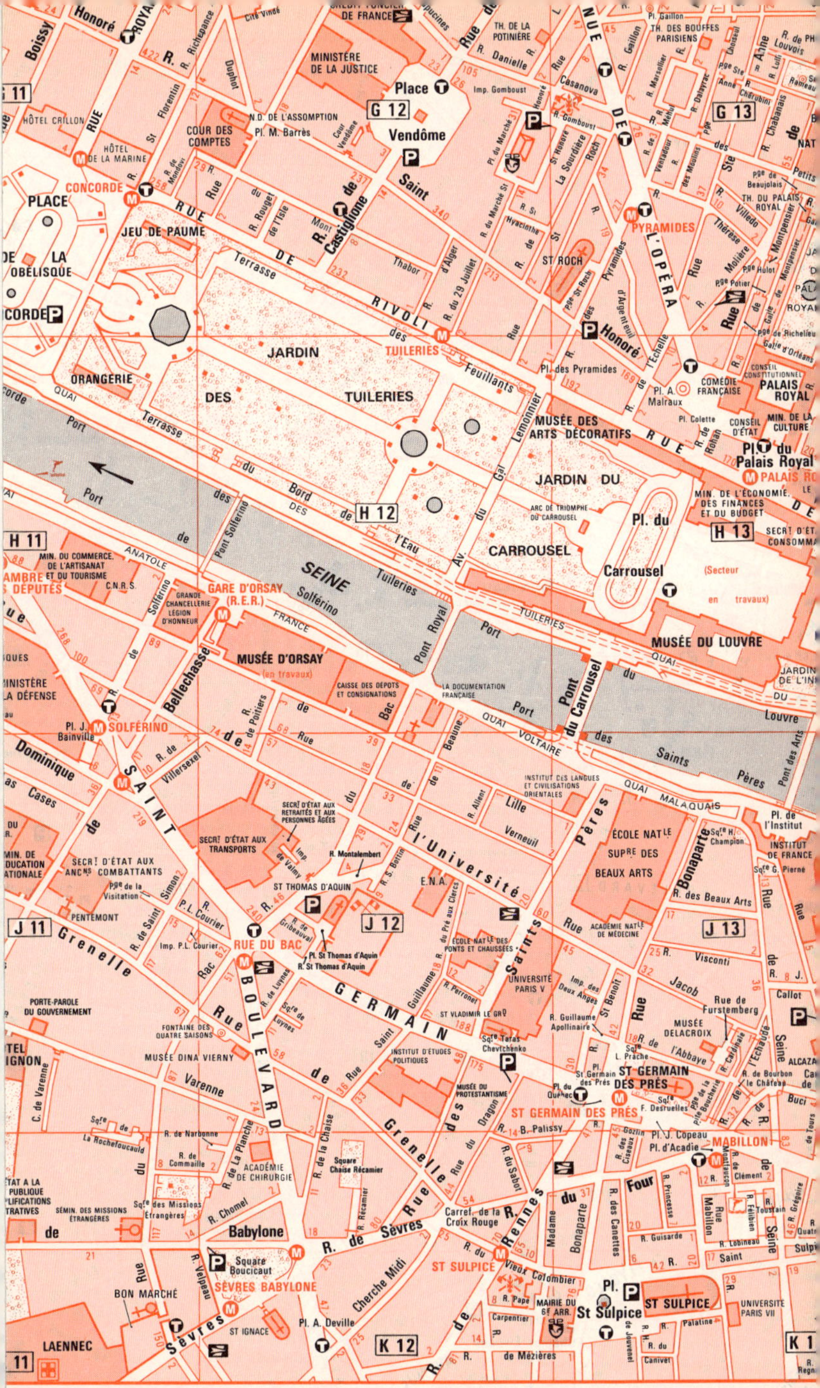

MINISTÈRE DE LA JUSTICE
Place Vendôme
G 11
G 12
G 13
HÔTEL CRILLON
HÔTEL DE LA MARINE
CONCORDE
PLACE DE LA CONCORDE
OBÉLISQUE
COUR DES COMPTES
N.D. DE L'ASSOMPTION
Pl. M. Barrès
TH. DE LA POTINIÈRE
TH. DES BOUFFES PARISIENS
Pl. Gaillon
JEU DE PAUME
RUE DE RIVOLI
R. de Castiglione
Saint Honoré
ST ROCH
PYRAMIDES
AVENUE DE L'OPÉRA
TH. DU PALAIS ROYAL
JARDIN DES TUILERIES
TUILERIES
ORANGERIE
Terrasse des Feuillants
Terrasse du Bord de l'Eau
Pl. des Pyramides
Pl. A. Malraux
COMÉDIE FRANÇAISE
CONSEIL CONSTITUTIONNEL
PALAIS ROYAL
MIN. DE LA CULTURE
CONSEIL D'ÉTAT
Pl. Colette
Pl. du Palais Royal
MUSÉE DES ARTS DÉCORATIFS
JARDIN DU CARROUSEL
ARC DE TRIOMPHE DU CARROUSEL
Pl. du Carrousel
MIN. DE L'ÉCONOMIE, DES FINANCES ET DU BUDGET
SECRT D'ÉTAT CONSOMMATION
(Secteur en travaux)
MUSÉE DU LOUVRE
H 11
H 12
H 13
SEINE
Port de la Concorde
Port des Tuileries
Port de Solférino
Port du Louvre
Pont Solférino
Pont Royal
Pont du Carrousel
Pont des Arts
QUAI ANATOLE FRANCE
QUAI VOLTAIRE
QUAI MALAQUAIS
Quai des Tuileries
Quai du Louvre
MIN. DU COMMERCE, DE L'ARTISANAT ET DU TOURISME
C.N.R.S.
CHAMBRE DES DÉPUTÉS
GRANDE CHANCELLERIE LÉGION D'HONNEUR
GARE D'ORSAY (R.E.R.)
MUSÉE D'ORSAY (en travaux)
CAISSE DES DÉPOTS ET CONSIGNATIONS
LA DOCUMENTATION FRANÇAISE
MINISTÈRE DE LA DÉFENSE
SOLFÉRINO
Pl. J. Bainville
Rue de Bellechasse
Rue de Lille
Rue de Verneuil
Rue de l'Université
Rue du Bac
Rue de Beaune
Rue des Saints Pères
INSTITUT DES LANGUES ET CIVILISATIONS ORIENTALES
ÉCOLE NATLE SUPRE DES BEAUX ARTS
Pl. de l'Institut
INSTITUT DE FRANCE
Sqre H. Champion
Sqre G. Pierné
R. des Beaux Arts
Rue Bonaparte
Rue de Seine
J 11
J 12
J 13
SECRT D'ÉTAT AUX RETRAITÉS ET AUX PERSONNES ÂGÉES
SECRT D'ÉTAT AUX TRANSPORTS
SECRT D'ÉTAT AUX ANCNS COMBATTANTS
MIN. DE L'ÉDUCATION NATIONALE
PENTEMONT
ST THOMAS D'AQUIN
R. Montalembert
E.N.A.
ÉCOLE NATLE DES PONTS ET CHAUSSÉES
UNIVERSITÉ PARIS V
ACADÉMIE NATLE DE MÉDECINE
R. Visconti
R. Jacob
Rue de Furstemberg
MUSÉE DELACROIX
R. de l'Abbaye
Rue Saint Dominique
Rue de Grenelle
Boulevard Saint Germain
RUE DU BAC
PORTE-PAROLE DU GOUVERNEMENT
FONTAINE DES QUATRE SAISONS
MUSÉE DINA VIERNY
Rue de Varenne
Boulevard Raspail
INSTITUT D'ÉTUDES POLITIQUES
MUSÉE DU PROTESTANTISME
ST VLADIMIR LE GRD
Sqre Taras Chevtchenko
ST GERMAIN DES PRÉS
Pl. du Québec
R. Guillaume Apollinaire
Pl. J. Copeau
Pl. d'Acadie
MABILLON
R. de Buci
ACADÉMIE DE CHIRURGIE
SÉMIN. DES MISSIONS ÉTRANGÈRES
Square Chaise Récamier
Rue de Babylone
Rue de Sèvres
Square Boucicaut
SÈVRES BABYLONE
BON MARCHÉ
LAENNEC
ST IGNACE
Pl. A. Deville
Rue du Cherche Midi
Carref. de la Croix Rouge
Rue de Rennes
ST SULPICE
Rue du Vieux Colombier
MAIRIE DU 6e ARR.
Pl. St Sulpice
Rue du Four
Rue Bonaparte
R. des Canettes
R. Princesse
R. Guisarde
R. Mabillon
R. Lobineau
Rue Saint Sulpice
UNIVERSITÉ PARIS VII
K 12
R. de Mézières
R. Palatine

BOURSE
SENTIER
G 14
G 15
Rue Réaumur
RÉAUMUR SÉBASTOPOL
BD SÉBASTOPOL
MAIRIE DU 2e ARR.
BASILIQUE N.D. DES VICTOIRES
R. du Mail
R. Léopold Bellan
R. Bachaumont
R. Montorgueil
R. Mandar
R. Montmartre
R. du Louvre
Pl. des Victoires
R. Étienne Marcel
BANQUE DE FRANCE
HÔTEL DES POSTES
CAISSE D'ÉPARGNE DE PARIS
R. Turbigo
R. St Sauveur
Cité Beaurepaire
R. Greneta
R. Tiquetonne
TOUR DE JEAN SANS PEUR
ÉTIENNE MARCEL
R. Pierre Lescot
R. St Denis
R. de Cygne
R. Quincampoix
R. St Martin
R. du Grenier St Lazare
R. Beaubourg
ST EUSTACHE
R. Rambuteau
LES HALLES
PAVILLON DES ARTS
MAISON DE LA POÉSIE
BOURSE DU COMMERCE
FORUM
R. Berger
H 14
H 15
ORATOIRE DU LOUVRE
R. St Honoré
R. de Rivoli
CHÂTELET LES HALLES (R.E.R.)
CENTRE NATL D'ART ET DE CULTURE G. POMPIDOU
Pl. Georges Pompidou
RAMBUTEAU
Sq. des Innocents
PALAIS DU LOUVRE
LOUVRE
MAIRIE DU 1ER ARR.
ST GERMAIN L'AUXERROIS
SAMARITAINE
R. du Pont Neuf
BD DE SÉBASTOPOL
CHÂTELET
ST MERRI
R. du Renard
R. du Temple
PONT NEUF
Pl. de l'École
TOUR ST JACQUES
TH. DU CHÂTELET
TH. DE LA VILLE
Pl. du Châtelet
AV. VICTORIA
HÔTEL DE VILLE
ASSISTANCE PUBLIQUE
MAIRIE DE PARIS
Quai de Gesvres
Quai de l'Horloge
Sq. du Vert Galant
CONCIERGERIE
J 14
J 15
PALAIS DE JUSTICE
Pl. Dauphine
HÔTEL DES MONNAIES
DIRECTION R.A.T.P.
STE CHAPELLE
TRIBUNAL DE COMMERCE
Pl. St Gervais
PRÉFECTURE DE POLICE
ÎLE DE LA CITÉ
HÔTEL DIEU
CITÉ
Quai des Grands Augustins
Quai St Michel
ST MICHEL (R.E.R.)
Place du Parvis Notre Dame
NOTRE DAME
Square Jean XXIII
Quai de Montebello
Quai d'Orléans
Pont Louis Philippe
ODÉON
Carref. de l'Odéon
UNIVERSITÉ PARIS V R. DESCARTES
UNIVERSITÉ PARIS VI (CORDELIERS)
Bd St Michel
Bd St Germain
R. St Jacques
Square de Cluny
MUSÉE DE CLUNY
ST SEVERIN
Sq. R. Viviani
ST JULIEN LE PAUVRE
MUSÉE DE L'ASSISTANCE PUBLIQUE
ÉCOLE SPÉCIALE DES TRAVAUX PUBLICS DU BÂTIMENT ET DE L'INDUSTRIE
Pl. Maubert
K 14
K 15

HOTELS, RESTAURANTS

Listed by districts and arrondissements

(List of Hotels and Restaurants in alphabetical order, see pp 5 to 8)

G 12: These reference letters and numbers correspond to the squares on the Michelin **Map of Paris** nº **10**, **Paris Atlas** nº **11**, **Map with street index** nº **12** and **Map of Paris** nº **14**.

Consult any of the above publications when looking for a car park nearest to a listed establishment.

Opéra, Palais-Royal,
Halles, Bourse.
1st et 2nd arrondissements.
1st : 75001
2nd : 75002

Ritz, 15 pl. Vendôme (1st) **42 60 38 30, Telex 220262, « Indoor garden »** – 30-80. AE E VISA. rest G 12
M Rest see **Ritz-Espadon** below – 80 – **164 rm** 1 955/2 415, 58 apartments.

Inter-Continental, 3 r. Castiglione (1st) **42 60 37 80, Telex 220114,** – 1000. AE E VISA. rest G 12
st. : Rôtiss. Rivoli M 250 - **café Tuileries M** 92 – 90 – **460 rm** 1 523/1 938, 40 apartments.

Meurice, 228 r. Rivoli (1st) **42 60 38 60, Telex 230673** – rest – 40-80. AE E VISA. rest G 12
st. : M a la carte 260/380 – 90 – **161 rm** 1 660/2 350, 31 apartments.

Lotti, 7 r. Castiglione (1st) **42 60 37 34, Telex 240066** – 25. AE E VISA. rest G 12
st. : M a la carte 220/300 – 86 – **126 rm** 1 185/1 690.

Westminster, 13 r. Paix (2nd) **42 61 57 46, Telex 680035** – rm – 80. AE E VISA G 12
st. : M Rest see **Le Céladon** below – 80 – **85 rm** 1 050/1 450, 18 apartments.

Résidence St-James et Albany M, 202 r. Rivoli (1st) **42 60 31 60, Telex 213031,** – 30-120 H 12
rest. **Le Noailles** – **105 rm**, 40 apartments.

Louvre-Concorde, pl. A.-Malraux (1st) **42 61 56 01, Telex 220412** – rest . AE E VISA H 13
st. : M a la carte 100/195 – 55 – **223 rm** 840/1 400.

Édouard VII, 39 av. Opéra (2nd) **42 61 56 90, Telex 680217** – 25. AE VISA G 13
M Rest see **Delmonico** below – **100 rm** 670/835, 4 apartments.

Mayfair M without rest, 3 r. Rouget-de-Lisle (1st) **42 60 38 14, Telex 240037** – . AE E VISA G 12
st. : 53 rm 630/900.

France et Choiseul, 239 r. St-Honoré (1st) **42 61 54 60, Telex 680959,** – – 30-200. AE E VISA. rest G 12
st. : M a la carte 120/180 – 40 – **120 rm** 750/1 000.

Novotel Paris Halles M, 8 pl. M. de Navarre (1st) **42 21 31 31, Telex 216389,** – – 40-100. AE E VISA H 14
M a la carte approx 115 – 45 – **271 rm** 610/640, 5 apartments.

Normandy, 7 r. Échelle (1st) **42 60 30 21, Telex 670250** – – 50. AE E VISA H 13
st. : M *(closed Saturday and Sunday)* 150 – 40 – **120 rm** 525/875, 8 apartments 875/1 025.

Cusset M without rest, 95 r. Richelieu (2nd) **42 97 48 90, Telex 670245** – . E VISA F 13
st. : 116 rm 380/550.

Cambon M without rest, 3 r. Cambon (1st) **42 60 38 09, Telex 240814** – . AE E VISA G 12
st. : 44 rm 620/880.

François without rest., 3 bd Montmartre (2nd) **42 33 51 53, Telex 211097** – . AE VISA. F 14
st. : 28 – **64 rm** 550/660, 11 apartments 770.

Favart without rest, 5 r. Marivaux (2nd) 42 97 59 83, Telex 213126 – wc wc – st. : **38 rm** 353/414. F 13

Montana H. Tuileries without rest, 12 r. St-Roch (1st) 42 60 35 10, Telex 204401 – wc wc . VISA G 12
st. : 30 – **25 rm** 360/495.

Duminy-Vendôme without rest, 3 r. Mont-Thabor (1st) 42 60 32 80, Telex 213492 – wc wc – 40. AE E VISA. G 12
st. : 79 rm 420/660.

Gaillon Opéra without rest, 9 r. Gaillon (2nd) 47 42 47 74, Telex 215716 – wc . AE E VISA G 13
st. : 25 – **26 rm** 450/480.

Richepanse without rest, 14 r. Richepanse (1st) 42 60 36 00, Telex 210811 – wc wc . AE. G 12
st. : 43 rm 380/420.

Louvre-Forum without rest, 25 r. du Bouloi (1st) 42 36 54 19, Telex 240288 – wc wc . AE VISA. H 14
st. : 20 – **28 rm** 280/350.

Du Piémont without rest, 22 r. Richelieu (1st) 42 96 44 50 – wc wc . AE E VISA G 13
st. : 21 – **28 rm** 250/420.

Ascot Opéra without rest, 2 r. Monsigny (2nd) 42 96 87 66, Telex 216679 – wc wc . AE E VISA G 13
st. : 25 – **36 rm** 175/420.

Gd H. Champagne without rest, 17 r. J.-Lantier (1st) 42 61 50 05, Telex 215955 – wc wc . AE VISA J 14
st. : 30 – **42 rm** 301/402.

Ducs de Bourgogne without rest, 19 r. Pont-Neuf (1st) 42 33 95 64, Telex 216367 – wc wc . VISA. H 14
st. : 20 – **49 rm** 240/290.

Ducs d'Anjou without rest, 1 r. Ste-Opportune (1st) 42 36 92 24 – wc wc . VISA – st. : 18,50 – **38 rm** 226/270 H 14

Family without rest, 35 r. Cambon (1st) 42 61 54 81 – wc wc G 12
st. : 17 – **25 rm** 148/310.

St-Romain without rest, 7 r. St-Roch (1st) 42 60 31 70 – wc wc G 13
st. : 26 – **33 rm** 450/600.

Ritz-Espadon, 15 pl. Vendôme (1st) 42 60 38 30, – AE E VISA. G 12
M a la carte 310/460
Spec. Omble chevalier (November-31 December), Canard, Crêpes flambées.

Grand Vefour, 17 r. Beaujolais (1st) 42 96 56 27, Pre-Revolutionary (late 18C) Café Style – . AE VISA. G 13
closed August, Saturday and Sunday – **M** a la carte 360/455
Spec. Foie gras au naturel, Bar farci, Tournedos à la moelle.

Carré des Feuillants (Dutournier), 14 r. Castiglione (1st) 42 86 82 82 – VISA G 12
closed Saturday and Sunday – **st. : M** a la carte 240/340
Spec. Escabèche de rouget, Volailles à la broche, Feuillantine aux fruits rouges.

Drouant, pl. Gaillon (2nd) 47 42 56 61 – . AE E VISA G 13
M a la carte 220/320.

Mercure Galant, 15 r. Petits-Champs (1st) 42 96 98 89 G 13
closed Saturday lunch, Sunday and Bank Holidays – **M** a la carte 200/280
Spec. Turbot aux écrevisses, Poêlée de foie de canard aux raisins, Mille et une feuilles.

Gérard Besson, 5 r. Coq Héron (1st) 42 33 14 74 – VISA H 14
closed 20 December-4 January, Saturday, Sunday and Bank Holidays – **M** 170 (lunch) and a la carte 170/270
Spec. Gibier (season), Poissons.

Le Céladon, 13 r. Paix (2nd) 42 61 57 46 G 12
closed August, Saturday and Sunday – **st. : M** a la carte 210/370
Spec. Salade tiède d'huîtres panées et rôties au curry, Escalope de bar à la moelle, Embeurée de cervelle de veau au porto.

Delmonico, 39 av. Opéra (2nd) 42 61 44 26, Telex 680217 – . AE VISA G 13
closed Sunday – **M** a la carte 190/290.

Chez Vong, 10 r. Grande-Truanderie (1st) 42 96 29 89, chinese and vietnamese cuisine – AE VISA H 15
closed Sunday – **M** a la carte 105/170.

Pierre "A la Fontaine Gaillon", pl. Gaillon (2nd) 42 65 87 04 – AE E VISA G 13
closed August, Saturday lunch and Sunday – **M** 120/195.

Goumard, 17 r. Duphot (1st) 42 60 36 07 – . AE E VISA G 12
closed 11 to 17 August, 22 December-5 January and Sunday – **M** a la carte 200/300
Spec. Feuilleté de langoustines, St-Jacques marinière (October to May), Fondant chocolat.

XX ✿ **Chez Pauline** (Génin), 5 r. Villedo (1st) ℘ 42 96 20 70 – ▤. VISA G 13
closed July, 22 December-2 January, Saturday dinner and Sunday – **M** (▤ 1st floor) a la carte 135/250
Spec. Ris de veau en croûte, Foie gras frais, Mariage de champignons sauvages et gibier (September-December).

XX Bistrot d'Honoré, 36 pl. Marché St-Honoré (1st) ℘ 42 60 03 00 G 12

XX **Aux Trois Turbigo,** 3 r. Turbigo (1st) ℘ 45 08 18 05 – AE D VISA H 14
closed August, Saturday lunch, Sunday and Bank Holidays – **st. : M** a la carte 140/220.

XX ✿ **Pierre Traiteur,** 10 r. Richelieu (1st) ℘ 42 96 09 17 – AE D VISA H 13
closed August, Saturday and Sunday – **M** a la carte 165/250
Spec. Terrine de foie gras, Rognon de veau rôti à l'échalote confite, Râble de lièvre (season).

XX **Velloni,** 22 r. des Halles (1st) ℘ 42 60 12 50, Italian cuisine – AE D VISA H 14
closed 10 to 17 August, Saturday lunch and Sunday – **st. : M** a la carte 140/200.

XX **Pavillon Baltard,** 9 r. Coquillière (1st) ℘ 42 36 22 00 – ▤. AE D E VISA H 14
st. : M a la carte 130/200.

XX **La Main à la Pâte,** 35 r. St-Honoré (1st) ℘ 48 08 85 73, Italian cuisine – AE D VISA H 14
closed Sunday – **st. : M** a la carte 155/225 🍷.

XX **Le Petit Coin de la Bourse,** 16 r. Feydeau (2nd) ℘ 45 08 00 08 – AE D VISA F 14
closed Saturday and Sunday – **M** a la carte 125/210.

XX **La Corbeille,** 154 r. Montmartre (2nd) ℘ 42 61 30 87 – VISA G 14
closed 1 to 15 July (except dinners from September-May) and Sunday – **st. : M** a la carte 180/300.

XX **La Barrière Poquelin,** 17 r. Molière (1st) ℘ 42 96 22 19 – AE D VISA G 13
closed 1 to 21 August, Saturday lunch and Sunday – **M** a la carte 150/245.

XX **Les Délices du Foie Gras,** 7 r. Gomboust (1st) ℘ 42 61 02 93 – AE VISA G 13
closed August, Saturday lunch and Sunday – **st. : M** (booking essential) a la carte 165/265.

XX **Pile ou Face,** 52 bis r. N.-D. des Victoires (2nd) ℘ 42 33 64 33 G 14
closed August, Saturday, Sunday and Bank Holidays – **M** a la carte 135/200.

XX **Le Soufflé,** 36 r. Mt-Thabor (1st) ℘ 42 60 27 19 – ▤. AE D E VISA G 12
closed Sunday and Bank Holidays – **M** a la carte 110/170.

XX **Saudade,** 34 r. Bourdonnais (1st) ℘ 42 36 30 71, Portuguese cuisine – AE D VISA H 14
closed 1 August-6 September, 23-27 December and Sunday – **st. : M** a la carte 115/185.

XX **Vaudeville,** 29 r. Vivienne (2nd) ℘ 42 33 39 31 – AE D VISA FG 14
M a la carte 90/152 🍷.

XX **La Ferme Irlandaise,** 30 pl. Marché St.-Honoré (1st) ℘ 42 96 02 99 – AE VISA G 12
closed 20 December-3 January and Monday – **st. : M** 130/200.

XX ✿ **Pharamond,** 24 r. Grande-Truanderie (1st) ℘ 42 33 06 72 – AE D VISA H 15
closed July, Monday lunch and Sunday – **M** a la carte 140/170
Spec. Tripes à la mode de Caen, St-Jacques au cidre (season), Grillades aux pommes soufflées.

XX **Pied de Cochon** (24hr service), 6 r. Coquillière (1st) ℘ 42 36 11 75 – AE D VISA H 14
M a la carte 115/190.

XX **Coup de Coeur,** 19 r. St-Augustin (2nd) ℘ 47 03 45 70 – AE D E VISA G 13
closed August, Saturday lunch and Sunday – **st. : M** a la carte 120/180.

XX **Kinugawa** 8 r. Mont-Thabor (1st) ℘ 42 60 65 07, Japanese cuisine – AE D VISA G 12
closed 10 August-1 September, 24 December-5 January and Sunday – **M** 74/265.

XX **Caveau du Palais,** 19 pl. Dauphine (1st) ℘ 43 26 04 28 – AE VISA J 14
closed Saturday and Sunday – **M** a la carte 140/220.

XX **Chez Gabriel,** 123 r. St-Honoré (1st) ℘ 42 33 02 99 – AE D VISA H 14
closed August, dinner Sunday and Monday – **M** a la carte 100/160.

XX **Pasadena,** 7 r. du 29-Juillet (1st) ℘ 42 60 68 96 – AE VISA G 12
closed August, Saturday dinner and Sunday – **M** a la carte 90/155 🍷.

XX **Le Saint-Amour,** 8 r. Port-Mahon (2nd) ℘ 47 42 63 82 – AE D VISA G 13
closed Saturday (except dinner from September to June), Sunday and Bank Holidays – **M** 130.

X ✿ **Aux Petits Pères** (Chez Yvonne), 8 r. N.-D.-des-Victoires (2nd) ℘ 42 60 91 73 – AE VISA G 14
closed August, February Holidays, Saturday and Sunday – **M** (booking essential) a la carte 115/170
Spec. St-Jacques à la provençale (October-April), Ris de veau toulousaine, Faisan (season) or pintade aux choux.

X Jéroboam, 8 r. Monsigny (2nd) ℘ 42 61 21 71 G 13

X **Chez Georges,** 1 r. Mail (2nd) ℘ 42 60 07 11 – ▤. AE D VISA G 14
closed Sunday and Bank Holidays – **M** a la carte 115/170.

X **Cochon Doré,** 16 r. Thorel (2nd) ℘ 42 33 29 70 – ▤ G 15
closed 10 August-6 September and Monday – **M** 62 b.i./128 b.i..

X **Louis XIV,** 1bis pl. Victoires (1st) ℘ 42 61 39 44 G 14
closed August, Saturday and Sunday – **M** a la carte 125/195.

X **Paul,** 15 pl. Dauphine (1st) ℘ 43 54 21 48 – AE J 14
closed August, Monday and Tuesday – **M** a la carte 110/135 🍷.

Bastille, République,
Hôtel de Ville.
3rd, 4th et 11th arrondissements.
3rd : 75003
4th : 75004
11th : 75011

Holiday Inn M, 10 pl. République (11th) 43 55 44 34, Telex 210651, – kitchenette – 150. AE E VISA G 17
st. : **Belle Époque** (Classic) **M** a la carte 140/220 – **Le Jardin d'hiver** (Coffee-Shop) **M** a la carte approx. 125 – **316 rm** 820/1 180, 17 apartments.

Atlantide without rest, 114 bd Richard-Lenoir (11th) 43 38 29 29, Telex 216907 – wc wc . AE E VISA H 18
closed August and 24 December to 2 January – **st. :** 28 – **27 rm** 400/480.

Méridional without rest, 36 bd Richard Lenoir (11th) 48 05 75 00, Telex 211324 – wc . AE E VISA. J 18
st. : 21 – **36 rm** 380/420.

Deux Iles M without rest, 59 r. St.-Louis-en-l'Ile (4th) 43 26 13 35 – wc wc – **st. :** 28 – **17 rm** 385/485. K 16

Lutèce M without rest, 65 r. St-Louis-en-l'Ile (4th) 43 26 23 52 – wc wc . – **st. :** 28 – **23 rm** 485/525 K 16

Bretonnerie without rest, 22 r. Ste-Croix-de-la-Bretonnerie (4th) 48 87 77 63 – wc wc . E. J 16
st. : 22 – **29 rm** 231/420.

Vieux Marais without rest, 2 r. Plâtre (4th) 42 78 47 22 – wc wc . H 16
st. : 30 rm 205/340.

Place des Vosges without rest, 12 r. Birague (4th) 42 72 60 46 – wc wc . AE E VISA J 17
st. : 21 – **16 rm** 175/290.

Nord et Est without rest, 49 r. Malte (11th) 47 00 71 70 – wc wc . VISA. G 17
closed August and 22 December-2 January – **st. :** 18 – **45 rm** 180/250.

Notre-Dame without rest, 51 r. Malte (11th) 47 00 78 76 – wc wc . G 17
closed end of July-end of August – **st. :** 17,50 – **54 rm** 104/218.

XXX **Ambassade d'Auvergne,** 22 r. Grenier St-Lazare (3rd) 42 72 31 82 – . VISA H 15
closed Sunday – **st. : M** a la carte 130/200.

XX ✿ **Quai des Ormes** (Masraff), 72 quai Hôtel de Ville (4th) 42 74 72 22 – . VISA J 15
closed August, Saturday and Sunday – **M** 140 (lunch) and a la carte 190/260
Spec. Ravioli de champignons des bois (from September to March), St-Pierre grillé au basilic, Chaud froid de poires aux pistaches.

XX **Le Dômarais,** 53 bis r. Francs-Bourgeois (4th) 42 74 54 17 – AE E VISA J 16
closed August, 23 December-2 January, Sunday and Monday – **st. : M** a la carte 170/255.

XX **Bofinger,** 5 r. Bastille (4th) 42 72 87 82 – AE E VISA J 17
M a la carte 125/180 .

XX ✿ **Chardenoux,** 1 r. J.-Vallès (11th) 43 71 49 52 – VISA K 20
closed Saturday, Sunday and Bank Holidays – **st. : M** a la carte 195/255.

XX ✿ **Péché Mignon** (Rousseau), 5 r. Guillaume-Bertrand (11th) 43 57 02 51 – . VISA
closed August, February holidays, Sunday and Monday – **st. : M** a la carte 160/210 H 19
Spec. Bavarois de crustacés au saumon fumé, Blanc de turbot à la vapeur, Aumonière de filet mignon au jus de morilles.

XX ✿ **A Sousceyrac** (Asfaux), 35 r. Faidherbe (11th) 43 71 65 30 – . AE VISA J 19
closed 22 to 31 March, August, Saturday and Sunday – **M** a la carte 150/200
Spec. Foie gras en terrine, Lièvre à la royale (Friday in season), Cassoulet (Wednesday and Friday).

XX **Repaire de Cartouche,** 8 bd Filles-du-Calvaire (11th) 47 00 25 86 – VISA H 17
closed 26 July-24 August, February Holidays, Saturday and Sunday – **M** a la carte 130/180.

XX **Coconnas,** 2 bis pl. Vosges (4th) 42 78 58 16 – AE VISA J 17
closed 15 December-15 January, Monday and Tuesday – **M** a la carte 200/260.

XX **Guirlande de Julie,** 25 pl. des Vosges (3rd) 48 87 94 07 – AE VISA J 17
closed February, Monday and Tuesday – **M** 166 b.i..

XX Wally, 16 r. Le Regrattier (4th) 43 25 01 39 K 15

XX **Pyrénées Cévennes,** 106 r. Folie-Méricourt (11th) ✆ 43 57 33 78 G 17
closed August, Saturday and Sunday – **M** a la carte 130/210.

XX **Taverne des Templiers,** 106 r. Vieille-du-Temple (3rd) ✆ 42 78 74 67 – AE VISA H 17
closed August, Saturday and Sunday – **M** a la carte 120/180.

XX **Au Gourmet de l'Isle,** 42 r. St-Louis-en-l'Ile (4th) ✆ 43 26 79 27 – ▤ K 16
closed 30 July-3 September, Monday and Thursday – **M** 85.

X ✿ **Benoît,** 20 r. St-Martin (4th) ✆ 42 72 25 76 – Ⓟ J 15
closed August, Saturday and Sunday – **st. : M** a la carte 225/300
Spec. Soupe de moules, Compotiers de boeuf en salade, Cassoulet maison.

Quartier Latin, Luxembourg,

Jardin des Plantes,

5th et 6th arrondissements.
5th : ✉ 75005
6th : ✉ 75006

Lutétia, 45 bd Raspail (6th) ✆ 45 44 38 10, Telex 270424 – |♦| ▤ TV ☎ – 25-600. AE ⓓ E VISA K 12
st. : M Rest see **Le Paris** below - **brasserie Lutetia M** a la carte approx. 150 ‡ – ☕ 50 – **286 rm** 750/1 400, 17 apartments.

Victoria Palace ⛰, 6 r. Blaise-Desgoffe (6th) ✆ 45 44 38 16, Telex 270557 – |♦| TV ☎ 🚗. AE VISA. ✻ L 11
st. : M 130 – **110 rm** ☕ 530/710.

Littré ⛰, 9 r. Littré (6th) ✆ 45 44 38 68, Telex 203852 – |♦| TV ☎ 🚗 – 25. AE E VISA. ✻ L 11
st. : M 120 – **96 rm** ☕ 530/660, 4 apartments 790.

Relais Christine Ⓜ ⛰ without rest, 3 r. Christine (6th) ✆ 43 26 71 80, Telex 202606 – |♦| ▤ TV ☎ 🚗 – 25. AE ⓓ VISA J 14
st. : ☕ 50 – **50 rm** 850/890.

Abbaye St-Germain Ⓜ ⛰ without rest, 10 r. Cassette (6th) ✆ 45 44 38 11, ≋ – |♦| ☎. ✻ K 12
st. : 45 rm ☕ 480/580.

Angleterre without rest, 44 r. Jacob (6th) ✆ 42 60 34 72 – |♦| ☎. AE ⓓ VISA. ✻ J 13
st. : ☕ 25 – **30 rm** 300/650.

Madison H. without rest, 143 bd St-Germain (6th) ✆ 43 29 72 50, Telex 201628 – |♦| ☎. AE VISA. ✻ J 13
st. : 57 rm ☕ 255/460.

Odéon H., Ⓜ without rest, 3 r. Odéon (6th) ✆ 43 25 90 67, Telex 206731 – |♦| ☎. AE VISA. ✻ K 13
st. : ☕ 25 – **34 rm** 370/540.

Scandinavia without rest, 27 r. Tournon (6th) ✆ 43 29 67 20, « Rural setting » – ⛀wc ☎. ✻ K 13
closed August – **st. :** ☕ 20 – **22 rm** 350/370.

St-Germain-des-Prés without rest, 36 r. Bonaparte (6th) ✆ 43 26 00 19 – |♦| TV ⛀wc ⛆wc ☎. AE. ✻ J 13
st. : ☕ 35 – **32 rm** 450/900.

Ferrandi without rest, 92 r. Cherche-Midi (6th) ✆ 42 22 97 40, Telex 205201 – |♦| ⛀wc ⛆wc ☎. AE VISA L 11
st. : ☕ 30 – **42 rm** ☕ 310/400.

Panthéon Ⓜ without rest, 19 pl. Panthéon (5th) ✆ 43 54 32 95 – |♦| TV ⛀wc ☎. AE ⓓ VISA. ✻ L 14
st. : ☕ 22 – **34 rm** 398/500.

Grands Hommes Ⓜ without rest 17 pl. Panthéon (5th) ✆ 46 34 19 60, Telex 200185 – |♦| TV ⛀wc ☎. AE ⓓ VISA. ✻ L 14
st. : ☕ 22 – **32 rm** 400/500.

des Saints-Pères without rest, 65 r. des Sts-Pères (6th) ✆ 45 44 50 00, Telex 205424 – |♦| ⛀wc ☎ ♿. ✻ J 12
st. : ☕ 35 – **37 rm** 350/1 000, 3 apartments 1 000.

Collège de France Ⓜ without rest, 7 r. Thénard (5th) ✆ 43 26 78 36 – |♦| TV ⛀wc ⛆wc ☎. AE. ✻ K 14
st. : ☕ 18,50 – **29 rm** 254/336.

Louis II without rest, 2 r. St.-Sulpice (6th) ✆ 46 33 13 80 – |♦| ⛀wc ⛆wc ☎. AE VISA K 13
st. : ☕ 25 – **22 rm** 400/550.

Pas-de-Calais without rest, 59 r. Sts-Pères (6th) ✆ 45 48 78 74 – |♦| ⛀wc ☎ J 12
st. : 41 rm ☕ 370/450.

Gd H. des Principautés Unies without rest, 42 r. Vaugirard (6th) ✆ 46 34 11 80 – ▯ TV wc wc ☎. ✗ K 13
closed August – **st.** : ☐ 25 – **29 rm** 140/360.

Marronniers ⛰ without rest, 21 r. Jacob (6th) ✆ 43 25 30 60, ☘ – ▯ wc wc ☎. ✗ – **st.** : ☐ 25 – **37 rm** 337/358 J 13

Aviatic without rest, 105 r. Vaugirard (6th) ✆ 45 44 38 21, Telex 200372 – ▯ TV wc ☎. AE ① VISA L 11
st. : **43 rm** ☐ 370/550.

Delavigne without rest, 1 r. C.-Delavigne (6th) ✆ 43 29 31 50, Telex 201579 – ▯ wc wc ☎. ✗ K 13
st. : ☐ 23 – **34 rm** 300/390.

Terminus Montparnasse without rest, 59 bd Montparnasse (6th) ✆ 45 48 99 10, Telex 202636 – ▯ TV wc wc ☎. E VISA L 11
closed August – **st.** : ☐ 29 – **63 rm** 346/446.

d'Isly without rest, 29 r. Jacob (6th) ✆ 43 26 32 39, Telex 643566 – ▯ wc wc ☎. ✗
st. : ☐ 25 – **37 rm** 200/360. J 13

Seine without rest, 52 r. Seine (6th) ✆ 46 34 22 80 – ▯ TV wc wc ☎. AE ① VISA. ✗
st. : **30 rm** ☐ 184/368. J 13

Rennes Montparnasse without rest, 151 bis r. Rennes (6th) ✆ 45 48 97 38, Telex 250048 – ▯ TV wc wc ☎. AE ① E VISA L 12
closed 1 to 28 August – **st.** : ☐ 30 – **35 rm** 220/420.

Nations without rest, 54 r. Monge (5th) ✆ 43 26 45 24, Telex 205139 – ▯ wc wc ☎. VISA. ✗ – **st.** : ☐ 25 – **38 rm** 310/425. L 15

Odéon without rest, 13 r. St-Sulpice (6th) ✆ 43 25 70 11, Telex 206731 – ▯ TV wc wc ☎. AE ① VISA K 13
st. : ☐ 26 – **26 rm** 420/540.

Gd H. Suez without rest, 31 bd St-Michel (5th) ✆ 46 34 08 02, Telex 202019 – ▯ TV wc wc ☎. AE ① E VISA. ✗ K 14
st. : **49 rm** ☐ 183/340.

Albe without rest, 1 r. Harpe (5th) ✆ 46 34 09 70 – ▯ wc wc ☎. ✗ K 14
st. : **41 rm** ☐ 239/299.

Muséum without rest, 9 r. Buffon (5th) ✆ 43 31 51 90 – ▯ TV wc wc ☎. VISA L 16
st. : ☐ 23 – **24 rm** 214/300.

Welcome Ⓜ without rest, 66 r. Seine (6th) ✆ 46 34 24 80 – ▯ wc wc ☎. ✗ J 13
st. : ☐ 21 – **30 rm** 190/325.

St-Sulpice without rest, 7 r. C.-Delavigne (6th) ✆ 46 34 23 90 – ▯ wc wc ☎. VISA
st. : ☐ 19 – **42 rm** 190/270. K 13

XXXXX ✿✿✿ **Tour d'Argent** (Terrail), 15 quai Tournelle (5th) ✆ 43 54 23 21, **« Little museum showing the development of eating utensils, ≤ Notre-Dame. In the cellar : an illustrated history of wine »** – AE ① VISA K 16
closed Monday – **M** 220 (lunch) and a la carte 390/585
Spec. Canard au sang Tour d'Argent.

XXXX ✿ **Le Paris,** 45 bd Raspail (6th) ✆ 45 44 38 10 – AE ① E VISA K 12
closed 2 August-2 September, Sunday and Monday – **st.** : **M** a la carte 235/340
Spec. Minute de bar en homardine, Tournedos à la croûte au pot, Chocolatine à la framboise.

XXX ✿✿ **Jacques Cagna,** 14 r. Gds-Augustins (6th) ✆ 43 26 49 39, **« Old Parisian house »** – ▤. VISA J 14
closed August, 24 December-2 January, Saturday and Sunday – **M** 190
Spec. Pétoncles en coquilles, Filet de barbue farci d'huîtres, Canard de Challans aux zestes d'orange et citron.

XXX ✿✿ **Relais Louis XIII,** 1 r. Pont de Lodi (6th) ✆ 43 26 75 96, **« 16C cellar, fine furniture »** – ▤. AE ① E VISA J 14
closed 3 August-1 September, 1 to 8 January, Monday lunch and Sunday – **M** a la carte 260/340
Spec. Dégustation de poissons de petite pêche, Millefeuille de rognons et ris de veau, Crème tiède aux framboises.

XXX ✿ **Villars Palace,** 8 r. Descartes (5th) ✆ 43 26 39 08 – AE ① E VISA L 15
closed Saturday lunch – **M** (rest.) a la carte 225/315 – **La Saumoneraie M** 71/100
Spec. Plâteau de poissons marinés, Saumon Villars fumé.

XXX ✿✿ **Duquesnoy,** 30 r. Bernardins (5th) ✆ 43 54 21 13 – AE VISA K 15
closed August, Saturday and Sunday – **M** 160 (lunch) and a la carte 210/330
Spec. Millefeuille de saumon fumé et caviar, Ravioli de tourteau et homard au basilic.

XXX **Chat Grippé,** 87 r. d'Assas (6th) ✆ 43 54 70 00 – ▤. AE VISA LM 13
closed August, 17 to 23 February, Saturday lunch and Monday – **M** a la carte 170/245 ♁.

XX **Aub. des Deux Signes,** 46 r. Galande (5th) ✆ 43 25 46 56, « Medieval decor » – AE ⓓ E VISA K 14
closed Sunday and Bank Holidays – **M** a la carte 200/300.

XX ✿ **Dodin-Bouffant,** 25 r. F.-Sauton (5th) ✆ 43 25 25 14 – ▤. ⓓ VISA K 15
closed August, Saturday and Sunday – **M** a la carte 170/240
Spec. Feuilleté aux huîtres, Timbale du pêcheur, Ragoût de canard et ris de veau.

XX ✿✿ **Ambroisie** (Pacaud), 65 quai de la Tournelle (5th) ✆ 46 33 18 65 – AE VISA K 15
closed 10 to 31 August, February Holidays, Sunday and Monday – **st. : M** 190 (lunch) and a la carte 245/360
Spec. Fonds d'artichaut au foie gras, Queue de boeuf en crépine, Pâtisseries.

XX **Le Pactole,** 44 bd St-Germain (5th) ✆ 46 33 31 31 – AE VISA K 15
closed Saturday lunch and Sunday – **st. : M** a la carte 215/275.

XX **Sud Ouest,** 40 r. Montagne Ste Geneviève (5th) ✆ 46 33 30 46, « 13C Crypt » – AE ⓓ E VISA – *closed August and Sunday* – **M** a la carte 125/155. K 15

XX ✿ **Miravile** (Keller), 25 quai de la Tournelle (5th) ✆ 46 34 07 78 – AE ⓓ VISA K 15
closed Sunday – **st. : M** a la carte 200/300
Spec. Terrine de brochet, Filet d'agneau sous croûte de sel, Feuilleté aux fruits.

XX **La Marlotte,** 55 r. Cherche-Midi (6th) ✆ 45 48 86 79 – ✻ K 12
closed August, Saturday and Sunday – **M** a la carte 145/200.

XX **Le Clos des Bernardins,** 14 r. Pontoise (5th) ✆ 43 54 70 07 – AE ⓓ VISA K 15
st. : M a la carte 165/220.

XX **Coupe-Chou,** 11 r. Lanneau (5th) ✆ 46 33 68 69 – VISA K 14
M a la carte 120/200.

XX **Atelier Maître Albert,** 1 r. Maître-Albert (5th) ✆ 46 33 13 78 – ▤ K 15
closed Sunday and Bank Holidays – **M** (dinner only) 140 b.i..

XX **La Truffière,** 4 r. Blainville (5th) ✆ 46 33 29 82 – ▤. AE ⓓ E VISA. ✻ L 15
closed 14 July-18 August, February holidays and Monday – **M** a la carte 160/300.

XX **L'Apollinaire,** 168 bd St.-Germain (6th) ✆ 43 26 50 30 – ▤. AE ⓓ E VISA J 12
closed 20 December-5 January – **M** a la carte 155/235.

XX **Taverne Basque,** 45 r. Cherche-Midi (6th) ✆ 42 22 51 07 – AE VISA K 12
closed 10 to 18 August, Sunday dinner and Monday – **M** a la carte 115/170.

XX **La Foux,** 2 r. Clément (6th) ✆ 43 54 09 53 – ▤. AE K 13
closed Sunday – **st. : M** a la carte 120/200.

XX **Les Arètes,** 165 bd Montparnasse (6th) ✆ 43 26 23 98 – AE VISA M 13
closed Saturday lunch and Monday – **st. : M** a la carte 170/265.

XX **Chez Tante Madée,** 11 r. Dupin (6th) ✆ 42 22 64 56 – AE ⓓ K 12
closed Saturday lunch and Sunday – **st. : M** a la carte 180/260.

XX **Le Sybarite,** 6 r. Sabot (6th) ✆ 42 22 21 56 – ▤. AE ⓓ VISA. ✻ K 12
closed Saturday lunch and Sunday – **st. : M** 138.

XX **Au Grilladin,** 13 r. Mézières (6th) ✆ 45 48 30 38 – VISA K 12
closed 22 March-1 April, August, 23 December-3 January, Monday lunch and Sunday – **st. : M** a la carte 130/210.

XX **Joséphine** (Chez Dumonet), 117 r. Cherche-Midi (6th) ✆ 45 48 52 40 – VISA L 11
closed July, 22 to 28 December, Saturday and Sunday – **M** a la carte 140/250.

XX **Dominique,** 19 r. Bréa (6th) ✆ 43 27 08 80, Russian cuisine – AE ⓓ E VISA L 12
closed July and February holidays – **M** a la carte 100/180.

X ✿ **Allard,** 41 r. St-André-des-Arts (6th) ✆ 43 26 48 23 – AE ⓓ E VISA K 14
closed August, 24 December-1 January, Saturday and Sunday – **st. : M** (booking essential) a la carte 180/270
Spec. St-Jacques au beurre blanc (10 October-15 May), Canard aux olives.

X **Balzar,** 49 r. Écoles (5th) ✆ 43 54 13 67 – VISA. ✻ K 14
closed August and Tuesday – **M** a la carte 120/165.

X **Moissonnier,** 28 r. Fossés-St-Bernard (5th) ✆ 43 29 87 65 K 15
closed August, Sunday dinner and Monday – **M** a la carte 100/150.

X **L'Ange Gourmand,** 31 quai Tournelle (5th) ✆ 43 54 11 31. AE K 15
closed Monday lunch – **st. : M** 135/180.

X **Au Charbon de Bois,** 16 r. Dragon (6th) ✆ 45 48 57 04 – ▤. AE ⓓ VISA J 12
closed Sunday – **st. : M** a la carte approx 140.

X **Chez Maître Paul,** 12 r. Monsieur-le-Prince (6th) ✆ 43 54 74 59 – AE ⓓ VISA K 13
closed August, 24 December-2 January, Sunday and Monday – **M** a la carte 110/150.

X **Xavier-Grégoire,** 80 r. Cherche-Midi (6th) ✆ 45 44 72 72 – AE VISA L 11
closed 10 to 30 August, Saturday lunch and Sunday – **st. : M** a la carte 155/230.

X **Moulin à Vent,** 20 r. Fossés-St-Bernard (5th) ✆ 43 54 99 37 – AE VISA K 15
closed August and Sunday – **M** a la carte 130/200.

X **L'Agronome,** 35 quai Tournelle (5th) ✆ 43 25 44 42 K 16
closed Saturday lunch and Sunday – **st. : M** a la carte 120/175.

X **Le Mange Tout,** 30 r. Lacépède (5th) ✆ 45 35 53 93 – ⓓ VISA L 15
closed 4 to 31 August, Monday lunch and Sunday – **st. : M** a la carte 100/130.

Faubourg-St-Germain,
Invalides,
École Militaire.

7th arrondissement.
7th : ✉ 75007

Pont Royal and rest. Les Antiquaires, 7 r. Montalembert ✆ 45 44 38 27, Telex 270113 – kitchenette – 50. AE ⓓ E VISA J 12
st. : **M** *(closed August and Sunday)* 190 b.i. – **75 rm** 720/1 600, 5 apartments.

Sofitel Bourbon M, 32 r. St-Dominique ✆ 45 55 91 80, Telex 250019 – – 50. AE ⓓ E VISA H 10
st. : **M** Rest. see **Le Dauphin** below – 70 – **112 rm** 1 020/1 250.

Cayré-Copatel M without rest, 4 bd Raspail ✆ 45 44 38 88, Telex 270577 – – 40. AE ⓓ E VISA J 12
st. : **130 rm** 724/751.

St-Simon without rest, 14 r. St-Simon ✆ 45 48 35 66, « Antique furniture » – . J 11
st. : 25 – **29 rm** 550/600, 5 apartments 800.

Université without rest, 22 r. Université ✆ 42 61 09 39 – . J 12
33 – **27 rm** 350/550.

Montalembert without rest, 3 r. Montalembert ✆ 45 48 68 11, Telex 200132 – . E J 12
st. : **61 rm** 520/690.

La Bourdonnais, 111 av. La Bourdonnais ✆ 47 05 45 42, Telex 201416 – . ⓓ VISA J 9
st. : **M** Rest. see **La Cantine des Gourmets** below – **56 rm** 310/420.

Suède without rest, 31 r. Vaneau ✆ 47 05 00 08, Telex 200596 – wc wc . AE. K 11
st. : **40 rm** 370/500.

De Varenne M without rest, 44 r. Bourgogne ✆ 45 51 45 55 – wc wc . AE J 10
st. : 24 – **24 rm** 239/360.

Résidence Elysées Maubourg M without rest, 35 bd Latour-Maubourg ✆ 45 56 10 78, Telex 206227 – wc . AE ⓓ E VISA. H 10
st. : **30 rm** 430/600.

Lenox without rest, 9 r. Université ✆ 42 96 10 95 – wc wc . AE E VISA J 12
st. : 25 – **32 rm** 295/420.

Académie without rest, 32 r. des Sts-Pères ✆ 45 48 36 22, Telex 205650 – wc wc . AE ⓓ E VISA J 12
st. : 25 – **34 rm** 360/440.

Beaugency M without rest, 21 r. Duvivier ✆ 47 05 01 63, Telex 201494 – wc wc . AE ⓓ E VISA. J 9
st. : **30 rm** 350/370.

St-Germain without rest, 88 r. Bac ✆ 45 48 62 92 – wc wc . AE. J 11
st. : 23 – **29 rm** 230/460.

Bourgogne et Montana, 3 r. Bourgogne ✆ 45 51 20 22, Telex 270854 – wc . AE E VISA H 11
st. : **M** *(closed Saturday and Sunday)* 125 – **30 rm** 330/560, 5 apartments 660.

Verneuil-St-Germain without rest, 8 r. Verneuil ✆ 42 60 24 16 – wc wc . AE VISA J 12
st. : 25 – **26 rm** 340/420.

Derby H. without rest, 5 av. Duquesne ✆ 47 05 12 05, Telex 206236 – wc wc – 30. AE ⓓ E VISA J 9
st. : 30 – **44 rm** 390/410.

Lindbergh without rest, 5 r. Chomel ✆ 45 48 35 53, Telex 201777 – wc wc . AE ⓓ E VISA K 12
st. : 23 – **26 rm** 270/350.

Tourville M without rest, 16 av. Tourville ✆ 47 05 52 15, Telex 250786 – wc wc . AE VISA J 9
st. : 18 – **30 rm** 221/288.

Londres without rest, ✆ 45 51 63 02, Telex 206398 – wc wc . AE E VISA.
st. : 25 – **30 rm** 390/490.

Solférino without rest, 91 r. Lille ✆ 47 05 85 54 – wc wc . VISA. H 11
closed 23 December-3 January – **st. : 34 rm** 303/360.

Chomel without rest, 15 r. Chomel 45 48 55 52, Telex 206522 – wc wc. AE E VISA. K 12
st. : 34 – **23 rm** 370/475.

Bersoly's without rest, 28 r. Lille 42 60 73 79 – wc wc. AE VISA. J 13
st. : 25 – **16 rm** 391/494.

Mars H. without rest, 117 av. La Bourdonnais 47 05 42 30 – wc wc J 9
st. : **24 rm**.

Kensington without rest, 79 av. La Bourdonnais 47 05 74 00 – wc wc. AE VISA J 9
st. : 18,50 – **26 rm** 197/258.

Turenne without rest, 20 av. Tourville 47 05 99 92, Telex 203407 – wc wc. AE VISA J 9
st. : 22 – **34 rm** 172/308.

Résidence d'Orsay without rest, 93 r. Lille 47 05 05 27 – wc wc. VISA. H 11
closed August – st. : 22 – **32 rm** 140/290.

Champ de Mars without rest, 7 r. Champ de Mars 45 51 52 30 – wc wc. VISA J 9
closed 15 to 28 August – st. : 18,50 – **25 rm** 260/280.

L'Empereur without rest, 2 r. Chevert 45 55 88 02 – wc wc J 9
st. : 19 – **34 rm** 226/300.

Muguet without rest, 11 r. Chevert 47 05 05 93 – wc wc J 9
closed 21 July-1 September – st. : 19 – **43 rm** 120/240.

XXXX **Le Divellec,** 107 r. Université 45 51 91 96 – AE VISA. H 10
closed August, Christmas, 1 January, Sunday and Monday – **M** a la carte 240/420
Spec. Huîtres raidies en cassolette, Escalopes de turbotin aux coques, Poêlée de langoustines au foie de canard.

XXXX **Jules Verne,** Eiffel Tower : 2nd platform, lift in south leg 45 55 61 44, Telex 205789, Paris – AE VISA. J 7
M a la carte 235/315
Spec. Fricassée de langoustines au curry, Pigeonneau rôti aux bolets, Grand dessert Jules Verne.

XXX **L'Argonne,** 84 r. Varenne 45 51 47 33 – AE VISA J 10
closed August, Saturday lunch and Sunday – st. : **M** a la carte 230/320
Spec. Filet de rouget, Aiguillette de caneton, Chaud et froid de poires.

XXX **Le Dauphin** (Sofitel Bourbon), 32 r. St-Dominique 45 55 91 80 – AE E VISA H 10
st. : **M** a la carte 225/295
Spec. Salade de langoustines au chou vert, Tronçons de colin rôti aux légumes, Fricassée de ris de veau.

XXX **Chez les Anges,** 54 bd Latour-Maubourg 47 05 89 86 – AE E VISA J 9
closed Sunday dinner and Monday – **M** a la carte 190/295
Spec. Oeufs en meurette, Feuillantine de bar et de saumon aux épinards, Foie de veau.

XXX **La Flamberge** (Albistur), 12 av. Rapp 47 07 91 37 – AE E VISA H 8
closed 2 to 18 August, Saturday lunch and Sunday – st. : **M** a la carte 205/275
Spec. Baron de lapereau à la menthe et pâtes fraîches (15 February-15 October), Gibier (season), Grande assiette de desserts.

XXX **La Cantine des Gourmets,** 113 av. de La Bourdonnais 47 05 47 96 – AE VISA J 9
closed Sunday and Monday – st. : **M** a la carte 195/300
Spec. Biscuit de sardines et olives, Paupiette de raie et saumon fumé, Consommé de ris de veau au potiron.

XXX **La Bourgogne,** 6 av. Bosquet 47 05 96 78 – AE VISA H 9
closed Saturday lunch and Sunday – **M** a la carte 145/230.

XXX **La Boule d'Or,** 13 bd Latour-Maubourg 47 05 50 18 – AE VISA H 10
closed August, Saturday lunch and Monday – **M** a la carte 170/240
Spec. Marbré de poissons aux avocats, Millefeuille de sole et langoustines, Soufflé chaud au citron.

XXX **Beato,** 8 r. Malar 47 05 94 27, Italian cuisine – AE VISA H 9
closed August, Christmas and 1 January – st. : **M** a la carte 180/260.

XX **Chez Françoise,** Aérogare des Invalides 47 05 49 03 – AE VISA H 10
closed August, Sunday dinner and Monday – **M** a la carte 125/195.

XX **Récamier** (Cantegrit), 4 r. Récamier 45 48 86 58 – E VISA K 12
closed Sunday – **M** a la carte 190/300
Spec. Oeufs en meurette, Mousse de brochet, Boeuf bourguignon.

XX **Ferme St-Simon** (Vandenhende), 6 r. St-Simon 45 48 35 74 – VISA J 11
closed 1 to 25 August, Saturday lunch and Sunday – **M** 144 b.i (lunch) and a la carte 165/240
Spec. Ravioli d'huîtres (end December-March), Grillandine Denise Fabre, Desserts.

XX ✿ **Labrousse,** 4 r. Pierre-Leroux ☎ 43 06 99 39 – ▤. AE VISA K 11
closed August, Sunday and Monday lunch – **M** a la carte 170/240
Spec. Ris de veau et langoustines en salade, Morue à l'ail doux, Pigeonneau en aumonière.

XX **Le Florence,** 22 r. Champ de Mars ☎ 45 51 52 69 – AE VISA J 9
closed July, Sunday and Monday – **M** 100/170.

XX **Le Galant Verre,** 12 r. Verneuil ☎ 42 60 84 56 – AE ① E VISA J 12
closed Saturday lunch and Sunday – **M** a la carte 170/285.

XX ✿ **Bistrot de Paris,** 33 r. Lille ☎ 42 61 16 83, bistro style – VISA J 12
closed Saturday lunch, Sunday and Bank Holidays – **M** a la carte 170/220
Spec. Salade de filets de canard au miel et soja, Daube de pieds de porc aux épices, Tournedos de canard et de volaille.

XX **Vert Bocage,** 96 bd Latour-Maubourg ☎ 45 51 48 54 – AE ① VISA J 9
closed August, Saturday and Sunday – **M** a la carte 165/250.

XX **Antoine et Antoinette,** 16 av. Rapp ☎ 45 51 75 61 – AE ① VISA H 8
closed Saturday and Sunday – **M** a la carte 145/215.

XX **Bellecour,** 22 r. Surcouf ☎ 45 51 46 93 – AE ① E VISA H 9
closed 15 August-1 September, Saturday (except dinner from 1 October to 1 June) and Sunday – **M** 185/270.

XX **Aux Délices de Szechuen,** 40 av. Duquesne ☎ 43 06 22 55, Chinese cuisine – ▤. AE VISA K 10
closed 5 to 22 August and Monday – **st. : M** a la carte 100/170 ♨.

XX **Chez Ribe,** 15 av. Suffren ☎ 45 66 53 79 – AE ① E VISA J 7
closed Saturday and Sunday – **M** a la carte 155/260.

XX ✿ **Gildo** (Bellini), 153 r. Grenelle ☎ 45 51 54 12, Italian cuisine J 9
closed 14 July-1 September, Christmas Holidays, Sunday and Monday – **M** a la carte 115/170
Spec. Ravioli, Tagliarini au safran, Rognonne trifolato.

XX **Le Champ de Mars,** 17 av. Motte-Picquet ☎ 47 05 57 99 – AE ① VISA J 9
closed 15 July-15 August, Tuesday dinner and Monday – **M** a la carte 100/170.

XX **Quai d'Orsay,** 49 quai d'Orsay ☎ 45 51 58 58 – AE ① VISA H 9
closed 1 to 24 August and Sunday – **M** a la carte 200/305.

X ✿ **Pantagruel** (Israël), 20 r. Exposition ☎ 45 51 79 96 – ① VISA J 9
closed August, February holidays, Saturday lunch and Sunday – **st. : M** a la carte 130/215
Spec. Cassolette d'escargots flambés, Soufflé aux oursins (October-March), Filets de sole aux oranges.

X ✿ **Tan Dinh,** 60 r. Verneuil ☎ 45 44 04 84, Vietnamese cuisine J 12
closed 15 to 31 August and Sunday – **M** a la carte 130/175
Spec. Ravioli vietnamiens, Pâtes fraîches aux crevettes piquantes, Emincé de filet de boeuf.

X **La Calèche,** 8 r. Lille ☎ 42 60 24 76 – AE ① E VISA J 12
closed 5 to 28 August, 24 December-5 January, Saturday and Sunday – **st. : M** a la carte 125/185.

X **Aub. Champ de Mars,** 18 r. Exposition ☎ 45 51 78 08 – AE ① VISA J 9
closed 4 to 31 August, Saturday lunch and Sunday – **M** a la carte 105/175.

X **Vin sur Vin,** 20 r. Monttessuy ☎ 47 05 14 20 H 8
closed 9 to 18 August, Saturday lunch and Sunday – **M** a la carte approx 140.

Champs-Élysées, St-Lazare, Madeleine.

8th arrondissement.

8th : ✉ 75008

Plaza-Athénée, 25 av. Montaigne ☎ 47 23 78 33, Telex 650092 – |‡| ▤ TV ☎ – 🛋 30-100. AE ① E VISA. ✱ rest G 9
M Rest. see **Régence and Relais Plaza** below – ☐ 70 – **174 rm** 1 650/1 950, 44 apartments.

Bristol, 112 fg St-Honoré ☎ 42 66 91 45, Telex 280961, ⛶, ⛱ – |‡| ▤ TV ☎ Ⓟ – 🛋 40-150. AE ① E VISA. ✱ F 10
st. : M Rest. see **Bristol** below – ☐ 80 – **155 rm** 1 150/2 600, 45 apartments.

Crillon, 10 pl. Concorde ☎ 42 65 24 24, Telex 290204, ⛱ – |‡| ▤ TV ☎ – 🛋 30-60. AE ① E VISA. ✱ rest G 11
st. : L'Obelisque M a la carte approx. 200 - Rest. see **Les Ambassadeurs** below – ☐ 80 – **146 rm** 1 510/2 200, 41 apartments.

George V, 31 av. George-V ☎ 47 23 54 00, Telex 650082, ⛱ – |‡| ▤ TV ☎ – 🛋 500. AE ① E VISA G 8
Rest. **Les Princes M** a la carte 280/440 – ☐ 70 – **289 rm** 1 990/2 860, 59 apartments.

Prince de Galles, 33 av. George-V ☎ 47 23 55 11, Telex 280627, ⛱ – |‡| ▤ TV ☎ – 🛋 40-200. AE ① E VISA. ✱ rest G 8
st. : M 210/340 – ☐ 90 – **150 rm** 1 550/2 450, 30 apartments.

Royal Monceau, 37 av. Hoche ✆ 45 61 98 00, Telex 650361, 🏊, ☐ – 🛗 ▤ 📺 ☎ – 🎤 500. AE ⓓ E VISA. ✗ rest E 8
st. : Le Jardin M a la carte 270/390 - **Le Carpaccio** *(closed August)* **M** a la carte 240/350 – ☕ 90 – **220 rm** 1 550/2 255, 40 apartments.

La Trémoille, 14 r. La Trémoille ✆ 47 23 34 20, Telex 640344 – 🛗 ▤ rest 📺 ☎. AE ⓓ E VISA G 9
M a la carte 130/180 🍷 – ☕ 40 – **97 rm** 950/1 620, 14 apartments.

Warwick Ⓜ, 5 r. Berri ✆ 45 63 14 11, Telex 642295 – 🛗 ▤ 📺 ☎ – 🎤 25-150. AE ⓓ E VISA F 9
st. : M Rest see **La Couronne** below – ☕ 75 – **144 rm** 1 280/1 950, 4 apartments.

Frantel-Windsor Ⓜ, 14 r. Beaujon ✆ 45 63 04 04, Telex 650902 – 🛗 ▤ rest 📺 ☎ – 🎤 25-120. AE ⓓ E VISA F 8
st. : M Rest. see **Le Clovis** below – ☕ 55 – **135 rm** 800/1 200.

Lancaster, 7 r. Berri ✆ 43 59 90 43, Telex 640991, 🏊 – 🛗 ▤ rm 📺 ☎. AE ⓓ E VISA F 9
M *(closed Saturday and Sunday)* a la carte 250/340 – ☕ 80 – **47 rm** 1 000/1 650, 10 apartments.

Claridge Bellman Ⓜ, 37 r. François 1er ✆ 47 23 90 03, Telex 641150 – 🛗 ▤ rest 📺 ☎. AE ⓓ VISA. ✗ G 9
st. : M *(closed Saturday and Sunday)* a la carte 170/250 – ☕ 49 – **42 rm** 625/875.

Château Frontenac, 54 r. P.-Charron ✆ 47 23 55 85, Telex 660994 – 🛗 📺 ☎ – 🎤 30. AE ⓓ E VISA. ✗ G 9
st. : Pavillon Russe M a la carte 185/315 – ☕ 48 – **103 rm** 640/890.

Napoléon, 40 av. Friedland ✆ 47 66 02 02, Telex 640609 – 🛗 kitchenette 📺 ☎ – 🎤 30-100. AE ⓓ E VISA F 8
st. : Rest. see **Napoléon Baumann** below – ☕ 40 – **108 rm** 650/1 020, 32 apartments.

Bedford, 17 r. Arcade ✆ 42 66 22 32, Telex 290506 – 🛗 ▤ rest 📺 ☎ – 🎤 80. E VISA. ✗ rest F 11
st. : M *(closed August, Saturday and Sunday)* (lunch only) 125 b.i. – **137 rm** ☕ 450/650, 10 apartments 930.

California without rest, 16 r. Berri ✆ 43 59 93 00, Telex 660634 – 🛗 📺 ☎ – 🎤 35-70 F 9
188 rm, 3 apartments.

Concorde-St-Lazare, 108 r. St-Lazare ✆ 42 94 22 22, Telex 650442 – 🛗 ▤ rest 📺 ☎ – 🎤 100. AE ⓓ E VISA E 12
st. : Café Terminus M 200 b.i./125 – ☕ 55 – **324 rm** 950/1 500.

Queen Elizabeth, 41 av. Pierre-1er-de-Serbie ✆ 47 20 80 56, Telex 641179 – 🛗 📺 ☎ – 🎤 25. AE ⓓ E VISA G 8
st. : M *(closed Sunday and dinner Monday to Friday)* 90 b.i./135 b.i. – ☕ 60 – **60 rm** 800/1 300, 7 apartments.

Etap St-Honoré Ⓜ without rest, 15 r. Boissy d'Anglas ✆ 42 66 93 62, Telex 240366 – 🛗 📺 ☎. AE ⓓ E VISA G 11
st. : ☕ 40 – **105 rm** 450/600, 8 apartments 800.

Royal Malesherbes Ⓜ, 24 bd Malesherbes ✆ 42 65 53 30, Telex 660190 – 🛗 📺 ☎ – 🎤 30. AE ⓓ E VISA F 11
st. : M a la carte approx. 160 🍷 – **101 rm** ☕ 690/770.

Royal-Madeleine Ⓜ without rest, 29 r. Arcade ✆ 42 66 13 81, Telex 641458 – 🛗 📺 ☎. AE ⓓ VISA. ✗ F 11
☕ 49 – **70 rm** 721/896.

Castiglione, 40 r. Fg-St-Honoré ✆ 42 65 07 50, Telex 240362 – 🛗 📺 ☎. AE ⓓ E VISA
M a la carte approx. 250 – **96 rm** 1 030/1 090, 16 apartments. G 11

Astor, 11 r. Astorg ✆ 42 66 56 56, Telex 642718 – 🛗 📺 ☎. AE ⓓ E VISA F 11
st. : M *(closed Sunday)* a la carte 190/275 – **128 rm** ☕ 720/830.

Résidence Champs-Elysées Ⓜ without rest, 92 r. La Boëtie ✆ 43 59 96 15, Telex 650695 – 🛗 📺 ☎. AE ⓓ E VISA F 9
st. : ☕ 38 – **84 rm** 597/850.

Elysées-Marignan without rest, 12 r. Marignan ✆ 43 59 58 61, Telex 660018 – 🛗 📺 ☎ – 🎤 100-130. AE ⓓ E VISA G 9
st. : ☕ 50 – **57 rm** 965/1 180, 22 apartments.

Printemps and rest. Chez Martin, 1 r. Isly ✆ 42 94 12 12, Telex 290744 – 🛗 📺 ☎ – 🎤 25. E F 12
st. : M *(closed Sunday)* 88 b.i. – **67 rm** ☕ 315/715.

Roblin and rest. Le Mazagran, 6 r. Chauveau-Lagarde ✆ 42 65 57 00, Telex 640154 – 🛗 📺 ☎. VISA F 11
M *(closed August, Saturday and Sunday)* a la carte 130/200 - **Grill** *(closed August, Saturday and Sunday)* **M** a la carte approx. 120 🍷 – **70 rm** ☕ 457/590.

Vernet, 25 r. Vernet ✆ 47 23 43 10, Telex 290347 – 🛗 ☎. AE ⓓ E VISA F 8
st. : M *(closed August, Saturday and Sunday)* 195 – ☕ 45 – **63 rm** 690/1 020.

Royal H. without rest, 33 av. Friedland ✆ 43 59 08 14, Telex 280965 – 🛗 📺 ☎. AE ⓓ E VISA. ✗ F 8
st. : ☕ 34 – **57 rm** 562/723.

Concortel without rest, 19 r. Pasquier ✆ 42 65 45 44, Telex 660228 – [lift] TV ☎. AE [Diners]
st. : ☕ 27 – **38 rm** 340/420, 8 apartments 520. F 11

Powers without rest, 52 r. François-1er ✆ 47 23 91 05, Telex 642051 – [lift] TV ☎. AE VISA. [no dogs]
st. : ☕ 30 – **56 rm** 450/610. G 9

Alison M without rest, 21 r. Surène ✆ 42 65 54 00, Telex 640435 – [lift] TV [bath]wc [shower]wc ☎. AE [Diners] E VISA. [no dogs]
st. : ☕ 30 – **35 rm** 280/480. F 11

L'Arcade without rest, 7 r. Arcade ✆ 42 65 43 85 – [lift] TV [bath]wc ☎
st. : **47 rm** ☕ 290/380. F 11

Bradford without rest, 10 r. St-Philippe-du-Roule ✆ 43 59 24 20, Telex 648530 – [lift] [bath]wc [shower]wc ☎. [no dogs]
st. : **48 rm** ☕ 360/460. F 9

Colisée M without rest, 6 r. Colisée ✆ 43 59 95 25, Telex 643101 – [lift] TV [bath]wc ☎. AE [Diners] E VISA
st. : **44 rm** ☕ 430/590. F 9

St Augustin without rest, 9 r. Roy ✆ 42 93 32 17, Telex 641919 – [lift] TV [bath]wc [shower]wc ☎. AE [Diners] E VISA
st. : ☕ 20 – **62 rm** 380/455. F 11

Plaza Haussmann M without rest, 177 bd Haussmann ✆ 45 63 93 83, Telex 673716 – [lift] TV [bath]wc ☎. AE [Diners] E VISA
st. : ☕ 20 – **41 rm** 395/480. F 9

Elysées Ponthieu M without rest, 24 r. Ponthieu ✆ 42 25 68 70, Telex 640053 – [lift] TV [bath]wc [shower]wc ☎. AE [Diners] E VISA
st. : ☕ 20 – **62 rm** 395/590. F 9

Angleterre-Champs-Élysées M without rest, 91 r. La Boétie ✆ 43 59 35 45, Telex 640317 – [lift] TV [bath]wc [shower]wc ☎. AE [Diners] VISA
st. : ☕ 23 – **40 rm** 225/338. F 9

Royal Alma without rest, 35 r. Jean-Goujon ✆ 42 25 83 30, Telex 641428 – [lift] [bath]wc [shower]wc ☎. AE VISA. [no dogs]
st. : ☕ 30 – **84 rm** 640/915. G 9

Astoria without rest, 42 r. Moscou ✆ 42 93 63 53, Telex 210408 – [lift] TV [bath]wc [shower]wc. AE [Diners] E VISA
st. : **82 rm** ☕ 560/590. D 11

Résidence Saint-Philippe without rest, 123 r. Fg-St-Honoré ✆ 43 59 86 99 – [lift] TV [bath]wc [shower]wc ☎. [no dogs]
st. : **38 rm** ☕ 340/530. F 9-10

Franklin Roosevelt without rest, 18 r. Clément-Marot ✆ 47 23 61 66, Telex 614797 – [lift] TV [bath]wc [shower]wc ☎. AE VISA. [no dogs]
st. : **45 rm** ☕ 470/500. G 9

Rond-Point des Champs-Elysées without rest, 10 r. Ponthieu ✆ 43 59 55 58, Telex 642386 – [lift] TV [bath]wc [shower]wc ☎. AE [Diners] E VISA. [no dogs]
st. : **46 rm** ☕ 355/475. F 10

West End without rest, 7 r. Clément-Marot ✆ 47 20 30 78, Telex 611972 – [lift] TV [bath]wc ☎. AE [Diners] VISA
st. : ☕ 35 – **60 rm** 550/850. G 9

Rochambeau without rest, 4 r. La Boétie ✆ 42 65 27 54, Telex 640030 – [lift] TV [bath]wc [shower]wc ☎. AE [Diners] E VISA
st. : **50 rm** ☕ 486/530. F 9

Brescia M without rest, 16 r. Edimbourg ✆ 45 22 14 31, Telex 660714 – [lift] TV [bath]wc [shower]wc ☎ [wheelchair]. AE [Diners] E VISA
st. : ☕ 23 – **38 rm** 200/280. E 11

Washington without rest, 43 r. Washington ✆ 45 61 10 76 – [lift] TV [bath]wc [shower]wc ☎. AE VISA. [no dogs]
st. : ☕ 22 – **23 rm** 200/350. F 9

Atlantic without rest, 44 r. Londres ✆ 43 87 45 40, Telex 650477 – [lift] [bath]wc [shower]wc ☎. AE VISA. [no dogs]
st. : ☕ 24 – **93 rm** 226/355. E 12

Queen Mary without rest, 9 r. Greffulhe ✆ 42 66 40 50, Telex 640419 – [lift] [bath]wc [shower]wc ☎. [no dogs]
st. : ☕ 30 – **36 rm** 330/450. F 12

Lido without rest, 4 passage Madeleine ✆ 42 66 27 37 – [lift] [bath]wc [shower]wc ☎. AE [Diners] E VISA
st. : ☕ 25 – **31 rm** 410/600. F 11

Lord Byron without rest, 5 r. Chateaubriand ✆ 43 59 89 98, Telex 649662, [phone line] – [lift] TV [bath]wc [shower]wc ☎. [no dogs]
st. : ☕ 26 – **30 rm** 355/630. F 9

Opal without rest, **19 r. Tronchet** ✆ **42 65 77 97, Telex 217152** – wc. AE VISA. F 12
st. : 22 – **36 rm** 400/470.

Élysées without rest, **100 r. La Boétie** ✆ **43 59 23 46** – wc wc. AE E VISA. F 9
st. : 30 rm 345/385.

Ministère without rest, **31 r. Surène** ✆ **42 66 21 43** – wc wc F 11
st. : 32 rm 175/385.

Lavoisier-Malesherbes without rest, **21 r. Lavoisier** ✆ **42 65 10 97** – wc wc. F 11
st. : 32 rm 240/296.

XXXXX ✿✿✿ **Lucas-Carton (Senderens), 9 pl. Madeleine** ✆ **42 65 22 90, « Fine 1900's decor »** – P. VISA. G 11
closed 2 to 26 August, 20 December-5 January Saturday and Sunday – **M** a la carte 365/520
Spec. Escalope de saumon fumé chaude, Foie gras de canard aux choux, Canard poché et rôti au miel.

XXXXX ✿✿ **Bristol, 112 r. Fg St-Honoré** ✆ **42 66 91 45** – P. AE E VISA. F 10
st. : M a la carte 335/420
Spec. Salade landaise, Escalope de turbot au Sauternes, Nage de St Pierre aux concombres et citronelle.

XXXXX ✿✿ **Lasserre, 17 av. Franklin-D.-Roosevelt** ✆ **43 59 53 43, Roof open in fine weather** – . G 10
closed 3 August-1 September, Sunday and Monday – **M** a la carte 320/420
Spec. Filets de sole marinière, Ailes de pigeon et chou garni aux cèpes, Charlotte chocolatée aux poires caramélisées.

XXXXX ✿✿✿ **Taillevent, 15 r. Lamennais** ✆ **45 61 12 90** – . F 9
closed 26 July-25 August, February Holidays, Saturday, Sunday and Bank Holidays – **M** (booking essential) a la carte 290/400
Spec. Cannelloni de céleri au jus de truffe, Poularde de Bresse Edouard Mignon, Diplomate aux griottes confites.

XXXXX ✿✿ **Les Ambassadeurs, 10 pl. Concorde** ✆ **42 65 24 24**, , **« 18C decor »** – AE E VISA. G 11
st. : M a la carte 320/500
Spec. Lamelles de St. Jacques Sonia Rykiel, Viennoise de Turbot aux pignes, Moëlleux de cacao aux quatre épices.

XXXXX ✿ **Ledoyen, carré Champs-Élysées** ✆ **42 66 54 77** – P G 10
closed August and Sunday – **M** a la carte 270/380
Spec. Civet de langouste à la crème d'estragon, Panaché de poissons vigneronne, Faisan en chartreuse à l'alsacienne (season).

XXXXX ✿ **Laurent, 41 av. Gabriel** ✆ **47 23 79 18** – AE . G 11
closed Saturday lunch, Sunday and Bank Holidays – **M** lunch 320 b.i. and a la carte 380/530
Spec. Salade de homard, Canard aux deux cuissons, Deux soufflés "Laurent".

XXXXX ✿ **Régence, 25 av. Montaigne** ✆ **47 23 78 33**, – AE E VISA. G 9
M a la carte 345/430
Spec. Soufflé de homard, Panaché de la mer, Aiguillettes de canard aux agrumes.

XXXXX ✿✿ **Pavillon Elysée** (Lenôtre), **10 av. Champs-Elysées (1st floor)** ✆ **42 65 35 10** – P. AE VISA G 10
closed August, Saturday, Sunday and Bank Holidays – **M** a la carte 350/430 and see **Les Jardins Lenôtre** (ground floor) below
Spec. Canard rouennais Madeleine Brument, Suprême de poule faisane (season), Saumon sauvage farci de pointes vertes (April-July).

XXXX ✿ **Lamazère, 23 r. Ponthieu** ✆ **43 59 66 66** – . AE E VISA. F 9
closed August and Sunday – **M** a la carte 260/400
Spec. Truffe Lamazère, Supprême Sole au foie gras, Cassoulet aux trois confits.

XXXX ✿✿ **Chiberta, 3 r. Arsène-Houssaye** ✆ **45 63 77 90** – . AE VISA F 8
closed 2 to 25 August, 25 December-1 January, Saturday, Sunday and Bank Holidays – **M** a la carte 260/370
Spec. Tartare de saumon, Etuvée de homard jardinière, Rognonnade de filet d'agneau au pistou.

XXXX ✿✿ **La Marée, 1 r. Daru** ✆ **47 63 52 42** – . AE E 8
closed August, Saturday and Sunday – **M** a la carte 240/360
Spec. Belons au champagne, Petite marmite marseillaise, Râble de lièvre à la caladoise (October-January).

XXXX ✿ **Fouquet's Élysées, 99 av. Champs-Élysées (1st floor)** ✆ **47 23 70 60, Telex 648227** – AE E VISA F 8
M *(closed 15 July-31 August, Saturday and Sunday)* a la carte 205/305
Spec. Fond d'artichaut et foie gras de canard, Aiguillettes de canard au citron vert, Gratin de langouste et langoustines aux pâtes fraîches.

XXX ❀ **La Couronne,** 5 r. Berri ✆ 45 63 14 11 – AE ◑ E VISA F 9
closed Sunday – **st. : M** 210
Spec. Ravioles d'écrevisses à l'estragon, Filet de boeuf au vin rouge et à la moelle, Chariot de desserts.

XXX ❀ **Les Jardins Lenôtre,** 10 av. Champs Élysées (ground-floor) ✆ 42 65 85 10 – P. AE ◑ VISA G 10
M 190
Spec. Petales de saumon galette bressane, Queue de boeuf en pot-au-feu, Charette jardinière de desserts.

XXX ❀ **Copenhague,** 142 av. Champs-Élysées ✆ 43 59 20 41, ☂ – ▤. AE ◑ E VISA. ✱ F 8
(closed 27 July-24 August, 1 to 8 January, Sunday and Bank Holidays) – **M** a la carte 190/280
Spec. Saumon mariné à l'aneth, Canard salé à la danoise, Filets de renne aux navets.

XXX ❀ **Clovis,** 4 r. B.-Albrecht ✆ 45 61 15 32 – AE ◑ E VISA F 8
closed August, 25 December-1 January, Saturday, Sunday and Bank Holidays – **st. : M** a la carte 240/300
Spec. Gelée de poireaux-langoustines et foie gras de canard, Blanc de turbot à la mousseline de crustacés, Emincé de canette de Barbarie rôtie.

XXX **Napoléon Baumann,** 38 av. Friedland ✆ 42 27 99 50 – ▤. AE ◑ E VISA F 8
M 188 ♁.

XXX **Le Marcande,** 52 r. Miromesnil ✆ 42 65 76 85 – AE ◑ VISA F 10
closed 1 to 25 August, Saturday and Sunday – **M** a la carte 260/335.

XXX **Chez Vong,** 27 r. Colisée ✆ 43 59 77 12, Chinese and Vietnamese cuisine – AE ◑ VISA F 10
closed Sunday – **M** 150/250.

XXX **Relais-Plaza,** 21 av. Montaigne ✆ 47 23 46 36 – ▤. AE ◑ E VISA. ✱ G 9
closed August – **M** a la carte 220/320.

XXX **Indra,** 10 r. Cdt-Rivière ✆ 43 59 46 40, Indian cuisine – AE ◑ E VISA F 9
closed Saturday lunch and Sunday – **st. : M** a la carte 150/190.

XXX **Au Vieux Berlin,** 32 av. George-V ✆ 47 20 88 96, German cuisine – ▤. AE ◑ E VISA G 8
closed Saturday and Sunday – **M** a la carte 165/220.

XX **Baumann Marbeuf,** 15 r. Marbeuf ✆ 47 20 11 11 – AE ◑ E VISA G 9
st. : M a la carte 140/200 ♁.

XX **Fermette Marbeuf,** 5 r. Marbeuf ✆ 47 20 63 53, « 1900's decor with genuine ceramics and leaded glass windows » – AE ◑ E VISA G 9
M a la carte 140/200 ♁.

XX **Le Boeuf sur le toit,** 34 r. Colisée ✆ 43 59 83 80 – AE ◑ E VISA
M a la carte 115/180.

XX **Le Petit Montmorency,** 5 r. Rabelais ✆ 42 25 11 19 – ▤. E VISA. ✱ F 10
closed August, Saturday from 1 April-31 July and Sunday – **st. : M** a la carte 220/350.

XX **Ruc,** 2 r. Pépinière ✆ 45 22 66 70 – ▤. AE ◑ E VISA F 11
M (1st floor) a la carte 180/240.

XX **Marius et Janette,** 4 av. George V ✆ 47 23 41 88 – AE VISA F 8
closed Saturday and Sunday – **M** a la carte 230/350.

XX **Le Grenadin,** 46 r. Naples ✆ 45 63 28 92 – AE VISA E 11
closed 8 August-3 September, 24 December-6 January, Saturday, Sunday and Bank Holidays – **M** a la carte 190/260.

XX **Chez Bosc,** 7 r. Richepanse ✆ 42 60 10 27 G 12
closed August, Saturday, Sunday and Bank Holidays – **M** a la carte 150/210.

XX **Chez Modeste,** 8 r. Miromesnil ✆ 42 65 20 39 – ▤. VISA F 10
closed Saturday, Sunday and Bank Holidays – **M** a la carte 170/240.

XX **Artois,** 13 r. Artois ✆ 42 25 01 10 F 9
closed 14 July-1 September, Saturday, Sunday and Bank Holidays – **M** (booking essential) a la carte 120/170.

XX **St Germain,** 74 av. Champs-Elysées ✆ 45 63 55 45 – AE ◑ E VISA G 9
closed Saturday, Sunday and Bank Holidays – **M** 150/240.

XX **La Dariole,** 49 r. Colisée ✆ 42 25 66 76 – AE ◑ VISA F 10
closed Saturday, Sunday and Bank Holidays – **st. : M** a la carte 170/240.

XX **Tong Yen,** 1 bis r. Jean-Mermoz ✆ 42 25 04 23, Chinese and Vietnamese cuisine – ▤. AE ◑ E VISA F 10
closed 1-22 August – **M** a la carte 150/220.

XX **Le Bonaventure,** 35 r. J. Goujon ✆ 42 25 02 58, ☂, ☂ – AE VISA. ✱ G 9
closed Saturday lunch and Sunday – **M** a la carte 140/200.

XX **Androuët,** 41 r. Amsterdam ✆ 48 74 26 93 – AE ◑ VISA E 12
closed Sunday – **M** a la carte 150/200.

XX **Le Sarladais,** 2 r. Vienne ✆ 45 22 23 62 – ▤. E VISA E 11
closed August, Saturday lunch, Sunday and Bank Holidays – **M** a la carte 115/195.

XX **Chez Max,** 19 r. Castellane ✆ 42 65 33 81 – VISA F 11
closed 31 July-3 September, 24 December-3 January, Thursday dinner, Saturday, Sunday and Bank Holidays – **M** a la carte 170/260.

l'Addition, 10 r. La Trémoille 47 23 53 53 – AE VISA G 9
M a la carte 150/200.

Le Manoir Normand, 77 bd Courcelles 42 27 38 97 – AE VISA E 8
M a la carte 130/190.

Rose des Sables, 19 r. Washington 45 63 36 73, Moroccan cuisine F 9
closed Saturday lunch and Sunday – **M** a la carte approx 125.

Annapurna, 32 r. Berri 45 63 91 56, Indian cuisine – AE VISA F 9
closed Saturday lunch and Sunday – **M** a la carte 120/185.

Bistro des Champs, 18 av. F. Roosevelt 45 62 08 37 – AE VISA F 10
M a la carte 150/200.

Olsson's, 62 r. P. Charron 45 61 40 11, Scandinavian cuisine – AE VISA
M a la carte 120/185.

Stresa, 7 r. Chambiges 47 23 51 62, Italian cuisine – AE G 9
closed 10 to 25 August, 20 December-5 January, Saturday dinner and Sunday – **M** a la carte 170/220.

Martin Alma, 44 r. J. Goujon 43 59 28 25, North African cuisine – VISA
closed August, Sunday dinner and Monday – **M** a la carte 95/150.

Le Capricorne, 81 r. Rocher 45 22 64 99 – VISA E 10-11
closed 29 March-6 April, 2 August-3 September, Saturday, Sunday and Bank Holidays – **M** a la carte 85/150.

Al Dente, 182 bd Haussmann 45 62 88 68, Italian cuisine – VISA F 8
closed 10 to 20 August, Sunday and Bank Holidays – **M** a la carte 105/160.

La Petite Auberge, 48 r. Moscou 43 87 91 84 – E VISA D 11
closed Saturday lunch and Sunday – **M** a la carte 130/190.

Opéra, Gare du Nord, Gare de l'Est, Grands Boulevards.

9th et 10th arrondissements.
9th : 75009
10th : 75010

Le Gd Hôtel, 2 r. Scribe (9th) 42 68 12 13, Telex 220875 – 25-500. AE E VISA. rest F 12
st. : Le Patio *(closed August)* **M** 195 b.i. and a la carte Sunday and see **Café de la Paix** below – 70 – **537 rm** 1 500/1 650, 19 apartments.

Scribe M, 1 r. Scribe (9th) 47 42 03 40, Telex 214653 – 150. AE E VISA. rest F 12
st. : M a la carte 175/255 – **le Jardin des Muses M** a la carte approx. 145 – 75 – **206 rm** 990/1 700, 11 apartments.

Ambassador, 16 bd Haussmann (9th) 42 46 92 63, Telex 650912 – 30. AE E VISA. F 13
st. : M *(closed July and 6 to 26 December)* a la carte approx. 180 – **300 rm** 1 200/1 600, 4 apartments.

Commodore, 12 bd Haussmann (9th) 42 46 72 82, Telex 280601 – AE E VISA. rest F 13
st. : M 160/300 – 42 – **150 rm** 785/950, 11 apartments.

Brébant M, 32 bd Poissonnière (9th) 47 70 25 55, Telex 280127 – rest. AE E VISA F 14
st. : M 70/85 – **129 rm** 510/595.

Terminus Nord without rest, 12 bd Denain (10th) 42 82 20 00, Telex 660615 – 40. AE E VISA. E 15-16
st. : 225 rm 390/520.

Astra without rest, 29 r. Caumartin (9th) 42 66 15 15, Telex 210408 – . AE E VISA F 15
st. : 85 rm 500/650.

Blanche Fontaine without rest, 34 r. Fontaine (9th) 45 26 72 32, Telex 660311 – . AE VISA. D 13
st. : 30 – **49 rm** 295/420.

St-Pétersbourg without rest, 33 r. Caumartin (9th) 42 66 60 38, Telex 680001 – . AE VISA F 12
st. : 25 – **120 rm** 495/520.

Paris Est M without rest, cour d'Honneur (10th) ✆ 42 41 00 33, Telex 217916 – TV ☎ – 50-450. E VISA
st. : ☕ 21 – **33 rm** 212/435. E 16

Franklin et du Brésil, 19 r. Buffault (9th) ✆ 42 80 27 27, Telex 640988 – TV ☎. AE ⓓ E VISA. rest
Les Années Folles *(closed 15 July-15 August, Saturday, Sunday and Bank Holidays)* **M** a la carte 135/185 – **64 rm** ☕ 480/599. E 14

Carlton's H. without rest, 55 bd Rochechouart (9th) ✆ 42 81 91 00, Telex 640649 – TV wc ☎. AE ⓓ E VISA.
st. : ☕ 26 – **94 rm** 335/370, 6 apartments 450/500. D 14

Gisendre without rest, 6 r. Fromentin (9th) ✆ 42 80 36 86, Telex 641797 – TV wc wc ☎. AE ⓓ E VISA.
st. : ☕ 21 – **32 rm** 275. D 13

Caumartin M without rest, 27 r. Caumartin (9th) ✆ 47 42 95 95, Telex 680702 – TV wc wc ☎. AE ⓓ E VISA
st. : **40 rm** ☕ 415/590. F 12

Alpha M without rest, 11 r. Geoffroy Marie (9e) ✆ 45 23 14 04, Telex 643939 – TV wc ☎. AE ⓓ E VISA.
28 rm ☕ 650. F 14

Athènes M without rest, 21 r. d'Athènes (9th) ✆ 48 74 00 55, Telex 640715 – TV wc wc ☎. AE ⓓ VISA.
st. : ☕ 27 – **36 rm** 380. E 12

Chamonix M without rest, 8 r. d'Hauteville (10th) ✆ 47 70 19 49, Telex 641177 – wc wc ☎. AE ⓓ E VISA.
st. : ☕ 27 – **35 rm** 460/600. F 15

Printania M without rest, 19 r. Chateau d'Eau (10e) ✆ 42 01 84 20, Telex 215425 – TV wc wc ☎. AE ⓓ E VISA.
st. : ☕ 25 – **51 rm** 400/500. F 16

Moris M without rest, 13 r. R.-Boulanger (10th) ✆ 46 07 92 08, Telex 212024 – TV wc wc ☎. AE ⓓ E VISA.
st. : ☕ 25 – **48 rm** 365/430. G 16

Florida without rest, 7 r. Parme (9th) ✆ 48 74 47 09, Telex 640410 – TV wc wc ☎. AE ⓓ VISA
st. : **31 rm** ☕ 290/450. D 12

Modern' Est without rest, 91 bd Strasbourg (10th) ✆ 46 07 24 72 – wc wc ☎.
st. : ☕ 24 – **30 rm** 240/300. E 16

Capucines without rest, 6 r. Godot-de-Mauroy (9th) ✆ 47 42 06 37 – wc wc ☎
st. : ☕ 18,50 – **46 rm** 183/300. F 12

Morny without rest, 4 r. Liège (9th) ✆ 42 85 47 92, Telex 660822 – TV wc ☎. AE ⓓ E VISA
st. : ☕ 20 – **43 rm** 414/454. E 12

London Palace without rest, 32 bd Italiens (9th) ✆ 48 24 54 64, Telex 642360 – wc wc ☎. AE ⓓ E VISA.
st. : ☕ 23 – **48 rm** 268/400. F 13

Gare du Nord without rest, 33 r. St-Quentin (10th) ✆ 48 78 02 92, Telex 642415 – wc wc ☎. AE E VISA.
st. : ☕ 22 – **49 rm** 185/380. E 16

Hélios without rest, 75 r. Victoire (9th) ✆ 48 74 28 64, Telex 641255 – wc wc ☎. AE ⓓ E VISA
st. : ☕ 25 – **50 rm** 288/418. F 13

Baccarat M without rest, 19 r. Messageries (10e) ✆ 47 70 96 92, Telex 648895 – TV wc wc ☎. AE ⓓ E VISA
st. : ☕ 25 – **31 rm** 250/550. E 15

Résidence Mauroy M without rest, 11 bis r. Godot-de-Mauroy (9th) ✆ 47 42 50 78 – TV wc wc ☎. AE ⓓ E VISA
closed August – **st. :** ☕ 25 – **26 rm** 220/400. F 12

Florence without rest, 26 r. Mathurins (9th) ✆ 47 42 63 47 – wc wc ☎. AE ⓓ
☕ 26 – **20 rm** 260/400. F 12

Royal Medoc without rest, 14 r. Geoffroy Marie (9e) ✆ 47 70 37 33, Telex 660053 – TV wc ☎. AE ⓓ E VISA.
41 rm ☕ 440.

Anjou-Lafayette without rest, 4 r. Riboutté (9th) ✆ 42 46 83 44, Telex 281001 – wc wc ☎. AE ⓓ E VISA
st. : **40 rm** ☕ 400/590. E 14

Montréal without rest, 23 r. Godot-de-Mauroy (9th) ✆ 42 65 99 54 – wc wc ☎. AE ⓓ E VISA
closed August – **st. :** ☕ 25 – **14 rm** 210/390, 5 apartments 490. F 12

Français without rest, 13 r. 8 Mai 1945 (10th) ✆ 46 07 42 02, Telex 230431 – wc wc. VISA E 16
st. : 18 – **71 rm** 200/255.

Peyris without rest, 10 r. Conservatoire (9th) ✆ 47 70 50 83 – wc wc. VISA F 14
st. : **50 rm** 240/300.

Gd H. Haussmann without rest, 6 r. Helder (9th) ✆ 48 24 76 10, Telex 650018 – TV wc wc. AE. F 13
st. : **59 rm** 289/404.

Pax H. without rest, 47 r. Trévise (9th) ✆ 47 70 84 75, Telex 650197 – wc wc. VISA E 14
st. : **52 rm** 255/300.

Gd H. Lafayette Buffault without rest, 6 r. Buffault (9th) ✆ 47 70 70 96, Telex 642180 – wc wc E 14
st. : 19 – **47 rm** 168/281.

Campaville Montmartre without rest, 21 bd Clichy (9th) ✆ 48 74 01 12, Telex 643572 – TV wc wc. VISA D 13
st. : 23 – **84 rm** 226/311.

Victor Massé without rest, 32 bis r. Victor-Massé (9th) ✆ 48 74 37 53 – wc wc. VISA. E 13
st. : 18,50 – **40 rm** 134/230.

Campaville-Montholon without rest, 11 r. P.-Sémard (9th) ✆ 48 78 28 94, Telex 643861 – TV wc wc. VISA E 15
st. : 23 – **45 rm** 226/311.

Ribouttė Lafayette without rest, 5 r. Riboutté (9e) ✆ 47 70 62 36 – wc wc
st. : 16 – **24 rm** 221/269.

Résidence Magenta without rest, 35 r. Y.-Toudic (10th) ✆ 46 07 63 13 – wc. AE F 17
st. : 16,50 – **29 rm** 195/226.

Laffon without rest, 25 r. Buffault (9th) ✆ 48 78 49 91 – wc wc. E VISA E 14
closed 25 July-25 August – **st. :** 17 – **46 rm** 91/249.

Fénelon without rest, 23 r. Buffault (9th) ✆ 48 78 32 18 – wc wc. VISA. E 14
st. : 17,50 – **36 rm** 127/254.

Blanche H. without rest, 69 r. Blanche (9th) ✆ 48 74 16 94 – wc. D 12
st. : 15 – **53 rm** 68/203.

XXXX ✿ **Café de la Paix,** pl. Opéra (9th) ✆ 47 42 97 02 – AE E VISA F 12
st. : Rest. Opéra *(closed August)* **M** a la carte 255/340 - Rest see **Café de la Paix - Relais Capucines** below
Spec. Chartreuse de rouget et homard sauce souveraine, Filet de canette pôelé aux aigres doux, Millefeuille praliné caramélisé.

XXX ✿ **Nicolas,** 12 r. Fidélité (10th) ✆ 42 46 84 74 – AE E VISA F 16
closed Saturday lunch – **M** a la carte 140/205
Spec. Foie gras frais, Canard aux fruits, Tournedos Nicolas.

XX ✿ **Au Chateaubriant,** 23 r. Chabrol (10th) ✆ 48 24 58 94, Collection of paintings – . AE VISA. E 15
closed August, 9 to 18 February, Sunday and Monday – **M** a la carte 115/235
Spec. Scampi fritti, Paglia e fieno alla Contadina, Roulades de sole au romarin.

XX ✿✿ **Chez Michel** (Tounissoux), 10 r. Belzunce (10th) ✆ 48 78 44 14 – . AE VISA E 15
closed 1 to 24 August, 31 January-15 February, Friday and Saturday – **M** (booking essential) a la carte 195/340
Spec. Foie gras de canard (September-June), Foie de veau au miel et citron, Crêpes soufflées.

XX **Café de la Paix-Relais Capucines,** pl. Opéra (9e) ✆ 47 42 97 02 – F 12
M Coffee shop a la carte approx. 140 .

XX **Grand Café Capucines,** 4 bd Capucines ✆ 47 42 75 77, (24 hr service), Early 20C decor – AE VISA F 13
M a la carte 125/220 .

XX **Mövenpick,** 12 bd Madeleine (9th) ✆ 47 42 47 93 – . AE E VISA G 12
M a la carte approx. 110 – **Café des Artistes M** a la carte 140/235.

XX **Atlantique,** 51 bd Magenta (10th) ✆ 42 08 27 20 – . AE E VISA. F 16
closed August, Sunday and Monday – **M** a la carte 180/275.

XX **Le Quercy,** 36 r. Condorcet (9th) ✆ 48 78 30 61 – AE VISA E 14
closed August and Sunday – **st. : M** a la carte 135/210.

XX **Rest. du Casino,** 41 r. Clichy (9th) ✆ 42 80 34 62 – AE E VISA E 12
closed Saturday, Sunday and Bank Holidays – **M** a la carte 170/240.

XX **Chez Casimir,** 6 r. Belzunce (10th) ✆ 48 78 32 53 – AE VISA E 15
closed Saturday lunch and Sunday – **st. : M** a la carte 185/250.

XX **Ty Coz,** 35 r. St-Georges (9th) ✆ 48 78 42 95, seafood only. AE ⓓ VISA — E 13
closed 11 to 17 August, Sunday and Monday – **st. : M** a la carte approx. 180.

XX **Le Saintongeais,** 62 r. Fg Montmartre (9th) ✆ 42 80 39 92 – AE VISA — E 14
closed 9 to 25 August, Saturday lunch and Sunday – **st. : M** a la carte 130/170.

XX **Julien,** 16 r. Fg St-Denis (10th) ✆ 47 70 12 06, Early 20C decor – AE ⓓ VISA — F 15
M a la carte 110/155 ♁.

XX **Petit Riche,** 25 r. Le Peletier (9th) ✆ 47 70 68 68, late 19C decor – AE VISA — F 13
closed 9 to 31 August and Sunday – **st. : M** a la carte 120/175 ♁.

XX **Brasserie Flo,** 7 cour Petites-Écuries (10th) ✆ 47 70 13 59, 1900 Setting – ▤. AE ⓓ VISA — F 15
M a la carte 90/165 ♁.

XX **Cartouche Edouard VII,** 18 r. Caumartin (9e) ✆ 47 42 08 82 – AE VISA — E 12
closed 2 to 17 August, Saturday and Sunday – **M** a la carte 120/180.

XX **Terminus Nord,** 23 r. Dunkerque (10th) ✆ 42 85 05 15 – AE ⓓ VISA — E 16
M a la carte approx. 150 ♁.

XX **Bistrot Papillon,** 6 r. Papillon (9e) ✆ 47 70 90 03 – AE ⓓ VISA — E 15
closed 31 March-6 April, August, Saturday, Sunday and Bank Holidays – **M** a la carte 130/190.

XX **Pagoda,** 50 r. Provence (9th) ✆ 48 74 81 48, Chinese and Vietnamese cuisine – VISA — F 13
closed Sunday in August – **M** a la carte 70/130.

XX **La P'tite Tonkinoise,** 56 Fg Poissonnière (10th) ✆ 42 46 85 98, Vietnamese cuisine – VISA — F 15
closed 1 August-15 September, Sunday and Monday – **M** a la carte 110/140.

X **Relais Beaujolais,** 3 r. Milton (9th) ✆ 48 78 77 91 — E 14
closed August, 24 to 30 March, Saturday, Sunday and Bank Holidays – **M** a la carte 85/160.

X **La Grille,** 80 Fg Poissonnière (10th) ✆ 47 70 89 73 – ⓓ — E 15
closed August, February Holidays, Saturday and Sunday – **st. : M** a la carte 100/140.

Bastille, Gare de Lyon,
Place d'Italie,
Bois de Vincennes.
12th et 13th arrondissements.
12th : ✉ 75012
13th : ✉ 75013

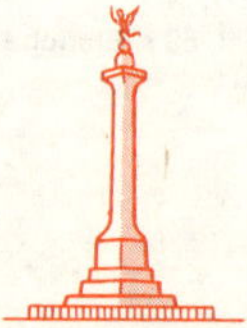

Équinoxe Ⓜ without rest, 40 r. Le Brun (13th) ✆ 43 37 56 56, Telex 201476 – 🛗 TV ☎ 🚗. AE ⓓ E VISA — N 15
49 rm ☕ 380/495.

Paris-Lyon-Palace without rest, 11 r. Lyon (12th) ✆ 43 07 29 49, Telex 213310 – 🛗 TV ☎ – 🎤 150. AE ⓓ E VISA — L 18
☕ 26 – **128 rm** 345/375.

Modern H. Lyon without rest, 3 r. Parrot (12th) ✆ 43 43 41 52, Telex 230369 – 🛗 TV ☎. AE VISA. ✗ — L 18
st. : ☕ 27 – **53 rm** 240/390.

Relais de Lyon Ⓜ without rest, 64 r. Crozatier (12th) ✆ 43 44 22 50, Telex 216690 – 🛗 TV ☎ – 🎤 25. AE ⓓ E VISA — K 19
st. : ☕ 20 – **34 rm** 350.

Terminus-Lyon without rest, 19 bd Diderot (12th) ✆ 43 43 24 03, Telex 230702 – 🛗 TV 🛁wc 🚿wc ☎. AE E VISA. ✗ — L 18
st. : ☕ 21 – **61 rm** 349/389.

Slavia without rest, 51 bd St-Marcel (13th) ✆ 43 37 81 25, Telex 205542 – 🛗 TV 🛁wc 🚿wc ☎. ✗ — M 16
st. : ☕ 17 – **37 rm** 220/270, 6 apartments 325/390.

Gd H. Gobelins without rest, 57 bd St-Marcel (13th) ✆ 43 31 79 89 – 🛗 TV 🛁wc 🚿wc ☎ — M 16
st. : ☕ 17 – **45 rm** 180/280.

Terrasses without rest, 74 r. Glacière (13th) ✆ 47 07 73 70 – 🛗 🛁wc 🚿wc ☎. VISA. ✗ — N 14
st. : ☕ 19 – **52 rm** 130/280.

Corail without rest, 23 r. Lyon (12 th) ✆ 43 43 23 54, Telex 212002 – 🛗 TV 🛁wc 🚿wc ☎. AE VISA — L 18
☕ 19 – **50 rm** 250/340.

Claret, 44 bd Bercy (12e) ✆ 46 28 41 31, Telex 217115 – 🛗 TV 🛁wc 🚿wc ☎ – 🎤 40. AE ⓓ E VISA — M 19
st. : M *(closed Sunday)* a la carte 90/120 ♁ – ☕ 30 – **52 rm** 380/600.

Hotels:

- **Marceau** without rest, 13 r. Jules-César (12th) ℘ 43 43 11 65 – lift, bath wc, shower wc, ☎. — K 17
  st. : breakfast 19 – **51 rm** 101/220.
- **Timhôtel** without rest, 22 r. Barrault (13th) ℘ 45 80 67 67, Telex 205461 – lift, TV, bath wc, shower wc, ☎. AE D E VISA — P 15
  st. : breakfast 25 – **73 rm** 261/305.
- **Viator** without rest, 1 r. Parrot (12th) ℘ 43 43 11 00 – lift, bath wc, shower wc, ☎. — L 18
  st. : breakfast 19 – **45 rm** 155/250.
- **Jules César** without rest, 52 av. Ledru-Rollin (12th) ℘ 43 43 15 88, Telex 670945 – lift, shower wc, ☎. — K 18
  st. : breakfast 19 – **48 rm** 180/220.
- Rubens without rest, 35 r. Banquier (13th) ℘ 43 31 73 30 – lift, bath wc, shower wc, ☎ — N 16
  63 rm.
- **Arts** without rest, 8 r. Coypel (13th) ℘ 47 07 76 32 – lift, shower wc, ☎ — N 16
  st. : breakfast 16 – **41 rm** 85/220.
- **Terminus et Sports** without rest, 96 cours Vincennes (12th) ℘ 43 43 97 93 – lift, TV, bath wc, shower wc, ☎. E VISA. — L 23
  st. : breakfast 18 – **43 rm** 130/260.
- **Résidence des Gobelins** without rest, 9 r. Gobelins (13th) ℘ 47 07 26 90, Telex 206566 – lift, TV, bath wc, shower wc, ☎. AE D VISA — N 15
  st. : breakfast 18,50 – **32 rm** 211/283.
- **Nouvel H.** without rest, 24 av. Bel Air (12th) ℘ 43 43 01 81, Telex 240139, garden – bath wc, shower wc, ☎. AE D VISA — L 21
  st. : breakfast 30 – **28 rm** 148/360.
- **Palym H.** without rest, 4 r. E.-Gilbert (12th) ℘ 43 43 24 48 – lift, shower wc, ☎ — L 18
  st. : breakfast 16 – **51 rm** breakfast 136/275.

Restaurants:

- XXX ✿ **Au Pressoir** (Seguin), 257 av. Daumesnil (12th) ℘ 43 44 38 21 – air-conditioned. VISA — M 22
  closed August, February Holidays, Saturday and Sunday – **st. : M** a la carte 190/340
  Spec. Damier de foie gras en chaud-froid, Bar en peau et rouelles de céleris, Lapin aux huîtres.
- XXX **Train Bleu,** Gare de Lyon (12th) ℘ 43 43 09 06, « Fine murals recalling the journey from Paris to the Mediterranean » – AE D E VISA — L 18
  M (1st floor) a la carte 150/205.
- XX **Au Trou Gascon,** 40 r. Taine (12th) ℘ 43 44 34 26 – air-conditioned. VISA — M 21
  closed 19 July-17 August, 27 December-5 January, Saturday and Sunday – **st. : M** (booking essential) a la carte 190/260.
- XX **Sologne,** 164 av. Daumesnil (12th) ℘ 43 07 68 97 – air-conditioned. VISA — M 21
  closed Sunday and Monday – **st. : M** a la carte 120/220.
- XX **La Gourmandise,** 271 av. Daumesnil (12e) ℘ 43 43 94 41 – AE D VISA — N 22
  closed 25 to 31 March, 15 to 31 August, Saturday lunch and Sunday – **st. : M** a la carte 165/220.
- XX **La Frégate,** 30 av. Ledru-Rollin (12th) ℘ 43 43 90 32 – VISA. — L 18
  closed August, February Holidays, Saturday and Sunday – **M** a la carte 160/200.
- XX **Le Traversière,** 40 r. Traversière (12th) ℘ 43 44 02 10 – AE D E VISA — K 18
  closed August and dinner Sunday and Bank Holidays – **M** a la carte 130/195.
- XX **L'Escapade en Touraine,** 24 r. Traversière (12e) ℘ 43 43 14 96 – E VISA — L 18
  closed August, Saturday, Sunday and Bank Holidays – **M** 100 b.i..
- XX **Potinière du Lac,** 4 pl. E.-Renard (12th) ℘ 43 43 39 98 – D VISA — N 23
  closed 5 to 15 September, 9 December-2 January, Sunday dinner and Monday – **M** a la carte 130/230.
- X **Petit Marguery,** 9 bd. Port-Royal (13th) ℘ 43 31 58 59 – AE D E VISA — M 15
  closed August, 23 December-3 January, Sunday and Monday – **st. : M** a la carte 150/225.
- X **Etchegorry,** 41 r. Croulebarbe (13th) ℘ 43 31 63 05 – AE D E VISA — N 15
  closed Sunday – **M** a la carte 105/165.
- X **Quincy,** 28 av. Ledru-Rollin (12th) ℘ 46 28 46 76 – AE D — L 17
  closed 10 August-15 September, Saturday, Sunday and Monday – **M** a la carte 120/190.
- X **Les Algues,** 66 av. Gobelins (13th) ℘ 43 31 58 22 – AE VISA — N 15
  closed August, 24 December-2 January, Sunday and Monday – **M** a la carte 145/190.
- X **Le Rhône,** 40 bd Arago (13th) ℘ 47 07 33 57, terrace – AE D VISA — N 14
  closed August, Saturday, Sunday and Bank Holidays – **M** (booking essential) a la carte 85/145 ₰.
- X **Relais du Périgord,** 15 r. Tolbiac (13th) ℘ 45 83 07 48, terrace – AE D VISA — P 18
  closed 15 August-15 September, Christmas Day-1 January, Saturday, Sunday and Bank Holidays – **M** (booking essential) a la carte 140/250.
- X **Michèle,** 39 r. Daviel (13th) ℘ 45 80 09 13 – AE VISA — P 14
  closed August and Sunday – **st. : M** a la carte 125/170 ₰.

Vaugirard,
Gare Montparnasse, Grenelle,
Denfert-Rochereau.

14th et 15th arrondissements.
14th : ✉ 75014
15th : ✉ 75015

Hilton M, 18 av. Suffren (15th) ✆ 42 73 92 00, Telex 200955, – 40 - 1200. AE E VISA J 7
st. : Rest : **Le Toit de Paris** ← Paris, *(closed August and Sunday)* **M** (dinner only) a la carte 260/340 - **Western M** 155 - **la Terrasse M** 98 b.i. – 70 – **450 rm** 1 263/2 031, 29 apartments.

Sofitel Paris M, 8 r. L.-Armand (15th) ✆ 45 54 95 00, Telex 200432, indoor pool overlooking Paris – – 30 - 1 200. AE E VISA N 5
st. : Rest. see **Le Relais de Sèvres** below - **La Tonnelle** (Brasserie) **M** a la carte approx. 160 – 57 – **618 rm** 750/1 100, 17 apartments.

Nikko M, 61 quai Grenelle (15th) ✆ 45 75 62 62, Telex 260012, ←, – – 40 - 800. AE E VISA K 6
st. : Rest. see **Les Célébrités** below - **Brasserie Pont Mirabeau M** a la carte approx. 200 **Japanese rest. Benkay M** a la carte 185/295 – 60 – **755 rm** 900/1 500, 9 apartments.

Montparnasse Park H. M, 19 r. Cdt-Mouchotte (14th) ✆ 43 20 15 51, Telex 200135, ←, – – 25 - 1 400. AE E VISA. rest M 11
st. : Montparnasse 25 *(closed August)* **M** a la carte 220/340 - **La Ruche M** 135 – 66 – **1 000 rm** 995/1 500, 33 apartments.

P.L.M. St-Jacques M, 17 bd St-Jacques (14th) ✆ 45 89 89 80, Telex 270740 – – 40 - 1000. AE E VISA N 13-14
st. : Café Français (1st floor) **M** 165/220 - **Le Patio** (3rd floor) **M** a la carte approx. 115 – 44 – **783 rm** 806/900, 14 apartments 1 117/1 300.

Mercure Paris Porte de Versailles M, at Vanves r. Moulin ✉ 92170 Vanves ✆ 46 42 93 22, Telex 202195 – – 350. AE E VISA P 7
M (brasserie) a la carte approx. 120 – 40 – **395 rm** 515/545.

L'Aiglon without rest., 232 bd Raspail (14th) ✆ 43 20 82 42 – . AE VISA. M 12
st. : 24 – **42 rm** 320/380, 8 apartments 480.

Holiday Inn M, porte Versailles (15th) ✆ 45 33 74 63, Telex 260844 – – 130. AE E VISA N 7
st. : M 90/160 – 44 – **90 rm** 600/1 000.

Montcalm M without rest., 50 av. F.-Faure (15th) ✆ 45 54 97 27, Telex 203174, – . AE E VISA M 6
st. : 41 rm 460/520.

Lenox M without rest, 15 r. Delambre (14th) ✆ 43 35 34 50, Telex 260745 – . AE VISA M 12
st. : 25 – **52 rm** 360/520.

Orléans Palace H. without rest, 185 bd Brune (14th) ✆ 45 39 68 50, Telex 260725 – – 35. AE E VISA R 11
st. : 22 – **92 rm** 270/360.

Wallace M without rest, 39 r. Fondary (15e) ✆ 45 78 83 30, Telex 205277 – wc . AE E VISA L 8
st. : 22 – **35 rm** 400/434.

Waldorf M without rest, 17 r. Départ (14th) ✆ 43 20 64 79, Telex 201677 – wc wc . AE VISA. L 11
st. : 25 – **30 rm** 360/480.

Versailles M without rest, 213 r. Croix-Nivert (15e) ✆ 48 28 48 66, Telex 200473 – wc wc . AE VISA N 7
st. : 25 – **41 rm** 380/450.

Messidor M without rest, 330 r. Vaugirard (15th) ✆ 48 28 03 74, Telex 204606, – wc wc . VISA M 8
st. : 74 rm 240/480.

Arès without rest., 7 r. Gén. de Larminat (15th) ✆ 47 34 74 04, Telex 206083 – wc wc . VISA K 8
st. : 20 – **43 rm** 270/325.

Châtillon H. without rest, 11 square Châtillon (14th) ✆ 45 42 31 17 – wc wc . P 11
closed August – **st. :** 16 – **31 rm** 170/200.

France without rest, 46 r. Croix-Nivert (15th) ✆ 47 83 67 02, Telex 206453 – wc wc st. : 21 – **30 rm** 221/310. L 8

Joigny without rest, 8 r. St-Charles (15th) ✆ 45 79 33 35, Telex 204057 – wc wc. AE E VISA. st. : 30 – **39 rm** 270/360. K 7

Tourisme without rest, 66 av. La-Motte-Picquet (15th) ✆ 47 34 28 01 – wc wc. st. : 13,50 – **60 rm** 190/250. K 8

Campaville Paris Tour Eiffel M without rest, 21 r. Sextius Michel (15th) ✆ 45 78 61 33, Telex 203086 – wc wc. VISA st. : 23 – **75 rm** 226/311. K 7

Pasteur M without rest, 33 r. Dr.-Roux (15th) ✆ 47 83 53 17 – wc wc. E VISA – *closed August* – **st.** : 18 – **19 rm** 190/300 M 10

Fondary without rest, 30 r. Fondary (15th) ✆ 45 75 14 75 – wc. st. : 20 – **23 rm** 240/290. L 8

Virgina without rest, 66 r. Père Corentin (14th) ✆ 45 40 70 90 – wc wc. AE. – **st.** : 18 – **54 rm** 95/220 R 12

Pacific H. without rest, 11 r. Fondary (15th) ✆ 45 75 20 49, Telex 201346 – wc wc. E. st. : **66 rm** 118/240. K 7

Atlantique without rest, 54 r. Falguière (15 th) ✆ 43 20 70 70 – wc wc. VISA st. : 20 – **26 rm** 160/320.

Baldi without rest, 42 bd Garibaldi (15th) ✆ 47 83 20 10 – wc wc st. : 18,50 – **28 rm** 220/280. L 9

XXXX ❀ **Les Célébrités,** 61 quai Grenelle (15th) ✆ 45 75 62 62, ← – AE E VISA K 6
st. : **M** 245 (lunch) and a la carte 310/455
Spec. Salade de langoustines rôties, Blanc de turbot au basilic, Fricassée de rognon et ris de veau truffés.

XXX ❀ **Morot Gaudry,** 6 r. Cavalerie (15th) (8th floor) ✆ 45 67 06 85, ←, open-air terrace, – . VISA K 8
closed Saturday and Sunday – **st.** : **M** a la carte 215/310
Spec. Cervelas de langoustines et crevettes, Mousseline d'huîtres au sabayon et Vermouth, Grouse rôtie (1 September-28 February).

XXX ❀ **Olympe,** 8 r. Nicolas Charlet (15th) ✆ 47 34 86 08 – . AE VISA L 10
closed 1 to 24 August, 22 December-4 January and Monday – **st.** : **M** a la carte 300/425
Spec. Ravioli de homard, Fricassée de pintade au beurre rouge, Gibier (season).

XXX **Armes de Bretagne,** 108 av. du Maine (14th) ✆ 43 20 29 50 – . AE E VISA N 11
closed 28 April-5 May, 4 to 24 August, 2 to 6 January, Sunday dinner and Monday except Bank Holidays – **M** a la carte 170/270.

XXX ❀ **Relais de Sèvres,** 8 r. L.-Armand (15th) ✆ 45 54 95 00 – . AE E VISA N 5
closed August, Christmas day, Saturday and Sunday – **st.** : **M** a la carte 210/305
Spec. Ravioles de petits gris, Fois gras chaud aux pommes de terre, Nage de rhubarbe à la vanille (April-October).

XXX ❀ Le Duc (Minchelli), 243 bd Raspail (14th) ✆ 43 22 59 59 M 12

XXX **Moniage Guillaume** with rm, 88 r. Tombe Issoire (14th) ✆ 43 22 96 15 – . AE E VISA P 12
closed Sunday – **M** 148 b.i/210 b.i. – 20 – **5 rm** 200/235.

XXX ❀ **Aquitaine** (Mme Massia), 54 r. Dantzig (15th) ✆ 48 28 67 38, – . AE E VISA N 8
closed Sunday and Monday – **st.** : **M** a la carte 225/295
Spec. Escalope de foie gras au chasselas (1 September-30 November), Panaché de poissons beurre blanc, Confit de Canard.

XX ❀ **Bistro 121,** 121 r. Convention (15th) ✆ 45 57 52 90 – . AE E VISA M 7
closed 13 July-19 August, 22 to 31 December, Sunday dinner and Monday – **M** a la carte 190/275
Spec. Foie de canard chaud au verjus, Filet de canard aux fruits de la passion, Lièvre à la royale (season).

XX **Le Pfister,** 1 r. Dr.-Jacquemaire-Clemenceau (15th) ✆ 48 28 51 38 L 8
closed August, Saturday lunch, Sunday and Bank Holidays – **st.** : **M** a la carte 185/255.

XX **Chez Albert,** 122 av. Maine (14th) ✆ 43 20 21 69 – AE E VISA N 11
closed August, Saturday lunch and Monday – **st.** : **M** a la carte 180/290.

XX ❀ **Gérard et Nicole,** 6 av. J.-Moulin (14th) ✆ 45 42 39 56 – VISA P 12
closed 11 to 17 August, Saturday and Sunday – **st.** : **M** a la carte 215/300
Spec. Ravioli de langoustines, Rougets à l'huile d'olive, Magret de mulard au gros sel.

XX ✿ **Le Dôme,** 108 bd du Montparnasse (14th) ✆ 43 35 25 81 – ▤. AE ⓓ VISA LM 12
closed Monday – **M** a la carte 185/275
Spec. Fricassée de langoustines à l'estragon, Ragoût de sole et foie gras, Coquilles St. Jacques à la Coque (Octobre-May).

XX **Maison Blanche,** 82 bd Lefèbvre (15e) ✆ 48 28 38 83 – AE P 7
closed 1 to 15 September, 24 December-3 January, Saturday lunch, Sunday and Monday – **st. : M** 180/300.

XX **Napoléon et Chaix,** 46 r. Balard (15th) ✆ 45 54 09 00 – ▤. AE E VISA M 5
closed 1 to 25 August, 1 to 7 January and Sunday – **M** a la carte 155/220.

XX **La Chaumière des Gourmets,** 22 pl. Denfert-Rochereau (14th) ✆ 43 21 22 59 – AE ⓓ VISA N 12
closed August, 1 to 7 March, Saturday, Sunday and Bank Holidays – **M** a la carte 180/255.

XX ✿ **Pierre Vedel,** 19 r. Duranton (15th) ✆ 45 58 43 17 – ⚘ M 6
closed 6 July-3 August, Christmas day-1 January, Saturday and Sunday – **st. : M** (booking essential) a la carte 150/210
Spec. Blanquette d'huîtres et St-Jacques au curry (October-March), Bourride de lotte, Tête de veau en pot-au-feu.

XX **Chaumière Paysanne,** 7 r. L.-Robert (14th) ✆ 43 20 76 55 – AE ⓓ E VISA M 12
closed August, Monday lunch and Sunday – **st. : M** a la carte 165/240.

XX **Vallon de Vérone,** 53 r. Didot (14th) ✆ 45 43 18 87 – VISA
closed August, Saturday lunch and Sunday – **st. : M** a la carte 130/210.

XX **Le Clos Morillons,** 50 r. Morillons (15th) ✆ 48 28 04 37 – VISA N 8
closed 20 July-17 August, Saturday lunch and Sunday – **st. : M** a la carte 170/225.

XX **Chez Maître Albert,** 8 r. Abbé Groult (15e) ✆ 48 28 36 98 – AE ⓓ E VISA L 7
closed Saturday – **st. : M** 150 b.i..

XX **Petite Bretonnière,** 2 r. Cadix (15th) ✆ 48 28 34 39 – AE VISA N 7
closed 10 to 28 August, Saturday lunch and Sunday – **st. : M** a la carte 150/215.

XX **La Giberne,** 42 bis av. Suffren (15th) ✆ 47 34 82 18 – AE ⓓ VISA J 8
closed August, Saturday and Sunday – **M** a la carte 125/215.

XX **La Gauloise,** 59 av. La Motte-Picquet (15e) ✆ 47 34 49 78 – AE VISA K 8
closed Saturday and Sunday – **st. : M** a la carte 180/235.

XX **Le Copreaux,** 15 r. Copreaux (15th) ✆ 43 06 83 35 – ▤. AE ⓓ E VISA M 9
closed August, 24 December-3 January, Saturday and Sunday – **M** a la carte 150/205.

XX **La Chaumière,** 54 av. F.-Faure (15th) ✆ 45 54 13 91 – AE ⓓ VISA M 7
closed August, Monday dinner and Tuesday – **M** a la carte 125/185.

XX **Le Caroubier,** 8 av. Maine (15th) ✆ 45 48 14 38, North African cuisine M 11
closed 15 July-31 August and Sunday – **M** a la carte 95/125.

XX **Les Brémailles,** 9 r. G.-Saché (14e) ✆ 45 39 05 55 – AE VISA N 11
closed Saturday lunch and Sunday – **st. : M** a la carte 140/200.

XX **Monsieur Lapin,** 11 r. R.-Losserand (14e) ✆ 43 20 21 39 – VISA N 11
closed August, February Holidays, Saturday lunch and Monday – **st. : M** a la carte 130/200.

X ✿ **La Cagouille,** 89 rue Daguerre (14th) ✆ 43 22 09 01 N 11
closed 27 July-10 September, Sunday and Monday – **st. : M** (booking essential) a la carte 135/200
Spec. Seafood.

X **La Bonne Table,** 42 r. Friant (14th) ✆ 45 39 74 91 – VISA R 11
closed July, 24 December-4 January, Saturday, Sunday and Bank Holidays – **st. : M** a la carte 125/210.

X **Senteurs de Provence,** 295 r. Lecourbe (15th) ✆ 45 57 11 98 – VISA M 6
closed 28 March-7 April, 26 July-25 August, Sunday and Monday – **M** a la carte approx. 170.

X **Bonne Auberge,** 33 r. Volontaires (15th) ✆ 47 34 65 49 – AE ⓓ E VISA M 9
closed August, February Holidays, Saturday and Sunday – **st. : M** a la carte 120/190.

X **Le Clos de la Tour,** 22 r. Falguière (15e) ✆ 43 22 34 73 – AE ⓓ E VISA L 10
closed August, 24 December-2 January, Saturday lunch and Sunday – **M** a la carte 130/190.

X **Chaumière du Petit Poucet,** 10 r. Desnouettes (15th) ✆ 48 28 60 91 – VISA N 7
closed July, Saturday dinner and Sunday – **M** a la carte 80/120 ♂.

X **La Rabolière,** 13 r. Mademoiselle (15th) ✆ 42 50 35 29 L 7
closed August, Sunday and Monday – **M** a la carte 110/170.

X **La Cour,** 12 r. Cepré (15th) ✆ 45 66 66 17 – AE ⓓ VISA L 9
closed 15 July-15 August and Sunday – **M** a la carte 110/160 ♂.

X **Trois Horloges,** 73 r. Brancion (15th) ✆ 48 28 24 08 – AE ⓓ E VISA N 9
st. : M a la carte 100/150.

X **La Datcha Lydie** 7 r. Dupleix (15e) ✆ 45 66 67 77, Russian cuisine – VISA K 8
closed 15 July-30 August and Wednesday – **st. :** a la carte 85/150.

Passy, Auteuil,
Bois de Boulogne,
Chaillot, Porte Maillot.
16th arrondissement.

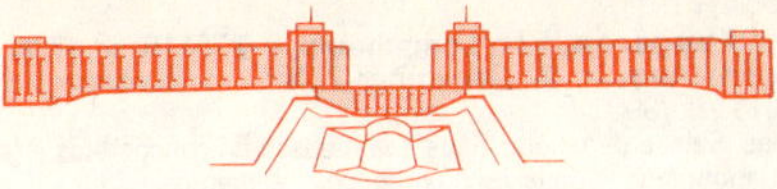

La Pérouse and rest. l'Astrolabe M, 40 r. La Pérouse ✉ 75116 ✆ 45 00 83 47, Telex 613420 – TV ☎. AE ⓓ E VISA F 7
st. : M *(closed Saturday, Sunday and Bank Holidays)* a la carte 240/360 – 50 – **11 rm** 950/1 100, 25 apartments.

Baltimore M, 88 bis av. Kléber, ✉ 75116, ✆ 45 53 83 33, Telex 611591 – TV ☎ – 30-100. AE ⓓ E VISA G 7
L'Estournel *(closed August, Saturday and Bank Holidays)* **M** a la carte 200/300 – **118 rm** 915/1 180.

Résidence du Bois without rest, 16 r. Chalgrin, ✉ 75116, ✆ 45 00 50 59, « Refined decor, garden » – TV ☎ F 7
st. : 16 rm 750/1 090, 3 apartments.

Alexander M without rest, 102 av. Victor-Hugo, ✉ 75116, ✆ 45 53 64 65, Telex 610373 – TV ☎. G 6
st. : 60 rm 470/725.

Union H. Étoile M without rest, 44 r. Hamelin, ✉ 75116, ✆ 45 53 14 95, Telex 611394 – kitchenette TV ☎. AE G 7
st. : 32 – **29 rm** 450/500, 13 apartments 650/800.

Victor Hugo without rest, 19 r. Copernic, ✉ 75116, ✆ 45 53 76 01, Telex 630939 – TV ☎ – 25. AE ⓓ E VISA. G 7
st. : 30 – **75 rm** 400/520.

Rond-Point de Longchamp and rest Belles Feuilles M, 86 r. Longchamp, ✉ 75116, ✆ 45 05 13 63, Telex 620653 – rest TV ☎. AE ⓓ G 6
st. : M *(closed August, Saturday and Sunday)* a la carte 160/260 – 32 – **59 rm** 461/485.

Régina de Passy without rest, 6 r. Tour, ✉ 75116, ✆ 45 24 43 64, Telex 630004 – kitchenette TV ☎. AE ⓓ VISA. H6-J6
st. : 25 – **55 rm** 390.

Majestic without rest, 29 r. Dumont-d'Urville, ✉ 75116, ✆ 45 00 83 70 – TV ☎. AE ⓓ E VISA F 7
st. : 27 rm 650/840, 3 apartments 1 100.

Fremiet without rest, 6 av. Fremiet, ✉ 75016, ✆ 45 24 52 06, Telex 630329 – TV ☎ ♿. AE ⓓ E VISA J 6
st. : 20 – **34 rm** 395/530.

Massenet without rest, 5 bis r. Massenet, ✉ 75116, ✆ 45 24 43 03, Telex 620682 – TV ☎. AE ⓓ E VISA. J 6
st. : 41 rm 240/560.

Elysées Bassano M without rest, 24 r. Bassano ✉ 75116 ✆ 47 20 49 03, Telex 611559 – TV ☎ – **40 rm.** G 8

Floride Etoile M without rest, 14 r. St-Didier ✉ 75116 ✆ 47 27 23 36, Telex 615087 – TV ☎ – 40. AE ⓓ E VISA. G 7
st. : 30 – **60 rm** 440/485.

Residence Foch without rest, 10 r. Marbeau ✉ 75116 ✆ 45 00 46 50, Telex 630886 – TV ☎. AE ⓓ E VISA F 6
st. : 25 – **21 rm** 425/510, 4 apartments.

Kléber without rest, 7 r. Belloy, ✉ 75116, ✆ 47 23 80 22, Telex 612830 – TV ☎. AE ⓓ E – **st. : 21 rm** 459/554 G 7

Sévigné without rest 6 r. Belloy ✉ 75116, ✆ 47 20 88 90, Telex 610219 – TV ☎. AE ⓓ E – **st. : 30 rm** 401/516. G 7

Sylva without rest, 3 r. Pergolèse, ✉ 75116, ✆ 45 00 38 12, Telex 612245 – TV wc ☎. AE ⓓ E VISA E 6
st. : 25 – **37 rm** 390/430.

Ambassade M without rest, 79 r. Lauriston ✉ 75116 ✆ 45 53 41 15, Telex 613643 – TV wc wc ☎. AE ⓓ E VISA. G 7
closed Christmas Holidays – **st. :** 27 – **38 rm** 350/410.

Passy Eiffel M without rest, 10 r. Passy ✉ 75016 ✆ 45 25 55 66, Telex 612753 – wc wc ☎. AE ⓓ E VISA J 6
st. : 23 – **50 rm** 340/390.

Longchamp without rest, 68 r. Longchamp ✉ 75116 ✆ 47 27 13 48, Telex 610342 – TV wc wc ☎. AE ⓓ E VISA G 6
st. : 25 – **23 rm** 450/500.

Queen's H. M without rest, 4 r. Bastien Lepage ✉ 75016 ✆ 42 88 89 85 – TV wc wc ☎. – **st. :** 17 – **22 rm** 180/400. K 4

Eiffel Kennedy without rest, 12 r. Boulainvilliers ✉ 75016 ✆ 45 24 45 75, Telex 614895 – TV wc wc ☎. AE ⓓ VISA. J 5
st. : 23 – **30 rm** 367/397.

XXXX ✻✻ **Faugeron,** 52 r. Longchamp, ✉ 75116, ✆ 47 04 24 53 – ▤. ✻ G 7
closed August, 24 December-2 January, Saturday, Sunday and Bank Holidays – **M** a la carte 280/390
Spec. Salade de langoustines à la mousse de concombres (May-September), Grenouilles et mousse tiède estragonnette, Parfaits "Epoux" chocolat et menthe.

XXXX ✻✻✻ **Jamin** (Robuchon), 32 r. Longchamp, ✉ 75116, ✆ 47 27 12 27 – ▤ G 7
closed July, Saturday and Sunday – **M** (booking essential) a la carte 300/440
Spec. Rouelles de homard à la vapeur, Bar cuit en peau sauce verjutée, Ravioli de ris de veau.

XXXX ✻✻ **Vivarois** (Peyrot), 192 av. V.-Hugo, ✉ 75116, ✆ 45 04 04 31 – ▤. AE ⓓ VISA. ✻ G 5
closed August, Saturday and Sunday – **M** a la carte 230/300
Spec. Canard au miel et citron vert, Poissons, Pâtisseries.

XXX ✻ **Toit de Passy** (Jacquot) (6th floor), 94 av. P.-Doumer ✉ 75016, ✆ 45 24 55 37, ⛱ – ▤ Ⓟ. VISA H J 5
closed 9 to 18 August, 20 December-12 January, Saturday from 23 September-20 December, Sunday and Bank Holidays – **M** 170 (lunch) and a la carte 250/320
Spec. Soupe d'huîtres (1 October-15 April), Pigeon en croûte de sel, Millefeuille aux fruits rouges (15 May-30 September).

XXX **Tsé-Yang,** 25 av. Pierre 1er de Serbie ✉ 75016 ✆ 47 20 68 02, Chinese cuisine – ▤. AE ⓓ E VISA G 8
st. : **M** a la carte 200/265.

XXX **Pavillon des Princes,** 69 av. Porte d'Auteuil ✉ 75016 ✆ 46 05 65 50, ⛱ – AE ⓓ VISA K 1
st. : **M** 212.

XXX ✻ **Ferrero,** 38 r. Vital ✉ 75016 ✆ 45 04 42 42 – AE ⓓ VISA H 5
closed 14 August-3 September, 23 December-6 January, Saturday, Sunday and Bank Holidays – **M** a la carte 245/290
Spec. Pâtes fraîches au foie gras, Champignons (season), Bar en croûte.

XXX **Sully d'Auteuil,** 78 r. d'Auteuil ✉ 75016 ✆ 46 51 71 18, ⛱ – ▤. AE VISA K 3
closed August, Saturday lunch and Sunday – **M** 250 b.i./350 b.i..

XXX **Morens,** 10 av. New-York, ✉ 75116, ✆ 47 23 75 11 – AE ⓓ VISA H 8
closed August, 24 December-2 January, Friday dinner and Saturday – **M** a la carte 150/255.

XXX **Ramponneau,** 21 av. Marceau ✉ 75116 ✆ 47 20 59 51 – AE ⓓ VISA G 8
closed August – **M** a la carte 150/245.

XXX ✻✻ **Le Petit Bedon** (Ignace), 38 r. Pergolèse ✉ 75116 ✆ 45 00 23 66 – ▤. AE ⓓ VISA F 6
closed August, Saturday and Sunday – **M** a la carte 185/290
Spec. Foie gras frais de canard, Filet de sole au coulis de moules, Pigeon au vinaigre de miel.

XXX ✻ **Michel Pasquet,** 59 r. La-Fontaine, ✉ 75016, ✆ 42 88 50 01 – AE ⓓ VISA K 4
closed August, Christmas Day, Saturday except dinner from 1 September to 30 April and Sunday – st. : **M** a la carte 240/315
Spec. Salade tiède de St-Jacques (October-March), Turbot rôti à la crème de ciboulette, Homard grillé au beurre de corail.

XXX ✻✻ **Guy Savoy,** 28 r. Duret ✉ 75116 ✆ 45 00 17 67 – ▤. VISA. ✻ F 6
closed 14 July-5 August, Saturday and Sunday – **M** a la carte 205/355
Spec. Huîtres en nage glacée, Filets de rougets au foie de poularde, Chaussons de pommes de terre et truffes (January-April).

XX **Al Mounia,** 16 r. Magdebourg, ✉ 75116, ✆ 47 27 57 28, Moroccan specialities – AE. ✻ G 7
closed 15 July-31 August and Sunday – **M** a la carte approx. 150.

XX ✻ **Paul Chêne,** 123 r. Lauriston, ✉ 75116, ✆ 47 27 63 17 – ▤. AE ⓓ VISA G 6
closed August, 24 December-3 January, Saturday and Sunday – **M** a la carte 170/270
Spec. Brouillade aux truffes, Filets de sole soufflés aux écrevisses, Daube de boeuf.

XX **Relais d'Auteuil,** 31 bd Murat ✉ 75016 ✆ 46 51 09 54 – AE E VISA L 3
closed Saturday lunch and Sunday – st. : **M** 163/228.

XX ✻ **Conti,** 72 r. Lauriston ✉ 75116 ✆ 47 27 74 67 – ▤. AE VISA. ✻ G 7
closed August, Saturday, Sunday and Bank Holidays – **M** a la carte 170/260
Spec. Ravioli de chou aux grillons de ris de veau (November-February), Lasagne de foie gras, Sabayon au porto.

XX Amazigh, 2 r. La Pérouse ✉ 75116 ✆ 47 20 90 38, Moroccan cuisine.

XX **Palais du Trocadéro,** 7 av. d'Eylau ✉ 75016 ✆ 47 27 05 02, Chinese cuisine – ▤. AE ⓓ VISA H 6
M a la carte approx. 180.

XX **Le Gd Chinois,** 6 av. New York, ✉ 75116, ✆ 47 23 98 21, Chinese and Vietnamese cuisine – AE ⓓ H 8
closed 11 to 26 August and Monday – **M** a la carte 100/160.

XX Le Moï, 7 r. G. Courbet ✉ 75016 ✆ 47 04 95 10 G 6

X **Au Clocher du Village,** 8 bis r. Verderet, ✉ 75016, ✆ 42 55 35 87 – VISA L 4
closed August, Saturday lunch and Sunday – **M** a la carte 115/160.

X **Le Valéry,** 55 r. Lauriston, ✉ 75016, ✆ 45 53 55 48 – VISA F 7
closed August, Saturday and Sunday – st. : **M** a la carte 135/245.

in the Bois de Boulogne :

XXXX ⚙⚙ **Pré Catelan,** ✉ 75016, ☎ 45 24 55 58, 🍽, 🛥 – **P**. AE ◑ VISA H 2
closed February Holidays, Sunday dinner and Monday – **M** a la carte 280/400
Spec. Soufflé d'oursins, Filets d'agneau au thym, Gratin rouge.

XXXX ⚙ **Grande Cascade,** ✉ 75016, ☎ 45 06 33 51, ←, 🍽 – **P**. AE ◑ E VISA
closed 20 December-20 January – **M** *(lunch only from 1 October to 14 April)* 190 (lunch) and a la carte 240/330
Spec. Langoustines rôties (May-September), Aiguillettes de St-Pierre aux écrevisses (October-May), Emincé de rognon aux échalottes confites.

Clichy, Ternes, Wagram.

17th arrondissement.
17th : ✉ *75017*

Méridien M, 81 bd Gouvion-St-Cyr (pte Maillot) ☎ 47 58 12 30, Telex 290952 – 🛗 ▤ TV ☎ 🚗 – 🏛 100-900 E 6
st. : Rest. see **Le Clos de Longchamp** below - **Café l'Arlequin M** a la carte approx. 130 🌡 – **Le Yamato** (Japanese rest) - **La Maison Beaujolaise** – **1 011 rm**, 16 apartments.

Concorde Lafayette M, 3 pl. Gén.-Koenig ☎ 47 58 12 84, Telex 650892, « Bar with ✳ on 34th floor » – 🛗 kitchenette ▤ TV ☎ – 🏛 4 000. AE ◑ E VISA E 6
st. : Rest. see **L'Étoile d'Or** below – **L'Arc-en-Ciel M** 157 🌡 - Coffee Shop **Les Saisons M** a la carte approx. 135 🌡 – ☕ 55 – **965 rm** 1 100/1 450, 25 apartments.

Splendid Etoile M without rest, 1 bis av. Carnot ☎ 47 66 41 41, Telex 280773 – 🛗 TV ☎. AE ◑ E VISA. 🚫 F 7
st. : ☕ 48 – **57 rm** 540/790, 3 apartments 890.

Regent's Garden 🔇 without rest, 6 r. P.-Demours ☎ 45 74 07 30, Telex 640127, « Garden » – 🛗 TV ☎. AE ◑ E VISA E 7
st. : ☕ 25 – **41 rm** 520/690.

Mercure M without rest, 27 av. Ternes ☎ 47 66 49 18, Telex 650679 – 🛗 ▤ TV ☎ **P**. AE ◑ E VISA E 8
st. : ☕ 32 – **56 rm** 435/456.

Balmoral without rest, 6 r. Gén.-Lanrezac ☎ 43 80 30 50, Telex 642435 – 🛗 TV ☎. AE ◑ VISA – **st.** : ☕ 25 – **57 rm** 350/450. E 7

Magellan 🔇 without rest, 17 r. J.B.-Dumas ☎ 45 72 44 51, Telex 660728, 🛥 – 🛗 ☎. AE ◑ E VISA D 7
st. : ☕ 18 – **75 rm** 309.

Pierre M without rest, 25 r. Th.-de-Bainville ☎ 47 63 76 69, Telex 643003 – 🛗 TV 🛁wc ☎ ♿ – 🏛 50. AE ◑ E VISA D 8
st. : ☕ 30 – **50 rm** 500/570.

Courcelles M without rest, 184 r. Courcelles ☎ 47 63 65 30, Telex 642252 – 🛗 TV 🛁wc 🚿wc ☎. AE ◑ E VISA D 8
st. : ☕ 25 – **42 rm** 410/470.

Banville without rest, 166 bd Berthier ☎ 42 67 70 16, Telex 643025 – 🛗 🛁wc 🚿wc ☎. VISA – **st.** : **40 rm** ☕ 360/380 D 8

Belfast without rest, 10 av. Carnot ☎ 43 80 12 10, Telex 642777 – 🛗 TV 🛁wc 🚿wc ☎. AE ◑ VISA. 🚫 E 7
st. : ☕ 30 – **54 rm** 360/530.

Mercédès without rest, 128 av. Wagram ☎ 42 27 77 82, Telex 660751 – 🛗 TV 🛁wc 🚿wc ☎. AE VISA D 9
st. : ☕ 23 – **37 rm** 340.

Régence-Étoile without rest, 24 av. Carnot ☎ 43 80 75 60, Telex 641914 – 🛗 TV 🛁wc 🚿wc ☎. AE VISA. 🚫 E 7
st. : ☕ 28 – **38 rm** 320/430.

Royal Magda without rest, 7 r. Troyon ☎ 47 64 10 19, Telex 641068 – 🛗 TV 🛁wc ☎. AE ◑ VISA E 8
st. : **28 rm** ☕ 406/427, 10 apartments 555/691.

Stella without rest, 20 av. Carnot ☎ 43 80 84 50, Telex 660845 – 🛗 TV 🛁wc 🚿wc ☎. AE ◑ VISA. 🚫 E 7
st. : ☕ 20 – **36 rm** 240/380.

Empire H. without rest, 3 r. Montenotte ☎ 43 80 15 55, Telex 643232 – 🛗 TV 🛁wc 🚿wc ☎. AE ◑ E VISA E 8
st. : ☕ 30 – **47 rm** 265/510.

Trois Couronnes M without rest, 30 r. Arc de Triomphe ☎ 43 80 46 81, Telex 660182 – 🛗 TV 🛁wc 🚿wc ☎. AE ◑ E VISA E 7
closed 24 December-1 January – **st.** : ☕ 20 – **20 rm** 375/385.

Tivoli Étoile without rest, 7 r. Brey ✆ 43 80 31 22, Telex 643107 – |‡| TV ⛀wc ☎. AE ⓓ E VISA. 🚫 E 8
st. : ☕ 22 – **30 rm** 400/460.

Astor without rest, 36 r. P.-Demours ✆ 42 27 44 93, Telex 650078 – |‡| TV ⛀wc ⋔wc ☎. AE VISA. 🚫 D 8
st. : ☕ 21 – **48 rm** 270/360.

Palma without rest, 46 r. Brunel ✆ 45 74 29 93, Telex 660183 – |‡| TV ⛀wc ⋔wc ☎. 🚫
st. : ☕ 18 – **37 rm** 210/240. E 7

Prima H., 167 r. Rome ✆ 46 22 21 09, Telex 642186 – |‡| TV ⛀wc ⋔wc ☎ C 10
st. : M a la carte approx. 130 🍷 – ☕ 20 – **30 rm** 190/250.

Astrid without rest, 27 av. Carnot ✆ 43 80 56 20, Telex 642065 – |‡| ⛀wc ⋔wc ☎. 🚫
st. : 40 rm ☕ 230/350. E 7

Néva without rest, 14 r. Brey ✆ 43 80 28 26, Telex 649041 – |‡| TV ⛀wc ⋔wc ☎. AE VISA. 🚫 E 8
☕ 20 – **35 rm** 290/350.

Bel'Hôtel without rest, 20 r. Pouchet ✆ 46 27 34 77, Telex 642396 – |‡| TV ⛀wc ☎ 🚗. VISA B 11
closed August – **st. :** ☕ 18 – **30 rm** 85/260.

XXXX ✿✿ **Michel Rostang,** 20 r. Rennequin ✆ 47 63 40 77, Telex 649629 – ▤. VISA D 8
closed 25 July-25 August, Saturday (except dinner from October to March), Sunday and Bank Holidays – **M** 200 (lunch) and a la carte 235/350
Spec. Oeufs de caille en coque d'oursins (October-March), Fricassée de soles aux choux verts, Canette de Bresse au sang (May-December).

XXX ✿ **Clos de Longchamp,** 81 bd. Gouvion-St-Cyr (Pte Maillot) ✆ 47 58 12 30 E 6

XXX ✿✿ **Le Bernardin** (Le Coze), 18 r. Troyon ✆ 43 80 40 61, Seafood – VISA E 8
closed August, Sunday and Monday – **M** a la carte 210/355
Spec. Oursins chauds au beurre d'oursins (October-March), Saumon à la menthe fraîche, Ravioli de langoustines.

XXX ✿ **Étoile d'Or,** 3 pl. Gén.-Koenig ✆ 47 58 12 84, Telex 650905 – ▤. AE ⓓ E VISA E 6
st. : M a la carte 240/295
Spec. Tartare de poissons crus au caviar, Sole soufflée au foie de canard, Civet de caneton à la cuillère.

XXX ✿ **Michel Comby,** 116 bd Péreire ✆ 43 80 88 68 – AE ⓓ VISA D 8
closed 12 July-3 August, 23 February-9 March, Saturday and Sunday – **M** a la carte 180/260
Spec. Feuilleté de grenouilles au confit de poireaux, Délice de sole Madeleine, Rognon de veau.

XXX ✿ **Timgad** (Laasri), 21 r. Brunel ✆ 45 74 23 70, « Moorish decor » – ▤. AE ⓓ E VISA. 🚫
M a la carte 135/180 E 7
Spec. Tagine, Couscous, Méchoui.

XXX ✿ **Manoir de Paris,** 6 r. Pierre-Demours ✆ 45 72 25 25 – AE ⓓ VISA E 7
closed 5 July-10 August, Saturday and Sunday – **M** a la carte 210/330
Spec. Ravioli de saumon au caviar, Braisé de pied de porc à la sauge (October-May), Coquille St-Jacques à la mode de Gevrey (season).

XXX ✿ **Sormani,** 4 r. Gén.-Lanrezac ✆ 43 80 13 91 – VISA. 🚫 E 7
closed 28 March-5 April, 2 to 25 August, 24 December-5 January, Saturday, Sunday and Bank Holidays – **M** a la carte 195/275
Spec. Filetto alla Carpaccio, Tagliarini aux coques et jus de truffes, Foie de veau à la vénitienne.

XXX ✿ **Apicius** (Vigato), 122 av. Villiers ✆ 43 80 19 66 – AE VISA D 8
closed August, Saturday and Sunday – **M** a la carte 205/270
Spec. Marbré de ris de veau et homard, Saumon sauvage aux truites frémies, Grand dessert au chocolat amer.

XXX **Chez Laudrin,** 154 bd Péreire ✆ 43 80 87 40 – AE VISA D 7
closed 24 to 31 March, Saturday and Sunday – **st. : M** a la carte 175/265

XXX **Lacanthe,** 123 av. Wagram ✆ 42 27 61 50 – AE E VISA D 8
closed Saturday lunch and Sunday – **st. : M** a la carte 150/215.

XX **Baumann,** 64 av. Ternes ✆ 45 74 16 66 – ▤. AE ⓓ E VISA E 7
st. : M a la carte 120/195 🍷.

XX **L'Écrevisse,** 212 bis bd Péreire ✆ 45 72 17 60 – ▤ Ⓟ. AE ⓓ VISA E 6
closed August, Saturday and Sunday – **M** a la carte 170/240.

XX ✿ **Le Petit Colombier** (Fournier), 42 r. Acacias ✆ 43 80 28 54 – VISA E 7
closed 26 July-18 August, 24 December-3 January, Sunday lunch and Saturday – **M** a la carte 160/230
Spec. Gâteau de brochet au beurre de caviar, Rognon de veau Palais Royal, Pigeonneau fermier à la croque au sel.

XX ✿ **Paul et France,** 27 av. Niel ℘ 47 63 04 24 – AE ⓓ VISA D 8
closed 15 July-15 August, Saturday and Sunday – **M** a la carte 165/240
Spec. Oeufs brouillés aux oursins (October-February), Barbue au beurre de poivron rouge, Ris de veau aux pâtes fraîches.

XX **Epicure 108,** 108 r. Cardinet ℘ 47 63 50 91 – E VISA D 10
closed Sunday, Monday and Bank Holidays – **M** a la carte 150/225.

XX ✿ **La Coquille,** 6 r. Débarcadère ℘ 45 74 25 95 – ▤. VISA E 7
closed August, 24 December-1 January, Sunday, Monday and Bank Holidays – **M** a la carte 160/240
Spec. St-Jacques au naturel (1 October-30 May), Sole aux morilles fraîches, Soufflé au praslin de noisettes.

XX La Truite Vagabonde, 17 r. Batignolles ℘ 43 87 77 80, ☂ D 11

XX ✿ **Chez Guyvonne** (Cros), 14 r. Thann ℘ 42 27 25 43 D 9-10
closed 12 July-4 August, 24 December-6 January, Saturday, Sunday and Bank Holidays – **M** a la carte 170/250
Spec. Salade de truffes, St Jacques et foie gras (December-February), Turbotin au persil, Entremets aux noisettes et amandes.

XX **Lajarrige,** 16 av. Villiers ℘ 47 63 25 61 – AE VISA D 10
closed August, Saturday lunch and Sunday – **M** a la carte 155/235.

XX ✿ **Chez Augusta,** 98 r. Tocqueville ℘ 47 63 39 97 – AE ⓓ E VISA C 9
closed August, Sunday and Bank Holidays – **M** a la carte 175/250
Spec. Salade Augusta, Bouillabaisse, Rougets de roches.

XX **Ma Cuisine,** 18 r. Bayen ℘ 45 72 02 19 – AE ⓓ VISA E 8
closed Saturday lunch and Sunday – **M** 185.

XX **La Braisière,** 54 r. Cardinet ℘ 47 63 40 37 – VISA D 9
closed Easter, August, Saturday lunch from 1 October-30 April and Sunday – **st. : M** a la carte 170/240.

XX **Chez Georges,** 273 bd Pereire ℘ 45 74 31 00 – VISA E 6
closed August – **M** a la carte 135/200.

XX ✿ **La Petite Auberge** (Harbonnier), 38 r. Laugier ℘ 47 63 85 51 – ⓓ VISA D 7-8
closed 3 August-2 September, Sunday, Monday and Bank Holidays – **M** (booking essential) a la carte 170/235
Spec. Turbot Camille Renault, Carré d'agneau Emile Compard, Tarte aux pommes.

XX **La Toque,** 16 r. Tocqueville ℘ 42 27 97 75 – VISA D 10
closed 18 July-15 August, 24 December-4 January, Saturday and Sunday – **st. : M** a la carte 125/180.

XX **Chez Léon,** 32 r. Legendre ℘ 42 27 06 82 – ⓓ VISA D 10
closed 31 July-31 August, February Holidays, Saturday, Sunday and Bank Holidays – **st. : M** a la carte 125/225.

X **Le Beudant,** 97 r. des Dames ℘ 43 87 11 20 – AE ⓓ VISA D 11
closed Saturday lunch and Sunday – **M** a la carte 170/250.

X **La Soupière,** 154 av. Wagram ℘ 42 27 00 73 – ▤. AE VISA D 9
closed 8 to 24 August, Christmas Day-1 January, Saturday and Sunday – **st. : M** a la carte 160/220.

X ✿ **Mère Michel** (Gaillard), 5 r. Rennequin ℘ 47 63 59 80 – VISA E 8
closed August, Saturday, Sunday and Bank Holidays – **st. : M** (booking essential) a la carte 155/215
Spec. Cressonnette de foies de volaille au Xérès, Poissons beurre blanc, Omelette soufflée.

X **Le Pain et le Vin,** 1 r. d'Armaillé ℘ 47 63 88 29 – VISA E 7
st. : M a la carte approx. 120.

Montmartre, La Villette, Belleville.

18th, 19th et 20th arrondissements.

18th : ✉ 75018
19th : ✉ 75019
20th : ✉ 75020

Terrass'H. Ⓜ, 12 r. J.-de-Maistre (18th) ℘ 46 06 72 85, Telex 280830 – |♦| ▤ rest ▣ ☎ ♿ – 🏛 30. AE ⓓ E VISA C 13
st. : Le Guerlande M a la carte 215/300 - **l'Albaron M** a la carte approx. 120 ♨ – **95 rm** ☕ 440/730, 13 apartments 690/800 – P 610/810.

Mercure Paris Montmartre Ⓜ without rest, 1 r. Caulaincourt (18th) ℘ 42 94 17 17, Telex 640605 – |♦| ▣ ☎ ♿. AE ⓓ E VISA D 12
st. : ☕ 39 – **308 rm** 520/550.

Mercure Porte de Pantin Ⓜ, à Pantin, 25 r. Scandicci ✉ 93500 Pantin ℘ 48 46 70 66, Telex 230742 – |♦| ▤ ▣ ☎ 🚗 – 🏛 25-150. AE ⓓ E VISA B 21
st. : M a la carte approx. 150 – ☕ 37 – **129 rm** 445/475, 9 appartments 750.

H. Le Laumière without rest, 4 r. Petit (19th) ✆ 42 06 10 77 – wc wc – st. : 16,50 – **54 rm** 92/231. D 19

Super H., 208 r. Pyrénées (20th) ✆ 46 36 97 48 – rest wc wc. VISA – *closed August* – **st. : M** *(closed Sunday)* 71/150 – **28 rm** 145/370. G 21

Regyn's Montmartre without rest, 18 pl. Abbesses (18th) ✆ 42 54 45 21 – TV wc wc. AE VISA – **st. :** 18 – **22 rm** 280/350. D 13

Pyrénées Gambetta without rest, 12 av. Père Lachaise (20th) ✆ 47 97 76 57 – wc wc – **st. : 30 rm** 125/290. H 21

Prima-Lepic without rest, 29 r. Lepic (18th) ✆ 46 06 44 64 – wc wc. AE. – **st. :** 19 – **38 rm** 145/220. D 13

Capucines Montmartre without rest, 5 r. A.-Bruant (18th) ✆ 42 52 89 80 – TV wc wc. AE – 17 – **30 rm** 198/300. D 13

Eden H. without rest, 90 r. Ordener (18th) ✆ 42 64 61 63 – TV wc wc. AE. – **st. :** 19 – **35 rm** 160/240. B 14

Luxia without rest, 8 r. Seveste (18th) ✆ 46 06 84 24 – wc wc. AE – **st. :** 17 – **48 rm** 170/270. D 14

XXX ✿ **Beauvilliers** (Carlier), 52 r. Lamarck (18th) ✆ 42 54 54 42, « **1900's decor, terrace** » – VISA. – *closed 1 to 16 September, Monday lunch and Sunday* – **M** a la carte 230/305 C 14
Spec. Râgout de St Jacques au curry (15 October-25 April), Boudin de faisan (1 October-15 March), Aiguillettes de canard.

XXX ✿ **Cochon d'Or,** 192 av. Jean-Jaurès (19th) ✆ 46 07 23 13 – AE E VISA – **M** a la carte 175/245 C 20
Spec. Grillades, Filets de barbue au Chablis et blancs de poireaux, Tête de veau ravigote.

XXX **Charlot 1er "Merveilles des Mers",** 128 bis bd Clichy (18th) ✆ 45 22 47 08 – AE E VISA – *closed 20 July-20 August* – **M** a la carte 195/260. D 12

XXX Dagorno, 190 av. J.-Jaurès (19th) ✆ 46 07 02 29 C 20

XXX ✿ **Relais Pyrénées** (Marty), 1 r. Jourdain (20th) ✆ 46 36 65 81 – AE E VISA – *closed August and Saturday* – **M** a la carte 170/225 F 20
Spec. Foie gras frais de canard, Saumon frais au Champagne, Confit d'oie.

XX **Petit Pré,** 1 r. Bellevue (19th) ✆ 42 08 92 62 – *closed August, Saturday, Sunday and Bank Holidays* – **st. : M** a la carte 210/260. E 21

XX **Le Clodenis,** 57 r. Caulaincourt (18th) ✆ 46 06 20 26 – AE VISA. – *closed Sunday* – **M** a la carte 210/275. C 13

XX **Chez le Baron,** 65 r. Manin (19th) ✆ 42 05 72 72 – AE VISA – *closed 10 to 20 August, Saturday lunch and Sunday* – **M** a la carte 175/250. D 19

XX **Sanglier Bleu,** 102 bd Clichy (18th) ✆ 46 06 07 61 – . AE E VISA – *closed 15 July-15 August and Saturday lunch* – **M** a la carte 130/220. D 12

XX **Deux Taureaux,** 206 av. J.-Jaurès (19th) ✆ 46 07 39 31 – AE VISA – *closed 25 to 31 December, Saturday and Sunday* – **st. : M** a la carte 150/200. C 21

XX **Boeuf Couronné,** 188 av. J.-Jaurès (19th) ✆ 46 07 89 52 – AE E VISA – *closed Sunday* – **M** a la carte 140/200. C 20

XX **Au Clair de la Lune,** 9 r. Poulbot (18th) ✆ 42 58 97 03 – AE VISA – *closed February Holidays, Monday lunch and Sunday* – **M** a la carte 165/250. D 14

XX **Grandgousier,** 17 av. Rachel (18th) ✆ 43 87 66 12 – AE E VISA – *closed 10 to 18 August, Saturday lunch and Sunday* – **M** a la carte 150/200. D 12

XX **La Chaumière,** 46 av. Secrétan (19th) ✆ 46 07 98 62 – AE E VISA – *closed August and Sunday* – **st. : M** a la carte 125/205. E 18

XX **Chez Frézet,** 181 r. Ordener (18th) ✆ 46 06 64 20 – AE VISA – *closed August, Saturday and Sunday* – **M** a la carte 115/205 . B 13

X **Le Pichet,** 174 r. Ordener (18th) ✆ 46 27 85 28 – VISA – *closed August and Sunday* – **M** a la carte 95/140 . B 13

X **Relais Normand,** 32 bis r. d'Orsel (18th) ✆ 46 06 92 57 – AE E VISA – *closed 5 to 27 August, February Holidays, Friday dinner and Saturday* – **st. : M** 58/102. D 14

X **Marie-Louise,** 52 r. Championnet (18th) ✆ 46 06 86 55 – VISA – *closed 31 July-1 September, Sunday, Monday and Bank Holidays* – **M** a la carte 90/140. B 15

X **Le Sancerre,** 13 av. Corentin Cariou (19th) ✆ 46 07 80 44 – *closed August, Saturday and Sunday* – **M** a la carte 110/155. B 19 B

Environrons

Bagnolet 93170 Seine-St-Denis 101 ⑯ – pop. 32 557 – alt. 86.

Paris 6 – Bobigny 10 – Lagny 27 – Meaux 40.

Novotel Paris Bagnolet M, av. République, Porte de Bagnolet interchange ✆ 43 60 02 10, Telex 670216, – – 25 - 800. AE E VISA
Le Clos Gourmand M a la carte approx. 160 - **Snack M** a la carte approx. 100 – 39 – **611 rm** 477/510.

Bougival 78380 Yvelines 101 ⑬ – pop. 8 487 – alt. 40.

Paris 18 – Rueil-Malmaison 3,5 – St-Germain-en-Laye 7 – Versailles 7 – Le Vésinet 4.

XXXX ❀ **Coq Hardy,** 16 quai Rennequin-Sualem (N 13) ✆ 36 69 01 43, « Terraced flower gardens, elegant setting » – . AE VISA
closed Wednesday – **M** (Sunday booking essential) 300/400
Spec. Foie gras de canard, Poulet de Bresse à l'estragon, Paupiette de sole et saumon au coulis d'écrevisses.

XXXX **Château de la Jonchère** M with rm, 10 côte la Jonchère ✆ 39 18 57 03, Telex 699491, , parc, – wc – 30. AE E VISA
st. : M 150/300 – 40 – **8 rm** 700/800.

XXX ❀ **Le Camelia** (Delaveyne), 7 quai G.-Clemenceau ✆ 39 69 03 02 – AE VISA.
closed Sunday dinner and Monday – **M** a la carte 255/330
Spec. Champignons, Beignets d'huîtres sauce citron miel, Boeuf braisé à la mode de chez Fournaise.

XX **L'Huître et la Tarte,** 6 quai Clemenceau ✆ 39 18 45 55 – VISA
closed August, Sunday and Monday – **st. : M** a la carte 100/130.

XX **Cheval Noir,** 14 quai G.-Clemenceau ✆ 39 69 00 96, – VISA
closed August, Wednesday dinner and Thursday – **M** a la carte 100/160.

Boulogne-Billancourt 92100 Hauts-de-Seine 101 ㉔ – pop. 102 595 – alt. 35.

See : Bois de Boulogne★★ : Municipal Floral Garden★ (Fleuriste municipal) – Albert Kahn Gardens★ – Paul Landowski Museum★.

Paris (by Porte de St-Cloud) 10 – Nanterre 7 – Versailles 11.

Sélect H. M without rest, 66 av. Gén.-Leclerc ✆ 46 04 70 47, Telex 206029 – wc wc . VISA
st. : 18,50 – **64 rm** 236/270.

Excelsior without rest, 12 r. Ferme ✆ 46 21 08 08, Telex 203114 – wc . AE
st. : 16 – **52 rm** 184/302.

XXXX ❀ **Au Comte de Gascogne,** 89 av. J.-B.-Clément ✆ 46 03 47 27, « Winter garden » – . AE VISA
closed August, Saturday, Sunday and Banks Holidays – **M** a la carte 230/290
Spec. Foie frais de canard, Panaché de poissons, Râble de lapereau.

XX **L'Avant Seine,** 1 rond point Rhin et Danube ✆ 48 25 58 00 – . VISA
M 85/150.

XX ❀ **La Bretonnière,** 120 av. J.-B.-Clément ✆ 46 05 73 56 – AE VISA
closed Saturday and Sunday – **M** a la carte 190/270
Spec. Filets de rougets de roche aux oursins, Fricassée de rascasse aux nouillettes et safran, Ris de veau à l'ancienne au jus de truffes.

XX **La Bergerie,** 87 av. J.-B.-Clément ✆ 46 05 39 07 – AE VISA
closed 9 to 25 August, Monday dinner and Sunday – **M** a la carte 180/230.

XX **La Petite Auberge Franc Comtoise,** 86 av. J.-B.-Clément ✆ 46 05 67 19 – AE E VISA
closed 4 August-1 September, Sunday and Bank Holidays – **M** a la carte 145/215.

XX **Laux... à la Bouche,** 117 av. J.-B.-Clément ✆ 48 25 43 88 – VISA
closed Saturday and Sunday in July and August – **M** a la carte 110/180.

X **La Galère,** 112 r. Gén.-Gallieni ✆ 46 05 64 51 – VISA.
closed August, Saturday and Sunday – **M** a la carte 100/145.

Le Bourget 93350 Seine-St-Denis 101 ⑰ – pop. 11 021 – alt. 66.

See : Aviation Museum★.

Paris 15 – Bobigny 5 – Chantilly 34 – Meaux 38 – St-Denis 6,5 – Senlis 36.

Novotel M, at Blanc-Mesnil ZA pont Yblon ✉ 93150 Le Blanc-Mesnil ✆ 48 67 48 88, Telex 230115, , – – 25-250. AE E VISA
M a la carte approx. 115 – 34 – **143 rm** 320/341.

Châteaufort **78117** Yvelines 101 ㉒ – pop. 780 – alt. 153.

Paris 27 – Arpajon 28 – Rambouillet 25 – Versailles 10.

XXX ✿ **La Belle Epoque** (Peignaud), 10 pl. Mairie ☎ 39 56 21 66, ⛱, « Country inn overlooking a small valley » – AE ⓓ E VISA
closed 12 August-11 September, 22 December-6 January and Sunday dinner – **M** a la carte 200/300
Spec. Potiche de grenouilles au gingembre, Lichettes de foie de canard aux salicornes, Compotée de perdrix aux choux (1 October-late December).

Clichy **92110** Hauts-de-Seine 101 ⑮ – pop. 47 000 – alt. 30.

Paris 6,5 – Argenteuil 7 – Nanterre 10 – Pontoise 27 – St-Germain-en-Laye 17.

XXX ✿ **Barrière de Clichy,** 1 r. de Paris ☎ 47 37 05 18 – ▤. AE ⓓ VISA
closed Saturday lunch and Sunday – **M** a la carte 200/280
Spec. Huîtres chaudes (September-April), Encornets farcis, Pigeonneau rôti aux choux.

Courbevoie **92400** Hauts-de-Seine 101 ⑭ – pop. 59 931 – alt. 34.

See : La Défense★★ : Exhibition (National Centre for Industry and Technology), Manhattan Tower★★★, Fiat Tower★, GAN Tower★, – Perspective★ from the parvis.

Paris (by Porte Champerret) 11 – Asnières 3 – Levallois-Perret 3,5 – Nanterre 4 – St-Germain-en-Laye 14.

the Défense quarter

Novotel Paris La Défense Ⓜ, 2 bd Neuilly ☎ 47 78 16 68, Telex 630288, ← – ▤ ▤ TV ☎ ♿ 🚗 – 25-150. AE ⓓ E VISA
M a la carte approx. 100 ⚲ – ☕ 42 – **276 rm** 545/575.

the Charras quarter

Penta, 18 r. Baudin ☎ 47 88 50 51, Telex 610470 – ▤ ▤ rest TV wc ☎ 🚗 – 25 - 300. AE ⓓ E VISA. ✻ rest
st. : l'Atelier M a la carte 110/160 ⚲ – ☕ 8,50 – **494 rm** 450/480.

Créteil P **94000** Val-de-Marne 101 ㉗ – pop. 71 705 – alt. 49.

See : Town Hall★ : parvis★.

ℹ 1 r. F.-Mauriac ☎ 48 98 58 18.

Paris 12 – Bobigny 19 – Évry 22 – Lagny 26 – Melun 36.

Novotel Ⓜ, ☎ 42 07 91 02, Telex 670396, ⛱, ⛱ – ▤ ▤ TV ☎ P – 25 - 200. AE ⓓ E VISA
M a la carte approx. 115 ⚲ – ☕ 34 – **110 rm** 325/346.

Écouen **95440** Val d'Oise 101 ⑥ – pop. 4 386 – alt. 150.

See : Château★★ : Renaissance Museum★★ (tapestry of David and Bathsheba★★★).

Enghien-les-Bains **95880** Val d'Oise 101 ⑤ – pop. 9 739 – alt. 50 – Spa – Casino.

See : Lake★ – 18 of Domont ☎ 39 91 07 50, N : 8 km.

ℹ 2 bd Cotte ☎ 34 12 41 15.

Paris 18 – Argenteuil 6 – Chantilly 32 – Pontoise 20 – St-Denis 6 – St-Germain-en-Laye 23.

Grand Hôtel, 85 r. Gén.-de-Gaulle ☎ 34 12 80 00, Telex 697842, ←, ⛱, « Attractive flower garden » – ▤ TV ☎ P – 35. AE ⓓ VISA. ✻ rest
closed 2 to 31 January – **st. : M** 125/200 – ☕ 38 – **48 rm** 345/505, 3 apartments 715 – P 631/731.

Villa Marie Louise without rest, 49 r. Malleville ☎ 39 64 82 21, ⛱ – ▤ wc wc ☎
st. : ☕ 16 – **22 rm** 140/210.

XXXX ✿✿ **Duc d'Enghien,** at the Casino ☎ 34 12 90 00, ← lake – ▤. AE ⓓ VISA. ✻
closed 2 to 30 January, Sunday dinner and Monday – **M** a la carte 205/315
Spec. Raviole de langouste aux truffes (November-April), Blanc de turbot aux langoustines, Pigeon et foie gras en paupiette de chou.

XX **Aub. Landaise,** 32 bd d'Ormesson ☎ 34 12 78 36 – AE VISA
closed August, February Holidays, Sunday dinner and Wednesday – **st. : M** a la carte 110/155.

XX **A la Carpe d'Or,** 91 r. Gén.-de-Gaulle ☎ 34 12 79 53, ← – AE ⓓ VISA
M a la carte 130/210 ⚲.

Gennevilliers **92230** Hauts-de-Seine 101 ⑮ – pop. 45 445 – alt. 29.

ℹ 177 av. Gabriel Péri (closed morning) ☎ 47 99 33 92.

Paris 11 – Nanterre 12 – Pontoise 23 – St-Denis 4 – St-Germain-en-Laye 20.

XX ✿ **Julius,** 6 bd Camélinat ☎ 47 98 79 37 – ▤. VISA
closed Saturday lunch and Sunday – **M** a la carte 180/235
Spec. Poissons, Marmitte de ris d'agneau, Mousseline de fromage blanc.

Grigny 91350 Essonne 101 ㉛ – pop. 26 181.

Paris 26 – Evry 7 – Versailles 32.

XXX **Château du Clotay** with rm, 8 r. du Port ✆ 69 06 89 70, park, – wc ☎ **P**. AE ⓓ E VISA
closed February Holidays, Sunday dinner and Monday – **M** 140/380 – 35 – **10 rm** 350/450.

Livry-Gargan 93190 Seine-St-Denis 101 ⑱ – pop. 32 806 – alt. 63.

pl. H. de Ville (closed morning) ✆ 43 30 61 60.

Paris 19 – Aubervilliers 13 – Aulnay-sous-Bois 5,5 – Bobigny 7,5 – Meaux 28 – Senlis 42.

XXX **Aub. St-Quentinoise,** 23 av. République ✆ 43 81 13 08, – AE VISA
closed Sunday dinner and Monday – **st.** : **M** (booking essential for dinner) 125 (lunch) and a la carte 190/245.

Longjumeau 91160 Essonne 101 ㉟ – pop. 18 395 – alt. 72.

Paris 21 – Chartres 70 – Dreux 82 – Évry 16 – Melun 39 – Orléans 96 – Versailles 21.

Relais des Chartreux M, at Saulxier SW : 2 km ✉ 91160 Longjumeau ✆ 69 09 34 31, Telex 691245, <, , , , – ☎ **P** – 150 – **100 rm**.

Relais St-Georges M , at Saulx-les-Chartreux SW : 3 km ✉ 91160 Longjumeau ✆ 64 48 36 40, Telex 603038, <, park – ☎ **P** – 80. AE ⓓ E VISA
closed August – **st.** : **M** 120/220 – 20 – **40 rm** 220/300 – P 340/410.

Maisons-Laffitte 78600 Yvelines 101 ⑬ – pop. 22 892 – alt. 40.

See : Château★.

Paris 21 – Argenteuil 8,5 – Mantes-la-Jolie 37 – Poissy 8 – Pontoise 18 – St-Germain 8 – Versailles 24.

XXX ✿✿ **Le Tastevin** (Blanchet), 9 av. Eglé ✆ 39 62 11 67, , – **P**. AE ⓓ VISA
closed 16 August-12 September, February Holidays, Monday dinner and Tuesday – **st.** : **M** a la carte 200/270
Spec. Ragoût de pieds de porc aux huîtres (September-March), Escalope de foie gras chaud, Sanciaux aux pommes (season).

XXX ✿✿ **Vieille Fontaine** (Clerc), 8 av. Gretry ✆ 39 62 01 78, « Garden » – AE ⓓ VISA
closed August, Sunday and Monday – **M** a la carte 250/335
Spec. Aumônières de caviar, Rognonnade de St Jacques (October-March), Rognon de veau au Chiroubles.

XX **Le Laffitte,** 5 av. St-Germain ✆ 39 62 01 53 – AE VISA
closed August, Tuesday dinner and Wednesday – **st.** : **M** 160 b.i./250 b.i..

Marne-la-Vallée 77206 S.-et-M. 101 ⑲

Paris 26 – Meaux 28 – Melun 35.

S.E : 6 km by Lagny traffic interchange A 4 :

Novotel M, ✆ 60 05 91 15, Telex 691990, , – ☎ **P** – 150. AE ⓓ E VISA – **M** a la carte approx. 100 – 31 – **92 rm** 330/346.

Meudon 92190 Hauts-de-Seine 101 ㉔ – pop. 49 004 – alt. 100.

See : Terrace★ : ★ – Meudon Forest★.

Paris 12 – Boulogne-Billancourt 3 – Clamart 3,5 – Nanterre 11 – Versailles 10.

XXX ✿ **Relais des Gardes,** at Bellevue, 42 av. Gallieni ✆ 45 34 11 79 – AE ⓓ VISA
closed August, Sunday dinner and Saturday – **st.** : **M** a la carte 180/240
Spec. Civet de sole, Pot-au-feu de canard (except in summer), Baba au rhum.

Montrouge 92120 Hauts-de-Seine 101 ㉕ – pop. 38 632 – alt. 74.

Paris (by Porte d'Orléans) 6 – Boulogne-Billancourt 6,5 – Longjumeau 14 – Nanterre 15 – Versailles 16.

Mercure M, 13 r. F.-Ory ✆ 46 57 11 26, Telex 202528 – rest ☎ **P**. AE ⓓ E VISA – **st.** : **M** a la carte approx. 130 – 42 – **186 rm** 495/525.

Neuilly-sur-Seine 92200 Hauts-de-Seine 101 ⑮ – pop. 64 450 – alt. 36.

See : Bois de Boulogne★★ : Jardin d'acclimatation★, (Children's Amusement Park, Miniature Railway and Zoo in the Bois de Boulogne), Bagatelle★ (Park and Garden) National Museum of Popular Art and Traditions★★ – Palais des Congrès★ : main conference hall★★, <★ from hotel Concorde-Lafayette.

Paris (by Porte Neuilly) 8 – Argenteuil 12 – Nanterre 5,5 – Pontoise 37 – St-Germain 14 – Versailles 18.

H.Club Méditerranée M, 58 bd. V.-Hugo ✆ 47 58 11 00, Telex 610971, , Club atmosphere, – rm ☎ – 150 – **335 rm**.

Parc Neuilly without rest, 4 bd Parc ✆ 46 24 32 62, Telex 613689 – wc wc ☎ **st.** : 17 – **71 rm** 196/250.

Roule without rest, 37 bis av. du Roule ✆ 46 24 60 09 – wc wc ☎ **st.** : 18 – **35 rm** 160/290.

XXX ✿ **Jacqueline Fénix,** 42 av. Ch.-de-Gaulle ✆ 46 24 42 61 – ▤. VISA
closed August, Saturday and Sunday – **st. : M** a la carte 210/335
Spec. Millefeuille lapereau, Filet d'agneau et rognon de veau au beurre de persil, Meringué aux noix.

XXX **Le Manoir,** r. Église ✆ 46 24 04 61 – ▤. AE VISA
closed Sunday dinner and Saturday – **st. : M** a la carte 200/280.

XX **Jarrasse,** 4 av. Madrid ✆ 46 24 07 56 – AE ⓓ VISA
closed 7 July-1 September, Sunday dinner and Monday – **M** a la carte 170/290.

XX **Tonnelle Saintongeaise,** 32 bd Vital Bouhot ✆ 46 24 43 15, 🏖
closed Easter Holidays, 8-30 August, 22 December-6 January, Saturday and Sunday – **M** a la carte 110/150.

XX **Bourrier,** 1 pl. Parmentier ✆ 46 24 11 19 – VISA
closed 1 to 20 August, 20 December-5 January, Saturday (except dinners from 1 October-Easter) and Sunday – **st. : M** 200/250.

XX **Chau'veau,** 59 r. Chauveau ✆ 46 24 46 22 – ⓓ VISA
closed August, Saturday and Sunday – **M** a la carte 90/170.

XX **Truffe Noire,** 2 pl. Parmentier ✆ 46 24 94 14 – AE E VISA
closed August, February Holidays, Friday dinner and Saturday – **M** a la carte 140/205.

XX **Focly,** 10 r. P.-Chatrousse ✆ 46 24 43 36, Chinese cuisine – AE VISA
closed 14 to 28 July – **M** a la carte 80/135.

XX **Carpe Diem,** 10 r. Église ✆ 46 24 95 01 – ⓓ VISA
closed August, Saturday lunch and Sunday – **st. : M** a la carte 175/235.

X **Chez Livio,** 6 r. longchamp ✆ 46 24 81 32, Italian cuisine
closed 1 to 29 August and 24 December-2 January – **M** 46 b.i./120 🍷 b.i..

Nogent-sur-Marne

<SP> 94130 Val-de-Marne 101 ㉗ – pop. 24 696 – alt. 56.

ℹ 5 av. Joinville (closed morning) ✆ 48 73 75 90.

Paris 14 – Créteil 6,5 – Montreuil 5 – Vincennes 4.

🏨 **Nogentel** Ⓜ, 8 r. Port ✆ 48 72 70 00, Telex 210116, ← – 🛗 TV ☎ – 🏛 250. AE ⓓ E VISA
rest. **Le Panoramic** *(closed August)* **M** a la carte 180/240 - Grill **Le Canotier M** a la carte approx. 100 🍷 – ☕ 32 – **61 rm** 330/360.

Orly (Paris Airport)

94396 Val-de-Marne 101 ㉖ – pop. 23 886 – alt. 89.

✈ Information : ✆ 48 84 32 10.

Paris 16 – Corbeil-Essonnes 17 – Longjumeau 9 – Villeneuve-St-Georges 12.

🏨 **Hilton Orly** Ⓜ, near air terminal ✆ 46 87 33 88, Telex 250621, ← – 🛗 ▤ TV ☎ ♿ Ⓟ – 🏛 300. AE ⓓ E VISA. ✗ rest
st. : Le Café du Marché M a la carte approx. 150 🍷 - **La Louisiane** *(closed August, Saturday and Sunday)* **M** a la carte 160/210 – ☕ 35 – **380 rm** 470/900.

Orly Airport South :

XX **Le Grillardin,** ✆ 46 87 24 25, ← – ▤. AE ⓓ E VISA
st. : M (lunch only) 135.

Orly Airport West :

XXX **Maxim's,** ✆ 46 87 16 16, ← – ▤. AE ⓓ VISA
st. : M 190 and a la carte.

XX **Jardin d'Orly,** ✆ 46 87 16 16, ← – ▤. AE VISA
closed August, Saturday and Sunday – **st. : M** a la carte 135/175.

X **La Galerie,** ✆ 46 87 16 16, ← – ▤. VISA
st. : M a la carte approx. 130 🍷.

Pontoise

<SP> 95300 Val-d'Oise 196 ⑤⑥ – pop. 29 411 – alt. 27.

ℹ 6 pl. Petit Martroy ✆ 30 38 24 25.

Paris 34 – Beauvais 55 – Dieppe 135 – Mantes-la-Jolie 39 – Rouen 91.

at Cormeilles-en-Vexin NW by D 915 – ✉ **95830** Cormeilles-en-Vexin :

XXX ✿✿ **Relais Ste-Jeanne** (Cagna), on D 915 ✆ 34 66 61 56, 🏖, « Garden » – Ⓟ. AE ⓓ VISA
closed August, Christmas Day, February Holidays, Tuesday dinner (except April-July), Sunday dinner and Monday – **st. : M** (booking essential) 200/300 and a la carte
Spec. Ris de veau au coulis de truffes, Gourmandise de Delphine, Huîtres chaudes au Champagne (September-June).

Le Pré St-Gervais

93310 Seine-St-Denis 101 ⑯ – pop. 13 313 – alt. 71.

Paris (by Porte de Pantin) 7 – Bobigny 5 – Lagny 27 – Meaux 38 – Senlis 44.

X ✿ **Au Pouilly Reuilly** (Thibault), 68 r. A.-Joineau ✆ 48 45 14 59 – AE ⓓ VISA
closed 1 August-5 September, Sunday and Bank Holidays – **M** a la carte 105/180
Spec. Pâté de grenouilles, Foie de veau aux girolles, Rognon de veau dijonnaise.

Puteaux 92800 Hauts-de-Seine 101 ⑭ – pop. 36 143 – alt. 36.

See : La Défense★★ : C.N.I.T.★ Exhibition Hall (National Centre for Industry and Technology), Manhattan Tower★★★, Fiat Tower★, GAN Tower★ – Perspective★ of the parvis.

Paris 10 – Nanterre 3 – Pontoise 35 – St-Germain-en-Laye 11 – Versailles 14.

XX ✿ **Gasnier,** 7 bd Richard-Wallace ✆ 45 06 33 63 – AE ⊙ VISA
closed 27 June-4 August, February Holidays, Saturday, Sunday and Bank Holidays – **st. :** **M** (booking essential) a la carte 200/300
Spec. Foie gras frais de canard, Cassoulet, Confit de canard aux cèpes.

Roissy-en-France 95 Val-d'Oise 101 ⑧ – pop. 1 411 – ✉ **95500** Gonesse.

✈ **Charles de Gaulle** ✆ **48 62 22 80.**

Paris 26 – Chantilly 28 – Meaux 36 – Pontoise 44 – Senlis 28.

in the airport area :

Sofitel M, ✆ 48 62 23 23, Telex 230166, ◫, ✂ – 🛗 ▤ TV ☎ ♿ P – 🎪 25 - 500. AE ⊙ E VISA. ✻ rest
Panoramic rest. **Les Valois** *(closed lunch Saturday, Sunday and in August)* **M** 180 - **Le Jardin** (brasserie) (ground floor) **M** a la carte approx. 130 🍷 - – ☕ 42 – **344 rm** 515/685, 8 apartments 995.

in the airport nr. 1 :

XXXX ✿ **Maxim's,** ✆ 48 62 16 16 – ▤. AE VISA
st. : M (lunch only) a la carte 300/420
Spec. Etuvée de langoustines et sole, Volaille de Bresse au vin jaune, Noisettes d'agneau à la truffe.

XX **Grill Maxim's,** ✆ 48 62 16 16 – ▤. AE VISA
st. : M a la carte 190/285.

Rueil-Malmaison 92500 Hauts-de-Seine 101 ⑬ – pop. 64 545 – alt. 15 – **See : Château de Bois-Préau★ – Church (organ-corse★) – Malmaison (château : museum★★).**

Paris 15 – Argenteuil 12 – Nanterre 1,5 – St-Germain-en-Laye 7,5 – Versailles 11.

XXX ✿ **El Chiquito,** 126 av. Paul-Doumer ✆ 47 51 00 53, 🌳, « Garden » – P. VISA
closed August, Saturday, Sunday and Bank Holidays – **M** a la carte 205/255
Spec. Médaillon de lotte au vinaigre et miel, Filet de rouget à l'oseille, Feuilleté de bar.

XXX **Pavillon Joséphine,** 191 av. N. Bonaparte ✆ 47 51 01 62 – AE ⊙ VISA
closed dinner Sunday and Monday – **M** 120 b.i./250 b.i..

XX Relais de St-Cucufa, 114 r. Gén.-Miribel ✆ 47 49 79 05, 🌳.

at Nanterre P N : 2 km – pop. 90 371 – ✉ **92000** Nanterre :

XXX **Ile de France,** 83 av. Mar. Joffre ✆ 47 24 10 44, 🌳 – P. AE ⊙ VISA
closed August and Sunday – **M** a la carte 160/225.

Rungis 94150 Val-de-Marne 101 ㉖ – pop. 2 650 – alt. 80 - Main wholesale produce market for Paris – Paris 13 – Antony 5,5 – Corbeil-Essonnes 26 – Créteil 11 – Longjumeau 10.

Frantel Rungis Orly M Access : from Paris, Highway A6 and take Orly Airport exit, from outside of Paris, A6 and Rungis-Orly exit, 20 av. Ch.-Lindbergh ✉ 94656 ✆ 46 87 36 36, Telex 260738, ←, ⛱ – 🛗 ▤ TV ☎ ♿ 🚗 P – 🎪 50 - 300. AE ⊙ E VISA
st. : rest. **La Rungisserie M** a la carte 160/230 🍷 – ☕ 45 – **206 rm** 419/578.

Holiday Inn M Access : from Paris, Highway A6 and take Orly Airport exit, from outside of Paris, A6 and Rungis-Orly exit ✆ 46 87 26 66, Telex 204679, ⛱ – 🛗 ▤ TV ☎ ♿ P – 🎪 50 - 250. AE ⊙ E VISA
st. : M a la carte approx. 200 🍷 – ☕ 55 – **171 rm** 517/594.

XXX **Le Charolais,** 13 r. N-Dame at Rungis Ville ✆ 46 86 16 42 – AE ⊙ VISA
closed 11 to 31 August, 22 December-5 January, Saturday and Sunday – **M** (lunch only) a la carte 170/230.

Saclay 91400 Essonne 101 ㉓ – pop. 1 865 – alt. 157.

18 St-Aubin ✆ 69 41 25 19, SW : 2,5 km.

Paris 21 – Arpajon 22 – Chartres 68 – Evry 28 – Rambouillet 30 – Versailles 11.

Novotel M, near Christ-de-Saclay circle ✆ 69 41 81 40, Telex 691856, 🌳, ⛱, ✂ – 🛗 ▤ TV ☎ ♿ P – 🎪 300. AE ⊙ E VISA
M Snack a la carte approx. 100 🍷 – ☕ 34 – **134 rm** 330/355.

St-Cloud 92210 Hauts-de-Seine 101 ⑭ – pop. 28 760 – alt. 60.

See : Park ★★ – Stella Matutina Church ★.

18 18 ✆ **47 01 01 85, Buzenval Park at Garches, W : 4 km.**

Paris 12 – Nanterre 5 – Rueil-Malmaison 5,5 – St-Germain 16 – Versailles 10.

XXX ✿ **Le Florian** (Mme Carini), 14 r. Eglise ✆ 47 71 29 90 – AE VISA. ✻
closed 3 to 31 August, Saturday lunch and Sunday – **st. : M** a la carte 200/270
Spec. Salades tièdes Florian, Ravioli de pigeon et canard, Ragoût de St Jacques et sole au Noilly.

St-Germain-en-Laye ⟨SP⟩ 78100 Yvelines 101 ⑫ – pop. 40 829 – alt. 78.

See: Terrace** BY – English Garden* BY – Château * BZ : Museum of National Antiquities ** – Priory Museum * AZ.

⛳9 ; ⛳18 ☎ 34 51 75 90 by ④ : 3 km ; ⛳9 ; ⛳9 ; ⛳9 of Fourqueux ☎ 34 51 41 47 by r. de Mareil AZ - 4 km.

ℹ 1 bis r. République ☎ 44 51 05 12.

Paris 21 ② – Beauvais 73 ① – Chartres 81 ③ – Dreux 70 ③ – Mantes-la-J. 34 ④ – Versailles 13 ③.

ST-GERMAIN EN-LAYE

Bonnenfant (R. A.) ..... AZ 3
Marché-Neuf (Pl. du) ..... AZ 17
Pain (R. au) ..... AZ 20
Paris (R. de) ..... AZ
Poissy (R. de) ..... AZ 22
Vieux-Marché (R. du) ..... AZ 33

Alain (Pl. Jéhan) ..... AY 2
Coches (R. des) ..... AZ 4
Denis (R. M.) ..... AZ 5
Detaille (Pl.) ..... AY 6
Gaulle (Pl. Ch. de) ..... BZ 7
Giraud-Teulon (R.) ..... BZ 9
Gde-Fontaine (R.) ..... AZ 10
Gréban (R. R.) ..... AZ 12
Lattre-de-T. (Av. Mar. de) ..... BZ 13
Loges (Av. des) ..... AY 14
Lyautey (R. Mar.) ..... BZ 15
Malraux (Pl. A.) ..... BZ 16
Mareil (Pl.) ..... AZ 19
Pologne (R. de) ..... AY 23
Pontoise (R. de) ..... AY 25
St-Louis (R.) ..... BZ 26
Victoire (Pl. de la) ..... AY 30
Vieil-Abreuvoir (R. du) ..... AZ 32

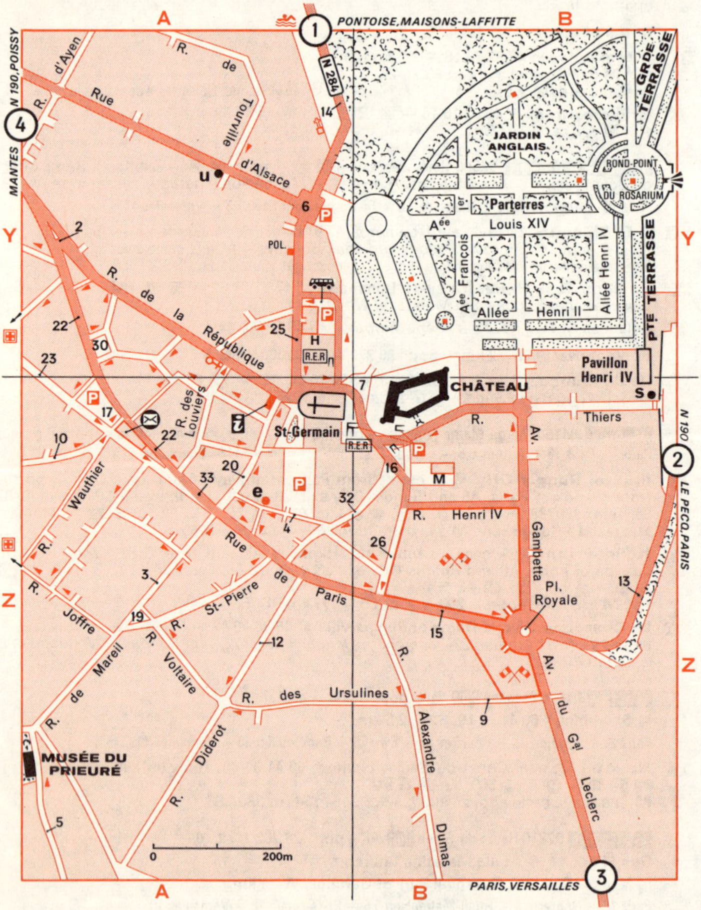

The names of main shopping streets are printed in red at the beginning of the list of streets.

Pavillon Henri IV M, 21 r. Thiers ✆ 34 51 62 62, Telex 695822, ≤ Paris and the River Seine, – – AE E VISA — BZ s
st. : **M** a la carte 270/440 – **42 rm** 500/1 400, 3 apartments.

Le Cèdre, 7 r. Alsace ✆ 34 51 84 35, – wc . — AY u
closed 1 February-8 March – **st. : M** 81/93 – **31 rm** 165/250 – P 245/350.

XXX **Le 7 Rue des Coches,** 7 r. Coches ✆ 39 73 66 40 – AE E VISA — AZ e
closed 5 to 25 August, Sunday dinner and Monday – **st. : M** a la carte 185/240.

X **Petite Auberge,** 119 bis r. L.-Desoyer by r. Joffre - AZ - ✆ 34 51 03 99
closed 15 to 25 March, July, Tuesday dinner and Wednesday – **st. : M** (booking essential) a la carte 95/135.

X **La Résidence,** 149 r. Pdt Roosevelt by r. Joffre - AZ - ✆ 34 51 03 07, – VISA
closed Sunday dinner and Monday – **st. : M** a la carte 130/190.

to the NW by ① : 2,5 km on N 284 and route des Mares – ✉ **78100** St-Germain-en-Laye :

La Forestière M, 1 av. Prés.-Kennedy ✆ 39 73 36 60, Telex 696055, – TV – 40. VISA
st. : M Rest. see **Cazaudehore** below – 38 – **30 rm** 490/560, 6 apartments 660/720.

XXX ✿ **Cazaudehore,** 1 av. Prés.-Kennedy ✆ 34 51 93 80, , « Rustic decor, flower garden in woods » – . VISA
closed Monday except Bank Holidays – **M** a la carte 170/230
Spec. Foie gras de canard, Feuilleté de haddock au beurre d'aneth, Aiguillettes de canard à l'orange.

Vélizy-Villacoublay

78140 Yvelines 101 ㉓ – pop. 23 886 – alt. 174.

Paris 18 – Antony 11 – Chartres 79 – Meudon 7,5 – Versailles 6,5.

Holiday Inn M, av. Europe, near commercial centre Vélizy II ✆ 39 46 96 98, Telex 696537, – TV – 300. AE E VISA
st. : M 70/170 – 50 – **183 rm** 624/715.

Versailles

P 78000 Yvelines 101 ㉒ – pop. 95 240 – alt. 132.

See : Château★★★ Y – Gardens★★★ fountain display★★★ (grandes eaux) and illuminated night performances★★★ (grandes fêtes de nuit) in summer – Grand Canal★★ – The Trianons★★ – Lambinet Museum★ Y **M.**

18 18 9 Racing Club France ✆ 39 50 59 41 by ③ : 2,5 km.

7 r. Réservoirs ✆ 39 50 36 22 and Pl. d'Armes (June-September).

Paris 22 ① – Beauvais 92 ⑦ – Dreux 62 ⑥ – Évreux 85 ⑦ – Melun 59 ③ – Orléans 121 ③.

Plan on next page

Trianon Palace, 1 bd Reine ✆ 39 50 34 12, Telex 698863, , park – TV – 80. AE E VISA. rest — X r
st. : M 162/220 – 55 – **120 rm** 440/1 020, 10 apartments – P 822/1 092.

Mercure M without rest, r. Marly-le-Roi at the Chesnay, across from Parly 2 Shopping mall ✉ 78150 Le Chesnay ✆ 39 55 11 41, Telex 695205 – TV wc . AE E VISA
st. : 30 – **78 rm** 324/350.

Bellevue M without rest, 12 av. Sceaux ✆ 39 50 13 41, Telex 695613 – TV wc . AE E VISA — Z a
st. : 21 – **24 rm** 168/279.

Le Versailles without rest, r. Ste-Anne (Petite Place) ✆ 39 50 64 65 – TV wc . AE VISA — Y m
st. : 19 – **48 rm** 220/298.

XXXX ✿✿ **Trois Marches** (Vié), 3 r. Colbert ✆ 39 50 13 21, , « Elegant 18C hotel » – . AE E VISA — Y u
closed Sunday and Monday – **M** 200 (lunch) and a la carte 250/400
Spec. Homard au jus de carottes (1 May-31 October), Pigeon fumé et rôti avec sa galette de choux, Mousse glacée de fruits rouges (1 June-10 October).

XXX **Rescatore,** 27 av. St-Cloud ✆ 39 50 23 60 – AE VISA — Y s
closed Saturday lunch and Sunday – **M** a la carte 195/250.

XXX **Boule d'Or,** 25 r. Mar.-Foch ✆ 39 50 22 97, « Antique setting » – AE VISA — Y a
M a la carte 160/250.

Viry-Châtillon

91170 Essonne 101 ㊱ – pop. 30 290 – alt. 36.

Paris 26 – Corbeil-Essonnes 11 – Évry 8,5 – Longjumeau 8,5 – Versailles 29.

XX ✿ **La Dariole de Viry** (Richard), 21 r. Pasteur ✆ 69 44 22 40 – . AE VISA
closed 7 July-4 August, Saturday lunch, Sunday and Bank Holidays – **st. : M** a la carte 160/215
Spec. Blinis aux escargots de Bourgogne, Rouelles de rognon de veau à la crème d'échalotes, Coupe "Béatrice".

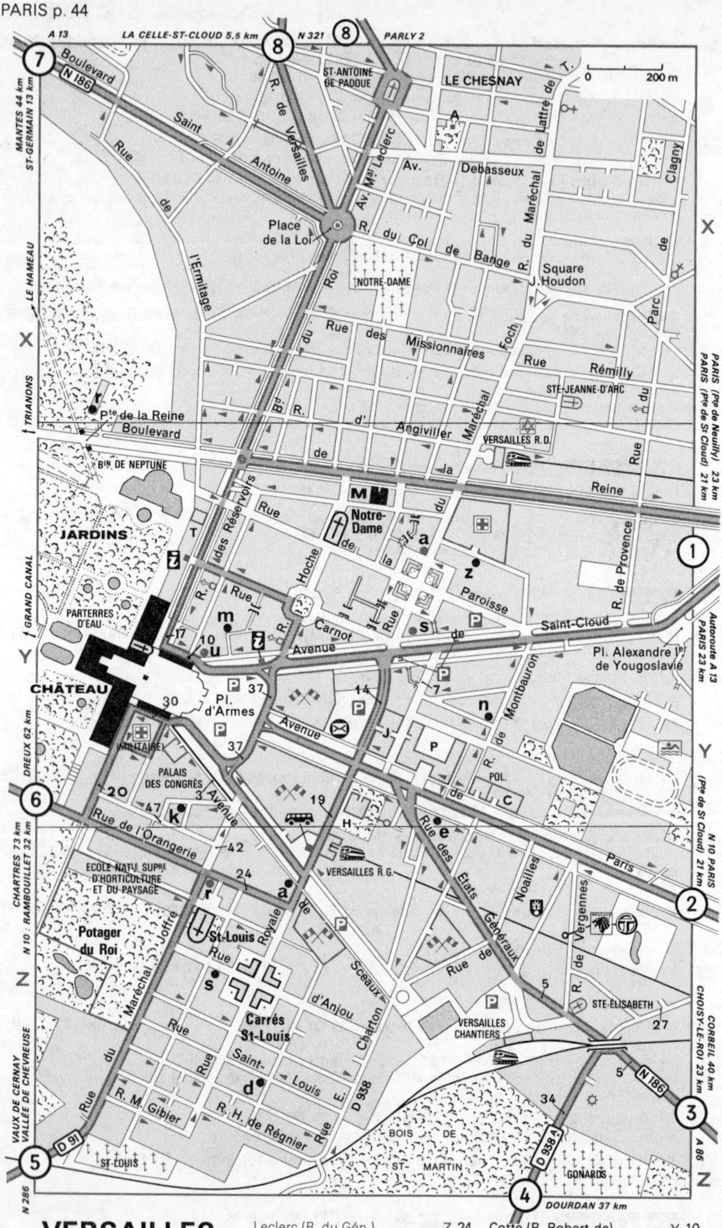
A 13
LA CELLE-ST-CLOUD 5,5 km
N 321
PARLY 2
MANTES 44 km
ST-GERMAIN 13 km
LE HAMEAU
TRIANONS
GRAND CANAL
DREUX 62 km
CHARTRES 73 km
N 10 : RAMBOUILLET 32 km
VAUX DE CERNAY
VALLÉE DE CHEVREUSE
N 286
DOURDAN 37 km
PARIS (Pte de Neuilly) 23 km
PARIS (Pte de St Cloud) 21 km
Autoroute A 13
PARIS 23 km
N 10 PARIS
(Pte de St Cloud) 21 km
CORBEIL 40 km
CHOISY-LE-ROI 23 km
A 86
0
200 m
Boulevard
N 186
Saint
Antoine
Rue
de
l'Ermitage
R. de Versailles
ST-ANTOINE DE PADOUE
LE CHESNAY
Av. Mal Leclerc
Av.
Debasseux
Rue du Maréchal de Lattre de T.
Clagny
Place de la Loi
R. du Col de Bange
NOTRE-DAME
Square J.Houdon
Parc de
Rue des Missionnaires
Foch
Rue Rémilly
STE-JEANNE-D'ARC
Bd. du Roi
R. d' Angiviller
Maréchal
Pte de la Reine
Boulevard de la Reine
VERSAILLES R.D.
BIN DE NEPTUNE
Rue des Réservoirs
Rue
JARDINS
Notre-Dame
de la Paroisse
R. de Provence
Rue Hoche
PARTERRES D'EAU
Rue Carnot
Rue
Avenue de Saint-Cloud
Pl. Alexandre Ier de Yougoslavie
CHÂTEAU
Pl. d'Armes
Avenue
(MILITAIRE)
de Montbauron
R. POL.
PALAIS DES CONGRÈS
Avenue
de Paris
Rue de l'Orangerie
Rue des États Généraux
Noailles
ÉCOLE NATLE SUPRE D'HORTICULTURE ET DU PAYSAGE
VERSAILLES R.G.
Royale
de Sceaux
R. de Vergennes
Potager du Roi
St-Louis
Rue d'Anjou
Rue de
Maréchal Joffre
Rue du
Carrés St-Louis
Charton
VERSAILLES CHANTIERS
STE-ÉLISABETH
Rue Saint-Louis
D 938
N 186
R. M. Gibier
R. H. de Régnier
Rue E.
BOIS DE ST- MARTIN
D 938 A
GONARDS
ST-LOUIS
D 91
X
Y
Z

VERSAILLES

and beyond...

La Ferté-sous-Jouarre 77260 S.-et-M. 56 ⑬, 196 ㉔ – pop. 7 020 – alt. 62.

See : Jouarre : crypt★ of the abbey (S : 3 km).

Paris 66 – Melun 63 – Reims 82 – Troyes 117.

XXXX ✿✿ **Auberge de Condé** (Tingaud), 1 av. Montmirail ✆ 60 22 00 07 – Ⓟ. AE ⓓ E VISA
closed 4 to 20 February, Monday dinner and Tuesday – **M** (booking essential on Sunday) 210/280 and a la carte
Spec. Foie gras, Filet de bar aux noisettes, Filet et ris de veau au champagne rosé. **Wines** Bouzy.

Joigny 89300 Yonne 65 ④ – pop. 10 488 alt. 101.

See : Vierge au Sourire★ in St-Thibault's Church – Côte St-Jacques ≤★ 1,5 km by D 20.

ℹ quai H.-Ragobert ✆ 86 62 11 05.

Paris 148 – Auxerre 27 – Gien 74 – Montargis 59 – Sens 30 – Troyes 76.

XXXX ✿✿✿ **A la Côte St-Jacques** (Lorain) with rm, 14 fb Paris ✆ 86 62 09 70, Telex 801458, « Fine decor », – TV wc wc ☎ Ⓟ. AE ⓓ VISA
closed 5 to 27 January – **M** (Sunday booking essential) 360/380 and a la carte – ☕ 55 – **18 rm** 250/420
Spec. Saumon sauvage en Vessie (season), Bar au beurre de truffes, Trois desserts au chocolat. **Wines** Chablis.

Rheims SP 51100 Marne 56 ⑥⑯ – pop. 181 985 – alt. 83.

See : Cathédral★★★ : tapestries★★ – St-Remi Basilica★★ : interior★★★ – Palais du Tau★★ – Champagne cellars★ – Place Royale★ – Porte Mars★ – Hôtel de la Salle★ – Foujita Chapel★ – Library★ of Ancient College de Jésuites – Museum St-Rémi★★ – Hôtel le Vergeur Museum★ – St-Denis Museum★ – Historical centre of the French motor industry.

Envir. : Fort de la Pompelle : German helmets ★ 9 km to the SE by N 44.

18 ✆ 26 03 60 14 at Gueux to the NW by N 44 : 9,5 km.

✆ 26 88 50 50.

ℹ and Accueil de France (Information facilities and hotel reservations - not more than 5 days in advance) 1 r. Jadart ✆ 26 47 25 69, Telex 830631 A.C. 7 bd Lundy ✆ 26 47 34 76.

Paris 142 – Bruxelles 214 – Châlons-sur-Marne 45 – Lille 205 – Luxembourg 232.

✿✿✿ **Boyer "Les Crayères"** M, 64 bd Vasnier ✆ 26 82 80 80, Telex 830959, ≤, « Elegant mansion in park », – ☎ – Ⓟ – 30. AE ⓓ E VISA
closed 22 December-12 January – **M** (closed Tuesday lunch and Monday) (booking essential) a la carte 240/340 – ☕ 55 – **16 rm** 695/960
Spec. Feuilleté de foie gras aux champignons des bois, Petit chou farci aux langoustines, Filet de canard rouennais aux poires et gingembre. **Wines** Chouilly blanc, Rilly rouge.

Vézelay 89450 Yonne 65 ⑮ – pop. 582 – alt. 302 – Pilgrimage (22 July).

See : Ste-Madeleine Basilica★★★ : tower ✲★.

Envir. : Site★ of Pierre-Perthuis SE : 6 km.

ℹ r. St-Pierre (Easter-30 September) ✆ 86 33 23 69.

Paris 217 – Auxerre 51 – Avallon 15 – Château-Chinon 60 – Clamecy 23.

at St-Père SE : 3 km by D 957 – alt. 148 – ✉ **89450** Vézelay.

See : Church of N.-Dame★.

✿✿✿ **Espérance** (Meneau), ✆ 86 33 20 45, Telex 800005, ≤, « country garden » – TV Ⓟ. AE ⓓ VISA
closed early January-early February and 23 to 27 June – **M** *(closed Wednesday lunch and Tuesday)* (booking essential) 190 (lunch only)/400 and a la carte – ☕ 65 – **17 rm** 450/800, 4 apartments
Spec. Cromesquis de foie gras, Turbot rôti au jus de viande, Salmigondi de pigeon au cresson. **Wines** Chablis, Irancy.

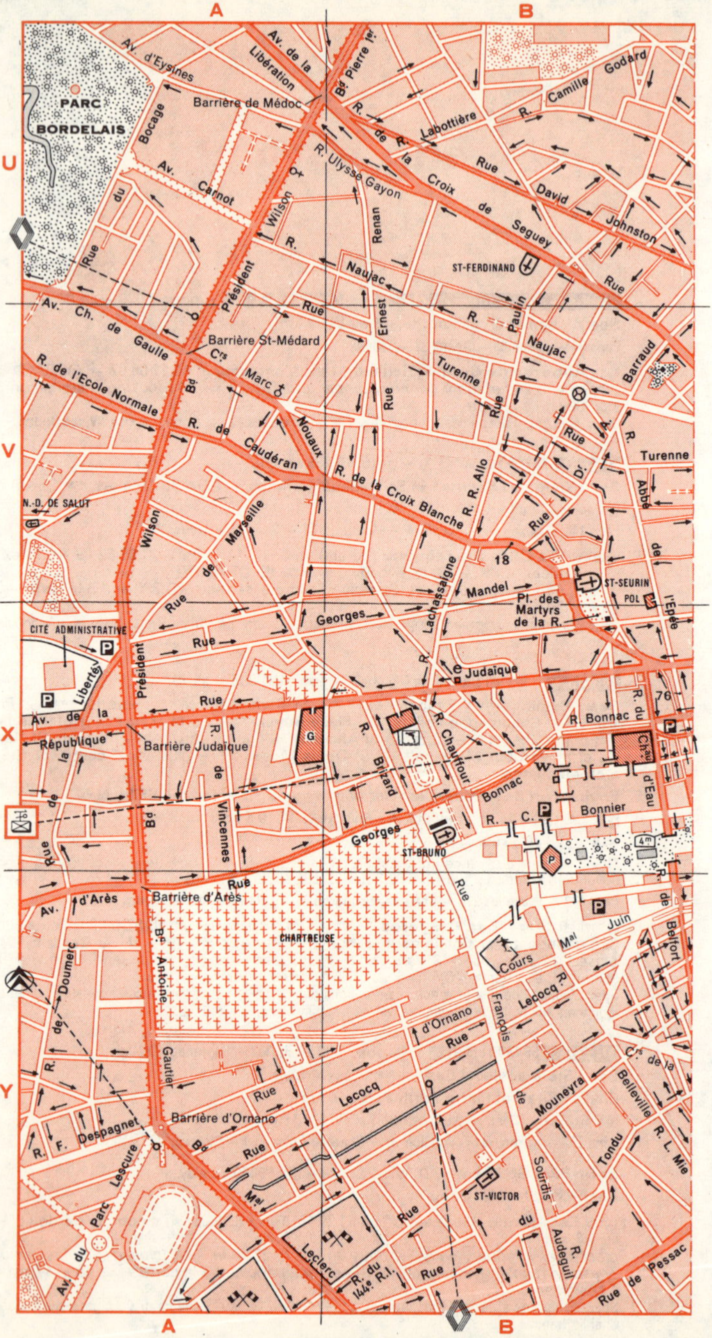
A
B
PARC BORDELAIS
Av. d'Eysines
Barrière de Médoc
Av. de la Libération
Bd Pierre 1er
Bocage
Av. Carnot
du
Rue
R. Ulysse Gayon
R. Labottière
R. Camille Godard
Rue David Johnston
R. de la Croix de Seguey
Président Wilson
Renan
R. Naujac
ST-FERDINAND
Rue Ernest
Rue Paulin
U
Av. Ch. de Gaulle
Barrière St-Médard
Crs Marc Nouaux
R. de l'Ecole Normale
R. de Caudéran
R. Naujac
Turenne
Barraud
Rue
R. de la Croix Blanche
R. R. Allo
Rue Dr. A.
R. Abbé de l'Epée
Turenne
V
N.-D. DE SALUT
Wilson
Rue de Marseille
18
Lachassaigne
ST-SEURIN
POL
Mandel
Pl. des Martyrs de la R.
Rue Georges
Rue
Judaïque
CITÉ ADMINISTRATIVE
P
Président
Liberté
Av. de la République
Barrière Judaïque
X
R. de Vincennes
R. Bizard
R. Chauffour
G
R. Bonnac
R. du Chau d'Eau
76
Bonnac
Bonnier
R. C.
Rue de la
Bd
Georges
ST-BRUNO
4m
R. de Belfort
Rue d'Arès
Barrière d'Arès
Av.
Rue
CHARTREUSE
Doumerc
Bd Antoine Gautier
Cours Mal Juin
Lecocq R.
François
d'Ornano
Rue
Crs de la
Belleville
Y
R. de
Rue
Lecocq
Mouneyra
de
R. F. Despagnet
Barrière d'Ornano
Bd
Rue
Tondu
R. L. Mie
Lescure
Parc
Mal
ST-VICTOR
Sourdis
Rue
du
R. Audeguil
Av. du
Leclerc
R. du 144e R.I.
Rue
Rue de Pessac
A
B

BORDEAUX

Capdeville (R.)	BV	18
Chapeau-Rouge (Cours)	DX	20
Comédie (Pl. de la)	CX	21
Docteur-Nancel-Pénard (R.)	CX	24
Duffour-Dubergier (R.)	CY	26
Esprit-des-Lois (R.)	DV	27
Gaspard-Philippe (R.)	DY	37
Hamel (R. du)	DY	43
Montbazon (R.)	CX	58
Parlement (Pl. du)	DX	65
Philippart (R. F.)	DX	69
République (Pl.)	CY	73
St-Sernin (R.)	BX	76
Tournon (Crs de)	CV	83
Tourny (Pl. de)	CV	84
Villedieu (R.)	CY	88

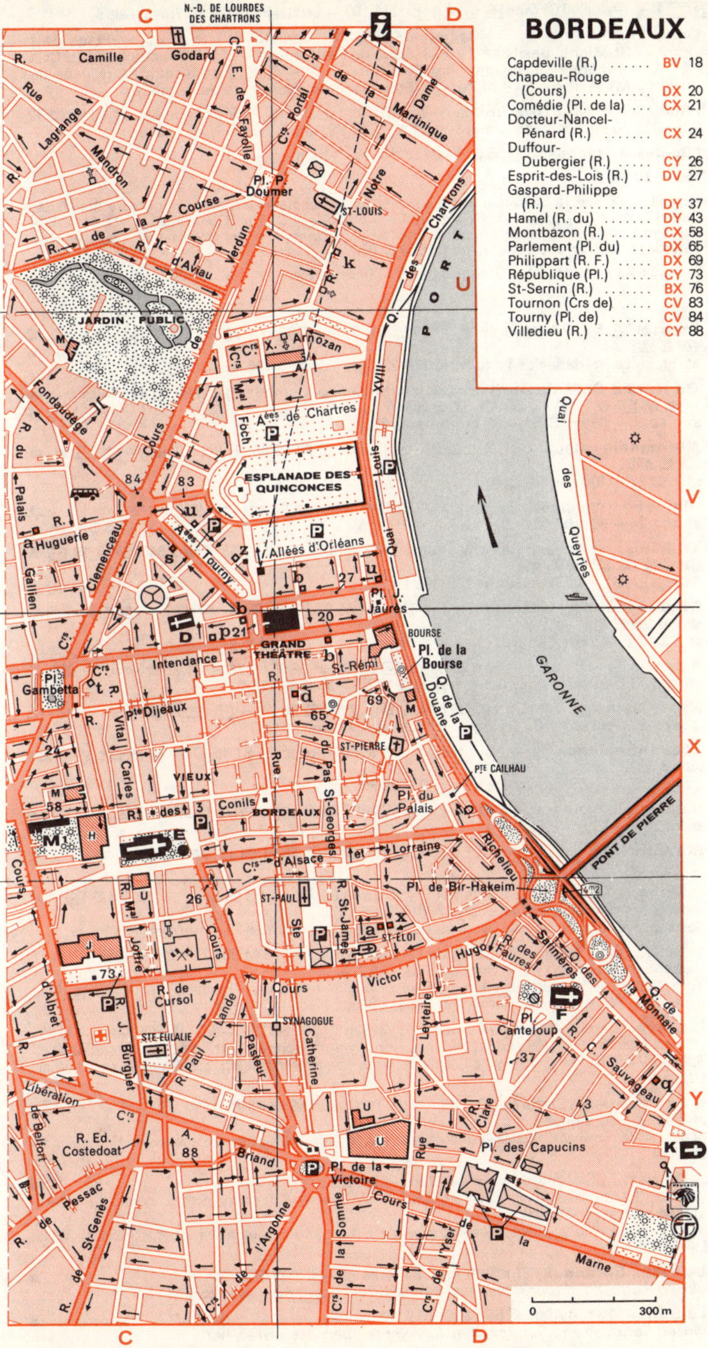

BORDEAUX P 33000 Gironde 71 ⑨ – pop. 211 197 – Greater Bordeaux 617 705 h. – alt. 5.

See : Grand Théâtre★★ CDVX – Cathedral★ and Pey Berland Belfry★ CX **E** – Place de la Bourse★ DX – St-Michel Basilica★ DY **F** – Place du Parlement★ DX **65** – Facade★ of Ste-Croix Church DY **K** – Façade★ of the church of N.-Dame CX **D** – Fine Arts Museum★★ (Musée des Beaux Arts) CX **M1** – The mint★ of Pessac (Établissement monétaire de Pessac).

Golf Bordelais ✆ 58 28 56 04, to the NW by D 109 : 4 km ; de Bordeaux Lac ✆ 56 50 92 72, to theN by D2 : 10 km ; de Cameyrac ✆ 36 72 96 79, to the NE by N 89 : 18 km.

of Bordeaux-Mérignac : ✆ 56 34 84 84 to the W : 11 km.

✆ 56 92 50 50.

and Accueil de France, (Information, exchange facilities and hotel reservations - not more than 5 days in advance) 12 cours 30 - juillet ✆ 56 44 28 41, Telex 570362 - A.C. 8 pl. Quinconces ✆ 56 44 22 92 – Bordeaux wine Exhibition (Maison du vin de Bordeaux), 1 cours 30-juillet (Information, wine-tasting - closed Saturday afternoon and Sunday) – ✆ 56 52 82 82 CV **Z.**

Paris 579 – Lyon 545 – Nantes 325 – Strasbourg 1 060 – Toulouse 244.

Plan on preceding pages

Frantel M, 5 r. R-Lateulade ✆ 56 90 92 37, Telex 540565 – 350. AE E VISA — BX **w**
st. : rest. Le Mériadeck **M** a la carte 170/235 – 45 – **196 rm** 430/680.

Gd H. and Café de Bordeaux without rest, 2 pl Comédie ✆ 56 90 93 44, Telex 541658 – 30-50. AE E VISA — CVX **b**
st. : 30 – **95 rm** 315/440, 3 apartments 750.

Normandie without rest, 7 cours 30-Juillet ✆ 56 52 16 80, Telex 570481 – AE E VISA — CV **z**
st. : 25 – **100 rm** 170/310.

Majestic without rest, 2 r. Condé ✆ 56 52 60 44 – VISA — DV **b**
st. : 24 – **50 rm** 200/300.

Terminus, at St-Jean Railway station ✉ 33800 ✆ 56 92 71 58, Telex 540264 – – 60. AE E VISA
M 88 b.i./120 – 29 – **80 rm** 208/395.

Royal Médoc M without rest, 3 r. Sèze ✆ 56 81 72 42, Telex 571042 – wc wc . AE E VISA. — CV **u**
st. : 25 – **45 rm** 230/270.

Atlantic M without rest, 69 r. E. Leroy ✉ 33800 ✆ 56 92 92 22 – wc . AE VISA
closed 24 December-2 January – **st.** : 18,50 – **36 rm** 144/227.

Notre Dame M without rest, 36 r. N. Dame ✆ 56 52 88 24 – wc — DU **k**
closed 22 December-6 January – **st.** : 18 – **12 rm** 160/200.

Tour Intendance M without rest, 16 r. Vieille Tour ✆ 56 81 46 27 – wc wc . AE VISA — CX **t**
closed 25 July-25 August – **st.** : 20 – **20 rm** 140/235.

Bayonne without rest, 4 r. Martignac ✆ 56 48 00 88 – wc . AE VISA — CX **p**
st. : 21 – **37 rm** 106/210.

Modern'H without rest, 21 r. P.-Loti ✉ 33800 ✆ 56 91 66 11, – wc.
st. : 15,50 – **19 rm** 100/160.

XXXX ✿ **Dubern** (Clément), 42 allées Tourny ✆ 56 48 03 44, « 18 C Decor » – AE E VISA — CV **s**
closed Sunday – **st.** : **M** a la carte 205/275
Spec. Huîtres tièdes au sabayon de citron vert, Rougets au foie gras frais, Pigeon au caramel d'épices.

XXX ✿ **Le Rouzic** (Gautier), 34 Cours du Chapeau rouge ✆ 56 44 39 11 – AE VISA — DX **b**
closed lunch Saturday and Sunday – **st.** : **M** 220/280
Spec. Queues de langoustines en feuilleté aux morilles et ris d'agneau, Lamproie à la bordelaise (April-September), Râble de lapereau au romarin. **Wines** Médoc.

XXX ✿ **Clavel** (Garcia), 44 r. Ch.-Domercq ✉ 33800 ✆ 56 92 91 52 – AE VISA.
closed 10 to 30 July, February Holidays, Sunday and Monday – **st.** : **M** a la carte 205/300
Spec. Gratin d'huîtres au foie gras, Galette de cèpes (September-January), Lapereau à la royale. **Wines** Listrac, St-Julien.

XXX ✿ **La Chamade** (Carrere), 20 r. Piliers de Tutelle ✆ 56 48 13 74 – . AE — DX **d**
st. : **M** 135/190 dinner a la carte
Spec. Salade "Chamade", Ris de veau pochés et poêlés, Aiguillettes de canard aux raisins. **Wines** Blayais, St Julien.

XXX ✿ **Ramet,** 7 pl. J. Jaurès ✆ 56 44 12 51 – . VISA — DV **u**
closed 31 March-13 April, 11-24 August, 29 December-3 January, Saturday and Sunday – **st.** : **M** a la carte 185/290
Spec. Feuilleté d'huîtres tièdes, Gratin d'asperges aux langoustines (April-July), Gibier (season). **Wines** Médoc, Graves.

XX **Le Vieux Bordeaux,** 27 r. Buhan ✆ 56 52 94 36 – AE VISA. — DY **a**
closed August, February Holidays, Saturday lunch and Sunday – **st.** : **M** 95/176.

XX **Le Buhan,** 28 r. Buhan ✆ 56 52 80 86 – AE . — DY **x**
closed Saturday and Sunday from July-September – **st.** : **M** 80/190.

XX **La Jabotière,** 86 r. Bègles ✉ 33800 ✆ 56 91 69 43 – AE ⓓ VISA
closed August, Monday dinner, Saturday lunch and Sunday – **st. : M** 90/140.

XX **Chez le Chef,** 57 r. Huguerie ✆ 56 81 67 07, 🍽. VISA — CV a
closed 1 to 31 October, Sunday dinner and Monday – **st. : M** 75/180.

X **Tupina,** 6 r. Porte de la Monnaie ✆ 56 91 56 37 – VISA — DY q
closed Sunday and Bank Holidays – **M** a la carte 110/175.

X **l'Alhambra,** 111 bis r. Judaïque ✆ 56 96 06 91 – — BX e
closed 14 July-15 August, Saturday lunch and Sunday – **st. : M** 85/130.

at Parc des Expositions : North of the town – ✉ **33300** Bordeaux :

Sofitel Aquitania M, ✆ 56 50 83 80, Telex 570557, ←, 🏊 – 🛗 ▤ TV ☎ ♿ P – 🏛 25-600. AE ⓓ E VISA
rest. **Le Flore** *(closed August, Sunday and Bank Holidays)* **M** a la carte 120/180 – **le Pub M** a la carte approx. 100 🍷 – ☕ 42 – **204 rm** 425/530, 8 apartments 680/900.

Mercure M, ✆ 56 50 90 14, Telex 540097, 🍽, 🏊, 🎾 – 🛗 ▤ TV ☎ ♿ P – 🏛 120
rest. **La Pinasse** – **95 rm**, 5 apartments.

Novotel-Bordeaux le Lac M, ✆ 56 50 99 70, Telex 570274, 🍽, 🏊 – 🛗 ▤ TV ☎ ♿ P – 🏛 350. AE ⓓ E VISA
M a la carte approx. 115 🍷 – ☕ 34 – **173 rm** 309/320.

Mercure M, ✆ 56 50 90 30, Telex 540077, 🍽 – 🛗 ▤ TV 🛁wc ☎ ♿ P – 🏛 250. AE ⓓ E VISA
M a la carte approx. 110 🍷 – ☕ 32 – **108 rm** 284/315, 3 apartments 425.

at Bouliac – ✉ **33270** Floirac :

XXX ✿✿ **Le St-James** (Amat), pl. C. Hosteins, near church ✆ 56 20 52 19, ←, 🍽, « shady terrace overlooking the Garonne River and Bordeaux », 🅿 – AE ⓓ VISA.
M 110/290 and a la carte
Spec. Fondant d'aubergines au cumin, Langoustines aux ravioli d'huîtres, Noisette de mouton à la crème d'ail. **Wines** 1ères Côtes de Bordeaux.

to the S :

at Talence : 6 km – ✉ **33400** Talence :

Guyenne (Hotel School) M, av. F.-Rabelais ✆ 56 80 75 08 – 🛗 TV 🛁wc ☎ P
27 rm, 3 apartments.

to the W :

at l'Alouette : 9 km – ✉ **33600** Pessac :

✿ **La Réserve** M 🐎, av. Bourgailh ✆ 56 07 13 28, Telex 560585, « park », 🎾 – TV ☎ P – 🏛 80. AE ⓓ E VISA
Easter-1 November – **st. : M** 200/330 – ☕ 35 – **19 rm** 350/550
Spec. Lamproie (season), Agneau du Médoc. **Wines** Graves, Médoc.

at the airport : 11 km by D 106E – ✉ **33700** Mérignac :

Novotel-Mérignac M, ✆ 56 34 10 25, Telex 540320, 🍽, 🏊, 🅿 – ▤ rm TV ☎ ♿ P – 🏛 25-200. AE ⓓ E VISA
M a la carte approx. 100 🍷 – ☕ 34 – **100 rm** 283/330.

Eugénie-les-Bains

40 Landes **82** ① – pop. 408 – alt. 90 – Spa (8 March-31 Oct.) – ✉ **40320** Geaune.
Bordeaux 152.

✿✿✿ **Les Prés d'Eugénie** (Guérard) M 🐎, ✆ 58 51 19 01, Telex 540470, « 19C mansion, elegant decor, park », 🏊, 🎾 – 🛗 TV ☎ ♿ P. AE ⓓ.
10 March-12 November – **M** (low-calorie menu for residents only) 140/180 – **rest. Michel Guérard M** (booking essential) 360 and a la carte – ☕ 65 – **28 rm** 800, 7 apartments 1 000
Spec. Langoustines sautées aux mousserons (season), Hachis Parmentier à l'oie et aux truffes, Corne d'abondance aux fruits glacés. **Wines** Côtes de Gascogne, Tursan.

☛ *The hotels have entered into certain undertakings towards the readers of this Guide.*
Make it plain that you have the most recent Guide.

If you would like a more complete selection of hotels and restaurants, consult the ***Michelin Guides*** *for the following countries:*
Benelux, Deutschland, España Portugal, France, Great Britain and Ireland, Italia.

CANNES 06400 Alpes-Mar. [84] ⑨, [195] ㉟㊳ – pop. 72 787 – Casinos : Les Fleurs BZ, Palm Beach X, Municipal BZ.

See : Boulevard de la Croisette★★ BCZ – Pointe de la Croisette★ X – ≤★ from the Mount Chevalier Tower AZ V – La Castre Museum★ (Musée de la Castre) AZ M – Super Cannes Observatory ☼★★★ E : 4 km, VX B – Tour into the Hills★ (Chemin des Collines) NE : 4 km V – The Croix des Gardes V E ≤★ W : 5 km then 15 mn.

⛳9 ⛳18 Country-Club of Cannes-Mougins ✆ 93 75 79 13 by ⑤ : 9 km ; ⛳9 ⛳18 Golf-Club of Cannes-Mandelieu ✆ 93 49 55 39 by ② : 6,5 km ; ⛳18 Biot ✆ 93 65 08 48 by ⑤ : 14 km ; ⛳18 Valbonne ✆ 93 42 00 08 by ⑤ : 15 km.

ℹ and Accueil de France (Information, exchange facilities and hotel reservations not more than 5 days in advance), Railway Station S.N.C.F. ✆ 93 99 19 77 Télex 470795 and Palais des Festivals et des Congrès, 1 La Croisette ✆ 93 39 24 53, Telex 470479 - A.C. 21 quai St-Pierre ✆ 93 39 38 94.

Paris 901 ③ – Aix-en-Provence 146 ③ – Grenoble 316 ⑤ – Marseille 158 ③ – Nice 32 ⑤ – Toulon 123 ③.

CANNES - LE CANNET - VALLAURIS

André (R. du Cdt)	CZ	
Antibes (R. d')	BCZ	
Belges (R. des)	BZ	6
Chabaud (R.)	CZ	15
Croisette (Bd de la)	BCZ	
Félix-Faure (R.)	ABZ	
Foch (R. du Mar.)	BZ	25
Hôtel-de-Ville (Pl. de l')	AZ	33
Joffre (R. du Mar.)	BZ	35
Riouffe (R. Jean de)	BZ	64
Alexandre-III (Bd)	X	2
Amouretti (R. F.)	CZ	3
Anc.-Combattants d'Afrique du Nord (Av.)	AZ	4
Beau-Soleil (Bd)	V	5
Bellevue (Pl.)	V	7
Bréguières (Ch. des)	V	8
Broussailles (Av. des)	V	9
Buttura (R.)	BZ	10
Carnot (Bd)	V	13
Castre (Pl. de la)	AZ	14
Christ-Roi (⛪)	V	16
Clemenceau (Av. G.)	V	17
Coteaux (Av. des)	V	18
Dr-Pierre-Gazagnaire (R.)	AZ	20
Dollfus (R. Jean)	AZ	22
Ferrage (Bd de la)	BYZ	23
Fiesole (Av.)	V	24
Four-à-Chaux (Bd du)	V	25
Fournas (Av. de)	V	26
Gambetta (Bd)	V	27
Gaulle (Pl. Gén.-de)	BZ	28
Grasse (av. de)	V	29
Haddad-Simon (R. J.)	CY	30
Isnard (Pl. Paul)	V	34
Lacour (Bd A.)	V	36
Lattre-de-Tassigny (Av. J.-de)	ABY	37
Leader (Bd)	VX	38
Lérins (Av. de)	X	39
Macé (R.)	BZ	41
Monod (Bd Jacques)	V	42
Montaigne (R.)	BY	43
Mont-Chevalier (R. du)	AZ	44
Montfleury (Bd)	X	45
Myron-T.-Herrik (Bd)	V	46
N.-D.-de-Bon-Voyage (⛪)	BZ	49
N.-D.-d'Espérance (⛪)	AZ	50
N.-D.-des-Pins (⛪)	DZ	52
Observatoire (Bd de l')	X	54
Oxford (Bd d')	V	55
Pastour (R. L.)	AZ	56
Perier (Bd du)	V	57
Perrissol (R. L.)	AZ	59
Pins (Bd des)	X	60
République (Bd de la)	X	62
Rouguière (R.)	BZ	66
Rouvier (Bd M.)	V	67
St-Charles (⛪)	V	69
St-Joseph (⛪)	AY	70
St-Nicolas (Av.)	BY	71
St-Sauveur (R.)	V	72
Ste-Philomène (⛪)	V	73
Sardou (R. L.)	V	74
Serbes (R. des)	BZ	75
Souvenir (⛪)	CY	76
Tapis-Vert (Av. du)	V	77
Tuby (Bd Victor)	AZ	78
Vallauris (Av. de)	V	79
Victor-Hugo (R.)	V	80
Vidal (R. du Cdt)	CZ	82

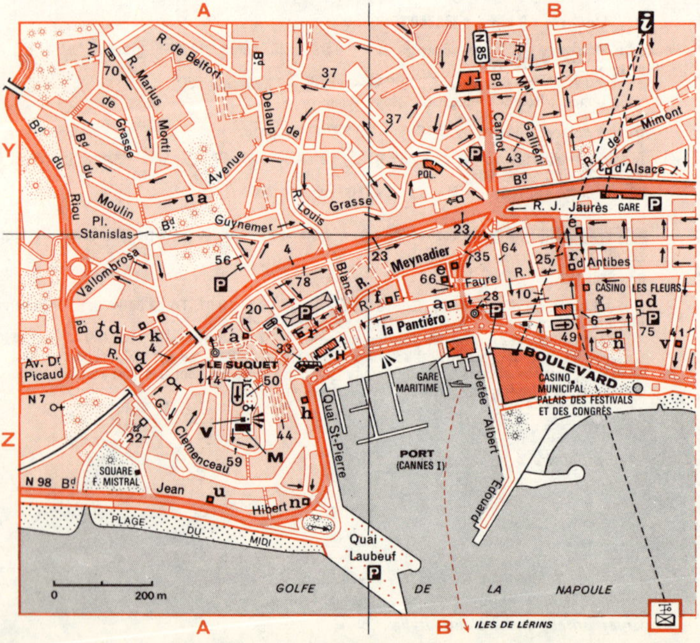

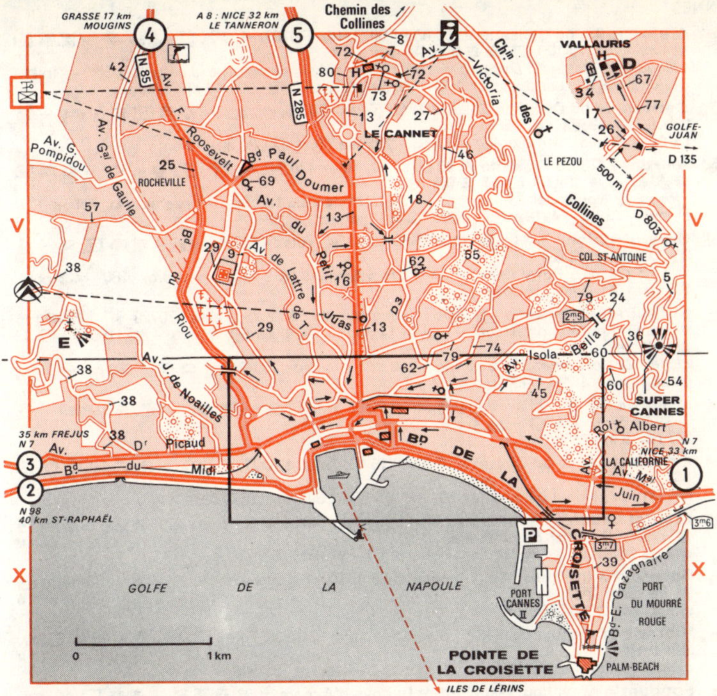
GRASSE 17 km
MOUGINS
A 8 : NICE 32 km
LE TANNERON
Chemin des Collines
VALLAURIS
LE CANNET
Av. Victoria
GOLFE-JUAN
D 135
LE PEZOU
500 m
Av. G. Pompidou
Av. Gal de Gaulle
Av. F. Roosevelt
Bd Paul Doumer
ROCHEVILLE
Collines
D 803
Av. du Petit Juas
Av. de Lattre de T.
Bd du Riou
COL ST ANTOINE
Isola Bella
Av. J. de Noailles
SUPER CANNES
35 km FREJUS
N 7
Av. Dr Picaud
Bd du Midi
Bd DE LA CROISETTE
Av. Roi Albert
LA CALIFORNIE
NICE 33 km
Av. Mal Juin
N 98
40 km ST-RAPHAËL
GOLFE DE LA NAPOULE
PORT CANNES II
PORT DU MOURRÉ ROUGE
Bd E. Gazagnaire
CROISETTE
0
1 km
POINTE DE LA CROISETTE
PALM-BEACH
ILES DE LÉRINS

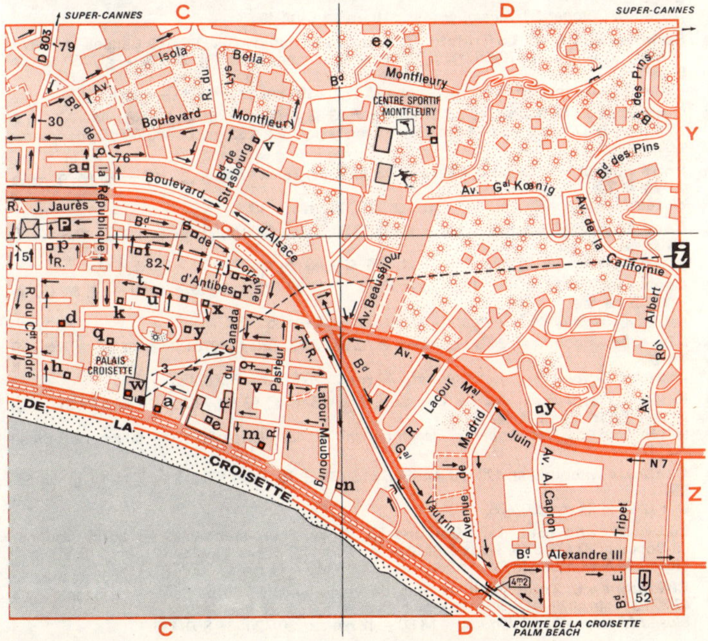
SUPER-CANNES
C
D
SUPER-CANNES
D 803
Isola Bella
Bd Montfleury
CENTRE SPORTIF MONTFLEURY
Bd des Pins
Boulevard Montfleury
Bd de la République
Bd de Strasbourg
Boulevard d'Alsace
Av. Gal Kœnig
Av. de la Californie
R. J. Jaurès
Bd de Lorraine
R. d'Antibes
Av. Beauséjour
R. du Canada
R. du Cdt André
PALAIS CROISETTE
R. Pasteur
R. Latour-Maubourg
Av. Mal Juin
R. Lacour
Av. de Madrid
Bd Gal Vautrin
Avenue
Av. A. Capron
Bd Alexandre III
R. Tripet
Av. Roi Albert
N 7
DE LA CROISETTE
Bd E.
52
POINTE DE LA CROISETTE
PALM BEACH
Y
Z

Majestic M, bd Croisette ✆ 93 68 91 00, Telex 470787, ≤, – 30-120. AE O E VISA. rest BZ n
closed 25 October-15 December – **M** (dinner only in summer) a la carte 220/360 – **Grill M** (lunch only) a la carte approx. 250 – ☐ 50 **262 rm** 1 000/1 600, 12 apartments.

Carlton, 58 bd Croisette ✆ 93 68 91 68, Telex 470720, ≤, – 250. AE O E VISA. rest CZ e
La Côte M a la carte 265/400 – ☐ 56 – **295 rm** 750/1 570, 30 apartments.

Martinez, 73 bd Croisette ✆ 93 68 91 91, Telex 470708, ≤, – 40-600. AE O E VISA CDZ n
closed 12 November-23 January – **st. : L'Orangeraie M** 185-and see also **La Palme d'Or** below – ☐ 60 – **421 rm** 750/2 000, 18 apartments.

Gray d'Albion M, 38 r. Serbes ✆ 93 68 54 54, Telex 470744, – 30-200. AE O E VISA BZ d
st. : M rest see **Royal Gray** below - **Les 4 Saisons M** a la carte approx. 180 – ☐ 60 – **187 rm** 1 200/1 400, 14 apartments.

Sofitel Méditerranée M, 2 bd J.-Hibert ✆ 93 99 22 75, Telex 470728, ≤, « Roof-top swimming pool and terrace ≤ bay of Cannes » – 150. AE O E VISA. rest AZ n
closed 22 November-23 December – **st. : M** a la carte 150/240 – ☐ 50 – **150 rm** 440/990, 4 apartments 1 290/1 450.

Montfleury M, 25 av. Beauséjour ✆ 93 68 91 50, Telex 470039, ≤, « Garden », – 400 DY r
227 rm, 8 apartments.

Gd Hôtel, 45 bd Croisette ✆ 93 38 15 45, Telex 470727, ≤, – AE VISA CZ q
M rest see **Lamour** below – ☐ 55 – **76 rm** 660/1 320 – P 780/1 685.

Frantel Beach M without rest, 13 r. Canada ✆ 93 38 22 32, Telex 470034, – 30-60. AE O E VISA CZ v
closed 1 November-25 January – **st. :** ☐ 50 – **94 rm** 675/990.

Splendid without rest, 4 r. F.-Faure ✆ 93 99 53 11, Telex 470990, ≤ – kitchenette. AE O E VISA BZ a
st. : 63 rm ☐ 300/650.

Victoria M without rest, 122 r. d'Antibes ✆ 93 99 36 36, Telex 470817, – . AE O VISA CZ x
closed 15 November-15 January – **st. :** ☐ 28 – **25 rm** 335/545.

Fouquet's M without rest, 2 Rd-pt Duboys-d'Angers ✆ 93 38 75 81 – . AE O E CZ y
closed 20 October-20 December – **st. : 10 rm** ☐ 540/940.

Solhotel and rest. Le Trident M, 61 av. Dr Picaud by ③ ✉ 06150 Cannes La Bocca ✆ 93 47 63 00, Telex 970956, – kitchenette – 150. AE O E VISA
closed 1 November-15 December – **st. : M** 110 – **101 rm** ☐ 360/530 – P 380/630.

Gonnet et de la Reine, 42 bd Croisette ✆ 93 38 40 00, ≤ – . AE VISA. CZ h
25 March-15 October – **st. : M** (closed to non residents) – **52 rm** ☐ 350/660, 6 apartments 1 000.

Paris without rest, 34 bd d'Alsace ✆ 93 38 30 89, Telex 470995, – 40. O E VISA. CY a
closed 31 October-25 January – **st. :** ☐ 20 – **48 rm** 368/488.

Beau Séjour M, 5 r. Fauvettes ✆ 93 39 63 00, Telex 470975, – . AE O E VISA. rest AZ d
closed 1 November-15 December – **st. : M** 90 – **46 rm** ☐ 235/500 – P 395/430.

Century M without rest, 133 r. d'Antibes ✆ 93 99 37 64, Telex 470090 – . AE O VISA CZ r
closed 20 November-10 January – **st. :** ☐ 25 – **35 rm** 355/458.

Abrial M without rest, 24 bd Lorraine ✆ 93 38 78 82, Telex 470761 – . AE O VISA CY s
closed 10 November-22 January – **st. : 48 rm** ☐ 260/410 – P 360/420.

Embassy and rest. As de Carreau, 6 r. Bône ✆ 93 38 79 02, Telex 470081 – rest . AE O E VISA CZ j
st. : M *(closed 20 November-20 December and Monday lunch)* 90/120 – **60 rm** ☐ 370/490 – P 425.

Canberra without rest, 120 r. d'Antibes ✆ 93 38 20 70, Telex 470817 – . AE O VISA CZ u
st. : ☐ 28 – **44 rm** 260/465.

Licorn'H. and rest. Les Saisons M, 23 av. Fr.-Tonner by ③ ✉ 06150 Cannes-La-Bocca ✆ 93 47 18 46, Telex 470818 – rest wc wc . AE O E VISA
closed 15 November-15 December – **st. : M** 85/140 – **45 rm** ☐ 285/420 – P 327/377.

Château de la Tour, 10 av. Font-de-Veyre by ③ ✉ 06150 Cannes-La-Bocca ✆ 93 47 32 23, Telex 470906, – wc wc . AE O VISA. rest
closed 15 November-1 January – **M** 86 – **42 rm** ☐ 250/420 – P 350/436.

🏨 **Des Congrès et Festivals** M without rest, 12 r. Teisseire 𝒫 93 39 13 81 – wc wc ☎. AE E VISA — CZ **p**
closed 1 December-15 January – **st. : 20 rm** 265/420.

🏨 **Ruc Hôtel** without rest, 15 bd Strasbourg 𝒫 93 38 64 32 – wc ☎. AE E VISA — CY **v**
closed 1 November-23 December – **st. : 30 rm** 260/420.

🏨 **La Madone** without rest, 5 av. Justinia 𝒫 93 43 57 87, « fine setting », – kitchenette wc wc ☎. AE E VISA — DZ **y**
st. : 30 – **23 rm** 350/470.

🏨 **Acapulco** M, 16 bd Alsace 𝒫 93 99 16 16, Telex 470929, – wc wc ☎. AE E VISA — BY **t**
st. : M 66/85 – **59 rm** 500/550 – P 665/840.

🏨 **Athénée** without rest, 6 rue Lecerf 𝒫 93 38 69 54, Telex 470978 – wc wc ☎. AE E VISA — CZ **f**
closed 1 November-15 January – **st. :** 27 – **15 rm** 253/460.

🏨 **Les Orangers,** 1 r. des Orangers 𝒫 93 39 99 92, Telex 470873, ←, – wc wc ☎. AE E VISA. rest — AZ **k**
closed 1 November-20 December – **st. : M** 105 – **40 rm** 270/435 – P 405.

🏨 **Host. de L'Olivier** without rest, 90 r. G.-Clemenceau 𝒫 93 39 53 28, – wc wc ☎ P. AE VISA — AZ **k**
23 rm 250/450.

🏨 **Provence,** 9 r. Molière 𝒫 93 38 44 35, – rm wc wc ☎. AE E VISA. rest — CZ **t**
st. : M *(Easter-end of September, Christmas and closed Sunday)* a la carte approx. 130 – 20 – **30 rm** 170/330.

🏨 **Univers** M without rest, 2 r. Mar.-Foch 𝒫 93 39 59 19, Telex 470972 – wc wc ☎. AE E VISA — BZ **r**
st. : – **68 rm** 320/518.

🏨 **Toboso** without rest, 7 allée des Oliviers 𝒫 93 38 20 05, – kitchenette wc ☎ P. — DY **e**
st. : 25 – **10 rm** 400.

🏨 **Roches Fleuries** without rest, 92 r. G.-Clemenceau 𝒫 93 39 28 78, – wc wc ☎ P. — AZ **q**
closed 15 November-27 December – **st. : 24 rm** 100/210.

🏨 **Campanile,** Aérodrome de Cannes-Mandelieu by ③ : 6 km ✉ 06150 Cannes-La-Bocca 𝒫 93 48 69 41, Telex 461570 – wc ☎ P – 30. VISA
st. : M 61 b.i./82 b.i. – 23 – **49 rm** 194/215.

🏨 **Festival** without rest, 3 r. Molière 𝒫 93 38 69 45 – kitchenette wc ☎ — CZ **k**
closed 25 November-20 December – **st. :** 15 – **17 rm** 130/300.

🏨 **Cheval Blanc** without rest, 3 r. de-Maupassant 𝒫 93 39 88 60 – wc wc ☎ — AY **a**
st. : 15 – **16 rm** 180/220.

🏨 **Wagram,** 140 r. d'Antibes 𝒫 93 94 55 53, – rm wc wc ☎. — CZ **x**
st. : M 88 – 22 – **23 rm** 166/413 – P 364/516.

✕✕✕✕ ✻ **La Palme d'Or,** 73 bd Croisette 𝒫 93 68 91 91 – P. AE E VISA — CDZ **n**
closed 12 November-23 January, Thursday (except dinner in July-August) and Friday lunch – **st. : M** a la carte 210/420
Spec. Blanc-manger de sole aux amandes, Pigeonneau au vieux vinaigre et au porto, Entremets Palme d'Or.

✕✕✕✕ ✻✻ **Royal Gray** 2 r. des Etats-Unis, 𝒫 93 68 54 54, « Tasteful, contemporary decor » – . AE E VISA — BZ **d**
closed February, Sunday (except July-August) and Monday – **M** a la carte 250/340
Spec. Salade tiède de St-Jacques, Papillote de langoustines chiffonnade de basilic, Fricassé de homard aux mousserons. **Wines** Flassans, Vidauban.

✕✕✕ **Félix,** 63 bd Croisette 𝒫 93 94 00 61, ←, – . AE VISA — CZ **m**
closed 1 November-24 December and Wednesday – **M** a la carte 185/275.

✕✕✕ **Gaston-Gastounette,** 7 quai St-Pierre 𝒫 93 39 47 92, ←, – . AE VISA — AZ **h**
closed 3 to 23 January – **M** 150/165.

✕✕✕ **Poêle d'Or,** 23 r. États-Unis 𝒫 93 39 77 65 – . AE VISA — BZ **v**
closed November and Monday – **st. : M** 120.

✕✕✕ **Le Festival,** 52 bd Croisette 𝒫 93 38 04 81, – . AE — CZ **a**
closed 26 November-26 December – **M** a la carte 180/225.

✕✕✕ **Rescator,** 7 r. Mar.-Joffre 𝒫 93 39 44 57 – . VISA — BZ **e**
closed Monday out of season – **M** (dinner only in July and August) 150/350.

✕✕✕ **Lamour,** 45 bd Croisette 𝒫 93 99 49 60, – AE VISA — CZ **q**
M 135.

✕✕ Blue Bar, Former festival Centre 𝒫 93 39 03 04, – — CZ **w**
closed 27 June-6 July and Tuesday except July-August.

✕✕ **Le Croquant,** 18 bd J.-Hibert 𝒫 93 39 39 79, ← – . AE E — AZ **u**
closed 15 February-1 March, Sunday dinner from 15 September-15 June and Monday – **M** (from 15 June-15 September dinner only) 90/210.

XX **La Mirabelle,** 24 r. St-Antoine ✆ 93 38 72 75 – AE VISA — AZ a
closed 1 to 15 March, 1-25 December and Tuesday – **M** (Dinner only) 200 b.i./350 b.i.

XX **Caveau Provençal,** 45 r. Félix-Faure ✆ 93 39 06 33, ≤, – ▤. AE ⓓ VISA — BZ f
M 76/180.

XX **Mère Besson,** 13 r. Frères-Pradignac ✆ 93 39 59 24, Provençal cuisine – AE VISA — CZ d
closed Sunday except July-August and Bank Holidays – **st. : M** (dinner only from July-August) a la carte 140/200.

X **L'Olivier,** 9 r. Rouguière ✆ 93 39 91 63 – AE ⓓ E VISA — BZ e
closed 15 December-15 January and Monday – **M** 60/90.

X **Le Monaco,** 15 r. 24-août ✆ 93 38 37 76 — BY e
closed 1 November-10 December and Sunday – **st. : M** 60/85 ₰.

X **Aux Bons Enfants,** 80 r. Meynadier – — AZ r
closed 30 March-15 April, 20 December-5 January, Wednesday dinner and Sunday – **st. : M** 65 ₰.

route de Pégomas by ③ : 8 km – ✉ **06150** Cannes-la-Bocca :

XXX L'Oriental, 286 av. M.-Jourdan – Entrance by Résidence Abadie ✆ 93 47 43 99, « Moorish décor », North African cuisine.

Antibes **06600** Alpes-Mar. **84** ⑨, **195** ㉟㊵
Cannes 11.

N : 4 km quartier de la Brague – ✉ **06600** Antibes :

XXXXX ✿✿ **La Bonne Auberge** (Rostang), on N 7 ✆ 93 33 36 65, Telex 470989, , « Provençal style dining room and flowered terrace » – Ⓟ. AE VISA
closed 15 November-15 December, 1 to 8 March and Monday (except Bank Holidays) dinner July-August – **M** 320/420 and a la carte
Spec. Minute de loup grillé, Daurade royale, Aile de volaille aux dés de tomates. **Wines** Côteaux d'aix.

Mougins **06250** Alpes-Mar. **84** ⑨, **195** ㉔㊳ – pop. 10 197 – alt. 260.
Cannes 7.

XXXX ✿✿✿ **Moulin de Mougins** (Vergé) with rm, **at Notre-Dame-de-Vie SE : 2,5 km by D 3** ✆ 93 75 78 24, Telex 970732, ≤, , – ▤ rest TV wc ☎ Ⓟ. AE ⓓ VISA
closed 15 November-23 December and 15 February-25 March – **M** *(closed Thursday lunch and Monday)* 400 and a la carte – **3 rm** 600/720
Spec. Poupeton de fleur de courgette aux truffes, Filets de rougets en barigoule de légumes, Noisettes d'agneau au coulis de truffes. **Wines** Rians.

La Napoule-Plage **06** Alpes-Mar. **84** ⑧, **195** ㉞㊲ – ✉ **06210** Mandelieu-La-Napoule.
Cannes 8.

XXXX ✿✿✿ **L'Oasis** (Outhier), ✆ 93 49 95 52, Telex 461389, « Shaded and flowered patio » – ▤
closed beginning November to 15 December, Monday dinner and Tuesday – **M** 350/380 and a la carte
Spec. Marjolaine de foie gras, Brochette de langoustines aux huîtres de Belon (December-June), Langouste aux herbes thaï. **Wines** Cassis, Bandol.

LYONS Ⓟ **69000** Rhône **74** ⑪⑫ – pop. 418 476 Greater Lyons 1 173 797 – alt. 169.

See : Site★★★ – Old Lyons★★ (Vieux Lyon) BX : Jewry Street★ (rue Juiverie) 65, rue St-Jean★ 92, Hotel de Gadagne★ **M1** , Maison du Crible★ **D** – St-Jean★ : Chancel★★ – Basilica of N.-D.-de-Fourvière ✻★★, ≤★ BX – Capitals★ of the Basilica St-Martin d'Ainay BYZ – Lanterne tower★ of St-Paul Church BV – Virgin with Child★ in the St-Nizier Church CX – Park of the Tête d'Or★ : Rose-garden★ (roseraie) – Fountain★ of the Place des Terreaux CV – Traboules★ of Quartier Croix-Rousse – Arches de Chaponost★ - Montée de Garillan★ BX – Punch and Judy Show (Théâtre de Guignol) BX **N** – Museums : Textile★★★ CZ**M2**, Gallo-Roman Civilization★★ (claudian table★★★) BX **M3**, Fine-Arts★★ CV **M4**, – Decorative Arts★★ CZ **M5**, Printing and Banking★★ CX **M6** , Guimet of Natural history★ – Puppet★ BX **M1**, Historic★ : lapidary★ BX **M1**, Apothecary's Shop★ (Civil Hospitals) CY **M8**.

Envir. : Rochetaillée : Automobile Museum Henri Malartre★ : 12 km.

9 9 9 Villette d'Anthon ✆ 78 31 11 33 to the E : 21 km ; 18 de Verger-Lyon ✆ 78 02 84 20 to the S.

✈ of Lyon-Satolas ✆ 78 71 92 21 to the E : 27 km.

✆ 78 92 50 50.

i and Accueil de France (Information, exchange facilities, hotel reservations - not more than 5 days in advance), pl. Bellecour ✆ 78 42 25 75, Télex 330032 and Centre d'Echange de Perrache A.C. 7 r. Grolée ✆ 78 42 51 01.

Paris 460 – Bâle 387 – Bordeaux 545 – Genève 159 – Grenoble 104 – Marseille 315 – St-Étienne 63 – Strasbourg 480 – Torino 300 – Toulouse 534.

Plan on following pages

Hotels

Town Centre (Bellecour-Terreaux) :

Sofitel M, 20 quai Gailleton, 69002, 78 42 72 50, Telex 330225, – – 200. AE E VISA. rest CY **k**
st. : rest. **Les Trois Dômes** (8th floor) **M** a la carte 230/320 - **Sofi Shop** (ground floor) **M** a la carte approx. 110 – 63 – **184 rm** 570/980, 6 apartments.

Gd Hôtel Concorde, 11 r. Grolée, 69002, 78 42 56 21, Telex 330244 – – 80. AE E VISA. rest DX **e**
st. : Le Fiorelle (Grill) *(closed Sunday)* **M** 70/95 – 38 – **140 rm** 310/630.

Royal, 20 pl. Bellecour, 69002, 78 37 57 31, Telex 310785 – rm – 40. AE E VISA CY **d**
st. : M Grill 85 – 34 – **95 rm** 240/580.

Gd H. des Beaux-Arts without rest, 75 r. Prés.-E.-Herriot, 69002, 78 38 09 50, Telex 330442 – . AE E VISA CX **t**
st. : 30 – **79 rm** 236/409.

Carlton without rest, 4 r. Jussieu, 69002, 78 42 56 51, Telex 310787 – rm . AE E VISA CX **y**
st. : 30 – **93 rm** 242/410.

La Résidence without rest, 18 r. Victor-Hugo, 69002, 78 42 63 28, Telex 900950 – wc wc – 40. AE VISA CY **s**
st. : 17 – **63 rm** 162/178.

Globe et Cécil without rest, 21 r. Gasparin 69002 78 42 58 95, Telex 305184 – wc wc – 60. AE VISA CY **b**
22 – **65 rm** 120/250.

Gd H. des Terreaux without rest, 16 r. Lanterne 69001 78 27 04 10, Telex 310273 – wc wc . AE E VISA CV **u**
st. : 24 – **50 rm** 87/255.

Moderne without rest, 15 r. Dubois, 69002, 78 42 21 83 – wc CX **n**
st. : 18,50 – **31 rm** 81/218.

Bayard without rest, 23 pl. Bellecour, 69002, 78 37 39 64 – wc . CY **g**
st. : 17 – **15 rm** 130/170.

Perrache :

Bordeaux without rest, 1 r. Bélier, 69002, 78 37 58 73, Telex 330355 – . AE E VISA BZ **y**
st. : 21 – **87 rm** 153/271.

Bristol without rest, 28 cours Verdun, 69002, 78 37 56 55, Telex 330584 – – 45. AE E VISA. BZ **y**
st. : 19 – **131 rm** 110/250.

Axotel and rest. Le Chalut M, 12 r. Marc-Antoine Petit 69002 78 42 17 18, Telex 380736, – wc – 25 - 130. AE E VISA
st. : M *(closed 1 to 30 August)* 110/148 – 21 – **130 rm** 195/240.

La Croix Rousse :

Lyon Métropole M, 85 quai J.-Gillet 69004 78 29 20 20, Telex 380198, , , – – 700. AE E VISA
Les Eaux Vives **M** 105/155 - **Le Grill M** a la carte approx 105 – 25 – **119 rm** 313/365.

Les Brotteaux :

Roosevelt M without rest, 25 r. Bossuet 69006, 78 52 35 67, Telex 300295 – kitchenette – 60. AE E VISA
st. : 25 – **87 rm** 252/315.

Olympique without rest, 62 r. Garibaldi 69006 78 89 48 04 – wc wc . VISA
st. : 15,50 – **23 rm** 161/178.

Britania without rest, 17 r. Prof.-Weill, 69006, 78 52 86 52 – wc wc
st. : 16,50 – **22 rm** 161/190.

La Part-Dieu :

Frantel M, 129 r. Servient (32nd floor) 69003 78 62 94 12, Telex 380088, Lyons, Valley of the Rhône – – 300. AE E VISA
st. : rest. **L'Arc-en-Ciel** *(closed 12 July-19 August, Monday lunch and Sunday)* **M** a la carte 185/245 - **La Ripaille** (Grill) (ground floor) *(closed Friday dinner and Saturday)* **M** 69 /115 – 45 – **242 rm** 475/600.

Mercure M, 47 bd Vivier Merle 69003 72 34 18 12, Telex 306469 – – 150. AE E VISA
M a la carte approx. 120 – 33 – **124 rm** 330/380.

Athéna La Part-Dieu M without rest, 45 bd Vivier Merle 69003 72 33 70 04, Telex 306412 – wc . VISA
st. : 24 – **122 rm** 230/245.

Créqui M without rest, 158 r. Créqui, 69003, 78 60 02 47 – wc . VISA
st. : 26 – **28 rm** 228/262.

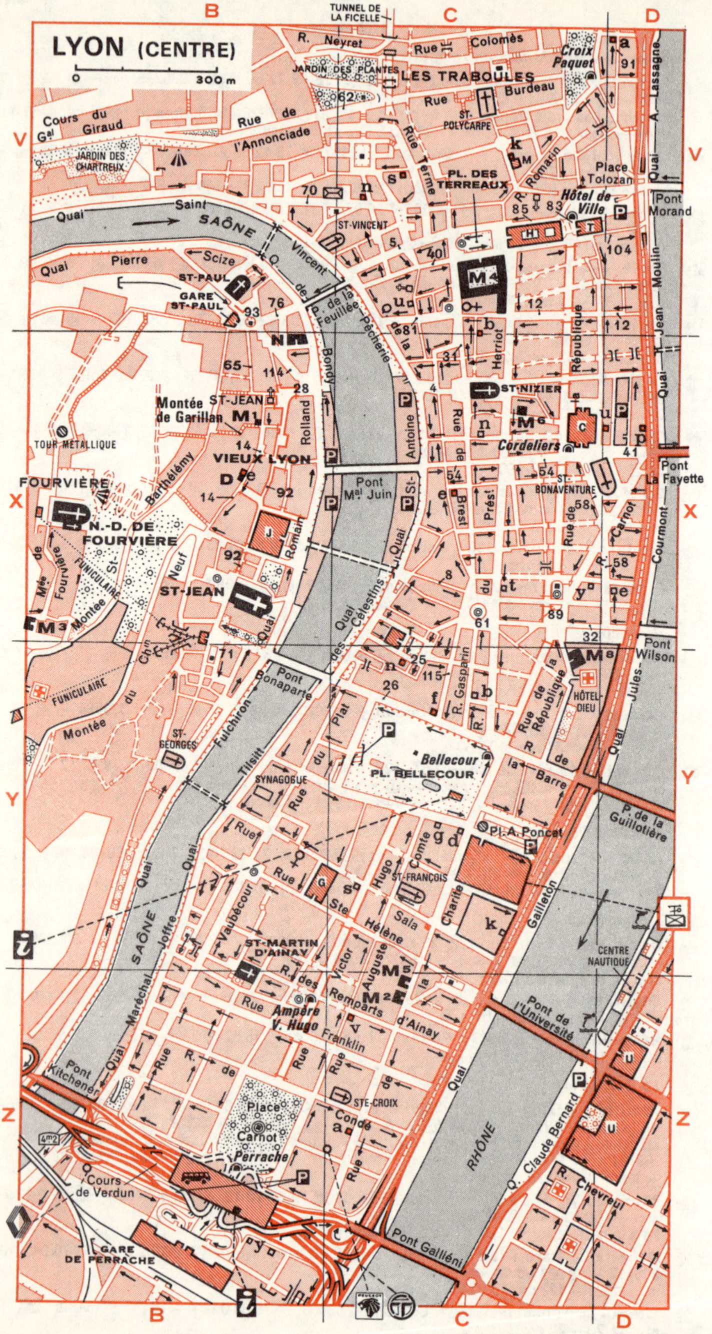

LYON (CENTRE)
300 m
B
C
D
V
X
Y
Z
TUNNEL DE LA FICELLE
R. Neyret
Rue Colomès
JARDIN DES PLANTES
LES TRABOULES
Croix Paquet
Rue Burdeau
A. Lassagne
ST. POLYCARPE
Cours du Gal Giraud
Rue de l'Annonciade
JARDIN DES CHARTREUX
Rue Terme
R. Romarin
Place Tolozan
PL. DES TERREAUX
Hôtel de Ville
Pont Morand
ST-VINCENT
Quai Saint Vincent
SAÔNE
Quai Pierre Scize
ST-PAUL
GARE ST-PAUL
P. de la Feuillée
Pêcherie
Quai Jean Moulin
Herriot
République
Bondy
Rolland
Montée de Garillan
ST-JEAN
TOUR MÉTALLIQUE
ST-NIZIER
Cordeliers
Antoine
Rue de Brest
VIEUX LYON
Pont La Fayette
FOURVIÈRE
Barthélemy
Pont Mal Juin
St-Antoine
Quai
Prést
ST-BONAVENTURE
N.-D. DE FOURVIÈRE
Romain
Carnot
Cournont
FUNICULAIRE
Fourvière
Montée St-Barthélemy
Neuf
ST-JEAN
Quai des Célestins
Pont Wilson
Chn
Pont Bonaparte
Fulchiron
R. Gasparin
Rue de la République
HÔTEL-DIEU
Quai Jules Courmont
FUNICULAIRE
Montée du Chemin Neuf
ST-GEORGES
Tilsitt
Rue du Plat
Bellecour
PL. BELLECOUR
R. de la Barre
SYNAGOGUE
Pl. A. Poncet
P. de la Guillotière
Quai Fulchiron
Rue Comte
Hugo
ST-FRANÇOIS
Rue Ste Hélène
Sala
Charité
Gailleton
Quai Tilsitt
Vaubecour
Victor
Auguste
CENTRE NAUTIQUE
ST-MARTIN D'AINAY
R. des Remparts d'Ainay
Ampère V. Hugo
Franklin
Pont de l'Université
Quai Maréchal Joffre
Pont Kitchener
Quai
R. de
Rue
STE-CROIX
Condé
Place Carnot
Perrache
Cours de Verdun
RHÔNE
Q. Claude Bernard
R. Chevreul
GARE DE PERRACHE
Pont Galliéni

STREET INDEX TO LYON TOWN PLAN

République (R.)	CX	
Terme (R.)	CV	
Victor-Hugo (R.)	CY	
Alnay (Remp. d')	CZ	
Albon (Pl.)	CX	4
Algérie (R. d')	CV	5
Anc.-Préfect. (R.)	CX	8
Annonciade (R.)	BV	
Barre (R. de la)	CY	
Bât-d'Argent (R.)	CV	12
Bellecour (Pl.)	CY	
Bœuf (R. du)	BX	14
Bonaparte (Pont)	BY	
Bondy (Quai de)	BX	
Brest (R. de)	CX	
Burdeau (R.)	CV	
Carnot (Pl.)	BZ	
Carnot (R.)	DX	
Célestins (Pl. des)	CY	25
Célestins (Q. des)	CX	
Chambonnet (R.)	CY	26
Change (Pl. du)	BX	28
Charité (R. de la)	CY	
Ch.-Neuf (Montée)	BX	
Chenevard (R. P.)	CX	31
Chevreul (R.)	DZ	
Childebert (R.)	CX	32
Cl.-Bernard (Quai)	CZ	
Colomès (R.)	CV	
Comte (R. A.)	CY	
Condé (R. de)	CZ	
Constantine (R.)	CV	40
Cordeliers (Pl.)	DX	41
Courmont (Quai J.)	DX	
Feuillée (P. de la)	BV	
Fourvière (Mtée de)	BX	
Franklin (R.)	CZ	
Fulchiron (Quai)	BY	
Gailleton (Quai)	CY	
Gallieni (Pont)	CZ	
Gasparin (R.)	CY	
Giraud (Crs Gén.)	BV	
Grenette (R.)	CX	54
Grolée (R.)	DX	58
Guillotière (P. de la)	DY	
Jacobins (Pl. des)	CX	61
Jardin-Plantes (R.)	CV	62
Joffre (Quai Mar.)	BZ	
Juin (Pont Mar.)	CX	
Juiverie (R.)	BX	65
Kitchener (Pont)	BZ	
La Fayette (Pont)	DX	
Lassagne (Quai A.)	DV	
Martinière (R.)	BV	70
Max (Av. Adolphe)	BY	71
Morand (Pont)	DV	
Moulin (Quai J.)	DV	
Neyret (R.)	BV	
Octavio-Mey (R.)	BV	76
Pêcherie (Quai)	CX	
Plat (R. du)	BY	
Platière (R. de la)	CV	81
Poncet (Pl. A.)	CY	
Pradel (Pl. Louis)	CV	83
Prés.-Herriot (R.)	CX	
Puits-Gaillot (R.)	CV	85
République (Pl.)	CX	89
Rom.-Rolland (Quai)	BX	
Romarin (R.)	CV	
Royale (R.)	DV	91
St-Antoine (Quai)	CX	
St-Barthélemy (Montée)	BX	
St-Jean (R.)	BX	92
St-Paul (Pl.)	BV	93
St-Vincent (Quai)	BV	
Ste-Hélène (R.)	CY	
Sala (Rue)	CY	
Scize (Quai Pierre)	BV	
Serlin (R. J.)	DV	104
Terreaux (Pl. des)	CV	
Tilsitt (Quai)	BY	
Tolozan (Pl.)	DV	
Université (P. de l')	CZ	
Vaubécour (R.)	BY	
Verdun (Cours de)	BZ	
Vernay (R. Fr.)	BX	114
Wilson (Pont)	DX	
Zola (R. Émile)	CY	115

La Guillotière :

Gd H. Helder et Institut without rest, 38 r. de Marseille ✉ 69007 ☎ 78 72 09 39, Telex 306411 – wc wc. AE VISA d
st. : 110 rm 195/240.

Urbis Université M without rest, 51 r. Université, ✉ 69007, ☎ 78 72 78 42, Telex 340455 – TV wc wc. AE E VISA
st. : 26 – **53 rm** 234/268.

Gerland :

Mercure M, 70 av. Leclerc ✉ 69007 ☎ 78 58 68 53, Telex 305484, – TV – 450. AE E VISA
M a la carte approx. 120 – 32 – **194 rm** 330/450.

Monchat-Monplaisir :

Park H. P.L.M M, 4 r. Prof.-Calmette, ✉ 69008, ☎ 78 74 11 20, Telex 380230, – TV – 30. AE VISA
st. : le Patio *(closed Saturday, Sunday and Bank Holidays)* **M** 85 b.i. – 30 – **70 rm** 275/320.

Lyon-Est M without rest, 104 rte Genas, ✉ 69003, ☎ 78 54 64 53 – TV wc wc. AE E VISA
st. : 23 – **42 rm** 130/270.

à Villeurbanne :

Congrès et rest. Le Grand Camp M, pl. Cdt Rivière ✉ 69100 Villeurbanne ☎ 78 89 81 10, Telex 370216 – TV – 120. AE E VISA
M *(closed Sunday and Bank Holidays)* 63/155 – 20 – **132 rm** 250.

Athena-Tolstoï, 90 cours Tolstoï ✉ 69100 Villeurbanne ☎ 78 68 81 21, Telex 330574 – wc – 200. VISA. rest
st. : M *(closed Saturday and Sunday)* 70/106 – 19 – **137 rm** 190/231.

Restaurants

XXXXX ✿✿✿ **Paul Bocuse** bridge of **Collonges, 12 km by the banks of the River Saône (D443, D51)** ✉ **69660 Collonges-au-Mont-d'Or,** ☎ **78 24 01 40, Telex 375382, « Tasteful decor »** – . AE VISA
M 280/400 and a la carte
Spec. Soupe aux truffes noires, Loup farci à la mousse de homard, Volaille de Bresse en vessie. **Wines** Pouilly-Fuissé, Brouilly.

XXX ✿ **Tour Rose** (Chavent), 16 r. Boeuf, ✉ 69005, ☎ 78 37 25 90, « 17C house in the old part of Lyons » – . AE E VISA BX e
closed Sunday – **M** 180/350
Spec. Saumon mi-cuit au fumoir, Bisque d'Oursins, Noisettes d'agneau rôties. **Wines** St-Véran, Brouilly.

XXX ✿✿ **Orsi,** 3 pl. Kléber, ✉ 69006, ☎ 78 89 57 68, Telex 305965, « Elegant setting » – . AE VISA
closed August, Saturday from 1 May-31 July, Sunday and Bank Holidays – **st. : M** 180/260 and a la carte
Spec. Aiguillettes de canard aux champignons, Filets de sandre en papillote, Pigeonneau de Bresse en cocotte. **Wines** St-Véran, St-Amour.

XXX ✿✿ **Vettard,** 7 pl. Bellecour, ✉ 69002, ✆ 78 42 07 59 – ▤. AE ① VISA CY **f**
closed 19 July-18 August, Saturday dinner in June, July and Sunday – **M** (at rest.) 210/300 and a la carte - **Café Neuf M** a la carte approx. 125
Spec. Loup à l'huile d'olive et vinaigre de Xérès, Quenelle de brochet, Poulet de Bresse en chemise. **Wines** Chiroubles, Mâcon Vire.

XXX ✿ **Henry, 27 r. Martinière, ✉ 69001, ✆ 78 28 26 08, mural paintings** – ▤ CV **n**

XXX ✿✿ **Nandron,** 26 quai J.-Moulin, ✉ 69002, ✆ 78 42 10 26 – ▤. AE ① E VISA DX **p**
closed 26 July-24 August, Friday dinner and Saturday – **M** 150/300 and a la carte
Spec. Quenelles de brochet, Terrine de champignons, Ris de veau aux truffes. **Wines** Brouilly, St-Véran.

XXX ✿ **Bourillot,** 8 pl. Célestins, ✉ 69002, ✆ 78 37 38 64 – ▤. AE ① VISA CY **n**
closed 30 June-29 July, 24 December-2 January, Sunday and Bank Holidays – **M** 150/200
Spec. Homard sauté en escabèche, Volaille de Bresse Marie, Soufflé glacé au chocolat.. **Wines** Côteaux du Lyonnais.

XXX ✿✿ **Léon de Lyon** (Lacombe), 1 r. Pleney, ✉ 69001, ✆ 78 28 11 33, « typical local establishment » – ▤. VISA CVX **b**
closed 23 December-8 January, Monday lunch, Sunday and Bank Holidays – **M** 150/310 and a la carte
Spec. Filets de rouget poêlés, Chartreuse de ris de veau aux choux, Aile de poularde farcie au foie gras. **Wines** Beaujolais-Village, Mâçonnais.

XXX ✿ **Mère Brazier,** 12 r. Royale, ✉ 69001, ✆ 78 28 15 49, « typical local establishment » – ▤. AE ① VISA DV **a**
closed August, Saturday lunch and Sunday – **M** (▤ 1st floor) 175/200
Spec. Fonds d'artichaut au foie gras, Quenelle au gratin, Volaille demi-deuil. **Wines** St Joseph, Montagnieu.

XXX ✿ **Aub. de Fond-Rose** (Brunet), 23 quai Clemenceau, ✉ 69300, Caluire ✆ 78 29 34 61, 🍽, « Garden » – ℗. AE ① E VISA
closed February, Monday from 1 October-30 April and Sunday dinner – **M** 165/320
Spec. Marinade de rouget, Filet de loup aux herbes, Cuisses de canard aux poires. **Wines** St-Véran, Brouilly.

XXX **Cazenove,** 75 r. Boileau ✉ 69006 ✆ 78 89 82 92 – ▤. AE VISA
closed August, Saturday and Sunday – **st. : M** a la carte 140/240.

XXX ✿ **Daniel et Denise** (Léron), 2 r. Tupin, ✉ 69002, ✆ 78 37 49 98 – ▤. AE ① VISA CX **e**
closed August, Sunday, Monday lunch and Bank Holidays – **M** 115/300
Spec. Terrine de homard, Gratin de queues d'écrevisses (July-April), Filet d'agneau en croûte. **Wines** Chiroubles,St-Joseph.

XXX **Le Rocher,** quartier St-Rambert, 8 quai R.-Carrié, ✉ 69009, ✆ 78 83 99 72, 🍽 – ℗. VISA
closed 12 August-2 September, 24 December-6 January, Saturday (except dinner from May to October) and Sunday – **st. : M** 103/243.

XXX ✿ **Le Quatre Saisons** (Bertoli), 15 r. Sully ✉ 69006 ✆ 78.93.76.07 – ▤. AE ① VISA
closed August, Saturday except dinner from 1 August-31 May, Sunday and Bank Holidays – **M** 150/210
Spec. Foie gras, Rognon de veau cuit dans sa graisse, Nougatine glacée. **Wines** Chiroubles, St-Véran.

XXX ✿ **Les Fantasques,** 47 r. Bourse, ✉ 69002, ✆ 78 37 36 58 – ▤. AE VISA DX **u**
closed 9 to 25 August and Sunday – **M** 145/250
Spec. Terrine de homard, Rouget en papillote, St-Jacques. **Wines** Mâcon, Brouilly.

XX **Le Gourmandin,** 156 r. P.-Bert ✉ 69003 ✆ 78 62 78 77 – ▤. AE ① VISA
closed 25 July-28 August, Saturday, Sunday and Bank Holidays – **st. : M** 108/240.

XX ✿ **Chez Gervais** (Lescuyer), 42 r. P.-Corneille, ✉ 69006, ✆ 78 52 19 13 – ▤. AE ① E VISA
closed July, Saturday 1er May to 15 September, Sunday and Bank Holidays – **st. : M** 135/350
Spec. Salade de ris de veau, Fricassée de volaille au vinaigre de framboises, Coupe Florence. **Wines** Chiroubles, St-Joseph.

XX **Tante Alice,** 22 r. Remparts-d'Ainay ✉ 69002 ✆ 78 37 49 83 – ▤. AE CZ **v**
closed Easter, 18 July-25 August, 25 December-2 January, Friday dinner and Saturday – **M** 64/140 🍷.

XX **Chevallier,** 40 r. du Sergent-Blandan, ✉ 69001, ✆ 78 28 19 83 – VISA CV **s**
closed September, 15 to 27 February, Tuesday and Wednesday – **st. : M** 74/134.

XX **Les Grillons,** 18 r. D.-Vincent at Champagne-au-Mont-d'Or ✉ 69410 Champagne, ✆ 78 35 04 78, 🍽 – ℗. AE ① E VISA
closed 3-21 November, Sunday dinner and Monday – **M** 95/179.

XX **Au Petit Col,** 68 r. Charité, ✉ 69002, ✆ 78 37 25 18 – ▤. AE VISA CZ **a**
closed 19 July-21 August, 24 December-2 January, Sunday dinner and Monday – **st. : M** 71/134.

X **La Bonne Auberge "Chez Jo",** 48 av. Félix-Faure, ✉ 69003, ✆ 78 60 00 57 – ▤. AE ① VISA
closed August, Saturday dinner and Sunday – **st. : M** 80/120.

X **Pied de Cochon,** 9 r. St-Polycarpe, ✉ 69001, ✆ 78 28 15 31 – AE ① CV **k**
closed August, Saturday (except dinner out of season) and Sunday – **st. : M** 83/195.

Environs

at Bron – pop. 41 500 . – ✉ **69500** Bron :

Novotel Ⓜ, r. Lionel Terray ✆ 78 26 97 48, Telex 340781, – 25 - 700. AE ⓓ E VISA
M a la carte approx. 115 – 35 – **196 rm** 312.

Dau Ly without rest, 28 r. de Prévieux ✆ 78 26 04 37 – wc wc . AE VISA
st. : 18 – **22 rm** 162/225.

at Tassin-la-Demi-Lune 5 km by D 407 – pop. 15 034 – ✉ **69160** Tassin-la-Demi-Lune :

XXX **Les Tilleuls,** 146 av. Ch.-de-Gaulle ✆ 78 34 19 58, – . AE VISA
closed 16 to 26 August, February Holidays, Sunday dinner and Monday except Bank Holidays – **st. : M** 85/210.

to the NE :

at Crépieux-la-Pape : 7 km by N 83 and N 84 – ✉ **69140** Rillieux-la-Pape :

XXX ✿ **Larivoire** (Constantin), ✆ 78 88 50 92, ←, – . AE ⓓ VISA
closed 2 to 9 September, 11 February-4 March, Monday dinner and Tuesday – **st. : M** 125/210
Spec. Huîtres chaudes au Montagnieu (September to April), Fricassée de volaille au vinaigre, Pigeonneau aux raisins. **Wines** Montagnieu, Côteaux du Lyonnais.

by the SE :

at St-Priest : 12 km by N 6 and D 148 – pop. 42 913 – ✉ **69800** St-Priest :

Moderne Ⓜ, 64 rte Heyrieux ✆ 78 20 47 46 – wc . AE ⓓ VISA
closed August – **st. :** 20 – **35 rm** 210/300.

at the airport of Satolas : 27 km by A 43 – ✉ **69125** Lyon Satolas Airport :

Méridien Ⓜ, 3rd floor ✆ 78 71 91 61, Telex 380480, ← – – 250. AE ⓓ E VISA
st. : M rest. see **La Gde Corbeille** below – 39 – **120 rm** 390/480.

XXX **La Gde Corbeille,** 1st floor ✆ 78 71 91 62, ← – . AE ⓓ VISA
closed August and Saturday – **st. : M** 155/190.

to the W :

at Charbonnières-les-Bains : 8 km by N 7 – pop. 3 973 – alt. 240 – Spa – Casino – ✉ **69260** Charbonnières-les-Bains :

Mercure Ⓜ, N 7 ✆ 78 34 72 79, Telex 900972, – wc – 25 - 75. AE ⓓ E VISA
M *(closed Saturday and Sunday)* (dinner only) a la carte approx. 120 – 27 – **60 rm** 229/275.

Beaulieu without rest, 19 av. Gén.-de-Gaulle ✆ 78 87 12 04 – wc – 100. AE ⓓ
st. : 17,50 – **40 rm** 141/179.

XX **Gigandon,** 5 av. Gén.-de-Gaulle ✆ 78 87 15 51 – AE VISA
closed August, 24 December-1 January, Sunday dinner and Monday – **st. : M** 75/190.

Porte de Lyon - motorway junction A 6 N 6 Exit road signposted Limonest N : 10 km – ✉ **69570** Dardilly :

Novotel Lyon-Nord Ⓜ , ✆ 78 35 13 41, Telex 330962, , , – – 150. AE ⓓ E VISA
M a la carte approx 100 – 35 – **107 rm** 309/320.

Best Western Ⓜ, ✆ 78 35 70 20, Telex 900006, – – 350. AE ⓓ E VISA
st. : Grill la Braise **M** 80/250 – 39 – **204 rm** 320/450.

Mercure Ⓜ, ✆ 78 35 28 05, Telex 330045, , – rest – 250. AE ⓓ E VISA
M a la carte approx 120 – 33 – **175 rm** 205/285.

Campanile, ✆ 78 35 48 44, Telex 310155 – wc . VISA
st. : M 61 b.i./82 b.i. – 23 – **46 rm** 194/215.

XX **Le Panorama,** at Dardilly-le-Haut, near the church, ✉ 69570 Dardilly, ✆ 78 47 40 19, , – AE VISA
closed July, February holidays, Tuesday, dinner Sunday and Monday – **st. : M** 161/300.

Michelin puts no plaque or sign
on the hotels and restaurants mentioned in this Guide.

Chagny 71150 S.-et-L. 69 ⑨ – pop. 5 604 – alt. 216.
Lyon 143.

❀❀❀ **Lameloise** Ⓜ, pl. d'Armes ✆ 85 87 08 85, « Old Burgundian house, tasteful decor » – rest
closed 9 December-8 January, Thursday lunch and Wednesday – **M** (booking essential) a la carte 220/350 – ☕ 45 – **20 rm** 280/700
Spec. Ravioli d'escargots, Pigeon de Bresse en vessie, Assiette du chocolatier. **Wines** Rully, Chassagne-Montrachet.

Condrieu 69420 Rhône 74 ⑪ – pop. 3 158 – alt. 150.
Lyon 40.

❀❀ **Hôt. Beau Rivage (Mme Castaing)** Ⓜ, ✆ 74 59 52 24, Telex 308946, « Terrace with view of Rhône River », – Ⓟ. AE ⓓ E VISA
closed 5 January-15 February – **M** 180/260 and a la carte – ☕ 36 – **22 rm** 200/380
Spec. Boudin de brochet au coulis de homard, Rouelle d'anguille à la mousse de cresson, Paupiette de boeuf au foie gras. **Wines** Viognier, St-Joseph.

Fleurie 69820 Rhône 74 ① – pop. 1 151 – alt. 295.
Lyon 58.

XXX ❀❀ **Aub. du Cep** (Cortembert), pl. de l'Eglise ✆ 74 04 10 77, – AE E VISA
closed December, Sunday dinner and Monday – **st. : M** (dinner : booking essential) 150/350 and a la carte
Spec. Mousseline de sandre, Fricassée de volaille au Fleurie, Entremets glacé moka nougatine. **Wines** Beaujolais, Fleurie.

Mionnay 01 Ain 74 ② – pop. 796 – alt. 288 – ✉ 01390 St-André-de-Corcy.
Lyon 20.

XXXX ❀❀❀ **Alain Chapel** with rm, ✆ 78 91 82 02, Telex 305605, « flowered garden » – wc Ⓟ
closed January, Tuesday lunch and Monday except Bank Holidays – **M** 280/500 and a la carte – ☕ 70 – **13 rm** 550/725
Spec. Gratin de cèpes (15 September-15 November), Petite tripière de pieds et ris de veau (15 April-15 October). **Wines** Chardonnay du Bugey, Fleurie.

Montrond-les-Bains 42210 Loire 73 ⑱ – pop. 3 194 – alt. 356.
Lyon 68.

❀❀ **Host. La Poularde** (Randoing), ✆ 77 54 40 06 – Ⓟ – 40. AE ⓓ VISA. rest
closed 2-15 January, Monday dinner and Tuesday lunch – **st. : M** (Sunday : booking essential) 135/350 and a la carte – ☕ 35 – **15 rm** 180/320
Spec. Feuilleté d'amourettes, ris de veau et crêtes de coq, Escalope de foie chaud aux navets, Coeur de charolais aux échalotes. **Wines** Chassagne-Montrachet, Fleurie.

Roanne 42300 Loire 73 ⑦ – pop. 49 638 – alt. 279.
Lyon 86.

❀❀❀ **H. des Frères Troisgros** Ⓜ, pl. Gare ✆ 77 71 66 97, Telex 307507 – rest Ⓟ. AE ⓓ VISA
closed 4 to 20 August, January, Wednesday lunch and Tuesday – **M** (booking essential) 200/380 and a la carte – ☕ 55 – **18 rm** 420/520, 6 apartments 720/850
Spec. Aubergines aux queues d'écrevisses (Spring-Summer), Filets de Sole, Soufflé tiède au caramel. **Wines** Beaujolais, Vins de Bourgogne.

St-Étienne 42000 Loire 73 ⑲, 76 ⑨ – pop. 206 087 – alt. 517 – Lyon 63.

XXX ❀❀ **Pierre Gagnaire** 3 r. G.-Teissier ✆ 77 37 57 93 – AE ⓓ VISA
closed August, February Holidays, Sunday and Monday – **st. : M** 160/330
Spec. Poëlée d'asperges et pommes de terre nouvelles au beurre de truffes (April-June), Produits de la mer, Confit de pigeon. **Wines** St-Joseph.

Valence Ⓟ 26000 Drôme 77 ⑫ – pop. 68 157 – alt. 123 – Lyon 99.

XXXX ❀❀❀ **Pic** with rm 285 av. Victor-Hugo, Motorway exit sign-posted Valence-Sud ✆ 75 44 15 32, « Shaded garden » – rest wc Ⓟ. AE ⓓ
closed 4 to 27 August, February Holidays, Sunday dinner and Wednesday – **st. : M** (Sunday : booking essential) 320/400 – ☕ 40 – **5 rm** 350/750
Spec. Menu Rabelais. **Wines** Crozes-Hermitage, St Péray.

at Pont de l'Isère – ✉ **2660010** Tain-l'Hermitage

XXX ❀❀ **Chabran** Ⓜ with rm, N7, Motorway exit sign-posted Valence-Nord ✆ 75 84 60 09, – wc Ⓟ. VISA
closed Sunday dinner, Monday and Tuesday lunch in season – **st. : M** 180/360 and a la carte – ☕ 40 – **12 ch** 220/400
Spec. Filets de rouget tièdes, Saumon rôti, Canette rôtie. **Wines** Hermitage, St-Joseph.

Vienne 38200 Isère 74 ⑪⑫ – pop. 29 050 – alt. 158.

Lyon 30.

XXXX ✿✿✿ **Pyramide** (Mme Point), bd F.-Point ✆ 74 53 01 96, « flowered garden » – ▤ Ⓟ. AE ⓓ
closed February, Monday dinner and Tuesday – **M** (booking essential) 340/400 and a la carte
Spec. Assiette de marée, Filet de turbot au champagne,. **Wines** Condrieu, Côte Rôtie.

Vonnas 01540 Ain 74 ② – pop. 2 505 – alt. 189.

Lyon 66.

✿✿✿ **Georges Blanc** Ⓜ, ✆ 74 50 00 10, Telex 380776, ⛱, ⛉, ⚘ – ▤ rest TV ☎ ⇔ Ⓟ. AE ⓓ VISA
closed 2 January-10 February – **M** *(closed Thursday except dinner from 15 June-15 September and Wednesday except Bank Holidays)* (booking essential) 240/360 and a la carte – ☕ 46 – **24 rm** 460/1 100, 6 apartments
Spec. Crêpe parmentière au saumon et caviar, Bar à la marinière, Poularde de Bresse aux gousses d'ail et au foie gras. **Wines** Mâcon blanc, Chiroubles.

MARSEILLES

Ⓟ 13 B.-du-R. 84 ⑬ – pop. 878 689.

See : N.-D.-de-la-Garde Basilica ☼* BY – La Canebière** CV – Old Port** ABVX – Corniche Président-J.-F.-Kennedy** – Modern Port** – Palais Longchamp* DU – St-Victor Basilica* : crypt** AX – Old Major Cathedral* AU N – Pharo Parc ≤* AX – St-Laurent Belvedere ≤* AV E – Museum : Grobet-Labadié** DU M4, Cantini* : Marseilles and Moustiers pottery** (galerie de la Faïence de Marseille et de Moustiers) CX M3 – Fine Arts* and Natural History Museum* (Longchamp Palace) DU M, – Mediterranean Archeology* Egyptian antiquities** (Château Borely), Roman Docks* ABV M2, – Old Marseilles* AV M1.**

Envir. : Corniche road of Callelongue S : 13 km.**

Exc. : Château d'If (☼***) 1 h 30.**

⛳18 of Aix-Marseilles ✆ 24 20 41 to the North : 22 km.

✈ Marseille-Provence Air France ✆ 91 89 90 10 to the North : 28 km.

🚗 ✆ 91 08 50 50.

⛴ for Corsica : Société Nationale Maritime Corse-Méditerranée, 61 bd des Dames (2e) ✆ 91 56 32 00 AU.

ℹ and Accueil de France (Information and hotel reservations - not more than 5 days in advance), 4 Canebière, 13001, ✆ 91 54 91 11, Telex 430402 - and at St-Charles railway Station ✆ 91 50 59 18 – A.C. 143 cours Lieutaud, 13006, ✆ 91 47 86 23.

Paris 776 – Lyon 315 – Nice 187 – Torino 407 – Toulon 64 – Toulouse 404.

Plan on following pages

Sofitel Vieux Port Ⓜ, 36 bd Ch.-Livon, ✉ 13007, ✆ 91 52 90 19, Telex 401270, panoramic restaurant ≤ old port, ⛱ – 🛗 ▤ TV ☎ ♿ ⇔ Ⓟ – 🎤 100 - 450. AE ⓓ E VISA AX **n**
rest. **les Trois Forts** *(closed August)* **M** a la carte 185/260 - **Le Jardin** *(closed Saturday and Sunday from 15 September-15 June)* **M** a la carte approx. 120 🍷 – ☕ 45 – **219 rm** 415/855, 3 apartments.

Frantel Ⓜ, r. Neuve St-Martin, ✉ 13001, ✆ 91 91 91 29, Telex 401886, ⛱ – 🛗 ▤ TV ☎ ♿ – 🎤 400. AE ⓓ E VISA BUV **g**
st. : rest. **L'Oursinade** *(closed 25 July-1 September, Sunday and Bank Holidays)* **M** a la carte 185/250 - **L'Oliveraie** (Grill) *(closed dinner Friday and Saturday)* **M** a la carte approx. 100 – ☕ 42 – **200 rm** 440/546, 4 apartments 900.

P.L.M. Beauvau without rest, 4 r. Beauvau ✉ 13001 ✆ 91 54 91 00, Telex 401778 – 🛗 ▤ TV ☎. AE ⓓ E VISA BV **r**
st. : ☕ 50 – **71 rm** 450/570.

Concorde-Prado Ⓜ, 11 av. Mazargues, ✉ 13008, ✆ 91 76 51 11, Telex 420209 – 🛗 ▤ TV ☎ ⇔ – 🎤 80. AE ⓓ E VISA
st. : **M** 100/150 🍷 – ☕ 42 – **100 rm** 425/468.

Résidence Bompard 🐎 without rest, 2 r. Flots-Bleus, ✉ 13007, ✆ 91 52 10 93, Telex 400430, ⛉ – 🛗 kitchenette TV ☎ ♿ Ⓟ – 🎤 40. AE ⓓ
st. : ☕ 25 – **47 rm** 225/295.

Gd H. Noailles, 66 Canebière, ✉ 13001, ✆ 91 54 91 48, Telex 430609 – 🛗 ▤ rm TV ☎ – 🎤 30 - 60. AE ⓓ E VISA CV **x**
st. : **M** *(closed Sunday)* 160 – ☕ 30 – **70 rm** 250/460, 4 apartments 550.

Gd H. Genève without rest, 3 bis r. Reine-Élisabeth, ✉ 13001, ✆ 91 90 51 42, Telex 440672 – 🛗 TV ☎. ⓓ VISA. ✂ BV **e**
st. : ☕ 21 – **45 rm** 128/286, 4 apartments 337.

Castellane Ⓜ without rest, 31 r. Rouet ✉ 13006 ✆ 91 79 27 54 – 🛗 TV 🛁wc ☎ ⇔. AE VISA DY **f**
st. : ☕ 28 – **55 rm** 221/291.

Européen without rest, 115 r. Paradis, ✉ 13006, ✆ 91 37 77 20 – 🛗 ▤ 🛁wc 🚿wc ☎ CY **u**
closed August – **st.** : ☕ 18 – **43 rm** 120/210.

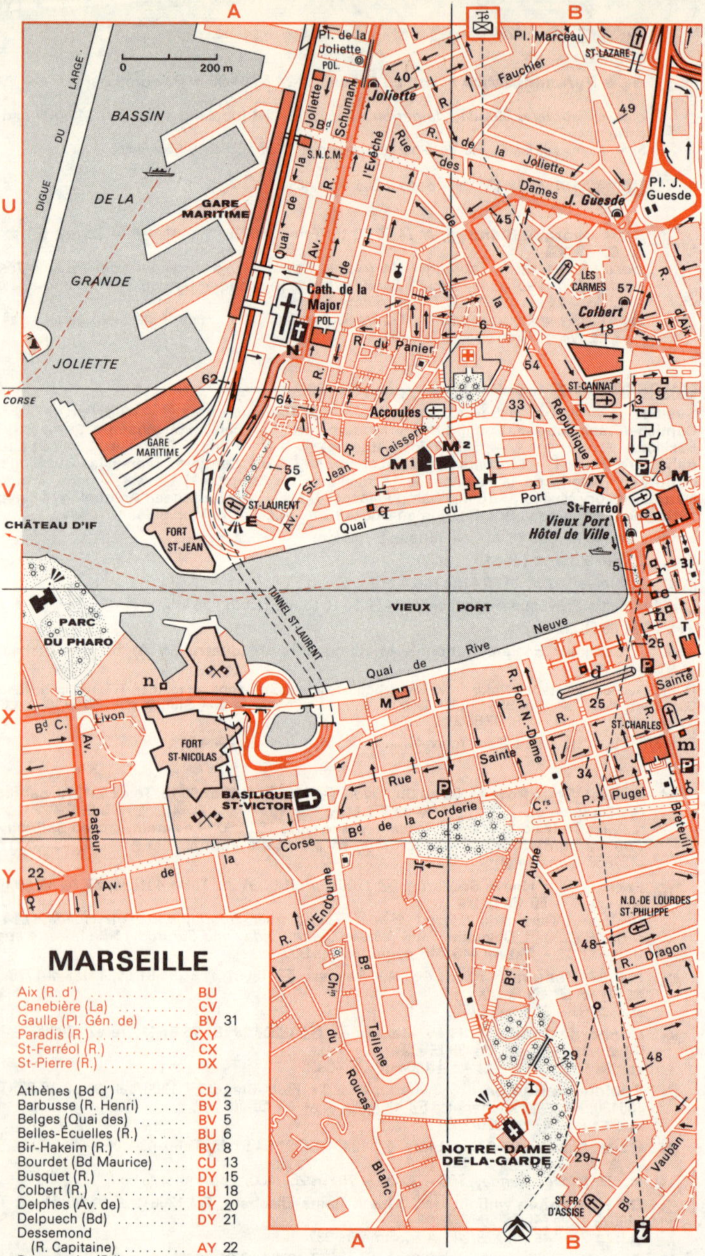

MARSEILLE

Aix (R. d') .... BU
Canebière (La) CV
Gaulle (Pl. Gén. de) ...... BV 31
Paradis (R.) .... CXY
St-Ferréol (R.) CX
St-Pierre (R.) .... DX

Athènes (Bd d') .... CU 2
Barbusse (R. Henri) ...... BV 3
Belges (Quai des) .... BV 5
Belles-Écuelles (R.) ...... BU 6
Bir-Hakeim (R.) .... BV 8
Bourdet (Bd Maurice) .... CU 13
Busquet (R.) .... DY 15
Colbert (R.) .... BU 18
Delphes (Av. de) .... DY 20
Delpuech (Bd) .... DY 21
Dessemond (R. Capitaine) .... AY 22
Dugommier (Bd) .... CV 23
Estienne-d'Orves (Cours) .... BX 25
Fabres (R. des) .... CV 27
Fort-du-Sanctuaire (R. du) .... BY 29
Garibaldi (Bd) .... CV 30
Grand'Rue .... BV 33
Grignon (R.) .... BX 34
Iéna (R. d') .... DY 35
Leblanc (R. V.) .... AU 40
Liberté (Bd de la) ...... CU 42
Moisson (R. F.) .... BU 45
Montricher (Bd) .... DU 46

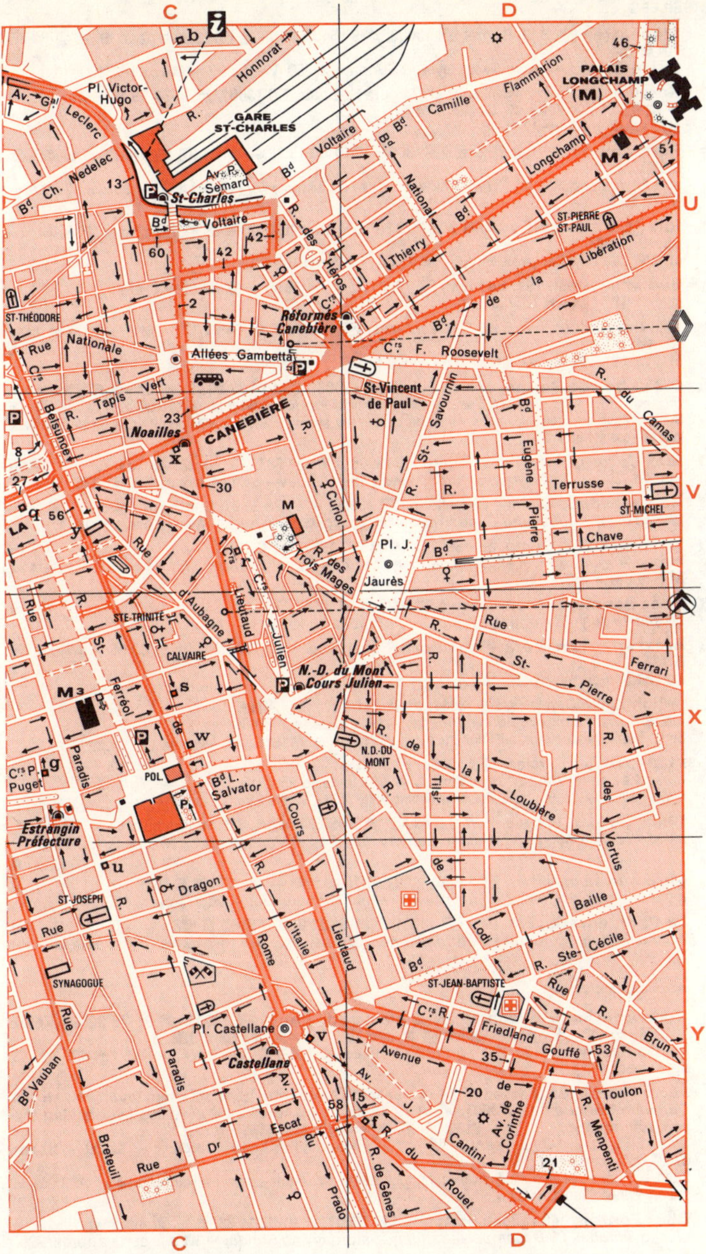

Notre-Dame (Bd)	BY	48	Sadi-Carnot (Pl.)	BU	54	Ste-Philomène (R.)	CY	58
Pelletan (Av. C.)	BU	49	St-Laurent (R.)	AV	55	Sembat (R. Marcel)	CU	60
Philipon (Bd)	DU	51	St-Louis (Crs)	CV	56	Tourette (Quai)	AU	62
Raynouard (Traverse)	DY	53	Ste-Barbe (R.)	BU	57	Vaudoyer (Av.)	AV	64

Manhattan M, 3 pl. Rome, ✉ 13006, ✆ 91 54 35 95 – |‡| TV ⊏wc ⋒wc ☎ – 🅰 80. AE ◑ E VISA CX **w**
st. : M *(closed August, Saturday and Sunday)* 68/250 ⅉ – ⊐ 22 – **41 rm** 190/280.

Rome et St Pierre without rest, 7 cours St-Louis, ✉ 13001, ✆ 91 54 19 52, Telex 430641 – |‡| TV ⊏wc ⋒wc ☎. AE ◑ E VISA CV **y**
st. : ⊐ 22 – **63 rm** 114/278.

Petit Louvre, 19 Canebière, ✉ 13001, ✆ 91 90 13 78 – |‡| ▤ TV ⊏wc ⋒wc ☎. AE ◑ E VISA. ✖ rest CV **q**
st. : M *(closed Sunday from 1 November to 31 March)* 75/110 – ⊐ 22 – **33 rm** 174/278 – P 310/360.

Ibis M, 6 r. Cassis ✉ 13008 ✆ 91 78 59 25, Telex 400362 – |‡| ▤ TV ⊏wc ☎ ♿ 🚗 – 🅰 40. E VISA
st. : M a la carte approx. 85 ⅉ – ☕ 19.50 – **119 rm** 190/241.

Sud without rest, 18 r. Beauvau ✉ 13001 ✆ 91 54 38 50 – |‡| ▤ ⊏wc ☏ BX **n**
st. : ⊐ 18 – **24 rm** 165/230.

Martini without rest, 5 bd G.-Desplaces, ✉ 13003, ✆ 91 64 11 17 – |‡| ⊏ ⋒wc ☎ 🚗. AE. ✖ CU **b**
st. : ⊐ 18 – **40 rm** 107/196.

XXX ❀ **Jambon de Parme,** 67 r. La Palud, ✉ 13006, ✆ 91 54 37 98 – ▤. AE ◑ E VISA
closed 12 July-18 August, Sunday dinner and Monday – **M** a la carte 150/220 CX **s**
Spec. Salade aux deux saumons, Filets de chapon au safran, Blancs de volaille au sabayon de poireaux. Wines Cassis, Bandol.

XXX **Max Caizergues,** 11 r. G.-Ricard ✉ 13006 ✆ 91 33 58 07 – ▤. AE ◑ VISA. ✖ CX **g**
closed 15 July-15 August, Saturday lunch and Sunday – **st. : M** a la carte 160/270.

XXX **Au Pescadou,** 19 place Castellane, ✉ 13006, ✆ 91 78 36 01, Seafood – ▤ CY **v**
closed July, August and Sunday dinner from November-June – **M** a la carte 110/220.

XXX **La Ferme,** 23 r. Sainte, ✉ 13001, ✆ 91 33 21 12 – ▤. AE VISA BX **m**
closed August, 29 December-4 January, Saturday lunch, Sunday and Bank Holidays – **st. : M** a la carte 160/210.

XXX **Chez Benoît,** 26 cours Julien ✉ 13006 ✆ 91 92 47 47 – ▤. VISA CV **r**
closed 13 July-18 August, Sunday and Monday Lunch. – **st. : M** 85.

XXX **Brasserie New-York Vieux Port,** 7 quai Belges ✉ 13001 ✆ 91 33 60 98 – ▤. AE ◑ E VISA BX **e**
st. : M a la carte approx. 160 ⅉ.

XX ❀ **Michel,** 6 r. Catalans, ✉ 13007, ✆ 91 52 64 22, ≤ – VISA
closed July, Tuesday and Wednesday – **M** a la carte 255/400
Spec. Bouillabaisse, Bourride, Poissons et langouste grillés. Wines Cassis, Meyreuil.

XX ❀ **Calypso,** 3 r. Catalans, ✉ 13007, ✆ 91 52 64 00, ≤ – VISA
closed August, Sunday and Monday – **M** a la carte 250/310
Spec. Bouillabaisse, Bourride, Poissons et langouste grillés. Wines Palette Cassis.

XX **Chez Caruso,** 158 quai Port, ✉ 13002, ✆ 91 90 94 04, ≤, ☂, Italian cuisine – AE
closed 15 October-15 November, Sunday dinner and Monday – **st. : M** a la carte 140/190. AV **q**

XX **Miramar,** 12 quai Port, ✉ 13002, ✆ 91 91 10 40, ☂ – ▤. AE ◑ E VISA BV **v**
closed 2 to 25 August, 23 December-8 January and Sunday – **M** a la carte 150/240 ⅉ.

X **La Charpenterie,** 22 r. Paix ✉ 13001 ✆ 91 54 22 89 – AE ◑ E VISA BX **d**
closed 14 July-15 August, Saturday lunch, Sunday and Bank Holidays – **st. : M** a la carte 70/140.

at the Corniche :

Concorde-Palm Beach M ⛵, 2 promenade Plage, ✉ 13008, ✆ 91 76 20 00, Telex 401894, ≤, ☂, 🏊, ⛺ – |‡| ▤ TV ☎ 🚗 Ⓟ – 🅰 450. AE ◑ E VISA
st. : La Réserve M 120/180 - **grill Les Voiliers M** 100/110 ⅉ – ⊐ 42 – **145 rm** 425/468, 3 apartments.

❀❀ **Le Petit Nice** (Passedat) M ⛵, anse de Maldormé (turn off when level with no 160 Corniche Kennedy) ✉ 13007, ✆ 91 52 19 39, Telex 401565, ☂, « Villas overlooking the sea, refined decor », 🏊 – |‡| ▤ rm TV ☎ 🚗 Ⓟ. AE VISA. ✖ rest
closed 1 January-8 February – **M** *(closed Monday)* 350 and a la carte – ⊐ 59 – **10 rm** 670/1 000, 8 apartments
Spec. Loup de ligne en huile d'olive, Ragoût phocéen aux pistils de safran, Feuillant caramélisé aux fruits de saison. Wines Bandol, Coteaux d'Aix.

XX **Chez Fonfon,** 140 vallon des Auffes, ✉ 13007, ✆ 91 52 14 38, ≤ – AE ◑ VISA
closed October, 23 December-2 January, Saturday and Sunday – **M** a la carte approx. 225.

to the E 10 km, exit road sign-posted La Penne-St-Menet :

Novotel M, at St-Menet, ✉ 13011, ✆ 91 43 90 60, Telex 400667, ☂, 🏊, ✂ – |‡| ▤ TV ☎ ♿ Ⓟ – 🅰 250. AE ◑ E VISA
M (coffee shop only) a la carte approx. 100 ⅉ – ⊐ 32 – **131 rm** 289/315.

Les Baux-de-Provence 13 B.-du-R. 84 ① – pop. 433 – alt. 280 – ✉ **13520** Maussane-les-Alpilles.

Marseille 86.

in the Vallon :

XXXXX ✿✿✿ **Oustaù de Baumanière** (Thuilier) Ⓜ with rm, ℘ **90 54 33 07, Telex 420203,** < « Tastefully decorated mansions, flowered terraces, ⛱, ✂, 🏊, Riding club », 🌳 – ▤ rm TV ⌂wc ☎ 🚗 P. AE ⓓ E VISA
closed 15 January-1 March, Thursday lunch and Wednesday from 31 October-31 March – **M** a la carte 260/395 – ☕ 65 – **14 rm** 725, 11 apartments 1 000
Spec. Soufflé de homard, Filets de rougets au vin rouge, Noisettes d'agneau Beaumanière. **Wines** Gigondas, Coteaux des Baux.

XXX ✿ **La Riboto de Taven,** ℘ 90 97 34 23, ⛱, « Shady terrace and flowered garden near the rocks » – P. AE ⓓ VISA
closed 6 January-25 February, Sunday dinner out of season and Monday – **st. : M** a la carte 245/340
Spec. Gratin de homard, Filet de loup à l'huile d'olive et gros sel, Selle carré d'agneau des Alpilles à la sauge. **Wines** Coteaux des Baux.

XXX ✿ **La Cabro d'Or** Ⓜ with rm, ℘ 90 54 33 21, Telex 401810, <, ⛱, « Shaded terraces, lake », 🏊, 🌳, ✂ – TV ⌂wc ☎ P – 🪑 80. AE ⓓ E VISA
closed 15 November-20 December, Tuesday lunch and Monday from 15 October-31 March – **st. : M** 200/235 – ☕ 45 – **22 rm** 380/600 – P 650/750
Spec. Salade du pêcheur, Filet de loup en papillote, Noisettes d'agneau aux primeurs. **Wines** Coteaux des Baux, Girondas.

MONACO (Principality of) 84 ⑩, 195 ㉗㉘ – pop. 27 800 – alt. 65 – Casino.

Paris 958 – Menton 9 – Nice (by the Moyenne Corniche) 18 – San Remo 44.

Monaco Capital of the Principality – ✉ Monaco.

See : Tropical Garden★★ (Jardin exotique) : <★ – Observatory Caves★ (Grotte de l'Observatoire) – St-Martin Gardens★ – Early paintings of the Nice School★★ in Cathedral – Recumbent Christ★ in the Misericord Chapel – Place du Palais★ – Prince's Palace★ – Museums : oceanographic★★ (aquarium★★, <★★ from the terrace), Prehistoric Anthropology★ – Museum of Napoleon and Monaco History★.

Urban racing circuit - A.C. M. 23 bd Albert-1er ℘ 93 30 32 20, Télex 469003.

Monte-Carlo Fashionable resort of the Principality - Grand casino, Casino of Sporting Club, Casino Loews – ✉ Monte-Carlo.

See : Terrace★★ of the Grand casino – Museum of Dolls and Automata★.

18 Monte-Carlo Golf Club ℘ 93 41 09 11 to the S by N7 : 11 km.

ℹ Direction Tourisme et Congrès, 2 A bd Moulins ℘ 93 30 87 01, Télex 469760.

✿ **Paris,** pl. Casino ℘ 93 50 80 80, Telex 469925, <, ⛱, « Empire style dining room », 🏊, 🌳 – ⇅ ▤ rm TV ☎ ♿ P – 🪑 50. AE ⓓ E VISA. ✗ rest
M *(closed 30 September-4 December, 7 January-15 April and Wednesday)* 380/480 – see **Grill** below – ☕ 75 – **210 rm** 1 300/1 600, 38 apartments
Spec. Millefeuille de truffe, Papillote de filets de loup à l'échalote, Filet d'agneau à la crème d'estragon. **Wines** Cuers, La Londe.

Hermitage, square Beaumarchais ℘ 93 50 67 31, Telex 479432, <, ⛱, « Dining room in Baroque style », 🏊 – ⇅ ▤ TV ☎ P – 🪑 80. AE ⓓ E VISA. ✗ rest
M 205/270 – ☕ 75 – **244 rm** 900/1 400, 16 apartments.

Loews Ⓜ, av. Spélugues ℘ 93 50 65 00, Telex 479435, <, Casino and cabaret, 🏊 – ⇅ ▤ TV ☎ 🚗 – 🪑 50-1 100
Le Foie Gras – L'Argentin – Le Pistou – Café de la mer – 580 rm, 68 apartments.

✿ **Mirabeau** Ⓜ, 1 av. Princesse-Grace ℘ 93 25 45 45, Telex 479413, <, 🏊 – ⇅ ▤ TV ☎ 🚗 – 🪑 80. AE ⓓ E VISA. ✗ rest
M 175/270 – ☕ 70 – **96 rm** 750/1 150, 5 apartments
Spec. Fetuccini aux langoustines, Filets de rougets en matelote, Suprêmes de pigeon en coeur.

Beach Plaza Ⓜ, av. Princesse-Grace, à la Plage du Larvotto ℘ 93 30 98 80, Telex 479617, <, ⛱, « Fashionable resort with good bathing facilities », 🏊, ⛵ – ⇅ ▤ TV ☎ ♿ 🚗 – 🪑 30-300. AE ⓓ E VISA. ✗ rest
st. : M 200/300 – ☕ 70 – **311 rm** 900/1 350, 9 apartments.

Balmoral without rest, 12 av. Costa ℘ 93 50 62 37, Telex 479436, < – ⇅ ▤ rm TV ☎. AE ⓓ E VISA. ✗
st. : ☕ 35 – **68 rm** 250/500.

Louvre without rest, 16 bd Moulins ℘ 93 50 65 25, Telex 479645 – ⇅ ▤ rm TV ⌂wc ☎. ⓓ E VISA. ✗
st. : – **35 rm** ☕ 467/555.

Alexandra without rest, 35 bd Princesse-Charlotte ℘ 93 50 63 13, Telex 489286 – ⇅ ⌂wc 🚿 ☎. AE ⓓ VISA
st. : ☕ 29 – **55 rm** 159/396.

XXXX ✿ **Dominique Le Stanc,** 18 bd Moulins ✆ 93 50 63 37 – AE ⓓ VISA
closed 1 to 15 November, Monday (except dinner in July-August) and Sunday lunch – **M** (dinner only in July-August) 280/360
Spec. Ravioli aux artichauts, asperges et langoustines (January-May), Courgettes au homard et truffes (May-October), Pêches rôties aux pistaches (May-October). **Wines** Bellet, Côtes de Provence.

XXX **Grill de l'Hôtel de Paris,** pl. Casino ✆ 93 50 80 80, « Roof-top grill (open air) with ≤ over the Principality » – ▤ Ⓟ. AE ⓓ E VISA. ⛝
closed 8 to 22 December and Monday except in July and August – **M** (dinner only from 1 June-5 September) a la carte 300/400.

XXX **Bec Rouge,** 11 av. Gde Bretagne ✆ 93 30 74 91 – ▤. AE ⓓ E VISA
closed 20-30 June and 4-31 January – **M** a la carte 190/285.

XX Toula, 20 bd de Suisse ✆ 93 50 02 02, ☂, Italian cuisine – ▤.

XX Rampoldi, 3 av. Spélugues ✆ 93 30 70 65 – ▤.

XX **Chez Gianni,** 39 av. Princesse Grace ✆ 93 30 46 33, Italian cuisine – AE ⓓ VISA
closed February and Tuesday – **st. : M** a la carte 170/255.

XX **du Port,** quai Albert 1er ✆ 93 50 77 21, ≤, ☂, Italian cuisine – ▤. AE ⓓ E VISA
closed 4 November-4 December and Monday – **st. : M** 150/320 Sunday, Bank holidays a la carte.

at Monte-Carlo Beach (06 Maritime Alps) at : 2,5 km – ✉ **06190** Roquebrune-Cap-Martin :

Monte-Carlo Beach H. Ⓜ, ✆ 93 78 21 40, ≤ sea and Monaco, « Fashionable resort with good bathing facilities, ⛱, ⛺ » – 🛗 ▤ rm 📺 ☎ Ⓟ – 🏛 30. AE ⓓ E VISA. ⛝ rest
29 March-13 October – **M** a la carte 180/310 – ☕ 75 – **46 rm** 1 250/1 400.

NICE Ⓟ **06000** Maritime Alps **84** ⑨⑩, **195** ㉖㉗ – pop. **338 486** – alt. at château 92.

See : Site★★ – Promenade des Anglais★★ EFZ – Old Nice★ : Château ≤★★ JZ, Interior★ of church of St-Martin and St-Augustin HY **D**, – Balnstraded staircase★ of the Palais Lascaris HZ **K**, Interior★ of Ste-Reparate Cathedral, – HZ **L** St-Jacques Church★ HZ **N**, Decoration of St-Giaumes-Chapel HZ **R** – Mosaic★ by Chagall in Law Faculty DZ **U** – Cimiez : Monastery★ (Masterpieces★★ of the early Nice School in the church) HV **Q**, Roman Ruins★ HV – Museums : MarcChagall★★ GX, Matisse★ HV **M2** Fine Arts Museum★★ DZ **M**, Masséna★ FZ **M1** – International Naive Style Museum★ – Carnival★★★ (before Shrove Tuesday) – Mount Alban ≤★★ 5 km – Mount Boron ≤★ 3 km – St-Pons Church★ : 3 km.

Envir. : St-Michel Plateau ≤★★ 9,5 km.

⛳18 Biot ✆ 93 65 08 48 : 22 km.

✈ of Nice-Côte d'Azur ✆ 93 21 30 30 : 7 km.

🚗 ✆ 93 87 50 50.

⛴ for Corsica : Société Nationale Maritime Corse-Méditerranée, 61 bd des Dames (Marseille), ✆ 91 56 32 00 FZ **D**.

ℹ Accueil de France (hotel reservations - not more than 7 days in advance) av. Thiers ✆ 93 87 07 07, Telex 460042 ; Acropolis, Esplanade Kennedy ✆ 93 92 82 82 5 av. Gustave-V ✆ 93 87 60 60 and Nice-Parking near the Airport ✆ 93 83 32 64 - A.C. 9 r. Massenet ✆ 93 87 18 17.

Paris 931 – Cannes 32 – Genova 194 – Lyon 470 – Marseille 187 – Turino 220.

Plan on following pages

Négresco, 37 prom. des Anglais ✆ 93 88 39 51, Telex 460040, ≤, « Public rooms and bedrooms, in period style : 16C and 18C, Empire and Napoléon III » – 🛗 ▤ 📺 ☎ ♿ – 🏛 50-400. AE ⓓ E VISA — FZ **k**
st. : La Rotonde M a la carte 150/215 ♨ and see rest. **Chantecler** below – ☕ 70 – **140 rm** 1 150/1 800, 10 apartments.

Sofitel Splendid Ⓜ, 50 bd Victor-Hugo ✆ 93 88 69 54, Telex 460938, « ⛱ on 8th floor, ≤ Nice » – 🛗 ▤ 📺 ☎ 🚗 – 🏛 30-100. AE ⓓ E VISA. ⛝ rest — FYZ **g**
st. : M a la carte 115/165 ♨ – **116 rm** ☕ 440/820, 12 apartments 900/1 200 – P 640/710.

Méridien Ⓜ, 1 prom. des Anglais ✆ 93 82 25 25, Telex 470361, ☂, « Roof-top swimming pool, ≤ bay » – 🛗 ▤ 📺 ☎ ♿ – 🏛 30-400. AE ⓓ E VISA — FZ **d**
st. : M a la carte 185/285 – ☕ 65 – **314 rm** 700/1 300, 25 apartments.

Beach Régency Ⓜ, 223 prom. des Anglais ✆ 93 83 91 51, Telex 461635, « ⛱ on the roof, ≤ the bay », ☂ – 🛗 ▤ 📺 ☎ 🚗 – 🏛 50-400. AE ⓓ E VISA
st. : Le Regency M a la carte 190/250 - **La Promenade** (coffee shop only) **M** a la carte approx. 170 – ☕ 60 – **305 rm** 720/1 230, 17 apartments.

Frantel Ⓜ without rest, 28 av. Notre-Dame ✆ 93 80 30 24, Telex 470662, « ⛱ on 8th floor, hanging gardens on 2nd floor, ≤ » – 🛗 ▤ 📺 ☎ ♿ – 🏛 25-120. AE ⓓ E VISA
st. : ☕ 38 – **200 rm** 370/650. — FXY **q**

Plaza, 12 av. Verdun ✆ 93 87 80 41, Telex 460979, ≤, « Roof-top terrace » – 🛗 ▤ 📺 ☎ – 🏛 30-550. AE ⓓ E VISA. ⛝ rest — GZ **f**
st. : M 130 – ☕ 45 – **186 rm** 600/850 – P 710/1 370.

Continental-Masséna M without rest, 58 r. Gioffredo ✆ 93 85 49 25, Telex 470192 – ▮ ▤ TV ☎ ⇔ – 60. AE ◑ E VISA GZ **k**
st. : 30 – **116 rm** 200/465.

La Pérouse ⚘, 11 quai Rauba-Capeù ✉ 06300 ✆ 93 62 34 63, Telex 461411, « < Nice and promenade des Anglais », ⛱ – ▮ ▤ rm TV ☎ – 30. AE ◑ E VISA. ✂ rest HZ **k**
st. : **M** (coffee shop only in summer) – 25 – **66 rm** 400/750, 3 apartments 900.

La Malmaison, 48 bd V.-Hugo ✆ 93 87 62 56, Telex 470410 – ▮ TV ☎. AE ◑ E VISA. ✂ rest FYZ **e**
st. : **M** 100/150 – **50 rm** 280/440 – P 370/480.

Ambassador M without rest, 8 av. Suède ✆ 93 87 90 19, Telex 460025, < – ▮ TV ☎ ♿. AE ◑ E VISA FZ **x**
15 February-15 November – **st. :** 29 – **45 rm** 375/440.

Grand H. Aston M, 12 av. F.-Faure ✆ 93 80 62 52, Telex 470290, ⛱, « Roof-top terrace » – ▮ ▤ rm TV ☎ – 50-180. AE ◑ E VISA. ✂ rest HZ **u**
st. : **M** 105/135 – 40 – **157 rm** 780.

Napoléon without rest, 6 r. Grimaldi ✆ 93 87 70 07, Telex 460949 – ▮ ▤ TV ☎ ♿. AE ◑ E VISA FZ **r**
closed November – **st. :** 22 – **80 rm** 250/370.

Atlantic, 12 bd Victor-Hugo ✆ 93 88 40 15, Telex 460840 – ▮ TV ☎ P – 30-80. AE ◑ E VISA FY **d**
st. : **M** 95 – 35 – **123 rm** 340/490 – P 435/720.

Park and rest. Le Passage, 6 av. de Suède ✆ 93 87 80 25, Telex 970176, < – ▮ ▤ rest TV ☎ ♿ – 80. AE ◑ E VISA FZ **x**
st. : **M** *(closed Sunday)* 110 – 40 – **148 rm** 500/630 – P 535/590.

Victoria without rest, 33 bd V.-Hugo ✆ 93 88 39 60, Telex 461337, ⛱ – ▮ TV ☎. AE ◑ E VISA FYZ **z**
st. : **40 rm** 280/420.

Westminster Concorde, 27 prom. des Anglais ✆ 93 88 29 44, Telex 460872, <, ⛱ – ▮ ▤ rest TV ☎ – 40-350. AE ◑ E VISA FZ **m**
st. : Le Farniente *(closed 1 November-10 December)* **M** 160/200 – 50 – **110 rm** 500/900.

Gd Hôtel de Florence M without rest, 3 r. P.-Deroulède ✆ 93 88 46 87, Telex 470652 – ▮ ▤ TV ☎. AE ◑ VISA. ✂ GY **r**
st. : **53 rm** 300/420.

Locarno without rest, 4 av. Baumettes ✆ 93 96 28 00, Telex 970015 – ▮ ▤ TV ⇔. AE ◑ E VISA DEZ **t**
st. : 20 – **48 rm** 195/310.

Lausanne, 36 r. Rossini ✆ 93 88 85 94, Telex 461269 – ▮ TV ⛀wc ⛆wc ☎. AE ◑ E VISA FY **t**
st. : **M** *(closed November and Wednesday)* 95/130 – 35 – **40 rm** 300/350 – P 395/420.

Gounod without rest, 3 r. Gounod ✆ 93 88 26 20, Telex 461705 – ▮ ▤ TV ⛀wc ⛆wc ☎ ⇔. AE ◑ VISA FYZ **g**
st. : **45 rm** 300/420, 5 apartments 520.

Georges M ⚘ without rest, 3 r. H.-Cordier ✆ 93 86 23 41 – ▮ TV ⛀wc ☎. AE VISA DZ **e**
st. : 20 – **18 rm** 210/320.

Suisse without rest, 15 quai Rauba-Capeu ✉ 06300 ✆ 93 62 33 00, < – ▮ ▤ ⛀wc ⛆wc ☎ HZ **r**
st. : 16 – **40 rm** 254.

Windsor without rest, 11 r. Dalpozzo ✆ 93 88 59 35, Telex 970072, ⛱, ⛱ – ▮ TV ⛀wc ⛆wc ☎. AE ◑ E VISA FZ **f**
st. : 25 – **60 rm** 210/380.

Avenida without rest, 41 av. J.-Médecin ✆ 93 88 55 03 – ▮ kitchenette ▤ TV ⛀wc ⛆wc ☎. AE ◑ VISA – 15 – **35 rm** 145/220. FY **m**

Brice, 44 r. Mar.-Joffre ✆ 93 88 14 44, Telex 470658, ⛱, ⛱ – ▮ TV ⛀wc ⛆wc ☎ – 30. ◑ E VISA. ✂ rest FZ **b**
st. : **M** 100 – **65 rm** 260/420 – P 380/460.

Carlton without rest, 26 bd V.-Hugo ✆ 93 88 87 83 – ▮ ⛀wc ⛆wc ☎. AE ◑ E VISA FY **f**
st. : 19 – **29 rm** 125/285.

New York without rest, 44 av. Mar.-Foch ✆ 93 92 04 19, Telex 470215 – ▮ ⛀wc ⛆wc ☎. AE ◑ VISA – **st. :** 22 – **52 rm** 270/368. GY **g**

Chatham without rest, 9 r. A.-Karr ✆ 93 87 80 61 – ▮ ⛀wc ⛆wc ☎. AE ◑ E VISA FY **x**
st. : 15 – **50 rm** 220/300.

Durante ⚘ without rest, 16 av. Durante ✆ 93 88 84 40, ⛱ – kitchenette TV ⛀wc ⛆wc ☎. ✂ – *closed 27 October-3 December* – **st. :** 25 – **27 rm** 150/250. FY **b**

Cigognes without rest, 16 r. Maccarani ✆ 93 88 65 02 – ▮ TV ⛀wc ⛆wc ☎. ✂ FY **s**
st. : **32 rm** 240/255.

Star H. M without rest, 14 r. Biscarra ✆ 93 85 19 03 – ⛀wc ⛆wc ☎. AE ◑ GY **k**
st. : 20 – **19 rm** 112/276.

Trianon without rest, 15 av. Auber ✆ 93 88 30 69 – ▮ TV ⛀wc ⛆wc ☎. AE ◑ E VISA FY **u**
st. : 15 – **32 rm** 176/229.

NICE

Félix-Faure (Av.) .... GZ 21
France (R. de) .... DFZ
Gambetta (Bd) .... EXZ
Gioffredo (R.) .... HY
Hôtel-des-Postes (R. de l') .... HY 30
Liberté (R. de la) .... GZ 35
Masséna (Espace, Pl.) ... GZ
Masséna (R.) .... GZ 43
Médecin (Av. J.) .... GY 44
Paradis (R.) .... GZ 56
Pastorelli (R.) .... GY 58
République (R.) .... JX 64

Alberti (R.) .... GHY 2
Alsace-Lorraine (Jardin d') .... EZ 3
Armée-du-Rhin (Pl.) ..... JX 5
Auriol (Pont V) .... JV 7
Carnot (Bd) .... JZ 14
Desambrois (Av.) ...... GHX 18
Diables-Bleus (Av. des) .. JX 19
Du Gésu (St-Jacques ⊞) .... HZ **N**
Église Russe (⊞)........ EX **X**
Gautier (Pl. P.) .... HZ 25
Ile-de-Beauté (Pl. de l') ... JZ 32
Lunel (Quai) .... JZ 37
Meyerbeer (R.) .... FZ 45
Monastère (Av. et Pl. du) . HV 46
Moulin (Pl. J.) .... HY 47
N.-D.-de-Cimiez (⊞) .. HJV **Q**
N.-D.-du-Port (⊞) ..... JY 52
Phocéens (Av. des) ..... GZ 59
Rivoli (R. de) .... FZ 65
Sacré-Cœur (⊞) ...... FZ 67
St-Augustin (⊞)....... HY **D**
St-Barthélémy (⊞) ..... EV **C**

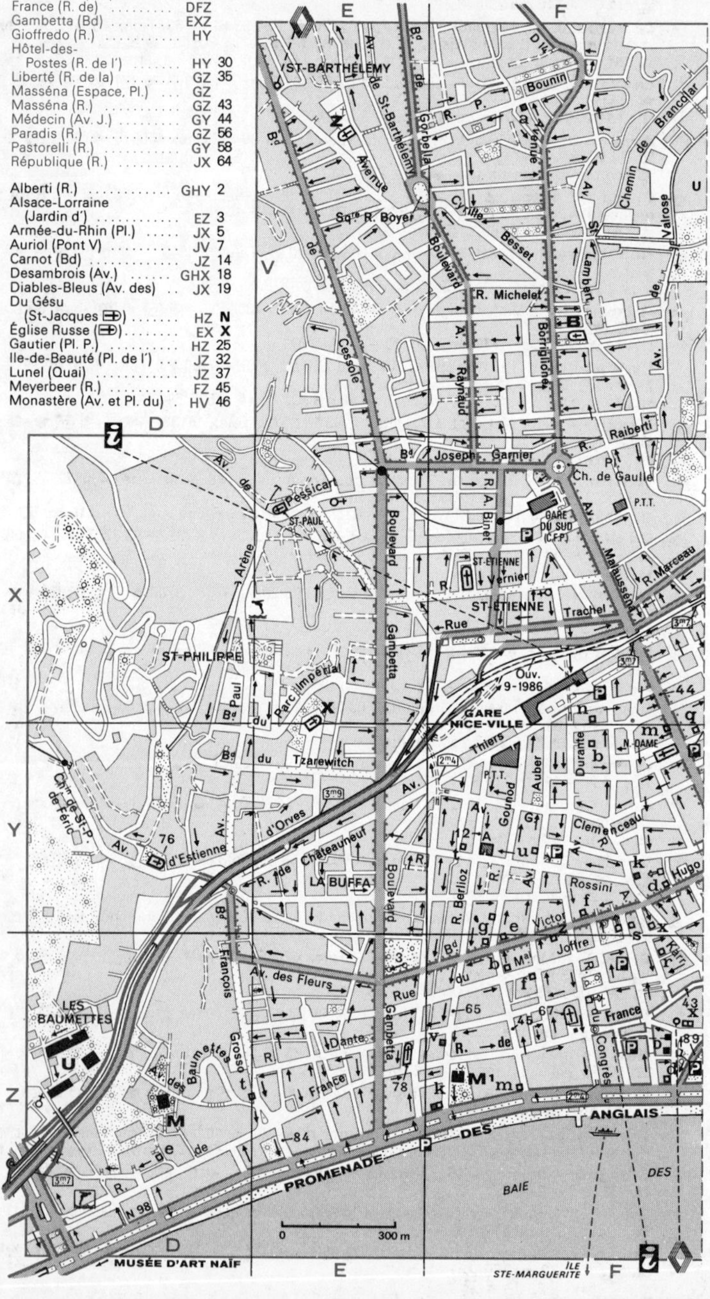

St-Jean-Baptiste (Av. ⊞) .... HY 73
St-Philippe (⊞) .... DY 76
St-Pierre-d'Arène (⊞) .. EZ 78

Ste-Jeanne-d'Arc (⊞) .... FV B
Ste-Réparate (Cath. ⊞) .... HZ L

Saleya (Cours) .... HZ 83
Sauvan (R. H.) .... EZ 84
Verdun (Av. de) .... FGZ 89
Wilson (Pl.) .... HY 92

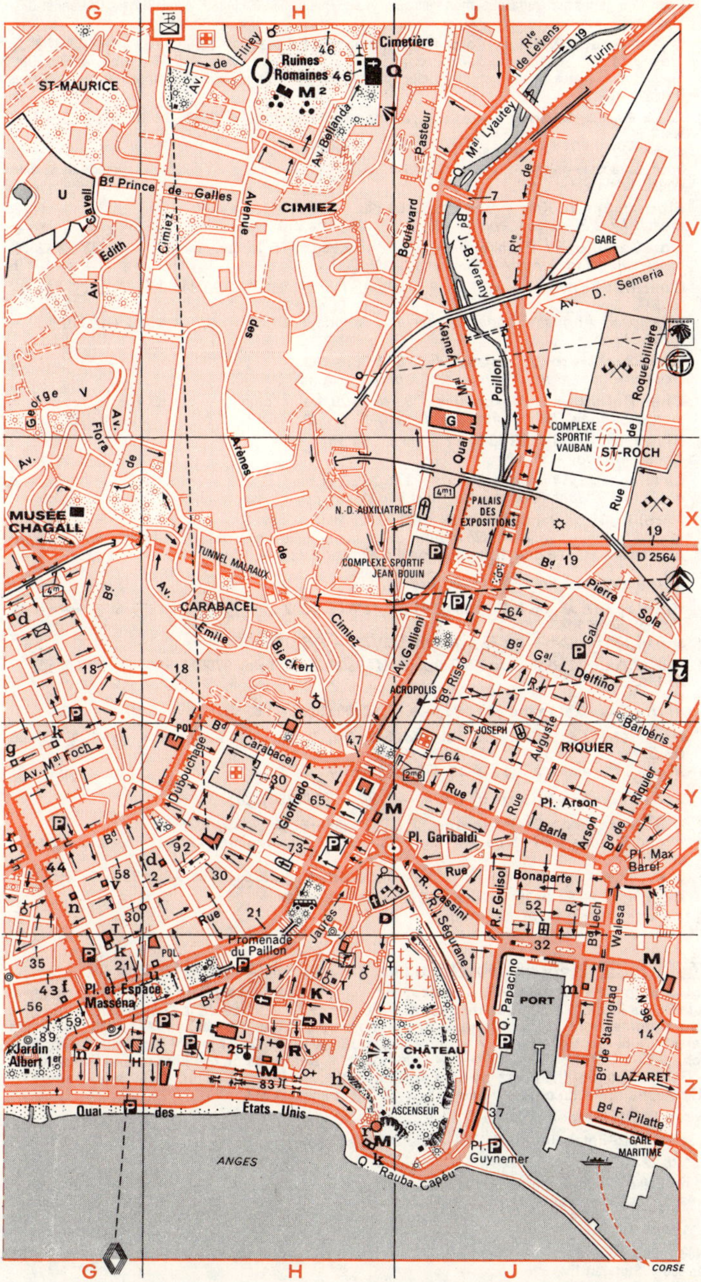

XXXX ✿✿ **Chantecler** (Maximin), 37 prom. des Anglais ✆ 93 88 39 51 – ▤. AE ⊙ E VISA
closed November – **st. : M** 280/430 and a la carte FZ **k**
Spec. Courgettes aux truffes, Saumon frais au gros sel, Tian de filet d'agneau. **Wines** Cassis, Le Cannet-des-Maures.

XXX ✿ **Ane Rouge** (Vidalot), 7 quai Deux-Emmanuel ✉ 06300 ✆ 93 89 49 63 – AE ⊙ VISA
closed 14 July-1 September, Saturday, Sunday and Bank Holidays – **M** a la carte 190/295
Spec. Huîtres plates au champagne, Homard ou Langouste Ane Rouge, Ris de veau des gourmets. **Wines** Bellet, Palette. JZ **m**

XXX ✿ **La Poularde chez Lucullus** (Normand), 9 r. Deloye ✆ 93 85 22 90 – ▤. AE ⊙ E VISA GY **n**
closed 12 July-17 August and Wednesday – **M** 140/200
Spec. Langouste grillée aux herbes (15 March-30 October), Rougets à la sauvage, Capilotade de volaille. **Wines** Gassin, Bellet.

XXX **Florian,** 22 r. A.-Karr ✆ 93 88 86 60. AE VISA FY **k**
closed 15 to 30 August and Sunday – **M** a la carte 210/290.

XX **Don Camillo,** 5 r. Ponchettes ✉ 06300 ✆ 93 85 67 95, Italian cuisine – ▤. AE ⊙ E VISA
closed July and Sunday – **M** a la carte 115/200. HZ **h**

XX **Gourmet Lorrain** with rm, 7 av. Santa-Fior ✉ 06100 ✆ 93 84 90 78 – ▤ TV ☎. AE VISA FV **a**
M *(closed August, Sunday dinner and Monday)* 70/130 – ☐ 14 – **15 rm** 110/160 – P 264/313.

XX **Bon Coin Breton,** 5 r. Blacas ✆ 93 85 17 01 – ▤ GY **v**
closed August, Sunday dinner and Monday – **st. : M** 60/140.

XX **Chez Rolando,** 3 r. Desboutins ✆ 93 85 76 79, Italian cuisine – ▤. AE VISA GZ **n**
closed Sunday, Bank Holidays and lunch in July and August – **M** a la carte 110/160 ♁.

X **Rivoli,** 9 r. Rivoli ✆ 93 88 12 62 – ▤. AE ⊙ VISA FZ **v**
closed Monday – **st. : M** 90/150 ♁.

X **La Nissarda,** 17 r. Gubernatis ✆ 93 85 26 29 – VISA HY **d**
closed 15-31 July, February Holidays and Wednesday – **st. : M** 65.

X **Mireille,** 19 bd Raimbaldi ✆ 93 85 27 23 ▤. VISA GX **d**
closed 2 June-2 July, 3-9 November, Monday and Tuesday except July-August and Bank Holidays – **st. : M** one dish only : paella a la carte approx. 95.

at the airport 7 km – ✉ **06200** Nice :

Holiday Inn [M], on N 7 ✆ 93 83 91 92, Telex 970202, ☂, ⛱ – ⇅ ▤ TV ☎ ♿ 🚗 – 250. AE ⊙ E VISA
st. : M 135 b.i./295 – ☐ 70 – **151 rm** 550/770 – P 660/990.

XXX **Ciel d'Azur,** 2nd floor in Air Terminal ✆ 93 21 36 36, Telex 970011, ⋞ – ▤. AE ⊙ VISA
M 140/200.

at the Cap 3000 to the SW : 8 km – ✉ **06700** St-Laurent-du-Var :

Novotel [M], ✆ 93 31 61 15, Telex 470643, ☂, ⛱, – ⇅ ▤ TV ☎ ♿ Ⓟ – 250. AE ⊙ E VISA
M a la carte approx. 100 ♁ – ☐ 37 – **103 rm** 346/417.

at St-Pancrace N : 8 km by D 914 – alt. 302 – ✉ **06100** Nice :

XXX ✿ **Rôtisserie de St-Pancrace,** ✆ 93 84 43 60, ⋞, ☂ – Ⓟ. VISA
closed 6 January-6 February and Monday except July-August and bank Holidays – **M** a la carte 200/300
Spec. Frivolités de St Pancrace, Terrine de Scampi, Rosette d'agneau au basilic. **Wines** Bellet, Bandol.

XX **Cicion,** ✆ 93 84 49 29, ⋞ Nice and seaside, ☂ – Ⓟ
closed dinner (except July-August) – **M** 105/130.

STRASBOURG

[P] **67000** B.-Rhin **62** ⑩ – pop. **252 264** Greater Strasbourg 409 161 alt. 139.

See : Cathédral* : Astronomical clock*, ⋞* CX – ⋞* of rue Mercière CX 53 – Old City*** BCX : la Petite France** BX, Rue du Bain-aux-Plantes** BX 7, Place de la Cathédrale* CX 17, – Maison Kammerzell* CX e, Château des Rohan* CX, Cour du Corbeau* CX 18, – Ponts couverts* BX B, Place Kléber* CV – Barrage Vauban ⋇** BX D – Mausoleum** in St-Thomas Church CX E – Hôtel de Ville * CV H – Orangery* – Boat trips on the Ill river and the canals* CX – Guided tours of the Port* by boat – Historical* CX M3 – Museum : Oeuvre N.-Dame*** CX M1, Museums** du château des Rohan CX, Alsatian* CX M2.**

18 Illkirch-Graffenstaden ✆ 88 66 17 22.

✈ Strasbourg-Entzheim ✆ 88 32 99 74 by D 392 : 12 km.

🚗 ✆ 88 22 50 50.

ℹ and Accueil de France (Information and hotel reservations, not more than 5 days in advance), Palais des Congrès av. Schutzenberger ✆ 88 35 03 00, Télex 870860 ; pl. Gare ✆ 88 32 51 49 and pl. Gutenberg ✆ 88 32 57 07 – Bureau d'accueil, pont Europe (exchange facilities) ✆ 88 61 39 23 - A.C. 5 av. Paix ✆ 88 36 04 34.

Paris 488 – Bâle 145 – Bonn 360 – Bordeaux 921 – Frankfurt 218 – Karlsruhe 81 – Lille 554 – Luxembourg 221 – Lyon 480 – Stuttgart 154.

STRASBOURG

Alsace (Av. d')	CV	2
Arc-en-ciel (R. de l')	CV	3
Austerlitz (R. d')	CX	4
Bains-aux-Plantes (R. du)	BX	7
Castelnau (R. Général de)	CV	16
Cathédrale (Pl. de la)	CX	17
Corbeau (Cour du)	CX	18
Corbeau (Pl. du)	CX	19
Course (Petite Rue de la)	BV	20
Desaix (Quai)	BV	22
Finkmatt (Quai)	CV	24
Finkwiller (Quai)	BX	25
Foch (R. du Mar.)	CV	26
Fossé-des-Tanneurs (R. du)	BX	27
Fossé-des-Treize (R. du)	CV	29
Francs-Bourgeois (R. des)	CX	30
Frey (Quai Ch.)	CX	32
Gutenberg (Pl. et R.)	CX	36
Haute-Montée (R.)	CV	40
Homme de fer (Pl.)	CV	41
Kuss (Pont)	BV	46
Liberté (Av. de la)	CV	47
Maire Kuss (R. du)	BV	48
Mercière (R.)	CX	53
Mésange (R. de la)	CV	54
Noyer (R. du)	BV	55
Paix (Av. de la)	CV	58
Parchemin (R. du)	CV	60
Pierre (R. du Fg de)	CV	61
Recollets (R. des)	CV	70
St-Jean (Quai)	BV	76
St-Michel (R.)	BX	77
Sébastopol (R. de)	BV	83
Temple Neuf (Pl.)	CV	88
Temple Neuf (R.)	CV	89
Turckheim (Quai)	BX	91
Vieux-Marché-aux-Poissons (R. du)	CX	94
1re Armée (R.)	CX	99

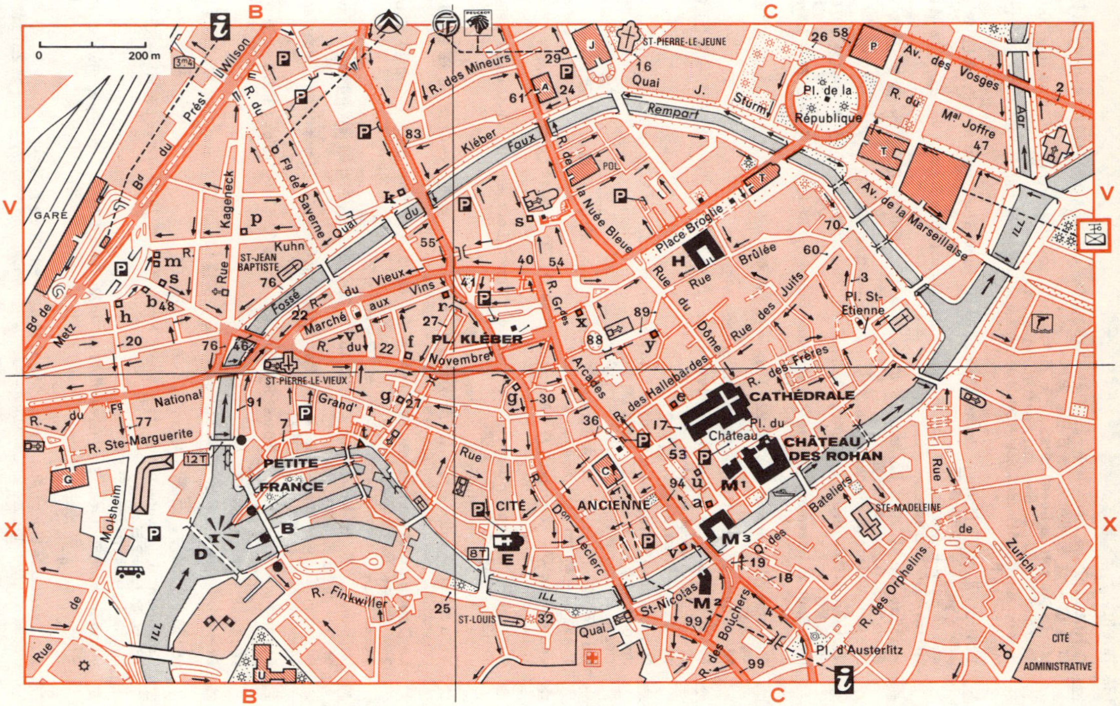

Hilton M, av. Herrenschmidt 88 37 10 10, Telex 890363, – kitchenette – 30-450. rest
st. : **La Maison du Boeuf** (closed 1 to 24 August, *1 to 8 January)* **M** a la carte 180/260 **Le Jardin M** 100 – 55 – **253 rm** 505/690, 5 apartments
Spec. Poissons fumés maison, Soufflé chaud de grenouilles, Filet de boeuf au pinot noir. **Wines** Gewurztraminer, Pinot gris.

Sofitel M, pl. St-Pierre-le-Jeune 88 32 99 30, Telex 870894, patio – – 100. rest CV **s**
st. : **Le Saint-Pierre** *(closed 1 to 15 August and Sunday)* **M** a la carte 180/250 – 44 – **180 rm** 460/720, 5 apartments.

Holiday Inn M, 20 pl. Bordeaux 88 35 70 00, Telex 890515, – – 50-600.
st. : **La Louisiane M** a la carte 160/230 – 55 – **170 rm** 588/682.

Terminus-Gruber, 10 pl. Gare 88 32 87 00, Telex 870998 – – 60. BV **m**
rest. **Cour de Rosemont** *(closed 22 December-5 January)* **M** 130/170 – 35 – **72 rm** 230/480, 6 apartments 520/580 – P 380/490.

Novotel M, quai Kléber 88 22 10 99, Telex 880700 – – 30-200. BV **k**
M a la carte approx. 100 – 34 – **97 rm** 388/441.

France M without rest, 20 r. Jeu-des-Enfants 88 32 37 12, Telex 890084 – – 30. BV **v**
st. : 24 – **70 rm** 270/380.

Monopole-Métropole without rest, 16 r. Kuhn 88 32 11 94, Telex 890366, « Alsatian decor » – . BV **p**
closed Christmas Day-1 January – **st. : 94 rm** 250/390.

Gd Hôtel without rest, 12 pl. Gare 88 32 46 90, Telex 870011 – .
st. : 32 – **90 rm** 300/380, 4 apartments 400. BV **m**

des Rohan M without rest, 17 r. Maroquin 88 32 85 11 – . CX **u**
st. : 30 – **36 rm** 225/400.

Nouvel H. Maison Rouge without rest, 4 r. Francs-Bourgeois 88 32 08 60, Telex 880130 – . CX **g**
st. : 30 – **130 rm** 270/350, 6 apartments 430.

Villa d'Est M without rest, 12 r. J.-Kablé 88 36 69 02 – wc .
closed 23 December-2 January – **st. :** 27 – **32 rm** 310/350.

La Dauphine M without rest, 30 r. 1e Armée 88 36 26 61, Telex 880766 – wc wc .
closed 23 December-2 January – **st. :** 23 – **45 rm** 285/300.

Hannong, 15 r. 22-Novembre 88 32 16 22, Telex 890551 – rest wc wc – 50. BV **f**
closed 20-27 December – **st. : Wyn's Bar** *(closed August, 20-27 December, Sunday and Monday)* **M** a la carte approx. 140 – 28 – **70 rm** 240/380.

Europe without rest, 38 r. Fossé-des-Tanneurs 88 32 17 88, Telex 890220 – wc wc . BX **g**
st. : 19 – **61 rm** 133/279.

Bristol, 4 pl. Gare 88 32 00 83, Telex 890317 – rest wc wc . BV **h**
st. : **M** 100/180 – 25 – **40 rm** 250/350 – P 350/380.

Continental M without rest, 14 r. Maire Kuss 88 22 28 07, Telex 880881 – wc . BV **s**
st. : 17 – **48 rm** 188/255.

Vendôme without rest, 9 pl. Gare 88 32 45 23, Telex 890850 – wc wc . BV **b**
st. : 17 – **48 rm** 135/210.

XXXX **Crocodile** (Jung), 10 r. Outre 88 32 13 02 – . CV **x**
closed 6 July-4 August, 21 December-1 January, Sunday and Monday – **st. : M** 280 and a la carte
Spec. Foie gras d'oie à l'ancienne, Gratin de langouste, Canard sauvage à la presse (season). **Wines** Riesling, Pinot gris.

XXX **Buerehiesel** (Westermann), Set in the Orangerie Park 88 61 62 24, « Attractive Alsatian mansion in a park » – .
closed 7-21 Aug., 23 Dec.-3 Jan., Feb. holidays, Tuesday except lunch from 1 March and Wednesday – **st. : M** 195/310 and a la carte
Spec. Fritot de foie d'oie et salade de ris de veau, Rouget et langoustines au chou vert, Sot-l'y-laisse à la purée de persil et truffes. **Wines** Muscat, Pinot gris.

XXX **Valentin-Sorg** (14th floor), 6 pl. Homme-de-Fer 88 32 12 16, < Strasbourg – BV **r**
closed 15-31 August, 15-28 February, Sunday dinner and Tuesday – **st. : M** 130/200
Spec. Compote de lapereau en gelée, Lotte au basilic, Crêpes au kirsch. **Wines** Riquewihr, Pinot blanc.

XXX ❀ **Maison Kammerzell,** 16 pl. Cathédrale ✆ 88 32 42 14, Telex 890221, « Attractive 16C Alsatian house » – AE ⓓ E VISA CX e
closed 24 February-15 March and Wednesday – **st. :** upstairs **M** 196/302 - **Leo Schnug** ground floor **M** 175 b.i./153
Spec. Parfait de foie gras, Filet de sandre au Pinot noir, Choucroute. **Wines** Klevner, Pinot noir.

XXX **Maison des Tanneurs dite "Gerwerstub",** 42 r. Bain-aux-Plantes ✆ 88 32 79 70, « Old Alsatian house on the banks of the River Ill » – AE ⓓ BX t
closed 29 June-14 July, 21 December-22 January, Sunday and Monday – **st. : M** a la carte 130/210.

XX **Zimmer,** 8 r. Temple-Neuf ✆ 88 32 35 01 – AE ⓓ VISA CV y
closed 1-25 August, Saturday and Sunday – **st. : M** 145 b.i./225.

XX **La Volière,** 1 av. Gén.-de-Gaulle ✆ 88 61 05 79 – ▤. AE ⓓ E VISA
closed 14 July-12 August, Saturday lunch and Sunday – **st. : M** 146/230.

XX ❀ **La Table Gourmande** (Reix), 43 rte Gén.-de-Gaulle ✉ 67300 Schiltigheim ✆ 88 83 61 67 – ▤. AE ⓓ VISA
closed 20 July-12 August, 24 December-7 January, Monday lunch and Sunday – **st. : M** a la carte 190/255
Spec. Huîtres tièdes à la coque, Blanc de St-Pierre au naturel, Confit de canard. **Wines** Sylvaner, Pinot noir.

X **A l'Ancienne Douane,** 6 r. Douane ✆ 88 32 42 19, ⛱, « Riverside terrace ». AE
st. : M 43/78 ♁. CX v

X **Strissel,** 5 pl. Grande-Boucherie ✆ 88 32 14 73, Restaurant with wine tasting, rustic decor – ▤. VISA CX a
closed 6 to 31 July, February holidays, Sunday except Bank Holidays and Monday – **st. : M** 37/72 ♁.

at pont de l'Europe :

🏨 **P.L.M. Motel du Pont de l'Europe** Ⓜ ⛵, ✆ 88 61 03 23, Telex 870833, ⛱ – TV ☎ Ⓟ – 🎤 100-400. AE ⓓ E VISA
st. : M 51/93 ♁ – ☕ 32 – **88 rm** 294/336, 5 apartments 421.

at Illkirch-Graffenstaden 8 km – ✉ **67400** Illkirch-Graffenstaden :

🏨 **Alsace** Ⓜ, 187 rte Lyon ✆ 88 66 41 60, Telex 870706 – |‡| ⊟wc ☎ Ⓟ – 🎤 60. VISA. ✂ rm – *closed 24 December-2 January* – **st. : M** *(closed Saturday lunch and Sunday)* 79/150 ♁ – ☕ 18,50 – **40 rm** 210/246 – P 280.

near Colmar interchange A 35 10 km – ✉ **67400** Illkirch-Graffenstaden :

🏨 **Novotel** Ⓜ, ✆ 88 66 21 56, Telex 890142, ⛱, ⛱, 🌳 – ▤ rest TV ☎ ♿ Ⓟ – 🎤 25 à 120. AE ⓓ E VISA
M a la carte approx. 100 ♁ – ☕ 32 – **76 rm** 278/304.

🏨 **Mercure** Ⓜ, ✆ 88 66 03 00, Telex 890277, ⛱, ⛱ – |‡| ▤ rest TV ☎ ♿ Ⓟ – 🎤 25-200. AE ⓓ E VISA
M a la carte approx. 120 ♁ – ☕ 30 – **91 rm** 290/330.

at La Wantzenau NE by D 468 – pop. 4 084 – ✉ **67610** La Wantzenau :

🏨 **H. Au Moulin** Ⓜ ⛵ without rest, S : 1,5 km by D 468 ✆ 88 96 27 83, <, « ancient watermill on a branch of the River Ill », 🌳 – |‡| TV ⊟wc ⫛wc ☎ Ⓟ. AE VISA
closed 24 December-2 January – **st. :** ☕ 25 – **19 rm** 185/285.

🏨 **A la Gare,** 32 r. Gare ✆ 88 96 63 44 – ⊟wc ⫛wc ☎ Ⓟ. VISA. ✂ rm
st. : M *(closed 28 July-17 August, 3-10 March, Sunday dinner and Friday)* 58/96 ♁ – ☕ 16 – **19 rm** 110/150.

XXX ❀ **A la Barrière** (Aeby), 3 rte Strasbourg ✆ 88 96 20 23, ⛱ – Ⓟ. AE ⓓ E VISA
closed 15 August-5 September, February holidays, Wednesday dinner and Thursday – **st. : M** (Sunday: booking essential) a la carte 190/280 ♁
Spec. Escalope de foie d'oie poêlée, Barbue et saumon à la vapeur, Paupiette de volaille et ris de veau. **Wines** Riesling, Kaefferkopf.

XX ❀ **Zimmer,** 23 r. Héros ✆ 88 96 62 08 – AE ⓓ E VISA
closed 1-17 August, Sunday dinner and Monday – **st. : M** 85/160
Spec. Foie chaud aux reinettes (September to March), Turbot à l'oseille, Rognon et ris de veau au vinaigre. **Wines** Pinot noir, Edelzwicker.

Ammerschwihr 68770 H.-Rhin 62 ⑱⑲ – pop. 1 639 – alt. 230 – Strasbourg 74.

XXX ❀❀ **Aux Armes de France** (Gaertner) with rm, ✆ 89 47 10 12 – ⊟wc ☎ Ⓟ. AE ⓓ E VISA. ✂ rm
closed January, Thursday lunch and Wednesday – **M** (booking essential) 250/330 and a la carte ♁ – ☕ 30 – **10 rm** 180/400
Spec. Foie gras d'oie, Timbale d'écrevisses au gratin, Canette de Barbarie aux épices et au miel. **Wines** Riesling, Gewurztraminer.

Colmar 68000 H.-Rhin 62 ⑲ – pop. 63 764 alt. 193 – Strasbourg 71.

XXXX ❀❀ **Schillinger,** 16 r. Stanislas ✆ 89 41 43 17, « Fine decor » – AE ⓓ VISA
closed 7 July-1 August, Sunday dinner and Monday except Bank Holidays – **M** 150/290 and a la carte ♁
Spec. Foie gras frais, Caneton au citron. **Wines** Pinot Blanc.

Colroy-la-Roche 67 B.-Rhin 62 ⑧ – pop. 431 alt. 424 – ✉ **67420** Saales – Strasbourg 62.

✿✿ **Host. la Cheneaudière** M, ✆ 88 97 61 64, Telex 870438, ←, « Fashionable country inn in a garden », – TV ☎ P. AE ⓞ E VISA
closed January and February – **st. : M** 180/280 and a la carte – ☐ 55 – **25 ch** 360/480, 4 apartments – P 580/660
Spec. Millefeuille de foie gras et truffes, Tartare de saumon sauvage, Selle de chevreuil à la fondue d'échalotes (June-December). **Wines** Pinot noir, Tokay.

Illhaeusern 68 H.-Rhin 62 ⑲ – pop. 557 – alt. 176 – ✉ **68150** Ribeauvillé – Strasbourg 60.

La Clairière M without rest, **rte Guémar** ✆ **87 71 80 80**, – TV ☎ P
closed January, February and Monday evening in November, December and March – **st. :** ☐ 30 – **24 rm** 270/400.

→

TOURS

Bordeaux (R. de) .... DY 8
Commerce (R. du) ..... CDX 28
Grammont (Av. de) ..... DEZ
Halles (Pl. et R.) .... CY
Marceau (R.) .... CDY
Nationale (R.) .... DXY
Scellerie (R. de la) .... DY 91

Anatole-France (Pl.) ..... DX 4
Béranger (Bd) .... BCDY
Blanqui (R. A.) .... EFX
Boisdenier (R. de) ...... CDZ
Boyer (R. Léon) .... BY
Bretonneau (R.) .... CXY
Briçonnet (R.) .... CX 15
Buffon (R.) .... DY
Cathédrale (Pl.) .... EX 18
Chanoineau (R.) .... CY 20
Chanzy (R. du Gén.) ..... BY
Charpentier (R. J.) ...... BCY
Chevallier (R. A.) .... BCZ
Colbert (R.) .... DX
Constantine (R.) .... CX 29
Corneille (R.) .... DY 30
Courteline (R. G.) .... BY
Descartes (R.) .... CY 33
Desmoulins (R. C.) ...... EFY
Dr-Fournier (R. du) ...... FZ
Docks (R. des) .... EFY
Entraigues (R. d') .... BCYZ
Foire-le-Roi (Pl.) .... DX 38
Fouquet (R. Jehan) ...... CYZ
Fuye (R. de la) .... FYZ
Galpin-Thiou (R.) .... DEZ
Gaulle (Av. Gén.-de) .... EFZ
George Sand (R.) .... DYZ
Gille (R. Charles) .... DY
Giraudeau (R.) .... BYZ
Grandière (R. de la) ...... CY 41
Gd-Marché (Pl.) .... CY 42
Gd-Marché (R.) .... CY 44
Grégoire-de-Tours (Pl.) ... EX 47
Heurteloup (Bd) .... EFY
Jaurès (Pl. Jean) .... DY
Jolivet (R.) .... FZ
Lakanal (R.) .... CZ
Lattre-de-T. (Bd de) ...... EZ
Lavoisier (R.) .... DEX 54
Leclerc (Pl. du Mar.) ..... EY
Lobin (R.) .... FX
Meusnier (R. du Gén.) .. EXY 57
Michelet (R.) .... DYZ
Mirabeau (R.) .... FXY
Néricault-Destouches (R.) .... CDY 60
N.-D. de la Riche (⊞) ... BY
Orléans (Quai d') .... DEX
Paillhou (Pl. Gaston) ..... CY
Palissy (R. Bernard) ...... EY
Pascal (R. Blaise) .... EYZ
Petit-Pré (R. du) .... EY
Plantin (R.) .... FY 66
Plat-d'Étain (R. du) ...... BZ
Plumereau (Pl.) .... CY 67
Pompidou (Av. G.) .... FXY 69
Pont-Neuf (Q. du) .... BCX 70
Preuilly (Bd) .... BY
Proudhon (Av.) .... BX 73
Rabelais (Pl.) .... BZ
Rempart (R. du) .... FY 74

Renault (R. du Gén.) ... BCZ
Résistance (Pl. de la) ... DY 75
Rouget-de-Lisle (R.) .... BY
Sacré-Cœur (⊞) ..... FZ
St-Étienne (⊞) .... DY 80
St-Gatien (Cathédrale) .... EX
St-Julien (⊞) .... DX X
St-Martin (⊞) .... CY W
St-Paul (⊞) .... EZ 83

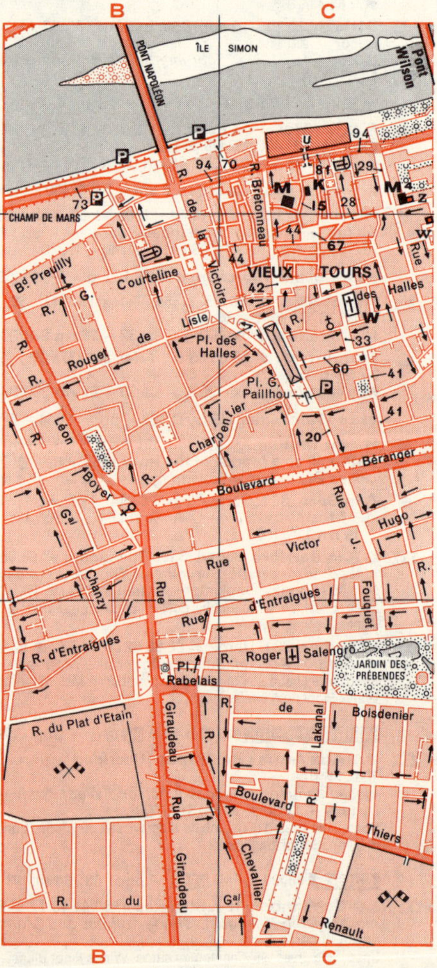

XXXXX ✿✿✿ **Aub de l'Ill** (Haeberlin), ✆ **89 71 83 23, « Tasteful decor, set on the banks of the River Ill, < over flower gardens »** – ▤ Ⓟ. AE ⓓ
closed 30 June-10 July, 2 February-2 March, Monday (except lunch in summer) and Tuesday – **M** (booking essential) a la carte 235/305
Spec. Salade de joues de porc au foie d'oie et lentilles vertes, Suprême de sandre piqué de saumon fumé, Filet de chevreuil aux champignons des bois (Jun-Jan.). **Wines** Riesling, Sylvaner.

Marlenheim **67520** B.-Rhin 62 ⑨ – pop. **2 822** alt. **184** – Strasbourg **20**.

XXX ✿✿ **Host. du Cerf** (Husser) with rm, ✆ **88 87 73 73**, 🍴 – ⇔wc ⋒wc ☎ Ⓟ – 🏛 25. AE ⓓ VISA
closed 6 to 22 January, Monday and Tuesday – **st. : M** 220/310 and a la carte 🌡 – ☕ 30 – **19 ch** 120/250
Spec. Roulades de turbot aux vermicelles, Millefeuille de filet de boeuf à la duxelle de champignons, Crêpes chaudes farcies aux griottes. **Wines** Edelzwicker, Vorlauf.

St-Pierre (⊞)	FX		Simon (R. Jules)	EY		Vaillant (R. E.)	EFYZ	
St-Saturnin (⊞)	CX		Tanneurs (R. des)	BX	94	Victoire (R. de la)	BXY	
Ste-Jeanne d'Arc (⊞)	CZ		Thiers (Bd et Pl.)	CDZ		Victor-Hugo (R.)	BCY	
Salengro (R. Roger)	CDZ		Thomas (R. A.)	EX		Voltaire (R.)	DXY	96
Sicard (Pl. François)	EY	92	Ursulines (R. des)	EXY		Zola (R. Émile)	DY	

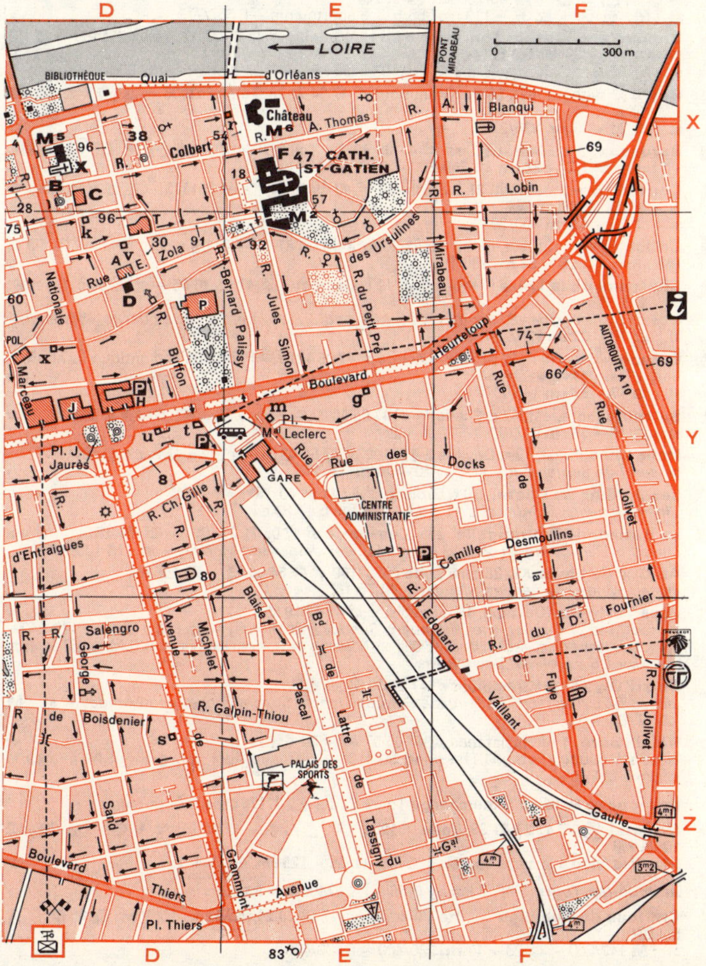

Tours P **37000** I.-et-L. 64 ⑮ – pop. 136 483 Greater Tours 251 320 – alt. 48.

See : Cathedral quarter** : Cathedral** EX, Fine Arts Museum** EXY **M2** – The Psalette* EX **F**, Historial de Touraine* EX **M6**, Place Grégoire de Tours* EX47 – Old Tours** : Place Plumereau* CY 67, hôtel Gouin* CX **M4**, rue Briçonnet* CX 15 – St-Julien quarter* : Craft Guilds Museum** (Musée du Compagnonnage) DX **M5**, Beaune-Semblançay Gardens* DX **B**, – Staircase bannister* of hôtel Mame DY **D** – St-Cosme Priory* W : 3 km – Meslay Tithe Barn* (Grange de Meslay) NE : 10 km.

18 of Touraine 47 53 20 28 ; domaine de la Touche at Ballan-Miré : 14 km.

of Tours-St-Symphorien : T.A.T 47 54 21 45 NE : 7 km.

47 20 23 43.

and Accueil de France (Information, exchange facilities and hotel reservations - not more than 5 days in advance), pl. Gare 47 05 58 08, Télex 750008 – Automobile Club de l'Ouest 4 pl. J.-Jaurès 47 05 50 19.

Paris 234 – Angers 108 – Bordeaux 345 – Chartres 140 – Clermont-Ferrand 307 – Limoges 204 – Le Mans 82 – Orléans 112 – Rennes 236 – St-Étienne 424.

Plan on preceding pages

Méridien M, 292 av. Grammont 37200 47 28 00 80, Telex 750922, ←, , , – AE E VISA
st. : M 105/150 – 37 – **119 rm** 355/530, 6 apartments – P 657/772.

Univers and rest. la Touraine, 5 bd Heurteloup 47 05 37 12, Telex 751460 – – 30. AE E VISA DY **u**
st. : M *(closed Saturday)* 105/140 – 33 – **88 rm** 254/357, 3 apartments 570.

Royal M without rest, 65 av. Grammont 47 64 71 78, Telex 752006 – . AE VISA. DZ **s**
st. : 26 – **35 rm** 236/272.

Bordeaux, 3 pl. Mar.-Leclerc 47 05 40 32, Telex 750414 – . AE E VISA. rm – **M** 120 – **52 rm** 265/300 – P 370/540 DY **t**

Central H. without rest, 21 r. Berthelot 47 05 46 44, Telex 751173 – wc wc . AE E VISA DY **k**
st. : 25 – **42 rm** 150/290.

Criden M without rest, 65 bd Heurteloup 47 20 81 14 – wc . AE E VISA – **st. :** 20 – **32 rm** 235/350 EY **g**

Châteaux de la Loire without rest, 12 r. Gambetta 47 05 10 05 – wc wc . AE E VISA DY **x**
closed 20 December-20 January, Saturday and Sunday from 1 November to 15 March – **st. :** 18 – **32 ch** 129/214.

Europe without rest, 12 pl. Mar.-Leclerc 47 05 42 07, « Paintings and antique furniture » – wc wc EY **m**
st. : 17 – **53 rm** 140/220.

Balzac without rest, 47 r. Scellerie 47 05 40 87 – wc wc . AE E VISA DY **v**
st. : 17 – **18 rm** 91/190.

Italia without rest, 19 r. Devilde 37100 47 54 43 01 – wc wc . VISA.
closed 1-15 September – **st. :** 20 – **20 rm** 95/173.

XXX **Les Jardins du Castel,** 10 r. Groison 47 41 94 40, , – AE
Closed January, Sunday and Monday – **M** 145 b.i./180 b.i..

XXX **La Rôtisserie Tourangelle,** 23 r. Commerce 47 05 71 21, – AE VISA CX **z**
closed 14 July-5 August, 2 to 16 March, Sunday dinner and Monday – **st. : M** 135/260.

XXX **Au Gué de Louis XI,** 36 quai Loire 37100 47 54 00 43 – AE VISA
closed Sunday dinner and Monday – **M** 75/165.

XX ✿ **Les Tuffeaux** (Devaux), 19 r. Lavoisier 47 47 19 89 EX **r**
closed 13 to 27 August, 4 to 26 January, Sunday and Monday – **st. : M** a la carte 175/240
Spec. Bouilleture de poissons blancs au Chinon, Noisettes de lapereau aux pruneaux (1 March-30 September), Nougat glacé. **Wines** Chinon, Vouvray.

XX **Coq d'Or,** 272 av. Grammont 47 20 39 51 – VISA
closed 5-25 August, 6-12 January, Saturday lunch, Sunday dinner and Monday – **st. : M** 110 b.i./85.

XX **Relais Buré,** 1 pl. Résistance 47 05 67 74 – AE VISA CXY **w**
closed Monday – **st. : M** (1st floor) 90/110 - (ground floor coffee shop) **M** a la carte approx. 120 .

exit road to Poitiers : interchange Tours Sud – **37170** Chambray-les-Tours :

Novotel M, 47 27 41 38, Telex 751206, , , – – 200. AE E VISA
M coffee shop a la carte approx. 100 – 35 – **125 rm** 298/344.

at Joué-lès-Tours SW : 5 km by D 86 – **37300** Joué-les-Tours :

Château de Beaulieu , rte Villandry 47 53 20 26, ←, park – wc – 50. VISA
st. : M 142/260 – 28 – **17 rm** 230/400 – P 400/480.

Bracieux **41250** L.-et-Ch. 64 ⑱ – pop. **1 150** – alt. 81.
Tours 81.

XXXX ✿✿ **Le Relais** (Robin), 1 av. Chambord ✆ 54 46 41 22, ≤ – P. AE ⓓ VISA
closed 17 December-25 January, Monday dinner and Wednesday – **st. : M** (booking essential) 170/280 and a la carte
Spec. Gelée de lapin aux herbes potagères, Carpe à la Chambord (season), Rognons et pied de veau au persil. **Wines** Cheverny, Côteaux du Giennois.

Montbazon **37250** I.-et-L. 64 ⑮ **G. Châteaux de la Loire** – pop. **3 011** – alt. 71.
ℹ Mairie ✆ 47 26 01 30.
Paris 247 – Châtellerault 60 – Chinon 41 – Loches 32 – Montrichard 40 – Saumur 67 – Tours 13.

✿ **Château d'Artigny** ⛰, SW : 2 km by D 17 ✆ **47 26 24 24, Telex 750900, « Garden, park, ≤ River Indre, riverside annex with 8 rm »,** ⛱, ✂ – ▯ ☎ P – 🏟 30-70. VISA
closed 1 December-10 January – **st. : M** 200/350 – ☕ 53 – **48 rm** 495/960, 7 apartments 660/1 100
Spec. Homard au Chinon et à la moëlle, Veau de lait rôti et Chartreuse d'écrevisses, Charlotte aux fruits rouges. **Wines** Sauvignon de Touraine, Chinon.

✿ **Domaine de la Tortinière** ⛰, **N : 2 km by N 10 and D 287** ✆ **47 26 00 19, « in a park ≤ valley of River Indre »,** ⛱, ✂ – ☎ P – 🏟 30. E VISA. ✱ rest
1 March-15 November – **st. : M** *(closed Tuesday lunch and Monday in March and from 15 October to 15 November)* a la carte 190/265 – ☕ 40 – **14 rm** 300/540, 7 apartments 550/650
Spec. Escalope de sandre à la graine de moutarde, Pigeonneau de Touraine rôti, Gratin de fruits de saison. **Wines** Vouvray, Chinon.

Relais de Touraine M ⛰, **N : 2 km rte Tours** ✆ **47 26 06 57,** ⛱, **park** – ⌂wc ⌂wc ☎ P – 🏟 50. AE E VISA
st. : M *(closed Sunday dinner and Monday)* 100/240 – ☕ 25 – **21 rm** 220/260 – P 380/400.

XXX ✿ **La Chancelière, 1 pl. Marronniers** ✆ **47 26 00 67** – AE VISA
closed 12 November-1 December, 2 to 12 January, Sunday dinner and Monday except Bank Holidays – **st. : M** a la carte 200/310
Spec. Langoustes aux huiles parfumées, Dos de saumon à la fleur de sel, Pigeon rôti aux figues (September-late October). **Wines** Chinon, Vouvray.

to W : 5 km by N 10, D 287 and D 87 – ✉ **37250** Montbazon :

XX **Moulin fleuri** ⛰ with rm, ✆ **47 26 01 12,** ≤, **« Terrace overlooking the River Indre »,** ⛱ – ⌂ P. AE VISA
closed 15-30 October, 1-20 February and Monday except Bank Holidays – **st. : M** a la carte 100/185 – ☕ 22 – **10 rm** 59/171 – P 178/257.

Romorantin-Lanthenay ⟨SP⟩ **41200** L.-et-Ch. 64 ⑱ – pop. **18 187** – alt. 88.
Tours 90.

✿✿ **Gd H. Lion d'Or** M, **69 r. Clemenceau** ✆ **54 76 00 28, Telex 750990, « flowered terrace »** – ▯ TV ☎ ♿ P – 🏟 50. AE ⓓ E VISA
closed early January-mid February – **st. : M** (booking essential) 220/265 and a la carte – ☕ 45 – **8 rm** 370/430
Spec. Feuilleté d'asperges (April-June), Langoustines rôties, Pannequets de Framboises. **Wines** Vouvray, Bourgueil.

Germany
Deutschland

Berlin
Cologne
Düsseldorf
Frankfurt am Main
Hamburg
Hanover
Munich
Stuttgart

PRACTICAL INFORMATION

LOCAL CURRENCY

Deutsche Mark : 100 DM = 40.57 US $ (Jan. 86)

TOURIST INFORMATION

Deutsche Zentrale für Tourismus (DZT)
Beethovenstr. 69, 6000 Frankfurt 1, ✆ 069/7 57 20
Telex 4189178

Hotel booking service
Allgemeine Deutsche Zimmerreservierung (ADZ)
Beethovenstr. 69, 6000 Frankfurt 1, ✆ 069/74 07 67
Telex 416666

AIRLINES

DEUTSCHE LUFTHANSA AG : Von-Gablenz-Str. 2, 5000 Köln 21, ✆ 0221/82 61

AIR CANADA : 6000 Frankfurt, Friedensstr. 7, ✆ 069/23 40 32

AIR FRANCE : 6000 Frankfurt, Friedensstr. 11, ✆ 069/2 56 61

AMERICAN AIRLINES : 6000 Frankfurt, Wiesenhüttenplatz 26, ✆ 069/23 20 71

BRITISH AIRWAYS : 1000 Berlin 15, Kurfürstendamm 178, ✆ 030/8 82 30 67

JAPAN AIRLINES : 6000 Frankfurt, Goethestr. 9, ✆ 069/1 36 00

PAN AMERICAN : 1000 Berlin 30, Europacenter, ✆ 030/4 10 44 15

TWA : 6000 Frankfurt 90, Hamburger Allee 2, ✆ 069/70 90 97

FOREIGN EXCHANGE

Is possible in banks, saving banks and at exchange offices.
Hours of opening from Monday to Friday 8.30am to 12.30pm and 2.30pm to 4pm except Thursday 2.30pm to 6pm.

SHOPPING

In the index of street names, those printed in red are where the principal shops are found.

BREAKDOWN SERVICE

ADAC : for the addresses see text of the towns mentioned

AvD : Lyoner Str. 16, 6000 Frankfurt 71-Niederrad, ✆ 069/6 60 63 00

In Germany the ADAC, and the AvD, make a special point of assisting foreign motorists. They have motor patrols covering main roads.

TIPPING

In Germany, prices include service and taxes. You may choose to leave a tip if you wish but there is no obligation to do so.

SPEED LIMITS

The speed limit, generally, in built up areas is 50 km/h - 31 mph and on all other roads it is 100 km/h - 62mph. On motorways and dual carriageways, the recommended speed limit is 130 km/h - 80 mph.

SEAT BELTS

The wearing of seat belts is compulsory for drivers and front seat passengers.

BERLIN

SIGHTS

West Berlin

Kurfürstendamm** BDX and Memorial Church (Kaiser-Wilhelm-Gedächtniskirche) DEV – Brandenburg Gate** (Brandenburger Tor) (East-Berlin) GU – Zoological Park** (Zoologischer Garten, Aquarium) EV.
Dahlem Museums (Museum Dahlem)*** (Painting Gallery, Ethnographic Museum**) – Chateau of Charlottenburg** (Schloß Charlottenburg) BU (at the Knobelsdorff-Wing : Painting Collection**, Golden Gallery**, Museum of Decorative Arts* with Guelph treasure**) – Antique Museum* (Antikenmuseum) (ancient treasure***) BU **M3** – Egyptian Museum* (Ägyptisches Museum) bust of Queen Nefertiti*) BU **M4** – National Gallery* (Nationalgalerie) FV **M6**.
Olympic Stadium* (Olympia-Stadion) – Radio Tower** (Funkturm) AV – Botanical Gardens** (Botanischer Garten).
Havel* and Peacock Island* (Pfaueninsel) – Wannsee**.
Church of Maria Regina Martyrum* (Maria-Regina-Martyrum-Kirche) BU **D** and Plötzensee Memorial (Gedenkstätte von Plötzensee) DU.

East-Berlin

Brandenburg Gate** (Brandenburger Tor) GU – Unter den Linden* GUV (State Opera House* GHU **C**, Neue Wache* HU **D**, Arsenal** GHU) – Platz der Akademie* GV.
Museum Island (Museumsinsel) (Pergamon-Museum*** GHU **M7** with Pergamon-Altar, National Gallery** HU **M8**).
Alexanderplatz** HU – Television Tower** (Fernsehturm) (☼) HU **K** – Karl-Marx-Allee* HU – Soviet Memorial* (Sowjetisches Ehrenmal).

BERLIN **West Berlin 1000.** **987** ⑰ – **Pop. 1 960 000 – alt. 40 m** – ☎ **030.**
✈ **Tegel,** ☎ **41 01 31 45.**
🚗 **Berlin - Wannsee,** ☎ **3 13 81 30.**
Exhibition Grounds (Messegelände) AV, ☎ **3 03 81, Telex 182908.**
ℹ Berlin Tourist-Information, Europa-Center (Budapester Straße), ☎ 2 62 60 31, Telex 18 3356 ;
ℹ Tourist Information, at Tegel Airport, ☎ 41 01 31 45.
ADAC, Berlin-Wilmersdorf, Bundesallee 29 (B 31), ☎ 8 68 61, Telex 183513.

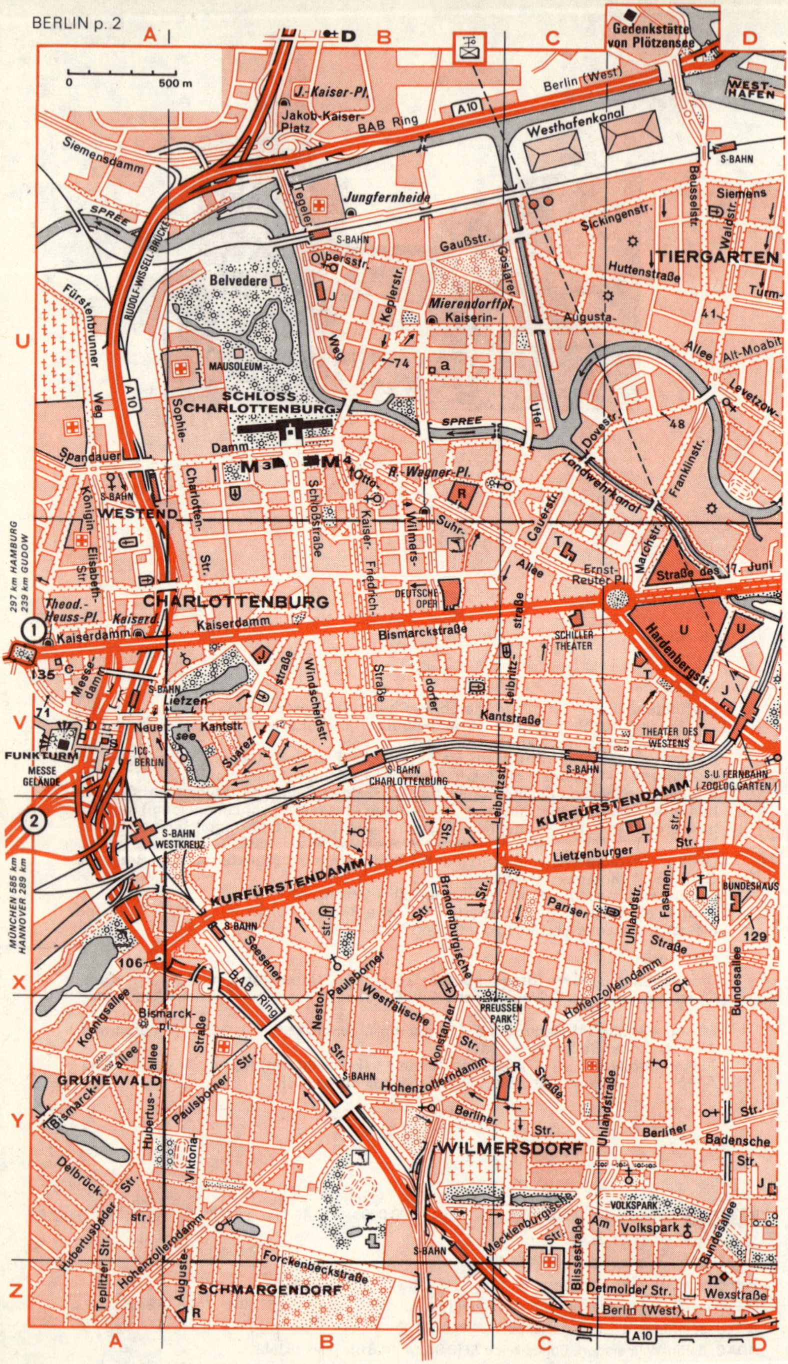
A
B
C
D
U
V
X
Y
Z
0
500 m
Gedenkstätte von Plötzensee
WEST-HAFEN
Berlin (West)
A 10
BAB Ring
J.-Kaiser-Pl.
Jakob-Kaiser-Platz
Westhafenkanal
S-BAHN
Siemensdamm
SPREE
Jungfernheide
Tegeler
Beusselstr.
Siemens
Waldstr.
Sickingenstr.
Gaußstr.
Goslarer
Olbersstr.
RUDOLF-WISSELL-BRÜCKE
TIERGARTEN
Huttenstraße
Turm-
Belvedere
Keplerstr.
Mierendorffpl.
Kaiserin-
Augusta-
Allee
Alt-Moabit
Levetzow-
Fürstenbrunner
Weg
MAUSOLEUM
SCHLOSS CHARLOTTENBURG
74
a
48
Ufer
Dovestr.
Franklinstr.
Spandauer
Damm
Sophie-
Charlotten-
Str.
R.-Wagner-Pl.
Otto-
Landwehrkanal
Schloßstraße
Kaiser-
Friedrich-
Wilmers-
dorfer
Suhr-
Cauerstr.
Marchstr.
Straße des 17. Juni
Ernst-Reuter-Pl.
WESTEND
Königin-
Elisabeth-
Str.
297 km HAMBURG
239 km GUDOW
CHARLOTTENBURG
Theod.-Heuss-Pl.
Kaiserd.
Kaiserdamm
1
DEUTSCHE OPER
Bismarckstraße
Leibnitz-
straße
SCHILLER THEATER
Hardenbergstr.
135
C
Messe-
damm
Lietzen-
see
Neue
Kantstr.
Windscheidstr.
Kantstraße
THEATER DES WESTENS
71
b
FUNKTURM
MESSE GELÄNDE
ICC-BERLIN
Suarez-
S-BAHN CHARLOTTENBURG
S-U. FERNBAHN (ZOOLOG GARTEN)
2
S-BAHN WESTKREUZ
KURFÜRSTENDAMM
Lietzenburger
Str.
MÜNCHEN 585 km
HANNOVER 289 km
Brandenburgische
Pariser
Uhlandstr.
Fasanen-
BUNDESHAUS
129
Seesener
106
Paulsborner
Nestor-
Westfälische
PREUSSEN PARK
Hohenzollerndamm
Bundesallee
Koenigsallee
Bismarck-pl.
Bismarck-allee
Hubertus-allee
GRUNEWALD
Konstanzer
Berliner
WILMERSDORF
Uhlandstraße
Badensche
Delbrück-
Viktoria
Hubertusbader
VOLKSPARK
Am Volkspark
Mecklenburgische
Blissestraße
Teplitzer Str.
Auguste-
Forckenbeckstraße
SCHMARGENDORF
Detmolder Str.
Wexstraße
R
T
J

BERLIN

Street index : See pp 5 and 8

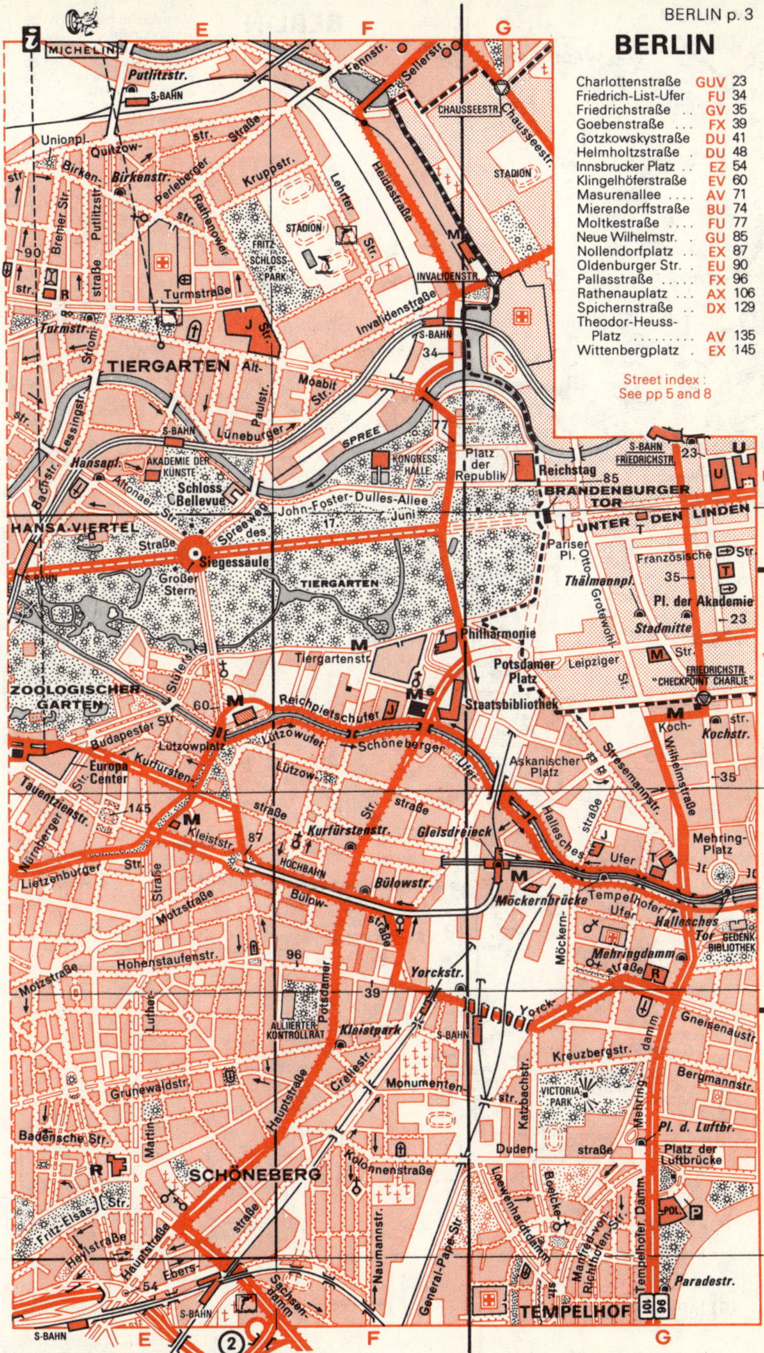

BERLIN

Brückenstraße	HV	17
Charlottenstraße	GUV	23
Fontanepromenade	HY	31
Gertraudenstraße	HV	38
Grunerstraße	HU	44
Holzmarktstraße	HV	53
Littenstraße	HU	66
Marx-Engels-Pl.	HU	70
Neue Wilhelmstr.	GU	85

Street index : See pp 5 and 8

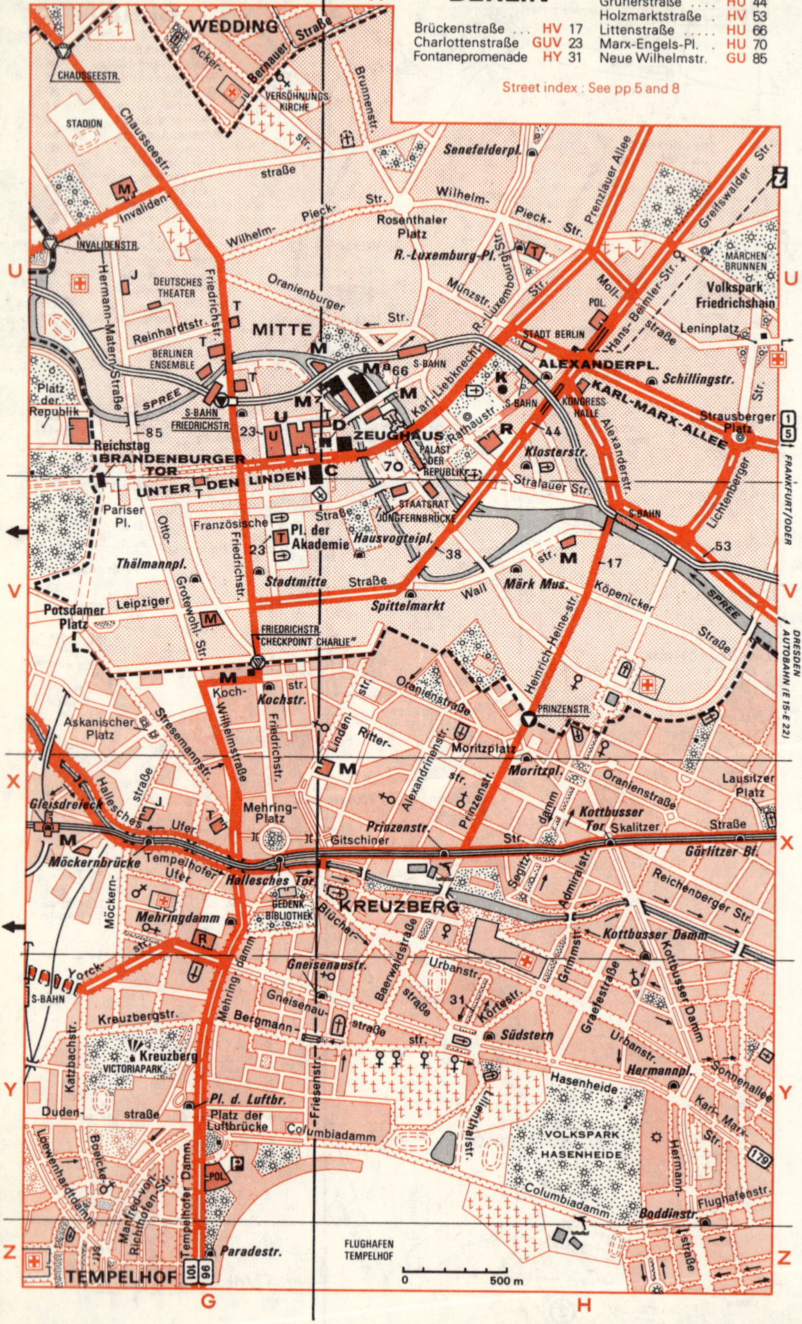

Continued p. 8

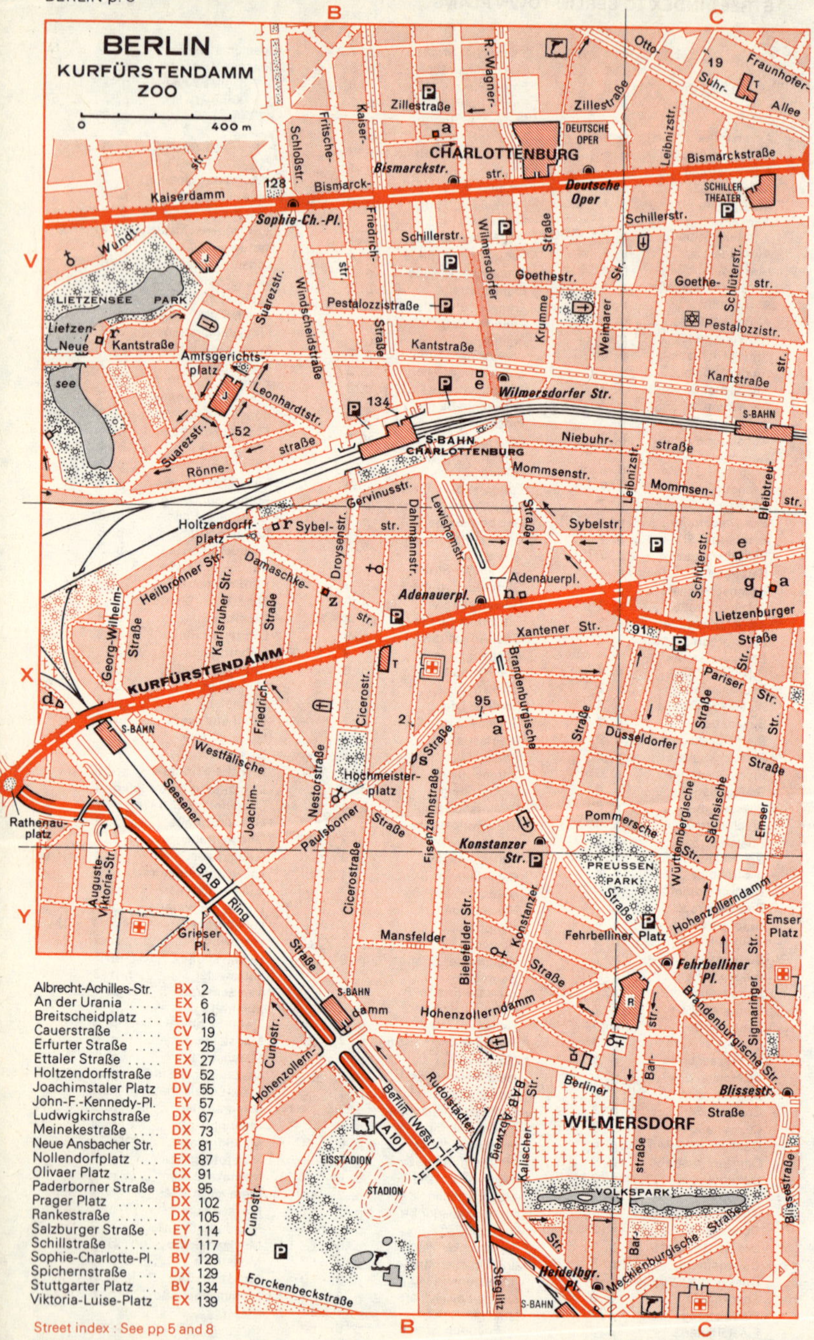

Albrecht-Achilles-Str.	BX	2
An der Urania	EX	6
Breitscheidplatz	EV	16
Cauerstraße	CV	19
Erfurter Straße	EY	25
Ettaler Straße	EX	27
Holtzendorffstraße	BV	52
Joachimstaler Platz	DV	55
John-F.-Kennedy-Pl.	EY	57
Ludwigkirchstraße	DX	67
Meinekestraße	DX	73
Neue Ansbacher Str.	EX	81
Nollendorfplatz	EX	87
Olivaer Platz	CX	91
Paderborner Straße	BX	95
Prager Platz	DX	102
Rankestraße	DX	105
Salzburger Straße	EY	114
Schillstraße	EV	117
Sophie-Charlotte-Pl.	BV	128
Spichernstraße	DX	129
Stuttgarter Platz	BV	134
Viktoria-Luise-Platz	EX	139

Street index : See pp 5 and 8

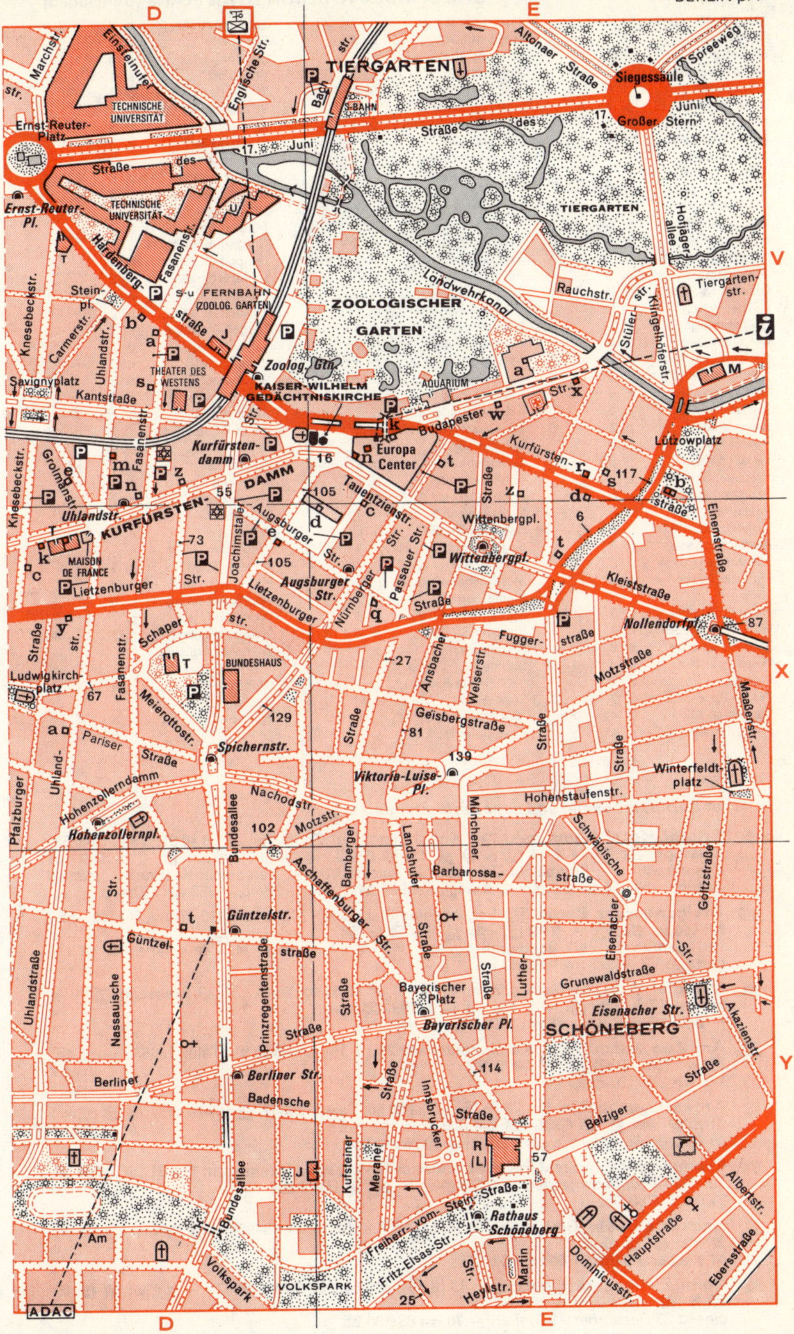

STREET INDEX TO BERLIN TOWN PLANS (Concluded)

The reference (B 15) at the end of the address is the postal district : Berlin 15

at Kurfürstendamm and near Kurfürstendamm :

Bristol-Hotel Kempinski, Kurfürstendamm 27 (B 15), 88 10 91, Telex 183553, Massage, – . AE ① E VISA. rest — DV n
Restaurants : – **Kempinski-Grill M** a la carte 40/85 – **Kempinski-Restaurant** *(closed Monday)* **M** a la carte 36/75 – **Kempinski-Eck M** a la carte 28/45 – **358 rm** 230/400.

Steigenberger Berlin, Los-Angeles-Platz 1 (B 30), 2 10 80, Telex 181444, Massage, – . AE ① E VISA — EX d
Restaurants : – **Park-Restaurant** *(dinner only)* **M** a la carte 47/74 – **Berliner Stube M** a la carte 23/52 – **377 rm** 190/360 Bb.

Mondial, Kurfürstendamm 47 (B 15), 88 41 10, Telex 182839, Massage, – rest (with). AE ① E VISA. rest — CX e
M a la carte 28/60 – **75 rm** 145/210 Bb.

Am Zoo without rest, Kurfürstendamm 25 (B 15), 88 30 91, Telex 183835 – wc wc . AE ① E VISA — DV z
145 rm 110/170 Bb.

Arosa, Lietzenburger Str. 79 (B 15), 88 00 50, Telex 183397, (heated) – wc wc . AE ① E VISA. rest — DX y
M *(closed Sunday)* a la carte 26/55 – **90 rm** 110/185 Bb.

Kronprinz without rest (restored house of 1894), Kronprinzendamm 1 (B 31), 89 60 30, Telex 181459, beer-garden – wc . AE ① E VISA — BX d
53 rm 85/165 Bb.

Hecker's Deele, Grolmanstr. 35 (B 12), 8 89 01, Telex 184954 – rest wc . AE ① E — DV e
M a la carte 23/63 – **60 rm** 108/177.

Domus without rest, Uhlandstr. 49 (B 15), 88 20 41, Telex 185975 – wc . AE ① E VISA — DX a
closed 23 December - 1 January – **76 rm** 88/130 Bb.

Kurfürstendamm am Adenauerplatz without rest, Kurfürstendamm 68 (B 15), 88 28 41, Telex 184630 – wc wc . BX n
33 rm 69/195.

Berlin-Plaza without rest, Knesebeckstr. 63 (B 15), 88 41 30, Telex 184181 – wc wc . DX c
131 rm 98/144 Bb.

Bremen without rest, Bleibtreustr. 25 (B 15), 8 81 40 76, Telex 184892 – wc . CX g
closed 21 to 28 December – **48 rm** 120/180.

Ristorante Anselmo, Damaschkestr. 17 (B 31), 3 23 30 94, « Modern Italian rest. » – BX z
closed Monday – **M** a la carte 38/71.

Tessiner Stuben, Bleibtreustr. 33 (B 15), 8 81 36 11 – CX a
closed lunch Saturday and Sunday – **M** a la carte 36/77 (booking essential).

Kopenhagen (Danish Smörrebröds), Kurfürstendamm 203 (B 15), 8 83 25 03 – . DX k
M a la carte 29/55.

Hongkong (Chinese rest.), Kurfürstendamm 210 (2nd floor,) (B 15), 8 81 57 56 – DX T
M a la carte 23/38.

Friesenhof, Uhlandstr. 185 (B 12), 8 83 60 79 – DV m
M a la carte 17.50/45.

near Memorial Church and Zoological Park :

Inter-Continental, Budapester Str. 2 (B 30), 2 60 20, Telex 184380, Massage, , – . rest EV a
M a la carte 45/79 – **Brasserie M** a la carte 34/55 – **600 rm** 181/382 Bb.

Schweizerhof, Budapester Str. 21 (B 30), 2 69 60, Telex 185501, Massage, , – rest (with). . rest EV w
M a la carte 36/75 – **431 rm** 168/314.

Palace - Restaurant La Réserve, Budapester Str. 42 (Europa-Centre) (B 30), 26 20 11, Telex 184825 – rest . . rest EV k
M a la carte 48/85 – **175 rm** 161/384 Bb.

Alsterhof, Augsburger Str. 5 (B 30), 21 99 60, Telex 183484, , Massage, , – . EX q
M a la carte 25/60 – **141 rm** 123/192 Bb.

Berlin-Penta Hotel , Nürnberger Str. 65 (B 30), 24 00 11, Telex 182877, Massage, , – . . rest EV t
M a la carte 30/66 – **425 rm** 177/229 Bb.

Savoy, Fasanenstr. 9 (B 12), 31 06 54, Telex 184292 – . . rest DV s
M a la carte 30/60 – **115 rm** 148/260 Bb.

Berlin, Kurfürstenstr. 62 (B 30), 26 92 91, Telex 184332, – rest (with). . rest EV b
M a la carte 27/60 (see also **Berlin Grill**) – **255 rm** 105/178 Bb.

Berlin Excelsior Hotel, Hardenbergstr. 14 (B 12), 3 19 91, Telex 184781 – rest . . rest DV b
M a la carte 29/68 – **320 rm** 142/192 Bb.

Ambassador - Restaurant Conti-Fischstuben, Bayreuther Str. 42 (B 30), 21 90 20, Telex 184259, Massage, , – rest wc wc . . rest EV z
M *(closed Sunday)* a la carte 35/75 – **200 rm** 125/220 Bb.

Hamburg, Landgrafenstr. 4 (B 30), 26 91 61, Telex 184974 – wc . . rest EV s
M a la carte 23/58 – **240 rm** 118/168 Bb.

Sylter Hof, Kurfürstenstr. 116 (B 30), 2 12 00, Telex 183317 – wc . EV d
M *(closed Sunday dinner)* a la carte 25/56 – **131 rm** 120/280 Bb – 25 apartments 180/280.

President without rest, An der Urania 16 (B 30), 21 90 30, Telex 184018, – wc wc . EX t
60 rm 110/200 Bb.

Astoria without rest, Fasanenstr. 2 (B 12), 3 12 40 67, Telex 181745 – wc wc . DV a
32 rm 65/150.

Remter without rest, Marburger Str. 17 (B 30), 24 60 61, Telex 183497 – wc wc . EVX c
33 rm 75/130 Bb.

Berlin-Grill, Kurfürstenstr. 62 (at Berlin Hotel) (B 30), 26 92 91 – . – *closed Sunday* – **M** a la carte 43/84 (booking essential) EV b

Ritz, Rankestr. 26 (B 30), 24 72 50 – DX e
closed 4 weeks July - August, Sunday and Bank Holidays – **M** a la carte 36/66.

XX **Mövenpick - Café des Artistes**, Europa-Centre (1st floor) (B 30), ✆ 2 62 70 77, ←, ☂ – ▤. AE ⓓ E EV **n**
M a la carte 32/64 – **Mövenpick-Restaurant M** a la carte 22/42.

XX **Du Pont**, Budapester Str. 1 (B 30), ✆ 2 61 88 11 – AE ⓓ E EV **x**
closed 24 December - 2 January, Saturday lunch, Sunday and Bank Holidays – **M** a la carte 35/72.

XX **Daitokai** (Japanese rest.), Tauentzienstr. 9 (Europa Centre, 1st floor) (B 30), ✆ 2 61 80 99 – AE ⓓ E VISA. ✻ EV **n**
closed Monday – **M** a la carte 33/68.

XX **Ristorante Il Sorriso** (Italian rest.), Kurfürstenstr. 76 (B 30), ✆ 2 62 13 13 – AE ⓓ E. ✻ – *closed Sunday* – **M** a la carte 27/54 (booking essential) EV **r**

at Berlin-Charlottenburg :

Seehof ⛰, Lietzensee-Ufer 11 (B 19), ✆ 32 00 20, Telex 182943, ←, ☂, ≘s, ▣ – 🛗 TV 🚗 🏔 (with ▤). AE ⓓ E VISA. ✻ rest BV **r**
M a la carte 36/72 – **77 rm** 120/210 Bb.

Kanthotel without rest, Kantstr. 111 (B 12), ✆ 32 30 26, Telex 183330 – 🛗 TV 🛁wc 🚿wc ☎ Ⓟ. AE ⓓ E VISA BV **e**
55 rm 119/169 Bb.

Ibis without rest, Messedamm 10 (B 19), ✆ 30 20 11, Telex 182882 – 🛗 🛁wc 🚿wc ☎ 🏔 AV **b**
191 rm Bb.

Econtel without rest (modern economy-hotel), Sömmeringstr. 24 (B 10), ✆ 34 40 01 – 🛗 🚿wc ☎ Ⓟ 🏔. E BU **a**
205 rm 77/117.

Kardell, Gervinusstr. 24 (B 12), ✆ 3 24 10 66 – 🛗 🛁wc 🚿wc ☎ Ⓟ. AE ⓓ E VISA BX **r**
M *(closed Saturday lunch)* a la carte 29/65 – **33 rm** 80/150 Bb.

Am Studio without rest, Kaiserdamm 80 (B 19), ✆ 30 20 81, Telex 182825 – TV 🛁wc ☎ 🚗. AE ⓓ E VISA AV **c**
78 rm 75/115 Bb.

XX ✿ **Ponte Vecchio** (Tuscan rest.), Spielhagenstr. 3 (B 10), ✆ 3 42 19 99 – ⓓ BV **a**
closed Tuesday and 4 weeks July - August – **M** *(dinner only)* a la carte 32/59 (booking essential)
Spec. Carpaccio "a modo mio", Spaghetti "al Rosa Nero", Medaglioni d'agnello "alla Fiorentina".

XX **Pullman**, Messedamm 11 (Congress Centre) (B 19), ✆ 30 38 39 46, ← – 🛗 ▤ ♿ 🏔. AE ⓓ E. ✻ AV **s**
closed Sunday dinner and 4 weeks July - August – **M** a la carte 22/61.

at Berlin-Dahlem by ② EZ :

Forsthaus Paulsborn ⛰, Am Grunewaldsee (B 33), ✆ 8 13 80 10, ☂ – TV 🛁wc 🚿wc ☎ Ⓟ. AE ⓓ E VISA
M *(closed Monday)* a la carte 22/54 – **11 rm** 85/120.

XX **Alter Krug**, Königin-Luise-Str. 52 (B 33), ✆ 8 32 50 89, « Terrace » – Ⓟ. ⓓ E VISA
closed Thursday – **M** a la carte 21/61.

at Berlin-Nikolassee by ② EZ :

XX **An der Rehwiese**, Matterhornstr. 101 (B 38), ✆ 8 03 27 20 – ⓓ
closed Tuesday and 3 weeks July – **M** (dinner only) a la carte 37/75 (booking essential).

at Berlin-Reinickendorf by Sellerstr. FU :

Rheinsberg am See, Finsterwalder Str. 64 (B 26), ✆ 4 02 10 02, Telex 185972, ☂, Massage, ≘s, ⛱, ▣, 🛶 – 🛗 TV 🚿wc ☎ Ⓟ
M a la carte 25/60 – **75 rm** 65/142 Bb.

at Berlin-Steglitz by Hauptstr. EYZ :

Steglitz International Ⓜ, Albrechtstr. 2 (B 41), ✆ 79 10 61, Telex 183545, Massage, ≘s – 🛗 TV ♿ 🏔. AE ⓓ E VISA
M a la carte 29/58 – **212 rm** 120/190 Bb.

at Berlin-Tegel by Jakob-Kaiser-Platz BU :

Novotel Berlin Airport Ⓜ, Kurt-Schumacher-Damm 202 (by airport approach) (B 51), ✆ 4 10 60, Telex 181605, ≘s, ⛱ (heated) – 🛗 ▤ TV 🛁wc ☎ ♿ Ⓟ 🏔. AE ⓓ VISA
M a la carte 25/47 – **187 rm** 135/183 Bb.

at Berlin-Waidmannslust by Sellerstr. FU :

XXX ✿ **Rockendorf's Restaurant** (elegant installation), Düsterhauptstr. 1 (B 28), ✆ 4 02 30 99 – AE ⓓ
closed Sunday, Monday, Bank Holidays, 3 weeks August and Christmas - New Year – **M** a la carte 48/92 (booking essential)
Spec. Parfait von Tomaten und Joghurt mit warmem Hummer, Wildentenbrust in Gänsestopflebersauce (October - November), Terrine von Datteln und Feigen mit Zimtsauce und Honigeis.

at Berlin-Wilmersdorf :

Crest Motor Hotel without rest, Güntzelstr. 14 (B 31), ✆ 87 02 41, Telex 182948 – wc wc . AE E VISA DY **t**
110 rm 145/189 Bb.

Franke, Albrecht-Achilles-Str. 57 (B 31), ✆ 8 92 10 97, Telex 184857 – wc BX **s**
67 rm.

Lichtburg, Paderborner Str. 10 (B 15), ✆ 8 91 80 41, Telex 184208 – wc . AE E VISA BX **a**
M a la carte 20/37 – **62 rm** 100/153.

Medel, Durlacher Str. 25 (B 31), « Furnished in Tyrolean chalet-style » – AE E DZ **n**
closed lunch Monday to Saturday – **M** a la carte 32/63.

COLOGNE (KÖLN) 5000. Nordrhein-Westfalen 987 ㉓ ㉔ – pop. 1 008 700 – alt. 65 m – ✆ 0221.

See : Cathedral (Dom)★★★ (Magi's Shrine★★★) DV **– Roman-Germanic Museum (Römisch-Germanisches Museum)★★★ (Dionysos Mosaic)** DV **– Wallraf-Richartz-Museum (14 - 16 C pictures by Cologne Masters) and Museum Ludwig★★★** DVX **– Schnütgen-Museum★★ (Madonnas of Cologne)** DX **M2 – St. Columbia (St. Kolumba)★** DX **V – St. Alban the New (Neu St. Alban)★ – St. Maria of the Capitol (St. Maria im Kapitol) (wooden doors★★)** DX **D – Holy Apostles (St. Aposteln) (apse★)** CX **N – St. Severinus (St. Severin) (inside★)** DY **K – Rhine Park (Rheinpark)★.**

Köln-Bonn at Wahn (SE : 17 km), ✆ (02203) 4 01.

✆ 1 41 56 66.

Exhibition Centre (Messegelände), ✆ 82 11, Telex 8873426.

Tourist office (Verkehrsamt), Am Dom, ✆ 2 21 33 40, Telex 8883421.

ADAC, Köln 51-Bayenthal, Alteburger Str. 375, ✆ 3 79 90.

Düsseldorf 39 – Aachen 70 – Bonn 27 – Essen 68.

Plans on following pages

The reference (K 15) at the end of the address is the postal district : Köln 15

Excelsior Hotel Ernst - Restaurant Hanse Stube, Trankgasse 1 (K 1), ✆ 27 01, Telex 8882645 – rest (with). AE E. rest DV **a**
M a la carte 36/83 – **146 rm** 208/425 Bb.

Dom-Hotel , Domkloster 2a (K 1), ✆ 23 37 51, Telex 8882919, « Terrace with < » – . AE E VISA. rest DV **d**
M a la carte 35/90 – **126 rm** 185/370 Bb.

Inter-Continental, Helenenstr. 14 (K 1), ✆ 22 80, Telex 8882162, Massage, , – . AE E VISA. rest CV **p**
M a la carte 40/100 – **300 rm** 227/440 Bb.

Consul, Belfortstr. 9 (K 1), ✆ 7 72 10, Telex 8885242, , – . AE E VISA. rest DU **v**
M *(closed Sunday and Bank Holidays)* a la carte 27/56 – **122 rm** 137/250 Bb.

Mondial, Bechergasse 10 (K 1), ✆ 21 96 71, Telex 8881932 – . AE E VISA. rest DV **f**
M a la carte 32/62 – **204 rm** 140/215 Bb.

Savoy without rest, Turiner Str. 9 (K 1), ✆ 12 04 66, Telex 8886360 – wc wc . AE E DU **s**
69 rm 110/265 Bb.

Haus Lyskirchen, Filzengraben 28 (K 1), ✆ 23 48 91, Telex 8885449, – wc wc . AE E VISA DY **u**
closed 23 December - 2 January – **M** *(dinner only, closed Sunday and Bank Holidays)* a la carte 28/58 – **95 rm** 90/190 Bb.

Bristol without rest, Kaiser-Wilhelm-Ring 48 (K 1), ✆ 12 01 95, Telex 8881146, « Antique furnished rooms » – wc wc . AE E VISA CU **m**
44 rm 95/205.

Ascot Hotel (rest. in bistro-style), Hohenzollernring 95 (K 1), ✆ 52 10 76, Telex 8883018 – wc wc . AE E VISA CV **a**
M *(closed lunch Saturday and Sunday)* a la carte 20/47 – **52 rm** 88/225 Bb.

Königshof without rest, Richartzstr. 14 (K 1), ✆ 23 45 83, Telex 8881318 – wc wc . AE E VISA DV **n**
95 rm 105/235 Bb.

Eden-Hotel without rest, Am Hof 18 (K 1), ✆ 23 61 23, Telex 8882889 – wc wc . AE E DV **w**
33 rm 138/220 Bb.

Kolpinghaus International, St.-Apern-Str. 32 (K 1), ✆ 21 03 53 – wc . AE CVX **q**
M a la carte 18/50 – **48 rm** 80/110.

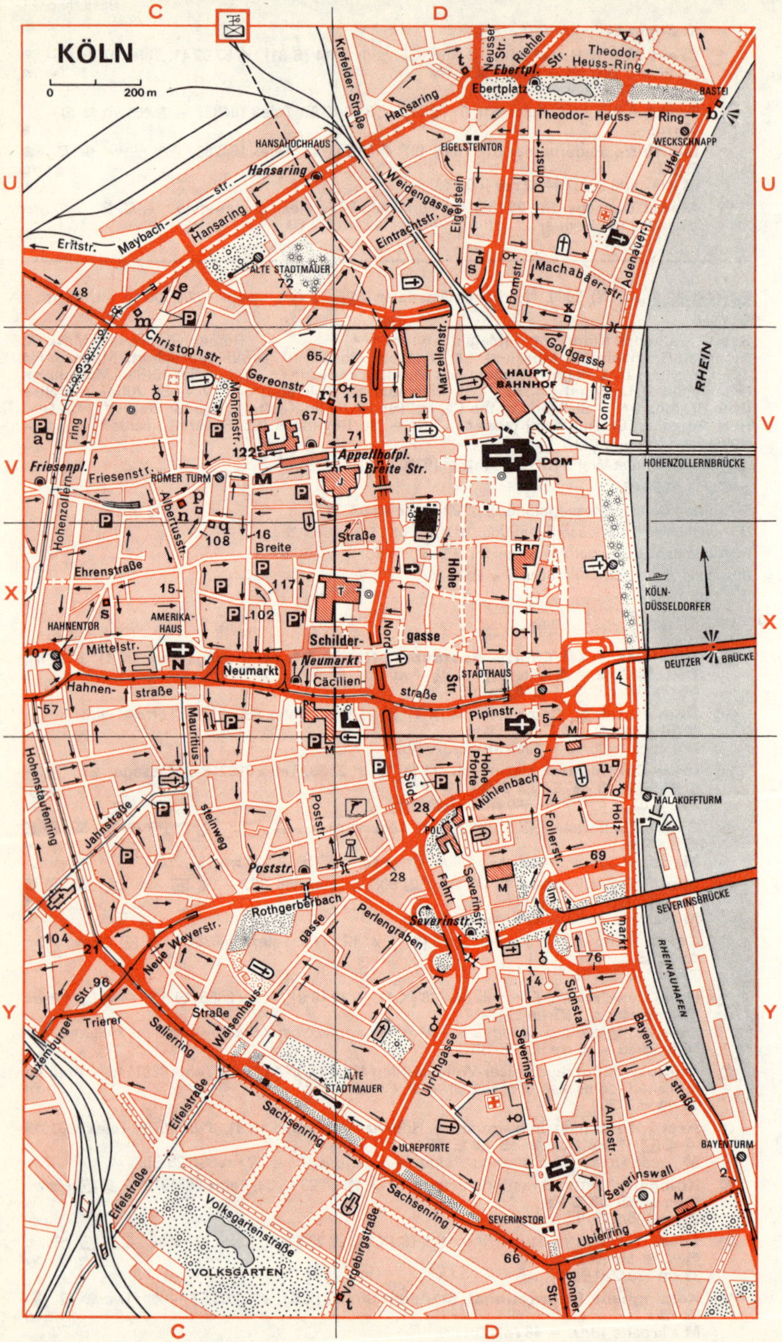
KÖLN
0
200 m
C
D
U
V
X
Y
Krefelder Straße
Neusser Str.
Riehler Str.
Theodor-Heuss-Ring
Ebertpl.
Ebertplatz
BASTEI
Hansaring
HANSAHOCHHAUS
EIGELSTEINTOR
WECKSCHNAPP
Theodor-Heuss-Ring
Weidengasse
Eigelstein
Domstr.
Adenauer-Ufer
Maybach-str.
Eritstr.
ALTE STADTMAUER
Eintrachtstr.
Machabäer-str.
Goldgasse
Christophstr.
Gereonstr.
Marzellenstr.
HAUPT-BAHNHOF
Konrad-
RHEIN
Friesenpl.
Friesenstr.
RÖMER TURM
Mohrenstr.
Appellhofpl.
Breite Str.
DOM
HOHENZOLLERNBRÜCKE
Hohenzollernring
Albertusstr.
Breite
Straße
Hohe
Ehrenstraße
KÖLN-DÜSSELDORFER
HAHNENTOR
AMERIKA-HAUS
Mittelstr.
Schilder-gasse
Nord-
Str.
Neumarkt
Neumarkt
Cäcilien-straße
STADTHAUS
DEUTZER BRÜCKE
Hahnen-straße
Mauritius-
Pipinstr.
Hohenstaufenring
Hohe Pforte
Jahnstraße
steinweg
Poststr.
Süd-
Mühlenbach
Follerstr.
Holz-
MALAKOFFTURM
POL.
Poststr.
Fahrt
Severinstr.
SEVERINSBRÜCKE
Rothgerberbach
Perlengraben
Severinstr.
Im-
markt
Neue Weyerstr.
gasse
RHEINAUHAFEN
Luxemburger Str.
Trierer
Straße
Waisenhaus-
Salierring
Ulrichgasse
Sionstal
Bayen-straße
Severinstr.
ALTE STADTMAUER
Eifelstraße
Sachsenring
ULREPFORTE
Annostr.
BAYENTURM
Severinswall
Eifelstraße
Volksgartenstraße
Sachsenring
SEVERINSTOR
Ubierring
VOLKSGARTEN
Vorgebirgstraße
Bonner Str.

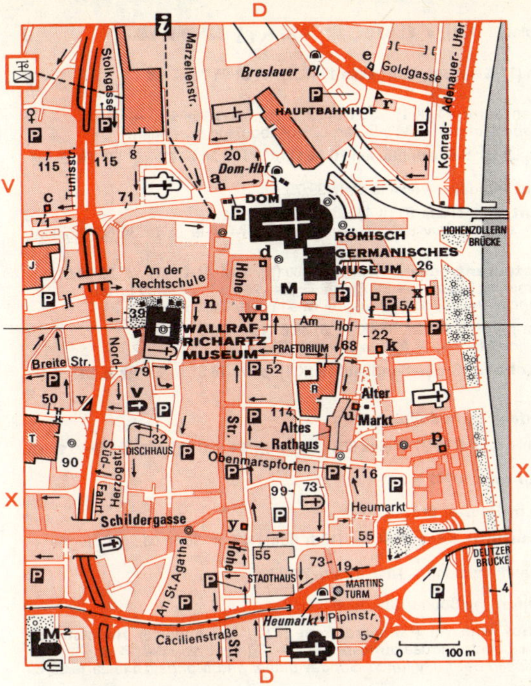

🏨 **Kommerzhotel** without rest, Breslauer Platz (K 1), ✆ 12 40 86, 🛏 – 🛗 📺 🛁wc 🚿wc ☎. AE ⓓ E VISA — DV r
57 rm 105/190 Bb.

🏨 **PLM-Hotel Baseler Hof**, Breslauer Platz 2 (K 1), ✆ 1 65 40, Telex 8886982 – 🛗 📺 🛁wc 🚿wc ☎ 🅰. AE ⓓ E VISA — DV e
M *(lunch only, closed Saturday, Sunday and Bank Holidays)* a la carte 34/51 – **108 rm** 128/210 Bb.

🏨 **Windsor** without rest, Von-Werth-Str. 36 (K 1), ✆ 13 40 31 – 🛗 🚿wc ☎. AE ⓓ E VISA
closed 20 December - 1 January – **37 rm** 70/190. — CU e

🏨 **Ludwig** without rest, Brandenburger Str. 24 (K 1), ✆ 12 30 31, Telex 8885326 – 🛗 📺 🛁wc 🚿wc ☎ 🚗. AE ⓓ E VISA — DU x
closed 23 December - 1 January – **61 rm** 95/165 Bb.

XXXX ✿ **Chez Alex**, Mühlengasse 1 (K 1), ✆ 23 05 60, « Elegant furniture » – ▤. AE ⓓ E
closed Saturday lunch, Sunday and Bank Holidays – **M** a la carte 58/110 (booking essential) — DX k
Spec. Mousse et tatar de saumon, Escalope de turbot au basilic, Foie gras chaud aux girolles.

XXX ✿ **Rino Casati**, Ebertplatz 3 (K 1), ✆ 72 11 08 – ⓓ E VISA. ✈ — DU t
closed Sunday and 3 weeks June - July – **M** a la carte 40/90 (booking essential)
Spec. Nudelgerichte, Babysteinbutt mit Champagnersauce, Ente mit Pflaumensauce.

XXX **Die Bastei**, Konrad-Adenauer-Ufer 80 (K 1), ✆ 12 28 25, ≤ Rhein – AE ⓓ E. ✈
closed Saturday lunch – **M** a la carte 45/92. — DU b

XXX **Franz Kellers Restaurant**, Aachener Str. 21 (K 1), ✆ 21 95 49, 🍽 – Ⓟ. AE ⓓ E
M *(dinner only, closed Sunday)* a la carte 57/90 (booking essential) – **Kellers Keller** *(lunch also, closed Sunday until 7 p. m.)* **M** à la carte 33/72. by Rudolfplatz CX

XXX ✿ **Restaurant Bado - La poêle d'or**, Komödienstr. 52 (K 1), ✆ 13 41 00 – ⓓ E
closed Monday lunch, Sunday, Bank Holidays, 3 weeks July - August and Christmas - New Year – **M** a la carte 56/99 – **Bistro M** a la carte 20/47 — DV c
Spec. Foie gras poelé à la graine de moutarde et raisins, St. Pierre aux zestes d'orange et endives, Canette de Barbarie aux deux cuissons.

XX **Ristorante Alfredo**, Tunisstr. 3 (K 1), ✆ 24 43 01 – AE — DX v
closed Saturday dinner, Sunday and 3 weeks July - August – **M** a la carte 44/74 (booking essential).

XX **St. Georg**, Magnusstr. 3 (K 1), ✆ 21 84 18, 🍽 – AE ⓓ E VISA — CV n
closed Sunday and Bank Holidays except exhibitions – **M** a la carte 48/93.

XX **Ratskeller**, Rathausplatz 1 (K 1), ✆ 21 83 01, – ▤ ♿ AE ⓓ E VISA — DX u
M a la carte 26/70.

XX **Weinhaus im Walfisch (17 C house)**, Salzgasse 13 (K 1), ✆ 21 95 75 – ✻ (booking essential). — DX p

XX **Em Krützche**, Am Frankenturm 1 (K 1), ✆ 21 14 32, « Terrace with ≤ » – ⓓ — DV x
closed April - 15 June and Monday – **M** a la carte 29/64 (booking essential).

XX **Börsen-Restaurant**, Unter Sachsenhausen 10 (K 1), ✆ 13 56 26 – ▤. AE ⓓ E VISA. ✻ — CV r
closed Sunday and Bank Holidays – **M** a la carte 39/75.

XX **Elsbeth's Restaurant**, Benesisstr. 57 (K 1), ✆ 21 42 78 – ✻ — CX s
closed Saturday lunch and Sunday except exhibitions – **M** a la carte 34/66 (booking essential).

XX **Colonius - Turmrestaurant**, Innere Kanalstr. 100 (▮, DM 4) (K 1), ✆ 52 20 61, ✻ Cologne, « Revolving rest. at 166 m » – ▤ Ⓟ. ⓓ E VISA. ✻ — by Erftstr. CU
closed Monday, and lunch Tuesday to Saturday – **M** a la carte 20/58.

X **La Baurie** (French rest.), Vorgebirgstr. 35 (K 1), ✆ 38 61 49 – VISA — DY t
closed Saturday lunch and Monday – **M** a la carte 42/72.

X **China-Restaurant Tchang**, Große Sandkaul 19 (K 1), ✆ 21 76 51 – AE ⓓ E VISA — DX y
M a la carte 21/43.

at Cologne 41-Braunsfeld by Rudolfplatz CX :

Regent, Melatengürtel 15, ✆ 5 49 91, Telex 8881824 – ▮ ▤ rest TV ⇔wc ⋒wc ☎ Ⓟ. AE ⓓ E VISA
M a la carte 32/63 – **157 rm** 129/242 Bb.

at Cologne 21-Deutz by Deutzer Brücke DX :

XX **Restaurant im Messeturm**, Kennedy-Ufer (18th floor, ▮), ✆ 88 10 08, ≤ Cologne – ▤. AE ⓓ E. ✻
closed Saturday lunch and Thursday – **M** a la carte 36/72.

at Cologne 50-Immendorf by Bonner Str. DZ :

XX **Weinstuben Bitzerhof** with rm (farmyard from 1821), Immendorfer Hauptstr. 21, ✆ (02236) 6 19 21, « Country house atmosphere » – TV ⋒wc ☎. ✻ rm
closed August – **M** *(closed Saturday lunch, Sunday dinner and Monday)* a la carte 33/60 – **3 rm** 80/130.

at Cologne 41-Lindenthal by Rudolfplatz and B 264 CX :

Crest-Hotel Köln, Dürener Str. 287, ✆ 46 30 01, Telex 8882516, « Garden with » – ▮ ▤ rest TV ♿ Ⓟ (with ▤). ✻ rest
152 rm Bb.

Bremer, Dürener Str. 225, ✆ 40 50 13, Telex 8882063, – ▮ ▤ rest TV ⇔wc ⋒wc ☎. AE ⓓ E VISA. ✻
closed 20 December - 4 January – **M** a la carte 38/78 (booking essential) – **König-Pub M** a la carte 25/56 – **75 rm** 95/165 Bb.

at Cologne 40-Marsdorf by Rudolfplatz and B 264 CX :

Novotel Köln-Westkreuz, Horbeller Str. 1, ✆ (02234) 1 60 81, Telex 8886355, (heated), – ▮ ▤ rest TV ⇔wc ☎ ♿ Ⓟ with ▤. AE ⓓ E VISA
M a la carte 32/62 – **140 rm** 149/197.

at Cologne 91-Merheim by Deutzer Brücke DX :

XXXX ✿✿✿ **Goldener Pflug**, Olpener Str. 421 (B 55), ✆ 89 55 09 – Ⓟ
closed Saturday lunch, Sunday, Bank Holidays and 3 weeks July - August – **M** a la carte 75/180
Spec. Salat von Langustinos und Rouget mit zwei Selleries, Schottischer Wildlachs im Gemüsesud, Kalbsbries mit Trüffeln.

at Cologne 90- Porz-Wahnheide SE : 17 km by A 59 – ✆ 02203 :

Holiday Inn, Waldstr. 255, ✆ 56 10, Telex 8874665, – ▮ ▤ TV Ⓟ AE ⓓ E VISA. ✻ rest
M a la carte 23/57 – **113 rm** 164/252 Bb.

Aachen

5100. Nordrhein-Westfalen 987 ㉓, 213 ㉔, 409 ⑯ – pop. 245 000 – alt. 174 m – ✆ 0241.

Köln 70.

XXXX ✿✿ **Gala**, Monheimsallee 44 (at Casino), ✆ 15 30 13, « Modern-elegant furniture » – ▤. AE ⓓ E VISA
closed Monday – **M** (dinner only) a la carte 55/115 (booking essential)
Spec. Seezunge mit Kapernknospen, Kalbsfilet mit Hummer, Aachener Printenauflauf.

DÜSSELDORF 4000. Nordrhein-Westfalen 987 ㉓㉔ – pop. 569 000 – alt. 40 m – ☎ 0211.

See : Königsallee★ – Hofgarten★ – Hetjensmuseum★ BX **M2** – Land Economic Museum (Landesmuseum Volk u. Wirtschaft)★ BV **M1** – Goethemuseum★ CV **M3** – Thyssen building (Thyssenhaus)★ CVX **E.**

Envir. : Chateau of Benrath (Schloß Benrath) (Park★) S : 10 km by Kölner Str. DXY.

✈ Düsseldorf-Lohausen (N : 8 km), ✆ 42 12 23.

🚗 ✆ 3 68 04 68.

Exhibition Centre (Messegelände), ✆ 4 56 01, Telex 8584853.

ℹ Tourist office, K.-Adenauer-Platz 12 and at the Main Station, (Hauptbahnhof) ✆ 35 05 05, Telex 8587785.

ADAC, Kaiserswerther Str. 207, ✆ 43 49 51.

Amsterdam 225 – Essen 31 – Köln 39 – Rotterdam 237.

Plan on following pages

The reference (D 15) at the end of the address is the postal district : Düsseldorf 15

Breidenbacher Hof, Heinrich-Heine-Allee 36 (D 1), ✆ 86 01, Telex 8582630 – AE E VISA. BX **a**
Restaurants : – **Grill Royal** *(closed Saturday lunch and Sunday)* **M** a la carte 53/102 – **Breidenbacher Eck M** a la carte 37/73 – **160 rm** 245/470.

Steigenberger Parkhotel, Corneliusplatz 1 (D 1), ✆ 86 51, Telex 8582331, – AE E VISA. rest CX **p**
M a la carte 40/89 – **160 rm** 219/420 Bb.

Nikko M, Immermannstr. 41 (D 1), ✆ 86 61, Telex 8582080, Massage, – AE E VISA. rest DX **a**
Restaurants : – **Benkay** (Japanese rest.) **M** a la carte 30/80 – **Travellers M** a la carte 37/75 – **301 rm** 221/387 Bb.

Excelsior without rest, Kapellstr. 1 (D 30), ✆ 48 60 06, Telex 8584737 – AE E VISA – **65 rm** 138/268 CV **a**

Savoy, Oststr. 128 (D 1), ✆ 36 03 36, Telex 8584215, Massage, – rest AE E VISA CX **w**
M a la carte 32/70 – **130 rm** 165/320 Bb.

Holiday Inn, Graf-Adolf-Platz 10 (D 1), ✆ 37 70 53, Telex 8586359, – AE E VISA CY **r**
Restaurants : – **Suppentopf** *(lunch only, closed Sunday)* **M** a la carte 21/38 – **La Rhénane M** a la carte 30/70 – **120 rm** 214/278 Bb.

Uebachs, Leopoldstr. 5 (D 1), ✆ 36 05 66, Telex 8587620 – AE E VISA. rest DX **r**
M *(closed Sunday except exhibitions)* a la carte 35/68 – **82 rm** 130/220 Bb.

Graf Adolf without rest, Stresemannplatz 1 (D 1), ✆ 36 05 91, Telex 8587844 – wc wc ☎. AE E CX **e**
closed 21 December - 2 January – **100 rm** 70/185 Bb.

Ambassador without rest, Harkortstr. 7 (D 1), ✆ 37 00 03, Telex 8586286 – wc wc ☎. AE E VISA DY **a**
60 rm 90/180 Bb.

Lindenhof without rest, Oststr. 124 (D 1), ✆ 36 09 63, Telex 8587012 – wc wc ☎. AE E VISA CX **u**
43 rm 120/185.

National without rest, Schwerinstr. 16 (D 30), ✆ 49 90, Telex 8586597, – wc wc ☎. AE E by Duisburger Str. CV
35 rm 105/205 Bb.

Madison without rest, Graf-Adolf-Str. 47 (D 1), ✆ 37 02 96 – wc ☎. AE E. CY **x**
24 rm 120/155 Bb.

City without rest, Bismarckstr. 73 (D 1), ✆ 36 50 23, Telex 8587362 – wc wc ☎. AE E VISA CX **d**
52 rm 110/170.

Börsenhotel without rest, Kreuzstr. 19a, ✆ 36 30 71, Telex 8587323 – wc wc ☎. AE E VISA CX **n**
76 rm 130/240 Bb.

Eden, Adersstr. 29, ✆ 38 10 60, Telex 8582530 – wc wc ☎. AE E VISA CY **m**
(rest. for residents only) – **90 rm** 127/210 Bb.

Minerva without rest, Cantadorstr. 13a (D 1), ✆ 35 09 61, Telex 8586888 – wc wc ☎. AE E. DX **m**
12 rm 110/150.

Astor without rest, Kurfürstenstr. 23 (D 1), ✆ 36 06 61, – wc ☎. AE E DX **k**
16 rm 75/145.

Großer Kurfürst without rest, Kurfürstenstr. 18 (D 1), ✆ 35 76 47 – wc wc ☎. AE E DX **s**
22 rm 75/145.

Regina without rest, Scheurenstr. 3 (D 1), ✆ 37 04 46 – wc ☎. AE E. CY **n**
closed August – **35 rm** 85/115.

Am Wehrhahn	DV	
Berliner Allee	CX	
Flinger Straße	BX	28
Graf-Adolf-Straße	CY	
Königsallee	CX	
Schadowstraße	CX	94
Blumenstraße	CX	7
Bolkerstraße	BX	8
Citadellstraße	BX	13
Elberfelder Straße	CX	21
Ernst-Reuter-Platz	CY	23
Fischerstraße	BV	27
Friedrich-Ebert-Straße	CX	29
Fürstenplatz	CY	30
Grabbeplatz	BX	32
Graf-Adolf-Platz	CX	33
Heinrich-Heine-Allee	BX	42
Hofgartenrampe	BV	45
Jan-Wellem-Platz	CX	51
Konrad-Adenauer-Platz	DX	59
Markplatz	BX	68
Martin-Luther-Platz	CX	69
Maximilian-Weyhe-Allee	CV	70
Mühlenstraße	BX	72
Oberbilker Markt	DY	80
Ratinger Straße	BV	88
Schadowplatz	CX	93
Schneider-Wibbel-Gasse	BX	95
Schwanenmarkt	BX	96
Tonhallenstraße	CX	99
Vagedesstraße	CV	104
Venloer Straße	CV	105

When in Europe

never be without:

the Michelin Map no 920

and

the Michelin Green Guides

Austria

England:

Scotland

The West Country

Germany

Italy

London

Paris

Portugal

Rome

Spain

Switzerland

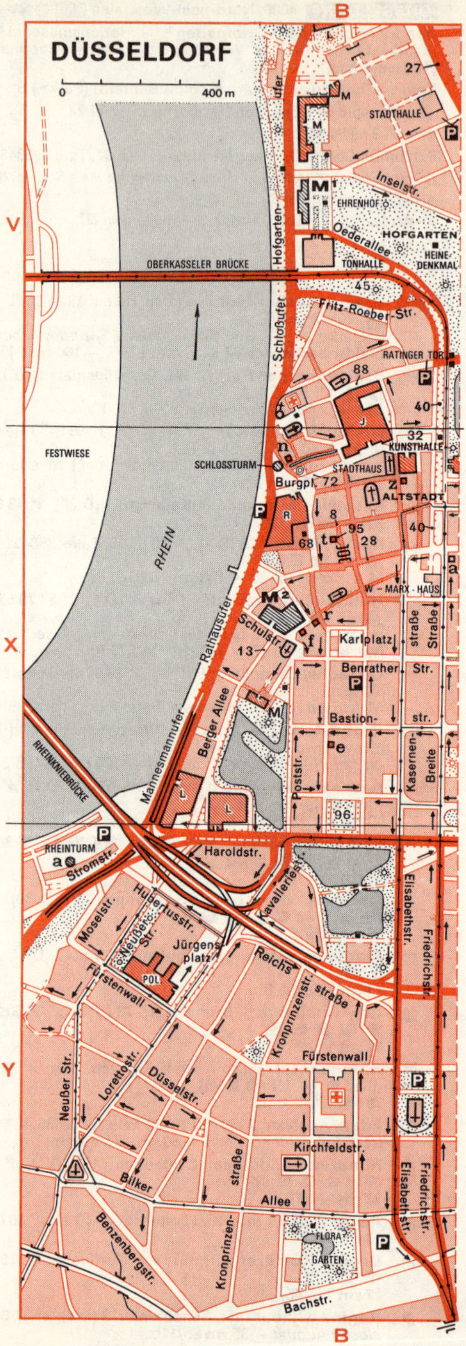

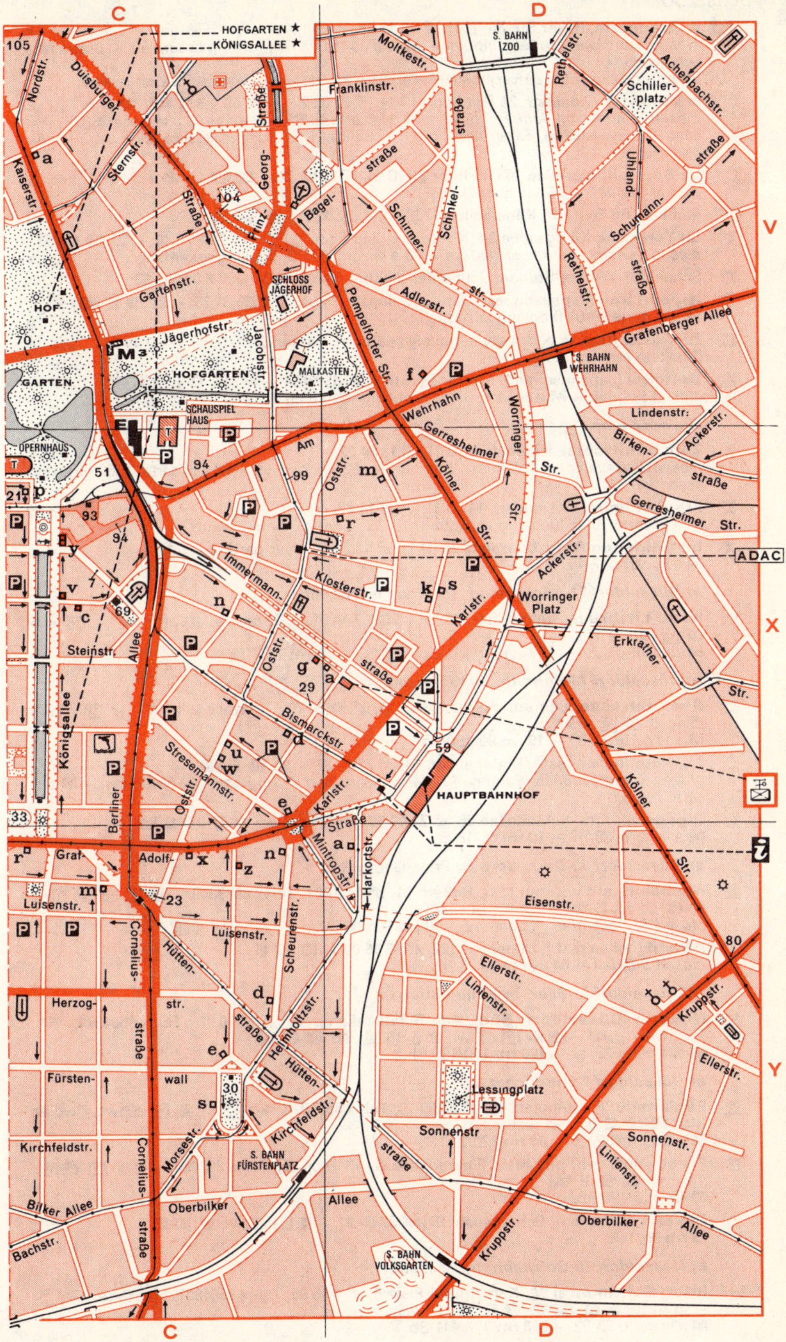
C
D
HOFGARTEN ★
KÖNIGSALLEE ★
105
Nordstr.
Duisburger
Kaiserstr.
Sternstr.
Straße
104
Georg-
Straße
Prinz-
Bagel-
Moltkestr.
Franklinstr.
straße
Schirmer-
Schinkel-
straße
S. BAHN ZOO
Rethelstr.
Schiller-
platz
Achenbachstr.
Uhland-
straße
Schumann-
straße
Rethelstr.
V
HOF
GARTEN
70
Gartenstr.
Jägerhofstr.
M³
SCHLOSS JÄGERHOF
Jacobistr.
HOFGARTEN
MALKASTEN
Pempelforter Str.
Adlerstr.
str.
Grafenberger Allee
S. BAHN WEHRHAHN
f
OPERNHAUS
SCHAUSPIEL HAUS
E
T
51
21
p
93
94
Am
Wehrhahn
99
Gerresheimer
Oststr.
m
Kölner
Str.
Worringer
Str.
Lindenstr.
Birken-
straße
Ackerstr.
Gerresheimer
Str.
r
ADAC
y
v
c
7
69
94
Immermann-
Klosterstr.
n
k
s
Karlstr.
Ackerstr.
Worringer
Platz
X
Steinstr.
Allee
Oststr.
g
a
29
straße
Erkrather
Str.
Königsallee
Bismarckstr.
d
u
w
Stresemannstr.
Oststr.
59
HAUPTBAHNHOF
Kölner
Str.
33
Berliner
e
Karlstr.
Straße
Mintropstr.
Harkortstr.
a
r
Graf-
Adolf-
x
z
n
m
Luisenstr.
23
Luisenstr.
Scheurenstr.
Cornelius-
Hütten-
Eisenstr.
80
Herzog-
str.
straße
d
Helmholtzstr.
straße
Hütten-
e
Ellerstr.
Linienstr.
Kruppstr.
Ellerstr.
Y
Fürsten-
wall
30
s
Kirchfeldstr.
Lessingplatz
Sonnenstr
Kirchfeldstr.
Morsestr.
S. BAHN FÜRSTENPLATZ
straße
Sonnenstr.
Linienstr.
Cornelius-
straße
Bilker Allee
Oberbilker
Allee
Oberbilker
Allee
Kruppstr.
Bachstr.
S. BAHN VOLKSGARTEN
C
D

XXXX ✿ **Orangerie,** Bilker Str. 30 (D 1), ✆ 13 18 28 – ⓓ BX **e**
closed Sunday except exhibitions – **M** a la carte 50/105 (booking essential) – **Bistro M** a la carte 33/66
Spec. Carpaccio von Gänseleber mit Ingwer, Pot au feu von Edelfischen, Wachteln in Madeirasauce.

XXX ✿ **Victorian,** Königstr. 3a (1st floor) (D 1), ✆ 32 02 22 – ▤. AE ⓓ E VISA. ✱ CX **c**
closed Sunday and Bank Holidays – **M** a la carte 48/85 – **Lounge M** a la carte 26/63
Spec. Gänseleberterrine, Safrannudeln mit Meeresfrüchten in Champagnersauce, Kalbsfilet in weißer Baumpilzbutter.

XXX **La Scala,** Königsallee 14 (1st floor |‡|) (D 1), ✆ 32 68 32 – AE ⓓ E. ✱ CX **y**
closed Sunday – **M** a la carte 37/69.

XXX Müllers und Fest KD, Königsallee 12 (D 1), ✆ 32 60 01, ☂ – ✱ CX **y**

XX **La Terrazza,** Königsallee 30 (Kö-Centre, 2nd floor, |‡|) (D 1), ✆ 32 75 40 – AE ⓓ E VISA
closed Sunday and Bank Holidays – **M** a la carte 37/70 (booking essential). CX **v**

XX Schneider-Wibbel-Stuben, Schneider-Wibbel-Gasse 7 (D 1), ✆ 8 00 00, ☂ BX **t**

XX **Nippon Kan** (Japanese rest.), Immermannstr. 35 (D 1), ✆ 35 31 35 – AE ⓓ E VISA. ✱
M a la carte 38/61 (booking essential). CX **g**

XX Zur Auster (rest. in bistro-style, mainly seafood), Berger Str. 9 (D 1), ✆ 32 44 04 BX **r**
(booking essential).

XX **Daitokai** (Japanese rest), Mutter-Ey-Str. 1, ✆ 32 50 54 – ▤. AE ⓓ E VISA. ✱ BX **z**
closed Sunday – **M** a la carte 33/68 (booking essential).

Brewery-inns :

X **Zum Schiffchen,** Hafenstr. 5 (D 1), ✆ 13 24 22 BX **f**
closed 25 December - 1 January, Sunday and Bank Holidays – **M** a la carte 22/52 (booking essential).

X **Frankenheim,** Wielandstr. 14 (D 1), ✆ 35 14 47 DV **f**
M a la carte 16/45 (booking essential).

X **Im Goldenen Ring,** Burgplatz 21 (D 1), ✆ 13 31 61, beer-garden – ⛹ BX **n**
M a la carte 17/46.

at Düsseldorf 31-Angermund N : 15 km by Fischerstr. BV :

🏨 **Haus Litzbrück,** Bahnhofstr. 33, ✆ (0203) 7 44 81, « Terrace », ≘s, ⛆, ⛱ – TV ⛟ Ⓟ ⛹. AE ⓓ E
M *(closed 15 July - 15 August)* a la carte 36/69 – **23 rm** 115/185.

at Düsseldorf 13-Benrath by Kölner Str. DXY :

🏨 **Rheinterrasse,** Benrather Schloßufer 39, ✆ 71 20 70, « Terrace with ≤ » – TV ⛀wc ⋔wc ☎ Ⓟ ⛹. ⓓ E
M a la carte 21/65 – **19 rm** 90/180 Bb.

XX **Lignano** (Italian rest.), Hildener Str. 43, ✆ 71 19 36 – AE ⓓ E VISA. ✱
closed Saturday lunch, Sunday, 18 May - 1 June and 31 August - 14 September – **M** a la carte 29/66.

XX **Pigage** with rm, Schloßallee 28, ✆ 71 40 66 – ⛀wc ⋔wc ☎ Ⓟ. ⓓ E VISA
M a la carte 28/67 – **10 rm** 65/180.

at Düsseldorf 30-Derendorf by Prinz-Georg-Str. CV :

🏨 **Michelangelo** without rest, Roßstr. 61, ✆ 48 01 01, Telex 8588649 – |‡| TV ⛀wc ⋔wc ☎ Ⓟ. AE ⓓ E VISA
closed 24 December - 1 January – **70 rm** 105/305 Bb.

XXX **Amalfi** (Italian rest.), Ulmenstr. 122, ✆ 43 38 09 – AE ⓓ E
closed Sunday – **M** a la carte 26/60.

at Düsseldorf 13-Eller by Kölner Str. DXY :

🏨 **Novotel Düsseldorf Süd,** Am Schönenkamp 9, ✆ 74 10 92, Telex 8584374, ☂, ⛆ (heated), ⛱ – |‡| ▤ TV ⛀wc ☎ ♿ Ⓟ ⛹. AE ⓓ E VISA
M a la carte 23/57 – **120 rm** 140/193 Bb.

at Düsseldorf 1-Friedrichstadt :

🏨 **Esplanade,** Fürstenplatz 17, ✆ 37 50 10, Telex 8582970, ≘s, ⛆ – |‡| TV ⛀wc ⋔wc ☎ ⛟. AE ⓓ E VISA. ✱ rest CY **s**
M a la carte 32/65 – **80 rm** 120/220 Bb.

🏨 **Fürstenhof** without rest, Fürstenplatz 3, ✆ 37 05 45, Telex 8586540 – |‡| TV ⛀wc ⋔wc ☎. AE ⓓ E VISA CY **e**
43 rm 115/198 Bb.

🏨 **Beyer** without rest, Scheurenstr. 57, ✆ 37 09 91 – |‡| TV ⛀wc ☎. AE E CY **d**
19 rm 65/145.

at Düsseldorf 30-Golzheim by Fischerstr. BV :

🏨 **Inter-Continental** Ⓜ, Karl-Arnold-Platz 5, ✆ 4 55 30, Telex 8584601, Massage, ≘s, ⛆ – |‡| ▤ TV ♿ Ⓟ ⛹. AE ⓓ E VISA. ✱ rest
M a la carte 38/82 – **310 rm** 317/441 Bb.

Düsseldorf Hilton, Georg-Glock-Str. 20, ✆ 43 49 63, Telex 8584376, Massage, – AE E VISA. rest
Restaurants : – **Hofgarten M** a la carte 24/56 – **San Francisco** (see below) – **383 rm** 211/455.

Golzheimer Krug, Karl-Kleppe-Str. 20, ✆ 43 44 53, Telex 8588919, – wc wc. AE E VISA
M *(closed Friday except exhibitions)* a la carte 31/65 – **27 rm** 115/230 Bb.

Rheinpark without rest, Bankstr. 13, ✆ 49 91 86 – wc.
30 rm 50/105.

XXXX **San Francisco**, Georg-Glock-Str. 20 (at Hilton-Hotel), ✆ 43 49 63 – . AE E VISA.
M a la carte 50/85 (booking essential for dinner)
Spec. Gänseleberterrine, Steinbuttmedaillon in Rotweinbutter, Kalbsfilet in weißer Trüffelsauce.

XX **Fischer-Stuben-Mulfinger**, Rotterdamer Str. 15, ✆ 43 26 12, « Terrace »
closed Friday dinner and Saturday – **M** a la carte 34/70 (booking essential).

XX **Rosati** (Italian rest), Felix-Klein-Str. 1, ✆ 4 36 05 03, – . AE E.
closed Sunday – **M** a la carte 39/70 (booking essential).

at Düsseldorf 31-Kaiserswerth by Fischerstr. BV :

Barbarossa without rest, Niederrheinstr. 365 (B 8), ✆ 40 27 19 – wc wc. AE E
closed 20 December - 5 January – **33 rm** 85/135.

XXX **Im Schiffchen** (1733 house with beautiful facade), Kaiserswerther Markt 9, ✆ 40 10 50 – AE E
closed Sunday, Bank Holidays and 4 weeks July - August – **M** (dinner only) a la carte 76/105 (booking essential)
Spec. Gefüllte Cannelloni in Trüffelbutter, kleiner Hummer in Kamillenblüten gedämpft, Eisauflauf mit Bergkräutern.

at Düsseldorf 30-Lohausen by Fischerstr. BV :

XX **Flughafen Grill-Restaurant**, Terminal 2 (4th floor), ✆ 4 21 60 97, ← – AE E VISA.
M a la carte 30/64.

at Düsseldorf 30-Mörsenbroich by Rethelstr. DV :

Ramada-Renaissance-Hotel M, Nördlicher Zubringer 6, ✆ 6 21 60, Massage, – . AE E VISA. rest
M a la carte 35/75 – **250 rm** 216/392 Bb.

Merkur without rest, Mörsenbroicher Weg 49, ✆ 63 40 31 – wc. AE E
28 rm 68/140 Bb.

at Düsseldorf 11-Oberkassel by Hofgartenrampe BV :

Ramada, Am Seestern 16, ✆ 59 10 47, Telex 8585575, – . AE E VISA. rest
M a la carte 42/82 – **222 rm** 182/329 Bb.

Rheinstern Penta-Hotel, Emanuel-Leutze-Str. 17, ✆ 5 99 70, Telex 8584242, – rest (with). AE E VISA.
M a la carte 31/64 – **182 rm** 181/287 Bb.

Hanseat without rest, Belsenstr. 6, ✆ 57 50 69 – wc. AE E VISA
28 rm 110/220 Bb.

Arosa without rest, Sonderburgstr. 48, ✆ 55 40 11, Telex 8582242 – wc wc. AE
closed 22 December - 1 January – **32 rm** 100/160.

XXX **De' Medici** (Italian rest.), Amboßstr. 3, ✆ 59 41 51 – AE E VISA
closed Saturday lunch, Sunday and Bank Holidays except exhibitions – **M** a la carte 31/70 (booking essential for dinner).

at Düsseldorf 1-Unterbilk :

XXX **Savini** (Italian rest.), Stromstr. 47, ✆ 39 39 31 –
closed Saturday lunch and Sunday – **M** a la carte 43/83 (booking essential).

XX **Rheinturm Top 180**, Stromstr. 20, ✆ 8 48 58, Düsseldorf and Rhein, « Revolving restaurant at 172 m », (4 DM) – . AE E. BY a
M a la carte 32/64.

Grevenbroich **4048**. Nordrhein-Westfalen 987 ㉓ – pop. 57 000 – alt. 60 m – 02181 – Düsseldorf 28.

XXX **Zur Traube** with rm, Bahnstr. 47, ✆ 6 87 67, remarkable wine-list – wc wc. AE E
closed 23 to 31 March, 2 weeks July and 22 December - 15 January – **M** *(closed Sunday and Monday)* a la carte 49/98 (booking essential) – **5 rm** 125/270
Spec. Parfait vom Stör mit Kaviar, Taubenbrüstchen mit Zwergorangensauce, Tannenhonigparfait mit Walderdbeerenmus.

FRANKFURT AM MAIN 6000. Hessen 987 ㉕ – pop. 612 600 – alt. 91 m – ☎ 069.

See : Zoo*** FX – Goethe's House (Goethehaus)** and Goethemuseum* DEY **M1** – Cathedral (Dom)* (Tower**, Treasure*, Choir-stalls*) EY – Tropical Garden (Palmengarten)* CV – Senckenberg-Museum* (Palaeontology department**) CX **M8** – Städel Museum (Städelsches Kunstinstitut)* (Collection** of flemish Primitives and German Masters of the 16 C) DY **M2** – Museum of Applied Arts (Museum für Kunsthandwerk)* EY **M4** – St. Catherine's Church (Katharinenkirche) (windows*) EX **A** – Henninger Turm ** DZ.

Rhein-Main (by ⑤ : 12 km), ☎ 6 90 25 95.

at Neu-Isenburg, ☎ (06102) 85 75.

Exhibition Centre (Messegelände) (CY), ☎ 7 57 51, Telex 411558.

Tourist Information, Main Station (Hauptbahnhof), ☎ 2 12 88 49.

Subway-Station Hauptwache, B-floor, ☎ 2 12 87 08.

ADAC, Schumannstr. 4, ☎ 7 43 00.

Wiesbaden 39 ⑤ – Bonn 176 ⑤ – Nürnberg 223 ④ – Stuttgart 205 ⑤.

Plans on following pages

The reference (F 15) at the end of the address is the postal district : Frankfurt 15

Steigenberger-Hotel Frankfurter Hof, Bethmannstr. 33 (F 16), ☎ 2 02 51, Telex 411806, – rest . rest DY **e**
M *(closed Saturday) (see also* **rest. Français and Frankfurter Stubb**) a la carte 32/74 – **400 rm** 189/380 Bb.

Hessischer Hof, Friedrich-Ebert-Anlage 40 (F 97), ☎ 7 54 00, Telex 411776, « Rest. with collection of Sèvres porcelain » – . rest CY **p**
M a la carte 52/86 – **161 rm** 289/448.

Frankfurt Intercontinental, Wilhelm-Leuschner-Str. 43 (F 1), ☎ 23 05 61, Telex 413639, < Frankfurt, Massage, , – . rest
Restaurants : – **Rôtisserie** *(closed Saturday lunch)* **M** a la carte 44/90 – **Brasserie M** a la carte 25/58 – **Bierstube** *(closed Saturday, Sunday and Bank Holidays)* **M** a la carte 17/32 – **800 rm** 299/414 Bb. CY **a**

CP Frankfurt Plaza M, Hamburger Allee 2, ☎ 77 07 21, Telex 412573, < Frankfurt, – . rest CX **a**
Restaurants : – **Geheimratsstube** – **Bäckerei** – **591 rm** Bb.

Parkhotel Frankfurt, Wiesenhüttenplatz 36 (F 1), ☎ 2 69 70, Telex 412808, Massage, – CY **k**
Restaurants : – **La Truffe** *(closed Saturday lunch, Sunday and Bank Holidays)* **M** a la carte 45/90 – **Die Parkstube** *(regional german cooking)* **M** a la carte 30/60 – **280 rm** 270/590 Bb.

Savigny, Savignystr. 14 (F 1), ☎ 7 53 30, Telex 412061 – . CY **f**
closed 20 December - 2 January – **M** a la carte 28/72 – **122 rm** 160/300 Bb.

National, Baseler Str. 50 (F 1), ☎ 23 48 41, Telex 412570 – . rest CY **x**
M a la carte 27/60 – **95 rm** 65/210 Bb.

Imperial, Sophienstr. 40 (F 90), ☎ 7 93 00 30, Telex 4189636 – wc . CV **t**
M a la carte 23/47 – **60 rm** 138/270 Bb.

Savoy, Wiesenhüttenstr. 42 (F 16), ☎ 23 05 11, Telex 416394, Massage, , – rest wc wc . rest CY **s**
M a la carte 38/70 – **151 rm** 155/205 Bb.

Turmhotel - Restaurant Sudpfanne, Eschersheimer Landstr. 20 (F 1), ☎ 55 00 01 – wc . EX **b**
M *(closed Saturday)* a la carte 24/53 – **75 rm** 98/183 Bb.

An der Messe without rest, Westendstr. 102 (F 1), ☎ 74 79 79, Telex 4189009 – wc wc . CX **e**
46 rm 140/250 Bb.

Continental, Baseler Str. 56 (F 1), ☎ 23 03 41, Telex 412502 – wc wc . CY **y**
M *(closed Sunday and Bank Holidays)* a la carte 19/45 – **80 rm** 98/160.

Mozart without rest, Parkstr. 17 (F 1), ☎ 55 08 31 – wc wc . CV **p**
closed 22 December - 2 January – **35 rm** 115/185.

Falk without rest, Falkstr. 38a (F 90), ☎ 70 80 94 – wc wc CV **n**
closed 22 December - 2 January – **32 rm** 88/155.

Jaguar without rest, Theobald-Christ-Str. 19 (F 1), ☎ 43 93 01 – wc FX **y**
37 rm.

Am Zoo, Alfred-Brehm-Platz 6 (F 1), ☎ 49 07 71, Telex 4170082 – wc wc . FX **q**
M *(dinner only, closed Sunday)* a la carte 20/47 – **85 rm** 79/125 Bb.

Tatra without rest, Kreuznacher Str. 37 (F 90), ☎ 77 20 71 – wc wc . CX **u**
closed 20 December - 6 January – **25 rm** 95/140 Bb.

Am Dom without rest, Kannengießergasse 3 (F 1), ☏ 28 21 41, Telex 414955 – 🛗 📺 ⛀wc ⋒wc ☎ EY s
30 rm 100/180 Bb.

Admiral without rest, Hölderlinstr. 25 (F 1), ☏ 44 80 21 – 🛗 📺 ⛀wc ⋒wc ☎ Ⓟ. AE Ⓓ E FX w
47 rm 70/130.

XXXX ❀ **Restaurant Français,** Bethmannstr. 33 (at Steigenberger-H. Frankfurter Hof) (F 16), ☏ 2 02 51 – ▤. AE Ⓓ E VISA. ⚹ DY e
closed 4 weeks July - August, Sunday and Bank Holidays – **M** a la carte 40/90 (booking essential)
Spec. Terrine von Krustentieren, Wolfsbarschfilet mit Limonen-Kräutervinaigrette, Kalbsmedaillon mit Morcheln in Kaviarsauce.

XXX **Weinhaus Brückenkeller,** Schützenstr. 6 (F 1), ☏ 28 42 38, « Old vaulted cellar with precious antiques » – ▤ Ⓟ. AE Ⓓ E VISA FY a
closed Sunday and Bank Holidays except exhibitions – **M** (dinner only) a la carte 47/94 (booking essential).

XXX **Mövenpick - Baron de la Mouette,** Opernplatz 2 (F 1), ☏ 2 06 80, 🍽 – ▤ DX f
M a la carte 35/76 – **Orangerie M** a la carte 24/47.

XXX ❀ **Humperdinck,** Grüneburgweg 95 (F 1), ☏ 72 21 22 – AE Ⓓ E VISA CV a
closed Saturday lunch and Sunday – **M** a la carte 65/91
Spec. Lachsroulade mit Vermouth, Pochierter Lammrücken auf Lauchstreifen, Limonencreme mit zwei Saucen.

XXX **Tse-Yang** (Chinese rest.), Kaiserstr. 67 (F 1), ☏ 23 25 41 – AE Ⓓ E VISA. ⚹ CY v
M a la carte 27/62.

XX **Le Midi,** Liebigstr. 47 (F 1), ☏ 72 14 38, 🍽 – AE Ⓓ E VISA CV b
closed Saturday lunch, Sunday and 2 to 18 August – **M** a la carte 31/64.

XX **Da Bruno** (Italian rest.), Elbestr. 15 (F 1), ☏ 23 34 16 – ▤. AE Ⓓ E CY t
closed Sunday, Bank Holidays and mid July - mid August – **M** a la carte 37/65.

XX **Frankfurter Stubb** (Rest. in the vaulted cellar of Hotel Frankfurter Hof), Bethmannstr. 33 (F 16), ☏ 21 56 79 – ▤. AE Ⓓ E VISA. ⚹ DY e
closed Sunday, Bank Holidays and 3 weeks August – **M** a la carte 25/55 (booking essential).

XX La Galleria (Italian rest.), Theaterplatz 2 (BFG-Haus) (F 1), ☏ 23 56 80 – ▤ DY u
(booking essential).

XX **Firenze** (Italian rest.), Berger Str. 30 (F 1), ☏ 43 39 56 – ▤. AE Ⓓ E. ⚹ FX s
closed Monday except exhibitions – **M** a la carte 37/72 (booking essential).

XX **Börsenkeller,** Schillerstr. 11 (F 1), ☏ 28 11 15 – ▤ 🏛. AE Ⓓ E VISA EX z
closed Sunday – **M** a la carte 20/60.

X ❀ **Ernos Bistro** (French rest.), Liebigstr. 15 (F 1), ☏ 72 19 97, 🍽 – AE Ⓓ E VISA CX s
closed Saturday and Sunday except exhibitions and 16 to 21 July – **M** a la carte 51/94 (booking essential)
Spec. Foie d'oie frais, Ragout de Lotte et de Saumon, Canard de Challans aux baies de Cassis.

at Frankfurt 80-Griesheim by ⑥ :

Ramada-Caravelle, Oeserstr. 180, ☏ 3 90 50, Telex 416812, ⛆, 🏊 – 🛗 ▤ rest 📺 Ⓟ 🏛. AE Ⓓ E VISA
M a la carte 38/76 – **236 rm** 163/304 Bb.

at Frankfurt 71-Niederrad by ⑤ :

Arabella-Hotel Frankfurt, Lyoner Str. 44, ☏ 6 63 30, Telex 416760, 🍽, ⛆, 🏊 – 🛗 ▤ 📺 ♿ Ⓟ 🏛. AE Ⓓ E VISA. ⚹ rest
M a la carte 28/57 – **400 rm** 150/265 Bb.

Crest-Hotel Frankfurt, Isenburger Schneise 40, ☏ 6 78 40, Telex 416717 – 🛗 ▤ 📺 Ⓟ 🏛. AE Ⓓ E VISA
M a la carte 24/65 – **283 rm** 172/249 Bb.

XX **Weidemann,** Kelsterbacher Str. 66, ☏ 67 59 96, 🍽 – Ⓟ. AE Ⓓ E VISA
closed Saturday, Sunday and Bank Holidays lunch – **M** a la carte 45/70 (booking essential).

at Frankfurt 70 - Sachsenhausen :

Holiday Inn-City Tower Ⓜ, Mailänder Str. 1, ☏ 68 00 11, Telex 411805, ⛆ – 🛗 ▤ 📺 Ⓟ 🏛. AE Ⓓ E VISA. ⚹ by ④
Restaurants : – **Le Ballon M** a la carte 26/62 – **Kaffeemühle M** a la carte 23/43 – **405 rm** 186/334 Bb.

Mühlberg without rest, Offenbacher Landstr. 56, ☏ 61 30 63 – 🛗 ⋒wc ☎ 🚗. AE Ⓓ FY h
closed end December - beginning January – **69 rm** 50/140.

XX **Bistrot 77** (modern Bistro), Ziegelhüttenweg 1, ☏ 61 40 40, 🍽 – AE Ⓓ E EZ a
closed Saturday lunch, Sunday and mid June - mid July – **M** a la carte 50/90.

X **Henninger Turm - Museums Stubb** (🛗 DM 3), Hainer Weg 60, ☏ 6 06 36 00, ≤ Frankfurt, « Revolving rest. at 101 m » – ▤ Ⓟ 🏛 FZ
closed Monday except exhibitions – **M** a la carte 17.50/52.

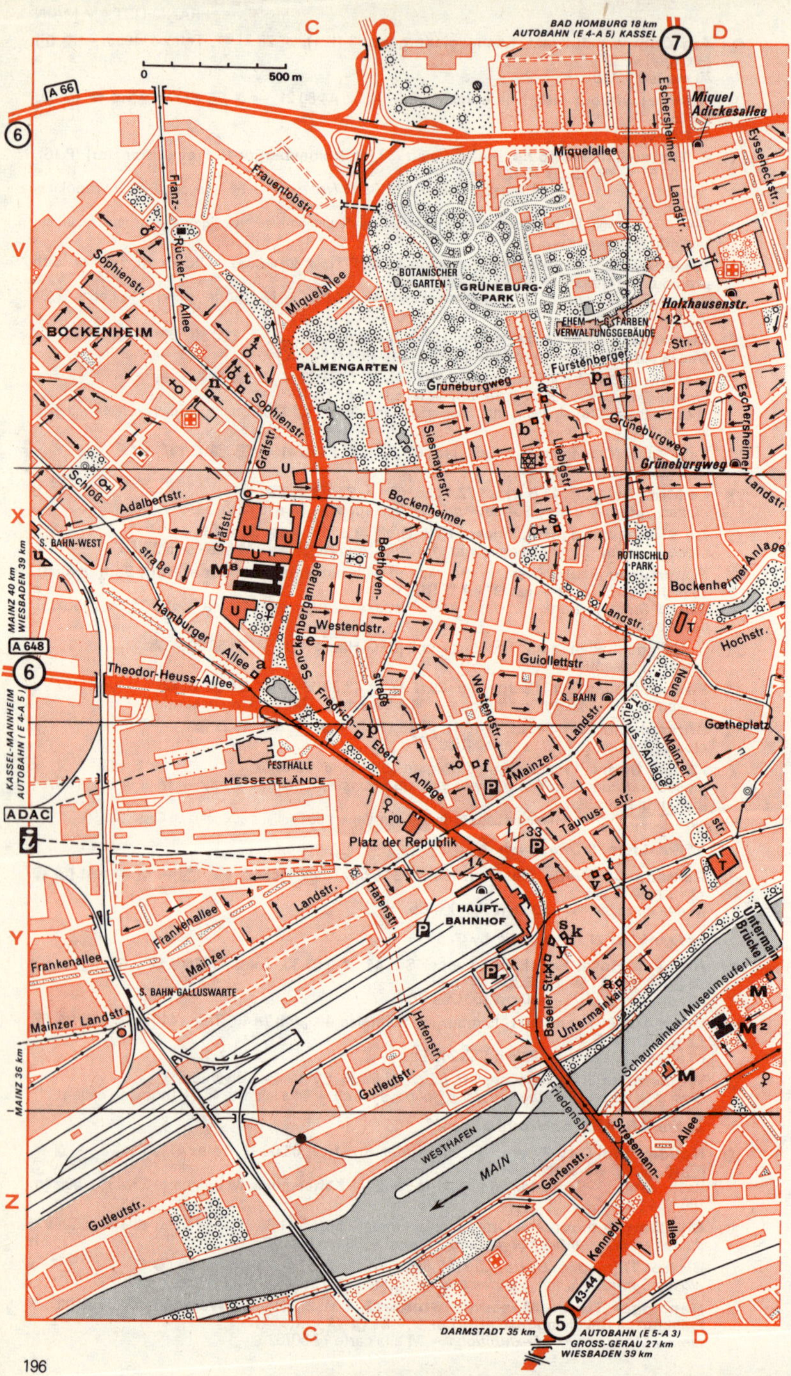
C
D
BAD HOMBURG 18 km
AUTOBAHN (E 4-A 5) KASSEL
7
0
500 m
A 66
6
Miquel Adickesallee
Eschersheimer
Landstr.
Eysseneckstr.
Miquelallee
Frauenlobstr.
Franz-Rücker-Allee
V
Sophienstr.
BOCKENHEIM
Miquelallee
BOTANISCHER GARTEN
GRÜNEBURG-PARK
EHEM. I. G. FARBEN VERWALTUNGSGEBÄUDE
Holzhausenstr.
12
Str.
Fürstenberger
PALMENGARTEN
Grüneburgweg
Grüneburgweg
Grüneburgweg
Eschersheimer Landstr.
Siesmayerstr.
Liebigstr.
Sophienstr.
Gräfstr.
Schloß-
Adalbertstr.
Bockenheimer
X
S. BAHN-WEST
Gräfstr.
Beethovenstr.
straße
M8
ROTHSCHILD PARK
Bockenheimer Anlage
Landstr.
Senckenberganlage
Westendstr.
Hamburger Allee
Hochstr.
MAINZ 40 km
WIESBADEN 39 km
A 648
6
Theodor-Heuss-Allee
Guiollettstr
S. BAHN
Neue
Taunus Anlage
Westendstr.
Friedrich-Ebert-Anlage
Mainzer Landstr.
Goetheplatz
KASSEL-MANNHEIM
AUTOBAHN (E 4-A 5)
FESTHALLE
MESSEGELÄNDE
Mainzer
Taunus-str.
str.
ADAC
POL.
Platz der Republik
33
14
Hafenstr.
Landstr.
Frankenallee
HAUPT-BAHNHOF
Y
Untermain Brücke
Frankenallee
Mainzer
S. BAHN-GALLUSWARTE
Baseler Str.
Untermainkai
Schaumainkai (Museumsufer)
Mainzer Landstr.
Hafenstr.
M
M2
M
MAINZ 36 km
Gutleutstr.
Friedensbr.
Stresemann-Allee
WESTHAFEN
MAIN
Gartenstr.
Z
Gutleutstr.
Kennedy-allee
43-44
C
D
5
DARMSTADT 35 km
AUTOBAHN (E 5-A 3)
GROSS-GERAU 27 km
WIESBADEN 39 km

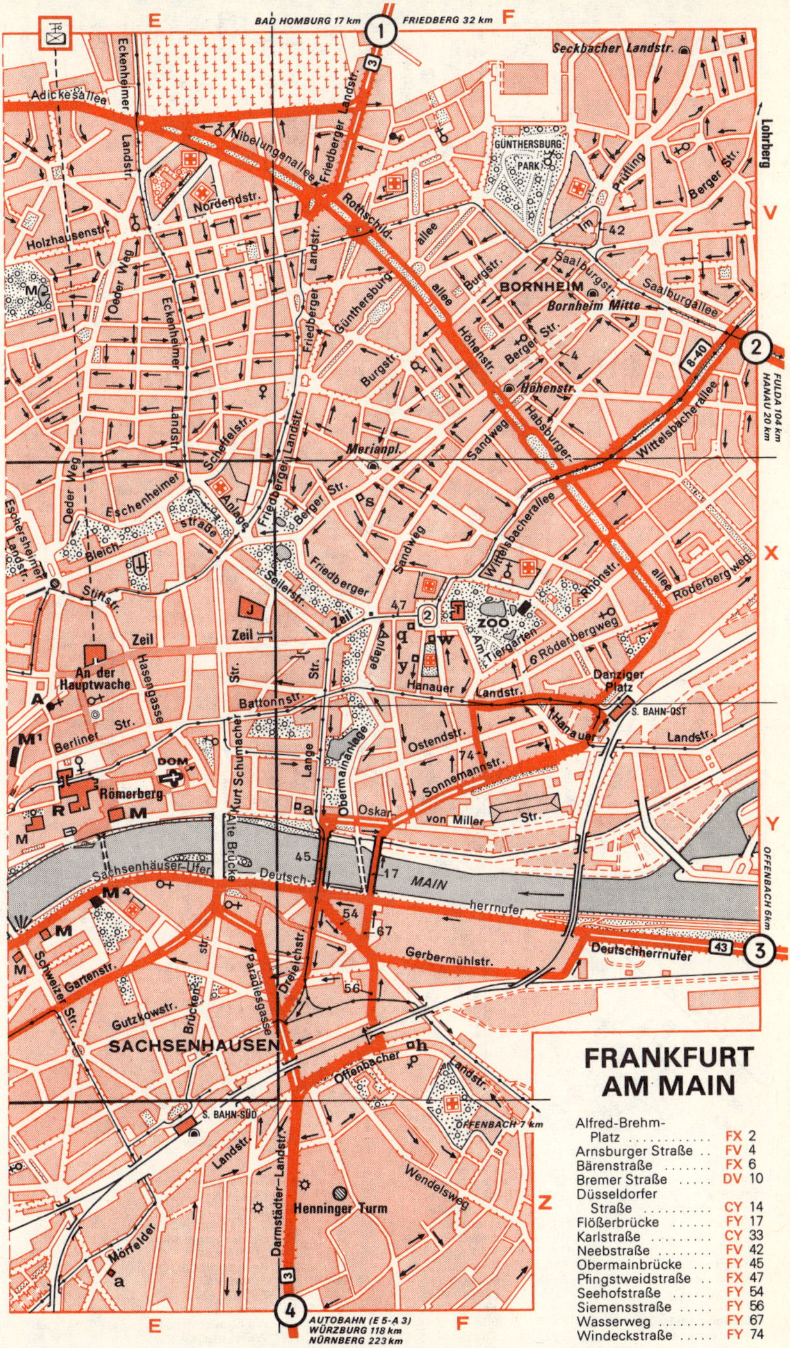

FRANKFURT AM MAIN

Alfred-Brehm-Platz	FX	2
Arnsburger Straße	FV	4
Bärenstraße	FX	6
Bremer Straße	DV	10
Düsseldorfer Straße	CY	14
Flößerbrücke	FY	17
Karlstraße	CY	33
Neebstraße	FV	42
Obermainbrücke	FY	45
Pfingstweidstraße	FX	47
Seehofstraße	FY	54
Siemensstraße	FY	56
Wasserweg	FY	67
Windeckstraße	FY	74

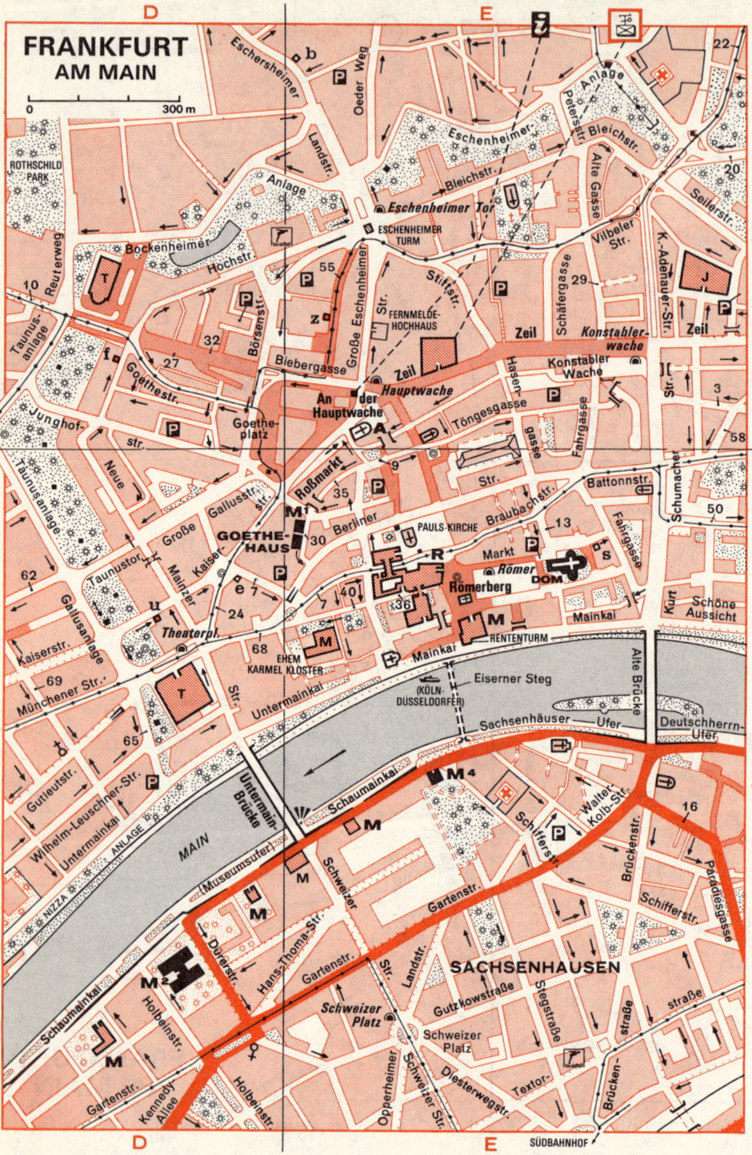

An der Hauptwache ...... EX
Goethestraße ...... DX
Gr. Bockenheimer Straße ...... DX 27
Kaiserstraße ...... DY
Münchener Straße ...... DY
Roßmarkt ...... EY
Schillerstraße ...... EX 55
Zeil ...... EX

Allerheiligenstraße ...... EX 3
Bethmannstraße ...... DY 7
Bleidenstraße ...... EY 9
Bockenheimer Landstraße ...... DX 10
Domstraße ...... EY 13
Elisabethenstraße ...... EY 16
Friedberger Anlage ...... EX 20
Friedberger Landstraße ...... EX 22
Friedensstraße ...... DY 24
Große Friedberger Straße ...... EX 29
Großer Hirschgraben ...... EY 30
Kalbächer Gasse ...... DX 32
Kleiner Hirschgraben ...... EY 35
Limpurgergasse ...... EY 36
Münzgasse ...... EY 40
Rechneigrabenstr. ...... EY 50
Stolzestraße ...... EX 58
Taunusstraße ...... DY 62
Untermainanlage ...... DY 65
Weißfrauenstraße ...... DY 68
Weserstraße ...... DY 69

***at Eschborn* 6236** NW : 12 km :

Novotel, Philipp-Helfmann-Str. 10, ✆ (06196) 4 28 12, Telex 415655, (heated), – wc . **E** by A 66 CV
M a la carte 22/41 – **227 rm** 138/185 Bb.

near Main-Taunus-Einkaufszentrum W : 14 km by ⑥ :

Holiday Inn, Am Main-Taunus-Zentrum 1, ✉ 6231 Sulzbach, ✆ (06196) 78 78, Telex 410373, , – . **E** VISA
M a la carte 32/64 – **291 rm** 180/240 Bb.

***at Neu-Isenburg 2-Gravenbruch* 6078** SE : 11 km by ④ :

Gravenbruch-Kempinski-Frankfurt M, ✆ (06102) 50 50, Telex 417673, , « Park », Massage, , (heated), , , – . **E** VISA. rest
M (*see also* **Gourmet-Restaurant below**) a la carte 36/79 – **317 rm** 171/372 Bb.

XXXX ❁ **Gourmet-Restaurant** (at hotel Gravenbruch-Kempinski), ✆ (06102) 50 50 – . **E** VISA.
closed Saturday, Sunday, Bank Holidays except exhibitions and 4 weeks July - August – **M** (dinner only) a la carte 45/116 (booking essential)
Spec. Hummerragout mit Nudeln, Gratinierter Lammrücken, Getrüffelte Maispoularde.

near Rhein-Main airport SW : 12 km by ⑤ (near motorway Flughafen exit) – ✉ 6000 Frankfurt 75 – ☎ 069 :

Sheraton M, Am Flughafen (Terminal Mitte), ✆ 6 97 70, Telex 4189294, , – . **E** VISA. rest
Restaurants : – **Papillon** (*closed lunch Saturday, Sunday and Bank Holidays*) **M** a la carte 47/99 – **Maxwell's Bistro M** a la carte 31/60 – **Taverne** (*closed Saturday and Sunday*) **M** a la carte 23/63 – **819 rm** 256/416 Bb.

Steigenberger Airporthotel, Unterschweinstiege 16, ✆ 6 98 51, Telex 413112, , , free shuttle-service to the airport – . **E** VISA
Restaurants : – **Grill-Restaurant** (*closed Saturday, Sunday and Bank Holidays*) **M** a la carte 35/70 – **Pergola M** a la carte 27/52 – **350 rm** 181/335 Bb.

XXX **Rôtisserie 5 Continents**, im Flughafen, Ankunft Ausland B (Besucherhalle, Ebene B), ✆ 6 90 34 44, ← – . **E** VISA
M a la carte 36/76.

XX **Waldrestaurant Unterschweinstiege**, Unterschweinstiege 16, ✆ 69 25 03, « Terrace, country house atmosphere » – . **E** VISA
M a la carte 31/69 (for lunch cold-warm buffet, booking essential).

on the road from Neu-Isenburg to Götzenhain by ④ : 13 km by A 661 and motorway-exit Dreieich :

XXX Gutsschänke Neuhof, ✉ 6072 Dreieich-Götzenhain, ✆ (06102) 32 14, « Country house atmosphere, terrace » – .

***at Maintal* 6457** by ② : 13 km :

XXX ❁ **Hessler**, Am Bootshafen 4 (Dörnigheim), ✆ (06181) 49 29 51 –
closed Sunday lunch, Monday and 3 weeks July - August – **M** a la carte 52/96 (booking essential)
Spec. Rotbarbe in Sesammantel, Lammrücken in Thymiankruste, Dreierlei von Mousse au chocolat.

Wertheim **6980.** Baden-Württemberg 987 ㉕ – pop. 20 000 – alt. 142 m – ☎ 09342.
Frankfurt am Main 87.

XXXX ❁❁ **Schweizer Stuben** with rm, at Wertheim-Bettingen (E : 10 km), Geiselbrunnweg 11, ✆ 43 51, Telex 689123, ←, , , , , (indoor) – wc wc .
M (*closed lunch Sunday to Monday*) a la carte 77/135 (booking essential) – **16 rm** 155/350
Spec. Gugelhupf von Gänsestopfleber mit Weinbeerensauce, Steinbutt mit Hummerravioli und Pimentosauce, Täubchenbrust in Blätterteig mit Perigordtrüffel.

HAMBURG **2000.** Hamburg 987 ⑤ – pop. 1 640 000 – alt. 10 m – ☎ 040.
See : Rathausmarkt★ and Jungfernstieg★ DY – Außenalster★★★ (trip by boat★★★) EX – Hagenbeck Zoo (Tierpark Hagenbeck)★★ – Television Tower (Fernsehturm)★★ (☀★★) BX – Art Gallery (Kunsthalle)★★ (19C German painting) EY M1 – St. Michael's church (St. Michaelis)★ (tower ☀★) BZ – Stintfang (←★) BZ – Port (Hafen)★★ (trip by boat★★) BZ.
✈ Hamburg-Fuhlsbüttel (N : 15 km), ✆ 50 80, City-Centre Airport (Air Terminal at ZOB FY), Brockesstraße, ✆ 50 85 57 – ✆ 39 18 65 56.
Exhibition Centre (Messegelände) (BX), ✆ 3 56 91, Telex 212609.
Tourist-Information, Hachmannplatz 1, ✆ 24 87 00, Telex 2163036.
Tourist-Information at the airport (Ankunftshalle), ✆ 24 87 00.
ADAC, Amsinckstr. 39 (H 1), ✆ 2 39 91.
Berlin 297 – Bremen 118 – Hannover 152.

Plan on following pages

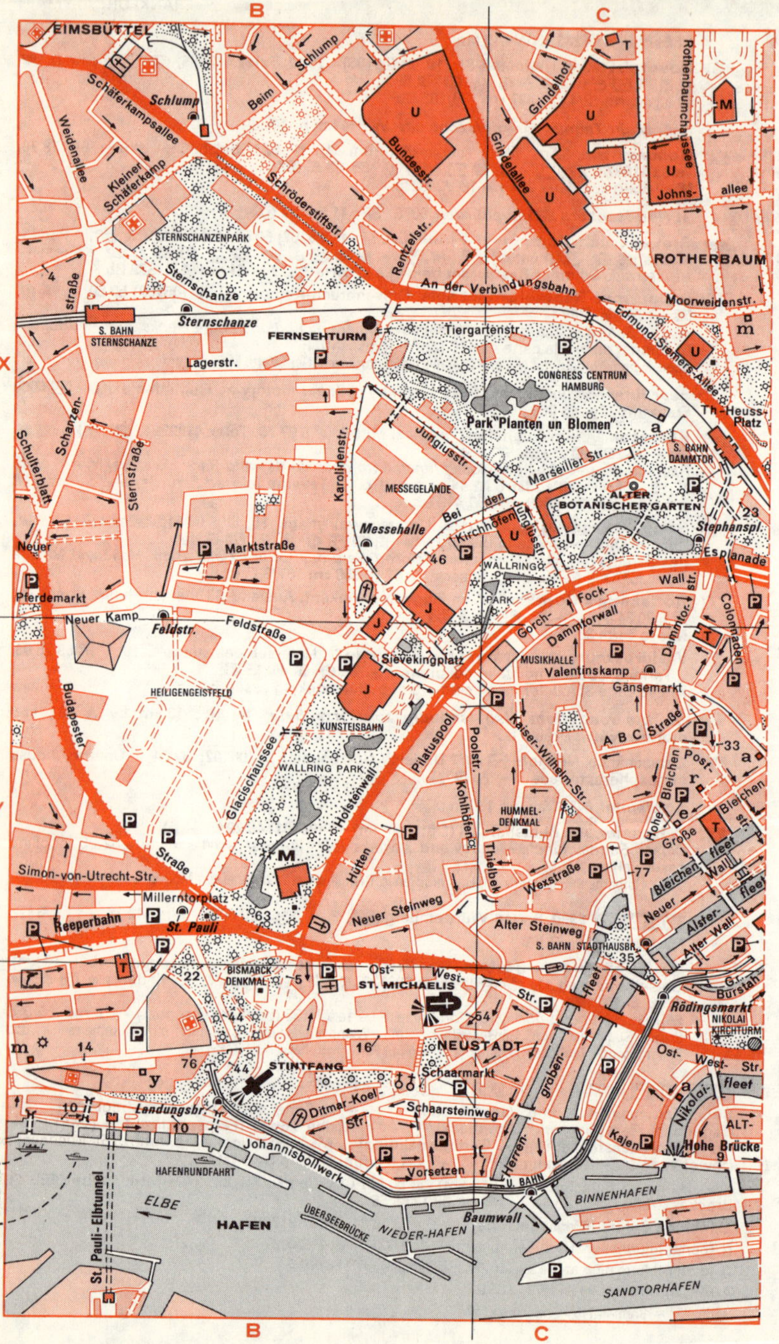
B
C
EIMSBÜTTEL
Schlump
Beim
Schlump
Grindelhof
Rothenbaumchaussee
Schäferkampsallee
Weidenallee
Kleiner Schäferkamp
Schröderstiftstr.
Bundesstr.
Grindelallee
Johns-
allee
STERNSCHANZENPARK
Rentzelstr.
Sternschanze
An der Verbindungsbahn
ROTHERBAUM
Moorweidenstr.
Edmund-Siemers-Allee
straße
S. BAHN STERNSCHANZE
Sternschanze
FERNSEHTURM
Tiergartenstr.
X
Lagerstr.
CONGRESS CENTRUM HAMBURG
Th.-Heuss-Platz
Schanzen-
Jungiusstr.
Park "Planten un Blomen"
S. BAHN DAMMTOR
Schulterblatt
Sternstraße
Karolinenstr.
MESSEGELÄNDE
Marseiller Str.
ALTER BOTANISCHER GARTEN
Bei den Kirchhöfen
Jungiusstr.
Stephanspl.
Messehalle
Neuer
Marktstraße
WALLRING
Esplanade
Pferdemarkt
PARK
Wall
Fock-
Dammtor-str.
Colonnaden
Neuer Kamp
Feldstr.
Feldstraße
Gorch-
Dammtorwall
Sievekingplatz
MUSIKHALLE
Valentinskamp
HEILIGENGEISTFELD
Gänsemarkt
Budapester
KUNSTEISBAHN
Kaiser-Wilhelm-Str.
ABC Straße
Glacischaussee
WALLRING PARK
Pilatuspool
Poolstr.
Post-
Y
Holstenwall
Kohlhöfen
HUMMEL-DENKMAL
Hohe Bleichen
Große Bleichen
Straße
Hütten
Thielbek
Wexstraße
Bleichen-fleet
Simon-von-Utrecht-Str.
Neuer Steinweg
Neuer Wall
Alster-
Millerntorplatz
Alter Steinweg
Alter Wall
Reeperbahn
St. Pauli
S. BAHN STADTHAUSBR.
BISMARCK-DENKMAL
Ost-
West-
ST. MICHAELIS
Str.
fleet
Gr. Burstah
Rödingsmarkt
NIKOLAI-KIRCHTURM
NEUSTADT
Ost-
West-
Str.
fleet
STINTFANG
Schaarmarkt
graben-
Nikolai-
Landungsbr.
Ditmar-Koel-Str.
Schaarsteinweg
ALT-
Z
Kajen
Hohe Brücke
Johannisbollwerk
Vorsetzen
Herren-
U. BAHN
HAFENRUNDFAHRT
BINNENHAFEN
HELGOLAND ENGLAND
ELBE
HAFEN
ÜBERSEEBRÜCKE
NIEDER-HAFEN
Baumwall
St. Pauli-Elbtunnel
SANDTORHAFEN
B
C

HAMBURG

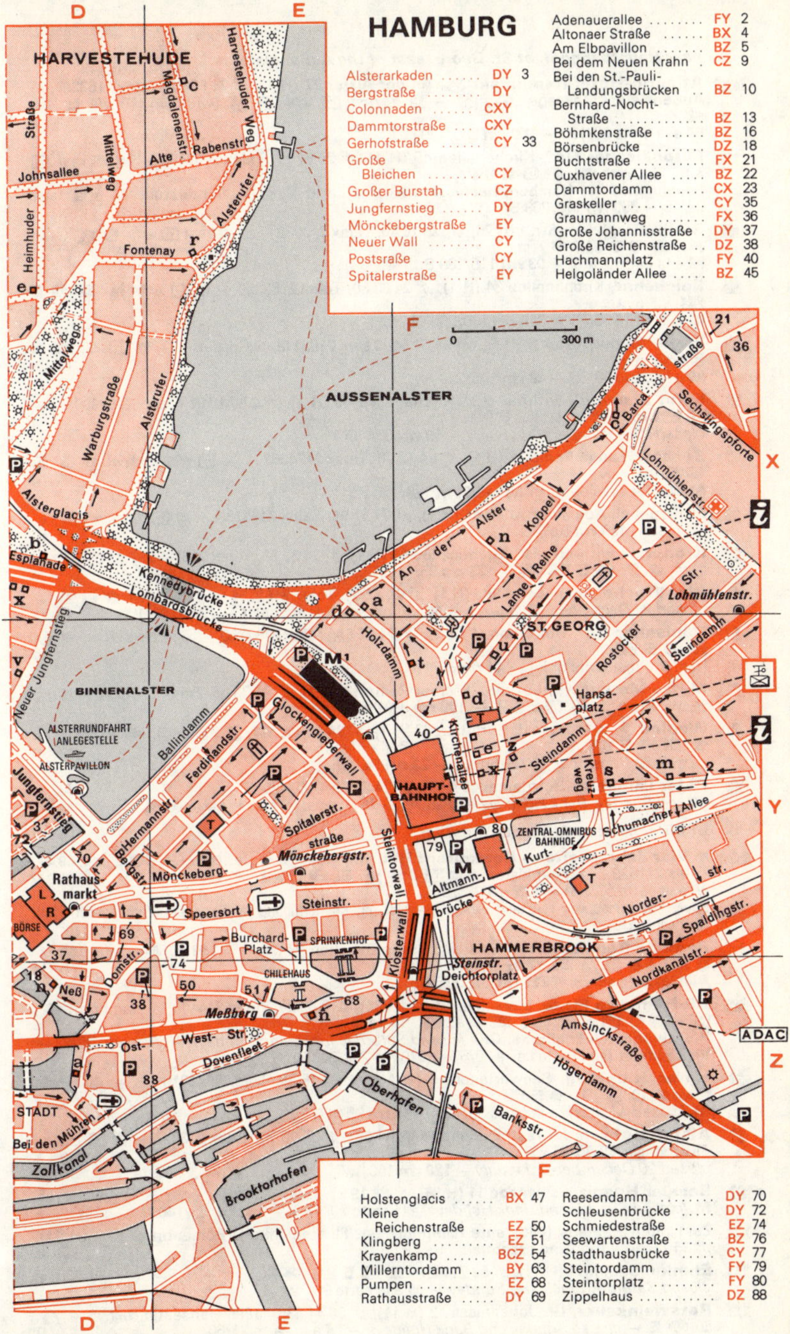

D
E
F
X
Y
Z
HARVESTEHUDE
AUSSENALSTER
BINNENALSTER
ST. GEORG
HAMMERBROOK
ALSTERRUNDFAHRT ANLEGESTELLE
ALSTERPAVILLON
HAUPT-BAHNHOF
ZENTRAL-OMNIBUS BAHNHOF
BÖRSE
SPRINKENHOF
CHILEHAUS
ADAC
STADT
0
300 m
Harvestehuder Weg
Magdalenenstr.
Rabenstr.
Alte
Mittelweg
Johnsallee
Heimhuder
Fontenay
Alsterufer
Warburgstraße
Alsterglacis
Esplanade
Kennedybrücke
Lombardsbrücke
Neuer Jungfernstieg
Ballindamm
Jungfernstieg
Ferdinandstr.
Glockengießerwall
Hermannstr.
Bergstr.
Rathausmarkt
Mönckeberg-
Mönckebergstr.
Spitalerstr.
Speersort
Steinstr.
Burchard-Platz
Domstr.
Neß
Meßberg
Ost-West-Str.
Dovenfleet
Bei den Mühren
Zollkanal
Brooktorhafen
Oberhafen
Banksstr.
Högerdamm
Amsinckstraße
Deichtorplatz
Steinstr.
Klosterwall
Steintorwall
Altmann-brücke
Kurt-Schumacher-Allee
Norder-str.
Spaldingstr.
Nordkanalstr.
Steindamm
Kreuzweg
Kirchenallee
Holzdamm
Lange Reihe
An der Alster
Koppel
Rostocker
Hansaplatz
Lohmühlenstr.
Sechslingspforte
Barca
straße
Str.
M
M¹

The reference (H 15) at the end of the address is the postal district : Hamburg 15

near Hauptbahnhof, at St. Georg, east of the Außenalster :

Atlantic-Hotel Kempinski, An der Alster 72 (H 1), 24 80 01, Telex 2163297, < Außenalster, Massage, , – rest (with). AE E VISA. rest EX a
M a la carte 50/100 – **300 rm** 280/420.

Europäischer Hof, Kirchenallee 45 (H 1), 24 81 71, Telex 2162493 – rest (with). AE E VISA FY e
Restaurants : – **Hamburg-Restaurant M** a la carte 30/69 – **Bürgerstube M** a la carte 22/45 – **350 rm** 118/268 Bb.

Berlin, Borgfelder Str. 1 (H 26), 25 16 40, Telex 213939 – rest (with). AE E VISA. rest by Kurt-Schumacher-Allee FY
M a la carte 28/57 – **93 rm** 115/180 Bb.

Reichshof, Kirchenallee 34 (H 1), 24 83 30, Telex 2163396 – . AE E VISA. rest FY d
M a la carte 35/74 – **310 rm** 130/260 Bb.

Prem, An der Alster 9 (H 1), 24 54 54, Telex 2163115, « Garden » – . AE E VISA. rest FX c
M a la carte 39/85 – **48 rm** 145/290 Bb.

Fürst Bismarck without rest, Kirchenallee 49 (H 1), 2 80 10 91, Telex 2162980 – wc wc . AE E VISA FY x
closed 23 December - 1 January – **59 rm** 80/145.

Senator, Lange Reihe 18 (H 1), 24 12 03, Telex 2174002 – wc wc . AE E VISA FY u
M (dinner - residents only) – **56 rm** 128/176 Bb.

St. Raphael, Adenauer-Allee 41 (H 1), 24 11 91, Telex 2174733 – wc . rest – **120 rm** Bb FY m

Kronprinz without rest, Kirchenallee 46 (H 1), 24 32 58, Telex 2161005 – wc wc . AE E VISA. – **73 rm** 95/145 Bb. FY e

Alte Wache, Adenauer-Allee (H 1), 24 12 91, Telex 2162254 – wc
closed 24 December - 2 January – **M** (dinner - residents only) – **72 rm** 98/150. FY s

Dänischer Hof, Holzdamm 4 (H 1), 24 55 56, Telex 2162760 – wc wc . AE E VISA EXY d
(rest. for residents only) – **44 rm** 80/170.

Metro Merkur without rest, Bremer Reihe 12 (H 1), 24 33 83, Telex 2162683 – wc wc . AE E VISA – **109 rm** 80/135. FY z

Wedina without rest, Gurlittstr. 23 (H 1), 24 30 11, , (heated), – wc . AE E VISA FX n
closed 22 December - 10 February – **23 rm** 54/115.

XX **Peter Lembcke**, Holzdamm 49 (H 1), 24 32 90 – AE E FY t
closed Sunday, Bank Holidays and 28 July - 16 August – **M** a la carte 46/81.

at Binnenalster, Altstadt, Neustadt :

Vier Jahreszeiten - Restaurant Haerlin, Neuer Jungfernstieg 9 (H 36), 3 49 41, Telex 211629, < Binnenalster – . AE E VISA. DY v
M a la carte 50/100 – **175 rm** 235/516
Spec. Pot au feu von Hummer, Lammrückenfilet mit Kräuterfüllung in Blätterteig, Zitronensoufflé mit Himbeersauce.

Ramada Renaissance Hotel M, Große Bleichen (H 36), 34 91 80, Massage, – . AE E VISA. rest CY e
M a la carte 46/79 – **211 rm** 247/385 Bb.

CP Hamburg Plaza, Marseiller Str. 2 (H 36), 3 50 20, Telex 214400, < Hamburg, , – . AE E VISA. rest CX a
Restaurants : – **Englischer Grill** *(closed Saturday lunch and Sunday)* **M** a la carte 37/77 – **Vierländerstube M** a la carte 28/57 – **570 rm** 200/340 Bb.

Hafen Hamburg, Seewartenstr. 9 (H 11), 31 15 25, Telex 2161319, < – wc wc . AE E VISA BZ y
M *(closed Monday)* a la carte 35/72 – **155 rm** 95/150 Bb.

Alster-Hof without rest, Esplanade 12 (H 36), 35 00 70, Telex 213843 – wc wc . AE E VISA DX x
closed 20 December - 2 January – **120 rm** 100/190.

Baseler Hospiz, Esplanade 11 (H 36), 34 19 21, Telex 2163707 – wc wc DX x
M *(closed Sunday and Bank Holidays)* a la carte 20/47 – **160 rm** 55/140.

XXX Zum alten Rathaus (with entertainment-rest. Fleetenkieker), Börsenbrücke 10 (H 11), 36 75 70 – (booking essential) DZ n

XXX **Ehmke**, Grimm 14 (H 11), 32 71 32 – AE E VISA. DZ a
closed Saturday lunch and Sunday – **M** a la carte 36/72.

XXX **Ratsweinkeller**, Gr. Johannisstr. 2 (H 11), 36 41 53, « 1896 Hanseatic rest. » – . AE E – *closed Sunday and Bank Holidays* – **M** a la carte 25/60. DY R

XX **Deichgraf**, Deichstr. 23 (H 11), ✆ 36 42 08 – AE ⓓ E VISA CZ **a**
closed Saturday lunch, Sunday and Bank Holidays – **M** a la carte 28/79 (booking essential).

XX Harmonie, Ost-West-Str. 12 (H 1), ✆ 32 71 91 EZ **n**

XX **Mövenpick - Café des Artistes**, Große Bleichen 36 (H 36), ✆ 35 16 35 – ▮. AE ⓓ E VISA – **M** a la carte 34/66 – **Mövenpick-Restaurant M** a la carte 20/52 CY **r**

XX **Schümann's Austernkeller**, Jungfernstieg 34 (H 36), ✆ 34 62 65, « Rest. from the turn of the century with private dining rooms » – ✻ CY **a**
closed Sunday and Bank Holidays – **M** a la carte 44/105.

XX **Restaurant im Finnlandhaus**, Esplanade 41 (12th floor, ▮) (H 36), ✆ 34 41 33, ≤ Hamburg, Binnen- and Außenalster – ▤. AE ⓓ E VISA. ✻ DX **b**
closed Saturday, Sunday and Bank Holidays dinner – **M** a la carte 34/73.

at Hamburg-Altona by Reeperbahn BY :

Raphael Hotel Altona, Präsident-Krahn-Str. 13 (H 50), ✆ 38 12 39 – ▮ wc ☎ Ⓟ. AE ⓓ E. ✻ rest
M *(dinner only, closed Saturday and Sunday)* a la carte 20/36 – **54 rm** 55/140 Bb.

XXXX ✿ **Landhaus Scherrer**, Elbchaussee 130 (H 50), ✆ 8 80 13 25 – Ⓟ. AE ⓓ E
closed Sunday, Bank Holidays and 14 to 27 July – **M** a la carte 55/105(booking essential) – **Bistro-Rest.** *(lunch only)* **M** a la carte 30/60
Spec. Marinierter Stör mit Languste in Algenvinaigrette, Gepökelter Kalbskopf mit Graupen-Kerbelbutter, Vierländer Entenbrust auf Wirsing.

XXX **Fischereihafen-Restaurant Hamburg**, Große Elbstr. 143 (H 50), ✆ 38 18 16, ≤ – Ⓟ. ⓓ E
M a la carte 30/93 (booking essential).

at Hamburg-Billstedt by Nordkanalstr. FZ :

Panorama without rest, Billstedter Hauptstr. 44 (H 74), ✆ 73 17 01, Telex 212162 – ▮ TV Ⓟ. AE ⓓ E VISA
closed 24 December - 2 January – **111 rm** 120/220 Bb.

at Hamburg-Blankenese W : 16 km by Reeperbahn BY :

Strandhotel, Strandweg 13 (H 55), ✆ 86 09 93, ≤, « Villa with elegant installation, painting collection », – TV wc wc ☎ Ⓟ. AE ⓓ E VISA
M *(closed Sunday dinner and Monday)* a la carte 37/76 – **13 rm** 105/325 Bb.

XXX **Sagebiels Fährhaus**, Blankeneser Hauptstr. 107 (H 55), ✆ 86 15 14, « Garden with ≤ » – Ⓟ. AE ⓓ E VISA
closed Monday October - March – **M** a la carte 31/75.

XXX **Süllberg**, Süllbergterrasse 2 (H 55), ✆ 86 16 86, « Terraced garden with ≤ » – Ⓟ. AE ⓓ E VISA
M a la carte 36/76.

X **Strandhof** (Bistro-rest.), Strandweg 27 (H 55), ✆ 86 52 36, ≤, – AE ⓓ
closed Monday and 3 to 31 January – **M** (dinner only) a la carte 40/89.

at Hamburg-City North by Buchtstr. FX :

Crest-Hotel Hamburg, Mexicoring 1 (H 60), ✆ 6 30 50 51, Telex 2174155 – ▮ ▤ rest TV Ⓟ (with ▤). AE ⓓ E VISA. ✻ rest
M a la carte 30/60 – **185 rm** 171/256 Bb.

Alsterkrug-Hotel, Alsterkrugchaussee 277 (H 60), ✆ 51 30 30, Telex 2173828, – ▮ TV wc ☎ Ⓟ. AE ⓓ E VISA. ✻ rest
M a la carte 28/53 – **80 rm** 129/187 Bb.

at Hamburg-Eppendorf by Grindelallee CX :

XXX ✿ **Le Canard**, Martinistr. 11 (H 20), ✆ 4 60 48 30 – AE ⓓ. ✻
closed Sunday – **M** a la carte 57/100 (booking essential)
Spec. Parfait von Räucheraal, Champagnersuppe mit Hummer, Barberie-Entenbrust in Beaujolais.

XX **Fisch Sellmer** (mainly seafood), Ludolfstr. 50 (H 20), ✆ 47 30 57 – Ⓟ. AE. ✻
M a la carte 29/76.

at Hamburg-Harvestehude :

Inter-Continental, Fontenay 10 (H 36), ✆ 41 41 50, Telex 211099, ≤ Hamburg and Alster, Massage, – ▮ ▤ TV Ⓟ. AE ⓓ E VISA. ✻ rest EX **r**
Restaurants : – **Fontenay-Grill** *(closed Saturday lunch)* **M** a la carte 47/96 – **Hulk-Brasserie** *(buffet lunch)* **M** a la carte 33/58 – **300 rm** 245/345 Bb.

Smolka, Isestr. 98 (H 13), ✆ 47 50 50, Telex 215275 – ▮ TV. AE ⓓ E VISA. ✻ rest
M *(closed Saturday dinner, Sunday and Bank Holidays)* a la carte 24/63 – **40 rm** 105/205 Bb. by Rothenbaumchaussee CX

Garden-Hotel Pöseldorf without rest, Magdalenenstr. 60 (H 13), ✆ 44 99 59, Telex 212621, « Elegantly furnished », – ▮ TV wc wc ☎. AE ⓓ E VISA EX **c**
70 rm 133/306.

Mittelweg without rest, Mittelweg 59 (H 13), ✆ 45 32 51, Telex 2165663 – TV wc wc ☎ Ⓟ by Mittelweg DX
38 rm 92/174.

XX La vite (Italian rest.), Heimhuder Str. 5 (H 13), ✆ 45 84 01, – (booking essential). DX e

XX **Daitokai** (Japanese rest.), Milchstr. 1 (H 13), ✆ 4 10 10 61 – AE E. *closed Sunday* – **M** a la carte 33/68 (booking essential). by Mittelweg DX

at Hamburg-Nienstedten W : 13 km by Reeperbahn BY :

XXX Jacob with rm, Elbchaussee 401 (H 52), ✆ 82 93 52, ⋞, « Elbe-side setting terrace » – wc
14 rm.

XX ⚡ **Landhaus Dill,** Elbchaussee 404 (H 52), ✆ 82 84 43 – . AE E VISA
closed lunch Tuesday to Friday and Monday – **M** a la carte 42/84
Spec. Marinierter Lachs auf Reibekuchen, Seeteufelmedaillons mit Pinot-Noir-Sauce, Lammrücken in Safransauce.

at Hamburg-Rotherbaum :

Elysee M, Rothenbaumchaussee 10, ✆ 41 41 20, Telex 212455, – . AE VISA CX m
Restaurants : – **Piazza Romana M** a la carte 35/59 – **Brasserie M** a la carte 25/45 – **299 rm** 175/310 Bb.

XX ⚡ **L'auberge française** (French rest.), Rutschbahn 34 (H 13), ✆ 4 10 25 32 –
closed July and Sunday October - December, Saturday and Sunday January - September – **M** a la carte 42/72 (booking essential) by Grindelhof CX
Spec. Foie d'oie poêlé sauce truffes et pommes, Salade tiède de scampi au beurre de basilic, Filets de rougets "Antibes".

XX **Fernsehturm-Restaurant,** Lagerstr. 2 (, 3,75 DM) (H 6), ✆ 43 80 24, ✻ Hamburg, « Revolving rest. at 132 m » – . AE E VISA. BX
M a la carte 40/70 (booking essential).

at Hamburg-St. Pauli :

XX **Bavaria-Blick,** Bernhard-Nocht-Str. 99 (7th floor,) (H 4), ✆ 31 48 00, ⋞ port – . AE E VISA BZ m
M a la carte 28/68 (booking essential).

at Hamburg-Schnelsen by Grindelallee CX :

Novotel, Oldesloer Str. 166 (H 61), ✆ 5 50 20 73, Telex 212923, (heated), – wc . AE E VISA
M a la carte 23/53 – **124 rm** 142/185 Bb.

at Hamburg-Stellingen by Schäferkampsallee BX :

Helgoland without rest (hospice), Kieler Str. 177 (H 54), ✆ 85 70 01 – wc wc . AE E VISA
109 rm 104/182 Bb.

Falck, Kieler Str. 333 (H 54), ✆ 5 40 20 61, Telex 213664, – wc wc . AE E VISA
M a la carte 31/67 – **83 rm** 105/190 Bb.

at Hamburg-Uhlenhorst by Buchtstraße FX :

Parkhotel Alster-Ruh without rest, Am Langenzug 6 (H 76), ✆ 22 45 77 – wc wc . AE E
27 rm 97/204 Bb.

XX **Ristorante Roma** (Italian rest.), Hofweg 7 (H 76), ✆ 2 20 25 54 – AE
closed Sunday lunch and Saturday – **M** a la carte 35/59.

at Hamburg-Veddel by Amsinckstr. FZ :

Carat-Hotel M, Sieldeich 9 (H 28), ✆ 78 96 00, Telex 2163354 – wc wc . AE E VISA
M a la carte 29/57 – **93 rm** 125/165 Bb.

HANOVER (HANNOVER) 3000. Niedersachsen 987 ⑮ – pop. 550 000 – alt. 55 m – 0511.

See : Herrenhausen Gardens (Herrenhäuser Gärten)★★ (Großer Garten★★, Berggarten★) CV – Kestner-Museum★ DY M1 – Market Church (Marktkirche) (Altarpiece★★) DY A – Museum of Lower Saxony (Niedersächsisches Landesmuseum) (Prehistorical department★) EZ M2.

Hanover-Langenhagen (① : 11 km), ✆ 7 30 51.

✆ 1 98 54 52.

Exhibition Centre (Messegelände), (by ② and B 6) ✆ 8 91, Telex 922728.

Tourist office, Ernst-August-Platz 8, ✆ 1 68 23 19.

City-Air-Terminal, Raschplatz 1PQ, ✆ 1 68 28 01.

ADAC, Hindenburgstr. 37, ✆ 8 50 00.

Berlin 289 ② – Bremen 123 ① – Hamburg 151 ①.

Plan on following pages

Maritim [M], Hildesheimer Str. 34, ✆ 1 65 31, Telex 9230268, ≘s, [pool] – |‡| ▤ [TV] ♿ Ⓟ 🏛. AE Ⓓ E VISA. ✈ rest EZ **b**
M a la carte 31/82 – **293 rm** 148/325 Bb.

Inter-Continental, Friedrichswall 11, ✆ 1 69 11, Telex 923656 – |‡| ▤ rest [TV] ♿ 🏛 (with ▤). ✈ rest – **285 rm** Bb. DY **a**

✿ **Schweizerhof Hannover - Schu's Restaurant** [M], Hinüberstr. 6, ✆ 3 49 50, Telex 923359 – |‡| [TV]. AE Ⓓ E VISA EX **d**
M *(closed Saturday until 6 p.m.)* a la carte 50/85 (remarkable wine-list) – **Gourmet's Buffet M** a la carte 27/59 – **84 rm** 174/278 Bb.

Kastens Hotel Luisenhof, Luisenstr. 2, ✆ 1 61 51, Telex 922325 – |‡| [TV] ♿ 🚗 Ⓟ 🏛. AE Ⓓ E VISA. ✈ rest EX **b**
M *(closed Sunday July to August)* a la carte 36/70 – **200 rm** 129/260 Bb.

Congress-Hotel am Stadtpark, Clausewitzstr. 6, ✆ 2 80 55 57, Telex 921263, [terrace], Massage, ≘s, [pool] – |‡| [TV] 🚗 Ⓟ 🏛 – **252 rm** Bb. by ②

Grand Hotel Mussmann without rest, Ernst-August-Platz 7, ✆ 32 79 71, Telex 922859 – |‡| [TV] Ⓟ 🏛. AE Ⓓ E VISA EX **v**
100 rm 128/318 Bb.

Königshof [M] without rest, Königstr. 12, ✆ 31 20 71, Telex 922306 – |‡| ⛀wc ⛆wc ☎ ♿ Ⓟ. AE E – **84 rm** 98/180 Bb. EX **c**

Central-Hotel Kaiserhof, Ernst-August-Platz 4, ✆ 32 78 11, Telex 922810 – |‡| [TV] ⛀wc ⛆wc ☎ 🏛. ✈ rest – **70 rm** Bb. EX **a**

Am Funkturm - Ristorante Milano, Hallerstr. 34, ✆ 31 70 33 (hotel) 33 23 09 (rest.) – |‡| ⛀wc ⛆wc ☎ ♿ Ⓟ. AE E EV **s**
M a la carte 23/50 – **40 rm** 60/140 Bb.

Hospiz Loccumer Hof, Kurt-Schumacher-Str. 16, ✆ 32 60 51 – |‡| [TV] ⛀wc ⛆wc ☎ 🚗 🏛. AE Ⓓ E VISA. ✈ DX **s**
M *(closed Saturday and Sunday for dinner)* a la carte 21/60 – **70 rm** 70/160 Bb.

Am Rathaus, Friedrichswall 21, ✆ 32 62 68, Telex 923865, ≘s – |‡| ⛀wc ⛆wc ☎. E VISA – **M** *(closed Sunday)* a la carte 23/55 – **53 rm** 86/240 Bb EY **y**

Intercity-Hotel, Ernst-August-Platz 1, ✆ 32 74 61, Telex 921171 – |‡| ▤ rest [TV] ⛆wc ☎ 🏛 (with ▤). AE E EX **r**
M a la carte 15/45 – **57 rm** 78/140.

Thüringer Hof without rest, Osterstr. 37, ✆ 32 64 37 – |‡| ⛀wc ⛆wc ☎. AE Ⓓ E
closed 24 December - 1 January – **59 rm** 75/200. EY **e**

Atlanta without rest, Hinüberstr. 1, ✆ 34 29 39, Telex 924603 – |‡| ⛀wc ⛆wc ☎ 🚗. E. ✈ – **39 rm** 55/210 Bb. EX **t**

XXXX ✿ **Landhaus Ammann** with rm, Hildesheimer Str. 185, ✆ 83 08 18, Telex 9230900, [terrace], « Elegant installation, patio with terrace » – |‡| [TV] ⛀wc ⛆wc ☎ ♿ Ⓟ 🏛. AE Ⓓ E. ✈ rest by ③
M a la carte 40/90 (remarkable wine-list) – **Nudelstubb M** a la carte 30/54 – **14 rm** 165/320
Spec. Gemüseterrine mit Hummermedaillons, Seezunge mit Safrannudeln und Artischockensauce, Entenbrust mit Rotwein-Preißelbeeren.

XXX **Bakkarat im Casino am Maschsee**, Arthur-Menge-Ufer 3 (1st floor), ✆ 80 10 20, ≤, [terrace] – AE Ⓓ E VISA DZ **a**
M a la carte 33/68.

XXX ✿ **Georgenhof** 🐇 with rm, Herrenhäuser Kirchweg 20, ✆ 70 22 44, « Lower Saxony country house in park, terrace » – ⛀wc ⛆wc ☎ Ⓟ by Engelbosteler Damm CV
M a la carte 42/102 (remarkable wine-list) – **17 rm** 65/180
Spec. Pörkölt vom Donauwaller (January to May), Heidelammkotelett in Blätterteig, Soufflé von Perlhuhnbrust in Portweinsauce.

XXX **Zur Brügge's Restaurant**, Bödekerstr. 29, ✆ 31 90 05 FV **a**
closed Sunday, Bank Holidays and 2 weeks August – **M** a la carte 43/79.

XXX **Mövenpick - Baron de la Mouette**, Georgenstr. 35 (1st floor), ✆ 32 62 85 – ▤. AE Ⓓ E VISA EX **x**
M a la carte 35/60.

XX **Ratskeller**, Köbelinger Str. 60, ✆ 1 53 63 – 🏛 DY **n**
closed Sunday, Monday and Bank Holidays – **M** a la carte 23/60.

XX ✿ **Clichy**, Weiße Kreuzstr. 31, ✆ 31 24 47 EV **m**
closed Sunday, Bank Holidays and 3 weeks July - August – **M** a la carte 39/75 (booking essential)
Spec. Steinbutt im Wirsingblatt, Lachsroulade in Sauerampfersauce, Lammnüßchen mit Paprikabutter.

XX ✿ **Stern's Restaurant Härke-Stuben**, Marienstr. 104, ✆ 81 73 22 – AE Ⓓ E FY **b**
closed Saturday until 7 p.m. – **M** a la carte 41/91
Spec. Kaninchenterrine mit Pilzsalat, Heidschnuckenrücken im Kartoffelmantel, Kalbsbries mit Himbeeressigsauce.

XX **Rôtisserie Helvetia**, Georgsplatz 11, ✆ 1 48 41 – Ⓓ E VISA EY **k**
M a la carte 23/55.

X **Härke-Klause** (brewery - inn), Ständehausstr. 4, ✆ 32 11 75 – AE Ⓓ E EY **b**
closed Sunday and Bank Holidays – **M** a la carte 15/46 (also diet).

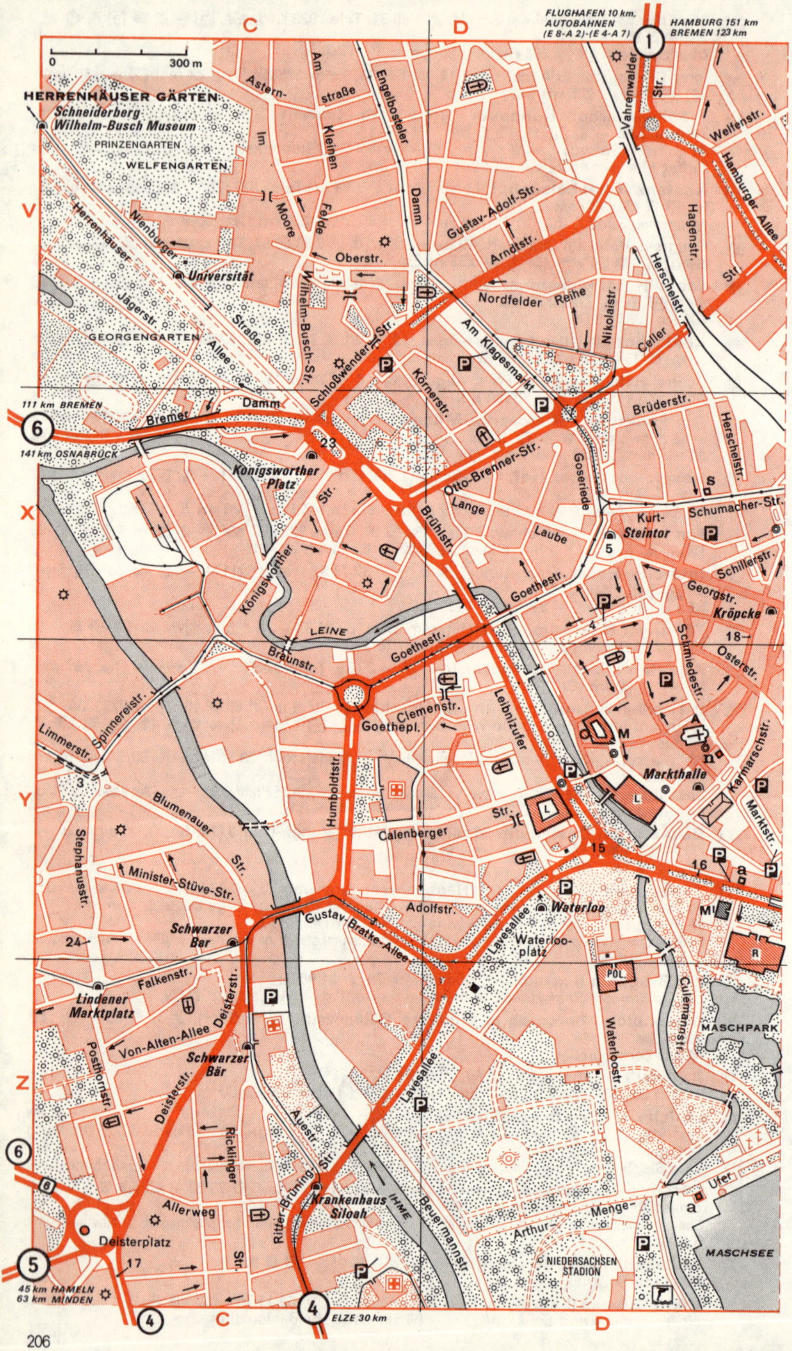
FLUGHAFEN 10 km.
AUTOBAHNEN
(E 8-A 2)-(E 4-A 7)
HAMBURG 151 km
BREMEN 123 km
C
D
1
0
300 m
HERRENHÄUSER GÄRTEN
Schneiderberg
Wilhelm-Busch Museum
PRINZENGARTEN
WELFENGARTEN
Astern-
Am
straße
Kleinen
Engelbosteler
Damm
Im
Moore
Felde
Vahrenwalder
Str.
Welfenstr.
Hamburger Allee
Hagenstr.
Str.
Gustav-Adolf-Str.
Arndtstr.
Oberstr.
V
Herrenhäuser
Nienburger
Universität
Jägerstr.
GEORGENGARTEN
Straße
Allee
Wilhelm-Busch-Str.
Schloßwender Str.
Nordfelder Reihe
Am Klagesmarkt
Nikolaistr.
Herschelstr.
Celler
111 km BREMEN
6
141 km OSNABRÜCK
Bremer
Damm
23
Körnerstr.
Brüderstr.
Herschelstr.
Königsworther Platz
Str.
Otto-Brenner-Str.
Lange
Goseriede
S
Kurt-Schumacher-Str.
X
Brühlstr.
Laube
Steintor
5
Schillerstr.
Königsworther
Goethestr.
Georgstr.
Kröpcke
4
18
LEINE
Goethestr.
Braunstr.
Schmiedestr.
Osterstr.
Spinnereistr.
Limmerstr.
Goethepl.
Clemenstr.
Leibnizufer
M
Karmarschstr.
3
Y
Blumenauer
Humboldtstr.
Markthalle
Marktstr.
Stephanusstr.
Str.
Calenberger
Str.
L
L
15
16
a
Minister-Stüve-Str.
Adolfstr.
Waterloo
M
Gustav-Bratke-Allee
Lavesallee
Waterlooplatz
R
24
Schwarzer Bär
POL.
Falkenstr.
Lindener Marktplatz
Deisterstr.
Von-Alten-Allee
Culemannstr.
MASCHPARK
Posthornstr.
Schwarzer Bär
Waterloostr.
Z
Lavesallee
Deisterstr.
Auestr.
6
Ricklinger
Str.
Ufer
a
Allerweg
Ritter-Brüning-Str.
Krankenhaus Siloah
IHME
Beuermannstr.
Arthur-Menge-
5
Deisterplatz
Str.
NIEDERSACHSEN STADION
MASCHSEE
17
45 km HAMELN
63 km MINDEN
4
C
4
ELZE 30 km
D

HANNOVER

Bahnhofstraße ..... EX 7
Georgstraße ...... DEX
Große Packhofstraße DX 18
Karmarschstraße ... DY

Aegidientorplatz ... EY 2
Am Küchengarten .. CY 3
Am Marstall .... DX 4
Am Steintor .... DX 5
Bischofsholer Damm FY 8
Braunschweiger Platz FY 9
Emmichplatz ...... FX 12
Ernst-August-Platz . EX 13
Friederikenplatz .... DY 15
Friedrichswall ...... DY 16
Göttinger Straße ... CZ 17
Hans-Böckler-Allee . FY 19
Hartmannstraße .... FZ 20
Joachimstraße ..... EX 21
Königsworther Platz CX 23
Lindener Marktplatz CY 24
Opernplatz .... EY 25
Scharnhorststraße .. FX 28
Thielenplatz .... EX 29
Volgersweg .... EX 30

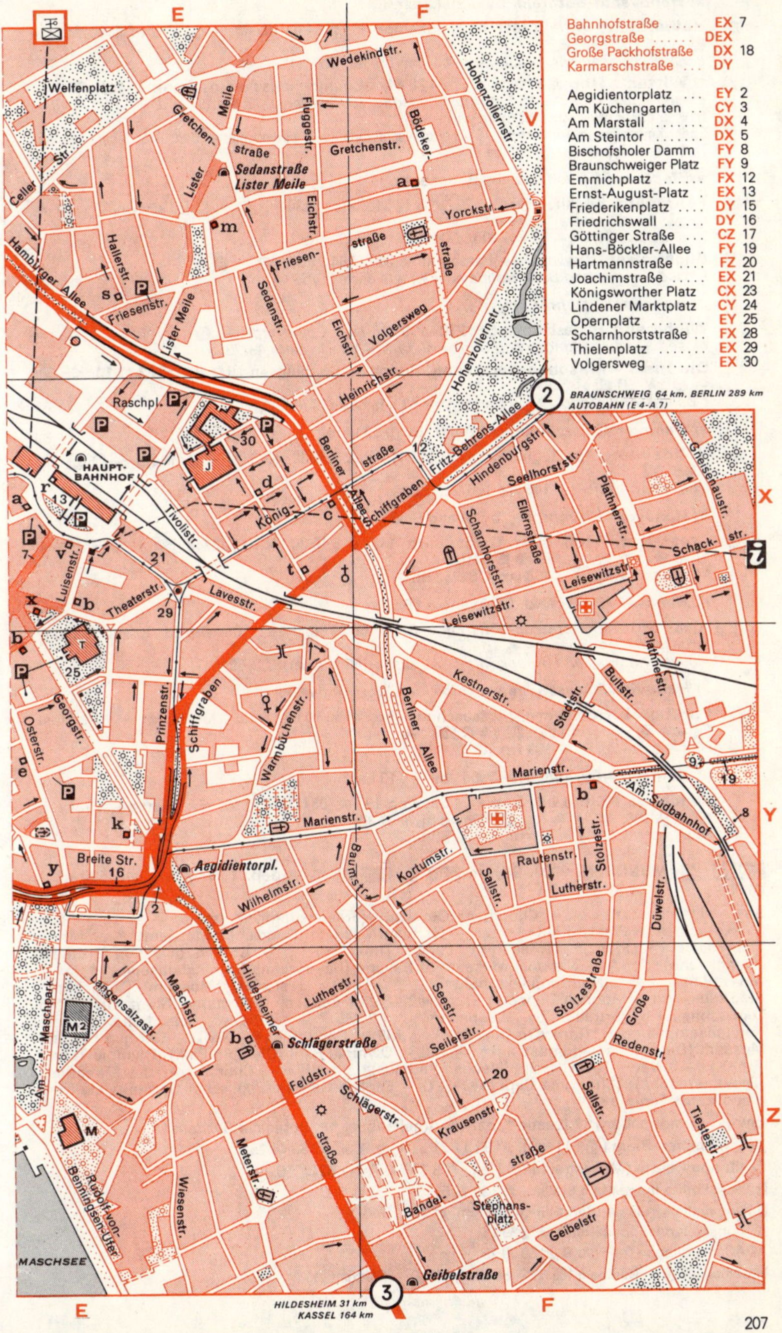

at Hanover 51-Bothfeld by Bödekerstr. FV :

Halberstadt without rest, Im Heidkampe 80, ✆ 64 01 18, – TV wc wc ☎ P
closed 23 December - 2 January – **36 rm** 65/140 Bb.

XXX ✿ **Witten's Hop**, Gernsstr. 4, ✆ 64 88 44, **« Country house atmosphere »** – P.
closed lunch Monday to Saturday, Tuesday, 16 February - 12 March and 17 to 24 April –
M a la carte 55/96 (remarkable wine-list)
Spec. Knurrhahn in Trüffelkruste, Sautierte Wachtelbrüstchen mit pochierter Gänsestopfleber, Gefülltes Täubchen in Trockenbeerenauslese.

at Hanover 51-Buchholz by Bödekerstr. FV :

Föhrenhof, Kirchhorster Str. 22, ✆ 6 17 21, Telex 923448, – TV wc wc ☎ P. AE. rest
M a la carte 24/54 – **77 rm** 105/200 Bb.

XX **Buchholzer Windmühle**, Pasteurallee 30, ✆ 64 91 38, – P
closed Sunday and Bank Holidays – **M** a la carte 25/53.

at Hanover 81-Döhren by ③ :

XXX **Wichmann**, Hildesheimer Str. 230, ✆ 83 16 71, **« Courtyard »** – P
closed Sunday, Monday and Bank Holidays – **M** a la carte 43/78.

XX **Die Insel - Maschseeterrassen**, Rudolf-von-Bennigsen-Ufer 81, ✆ 83 12 14, ←, – P. AE E
closed Monday and 2 to 21 January – **M** a la carte 24/60.

at Hanover 42-Flughafen (Airport) by ① : 11 km :

Holiday Inn, Am Flughafen, ✆ 73 01 71, Telex 924030, , – TV P. AE E VISA
M a la carte 26/64 – **146 rm** 185/235 Bb.

at Hanover 71-Kirchrode by ② and B 65 :

Crest-Hotel Hannover, Tiergartenstr. 117, ✆ 5 10 30, Telex 922748, – TV wc wc ☎ P. AE E VISA
M a la carte 30/62 – **108 rm** 173/232 Bb.

at Hanover 71-Kleefeld by ② and B 65 :

XX **Alte Mühle**, Hermann-Löns-Park 3, ✆ 55 94 80, ←, **« Converted lower Saxony farm-house, terrace »** – P. AE
closed Thursday and 3 weeks July - August – **M** a la carte 25/68.

at Hanover 72-Messe (near exhibition Centre) by ② :

Parkhotel Kronsberg, Messeschnellweg, ✆ 86 10 86, Telex 923448, – rest TV P (with). AE E VISA. rest
M a la carte 29/72 – **109 rm** 105/200 Bb.

***at Garbsen 4-Berenbostel* 3008** by ⑥ : 13 km :

Landhaus Köhne am See , Seeweg 19, ✆ (05131) 9 10 85, ←, **« Garden terrace »**, , , , – rest TV wc wc ☎ P
M a la carte 23/64 – **19 rm** 76/160 Bb.

MUNICH (MÜNCHEN) 8000. Bayern 987 ㊲, 426 ④ ⑰ – pop. 1 297 000 – alt. 520 m – ☎ 089.

See : Marienplatz★ KLY – Church of Our Lady (Frauenkirche)★★ (tower ★) KY – Old Pinakothek (Alte Pinakothek)★★★ KY – German Museum (Deutsches Museum)★★ LZ **M1** – The Palace (Residenz)★ (Treasury★★ Palace Theatre★) LY – Church of Asam Brothers (Asamkirche)★ KZ **A** – National Museum of Bavaria (Bayerisches Nationalmuseum)★★ HV – New Pinakothek (Neue Pinakothek)★ GU – City Historical Museum (Münchener Stadtmuseum)★ (Moorish Dancers★★) KZ **M2** – Villa Lenbach Collections (Städt. Galerie im Lenbachhaus) (Portraits by Lenbach★) KY **M5** – Antique Collections (Staatl. Antikensammlungen)★(Etruscan trinkets★) KY **M6** – Glyptothek★ KY **M7** – German Hunting Museum (Deutsches Jagdmuseum)★ KY **M8** – Olympic Park (Olympia-Park) (Olympic Tower ★★★) – New Town Hall (Neues Rathaus)★ LY **R** – Church of the Theatines (Theatinerkirche)★(Choir and Cupola★) LY **D** – English Garden (Englischer Garten)(view from Monopteros Temple★) HU.

Envir. : Nymphenburg★★ (castle★, park★, Amalienburg★★, Botanical Gardens★★).

✈ München-Riem (③ : 11 km), ✆ 92 11 21 27 – ✆ 12 88 44 25.

Exhibition Centre (Messegelände) (EX), ✆ 5 10 71, Telex 5212086.

Tourist office in the Main Station, ✆ 2 39 12 56.

Tourist office in the Airport München-Riem, ✆ 2 39 12 66.

Tourist information, Rathaus, ✆ 2 39 11.

ADAC, Sendlinger-Tor-Platz 9, ✆ 59 39 79.

Innsbruck 149 ⑤ – Nürnberg 165 ② – Salzburg 140 ④ – Stuttgart 219 ⑦.

Plans on following pages

The reference (M 15) at the end of the address is the postal district : Munich 15

Vier Jahreszeiten Kempinski - Restaurant Walterspiel, Maximilianstr. 17 (M 22), 23 03 90, Telex 523859, Massage, – . AE E VISA. rest LY a
M *(closed lunch Monday, Saturday lunch and August)* a la carte 64/115 – **Jahreszeiten-Eck** *(closed Sunday)* **M** a la carte 32/65 – **365 rm** 248/466
Spec. Filet vom Meerwolf in Rotwein mit Rindermark, Bresse-Poularde mit Brunnenkresseschaum, Himbeeren Walterspiel.

Königshof, Karlsplatz 25 (M 2), 55 84 12, Telex 523616 – . AE E VISA. rest KY s
M a la carte 48/112 (booking essential) – **120 rm** 174/318
Spec. Lasagne mit Seezunge und Langustinen, Gefüllte Hechtklößchen in brauner Noilly-Prat-Sauce, Entenbrust in Honig-Cidre-Sauce.

Hilton, Am Tucherpark 7 (M 22), 3 84 50, Telex 5215740, beer-garden, Massage, , – . AE E VISA HU n
Restaurants : – **Hilton Grill M** a la carte 36/80 – **Isar-Terrassen** (also diet) **M** a la carte 26/56 – **485 rm** 202/414.

Bayerischer Hof-Palais Montgelas, Promenadeplatz 6 (M 2), 2 12 00, Telex 523409, Massage, , – rest . AE E VISA KY y
Restaurants : – **Grill M** a la carte 33/75 – **Trader Vic's** *(dinner only)* **M** a la carte 28/70 – **Palais Keller M** a la carte 17/48 – **442 rm** 163/413.

Continental, Max-Joseph-Str. 5 (M 2), 55 79 71, Telex 522603, , « Antique furniture » – . AE E VISA KY f
M a la carte 43/83 – **160 rm** 200/350 Bb.

Arabella-Westpark-Hotel, Garmischer Str. 2 (M 2), 5 19 60, Telex 523680, , – . AE E VISA by Heimeranstr. EX
M a la carte 24/60 – **258 rm** 160/270 Bb.

Excelsior, Schützenstr. 11 (M 2), 55 79 06, Telex 52419 – rest . AE E VISA JY z
M a la carte 31/68 – **118 rm** 149/258.

Eden-Hotel-Wolff, Arnulfstr. 4 (M 2), 55 82 81, Telex 523564 – . AE E VISA JY p
M a la carte 25/60 – **214 rm** 150/280 Bb.

Drei Löwen - Rest.Strawberry, Schillerstr. 8 (M 2), 59 55 21, Telex 523867 – . AE E VISA. rest JY e
M *(closed Sunday)* a la carte 26/50 – **130 rm** 118/198 Bb.

Metropol, Bayerstr. 43, (Entrance Goethestr.) (M 2), 53 07 64, Telex 522816 – rest . AE E JY k
M a la carte 21/53 – **272 rm** 67/153.

Europe M, Erzgießereistr. 15 (M 1), 18 60 55, Telex 5214977 – wc . AE E VISA EU a
M a la carte 30/62 – **106 rm** 170/210.

Germania, Schwanthaler Str. 28 (M 2), 5 16 80, Telex 523790 – wc wc . AE E VISA JY a
M a la carte 21/50 (mainly grills) – **100 rm** 148/218 Bb.

Bundesbahnhotel, Bahnhofplatz 2 (M 2), 55 85 71, Telex 523174 – wc wc . AE E VISA JY u
M a la carte 22/47 – **217 rm** 80/170 Bb.

Reinbold without rest, Adolf-Kolping-Str. 11 (M 2), 59 79 45, Telex 522539 – wc . AE E VISA JY t
56 rm 77/184.

Deutscher Kaiser, Arnulfstr. 2 (M 2), 55 83 21, Telex 522650, rest. on the 15th floor with < Munich – wc wc . AE E VISA. rest JY s
M a la carte 32/60 – **156 rm** 112/195 Bb.

Apollo without rest, Mittererstr. 7 (M 2), 53 95 31, Telex 5212981 – wc . AE E VISA JY w
closed 23 December - 7 January – **74 rm** 160/205 Bb.

Central-Hotel without rest, Schwanthalerstr. 111 (M 2), 50 60 81, Telex 5216031 – wc . AE E VISA EV s
60 rm 140/195 Bb.

Admiral without rest, Kohlstr. 9 (M 5), 22 66 41, Telex 529111 – wc . AE E VISA LZ b
closed 22 December - 5 January – **30 rm** 125/220 Bb.

Bristol without rest, Pettenkoferstr. 2 (M 2), 59 51 51, Telex 524767 – wc . AE E KZ f
closed 22 December - 6 January – **57 rm** 110/240.

Splendid without rest, Maximilianstr. 54 (M 22), 29 66 06, Telex 522427 – wc . AE – **40 rm** 92/289 Bb. HV d

Adria without rest, Liebigstr. 8a (M 22), 29 30 81 – wc wc . AE E VISA HV a
closed 23 December - 7 January – **54 rm** 60/180.

Am Gasteig .... HX 4
Baldeplatz .... GX 14
Baumgartnerstraße ... EX 17
Biedersteiner Straße .... HU 25
Bonner Straße .... GU 26
Denninger Straße .... HU 34
Elsässer Straße .... HX 42
Emil-Riedel-Straße .... HV 45
Flurstraße .... HX 49
Friedrichstraße .... GU 52
Galileiplatz .... HV 53
Gebsattelstraße ...... HX 55
Georgenstraße .... GU 59
Giselastraße .... GU 60
Gohrenstraße .... HU 61
Grasserstraße .... EV 63
Hackerbrücke .... EV 65
Herkomerplatz .... HU 71
Hiltenspergerstraße ... GU 74
Hompeschstraße ..... HV 76
Humboldtstraße ...... GX 77
Innere Wiener Straße .... HX 79
Johann-Fichte-Straße .... HU 82
Josephsplatz .... FU 83
Kaiserstraße .... GU 86
Kißkaltplatz .... GU 94
Kölner Platz .... GU 95
Kunigundenstraße .... HU 97
Kurfürstenplatz .... GU 99
Lerchenfeldstraße .... HV 102
Maillingerstraße ..... EV 109
Maria-Theresia-Straße .... HV 111
Marschallstraße ...... HU 112
Martin-Greif-Straße .... EV 115
Martiusstraße .... GU 116
Maßmannstraße ...... FU 118
Maximiliansbrücke .... HV 119
Max-Josephs-Brücke .... HV 124
Max-Planck-Straße .... HV 129
Messeplatz .... EV 133
Metzgerstraße .... HX 134
Möhlstraße .... HV 137
Mozartstraße .... EX 138
Münchener-Freiheit .... HU 140
Oettingenstraße ...... HV 151
Pappenheimstraße .... EV 163
Potsdamer Straße .... HU 167
Prinzregentenbrücke .. HV 169
Prinzregentenstraße ... HV 170
Radlkoferstraße ...... EX 174
Regerplatz .... HX 175
Rosenheimer Platz .... HX 181
Sandstraße .... FU 186
Schießstättstraße ..... EV 189
Stengelstraße .... HU 201
Sternstraße .... HV 202
Sternwartstraße ...... HV 204
Theresienhöhe .... EX 207
Thiemestraße .... HU 208
Tivolistraße .... HU 211
Triftstraße .... HV 214
Trogerstraße .... HV 215
Tumblingerstraße ..... FX 218
Veterinärstraße .... GU 221
Viktoriastraße .... GU 223
Wagmüllerstraße ..... HV 224
Wittelsbacherstraße .. GX 231
Wredestraße .... EV 232
Zirkus-Krone-Straße .... EV 236

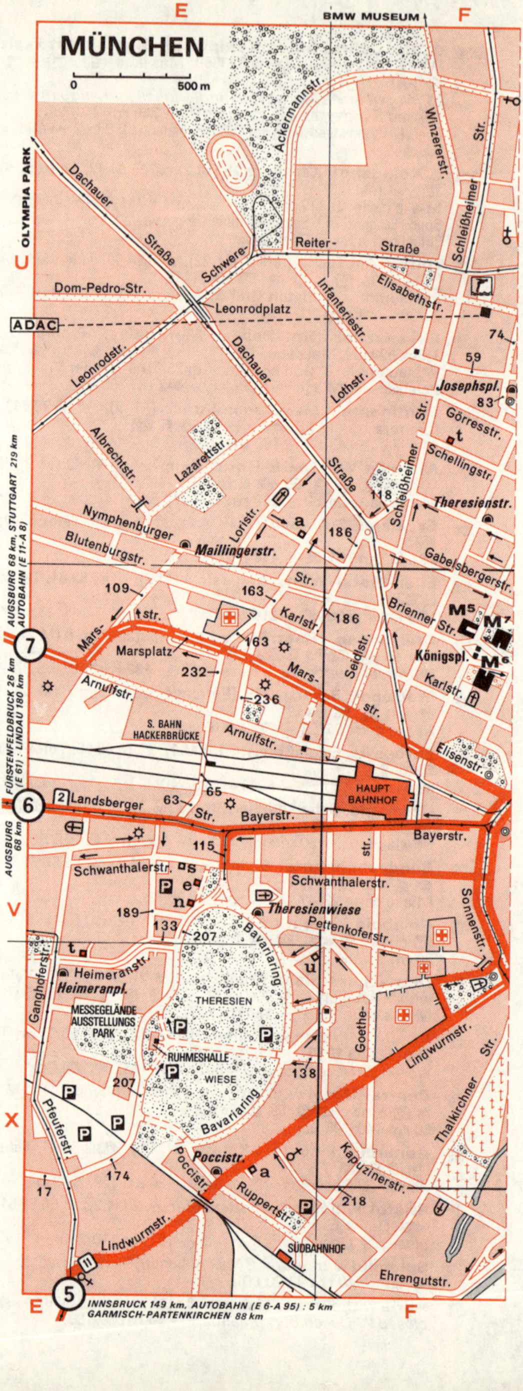

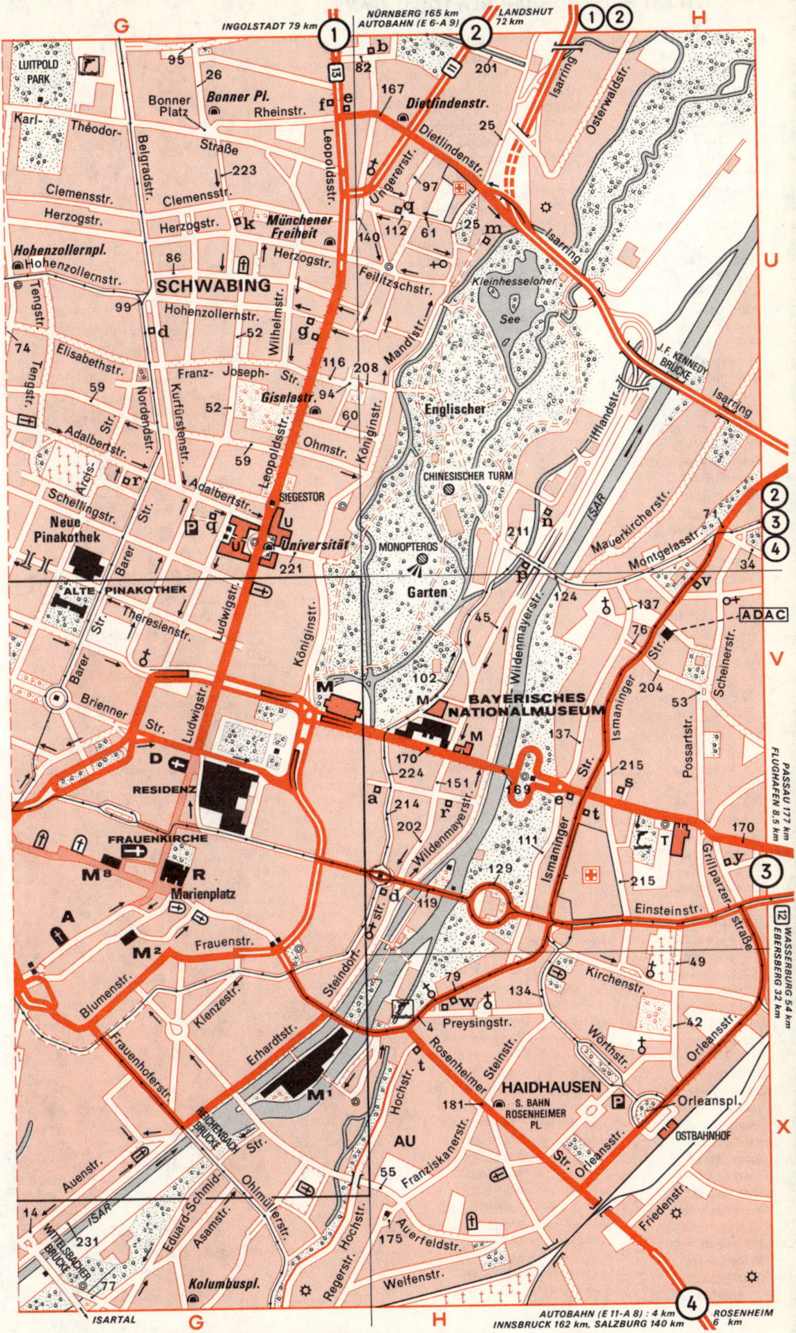
INGOLSTADT 79 km
NÜRNBERG 165 km
AUTOBAHN (E 6-A 9)
LANDSHUT 72 km
G
H
U
V
X
LUITPOLD PARK
Bonner Pl.
Bonner Platz
Rheinstr.
Dietlindenstr.
Karl-Theodor-Straße
Belgradstr.
Leopoldstr.
Ungererstr.
Isarring
Osterwaldstr.
Clemensstr.
Herzogstr.
Münchener Freiheit
Hohenzollernpl.
Hohenzollernstr.
SCHWABING
Feilitzschstr.
Kleinhesseloher See
Tengstr.
Wilhelmstr.
Elisabethstr.
Franz-Joseph-Str.
Giselastr.
Mandlstr.
J.F. KENNEDY BRÜCKE
Nordendstr.
Kurfürstenstr.
Ohmstr.
Königinstr.
Englischer Garten
Ifflandstr.
Adalbertstr.
Arcisstr.
CHINESISCHER TURM
Schellingstr.
SIEGESTOR
Neue Pinakothek
Universität
MONOPTEROS
ISAR
Mauerkircherstr.
Montgelasstr.
Barer Str.
ALTE PINAKOTHEK
Theresienstr.
Ludwigstr.
Wildenmayerstr.
ADAC
Scheinerstr.
Brienner Str.
BAYERISCHES NATIONALMUSEUM
Ismaninger Str.
Possartstr.
RESIDENZ
FRAUENKIRCHE
Marienplatz
Widenmayerstr.
Grillparzerstraße
Einsteinstr.
PASSAU 177 km
FLUGHAFEN 8,5 km
WASSERBURG 54 km
EBERSBERG 32 km
Frauenstr.
Steindorfstr.
Kirchenstr.
Blumenstr.
Klenzestr.
Preysingstr.
Wörthstr.
Orleansstr.
Erhardtstr.
Rosenheimer Str.
Steinstr.
HAIDHAUSEN
S. BAHN ROSENHEIMER PL.
Orleanspl.
OSTBAHNHOF
Frauenhoferstr.
REICHENBACH BRÜCKE
Hochstr.
AU
Auenstr.
Ohlmüllerstr.
Franziskanerstr.
Orleansstr.
Friedenstr.
WITTELSBACHER BRÜCKE
Eduard-Schmid-Str.
Asamstr.
Regerstr.
Auerfeldstr.
Welfenstr.
Kolumbuspl.
ISARTAL
AUTOBAHN (E 11-A 8) : 4 km
INNSBRUCK 162 km, SALZBURG 140 km
ROSENHEIM 6 km

STREET INDEX TO MÜNCHEN TOWN PLANS

Continued after town plan

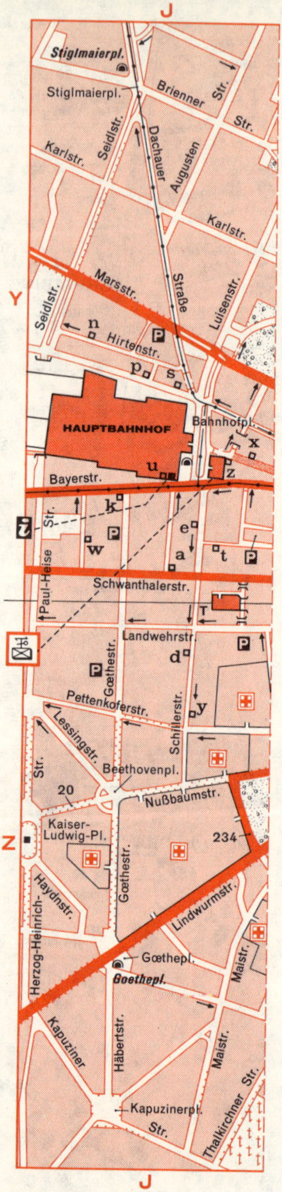

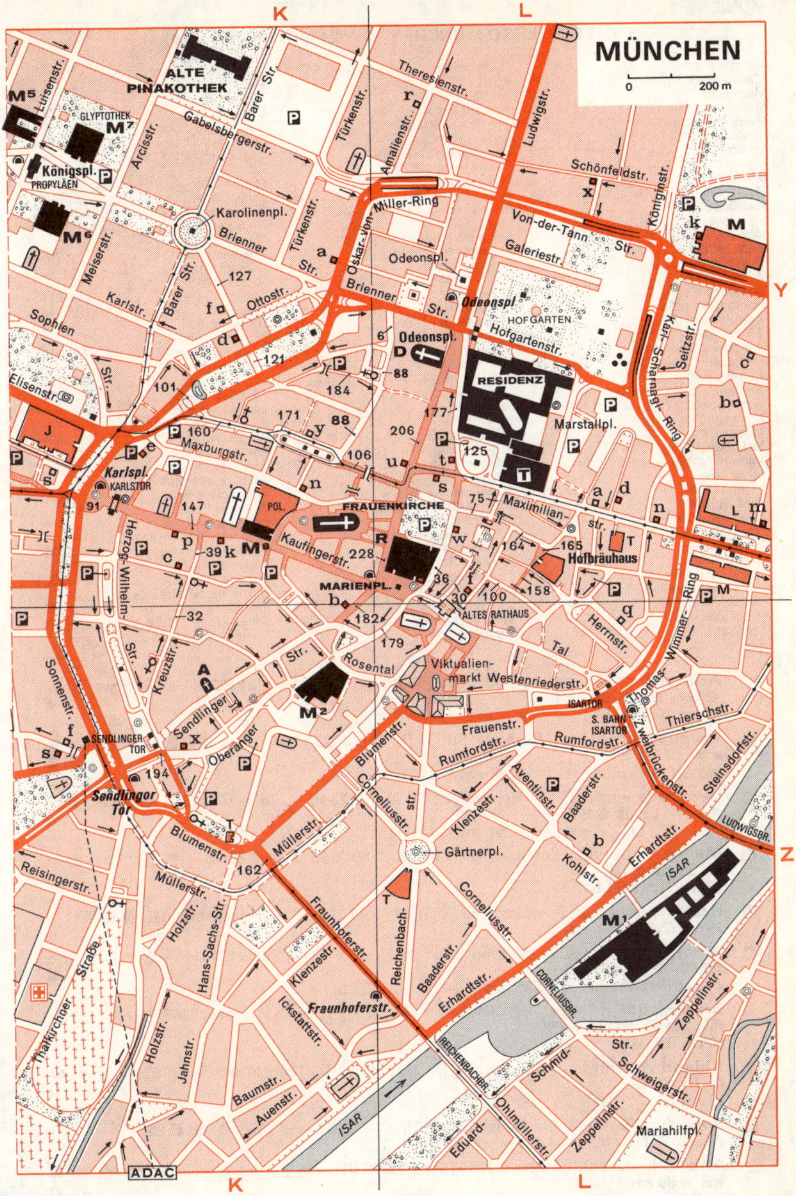

Theatinerstraße .... LY 206	Kardinal-Faulhaber-Straße . KY 88	Papa-Schmid-Straße .... KZ 162
Weinstraße .... KY 228	Ledererstraße .... LY 100	Pfisterstraße .... LY 164
	Lenbachplatz .... KY 101	Platzl .... LY 165
Amiraplatz .... LY 6	Maffeistraße .... KY 106	Promenadeplatz .... KY 171
Beethovenstraße .... JZ 20	Maximiliansplatz .... KY 121	Rindermarkt .... LZ 179
Burgstraße .... LY 30	Max-Joseph-Platz .... LY 125	Rosenstraße .... KZ 182
Damenstiftstraße .... KZ 32	Max-Joseph-Straße .... KY 127	Salvatorstraße .... KY 184
Eisenmannstraße .... KY 39	Orlandostraße .... LY 158	Sendlinger-Tor-Platz .... KZ 194
Hofgraben .... LY 75	Pacellistraße .... KY 160	Ziemssenstraße .... JZ 234

STREET INDEX TO MÜNCHEN TOWN PLANS (Concluded)

Street	Plan	No.
Marstallplatz	LY	
Martin-Greif-Straße	EV	115
Martiusstraße	GU	116
Maßmannstraße	FU	118
Mauekircherstraße	HU	
Maxburgstraße	KY	
Maximiliansbrücke	HV	119
Maximiliansplatz	KY	121
Maximilianstraße	LY	
Max-Josephs-Brücke	HV	124
Max-Joseph-Platz	LY	125
Max-Joseph-Straße	KY	127
Max-Planck-Straße	HV	129
Meiserstraße	KY	
Messeplatz	EV	133
Metzgerstraße	HX	134
Möhlstraße	HV	137
Montgelasstraße	HU	
Mozartstraße	EX	138
Müllerstraße	KZ	
Münchener Freiheit	HU	140
Neuhauser Straße	KY	147
Nordendstraße	GU	
Nußbaumstraße	JZ	
Nymphenburger Straße	EUV	
Oberanger	KZ	
Odeonsplatz	LY	
Oettingenstraße	HV	151
Ohlmüllerstraße	LZ	
Ohmstraße	GU	
Orlandostraße	LY	158
Orleansstraße	HX	
Oskar-von-Miller-Ring	KLY	
Osterwaldstraße	HU	
Ottostraße	KY	
Pacellistraße	KY	160
Papa-Schmid-Straße	KZ	162
Pappenheimstraße	EV	163
Paul-Heyse-Straße	JZ	
Pettenkoferstraße	JZ	
Pfeuferstraße	EX	
Pfisterstraße	LY	164
Platzl	LY	165
Poccistraße	EX	
Possartstraße	HV	
Potsdamer Straße	HU	167
Preysingstraße	HX	
Prinzregentenbrücke	HV	169
Prinzregentenstraße	HV	170
Promenadeplatz	KY	171
Radlkoferstraße	EX	174
Regerplatz	HX	175
Regerstraße	GX	
Reichenbachbrücke	LZ	
Reichenbachstraße	LZ	
Reisingerstraße	KZ	
Residenzstraße	LY	177
Rheinstraße	GU	
Rindermarkt	LZ	179
Rosenheimer Platz	HX	181
Rosenheimer Straße	HX	
Rosenstraße	KZ	182
Rosental	KZ	
Rumfordstraße	LZ	
Ruppertstraße	EX	
Salvatorstraße	KY	184
Sandstraße	FU	186
Scheinerstraße	HV	
Schellingstraße	FU	
Schießstättstraße	EV	189
Schillerstraße	JZ	
Schleißheimer Straße	FU	
Schönfeldstraße	LY	
Schützenstraße	KY	
Schwanthalerstraße	JY	
Schweigerstraße	LZ	
Schwere-Reiter-Straße	EFU	
Seidlstraße	JY	
Seitzstraße	LY	
Sendlinger Straße	KZ	
Sendlinger-Tor-Platz	KZ	194
Sonnenstraße	KZ	
Sophienstraße	KY	
Steinsdorfstraße	LZ	
Steinstraße	HX	
Stengelstraße	HU	201
Sternstraße	HV	202
Sternwartstraße	HV	204
Stiglmaierplatz	JY	
Tal	LZ	
Tengstraße	GU	
Thalkirchner Straße	JZ	
Theatinerstraße	LY	206
Theresienhöhe	EX	207
Theresienstraße	LY	
Thiemestraße	HU	208
Thierschstraße	LZ	
Thomas-Wimmer-Ring	LZ	
Tivolistraße	HU	211
Trifstraße	HV	214
Trogerstraße	HV	215
Türkenstraße	KY	
Tumblingerstraße	FX	218
Ungererstraße	HU	
Veterinärstraße	GU	221
Viktoriastraße	GU	223
Viktualienmarkt	LZ	
Von-der-Tann-Straße	LY	
Wagmüllerstraße	HV	224
Waltherstraße	JZ	
Weinstraße	KY	228
Westenriederstraße	LZ	
Widenmayerstraße	HV	
Wilhelmstraße	GU	
Winzererstraße	FU	
Wittelsbacherbrücke	GX	
Wittelsbacherstraße	GX	231
Wörthstraße	HX	
Wredestraße	EV	232
Zeppelinstraße	LZ	
Ziemssenstraße	JZ	234
Zirkus-Krone-Straße	EV	236
Zweibrückenstraße	LZ	

Ariston without rest, Unsöldstr. 10 (M 22), 22 26 91, Telex 522437 – wc wc . AE E — LY **c**
63 rm 105/160 Bb.

Domus without rest, St.-Anna-Str. 31 (M 22), 22 17 04, Telex 529835 – wc . AE E — LY **b**
closed 22 to 26 December – **45 rm** 120/220 Bb.

Concorde without rest, Herrnstr. 38 (M 22), 22 45 15, Telex 522002 – wc wc . AE E VISA — LZ **q**
closed 23 to 27 December – **51 rm** 110/190 Bb.

Meier without rest, Schützenstr. 12 (M 2), 59 56 23, Telex 529126 – TV wc wc . AE E VISA — JY **x**
59 rm 118/189 Bb.

Kraft without rest, Schillerstr. 49 (M 2), 59 48 23 – wc wc . AE E VISA — JZ **y**
39 rm 65/170.

Brack without rest, Lindwurmstr. 153 (M 2), 77 10 52, Telex 524416 – wc wc . AE E VISA — EX **a**
closed 16 December - 3 January – **54 rm** 85/150 Bb.

Brunnenhof without rest, Schillerstr. 36 (M 2), 55 49 21, Telex 524917 – wc wc . AE E VISA — JZ **d**
60 rm 85/190.

Uhland without rest, Uhlandstr. 1 (M 2), 53 92 77, Telex 528368 – wc wc . AE E — EX **u**
25 rm 75/150 Bb.

Bosch without rest, Amalienstr. 25 (M 2), 28 10 61 – wc . AE E VISA — LY **r**
closed 22 December - 4 January – **75 rm** 75/170.

Alfa without rest, Hirtenstr. 22 (M 2), 59 84 61 – TV wc wc . AE E VISA – **80 rm** 60/190 — JY **n**

XXXX **Aubergine**, Maximiliansplatz 5 (M 2), 59 81 71 – E — KY **d**
closed Sunday, Monday, Bank Holidays and 4 to 24 August – **M** a la carte 64/145 (booking essential)
Spec. Hummer in Rotweinbuttersauce, Kalbsbriesschnitten auf Artischockensalat, Quarkgratin mit Orangen.

XXX **Le Gourmet**, Ligsalzstr. 46 (M 2), 50 35 97, « Small rest, elegant installation » – E — EX **t**
closed Sunday and 19 May - 8 June – **M** (dinner only) a la carte 60/100 (booking essential)
Spec. Falsche Prinzregententorte, Seestern auf Basilikumcreme, Krautwickel vom Lammrücken.

XXX **La Piazzetta**, Oskar-v.-Miller-Ring 3 (M 2), ✆ 28 29 90, beer-garden, « Modern Italian rest, Florentine style » – AE ◑ E VISA KY a
closed Saturday lunch – **M** a la carte 33/63 – **Rosticceria M** a la carte 18/47.

XXX ✿ **Sabitzer**, Reitmorstr. 21 (M 22), ✆ 29 85 84 – ◑ E HV r
closed Saturday lunch, Sunday, Saturday during July and August and Bank Holidays lunch – **M** a la carte 55/97 (booking essential)
Spec. Gänsestopfleber mit Johannisbeeren, Steinbutt in Kerbelschaum, Lamm- und Wildgerichte.

XX ✿ **Boettner** (Small old Munich rest.), Theatinerstr. 8 (M 2), ✆ 22 12 10 – ▤. AE ◑ E VISA
closed Saturday dinner, Sunday and Bank Holidays – **M** a la carte 57/112 (booking essential) LY u
Spec. Hechtsouffle mit Sauce Nantua, Hummereintopf "Hartung", Rote Grütze.

XX **La Belle Epoque**, Maximilianstr. 29 (M 22), ✆ 29 33 11, 🏶 LY n
closed Saturday until 6 p.m, Sunday and 4 to 25 August – **M** a la carte 33/73 (booking essential).

XX **Weinhaus Schwarzwälder** (old Munich wine-restaurant), Hartmannstr. 8 (M 2), ✆ 22 72 16 – AE ◑ E VISA KY n
M a la carte 35/74.

XX **Chesa Rüegg**, Wurzerstr. 18 (M 22), ✆ 29 71 14, « Country house furniture » – ▤. AE ◑ E VISA LY d
closed Saturday, Sunday and Bank Holidays – **M** a la carte 30/65 (booking essential).

XX **Weinhaus Neuner** (Typical 1852 wine-rest.), Herzogspitalstr. 8 (M 2), ✆ 2 60 39 54 – AE ◑ E KY c
closed Sunday and Bank Holidays – **M** a la carte 31/65.

XX **El Toula**, Sparkassenstr. 5 (M 2), ✆ 29 28 69 – AE ◑ E VISA LY f
closed Monday and end July - end August – **M** a la carte 47/91 (booking essential for dinner).

XX **Zum Bürgerhaus**, Pettenkoferstr. 1 (M 2), ✆ 59 79 09, 🏶, « Bavarian farm-house furniture » – ◑ E KZ s
closed Saturday until 6 p.m, Sunday and Bank Holidays – **M** a la carte 28/70 (booking essential).

XX **Dallmayr**, Dienerstr. 14 (1st floor) (M 2), ✆ 2 13 51 00 – AE ◑ LY w
closed Saturday dinner, Sunday and for dinner in August – **M** a la carte 27/70.

XX **Halali**, Schönfeldstr. 22 (M 22), ✆ 28 59 09 LY x
closed 2 weeks from Whitsuntide, Saturday until 6 p.m, Sunday and Bank Holidays – **M** a la carte 32/56 (booking essential).

XX **Tivoli** (Italian rest.), Widenmayerstr. 52 (M 22), ✆ 22 12 74, 🏶 – AE ◑ E VISA. ✂
closed Saturday – **M** a la carte 32/66 (booking essential). HU p

XX **Mövenpick im Künstlerhaus**, Lenbachplatz 8 (M 2), ✆ 55 78 65, 🏶 – AE ◑ E VISA
M a la carte 20/58. KY e

XX **Csarda Piroschka** (Hungarian rest. with gipsy-music), Prinzregentenstr. 1 (M 22), ✆ 29 54 25 – Ⓟ. AE ◑ E LY k
closed until 6.30 p.m and Sunday – **M** a la carte 30/65 (booking essential).

X **Goldene Stadt** (Bohemian cooking), Oberanger 44 (M 2), ✆ 26 43 82 – AE ◑ E
closed Sunday – **M** a la carte 20/53 (booking essential for dinner). KZ x

X **Zum Klösterl**, St.-Anna-Str. 2 (M 22), ✆ 22 50 86 LY m
closed Saturday and Bank Holidays – **M** (dinner only) a la carte 20/55 (booking essential).

X **Ratskeller**, Marienplatz 8 (M 2), ✆ 22 03 13 – AE ◑ E LY R
M a la carte 18/42.

Brewery - inns :

XX **Spatenhaus-Bräustuben**, Residenzstr. 12 (M 2), ✆ 22 78 41, 🏶, « Furnished in traditional alpine style » – AE E VISA LY t
M a la carte 29/65.

X **Franziskaner - Fuchs'n Stub'n**, Perusastr. 5 (M 2), ✆ 22 50 02, 🏶 – AE ◑ LY s
M a la carte 23/61.

X **Augustiner - Gaststätten**, Neuhauser Str. 16 (M 2), ✆ 2 60 41 06, « Beer-garden » – ◑ KY p
M a la carte 17/48.

X **Zum Spöckmeier**, Rosenstr. 9 (M 2), ✆ 26 80 88 – AE ◑ KY b
closed Sunday June - August – **M** a la carte 20/52 ♫.

X **Zum Pschorrbräu**, Neuhauser Str. 11 (M 2), ✆ 2 60 30 01, 🏶 – AE ◑ E VISA KY k
M a la carte 19/43.

X **Pschorr-Keller**, Theresienhöhe 7 (M 2), ✆ 50 10 88, beer-garden – 🏔. ◑ E EV n
M a la carte 18/43.

X **Hackerkeller und Schäfflerstuben**, Theresienhöhe 4 (M 2), ✆ 50 70 04, beer-garden – AE ◑ E VISA EV e
M a la carte 16/44.

at Munich-Bogenhausen :

Sheraton, Arabellastr. 6 (M 81), ☎ 92 40 11, Telex 522391, < Munich, beer-garden, Massage, ≘s, ⊠, ⚘ – ⛫ ▤ 📺 ♿ ⇔ 🅿 ⛶. ✂ by Isarring HU
Restaurants : – **Atrium** – **Alt Bayern Stube** *(dinner only)* – **Sandwich Bar** – **650 rm.**

Prinzregent Ⓜ without rest, Ismaninger Str. 42 (M 80), ☎ 4 70 20 81, Telex 524403, « Elegant, rustic installation », ≘s – ⛫ 📺 ⇔. AE ⓓ E VISA HV t
closed Christmas - 6 January – **66 rm** 166/260 Bb.

Crest-Hotel, Effnerstr. 99 (M 81), ☎ 98 25 41, Telex 524757 – ⛫ ▤ 📺 🅿 ⛶. AE ⓓ E VISA. ✂ rest by Isarring HU
M a la carte 26/54 – **155 rm** 177/239 Bb.

Arabella-Hotel, Arabellastr. 5 (M 81), ☎ 9 23 21, Telex 529987, < Munich, Massage, ≘s, ⊠ – ⛫ ▤ rest 📺 ♿ ⇔ ⛶ (with ▤). AE ⓓ E VISA by Isarring HU
M a la carte 27/57 – **285 rm** 145/250 Bb – 90 apartments 250/350.

XXX ✿ **Käfer-Schänke**, Schumannstr. 1 (M 80), ☎ 4 16 81, Telex 523073, ⚘, « Several rooms with rustic and elegant installations » – AE ⓓ E. ✂ HV s
closed Sunday and Bank Holidays – **M** a la carte 40/90 (booking essential)
Spec. Vorspeisen vom Schaubuffet, Mit weißen Trüffeln gefüllte Ravioli(November-March), Ragout von Krebsen, Entenbrust und -leber in Nelkenpfeffersauce.

XXX **Da Pippo** (Italian rest.), Mühlbaurstr. 36 (M 80), ☎ 4 70 48 48, ⚘ – ⓓ E. ✂
closed 1 to 21 August, Sunday and Bank Holidays – **M** a la carte 38/65.
by Prinzregentenstr. HV

XX Tai Tung (Chinese rest.), Prinzregentenstr. 60 (Villa Stuck) (M 80), ☎ 47 11 00 HV e

XX **Mifune** (Japanese rest.), Ismaninger Str. 136 (M 80), ☎ 98 75 72 – AE ⓓ E. ✂ HV v
closed 2nd Sunday of month, all other Sundays for lunch and 1 week June – **M** a la carte 23/60.

X **Zum Klösterl**, Schneckenburger Str. 31 (M 80), ☎ 47 61 98 HV y
closed Saturday – **M** a la carte 20/55.

at Munich 80-Haidhausen :

Preysing (see also **Preysing-Keller** rest. below), Preysingstr. 1, ☎ 48 10 11, Telex 529044, « Rustic, elegant installation », ≘s, ⊠ – ⛫ ▤ 📺 ⇔ ⛶ HX w
– **Preysing-Pub** *(dinner only)* – **73 rm.**

München Penta Hotel, Hochstr. 3, ☎ 4 48 55 55, Telex 529046, Massage, ≘s, ⊠ – ⛫ ▤ 📺 🅿 ⛶. AE ⓓ E VISA HX t
M a la carte 34/68 – **583 rm** 183/266 Bb.

XXX ✿ Preysing-Keller, Innere-Wiener-Str. 6, ☎ 48 10 15, « Vaulted cellar, country-house furniture » – ▤ HX w
dinner only – (remarkable wine-list)
Spec. Suppe von Donau-Waller mit Gurken, Kalbsniere mit Pilzduxelles gefüllt, Pot-au-feu vom Lamm.

at Munich 83-Neu Perlach by ④ :

Orbis Hotel München Ⓜ, Karl-Marx-Ring 87, ☎ 6 32 70, Telex 5213357, ≘s, ⊠ – ⛫ ▤ rest 📺 ⇔ 🅿 ⛶ (with ▤). AE ⓓ E VISA
M a la carte 24/58 – **185 rm** 130/190 Bb.

Novotel, Rudolf-Vogel-Bogen 3, ☎ 63 80 00, Telex 522030, ⚘, ≘s, ⊠ – ⛫ 📺 ♿ 🅿 ⛶. AE ⓓ E VISA
M a la carte 24/54 – **254 rm** 140/185 Bb.

at Munich 40-Oberwiesenfeld by Schleissheimer Str. FU :

Olympiapark-Hotel, Helene-Mayer-Ring 12, ☎ 3 51 60 71, Telex 5215231, free entrance to the ⊠ in the recreation centre – ⛫ 📺 🅿 ⛶. AE ⓓ E VISA. ✂ rest
closed 24 December - 2 January – **M** a la carte 19/42 – **100 rm** 125/195 Bb.

at Munich 40-Schwabing :

Holiday Inn, Leopoldstr. 194, ☎ 34 09 71, Telex 5215439, Massage, ≘s, ⊠ – ⛫ ▤ 📺 ⇔ ⛶. AE ⓓ E VISA by ①
Restaurants : – **Almstuben-Grill** *(dinner only)* **M** a la carte 32/63 – **Oma's Küche M** a la carte 22/44 – **360 rm** 190/310 Bb.

Residence, Arthur-Kutscher-Platz 4, ☎ 38 17 80, Telex 529788, ⚘, ⊠ – ⛫ ⇔ ⛶. AE ⓓ E VISA. ✂ rest HU q
M a la carte 30/60 – **150 rm** 178/248.

Weinfurtners Garden-Hotel without rest, Leopoldstr. 132, ☎ 36 80 04, Telex 5214315 – ⛫ 📺 ⛀wc ⛆wc ☎ ⇔ 🅿 ⛶ – **180 rm** 122/174 Bb. GU e

International - Hotel Auer without rest, Hohenzollernstr. 5, ☎ 33 30 43, Telex 529148 – ⛫ 📺 ⛀wc ☎ ⇔ – **70 rm.** GU g

Biederstein ⛰ without rest, Keferstr. 18, ☎ 39 50 72, ⚘ – ⛫ ⛀wc ☎ ⇔. AE
31 rm 85/140. HU m

Consul without rest, Viktoriastr. 10, ☎ 33 40 35 – ⛫ 📺 ⛀wc ☎ ⇔ 🅿 GU k
27 rm 70/150 Bb.

Leopold, Leopoldstr. 119, ☎ 36 70 61, Telex 5215160 – ⛫ 📺 ⛀wc ⛆wc ☎ ♿ ⇔ 🅿. AE ⓓ E VISA – **M** *(closed Saturday)* a la carte 25/49 – **85 rm** 95/160 Bb. GU f

XXXX ✿✿✿ **Tantris**, Johann-Fichte-Str. 7, ☎ 36 20 61, « Modern rest., fashionable decoration » – ▤ Ⓟ. AE ⓓ E. ✈ HU **b**
closed lunch Saturday and Monday, Sunday, Bank Holidays and Whitsuntide - early June – **M** a la carte 69/131 (booking essential)
Spec. Hummer in Basilikum, Taubenbrust auf Lauch und Pfifferlingen, Quark-Soufflé mit Walderdbeeren und Birnensauce.

XXX ✿ **La Mer**, Schraudolphstr. 24, ☎ 2 72 24 39, « Opulent decor » – AE ⓓ E. ✈ GU **r**
closed Monday and end July - end August – **M** (dinner only) a la carte 53/95 (booking essential)
Spec. Marinierte Gänseleber mit Trüffel, Eintopf von Hummer und Jakobsmuscheln, Gratin von Früchten.

XXX ✿ **Savarin**, Schellingstr. 122, ☎ 52 53 11 – ⓓ E FU **t**
closed Saturday lunch, Sunday, Monday and 3 weeks August – **M** a la carte 47/78 (booking essential)
Spec. Hechtklößchen in Dillrahm, Zicklein mit Rosmarinsauce, Dessert Savarin Surprise.

XX **Walliser Stuben**, Leopoldstr. 33, ☎ 34 80 00, beer-garden – AE ⓓ E VISA GU **g**
closed Sunday and Bank Holidays – **M** (dinner only) a la carte 30/60.

XX **Daitokai** (Japanese rest), Nordendstr. 64 (entrance Kurfürstenstr.), ☎ 2 71 14 21 – ▤. AE ⓓ E VISA. ✈ GU **d**
closed Sunday – **M** a la carte 33/68.

XX **Bistro Terrine** (French rest), Amalienstr. 89 (Amalien-Passage), ☎ 28 17 80 – AE E. ✈
closed lunch Monday and Saturday, Sunday, Bank Holidays and 17 May - 2 June – **M** a la carte 34/65 (booking essential). GU **q**

X **Ristorante Bei Grazia**, Ungererstr. 161, ☎ 36 69 31 by ②
closed Friday dinner and Saturday – **M** a la carte 24/46 (booking essential).

at Munich 50-Untermenzing by ⑦ :

Insel-Mühle, von-Kahr-Str. 87, ☎ 8 10 10, Telex 5218292, « Würm-side setting, terrace » – TV ⇔wc ⋒wc ☎ ⇔ Ⓟ. ⓓ E
M *(closed Sunday and Bank Holidays)* a la carte 33/64 – **37 rm** 120/240.

at Neuried **8027** by ⑤ :

XX **Neurieder Hof**, Münchner Str. 2, ☎ (089) 7 55 82 72, beer-garden – Ⓟ. AE ⓓ E VISA
closed Monday lunch and Tuesday – **M** a la carte 27/60 (booking essential for dinner).

at Aschheim **8011** ③ : 13 km by Riem :

Zur Post, Ismaninger Str. 11 (B 471), ☎ (089) 9 03 20 27, – ⫼ ⇔wc ⋒wc ☎ ⇔ Ⓟ
M a la carte 14/42 – **50 rm** 43/130 Bb.

STUTTGART 7000. Baden-Württemberg 987 ㉟ – pop. 555 000 – alt. 245 m – ☎ 0711.

See : Site (Lage)★★ – Killesberg Park (Höhenpark Killesberg)★★ BU – Television Tower (Fernsehturm)★★ (✳★★) DZ – Birkenkopf ✳★★ AY – Congress- and Concert Hall (Liederhalle)★ BX – Old Castle (Altes Schloß) (Renaissance courtyard★) CX – Stuttgart State Gallery (Staatsgalerie)★ CX **M1** – Collegiate Church (Stiftskirche) (Commemorative monuments of dukes★) CX **A** – Württemberg Regional Museum (Württembergisches Landesmuseum) (Medieval art objects★★) CX **M2** – Daimler-Benz Museum★ EX **M** – Porsche-Museum★ by ⑧.

Envir. : Bad Cannstatt Spa Park (Kurpark)★ E : 4 km EU.

✈ Stuttgart-Echterdingen, by ③ ☎ 7 90 11, City Air Terminal, Stuttgart, Lautenschlagerstr. 14, ☎ 22 12 64..

Exhibition Centre (Messegelände Killesberg) (BU), ☎ 2 58 91, Telex 722584.

ℹ Tourist-Information, Klett-Passage (subway to the Main Station), ☎ 2 22 82 40, Telex 723854.

ADAC, Am Neckartor 2, ☎ 2 80 00.

Frankfurt am Main 205 ⑧ – Karlsruhe 82 ⑥ – München 219 ④ – Strasbourg 154 ⑥.

Plans on following pages

✿ **Steigenberger-Hotel Graf Zeppelin** ⛐, Arnulf-Klett-Platz 7, ☎ 29 98 81, Telex 722418, Massage, ⛆, ▢ – ⫼ ▤ TV ♿ 🏛. AE ⓓ E VISA CX **s**
M *(closed Saturday, Sunday, Bank Holidays and 12 July - 3 August)* a la carte 43/85 (booking essential) – **280 rm** 199/380 Bb
Spec. Zanderfilet in Burgunderbutter, Kalbsbries in weißem Portwein mit Leipziger Allerlei, Kaninchenrücken in Trollinger mit Lauchspätzle.

Am Schloßgarten, Schillerstr. 23, ☎ 29 99 11, Telex 722936, « Terrace with ≤ » – ⫼ TV ⇔ 🏛. AE ⓓ E VISA CX **u**
M a la carte 39/78 – **125 rm** 165/270 Bb.

Royal, Sophienstr. 35, ☎ 62 50 50, Telex 722449 – ⫼ ▤ rest TV ⇔ Ⓟ 🏛. AE ⓓ E VISA BY **b**
M a la carte 34/64 – **85 rm** 175/260.

Park-Hotel, Villastr. 21, ☎ 28 01 61, Telex 723405, – ⫼ ▤ rest TV Ⓟ 🏛 (with ▤). AE ⓓ E VISA DV **r**
M a la carte 35/61 – **Radiostüble** *(dinner only)* **M** a la carte 21/49 – **81 rm** 140/240 Bb.

STUTTGART

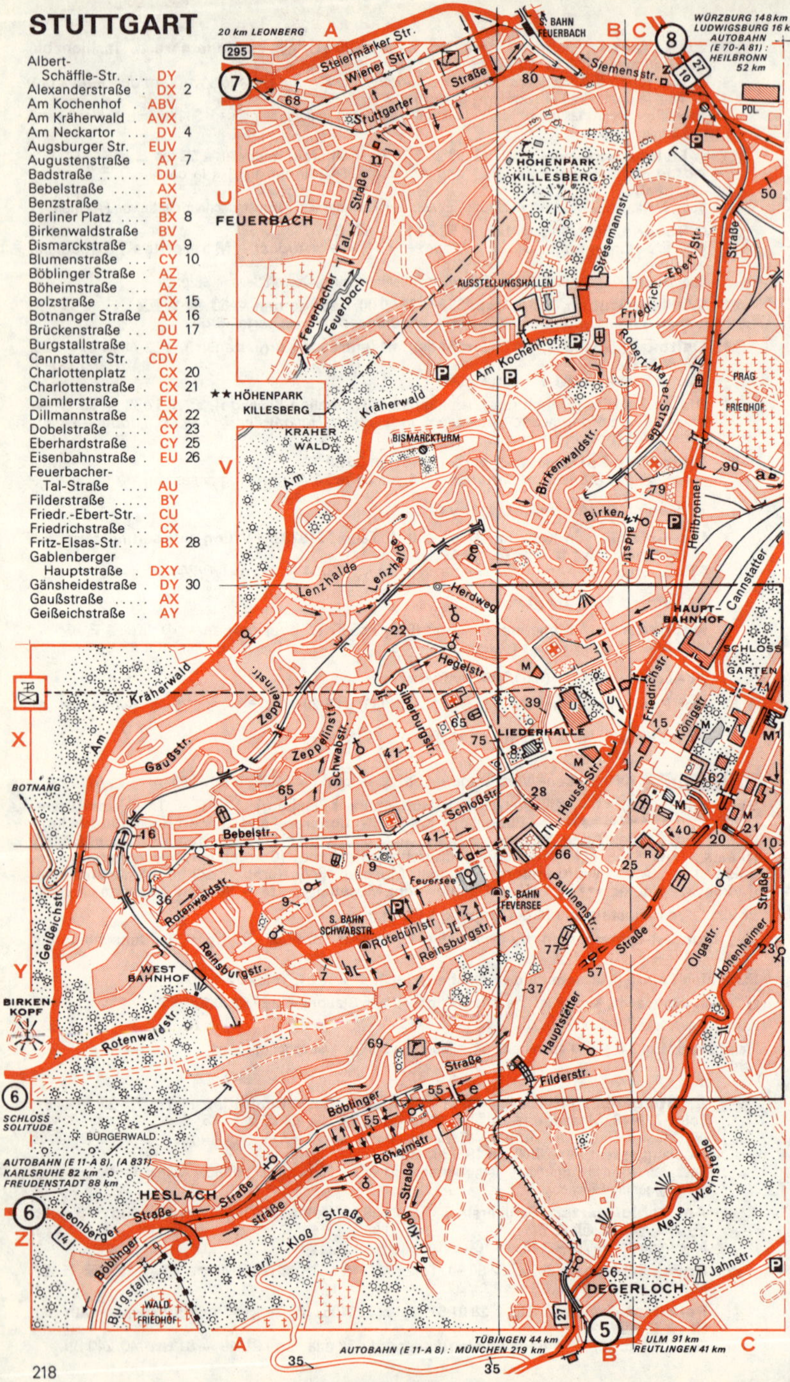

20 km LEONBERG
A
B
C
BAHN FEUERBACH
WÜRZBURG 148 km
LUDWIGSBURG 16 km
AUTOBAHN (E 70-A 81) : HEILBRONN 52 km
295
7
8
10
27
Steiermärker Str.
Wiener Str.
Stuttgarter Straße
Siemensstr.
68
80
POL
HÖHENPARK KILLESBERG
U
FEUERBACH
Tal-Straße
50
Feuerbacher Tal
Feuerbach
Stresemannstr.
Friedrich-Ebert-Str.
Straße
AUSSTELLUNGSHALLEN
Am Kochenhof
Robert-Mayer-Straße
PRAG FRIEDHOF
★★ HÖHENPARK KILLESBERG
KRAHER WALD
Kräherwald
BISMARCKTURM
V
Am
Birkenwaldstr.
Birkenwaldstr.
90
79
Heilbronner
Lenzhalde
Lenzhalde
Herdweg
Cannstatter
HAUPT-BAHNHOF
SCHLOSS GARTEN
22
Hegelstr.
Kräherwald
Zeppelinstr.
Silberburgstr.
39
Friedrichstr.
Königstr.
71
X
Am
Zeppelinstr.
Schwabstr.
41
65
75
LIEDERHALLE
15
M1
BOTNANG
Gaußstr.
65
Schloßstr.
28
Th. Heuss-Str.
62
16
Bebelstr.
41
66
40
20
21
10
9
Feuersee
25
S. BAHN FEUERSEE
Paulinenstr.
Rotenwaldstr.
36
9
S. BAHN SCHWABSTR.
Rotebühlstr.
Reinsburgstr.
7
77
57
Straße
Olgastr.
Hohenheimer Straße
23
Y
Geißeichstr.
WEST BAHNHOF
Reinsburgstr.
7
37
BIRKEN-KOPF
Rotenwaldstr.
69
Hauptstätter
Straße
Filderstr.
6
55
SCHLOSS SOLITUDE
BÜRGERWALD
Böblinger
55
AUTOBAHN (E 11-A 8), (A 831) : KARLSRUHE 82 km
FREUDENSTADT 88 km
Böheimstr.
Straße
HESLACH
Straße
Neue Weinsteige
6
Leonberger
Straße
Z
14
Karl-Kloß-Straße
Karl-Kloß
Böblinger
Burgstall
WALD FRIEDHOF
56
DEGERLOCH
Jahnstr.
27
5
A
TÜBINGEN 44 km
AUTOBAHN (E 11-A 8) : MÜNCHEN 219 km
B
ULM 91 km
REUTLINGEN 41 km
C
35
35

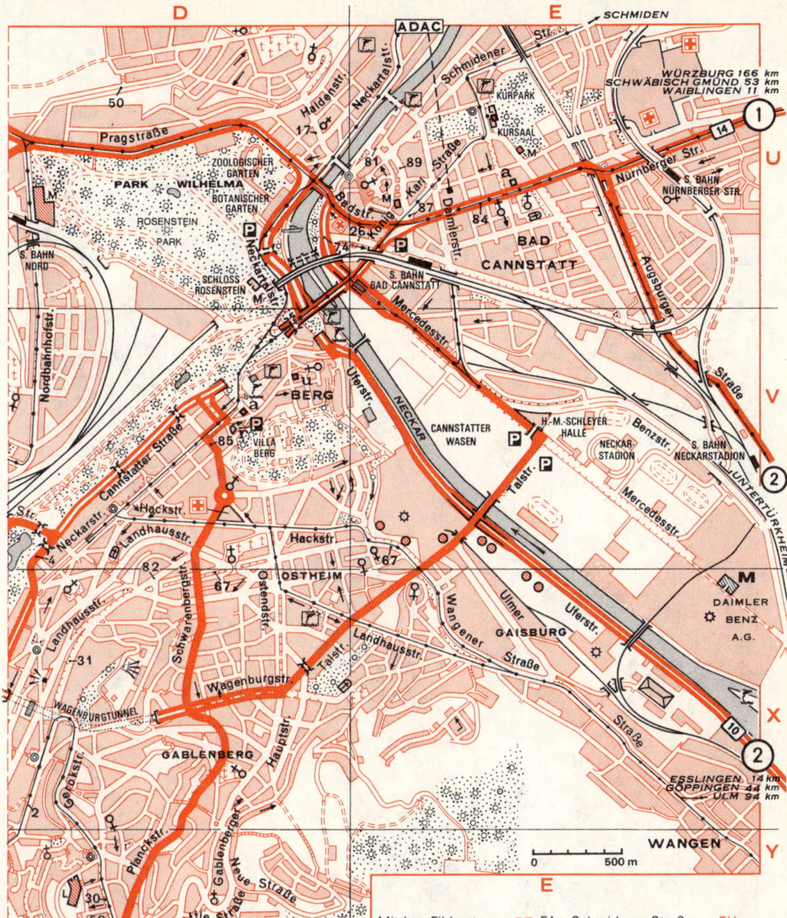
D
E
ADAC
SCHMIDEN
WÜRZBURG 166 km
SCHWÄBISCH GMÜND 53 km
WAIBLINGEN 11 km
Pragstraße
Haldenstr.
Neckartalstr.
Schmidener Str.
KURPARK
KURSAAL
ZOOLOGISCHER GARTEN
PARK WILHELMA
BOTANISCHER GARTEN
ROSENSTEIN PARK
SCHLOSS ROSENSTEIN
S. BAHN NORD
Nordbahnhofstr.
Badstr.
König-Karl-Straße
Daimlerstr.
Nürnberger Str.
S. BAHN NÜRNBERGER STR.
BAD CANNSTATT
S. BAHN BAD CANNSTATT
Mercedesstr.
Augsburger Straße
BERG
Uferstr.
NECKAR
CANNSTATTER WASEN
H.-M.-SCHLEYER-HALLE
NECKAR-STADION
Benzstr.
S. BAHN NECKARSTADION
UNTERTÜRKHEIM
VILLA BERG
Cannstatter Straße
Neckarstr.
Hackstr.
Landhausstr.
Talstr.
Mercedesstr.
OSTHEIM
Ostendstr.
Schwarenbergstr.
Wangener Straße
Ulmer Straße
GAISBURG
Uferstr.
DAIMLER BENZ A.G.
Landhausstr.
Wagenburgstr.
WAGENBURGTUNNEL
GABLENBERG
Hauptstr.
Gerokstr.
Planckstr.
Gablenberger
Neue Straße
Albert-Schäffle-Straße
Straße
ESSLINGEN 14 km
GÖPPINGEN 44 km
ULM 94 km
WANGEN
0
500 m
U
V
X
Y

Sonnenbergstr.
WERNHALDE
Jahnstr.
FERNSEHTURM ★★
Z
NEUHAUSEN
Guts-Muths-Weg
REUTLINGEN 41 km
D

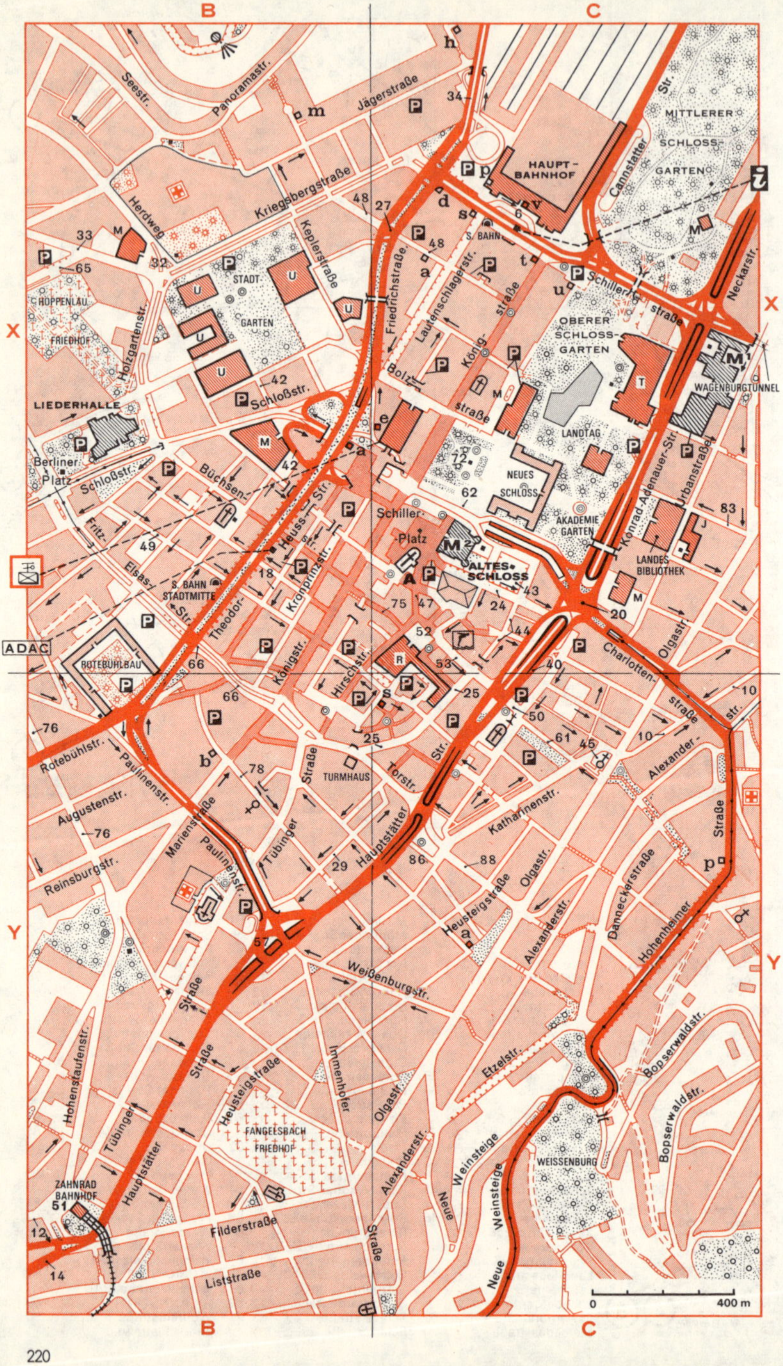
B
C
X
Y
Seestr.
Panoramastr.
Jägerstraße
Kriegsbergstraße
Herdweg
Keplerstraße
HOPPENLAU FRIEDHOF
Holzgartenstr.
STADT-GARTEN
LIEDERHALLE
Berliner Platz
Schloßstr.
Büchsen-
Friedrichstraße
Lautenschlagerstr.
Königstraße
Bolzstraße
HAUPT-BAHNHOF
S. BAHN
Cannstatter Str.
MITTLERER SCHLOSS-GARTEN
Schillerstraße
OBERER SCHLOSS-GARTEN
LANDTAG
NEUES SCHLOSS
AKADEMIE GARTEN
WAGENBURGTUNNEL
Neckarstr.
Konrad-Adenauer-Str.
Urbanstraße
LANDES BIBLIOTHEK
Schiller-Platz
ALTES SCHLOSS
Fritz-Elsas-Str.
S. BAHN STADTMITTE
Theodor-Heuss-Str.
Kronprinzstr.
Königstr.
Hirschstr.
ADAC
ROTEBÜHLBAU
Rotebühlstr.
Paulinenstr.
Augustenstr.
Reinsburgstr.
Marienstraße
Tübinger Straße
TURMHAUS
Torstr.
Hauptstätter Str.
Charlottenstraße
Olgastr.
Alexanderstr.
Katharinenstr.
Straße
Heusteigstraße
Dannecker straße
Hohenheimer Straße
Weißenburgstr.
Immenhofer
Etzelstr.
Bopserwaldstr.
Hohenstaufenstr.
FANGELSBACH FRIEDHOF
Neue Weinsteige
WEISSENBURG
Filderstraße
Liststraße
ZAHNRAD BAHNHOF
0
400 m

STUTTGART

Charlottenplatz .... CX 20
Eberhardstraße .... CY
Königstraße .... BCX
Schulstraße .... CX 75
Theodor-Heuss-Straße .... BX

Alexanderstraße .... CY
Arnulf-Klett-Platz .... CX 6
Augustenstraße .... BY
Blumenstraße .... CY 10
Böblinger Straße .... BY 12
Böheimstraße .... BY 14
Bolzstraße CX
Bopserwaldstraße .... CY
Büchsenstraße .... BX
Calwer Straße .... BX 18
Charlottenstraße .... CXY
Danneckerstraße .... CY
Dorotheenstraße .... CX 24
Eberhardstraße .... CY 25
Etzelstraße .... CY
Filderstraße .... BY
Friedrichsplatz .... CX 27
Friedrichstraße CX
Fritz-Elsas-Straße .... BX
Gerberstraße .... BY 29
Hauptstätter Straße .... BCY
Hegelplatz .... BX 32
Hegelstraße .... BX 33
Heilbronner Straße .... CX 34
Herdweg .... BX
Heusteigstraße .... BCY
Hirschstraße .... BXY
Hohenheimer Straße .... CY
Hohenstaufenstraße .... BY
Holzgartenstraße .... BX
Holzstraße .... CX 40
Immenhofer Straße .... BY
Jägerstraße .... BCX
Kanzleistraße .... BX 42
Karlsplatz .... CX 43
Karlstraße .... CX 44
Katharinenplatz .... CY 45
Katharinenstraße .... CY
Keplerstraße .... BX
Kirchstraße .... CX 47
Konrad-Adenauer-Straße CX
Kriegsbergstraße .... BX
Kronenstraße .... CX 48
Kronprinzstraße .... BX
Lange Straße .... BX 49
Lautenschlagerstraße CX
Leonhardsplatz .... CY 50
Liststraße .... BY
Marienplatz .... BY 51
Marienstraße .... BY
Marktplatz .... CX 52
Marktstraße .... CX 53
Neckarstraße CX
Neue Weinsteige .... CY
Österreichischer Platz .... BY 57
Olgastraße .... CXY
Panoramastraße .... BX
Paulinenstraße .... BY
Pfarrstraße .... CY 61
Planie .... CX 62
Reinsburgstraße .... BY
Rosenbergstraße .... BX 65
Rotebühlplatz .... BX 66
Rotebühlstraße .... BY
Schillerplatz CX
Schillerstraße CX
Schloßplatz .... CX 72
Schloßstraße .... BX
Seestraße .... BX
Silberburgstraße .... BY 76
Sophienstraße .... BY 78
Tübinger Straße .... BY
Ulrichstraße .... CX 83
Urbanstraße CX
Weißenburgstraße .... BCY
Wilhelmsplatz .... CY 86
Wilhelmstraße .... CY 88

Ruff, Friedhofstr. 21, ✆ 25 01 61, Telex 721645, – AE E VISA — CV **a**
closed 21 December - 2 January – **M** *(closed Saturday)* a la carte 20/49 – **85 rm** 85/145 Bb.

Intercity-Hotel without rest, Arnulf-Klett-Platz 2, ✆ 29 98 01, Telex 723543 – wc wc. AE E VISA — CX **p**
104 rm 75/165.

Kronen-Hotel without rest, Kronenstr. 48, ✆ 29 96 61, Telex 723632, – wc. AE E VISA — BX **m**
closed 20 December - 7 January – **90 rm** 85/170 Bb.

Azenberg, Seestr. 116, ✆ 22 10 51, Telex 721819, – wc wc. AE E VISA — AV **e**
(closed dinner to non-residents) – **55 rm** 110/180.

Unger without rest, Kronenstr. 17, ✆ 29 40 41, Telex 723995 – wc wc. AE E VISA — CX **a**
80 rm 111/205 Bb.

Rieker without rest, Friedrichstr. 3, ✆ 22 13 11 – wc wc. AE E VISA — CX **d**
63 rm 96/154.

Am Feuersee, Johannesstr. 2, ✆ 62 61 03 – wc — AY **t**
M *(dinner only)* – **38 rm** Bb.

Wörtz-Zur Weinsteige, Hohenheimer Str. 30, ✆ 24 53 96, Telex 723821, « Terrace » – wc wc. AE E VISA — CY **p**
closed 15 December - 15 January – **M** *(closed Saturday, Sunday and Bank Holidays)* a la carte 22/55 – **25 rm** 56/150.

Mack und Pflieger without rest, Kriegerstr. 7, ✆ 29 19 27 – wc — CX **h**
closed 23 December - 2 January – **94 rm** 58/160 Bb.

XXX ✿ **Alte Post**, Friedrichstr. 43, ✆ 29 30 79 – — CX **e**
closed Sunday, Bank Holidays, end July - mid August and lunch Monday and Saturday – **M** a la carte 47/90 (booking essential)
Spec. Essenz von Tomaten und Estragon, St. Petersfisch in Rote Beetebutter, Suprême von Poularde in grüner Pfeffercrème.

XXX **Mövenpick-Rôtisserie Baron de la Mouette**, Kleiner Schloßplatz 11 (entrance Theodor-Heuss-Str.), ✆ 22 00 34 – . AE E VISA — BX **a**
M a la carte 32/70 – **Boulevard Café M** a la carte 19/48.

XX **Der Goldene Adler**, Böheimstr. 38, ✆ 64 17 62 – . AE E — AY **e**
closed Monday – **M** a la carte 24/67.

XX **Martin's Stuben**, Karl-Schurz-Str. 15, ✆ 26 16 31 – AE E — DV **u**
closed lunch Saturday and Monday – **M** a la carte 39/75.

XX **Schwyzer Eck**, Neckarstr. 246, ✆ 2 62 26 94 – E — DV **a**
closed Saturday and 1 to 7 January – **M** a la carte 40/72.

XX Intercity-Restaurant, Arnulf-Klett-Platz 2, ✆ 29 49 46 — CX **v**

XX **Greiner Stuben**, Arnulf-Klett-Platz 1, ✆ 29 51 21 – AE E — CX **t**
M a la carte 25/51 – **Bräustüble M** a la carte 13,50/37.

X **Kupferschmiede**, Christophstr. 45, ✆ 23 35 30, Terrace – AE E — CY **a**
closed Saturday and Bank Holidays – **M** a la carte 27/58.

X **Come Prima** (Italian rest.), Steinstr. 3, ✆ 24 34 22 – AE E — CY **s**
closed Monday – **M** a la carte 25/52.

at Stuttgart 50 - Bad Cannstatt :

Spahr without rest, Waiblinger Str. 63 (B 14), 55 20 00, Telex 7254608 – wc wc. AE E VISA EU a
closed 23 December - 7 January – **59 rm** 100/195.

Alt-Cannstatt, Königsplatz 1 (Kursaal), 56 11 15, – . AE E EU
closed Monday – **M** a la carte 23/53.

at Stuttgart 70 - Degerloch :

Waldhotel Degerloch, Guts-Muths-Weg 18, 76 50 17, Telex 7255728, , – wc wc . AE E VISA by Guts-Muths-Weg DZ
M a la carte 22/50 – **52 rm** 90/190 Bb.

Turmrestaurant (Television Tower, 144 m, 4 DM), Jahnstr. 120, 24 61 04, Stuttgart and environs – . AE E VISA DZ
M a la carte 24/58.

at Stuttgart 30 - Feuerbach :

Europe, Siemensstr. 26, 81 50 91, Telex 723650 – . AE E VISA. rest – **M** a la carte 34/63 – **200 rm** 145/190 Bb CU z

Lamm, Mühlstr. 24, 85 36 15 – AU n
closed Saturday lunch, Sunday, Bank Holidays and 22 December - 6 January – **M** a la carte 55/85 (booking essential)
Spec. Lachsgratin, Kaninchenrücken in Senfrahm, Lammrücken provençale.

at Stuttgart 23 - Flughafen (Airport) ④ : 15 km :

Airport-Hotel Mövenpick, Randstraße, 7 90 70, Telex 7245677 – rest wc (with). AE E VISA. rest
M a la carte 26/65 – **128 rm** 169/211 Bb.

at Stuttgart 80 - Möhringen ⑤ : 7 km :

Stuttgart International, Plieninger Str. 100, 7 20 21, Telex 7255763, entrance to the Römerbad (with ,) – rest (with). AE E VISA. rest
Restaurants : – **Kopenhagen** *(lunch only)* **M** a la carte 30/65 – **Paris Grill** *(dinner only)* **M** a la carte 35/75 – **Schwabenbräu-Stuben M** a la carte 17/48 – **200 rm** 158/285 Bb.

Gloria - Restaurant Möhringer Hexle, Sigmaringer Str. 59, 71 30 59, – wc
M a la carte 19/47 – **70 rm** 85/129 Bb.

Neotel without rest, Vaihinger Str. 151, 7 80 06 35, Telex 7255179 – wc wc . AE E VISA
71 rm 119/189 Bb.

Anker, Vaihinger Str. 76, 71 30 31 – wc . AE E VISA.
closed 2 weeks August – **M** *(closed Saturday and Sunday lunch)* a la carte 20/42 (Swabian specialities) – **24 rm** 75/120 Bb.

Hirsch-Weinstuben, Maierstr. 3, 71 13 75 – .
closed Saturday lunch, Sunday, Bank Holidays and 2 weeks March - April – **M** a la carte 27/64 (booking essential)
Spec. Terrine von Gänsestopfleber, Salat von Kalbskopf in Gemüsevinaigrette, Seeteufel auf Linsen mit Safransauce.

Landgasthof Riedsee, Elfenstr. 120, 71 24 84, – . AE E VISA
closed Sunday dinner, Monday and 2 to 14 January – **M** a la carte 26/62.

at Stuttgart 50 - Mühlhausen by Neckartalstraße EU :

Öxle's Löwen, Veitstr. 2, 53 22 26 – AE E
closed lunch Monday and Saturday, Sunday and Bank Holidays – **M** a la carte 37/76
Spec. Pasteten und Terrinen, Zephyr vom Hummer mit Kaviarvinaigrette, Kräuterroulade vom Kaninchenrücken.

at Stuttgart 61 - Obertürkheim by ② :

Weinstube Paule, Augsburger Str. 643, 32 14 71 – . AE
closed Thursday and last Sunday in the month – **M** a la carte 29/55 .

Wirt am Berg, Uhlbacher Str. 14, 32 12 26
closed Sunday, Bank Holidays, first Saturday in the month and 3 weeks July - August – **M** a la carte 29/52 .

at Stuttgart 70 - Plieningen ④ : 13 km :

Traube, Brabandtgasse 2, 45 48 33, – wc wc
closed 22 December - 6 January – **M** *(closed Saturday and Sunday)* a la carte 31/88 (booking essential) – **22 rm** 65/180.

Fissler-Post, Schoellstr. 4, 45 50 74 – wc wc . AE E VISA
M *(closed Sunday dinner)* a la carte 29/56 (booking essential) – **63 rm** 68/105.

Recknagel's Nagelschmiede, Brabandtgasse 1, 45 74 54 –
closed lunch Monday to Saturday, Tuesday and 22 August - 15 September **M** a la carte 24/50.

at Stuttgart 40 - Stammheim by ⑧ :

Novotel, Korntaler Str. 207, ✆ 80 10 65, Telex 7252137, (heated) – wc
M a la carte 22/46 – **117 rm** 130/165 Bb.

***at Fellbach* 7012** by ① 8 km : – 0711 (Stuttgart)

Kongresshotel M, Tainer Str. 7, ✆ 5 85 90, Telex 7254900, – AE E VISA
M (rest. see **Alt Württemberg below**) – **155 rm** 160/230 Bb.

Am Kappelberg M without rest, Karlstr. 37, ✆ 58 50 41, Telex 7254486, – wc AE E
closed 22 December - 10 January – **41 rm** 100/155 Bb.

Alt Württemberg, Tainer Str. 7 (Schwabenlandhalle), ✆ 58 00 88 – AE E VISA
M a la carte 30/57.

Weinkeller Häusermann (vaulted cellar of 1732), Kappelbergstr. 1, ✆ 58 77 75 –
closed Sunday, Bank Holidays and 24 December - 3 January – **M** a la carte 22/51.

***at Gerlingen* 7016** ⑦ : 14 km :

Krone, Hauptstr. 28, ✆ (07156) 2 10 04 – wc wc AE E VISA
M *(closed Wednesday dinner, Sunday, Bank Holidays and 25 July - 15 August)* a la carte 27/64 (booking essential) – **35 rm** 94/178 Bb.

Balogh without rest, Max-Eyth-Str. 16, ✆ (07156) 2 30 95 – wc AE
48 rm 70/135.

***at Korntal-Münchingen 2* 7015** ⑧ : 9 km, near motorway exit S-Zuffenhausen :

Mercure, Siemensstr. 50, ✆ (07150) 1 30, Telex 723589, beer-garden, – AE E VISA
M a la carte 29/60 – **215 rm** 151/238 Bb.

Strohgäu Hotel, Stuttgarter Str. 60, ✆ (07150) 60 81 – wc AE E VISA
M a la carte 25/47 – **22 rm** 96/135 Bb.

***at Leinfelden-Echterdingen 1* 7022** by ⑤ :

Drei Morgen without rest, Bahnhofstr. 39, ✆ (0711) 75 10 85 – wc AE E
25 rm 75/130 Bb.

Filderämtle, Bahnhofstr. 16 (Filderhalle), ✆ (0711) 75 02 51 – AE E
closed Monday – **M** a la carte 22/45.

***at Leinfelden-Echterdingen 2* 7022** by ⑤ :

Lamm, Hauptstr. 98, ✆ (0711) 79 33 26, Telex 7255686 – wc AE E
M a la carte 32/64 – **20 rm** 80/110.

Adler, Obergasse 16, ✆ (0711) 79 35 90, – wc wc
M *(closed Sunday, Monday lunch and 3 weeks July - August)* a la carte 23/54 – **19 rm** 85/125.

Baiersbronn 7292. Baden-Württemberg 987 ㉟ – pop. 14 000 – alt. 550 m – 07442.

Stuttgart 100.

✿✿ **Restaurant Bareiss**, Gärtenbühlweg 14 (Mitteltal), ✆ 4 71, ← – .
closed Monday, Tuesday, 20 May - 13 June and 24 November - 24 December – **M** a la carte 49/84 (wine-list with 350 wines)
Spec. Cassolette von Wachtel und Gänseleber, St. Peters-Fisch mit Jakobsmuscheltatar, Gefüllter Kaninchenrücken mit Sauce von schwarzen Oliven.

✿✿ **Schwarzwaldstube in der Traube-Tonbach**, Tonbachstr. 237 (Tonbach), ✆ 49 20, ← – AE E.
closed Thursday, Friday lunch, 13 January - 6 February and 10 to 24 July – **M** a la carte 43/92 (booking essential)
Spec. Hummer-Cassolette in Sauternes, Rotbarbe mit Kräutern in Knoblauchsauce, Gefüllte Taubenbrust im Netz.

Bühl 7580. Baden-Württemberg 987 ㉞, 57 ⑳ – pop. 22 800 – alt. 135 m – 07223.

Stuttgart 117 .

✿✿ **Burg Windeck**, Kappelwindeckstr. 104 (SE : 4 km, near the castle ruins Altwindeck), ✆ 2 36 71, ← Bühl and Rhine-plain – E
closed Monday, Tuesday and January - 22 February – **M** a la carte 53/108 (remarkable wine-List)
Spec. Taubensalat mit Gänseleber, Hummer auf Linsen, Perlhuhnbrust mit Orangensenfsauce.

Republic of Ireland

Dublin

Republic of IRELAND

PRACTICAL INFORMATION

LOCAL CURRENCY

Punt (Irish Pound) : 1 punt = 1.24 US $ (Jan. 86)

TOURIST INFORMATION

The telephone number and address of the Tourist Information office is given in the text under ℹ.

FOREIGN EXCHANGE

Banks are open 10am to 12.30pm and 1.30pm to 3pm on weekdays only.

Banks in Dublin stay open to 5pm on Thursdays and banks at Dublin and Shannon airports are open on Saturdays and Sundays.

SHOPPING IN DUBLIN

In the index of street names those printed in red are where the principal shops are found.

CAR HIRE

The international car hire companies have branches in each major city. Your hotel porter will be able to give details and help you with your arrangements.

TIPPING

Many hotels and restaurants include a service charge but where this is not the case an amount equivalent to between 10 and 15 per cent of the bill is customary. Additionally doormen, baggage porters and cloakroom attendants are generally given a gratuity.

Taxi drivers are customarily tipped between 10 and 15 per cent of the amount shown on the meter in addition to the fare.

SPEED LIMITS

The maximum permitted speed in the Republic is 55 mph (88 km/h) except where a lower speed limit is signposted.

SEAT BELTS

The wearing of seat belts is compulsory for drivers and front seat passengers.

ANIMALS

It is forbildden to bring domestic animals (dogs, cats...) into the Republic of Ireland.

DUBLIN

SIGHTS

See : National Gallery★★★ BY – Castle (State apartments★★★ *AC*) BY – Christ Church Cathedral★★ 12C BY – National Museum (Irish antiquities, Art and Industrial)★★ BY **M2** – Trinity College★ (Library★★) BY – National Museum (Zoological Collection)★ BY **M1** – Municipal Art Gallery★ BX **M3** – O'Connell Street★ (and the General Post Office) BXY – St. Stephen's Green★ BZ – St. Patrick's Cathedral (interior★) BZ – Phoenix Park (Zoological Gardens★).

Envir. : St. Doolagh's Church★ 13C (open Saturday and Sunday, afternoon only) NE : 7 m. by L 87.

DUBLIN Dublin 405 N 7 – pop. 567 866 – 01.

18 Edmondstown, Rathfarnham 907461, S : 3 m. by N 81 – 18 Elm Park, Nutley House, Donnybrook 693438, S : 3 m. – 18 Lower Churchtown Rd, Milltown 977060, S : by T 43.

379900, N : 5 ½ m. by N 1 – **Terminal :** Busaras (Central Bus Station) Store St.

to Liverpool (B & I Line) 1 nightly (8 h) – to Holyhead (B & I Line) 1-2 daily (3 h 30 mn) – to the Isle of Man : Douglas (Isle of Man Steam Packet Co.) June to September 1-3 weekly (4 h 30 mn).

14 Upper O'Connell St. 747733 – Dublin Airport 376387 and 375533.

Belfast 103 – Cork 154 – Londonderry 146.

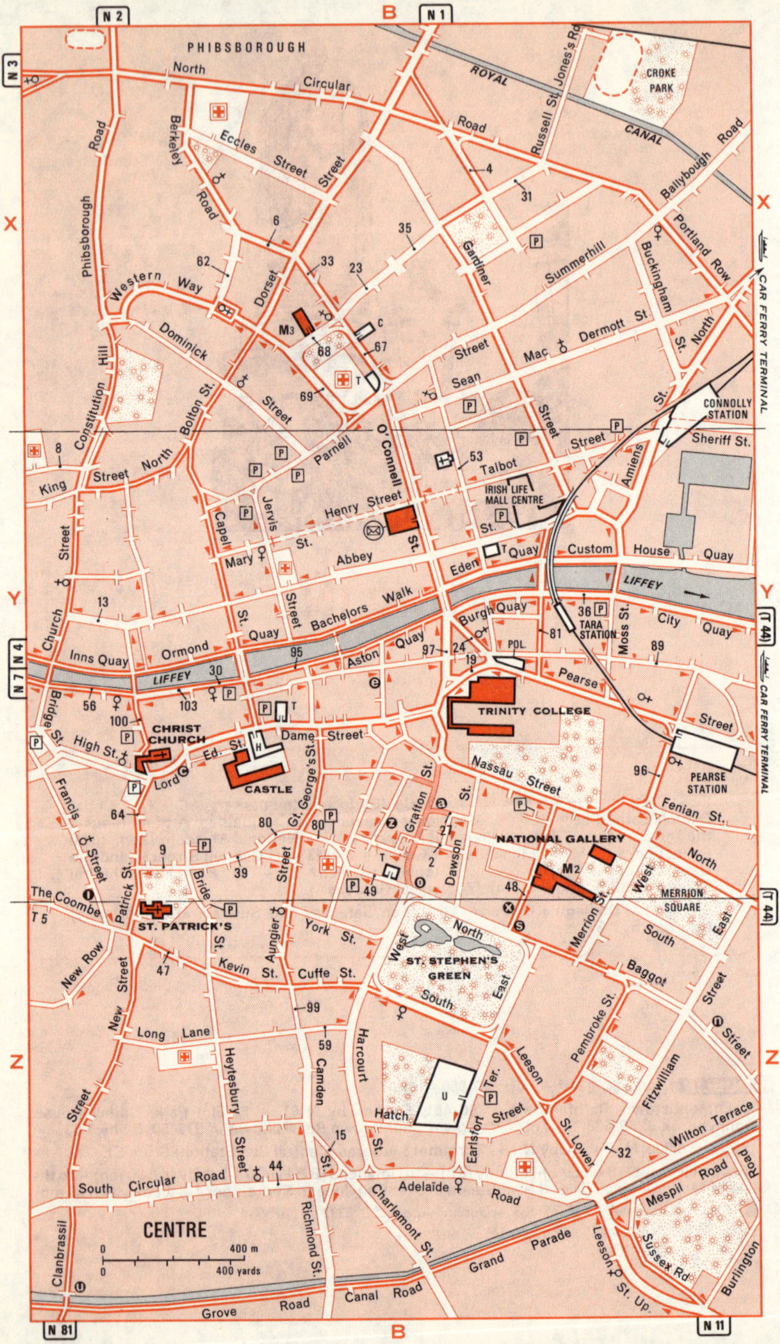

PHIBSBOROUGH
North Circular Road
ROYAL CANAL
CROKE PARK
Eccles Street
Berkeley Road
Phibsborough Road
Western Way
Dorset St.
Gardiner Street
Summerhill
Buckingham St.
Portland Row
Ballybough Road
Russell St.
Jones's Rd
Dominick Street
Constitution Hill
Bolton St.
Sean Mac Dermott St.
CONNOLLY STATION
CAR FERRY TERMINAL
O' Connell St.
Parnell Street
Talbot Street
Amiens St.
Sheriff St.
IRISH LIFE MALL CENTRE
King Street North
Henry Street
Capel St.
Jervis St.
Mary St.
Abbey St.
Eden Quay
Custom House Quay
Church Street
Bachelors Walk
Burgh Quay
LIFFEY
City Quay
TARA STATION
Moss St.
Inns Quay
Ormond Quay
Aston Quay
POL
Pearse Street
TRINITY COLLEGE
CHRIST CHURCH
High St.
Bridge St.
Lord Ed. St.
Dame Street
CASTLE
Nassau Street
PEARSE STATION
Fenian St.
Francis Street
Gt. George's St.
Grafton St.
Dawson St.
NATIONAL GALLERY
Merrion St.
MERRION SQUARE
North
West
South
East
The Coombe
Patrick St.
Bride St.
ST. PATRICK'S
Aungier Street
York St.
ST. STEPHEN'S GREEN
Kevin St.
Cuffe St.
Baggot Street
New Row
New Street
Long Lane
Heytesbury Street
Camden St.
Harcourt St.
Leeson St. Lower
Pembroke St.
Fitzwilliam Street
Hatch Street
Earlsfort Ter.
Wilton Terrace
South Circular Road
Adelaide Road
Charlemont St.
Richmond St.
Mespil Road
Sussex Rd
Burlington Road
Grand Parade
Leeson St. Up.
Clanbrassil Street
Grove Road
Canal Road
CENTRE
0 400 m
0 400 yards
N 1
N 2
N 3
N 4
N 7
N 11
N 81
T 5
T 44
B
X
Y
Z
M3
M2
C
T
H
U

DUBLIN

Anne Street South	BY	2
Dawson Street	BY	
Duke Street	BY	27
Grafton Street	BY	
Henry Street	BY	
Irish Life Mall Centre	BY	
O'Connell Street	BXY	
Belvidere Place	BX	4
Blessington Street	BX	6
Brunswick Street North	BY	8
Bull Alley	BY	9
Chancery Street	BY	13
Charlotte Street	BZ	15
College Street	BY	19
Denmark Street	BX	23
D'Olier Street	BY	24
Essex Quay	BY	30
Fitzgibbon Street	BX	31
Fitzwilliam Place	BZ	32
Frederick Street North	BX	33
Gardiner Place	BX	35
George's Quay	BY	36
Golden Lane	BY	39
Harrington Street	BZ	44
Kevin Street Upper	BZ	47
Kildare Street	BYZ	48
King Street South	BY	49
Malborough Street	BY	53
Merchants Quay	BY	56
Montague Street	BZ	59
Mountjoy Street	BX	62
Nicholas Street	BY	64
Parnell Square East	BX	67
Parnell Square North	BX	68
Parnell Square West	BX	69
Stephen Street	BY	80
Tara Street	BY	81
Townsend Street	BY	89
Wellington Quay	BY	95
Westland Row	BY	96
Westmoreland Street	BY	97
Wexford Street	BZ	99
Winetavern Street	BY	100
Wood Quay	BY	103

Berkeley Court, Lansdowne Rd, Ballsbridge, ☎ 601711, Telex 30554, – AE VISA.
M 15.00/18.00 **t.** and a la carte 🍷 5.00 – ☕ 6.50 – **200 rm** 69.00/88.00 **t.**

Westbury, Grafton St., ☎ 791122, Telex 91091 – rest wc ☎ — BY **z**
146 rm.

Jury's, Pembroke Rd, Ballsbridge, ☎ 605000, Telex 25304, heated, – AE VISA
M 15.00/16.00 **t.** and a la carte 🍷 7.50 – ☕ 7.50 – **300 rm** 63.00/82.50 **t.**

Shelbourne (T.H.F.), 27 St. Stephen's Green, ☎ 766471, Telex 25184 – ☎. AE VISA — BZ **s**
M 18.00/21.00 **t.** and a la carte 🍷 6.40 – ☕ 8.00 – **167 rm** 75.00/97.00 **t.**

Blooms, Anglesea St., ☎ 715622, Telex 31688 – ☎. AE VISA — BY **e**
M (buffet lunch)/dinner 14.00 **t.** and a la carte 🍷 4.50 – **84 rm** 66.00/85.00 **t.**

Le Coq Hardi, 35 Pembroke Rd, ☎ 689070 – .

Patrick Guilbaud, 46 St. James's Pl., St. James' St., off Lower Baggot St., ☎ 764192, French rest. – . AE VISA — BZ **n**
closed Saturday lunch, Sunday, 24 to 28 December, 1 January and Bank Holidays – **M** 12.75 **t.** and a la carte.

Bailey, 2-4 Duke St., ☎ 770600 – AE VISA — BY **a**
closed Saturday lunch, Sunday and Bank Holidays – **M** 12.50/14.95 **t.** and a la carte 🍷 5.95.

Locks, 1 Windsor Terr., Portobello, ☎ 752025 – AE VISA — BZ **u**
closed Saturday lunch, Sunday, 24 December-2 January and Bank Holidays – **M** 11.50 **t.** (lunch) and a la carte 15.50/20.50 **t.** 🍷 3.60.

Park, 26 Main Street, Blackrock, SE : 4 ½ m. on T 44 ☎ 886177 – AE VISA
closed Saturday lunch, Sunday, 3 days at Christmas and Bank Holidays – **M** (booking essential) 8.50/20.00 **t.** 🍷 2.60.

Old Dublin, 90-91 Francis St., ☎ 751173, Scandinavian rest. – AE VISA — BY **i**
closed Saturday lunch, Sunday and Bank Holidays – **M** 9.50/14.75 **t.** and a la carte 🍷 4.25.

Lord Edward, 23 Christchurch Pl., ☎ 752557, Seafood – AE VISA — BY **c**
closed Saturday lunch, Sunday and Bank Holidays – **M** a la carte 15.50/25.15 **t.** 🍷 4.25.

Small Home, 41-43 Shelbourne Rd, Ballsbridge, ☎ 608087 – AE VISA
closed Saturday lunch and Sunday – **M** 10.50/14.95 **t.** and a la carte.

Bentleys, 46 Upper Baggot St., ☎ 682760 – AE VISA
closed Monday dinner, Sunday, 2 weeks July and Bank Holidays – **M** a la carte 11.75/19.00 **t.** 🍷 3.95.

Dobbin's, 15 Stephen's Lane, ☎ 764679, Bistro.

Mitchell's Cellars, 21 Kildare St., ☎ 680367 – AE VISA — BZ **x**
closed Saturday June-September, Sunday, 28-29 March, 23 December-2 January and Bank Holidays – **M** (lunch only) a la carte 8.00/8.95 **t.** 🍷 3.85.

Cafe de Paris, The Galleria, 6 St. Stephen's Green, ☎ 778499 – VISA — BY **o**
closed lunch Sunday and Bank Holiday Mondays, 25-26 December and 1 January – **M** a la carte 9.55/13.25 **t.** 🍷 4.05.

at Dublin Airport N : 6 ½ m. by N 1 – ✉ 01 Dublin :

Dublin International (T.H.F.), ☎ 379211, Telex 24612 – wc ☎ . AE VISA
M 12.75/11.00 **st.** and a la carte 🍷 4.25 – ☕ 6.00 – **195 rm** 57.00/69.50 **st.**

Italy
Italia

Rome
Florence
Milan
Naples - Capri
Palerme
Taormina
Turin
Venice

PRACTICAL INFORMATION

LOCAL CURRENCY

Italian Lire : 1000 lire = 0.60 US $ (Jan. 86)

TOURIST INFORMATION

Welcome Office (Ente Provinciale per il Turismo), closed Saturday and Sunday :
- Via Parigi 5 - 00185 ROMA, ✆ 06/463748
- Via Marconi 1 - 20123 MILANO, ✆ 02/809662

See also telephone number and address of other Tourist Information offices in the text of the towns under ☐.

American Express :
- Piazza di Spagna 38 - 00187 ROMA, ✆ 06/67641
- Via Brera 3 - 20121 MILANO, ✆ 02/85571

AIRLINES

ALITALIA : Via Bissolati 13 - 00187 ROMA, ✆ 06/46881
Piazzale Pastore o dell'Arte (EUR) - 00144 ROMA, ✆ 06/54441
Via Albricci 5 - 20122 MILANO, ✆ 02/6281
AIR FRANCE : Via Vittorio Veneto 93 - 00187 ROMA, ✆ 06/4758741
Piazza Cavour 2 - 20121 MILANO, ✆ 02/77381
PAN AM : Via Bissolati 46 - 00187 ROMA, ✆ 06/4773
Piazza Velasca 5 - 20122 MILANO, ✆ 02/877241
TWA : Via Barberini 59/67 - 00187 ROMA, ✆ 06/47211
Corso Europa 9/11 - 20122 MILANO, ✆ 02/77961

FOREIGN EXCHANGE

Money can be changed at the Banca d'Italia, other banks and authorised exchange offices (Banks close at 1.15pm and at weekends

POSTAL SERVICES

Local post offices : open Monday to Saturday 8.00am to 2.00pm

General Post Office (open 24 hours only for telegrams) :
- Piazza San Silvestro 00187 ROMA – Piazza Cordusio 20123 MILANO

SHOPPING

In the index of street names those printed in red are where the principal shops are found. In Rome, the main shopping streets are : Via del Babuino, Via dei Condotti, Via Frattina, Via Vittorio Veneto ; in Milan : Via Dante, Via Manzoni, Via Monte Napoleone, Corso Vittorio Emanuele.

BREAKDOWN SERVICE

Certain garages in the centre and outskirts of towns operate a 24 hour breakdown service. If you breakdown the police are usually able to help by indicating the nearest one.

A free car breakdown service (a tax is levied) is operated by the A.C.I. for foreign motorists carrying the fuel card (Carta Carburante). The A.C.I. also offers telephone information in English (8am to 5pm) for road and weather conditions and tourist events : 06/4212.

TIPPING

As well as the service charge, it is the custom to tip employees. The amount can vary with the region and the service given.

SPEED LIMITS

Speed limits applicable on trunk roads and motorways are according to engine capacity : 80-90 km/h or 50-56 mph (600 cc) to 110-140 km/h or 68-87 mph (over 1300 cc).

ROME

SIGHTS

Rome's most famous sights are indicated on the town plans pp. 2 to 5. For a more complete visit see the Green Guide to Italy.

ROME (ROMA) 00100 988 ㉖ – Pop. 2 830 650 – alt. 20 – ☎ 06.

18 (closed Monday) at Acquasanta ✉ 00178 Roma ☎ 783407, SE : 12 km.

9 Fioranello (closed Wednesday) at Santa Maria delle Mole ✉ 00040 Roma ☎ 608291.

18 and 9 (closed Monday) at Olgiata ✉ 00123 Roma ☎ 3789141.

Ciampino SE : 15 km ☎ 4694 and Leonardo da Vinci di Fiumicino ☎ 601437 – Alitalia, via Bissolati 13 ✉ 00187 ☎ 46881 and piazzale Pastore o dell'Arte (EUR) ✉ 00144 ☎ 54441.

Termini ☎ 464923 – Tiburtina ☎ 4956626.

via Parigi 5 ✉ 00185 ☎ 463748 ; at Termini station ☎ 465461 ; on the motorways : A1 Roma North ☎ 6919958 and A2 Roma South ☎ 9464341.

A.C.I. via Cristoforo Colombo 261 ✉ 00147 ☎ 5106 and via Marsala 8 ✉ 00185 ☎ 4998, Telex 610686.

Distances from Rome are indicated in the text of the other towns listed in this Guide.

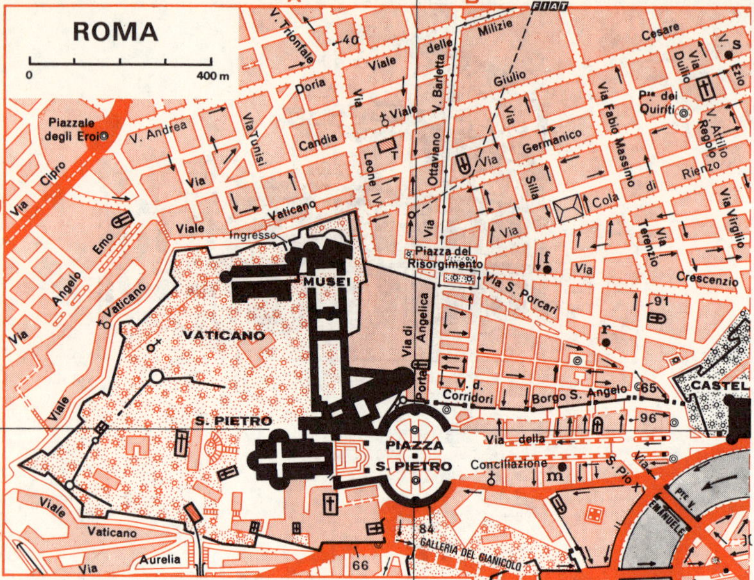

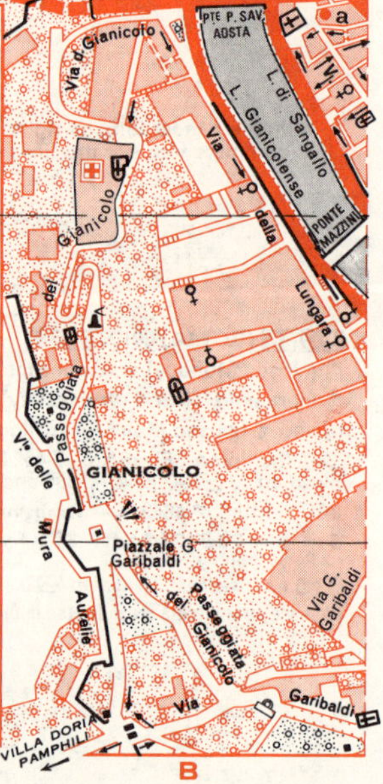

A

ROMA ANTICA

COLONNA TRAIANA ★★★ ____ EX L
FORO ROMANO ★★★ ____ EX
PALATINO ★★★ ____ EY
PANTHEON ★★★ ____ DV
ARA PACIS AUGUSTAE ★★ ____ DU N
AREA SACRA LARGO ARGENTINA ★★ ____ DX R
TEATRO DI MARCELLO ★★ ____ DX V
TEMPIO DI APOLLO SOSIANO ★★ ____ DX S
COLONNA DI MARCO AURELIO ★ ____ DEV W
ISOLA TIBERINA ★ ____ DY
TEMPIO DELLA FORTUNA VIRILE ★ ____ EY X
TEMPIO DI VESTA ★ ____ EY Y

ROMA CRISTIANA

GESÙ ★★★ ____ DEX
S. LUIGI DEI FRANCESI ★★ ____ DV A
S. MARIA D'ARACOELI ★★ ____ EX B
S. MARIA DEL POPOLO ★★ ____ DU C
CAPELLA DEL MONTE DI PIETÀ ★ ____ DX F
CHIESA NUOVA ★ ____ CV D
ORATORIO DEL CROCIFISSO ★ ____ EV E
S. AGOSTINO ★ ____ DV K
S. ANDREA DELLA VALLE ★ ____ DX G
S. CECILIA IN TRASTEVERE ★ ____ DY W
S. GIOVANNI DECOLLATO ★ ____ EY R
S. IGNAZIO ★ ____ DEV L
S. IVO ★ ____ DV N
S. LUCA E S. MARTINA ★ ____ EX S
S. PIETRO IN MONTORIO ★ : ____ BCY V
SPIANATA : ⋘ ★★★
S. MARIA IN COSMEDIN ★ ____ EY Z
S. MARIA SOPRA MINERVA ★ ____ DV X
S. MARIA DELLA PACE ★ ____ CV Y
S. MARIA IN TRASTEVERE ★ ____ CY A
SANTI APOSTOLI ★ ____ EV B

PALAZZI E MUSEI

CASTEL SANT'ANGELO ★★★ : ____ BCU
TERRAZZA : ⋘ ★★★
MUSEO DEL PALAZZO DEI CONSERVATORI ★★★ ____ EX M5
PALAZZO FARNESE ★★★ ____ CX
PALAZZO NUOVO ★★★ :
MUSEO CAPITOLINO ★★ ____ EX M6
PALAZZO SENATORIO ★★★ ____ EX H
PALAZZO DELLA CANCELLERIA ★★ ____ CV E
PALAZZO DEL QUIRINALE ★★ ____ EV
VILLA FARNESINA ★★ ____ CX F
GALLERIA NAZIONALE DI PITTURA ★ ____ CX M7
GALLERIA DEL PALAZZO COLONNA ★ ____ EV M8
MUSEO DEL RISORGIMENTO ★ ____ EX M9
PALAZZO BRASCHI ★ ____ CV M10
PALAZZO E GALLERIA DORIA PAMPHILI ★ ____ EV M12
PALAZZO SPADA ★ ____ CX M13
PALAZZO VENEZIA ★ ____ EX M14

CITTÀ DEL VATICANO

BASILICA DI S. PIETRO ★★★ : ____ AV
DUOMO : ⋘ ★★★ ____ AV
PIAZZA S. PIETRO ★★★ ____ ABV
GIARDINI DEL VATICANO ★★★ ____ AUV
MUSEI DEL VATICANO ★★★ : ____ AU
CAPPELLA SISTINA ★★★

PASSEGGIATE

FONTANA DEI FIUMI ★★★ ____ DV G
FONTANA DI TREVI ★★★ ____ EV
PIAZZA DEL CAMPIDOGLIO ★★★ ____ EX
PINCIO : ⋘ ★★★ ____ DU
MONUMENTO VITTORIO EMANUELE : ⋘ ★★ ____ EX N
PIAZZA NAVONA ★★ ____ CDV
PIAZZA DEL POPOLO ★★ ____ DU
PIAZZA DEL QUIRINALE ★★ ____ EV
PIAZZA DI SPAGNA ★★ ____ EU
VIA DEL CORSO ★★ ____ DU EV
FONTANA DELLE TARTARUGHE ★ ____ DX L
GIANICOLO ★ ____ BX
PIAZZA BOCCA DELLA VERITÀ ★ ____ EY
PIAZZA CAMPO DEI FIORI ★ ____ CDX
PIAZZA COLONNA ★ ____ EV
PIAZZA VENEZIA ★ ____ EX
PONTE S. ANGELO ★ ____ CV
VIA DEI CORONARI ★ ____ CV
VIA GIULIA ★ ____ CVX

Banco di S. Spirito (V. del) .... CV 8
Battisti (Via Cesare) .... EV 10
Caravita (Via del) .... EV 15
Chigi (Largo) .... EV 20
Clementino (Via del) .... DU 23
Consolazione (Via della) ... EX 25
Crescenzi (Salita de') .... DV 27
Dogana Vecchia (Via della) .... DV 29
Fori Imperiali (Via dei) .... EX 35
Giubbonari (Via dei) .... CX 39
Lucchesi (Via dei) .... EV 45
Mercede (Via della) .... EU 49
Orsini (Via V.) .... CU 54
Porta Castello (Via di) .... BU 65
Porta Cavalleggeri (Largo di) .... AV 66
Portico d'Ottavia (Via del) ... DX 69
S. Agostino (Via di) .... DV 77
S. Maria del Pianto (Via di) .... DX 79
S. Maria in Via (Via di) ... EV 80
S. Uffizio (Via del) .... BV 84
S. Vincenzo (Via di) .... EV 85
Sforza Pallavicini (Via) ... BU 91
Stamperia (Via della) .... EV 93
Traspontina (Via della) ... BU 96
Tulliano (Via del) .... EX 99
Zanardelli (Via G.) .... CV 103

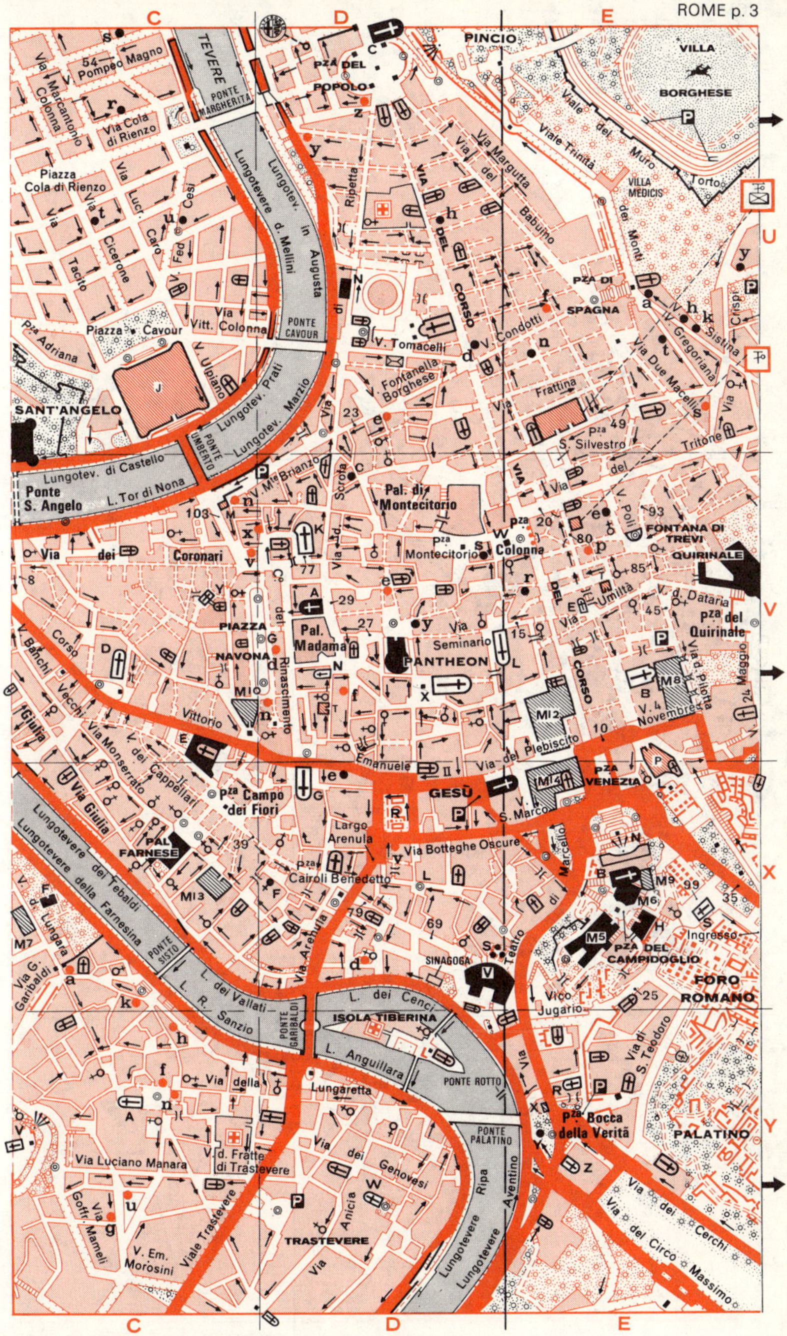
C
D
E
U
V
X
Y
PINCIO
VILLA BORGHESE
Pza DEL POPOLO
TEVERE
PONTE MARGHERITA
Via Marcantonio Colonna
Pompeo Magno
Via Cola di Rienzo
Piazza Cola di Rienzo
Lungotevere d. Mellini
Lungotev. in Augusta
Ripetta
VIA DEL CORSO
Via Margutta
Via del Babuino
Viale Trinità
Viale del Muro Torto
VILLA MEDICIS
dei Monti
Pza DI SPAGNA
V. Gregoriana
Sistina
Crispi
Cicerone
Tacito
Cesi
Piazza Cavour
Via Vitt. Colonna
PONTE CAVOUR
Pza Adriana
V. Tomacelli
V. Condotti
Fontanella Borghese
Frattina
Via Due Macelli
Tritone
Pza S. Silvestro
SANT'ANGELO
Lungotev. Prati
Lungotev. Marzio
PONTE UMBERTO
Lungotev. di Castello
Ponte S. Angelo
L. Tor di Nona
Scrofa
Pal. di Montecitorio
Pza Montecitorio
Pza Colonna
FONTANA DI TREVI
QUIRINALE
Via dei Coronari
PIAZZA NAVONA
Pal. Madama
PANTHEON
Seminario
Umiltà
V. d. Dataria
Pza del Quirinale
V. 4 Novembre
Via della Pilotta
24 Maggio
V. Banchi Vecchi
Corso Vittorio Emanuele
Rinascimento
Via del Plebiscito
Giulia
Via Monserrato
V. dei Cappellari
Pza Campo dei Fiori
GESÙ
Pza VENEZIA
V. S. Marco
PAL FARNESE
Largo Arenula
Via Botteghe Oscure
Pza Cairoli Benedetto
Via Arenula
Marcello
Lungotevere dei Tebaldi
Lungotevere della Farnesina
PONTE SISTO
Via della Lungara
Via G. Garibaldi
L. dei Vallati
L. R. Sanzio
PONTE GARIBALDI
L. dei Cenci
ISOLA TIBERINA
SINAGOGA
Teatro di Marcello
Pza DEL CAMPIDOGLIO
Ingresso
FORO ROMANO
Vico Jugario
Via di S. Teodoro
L. Anguillara
Lungaretta
Via della
PONTE ROTTO
Pza Bocca della Verità
PALATINO
PONTE PALATINO
V. d. Fratte di Trastevere
Via Luciano Manara
Via dei Genovesi
Anicia
Lungotevere Ripa
Lungotevere Aventino
Via dei Cerchi
Via del Circo Massimo
Via Goffr. Mameli
V. Em. Morosini
Viale Trastevere
TRASTEVERE

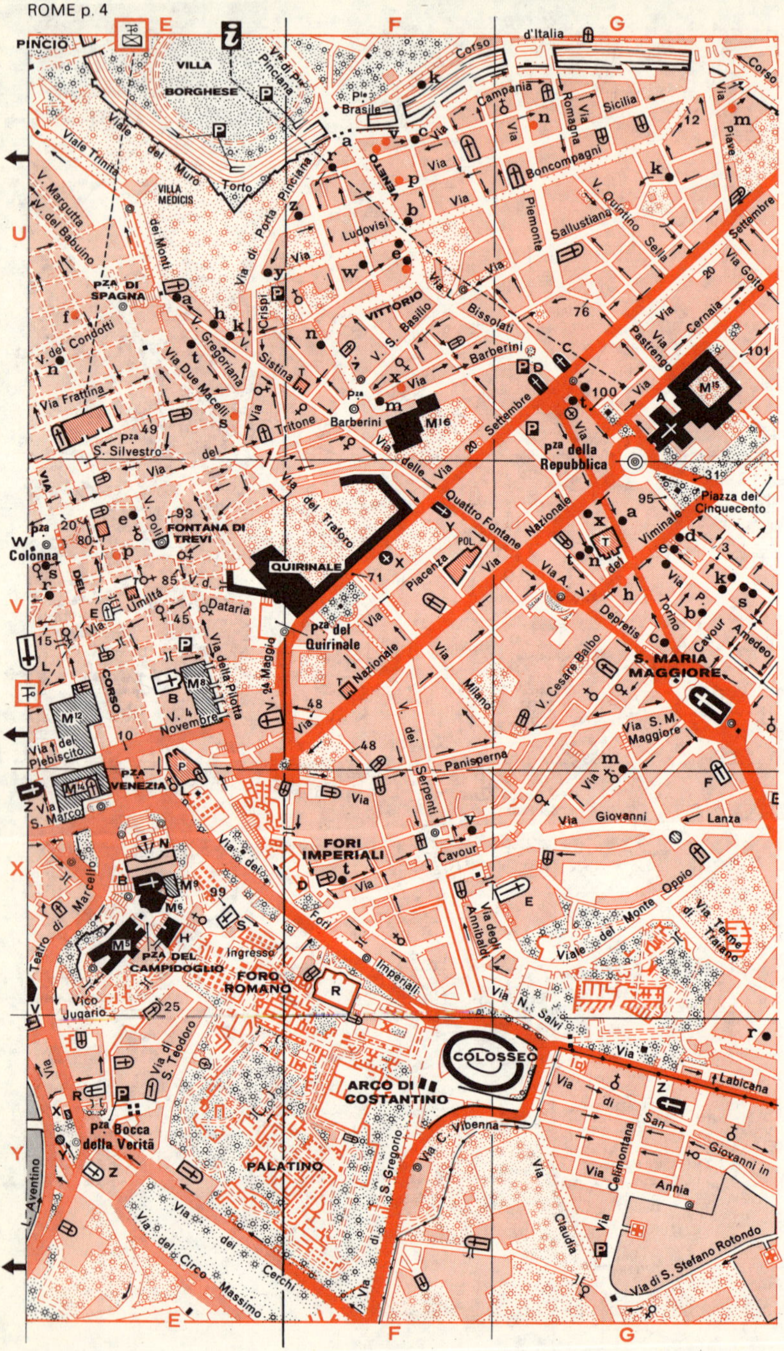

PINCIO
VILLA BORGHESE
VILLA MEDICIS
Viale Trinità
Viale del Muro Torto
V. Margutta
V. del Babuino
Pza DI SPAGNA
V. dei Condotti
Via Frattina
Pza S. Silvestro
Via Due Macelli
V. Gregoriana
Via Sistina
Via Crispi
Via di Porta Pinciana
Via Veneto
Via Ludovisi
Via Boncompagni
Via Sicilia
Via Campania
Via Romagna
Via Piemonte
Via Sallustiana
V. Quintino Sella
Via Piave
Corso d'Italia
Pte Brasile
Via Bissolati
Via S. Basilio
VITTORIO
Via Barberini
Pza Barberini
Via del Tritone
Via delle Quattro Fontane
Via XX Settembre
Via Pastrengo
Via Cernaia
Via Goito
Pza della Repubblica
Piazza dei Cinquecento
Via Viminale
Via Nazionale
FONTANA DI TREVI
QUIRINALE
Via del Traforo
Pza del Quirinale
Via Dataria
Via della Pilotta
V. 4 Novembre
V. 24 Maggio
Pza Colonna
Via del Corso
Via del Plebiscito
Pza VENEZIA
Via S. Marco
Via Piacenza
Via Milano
Via Depretis
Via Torino
Via Cavour
Via Amedeo
S. MARIA MAGGIORE
Via S. M. Maggiore
V. Cesare Balbo
Via Panisperna
V. dei Serpenti
Via Giovanni Lanza
FORI IMPERIALI
Via dei Fori Imperiali
Via degli Annibaldi
Viale del Monte Oppio
Via Terme di Traiano
Via N. Salvi
Via del Teatro di Marcello
Pza DEL CAMPIDOGLIO
FORO ROMANO
Ingresso
Vico Jugario
Via di S. Teodoro
COLOSSEO
ARCO DI COSTANTINO
Via Labicana
Via C. Vibenna
Via di S. Gregorio
Via Claudia
Via Celimontana
Via di S. Giovanni in Laterano
Via Annia
Via di S. Stefano Rotondo
PALATINO
Pza Bocca della Verità
Via del Circo Massimo
Via dei Cerchi
L. Aventino

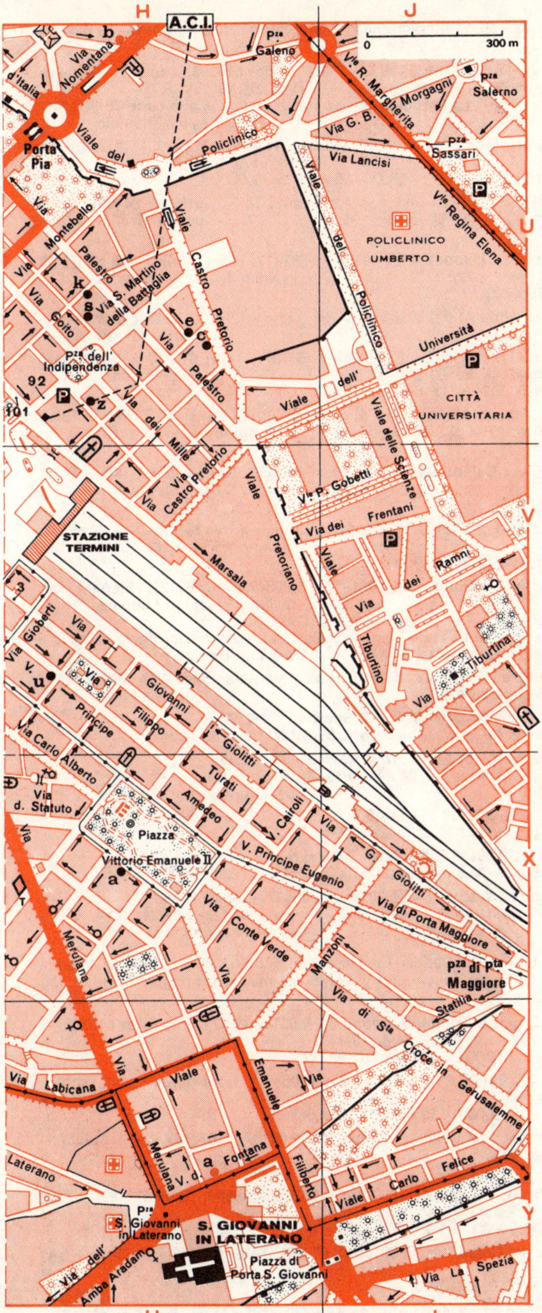

ROMA

ROMA ANTICA

ARCO DI COSTANTINO ★★★	FY	
BASILICA DI MASSENZIO ★★★	FX	R
COLONNA TRAIANA ★★★	EX	L
COLOSSEO ★★★	FGY	
FORI IMPERIALI ★★★	FX	
FORO ROMANO ★★★	EX	
PALATINO ★★★	EFY	
TEATRO DI MARCELLO ★★	EX	V
COLONNA DI MARCO AURELIO ★	EV	W
TEMPIO DELLA FORTUNA VIRILE ★	EY	X
TEMPIO DI VESTA ★	EY	Y

ROMA CRISTIANA

GESÙ ★★★	EX	Z
S. GIOVANNI IN LATERANO ★★★	HY	
S. MARIA MAGGIORE ★★★	GV	
S. ANDREA AL QUIRINALE ★★	FV	X
S. CARLO ALLE QUATTRO FONTANE ★★	FV	Y
S. CLEMENTE ★★	GY	Z
S. MARIA DEGLI ANGELI ★★	GU	A
S. MARIA D'ARACOELI ★★	EX	B
S. MARIA DELLA VITTORIA ★★	GU	C
S. SUSANNA ★★	GU	D
ORATORIO DEL CROCIFISSO ★	EV	E
S. IGNAZIO ★	EV	L
S. GIOVANNI DECOLLATO ★	EY	R
S. LUCA E S. MARTINA ★	EX	S
S. MARIA IN COSMEDIN ★	EY	Z
S. PIETRO IN VINCOLI ★	GX	E
S. PRASSEDE ★	GVX	F
SANTI APOSTOLI ★	EV	B

PALAZZI E MUSEI

MUSEO NAZIONALE ROMANO ★★★	GU	M15
MUSEO DEL PALAZZO DEI CONSERVATORI ★★★	EX	M5
PALAZZO NUOVO ★★★ : MUSEO CAPITOLINO ★★	EX	M6
PALAZZO SENATORIO ★★★	EX	H
PALAZZO BARBERINI ★★	FU	M16
PALAZZO DEL QUIRINALE ★★	EV	
GALLERIA DEL PALAZZO COLONNA ★	EV	M8
MUSEO DEL RISORGIMENTO ★	EX	M9
PALAZZO E GALLERIA DORIA PAMPHILI ★	EV	M12
PALAZZO VENEZIA ★	EX	M14

PASSEGGIATE

FONTANA DI TREVI ★★★	EV	
PIAZZA DEL CAMPIDOGLIO ★★★	EX	
MONUMENTO VITTORIO EMANUELE : ⋞ ★★	EX	N
PIAZZA DEL QUIRINALE ★★	FV	
PIAZZA DI SPAGNA ★★	EU	
VIA VITTORIO VENETO ★★	FU	
PIAZZA BOCCA DELLA VERITÀ ★	EY	
PIAZZA COLONNA ★	EV	
PIAZZA DI PORTA MAGGIORE ★	JX	
PIAZZA VENEZIA ★	EX	
PORTA PIA ★	HU	

Amendola (Via Giovanni)	GV	3
Battisti (Via Cesare)	EV	10
Calabria (Via)	GU	12
Caravita (Via del)	EV	15
Chigi (Largo)	EV	20
Consolazione (Via della)	EX	25
Einaudi (Viale Luigi)	GV	31
Lucchesi (Via dei)	EV	45
Mazzarino (Via)	FV	48
Mercede (Via della)	EU	49
Quirinale (Via del)	FV	71
Salandra (Via A.)	GU	76
S. Maria in Via (Via di)	EV	80
S. Vincenzo (Via di)	EV	85
Solferino (Via)	HU	92
Stamperia (Via della)	EV	93
Terme Diocleziano (Via)	GV	95
Tulliano (Via del)	EX	99
Vittorio Emanuele Orlando (Via)	GU	100
Volturno (Via)	GU	101

North area Monte Mario, Stadio Olimpico, via Flaminia-Parioli, Villa Borghese, via Salaria, via Nomentana (Plans : Rome pp. 2 to 5) :

Cavalieri Hilton, via Cadlolo 101 ⊠ 00136 𝒫 3151, Telex 610296, ≤ town, « Terraces and park », – AE E VISA. rest
M a la carte 49/75000 and rest. **La Pergola** *(closed 1 to 20 January)* a la carte 75/90000 – 20000 – **387 rm** 260/360000. by via Trionfale AU

Lord Byron, via De Notaris 5 ⊠ 00197 𝒫 3609541, Telex 611217, – AE E VISA. by lungotevere in Augusta DU
M see rest. Relais le Jardin below – 16500 – **50 rm** 275/380000.

Aldrovandi Palace Hotel without rest., via Aldrovandi 15 ⊠ 00197 𝒫 841091, Telex 616141, – AE VISA. by viale Trinità EU
139 rm 185/223000.

Borromini without rest., via Lisbona 7 ⊠ 00198 𝒫 841321, Telex 680485 – AE E VISA. by viale Regina Margherita JU
14000 – **75 rm** 155/195000.

Albani, without rest., via Adda 41 ⊠ 00198 𝒫 84991, Telex 612414 – – **157 rm** by via Piave GU

Parco dei Principi, via Frescobaldi 5 ⊠ 00198 𝒫 841071, Telex 610517, « Small park with » – AE VISA. rest by via Piemonte GU
M (residents only) 36000 – **203 rm** 170/250000.

Fleming without rest., piazza Monteleone di Spoleto 20 ⊠ 00191 𝒫 3276741, Telex 610640 – wc wc – AE VISA. by lungotevere in Augusta DU
270 rm 83/133000.

Panama without rest., via Salaria 336 ⊠ 00199 𝒫 862558, Telex 620189, – wc wc. by viale Regina Margherita JU
43 rm 78/132000, 10000.

Degli Aranci, via Oriani 11 ⊠ 00197 𝒫 870202, « Orange-grove terrace » – wc wc – AE. by lungotevere in Augusta DU
M 15/28000 – **47 rm** 80/110000 – P 95000.

Relais Le Jardin, via De Notaris 5 ⊠ 00197 𝒫 3609541, Telex 611217, Elegant rest. – AE E VISA. by lungotevere in Augusta DU
closed Sunday – **M** (booking essential) a la carte 58/103000
Spec. Ravioli con melanzane e scampi alla menta (April-June), Delizia di rombo con funghi porcini, Rognone di vitello alle bacche di ginepro e fegato d'oca. **Wines** Fiano di Avellino, Torre Ercolana.

Al Fogher, via Tevere 13/b ⊠ 00198 𝒫 857032, Typical Venetian rest. – AE.
closed Sunday – **M** a la carte 33/42000. by via Piave GU

Loreto, via Valenziani 19 ⊠ 00187 𝒫 4742454, Seafood – . GU **m**
closed Sunday and 10 to 28 August – **M** a la carte 33/51000.

Il Caminetto, viale dei Parioli 89 ⊠ 00197 𝒫 803946 – AE
closed Thursday and 12 to 18 August – **M** a la carte 24/34000. by lungotevere in Augusta DU

Da Paola, via Lanciani 77 ⊠ 00162 𝒫 8392452 by via Nomentana HU
closed Monday and August – **M** a la carte 25/35000.

Al Ceppo, via Panama 2 ⊠ 00198 𝒫 8449696, Typical rest. – AE VISA
closed Monday and August – **M** a la carte 23/37000. by viale Regina Margherita JU

Delle Vittorie, via Monte Santo 62/64 ⊠ 00195 𝒫 386847 – AE E VISA.
closed Sunday, 1 to 20 August and 23 December-3 January – **M** a la carte 24/35000. by via Marcantonio Colonna CU

Middle-western area San Pietro (Vatican City), Gianicolo, corso Vittorio Emanuele, piazza Venezia, Pantheon and Quirinale, Pincio and Villa Medici, piazza di Spagna, Palatino and Fori (Plans : Rome pp. 2 and 3) :

Hassler-Villa Medici, piazza Trinità dei Monti 6 ⊠ 00187 𝒫 6792651, Telex 610208, ≤ town from roof-garden rest. – . EU **a**
M a la carte 87/134000 – 20000 – **107 rm** 310/420000.

Eden, via Ludovisi 49 ⊠ 00187 𝒫 4743551, Telex 610567, « Roof-garden rest. with ≤ town » – . EU **y**
M a la carte 49/63000 – 12000 – **110 rm** 230/340000.

D'Inghilterra without rest., via Bocca di Leone 14 ⊠ 00187 𝒫 672161, Telex 614552 – AE E VISA. EU **n**
102 rm 200/270000.

Jolly Leonardo da Vinci, via dei Gracchi 324 ⊠ 00192 𝒫 39680, Telex 611182 – AE E VISA. rest CU **r**
M 40000 – **245 rm** 145/200000 – P 215000.

Plaza without rest., via del Corso 126 ⊠ 00186 𝒫 672101, Telex 624669 – AE E VISA. DU **d**
11500 – **207 rm** 116/179000, 10000.

Gd H. de la Ville, via Sistina 69 ⊠ 00187 𝒫 6733, Telex 620836 – – **189 rm**. EU **h**

Visconti Palace without rest., via Cesi 37 ✉ 00193 ✆ 3684, Telex 680407 – AE E VISA. CU u
247 rm 160/220000.

Cicerone, via Cicerone 55 ✉ 00193 ✆ 3576, Telex 680514 – AE E VISA. CU t
M a la carte 30/46000 – **237 rm** 165/240000 – P 173/218000.

Colonna Palace without rest., piazza Montecitorio 12 ✉ 00186 ✆ 6781341, Telex 621467 – AE E VISA. DV s
12000 – **100 rm** 145/190000.

Giulio Cesare without rest., via degli Scipioni 287 ✉ 00192 ✆ 310244, Telex 613010 – P – AE VISA. CU s
22000 – **86 rm** 170/245000.

Atlante, via Vitelleschi 34 ✉ 00193 ✆ 6564196, Telex 680258, « Roof-garden rest. with ← St. Peter's Basilica » – rm. AE E VISA BU r
M *(closed January-February)* a la carte 46/65000 – **61 rm** 230/290000.

Delle Nazioni without rest., via Poli 7 ✉ 00187 ✆ 6792441, Telex 614193 – AE E VISA. EV e
74 rm 165/245000.

Gregoriana without rest., via Gregoriana 18 ✉ 00187 ✆ 6794269 – wc wc EU t
19 rm 90/150000.

Garden Atlante without rest., via Crescenzio 78/a ✉ 00193 ✆ 3598884 – wc wc. AE E VISA BU f
43 rm 230/290000.

Columbus, via della Conciliazione 33 ✉ 00193 ✆ 6565435, Telex 620096, « Beautiful decor in 15C style building » – wc wc P – AE E VISA. rest
M a la carte 36/50000 – **107 rm** 95/135000 – P 125/150000. BV m

Internazionale without rest., via Sistina 79 ✉ 00187 ✆ 6793047, Telex 614333 – wc wc. AE E VISA. EU k
38 rm 115/180000.

Gerber without rest., via degli Scipioni 241 ✉ 00192 ✆ 3595148 – wc wc. AE VISA. BU s
28 rm 54/90000.

Della Torre Argentina without rest., corso Vittorio Emanuele 102 ✉ 00186 ✆ 6548251 – wc wc. AE VISA. DX e
32 rm 66/109000.

Senato without rest., piazza della Rotonda 73 ✉ 00186 ✆ 6793231, ← Pantheon – wc wc. DV y
48 rm 91000.

Mozart without rest., via dei Greci 23/b ✉ 00187 ✆ 6787422 – wc wc. AE E VISA. DU h
31 rm 62/100000.

Adriano without rest., via di Pallacorda 2 ✉ 00186 ✆ 6542451 – wc wc. DV c
7000 – **82 rm** 52/90000.

Cesàri without rest., via di Pietra 89/a ✉ 00186 ✆ 6792386 – wc. AE E VISA EV r
7000 – **50 rm** 60/75000.

XXXX Hostaria dell'Orso, via Monte Brianzo 93 ✉ 00186 ✆ 6564250, Elegant rest. - night club, « Building and decorations in 15C style » – CV n
dinner only (booking essential).

XXXX ✲ **El Toulà,** via della Lupa 29 ✉ 00186 ✆ 6781196, Elegant rest. – AE E VISA.
closed Saturday lunch, Sunday, August and 24 to 26 December – **M** (booking essential) a la carte 42/56000 (15%) DU e
Spec. Risotto al nero di seppia, Rombo alle mandorle, Radicchio di Treviso ai ferri. **Wines** Sauvignon del Collio, Refosco.

XXX **Passetto,** via Zanardelli 14 ✉ 00186 ✆ 6543696 – AE VISA. CV v
closed Sunday – **M** a la carte 36/58000.

XXX **Ranieri,** via Mario de' Fiori 26 ✉ 00187 ✆ 6791592 – AE E VISA EU f
closed Sunday – **M** (booking essential) a la carte 32/64000.

XXX **4 Colonne,** via della Posta 4 ✉ 00186 ✆ 6547152 – DV n
closed Sunday and 5 to 31 August – **M** (booking essential) a la carte 35/47000.

XX ✲ **Piperno,** Monte de' Cenci 9 ✉ 00186 ✆ 6540629, Roman rest. – DX d
closed Sunday dinner, Monday, Easter, August and 23 December-2 January – **M** a la carte 33/56000
Spec. Pasta e ceci, Filetti di baccalà con fritto vegetariano, Coda alla vaccinara, Agnello al forno. **Wines** Frascati, Rosso Tapino.

XX **Mastrostefano,** piazza Navona 94 ✉ 00186 ✆ 6541669, Rest.-American bar, « Outdoor service in Summer with ← Bernini fountain » – DV d

XX **Taverna Giulia,** vicolo dell'Oro 23 ✉ 00186 ☎ 6569768, Ligurian rest. – ▤. AE ⓓ
closed Sunday and August – **M** (booking essential) a la carte 31/47000 (15%). BV **a**

XX **Dal Bolognese,** piazza del Popolo 1 ✉ 00187 ☎ 3611426, Bolognese rest., « Collection of paintings » – ▤. AE ⓓ. ✻ DU **z**
closed Sunday dinner, Monday, 6 to 28 August and 23 December-2 January – **M** a la carte 31/48000.

XX **Eau Vive,** via Monterone 85 ✉ 00186 ☎ 6541095, Catholic missionaries; international cuisine, « 16C building » – ▤. AE. ✻ DV **f**
closed Sunday and August – **M** (booking essential) a la carte 22/36000.

XX **La Maiella,** piazza Sant'Apollinare 45/46 ✉ 00186 ☎ 6564174, Abruzzi rest. – ▤. AE ⓓ E VISA. ✻ CDV **x**
closed Sunday and 10 to 20 August – **M** a la carte 37/49000.

XX **Nuovo Calafuria,** viale Tiziano 91 ✉ 00196 ☎ 3962377 – AE ⓓ E VISA. ✻
closed Monday – **M** a la carte 29/42000 (15%). by lungotevere in Augusta DU

X ✿ **La Rosetta,** via della Rosetta 9 ✉ 00187 ☎ 6561002, Sicilian and seafood trattoria – ▤. AE ⓓ DV **e**
closed Sunday, Monday lunch and August – **M** 60000 (15%)
Spec. Tonnarelle con capesante e basilico, Rombo in salsa di ostriche, Spigola o salmone in salsa. **Wines** Jerman.

X **Al 59,** via Brunetti 59 ✉ 00186 ☎ 3619019, Bolognese rest. – ▤. ✻ DU **y**
closed August, Sunday and Saturday from June-July – **M** a la carte 29/48000.

X **Al Salanova,** via Florida 23 ✉ 00186 ☎ 6561409 – AE ⓓ E VISA. ✻ DX **v**
closed Monday, 4 to 20 January and 4 to 20 September – **M** a la carte 24/46000 (10%).

X **Al Moro,** vicolo delle Bollette 13 ✉ 00187 ☎ 6783495, Roman trattoria – ▤. ✻ EV **p**
closed Sunday and August – **M** (booking essential) a la carte 32/68000.

X **La Cantinella,** via Crispi 19 ✉ 00187 ☎ 6795069, Habitués' trattoria with Sardinian specialities – ▤. AE ⓓ E VISA. ✻ EU **s**
closed Wednesday and August – **M** a la carte 20/33000.

Central eastern area via Vittorio Veneto, via Nazionale, Viminale, Santa Maria Maggiore, Colosseum, Porta Pia, via Nomentana, Stazione Termini, Porta San Giovanni (Plans : Rome pp. 4 and 5) :

🏨🏨🏨🏨🏨 **Le Grand Hotel,** via Vittorio Emanuele Orlando 3 ✉ 00185 ☎ 4709, Telex 610210 – ⧉ ▤ TV ☎ ♿ – 🏛. AE ⓓ E VISA. ✻ GU **t**
M a la carte 70/110000 – ☕ 20000 – **160 rm** 325/461000.

🏨🏨🏨🏨🏨 Excelsior, via Vittorio Veneto 125 ✉ 00187 ☎ 4708, Telex 610232 – ⧉ ▤ TV ☎ – 🏛 FU **b**
363 rm.

🏨🏨🏨🏨 **Ambasciatori Palace,** via Vittorio Veneto 70 ✉ 00187 ☎ 473831, Telex 610241 – ⧉ ▤ TV ☎ ♿ – 🏛. AE ⓓ E VISA FU **e**
M rest. see Grill Bar ABC below – ☕ 18000 – **145 rm** 236/378000.

🏨🏨🏨🏨 **Bernini Bristol,** piazza Barberini 23 ✉ 00187 ☎ 463051, Telex 610554 – ⧉ ▤ TV ☎ ♿ – 🏛. AE ⓓ E. ✻ FU **m**
M *(closed Sunday dinner and Monday)* a la carte 42/71000 – ☕ 15000 – **125 rm** 250/350000.

🏨🏨🏨🏨 **Jolly Vittorio Veneto,** corso d'Italia 1 ✉ 00198 ☎ 8495, Telex 612293 – ⧉ ▤ TV ☎ 🚗 – 🏛. AE ⓓ E VISA. ✻ rest FU **k**
M 40000 – **200 rm** ☕ 160/220000 – P 228000.

🏨🏨🏨🏨 **Regina Carlton,** via Vittorio Veneto 72 ✉ 00187 ☎ 476851, Telex 620863 – ⧉ ▤. AE ⓓ E VISA. ✻ FU **e**
M a la carte 40/60000 – ☕ 11000 – **134 rm** 155/220000 – P 195/240000.

🏨🏨🏨🏨 **Mediterraneo,** via Cavour 15 ✉ 00184 ☎ 464051 – ⧉ ▤ TV ☎ – 🏛. AE ⓓ E VISA. ✻
M *(closed Friday and Saturday)* 29000 – **272 rm** ☕ 157/224000. GV **k**

🏨🏨🏨 **Victoria,** via Campania 41 ✉ 00187 ☎ 473931, Telex 610212 – ⧉ ▤ ☎ ♿. AE E. ✻ rest
M a la carte 31/51000 – **110 rm** ☕ 130/230000. FU **c**

🏨🏨🏨 **Genova** without rest., via Cavour 33 ✉ 00184 ☎ 476951, Telex 621599 – ⧉ ▤ TV ☎ ♿. AE ⓓ VISA. ✻ GV **b**
91 rm ☕ 190/254000.

🏨🏨🏨 **Londra e Cargill,** piazza Sallustio 18 ✉ 00187 ☎ 473871, Telex 680412 – ⧉ ▤ TV ☎ 🚗 – 🏛. AE ⓓ. ✻ GU **k**
M 35/40000 – **105 rm** ☕ 155/215000 – P 170/180000.

🏨🏨🏨 **Massimo D'Azeglio,** via Cavour 18 ✉ 00184 ☎ 460646, Telex 610556 – ⧉ ▤ TV ☎ – 🏛. AE ⓓ E VISA. ✻ GV **s**
M *(closed Sunday)* 29000 – **210 rm** ☕ 135/192000.

🏨🏨🏨 **Quirinale,** via Nazionale 7 ✉ 00184 ☎ 4707, Telex 610332 – ⧉ ▤ ☎ ♿. AE ⓓ E. ✻
M 35/40000 – **193 rm** ☕ 160/220000 – P 240000. GV **x**

🏨🏨🏨 **Forum,** via Tor de' Conti 25 ✉ 00184 ☎ 6792446, Telex 622549, « Roof-garden rest. with ≤ Imperial Forums » – ⧉ ▤ ☎ 🚗 – 🏛. AE ⓓ E VISA. ✻ FX **t**
M *(closed Sunday)* a la carte 60/98000 – ☕ 15000 – **81 rm** 180/250000.

Eliseo, via di Porta Pinciana 30 ✉ 00187 ℘ 460556, Telex 610693, « Roof-garden rest. with ≤ Villa Borghese » – 🛗 ▤ TV ☎ – 🏛. AE ⓓ E VISA. ※ FU r
M 37000 – **50 rm** ☕ 145/222000.

P.L.M. Etap Boston, via Lombardia 47 ✉ 00187 ℘ 473951, Telex 680460 – 🛗 ▤ ☎ ♿. AE ⓓ E. ※ rest FU z
M 27000 – **121 rm** ☕ 135/215000 – P 162000.

Imperiale, via Vittorio Veneto 24 ✉ 00187 ℘ 4756351, Telex 621071 – 🛗 ▤ ☎ ♿. AE ⓓ E VISA. ※ FU n
M 35000 – **84 rm** ☕ 135/198000 – P 169/205000.

Napoleon, piazza Vittorio Emanuele 105 ✉ 00185 ℘ 737646, Telex 611069 – 🛗 ▤ – 🏛. AE ⓓ E VISA. ※ HX a
M (residents only) (closed lunch) 22/25000 – ☕ 10000 – **80 rm** 80/125000.

San Giorgio without rest., via Amendola 61 ✉ 00185 ℘ 4751341 – 🛗 ▤ TV. AE ⓓ E VISA. ※ GV s
186 rm ☕ 116/166000.

Mondial without rest., via Torino 127 ✉ 00184 ℘ 472861, Telex 612219 – 🛗 ▤ TV ☎ ♿. AE E. ※ GV a
☕ 12000 – **77 rm** 120/175000.

Atlantico without rest., via Cavour 23 ✉ 00184 ℘ 485951 – 🛗 ▤ TV ☎. AE ⓓ E VISA. ※ GV k
83 rm ☕ 116/166000.

Universo, via Principe Amedeo 5 ✉ 00185 ℘ 476811, Telex 610342 – 🛗 ▤ ♿ – 🏛. AE ⓓ E. ※ GV e
M *(closed Saturday dinner)* 31000 – **206 rm** ☕ 125/187000 – P 146000.

Commodore without rest., via Torino 1 ✉ 00184 ℘ 485656, Telex 612170 – 🛗 ▤ ☎ ♿. AE ⓓ E VISA. ※ GV c
☕ 10000 – **65 rm** 90/140000.

La Residenza without rest., via Emilia 22 ✉ 00187 ℘ 6799592 – 🛗 ▤ TV 🛁wc 🚿wc ☎ Ⓟ FU w
27 rm ☕ 78/122000.

Britannia without rest., via Napoli 64 ✉ 00184 ℘ 463153, Telex 611292 – 🛗 ▤ 🛁wc 🚿wc ☎ Ⓟ. AE ⓓ E VISA GV t
32 rm ☕ 105/165000.

Diana, via Principe Amedeo 4 ✉ 00185 ℘ 4751541, Telex 611198 – 🛗 ▤ rest 🛁wc 🚿wc ☎. AE E VISA. ※ rest GV e
M (residents only) 24000 – ☕ 8500 – **187 rm** 63/104000.

Nord-Nuova Roma without rest., via Amendola 3 ✉ 00185 ℘ 465441 – 🛗 ▤ 🛁wc 🚿wc ☎ ♿. AE ⓓ E VISA. ※ GV d
156 rm ☕ 86/130000.

Sitea without rest., via Vittorio Emanuele Orlando 90 ✉ 00185 ℘ 4751560, Telex 614163 – 🛗 ▤ 🛁wc 🚿wc ☎. AE ⓓ E GU t
37 rm ☕ 115/180000.

Milani without rest., via Magenta 12 ✉ 00185 ℘ 4940051, Telex 614356 – 🛗 🛁wc 🚿wc ☎. ※ HU z
78 rm ☕ 71/112000.

Alpi without rest., via Castelfidardo 84/a ✉ 00185 ℘ 464618, Telex 611677 – 🛗 ▤ 🛁wc ☎. AE ⓓ E VISA. ※ HU s
46 rm ☕ 65/103000, ▤ 5000.

Galles without rest., viale Castro Pretorio 66 ✉ 00185 ℘ 4954741, Telex 622041 – 🛗 ▤ 🛁wc 🚿wc ☎ ♿. AE ⓓ E VISA. ※ HU c
45 rm ☕ 62/99000, ▤ 6000.

Edera 🌿 without rest., via Poliziano 75 ✉ 00184 ℘ 738355, Telex 621472, 🌳 – 🛗 🛁wc 🚿wc ☎ Ⓟ. AE ⓓ E VISA. ※ GY r
38 rm ☕ 88/130000.

Siviglia without rest., via Gaeta 12 ✉ 00185 ℘ 4750004, Telex 612225 – 🛗 🛁wc 🚿wc ☎. AE ⓓ VISA. ※ HU k
41 rm ☕ 69/107000.

Colosseum without rest., via Sforza 10 ✉ 00184 ℘ 4751228 – 🛗 🚿wc ☎. AE ⓓ E VISA GVX m
50 rm ☕ 54/93000.

Igea without rest., via Principe Amedeo 97 ✉ 00185 ℘ 7311212 – 🛗 🚿wc ☎. ※ HV u
☕ 5000 – **42 rm** 35/55000.

Centro without rest., via Firenze 12 ✉ 00184 ℘ 464142, Telex 612125 – 🛗 ▤ 🛁wc 🚿wc ☎. AE ⓓ VISA. ※ GV n
36 rm ☕ 70/102000.

Canada without rest., via Vicenza 58 ✉ 00185 ℘ 4957385, Telex 613037 – 🛗 ▤ 🛁wc 🚿wc ☎. AE ⓓ E VISA. ※ HU e
48 rm ☕ 77/112000, ▤ 8000.

Alba without rest., via Leonina 12 ✉ 00184 ℘ 484471 – 🛗 🛁wc 🚿wc ☎ ♿ – 🏛. AE ⓓ E VISA FX v
25 rm ☕ 45/65000.

XXXX ✿ **Sans Souci,** via Sicilia 20/24 ✉ 00187 ✆ 493504, Elegant tavern, late night dinners – ▤. AE ◑ E VISA. ✻ FU p
closed Monday and August – **M** (dinner only) (booking essential) a la carte 55/92000
Spec. I nostri risotti, Filetti di sogliola al Berlucchi e fragole, Medaglioni di vitella al tartufo nero di Norcia.
Wines Sauvignon del Collio, Rubesco.

XXX **Grill Bar ABC,** via Vittorio Veneto 66 ✉ 00187 ✆ 4740950, Elegant rest. – ▤. AE ◑ E VISA. ✻ – **M** (booking essential) a la carte 50/78000. FU e

XXX **Harry's Bar,** via Vittorio Veneto 150 ✉ 00187 ✆ 4745832 – AE ◑. ✻ FU a
M (booking essential) a la carte 42/71000.

XX **Cesarina,** via Piemonte 109 ✉ 00187 ✆ 460828, Bolognese rest. – ▤. AE ◑ VISA. ✻
closed Sunday – **M** a la carte 30/48000. GU n

XX **Leon d'Oro,** via Cagliari 25 ✉ 00198 ✆ 861847, Seafood – ▤. AE ◑ E. ✻
closed Sunday – **M** a la carte 32/57000. by viale Regina Margherita JU

XX **Andrea,** via Sardegna 28 ✉ 00187 ✆ 493707 – ▤. AE ◑ E VISA FU v
closed Sunday and 5 to 25 August – **M** (booking essential) a la carte 35/55000.

XX ✿ **Girarrosto Toscano,** via Campania 29 ✉ 00187 ✆ 493759, Modern tavern – ▤. AE ◑ VISA. ✻ FU v
closed Wednesday – **M** a la carte 36/55000
Spec. Antipasto misto della Casa, Trittico di paste fresche, Bistecca alla fiorentina, Crostate ai frutti di bosco. Wines Frascati, Chianti.

X **Tullio,** via di San Nicola da Tolentino 26 ✉ 00187 ✆ 4758564, Tuscan trattoria – ▤. AE ◑ VISA. ✻ – *closed Sunday and August* – **M** a la carte 26/43000. FU x

X **La Matriciana,** via del Viminale 40/44 ✉ 00184 ✆ 461775 – ▤. AE ◑ VISA GV h
closed Saturday and 11 to 16 August – **M** a la carte 22/33000.

X **Cannavota,** piazza San Giovanni in Laterano 20 ✉ 00184 ✆ 775007, Roman trattoria – AE ◑. ✻ HY a
closed Wednesday and 1 to 20 August – **M** a la carte 20/35000.

X **Costa Balena,** via Messina 5/7 ✉ 00198 ✆ 857686, Seafood trattoria – ▤. AE ◑ E VISA. ✻ – *closed Sunday and August* – **M** a la carte 28/43000. HU b

Southern area Aventino, Porta San Paolo, Terme di Caracalla, via Appia Nuova (Plans : Rome pp. 2 to 5) :

Santa Prisca, largo Manlio Gelsomini 25 ✉ 00153 ✆ 571917 – ▤ ▤ rest ⋔wc ☎ Ⓟ
45 rm. by lungotevere Aventino DEY

Villa San Pio without rest., via di Sant'Anselmo 19 ✉ 00153 ✆ 5755231, ⚘ – ▤ ⌂wc ⋔wc ☎ ♿. ✻ – **59 rm** ⊒ 52/75000. by lungotevere Aventino DEY

Domus Maximi ⊗ without rest., via Santa Prisca 11/b ✉ 00153 ✆ 5782565 – ⌂wc ⋔wc ☎. ✻ – **21 rm** ⊒ 55/82000. by via del Circo Massimo EY

Sant'Anselmo without rest., piazza Sant'Anselmo 2 ✉ 00153 ✆ 573547 – ⌂wc ☎ ♿. ✻ – **26 rm** ⊒ 51/75000. by lungotevere Aventino DY

XX **Severino,** piazza Zama 5/c ✉ 00183 ✆ 7550872 – ▤. AE ◑ VISA
closed Sunday dinner, Monday, 1 to 22 August and 24 to 30 December –
M a la carte 33/47000. by via dell'Amba Aradam HY

XX **Apuleius,** via Tempio di Diana 15 ✉ 00153 ✆ 572160, « Ancient Rome style decor tavern » – AE. ✻ by via del Circo Massimo EY
closed Sunday and 13 to 28 August – **M** a la carte 27/44000.

Trastevere area (typical district) (Plan : Rome p. 3) :

XX ✿ **Alberto Ciarla,** piazza San Cosimato 40 ✉ 00153 ✆ 5818668 – ▤. AE ◑ VISA. ✻
closed Sunday, 5 to 25 August and 23 December-10 January – **M** (dinner only) (booking essential) a la carte 45/62000 CY u
Spec. Insalate di pesce crudo, Zuppa di pasta e fagioli ai frutti di mare, Filetti di spigola alle mandorle.
Wines Jerman.

XX **Corsetti-il Galeone,** piazza San Cosimato 27 ✉ 00153 ✆ 5816311, Typical seafood – ▤. AE ◑ E VISA. ✻ CY g
closed Wednesday and 2 to 26 July – **M** a la carte 23/42000.

XX Sabatini a Santa Maria in Trastevere, piazza di Santa Maria in Trastevere 10 ✉ 00153 ✆ 582026, Roman and seafood rest. CY n

XX **Galeassi,** piazza di Santa Maria in Trastevere 3 ✉ 00153 ✆ 5803775, Roman and seafood rest. – ▤. AE ◑ E VISA. ✻ CY f
closed Monday and 20 December-20 January – **M** a la carte 23/42000.

XX **Checco er Carettiere,** via Benedetta 10 ✉ 00153 ✆ 5817018, Typical Roman and seafood rest. – ▤ CX k
closed Sunday dinner, Monday and 10 August-1 September – **M** a la carte 26/41000.

XX **Taverna Trilussa,** via del Politeama 23 ✉ 00153 ✆ 5818918, Typical Roman rest. – ▤. AE ◑ VISA CY h
closed Sunday dinner, Monday and 30 July-28 August – **M** a la carte 20/31000.

X **Romolo,** via di Porta Settimiana 8 ✉ 00153 ✆ 5818284, Typical trattoria, « Summer service in a cool little court-yard » – AE VISA CX a
closed Monday and August – **M** a la carte 32/47000.

Outskirts of Rome

on national road 1 - Aurelia :

Villa Pamphili, via della Nocetta 105 ✉ 00164 ☎ 5862, Telex 611675, (covered in winter), – . AE E VISA. rest — by via Garibaldi BY
M 38000 – **253 rm** 115/170000.

Holiday Inn St. Peter's, via Aurelia Antica 415 ✉ 00165 ☎ 5872, Telex 625434, – . AE E VISA. rest — by via Garibaldi BY
M a la carte 38/44000 – 10000 – **330 rm** 130/190000.

MotelAgip, ✉ 00163 ☎ 6379001, Telex 613699, – wc – . AE E VISA. — by via Aurelia AV
M 22/25000 – **222 rm** 63/99000.

La Maielletta, via Aurelia Antica 270 ✉ 00165 ☎ 6374957, Typical Abruzzi rest. – . AE — by via Aurelia AV
closed Monday – **M** a la carte 26/41000.

on the Ancient Appian way :

Cecilia Metella, via Appia Antica 125/127 ✉ 00179 ☎ 5136743, « Shaded garden » – . AE. — by via Claudia GY
closed Monday – **M** a la carte 25/36000.

Quo Vadis, via Appia Antica 38 ✉ 00179 ☎ 5136795, – . .
closed Tuesday and 2 to 22 August – **M** (lunch only) a la carte 28/42000. — by via Claudia GY

on via Cristoforo Colombo :

Caravel, without rest., via Colombo 124/c ✉ 00147 ☎ 5115046 – wc wc — by via Claudia GY
83 rm.

to E.U.R. Garden City :

Sheraton, viale del Pattinaggio ✉ 00144 ☎ 5453, Telex 614223, – – . AE E VISA. — by via di San Gregorio FY
M a la carte 41/82000 – **615 rm** 221/307000.

Shangri Là-Corsetti, viale Algeria 141 ✉ 00144 ☎ 5916441, Telex 614664, heated, – – . AE E VISA. — by via di San Gregorio FY
M a la carte 23/42000 – 9000 – **52 rm** 120/170000.

Dei Congressi without rest., viale Shakespeare 29 ✉ 00144 ☎ 5926021, Telex 614140 – – . AE E. — by via di San Gregorio FY
96 rm 100/130000.

Vecchia America-Corsetti, piazza Marconi 32 ✉ 00144 ☎ 5926601, Typical rest. and ale house – . AE E VISA — by via di San Gregorio FY
closed Tuesday – **M** a la carte 23/39000.

on the motorway to Fiumicino close to the ring-road :

Holiday Inn-Parco dei Medici, viale Castello della Magliana 65 ✉ 00148 ☎ 5475, Telex 613302, – – . AE E VISA.
M 36000 – 13000 – **324 rm** 133/189000 – P 218000. — by viale Trastevere CY

FLORENCE (FIRENZE) 50100 P 988 ⑮ – pop. 440 910 alt. 49 – ☎ 055.

See : Monuments of Piazza del Duomo*** : Cathedral** (exterior of the apse***, dome*** : ※** – bell tower** (※**) – Baptistry** (doors***, mosaics***) – Museum of the Cathedral building and its possessions** (Pietà** by Michelangelo, choristers' tribunes*** by Luca della Robbia and Donatello, bas-reliefs** from the bell tower) – Uffizi Gallery*** (Botticelli room***) – Piazza della Signoria** : Palazzo Vecchio*** (cabinet**) – Loggia della Signoria** (Perseus*** by B. Cellini) – Ponte Vecchio* – Pitti Palace** : Palatine Gallery** (collection*** of Titian and Raphael) – The Bargello Palace and museum** (courtyard**, works by Donatello***) – Museum of St. Mark** (works by Fra Angelico***) – Academy Gallery** (works by Michelangelo***) – San Lorenzo** : church*, Laurentian Library**, Medici chapels** (Medici tombs***) – Santa Maria Novella** : church* (frescoes*** of the chapel by Domenico Ghirlandaio, Crucifix** by Brunelleschi); Spaniard's chapel (frescoes**) – Santa Croce** : church* (interior** : bas relief of the Annunciation* by Donatello, frescoes by Giotto depicting the life of St. Francesco**) ; Pazzi chapel** – Medici Riccardi Palace** (frescoes*** by Benozzo Gozzoli, Luca Giordano Gallery**) – Strozzi Palace** BY F – Trip to the Hills** : from Piazzale Michelangiolo ※**; church of San Miniato al Monte** DZ – Boboli Garden*, ※** from the Citadel Belvedere ABZ – Orsanmichele* (tabernacle** by Orcagna) BCY G – Church of Santa Maria del Carmine : frescoes** by Masaccio AY Z.

18 Dell'Ugolino (closed Monday), to Grassina ✉ 50015 ☎ 2051009, S : 12 km.

Galileo Galilei of Pisa to ⑦ : 95 km ☎ (050) 28088 – Alitalia, lungarno Acciaiuoli 10/12, ✉ 30123 ☎ 263051.

via Manzoni 16 ✉ 50121 ☎ 678841 – via de' Tornabuoni 15 ✉ 50123 ☎ 216544, Telex 572263.

A.C.I. viale Amendola 36 ✉ 50121 ☎ 27841, Telex 571202.

Roma 277 ③ – Bologna 105 ⑧ – Milano 298 ⑧.

FIRENZE

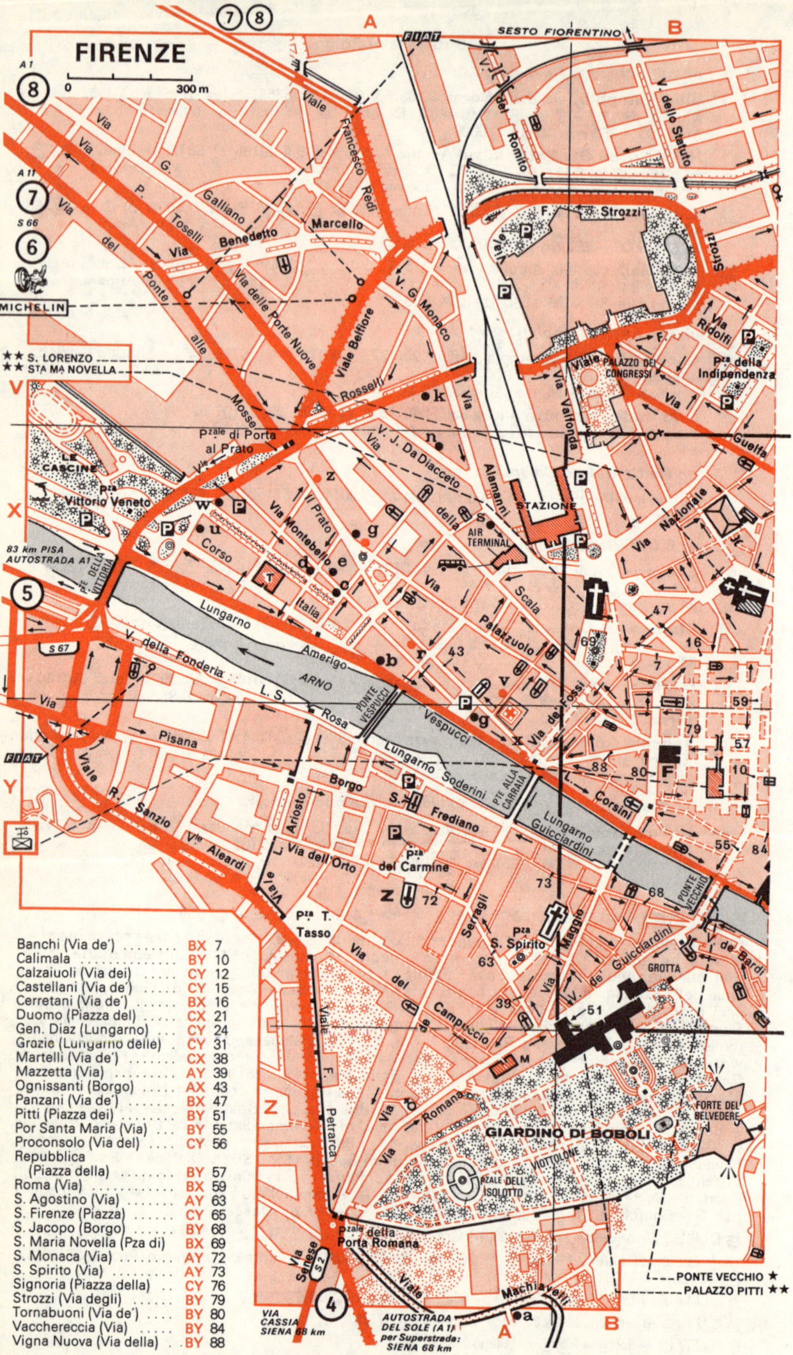

Banchi (Via de')	BX	7
Calimala	BY	10
Calzaiuoli (Via dei)	CY	12
Castellani (Via de')	CY	15
Cerretani (Via de')	BX	16
Duomo (Piazza del)	CX	21
Gen. Diaz (Lungarno)	CY	24
Grazie (Lungarno delle)	CY	31
Martelli (Via de')	CX	38
Mazzetta (Via)	AY	39
Ognissanti (Borgo)	AX	43
Panzani (Via de')	BX	47
Pitti (Piazza dei)	BY	51
Por Santa Maria (Via)	BY	55
Proconsolo (Via del)	CY	56
Repubblica (Piazza della)	BY	57
Roma (Via)	BX	59
S. Agostino (Via)	AY	63
S. Firenze (Piazza)	CY	65
S. Jacopo (Borgo)	BY	68
S. Maria Novella (Pza di)	BX	69
S. Monaca (Via)	AY	72
S. Spirito (Via)	AY	73
Signoria (Piazza della)	CY	76
Strozzi (Via degli)	BY	79
Tornabuoni (Via de')	BY	80
Vacchereccia (Via)	BY	84
Vigna Nuova (Via della)	BY	88

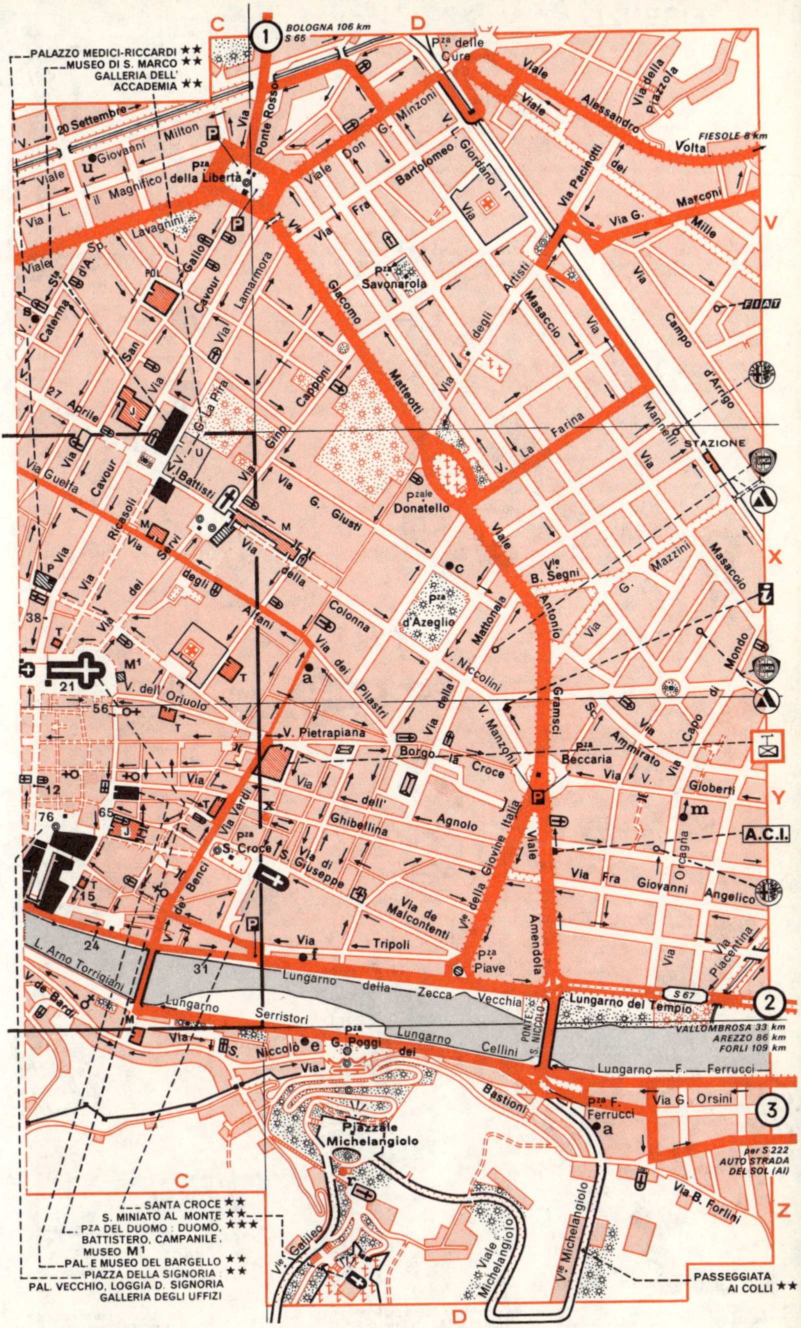

C
D
BOLOGNA 106 km
S 65
PALAZZO MEDICI-RICCARDI ★★
MUSEO DI S. MARCO ★★
GALLERIA DELL' ACCADEMIA ★★
Pza delle Cure
Viale Alessandro Volta
Via della Piazzola
FIESOLE 8 km
Ponte Rosso
Pza della Libertà
Viale Don G. Minzoni
V. L. Giordano
Via Bartolomeo
Viale Giovanni Milton
20 Settembre
Viale il Magnifico
Lavagnini
Via Pacinotti
Via G. Marconi
Mille
Via Fra
Pza Savonarola
Viale Giacomo Matteotti
Via degli Artisti
Masaccio
Via Campo d'Arrigo
FIAT
Via Cavour
Via Lamarmora
Via S. Caterina
Via San Gallo
27 Aprile
G. La Pira
Gino Capponi
La Farina
Mannelli
STAZIONE
V. Battisti
Via Guelfa
Via Ricasoli
Via dei Servi
Via G. Giusti
Pzale Donatello
Viale Antonio
Vle B. Segni
Mazzini
Masaccio
Via degli Alfani
Via della Colonna
Pza d'Azeglio
Via dei Pilastri
Mattonaia
V. Niccolini
Via Capo di Mondo
V. dell' Oriuolo
V. Pietrapiana
Borgo la Croce
V. Manzoni
Via della
Gramsci
Pza Beccaria
Via V. Gioberti
Via Ammirato
Via dell' Agnolo
Ghibellina
Via Verdi
Pza S. Croce
Via di S. Giuseppe
Viale della Giovine Italia
Viale Amendola
Via Orcagna
A.C.I.
Via Fra Giovanni Angelico
Via de' Benci
Via de Malcontenti
Via Tripoli
Pza Piave
Via Piacentina
L. Arno Torrigiani
V. de Bardi
Lungarno della Zecca Vecchia
Lungarno del Tempio
S 67
VALLOMBROSA 33 km
AREZZO 86 km
FORLI 109 km
Lungarno Serristori
Pza G. Poggi
Lungarno Cellini
PONTE S. NICCOLÒ
Via S. Niccolò
Via dei Bastioni
Lungarno F. Ferrucci
Pza F. Ferrucci
Via G. Orsini
per S 222
AUTO STRADA DEL SOL (A1)
Piazzale Michelangiolo
Viale Michelangiolo
Vle Galileo
Via B. Forlini
SANTA CROCE ★★
S. MINIATO AL MONTE ★★
PZA DEL DUOMO : DUOMO, BATTISTERO, CAMPANILE, MUSEO M1 ★★★
PAL. E MUSEO DEL BARGELLO ★★
PIAZZA DELLA SIGNORIA : PAL. VECCHIO, LOGGIA D. SIGNORIA GALLERIA DEGLI UFFIZI ★★
PASSEGGIATA AI COLLI ★★
V
X
Y
Z
1
2
3

FIRENZE

Calimala ..... BY 10
Calzaiuoli (Via dei) ..... CY
Guicciardini (Via) ..... BY
Ponte Vecchio ..... BY
Por Santa Maria (Via) ..... BY 55
Porta Rossa (Via) ..... BY
Roma (Via) ..... BXY
S. Jacopo (Borgo) ..... BY
Strozzi (Via degli) ..... BY
Tornabuoni (Via de') ..... BXY

Archibusieri (Lungarno degli) ..... BY 4
Avelli (Via degli) ..... BX 6
Baroncelli (Chiasso dei) ..... BCY 8
Canto de' Nelli (Via) ..... BX 13
Castellani (Via de') ..... CY 15
Duomo (Piazza del) ..... CX 21
Leoni (Via dei) ..... CY 33
Medici (Lungarno A.M.Luisa de') ..... CY 40
Pellicceria (Via) ..... BY 49
Repubblica (Piazza della) ..... BY 57
Rondinelli (Via de') ..... BX 60
S. Firenze (Piazza) ..... CY 65
S. Giovanni (Piazza) ..... BX 67
S. Maria Nuova (Piazza di) ..... CX 69
Sassetti (Via de') ..... BY 73
Signoria (Piazza della) ..... CY 76
Speziali (Via degli) ..... BCY 77
Trebbio (Via del) ..... BX 81
Uffizi (Piazzale degli) ..... CY 83
Vacchereccia (Via) ..... BY 84
Vecchietti (Via de') ..... BXY 85

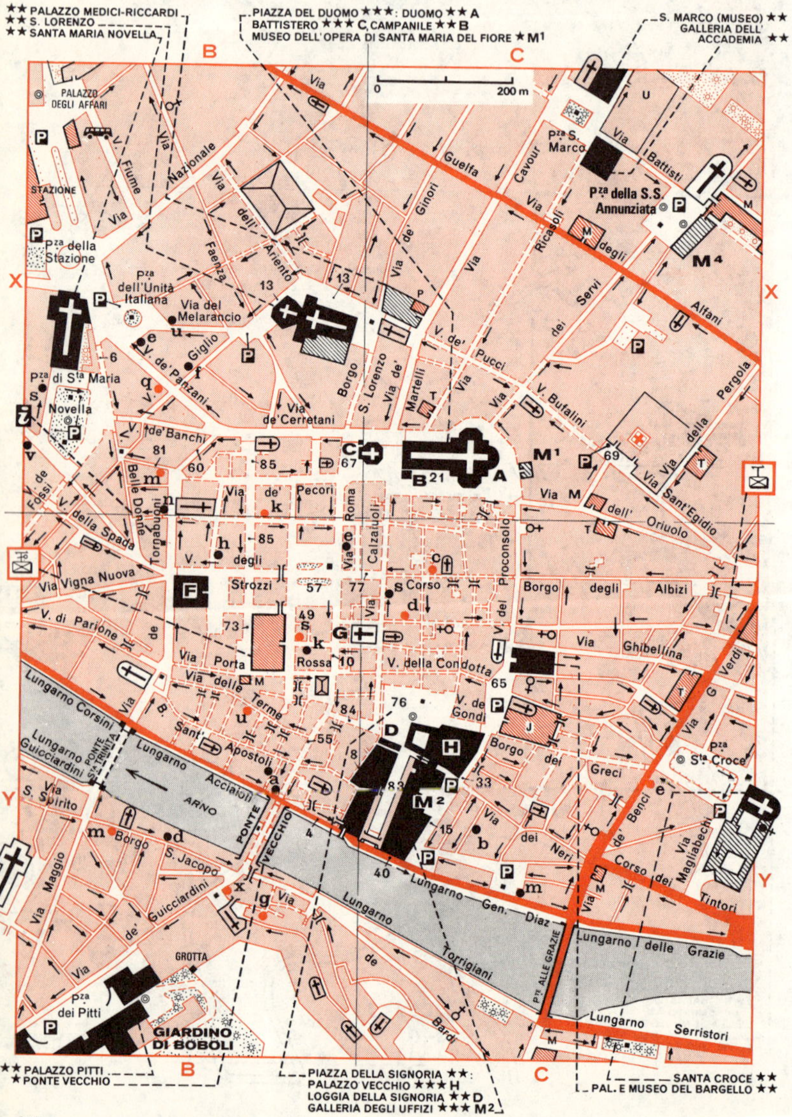

Excelsior, piazza Ognissanti 3 ✉ 50123 ☎ 264201, Telex 570022, « Rest. with summer service on terrace with ≤ » – |‡| ▤ TV ☎ ♿ – 🔔. AE ⊕ E VISA. ✻ rest AY **g**
M a la carte 76/115000 – ☐ 18000 – **205 rm** 309/488000.

Savoy, piazza della Repubblica 7 ✉ 50123 ☎ 283313, Telex 570220 – |‡| ▤ TV ☎ ♿ – 🔔. AE ⊕ E VISA. ✻ rest BY **e**
M a la carte 58/79000 – ☐ 18000 – **101 rm** 300/400000.

Villa Medici, via Il Prato 42 ✉ 50123 ☎ 261331, Telex 570179, 🏊 – |‡| ▤ TV ☎ – 🔔. AE ⊕ E AX **g**
M rest. see Lorenzaccio below – ☐ 15000 – **107 rm** 265/425000.

Regency, piazza Massimo D'Azeglio 3 ✉ 50121 ☎ 245247, Telex 571058, « Beautiful garden » – |‡| ▤ TV ☎ ♿ 🚗. AE ⊕ E VISA. ✻ rest DX **c**
M *(closed Sunday)* a la carte 45/60000 – ☐ 16500 – **31 rm** 275/380000 – P 422000.

Baglioni, piazza Unità Italiana 6 ✉ 50123 ☎ 218441, Telex 570225, « Roof-garden rest. with ≤ » – |‡| ▤ TV ☎ ♿ – 🔔. AE ⊕ E VISA. ✻ rest BX **e**
M a la carte 39/52000 – **195 rm** ☐ 158/225000.

Jolly, piazza Vittorio Veneto 4/a ✉ 50123 ☎ 2770, Telex 570191, « 🏊 on panoramic terrace » – |‡| ▤ TV ☎ – 🔔. AE ⊕ E VISA. ✻ rest AX **u**
M 37000 – **165 rm** ☐ 130/204000 – P 194000.

Majestic, via del Melarancio 1 ✉ 50123 ☎ 264021, Telex 570628 – |‡| ▤ TV ☎ ♿ 🚗 – 🔔. AE E VISA. ✻ rest BX **u**
M *(closed Sunday)* 35/40000 – ☐ 15000 – **104 rm** 140/190000 – P 180/220000.

Plaza Hotel Lucchesi, lungarno della Zecca Vecchia 38 ✉ 50122 ☎ 264141, Telex 570302, ≤ – |‡| ▤ ☎ ♿ – 🔔. AE ⊕ E VISA. ✻ rest DY **f**
M a la carte 40/45000 (15%) – **104 rm** ☐ 162/228000.

Gd H. Minerva, piazza Santa Maria Novella 16 ✉ 50123 ☎ 284555, Telex 570414, 🏊 – |‡| ▤ TV ☎ ♿ – 🔔. AE E. ✻ rest BX **s**
M a la carte 35/52000 – ☐ 16000 – **107 rm** 145/192000 – P 150/215000.

Etap Astoria, via del Giglio 9 ✉ 50123 ☎ 298095, Telex 571070 – |‡| ▤ TV ☎ ♿. AE ⊕ E VISA. ✻ rest BX **f**
M a la carte 33/52000 – **90 rm** ☐ 135/210000.

De la Ville, piazza Antinori 1 ✉ 50123 ☎ 261805, Telex 570518 – |‡| ▤ TV ☎ ♿. AE ⊕ E VISA. ✻ rest BX **n**
M *(closed lunch and Sunday)* a la carte 41/60000 – **75 rm** ☐ 160/227000.

Croce di Malta and Rest. il Coccodrillo, via della Scala 7 ✉ 50123 ☎ 282600, Telex 570540, 🏊, 🌳 – |‡| ▤ TV ☎ ♿ – 🔔. AE VISA. ✻ rest BX **v**
M *(closed Sunday and Monday lunch)* a la carte 36/50000 – ☐ 15000 – **100 rm** 145/194000 – P 150/220000.

Augustus without rest., piazzetta dell'Oro 5 ✉ 50123 ☎ 283054, Telex 570110 – |‡| ▤ TV ☎ ♿ – 🔔. AE ⊕ E VISA. ✻ BY **a**
☐ 12000 – **67 rm** 130/175000.

Kraft, via Solferino 2 ✉ 50123 ☎ 284273, Telex 571523, « Roof-garden rest. with ≤ », 🏊 – |‡| ▤ TV ☎ – 🔔. AE ⊕ E VISA. ✻ rest AX **c**
M 30/40000 – ☐ 15000 – **66 rm** 130/185000.

Anglo American, via Garibaldi 9 ✉ 50123 ☎ 282114, Telex 570289 – |‡| ▤ ☎ ♿ – 🔔. AE E VISA. ✻ rest AX **d**
M *(closed Sunday)* 40/45000 – **118 rm** ☐ 157/220000.

Londra, via Jacopo da Diacceto 16 ✉ 50123 ☎ 262791, Telex 571152 – |‡| ▤ TV ☎ ♿ 🚗 – 🔔. AE E VISA. ✻ rest AX **n**
M a la carte 36/57000 – ☐ 15500 – **105 rm** 145/192000 – P 149/212000.

Lungarno without rest., borgo Sant'Jacopo 14 ✉ 50125 ☎ 264211, Telex 570129, ≤, « Collection of modern pictures » – |‡| ▤ TV – 🔔. AE ⊕ E VISA. ✻ BY **d**
☐ 12000 – **71 rm** 130/190000.

Michelangelo, via Fratelli Rosselli 2 ✉ 50123 ☎ 278711, Telex 571113 – |‡| ▤ TV ☎ 🚗 – 🔔. AE ⊕ E VISA. ✻ rest AX **w**
M (residents only) a la carte 28/41000 – **138 rm** ☐ 143/198000 – P 187000.

Crest and Rest. la Tegolaia, viale Europa 205 ✉ 50126 ☎ 686841, Telex 570376, 🏊 heated, 🌳 – |‡| ▤ TV ☎ Ⓟ – 🔔. AE ⊕ E VISA. ✻ rest by ③
M 30/35000 – ☐ 15000 – **92 rm** 160/190000.

Pierre without rest., via de' Lamberti 5 ✉ 50123 ☎ 217512, Telex 573175 – |‡| ▤ ☎. AE ⊕ VISA BY **k**
☐ 14500 – **39 rm** 140/196000.

Montebello Splendid, via Montebello 60 ✉ 50123 ☎ 298051, Telex 574009, 🌳 – |‡| ▤ TV ☎. AE ⊕ E. ✻ AX **e**
M (residents only) 20/30000 – ☐ 15000 – **48 rm** 120/160000.

Principe without rest., lungarno Vespucci 34 ✉ 50123 ☎ 284848, Telex 571400, ≤, 🌳 – |‡| ▤ Ⓟ AX **b**
☐ 13000 – **21 rm** 105/175000.

Continental without rest., lungarno Acciaiuoli 2 ✉ 50123 ☎ 282392, Telex 580525, « Flowered terrace with ≤ » – AE E VISA BY a
11000 – **62 rm** 90/130000.

Alexander, viale Guidoni 101 ✉ 50127 ☎ 4378951, Telex 574026 – TV wc wc AE E VISA. by ⑧
M a la carte 25/40000 – 12500 – **88 rm** 136/188000.

Ville sull'Arno without rest., lungarno Colombo 5 ✉ 50136 ☎ 670971, Telex 573297, ≤, heated – wc wc AE VISA by ②
12000 – **47 rm** 100/165000.

Calzaiuoli without rest., via Calzaiuoli 6 ✉ 50122 ☎ 212456 – wc AE E VISA. CY s
8000 – **37 rm** 60/89000.

Golf without rest., viale Fratelli Rosselli 56 ✉ 50123 ☎ 293088, Telex 571630 – wc wc AE E. AV k
9000 – **39 rm** 69/104000, 5000.

Columbus, lungarno Colombo 22/a ✉ 50136 ☎ 677251, Telex 570273 – wc wc AE E VISA. rest by ②
M (residents only) 28/31000 – 9000 – **99 rm** 65/97000.

Helvetia e Bristol without rest., via de' Pescioni 2 ✉ 50123 ☎ 287814 – wc wc AE E VISA BY h
7000 – **62 rm** 61/93000.

Balestri without rest., piazza Mentana 7 ✉ 50122 ☎ 214743 – wc wc AE VISA. CY m
March-November – 9000 – **49 rm** 65/95000, 5000.

David without rest., viale Michelangiolo 1 ✉ 50125 ☎ 6811696, Telex 574553 – wc wc AE E VISA. DZ a
9000 – **26 rm** 64/94000, 5000.

Caravel without rest., via Alamanni 9 ✉ 50123 ☎ 217651 – wc wc. AX s
8000 – **59 rm** 66/99000.

Franchi without rest., via Sgambati 28 ✉ 50127 ☎ 372425, Telex 580425 – wc AE E VISA by ⑧
7500 – **35 rm** 50/79000.

Rapallo, via di Santa Caterina d'Alessandria 7 ✉ 50129 ☎ 472412, Telex 574251 – wc wc AE E VISA. CV s
M (residents only) a la carte 23/34000 (12%) – 8000 – **31 rm** 70/104000 – P 84/113000.

Astor, viale Milton 41 ✉ 50129 ☎ 483391, Telex 573155 – rest wc wc AE E VISA. rest CV u
M (residents only) (closed lunch) 25000 – 9000 – **25 rm** 62/90000.

Fiorino without rest., via Osteria del Guanto 6 ✉ 50122 ☎ 210579 – wc wc CY b
6500 – **23 rm** 50/68000, 4000.

Ariston without rest., via Fiesolana 40 ✉ 50122 ☎ 2476980, Telex 571603 – wc DX a
26 rm 41/63000.

Jane without rest., via Orcagna 56 ✉ 50121 ☎ 677383 – wc wc. DY m
6500 – **28 rm** 39/58000, 3500.

San Remo without rest., lungarno Serristori 13 ✉ 50125 ☎ 213390 – wc wc AE E. DZ e
17 rm 58/88000, 5000.

XXXX ✿✿ **Enoteca Pinchiorri,** via Ghibellina 87 ✉ 50122 ☎ 242757, « Nightly service in a cool court-yard » – AE CDY x
closed Sunday, Monday lunch, August and 25 to 27 December – **M** (booking essential) a la carte 75/90000 (12%)
Spec. Code di spannocchie con purea di melanzane, pomodoro e basilico fresco, Maltagliate al ragù di anatra e olive nere, Petto di faraona al cartoccio. **Wines** Nosiola di Faedo, Sodaccio di Monte Vertine.

XXXX **Sabatini,** via de' Panzani 9/a ✉ 50123 ☎ 282802, Elegant traditional decor – AE E VISA. BX q
closed Monday – **M** a la carte 39/53000 (13%).

XXX **Da Dante-al Lume di Candela,** via delle Terme 23 r ✉ 50123 ☎ 294566 – AE VISA BY u
closed Sunday, Monday lunch and 10 to 25 August – **M** (booking essential) a la carte 29/46000 (16%).

XXX **Harry's Bar,** lungarno Vespucci 22 r ✉ 50123 ☎ 296700 – AE AY x
closed Sunday and 10 December-15 January – **M** (booking essential) a la carte 43/50000 (16%).

XXX **Gourmet,** via Il Prato 68 r ✉ 50123 ☎ 294766, Rest.-American bar – AE. AX z
closed Sunday – **M** (booking essential) a la carte 37/58000 (15%).

XXX **Lorenzaccio,** via Rucellai 1/a ✉ 50123 ☎ 217100 – AE E VISA AX g
M a la carte 38/73000 (15%).

XX **La Posta,** via de' Lamberti 20 r ✉ 50123 ✆ 212701 – ▤. AE ⓓ E VISA — BY **s**
closed Tuesday – **M** a la carte 26/43000 (13%).

XX **Al Campidoglio,** via del Campidoglio 8 r ✉ 50123 ✆ 287770 – ▤. AE ⓓ E VISA. ✻ — BXY **k**
closed Thursday and August – **M** a la carte 29/38000 (12%).

XX **La Loggia,** piazzale Michelangiolo 1 ✉ 50125 ✆ 287032, « Outdoor service in Summer with ← » – ▤ Ⓟ. AE ⓓ VISA. ✻ — DZ **r**
closed Wednesday and 10 to 25 August – **M** a la carte 24/36000 (13%).

XX **Il Profeta,** borgo Ognissanti 93 r ✉ 50123 ✆ 212265 – ▤. AE VISA — AX **r**
closed Sunday, Monday and August – **M** a la carte 21/31000 (12%).

XX **Buca Lapi,** via del Trebbio 1 r ✉ 50123 ✆ 213768, Typical tavern – ▤. AE VISA — BX **m**
closed Sunday and Monday lunch – **M** a la carte 26/41000 (12%).

XX **Il Paiolo,** via del Corso 42 r ✉ 50123 ✆ 215019 – ▤ — CY **c**
closed Sunday – **M** (booking essential) a la carte 25/40000 (12%).

XX **Paoli,** via dei Tavolini 12 r ✉ 50122 ✆ 216215, Typical rest., « Reproduction 14C style decor » – AE ⓓ E VISA — CY **d**
closed Tuesday – **M** a la carte 26/36000 (12%).

XX **13 Gobbi,** via del Porcellana 9 r ✉ 50123 ✆ 298769, Tuscan rest. – AE VISA. ✻ — AX **v**
closed Sunday, Monday and 27 July-25 August – **M** a la carte 25/35000 (10%).

X **Celestino,** piazza Santa Felicita 4 r ✉ 50125 ✆ 296574 – ▤ — BY **x**
closed Sunday and 30 July-23 August – **M** a la carte 23/38000 (12%).

X **Il Tirabusciò,** via de' Benci 34 r ✉ 50122 ✆ 2476225 – ▤ — CY **e**
closed Thursday and Friday – **M** (booking essential) a la carte 15/27000 (12%).

X **Bordino,** via Stracciatella 9 r ✉ 50125 ✆ 213048, Typical trattoria – ▤. AE ⓓ E VISA
closed lunch, Sunday, Monday, July and 23 to 31 December – **M** (booking essential) a la carte 17/37000. — BY **g**

X ✿ **Cammillo,** borgo Sant'Jacopo 57 r ✉ 50125 ✆ 212427, Typical florentine trattoria – ▤. AE ⓓ E VISA — BY **m**
closed Wednesday, Thursday, 20 December-15 January and 1 to 20 August – **M** a la carte 35/57000
Spec. Trippa alla fiorentina, Petti di pollo alla Cammillo, Scaloppine Capriccio. **Wines** Chianti.

on the hills S : 3 km :

Gd H. Villa Cora and Rest. Taverna Machiavelli ⛰, viale Machiavelli 18 ✉ 50125 ✆ 2298451, Telex 570604, « Floral park with ⛱ » – 🛗 ▤ TV ☎ ♿ Ⓟ – 🏛. AE ⓓ VISA. ✻ rest — by viale Machiavelli ABZ
M 57000 (15%) – ☕ 16000 – **48 rm** 224/356000.

Villa Carlotta ⛰, via Michele di Lando 3 ✉ 50125 ✆ 220530, Telex 573485, « Beautiful garden » – 🛗 ▤ TV ☎ Ⓟ – 🏛. AE ⓓ E VISA. ✻ rest — AZ **a**
M *(closed 15 November-1 March)* a la carte 32/44000 – ☕ 15000 – **26 rm** 140/190000 – P 170/190000.

Villa Belvedere ⛰, via Benedetto Castelli 3 ✉ 50124 ✆ 222501, ← town and hills, « Garden-park with ⛱ », 🎾 – 🛗 ▤ wc ☎ ♿ Ⓟ. ✻ — by ④
March-November – **M** coffee shop only – ☕ 9000 – **27 rm** 86/142000.

at Arcetri S : 5 km – ✉ **50125** Firenze :

X **Omero,** via Pian de' Giullari 11 r ✆ 220053, Rustic trattoria with ←, « Summer service on terrace » — by viale Galileo CDZ
closed Monday lunch, Tuesday and August – **M** a la carte 19/30000 (13%).

at Candeli – ✉ **50010** :

Villa La Massa and Rest. Il Verrocchio ⛰, ✆ 630051, Telex 573555, ←, « House and furnishing in 18C style », ⛱ heated, 🌳, 🎾 – 🛗 ▤ TV ☎ ♿ Ⓟ – 🏛. AE ⓓ E VISA. ✻ rest
M *(closed Monday and Tuesday lunch from November to March)* a la carte 50/65000 – **43 rm** ☕ 229/370000, ▤ 5500 – P 262/306000.

towards Trespiano N : 7 km :

Villa le Rondini ⛰, via Bolognese Vecchia 224 ✉ 50139 Firenze ✆ 400081, ← town, « Among the olive trees », ⛱, 🌳, 🎾 – wc wc ☎ ♿ Ⓟ – 🏛. AE ⓓ E VISA. ✻ rest
M 30/35000 – ☕ 10000 – **29 rm** 73/111000 – P 121000.

at Serpiolle N : 8 km – ✉ **50142** Firenze :

XX **Lo Strettoio,** ✆ 452344, « 17C Country house among the olive trees » – Ⓟ. ✻
closed Sunday, Monday and August – **M** (booking essential) a la carte 28/38000.

If you would like a more complete selection of hotels and restaurants, consult the MICHELIN Guides for the following countries :

Benelux, Deutschland, España Portugal, France, Great Britain and Ireland, and Italia,

all in annual editions.

MILAN (MILANO) 20100 P 988 ③, 219 ⑲ – pop. 1 561 438 alt. 122 – ✆ 02.

See : Cathedral*** (Duomo), Tour of the Cathedral terraces*** – Brera exhibition hall and art gallery*** – Sforza castle** (municipal Art collections**) – Poldi-Pezzoli museum** (Golden Hall : portrait of a woman***, Persian carpet*, Ecce Homo** by G. Bellini) CU **M1** – Via and piazza Mercanti* – La Scala Theatre* – Church of St. Maria delle Grazie (dome*, Leonardo da Vinci's Last Supper***) – Basilica of St. Ambrogio* (atrium**) – Galleria Vittorio Emanuele* CV – Ambrosian Library* (art gallery**, two portraits*** by Leonardo da Vinci, Raphael's cartoons*** for the fresco of the Athenian School, the Manger** by Barocci, the Mouse with a rose* by Velvet Breughel)BV – Leonardo da Vinci museum of Science and Technology* AV **M1** – Church of St. Eustorgio* (Portinari Chapel**) BY **B** – Church of St. Satiro* CV **C** – Maggiore Hospital* DX **U** – Church of St. Maurizio (frescoes by Luini*) BV **E** – Parco Sempione*.

Envir. : Chiaravalle Abbey* SE : 7 km – N : Lakes : Lake Como***, Lake Maggiore***, Lake Lugano**.

18, 9 (closed Monday) in Monza Park ✉ 20052 Monza ✆ (039) 303081, by ② : 20 km;

18 Molinetto (closed Monday) in Cernusco sul Naviglio ✉ 20063 ✆ (02) 9238500, by ⑤ : 14 km;

18 Barlassina (closed Wednesday) in Birago di Camnago ✉ 20030 ✆ (0362) 560621, by ① : 26 km;

9 Le Rovedine in Noverasco di Opera ✉ 20090 Opera ✆ (02) 5442730, S : 8 km by via Ripamonti.

Motor-Racing circuit in Monza Park by ② : 20 km, ✆ (039) 22366.

✈ Forlanini of Linate E : 8 km ✆ 74852200 and Malpensa by ⑫ : 45 km ✆ 74852200 – Alitalia, viale Luigi Sturzo 37 ✉ 20154 ✆ 6281 and via Albricci 5 ✉ 20122 ✆ 6281.

🚗 Porta Garibaldi ✆ 228274.

☐ via Marconi 1 ✉ 20123 ✆ 809662 – Central Station ✉ 20124 ✆ 6690532.

A.C.I. corso Venezia 43 ✉ 20121 ✆ 7745.

Roma 572 ⑦ – Genève 323 ⑫ – Genova 142 ⑨ – Torino 140 ⑫.

Plans on following pages

Northern area Piazza della Repubblica, Central Station, viale Zara, Porta Garibaldi Station, Porta Volta, corso Sempione (Plans : Milan pp. 2 and 3) :

Principe e Savoia, piazza della Repubblica 17 ✉ 20124 ✆ 6230, Telex 310052 – 🛗 ▤ TV ☎ ♿ P – 🏋. AE ⊙ E VISA. ✗ DS **x**
M a la carte 77/120000 – ☕ 19000 – **280 rm** 339/488000.

Palace, piazza della Repubblica 20 ✉ 20124 ✆ 6336 and rest. ✆ 650803, Telex 311026 – 🛗 ▤ TV ☎ ♿ P – 🏋. AE ⊙ E VISA. ✗ rest DS **t**
M Casanova rest. *(closed Saturday)* a la carte 65/80000 – ☕ 21000 – **187 rm** 280/410000.

Excelsior Gallia, piazza Duca d'Aosta 9 ✉ 20124 ✆ 6277, Telex 311160 – 🛗 ▤ TV ☎ – 🏋. AE ⊙ E VISA. ✗ rest DR **a**
M 50/60000 – **252 rm** ☕ 263/362000.

Milano Hilton, via Galvani 12 ✉ 20124 ✆ 6983, Telex 330433 – 🛗 ▤ TV ☎ ♿ 🚗 – 🏋. AE ⊙ E VISA. ✗ rest DR **t**
M a la carte 48/77000 – ☕ 21000 – **339 rm** 295/368000.

Executive, viale Luigi Sturzo 45 ✉ 20154 ✆ 6294, Telex 310191 – 🛗 ▤ TV ☎ ♿ – 🏋. AE ⊙ E VISA. ✗ rest CRS **v**
M 40000 – **420 rm** ☕ 185/225000.

Michelangelo, via Scarlatti 33 ✉ 20124 ✆ 6755, Telex 340330 – 🛗 ▤ TV ☎ 🚗 – 🏋. AE ⊙ E VISA. ✗ rest DR **c**
M 55/65000 – **278 rm** ☕ 225/280000 – P 225/275000.

Anderson without rest., piazza Luigi di Savoia 20 ✉ 20124 ✆ 6690141, Telex 321018 – 🛗 ▤ TV ☎ 🚗. AE E VISA DR **v**
closed August – ☕ 9500 – **102 rm** 130/170000.

Jolly Touring, via Tarchetti 2 ✉ 20121 ✆ 6335, Telex 320118 – 🛗 ▤ TV ☎ – 🏋. AE ⊙ E VISA. ✗ rest DT **v**
M 40000 – **270 rm** ☕ 160/205000 – P 235000.

Auriga without rest., via Pirelli 7 ✉ 20124 ✆ 6592851, Telex 350146 – 🛗 ▤ TV ☎. AE E VISA. ✗ DR **f**
closed August – ☕ 7500 – **65 rm** 120/150000.

Windsor without rest., via Galilei 2 ✉ 20124 ✆ 6346, Telex 330562 – 🛗 ▤ TV ☎ ♿ – 🏋. AE ⊙ E DS **j**
☕ 12000 – **114 rm** 118/128000.

Atlantic without rest., via Napo Torriani 24 ✉ 20124 ✆ 6691941, Telex 321451 – 🛗 ▤ TV ☎ ♿ 🚗. AE E VISA DS **q**
☕ 12000 – **62 rm** 140/190000.

Royal, via Cardano 1 ✉ 20124 ✆ 6709151, Telex 333167 – 🛗 ▤ ☎ – 🏋. AE ⊙ E VISA. ✗ rest DR **b**
closed August – **M** (residents only) (closed Saturday and Sunday) 33000 – ☕ 11000 – **110 rm** 130/170000 – P 207000.

Splendido without rest., viale Andrea Doria 4 ✉ 20124 ✆ 2050, Telex 321413 – |‡| ▤ TV – 🅐. AE ⓞ E VISA. ✻ DR x
129 rm ☕ 160/250000.

Bristol without rest., via Scarlatti 32 ✉ 20124 ✆ 6694141 – |‡| ▤ TV ☎ – 🅐. AE ⓞ E. ✻ DR u
closed August – ☕ 10000 – **71 rm** 121/163000.

Berna without rest., via Napo Torriani 18 ✉ 20124 ✆ 6691441, Telex 334695 – |‡| ▤ TV ☎ – 🅐. AE ⓞ E VISA. ✻ DS a
☕ 11000 – **83 rm** 112/152000.

Europeo without rest., via Canonica 38 ✉ 20154 ✆ 344041, Telex 321237, ✻ – |‡| ▤ TV ☎ 🚗 – 🅐. AE E VISA. ✻ AS f
☕ 17000 – **45 rm** 100/140000.

Lancaster without rest., via Abbondio Sangiorgio 16 ✉ 20145 ✆ 344705 – |‡| ▤ TV ⛀wc ⛆wc ☎. AE E VISA. ✻ AT v
closed July and August – ☕ 16000 – **29 rm** 100/135000.

Mediolanum without rest., via Mauro Macchi 1 ✉ 20124 ✆ 6705312, Telex 310448 – |‡| ▤ TV ⛀wc ⛆wc ☎ ♿. AE VISA DS r
52 rm ☕ 90/135000.

Club Hotel without rest., via Copernico 18 ✉ 20125 ✆ 606128, Telex 323816 – |‡| ▤ TV ⛀wc ⛆wc ☎. AE DR n
closed August – ☕ 10000 – **53 rm** 70/95000.

Augustus ✻ without rest., via Napo Torriani 29 ✉ 20124 ✆ 6575741, Telex 333112 – |‡| ▤ ⛀wc ⛆wc ☎. AE ⓞ E VISA DS h
56 rm ☕ 80/119000.

San Carlo without rest., via Napo Torriani 28 ✉ 20124 ✆ 6692431, Telex 314324 – |‡| ▤ ⛀wc ⛆wc ☎. AE ⓞ E VISA DS s
62 rm ☕ 80/120000.

Flora without rest., via Napo Torriani 23 ✉ 20124 ✆ 650242, Telex 312547 – |‡| ▤ TV ⛀wc ⛆wc ☎. AE ⓞ VISA. ✻ DS h
☕ 10000 – **45 rm** 70/100000.

New York without rest., via Pirelli 5 ✉ 20124 ✆ 650551, Telex 325057 – |‡| ⛀wc ☎. AE ⓞ E VISA DR f
closed 8 to 28 August – ☕ 8000 – **71 rm** 69/100000.

Sempione, via Finocchiaro Aprile 11 ✉ 20124 ✆ 6570323, Telex 340498 – |‡| ▤ rest TV ⛆wc ☎. ✻ DST u
M *(closed Saturday)* a la carte 21/33000 – ☕ 10000 – **38 rm** 75/110000 – P 100/110000.

Cervo, without rest., piazzale Principessa Clotilde 10 ✉ 20121 ✆ 666112 – |‡| ⛀wc ⛆wc ☎ DS d
59 rm.

Gala without rest., viale Zara 89 ✉ 20159 ✆ 6890867 – |‡| ▤ ⛀wc ⛆wc ☎. E VISA
closed August – ☕ 9000 – **22 rm** 55/85000. DQ j

XXX **Romani,** via Trebazio 3 ✉ 20145 ✆ 340738 – ▤. AE ⓞ AS m
closed Saturday lunch, Sunday and August – **M** a la carte 30/52000.

XXX Grattacielo, via Vittor Pisani 6 ✉ 20124 ✆ 6592359, ✻, « Collection of paintings by well-known artists » – ▤ DS y

XX **Tre Pini,** via Tullo Morgagni 19 ✉ 20125 ✆ 6898464, « Pergola-garden » – ⓞ. ✻
closed Friday lunch, Saturday and 5 to 31 August – **M** a la carte 26/50000. DQ n

XX ✻ **A Riccione,** via Taramelli 70 ✉ 20124 ✆ 6086807, Seafood – ▤ Ⓟ. AE ⓞ E VISA
closed Monday – **M** (booking essential) a la carte 40/55000 DQ a
Spec. Pasta fresca con sugo di cannelli e scampi, Paella valenciana, Orata al tegame, Grigliata mista di pesce alla brace. **Wines** del Collio, Barbaresco.

XX **Da Lino Buriassi,** via Lecco angolo via Casati 12 ✉ 20124 ✆ 273383 – ▤. AE VISA
closed Saturday lunch, Sunday and 10 to 28 August – **M** (booking essential) a la carte 33/37000. DT g

XX **Wan Tong,** via Paolo Sarpi ang. via Niccolini ✉ 20154 ✆ 3453633, Chinese rest. – ▤. AE ⓞ VISA. ✻ BS x
closed Sunday, Monday lunch, August and 24 December-3 January – **M** (booking essential) a la carte 40/50000 (10%).

XX **Pesce d'Oro,** via Cornalia 17 ✉ 20124 ✆ 6702532 – ▤. AE E VISA DR s
closed Saturday lunch, Sunday and August – **M** a la carte 22/35000 (12%).

XX ✻ **Alfredo-Gran San Bernardo,** via Borgese 14 ✉ 20154 ✆ 3319000 – ▤ AR f
closed Sunday, August and 21 December-19 January – **M** (booking essential) a la carte 36/45000
Spec. Risotto alla milanese ed al salto, Ossobuco in cremolata, Foiolo (trippa). **Wines** Pinot grigio, Barbera.

XX **Altopascio,** via Gustavo Fara 17 ✉ 20124 ✆ 6702458, Tuscan rest. – ▤. AE E DS e
closed Saturday, Sunday lunch and August – **M** a la carte 18/35000 (11%).

MILANO

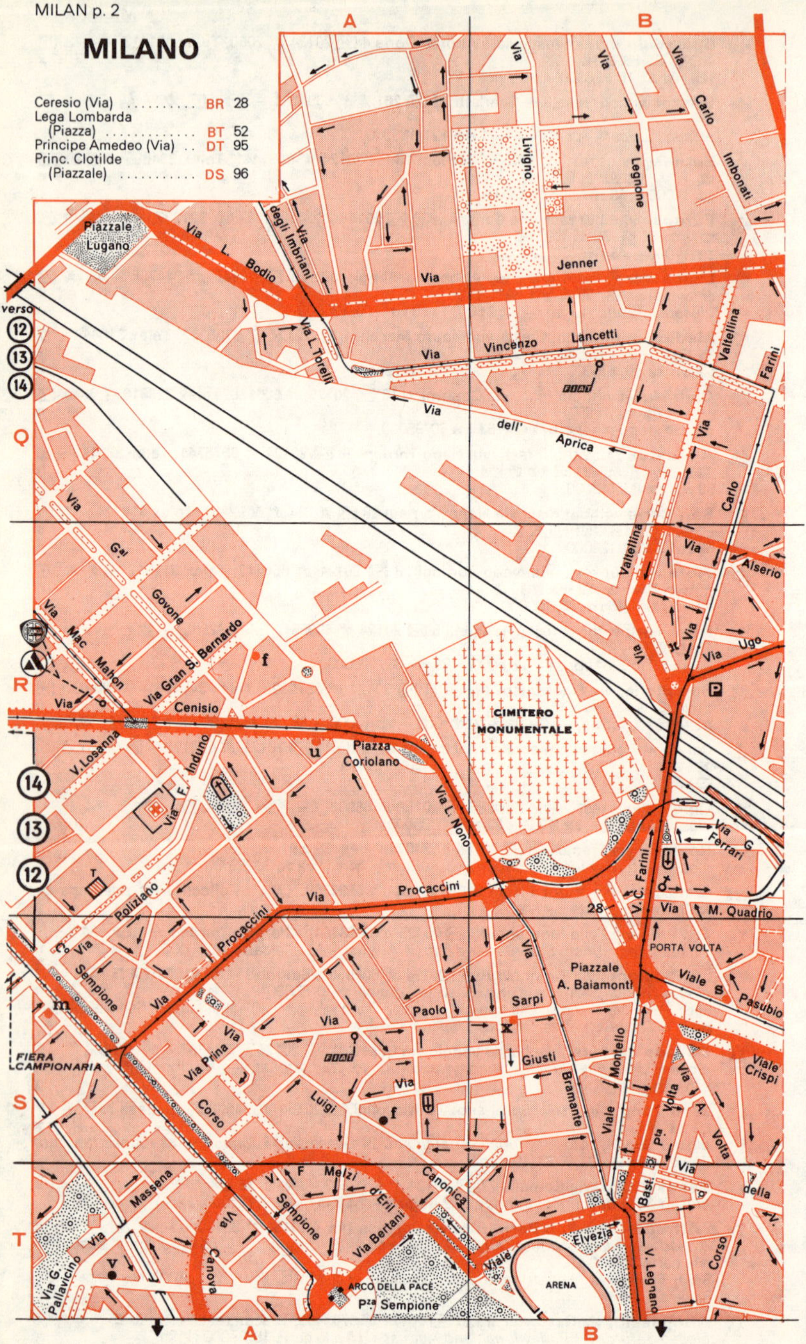

A
B
Q
R
S
T
verso
12
13
14
Piazzale Lugano
Via L. Bodio
Via degli Imbriani
Via L. Torelli
Via Jenner
Via Livigno
Via Legnone
Via Carlo Imbonati
Via Vincenzo Lancetti
Via dell' Aprica
Via Valtellina
Via Carlo Farini
Via Alserio
Via Ugo
Via Gal Govone
Via Mac Mahon
Via Gran S. Bernardo
Via Cenisio
V. Losanna
Via E. Induno
Piazza Coriolano
Via L. Nono
CIMITERO MONUMENTALE
Via G. Ferrari
V. C. Farini
Via M. Quadrio
PORTA VOLTA
Piazzale A. Baiamonti
Viale Pasubio
Viale Crispi
Via Procaccini
Via Poliziano
Co Sempione
Via Paolo Sarpi
Via Giusti
Via Prina
Corso
Via Luigi
Via Bramante
Viale Montello
Via Volta
Via A. Volta
Pta
Basti
Via della
FIERA CAMPIONARIA
Massena
V. F. Melzi d'Eril
Sempione
Via Bertani
Canonica
Via Canova
Via G. Pallavicino
ARCO DELLA PACE
Pza Sempione
Viale Elvezia
ARENA
V. Legnano
Corso
28
52

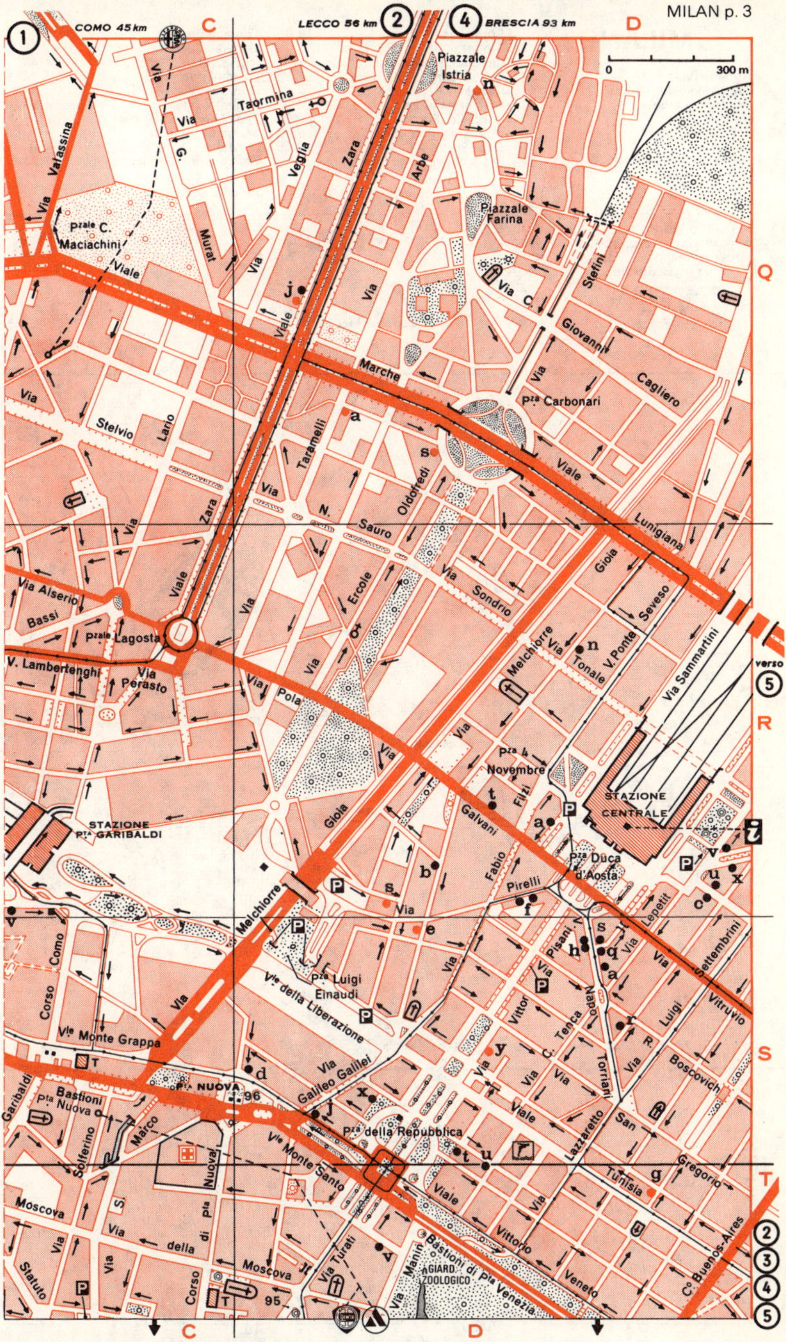
COMO 45 km
LECCO 56 km
BRESCIA 93 km
300 m
Piazzale Istria
Via Taormina
Via G.
Vatassina
Vegia
Zara
Arbe
Piazzale Farina
Pzale C. Maciachini
Viale
Murat
Via
Stefini
Via C. Giovanni
Cagliero
Pza Carbonari
Viale Marche
Taramelli
Stelvio
Lario
Via N. Sauro
Oldofredi
Viale Lunigiana
Gioia
Seveso
Via Sondrio
Ercole
Via Alserio
Bassi
Pzale Lagosta
V. Lambertenghi
Via Perasto
Via Pola
Melchiorre
Via Tonale
V. Ponte
Via Sammartini
verso
Pza 4 Novembre
Filzi
Galvani
STAZIONE CENTRALE
STAZIONE Pta GARIBALDI
Pza Duca d'Aosta
Fabio
Pirelli
Lepetit
Settembrini
Pisani
Napo
Vittor
Tenca
Torriani
Lazzaretto
Boscovich
Vitruvio
Pza Luigi Einaudi
Vle della Liberazione
Via Galileo Galilei
Corso Como
Vle Monte Grappa
Pta NUOVA
Bastioni Pta Nuova
Garibaldi
Solferino
Marco
Nuova
Vle Monte Santo
Pza della Repubblica
Viale Vittorio Veneto
Tunisia
Gregorio
San
Co Buenos-Aires
Moscova
Via della Moscova
Statuto
Corso
Via Turati
Via Manin
Bastioni di Pta Venezia
GIARD. ZOOLOGICO
95
96
C
D
Q
R
S
T

MILANO

Agnello (Via) . . . . DV 3
Arcivescovado (Via) . . . . CV 4
Augusto (Largo) . . . . DV 6
Battisti
(Via Cesare) . . . . DV 12
Beccaria
(Piazza e Via) . . . . DV 14
Borgogna (Via) . . . . DV 16
Broletto (Via) . . . . BCU 19
Cadorna (Piazzale) . . . . AU 22
Cairoli (Largo) . . . . BU 23
Cavallotti (Via Felice) . . . . . DV 27
Concordia (Corso) . . . . DU 30
Cordusio (Piazza) . . . . CV 32
De Marchi (Via Marco) . . . . DU 35
Diaz (Piazza A.) . . . . CV 36
Festa del Perdono (Via) . . . . DV 38
Fontana (Piazza) . . . . DV 40
Generale Cantore
(Piazzale) . . . . AX 43
Giardini (Via dei) . . . . DU 44
Gonzaga (Via Maurizio) . . . . CV 46
Laghetto (Via) . . . . DV 50
Lega Lombarda (Piazza) . . . . BT 52
Marco d'Oggiono
(Via) . . . . AX 63
Marconi (Via Guglielmo) . . . . CV 64

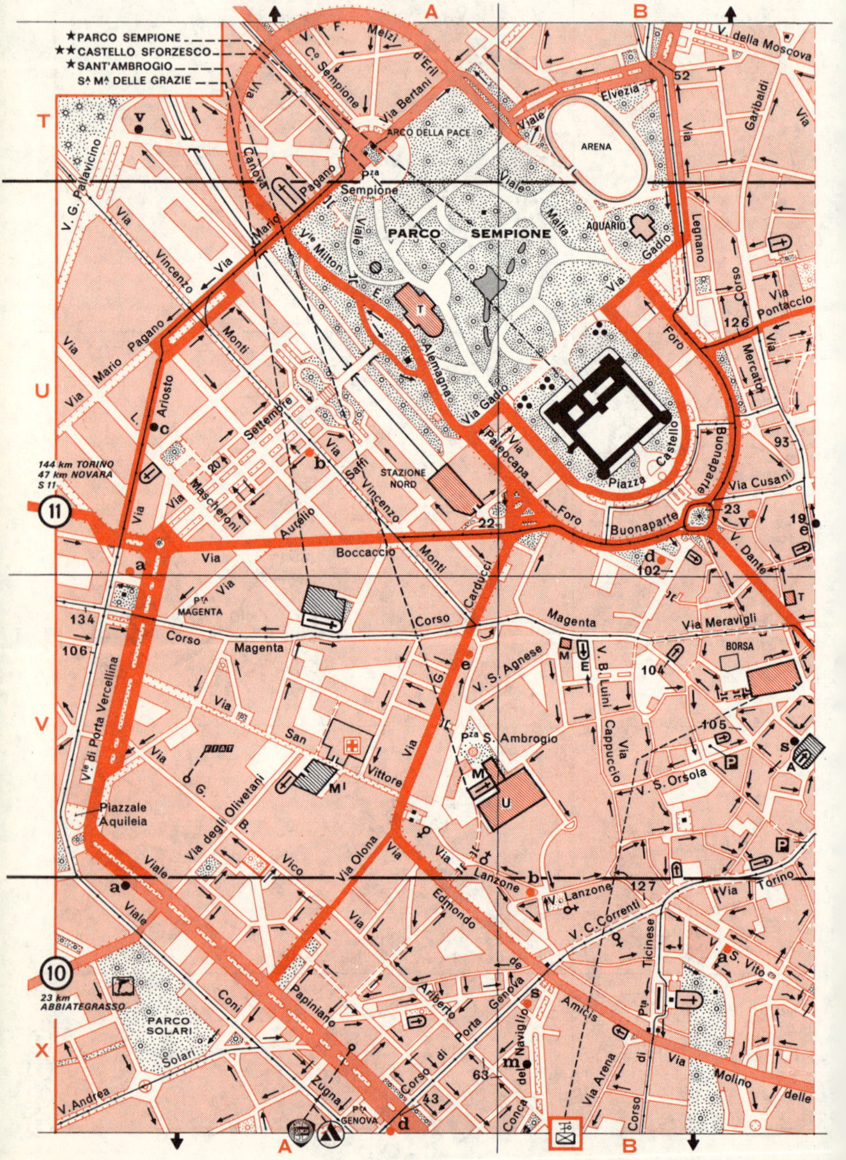

Mazzini (Via G.) .... CV 65
Mercanti (Piazza e Via) .... CV 66
Missori (Piazza) .... CV 73
Orefici (Via) .... CV 84
Ponte Vetero (Via) .... BU 93
Porrone (Via Bassano) .... CV 94
Principe Amedeo (Via) .... DT 95
S. Babila (Piazza) .... DV 99
S. Fedele (Piazza) .... CV 100

S. Giovanni sul Muro (Via) .... BU 102
S. Margherita (Via) .... CV 103
S. Maria alla Porta (Via) .... BV 104
S. Maria Fulcorina (Via) .... BV 105
S. Michele del Carso (Viale) .... AV 106
S. Paolo (Via) .... DV 108
S. Prospero (Via) .... CV 109
S. Protaso (Via) .... CV 112
S. Stefano (Piazza) .... DV 113

Scala (Piazza della) .... CV 115
Tivoli (Via) .... BU 126
Torchio (Via del) .... BX 127
Tricolore (Piazza del) .... DU 128
Vercelli (Corso) .... AV 134
Verziere (Via) .... DV 135
Visconti di Modrone (Via) .... DV 136
5 Giornate (Piazzale) .... DV 142
22 Marzo (Corso) .... DV 143

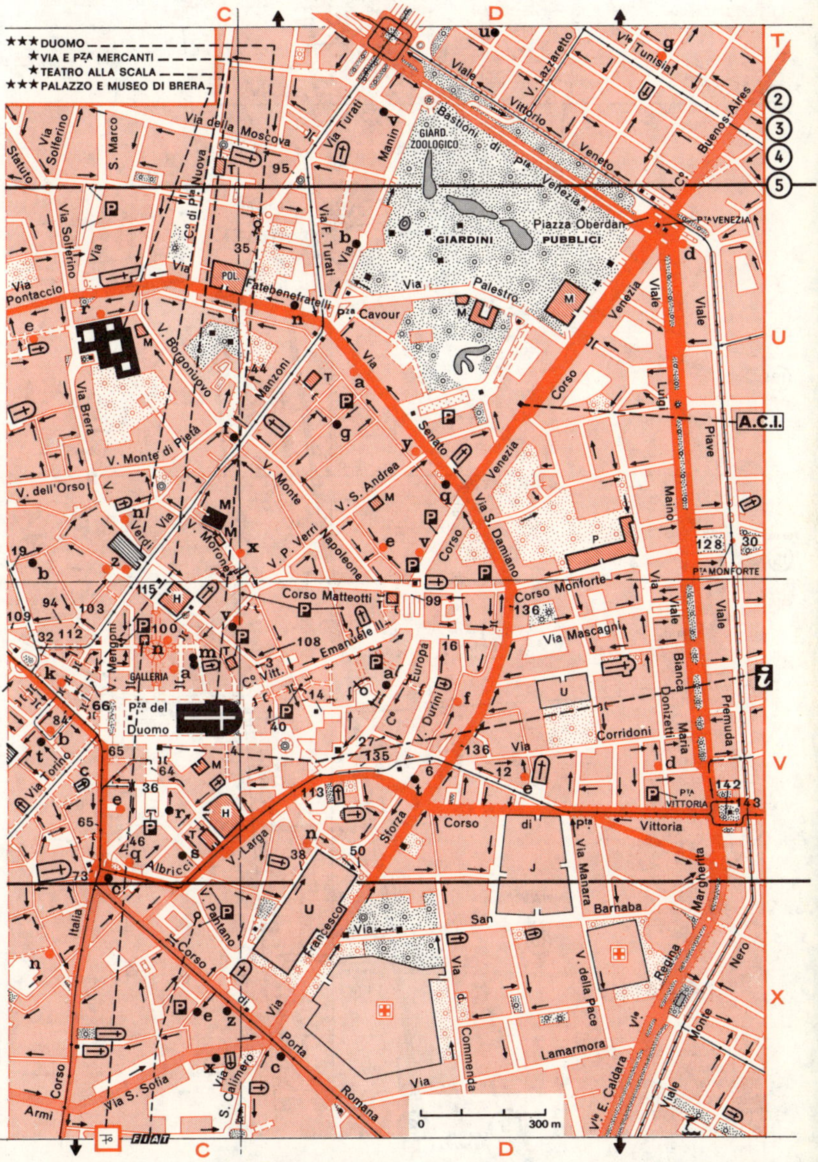

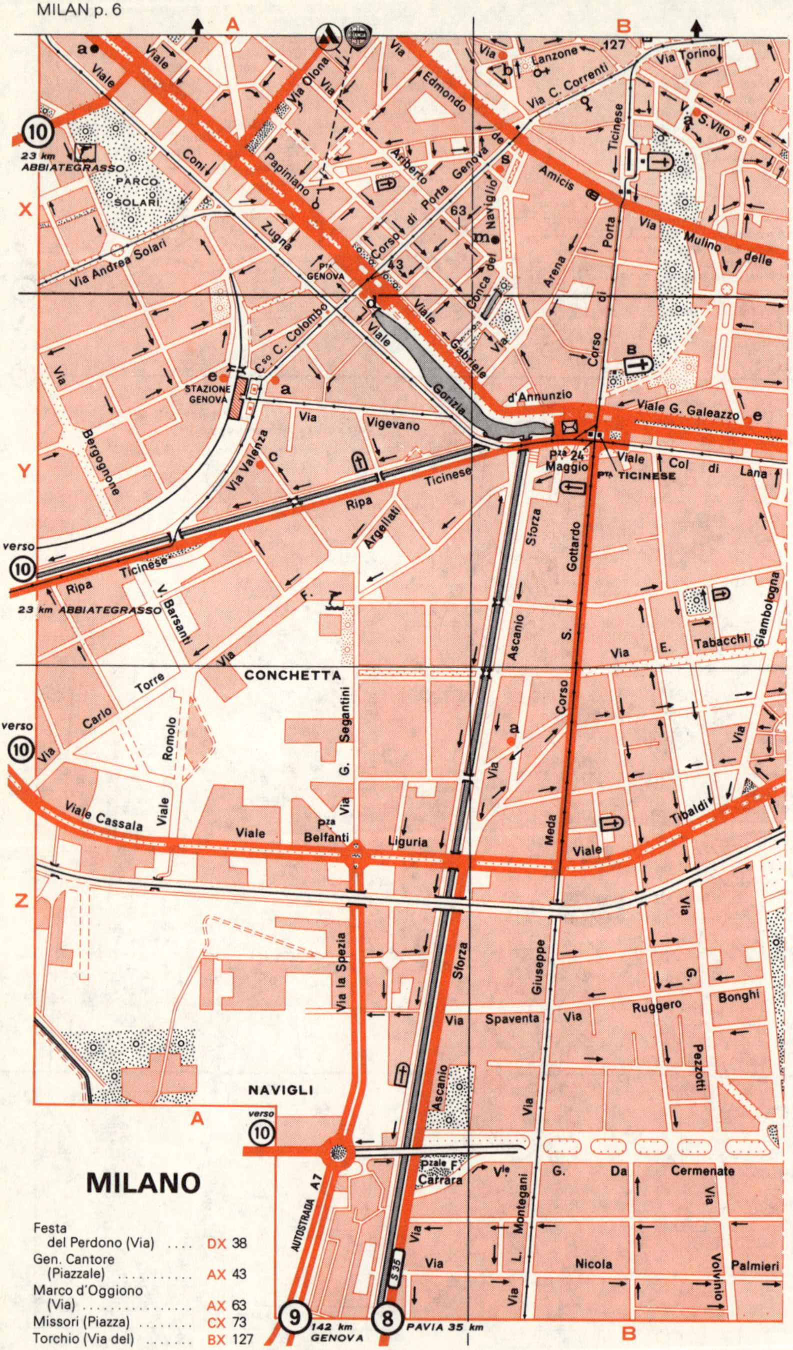
A
B
X
Y
Z
23 km ABBIATEGRASSO
PARCO SOLARI
Viale Coni Zugna
Via Andrea Solari
Via Olona
Via Papiniano
Corso di Porta Genova
Via Ariberto
Via Edmondo de Amicis
Via Lanzone
Via C. Correnti
Via Torino
V. S. Vito
Via Ticinese
Via Mulino delle Armi
Conca del Naviglio
Corso di Porta Ticinese
Via Arena
Pta GENOVA
Viale Gabriele d'Annunzio
Viale Gorizia
C.so C. Colombo
STAZIONE GENOVA
Via Vigevano
Via Bergognone
Via Valenza
Ripa Ticinese
Viale G. Galeazzo
Pza 24 Maggio
Pta TICINESE
Viale Col di Lana
verso 10
23 km ABBIATEGRASSO
V. Barsanti
Via Argelati
Viale Sforza
Ascanio Sforza
Corso S. Gottardo
Via E. Tabacchi
Via Giambologna
CONCHETTA
Via Carlo Torre
Romolo
Via G. Segantini
Viale Cassala
Viale Romolo
Viale Liguria
Pza Belfanti
Via Meda
Viale Tibaldi
Via la Spezia
Via Giuseppe Meda
Via Spaventa
Via Ruggero Bonghi
Via G. Pezzotti
NAVIGLI
Ascanio Sforza
Pzale F. Carrara
Vle G. Da Cermenate
Via L. Montegani
Via Nicola Palmieri
Via Volvinio
AUTOSTRADA A7
S 35
9 142 km GENOVA
8 PAVIA 35 km
MILANO
127
63
43
a
b
c
d
e
m

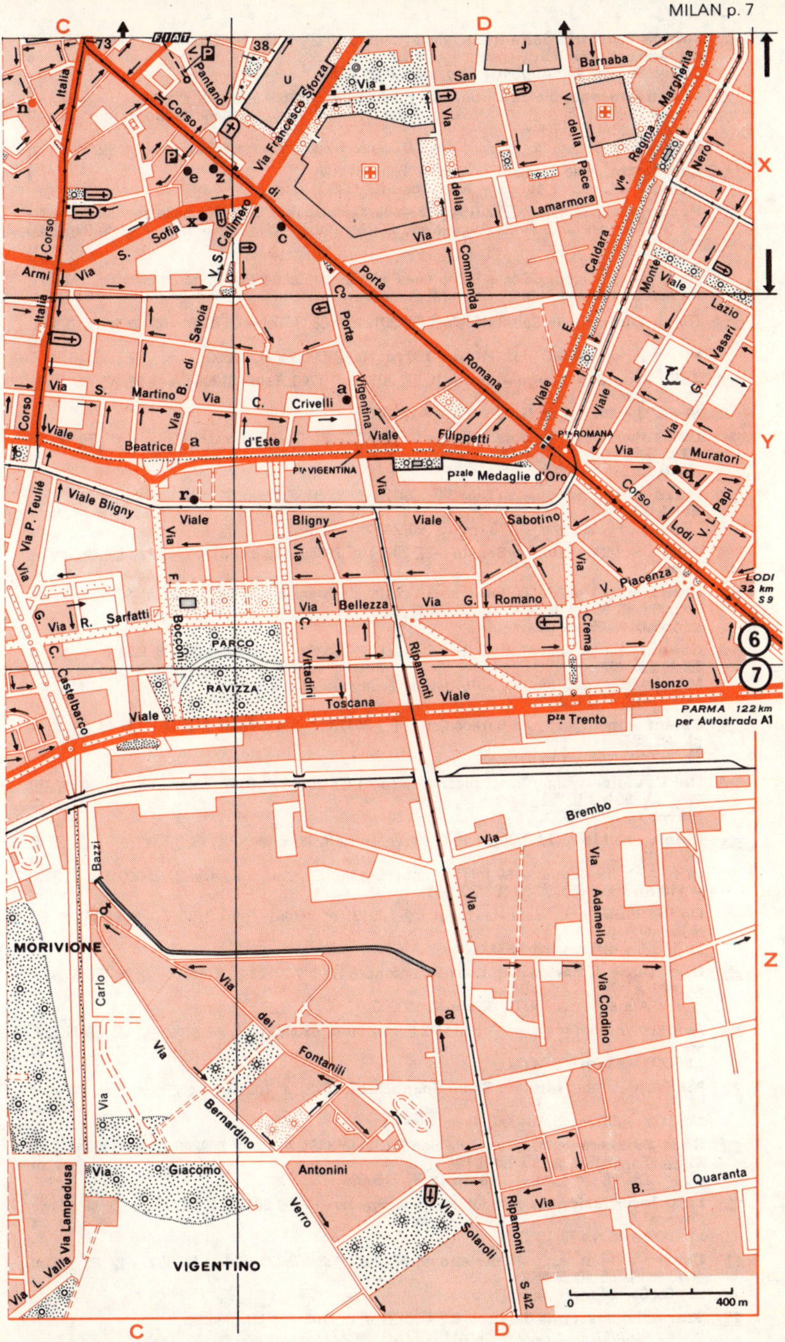
C
D
X
Y
Z
FIAT
73
38
Corso Italia
Pantano
Corso di Porta Romana
Via Francesco Sforza
Via San Barnaba
Via della Pace
Via della Commenda
Lamarmora
Viale Regina Margherita
Via Caldara
Nerd
Via Sofia
V. S. Calimero
Armi
Via S. Sofia
Corso Italia
Via Savoia
Co Porta Vigentina
Viale Monte Nero
Viale Lazio
Via Vasari
Via G.
Via S. Martino
Via B. di Savoia
Via C. Crivelli
Viale Beatrice d'Este
Viale Filippetti
P. Romana
P.ta Vigentina
Pzale Medaglie d'Oro
Via Muratori
Corso Lodi
V. L. Papi
Viale Bligny
Via P. Teulié
Via F. Bocconi
Viale Sabotino
Via Piacenza
Via Bellezza
Via G. Romano
Via Crema
Via R. Sarfatti
Parco Ravizza
Via C. Vittadini
Via Ripamonti
Viale Toscana
Viale Isonzo
Pza Trento
C. Castelbarco
LODI 32 km S 9
PARMA 122 km per Autostrada A1
6
7
Via Brembo
Via Adamello
Via Condino
Via Bazzi
Via Carlo Bazzi
MORIVIONE
Via dei Fontanili
Via Bernardino Verro
Via Giacomo Antonini
Via Solaroli
Via B. Quaranta
Via L. Valla
Via Lampedusa
VIGENTINO
S 412
0
400 m
C
D

X **Antica Trattoria della Pesa,** viale Pasubio 10 ✉ 20154 ✆ 6555741, Old Milan typical trattoria with Lombardy specialities – ▤ BS **s**
closed Sunday and August – **M** a la carte 25/38000.

X ✿ **Casa Fontana,** piazza Carbonari 5 ✉ 20125 ✆ 6892684 – ▤. AE VISA. ✻ DQ **s**
closed 15 June-25 August, Monday, Saturday lunch and Sunday – **M** (booking essential) a la carte 28/41000 (15%)
Spec. Risotti della Casa, Rognoncini di vitello al Cognac, Filetto alla menta. **Wines** Trebbiano, Sizzano.

X **La Villetta,** viale Zara 87 ✉ 20159 ✆ 6891981, ☂ DQ **j**
closed Tuesday and August – **M** a la carte 20/30000.

X **Pechino,** via Cenisio 7 ✉ 20154 ✆ 384668, Chinese rest. with Pekinese specialities – ▤
closed Monday, 15 July-22 August and 20 December-4 January – **M** a la carte 23/33000 (12%). AR **u**

Central area Duomo, Scala, Sempione Park, Sforza Castle, Public gardens, corso Venezia, via Manzoni, North Station, corso Magenta, Porta Vittoria (Plans : Milan pp. 4 and 5) :

Gd H. Duomo, via San Raffaele 1 ✉ 20121 ✆ 8833, Telex 312086 – ▤ ☎ ♿. E VISA. ✻ CV **m**
M a la carte 33/46000 – ☕ 11000 – **160 rm** 155/240000 – P 215000.

Jolly President, largo Augusto 10 ✉ 20122 ✆ 7746, Telex 312054 – ▤ TV ☎ – 🚶. AE ⓓ E VISA. ✻ rest DV **t**
M 45000 – **201 rm** ☕ 195/230000 – P 277000.

Galileo without rest., corso Europa 9 ✉ 20122 ✆ 7743, Telex 322095 – ▤ TV ☎. AE ⓓ E VISA. ✻ DV **a**
76 rm ☕ 210/270000.

Plaza without rest., piazza Diaz 3 ✉ 20123 ✆ 8058452, Telex 321162 – ▤ TV ☎ – 🚶. AE ⓓ. ✻ CV **r**
closed 1 to 21 August – **118 rm** ☕ 190/240000.

Carlton Hotel Senato, via Senato 5 ✉ 20121 ✆ 798583, Telex 331306 – ▤ TV ☎ 🚗
71 rm. DU **q**

Grand Hotel et de Milan without rest., via Manzoni 29 ✉ 20121 ✆ 870757, Telex 334505 – ▤ TV ☎ ♿ – 🚶. AE ⓓ E VISA CDU **f**
☕ 16500 – **105 rm** 185/265000.

Cavour, via Fatebenefratelli 21 ✉ 20121 ✆ 650983, Telex 320498 – ▤ TV ☎ ♿. AE ⓓ E VISA. ✻ rest DU **n**
M *(closed Friday dinner, Saturday and Sunday lunch)* 40000 – ☕ 12000 – **113 rm** 121/152000 – P 152/204000.

Select without rest., via Baracchini 12 ✉ 20123 ✆ 8843, Telex 312256 – ▤ TV ☎ – 🚶. AE VISA CV **s**
☕ 15000 – **140 rm** 150/250000.

Dei Cavalieri without rest., piazza Missori 1 ✉ 20123 ✆ 8857, Telex 312040 – ▤ TV ☎ – 🚶. AE ⓓ E VISA CVX **c**
169 rm ☕ 138/180000.

Manin, via Manin 7 ✉ 20121 ✆ 6596511, Telex 320385, 🌳 – ▤ TV ☎ ♿ – 🚶. AE E VISA. ✻ rest DU **b**
closed 3 to 19 August – **M** *(closed Saturday and Sunday)* a la carte 35/50000 – ☕ 13000 – **110 rm** 130/165000 – P 153/200000.

De la Ville without rest., via Hoepli 6 ✉ 20121 ✆ 867651, Telex 312642 – ▤ TV ☎. AE E VISA. ✻ CV **v**
☕ 14000 – **105 rm** 165/190000.

Gran Duca di York without rest., via Moneta 1/a ✉ 20123 ✆ 874863 – ▤ TV ☎ ♿ – 🚶. ✻ BV **s**
closed August – ☕ 7500 – **33 rm** 70/100000.

Ariosto without rest., via Ariosto 22 ✉ 20145 ✆ 490995 – ▤ ♿ – 🚶. AE ⓓ E VISA. ✻ AU **c**
☕ 7500 – **53 rm** 80/120000.

Manzoni without rest., via Santo Spirito 20 ✉ 20121 ✆ 705700 – 🛁wc 🚿wc ☎ 🚗. ✻ DU **g**
☕ 10000 – **52 rm** 71/104000.

Casa Svizzera without rest., via San Raffaele 3 ✉ 20121 ✆ 802246, Telex 316064 – ▤ TV 🛁wc 🚿wc ☎. AE ⓓ E VISA CV **m**
closed 28 July-24 August – **45 rm** ☕ 78/115000.

Lord Internazionale without rest., via Spadari 11 ✉ 20123 ✆ 803028 – ▤ 🛁wc 🚿wc ☎. AE CV **t**
☕ 7000 – **46 rm** 72/103000.

Centro without rest., via Broletto 46 ✉ 20121 ✆ 875232, Telex 332632 – ▤ 🛁wc 🚿wc ☎ ♿. AE ⓓ E VISA BU **e**
☕ 10000 – **54 rm** 67/99000.

Star without rest., via dei Bossi 5 ✉ 20121 ✆ 871703 – ▤ 🚿wc ☎ CU **b**
closed August – ☕ 7000 – **28 rm** 61/90000, ▤ 5000.

XXXXX ✿ **Savini,** galleria Vittorio Emanuele II° ✉ 20121 ✆ 8058343, Elegant traditional decor, « Winter garden » – ▤. AE ⓓ E VISA CV **n**
closed Sunday, 10 to 19 August and 23 December-3 January – **M** (booking essential) a la carte 55/85000 (15%)
Spec. Risotto alla milanese ed al salto, Costoletta alla milanese, Filetto di San Pietro alla Ca' d'Oro. **Wines** Gavi, Franciacorta rosso.

XXXX **El Toulà,** piazza Paolo Ferrari 6 ✉ 20121 ✆ 870302, Elegant installation – ▤. AE ⓓ E VISA CU **z**
closed 6 to 21 August, 23 December-6 January, Sunday and June to August also Saturday – **M** a la carte 55/79000 (13%).

XXXX **St. Andrews,** via Sant'Andrea 23 ✉ 20121 ✆ 793132, Elegant installation, late night dinners – ▤. AE ⓓ E VISA. ✂ DU **y**
closed Sunday and August – **M** (booking essential) a la carte 50/72000.

XXXX **Biffi Scala,** piazza della Scala ✉ 20121 ✆ 876332, Tea-room and late night dinners – ▤. AE ⓓ E VISA. ✂ CU **z**
closed Sunday and 1 to 20 August – **M** a la carte 39/61000 (13%).

XXX **Suntory,** via Verdi 6 ✉ 20121 ✆ 862210, Japanese rest. – ▤. AE ⓓ VISA. ✂ CU **n**
closed Sunday and 10 to 17 August – **M** a la carte 41/63000.

XXX **Canoviano,** via Hoepli 6 ✉ 20121 ✆ 8058472 – ▤. AE ⓓ E. ✂ CV **v**
closed Saturday and Sunday – **M** a la carte 32/53000.

XXX **Prospero,** via Chiossetto 20 ✉ 20122 ✆ 701345 – ▤. AE ⓓ E DV **e**
closed Saturday, Sunday and August – **M** a la carte 33/48000.

XXX **Luciano,** via Ugo Foscolo 1 ✉ 20121 ✆ 866818 – ▤. AE ⓓ E VISA CV **a**
closed Saturday and 10 to 28 August – **M** a la carte 43/62000 (12%).

XXX **Alfio,** via Senato 31 ✉ 20121 ✆ 780731 – ▤. AE ⓓ E VISA DU **a**
closed Saturday, Sunday lunch, 9 to 26 August and 23 December-3 January – **M** a la carte 35/53000.

XXX **Crispi,** corso Venezia 3 ✉ 20121 ✆ 782010, ☂ – ▤. AE ⓓ E VISA DU **v**
closed Monday and 11 to 31 August – **M** a la carte 37/58000 (12%).

XXX **Rigoletto,** via Vincenzo Monti 33 ✉ 20123 ✆ 4988687, Rest. and piano-bar – ▤. AE ⓓ VISA AU **b**
closed Sunday and August – **M** a la carte 32/55000.

XXX **L'Innominato,** via Fiori Oscuri 3 ✉ 20121 ✆ 8690552, Rest. and piano-bar – ▤. AE ⓓ E VISA. ✂ CU **r**
closed Sunday, 28 March-2 April, August and 24 to 29 December – **M** a la carte 35/60000.

XXX **Barbarossa,** via Cerva 10 ✉ 20122 ✆ 781418, Old Milan-style setting – ▤. AE ⓓ VISA
closed August, Sunday and Saturday in July – **M** a la carte 30/46000. DV **f**

XXX 4 Mori, via San Giovanni sul Muro 2 ✉ 20121 ✆ 870617, « Summer service in garden » – ▤ BU **d**

XXX **Boeucc,** piazza Belgioioso 2 ✉ 20121 ✆ 790224, ☂ – ▤. AE. ✂ CDU **x**
closed Friday dinner, Saturday and August – **M** (booking essential) a la carte 30/46000.

XXX **Peck,** via Victor Hugo 4 ✉ 20123 ✆ 876774 – ▤. AE ⓓ E VISA. ✂ CV **b**
closed Sunday – **M** a la carte 31/56000.

XX La Lanterna, via Novati 2 ✉ 20123 ✆ 8052497 – ▤ BX **b**

XX **Kota Radja,** piazzale Baracca 6 ✉ 20123 ✆ 468850, Chinese rest. – ▤. AE ⓓ VISA
closed Monday – **M** a la carte 17/48000 (12%). AU **a**

XX **Bagutta,** via Bagutta 14 ✉ 20121 ✆ 702767, ☂, Artists' meeting place, « Typical paintings and caricatures » – AE ⓓ E VISA DU **e**
closed Sunday, 7 to 31 August and 23 December-5 January – **M** a la carte 32/46000 (12%).

XX **Al Mercante,** piazza Mercanti 17 ✉ 20123 ✆ 8052198, « Outdoor service in summer » – AE. ✂ CV **k**
closed Sunday and 5 to 25 August – **M** a la carte 26/35000.

XX **Boccondivino,** via Carducci 17 ✉ 20123 ✆ 866040, Typical pork-butcher's meat, cheese and wines – ▤. ✂ AV **e**
closed Sunday and August – **M** (dinner only) (booking essential) a la carte 20/41000.

XX **La Muraglia,** piazza Oberdan 2 ✉ 20129 ✆ 279528, ☂, Chinese rest. – ▤. AE E VISA
closed Monday and 10 to 20 August – **M** a la carte 18/28000 (12%). DU **d**

XX **Albric,** via Albricci 3 ✉ 20122 ✆ 806356, « Collection of paintings » – ▤. AE ⓓ E VISA. ✂ CV **q**
closed Sunday and 25 July-25 August – **M** a la carte 30/40000.

X **Trattoria dell'Angolo,** via Fiori Chiari ang via Formentini ✉ 20121 ✆ 8058495 – ▤. AE
closed Saturday lunch, Sunday, 1 to 7 January and 10 to 18 August – **M** a la carte 28/41000. CU **e**

X **Trattoria al Piccolo Teatro,** via Rovello 21 angolo via Cusani ✉ 20121 ✆ 877127, Typical rest. – ▤. AE ⓓ E BU **v**
closed Saturday lunch, Sunday and August – **M** (booking essential) a la carte 30/38000.

Francesco, via Festa del Perdono 4 20122 8053071, – . AE E VISA DV n
closed Sunday, 12 to 24 August and 23 to 31 December – **M** a la carte 30/45000.

Allo Scudo, via Mazzini 7 20123 8052761, Habitués' rest. – . AE CV e
closed Sunday and August – **M** a la carte 21/34000 (10%).

Giacomo, via Donizzetti 11 20122 795020 – AE. DV d
closed Sunday – **M** a la carte 27/44000.

Southern area Porta Ticinese, Porta Romana, Genova Station, Navigli, Ravizza Park, Vigentino (Plans : Milan pp. 6 and 7) :

Lloyd, without rest., corso di Porta Romana 48 20122 867971, Telex 335028, « Collection of paintings by well-known artists » – – CX z
52 rm.

Ascot without rest., via Lentasio 3 20122 862946, Telex 311303 – . AE E VISA. CX e
closed August – 12000 – **57 rm** 118/169000.

Crivi's without rest., corso Porta Vigentina 46 20122 5463341, Telex 313255 – – . AE DY a
closed August – 10000 – **62 rm** 119/157000.

D'Este, without rest., viale Bligny 23 20136 5461041, Telex 324216 – – – **54 rm.** CY r

Sant'Ambroeus without rest., viale Papiniano 14 20123 4697451, Telex 313373 – – . AE E VISA. AX a
closed August – 7000 – **52 rm** 71/104000.

Ambrosiano without rest., via Santa Sofia 9 20122 580445 – . AE E VISA. CX x
closed 20 July-26 August and 24 December-7 January – 9000 – **68 rm** 72/105000.

Mediterraneo without rest., via Muratori 14 20135 5488151, Telex 335812 – wc wc – . AE E VISA DY q
closed 1 to 21 August – 7000 – **93 rm** 75/108000.

Adriatico without rest., via Conca del Naviglio 20 20123 8324141 – wc wc . AE E VISA BX m
closed 1 to 21 August – 7000 – **105 rm** 73/105000.

Imperial without rest., corso di Porta Romana 68 20122 5468241 – wc wc . AE E VISA. DX c
10000 – **36 rm** 68/99000.

Garden without rest., via Rutilia 6 20141 537368 – wc DZ a
closed August – 5500 – **23 rm** 40/55000.

La Nôs, via Amedei 2 20123 808077, , Elegant old Milan-style meeting-place, « 19C decor ». CX n

Vecchia Milano, viale Gian Galeazzo ang. via Aurispa 20136 8397365, Arabian rest. – . E VISA BY e
closed Sunday and 20 July-20 August – **M** a la carte 32/57000 (12%).

Malatesta, via Bianca di Savoia 19 20122 5461079 – . AE VISA. CY a
closed Saturday, Sunday and August – **M** a la carte 30/42000.

San Vito da Nino, via San Vito 5 20123 8377029 – . VISA. BX a
closed Monday and August – **M** (booking essential) a la carte 45/65000 (13%)
Spec. Gingillo tartufato, Pollo allo Champagne, Costa di manzo alla bourguignonne. **Wines** Greco di Tufo, Dolcetto d'Alba.

Scaletta, piazzale Stazione Genova 20144 8350290 – . AY a
closed Sunday, Monday, 5 to 16 April, August and 24 December-7 January – **M** (booking essential) a la carte 70/80000
Spec. Terrina di trippa in gelatina, Risotto al ragù di lumache, Insalata di scampi. **Wines** Pinot di Franciacorta, Pergole Torte.

Al Porto, piazzale Generale Cantore 20123 8321481, Seafood – AXY d
closed Sunday, Monday lunch, August and 24 December-3 January – **M** (booking essential) a la carte 33/44000
Spec. Orata al pepe rosa, Scamponi gratinati, Branzino al pepe verde. **Wines** Tocai, Sauvignon.

Giordano, via Torti angolo corso Genova 3 20123 8350824, Neo rustic Bolognese cuisine – . AE BX s
closed Sunday and 5 to 28 August – **M** a la carte 24/33000 (12%).

Al Genovese, via Conchetta 18 20136 8373180, Liguria rest. – AE VISA BZ a
closed Monday and Tuesday lunch from October to May; Sunday and Monday lunch from June to September – **M** a la carte 26/45000.

Osteria del Binari, via Tortona 1 20144 8390753, , Old Milan atmosphere – AE
closed Sunday and 10 to 17 August – **M** (dinner only) (booking essential) a la carte 30/35000. AY e

Osteria Via Pré, via Casale 4 20144 8373869, Typical trattoria Ligurian cuisine – . VISA AY c
closed Monday, Tuesday and August – **M** a la carte 23/37000.

Districts : Città Studi, Monforte, corso 22 Marzo, viale Corsica – E : by : Linate Airport, Idroscalo, strada Rivoltana : :

Zefiro without rest., via Gallina 12 ✉ 20129 ✆ 7384253 – |♦| ▤ ⌂wc ⋒wc ☎ – 🅐. ✻
closed August – ☕ 9000 – **55 rm** 65/93000. by corso Concordia DU

Vittoria without rest., via Pietro Calvi 32 ✉ 20129 ✆ 5459695 – |♦| ▤ ⌂wc ⋒wc ☎. AE. ✻ by corso 22 Marzo DV
closed 27 July-27 August and 23 December-1 January – ☕ 5000 – **18 rm** 57/86000.

Città Studi without rest., via Saldini 24 ✉ 20133 ✆ 744666 – |♦| ⌂wc ⋒wc ☎ ♿. AE VISA – ☕ 5000 – **45 rm** 38/56000. by corso Concordia DU

XXXX ❀ **Giannino,** via Amatore Sciesa 8 ✉ 20135 ✆ **5452948, Traditional style, « Original decor; winter garden »** – Ⓟ. AE ◑ E VISA. ✻ by corso 22 Marzo DV
closed Sunday and August – **M** a la carte 62/92000
Spec. Risotto alla Giannino, Baccalà in tre modi, Stinco di vitello alla casalinga, Ossobuco del buongustaio (15 September-April). Wines Collefino di Ghemme, Dolcetto di Ovada.

XXXX ❀❀❀ **Gualtiero Marchesi,** via Bonvesin de la Riva 9 ✉ 20129 ✆ **741246, Elegant installation** – ▤. AE. ✻ by corso 22 Marzo DV
closed holidays, Sunday, Monday lunch, August and 24 to 28 December – **M** (booking essential) a la carte 52/90000
Spec. Raviolo aperto, Scaloppine di vitello impanate con salsa agrodolce, pinoli e uvette, Filetti di triglia impanati al rosmarino e pomodori saltati. Wines Prosecco, Settefilari.

XX **La Bella Pisana,** via Pasquale Sottocorno 17 ✉ 20129 ✆ 708376, ☂ – ▤. AE
closed Sunday, Monday lunch, 4 to 31 August and 25 December-5 January – **M** a la carte 28/38000. by corso Concordia DU

XX **Hosteria del Cenacolo,** via Archimede 12 ✉ 20129 ✆ 5458962, « **Summer service in garden** » – AE. ✻ by corso 22 Marzo DV
closed Saturday lunch and Sunday – **M** a la carte 29/43000.

X **Sagittario,** via Eustachi 6 ✉ 20129 ✆ 220045 by corso 22 Marzo DV
closed Sunday and August – **M** a la carte 27/43000.

Districts : Fiera Campionaria, San Siro, Porta Magenta – NW : by ⑩ and ⑪ : Novara, Torino :

Gd H. Fieramilano, viale Boezio 20 ✉ 20145 ✆ 3105, Telex 331426, ☂ – |♦| ▤ TV ☎ ♿ – 🅐. AE ◑ E VISA. ✻ rest by via Vincenzo Monti AT
M a la carte 32/50000 – **238 rm** ☕ 185/225000.

Gd H. Brun, via Caldera ✉ 20153 ✆ 45271, Telex 315370 – |♦| ▤ TV ☎ ♿ – 🅐. AE ◑ E VISA. ✻ by corso Sempione AT
M a la carte 42/62000 – **330 rm** ☕ 195/255000.

Rubens without rest., via Rubens 21 ✉ 20148 ✆ 405051, Telex 333503 – |♦| ▤ TV ☎ Ⓟ – 🅐. AE E VISA. ✻ by corso Vercelli AV
closed 1 to 21 August – **76 rm** ☕ 130/170000.

Montebianco without rest., via Monte Rosa 90 ✉ 20149 ✆ 4697941 – |♦| ▤ ☎ Ⓟ. AE ◑ E VISA. ✻ by ⑪
closed August and Christmas – ☕ 7000 – **44 rm** 68/100000.

Capitol, via Cimarosa 6 ✉ 20144 ✆ 4988851, Telex 316150 – |♦| ▤ TV ☎ – 🅐. AE ◑ E. ✻ rest by corso Vercelli AV
M *(closed lunch and August)* coffee shop only – **96 rm** ☕ 123/180000.

Mini Hotel Tiziano, via Tiziano 6 ✉ 20145 ✆ 4988921, Telex 325420, « **Little park** » – |♦| ▤ ☎ Ⓟ – 🅐 – **54 rm**. by ⑪

Green House without rest., viale Famagosta 50 ✉ 20142 ✆ 8132451 – |♦| ▤ ⋒wc ☎ ♿ 🚗. Ⓟ. AE. ✻ by ⑩
☕ 7000 – **45 rm** 45/71000.

Fiera, without rest., via Spinola 9 ✉ 20149 ✆ 432374, « **Little garden** » – |♦| ⌂wc ⋒wc ☎ 🚗 – 🅐 – **29 rm**. by ⑪

Astoria, viale Murillo 9 ✉ 20149 ✆ 4046646, Telex 334201 – |♦| ▤ ⌂wc ⋒wc ☎ – 🅐. AE ◑ E VISA. ✻ by ⑪
M *(closed Sunday)* a la carte 25/35000 – ☕ 8000 – **72 rm** 80/120000 – P 100000.

Wagner without rest., via Buonarroti 13 ✉ 20149 ✆ 4696051 – |♦| ▤ ⌂wc ⋒wc ☎. AE ◑ E VISA by ⑪
closed 26 July-24 August – **49 rm** ☕ 73/108000.

XXX **La Corba,** via dei Gigli 14 ✉ 20147 ✆ 4158977, « **Summer service in garden** » – AE ◑ VISA – *closed Sunday dinner, Monday and 8 to 24 August* – **M** a la carte 30/43000. by ⑩

XX **Raffaello,** via Raffaello Sanzio 8 ✉ 20149 ✆ 4814227, ☂ – AE ◑ E VISA by ⑪
closed Friday, Saturday lunch and 5 to 22 August – **M** a la carte 25/46000.

XX ❀ **Da Aimo,** via Montecuccoli 6 ✉ 20147 ✆ 416886, ☂ – ▤. AE VISA. ✻ by ⑩
closed Saturday lunch, Sunday and August – **M** (booking essential) a la carte 51/82000
Spec. Ricotta calda con radicchietti amari, Risotto con fiori di zucca e tartufi, Capretto al ginger fresco (October-March).

XX **Da Gino e Franco,** largo Domodossola 2 ✉ 20145 ✆ 312003 – ▤. ✻
closed Monday and 25 July-25 August – **M** a la carte 23/36000 (12%). by corso Sempione AT

XX **Ribot,** via Cremosano 41 ✉ 20148 ✆ 390646, **« Summer service in garden »** – Ⓟ. AE VISA. ⊁ by ⑪
closed Monday and August – **M** a la carte 29/37000.

XX **Furio-Montebianco,** via Monte Bianco 2 ✉ 20149 ✆ 4814677, Tuscan rest. – ▤. AE ⓓ E VISA by ⑪
closed Monday and August – **M** a la carte 27/46000 (12%).

XX **Al Garfagnino,** via Cherubini 8 ✉ 20145 ✆ 4814191 – ▤. AE ⓓ E VISA. ⊁ by ⑪
closed Monday and July – **M** a la carte 21/31000.

X **Pace,** via Washington 74 ✉ 20146 ✆ 468567, ⛱, Habitués' rest. – VISA by ⑩
closed Tuesday dinner, Wednesday and 1 to 23 August – **M** a la carte 21/33000.

Districts : Sempione-Bullona, viale Certosa – NW : by ⑫ ⑬ and ⑭ :Varese, Como, Torino, Malpensa Airport : :

Raffaello without rest., **viale Certosa 108 ✉ 20156 ✆ 3270146, Telex 315499** – ⫼ ▤ TV ☎ ♿ – 🏊. AE E VISA. ⊁ by via Cenisio AR
⊒ 8000 – **109 rm** 70/99000.

Berlino without rest., **via Plana 33 ✉ 20155 ✆ 367732, Telex 312609** – ⫼ ▤ ⛀wc ⎍wc ☎. AE E VISA by via Cenisio AR
⊒ 8000 – **47 rm** 68/96000.

Corallo without rest., **via Cesena 20 ✉ 20155 ✆ 314074** – ⫼ TV ⛀wc ⎍wc ☎ ♿. AE VISA – ⊒ 6000 – **35 rm** 44/68000. by via Mach Mahon AR

XX **La Pobbia,** via Gallarate 92 ✉ 20151 ✆ 305641, Neo rustic rest., **« Outdoor service in summer »** – Ⓟ. AE. ⊁ by via Cenisio AR
closed Sunday and August – **M** a la carte 35/45000 (12%).

X Da Stefano il Marchigiano, via Plana angolo via Arimondi 1 ✉ 20155 ✆ 390863 by via Cenisio AR

X **Al Vöttantott,** corso Sempione 88 ✉ 20154 ✆ 3182114, Habitués trattoria – ▤. AE
closed Sunday and August – **M** a la carte 22/31000. by corso Sempione AS

Abbiategrasso 20081 Milano 988 ③, 219 ⑱ – pop. 27 401 – ☎ 02.
Roma 590 – Alessandria 74 – Milano 23 – Novara 29 – Pavia 33.

at Cassinetta di Lugagnano N : 3 km – ✉ **20081 :**

XXX ✿✿ **Antica Osteria del Ponte,** ✆ 9420034 – ▤ Ⓟ. AE. ⊁
closed Sunday, Monday, 1 to 15 January and August – **M** (booking essential) a la carte 60/91000
Spec. Foie gras fresco di anitra, Ravioli di aragosta e zucchine (April-September), Petto d'anitra salsa mirtilli e aceto balsamico (June-October). **Wines** Sauvignon, Dolcetto d'Alba.

NAPLES (NAPOLI) 80100 Ⓟ 988 ㉗ – **pop. 1 208 545 – h.s. April-October – ☎ 081.**

See : On the sea-front : Castel Nuovo★★ (triumphal arc★★) KZ, **San Carlo Theatre★** KZ **T, piazza del Plebiscito★** JKZ, **Royal Palace★** KZ – **Port of Santa Lucia★★ (⩤★★★ of the gulf) – Mergellina★ (⩤★★ of the gulf).**

National Archaeological Museum★★★ KY **: Graeco-Roman sculptures★★★; mosaics★★; collections★★ of small bronzes, paintings and various objects from Herculaneum and Pompeii – Carthusian Monastery of St. Martin★★** JZ **: historical collections (presepi★★), from Belvedere (room n° 25) ⩤★★★ of the Bay of Naples, Baroque church★ (the monks' chancel★★) – Capodimonte Palace and National Galleries★★ : picture gallery★★, Royal apartments (the porcelain room★★).**

Spacca-Napoli quarter★★ KY **: St. Chiara Church★** KY **C(tomb★★ of King Robert the Wise, the cloisters★) – Cathedral : Chapel of San Gennaro★** LY.

Envir. : Island of Capri★★★ – Island of Ischia★★★ – Vesuvius★★★ (ascent of the volcano★★★, ✳★★★), E : 23 km and chairlift – Pompeii★★★ (excavations), SE : 24 km – Herculaneum★★ (excavations), SE : 9 km.

✈ Ugo Niutta of Capodichino NE : 6 km ✆ 312200 – Alitalia, via Medina 41 ✉ 80133 ✆ 325325.

⛴ to Capri March-October daily (1 h 30 mn about) – Navigazione Libera del Golfo, molo Beverello ✉ 80133 ✆ 325589; to Capri (1 h 15 mn), Ischia (1 h 15 mn) and Procida (1 h), daily – Agency De Luca, molo Beverello ✉ 80133 ✆ 313882; to Cagliari Wednesday and Sunday (15 h) and Palermo daily (10 h); to Catania (15 h 15 mn) and Siracusa (18 h 45 mn), Thursday – Tirrenia Navigazione, Stazione Marittima, molo Angioino ✉ 80133 ✆ 7201111, Telex 710030; to Ischia daily (1 h 15 mn) – Libera Navigazione Lauro, via Caracciolo 11 ✆ 991889, Telex 720354 and Agency de Luca, molo Beverello ✉ 80133 ✆ 313882.

⛴ to Capri, Ischia and Procida daily (45 mn) – Agency De Luca, molo Beverello ✉ 80133 ✆ 313882; to Capri (45 mn) and Ischia (45 mn), daily – Alilauro, via Caracciolo 11 ✆ 682017, Telex 720354; to Capri daily (45 mn) – SNAV, via Caracciolo 10 ✆ 660444, Telex 720446.

ℹ via Partenope 10/a ✉ 80121 ✆ 406289 – piazza del Plebiscito (Royal Palace) ✉ 80132 ✆ 418744 – Central Station ✉ 80142 ✆ 268779 – Capodichino Airport ✉ 80133 ✆ 7805761.

A.C.I. piazzale Tecchio 49/d ✉ 80125 ✆ 611084.

Roma 219 ③ – Bari 261 ⑤.

Plans on following pages

Excelsior, via Partenope 48 ✉ 80121 ☏ 417111, Telex 710043, < gulf, Vesuvius and Castel dell'Ovo – AE E VISA. GX **w**
M a la carte 70/95000 – 16500 – **137 rm** 226/346000.

Vesuvio, via Partenope 45 ✉ 80121 ☏ 417044, Telex 710127, « Roof-garden rest. with < gulf and Castel dell'Ovo » – AE E VISA. rest FX **n**
M a la carte 38/56000 – **170 rm** 154/219000 – P 170/214000.

Jolly, via Medina 70 ✉ 80133 ☏ 416000, Telex 720335, « Roof-garden rest. with < town, gulf and Vesuvius » – AE E VISA. rest KZ **s**
M 35000 – **278 rm** 120/154000 – P 180000.

Royal, via Partenope 38 ✉ 80121 ☏ 400244, Telex 710167, < gulf, Posillipo and Castel dell'Ovo, – AE E VISA. rest FX **n**
M a la carte 34/60000 – **300 rm** 108/177000.

Britannique, corso Vittorio Emanuele 133 ✉ 80121 ☏ 660933, Telex 722281, <, – AE E VISA. EX **r**
M 27000 – 10000 – **80 rm** 104/140000, 10000 – P 140000.

San Germano, via Beccadelli 41 ✉ 80125 ☏ 7605422, Telex 720080, « Beautiful garden-park », – by ⑧
107 rm.

Serius, viale Augusto 74 ✉ 80125 ☏ 614844 – wc wc by ⑧
M 22000 – **69 rm** 57/85000, 9000 – P 84000.

Palace Hotel, piazza Garibaldi 9 ✉ 80142 ☏ 264575 – wc wc. AE VISA. rest MY **s**
M a la carte 25/37000 – 6500 – **102 rm** 46/72000, 6000 – P 82/93000.

Rex without rest., via Palepoli 12 ✉ 80132 ☏ 416388 – wc wc. AE E VISA GX **r**
5000 – **40 rm** 42/65000.

Domitiana without rest., viale Kennedy 143 ✉ 80125 ☏ 610560 – wc. AE E VISA by ⑧
8500 – **40 rm** 62/94000.

Miramare without rest., via Nazario Sauro 24 ✉ 80132 ☏ 427388 – wc wc. AE E VISA GX **e**
9000 – **26 rm** 71/83000, 8000.

XXX La Sacrestia, via Orazio 116 ✉ 80122 ☏ 664186, <, Elegant rest., – by piazza J. Sannazzaro EX

XX **Harry's Bar,** via Lucilio 11 ✉ 80132 ☏ 407810 – GX **a**
closed Sunday and August – **M** (booking essential) a la carte 24/33000 (12%).

XX ✲ **Giuseppone a Mare,** via Ferdinando Russo 13-Capo Posillipo ✉ 80123 ☏ 7696002, Seaside rest. with <, « In little harbour » – AE E VISA.
closed Sunday and 23 to 31 December – **M** a la carte 40/55000 (12%)
Spec. Linguine Riva Fiorita, Polipetti al pignatiello, Pesce all'acqua pazza. **Wines** Forastera.
by piazza J. Sannazzaro EX

XX ✲ **La Cantinella,** via Cuma 42 ✉ 80132 ☏ 404884, Typical seaside rest. – AE VISA.
closed Sunday and August – **M** a la carte 23/42000 (12%) GX **v**
Spec. Linguine al Mar Tirreno, Penne alla Cantinella, Grigliata mista di pesce. **Wines** Greco di Tufo, Tavrasi.

XX **Don Salvatore,** strada Mergellina 4/a ✉ 80122 ☏ 681817, Rest. and pizzeria – AE VISA by piazza J. Sannazzaro EX
closed Wednesday – **M** a la carte 25/42000 (12%).

X **San Carlo,** via Cesario Console 18/19 ✉ 80132 ☏ 417206 – AE E VISA. KZ **a**
closed Sunday and August – **M** (booking essential) 40/50000.

X **Al Sarago,** piazza Sannazzaro 201/b ✉ 80122 ☏ 685587 – EX **a**
closed Sunday – **M** a la carte 26/36000 (13%).

X **Sbrescia,** rampe Sant'Antonio a Posillipo 109 ✉ 80122 ☏ 669140, Typical Neapolitan trattoria with < – AE. by piazza J. Sannazzaro EX
closed Monday – **M** a la carte 18/34000 (12%).

When driving through towns
use the plans in the ***Michelin Guide*** *Features indicated include:*
throughroutes and by -passes;
traffic junctions and major squares,
new streets, car parks, pedestrian streets...
All this information is revised annually.

A complete list of cities included in this guide
will be found on pp. 4 and 5.

NAPOLI

Giordano (Via L.) .... EV 64
Scarlatti
(Via Alessandro) ...... EV 153

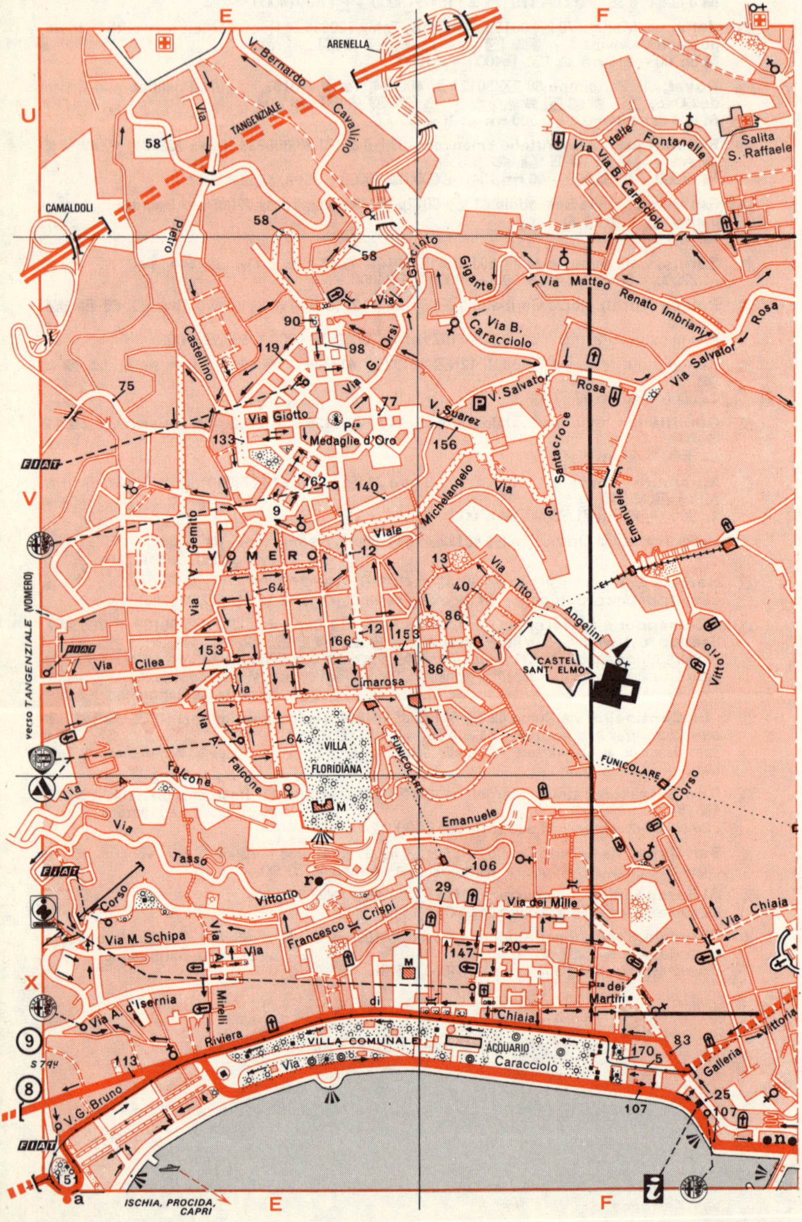

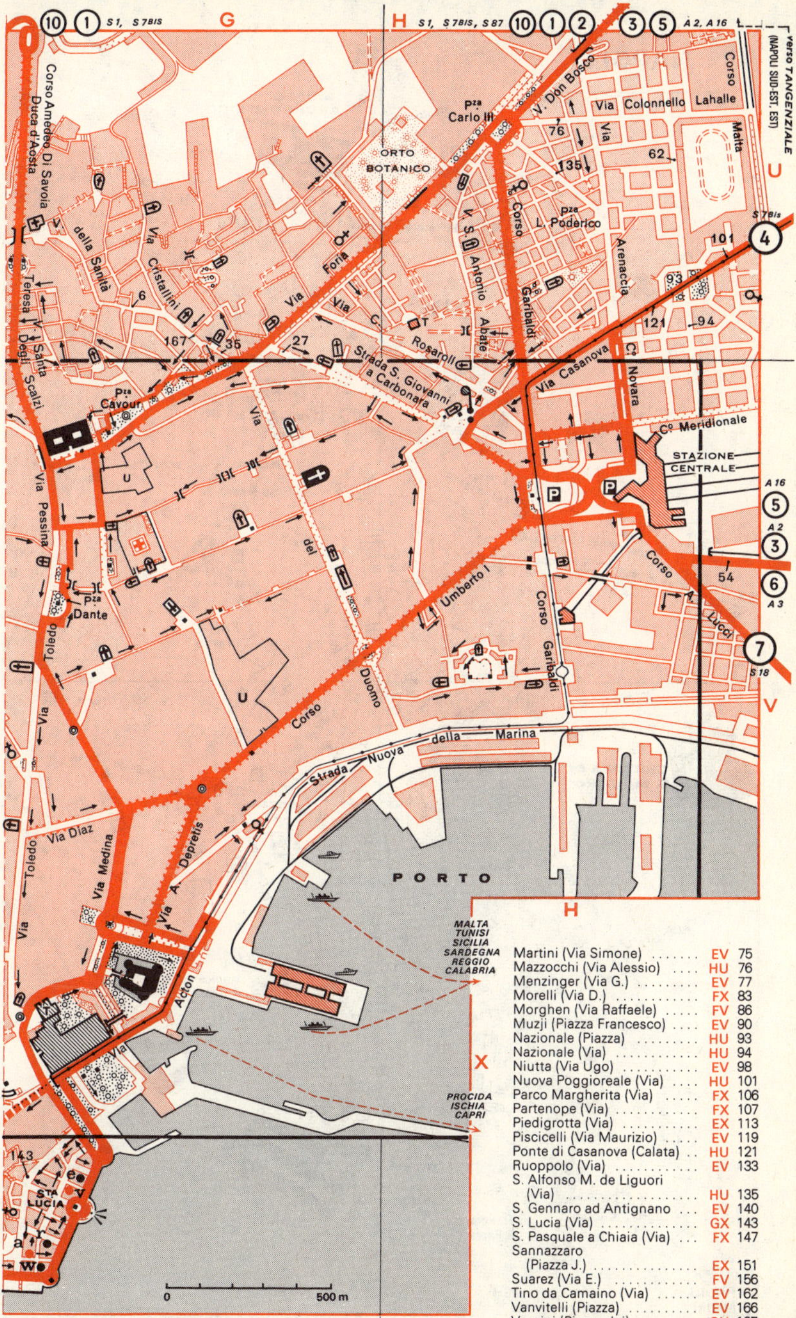

Martini (Via Simone)	EV	75
Mazzocchi (Via Alessio)	HU	76
Menzinger (Via G.)	EV	77
Morelli (Via D.)	FX	83
Morghen (Via Raffaele)	FV	86
Muzji (Piazza Francesco)	EV	90
Nazionale (Piazza)	HU	93
Nazionale (Via)	HU	94
Niutta (Via Ugo)	EV	98
Nuova Poggioreale (Via)	HU	101
Parco Margherita (Via)	FX	106
Partenope (Via)	FX	107
Piedigrotta (Via)	EX	113
Piscicelli (Via Maurizio)	EX	119
Ponte di Casanova (Calata)	HU	121
Ruoppolo (Via)	EV	133
S. Alfonso M. de Liguori (Via)	HU	135
S. Gennaro ad Antignano	EV	140
S. Lucia (Via)	GX	143
S. Pasquale a Chiaia (Via)	FX	147
Sannazzaro (Piazza J.)	EX	151
Suarez (Via E.)	FV	156
Tino da Camaino (Via)	EV	162
Vanvitelli (Piazza)	EV	166
Vergini (Piazza dei)	GU	167
Vittoria (Piazza)	FX	170

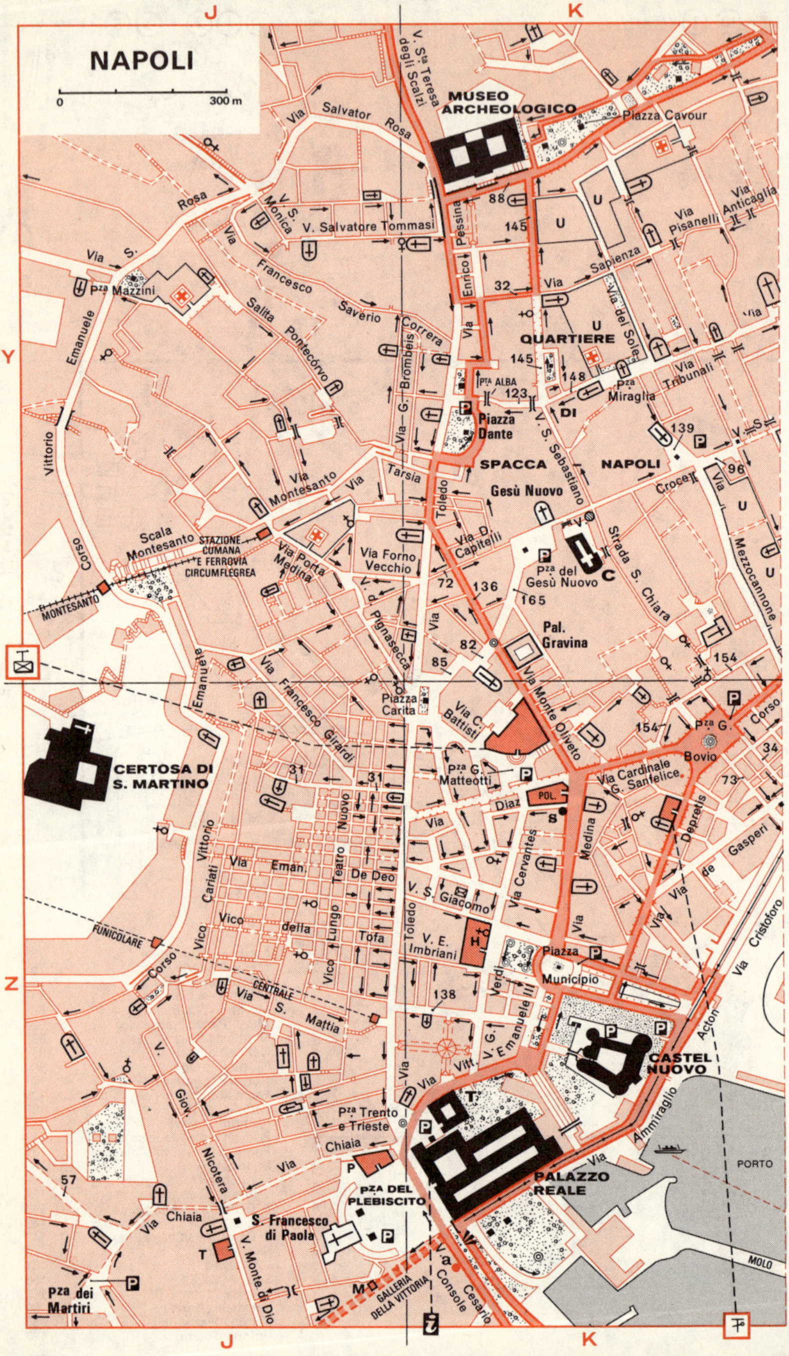
NAPOLI
0
300 m
J
K
Y
Z
MUSEO ARCHEOLOGICO
Piazza Cavour
V. Sta Teresa degli Scalzi
Via Salvator Rosa
V. S. Monica
V. Salvatore Tommasi
Via S. Rosa
Pza Mazzini
Via Francesco Saverio Correra
Salita Pontecorvo
Via Enrico Pessina
Via G. Brombeis
Via Sapienza
Via Pisanelli
Via Anticaglia
Via del Sole
QUARTIERE
Via Tribunali
Pza Miraglia
PTA ALBA
Piazza Dante
SPACCA
DI
NAPOLI
V. S. Sebastiano
Via Tarsia
Via Montesanto
Scala Montesanto
STAZIONE CUMANA E FERROVIA CIRCUMFLEGREA
MONTESANTO
Via Porta Medina
Via Forno Vecchio
Gesù Nuovo
Via D. Capitelli
Pza del Gesù Nuovo
Strada S. Chiara
Via Croce
Via Mezzocannone
Pal. Gravina
Via Pignasecca
Toledo
Corso Vittorio Emanuele
CERTOSA DI S. MARTINO
Via Francesco Girardi
Piazza Carita
Via C. Battisti
Via Monte Oliveto
Pza G. Bovio
Corso
Pza G. Matteotti
Via Diaz
POL.
Via Cardinale G. Sanfelice
Via Depretis
Via de Gasperi
Via Medina
Via Cervantes
Via Emanuele De Deo
Vico Cariati
Teatro Nuovo
V. S. Giacomo
Vico della Tofa
Vico Lungo
V. E. Imbriani
FUNICOLARE CENTRALE
Via S. Mattia
Verdi
Piazza Municipio
V. G. Emanuele III
Via Cristoforo
Acton
CASTEL NUOVO
Via Ammiraglio
PORTO
Via Chiaia
Pza Trento e Trieste
Via Toledo
Vitt.
PALAZZO REALE
PZA DEL PLEBISCITO
S. Francesco di Paola
V. Giov. Nicotera
V. Monte di Dio
Via Chiaia
Pza dei Martiri
GALLERIA DELLA VITTORIA
Via Console
Cesario
MOLO
U
H
T
P
C
S
M
88
145
32
145
148
123
139
96
72
136
165
82
85
154
154
34
73
31
31
138
57

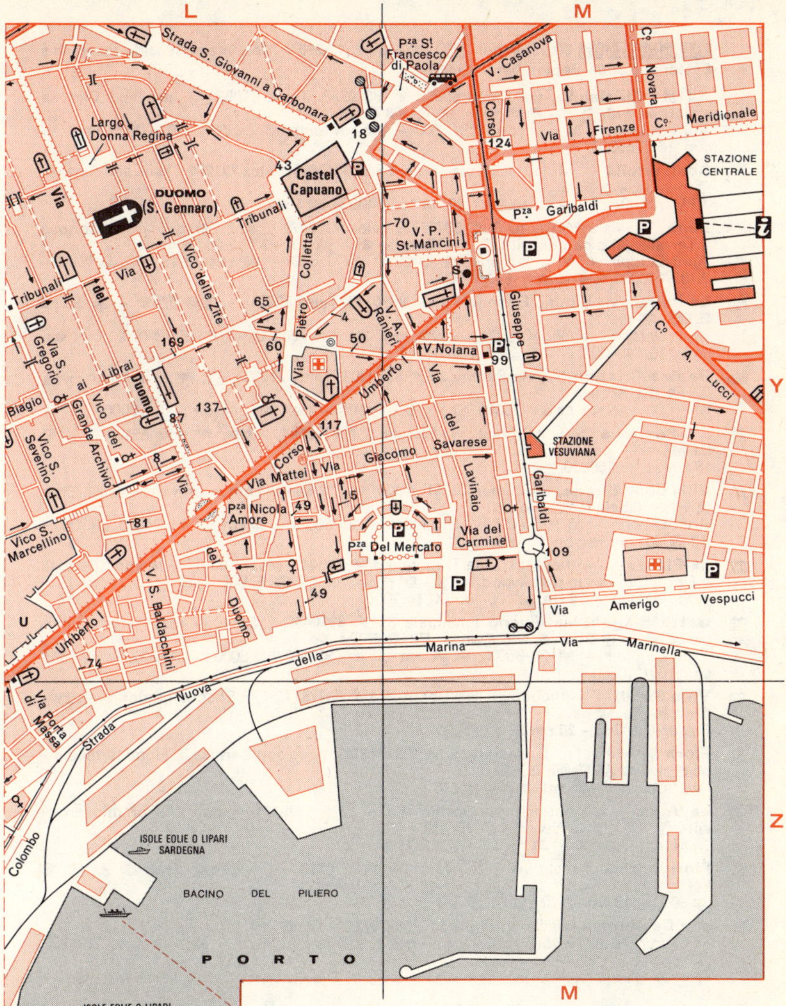

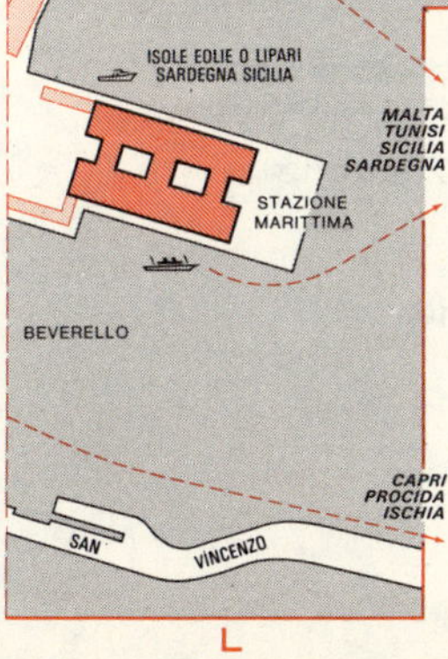

Chiaia (Via)	JZ	
Filangieri (Via Gaetano)	JZ	57
Toledo (Via)	KY	
Annunziata (Via dell')	LY	4
Arte della Lana (Via)	LY	8
Cangiani al Mercato (Vico)	LY	15
Capuana (Piazza)	LY	18
Concezione a Montecalvario (Via)	JZ	31
Conte di Ruvo (Via)	KY	32
Cortese (Via Giuio C.)	KZ	34
De Nicola (Piazza E.)	LY	43
Duca di S. Donato (Via)	LY	49
Egiziaca a Forcella (Via)	LY	50
Forcella (Via)	LY	60
Giudecca Vecchia (Via)	LY	65
Maddalena (Via)	MY	70
Maddaloni (Via)	KY	72
Marchese Campodisola (Via)	KZ	73
Marotta (Via G.)	LY	74
Miroballo al Pendino (Via)	LY	81
Monteoliveto (Piazza)	KY	82
Morgantini (Via M.)	KY	85
Museo Filangieri (Piazza)	LY	87
Museo Nazionale (Piazza)	KY	88
Nilo (Piazzetta)	KY	96
Nolana (Piazza)	MY	99
Pepe (Piazza Guglielmo)	MY	109
Pironti (Via M.)	LY	117
Porta Alba (Via)	KY	123
Principe Umberto (Piazza)	MY	124
S. Anna dei Lombardi (Via)	KY	136
S. Arcangelo a Baiano (Via)	LY	137
S. Brigida (Via)	KZ	138
S. Domenico Maggiore (Piazza)	KY	139
S. Maria di Costantinopoli (Via)	KY	145
S. Pietro a Maiella (Via)	KY	148
Sedile di Porto (Via del)	KYZ	154
Trinità Maggiore (Calata)	KY	165
Vicaria Vecchia (Via)	LY	169

Island of Capri 80073 Napoli 988 ㉗ – pop. 12 296 – Health and seaside resort, h.s. Easter and June-September – ✆ 081.

Gd H. Quisisana, via Camerelle 2 ✆ 8370788, Telex 710520, ≤ sea and Certosa, « Garden with ⛱ » – |$| ▤ ☎ – 🏊. AE ⓓ E VISA. ✻
April-October – **M** a la carte 55/82000 – **143 rm** (dinner included) 220/302000, low season 168/265000.

Scalinatella ⛵ without rest., via Tragara 8 ✆ 8370633, Telex 721204, ≤ sea and Certosa, ⛱ heated – |$| ▤ ☎
15 March-October – ☐ 16000 – **28 rm** 140/240000, ▤ 15000.

Luna ⛵, viale Matteotti 3 ✆ 8370433, Telex 721247, ≤ sea, Faraglioni and Certosa, « Terraces and garden with ⛱ » – |$| ▤ rm ☎ – 🏊. AE ⓓ E VISA. ✻ rest
April-October – **M** a la carte 39/50000 – ☐ 13500 – **48 rm** 78/180000, ▤ 7000 – P 132/176000, low season 110/155000.

La Palma, via Vittorio Emanuele 39 ✆ 8370133, Telex 722015 – |$| ▤ TV ☎ – 🏊. AE ⓓ E VISA. ✻ rest
April-October – **M** 40/50000 – **80 rm** ☐ 135/258000 – P 165/189000, low season 110/140000.

Regina Cristina ⛵, via Serena 20 ✆ 8370303, Telex 710531, ⛱, ⌂ – |$| ▤ rm – 🏊. AE ⓓ VISA. ✻ rest
M 35000 – **55 rm** ☐ 68/175000, ▤ 10000 – P 115/140000, low season 100/120000.

L'a Pazziella ⛵ without rest., via Giuliani 4 ✆ 8370044, ≤ sea, ⌂ – ▤ ⌸wc ⋒wc ☎. AE VISA. ✻
19 rm ☐ 85/160000.

Villa delle Sirene, via Camerelle 51 ✆ 8370102, ≤ sea, « Lemon-grove » – |$| ▤ ⌸wc ⋒wc ☎. AE ⓓ E VISA. ✻ rest
April-October – **M** *(closed Tuesday)* a la carte 26/38000 – **35 rm** ☐ 70/124000, ▤ 7000 – P 115000, low season 104000.

La Pineta ⛵ without rest., via Tragara 6 ✆ 8370644, Telex 710011, ≤ sea and Certosa, « Floral terraces in pine-wood », ⛱ – ▤ ⌸wc ☎. AE ⓓ E VISA
April-October – **54 rm** ☐ 105/165000, ▤ 10000.

Gatto Bianco, via Vittorio Emanuele 32 ✆ 8370446, « Summer rest. service under pergola » – |$| ▤ rm ⌸wc ⋒wc ☎. AE ⓓ E VISA. ✻
April-October – **M** 30/35000 – **44 rm** ☐ 64/108000, ▤ 8000 – P 124000, low season 100/110000.

Villa Sarah ⛵ without rest., via Tiberio 3/a ✆ 8377817, ≤, « Shaded garden » – ⌸wc ⋒wc ☎. AE. ✻
Easter-October – **25 rm** ☐ 46/76000.

Flora ⛵ without rest., via Serena 26 ✆ 8370211, ≤ sea and Certosa, « Floral terrace » – ▤ ⌸wc ☎ ♿. AE ⓓ E VISA
April-October – **25 rm** ☐ 68/115000.

La Vega ⛵ without rest., via Occhio Marino 10 ✆ 8370481, ≤ sea, « Panoramic terrace with ⛱ » – ⌸wc ⋒wc ☎. AE ⓓ VISA
15 March-October – **24 rm** ☐ 70/120000.

Florida without rest., via Fuorlovado 34 ✆ 8370710, ⌂ – ⌸wc ⋒wc ☎ ♿. AE ⓓ VISA
☐ 9000 – **19 rm** 37/70000.

XX ✿ **La Capannina,** via Le Botteghe 14 ✆ 8370732 – ▤. AE. ✻
15 March-10 November; closed Wednesday (except August) – **M** a la carte 26/42000 (13%)
Spec. Ravioli alla caprese, Linguine al sugo di scorfano, Grigliata mista di pesce. **Wines** Capri, Greco di Tufo.

XX **La Pigna,** via Lo Palazzo 30 ✆ 8370280, ≤ gulf of Naples, 🍽 – AE ⓓ E VISA. ✻
Easter-October; closed Tuesday during low season – **M** a la carte 25/35000 (15%).

XX **Aurora Grill,** via Le Botteghe 46 ✆ 8377642
closed Monday, January, February and March – **M** a la carte 22/36000 (12%).

X **La Sceriffa,** via Acquaviva 29 ✆ 8377953, ≤
April-October; closed Tuesday – **M** a la carte 23/36000.

X **Geranio,** viale Matteotti 8 ✆ 8370616, 🍽 – AE VISA
April-15 October; closed Thursday – **M** a la carte 25/40000 (11%).

Pleasant hotels and restaurants
are shown in the Guide by a red sign.
Please send us the names
of any where you have enjoyed your stay.
Your Michelin Guide will be even better.

XXXXX ... X

PALERME (PALERMO) (SICILY) 90100 P 988 ㉟ – pop. 712 342 – ☎ 091.

See : Town centre*** : Quattro Canti**, piazza Pretoria* (fountain**), piazza Bellini** (the Martorana**, church of St. Cataldo**) – Church of St. John of the Hermits** – Palace of the Normans** (the palatine Chapel***, King Roger's Room**) – Botanical garden** – Capuchin catacombs**.

Abbatellis Palace* : National Gallery of Sicily** (fresco of Death Triumphant***) – Archaeological Museum* (metopes from temples at Selinus**) BY **M** – Chiaramonte Palace* – Palazzo della Zisa* (temporarily closed for restoration work) – Cathedral* BZ **B** – St. Lawrence Oratory* CY **C** – St. Mary of the Chain* DY **D** – Garden of the Villa Bonanno* – Garibaldi gardens (ficus magnolioides**) – Villa Giulia (garden*) DZ.

Envir. : Park of the Favourite* 3 km – Monte Pellegrino (picturesque landscapes** and ≤**) N : 14 km – Monreale : Cathedral*** (mosaics***), Cloister*** 8 km by ②.

Exc : Ustica Island (ensemble ≤**, Blue grotto*) 2 h 30 mn by boat-service or 1 h 15 mn by hydrofoil speedboat.

✈ Punta Raisi by ③ : 30 km ☎ 591414 – Alitalia, via della Libertà 29 ✉ 90139 ☎ 584533.

⛴ to Genova : Tuesday, Friday and Sunday (22 h) and to Livorno : Monday, Wednesday and Friday (19 h) – Grandi Traghetti, via Mariano Stabile 179 ☎ 587939, Telex 910098; to Napoli daily (10 h), to Genova Monday, Wednesday, Friday and Sunday (23 h) and to Cagliari Monday (12 h 30 mn) – Tirrenia Navigazione, via Roma 385 ☎ 585733, Telex 910020; to Ustica daily (2 h 30 mn) – Prestifilippo Agency, via Crispi 124 ☎ 582403.

🚤 to Ustica daily (1 h 15 mn) – Prestifilippo Agency, via Crispi 124 ☎ 582403.

ℹ piazza Castelnuovo 35 ✉ 90141 ☎ 583847, Telex 910179 – Punta Raisi Airport ☎ 591405 – Central Station ✉ 90127 ☎ 233808.

A.C.I. viale delle Alpi 6 ✉ 90144 ☎ 266393.

Messina 235 ①.

Plan on following pages

Villa Igiea Gd H. 🌳, salita Belmonte 43 ✉ 90142 ☎ 543744, Telex 910092, ≤, 🌳, « Floral terraces overlooking the sea », 🏊, 🌳, 🎾 – 🛗 ▤ 📺 ☎ ♿ 🅟 – 🏛. AE ⓓ E VISA. 🚫 rest — by ③
M 60000 – ☕ 18000 – **118 rm** 158/244000 – P 216/276000.

Gd H. et des Palmes, via Roma 398 ✉ 90139 ☎ 583933, Telex 911082, « Roof-garden rest. nightly » – 🛗 ▤ 📺 ☎ ♿ – 🏛. AE ⓓ E VISA. 🚫 rest — BX **g**
M 32000 – ☕ 11000 – **184 rm** 77/101000 – P 126000.

President, via Crispi 230 ✉ 90133 ☎ 580733, Telex 910359, ≤, « Roof-garden rest. » – 🛗 ▤ 📺 ☎ ♿ – 🏛. VISA. 🚫 — BX **e**
M 15/18000 – ☕ 5000 – **129 rm** 57/74000 – P 63/76000.

Politeama Palace, piazza Ruggero Settimo 15 ✉ 90139 ☎ 322777, Telex 911053 – 🛗 ▤ 📺 ☎ – 🏛 — BX **a**
102 rm.

Jolly, Foro Italico 22 ✉ 90133 ☎ 235842, Telex 910076, ≤, 🏊, 🌳 – 🛗 ▤ 📺 ☎ 🅟 – 🏛. AE ⓓ E VISA. 🚫 rest — DY **s**
M 31000 – **290 rm** ☕ 90/130000 – P 139000.

Excelsior Palace, via Marchese Ugo 3 ✉ 90141 ☎ 266155, Telex 911149 – 🛗 ▤ 📺 ☎. VISA. 🚫 — AX **c**
M 20/25000 – ☕ 6000 – **86 rm** 69/85000 – P 80/95000.

Europa, via Agrigento 3 ✉ 90141 ☎ 266673 – 🛗 ▤ 📺 ☎. AE ⓓ E VISA. 🚫 rest — AX **r**
M 20000 – ☕ 6000 – **73 rm** 45/71000 – P 78000.

Mediterraneo, via Rosolino Pilo 43 ✉ 90139 ☎ 581133 – 🛗 ▤ 📺 ☎ ♿ – 🏛. AE ⓓ E VISA — BX **k**
M 20000 – ☕ 6000 – **106 rm** 45/71000 – P 70000.

Ponte, via Crispi 99 ✉ 90133 ☎ 583744 – 🛗 ▤ 📺 🛁wc 🚿wc ☎ — CX **x**
136 rm.

MotelAgip, viale della Regione Siciliana 2620 ✉ 90145 ☎ 552033, Telex 911196 – 🛗 ▤ 🚿wc ☎ ♿ 🅟 – 🏛. AE ⓓ E VISA. 🚫 — by ③
M 20/23000 – **105 rm** ☕ 50/90000.

Metropol, via Turrisi Colonna 4 ✉ 90141 ☎ 588608 – ▤ 🛁wc 🚿wc ☎. AE ⓓ E VISA. 🚫 rest — AX **a**
M (residents only) 18000 – ☕ 6000 – **44 rm** 33/60000, ▤ 6000 – P 57/70000.

Sausele without rest., via Vincenzo Errante 12 ✉ 90127 ☎ 237524 – 🛗 🛁wc 🚿wc ☎ 🚗. AE E VISA — CZ **u**
☕ 6000 – **40 rm** 30/44000.

Villa Archirafi without rest., via Lincoln 30 ✉ 90133 ☎ 285827, 🌳 – 🛗 🚿wc ☎ 🅟. E — DZ **m**
☕ 5000 – **30 rm** 31/46000.

Touring without rest., via Mariano Stabile 136 ✉ 90139 ☎ 584444 – 🛗 ▤ 🛁wc 🚿wc ☎. AE ⓓ VISA. 🚫 — BX **h**
☕ 5000 – **22 rm** 35/52000, ▤ 5500.

Liguria without rest., via Mariano Stabile 128 ✉ 90139 ☎ 581588 – 🚿wc ☎. ⓓ. 🚫 — BX **b**
☕ 3500 – **16 rm** 22/44000.

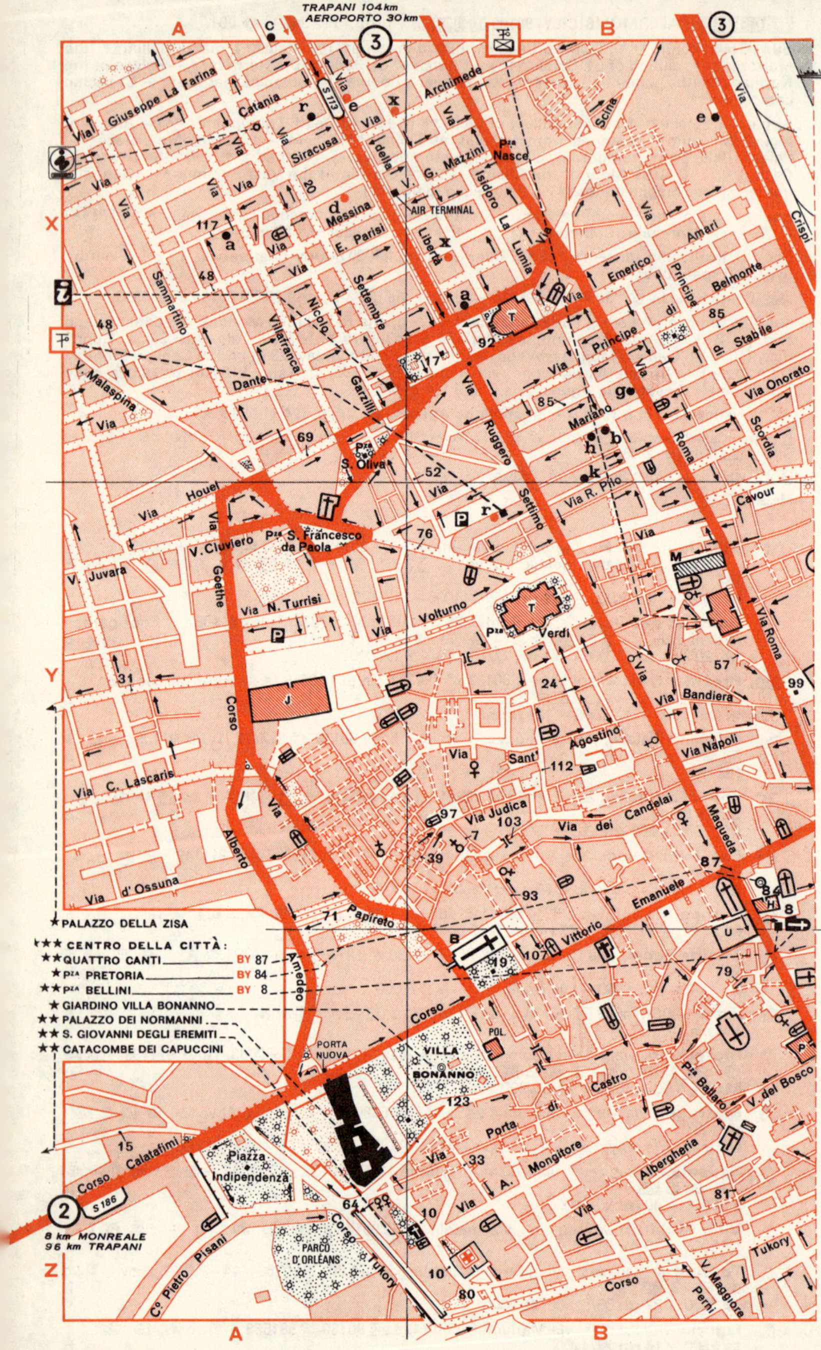

TRAPANI 104 km
AEROPORTO 30 km
A
B
X
Y
Z
Via Giuseppe La Farina
Catania
Via Siracusa
Via della Libertà
Archimede
Via G. Mazzini
Pza Nasce
Isidoro La Lumia
Via Messina
AIR TERMINAL
Via E. Parisi
Via Sammartino
Via Villafranca
Via Nicolò Garzilli
Via Settembre
Via Dante
V. Malaspina
Via Emerico Amari
Via Principe di Belmonte
Via Principe di Scordia
Via Stabile
Via Onorato
Via Ruggero Settimo
Via Mariano Stabile
Via R. Pilo
Via Roma
Via Crispi
Scina
Cavour
Pza S. Oliva
Via Houel
V. Cluviero
Pza S. Francesco da Paola
V. Juvara
Via N. Turrisi
Via Goethe
Volturno
Pza Verdi
Via Bandiera
Via Napoli
Via Sant' Agostino
Via Maqueda
Via Judica
Via dei Candelai
Via C. Lascaris
Corso Alberto Amedeo
Via d'Ossuna
Papireto
Corso Vittorio Emanuele
PORTA NUOVA
VILLA BONANNO
POL
Castro
Porta di Castro
Pza Ballarò
V. del Bosco
Via Albergheria
Via Porta Mongitore
Via A. Tukory
Corso Tukory
V. Maggiore Perni
Corso Calatafimi
Piazza Indipendenza
PARCO D'ORLÉANS
Co Pietro Pisani
S 186
S 113
8 km MONREALE
96 km TRAPANI
★PALAZZO DELLA ZISA
★★★ CENTRO DELLA CITTÀ:
★★QUATTRO CANTI BY 87
★Pza PRETORIA BY 84
★★Pza BELLINI BY 8
★GIARDINO VILLA BONANNO
★★PALAZZO DEI NORMANNI
★★S. GIOVANNI DEGLI EREMITI
★★CATACOMBE DEI CAPUCCINI

PALERMO

Maqueda (Via)	BY	
Roma (Via)	BXY	
Ruggero Settimo (Via)	BXY	
Vittorio Emanuele (Corso)	BY	
Aragona (Piazza)	CY	4
Aragona (Via)	CY	6
Beati Paoli (Via)	BY	7
Bellini (Piazza)	BY	8
Benedettini (Via dei)	BZ	10
Cappuccini (Via dei)	AZ	15
Cassa di Risparmio (Piazza)	CY	16
Castelnuovo (Piazza)	BX	17
Cattedrale (Piazza della)	BZ	19
Cervello (Via)	DY	20
Croce dei Vespri (Piazza della)	CY	21
Donizetti (Via Gaetano)	BY	24
Finocchiaro Aprile (Corso)	AY	31
Fonderia (Piazza)	CY	32
Generale Cadorna (Via)	BZ	33
Gioiamia (Via)	ABY	39
Giudici (Discesa dei)	CY	41
Loggia (Via della)	CY	45
Marconi (Via)	AX	48
Materassai (Via)	CY	51
Meccio (Via Salvatore)	BX	52
Monteleone (Via)	BY	57
Mura delle Cattive (Salita)	DY	60
Orleans (Piazza d')	AZ	64
Paternostro (V. Alessandro)	CY	68
Paternostro (Via Paolo)	AX	69
Peranni (Pza Domenico)	AYZ	71
Pignatelli d'Aragona (Via)	BY	76
Ponticello (Via)	BZ	79
Porta Montalto (Piazza)	BZ	80
Porta Sant'Agata (Via)	BZ	81
Porto Salvo (Via)	CY	83
Pretoria (Piazza)	BY	84
Principe Granatelli (Via)	BX	85
Quattro Canti	BY	87
Rivoluzione (Piazza)	CZ	91
Ruggero Settimo (Piazza)	BX	92
S. Agata (Via)	BY	93
S. Anna (Piazza)	CY	95
S. Antonino (Piazza)	CZ	96
S. Cosmo (Piazza)	BY	97
S. Domenico (Piazza)	BY	99
S. Francesco d'Assisi (Pza)	CY	100
S. Giorgio (Piazza)	CY	101
S. Isidoro (Via)	BY	103
S. Sebastiano (Via)	CY	104
S. Teresa (Piazzetta)	DY	105
Scuole (Via delle)	BZ	107
Spasimo (Piazza dello)	DY	108
Spasimo (Via dello)	DZ	109
Spirito Santo (Via dello)	BY	112
Squarcialupo (Via)	CY	113
Torremuzza (Via)	DY	116
Turrisi Colonna (Via)	AX	117
Valverde (Piazza)	CY	122
Vittoria (Piazza della)	BZ	123

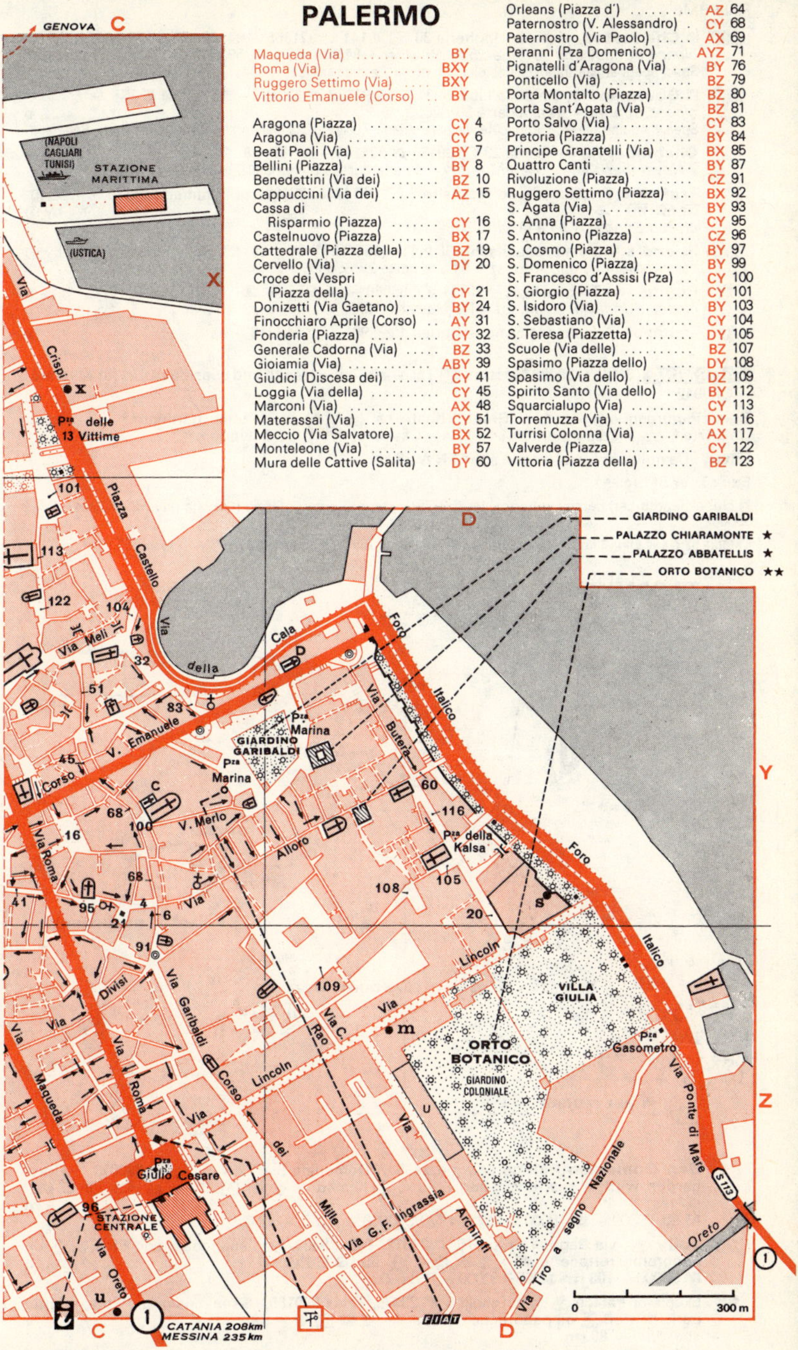

XXXX ✿ **Charleston,** piazzale Ungheria 30 ✉ 90141 ☎ 321366 – ▤. AE (D) E VISA. ✗ BY **r**
closed Sunday and 16 June-25 September – **M** a la carte 40/58000
Spec. Spaghetti all'aragosta, Costoletta di vitello, Cassata siciliana. **Wines** Corvo, Casteldaccia.

XXXX ✿ **Gourmand's,** via della Libertà 37/e ✉ 90139 ☎ 323431 – ▤. AE (D) E VISA. ✗
closed Sunday – **M** a la carte 36/52000 AX **e**
Spec. Linguine alla Lido, Entrecôte alla palermitana, Zuccotto alla mandorla. **Wines** Damaschino, Bonera.

XXX **Chamade,** via Torrearsa 22 ✉ 90139 ☎ 322204 – ▤. AE (D). ✗ BX **x**
2 November-May; closed Monday – **M** a la carte 22/43000 (15%).

XXX **Trattoria Trittico,** largo Montalto 7 ✉ 90147 ☎ 294809, « Summer service » – ▤ (P). AE (D) VISA. ✗ by ③
closed Sunday – **M** a la carte 30/43000.

XXX **Friend's Bar** via Brunelleschi 138 ✉ 90145 ☎ 201401 – ▤. AE (D) by ③
closed Monday and August – **M** a la carte 28/35000.

XX **Regine,** via Trapani 4/a ✉ 90141 ☎ 586566 – ▤. AE VISA. ✗ AX **d**
closed Sunday and August – **M** a la carte 19/26000.

XX Trattoria L'Angolo, via Simone Corleo 1 ✉ 90139 ☎ 585318 – ▤ AX **x**

TAORMINA **(SICILY) 98039 Messina 988 ㊲ – alt. 250 – Health and seaside resort (at Mazzarò) – ☎ 0942.**

See : Picturesque site★★★ – Greek Theatre★★ (≤★★★) B – Public gardens★★ B – Corso Umberto★ A – Piazza 9 Aprile★ (≤★★) A – Castle★ (≤★★) A – Belvedere★ A.

Envir. : Castelmola (picturesque site★) NW : 5 km A.

Exc : Tour of Etna★★.

ℹ (June-September) corso Umberto 144 ☎ 23751 – largo Santa Caterina (Corvaja palace) ☎ 23243, Telex 980062.

Catania 52 ② – Enna 135 ② – Messina 52 ① – Palermo 255 ② – Siracusa 111 ② – Trapani 359 ②.

TAORMINA

Umberto (Corso) .... A
Dionisio (Via) .... A 2
Duomo (Piazza) .... A 3
Rotabile Castelmola .... A 5
S. Antonio (Piazza) .... A 6
Vittorio Emanuele (Pza) .... B 8
9 Aprile (Piazza) .... A 9

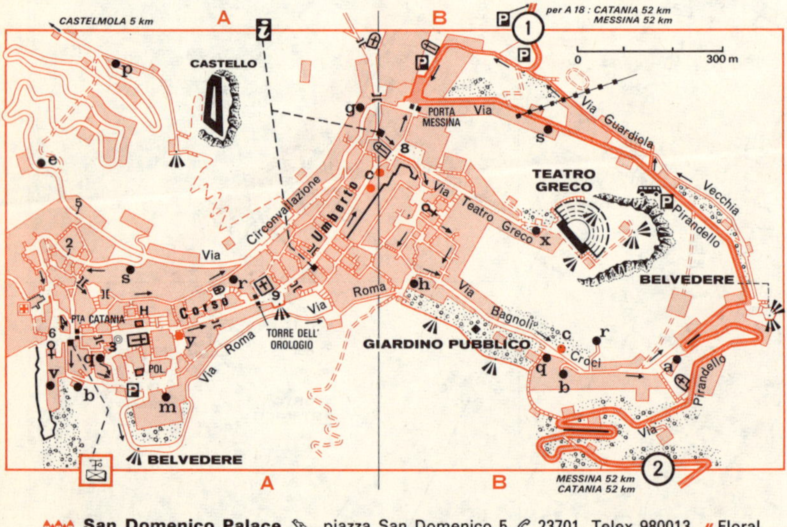

🏨 **San Domenico Palace** ⛰, piazza San Domenico 5 ☎ 23701, Telex 980013, « Floral garden with ≤ sea, coast and Etna », ⛱ heated – |♦| ▤ TV ☎ – 🏛. AE (D) E VISA. ✗ rest A **m**
M 60/70000 – ☕ 18000 – **117 rm** 170/300000 – P 285/409000.

🏨 **Jolly** ⛰, via Bagnoli Croce 75 ☎ 23312, Telex 980028, ≤ sea, coast and Etna, « ⛱ on panoramic terrace », 🌴 – |♦| ▤ (P) – 🏛. AE (D) E VISA. ✗ rest B **q**
M 35000 – **103 rm** ☕ 96/150000 – P 156000.

🏨 Excelsior Palace ⛰, via Toselli 8 ☎ 23975, Telex 980185, ≤ sea, coast and Etna, « Little park, heated ⛱ on panoramic terrace » – |♦| ▤ TV ☎ – 🏛 A **v**
seasonal – **89 rm.**

XXXX ✿ **Villa Sassi-El Toulà** ✧ with rm, **strada al Traforo del Pino 47 ✉ 10132 ✆ 890556, « 18C Country house in a spacious park » – ▤ rest ⇔wc ⋔wc ☎ P – ⛰. AE ⓓ E VISA. ✗** by ⑤
closed August – **M** *(closed Sunday)* a la carte 45/68000 (13%) – ☕ 15000 – **12 rm** 160/210000 – P 230000
Spec. Salmone marinato all'aceto di lamponi, Agnolotti alla Cavour, Petto d'anatra agli aromi. **Wines** Grignolino.

XXXX ✿ **Del Cambio,** piazza Carignano 2 ✉ 10123 ✆ 546690, Elegant traditional decor, « 19C Decoration » – ▤. AE ⓓ VISA. ✗ CX a
closed Sunday and 28 July-31 August – **M** (booking essential) a la carte 38/55000 (15%)
Spec. Gamberetti all'olio di basilico, Risotto allo spumante, Brasato al Barolo. **Wines** Bianco dei Roeri, Dolcetto.

XXXX **Tiffany,** piazza Solferino 16/h ✉ 10121 ✆ 540538 – ▤. AE. ✗ CX x
closed Sunday and August – **M** a la carte 36/50000 (15%).

XXX ✿ **Vecchia Lanterna,** corso Re Umberto 21 ✉ 10128 ✆ 537047, Elegant installation – ▤. AE E VISA. ✗ CY x
closed Saturday lunch, Sunday and August – **M** (booking essential) a la carte 43/60000 (10%)
Spec. Terrina d'anatra al fegato d'oca, Savarin di riso con crostacei alla d ogaressa, Sella di cervo alla Monviso. **Wines** Gavi, Barbaresco.

XXX ✿ **Al Gatto Nero,** corso Filippo Turati 14 ✉ 10128 ✆ 590414, Typical Tuscan decor and cuisine – ▤. AE ⓓ. ✗ BZ z
closed Sunday and August – **M** a la carte 35/50000
Spec. Insalata di pesce Gatto Nero, Costata di manzo alla fiorentina, Misto mare alla brace. **Wines** bianco e rosso Montecarlo.

XXX **Al Saffi,** via Aurelio Saffi 2 ✉ 10138 ✆ 442213, Elegant installation – ▤. AE ⓓ VISA AV n
closed Sunday and August – **M** (booking essential) a la carte 40/50000.

XXX **Due Lampioni,** via Carlo Alberto 45 ✉ 10123 ✆ 546721 – ▤. ✗ CY n
closed Sunday and August – **M** a la carte 50/56000.

XX Bridge, via Giacosa 2 bis ✉ 10125 ✆ 687609 – ▤ CZ v

XX La Smarrita, corso Unione Sovietica 244 ✉ 10134 ✆ 390657 – ▤ by ⑩

XX **La Cloche,** strada al Traforo del Pino 106 ✉ 10132 ✆ 894213, Typical atmosphere – ▤ P. AE ⓓ. ✗ by ⑤
closed Monday – **M** (surprise menu) 35/55000.

XX **Al Dragone,** via Pomba 14 ✉ 10123 ✆ 547019 – ✗ CY m
closed Saturday, Sunday and August – **M** a la carte 25/41000.

XX **Due Mondi-da Ilio,** via San Pio V n° 3 ✉ 10125 ✆ 682056 – ▤. AE VISA. ✗ CZ k
closed Monday and 25 July-20 August – **M** a la carte 25/35000.

XX **Al Bue Rosso,** corso Casale 10 ✉ 10131 ✆ 830753 – ▤ DY e
closed Monday, Saturday lunch and August – **M** a la carte 24/36000 (10%).

XX **Montecarlo,** via San Francesco da Paola 37 ✉ 10123 ✆ 541234 – ▤. AE ⓓ VISA ✗ DY c
closed Saturday lunch, Sunday and August – **M** (booking essential) a la carte 30/45000.

XX **Al Ghibellin Fuggiasco,** via Tunisi 50 ✉ 10134 ✆ 390750 – ▤. AE ⓓ VISA BZ b
closed Saturday, Sunday dinner and August – **M** a la carte 23/38000.

XX **Il Papavero,** corso Raffaello 5 ✉ 10126 ✆ 6505168 – AE ⓓ VISA CZ d
closed Sunday and 20 June-10 July – **M** (booking essential) a la carte 25/45000.

X **La Cuccagna,** corso Casale 371 ✉ 10132 ✆ 890069, Typical Romagnese rest. by ⑤
closed Monday and August – **M** (surprise menu) 18/28000.

X **Porta Rossa,** corso Appio Claudio 227 ✉ 10146 ✆ 790963, ☂ – AE VISA. ✗ by ⑪
closed Saturday lunch, Sunday and August – **M** (booking essential) a la carte 28/47000.

X ✿ **Ostu Bacu,** corso Vercelli 226 ✉ 10155 ✆ 264579, Modern Piedmontese trattoria – ▤
closed Sunday and July – **M** a la carte 32/45000 by corso Vercelli DV
Spec. Assaggi di pasta, Fritto misto piemontese, Coniglio con peperoni, Dolci piemontesi. **Wines** Arneis, Dolcetto.

X **C'era una volta,** corso Vittorio Emanuele 41 ✉ 10125 ✆ 655498, Typical Piedmontese rest. – ▤. AE ⓓ E VISA CZ k
closed lunch, Sunday and August – **M** (typical menu-booking essential) 35000.

X **Da Mauro,** via Maria Vittoria 21 ✉ 10123 ✆ 8397811, Tuscan habitués' trattoria – ▤. ✗ DY h
closed Monday and July – **M** a la carte 16/26000.

X **Trattoria della Posta,** strada Mongreno 16 ✉ 10132 ✆ 890193, Habitués' trattoria Piedmontese cheese – ▤. ✗ by ⑤
closed Sunday dinner, Monday and 10 July-20 August – **M** a la carte 19/30000.

X **Da Giudice,** strada Valsalice 78 ✉ 10131 ✆ 682488, « Summer service under pergola » – P. AE ⓓ E VISA. ✗ by ⑤
closed Tuesday, Wednesday lunch and August – **M** a la carte 23/35000.

TORINO

Carlo Felice (Piazza)	CY	15
Roma (Via)	CXY	
S. Carlo (Piazza)	CXY	45
Alfieri (Via)	CY	6
Cadorna (Lungo Po L.)	DY	10
Carignano (Piazza)	CX	12
Carlo Emanuele II (Pza)	DY	13
Casale (Corso)	DY	16
Castello (Piazza)	CX	17
Cesare Augusto (Piazza)	CV	19
Consolata (Via della)	CV	20
Diaz (Lungo Po A.)	DY	24
Gran Madre di Dio (Piazza)	DY	27
Milano (Via)	CV	32
Ponte Vittorio Emanuele I	DY	40
Repubblica (Piazza della)	CV	44
S. Francesco d'Assisi (Via)	CX	47
S. Giovanni (Piazza)	CX	48
Solferino (Piazza)	CX	55
Vitt. Emanuele II (Lgo)	BCY	67
4 Marzo (Via)	CX	69
20 Settembre (Via)	CXY	71

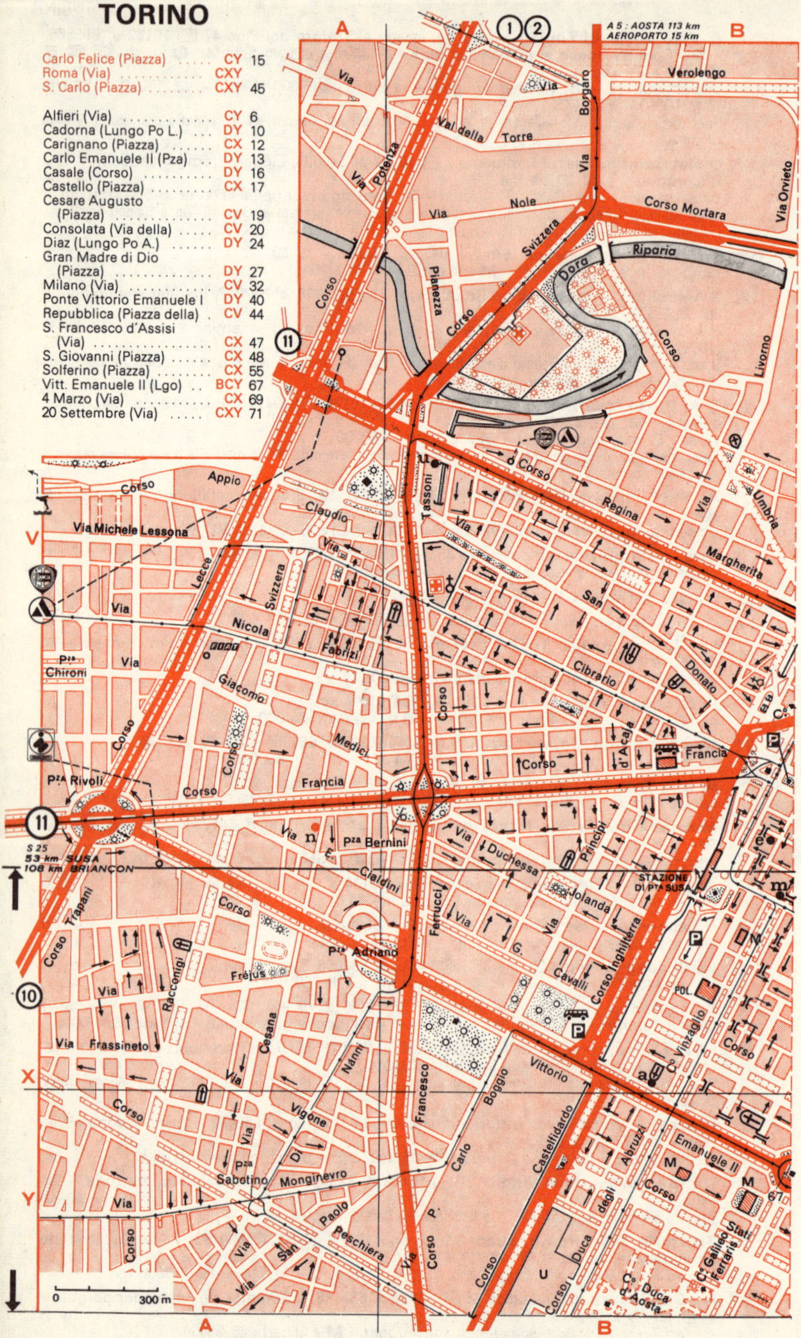

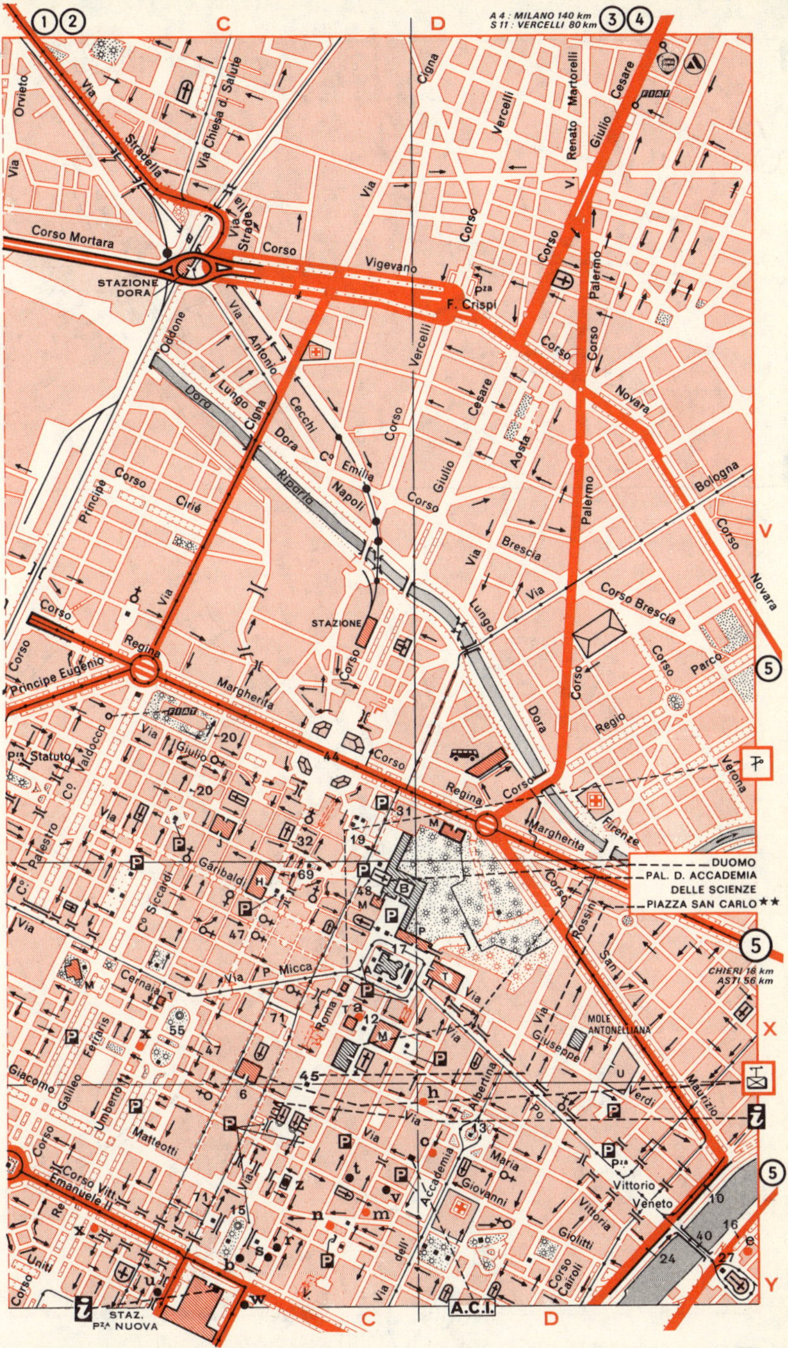
A 4 : MILANO 140 km
S 11 : VERCELLI 80 km
C
D
V
X
Y
Via Orvieto
Via Stradella
Via Chiesa d. Salute
Corso Mortara
STAZIONE DORA
Via Stradella
Corso Vigevano
Pza F. Crispi
Via Cigna
Corso Vercelli
Corso Renato Martorelli
Corso Giulio Cesare
FIAT
Via Oddone
Via Antonio Cecchi
Lungo Dora
Via Cigna
Corso Vercelli
Corso Giulio Cesare
Corso Palermo
Corso Novara
Corso Aosta
Lungo Dora Riparia
Co Emilia
Corso Napoli
Corso Principe
Corso Cirié
Via Brescia
Corso Brescia
Corso Bologna
Corso Novara
Corso Palermo
STAZIONE
Corso Regina Margherita
Corso Principe Eugenio
Corso Regina
Corso Parco
Corso Regio
Via Verona
Lungo Dora Firenze
FIAT
Via Giulio
Pza Statuto
Co Valdocco
Co Palestro
Via Garibaldi
Co Siccardi
Via Cernaia
Via P. Micca
Via Roma
Via Galileo Ferraris
Via Giacomo Matteotti
Corso Umberto
Corso Vitt. Emanuele II
Corso Re Umberto
Corso Uniti
Via Accademia
Via dell' Accademia
Via Po
Via Giuseppe Verdi
Via San Rossini
Via Maria Vittoria
Via Giovanni Giolitti
Corso Cairoli
Pza Vittorio Veneto
Corso San Maurizio
MOLE ANTONELLIANA
DUOMO
PAL. D. ACCADEMIA DELLE SCIENZE
PIAZZA SAN CARLO ★★
CHIERI 18 km
ASTI 56 km
A.C.I.
STAZ. PZA NUOVA
C
D

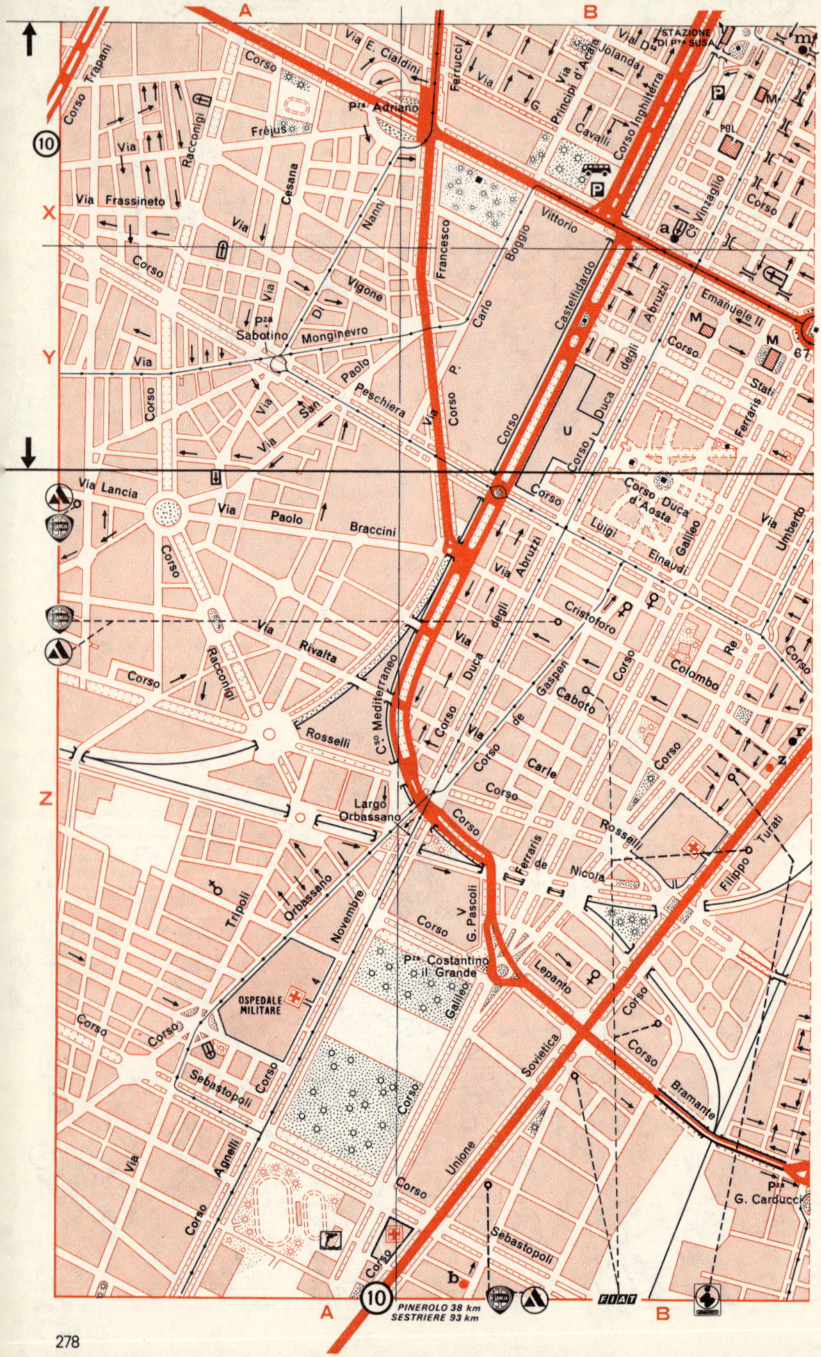
A
B
STAZIONE DI P.TA SUSA
Corso Trapani
Corso
Via E. Cialdini
Corso
Via Frejus
P.za Adriano
Ferrucci
Via G.
Via Principi d'Acaja
Via Jolanda
Via Duchessa
Corso Inghilterra
Cavalli
Via Racconigi
Via Frassineto
Via Cesana
Via Nanni
Corso Francesco
Vittorio
Boggio
Vinzaglio
Corso
Corso
Via Di Vigone
P.za Sabotino
Monginevro
Via Carlo
Corso Castellidardo
Abruzzi
Emanuele II
Corso
Via
Via Paolo
Peschiera
Via San
Via
Corso P.
Corso Duca degli
Stati
Ferraris
Via Lancia
Via Paolo Braccini
Corso
Corso
Corso Duca d'Aosta
Luigi Einaudi
Galileo
Via Umberto
Via Abruzzi
Cristoforo
Via Rivalta
Via Duca degli
Corso
Colombo
Re
Corso
Corso Racconigi
Corso Mediterraneo
Gasperi
Caboto
Via Rosselli
Corso Via de
Corso
Carle
Corso
Largo Orbassano
Corso
Corso Rosselli
Ferraris de Nicola
Filippo Turati
Via Tripoli
Orbassano
Novembre
Corso
V. G. Pascoli
P.za Costantino il Grande
Galileo
Lepanto
OSPEDALE MILITARE
Corso
Corso
Corso
Corso
Sebastopoli
Corso
Sovietica
Bramante
Via Agnelli
Corso
Unione
Corso
Corso
Sebastopoli
P.za G. Carducci
Corso
POL
X
Y
Z
10
67
10
PINEROLO 38 km
SESTRIERE 93 km
FIAT

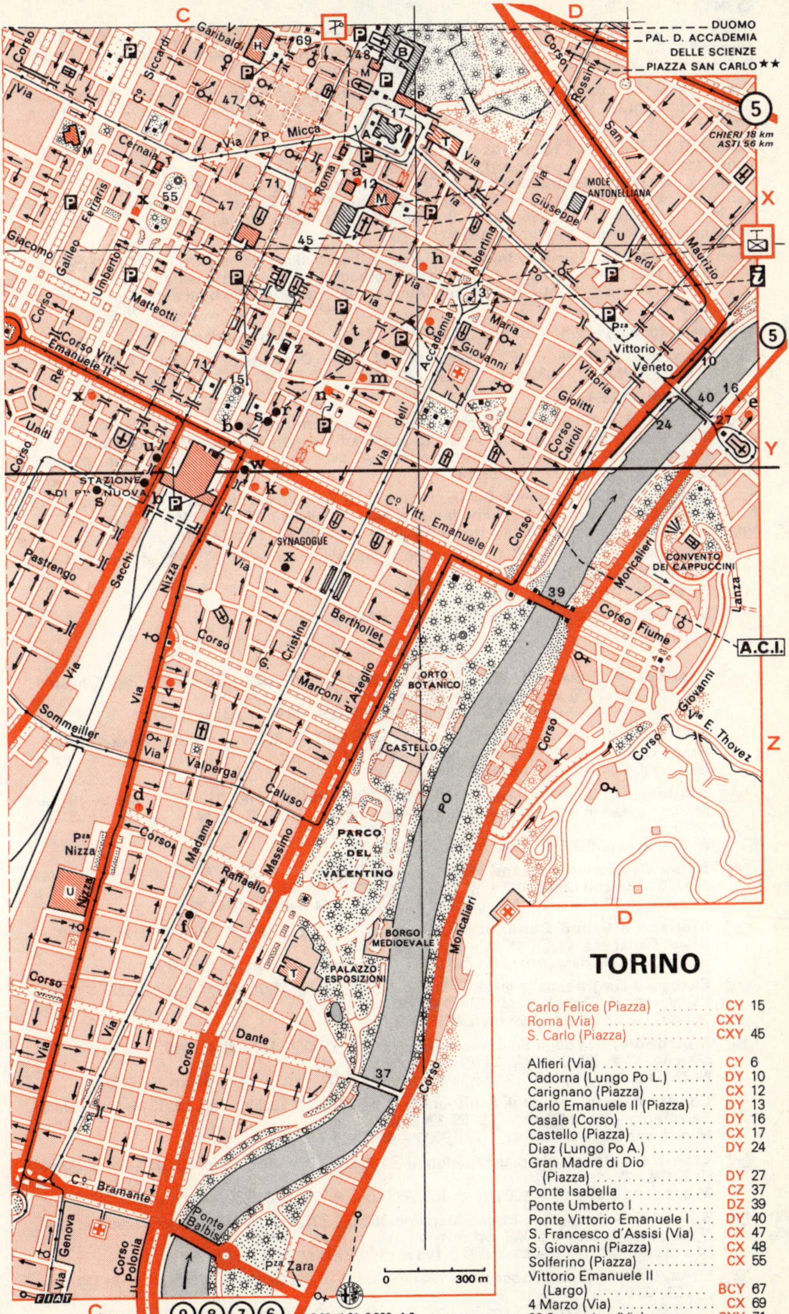

TORINO

Carlo Felice (Piazza) . . . . CY 15
Roma (Via) . . . . CXY
S. Carlo (Piazza) . . . . CXY 45

Alfieri (Via) . . . . CY 6
Cadorna (Lungo Po L.) . . . . . . DY 10
Carignano (Piazza) . . . . CX 12
Carlo Emanuele II (Piazza) . . DY 13
Casale (Corso) . . . . DY 16
Castello (Piazza) . . . . CX 17
Diaz (Lungo Po A.) . . . . DY 24
Gran Madre di Dio (Piazza) . . . . DY 27
Ponte Isabella . . . . CZ 37
Ponte Umberto I . . . . DZ 39
Ponte Vittorio Emanuele I . . . DY 40
S. Francesco d'Assisi (Via) . . CX 47
S. Giovanni (Piazza) . . . . CX 48
Solferino (Piazza) . . . . CX 55
Vittorio Emanuele II (Largo) . . . . BCY 67
4 Marzo (Via) . . . . CX 69
20 Settembre (Via) . . . . CXY 71

VENICE (VENEZIA) 30100 **P** 988 ⑤ – pop. 340 873 – h.s. April-October and Christmas – ✆ 041.

See : St. Mark's square*** FZ : St. Mark's basilica*** (mosaics***, Pala d'oro***, Treasury***), Bell tower* (※**), Clock tower*, Law courts*, Correr Museum**, Doges Palace***, Piazzetta*** (Old library*) – Bridge of sighs* GZ.

Grand Canal*** : Palazzo Venier (modern art gallery*) BV, Palazzo Rezzonico* (Museum of Eighteenth-Century Venetian Art) AU, Rialto bridge* FY, Cà d'Oro** EX – Academy of fine arts*** ABV.

School of St. Rocco*** (paintings by Tintoretto***) AT – School of St. Giorgio degli Schiavoni* (paintings by Carpaccio**) DT – School of Carmini* (paintings by Tiepolo*) AU – Church of St. Maria della Salute* BV – Church of St. Giorgio Maggiore* CV – Church of St. Zanipolo*, Equestrian statue of Bartolomeo Colleoni** GX – Church of St. Maria Gloriosa dei Frari* AT – Church of St. Zaccaria* GZ – Church of St. Maria dei Miracoli* FGX – Church of St. Sebastiano (ceiling by Veronese*) AU.

Envir. : Lido*** SE : 15 mn by boat – Murano* (Glass-making Museum*) NE : 15 mn by boat – Burano* NE : 30 mn by boat – Torcello** (Cathedral of St. Maria Assunta*, Church of St. Fosca*) NE : 45 mn by boat – Riviera del Brenta**, W : departure by boat and return by coach (whole day).

18 (closed Monday) al Lido Alberoni ✉ 30011 ✆ 731015, 15 mn by boat and 9 km.

✈ Marco Polo di Tessera, NE : 13 km ✆ 661111 (plan : Outskirts p. 3) – Alitalia, campo San Moisè 1483 ✉ 30124 ✆ 700355.

🚗 at Mestre ✆ 929472.

⛴ to Lido - San Nicolò from piazzale Roma (Tronchetto) daily (35 mn); to Punta Sabbioni from Riva degli Schiavoni daily (40 mn); to island of Pellestrina-Santa Maria del Mare from Lido Alberoni daily (1 h 15 mn) – Informarion : ACTV - Venetian Transport Union, piazzale Roma ✉ 30124 ✆ 5287886, Telex 223487.

⛴ to islands of Murano (10 mn), Burano (40 mn) and Torcello (45 mn) daily, from fondamenta Nuove; to Treporti-Cavallino from Fondamenta Nuove daily (1 h 10 mn) – Information : ACTV - Venetian Transport Union, piazzale Roma ✉ 30124 ✆ 5287886, Telex 223487.

i San Marco Ascensione 71/c ✉ 30124 ✆ 26356 – piazzale Roma 540/d ✉ 30125 ✆ 27402 – Santa Lucia Railway station ✉ 30121 ✆ 715016.

A.C.I. piazzale Roma ✉ 30125 ✆ 700300.

Roma 528 ① – Bologna 152 ① – Milano 267 ① – Trieste 158 ①.

Plans on following pages

Cipriani ⛱, isola della Giudecca 10 ✉ 30123 ✆ 707744, Telex 410162, <, heated, ⛱, – – ☎ ♿ – AE. rest CV **h**
28 February-24 November – **M** a la carte 90/120000 – **98 rm** 420/620000.

Gritti Palace, campo Santa Maria del Giglio 2467 ✉ 30124 ✆ 794611, Telex 410125, < Grand Canal – ☎ ♿ – AE E VISA. rest EZ **a**
M a la carte 80/100000 – **99 rm** 442/589000.

Danieli, riva degli Schiavoni 4196 ✉ 30122 ✆ 26480, Telex 410077, < canale di San Marco, « Hall in a small Venetian-style courtyard » – ☎ – AE E VISA. rest GZ **a**
M a la carte 68/100000 – **242 rm** 307/519000.

Bauer Grünwald e Grand Hotel, campo San Moisè 1459 ✉ 30124 ✆ 5231520, Telex 410075, < Grand Canal, – ♿ – AE E VISA. rest FZ **h**
closed 1 to 24 January – **M** a la carte 75/95000 – **214 rm** 273/452000.

Monaco e Grand Canal, calle Vallaresso 1325 ✉ 30124 ✆ 700211, Telex 410450, < Grand Canal – ☎ ♿ – AE VISA. rest FZ **e**
M Grand Canal Rest. a la carte 75/105000 – 19000 – **75 rm** 210/325000.

Europa e Regina, calle larga 22 Marzo 2159 ✉ 30124 ✆ 700477, Telex 410123, < Grand Canal – ☎ ♿ – AE E VISA. rest FZ **d**
M 54000 – 20500 – **199 rm** 226/370000.

Metropole, riva degli Schiavoni 4149 ✉ 30122 ✆ 705044, Telex 410340, < canale di San Marco – ☎ – AE E VISA. rest DU **t**
M Zodiaco Grill *(closed Tuesday)* a la carte 40/68000 – 16000 – **64 rm** 180/250000.

Londra Palace, riva degli Schiavoni 4171 ✉ 30122 ✆ 700533, Telex 431315, < canale di San Marco – ☎ – AE E VISA GZ **t**
M rest. see Do Leoni below – 19000 – **69 rm** 210/325000.

Etap-Park Hotel, giardini Papadopoli ✉ 30125 ✆ 5285394, Telex 410310 – ☎. AE E VISA. rest AT **k**
M a la carte 38/54000 – **100 rm** 160/260000 – P 175/205000, low season 115/145000.

Splendid-Suisse, San Marco-Mercerie 760 ✉ 30124 ✆ 700755, Telex 410590 – ☎ ♿ – AE E VISA. rest FY **n**
M a la carte 40/60000 – 15000 – **155 rm** 190/310000.

Luna, calle larga dell'Ascensione 1243 ✉ 30124 ✆ 89840, Telex 410236 – ☎ – AE. FZ **p**
M 55000 – 18000 – **125 rm** 192/330000 – P 275/302000, low season 194/216000.

Saturnia-International and Rest. il Cortile, calle larga 22 Marzo 2398 ✉ 30124 ✆ 708377, Telex 410355, « 14C Patrician building; outdoor rest. service in Summer » – |♦| ▤ TV ☎ – . AE ⊙ E VISA. ✻ rest EZ **n**
M *(closed Wednesday)* a la carte 48/70000 – **98 rm** ⊐ 190/290000.

Gabrielli Sandwirth, riva degli Schiavoni 4110 ✉ 30122 ✆ 5231580, Telex 410228, ← canale di San Marco, « Small courtyard and garden » – |♦| ▤ rest. AE ⊙ E VISA. ✻ rest
15 March-15 November – **M** 38/55000 – **110 rm** ⊐ 200/330000 – P 150/280000. DU **b**

La Fenice et des Artistes without rest., campiello de la Fenice 1936 ✉ 30124 ✆ 5232333, Telex 411150 – |♦| ▤. ✻ EZ **v**
⊐ 12000 – **68 rm** 89/127000, ▤ 8000.

Cavalletto e Doge Orseolo, calle del Cavalletto 1107 ✉ 30124 ✆ 700955, Telex 410684, ← – |♦| ☎. AE. ✻ FZ **f**
M 60000 – **80 rm** ⊐ 155/265000.

Concordia without rest., calle larga San Marco 367 ✉ 30124 ✆ 706866, Telex 411069 – |♦| wc ☎. AE VISA GZ **r**
60 rm ⊐ 105/160000.

Santa Chiara without rest., Santa Croce 548 ✆ 706955, Telex 215621 – |♦| ▤ TV wc ☎ ♿. AE VISA. ✻ AT **c**
26 rm ⊐ 90/135000.

Flora without rest., calle larga 22 Marzo 2283/a ✉ 30124 ✆ 705844, « Small flower garden » – |♦| ▤ wc wc ☎ ♿. AE ⊙ E VISA EZ **t**
February-15 November – **44 rm** ⊐ 98/158000, ▤ 10000.

San Cassiano without rest., Santa Croce 2232 ✉ 30125 ✆ 705477, Telex 223479, ← – ▤ TV wc ☎. AE ⊙. ✻ EX **f**
35 rm ⊐ 102/153000.

Ala without rest., campo Santa Maria del Giglio 2494 ✉ 30124 ✆ 708333, Telex 410275 – |♦| ▤ wc wc ☎. AE ⊙ E VISA EZ **e**
80 rm ⊐ 100/155000, ▤ 8000.

Abbazia without rest., calle Priuli 66 ✉ 30121 ✆ 717333 – wc wc ☎ AT **a**
37 rm ⊐ 51/89000.

Casanova without rest., San Marco-Frezzeria 1284 ✉ 30124 ✆ 706855, Telex 223553 – |♦| ▤ wc wc ☎. AE FZ **u**
45 rm ⊐ 106/161000, ▤ 12000.

Montecarlo without rest., calle dei Specchieri 463 ✉ 30124 ✆ 707144, Telex 411098 – |♦| ▤ wc wc ☎ ♿. AE ⊙ E VISA GY **q**
48 rm ⊐ 107/164000, ▤ 10000.

San Marco, calle dei Fabbri 877 ✉ 30124 ✆ 704277, Telex 215660 – |♦| wc wc ☎. AE ⊙ E VISA. ✻ rest FZ **r**
M *(closed Tuesday)* a la carte 28/47000 (12%) – **60 rm** ⊐ 110/170000 – P 110/130000, low season 90/110000.

Bonvecchiati, calle Goldoni 4488 ✉ 30124 ✆ 5285017, Telex 410560, « Modern art picture collection » – |♦| ▤ wc wc ☎. AE E. ✻ rest FZ **a**
M a la carte 32/44000 – ⊐ 9000 – **86 rm** 85/125000, ▤ 8000 – P 110/145000, low season 88/116000.

Scandinavia without rest., Santa Maria Formosa 5240 ✉ 30122 ✆ 5223507 – wc wc ☎ – **29 rm** ⊐ 52/91000. GY **s**

Nuovo Teson without rest., calle de la Pescaria 3980 ✉ 30122 ✆ 705555 – wc ☎. AE ⊙ E VISA DU **s**
30 rm ⊐ 50/88000.

Serenissima without rest., calle Goldoni 4486 ✉ 30124 ✆ 700011 – wc wc ☎. AE ⊙ – *10 March-5 November* – **34 rm** ⊐ 49/85000. FYZ **w**

Basilea without rest., rio Marin 817 ✉ 30125 ✆ 718477 – wc wc. AE VISA. ✻ AT **d**
⊐ 8000 – **30 rm** 40/68000.

La Residenza without rest., campo Bandiera e Moro 3608 ✉ 30122 ✆ 5285315, « 14C building » – ▤ TV wc wc ☎. AE ⊙ VISA. ✻ DU **n**
closed 8 January-15 February and 16 November-7 December – **14 rm** ⊐ 47/82000, ▤ 3500.

Paganelli, riva degli Schiavoni 4687 ✉ 30122 ✆ 5224324 – ▤ rest wc wc ☎. AE. ✻ GZ **t**
M *(closed Wednesday and 15 November-16 March)* a la carte 30/50000 – **23 rm** ⊐ 50/88000 – P 86/95000, low season 75/83000.

XXXX ✻ **Antico Martini,** campo San Fantin 1983 ✉ 30124 ✆ 5224121, Elegant rest. – ▤. AE ⊙ E VISA. ✻ EZ **x**
March-November; closed Tuesday and Wednesday lunch – **M** a la carte 56/93000 (15%)
Spec. Involtini di salmone, Chicche del nonno, Filetto di San Pietro alla Betty. **Wines** Malvasia, Cabernet.

XXX ✻✻ **Harry's Bar,** calle Vallaresso 1323 ✉ 30124 ✆ 5236797, American bar-rest. – ▤. AE ⊙ E VISA FZ **n**
closed 7 to 21 January, Monday, and Sunday dinner from October to March – **M** a la carte 65/110000 (20%)
Spec. Taglierini o risotto alle seppioline (15 July-15 October), Scampi alla Carlina, Pasticceria della Casa. **Wines** Soave, Cabernet.

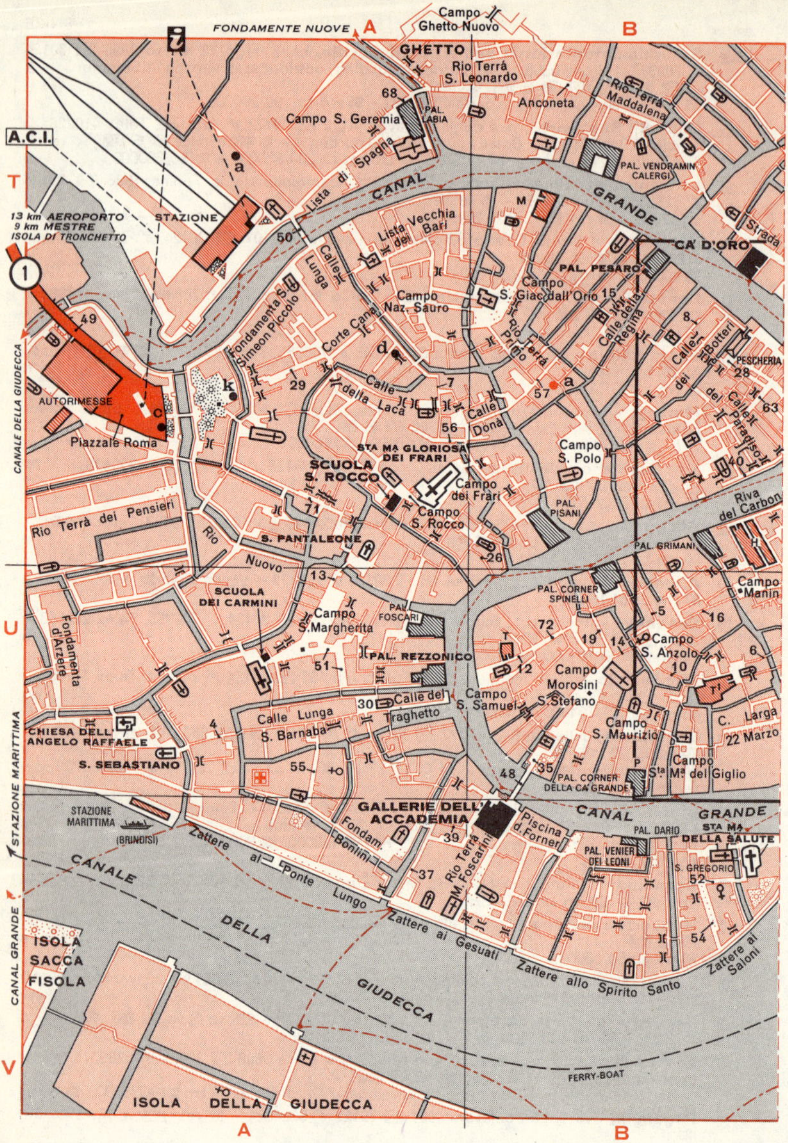

Calle larga S. Marco	CU	23
Calle larga 22 Marzo	BU	
Campo S. Bartolomeo	CT	31
Frezzeria	CU	41
Marzaria del Capitello	CT	42
Marzaria dell'Orologio	CU	43
Marzaria S. Salvador	CT	44
Marzaria S. Zulian	CT	45
Piazza S. Marco	CU	
Ponte di Rialto	CT	
Ruga degli Orefici	CT	62
Salizzada S. Moisé	CU	70
Via 2 Aprile	CT	74
Barbaria delle Tole	DT	2
Borgoloco S. Lorenzo	CT	3
Calle Avogaria	AU	4
Calle degli Avvocati	BU	5
Calle dei Barcaroli	BU	6
Calle del Caffettier	AT	7
Calle del Campanile	BT	8
Calle di Canonica	CU	9
Calle Caotorta	BU	10
Calle delle Carrozze	BU	12
Calle della Chiesa	AU	13
Calle dei Frati	BU	14
Calle Longo	BT	15
Calle della Mandola	BU	16
Calle larga Mazzini	CT	17
Calle dell'Ospedaletto	CT	18
Calle del Pestrin	BU	19
Calle del Pistor	CT	20
Calle delle Rasse	CU	22
Calle lunga S. M. Formosa	CT	24
Calle del Te Deum	DT	25
Calle del Traghetto Vecchio	BT	26
Campo Bandiera e Moro	DU	27
Campo delle Beccarie	BT	28
Campo della Lana	AT	29

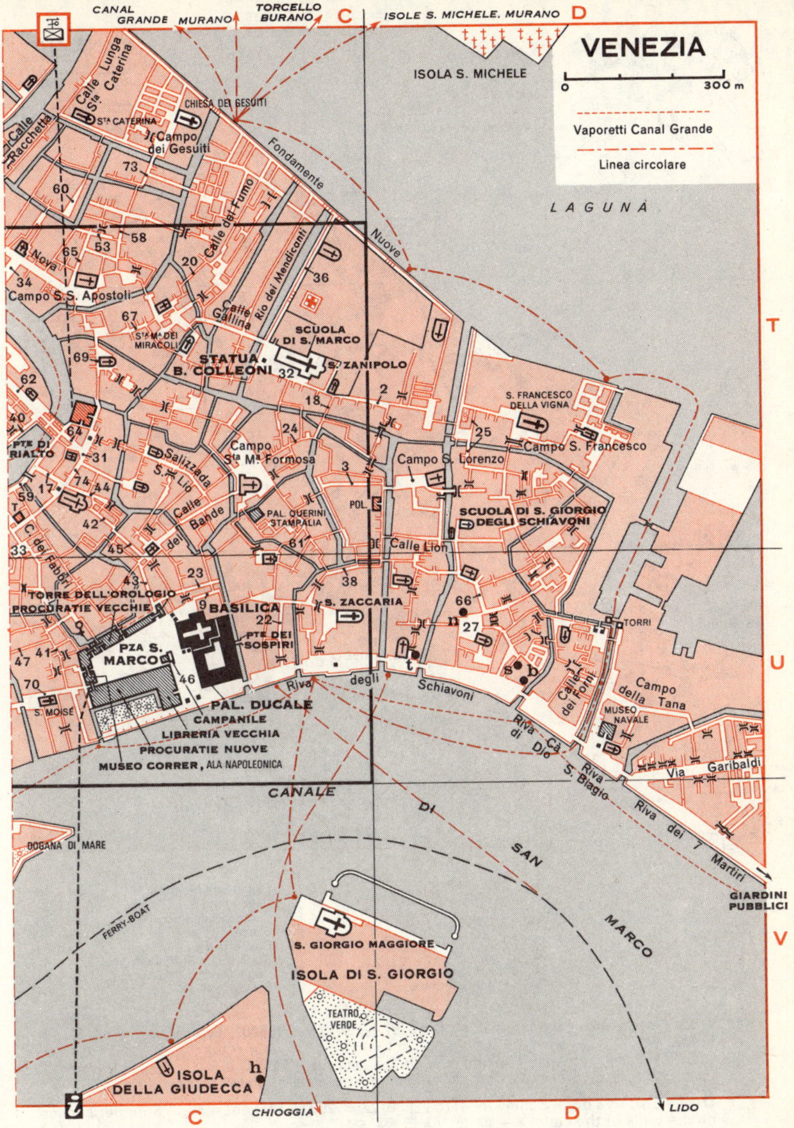

Campo S. Barnaba .... AU 30
Campo SS. Giovanni e Paolo .... CT 32
Campo S. Luca .... CT 33
Campo S. Sofia .... CT 34
Campo S. Vidal .... BU 35
Fondamenta dei Mendicanti .... CT 36
Fondamenta Nani .... AV 37
Fondamenta dell'Osmarin . CU 38
Fondamenta Priuli .... AV 39
Fondamenta del Vin ..... BCT 40
Piazzetta S. Marco .... CU 46

Piscina di Frezzeria .... CU 47
Ponte dell'Accademia ..... BU 48
Ponte della Libertà .... AT 49
Ponte degli Scalzi .... AT 50
Rio Terrà Canal .... AU 51
Rio Terrà dei Catecumeni .. BV 52
Rio Terrà dei Franceschi ... CT 53
Rio Terrà dei Saloni .... BV 54
Rio Terrà Ognissanti ...... AU 55
Rio Terrà S. Stin .... AT 56
Rio Terrà Secondo .... BT 57
Rio Terrà SS. Apostoli ..... CT 58
Riva del Ferro .... CT 59

Ruga Due Pozzi .... CT 60
Ruga Giuffa S. M. Formosa . CT 61
Ruga Vecchia S. Giovanni .. BT 63
Salizzada Pio X .... CT 64
Salizzada del Pistor .... CT 65
Salizzada S. Antonin .... DU 66
Salizzada S. Canciano ...... CT 67
Salizzada S. Geremia .... AT 68
Salizzada S. Giovanni Crisostomo .... CT 69
Salizzada S. Pantaleone .... AT 71
Salizzada S. Samuel .... BU 72
Salizzada Seriman .... CT 73

Calle larga S. Marco ..... GYZ 23
Calle larga 22 Marzo ...... EZ
Campo S. Bartolomeo ..... FY 31
Frezzeria .... FZ 41
Marzaria del Capitello ..... FY 42
Marzaria dell'Orologio .... FY 43
Marzaria S. Salvador ...... FY 44
Marzaria S. Zulian .... FY 45

Piazza S. Marco .... FZ
Ponte di Rialto .... FY
Ruga degli Orefici .... FX 62
Salizzada S. Moisé .... FZ 70
Via 2 Aprile .... FY 74

Calle degli Avvocati .... EZ 5
Calle di Canonica .... GZ 9

Calle larga Mazzini .... FY 17
Calle lunga S. M. Formosa .. GY 24
Campo delle Beccarie ...... EX 28
Piscina di Frezzeria .... FZ 47
Rio Terrà dei Franceschi .... FX 53
Ruga Giuffa S. M. Formosa . GY 61
Ruga Vecchia S. Giovanni .. EX 63
Salizzada Pio X .... FY 64

XXX ✿ **La Caravella,** calle larga 22 Marzo 2397 ✉ 30124 ✆ 708901, Typical rest. – ▤. AE ⓓ E VISA. ✈ EZ **m**
closed Wednesday – **M** (booking essential) a la carte 59/88000
Spec. Bigoli in salsa, Scampi allo Champagne, Filetto di bue Caravella. Wines Venegazzù, Barchessa.

XXX **Do Leoni,** riva degli Schiavoni 4175 ✉ 30122 ✆ 25032, Elegant rest., « Summer service on the bank of the canal » – ▤. AE ⓓ E VISA. ✈ GZ **t**
closed Tuesday and 15 November-15 December – **M** (booking essential) a la carte 76/115000.

XXX **Taverna La Fenice,** San Marco 1938 ✉ 30124 ✆ 5223856, ☂, Elegant rest. – ▤. AE ⓓ E VISA. ✈ EZ **v**
closed Sunday, Monday lunch and 2 January-5 February – **M** a la carte 40/70000 (15%).

XXX **Al Campiello,** calle dei Fuseri 4346 ✉ 30124 ✆ 706396, Rest.-American-bar-late night dinners – ▤. AE ⓓ E VISA FZ **z**
closed Monday and 8 to 22 August – **M** (booking essential) a la carte 33/50000 (13%).

XXX **Do Forni,** calle dei Specchieri 457/468 ✉ 30124 ✆ 5237729, New rustic rest. – ▤. AE ⓓ E VISA GY **c**
closed Thursday and 22 November-5 December – **M** a la carte 40/60000.

XX **Malamocco,** campiello del Vin 4650 ✉ 30122 ✆ 27438 – ▤ GZ **n**
closed Thursday and 9 January-14 February – **M** a la carte 37/60000 (15%).

XX ❁ **Al Graspo de Uva,** calle dei Bombaseri 5094 ✉ 30124 ✆ 5223647, Typical tavern – ▤. AE ◑ E VISA FY **x**
closed Monday, Tuesday and 20 December-3 January – **M** a la carte 35/54000 (12%)
Spec. Zuppa di pesce con crostoni, Rombo al pepe verde, Braciola di vitello alla vetraia. **Wines** Soave, Valpolicella.

XX ❁ **Noemi** with rm, **calle dei Fabbri 909** ✉ **30124** ✆ **25238** – ▤ rest ☎. AE ◑ E VISA
M *(closed Sunday dinner, Monday and 7 January-15 February)* a la carte 41/58000 (12%) – ☕ 6500 – **15 rm** 29/51000 FZ **g**
Spec. Cannelloni Smeraldina, Vermicelli neri alle seppie, Filetti di sogliola Casanova e Salmone fresco alla Sultanina. **Wines** Verduzzo, Cabernet.

XX **Al Giglio,** campo Santa Maria del Giglio 2477 ✉ 30124 ✆ 89456 – ▤. ✻ EZ **u**
closed Wednesday and December-14 February – **M** a la carte 43/60000 (15%).

XX **La Colomba,** piscina di Frezzeria 1665 ✉ 30124 ✆ 5221175, Typical trattoria, « Modern art picture collection » – ▤. AE ◑ E VISA FZ **m**
closed Wednesday in November-May – **M** a la carte 41/68000 (12%).

XX **Da Ivo,** calle dei Fuseri 1809 ✉ 30124 ✆ 5285004 – ▤. AE ◑ E VISA. ✻ FZ **s**
closed Sunday and January – **M** (booking essential) a la carte 43/65000 (13%).

X **Madonna,** calle della Madonna 594 ✉ 30125 ✆ 5223824, Venetian trattoria – ▤. ✻
closed Wednesday, 24 December-31 January and 4 to 17 August – **M** a la carte 20/32000 (11%). EY **e**

X **A la Vecia Cavana,** rio Terrà SS. Apostoli 4642 ✉ 30121 ✆ 5287106 – ▤. AE ◑ VISA FX **w**
closed Tuesday – **M** a la carte 29/42000.

X **Al Barcariol,** San Marco-calle dei Barcaroli ✉ 30124 ✆ 5224660 – ▤ EZ **g**
closed Tuesday – **M** a la carte 20/33000 (12%).

X **Da Bruno,** Castello-calle del Paradiso 5731 ✉ 30122 ✆ 5221480, Habitués' trattoria – ▤ GY **r**
closed Tuesday and 15 to 30 July – **M** a la carte 21/29000 (10%).

in Lido : 15 mn by boat from San Marco FZ – ✉ **30126** Venezia Lido.

🅸 Gran Viale S. M. Elisabetta 6 ✆ 765721 :

Excelsior, lungomare Marconi 41 ✆ 5260201, Telex 410023, ←, ⛱ heated, ▲ₑ, 🎾, 18 – |‡| ▤ TV ☎ ♿ – 🏛. AE ◑ E VISA. ✻ rest
15 April-20 October – **M** a la carte 85/137000 – ☕ 18000 – **230 rm** 400/500000.

Des Bains, lungomare Marconi 17 ✆ 765921, Telex 410142, ←, « Flower garden with heated ⛱ and 🎾 », ▲ₑ, 18 – |‡| ▤ TV ☎ Ⓟ – 🏛
seasonal – **254 rm**.

Quattro Fontane ♨, via 4 Fontane 16 ✆ 5260227, ⛱, 🎾 – ☎ Ⓟ. AE VISA. ✻ rest
20 April-September – **M** 55/75000 – ☕ 16000 – **70 rm** 150/245000 – P 205/245000, low season 180/220000.

Villa Mabapa, riviera San Nicolò 16 ✆ 5260590, Telex 440170, « Summer rest. in garden », ⛱ – |‡| ▤ ☎ ♿. AE ◑ E VISA. ✻ rest
M *(closed 3 November-15 March)* 26/32000 – **62 rm** ☕ 130/200000 – P 120/160000, low season 100/130000.

Villa Otello without rest., via Lepanto 12 ✆ 5260048 – |‡| ⛀wc ⛆wc ☎ Ⓟ. ✻
22 April-15 October – **34 rm** ☕ 90/135000.

Helvetia without rest., Gran Viale S. M. Elisabetta 4 ✆ 5260105, ⛱ – |‡| ⛀wc ⛆wc ☎ Ⓟ. ✻
April-October – **56 rm** ☕ 110/169000.

Byron Central Hotel, via Bragadin 30 ✆ 5260052, ⛱ – |‡| ▤ ⛀wc ⛆wc ☎. AE VISA. ✻
April-15 October – **M** 28/32000 – **36 rm** ☕ 89/128000, ▤ 10000 – P 95/120000, low season 75/90000.

Vianello, località Alberoni ✉ 30011 ✆ 731072, ⛱ – ⛀wc ⛆wc. ✻ rest
15 March-15 October – **M** *(closed September-May)* 18000 – ☕ 6000 – **20 rm** 38/66000 – P 45/55000.

X **Da Valentino,** via Sandro Gallo 81 ✆ 5260128, 🌳
closed Monday and November – **M** a la carte 32/47000 (10%).

X **Trattoria da Ciccio,** via S. Gallo 241-in direction of Malamocco ✆ 765489, 🌳 – Ⓟ
closed Tuesday and 15 to 30 November – **M** a la carte 25/40000 (12%).

in Torcello 50 mn by boat from fondamenta Nuove CT – ✉ **30012** Burano :

XX ❁ **Locanda Cipriani** ♨, ✆ 730757, Typical rest., « Floral setting » – AE VISA. ✻
19 March-10 November; closed Tuesday – **M** a la carte 57/85000 (15%)
Spec. Risotto alla torcellana (con verdure), Scampi alla Carlina, Zuppa di pesce. **Wines** Soave, Cabernet.

XX **Ostaria al Ponte del Diavolo,** ✆ 730401, 🌳 – AE
March-15 November; closed Thursday and dinner (except Saturday) – **M** a la carte 36/51000 (10%).

Norway
Norge

Oslo

PRACTICAL INFORMATION

LOCAL CURRENCY

Norwegian Kroner : 100 N-Kr = 13.20 US $ (Jan. 86)

TOURIST INFORMATION

The telephone number and address of the Tourist Information office is given in the text under ℹ.

FOREIGN EXCHANGE

In the Oslo area banks are usually open between 8.15am and 3.30pm, but in summertime, 15.5 - 31/8, they close at 3pm. Thursdays they are open till 5pm. Saturdays closed.

Most large hotels, main airports and railway stations have exchange facilities. At Fornebu Airport the bank is open from 6.30am to 10.30pm on weekdays and 7.00am to 10pm on Sundays, all the year round.

SHOPPING IN OSLO

(Knitted ware - silver ware)

Your hotel porter will be able to help you and give you information.

CAR HIRE

The international car hire companies have branches in each major city. Your hotel porter will be able to give details and help you with your arrangements.

TIPPING IN NORWAY

A service charge is included in hotel and restaurant bills and it is up to the customer to give something in addition if he wants to.

The cloakroom is sometimes included in the bill, sometimes you pay a certain amount.

Taxi drivers and baggage porters have no claim to be tipped. It is up to you if you want to give a gratuity.

SPEED LIMITS

The maximum permitted speed within congested areas is 50 km/h - 31mph. Outside congested areas it is 80 km/h - 50mph. Where there are other speed limits (lower or higher) it is signposted.

SEAT BELTS

The wearing of seat belts in Norway is compulsory for drivers and front seat passengers. All cars registered in Norway after 1/1-84 have got to have seat belts in the back seat too, and after 1/3-85 it is compulsory to use them.

ANIMALS

Very strict quarantine regulations for animals from all countries except Sweden and Finland. NO dispensations.

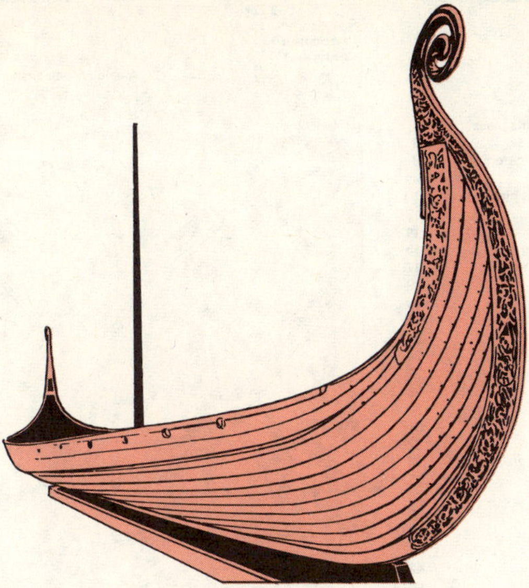

OSLO

SIGHTS

See : Bygdøy AZ : Viking Ships★★★ (Vikingeskipene), Folk Museum★★ (Norsk Folkemuseum), Kon-Tiki Museum★ (Kon-Tiki Museet), Fram Museum★ (Fram Museet), Maritime Museum★ (Norsk Sjøfartsmuseum) ; Frognerparken★ (Vigeland Sculptures★★) AX ; City Hall★ (Rådhuset) BY **H** ; Munch Museum★ (Munchmuseet) CY ; National Gallery★ (Nasjonalgalleriet) BY **M1** ; Akershus Castle★ (Akershus Festning) BZ ; Historical Museum★ (Historisk Museum) BY **M2**.

Outskirts : Holmenkollen★★ (NW : 10 km) : Ski Jump★, Ski Museum★ AX ; Tryvann Tower★★ (Tryvannstårnet) (NW : 14 km) : ☼★★ AX ; Sonja Henie-Onstad Centre★ (Henie-Onstads Kunstsenter) (W : 12 km) AY.

OSLO Norge 920 K 2 – pop. 447 512 – ☎ 02.

Oslo Golfklubb ☎ 50 44 02.

Fornebu SW : 8 km ☎ 59 67 16 – SAS : Ruseløkkveien 6 ☎ Business travel : 42 75 50 (Europe and Overseas) 42 79 00 (Domestics and Scandinavia), Vacation travel : 42 77 60 – Air Terminal : Havnegata, main railway station, seaside.

Copenhagen, Frederikshavn, Kiel : contact tourist information centre (see below).

Oslo Tourist Information, City Hall, seaside ☎ 42 71 70 – **KNA** (Kongelig Norsk Automobilklub) Royal Norwegian Automobile Club ☎ 56 26 90 – **NAF** (Norges Automobil Forbund) ☎ 42 94 00.

Hamburg 888 – København 583 – Stockholm 522.

OSLO

Karl Johans gate	BCY	
Lille Grensen	CY	37
Torggata	CY	
Apotekergata	CY	2
Arbeidersamfunnets plass	CY	3
Arne Garborgs plass	CY	5
Biskop Gunnerus' gate	CY	8
Bygdøy kappellvei	AZ	9
Christian Frederiks plass	CY	10
Christiania torv	CY	13
Dronningens gate	CYZ	14
Dronning Mauds gate	BY	16
Edvard Storms gate	BX	17
Elisenbergveien	AX	19
Fredriksborgveien	AZ	20
Fridtjof Nansens plass	BY	21
Frimanns gate	CX	23
Gimleveien	AX	24
Grubbegata	CY	27
Haakon VII's gate	BY	28
Industrigata	AX	30
Jernbanetorget	CY	31
Josefines gate	ABX	32
Kristian Augusts gate	BCY	34
Langes gate	CX	35
Lassons gate	AY	36
Løchenveien	AZ	38
Løkkeveien	ABY	39
Munchs gate	CY	41
Munkedamsveien	ABY	42
Nedre Slottsgate	CYZ	44
Nedre Vollgate	BY	45
Nygata	CY	47
Pløens gate	CY	48
Professor Aschehougs pl.	CY	49
Professor Dahls gate	AX	51
Riddervolds gate	AX	52
Roald Amundsens gate	BY	53
Ruseløkkveien	ABY	55
Rådhusplassen	BY	56
Schives gate	AX	57
Skillebekk plass	AY	59
Skovveien	AXY	60
Solli plass	AY	61
Stortingsgata	BY	62
Stortorvet	CY	63
Strandgata	CZ	64
Sven Bruns gate	BX	65
Thor Olsens gate	CX	67
Tullins gate	BX	68
Uelands gate	CX	69
Wilses gate	CX	71
Youngstorget	CY	72
Øvre Slottsgate	CY	73

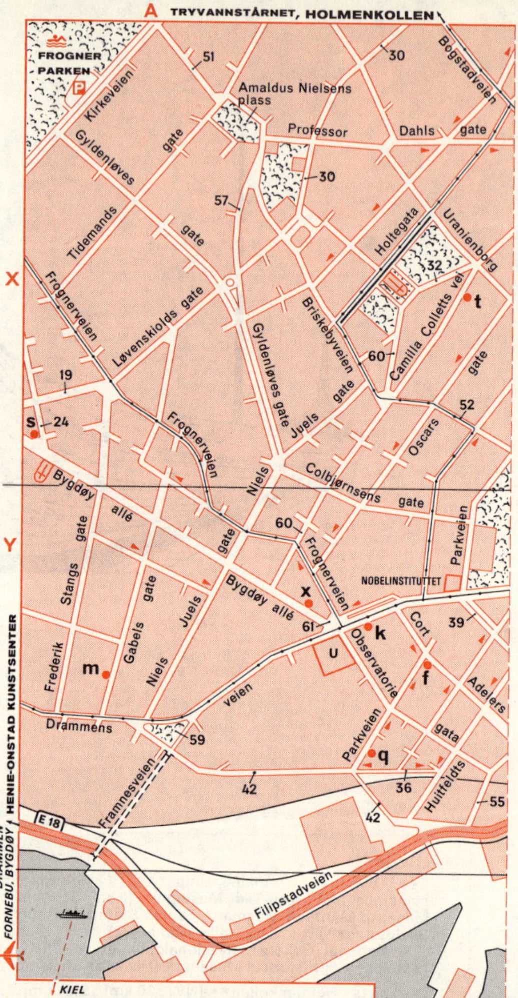

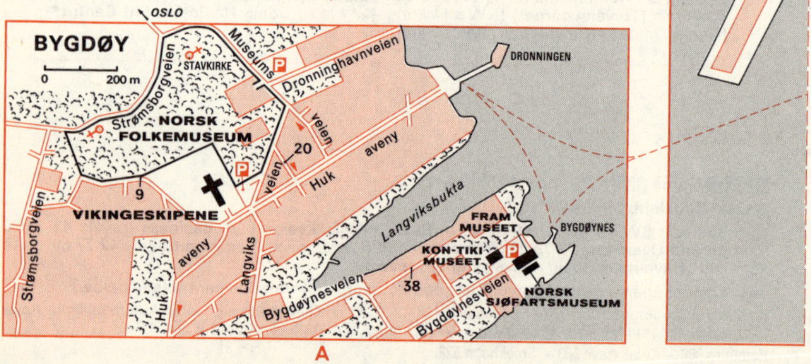

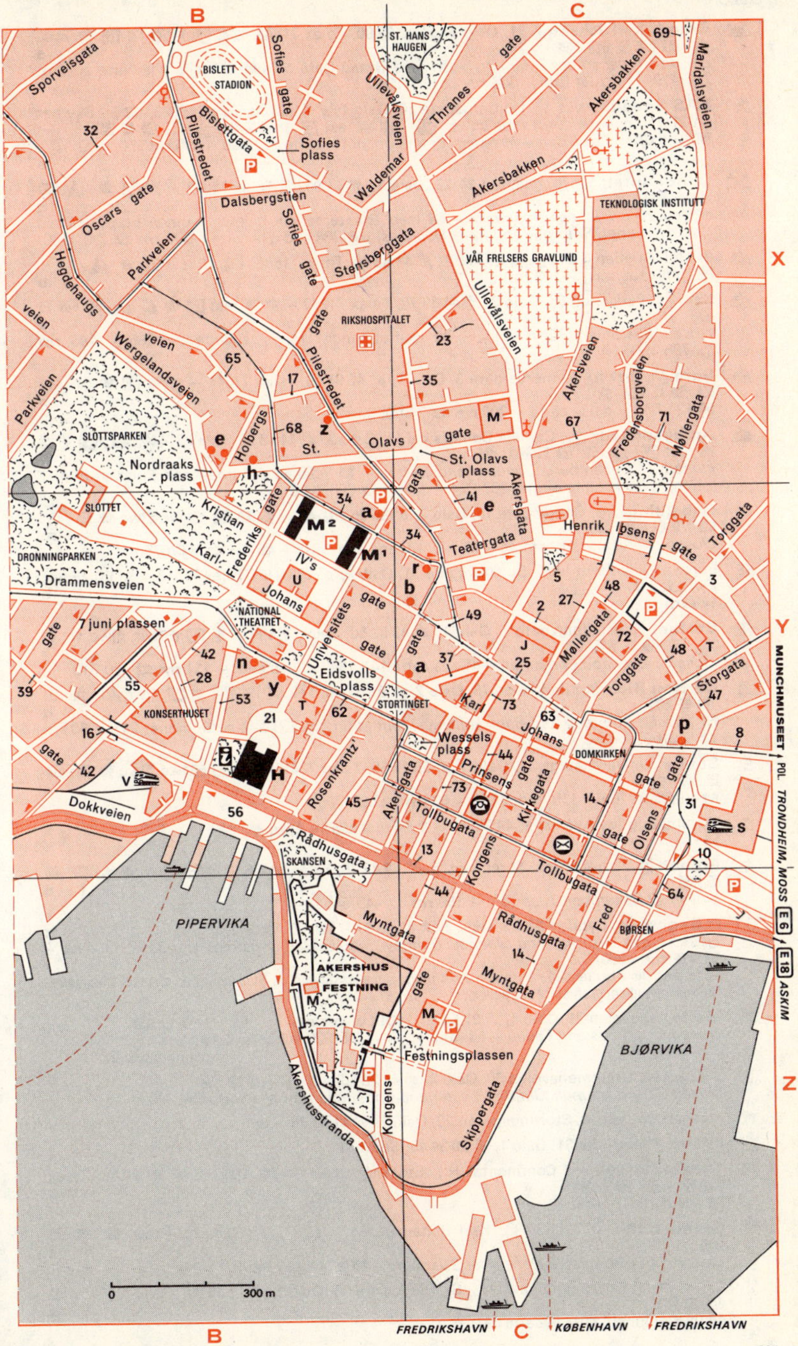
B
C
X
Y
Z
ST. HANS HAUGEN
BISLETT STADION
Sofies gate
Sofies plass
Sporveisgata
Bislettgata
Pilestredet
Ullevålsveien
Thranes gate
Akersbakken
Maridalsveien
Waldemar
Dalsbergstien
Oscars gate
Parkveien
Hegdehaugsveien
Stensberggata
TEKNOLOGISK INSTITUTT
VÅR FRELSERS GRAVLUND
RIKSHOSPITALET
Wergelandsveien
Akersveien
Fredensborgveien
Møllergata
SLOTTSPARKEN
Nordraaks plass
Holbergs gate
St. Olavs gate
St. Olavs plass
Akersgata
SLOTTET
Kristian
Frederiks gate
Karl
IV's
Johans gate
Teatergata
Henrik Ibsens gate
Torggata
DRONNINGPARKEN
Drammensveien
NATIONAL THEATRET
Universitets gate
7 juni plassen
Eidsvolls plass
STORTINGET
Karl Johans gate
KONSERTHUSET
Wessels plass
DOMKIRKEN
Storgata
MUNCHMUSEET
Prinsens gate
Kirkegata
Dokkveien
Rosenkrantz'
Tollbugata
Rådhusgata
SKANSEN
Kongens gate
Olsens gate
Fred
BØRSEN
POL. TRONDHEIM, MOSS
E 6
E 18
ASKIM
PIPERVIKA
Myntgata
AKERSHUS FESTNING
Festningsplassen
Akershusstranda
Skippergata
BJØRVIKA
0
300 m
FREDRIKSHAVN
KØBENHAVN
FREDRIKSHAVN

Grand, Karl Johansgt. 31, Oslo 1, 42 93 90, Telex 71683. AE E VISA. CY a
closed 21 December-2 January – **M** (see **Grand Café** below) – **Etoile** a la carte approx. 211/419 – **Fritzuer Grill** – **308 rm** 850/1090.

SAS Scandinavia M, Holbergsgate 30, Oslo 1, 11 30 00, Telex 19090, « Sky bar on 21st floor with < over the city », rest AE E VISA
M (see **Charly's** below) – **Holberg** (dinner only) a la carte 252/398 – **490 rm** 950/1100. BX e

Continental, Stortingsgaten 24-26, Oslo 1, 41 90 60, Telex 71012 – AE E VISA. BY n
closed 22 December-2 January – **M** (see **Theatercaféen** below) - **Annen Etage** *(closed Sunday dinner, Saturday and Bank Holidays)* 108/368 and a la carte – **170 rm** 790/1200.

Bristol, Kristian 4 des gate 7, Oslo 1, 41 58 40, Telex 71668 – rest
M (grill rest only) – **143 rm**. CY b

Kna M, Parkveien 68, Oslo 2, 44 69 70, Telex 71763 – rest AE E VISA. AY f
closed Easter and Christmas – **M** (buffet lunch) 140 a la carte 160/385 – **148 rm** 795/1900.

Sara M, Biskop Gunnerus gate 3, Oslo 1, 42 94 10, Telex 71342 – AE E VISA. CY p
M 125/535 and a la carte – **309 rm** 740/995.

Ambassadeur, Camilla Colletts vei 15, Oslo 2, 44 18 35, Telex 71446, rest AE E VISA. AX t
closed 21 December-2 January and Easter – **M** *(closed Saturday and Sunday)* (buffet lunch) 150 a la carte dinner 262/324 – **33 rm** 690/1300.

Gabelshus, Gabelsgate 16, Oslo 2, 56 25 90, wc wc AE E VISA. AY m
closed Easter and Christmas – **M** 350/420 and a la carte – **45 rm** 500/675.

Europa M without rest., St. Olavsgate 31, Oslo 1, 20 99 90, Telex 71512 – wc wc. BX h
148 rm.

Stefan, Rosenkrantzgate 1, Oslo 1, 42 92 50, Telex 19809 – wc wc. AE E VISA. CY r
closed Easter and Christmas – **M** a la carte 141/184 (unlicensed) – **131 rm** 710/810.

Carlton Rica, Parkveien 78, Oslo 2, 69 61 70, Telex 71902 – wc AE E VISA AY q
M *(closed Saturday and Bank Holidays)* (buffet lunch) 250 a la carte dinner 247 – **50 rm** 505/650.

Savoy, Universitetsgt. 11, Oslo 1, 20 26 55, Telex 76418 – wc wc AE E VISA. BY a
M a la carte lunch 115 /dinner 85 – **68 rm** 695/795.

Norum, Bygdøy Allé 53, 44 79 90 – rest wc wc. AX s
59 rm.

Munch M without rest., Munchsgt. 5, 42 42 75, Telex 74096 – wc AE E VISA CY e
closed 23 December-3 January – **180 rm** 445/545.

Bagatelle, Bygdøy Allé 3, Oslo 2, 44 63 97 – AE E VISA AY x
closed lunch Saturday and Monday, Sunday, July, Easter, Christmas and Bank Holidays – **M** a la carte 250/355
Spec. Raviolis à la brandade de morue aux truffes, Lamelles de noix de St. Jacques en chemise d'épinards, Huitres, coquillages, crustacés et poissons.

Mølla, Sagveien 21, Oslo 4, 37 54 50, « Old water-mill » – AE E VISA
closed Christmas and Easter – **M** (dinner only) 245/320 and a la carte.
by Maridalsveien CX

3 Kokker, Drammensveien 30, Oslo 2, 44 26 50 – AE E VISA AY k
closed Saturday lunch, Sunday, Easter and Christmas – **M** a la carte 350/300.

Frascati Rotisserie, Stortingsgaten 20, Oslo 1, 41 68 76 – BY y

La Mer, Pilestredet 31, Oslo 1, 20 34 45, Seafood BX z

Theatercaféen (at Continental H.), Stortingsgaten 24-26, Oslo 1, 41 90 60, Telex 71012 – AE E VISA BY n
M a la carte 160/250.

Grand Café (at Grand H.), Karl Johansgt. 31, Oslo 1, 33 48 70 – AE E VISA CY a
closed Saturday and 23 December-2 January – **M** a la carte 140/377.

Charlys (at SAS Scandinavia H.), St. Olavs gate 33, Oslo 1, 11 30 00, Telex 19090 – AE E VISA BX e
M (buffet lunch) 49/a la carte 69/133.

at Holmenkollen NW : 7 km by Bogstadveien – AX – and Holmenkollveien – ✉ ☎ 02 Oslo :

Holmenkollen Park Ⓜ, Kongeveien 26, Oslo 3, NW : 7 km by Hegdehaugsveien ☎ 14 60 90, Telex 72094, ≤ Oslo and fjord, – AE E VISA.
closed 21 December-4 January – **M De fem Stuer** buffet lunch 195/dinner a la carte 227/378 – **Bakeriet** a la carte 170/243 – **200 rm** 795/1035.

XXX **Frognerseteren,** Holmenkollveien 200, Oslo 3, NW : 10 km by Holmenkollveien ☎ 14 37 36, ≤ Oslo and fjord – E VISA
M a la carte 168/257.

at Fornebu Airport SW : 8 km by E 18 – AY – and Snarøyveien – ✉ ☎ 02 Oslo :

SAS Park Royal Ⓜ, Oslo-N-1324, Lysaker ☎ 12 02 20, Telex 78745, « Sea-side setting with private beach and tennis », park, – – **254 rm**.

at Sandvika SW : 18km by E 18 – ✉ ☎ 02 Oslo :

Sheraton Oslo Fjord Ⓜ, Sandviksveien 184, Oslo 1300, ☎ 54 57 00, Telex 74345, – AE E VISA
M a la carte 282/478 – **245 rm** 750/1095.

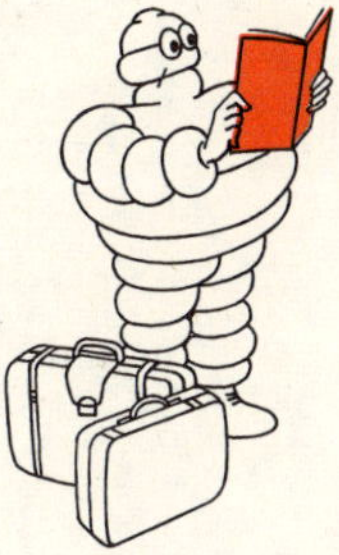

Portugal

Lisbon

PRACTICAL INFORMATION

LOCAL CURRENCY

Escudo : 100 Esc. = 0.62 US $ (Jan. 86)

FOREIGN EXCHANGE

Hotels, restaurants and shops do not always accept foreign currencies and the tourist is therefore advised to change cheques and currency at banks, saving banks and exchange offices - The general opening times are as follows: banks 8.30am to noon and 1 to 2.45pm (closed on Saturdays), money changers 9.30am to 6pm (usually closed on Saturday afternoons and Sundays).

SHOPPING IN LISBON

Shops and boutiques are generally open from 9am to 1pm and 3 to 7pm - In Lisbon, the main shopping streets are: Rua Augusta, Rua do Carmo, Rua Garrett (Chiado), Rua do Ouro, Rua da Prata, Av. da Roma.

TIPPING

A service charge is added to all bills in hotels, restaurants and cafés. It is usual, however, to give an additional tip for personal service ; 10 % of the fare or ticket price is also the usual amount given to taxi drivers and cinema and theatre usherettes.

SPEED LIMITS

The speed limit on motorways is 120 km/h - 74 mph, on other roads 90 km/h - 56 mph and in built up areas 60 km/h - 37 mph.

SEAT BELTS

Out of cities, it is compulsory for drivers and front seat passengers to wear seat belts.

THE FADO

The Lisbon Fado (songs) can be heard in restaurants in old parts of the town such as the Alfama, the Bairro Alto and the Mouraria. A selection of fado cabarets will be found at the end of the Lisbon restaurant list.

LISBON

SIGHTS

See : View : ** from the Suspension Bridge (Ponte de 25 Abril), ※ ** from Christ in Majesty (Cristo-Rei) S : 3,5 km.

CENTRE : POMBALINE LISBON

See : Rossio* (square) GY – Avenida da Liberdade* FX – Edward VII Park* (Cold Greenhouse) EX – St. Rock* (Igreja São Roque) FY **M¹** – Terreiro do Paço (square) GZ.

MEDIAEVAL LISBON

See : St. George's Castle** (Castelo de São Jorge) GY – Cathedral* (Sé) GZ – Santa Luzia Belvedere* (Miradouro de Santa Luzia) JY – Alfama** JYZ.

MANUELINE LISBON

See : Hieronymite Monastery** (Mosteiro dos Jerónimos : church**, cloister***) – Belém Tower** (Torre de Belém) – Monument to the Discoveries* (Padrão dos Descobrimentos).

MUSEUMS

Museum of Ancient Art** (Museu Nacional de Arte Antiga : polyptych by Nuno Gonçalves***) – Calouste Gulbenkian Museum*** (Art collection) – Azulejo Museum* and Church of the Mother of God** (Igreja da Madre de Deus) – Coach Museum** (Museu Nacional dos Coches) – Maritime Museum** (Museu de Marinha).

LISBON (LISBOA) 1100 37 ⑫ e ⑰ – Pop. 826 140 – alt. 111 – 01.

18, 9 Estoril Golf Club W : 25 km ✆ 268 01 76 Estoril – 18 Lisbon Sports Club NW : 20 km ✆ 96 00 77 – 18 Club de Campo de Lisboa S : 15 km ✆ 24 57 17 Aroeira, Fonte da Telha.

Lisboa Airport N : 8 km from city centre – T.A.P., Praça Marquês de Pombal 3, ✉ 1200, ✆ 54 40 80 and airport ✆ 88 91 81.

✆ 87 60 27 and 87 70 92.

to Madeira : E.N.M., Rua de São Julião 5, ✉ 1100, ✆ 87 01 21, and Rocha Conde de Óbidos, ✉ 1300.

Palácio Foz, Praça dos Restaudores ✆ 36 36 24, jardim de Regedor ✆ 36 35 21 and airport ✆ 89 43 23 – A.C.P. Rua Rosa Araújo 24, ✉ 1200, ✆ 56 39 31, Telex 12581 – A.C.P. Av. Barbosa do Bocage 23, ✉ 1000, ✆ 77 54 75, Telex 14070.

Madrid 648 – Bilbao 902 – Paris 1814 – Porto 330 – Sevilla 409.

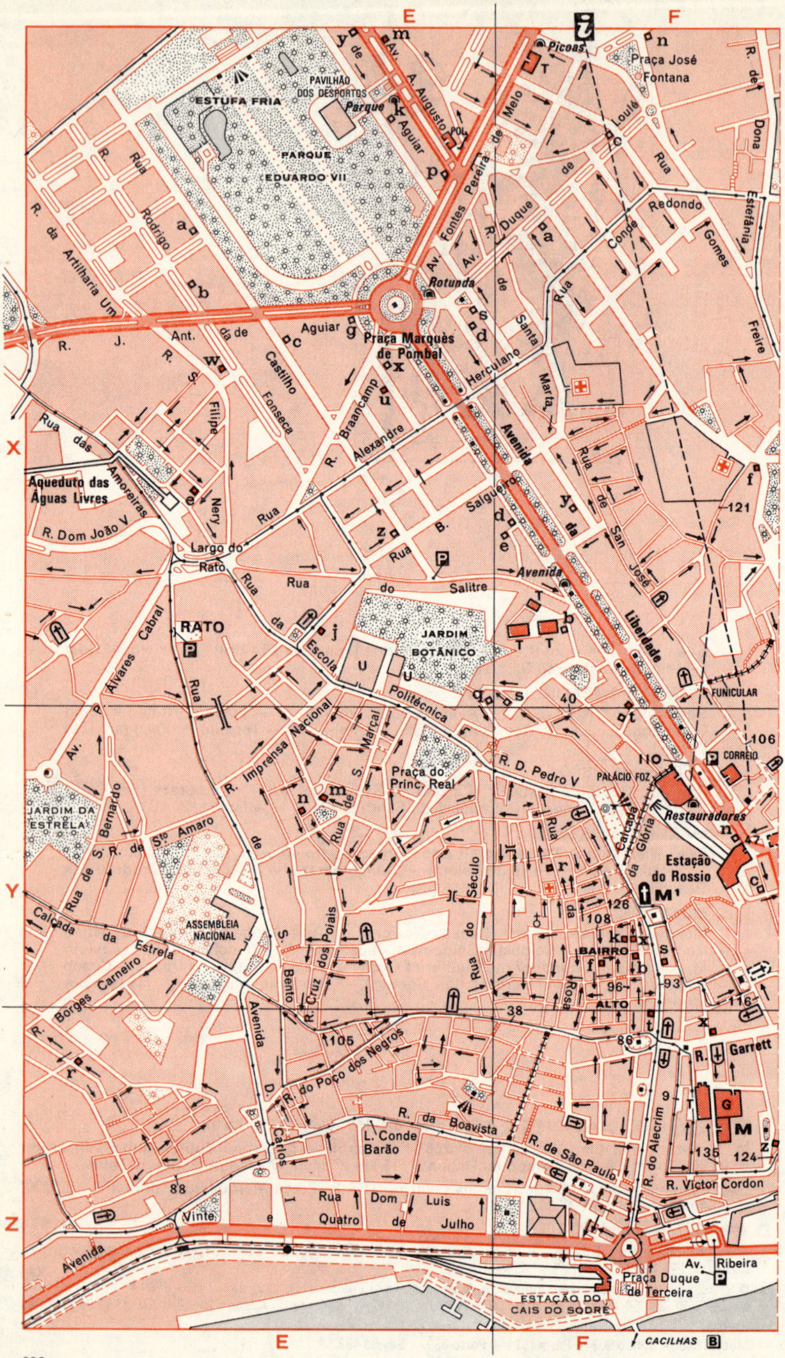
E
F
X
Y
Z
Picoas
Praça José Fontana
ESTUFA FRIA
PAVILHÃO DOS DESPORTOS
Parque
PARQUE EDUARDO VII
Rotunda
Praça Marquês de Pombal
Aqueduto das Águas Livres
Largo do Rato
RATO
JARDIM BOTÂNICO
FUNICULAR
CORREIO
PALÁCIO FOZ
Restauradores
Estação do Rossio
Praça do Princ. Real
JARDIM DA ESTRELA
ASSEMBLEIA NACIONAL
BAIRRO ALTO
L. Conde Barão
Praça Duque de Terceira
ESTAÇÃO DO CAIS DO SODRÉ
CACILHAS
Avenida da Liberdade
Av. Fontes Pereira de Melo
Av. A. Augusto de Aguiar
R. Duque de Loulé
R. Conde Redondo
Rua Gomes Freire
R. de Dona Estefânia
Rua Rodrigo da Fonseca
R. da Artilharia Um
R. J. Ant. de Aguiar
R. Castilho
R. S. Filipe Nery
Rua das Amoreiras
R. Dom João V
R. Braancamp
Rua Alexandre Herculano
Rua de Santa Marta
Rua B. Salgueiro
Rua do Salitre
Rua da Escola Politécnica
R. D. Pedro V
Rua de S. José
Calçada da Glória
Av. P. Álvares Cabral
Rua de S. Bernardo
R. de Sto Amaro
R. Imprensa Nacional
Rua de S. Marçal
Rua do Século
Rua da Misericórdia
Rua da Rosa
Calçada da Estrela
Borges Carneiro
Rua de S. Bento
R. Cruz dos Poiais
R. do Poço dos Negros
Avenida D. Carlos I
R. da Boavista
R. de São Paulo
R. do Alecrim
R. Garrett
R. Victor Cordon
Rua Dom Luís I
Avenida Vinte e Quatro de Julho
Av. Ribeira
M¹
G
M
40
106
121
126
108
93
96
116
38
86
105
88
9
135
124

LISBOA

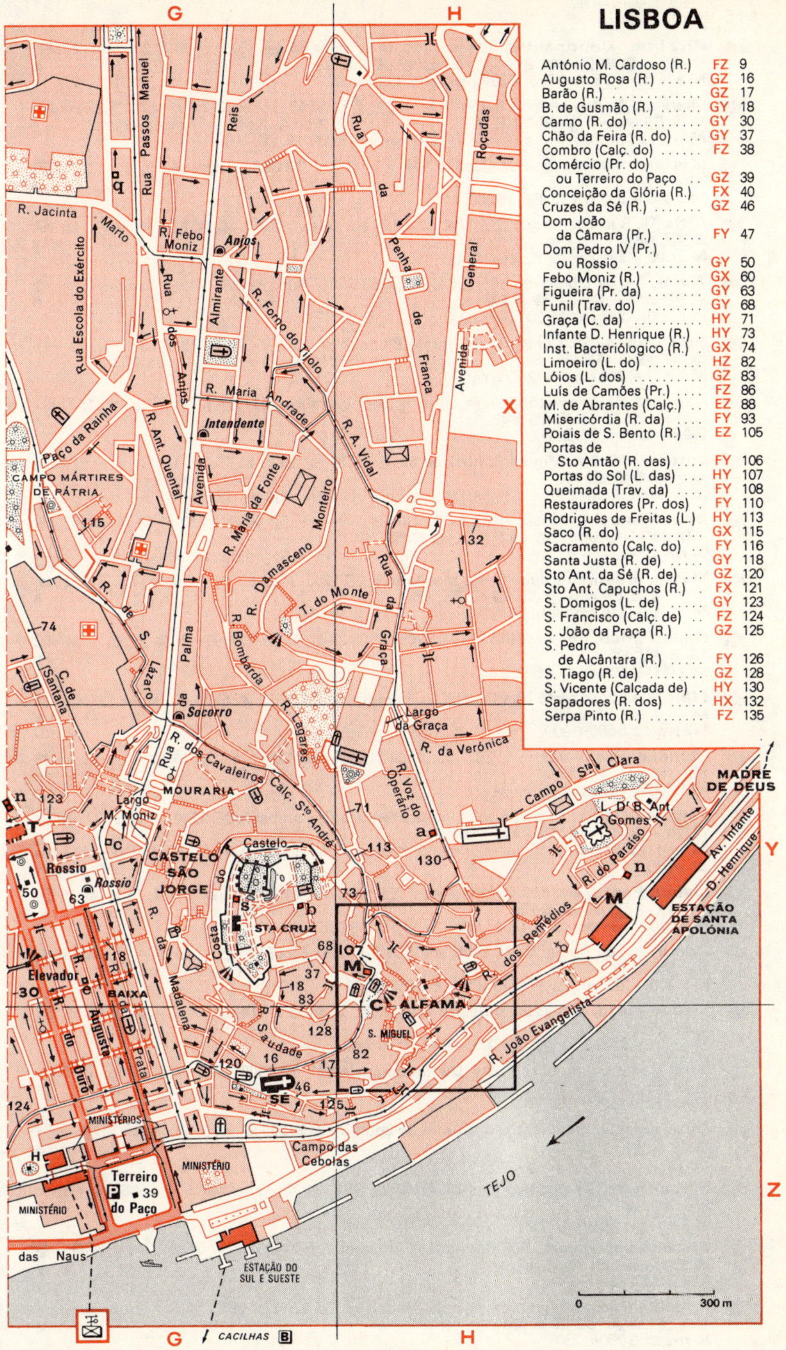

António M. Cardoso (R.)	FZ	9
Augusto Rosa (R.)	GZ	16
Barão (R.)	GZ	17
B. de Gusmão (R.)	GY	18
Carmo (R. do)	GY	30
Chão da Feira (R. do)	GY	37
Combro (Calç. do)	FZ	38
Comércio (Pr. do) ou Terreiro do Paço	GZ	39
Conceição da Glória (R.)	FX	40
Cruzes da Sé (R.)	GZ	46
Dom João da Câmara (Pr.)	FY	47
Dom Pedro IV (Pr.) ou Rossio	GY	50
Febo Moniz (R.)	GX	60
Figueira (Pr. da)	GY	63
Funil (Trav. do)	GY	68
Graça (C. da)	HY	71
Infante D. Henrique (R.)	HY	73
Inst. Bacteriólogico (R.)	GX	74
Limoeiro (L. do)	HZ	82
Lóios (L. dos)	GZ	83
Luís de Camões (Pr.)	FZ	86
M. de Abrantes (Calç.)	EZ	88
Misericórdia (R. da)	FY	93
Poiais de S. Bento (R.)	EZ	105
Portas de Sto Antão (R. das)	FY	106
Portas do Sol (L. das)	HY	107
Queimada (Trav. da)	FY	108
Restauradores (Pr. dos)	FY	110
Rodrigues de Freitas (L.)	HY	113
Saco (R. do)	GX	115
Sacramento (Calç. do)	FY	116
Santa Justa (R. de)	GY	118
Sto Ant. da Sé (R. de)	GZ	120
Sto Ant. Capuchos (R.)	FX	121
S. Domigos (L. de)	GY	123
S. Francisco (Calç. de)	FZ	124
S. João da Praça (R.)	GZ	125
S. Pedro de Alcântara (R.)	FY	126
S. Tiago (R. de)	GZ	128
S. Vicente (Calçada de)	HY	130
Sapadores (R. dos)	HX	132
Serpa Pinto (R.)	FZ	135

Ritz Inter-Continental, Rua Rodrigo da Fonseca 88, ✉ 1093, ✆ 69 20 20, Telex 12589, <, – ▤ – ✥ rest EX b
M a la carte 2 590/6 270 – **300 rm** ▭ 13 900/16 000.

Sheraton Ⓜ, Rua Latino Coelho 1, ✉ 1000, ✆ 57 57 57, Telex 12774, <, heated – by Av. Fontes Pereira de Melo EFX
M *(closed Saturday and Sunday)* – **390 rm** ▭ 16 000/19 000.

Meridien Lisboa Ⓜ, Rua Castillo 149, ✉ 1000, ✆ 69 09 00, Telex 64315, < – ✥ EX a
M 3 000 – **331 rm** 15 450/18 000.

Altis Ⓜ, Rua Castilho 11, ✉ 1200, ✆ 52 24 96, Telex 13314 – E VISA. ✥ EX z
M 2 000 – **225 rm** ▭ 10 000/12 000.

Tivoli, Av. da Liberdade 185, ✉ 1200, ✆ 53 01 81, Telex 12588, heated, – E VISA. ✥ FX d
M 2 000 – **342 rm** ▭ 10 500/12 000.

Alfa Lisboa, Av. Columbano Bordalo Pinheiro ✆ 72 21 21, Telex 18477, < – E VISA. ✥ rest NW : by Av. A. Augusto de Aguiar EX
M 1 800 – **260 rm** ▭ 12 300/15 000.

Avenida Palace without rest., Rua 1° de Dezembro 123, ✉ 1200, ✆ 36 01 51, Telex 12815 – E VISA. ✥ FY n
100 rm ▭ 10 000/12 000.

Lutécia, Av. Frei Miguel Contreiras 52, ✉ 1700, ✆ 80 31 21, Telex 12457, < – E VISA. ✥ N : by Av. Almirante Reis GX
M *(closed Sunday from December to February)* 1 600 – **150 rm** ▭ 6 500/7 500.

Dom Manuel I without rest., av. Duque d'Ávila 189, ✉ 1000, ✆ 57 61 60, Telex 43558, « Tasteful decor » – E VISA. ✥ N : by Av. Fontes Pereira de Melo EFX
64 rm ▭ 6 400/6 900.

Tivoli Jardim, Rua Julio Cesar Machado 7, ✉ 1200, ✆ 53 99 71, Telex 12172, heated, – E VISA. ✥ FX e
M 1 500 – **119 rm** ▭ 8 600/9 000.

Diplomático, Rua Castilho 74, ✉ 1200, ✆ 56 20 41, Telex 13713 – E VISA. ✥ EX c
M 1 600 – **90 rm** ▭ 6 500/9 600.

Flórida without rest., Rua Duque de Palmela 32, ✉ 1200, ✆ 57 61 45, Telex 12256 – E VISA EX x
112 rm ▭ 5 500/6 900.

Mundial, Rua D. Duarte 4, ✉ 1100, ✆ 86 31 01, Telex 12308, < – E VISA. ✥ rest GY c
M 1 600 – **147 rm** ▭ 7 200/9 000.

Fénix and Rest. El Bodegón, Praça Marquês de Pombal 8, ✉ 1200, ✆ 53 51 21, Telex 12170 – E VISA. ✥ EX g
M *(closed Saturday dinner, Sunday and Bank Holidays)* a la carte 1 600/2 910 – **112 rm** ▭ 7 000/8 000.

Lisboa Penta, Av. dos Combatentes, ✉ 1600, ✆ 72 50 50, Telex 18437, – E VISA NW : by Av. A. Augusto de Aguiar EX
M 2 200 – **588 rm** ▭ 8 150/11 085 – P 12 550/19 885.

Roma, Av. de Roma 33, ✉ 1700, ✆ 76 77 61, Telex 16586, <, – E VISA. ✥ N : by Av. Almirante Reis GX
M 1 300 – **263 rm** ▭ 3 500/5 100 – P 5 150/6 100.

Lisboa Plaza, Travessa do Salitre 7, ✉ 1200, ✆ 36 39 22, Telex 16402 – E VISA. ✥ FX b
M 1 600 – **93 rm** ▭ 7 800/9 000 – P 11 000/15 400.

Dom Carlos without rest., Av. Duque de Loulé 121, ✉ 1000, ✆ 53 90 71, Telex 16468 – E VISA. ✥ EX s
73 rm ▭ 4 500/5 750.

Embaixador, without rest., Av. Duque de Loulé 73, ✉ 1000, ✆ 53 01 71, Telex 13773, < – FX a
96 rm.

Miraparque, Av. Sidónio Pais 12, ✉ 1000, ✆ 57 80 70, Telex 16745 – rest wc wc. ✥ EX k
M 1 300 – **100 rm** ▭ 3 600/4 300 – P 4 750/6 200.

Britânia without rest., Rua Rodrigues Sampaio 17, ✉ 1100, ✆ 57 50 95, Telex 13733 – wc. E VISA. ✥ FX y
30 rm ▭ 4 300/5 500.

Príncipe Real without rest., Rua da Alegria 53, ✉ 1200, ✆ 36 01 16, « Tasteful decor » – wc. E VISA EX q
24 rm ▭ 6 750/8 250.

Eduardo VII, Av. Fontes Pereira de Melo 5, ✉ 1000, ✆ 53 01 41, Telex 18340, ≤ – |‡| ▤ TV ⊟wc ⋔wc ☎. AE ⓓ E VISA. ⁂ EX p
M a la carte 1 400/2 100 – **110 rm** ☕ 5 400/6 300 – P 6 350/8 600.

York House, Rua das Janelas Verdes 32, ✉ 1200, ✆ 66 25 44, « Former 16C Convent, Portuguese decor » – ⊟wc ⋔wc ☎. AE ⓓ E VISA. ⁂ rest
M 1 200 – **63 rm** ☕ 6 000/7 000. W : by calçada M., de Abrantes EZ

Botánico, without rest, Rua Mãe d'Água 16, ✉ 1200, ✆ 32 03 92, Telex 12308 – |‡| ▤ ⊟wc ⋔wc ☎. AE ⓓ E VISA. ⁂ FX s
30 rm ☕ 3 700/5 000.

Vip, without rest., Rua Fernão Lopes 25, ✉ 1000, ✆ 57 89 23, Telex 14194 – |‡| ⊟wc ☎ – ♨ FX n
54 rm.

Principe, Av. Duque d'Ávila 201, ✉ 1000, ✆ 53 61 51, Telex 43565 – |‡| ▤ ⊟wc ☎ Ⓟ
67 rm. NW : by Av. A. Augusto de Aguiar EX

Do Reno without rest., Av. Duque d'Ávila 195, ✉ 1000, ✆ 54 81 81, Telex 15893 – |‡| ⊟wc ⋔wc ☎ Ⓟ. AE ⓓ E VISA. ⁂ NW : by Av. A. Augusto de Aguiar EX
54 rm ☕ 3 000/4 000.

Excelsior without rest., Rua Rodrigues Sampaio 172, ✉ 1100, ✆ 53 71 51, Telex 14223 – |‡| ⊟wc ⋔wc ☎. AE ⓓ E VISA. ⁂ EX d
80 rm ☕ 4 500/5 500.

Nazareth 4th floor, without rest., Av. António Augusto de Aguiar 25, ✉ 1000, ✆ 54 20 16 – |‡| ⊟wc ☎. AE ⓓ E VISA. ⁂ EX y
32 rm ☕ 3 000/4 250.

São Pedro without rest., Rua Pascoal de Melo 130, ✉ 1000, ✆ 57 87 65 – |‡| ⊟wc ⋔wc ☎. ⁂ N : by Av. Almirante Reis GX
50 rm ☕ 3 200/3 500.

Insulana, 2nd floor, without rest., Rua da Assunção 52, ✉ 1100, ✆ 32 80 13 – |‡| ⊟wc ⋔wc ☎. ⁂ GY e
32 rm.

Alicante without rest., Av. Duque de Loulé 20, ✉ 1000, ✆ 57 38 70 – |‡| ⊟wc ⋔wc ☎. ⁂ FX c
36 rm ☕ 1 800/2 900.

Imperador without rest., Av. 5 de Outubro 55, ✉ 1000, ✆ 57 48 84 – |‡| ⊟wc ⋔wc ☎. ⁂ N : by Av. Fontes Pereira de Melo EFX
43 rm ☕ 2 500/3 100.

Roma 1st floor, without rest., Travessa da Glória 22-A, ✉ 1200, ✆ 36 05 57 – ⊟wc ⋔wc ☎. AE E VISA. ⁂ FY t
24 rm ☕ 3 000/4 000.

Americano without rest., Rua 1° de Dezembro 73, ✉ 1200, ✆ 32 75 19 – |‡| ⊟wc ⋔wc ☎ FY c
49 rm ☕ 2 900/3 600.

XXXX **Aviz,** Rua Serpa Pinto 12-B, ✉ 1200, ✆ 32 53 72 – ▤. AE ⓓ E VISA. ⁂ FZ x
closed Saturday lunch and Sunday – **M** a la carte 1 940/5 780.

XXXX ❀ **Tágide,** Largo da Academia Nacional de Belas Artes 18, ✉ 1200, ✆ 32 07 20, ≤ – ▤. AE ⓓ E VISA. ⁂ FZ z
closed Saturday dinner and Sunday – **M** a la carte 2 450/4 400
Spec. Paté de salmão, Cherne com molho de coentras, Churrasco de cabrito finas ervas.

XXXX **António Clara,** Av. da República 38, ✉ 1000, ✆ 76 63 80, Telex 62506, « Former old palace » – ▤ Ⓟ. AE ⓓ E N : by Av. Fontes Pereira de Melo EFX
closed Sunday – **M** a la carte 1 850/3 800.

XXXX **Clara,** Campo dos Martires da Patria 49, ✉ 1100, ✆ 55 73 41 – ▤. AE ⓓ E VISA. ⁂ FX f
closed Sunday – **M** a la carte 1 640/2 960.

XXXX **Tavares,** Rua da Misericórdia 37, ✉ 1200, ✆ 32 11 12, Late 19C decor – ▤. AE E VISA. ⁂ FZ t
closed Saturday and Sunday lunch – **M** a la carte 1 830/3 630.

XXX Cota D'Armas, Beco de São Miguel 7, ✉ 1100, ✆ 86 86 82, ♫, Tasteful decor and Fado cabaret at night – ▤ in Alfama

XXX **Gambrinus,** Rua das Portas de Santo Antão 25, ✉ 1100, ✆ 32 14 66 – ▤. AE VISA. ⁂ GY n
M a la carte 2 000/6 600.

XXX **Escorial,** Rua das Portas de Santo Antão 47, ✉ 1100, ✆ 36 44 29, Modern decor – ▤. AE ⓓ E VISA GY n
M a la carte 1 410/4 220.

XXX **Pabe,** Rua Duque de Palmela 27-A, ✉ 1200, ✆ 53 74 84, English pub style – ▤. AE ⓓ E VISA EX u
M a la carte 1 640/4 530.

XXX ✿ **Casa da Comida,** Travessa das Amoreiras 1, ✉ 1200, ✆ 68 53 76, « Patio with plants » – ▤. AE ⓓ E VISA. ✈ EX e
closed Saturday lunch and Sunday – **M** a la carte 2 100/4 800
Spec. Pregado com pimenta verde, Cherne com ananás, Pato com cepes.

XXX **Chester,** Rua Rodrigo da Fonseca 87-D, ✉ 1000, ✆ 68 78 11, Telex 13649, Meat specialities – ▤. AE ⓓ E VISA. ✈ EX w
closed Sunday – **M** a la carte 1 700/3 230.

XXX **Saraiva's,** Rua Eng. Canto Rosende 3, ✉ 1000, ✆ 53 19 87, Modern decor – ▤. AE ⓓ E VISA. ✈ N : by Av. A. Augusto de Aguiar EX
closed Saturday – **M** a la carte 1 380/3 160.

XXX **Conventual,** Praça das Flores 45, ✉ 1200, ✆ 60 91 96, Monastic decor and atmosphere, Traditional Portuguese cuisine – AE ⓓ E VISA EY m
closed Sunday – **M** a la carte 990/3 030.

XXX O Faz Figura, Rua do Paraiso 15 B, ✉ 1100, ✆ 86 89 31, ≤, 斎 – ▤ HY n

XXX **Bachus,** Largo da Trindade 9, ✉ 1200, ✆ 32 28 28 – ▤. AE ⓓ E VISA. ✈ FY s
M a la carte 1 280/2 700.

XX **A Góndola,** Av. de Berna 64, ✉ 1000, ✆ 77 04 26, 斎 – ▤. E VISA
closed Saturday dinner and Sunday – **M** a la carte 1 430/2 720.
N : by Av. A. Augusto de Aguiar EX

XX **Michel,** Largo de Santa Cruz do Castelo 5, ✉ 1100, ✆ 86 43 38, French rest. – ▤. AE ⓓ E VISA GY b
closed Saturday lunch, Sunday and Bank Holidays – **M** a la carte 1 880/4 680.

XX **São Jerónimo,** Rua dos Jerónimos 12, ✉ 1300, ✆ 64 87 97 – ▤. AE ⓓ E VISA
closed Sunday dinner and Monday – **M** a la carte 1 160/2 720.
W : by Av. 24 de Julho EZ

XX **Casa do Lẽao,** Castelo de São Jorge, ✉ 1100, ✆ 87 59 62, ≤ – ▤. AE ⓓ E VISA. ✈
M (lunch only) a la carte 2 500/4 200. GY s

XX **Petite Folie,** Av. António Augusto de Aguiar 74, ✉ 1000, ✆ 52 19 48, 斎, French rest. – AE ⓓ E VISA EX m
M a la carte 1 140/2 040.

XX Espelho d'Água, Av. de Brasilia, ✉ 1300, ✆ 61 73 73, ≤, 斎, Modern decor – ▤
W : by Av. 24 de Julho EZ

XX **Sancho,** Travessa da Glória 14, ✉ 1200, ✆ 36 97 80 – ▤. AE E VISA. ✈ FXY t
closed Sunday – **M** a la carte 760/1 430.

XX Fred basement, Av. da República 9-A, ✉ 1000, ✆ 53 04 11, Modern decor – ▤
N : by Av. Fontes Pereira de Melo EFX

X **O Vicentinho,** Rua Voz do Operario 1 B, ✉ 1100, ✆ 86 46 95 – ▤. AE ⓓ E VISA. ✈
closed Sunday lunch, Bank Holidays and Monday – **M** a la carte 1 080/2 260. HY a

X **Xêlê Bananas,** Praça das Flores 29, ✉ 1200, ✆ 67 05 15, Tropical style decor – ▤. AE ⓓ E VISA EY n
closed Sunday – **M** a la carte 1 270/2 950.

X **Sua Excelência,** Rua do Conde 42, ✉ 1200, ✆ 60 36 14 – ▤. AE ⓓ E VISA
closed Wednesday, Saturday lunch and September – **M** a la carte 1 600/2 850.
W : by calçada M. de Abrantes EZ

X **António,** Rua Tomás Ribeiro 63, ✉ 1000, ✆ 53 87 80 – ▤. AE ⓓ E VISA. ✈
M a la carte 915/2 890. N : by Av. A. Augusto de Aguiar EX

X **Mestre Cuco,** Rua Nova S. Mamede 16, ✉ 1200, ✆ 67 57 23 – ▤. AE ⓓ E VISA. ✈
closed Sunday – **M** a la carte 960/2 020. EX j

Typical restaurants.

XX **Arcadas do Faia,** Rua da Barroca 56, ✉ 1200, ✆ 32 67 42, Telex 13649, Fado cabaret – ▤. AE ⓓ E. ✈ FY f
closed Sunday – **M** (dinner only) a la carte 1 650/3 370.

XX **A Severa,** Rua das Gáveas 51, ✉ 1200, ✆ 36 40 06, Fado cabaret at dinner – ▤. AE ⓓ E VISA. ✈ FY b
closed Thursday – **M** a la carte 1 650/3 400.

XX Lisboa à Noite, Rua das Gáveas 69, ✉ 1200, ✆ 36 85 57, Fado cabaret at dinner – ▤ FY x

XX **Sr. Vinho,** Rua do Meio - à - Lapa 18, ✉ 1200, ✆ 67 26 81, Fado cabaret – ▤. AE ⓓ E VISA EZ r
closed Sunday – **M** (dinner only) a la carte 2 900/3 000.

X **Adega Machado,** Rua do Norte 91, ✉ 1200, ✆ 36 00 95, Fado cabaret – ▤. AE ⓓ E VISA. ✈ FY k
M (dinner only) a la carte 1 500/2 300.

X O Forcado, Rua da Rosa 221, ✉ 1200, ✆ 36 85 79, Fado cabaret – ▤ FY r
M (dinner only).

X Parreirinha de Alfama, Beco do Espírito Santo 1, ✉ 1100, ✆ 86 82 09, Fado cabaret
M (dinner only). in Alfama

Spain
España

Madrid
Barcelona
Malaga - Marbella
Sevilla
Valencia

PRACTICAL INFORMATION

LOCAL CURRENCY

Peseta : 100 ptas = 0.65 US $ (Jan. 86)

TOURIST INFORMATION

The telephone number and address of the Tourist Information offices is given in the text of the towns under ☒.

FOREIGN EXCHANGE

Banks are open from 9am to 2pm (12.30pm on Saturdays).
Exchange offices in Sevilla and Valencia airports open from 9am to 2pm, in Barcelona airport from 9am to 2pm and 7 to 11pm. In Madrid and Málaga airports, offices operate a 24 hour service.

TRANSPORT

Taxis may be hailed when showing the green light or sign "Libre" on the windscreen.
Madrid and Barcelona have a Metro (subway) network. In each station complete information and plans will be found.

SHOPPING

In the index of street names, those printed in red are where the principal shops are found.
The big stores are easy to find in town centres; they are open from 10am to 8pm.
Exclusive shops and boutiques are open from 10am to 2pm and 5 to 8pm - In Madrid they will be found in Serrano, Princesa and the Centre; in Barcelona, Passeig de Gracia, Diagonal and the Rambla de Catalunya.
Second-hand goods and antiques: El Rastro (Flea Market), Las Cortes, Serrano in Madrid; in Barcelona, Los Encantes (Flea Market), Barrio Gótico.

TIPPING

Hotel, restaurant and café bills always include service in the total charge. Nevertheless it is usual to leave the staff a small gratuity which may vary with the district and the service given. Doormen, porters and taxi-drivers are used to being tipped.

SPEED LIMITS

The maximum permitted speed on motorways is 120 km/h - 74 mph, and 90 km/h - 56 mph on other roads.

SEAT BELTS

The wearing of seat belts is compulsory for drivers and front seat passengers.

"TAPAS"

Bars serving "tapas" (typical spanish food to be eaten with a glass of wine or an aperitif) will usually be found in central, busy or old quarters of towns. In Madrid, idle your way to the Calle de la Cruz (Puerta del Sol) or to the Calle de Cuchilleros (Plaza Mayor).

MADRID

SIGHTS

See : The Prado Museum★★★ (Museo del Prado) NZ – Parque del Buen Retiro★★ HY – Paseo del Prado (Plaza de la Cibeles) NXYZ – Paseo de Recoletos NVX – Paseo de la Castellana NV – Puerta del Sol and Calle de Alcalá LMNY – Plaza Mayor★ KYZ – Royal Palace (Palacio Real)★★ KY – Descalzas Reales Convent★★ (Convento de las Descalzas Reales) KY **L** – San Antonio de la Florida (fresco by Goya★) DX **R.**

Other Museums : Archeological Museum★★ (Arqueológico Nacional) NV **M22** – Lázaro Galdiano★★ HV **M7** – The Américas Museum★ DV **M8** – Museum of Contemporary Spanish Art★ – Army Museum (del Ejército★) NY **M2.**

Envir. : El Pardo (Palacio★) NW : 13 km by C 601.

MADRID 444 y 447 K 19 – Pop. 3 188 297 – alt. 646 – ⊗ 91 – Bullring.

Racecourse of the Zarzuela – 18, 18 Puerta de Hierro ✆ 216 17 45 – 9, 18 Club de Campo ✆ 207 03 95 – 18 La Moraleja by ① : 11 km ✆ 650 07 00 – 9 Club Barberán by ⑥ : 10 km ✆ 218 85 05 – 9, 18 Las Lomas – El Bosque by ⑥ : 18 km ✆ 464 32 15 – 18 Real Automóvil Club de España by ① : 28 km ✆ 652 26 00 – 18 Nuevo Club de Madrid, Las Matas by ⑦ : 26 km ✆ 630 08 20 – 9 Somosaguas W : 10 km by Casa de Campo ✆ 212 16 47.

✈ Madrid-Barajas by ② : 13 km ✆ 222 11 65 – Iberia : pl. de Cánovas 5, ✉ 28014, ✆ 429 74 43 and Aviaco, Modesto Lafuente 76, ✉ 28003, ✆ 254 51 19.

🚗 Atocha ✆ 228 52 37 – Chamartín ✆ 733 11 22 – Príncipe Pío ✆ 248 87 16.

Shipping Companies : Cía. Trasmediterránea, Pedro Munõz Seca 2 NX, ✉ 1, ✆ 431 07 00, Telex 23189.

ℹ Princesa 1, ✉ 28008, ✆ 241 23 25, Medinaceli 2, ✉ 28006, ✆ 411 43 36 pl. Mayor 3, ✉ 28012, ✆ 266 48 74, Caballero de Gracia 7, ✉ 28013, ✆ 231 44 57 and Barajas airport ✆ 205 86 56 – R.A.C.E. José Abascal 10, ✉ 28003, ✆ 447 32 00, Telex 27341.

París (by Irún) 1317 ① – Barcelona 626 ② – Bilbao 401 ① – La Coruña 601 ⑦ – Lisboa 648 ⑥ – Málaga 546 ④ – Porto 602 ⑦ – Sevilla 547 ④ – Valencia 354 ③ – Zaragoza 321 ②.

Centre : Paseo del Prado, Puerta del Sol, Gran Vía, Alcalá, Paseo de Recoletos, Plaza Mayor, Leganitos (plan pp. 6 and 7).

Palace, pl. de las Cortes 7, ✉ 28014, ☎ 429 75 51, Telex 22272 – AE E VISA. rest — MY **e**
M 3 750 – ☐ 900 – **510 rm** 12 500/16 500.

Princesa Plaza M, Serrano Jover 3, ✉ 28008, ☎ 242 21 00, Telex 44378 – AE E VISA — KV **c**
M 3 650 – ☐ 790 – **406 rm** 11 280/14 100 – P 13 520/17 750.

Plaza without rest. coffee shop only, pl. España, ✉ 28013, ☎ 247 12 00, Telex 27383, ←, AE E VISA — KV **s**
☐ 630 – **306 rm** 8 320/10 400.

Emperador without rest, Gran Vía 53, ✉ 28013, ☎ 247 28 00, Telex 46261, AE E VISA — KX **n**
☐ 460 – **232 rm** 6 320/7 900.

Liabeny, Salud 3, ✉ 28013, ☎ 232 53 06, Telex 49024 – AE VISA — LY **e**
M 1 400 – ☐ 500 – **158 rm** 4 600/7 100.

Suecia and Rest. Bellman, Marqués de Casa Riera 4, ✉ 28014, ☎ 231 69 00, Telex 22313 – AE E VISA — MY **b**
closed August – **M** *(closed Saturday and Sunday)* 2 200 – ☐ 600 – **64 rm** 7 590/9 350 – P 9 675/12 590.

Victoria, pl. del Angel 7, ✉ 28012, ☎ 231 60 00 – AE E VISA — LZ **u**
M 1 375 – ☐ 300 – **114 rm** 3 550/5 450 – P 5 425/6 250.

Arosa without rest, coffee shop only, Salud 21, ✉ 28013, ☎ 232 16 00, Telex 43618 – AE E VISA — LX **q**
☐ 495 – **126 rm** 5 450/8 220.

El Prado without rest, Prado 11, ✉ 28014, ☎ 429 35 68 – AE VISA — LZ **z**
☐ 400 – **45 rm** 6 300/7 500.

Mayorazgo without rest, coffee shop only, Flor Baja 3, ✉ 28013, ☎ 247 26 00, Telex 45647 – AE E VISA — KX **b**
☐ 425 – **200 rm** 5 200/7 200.

El Coloso, Leganitos 13, ✉ 28013, ☎ 248 76 00, Telex 47017 – AE E VISA — KX **y**
M 1 250 – ☐ 460 – **84 rm** 6 350/7 950.

Casón del Tormes without rest, Río 7, ✉ 28013, ☎ 241 97 46 – wc VISA — KX **v**
☐ 250 – **61 rm** 2 950/4 300.

Mercator without rest, coffee shop only, Atocha 123, ✉ 28012, ☎ 429 05 00, Telex 46129 – wc P. AE E VISA — NZ **b**
☐ 280 – **90 rm** 2 925/4 425.

Atlántico 3rd floor, without rest, Gran Vía 38, ✉ 28013, ☎ 222 64 80 – wc AE E VISA — LX **e**
62 rm ☐ 3 560/5 350.

Lope de Vega 9th floor, without rest, Gran Vía 59, ✉ 28013, ☎ 247 70 00, ← – wc wc AE E VISA — KX **b**
☐ 250 – **47 rm** 2 500/4 000.

Carlos V without rest, Maestro Vitoria 5, ✉ 28013, ☎ 231 41 00, Telex 48547 – wc wc AE E VISA — KY **f**
☐ 275 – **67 rm** 3 750/4 950.

Moderno, without rest., Arenal 2, ✉ 28013, ☎ 231 09 00 – wc — LY **d**
98 rm.

Reyes Católicos without rest, Angel 18, ✉ 28005, ☎ 265 86 00, Telex 44474 – wc. AE — KZ **w**
☐ 350 – **38 rm** 3 060/4 750.

Fontela, 2nd floor, without rest, Gran Vía 11, ✉ 28013, ☎ 221 64 00 – wc — LX **u**
64 rm.

California without rest, Gran Vía 38, ✉ 28013, ☎ 222 47 03 – wc AE E VISA — LX **e**
☐ 255 – **27 rm** 2 600/4 100.

Amberes 7th floor, without rest, Gran Vía 68, ✉ 28013, ☎ 247 61 00 – wc AE VISA — KX **x**
☐ 230 – **42 rm** 3 750.

XXX ✿ **Clara's,** Arrieta 2, ✉ 28013, ☎ 242 09 45, Telex 23307, « Tasteful decor » – E VISA — KY **s**
closed Sunday – **M** a la carte 2 550/4 600
Spec. Broccoli y endivias supreme al sabor de trufas, Ragoût de rodaballo y vieiras con hortalizas, Cogollos de lechuga al higado de oca y salsa de manzana.

XXX ✿ **El Cenador del Prado,** Prado 4, ✉ 28014, ☎ 429 15 49 – AE E VISA — LZ **n**
closed Saturday dinner, Sunday, Bank Holidays and August – **M** a la carte 2 730/4 620
Spec. Patatas a la importancia con almejas, Caracoles con setas en hojaldre, Salmón escalfado con bígaros.

MADRID

Caídos de la División Azul	HS	6
Capitán Haya	GS	7
Comandante Zorita	FT	14
Costa Rica (Av. de)	HS	20
Cuatro Caminos (Glorieta de)	FU	21
Doctor Arce (Av. del)	HU	25
Doctor Fleming	GT	26
Enrique Larreta	HS	29
Estébanez Calderón	GS	30
Fray Bernardino Sahagún	HS	35
Gen. López Pozas	HS	37
Gen. Moscardó	FT	39
Jerez	HS	43
Pedro Teixeira	GT	58
Pinos Alta	FS	59
Pintor Juan Gris	FS	60
Presidente Carmona	FT	64
Raimundo Fernández Villaverde	FU	69
Ramón y Cajal (Av.)	HT	70
Reina Mercedes	FT	73
República Dominicana (Plaza)	HS	75
Rosa de Silva	FS	78
Rosario Pino	GS	79
San Amaro (Pl.)	FT	82
Segre	HT	96
Sor Angela de la Cruz	GS	99
Teruel	FT	100
Víctor Andrés Belaunde	HT	108
Víctor de la Serna	HT	110

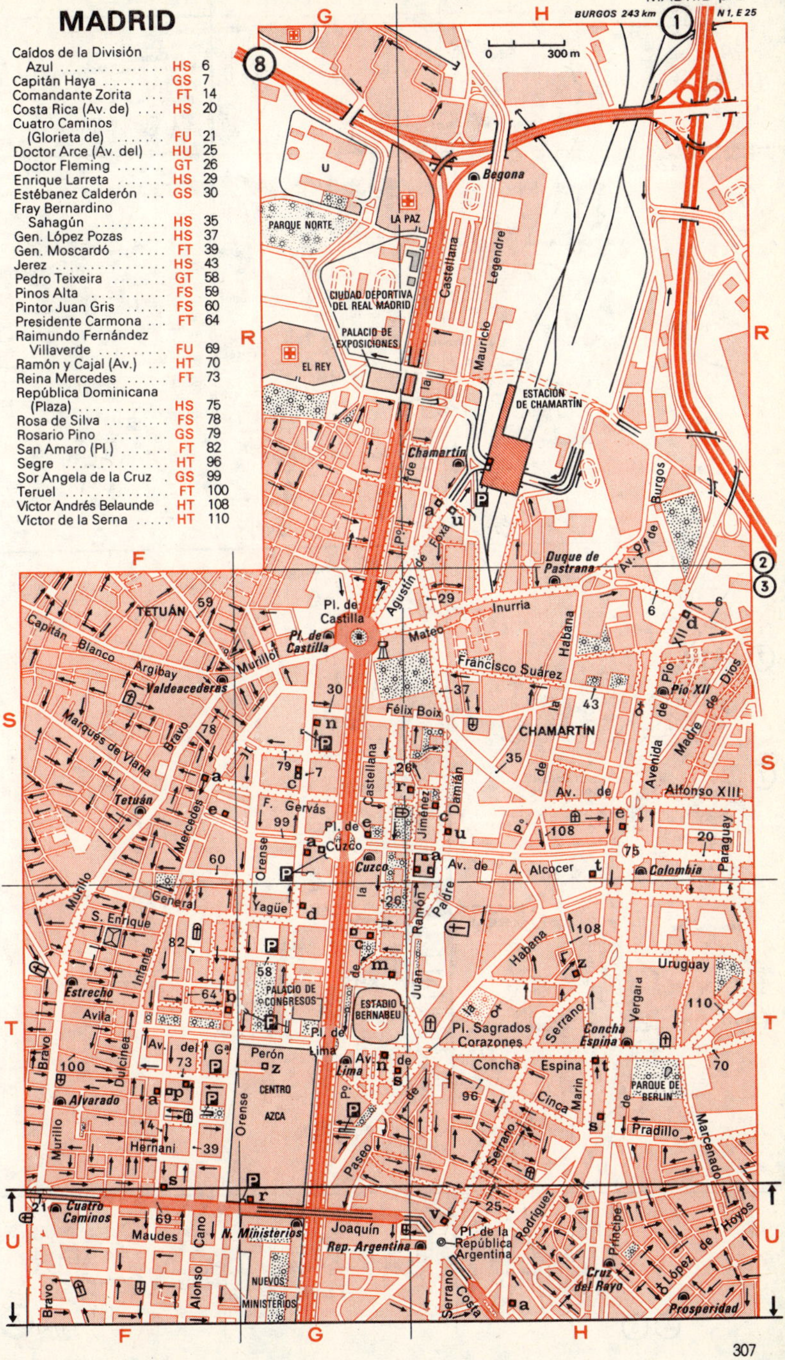

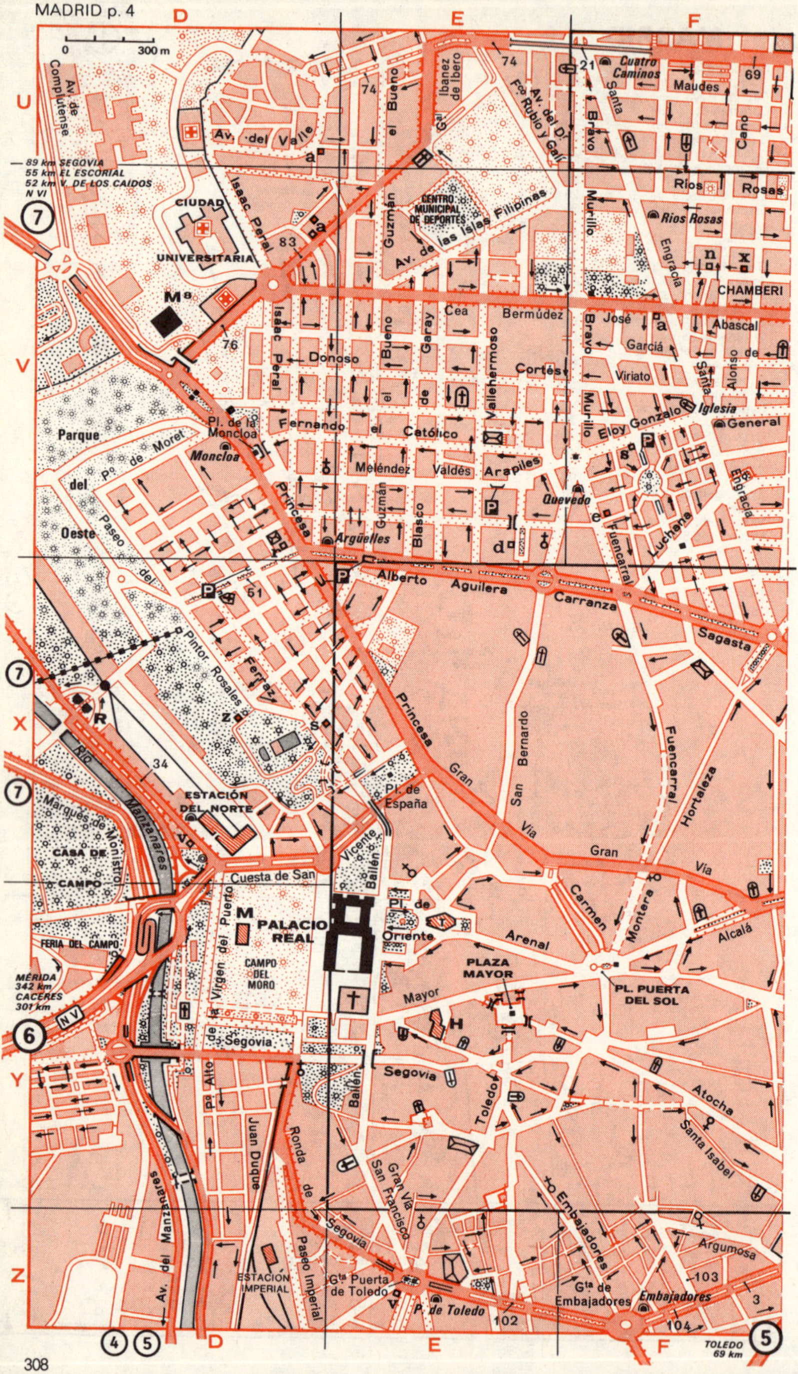
D
E
F
U
V
X
Y
Z
0
300 m
Av. de Complutense
89 km SEGOVIA
55 km EL ESCORIAL
52 km V. DE LOS CAIDOS
N VI
7
CIUDAD
UNIVERSITARIA
Av. del Valle
Isaac Peral
83
76
Cea
Bermúdez
José
Abascal
García
Donoso
Bueno
Garay
Vallehermoso
Cortés
Bravo
Murillo
Viriato
Santa
Iglesia
General
Alonso
Eloy Gonzalo
Fernando el Católico
Meléndez Valdés
Arapiles
Quevedo
Pl. de la Moncloa
Moncloa
Parque del Oeste
Po. de Moret
Paseo del Pintor Rosales
Princesa
Argüelles
Guzmán
Blasco
Luchana
Fuencarral
Engracia
Alberto Aguilera
Carranza
Sagasta
51
Ferraz
R
34
Río Manzanares
ESTACIÓN DEL NORTE
Marqués de Monistrol
CASA DE CAMPO
Pl. de España
Gran Vía
San Bernardo
Hortaleza
Vicente
Bailén
Cuesta de San
M
PALACIO REAL
CAMPO DEL MORO
Virgen del Puerto
Pl. de Oriente
Arenal
Carmen
Montera
Alcalá
PLAZA MAYOR
PL. PUERTA DEL SOL
Mayor
H
FERIA DEL CAMPO
MÉRIDA 342 km
CÁCERES 301 km
N V
6
Segovia
Po. Alto
Juan Duque
Ronda de Segovia
Toledo
Atocha
Santa Isabel
Gran Vía San Francisco
Embajadores
Argumosa
Av. del Manzanares
ESTACIÓN IMPERIAL
Paseo Imperial
Gta Puerta de Toledo
P. de Toledo
102
103
104
3
Gta de Embajadores
Embajadores
4
5
TOLEDO 69 km
CENTRO MUNICIPAL DE DEPORTES
Av. de las Islas Filipinas
Gal Ibañez de Ibero
Av. del Dr Fco Rubio y Galí
74
21
Cuatro Caminos
Maudes
Cano
69
Ríos Rosas
CHAMBERI
a
d
e
n
x
z
s

MADRID

Atocha (Ronda de)	FZ	3
Emperador Carlos V (Glorieta del)	GZ	28
Florida (Paseo de la)	DX	34
Infanta Isabel (Pas.)	GZ	42
Lagasca	HVX	44
Marqués de Salamanca (Pl.)	HV	50
Marqués de Urquijo	DX	51
Miguel Angel	GV	55
Reina Cristina (Pas.)	HZ	72
Reina Victoria (Av.)	EU	74
Reyes Católicos (Av.)	DV	76
San Francisco de Sales (Pas.)	DV	83
Toledo (Ronda de)	EZ	102
Valencia	FZ	103
Valencia (Ronda de)	FZ	104

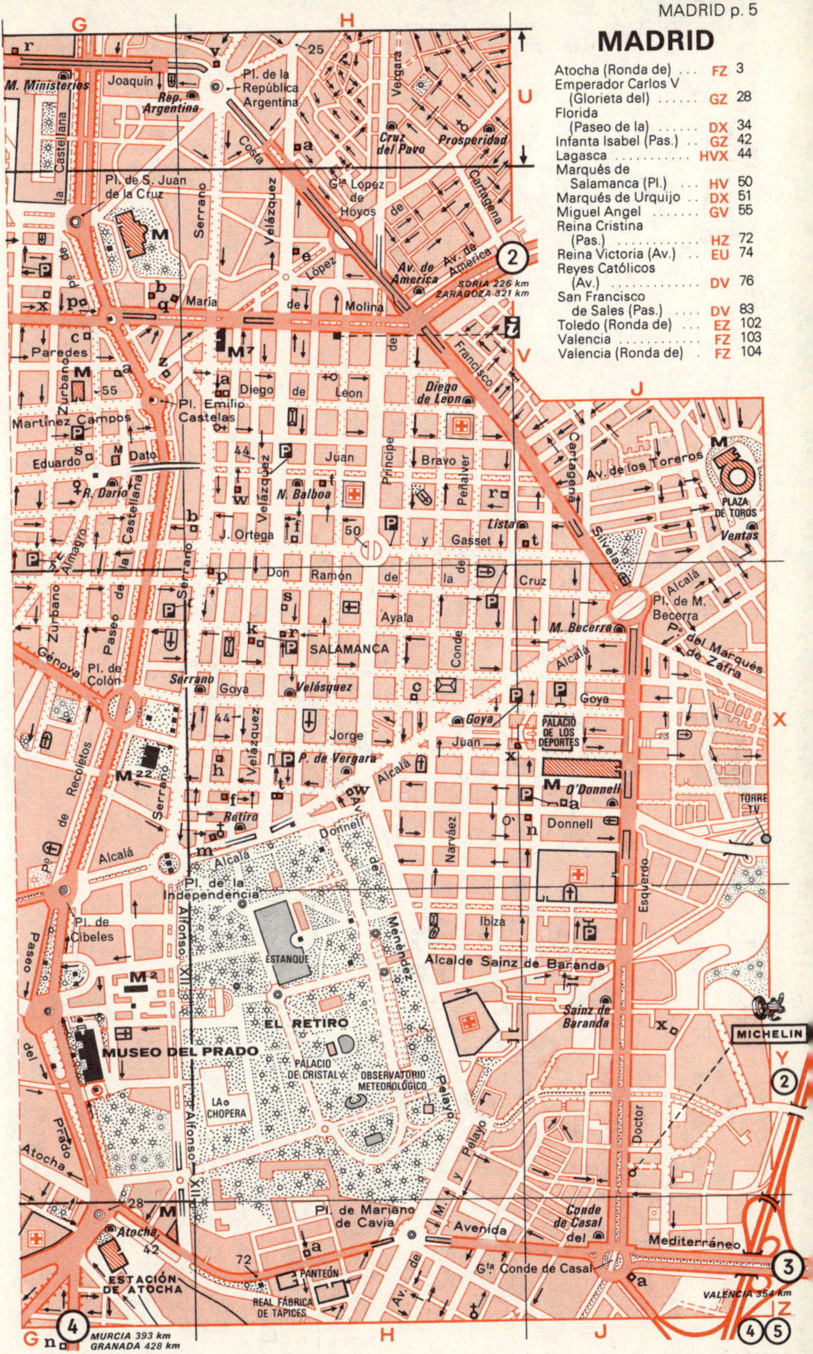

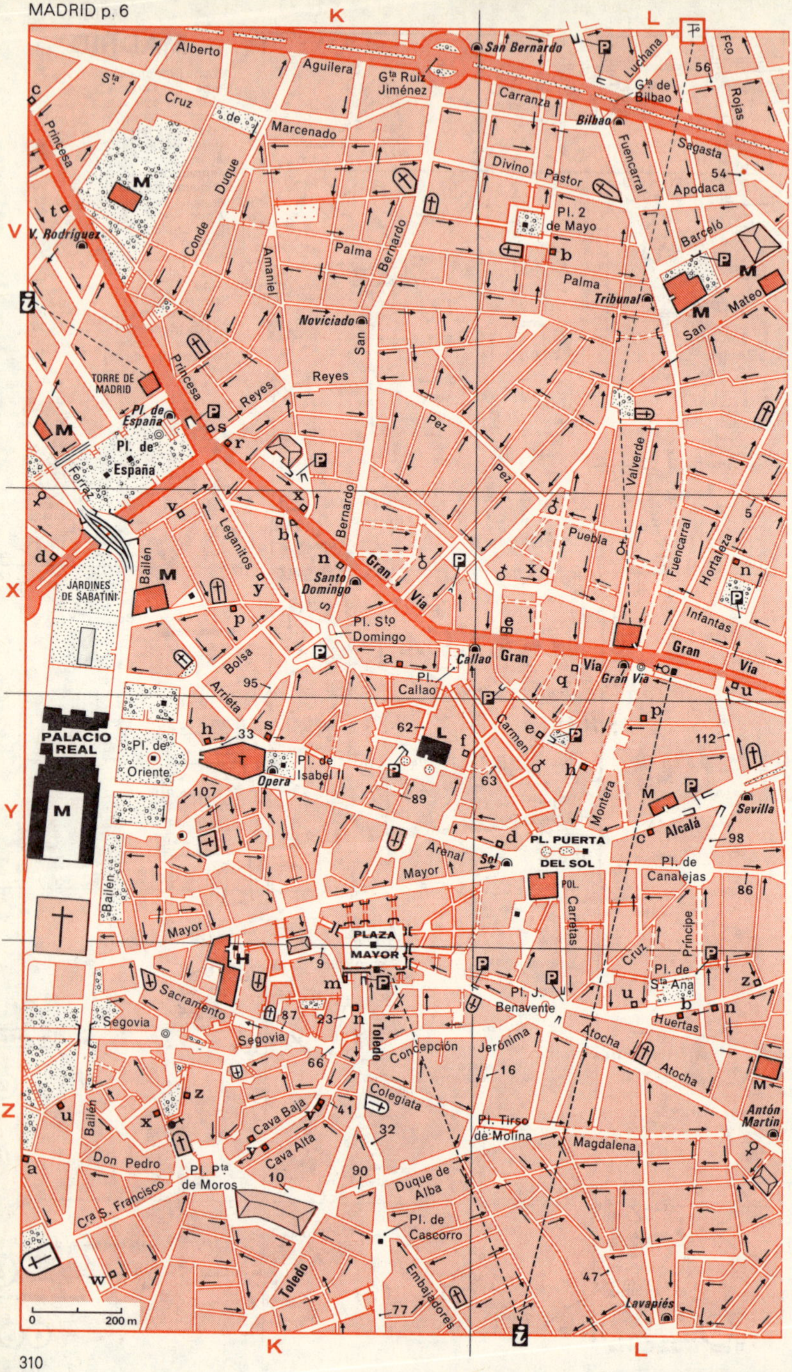
K
L
V
X
Y
Z
Alberto
Aguilera
Gta Ruiz Jiménez
San Bernardo
Luchana
Gta de Bilbao
Fco Rojas
56
Carranza
Bilbao
Sagasta
Sta Cruz de Marcenado
Princesa
Divino Pastor
Fuencarral
54
Apodaca
Duque
Conde
Pl. 2 de Mayo
Barceló
V. Rodríguez
Amaniel
Palma
Bernardo
San Mateo
Tribunal
Noviciado
San
Reyes
TORRE DE MADRID
Pl. de España
Pl. de España
Pez
Valverde
Ferraz
Leganitos
Bernardo
Puebla
Hortaleza
Gran Vía
Santo Domingo
Bailén
JARDINES DE SABATINI
Pl. Sto Domingo
Infantas
Bolsa
Arrieta
95
Pl. Callao
Callao
Gran Vía
Gran Vía
PALACIO REAL
Pl. de Oriente
33
Opera
Pl. de Isabel II
62
63
Carmen
112
107
89
Montera
Sevilla
Alcalá
98
PL. PUERTA DEL SOL
Arenal
Sol
Mayor
Pl. de Canalejas
POL.
86
Bailén
Mayor
Carretas
PLAZA MAYOR
Príncipe
Cruz
Pl. de Sta Ana
9
Pl. J. Benavente
Huertas
Sacramento
Segovia
87
Segovia
23
Toledo
Concepción
Jerónima
Atocha
Atocha
66
16
Colegiata
Antón Martín
41
Bailén
Cava Baja
Pl. Tirso de Molina
Magdalena
32
Cava Alta
Don Pedro
90
Duque de Alba
Pl. Pta de Moros
10
Cra S. Francisco
Pl. de Cascorro
Embajadores
47
Toledo
77
Lavapiés
0
200 m
K
L

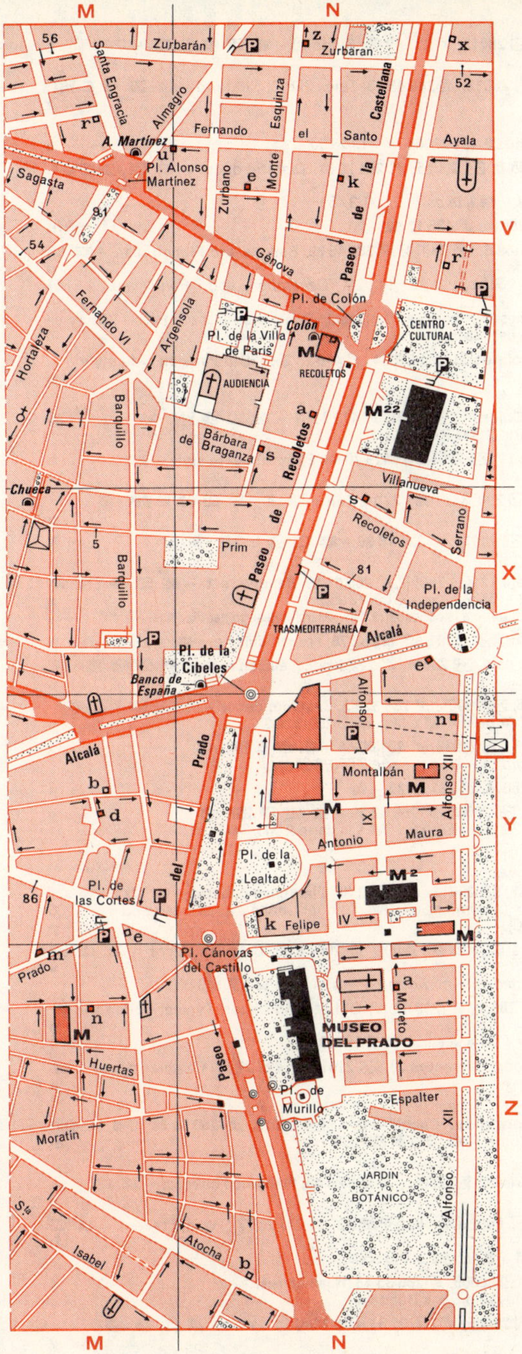

MADRID

When driving through towns use the plans in the **Michelin Guide**

Features indicated include : throughroutes and by -passes ; traffic junctions and major squares, new streets, car parks, pedestrian streets... All this information is revised annually.

XXX **Korynto,** Preciados 36, ⊠ 28013, ☎ 221 59 65, Seafood – ▤. AE ① E VISA. ✕ KX a
M a la carte 2 050/4 200.

XXX **Bajamar,** Gran Vía 78, ⊠ 28013, ☎ 248 48 18, Telex 22818, Seafood – ▤. AE ① E VISA. ✕ KV r
M a la carte 2 680/4 230.

XXX El Escuadrón, Tamayo y Baús 8, ⊠ 28004, ☎ 419 28 30 – ▤ NV s

XXX **El Landó,** pl. Gabriel Miró 8, ⊠ 28005, ☎ 266 76 81, Tasteful decor – ▤. AE ① E VISA. ✕ KZ a
closed Sunday and August – **M** a la carte 2 500/3 450.

XXX Medinaceli, Prado 27, ⊠ 28014, ☎ 429 13 92 – ▤ MZ m

XXX ✿ **Irizar** 1st floor, Jovellanos 3, ⊠ 28014, ☎ 231 45 69, Basque and French rest. – ▤. AE ① E VISA. ✕ MY d
closed Saturday lunch, Sunday, 23 to 29 December and Holy-Week – **M** a la carte 2 550/4 300
Spec. Ostras gratinadas a la muselina de limón (Sept.-April), Suprema de lubina al txacoli, Paletilla de cordero rellena en hojaldre salsa de finas hierbas.

XX **El Espejo,** paseo de Recoletos 31, ⊠ 28004, ☎ 410 25 25, « Old Parisian café style » – ▤. AE ① E VISA. ✕ NV a
M a la carte 2 175/3 140.

XX **El Descubrimiento,** pl. Colón 1, ⊠ 28001, ☎ 410 28 51 – ▤. AE ① VISA. ✕ NV M
closed Sunday – **M** a la carte 2 000/3 400.

XX Platerías, pl. de Santa Ana 11, ⊠ 28012, ☎ 429 70 48, Early 20C café style – ▤ LZ b
M (booking essential).

XX **La Grillade,** Jardines 3, ⊠ 28013, ☎ 221 22 17, Telex 43618 – ▤. AE ① E VISA. ✕ LY p
M a la carte 2 415/3 130.

XX **Valentín,** San Alberto 3, ⊠ 28014, ☎ 221 16 38 – ▤. AE ① E VISA. ✕ LY h
M a la carte 2 475/3 540.

XX ✿ **Gure-Etxea,** pl. de la Paja 12, ⊠ 28005, ☎ 265 61 49, Basque rest. – ▤. AE ① VISA. ✕ KZ x
closed Sunday and August – **M** a la carte 2 000/2 950
Spec. Angulas (Nov.-March), Txangurro a la donostiarra (Nov.-March), Besugo parrilla (Nov.-March).

X Pepe Botella, San Andrés 12, ⊠ 28004, ☎ 222 52 78, French cuisine – ▤ LV b

X **Pazo de Monterrey,** Alcalá 4, ⊠ 28014, ☎ 222 30 10, Galician rest. – ▤. AE ① VISA. ✕ LY c
M a la carte 2 050/3 150.

X **Casa Lucio,** Cava Baja 35, ⊠ 28005, ☎ 265 32 52, Castilian decor – ▤. AE ① VISA. ✕ KZ y
closed Saturday lunch and August – **M** a la carte 2 250/3 500.

X **La Gran Tasca,** Ballesta 1, ⊠ 28013, ☎ 231 00 44 – AE ① E VISA. ✕ LX x
closed Sunday and July-August – **M** a la carte 2 050/3 250.

X Berrio, San Marcos 8, ⊠ 28004, ☎ 221 20 35 – ▤ LX n

X **El Schotis,** Cava Baja 11, ⊠ 28005, ☎ 265 32 30 – ▤. AE ① VISA. ✕ KZ v
closed Sunday dinner and 25 July-August – **M** a la carte 2 000/3 600.

Typical atmosphere

XX **Café de Chinitas,** Torija 8, ⊠ 28013, ☎ 248 51 35, Flamenco cabaret – ▤. AE E. ✕ KX p
closed Sunday and 24 December – **M** (dinner only) a la carte 3 475/5 200 (extra charge for show 2 100).

XX **Posada de la Villa,** Cava Baja 9, ⊠ 28005, ☎ 266 18 60, Castilian decor – ▤. AE ① VISA. ✕ KZ v
closed Sunday dinner and mid July-mid August – **M** a la carte 1 775/3 600.

XX **Botín,** Cuchilleros 17, ⊠ 28005, ☎ 266 42 17, Old Madrid decor, Typical bodega – ▤. AE ① E VISA KZ n
closed dinner 24 December – **M** a la carte 1 915/3 140.

XX **Sixto Gran Mesón** 1st floor, Cervantes 28, ⊠ 28014, ☎ 429 22 55, Castilian decor – ▤. AE ① E VISA. ✕ MZ n
M a la carte 1 800/3 150.

XX **Las Cuevas de Luis Candelas,** Cuchilleros 1, ⊠ 28012, ☎ 266 54 28, Old Madrid decor - Staff in bandit costume – ▤. AE ① VISA. ✕ KZ m
M a la carte 1 725/3 900.

X Corral de la Morería, Morería 17, ⊠ 28005, ☎ 265 84 46, Flamenco cabaret – ▤. ✕ KZ u
M (dinner only).

X **Taberna del Alabardero,** Felipe V - 6, ⊠ 28013, ☎ 247 25 77, Typical tavern – ▤. AE ① E VISA. ✕ KY h
closed 15 to 30 August – **M** a la carte 2 050/3 850.

X El Cosaco, pl. de la Paja 2, ⊠ 28005, ☎ 265 35 48, Russian rest. KZ z
M (dinner only except Sunday and Bank Holidays).

X **Esteban,** Cava Baja 36, ⊠ 28005, ☎ 265 90 91, Old Madrid decor – ▤. AE ①. ✕ KZ y
M a la carte 2 350/3 750.

Retiro-Salamanca-Ciudad Lineal : Castellana, Velázquez, Serrano, Goya, Príncipe de Vergara, Narváez, Don Ramón de la Cruz (plan p. 5 except where otherwise stated).

Ritz, pl. de la Lealtad 5, ✉ 28014, ✆ 521 28 57, Telex 43986 – (in Palace H.). AE VISA. rest — plan p. 7 NY k
M 4 500 – 1 250 – **155 rm** 28 000/35 000.

Villa Magna M, paseo de la Castellena 22, ✉ 28046, ✆ 261 49 00, Telex 22914 – TV – . AE . — plan p. 7 NV x
M 5 700 – 1 200 – **200 rm** 19 000/26 000.

Wellington, Velázquez 8, ✉ 28001, ✆ 275 44 00, Telex 22700, – TV . AE E VISA. — HX t
M (rest see El Fogón below) – 780 – **291 rm** 8 500/13 500.

Sanvy without rest, Goya 3, ✉ 28001, ✆ 276 08 00, – . AE E VISA.
closed Sunday – 600 – **141 rm** 6 900/10 700. — plan p. 7 NV r

Convención without rest, coffee shop only, O'Donnell 53, ✉ 28009, ✆ 274 68 00, Telex 23944 – – . AE E VISA. — JX a
475 – **790 rm** 5 840/7 300.

Los Galgos and Rest. La Almoraima, Claudio Coello 139, ✉ 28006, ✆ 262 42 27, Telex 43957 – TV – . AE E VISA. — HV a
M 2 500 – **361 rm** 8 100/12 200.

G. H. Velázquez, Velázquez 62, ✉ 28001, ✆ 431 82 60, Telex 22779 – . AE E VISA. — HX s
M 1 775 – **144 rm** 6 450/8 400 – P 7 150/9 400.

G. H. Colón, Dr. esquerdo 119, ✉ 28007, ✆ 273 86 00, Telex 22984 – – . AE E VISA. — JY x
M 1 725 – 350 – **220 rm** 4 000/5 750 – P 6 105/7 230.

Alcalá and Rest. Basque, Alcalá 66, ✉ 28009, ✆ 435 10 60, Telex 48094 – . AE E VISA. — HX w
M *(closed Sunday)* 1 750 – 450 – **153 rm** 5 040/7 800.

Pintor without rest, coffee shop only, Goya 79, ✉ 28001, ✆ 435 75 45, Telex 23281 – – . AE. — HX c
500 – **176 rm** 5 025/7 620.

Emperatriz without rest, coffee shop only, López de Hoyos 4, ✉ 28006, ✆ 413 65 11, Telex 43640 – . AE E VISA. — GV z
415 – **170 rm** 5 000/8 150.

Agumar without rest, coffee shop only, paseo Reina Cristina 9, ✉ 28014, ✆ 252 69 00, Telex 22814 – . AE E VISA. — HZ a
475 – **252 rm** 5 280/6 610.

Serrano without rest, Marqués de Villamejor 8, ✉ 28006, ✆ 435 52 00 – . AE VISA. — HV b
34 rm 5 900/7 700.

Claridge without rest, coffee shop only, pl. del Conde de Casal 6, ✉ 28007, ✆ 251 94 00, Telex 45585 – wc wc . AE E VISA — JZ a
300 – **150 rm** 2 600/4 400.

Abeba without rest, Alcántara 63, ✉ 28006, ✆ 401 16 50 – TV wc . AE E VISA. — HV r
300 – **90 rm** 3 215/4 560.

Don Diego 5th floor, without rest, Velázquez 45, ✉ 28001, ✆ 435 07 60 – wc . — HX k
395 – **58 rm** 4 100/5 820.

XXXX ✻ **Horcher,** Alfonso XII - 6, ✉ 28014, ✆ 222 07 31, « Tasteful decor » – . AE . — plan p. 7 NY n
closed Sunday – **M** a la carte 2 985/4 450
Spec. Fondos de alcachofas con cangrejos, Higado a la berlinesa, Perdiz a la prensa (Game season).

XXX ✻ **Club 31,** Alcalá 58, ✉ 28014, ✆ 231 00 92 – . AE E VISA. — plan p. 7 NX e
closed August – **M** a la carte 3 500/5 400
Spec. Rodaballo al horno con setas de campo, Faisán al asador con salsa de uvas de Moscatel y foie de oca (Oct.-March), Chuletas de ternera de Ávila en papillotte.

XXX ✻ **El Amparo,** Puigcerdá 8, ✉ 28001, ✆ 431 64 56, Basque and French cuisine – . AE VISA. — HX h
closed Saturday lunch, Sunday, Holy-Week and August – **M** a la carte 3 175/4 900
Spec. Mousse de salmón con aguacate, Plato variado de pescados al vapor, Charlota de cordero con verduras frescas.

XXX **El Circo,** José Ortega y Gasset 29, ✉ 28006, ✆ 276 01 44, Modern decor, Pianist at dinner – . AE E VISA. — HV f
closed August – **M** a la carte 2 640/3 790.

XXX **Villa y Corte de Madrid,** Serrano 110, ✉ 28006, ✆ 261 29 77, Elegant decor – . AE . — HV a
closed Sunday and Bank Holidays in Summer – **M** a la carte 2 250/3 590.

XXX **El Gran Chambelán,** Ayala 46, ✉ 28001, ☎ 431 77 45 – ▤. AE VISA. ✱ HX r
closed Sunday and 9 August-9 September – **M** a la carte 2 325/4 350.

XXX **Balzac,** Moreto 7, ✉ 28014, ☎ 239 19 22 – ▤. AE ◑ VISA. ✱ plan p. 7 NZ a
closed Saturday lunch, Sunday and 25 March-1 April – **M** a la carte 2 950/4 950.

XX La Puerta de Madrid, Alcalá 79, ✉ 28009, ☎ 431 22 85 – ▤ HX m

XX **St.-James,** Juan Bravo 26, ✉ 28020, ☎ 275 60 10, 帝, Rice rest. – ▤. AE HV t
closed Sunday – **M** a la carte 1 700/3 600.

XX **Caruso,** Serrano 70, ✉ 28001, ☎ 435 52 62 – ▤. AE ◑ VISA. ✱ HVX p
closed Sunday and Bank Holidays – **M** a la carte 1 825/3 050.

XX **Schwarzwald (Selva Negra),** O'Donnel 46, ✉ 28009, ☎ 409 56 13, « Original decor » – ▤. AE ◑ E VISA JX n
M a la carte 1 900/3 000.

XX **Al Mounia,** Recoletos 5, ✉ 28001, ☎ 435 08 28, « Oriental atmosphere », North African rest. – AE ◑ E VISA. ✱ plan p. 7 NX s
closed Sunday, Monday and August – **M** a la carte 1 600/3 380.

XX **La Fonda,** Lagasca 11, ✉ 28001, ☎ 403 83 07, Catalonian rest – ▤. AE ◑ E VISA. ✱
M a la carte 1 820/2 875. HX f

XX **Ponteareas,** Claudio Coello 96, ✉ 28006, ☎ 275 58 73, Galican rest – ▤. AE ◑ VISA. ✱
closed Sunday, Bank Holidays and 10 August-10 September – **M** a la carte 2 240/4 780. HV w

XX El Fogón, Villanueva 34, ✉ 28001, ☎ 275 44 00, « Spanish rustic style decor » – ▤ HX t

X **Asador Velate,** Jorge Juan 91, ✉ 28009, ☎ 435 10 24, Basque rest. – ▤. VISA. ✱
closed Sunday and August – **M** a la carte 1 850/3 100. HJX x

X ✿ **El Pescador,** José Ortega y Gasset 75, ✉ 28006, ☎ 402 12 90, 帝, Seafood – ▤. ✱
closed Sunday and 10 August-15 September – **M** a la carte 1 900/3 000 JV t
Spec. Sopa El Pescador, Lenguado Evaristo, Langosta a la americana.

X ✿ **La Trainera,** Lagasca 60, ✉ 28001, ☎ 276 80 35, Seafood – ▤. VISA. ✱ HX k
closed Sunday and August – **M** a la carte 2 000/3 350
Spec. Sopa y crema de mariscos, Pescados y mariscos a la plancha, Langosta y bogavante a la americana.

Arganzuela, Carabanchel, Villaverde : Antonio López, paseo de Las Delicias, Santa María de la Cabeza.

🏨 **Praga** without rest, coffee shop only, Antonio López 65, ✉ 28019, ☎ 469 06 00, Telex 45248 – |♦| ▤ ⇔. AE ◑ E VISA. ✱ by ⑤
☕ 400 – **428 rm** 3 335/4 500.

🏨 **Aramo** without rest, coffee shop only, paseo Santa María de la Cabeza 73, ✉ 28045, ☎ 473 91 11, Telex 45885 – |♦| ▤ ⇔. AE ◑ E VISA by ⑤
☕ 350 – **105 rm** 4 000/5 800.

🏨 **Puerta de Toledo,** glorieta Puerta de Toledo 4, ✉ 28005, ☎ 474 71 00, Telex 22291 – |♦| ▤ ⇔. AE ◑ E VISA. ✱ plan p. 4 EZ v
M (rest see **Puerta de Toledo** below) – ☕ 275 – **152 rm** 2 750/5 060.

🏨 Carlton, paseo de las Delicias 26, ✉ 28045, ☎ 239 71 00, Telex 44571 – |♦| ▤
133 rm. plan p. 5 GZ n

XX **Puerta de Toledo,** glorieta Puerta de Toledo 4, ✉ 28005, ☎ 474 12 69 – ▤. ◑ E VISA. ✱ plan p. 4 EZ v
M a la carte 1 600/2 900.

Moncloa : Princesa, Rosales, paseo Florida, Casa de Campo (plan p. 4 except where otherwise stated)

🏨 **Meliá Madrid,** Princesa 27, ✉ 28028, ☎ 241 82 00, Telex 22537, 帝 – |♦| ▤ TV – 🏰. AE ◑ E VISA. ✱ plan p. 6 KV t
M 3 200 – ☕ 850 – **266 rm** 10 350/13 000 – P 12 660/16 510.

🏨 **Florida Norte** M, paseo de la Florida 5, ✉ 28008, ☎ 241 61 90, Telex 23675 – |♦| ▤ ⇔. AE ◑ E VISA. ✱ rest DX v
M 1 450 – ☕ 400 – **399 rm** 5 300/7 300 – P 6 950/8 600.

🏨 **Príncipe Pío,** cuesta de San Vicente 16, ✉ 28008, ☎ 247 08 00, Telex 42183 – |♦| ▤ ⇔. AE E VISA. ✱ rest plan p. 6 KX d
M 1 225 – ☕ 375 – **157 rm** 3 600/5 150 – P 4 900/5 925.

🏨 **Tirol** without rest., coffee shop only and no ☕, Marqués de Urquijo 4, ✉ 28008, ☎ 248 19 00 – |♦| ▤ ⊟wc ☎ ⇔. VISA. ✱ DV r
93 rm 3 200/4 715.

XXX Café Viena, Luisa Fernanda 23, ✉ 28008, ☎ 248 15 91, Pianist at dinner, « Old style café » – ▤ DX s

XXX **Los Porches,** paseo Pintor Rosales 1, ✉ 28008, ☎ 247 70 53, 帝 – ▤. AE ◑ E VISA. ✱
M a la carte 2 090/3 850. DX z

Chamberí : San Bernardo, Fuencarral, Alberto Aguilera, Santa Engracia (plan pp. 4 to 7)

Miguel Angel M, Miguel Angel 31, ✉ 28010, ✆ 442 00 22, Telex 44235, – AE E VISA. GV c
M 3 500 – 900 – **300 rm** 11 000/16 500.

Mindanao, paseo San Francisco de Sales 15, ✉ 28003, ✆ 449 55 00, Telex 22631, – AE E VISA. DV a
M 2 585 – 625 – **289 rm** 8 950/12 500.

Luz Palacio, paseo de la Castellana 57, ✉ 28046, ✆ 442 51 00, Telex 27207 – AE E VISA. GV p
M 3 030 – 660 – **182 rm** 10 000/10 500 – P 13 200/15 700.

Castellana without rest, coffee shop only, paseo de la Castellana 49, ✉ 28046, ✆ 410 02 00, Telex 27686 – AE E VISA. GV a
1 200 – **311 rm** 14 800/17 600.

Escultor, Miguel Angel 3, ✉ 28010, ✆ 410 42 03, Telex 44285 – AE E VISA. rest GV s
closed Sunday – **M** 2 400 – 650 – **82 apartments** 6 200/10 200 – P 11 100/15 100.

Las Alondras, without rest, coffee shop only, José Abascal 8, ✉ 28003, ✆ 447 40 00, Telex 49454 – AE E VISA. FV a
72 rm 6 550/8 900.

Bretón without rest, coffee shop only, Bretón de los Herreros 29, ✉ 28003, ✆ 442 83 00 – wc wc. AE E VISA. FV n
closed December – 450 – **56 rm** 4 500/6 500.

Conde Duque without rest, coffee shop only, pl. Conde Valle de Suchil 5, ✉ 28015, ✆ 447 70 00, Telex 22058 – wc. AE E VISA EV d
300 – **138 rm** 2 970/5 060.

Zurbano, Zurbano 79, ✉ 28003, ✆ 441 55 00, Telex 27578 – wc. AE E VISA. rest GV x
M 1 525 – 375 – **261 rm** 4 000/6 100 – P 5 850/6 800.

Embajada, without rest, Santa Engracia 5, ✉ 28010, ✆ 447 33 00 – wc MV r
65 rm.

Trafalgar without rest, Trafalgar 35, ✉ 28010, ✆ 445 62 00 – wc wc. AE E VISA. FV s
200 – **45 rm** 2 600/4 400.

XXXX ❀ **Jockey,** Amador de los Ríos 6, ✉ 28010, ✆ 419 24 35, « Tasteful decor » – AE E VISA. NV k
closed Sunday, Bank Holidays and August – **M** a la carte 3 100/5 500
Spec. Bogavante en hojaldre sobre fondo de puervos al cava, Lubina del Cantábrico en papillote, Ragoût de perdiz con verduras del tiempo (Game season).

XXX **Lur Maitea,** Fernando el Santo 4, ✉ 28010, ✆ 419 09 38, Basque rest. – AE E VISA. MNV u
closed Saturday lunch, Sunday, Bank Holidays and August – **M** a la carte 2 500/4 200.

XX **Aymar,** Fuencarral 138, ✉ 28010, ✆ 445 57 67, Seafood – AE E VISA. FV e
M a la carte 2 150/3 350.

XX **Las Reses,** Orfila 3, ✉ 28010, ✆ 419 33 15, Meat rest. – AE VISA. NV e
closed Sunday, Bank Holidays and August – **M** a la carte 1 950/3 515.

XX **L'Alsace,** Doménico Scarlatti 5, ✉ 28003, ✆ 244 40 75, « Alsatian decor » – AE E VISA DV a
M a la carte 1 850/3 100.

X **Quattrocento,** General Ampudia 18, ✉ 28003, ✆ 234 91 06, Italian rest. – AE VISA. DU a
closed Sunday dinner – **M** a la carte 1 700/3 400.

X La Parra, Monte Esquinza 34, ✉ 28010, ✆ 419 54 98 – NV z

X **Casa Félix,** Bretón de los Herreros 39, ✉ 28003, ✆ 441 24 79 – AE VISA. FV x
M a la carte 1 900/2 900.

Chamartín, Tetuán : Capitán Haya, Orense, Alberto Alcocer, paseo de la Habana (plan p. 3 except where otherwise stated)

Eurobuilding M, Padre Damián 23, ✉ 28036, ✆ 457 17 00, Telex 22548, « Garden with » – AE E VISA. HS a
M (rest see **Balthasar and La Taberna** below) – 850 – **555 rm** 10 850/14 450.

Meliá Castilla M, Capitán Haya 43, ✉ 28020, ✆ 270 80 00, Telex 23142, – AE E VISA. GS c
M 2 850 – 850 – **1 000 rm** 10 500/12 900.

Holiday Inn, av. General Perón, ✉ 28020, ✆ 456 70 14, Telex 44709, Pianist at dinner, – GT z
313 rm.

Cuzco without rest, coffee shop only, paseo de la Castellana 133, ✉ 28046, ✆ 456 06 00, Telex 22464 – . AE E VISA. GS a
600 – **330 rm** 7 100/9 200.

Chamartín without rest, estación de Chamartín (railway station), ✉ 28036, ✆ 733 90 11, Telex 49201 – . AE E VISA. HR
520 – **378 rm** 5 500/7 700.

Foxá 32 M without rest, coffee shop only, Agustín de Foxá 32, ✉ 28036, ✆ 733 10 60, Telex 49366 – . AE E VISA. HR u
250 – **161 rm** 6 200.

El Gran Atlanta without rest, Comandante Zorita 34, ✉ 28020, ✆ 253 59 00, Telex 45210 – . AE E VISA FT p
550 – **180 rm** 5 100/7 700.

Apart. Suite Foxá 25 M without rest, Agustín de Foxá 25, ✉ 28036, ✆ 733 70 64, Telex 44911 – HR a
121 rm.

Apartotel El Jardin M without rest, carret. N I (vía de servicio), ✉ 28034, ✆ 202 83 36, – by ①
41 rm.

Aitana without rest, coffee shop only, paseo de la Castellana 152, ✉ 28046, ✆ 250 71 07, Telex 49186 – . AE VISA. GT c
400 – **111 rm** 4 600/7 000.

Aristos and Rest El Chaflán, av. Pío XII-34, ✉ 28016, ✆ 457 04 50, – wc . AE VISA. HS d
M *(closed Sunday)* a la carte 2 125/3 450 – 325 – **25 rm** 3 650/5 950.

XXXXX ✿✿ **Zalacaín,** Álvarez de Baena 4, ✉ 28006, ✆ 261 48 40, , « Elegant decor » – . AE . plan p. 5 GV b
closed Saturday lunch, Sunday, Holy-Week and August – **M** a la carte 4 200/7 825.

XXXX **Balthasar,** Juan Ramón Jiménez 8, ✉ 28036, ✆ 457 91 91, Telex 22548, « Tasteful classic decor » – . AE E VISA. HS a
closed Sunday, Bank Holidays and August – **M** a la carte 2 975/5 175.

XXXX Mayte Commodore, pl. República Argentina 5, ✉ 28002, ✆ 261 86 06, , « Elegant decor » – HU v

XXXX ✿ **El Bodegón,** Pinar 15, ✉ 28006, ✆ 262 31 37 – . AE E VISA. plan p. 5 GV q
closed Sunday and August – **M** a la carte 2 620/3 830
Spec. Pastel de verduras caliente, Mero al horno con cebolletas nuevas, Plato de repostería variada.

XXXX ✿ **Príncipe de Viana,** Manuel de Falla 5, ✉ 28036, ✆ 259 14 48, Basque rest. – . AE . GT c
closed Saturday lunch, Sunday, Holy-Week and August – **M** a la carte 3 375/6 150.

XXXX **Wallis,** Raimondo Fernandéz Villaverde 65 - edificio Windsor, ✉ 28003, ✆ 456 71 70 – . AE E VISA. GU r
closed Sunday and August – **M** a la carte 3 400/4 250.

XXX **Nicolasa,** Velázquez 150, ✉ 28002, ✆ 261 99 85 – AE E VISA. HU a
closed Sunday and August – **M** a la carte 2 840/4 550.

XXX **Nuevo Valentín,** av. Concha Espina 8, ✉ 28036, ✆ 259 74 16, – . AE E VISA. GT n
M a la carte 2 840/3 470.

XXX **O'Pazo,** Reina Mercedes 20, ✉ 28020, ✆ 234 37 48, Seafood – . FT p
closed Sunday and August – **M** a la carte 2 150/4 925.

XXX **L'Albufera,** Capitán Haya 45, ✉ 28020, ✆ 270 84 00, Telex 23142, Pianist at dinner – . AE E VISA. GS c
closed August – **M** a la carte 3 000/3 350.

XXX **La Gabarra,** Santo Domingo de Silos 6, ✉ 28036, ✆ 458 78 97, Basque rest. – . AE E VISA. GT s
closed Saturday lunch, Sunday, Bank Holidays and August – **M** a la carte 2 450/4 050.

XXX **La Máquina,** Sor Angela de la Cruz 22, ✉ 28020, ✆ 270 61 23 – . AE E VISA FS e
closed Sunday and Bank Holidays dinner – **M** a la carte 2 650/3 400.

XXX **José Luis,** Rafael Salgado 11, ✉ 28036, ✆ 457 50 36, – . AE E VISA. GT m
closed Sunday and August – **M** a la carte 2 025/3 225.

XXX **La Boucade,** Capitán Haya 30, ✉ 28020, ✆ 456 02 45 – . AE E VISA. GS a
closed Sunday and 15 to 30 August – **M** a la carte 2 200/4 400.

XXX Cota 13, estación de Chamartín (railway station), ✉ 28036, ✆ 215 10 83, – HR

XXX **Bogavante,** Capitán Haya 20, ✉ 28020, ✆ 456 21 14, Seafood – . AE E VISA. GT d
closed Sunday – **M** a la carte 2 150/3 650.

XXX **Itxaso,** Capitán Haya 58, ✉ 28020, ✆ 450 64 64, Basque rest. – . AE E VISA GS n
closed Sunday and August – **M** a la carte 2 750/4 150.

XXX **Señorío de Bertiz,** Comandante Zorita 6, ✉ 28020, ☎ 233 27 57 – ▤. AE ⓓ VISA. ⚘
closed Saturday lunch, Bank Holidays and August – **M** a la carte 2 650/4 150. FT **s**

XXX Amalur, Padre Damián 37, ✉ 28036, ☎ 457 62 98 – ▤ HS **c**

XXX **Señorio de Alcocer,** Alberto Alcocer 1, ✉ 28036, ☎ 457 16 96 – ▤. AE ⓓ E VISA. ⚘
closed Sunday and August – **M** a la carte 2 300/3 250. GS **e**

XXX Gaztelupe, Comandante Zorita 37, ✉ 28020, ☎ 233 01 85 – ▤ FT **a**

XXX **La Taberna,** Padre Damian 23, ✉ 28036, ☎ 457 78 00, Telex 22548 – ▤ 🚗. AE ⓓ E VISA HS **a**
M a la carte 2 275/4 400.

XX El Hostal, Príncipe de Vergara 285, ✉ 28023, ☎ 259 11 94 – ▤ HS **e**

XX ⊛ **Cabo Mayor,** Juan Hurtado de Mendoza 11 (back), ✉ 28036, ☎ 250 87 76, Telex 49784, « Original decor » – ▤. AE ⓓ E VISA. ⚘ GHS **r**
closed Sunday, Holy-Week, 15 to 30 August and Christmas – **M** a la carte 2 600/3 600
Spec. Rollo de salmón y mero con mousse de judías verdes, Merluza al cava con trufas, Lomo de conejo a la mostaza.

XX El Faisán de Oro, Bolivia 11, ✉ 28016, ☎ 259 30 76 – ▤ HS **t**

XX Fass, Rodriguez Marín 84, ✉ 28022, ☎ 457 22 02, Bavarian decor, German cuisine – ▤ HT **t**

XX **Rugantino,** Velázquez 136, ✉ 28006, ☎ 261 02 22, Italian rest. – ▤. AE ⓓ E VISA. ⚘
M a la carte 1 620/3 870. plan p. 5 HV **e**

XX **De Funy,** Serrano 213, ✉ 28016, ☎ 259 72 25, ☂, Lebanese rest., Pianist at dinner – ▤. AE ⓓ E VISA. ⚘ HT **z**
M a la carte 1 950/3 100.

XX **Rheinfall,** Padre Damián 44, ✉ 28036, ☎ 457 82 88, German cuisine, « Regional decor » – ▤. AE ⓓ E VISA. ⚘ HS **u**
M a la carte 2 050/3 650.

X El Pajar, Orense 35, ✉ 28020, ☎ 455 00 09 – ▤ FT **b**

X **Asador Donostiarra,** Pedro Villar 14, ✉ 28020, ☎ 279 73 40, Basque rustic decor – ▤. AE ⓓ E VISA. ⚘ FS **a**
closed Sunday dinner – **M** a la carte 1 975/3 575.

X **Los Borrachos de Velázquez,** Príncipe de Vergara 205, ✉ 28002, ☎ 458 10 76, Andalusian rest. – ▤. AE ⓓ VISA. ⚘ HT **s**
closed Sunday – **M** a la carte 2 000/3 150.

Environs

at Ciudad Puerta de Hierro by ⑦ : 8 km by N VI and road to El Pardo – ✉ 28035 Madrid – ☎ 91 :

🏨 **Monte Real** ⛰, Arroyofresno 17, ✉ 28035, ☎ 216 21 40, Telex 22089, ☂, « Elegant decor, garden », 🏊 – |‡| ▤ 🚗 Ⓟ – 🏛. AE ⓓ E VISA. ⚘ rest
M 3 800 – ☕ 800 – **79 rm** 10 000/16 000 – P 15 600/17 600.

by ② ***: N II*** and Coslada - San Fernando Road E : 12 km – ✉ 28022 Madrid – ☎ 91 :

XX **Rancho Texano,** av. Aragón 364, ✉ 28022, ☎ 747 47 44, ☂, Grill rest., « Terrace » – ▤ Ⓟ. AE ⓓ E VISA. ⚘
closed Sunday dinner – **M** a la carte 2 175/3 340.

on the road to the Airport : 12,5 km – ✉ 28042 Madrid – ☎ 91 :

🏨 **Diana** without rest, Galeón 27 (Alameda de Osuna), ✉ 28042, ☎ 747 13 55, Telex 45688, 🏊 – |‡| ▤ – 🏛. AE ⓓ E VISA
☕ 290 – **271 apartments** 5 250/6 550.

at Barajas by ② : 14 km – 28042 Madrid – ☎ 91 :

🏨 **Barajas,** av. de Logroño 305 ☎ 747 77 00, Telex 22255, ☂, « Large lawn with 🏊 » – |‡| ▤ Ⓟ – 🏛. AE ⓓ E VISA. ⚘ rest
M 2 725 – ☕ 660 – **230 rm** 9 100/13 700 – P 12 040/14 290.

🏨 **Alameda** Ⓜ, av. de Logroño 100 ☎ 747 48 00, Telex 43809, 🏊 – |‡| ▤ 🚗 Ⓟ – 🏛. AE ⓓ E VISA. ⚘ rest
M 2 470 – ☕ 570 – **145 rm** 7 825/10 925 – P 10 140/12 505.

at San Sebastián de los Reyes by ① : 17 km – ✉ San Sebastián de los Reyes – ☎ 91

XXX **Mesón Tejas Verdes,** carret. N I ☎ 652 73 07, ☂, « Typical Castilian tavern, garden » – ▤ Ⓟ. AE ⓓ VISA
closed Sunday, Bank Holiday dinner and August – **M** a la carte 1 675/3 300.

If you would like a more complete selection of hotels and restaurants, consult the Michelin Guides for the following countries:
Benelux, Deutschland, España Portugal, France, Great Britain and Ireland, Italia.

BARCELONA 08000 43 ⑱ and 990 ⑳ – pop. 1 754 900 – ✆ 93 – Bullring.

See : Gothic Quarter** (Barrio Gótico) : Cathedral** MR, Federic Marés Museum** (Museo F. Marés) MR, Provincial Council* (Palau de la Generalitat) MR – Montjuic* (≤*) : Museum of Catalonian Art** (Museo d'Art de Catalunya) : Romanesque and Gothic department***, ceramic Museum* – Archeological Museum (Museo Arqueológico), Spanish Village* (Pueblo Español), Joan Miró Foundation* – Zoo* (Parque Zoológico) LV – Tibidabo* (※**) – Maritime Museum** (Drassanes i Museo Maritim) KZ **M6** – Cambo Collection (Palau de la Virreina)* JX **M7** – Picasso Museum* KV **M8** – Church of the Holy Family* (Sagrada Familia) JU **L**.

18, 9 of Prat by ⑤ : 16 km ✆ 379 02 78 – 18 of Sant Cugat by ⑦ : 20 km ✆ 674 39 58 – 18 of Vallromanas by ④ : 25 km ✆ 568 03 62.

✈ Barcelona by ⑤ : 12 km ✆ 317 01 12 – Iberia : pl. Espanya, ✉ 08004, ✆ 325 60 00 EZ Aviaco : aeropuerto ✆ 379 24 58.

✆ 310 00 30.

to the Balearic islands : Cía. Trasmediterránea, vía Laietana 2, ✉ 08003, ✆ 319 82 12, Telex 54629 KX.

Gran Via de les Corts Catalanes 658, ✉ 08010, ✆ 301 74 43, 317 22 46 - Palacio de Congresos, av. María Cristina, ✉ 08004, ✆ 323 31 01 and at Airport ✆ 325 58 29 – R.A.C.C. Santaló 8, ✉ 08006, ✆ 200 33 11, Telex 53056.

Madrid 626 ⑥ – Bilbao 606 ⑥ – Lérida/Lleida 169 ⑥ – Perpignan 185 ② – Tarragona 108 ⑥ – Toulouse 387 ② – Valencia 361 ⑥ – Zaragoza 307 ⑥.

Plans on following pages

Princesa Sofía M, pl. del Papa Pius XII, ✉ 08028, ✆ 330 71 11, Telex 51032, ≤, – AE E VISA. by ⑥
M 3 500 – **496 rm** 12 500/16 400 – P 13 750/18 050.

G. H. Sarriá M without rest, coffee shop only, av. de Sarriá 50, ✉ 08029, ✆ 239 11 09, Telex 51033, ≤ – – EU **n**
600 – **314 rm** 9 250/12 800.

Avenida Palace, Gran Vía 605, ✉ 08007, ✆ 301 96 00, Telex 54734, Pianist at dinner – – AE VISA. rest GV **r**
M 2 700 – **211 rm** 10 890/13 980 – P 11 330/15 230.

Ritz, Gran Vía de les Corts Catalanes 668, ✉ 08010, ✆ 318 52 00, Telex 52739, – – AE E VISA. JU **p**
M 4 300 – 975 – **197 rm** 11 000/16 500.

Presidente, av. de la Diagonal 570, ✉ 08021, ✆ 200 21 11, Telex 52180, – – AE VISA. rest EU **u**
M 2 500 – **161 rm** 10 020/12 900.

Majestic, passeig de Grácia 70, ✉ 08008, ✆ 215 45 12, Telex 52211, – – AE E VISA. GU **f**
M 2 300 – 500 – **330 rm** 9 200/11 500 – P 13 280/19 660.

Diplomatic and Rest. la Salsa, Pau Claris 122, ✉ 08009, ✆ 317 31 00, Telex 54701, – – AE E VISA. GU **e**
M a la carte 2 200/3 600 – 900 – **213 rm** 11 600/15 800.

Calderón, rambla Catalunya 26, ✉ 08007, ✆ 301 00 00, Telex 51549, – – AE E VISA. GV **t**
M 2 500 – 600 – **244 rm** 8 400/10 500.

Colón, av. de la Catedral 7, ✉ 08002, ✆ 301 14 04, Telex 52654 – – AE E VISA. rest KV **e**
M 1 930 – **161 rm** 5 120/9 160 – P 7 570/8 110.

Hesperia M without rest, coffee shop only, Los Vergós 20, ✉ 08017, ✆ 204 55 51, Telex 98403 – – AE E VISA. by ⑦
550 – **142 rm** 7 600/9 500.

Derby without rest, Loreto 21, ✉ 08029, ✆ 322 32 15, Telex 97429 – – AE E VISA EV **e**
570 – **116 rm** 5 700/8 950.

Cristal, Diputació 257, ✉ 08007, ✆ 301 66 00, Telex 54560 – – AE VISA. rest GV **t**
147 rm 7 000/9 500.

Gran Derby M without rest, Loreto 28, ✉ 08029, ✆ 322 32 15, Telex 97429 – – AE E VISA EV **g**
570 – **38 rm** 11 200.

Núñez Urgel, without rest, coffee shop only, Comptes de Urgell 232, ✉ 08036, ✆ 322 41 53 – EV **a**
121 rm.

Royal without rest, Ramblas 117, ✉ 08002, ✆ 301 94 00, Telex 97565 – AE E VISA. JX **e**
400 – **108 rm** 4 900/7 900.

Balmoral without rest, coffee shop only, vía Augusta 5, ✉ 08006, ✆ 217 87 00, Telex 54087 – – AE E VISA. FU **n**
495 – **94 rm** 5 700/8 800.

Regente, rambla de Catalunya 76, 08008, 215 25 70, Telex 51939, – GU z
78 rm.

Cóndor, without rest, coffee shop only, vía Augusta 127, 08006, 209 45 11, Telex 52925 – . EU z
550 – **78 rm** 5 800/8 000.

Arenas without rest, coffee shop only for dinner, Capitán Arenas 20, 08034, 204 03 00, Telex 54990 – – . . by ⑥
59 rm 7 400/9 600.

Astoria without rest, París 203, 08036, 209 83 11, Telex 97429 – . FU a
350 – **109 rm** 4 320/6 500.

G. H. Cristina without rest, coffee shop only, av. de la Diagonal 458, 08006, 217 68 00, Telex 54328 – . FU y
400 – **126 rm** 5 400/8 300.

Dante without rest, Mallorca 181, 08036, 323 22 54, Telex 52588 – – . FV e
350 – **81 rm** 4 200/7 200.

Numáncia without rest, coffee shop only, Numància 74, 08029, 242 15 11 – – . . by ⑥
375 – **140 rm** 3 800/5 800.

Expo H., without rest, coffee shop only, Mallorca 1, 08014, 325 12 12, Telex 54147, – – EY m
432 rm.

Euro-Park, without rest, coffee shop only, Aragó 325, 08009, 257 92 05 – JU e
66 rm.

Ficus, without rest, Mallorca 163, 08036, 253 35 00, Telex 98203 – wc wc FV u
74 rm.

Mitre without rest, Bertrán 15, 08023, 212 11 04, Telex 51531 – wc . by ⑦
375 – **57 rm** 4 300/6 300.

Gala Placidia, vía Augusta 112, 08006, 217 82 00, Telex 98820 – rest wc EU r
28 apartments.

Condado, Aribau 201, 08021, 200 23 11, Telex 54546 – rest wc wc . . EU g
M 1 375 – 300 – **89 rm** 3 415/5 975 – P 5 575/6 000.

Rialto without rest, coffee shop only, Fernando 42, 08002, 318 52 12, Telex 97206 – wc . MR s
320 – **53 rm** 4 025/5 850.

Taber without rest, Aragó 256, 08007, 318 70 50, Telex 93452 – wc . GV g
65 rm 3 625/6 350.

Terminal 7th floor, without rest, coffee shop only for dinner, Provença 1, 08029, 321 53 50, Telex 98213 – wc . . EY a
75 rm 5 150/6 700.

Tres Torres without rest, Calatrava 32, 08017, 247 73 00, Telex 54990 – wc – . by ⑦
56 rm 4 400/6 800.

Covadonga without rest, coffee shop only, av. de la Diagonal 596, 08021, 209 55 11 – wc wc . EU v
325 – **76 rm** 3 600/5 800.

Regencia Colón without rest, Sagristans 13, 08002, 318 98 58, Telex 98175 – wc wc . . KV r
315 – **55 rm** 3 315/5 500.

Wilson without rest, av. de la Diagonal 568, 08021, 209 25 11, Telex 54134 – wc wc . EU a
52 rm 5 150/6 700.

Gótico without rest, Jaime I - 14, 08002, 315 22 11, Telex 97206 – wc . MR a
320 – **72 rm** 3 500/5 850.

Las Corts without rest, coffee shop only, Travessera de Les Corts 292, 08029, 322 08 11, Telex 59001 – wc wc – . . by ⑥
275 – **79 rm** 3 200/4 600.

Bonanova Park, without rest, Capitán Arenas 51, 08034, 204 09 00, Telex 54990 – wc wc . by ⑥
275 – **60 rm** 3 100/4 800.

BARCELONA

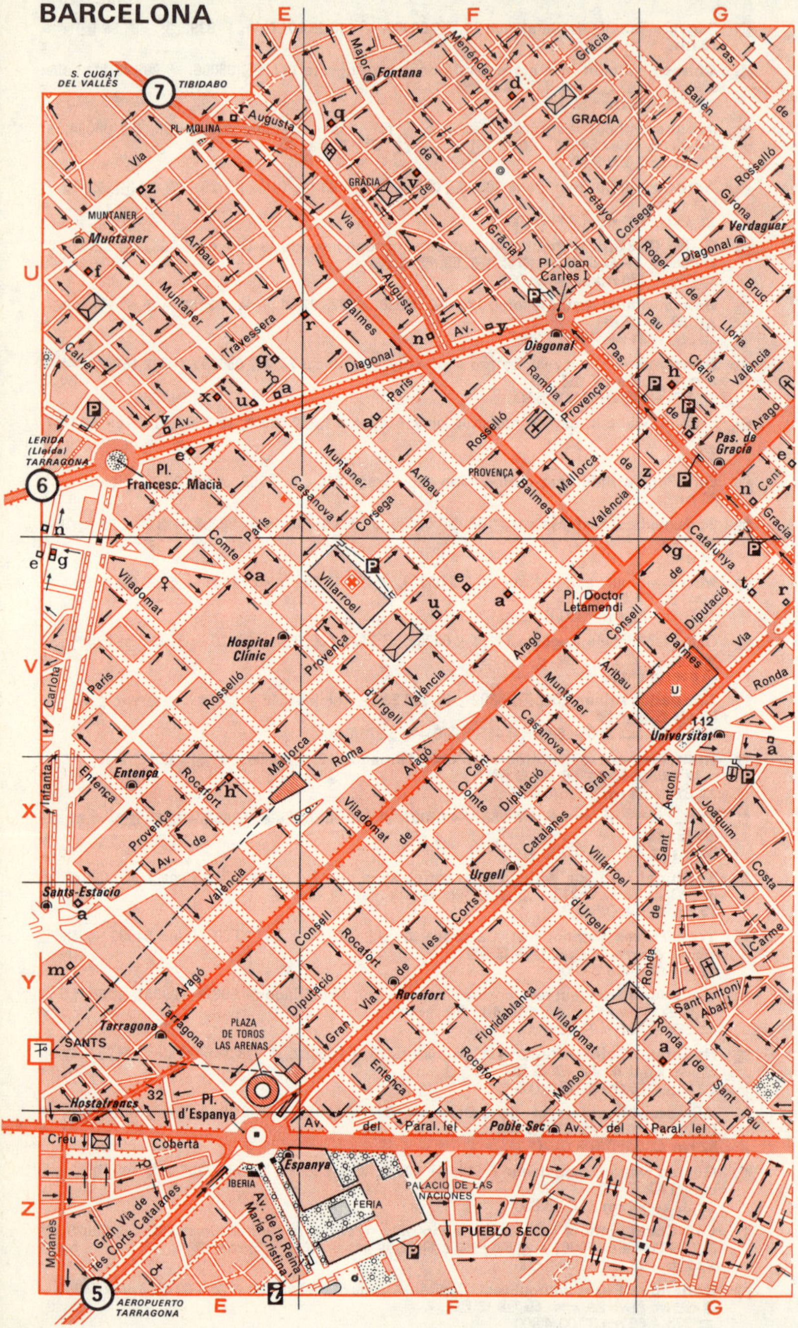

E
F
G
U
V
X
Y
Z
S. CUGAT DEL VALLÈS
TIBIDABO
PL. MOLINA
MUNTANER
Muntaner
Fontana
GRACIA
GRÀCIA
Verdaguer
Pl. Joan Carles I
Diagonal
LERIDA (Lleida) TARRAGONA
Pl. Francesc. Macià
PROVENÇA
Pas. de Gràcia
Pl. Doctor Letamendi
Hospital Clínic
Universitat
Entença
Urgell
Sants-Estació
Tarragona
SANTS
PLAZA DE TOROS LAS ARENAS
Rocafort
Hostafrancs
Pl. d'Espanya
Poble Sec
Espanya
IBERIA
FERIA
PALACIO DE LAS NACIONES
PUEBLO SECO
AEROPUERTO TARRAGONA

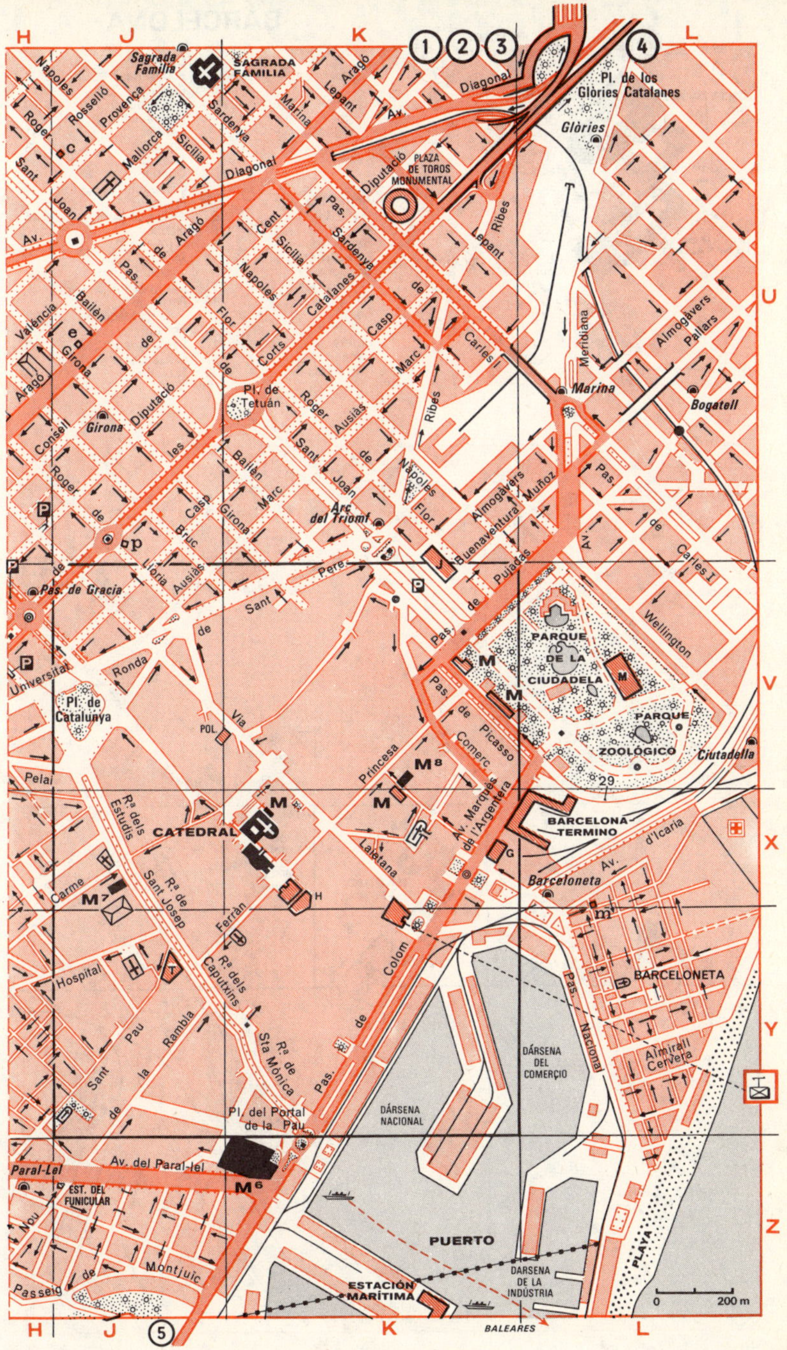

H
J
K
L
1
2
3
4
Sagrada Familia
SAGRADA FAMILIA
Pl. de les Glòries Catalanes
Glòries
Nàpoles
Rosselló
Provença
Roger
Mallorca
Sicília
Sardenya
Marina
Lepant
Aragó
Diagonal
Av.
Diputació
PLAZA DE TOROS MONUMENTAL
Ribes
Sant Joan
Av.
Pas. de Aragó
Cent
Pas. Sardenya
Sicília
Nàpoles
Catalanes
Casp
Carles
Meridiana
Almogàvers
Pallars
U
València
Bailèn
Girona
de
Flor
Corts
Marc
Aragó
Pl. de Tetuán
Roger
Ausiàs
Ribes
Marina
Bogatell
Consell
Girona
Diputació
les
Sant
de
Joan
Nàpoles
Almogàvers
Muñoz
Pas.
Roger
Bailèn
Casp
Marc
Arc del Triomf
Flor
Buenaventura
Av.
de
Carles I
de
Girona
P
p
Bruc
Llúria
Ausiàs
Sant
Pere
Pujadas
P
Pas. de Gracia
de
de
Wellington
P
Universitat
Ronda
Pas.
PARQUE DE LA CIUDADELA
M
M
M
V
Pl. de Catalunya
POL
Via
Pas.
de
Picasso
Comerç
PARQUE ZOOLÓGICO
Ciutadella
Pelai
Princesa
M8
Rª dels Estudis
M
M
29
CATEDRAL
Av. Marquès de l'Argentera
BARCELONA TERMINO
d'Icaria
X
Laietana
G
Av.
Carme
M7
Rª de Sant Josep
H
Barceloneta
m1
Ferran
Hospital
Rª dels Caputxins
Colom
Pas. Nacional
BARCELONETA
Y
Pau
Sant
la
Rambla
de
Rª de Sta Mònica
Pas.
DÁRSENA DEL COMERÇIO
Almirall Cervera
Pl. del Portal de la Pau
DÁRSENA NACIONAL
Paral-Lel
Av. del Paral-lel
M6
EST. DEL FUNICULAR
Z
Nou
PUERTO
Montjuïc
de
Passeig
ESTACIÓN MARÍTIMA
DARSENA DE LA INDUSTRIA
PLAYA
0
200 m
H
J
5
K
BALEARES
L

BARCELONA

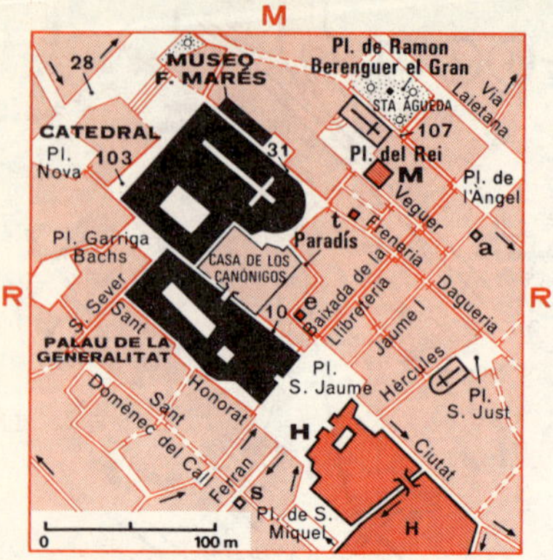

Caputxins (Rambla dels) JY
Catalunya (Pl. de) JV
Estudis (Rambla dels) JX
Sant Josep (Rambla de) JX
Santa Mònica (Rambla de) KY

Antoni Maura (Pl. d') KV 2
Avinyó KY 5
Banys Nous JX 6
Bisbe Irurita MR 10
Boqueria (Pl. de la) JY 11
Bòria KX 14
Born (Pas. del) KX 15
Boters JX 17
Canaletes (Rambla de) JV 20
Cardenal Casañas JX 24
Catedral (Av. de la) MR 28
Comercial (Pl.) KV 30
Comtes MR 31
Consolat KX 33
Cucurulla JX 36
Doctor Joaquim Pou KV 38
Francesc Cambó (Av.) KV 44
Isabel II (Pas. d') KX 54
Méndez Núñez KV 69
Montcada KX 71
Portal de Santa Madrona KY 83
Rec Comtal KV 87
Santa Anna JV 100
Santa Llúcia MR 103
Tapineria MR 104

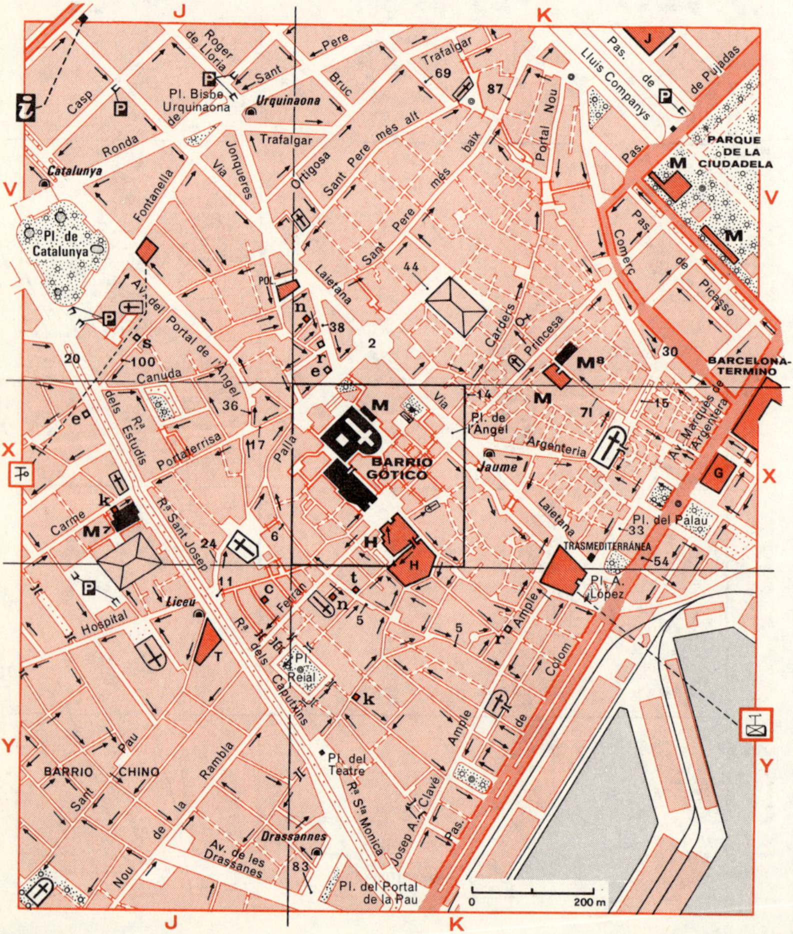

Lleó, Pelai 24, ✉ 08001, ✆ 318 13 12, Telex 98338 – wc. VISA. rest GV a
M 825 – 220 – **42 rm** 1 980/3 300 – P 3 230/3 560.

Torelló without rest, Ample 31, ✉ 08002, ✆ 315 40 11, Telex 54606 – wc wc. KY r
260 – **72 rm** 1 800/3 100.

Cortés, Santa Ana 25, ✉ 08002, ✆ 317 91 12, Telex 98215 – rest wc wc. AE E VISA. JV s
M *(closed Sunday)* 660 – 300 – **46 rm** 2 375/3 940.

L'Alguer without rest, passeig Pedro Rodriguez 20, ✉ 08028, ✆ 334 60 50 – wc. E VISA. by Creu Coberta EZ
250 – **33 rm** 1 950/3 400.

Classical and modern restaurants

XXXX ✿ **Ama Lur,** Mallorca 275, ✉ 08008, ✆ 215 30 24, « Garden-terrace » – . AE VISA. GU h
M a la carte 3 750/6 350
Spec. Pimientos del piquillo rellenos de zancarrón, Tronco de merluza estilo Ondárroa, Arroz con almejas en cazuelita.

XXXX ✿ **Reno,** Tuset 27, ✉ 08006, ✆ 200 91 29, « Elegant classical decor » – . AE E VISA. FU r
M a la carte 3 650/4 650
Spec. Marmita de faisán y trufas en hojaldre (Game season), Civet de langosta a la catalana, Costillar de corderito asado a las finas hierbas.

XXXX ✿ **Vía Veneto,** Ganduxer 10, ✉ 08021, ✆ 200 72 74, « Early 20C style » – . AE E VISA. by ⑥
M a la carte 3 055/4 375
Spec. Arroz con almejas al estilo Vía Veneto, Ravioli de langostinos con salsa de cangrejos de río, Pies de cerdo deshuesados y rellenos de ceps.

XXX **Finisterre,** av. de la Diagonal 469, ✉ 08036, ✆ 239 55 76 – . AE E VISA. EU e
M a la carte 3 250/4 700.

XXX ✿✿ **Neichel,** av. de Pedralbes 16 bis, ✉ 08034, ✆ 203 84 08 – . AE E VISA.
closed Sunday, Bank Holidays, Holy-Week, Christmas and August – **M** (booking essential) a la carte 3 000/4 500 by ⑥
Spec. Mousse fría de gazapo y foie gras de pato (Game season), Escalopa de lubina con muselina de trufas de Huesca, Pichoncito de masía relleno y braseado al Oporto.

XXX **Hostal del Sol** 1st floor, passeig de Gràcia 44, ✉ 08007, ✆ 215 62 25, Pianist at dinner – . AE E VISA. GU n
M a la carte 2 260/3 640.

XXX **El Túnel de Muntaner,** Sant Mario 22, ✉ 08022, ✆ 212 60 74 – . AE E VISA.
closed Sunday, Bank Holidays and 25 July-25 August – **M** a la carte 2 350/4 000. by ⑥

XXX ✿ **Botafumeiro,** Major de Grácia 81, ✉ 08012, ✆ 218 42 30, Seafood – . AE E VISA. FU v
closed Monday except Bank Holidays, day before Bank Holidays and August – **M** a la carte 2 600/4 050
Spec. Mariscada, Bullavesa, Lubina Reina Elisenda.

XX ✿ **La Odisea,** Copons 7, ✉ 08002, ✆ 302 36 92, Pianist at dinner – . AE VISA KV n
closed Sunday, Holy-Week and August – **M** a la carte 1 995/3 505
Spec. Sopa de ágatas con setas y trufas (Nov.-April), Solomillo Villete con hortalizas al calvados, Calamares rellenos con albóndigas.

XX **El Gran Café,** Avinyó 9, ✉ 08002, ✆ 318 79 86, Pianist at dinner, « Early 20C style » – . AE E VISA KY t
closed Sunday, Bank Holidays and August – **M** a la carte 1 750/3 650.

XX ✿ **Azulete,** Vía Augusta 281, ✉ 08017, ✆ 203 59 43, « Conservatory terrace with plants » – AE E VISA by ⑦
closed Saturday lunch, Sunday, Holy-Week, 1 to 15 August and 23 December-6 January – **M** a la carte 2 800/3 925
Spec. Ensalada templada de sesos y mollejas de ternera con setas, Filetes de salmonetes sobre lecho de hinojo, Corona de naranja.

XX ✿ **Ara-Cata,** Dr Ferràn 33, ✉ 08034, ✆ 204 10 53 – . AE E VISA by ⑥
closed Saturday, Bank Holidays dinner, Holy-Week and August – **M** a la carte 2 500/4 000
Spec. Judietas Judy, Rape al Fontenac, Tournedo José Torres.

XX ✿ **Eldorado Petit,** Dolors Monserdá 51, ✉ 08017, ✆ 204 51 53, « Terrace » – . AE E VISA by ⑦
closed Sunday – **M** a la carte 2 650/4 000
Spec. Ensalada de bacalao marinado al tomillo, San Pedro al horno de romero fresco, Filete de buey al adobo de mostaza.

XX Aitor, Carbonnell 5, ✉ 08003, ✆ 319 94 88, Basque rest. – LXY m

XX **Las Indias,** passeig Manuel Girona 38 bis, ✉ 08034, ✆ 204 48 00 – . AE VISA.
closed Sunday dinner – **M** a la carte 1 975/3 825. by ⑥

XX **El Dento,** Loreto 32, ✉ 08029, ✆ 321 67 56, Seafood – . AE E VISA. EV g
closed Saturday and August – **M** a la carte 1 520/3 360.

XX **Quo Vadis,** Carme 7, ✉ 08001, ☎ 317 74 47 – ▤. AE ⓓ E VISA JX k
closed Sunday – **M** a la carte 2 000/4 200.

XX **Chévere,** rambla del Prat 14, ✉ 08012, ☎ 217 03 59 – ▤ Ⓟ. AE ⓓ E VISA. ✻ FU q
closed Saturday lunch, Sunday and August – **M** a la carte 1 845/3 700.

XX Cathay, Santaló 86, ✉ 08021, ☎ 209 37 86, Chinese rest. – ▤ EU f

XX ✿ **Jaume de Provença,** Provença 88, ✉ 08029, ☎ 230 00 29, Modern decor – AE ⓓ E VISA. ✻ EX h
closed Sunday dinner, Monday and August – **M** a la carte 2 150/4 350
Spec. Huevos poches a las finas hierbas, Hojaldre de cigalas, Riñoncitos de lechal al Armañac.

XX **Alt Berlín,** Diagonal 633, ✉ 08028, ☎ 339 01 66, German rest. – ▤. AE ⓓ E VISA by ⑥
M a la carte 1 975/3 800.

XX ✿ **Hostal Sant Jordi,** Travessera de Dalt 123, ✉ 08024, ☎ 213 10 37 – ▤. AE ⓓ E VISA. ✻ by Travessera de Gràcia FU
closed Sunday dinner and August – **M** a la carte 1 940/2 990
Spec. Suquet de pescados de roca, Filete en papillot con salsa de mostaza y trufas a la crema, Filete de ciervo al agridulce (Oct.-March).

X **Can Jordi,** pasaje Marimón 18, ✉ 08021, ☎ 200 11 18 – ▤. AE VISA. ✻ EU x
closed Sunday – **M** a la carte 1 650/2 150.

X **La Balsa,** Infanta Isabel 4, ✉ 08022, ☎ 211 50 48, 🍽 – AE ⓓ VISA by ⑦
closed Sunday and Monday lunch – **M** a la carte 2 150/3 650.

X Tinell, Frenería 8, ✉ 08002, ☎ 315 46 04 – ▤ – **M** (buffet dinner only in August). MR t

X **Chicoa,** Aribau 71, ✉ 08036, ☎ 253 11 23, Rustic decor – ▤. AE E VISA FV a
closed Saturday dinner, Sunday and August – **M** a la carte 1 800/3 200.

X **La Senyora Grill,** Bori i Fontesta 45, ✉ 08017, ☎ 201 25 77, 🍽 – ▤. AE VISA. ✻ by ⑥
M a la carte 1 675/3 225.

Typical atmosphere restaurants

XX La Dida, Roger de Flor 230, ✉ 08025, ☎ 207 20 04, « Regional decor » – ▤ Ⓟ JU c

XX **Agut d'Avignon,** Trinidad 3 (Aviñó 8), ✉ 08002, ☎ 302 60 34, « Regional decor » – ▤. AE ⓓ E VISA. ✻ KY n
closed Sunday and Holy-Week – **M** a la carte 1 840/3 785.

XX **Font del Gat,** passeig Santa Madrona, Montjuic, ✉ 08004, ☎ 224 02 24, 🍽, Regional decor – Ⓟ. AE ⓓ. ✻ by av. Reina María Cristina EZ
M a la carte 1 600/3 450.

X **La Cuineta,** Paradís 4, ✉ 08002, ☎ 315 01 11, « In a 17C cellar » – ▤. AE ⓓ E VISA. ✻
closed Monday except Bank Holidays and day before holiday – **M** a la carte 1 850/3 775. MR e

X **Los Caracoles,** Escudellers 14, ✉ 08002, ☎ 301 20 41, Rustic regional decor – ▤. AE ⓓ E VISA. ✻ KY k
M a la carte 1 205/3 100.

X **Can Culleretes,** Quintana 5, ✉ 08002, ☎ 317 64 85 – ▤ JY c
closed Sunday dinner and Monday – **M** a la carte 975/1 925.

X **Pá i Trago,** Parlamento 41, ✉ 08015, ☎ 241 13 20 – ▤ Ⓟ. E VISA. ✻ GY a
M a la carte 1 525/2 650.

X **A la Menta,** passeig Manuel Girona 50, ✉ 08034, ☎ 204 15 49, Tavern – ▤. AE ⓓ VISA. ✻ – *closed Sunday in Summer and Sunday dinner all year* – **M** (booking essential) a la carte 1 650/3 225 by ⑥

X **L'Alberg,** Ramón y Cajal 13, ✉ 08012, ☎ 214 10 25, Rustic decor – ▤. E VISA. ✻
closed Sunday – **M** a la carte 1 250/2 750. FU d

at Esplugues de Llobregat by ⑥ – ✉ Esplugues de Llobregat – ✪ 93 :

XXX **La Masía,** av. Paisos Catalans 58 ☎ 371 37 42, 🍽, « Terrace under pine-trees » – ▤ Ⓟ. AE ⓓ E VISA. ✻
M a la carte 1 700/3 425.

X ✿ **Casa Quirze,** Laureano Miró 202 ☎ 371 10 84 – ▤ Ⓟ. AE VISA. ✻
closed Sunday dinner, Monday and Holy-Week – **M** a la carte 2 000/3 200
Spec. Mousseline de rascasse, Higado de oca al vinagre de Jerez, Muslo de pato braseado.

at the Tibidabo by ⑦ – ✉ 08022 Barcelona – ✪ 93 :

X **La Masía,** ☎ 247 63 50, < Town, sea and mountains – AE ⓓ E VISA
closed Monday from November-February – **M** (lunch only) a la carte 1 550/2 895.

on the road to Sant Cugat del Vallés by ⑦ : 11 km – ✉ 08023 Barcelona – ✪ 93 :

X **Can Cortés,** urbanización Ciudad Condal Tibidabo ☎ 674 17 04, <, 🍽, « Old masía, rustic decor », 🏊 admis. charge – Ⓟ. AE ⓓ E VISA. ✻
closed Sunday dinner – **M** a la carte 1 315/2 475.

Argentona Barcelona 43 ⑱ and 990 ⑳ – pop. 6 515 h. alt. 75 – ✪ 93 – Barcelona 27.

XX ✿✿ **Racó d'En Binu,** Puig i Cadafalch 14 ☎ 797 01 01 – ▤. AE E VISA. ✻
closed Sunday dinner, Monday and 19 May-19 June – **M** a la carte 2 800/4 800
Spec. Pasta de full d'esparrecs bladers (Nov.-May), Supreme de turbot Masse, Arco iris de frutas naturales con granizados y salsa de frambuesas (Summer only).

Málaga 29000 446 V16 – pop. 503 251 – ☎ 952 – Sea-side resort - Bullring.

See : Cathedral★ CY – Fine Arts Museum★ (Museo de bellas Artes) DY **M** – Alcazaba★ (museo★) DY – Gibralfaro ≤★★ DY.

Envir. : Finca de la Concepción★ by ④ : 7 km – Road from Málaga to Antequera ≤★★.

18 Club de Campo of Málaga by ② : 9 km ☎ 38 11 20 – 9 of El Candado by ① : 5 km ☎ 29 46 66.

✈ Málaga by ② : 9 km ☎ 31 19 44 – Iberia : Molina Larios 13, ✉ 29015, ☎ 31 37 31 and Aviaco : airport ☎ 31 78 58.

☎ 31 62 49.

to Melilla : Cia Trasmediterránea, Juan Díaz 4, ✉ 29015 (CZ), ☎ 22 43 93, Telex 77042.

Larios 5, ✉ 29015, ☎ 21 34 45 av. Cervantes, ✉ 29016 ☎ 22 86 00 and Airport ☎ 31 20 44 – R.A.C.E. (Automóvil Club de Málaga) pl. de las Flores 2, ✉ 29005, ☎ 21 42 60.

Madrid 546 ④ – Algeciras 133 ② – Córdoba 173 ④ – Sevilla 212 ④ – Valencia 655 ④.

Plan on next page

Centre :

Casa Curro without rest, Sancha de Lara 7, ✉ 29015, ☎ 22 72 00, Telex 77366 – lift, air cond. AE ⓓ E VISA. no dogs — CZ e
350 – **104 rm** 3 600/5 300.

Bahía Málaga, without rest, Somera 8, ✉ 29001, ☎ 22 43 05 – lift, bath wc, phone — CZ d
44 rm.

Venecia, without rest, no breakfast, Alameda Principal 9, ✉ 29001, ☎ 21 36 36 – lift, bath wc, phone — CZ u
40 rm.

Niza without rest, Larios 2, ✉ 29005, ☎ 22 77 04 – lift, bath wc, shower wc, phone. AE VISA — CY K
210 – **52 rm** 2 000/3 000.

La Alegría, Marín Garcia 10, ✉ 29005, ☎ 22 41 43 – air cond. AE ⓓ E VISA — CZ y
closed Saturday – **M** a la carte 2 000/3 525.

Cortijo de Pepe, pl. de la Merced 2, ✉ 29012, ☎ 22 40 71, terrace, Andalusian decor – air cond. — DY a

suburbs :

Las Vegas, paseo de Sancha 22, ✉ 29016, ☎ 21 77 12, ≤, terrace, pool, garden – lift, bath wc, phone, P. AE ⓓ VISA. no dogs rest — by ①
M 1 450 – 330 – **73 rm** 3 600/4 500 – P 4 950/6 300.

Los Naranjos without rest, paseo de Sancha 35, ✉ 29016, ☎ 22 43 19, Telex 77030 – lift, air cond., bath wc, shower wc, phone, garage. AE ⓓ E VISA. no dogs — by ①
500 – **41 rm** 4 700/6 980.

Apartogar La Maestranza without rest, no breakfast, av. Cánovas del Castillo 1, ✉ 29016, ☎ 21 36 10 – lift, bath wc, phone. AE ⓓ E VISA. no dogs — by ①
78 apartments 3 100/4 300.

Parador Nacional de Gibralfaro quiet, ✉ 29016, ☎ 22 19 02, terrace, « Beautiful location with ≤ bay and town » – bath wc, phone, P. AE ⓓ E VISA. no dogs — DY
M 1 800 – 600 – **12 rm** 6 000/7 500.

Olletas without rest, Cuba 3, ✉ 29013, ☎ 25 20 00 – lift, bath wc, phone, P. no dogs
200 – **66 rm** 1 800/2 800. — by Cristo de la Epidemia DX

Antonio Martín, paseo Marítimo 4, ✉ 29016, ☎ 22 21 13, ≤, terrace – P. AE ⓓ E VISA — by ①
closed Sunday dinner in winter – **M** a la carte 1 100/2 275.

Café de París, Vélez Málaga 8, ✉ 29016, ☎ 22 50 43 – air cond. AE ⓓ E VISA. no dogs — by ①
closed Tuesday and 10 June-5 July – **M** a la carte 1 375/4 200.

La Taberna del Pintor, Maestranza 6, ✉ 29016, ☎ 21 53 15, Typical decor – air cond. AE ⓓ E VISA — by ①
closed Sunday – **M** a la carte 1 050/1 800.

by the road to Cádiz by ② : 10 km – ✉ Málaga – ☎ 952 :

Guadalmar, urbanización Guadalmar, ✉ 29004, ☎ 31 90 00, Telex 77099, ≤, pool, garden, tennis – lift, air cond., TV, P – conference. AE ⓓ E VISA. no dogs rest
M 1 650 – 400 – **195 rm** 4 950/6 950 – P 6 680/8 150.

Do not mix up :

Comfort of hotels	: ... ,
Comfort of restaurants	: XXXXX ... X
Quality of the cuisine	: ✿✿✿, ✿✿, ✿

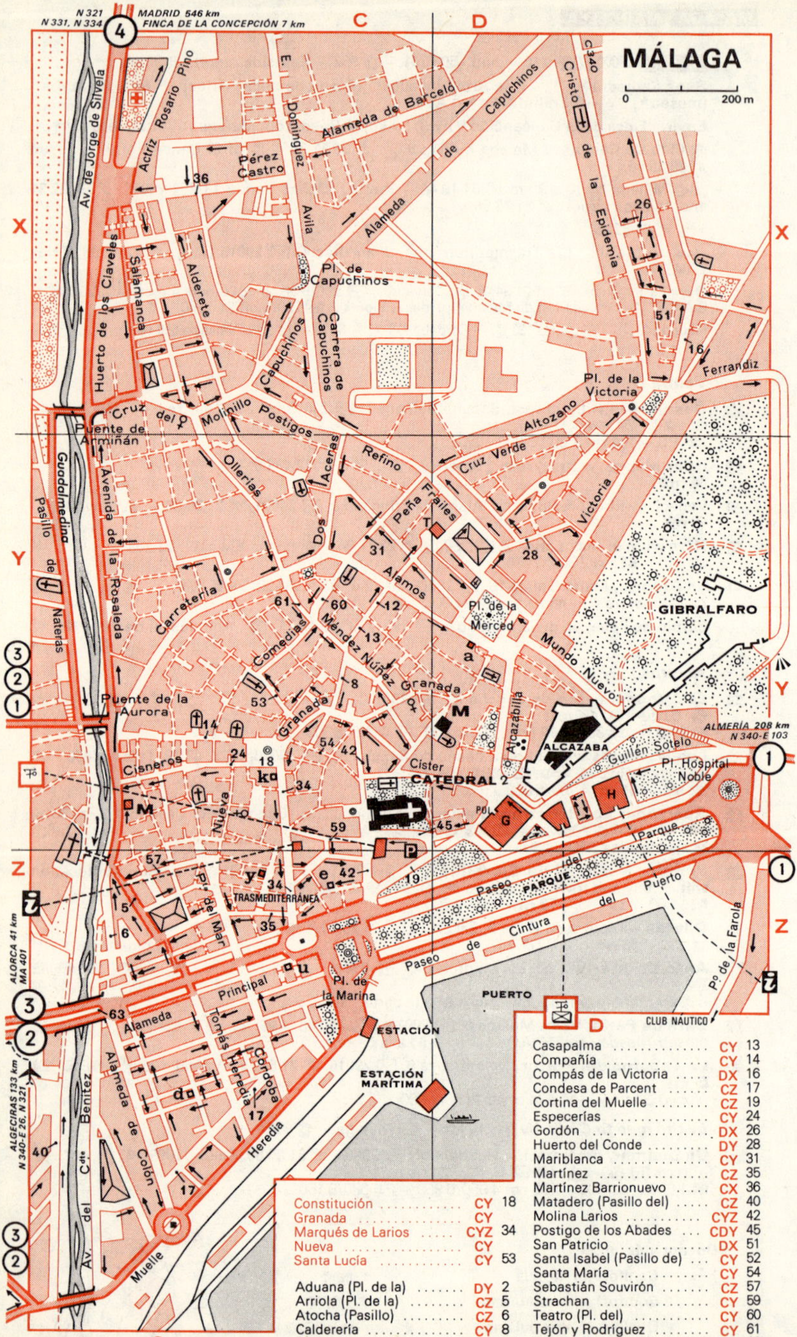

Constitución .... CY 18
Granada .... CY
Marqués de Larios .... CYZ 34
Nueva .... CY
Santa Lucía .... CY 53

Aduana (Pl. de la) .... DY 2
Arriola (Pl. de la) .... CZ 5
Atocha (Pasillo) .... CZ 6
Calderería .... CY 8
Cárcer .... CY 12
Casapalma .... CY 13
Compañía .... CY 14
Compás de la Victoria .... DX 16
Condesa de Parcent .... CZ 17
Cortina del Muelle .... CZ 19
Especerías .... CY 24
Gordón .... DX 26
Huerto del Conde .... DY 28
Mariblanca .... CY 31
Martínez .... CZ 35
Martínez Barrionuevo .... CX 36
Matadero (Pasillo del) .... CZ 40
Molina Larios .... CYZ 42
Postigo de los Abades .... CDY 45
San Patricio .... DX 51
Santa Isabel (Pasillo de) .... CY 52
Santa María .... CY 54
Sebastián Souvirón .... CZ 57
Strachan .... CY 59
Teatro (Pl. del) .... CY 60
Tejón y Rodríguez .... CY 61
Tetuán (Puente de) .... CZ 63

Marbella Málaga 446 W 15 – pop. 67 882 – ☎ 952 – Beach – Bullring.

⛳ Río Real-Los Monteros by ① : 5 km ✆ 77 37 76 – ⛳ Nueva Andalucía by ② : 5 km ✆ 81 22 00 – ⛳ Aloha golf, urbanización Aloha by ② : 8 km ✆ 78 23 88 – ⛳ golf Las Brisas, Nueva Andalucía by ② ✆ 78 03 00 – Iberia : paseo Marítimo ✆ 77 02 84.

🅸 Miguel Cano 1 ✆ 77 14 42.

Madrid 602 ① – Algeciras 77 ② – Málaga 56 ①.

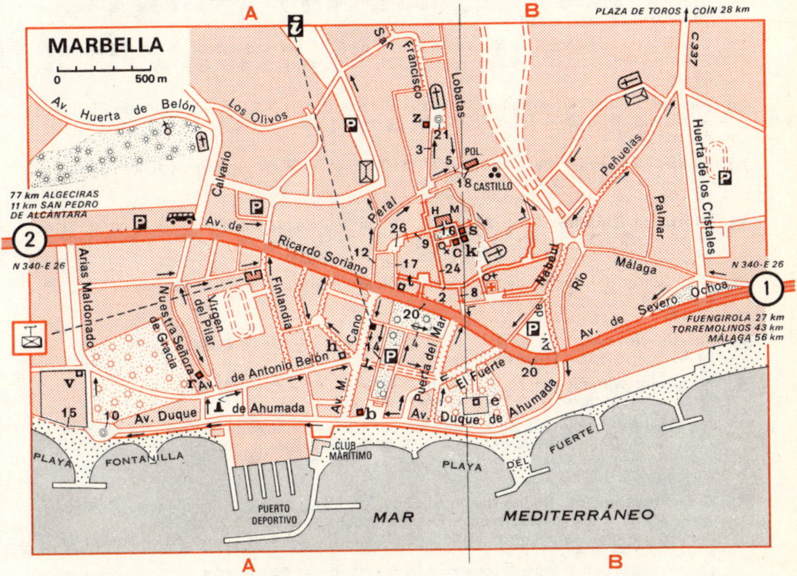

El Fuerte, Castillo San Luis ✆ 77 15 00, Telex 77523, ≤, 🌳, « Garden with palm-trees », 🏊 heated, 🎾 – 🛗 ▤ rest 🅿. AE ⓓ VISA. ✻ AB **e**
M 1 850 – **146 rm** ☕ 6 050/9 200 – P 7 660/9 110.

Skol, La Fontanilla ✆ 77 08 00, Telex 78631, ≤, 🏊, 🚗 – 🛗 ▤ rest. AE VISA. ✻ rest A **v**
M 1 400 – ☕ 400 – **300 apartments** 6 520/7 900 – P 6 450/9 020.

San Cristóbal without rest, coffee shop only, Ramón y Cajal 18 ✆ 77 12 50, Telex 77712 – 🛗 ▤ 🛁wc 🚿wc ☎. E VISA. ✻ A **t**
☕ 225 – **100 rm** 2 725/4 345.

Lima without rest, av. Antonio Belón 2 ✆ 77 05 00 – 🛗 🛁wc 🚿wc ☎. AE ⓓ E VISA. ✻ A **h**
☕ 300 – **64 rm** 3 000/4 650.

✻ **La Fonda,** pl. Santo Cristo 10 ✆ 77 25 12, 🌳, « Pretty Andalusian patio » – AE ⓓ VISA. ✻ A **z**
closed Sunday except August – **M** (dinner only) a la carte 2 400/4 445
Spec. Crepes de gambas con aguacates, Lenguado relleno, Pintada de Guinea al hojaldre.

Marcuño, Nuestra Señora de Gracia 26, Seafood – ▤ A **r**

Gran Marisquería Santiago, av. Duque de Ahumada 5 ✆ 77 00 78, 🌳, Seafood – ▤. AE ⓓ E VISA. ✻ A **b**
M a la carte 2 050/3 400.

Mena, pl. de los Naranjos 10 ✆ 77 15 97, 🌳 – AE ⓓ E VISA. ✻ A **c**
closed Sunday and December-February – **M** a la carte 1 700/3 550.

Plaza, General Chinchilla 6 ✆ 77 11 11, 🌳 – AE ⓓ E VISA. ✻ AB **s**
closed Sunday and 16 October-16 January – **M** a la carte 1 825/3 075.

Los Naranjos, pl. de los Naranjos ✆ 77 18 19, 🌳 – AE ⓓ E VISA. ✻ AB **k**
closed Sunday and 15 November-15 February – **M** a la carte 2 250/3 650.

on the road to Cádiz – ✉ Marbella – ☎ 952 :

Meliá Don Pepe and Grill la Farola, by ② : 1 km ✆ 77 03 00, Telex 77055, ≤ sea and mountains, Pianist at dinner, « Subtropical plants », heated, – AE E VISA.
M 3 800 – 950 – **218 rm** 13 000/21 000 – P 17 760/20 260.

Puente Romano M, by ② : 3,5 km ✆ 77 01 00, Telex 77399, « Elegant Andalusian complex in beautiful garden », heated, – AE E VISA. rest
M 4 000 – 1 000 – **196 rm** 20 000/25 000.

Del Golf, urbanización Nueva Andalucía by ② : 7 km and detour : 4 km, ✉ apartado 2 Nueva Andalucía, ✆ 78 03 00, Telex 77783, ≤, – –
80 rm.

Andalucía Plaza, urbanización Nueva Andalucía by ② : 7,5 km, ✉ apartado 21 Nueva Andalucía, ✆ 78 20 00, Telex 77086, heated, – –
418 rm.

Marbella Club, by ② : 3 km ✆ 77 13 00, Telex 77319, « Elegant decor ; garden », heated – rm. AE E VISA. rest
M 4 000 – 1 100 – **71 rm** 17 200/21 500 – P 18 450/24 900.

Marbella Dinamar Club 24, by ② : 6 km, ✉ Nueva Andalucía, ✆ 78 05 00, Telex 77656, ≤, – – AE E VISA.
M 2 100 – 750 – **117 rm** 9 000/11 500 – P 9 750/13 000.

Las Fuentes del Rodeo, by ② : 8 km, ✉ Nueva Andalucía, ✆ 78 10 00, Telex 77340, « Garden », –
90 rm.

Guadalpín, by ② : 1,5 km ✆ 77 11 00, – AE E VISA. rest
M 1 175 – 300 – **110 rm** 3 850/5 600 – P 4 950/6 000.

Nagüeles without rest, by ② : 3,5 km ✆ 77 16 88, – wc wc.
15 March-15 October – 250 – **17 rm** 1 600/2 750.

La Meridiana, by ② : 3,5 km and detour 1 km - camino de la Cruz - Las Lomas ✆ 77 61 90, ≤, « Terrace-garden » – AE E VISA
closed Thursday lunch and 12 January-11 February – **M** (dinner only in Summer) a la carte 3 450/5 550.

✿ **Le Restaurant,** Rodeo Beach Club by ② : 8 km, ✉ Nueva Andalucía, ✆ 78 59 00, Telex 77340, ≤, French rest., « Elegant decor » – AE E VISA.
closed Sunday in Winter and November-15 December – **M** (dinner only) a la carte 2 900/5 800
Spec. Paupetón de trufa negra de Soria con salsa de champiñones, Filete de salmonete confitados en aceite con hierbas frescas, Solomillo de buey a la pimienta negra con pasas y salsa al armagnac.

El Girasole, urb. Aloha, ✉ Nuevo Andalucia, ✆ 78 38 59, –

Orquídea, urbanización Nueva Andalucía - calle 2 - 21 B by ② : 7,7 km, ✉ Nueva Andalucía, ✆ 78 16 99, French rest. – AE
closed Wednesday and January-February – **M** (dinner only) a la carte 1 450/2 625.

on the road to Málaga – ✉ Marbella – ☎ 952 :

✿ **Los Monteros and Grill El Corzo** M, by ① : 5,5 km ✆ 77 17 00, Telex 77059, ≤, Pianist at dinner, « Subtropical garden », heated, – AE E VISA.
M 5 000 – **170 rm** 18 700/24 300 – P 19 350/25 400
Spec. Filetes de lenguado con langostinos al champán, Vieiras en fondo de alcachofas a la crema de albahaca, Medallón de venado al vino de Málaga.

Don Carlos M, by ① : 10 km ✆ 83 11 40, Telex 74481, ≤, Pianist at dinner, « Large garden », heated, – –
231 rm.

Estrella del Mar, by ① : 9 km ✆ 83 12 75, Telex 76669, – rest. AE E VISA. rest
March-November – **M** 1 750 – 475 – **98 rm** 4 000/6 300 – P 6 525/7 375.

Bellamar (Trade School Hotel), by ① : 1,5 km ✆ 77 23 00, ≤, – rest. AE E VISA.
closed 21 to 31 December – **M** 1 320 – 330 – **60 rm** 2 750/4 400 – P 4 650/5 200.

Belarcos, by ① : 13,5 km ✆ 83 17 44, – wc
78 rm.

✿ **La Hacienda,** by ① : 11,5 km and detour 1,5 km ✆ 83 12 67, « Rustic decor - Patio » – AE E VISA.
closed Monday except August, Tuesday and 17 November-17 December – **M** (dinner only in August) a la carte 3 300/5 425
Spec. Blinis con coquinas y albahaca, Pintada la Hacienda, Souffle helado al vino Málaga.

Chez Charlemagne, by ① : 8 km ✆ 83 11 05, French rest. – AE
closed Wednesday – **M** (dinner only) a la carte 1 450/2 890.

SEVILLA 41000 P 446 T 11 12 – pop. 653 833 – alt. 12 – 954 – Bullring.

See : Cathedral*** CV – Giralda*** (<**) CV – Alcazar*** (gardens**, Admiral's Apartments : Virgin of the Navigators altarpiece*) CX – Maria Luisa Park** – Fine Arts Museum** AU M1 – Santa Cruz Quarter* CV – Pilate's House** (casa de Pilatos : azulejos**) DV R – Archeological Museum (Roman department*).

Envir. : Itálica <* 9 km by ⑤.

and Racecourse Club Pineda by ③ : 3 km 61 14 00.

Sevilla - San Pablo by ① : 14 km 51 65 98 – Iberia : Almirante Lobo 2, 41002 21 88 00.

22 03 70.

av. de la Constitución 21B 41004 22 14 04 and paseo de Las **Delicias** 41012 23 44 65 – R.A.C.E. (R.A.C. de Andalucía) av. Eduardo Dato 22, 41002 63 13 50.

Madrid 547 ① – La Coruña 959 ⑤ – Lisboa 409 ⑤ – Málaga 215 ② – Valencia 676 ①.

Plan on following pages

Alfonso XIII, San Fernando 2, 41004, 22 28 50, Telex 72725, , « Magnificent Andalusian building », , – AE VISA. CX c
M 2 750 – **148 rm** 11 000/15 000 – P 12 500/16 000.

Los Lebreros M, Luis Morales 2, 41007, 57 94 00, Telex 72772, – – AE E VISA. by Luis Montoto DV
M 2 700 (see also Rest. **La Dehesa below)** – **439 rm** 7 350/10 700.

Porta Coeli M without rest, coffee shop only, av. Eduardo Dato 49, 41005, 57 00 40, Telex 72913 – – AE E VISA by E. Dato DV
450 – **246 rm** 6 050/10 500.

Macarena, San Juan de Ribera 2, 41009, 37 57 00, Telex 72815, – – AE E VISA. CDT a
M 2 700 – **281 rm** 7 100/10 200.

Inglaterra, pl. Nueva 7, 41001, 22 49 70, Telex 72244 – . AE E VISA. BV a
M 1 900 – 400 – **120 rm** 7 700/11 500 – P 9 250/11 200.

Pasarela M without rest, av. de la Borbolla 11, 41004, 41 55 11, Telex 72486 – . AE E VISA. by Av. de Portugal DX
400 – **82 rm** 6 500/9 500.

Resid. and Rest. Fernando III, San José 21, 41004, 21 77 08, Telex 72491, – – . AE E VISA. rest CV z
M 1 500 – 300 – **156 rm** 3 300/4 900 – P 4 250/5 100.

Bécquer without rest, Reyes Católicos 4, 41001, 22 89 00, Telex 72884 – . AE E VISA. AV s
275 – **126 rm** 3 000/4 500.

América without rest, coffee shop only, Jesús del Gran Poder 2, 41002, 22 09 51, Telex 72709 – . E VISA. BU h
275 – **100 rm** 2 810/4 810.

Nuevo Lar, pl. Carmen Benítez 3, 41003, 41 03 61, Telex 72816 – – . E VISA. DV v
M 1 500 – 400 – **137 rm** 6 000/8 500.

Alcázar without rest, coffee shop only, Menéndez Pelayo 10, 41004, 41 20 11, Telex 72360 – . AE E VISA DX u
275 – **93 rm** 3 600/4 800.

Giralda Playa, Sierra Nevada 3, Puerta de Carmona, 41003, 41 66 61, Telex 72417 – – . AE E VISA. DV y
M 950 – 300 – **90 rm** 4 800/6 000 – P 4 760/6 560.

Doña María without rest, Don Remondo 19, 41004, 22 49 90, « Elegant classic decor - terrace with < Giralda », – . AE VISA. CV b
400 – **61 rm** 7 000/11 500.

Monte Carmelo without rest, Turia 9, 41011, 27 90 00 – . AE VISA. SW : by pl. de Cuba
250 – **68 rm** 3 000/4 500.

La Rábida, Castelar 24, 41001, 22 09 60, – wc . rest BV d
M 950 – 200 – **90 rm** 2 100/3 600 – P 3 385/3 885.

Corregidor without rest, Morgado 17, 41003, 38 51 11 – wc . AE VISA CTU g
295 – **69 rm** 3 200/6 000.

Venecia without rest, Trajano 31, 41002, 38 11 61 – wc wc . VISA BU n
250 – **24 rm** 2 700/4 500.

Reyes Católicos without rest, Gravina 57, 41001, 21 12 00 – wc wc . AE E VISA. AV n
250 – **26 rm** 2 900/4 500.

Murillo and apart. Murillo without rest, Lope de Rueda 9, 41004, 21 60 95 – wc – . AE E VISA. CV e
61 rm 3 450/5 800 – **14 apartments.**

Ducal without rest, pl. Encarnación 19, 41003, 21 51 07 – wc wc . AE E VISA. CU b
200 – **51 rm** 2 100/3 300.

SEVILLA

Francos	CV	29
Sierpes	BUV	
Tetuán	BV	62
Adriano	ABV	2
Alemanes	CV	3
Almirante Apodaca	CU	4
Almirante Lobo	BX	6
Caballerizas	CV	12
Cabeza Rey Don Pedro	CV	13
Campana	BU	16
Concordia (Pl.)	BU	19
Demetrio de los Rios	DVX	25
Fray Ceferino González	CX	30
García de Vinuesa	BV	32
Gerona	CU	34
Jerez (Puerta de)	CX	36
Julio César	AV	37
Martín Villa	BU	42
Mateos Gago	CV	43
O'Donnell	BU	45
Pastor y Landero	AV	46
Peñuelas	DU	48
Reyes Católicos	AV	53
Rioja	BUV	54
San Laureano	AU	57
Santa Maria la Blanca	DV	59
Santo Tomás	CX	61
Triunfo (Pl. del)	CX	63
Velázquez	BU	65

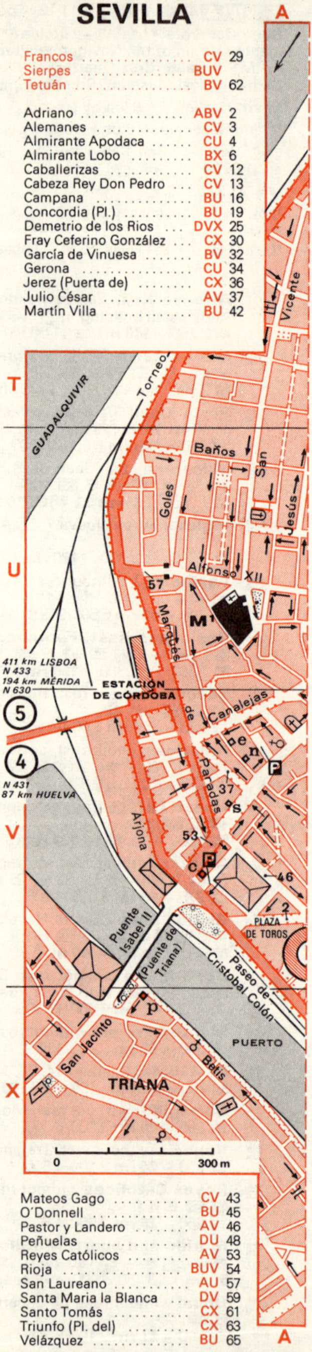

🏨 **Montecarlo,** Gravina 51, ✉ 41001, ☎ 21 75 02 – |‡| ⊟wc ⋔wc ☎. AE ◑ E VISA. ✗ AV **e**
M 1 000 – ☕ 250 – **25 rm** 2 100/3 600 – P 3 600/3 900.

🏨 **Sevilla** without rest, no ☕, Daoiz 5, ✉ 41003, ☎ 38 41 61 – |‡| ⊟wc ⋔wc ☎ BCU **w**
30 rm 2 100/3 150.

XXX **Paco Ramos** 1st floor, Reyes Católicos 25, ✉ 41001, ☎ 21 75 85 – ▤. AE ◑ E VISA AV **c**
closed Sunday and August – **M** a la carte 1 675/3 550.

XXX **San Marco,** Cuna 6, ✉ 41004, ☎ 21 24 40 – ▤. AE ◑ VISA. ✗ CU **x**
closed 23 July-August – **M** a la carte 1 900/3 760.

XXX **Or-Iza,** Betis 61, ✉ 41010, ☎ 27 95 85, Basque rest. – ▤. AE ◑ E VISA. ✗ BX **y**
closed Sunday and August – **M** a la carte 2 200/3 175.

XXX Maitres, av. República Argentina 54, ✉ 41011, ☎ 45 68 80 – ▤ SW : by pl. de Cuba BX

XXX **Río Grande,** Betis, ✉ 41010, ☎ 27 39 56, ≤, 🏖, « Large terraces on riverside » – ▤. AE ◑ E VISA BX **r**
M a la carte 1 800/3 350.

XXX Maitres, av. San Francisco Javier 16, ✉ 41005, ☎ 65 67 52 – ▤.

XXX **La Dehesa,** Luis Morales 2, ✉ 41005, ☎ 57 62 04, Telex 72772, Typical Andalusian decor - Grills – ▤. AE ◑ E VISA. ✗
closed August – **M** a la carte 1 700/2 900.
by Luis Montoto DV

XXX Rincón de Curro, Virgen de Luján 45, ✉ 41011, ☎ 45 02 38 – ▤ SW : by pl. de Cuba BX

XXX Figón del Cabildo, pl. del Cabildo, ✉ 41001, ☎ 22 01 17, 🏖 – ▤ BV **e**

XX **Jamaica,** Jamaica 16, ✉ 41012, ☎ 61 12 44 – ▤. AE ◑ VISA. ✗ by ③
closed Sunday dinner – **M** a la carte 1 250/2 850.

XX **La Raza,** av. Isabel la Católica, ✉ 41013, ☎ 23 20 24, ≤, 🏖 – ▤. AE ◑ E VISA CX **e**
M a la carte 1 550/2 840.

XX Bodegón El Riojano, Virgen de las Montañas 12, ✉ 41011, ☎ 45 06 82 – ▤ SW : by pl. de Cuba BX

XX **La Albahaca,** pl. Santa Cruz 12, ✉ 41004, ☎ 22 07 14, « Former manor house » – ▤. AE ◑ E VISA. ✗ CV **s**
closed Sunday – **M** a la carte 1 700/3 200.

XX José Luis Hernandez, av. República Argentina 13, ✉ 41011, ☎ 27 70 93 – ▤ SW : by pl. de Cuba BX

XX **El Mero,** Betis 1, ✉ 41010, ☎ 33 42 52, Seafood – ▤. ◑ E VISA. ✗ AX **p**
closed Tuesday – **M** a la carte 1 825/3 125.

X Cetaria, Luis de Morales - edificio Estadio, ✉ 41005, ☎ 57 87 28, Seafood – ▤ by av. E. Dato DX

X **La Parra,** Gustavo Gallardo 14, ✉ 41013, ☎ 61 29 59, 🏖, « Patio with pergola » – ▤. AE VISA. ✗ by av. de Portugal DX
closed Saturday lunch, Sunday and 10 August-10 September – **M** a la carte 1 400/2 430.

X **La Isla,** Arfe 25, ✉ 41001, ☎ 21 26 31 – ▤. AE ◑ E VISA BV **u**
closed August – **M** a la carte 1 700/2 900.

X **Los Alcázares,** Miguel de Mañara 10, ✉ 41004, ☎ 21 31 03, Regional decor – ▤. AE E VISA. ✗ CX **s**
closed Sunday – **M** a la carte 1 475/3 150.

X **Hostería del Laurel,** pl. de los Venerables 5, ✉ 41004, ☎ 22 02 95, Typical decor – ▤. AE VISA. ✗ CV **r**
M a la carte 1 150/2 450.

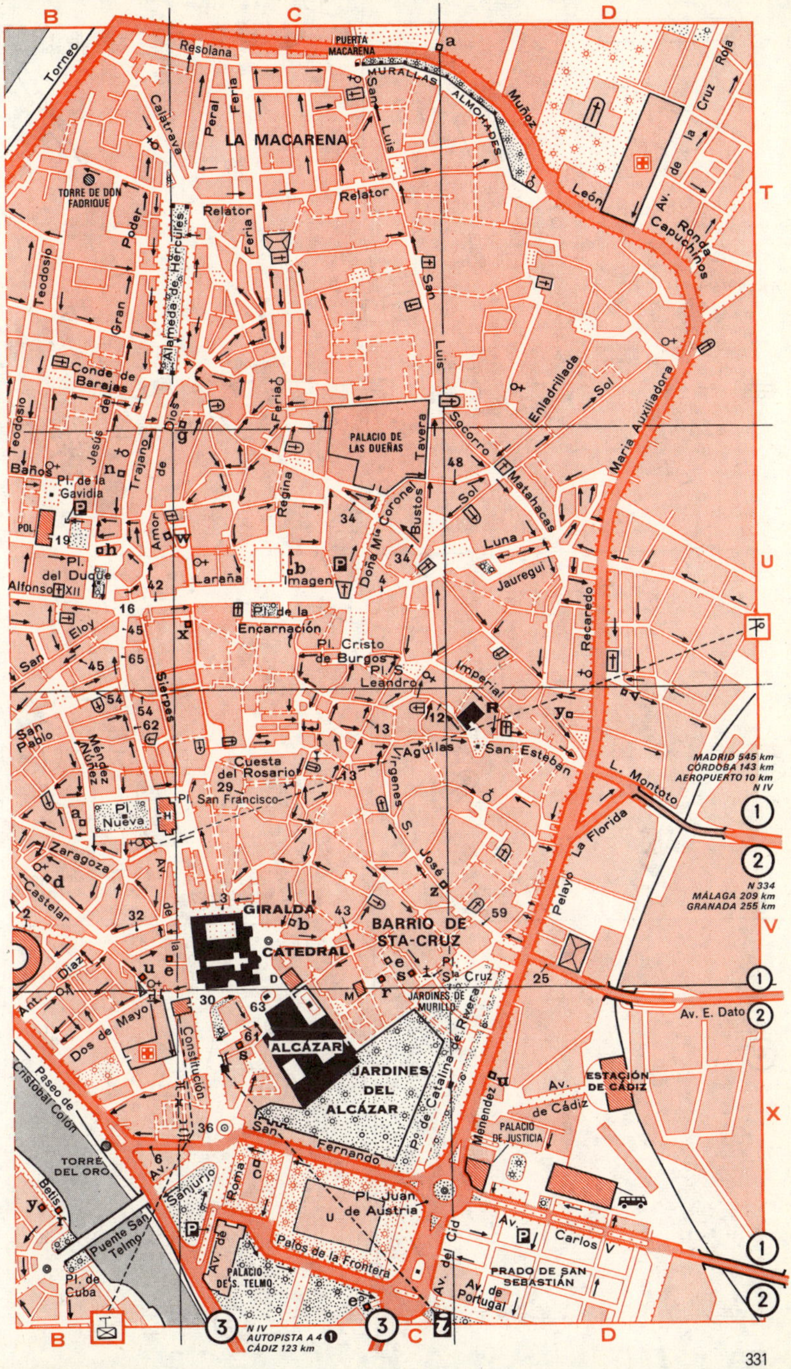

LA MACARENA
PUERTA MACARENA
MURALLAS ALMOHADES
TORRE DE DON FADRIQUE
Alameda de Hércules
PALACIO DE LAS DUEÑAS
Pl. de la Encarnación
Pl. Cristo de Burgos
Pl. S. Leandro
Cuesta del Rosario
Pl. San Francisco
Pl. Nueva
Pl. del Duque
Pl. de la Gavidia
GIRALDA
CATEDRAL
BARRIO DE STA-CRUZ
ALCÁZAR
JARDINES DEL ALCÁZAR
JARDINES DE MURILLO
TORRE DEL ORO
Puente San Telmo
Pl. de Cuba
Pl. Juan de Austria
PALACIO DE S. TELMO
PALACIO DE JUSTICIA
ESTACIÓN DE CÁDIZ
PRADO DE SAN SEBASTIÁN
MADRID 545 km
CÓRDOBA 143 km
AEROPUERTO 10 km
N IV
N 334
MÁLAGA 209 km
GRANADA 255 km
Av. E. Dato
N IV
AUTOPISTA A 4
CÁDIZ 123 km

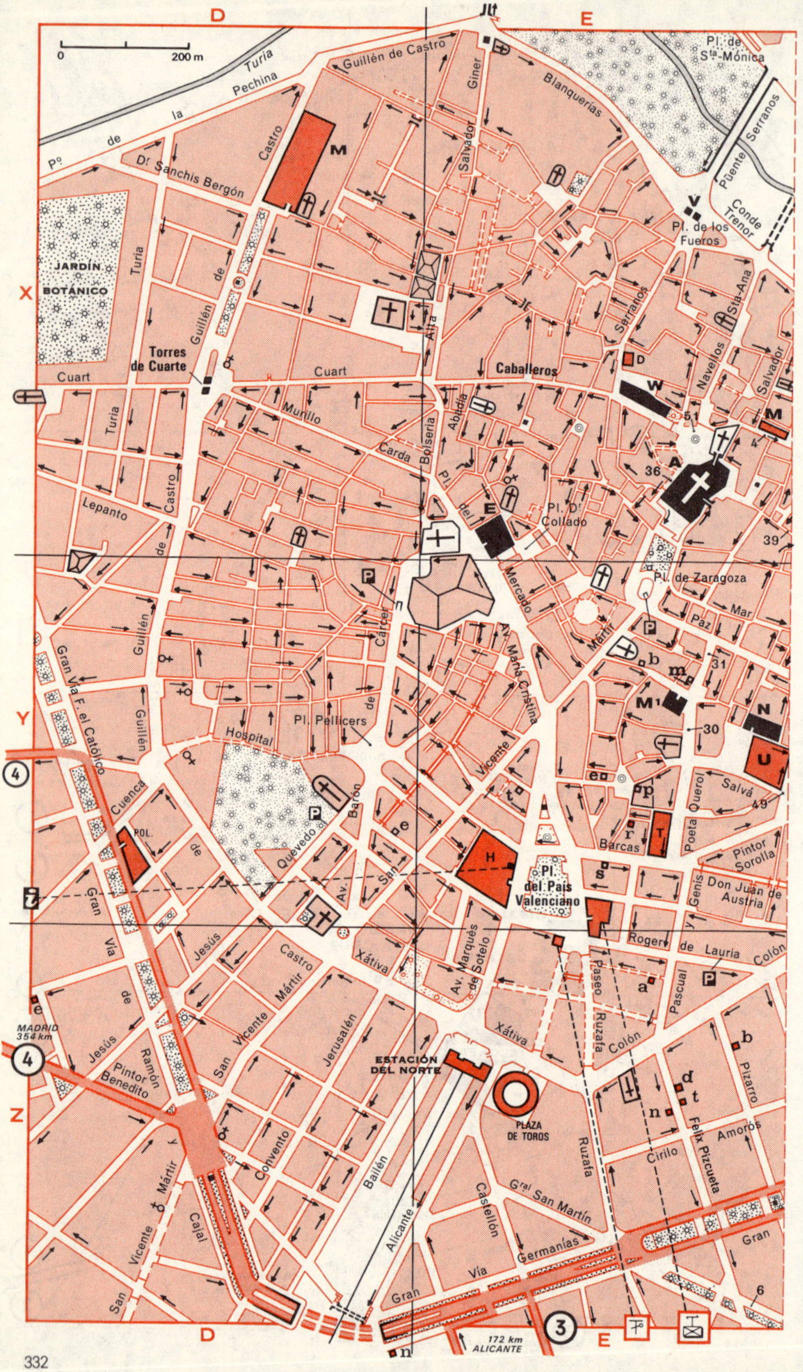
D
E
X
Y
Z
0
200 m
Turia
Pechina
Pº de la
Guillén de Castro
Giner
Blanquerías
Pl. de Sta Mónica
Serranos
Puente
Conde Trenor
Pl. de los Fueros
Dr Sanchis Bergón
Castro
M
Salvador
Alta
JARDÍN BOTÁNICO
Turia
Guillén de
Torres de Cuarte
Cuart
Caballeros
Serranos
Sta Ana
Navellos
Salvador
D
W
51
M
A
36
Murillo
Carda
Bolsería
Abadía
Pl. del
E
Pl. Dr Collado
Lepanto
Turia
Castro
de
Mercado
Pl. de Zaragoza
39
Paz
Mar
Cárcel
Av. María Cristina
Mártir
b
m
31
M1
N
30
U
Guillén
Gran Vía F. el Católico
Guillén
Hospital
Pl. Pellicers
de
Vicente
Salvá
49
Poeta Querol
Cuenca
POL.
de
Quevedo
Barón
San
Av.
t
e
p
r
T
Barcas
H
Pl. del País Valenciano
s
Pintor Sorolla
Genís
Don Juan de Austria
Gran
Vía
Jesús
Castro
Mártir
Xátiva
Av. Marqués de Sotelo
Roger de Lauria
Colón
Paseo
Ruzafa
a
Pascual y
MADRID 354 km
4
e
de
Jesús
Pintor Benedito
Ramón
San Vicente
Jerusalén
Xátiva
Colón
ESTACIÓN DEL NORTE
PLAZA DE TOROS
b
Pizarro
d
t
n
Félix Pizcueta
Amorós
Cirilo
Convento
Bailén
Ruzafa
Mártir
Vicente
San
Cajal
Alicante
Castellón
Gral San Martín
Germanías
Vía
Gran
Gran
6
n
172 km ALICANTE
3

VALENCIA

STREET INDEX

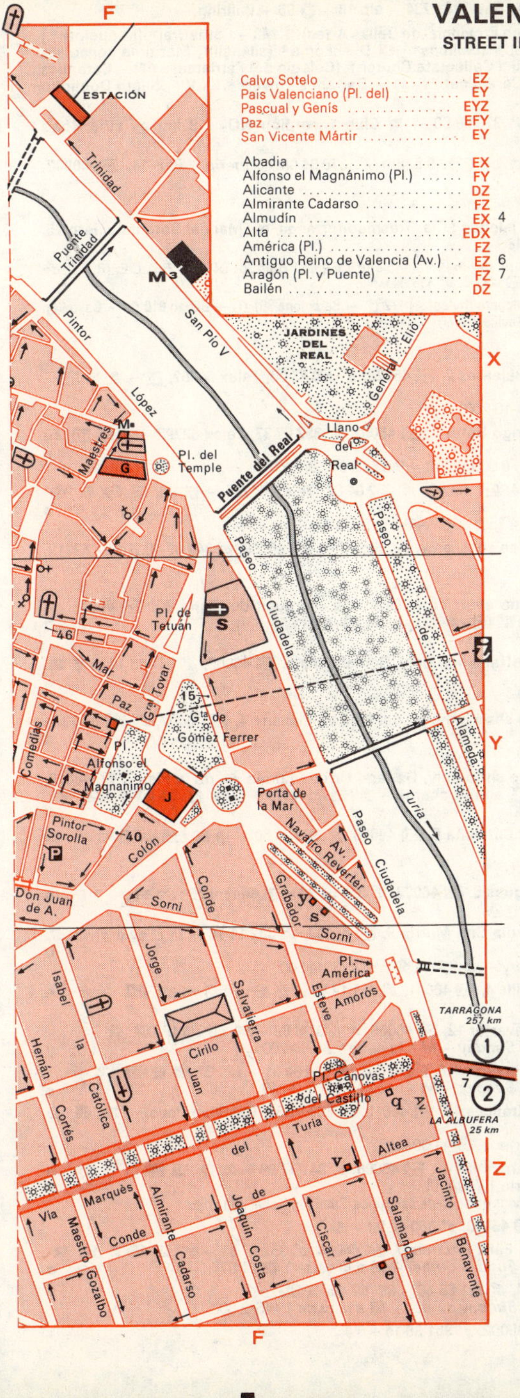

VALENCIA 46000 445 N 28 29 – pop. 751 734 – alt. 13 – 96 – Bullring.

See : Fine Arts Museum★★ (Museo Provincial de Bellas Artes) FX **M3** – Cathedral★ (Miguelete★) EX **A** – Palacio de la Generalidad★ (ceilings★) EX **D** – Lonja★ (silkhall★, Maritime consulate hall : ceiling★) EX **E** – Corpus Christi Collegiate Church★ (Colegio del Patriarca) EY **N** – Ceramics Museum★ (Museo Nacional de Cerámica) EY **M1** – Serranos Towers★ EX **V** – Santo Domingo Monastery (Royal Chapel★) FY **S**.

of Manises by ④ : 12 km 379 08 50 – Club Escorpión NO : 19 km by Liria Road 160 12 11.

Valencia - Manises Airport by ④ : 9,5 km 370 34 08 – Iberia : Paz 14, 46003, 352 05 00.

351 00 43.

To the Balearic and Canary Islands : Cía. Trasmediterránea, av. Manuel Soto Ingeniero 15, 46024, 367 06 04, Telex 62648.

Paz 46, 46003, 352 24 97 and pl. del País Valenciano 1 46016 351 04 17 – **R.A.C.E.** (R.A.C. de Valencia) av. Jacinto Benavente 25, 46005, 333 94 03.

Madrid 354 ④ – Albacete 184 ③ – Alicante (by coast) 172 ③ – Barcelona 361 ① – Bilbao 610 ① – Castellón de la Plana 75 ① – Málaga 654 ③ – Sevilla 676 ④ – Zaragoza 332 ①.

Plan on preceding pages

Rey Don Jaime M, av. Baleares 2, 46023, 360 73 00, Telex 64252, – AE E VISA.
M 2 700 – **314 rm** 7 000/10 200.

Astoria Palace, pl. Rodrigo Botet 5, 46002, 352 67 37, Telex 62722 – . AE E VISA. — EY **p**
M 1 950 – 500 – **207 rm** 6 000/9 270 – P 8 535/9 900.

Reina Victoria, Barcas 4, 46002, 352 04 87, Telex 64755 – . AE E VISA. rest — EY **s**
M 2 000 – 450 – **92 rm** 4 750/7 950 – P 7 525/8 300.

Expo H., without rest, coffee shop only, av. Pío XII-4, 46009, 347 09 09, Telex 63212, – –
396 rm.

Dimar without rest, coffee shop only, Gran Vía Marqués del Turia 80, 46005, 334 18 07, Telex 62952 – – . AE VISA. — FZ **q**
95 rm 6 205/8 045.

Excelsior without rest, coffee shop only, Barcelonina 5, 46002, 351 46 12 – . AE E VISA. — EY **e**
240 – **64 rm** 3 200/4 900.

Oltra without rest, coffee shop only, pl. del País Valenciano 4, 46002, 352 06 12 – . AE E VISA. — EY **t**
300 – **93 rm** 3 200/5 150.

Lehos without rest, coffee shop only, General Urrutia (angle av. de la Plata), 46013, 334 78 00, Telex 63055, admis. charge – wc wc . AE E VISA.
375 – **104 rm** 4 000/5 000.

Renasa without rest., av. Cataluña 5, 46010, 369 24 50 – wc wc . AE VISA
275 – **73 rm** 5000.

Inglés, Marqués de Dos Aguas 6, 46002, 351 64 26 – rest wc — EY **m**
55 rm.

Bristol without rest., Abadía San Martín 3, 46002, 352 11 76 – wc wc . AE E VISA — EY **b**
closed December-15 January – 250 – **40 rm** 2 730/4 500.

Florida without rest., Padilla 4, 46001, 351 12 84 – wc wc . VISA — DY **e**
250 – **45 rm** 2 400/4 500.

XXX **La Hacienda,** Navarro Reverter 12, 46006, 373 18 59 – . AE E VISA. — FY **y**
closed Saturday lunch and Sunday – **M** a la carte 1 950/4 200.

XXX **Los Azahares,** Navarro Reverter 16, 46004, 334 86 01 – . AE E VISA. — FY **s**
closed Saturday lunch and Sunday – **M** a la carte 2 100/3 740.

XXX **El Condestable,** Artes Gráficas 15, 46010, 369 92 50, Castilian decor – . AE E VISA
closed Sunday – **M** a la carte 1 025/4 000.

XXX ✿ **Ma Cuina,** Gran Vía Germanías 49, 46006, 341 77 99 – . AE VISA — DZ **n**
closed Sunday – **M** a la carte 1 750/4 050
Spec. Pimientos del piquillo rellenos en salsa de cangrejos, Cabritillo lechal, Mil hojas.

XXX Les Graelles, pl. Galicia, 46010, 360 47 00 – .

XXX **Mesón del Marisquero,** Félix Pizcueta 7, 46004, 352 97 91 – . AE E VISA. — EZ **d**
closed Saturday lunch and Sunday dinner – **M** a la carte 1 425/1 975.

XXX **Lionel,** Pizarro 9, 46004, 351 65 66 – . AE E VISA. — EZ **b**
closed Saturday lunch and Sunday dinner – **M** a la carte 1 445/2 800.

XXX Comodoro, Transits 3, 46002, 351 38 15 – — EY **r**

XX **El Cachirulo,** Cronista Almela y Vives 3, ✉ 46010, ☎ 360 10 84, Aragonese rest. – ▤. VISA. ✻
closed Sunday dinner – **M** a la carte 1 700/2 650.

XX El Timonel, Felix Pizcueta 13, ✉ 46004, ☎ 352 63 00 – ▤ EZ **t**

XX **Río Sil,** Mosén Femades 10, ✉ 46002, ☎ 352 97 64 – ▤. AE ⓓ E VISA. ✻ EZ **a**
M a la carte 1 600/3 500.

XX **Mey Mey,** Historiador Diago 19, ✉ 46007, ☎ 326 07 47, Chinese rest. – ▤. AE VISA. ✻
closed Holy-Week, Sunday dinner and Monday lunch – **M** a la carte 995/1 820. DZ **e**

XX Tres Escudos, Feliz Pizcueta 10, ✉ 46004, ☎ 352 66 57 – ▤ EZ **n**

X **Marisquería Ismael,** Burriana 40, ✉ 46005, ☎ 373 57 15 – ▤. AE ⓓ VISA. ✻ FZ **e**
closed Sunday dinner – **M** a la carte 1 875/3 500.

X **El Plat,** Conde de Altea 41, ✉ 46005, ☎ 334 96 38, Paella and rice rest. – ▤. VISA. ✻
closed Monday – **M** a la carte 1 500/3 200. FZ **v**

at Playa Puebla de Farnals by ① : 15 km – ✉ Playa Puebla de Farnals – ☎ 96 :

X **Bergamonte,** ☎ 144 16 12, ⛱, « Typical Valencian "barraca" », ⛱ admis. charge, ✻ – Ⓟ. AE VISA. ✻
closed Monday – **M** a la carte 1 400/2 500.

on the road to the Airport by ④ : 9,5 km – ✉ Manises – ☎ 96 :

🏨 Azafata Sol, ☎ 154 61 00, Telex 64036 – |¢| ▤ 🚗 Ⓟ – 🏔
130 rm.

Sweden
Sverige

Stockholm

SWEDEN

PRACTICAL INFORMATION

LOCAL CURRENCY

Swedish Kronor : 100 SEK = 13.15 US $ (Jan. 86)

TOURIST INFORMATION

The Tourist Centre is situated in the Sweden House, entrance from Kungsträdgården at Hamngatan. Open Mon-Fri 9am-5pm. Sat. and Sun. 9am-2pm. Telephone weekdays 08/789 20 00, weekends to Excursion Shop 08/789 24 15, to Tourist Centre 08/789 24 18.

FOREIGN EXCHANGE

Banks are open between 9.00am and 3.00pm on weekdays only. Some banks in the centre of the city are usually open weekdays 9am to 5.30pm. Most large hotels have exchange facilities, and Arlanda airport has banking facilities between 7am to 10pm seven days a week.

SHOPPING IN STOCKHOLM

The main shopping streets in the Centre are: Hamngatan, Biblioteksgatan, Drottninggatan.

In the Old Town mainly Västerlånggatan.

THEATRE BOOKINGS

Your hotel porter will be able to make your arrangements or direct you to Theatre Booking Agents.

In addition there is a kiosk at Norrmalmstorg selling tickets for the same day's performances with a reduction of approx. 25 per cent, no booking fee.

In the summer it's open 11am-7.30pm Tues.-Sat. and 11am-5pm Sun. and Mon. During the winter 12am-7.15pm Tues.-Sat., 12am-4pm Sun., 12am-5pm Mon.

CAR HIRE

The international car hire companies have branches in Stockholm city and at Arlanda airport. Your hotel porter will be able to give details and help you with your arrangements.

TIPPING

Hotels and restaurants normally include a service charge of 15 per cent. Doormen, baggage porters etc. are generally given a gratuity.

Taxi drivers are customarily tipped about 10 per cent of the amount shown on the meter in addition to the fare.

SPEED LIMITS - SEAT BELTS

The maximum permitted speed on motorways and dual carriageways is 110 km/h - 68 mph and 90 km/h - 56 mph on other roads except where a lower speed limit is signposted.

The wearing of seat belts in Sweden is compulsory for drivers and front seat passengers.

STOCKHOLM

SIGHTS

See : Old Town★★★ (Gamla Stan) : Stortorget★★, AZ, Köpmangatan★★ AZ **35**, Osterlanggatan★★ AZ ; Royal Warship Vasa★★★ (Wasavarvet) DYZ ; Skansen Open-Air Museum★★★ DY.
Royal Palace★★ (Kungliga Slottet) AZ ; Changing of the Guard★★ ; Apartments★★, Royal Armoury★★, Treasury★ ; Museum★ ; Great Church★★ (Storkyrkan) AZ ; Riddarholmen Church★★ (Riddarholmskyrkan) AZ ; Town Hall★★ (Stadshuset) BYH : ✲★★★, Djurgården DYZ : Waldemarsudde House★★, Rosendal Palace★, Thiel Gallery★ ; Gröna Lunds Tivoli★ DZ.
Kaknäs TV Tower★ (Kaknäs Tornet) ✲★★★ DY ; Gustav Adolf Square★ (Gustav Adolfs Torg) CY**16** ; Kings Gardens★ (Kungsträdgården) CY ; Riddarhouse★ (Riddarhuset) AZ ; German Church★ (Tyska Kyrkan) AZ ; Fjällgatan★ DZ ; Sergels Torg CY**54** – Hötorget★ CY 20.

Museums : Museum of National Antiquities★★★ (Historiska Museet) DY ; National Art Gallery★★ (National Museum) DY **M1** ; Nordic Museum★★ (Nordiska Museet) DY **M2** ; Museum of Far Eastern Antiquities★★ (Ostasiastiska Museet) DY **M3** ; Museum of Modern Art (Moderna Museet) DYZ **M4** ; National Maritime Museum★★ (Sjöhistoriska Museet) DY ; Halwyl Museum★ (Halwylska Museet) CY **M5** ; City Museum★ (Stads Museet) CZ **M6** ; Strindberg Museum★ BX **M7**.

Outskirts : Drottningholm Palace★★ (Drottningholms Slott) W : 12 km BY ; Apartments★★, Gardens★★, Court Theatre★, Chinese Pavilion★ ; Tours by boat★★ (in summer) : Under the Bridges★★ ; Archipelago★★ (Vaxholm, Möja, Sandhamn, Utö), Mälarenlake★ (Gripsholm, Skokloster) ; Haga Park and Pavilion of Gustav III★ (N : 4 km) BX ; Millesgården★ (E : 4 km) DX.

STOCKHOLM Sverige 920 MN2 – pop. 649 686 – ✆ 08.

Svenska Golfförbundet ✆ 753 02 65.

Stockholm-Arlanda N : 41 km ✆ (08) 780 30 30 – SAS : Flygcity, Sveavägen 22 ✆ 780 10 00 – Air Terminal : main railway station.

Motorail for Southern Europe : SJ Travel Agency, Vasagatan 22 ✆ 762 58 15.

To Finland and excursions by boat : contact Stockholm Information Service (see below).

Stockholm Information Service, Tourist Centre, Sverigehuset, Hamngatan 27 ✆ 789 20 00 – Motormännens Riksförbund Kungl. Automobilklubben (Royal Automobile Club) ✆ 67 05 80.

Hamburg 935 – København 630 – Oslo 522.

STOCKHOLM

Biblioteksgatan	CY	2
Drottninggatan	BX, CY	10
Gallerian	CY	14
Hamngatan	CY	
Kungsgatan	BCY	
Sergelgatan	CY	52
Västerlånggatan	AZ	
Österlånggatan	AZ	

Birger Jarlsgatan	CXY	3
Brunkebergstorg	CY	5
Brunnsgränd	AZ	6
Bryggargatan	BY	8
Djurgårdsbron	DY	9
Erstagatan	DZ	13
Gustav Adolfs Torg	CY	16
Götgatan	CZ	17
Herkulesgatan	CY	18
Hötorget	CY	20
Järntorget	AZ	21
Järntorgsgatan	AZ	23
Kindstugatan	AZ	24
Klarabergsgatan	CY	25
Klarabergsviadukten	BY	27
Kornhamnstorg	AZ	28
Kungsbron	BY	30
Kungsträdgårdsgatan	CY	32
Källargränd	AZ	34
Köpmangatan	AZ	35
Lilla Nygatan	AZ	37
Lill-Jans Plan	CX	38
Munkbrogatan	AZ	40
Myntgatan	AZ	41
Norrbro	CY	43
Norrlandsgatan	CY	44
Nybroplan	CY	46
Odenplan	BX	47
Riddarhusgränd	AZ	48
Riddarhustorget	AZ	50
Rådhusgränd	AZ	51
Sergels Torg	CY	54
Slottskajen	AZ	55
Slussplan	AZ	56
Stadshusbron	BY	57
Stallgatan	CY	59
Storkyrkobrinken	AZ	60
Strömbron	CY	61
Strömgatan	CY	63
Södermalmstorg	CZ	64
Södra Blasieholmshamnen	CY	66
Tegelbacken	CY	67
Tegnérlunden	BX	69
Triewaldsgränd	AZ	70
Tunnelgatan	BY	71
Tyska Brinken	AZ	73
Vasagatan	BY	75
Östermalmstorg	DY	76
Östra Järnvägsgatan	BY	78

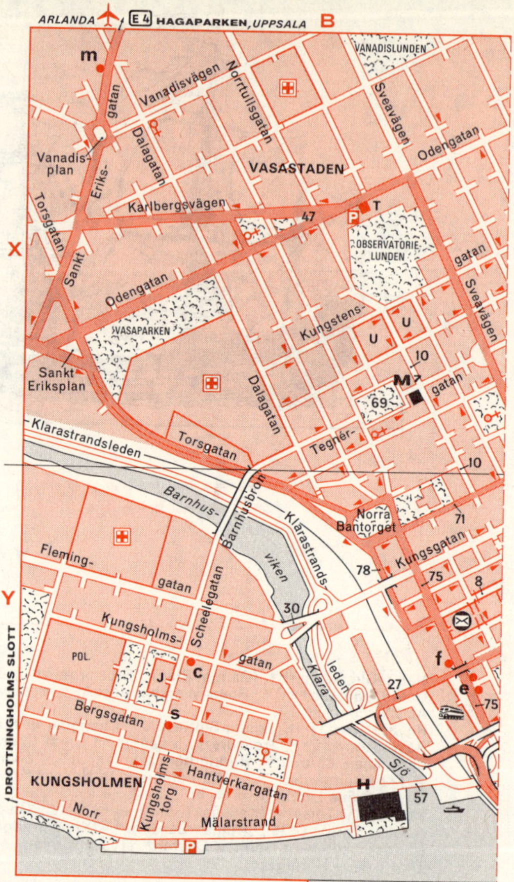

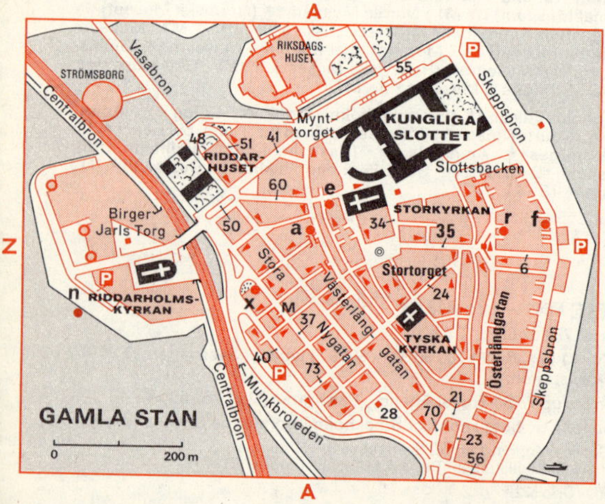

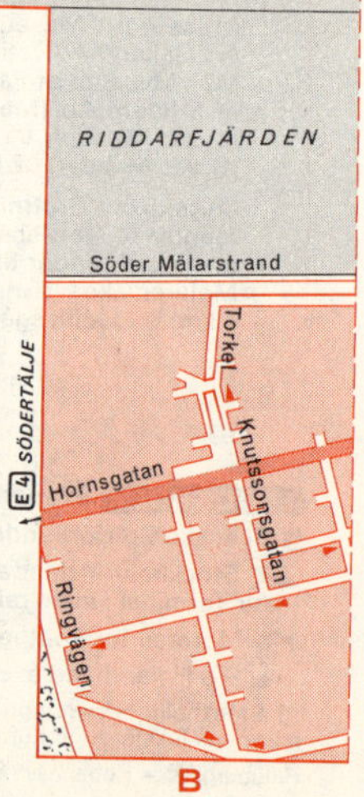

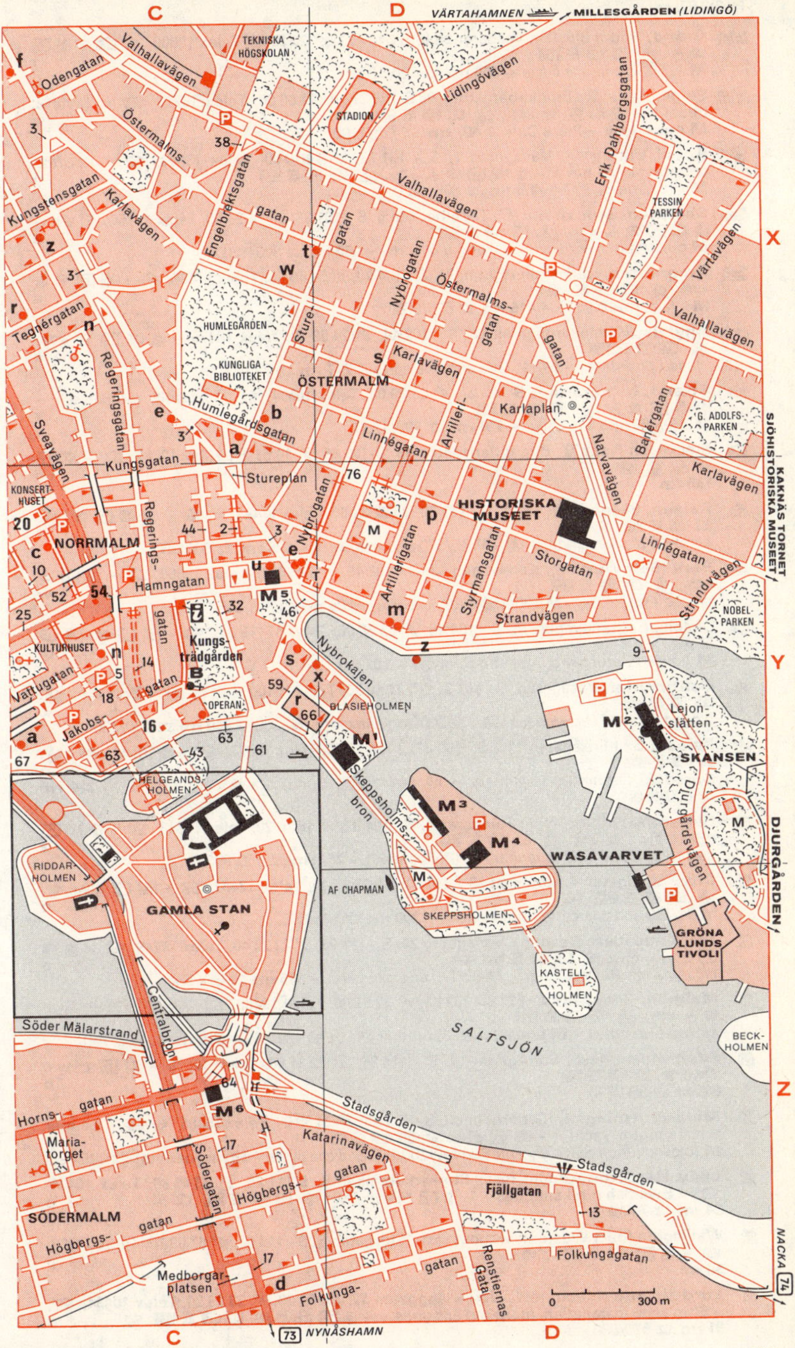
C
D
VÄRTAHAMNEN
MILLESGÅRDEN (LIDINGÖ)
TEKNISKA HÖGSKOLAN
Valhallavägen
Odengatan
Östermalms-
gatan
STADION
Lidingövägen
Erik Dahlbergsgatan
TESSIN PARKEN
Värtavägen
Kungstensgatan
Karlavägen
Engelbrektsgatan
Sture-
gatan
Nybrogatan
Östermalms-
gatan
Valhallavägen
Tegnérgatan
HUMLEGÅRDEN
KUNGLIGA BIBLIOTEKET
ÖSTERMALM
Karlavägen
Karlaplan
G. ADOLFS-PARKEN
Regeringsgatan
Humlegårdsgatan
Linnégatan
Artilleri-
Narvavägen
Banérgatan
Karlavägen
KAKNÄS TORNET
SJÖHISTORISKA MUSEET
Sveavägen
Kungsgatan
Stureplan
KONSERT-HUSET
NORRMALM
Regerings-
gatan
HISTORISKA MUSEET
Artillerigatan
Styrmansgatan
Storgatan
Linnégatan
Strandvägen
Hamngatan
Kungsträdgården
KULTURHUSET
Vattugatan
Jakobs-
gatan
Strandvägen
NOBEL-PARKEN
Nybrokajen
OPERAN
BLASIEHOLMEN
Lejonslätten
SKANSEN
HELGEANDS HOLMEN
Skeppsholmsbron
RIDDAR-HOLMEN
GAMLA STAN
AF CHAPMAN
SKEPPSHOLMEN
WASAVARVET
Djurgårdsvägen
DJURGÅRDEN
GRÖNA LUNDS TIVOLI
KASTELL HOLMEN
SALTSJÖN
BECK-HOLMEN
Söder Mälarstrand
Centralbron
Horns-
gatan
Maria-
torget
Stadsgården
Katarinavägen
Stadsgården
Södergatan
Högbergs-
gatan
Fjällgatan
SÖDERMALM
Högbergs-
gatan
Medborgar-
platsen
Folkunga-
gatan
Renstiernas Gata
Folkungagatan
0
300 m
NACKA
74
73
NYNÄSHAMN
X
Y
Z

Grand, Södra Blasieholmshamnen 8, S - 103 27, 22 10 20, Telex 19500, <, – TV AE E VISA CY **r**
M 175/295 and a la carte – **350 rm** 720/1030.

Sergel Plaza [M], Brunkebergstorg 9, S-103 27, 22 66 00, Telex 16711, « Tasteful decor » – TV AE E VISA CY **n**
M Anna Rella – Plaza Café – **407 rm** 725/1100.

Royal Viking [M], Vasagatan 1, S - 101 23, 14 10 00, Telex 13900, « Rooftop restaurant and bar » – TV AE E VISA BY **f**
M a la carte 81/327 – **400 rm** 805/1200.

Sheraton-Stockholm [M], Tegelbacken 6, S - 101 23, 14 26 00, Telex 17750, <, – TV AE E VISA CY **a**
M buffet lunch 65/dinner 150 and a la carte – **460 rm** 800/1200.

Amaranten, Kungsholmsgatan 31, S - 104 20, 54 10 60, Telex 17498, – TV AE E VISA BY **c**
M a la carte 100/215 – **415 rm** 535/855.

Anglais, Humlegårdsgatan 23, S - 102 44, 24 99 00, Telex 19475 – TV AE E VISA CX **a**
closed Christmas – **M** 115/185 and a la carte – **211 rm** 775/1100.

Strand, Nybrokajen 9, S-103 27, 22 29 00, Telex 10504, <, « Tastefully furnished » – TV AE E VISA CDY **x**
M 130/450 and a la carte – **134 rm** 790/1250.

Stockholm Plaza [M], Birger Jarlsgatan 29, S-103 95, 14 51 20, Telex 13982, – TV CX **e**
155 rm.

Reisen, Skeppsbron 12-14, S - 111 30, 22 32 60, Telex 17494, <, – TV AE E VISA AZ **f**
closed 3 days at Christmas – **M** 45/370 and a la carte – **125 rm** 800/950.

Park (Best Western), Karlavägen 43, S - 102 45, 22 96 20, Telex 10666, – TV AE E VISA CX **w**
closed Christmas – **M** 135/158 and a la carte – **205 rm** 845/975.

Diplomat, Strandvägen 7c, S - 104 40, 63 58 00, Telex 17119, <, – TV AE E VISA DY **m**
M *(closed Saturday dinner and Sunday)* – **132 rm** 675/1100.

Continental, Vasagatan, S - 101 21, 24 40 20, Telex 10100 – rest TV AE E VISA BY **e**
closed 23 to 27 December – **M** 100/300 and a la carte 180/250 – **250 rm** 750/1200.

Palace, S : t Eriksgatan 115, S - 100 31, 24 12 20, Telex 19877, – TV AE E VISA BX **m**
closed 23 December-1 January – **M** (bar menu Sunday)/a la carte 90/276 – **214 rm** 600/860.

Birger Jarl without rest., Tulegatan 8, S - 104 32, 15 10 20, Telex 11843, – TV wc wc AE E VISA CX **z**
closed 23 December-2 January – (unlicensed) – **252 rm** 550/800.

City, Slöjdgatan 7, Hötorget, S - 111 81, 22 22 40, Telex 12487, – TV wc AE E VISA CY **c**
M 84/150 and a la carte (unlicensed) – **300 rm** 545/695.

Terminus (Best Western), Vasagatan 20, S - 101 23, 22 26 40, Telex 11749, – TV wc wc AE E VISA BY **e**
closed 23 to 28 December – **M** 88/170 and a la carte – **155 rm** 665/840.

Malmen, Götgatan 49 - 51, S - 102 61, 22 61 80, Telex 19489, – TV wc wc AE E VISA CZ **d**
closed Christmas – **M** buffet lunch 32/dinner a la carte 139/200 – **280 rm** 590/760.

Eden without rest., Sturegatan 10, S - 114 36, 22 31 60, Telex 10570 – TV wc wc AE E VISA CX **b**
60 rm 350/890.

Mälardrottningen, Riddarholmen, S - 111 28, 24 36 00, Telex 15468, <, « Former private motor-yacht » – TV wc AE E VISA AZ **n**
M *(closed lunch Saturday and Sunday)* 250/685 and a la carte – **59 rm (cabins)** 395/895.

Lady Hamilton without rest., Storkyrkobrinken 5, S-111 28, 23 46 80, Telex 10434, « Swedish rural antiques » – TV wc wc AE E VISA AZ **e**
34 rm 760/975.

Wellington (Best Western) without rest., Storgatan 6, S - 114 51, 67 09 10, Telex 17963, – TV wc wc DY **p**
50 rm.

Lord Nelson without rest., Västerlånggatan 22, S-111 29, 23 23 90, Telex 10434, « Ship style installation, maritime antiques » – TV wc AE E VISA AZ **a**
31 rm 570/830.

XXXX **Operakällaren** (at Opera House), S-111 86, ☎ 24 27 00, « Opulent classical decor » – AE ⓓ E VISA CY
closed 30 June-27 July and Christmas Day – **M** a la carte 123/508.

XXX ✿ **Coq Blanc,** Regeringsgatan 111, S - 111 39, ☎ 11 61 53 – ▤. AE ⓓ E VISA CX **n**
closed Saturday except dinner September-May, Sunday, 5 July-5 August and Bank Holidays – **M** a la carte 175/335
Spec. Marinated tenderloin with herb sauce, Fillets of reindeer à la maison, Strawberry flambé du patron.

XXX ✿ **L'Escargot,** Scheelegatan 8, S - 112 23, ☎ 53 05 77 – AE ⓓ E VISA BY **s**
closed Sunday and Bank Holidays – **M** a la carte 190/341
Spec. Escargots beurre roquefort, Crêpe de pommes de terre au caviar Beluga chinois, Poisson et crustacés variés selon la saison.

XX **Teatergrillen,** Nybrogatan 3, S-114 34, ☎ 10 70 44, « Theatre atmosphere » – ▤. AE ⓓ E VISA CY **e**
closed lunch Saturday, Sunday and Bank Holidays, Christmas and July – **M** a la carte 160/360.

XX **Wärdshuset Stallmästaregården,** Norrtull, S-113 47, N : 2 km on E.4 ☎ 24 39 10, ←, « 17C Inn, Waterside setting », 🚗 – Ⓟ. AE ⓓ E VISA by Sveavägen BX
closed Christmas – **M** a la carte 200/350.

XX **Clas På Hörnet** with rm, Surbrunnsgatan 20, ☎ 16 51 30, « 18C atmosphere » – TV ⋒wc ☎. AE ⓓ E VISA. ✻ CX **f**
closed 23 to 26 December – **M** 115/207 and a la carte – **10 rm** ☐ 760/1300.

XX ✿ **Gourmet,** Tegnérgatan 10, S - 113 58, ☎ 31 43 98 – ▤. AE ⓓ E VISA CX **r**
closed Saturday lunch, Sunday and Bank Holidays – **M** a la carte 180/360
Spec. Flambéed sea-crayfish.

XX **Riche,** Birger Jarlsgatan 4, S-114 34, ☎ 23 68 40 – ▤. AE ⓓ E VISA CY **e**
closed lunch Sunday and Bank Holidays and Christmas – **M** 110 and a la carte 182/260.

XX **Paul and Norbert,** Strandvägen 9, S - 114 56, ☎ 63 81 83 – AE ⓓ E VISA DY **m**
closed Saturday, Sunday, 7 July-3 August, 24 December-6 January and Bank Holidays – **M** (booking essential) a la carte 180/325.

XX ✿ **Eriks,** Strandvägskajen 17, S - 114 56, ☎ 60 60 60, Seafood, « Converted barge » – AE ⓓ E VISA DY **z**
closed Sunday and Christmas-New Year – **M** 105/335 and a la carte
Spec. Shellfish consomme with quennelles, Turbot with saffron flavoured stuffing, Noilly Prat sauce and vegetables, Grand Dessert.

XX **Coq Roti,** Sturegatan 19, S - 114 36, ☎ 10 25 67 – ▤. AE ⓓ E VISA CDX **t**
closed Saturday lunch, Sunday and 3 weeks July-August – **M** 350/375 and a la carte.

XX **Källaren Aurora,** Munkbron 11, S-111 28, ☎ 21 93 59, « In the cellars of a 17C house » – ▤. AE ⓓ E VISA AZ **x**
closed Saturday lunch, Sunday, 23 to 28 December and Bank Holidays – **M** 180/260.

XX **Fem Små Hus,** Nygränd 10, S - 111 30, ☎ 10 87 75, « Cellars, antiques » – ▤. AE ⓓ E VISA AZ **r**
M a la carte 190/385.

X ✿ **Wedholms Fisk,** Nybrokajen 17 – AE ⓓ E CY **s**
closed Sunday and July – **M** a la carte 210/247
Spec. Seafood.

X **KB,** Smålandsgatan 7, S-111 46, ☎ 11 02 32 – ⓓ E VISA CY **u**
closed Saturday lunch and Sunday – **M** a la carte 275/335.

X **Ett Rum och Kök,** Nybrogatan 46, S-114 40, ☎ 61 12 02 – AE ⓓ E DX **s**
closed Saturday, Sunday, 15 July-15 August, 23 December-7 January and Bank Holidays – **M** a la carte 130/288.

at Arlanda Airport N : by E4 – BX – ✆ 0760 Arlanda :

🏨 SAS Arlandia, 190 45 Stockholm - Arlanda ☎ 618 00, Telex 13018, ≘s, ▣, ✂ – ⇅ ▤ TV ☎ ♿ Ⓟ. 🏛 – **300 rm**.

in Djurgården E : 2 km by Strandvägen – DY – ✉ ✆ 08 Stockholm :

XXX **Djurgårdsbrunns Wärdshus,** Djurgårdsbrunnsvägen 68, S - 115 25, ☎ 67 90 95, ←, « In Djurgården Park » – AE ⓓ E VISA
closed Sunday dinner – **M** a la carte 160/298.

at Solna NW : 5 km by Sveavägen – BX – and E 4 – ✉ Solna – ✆ 08 Stockholm :

XXX ✿ **Ulriksdals Wärdshus,** 171 71 Solna, N : 3 km in Ulriksdals Slottspark ☎ 85 08 15, ←, « Former inn in Royal Park », 🚗 – Ⓟ. AE ⓓ E VISA
closed 24 to 26 December – **M** a la carte 250/365
Spec. Avocado butterfly with Swedish roe, Noisettes of reindeer with Juniper cream sauce, Cloudberry parfait.

XX **Finsmakaren,** Råsundavägen 9, 171 52 Solna, ☎ 27 67 71 – AE ⓓ E
closed Saturday, Sunday, 30 June-4 August and 23 December-7 January – **M** a la carte 150/249.

Switzerland
Suisse
Schweiz
Svizzera

Basle
Geneva
Zürich

PRACTICAL INFORMATION

LOCAL CURRENCY

Swiss Franc : 100 F = 48.15 US $ (Jan. 86)

LANGUAGES SPOKEN

German, French and Italian are usually spoken in all administrative departments, shops, hotels and restaurants.

AIRLINES

A large number of international airlines operate out of the main Swiss airports. For general information ring the number given after the airport symbol and name in the text of each town.

POSTAL SERVICES

In large towns, post offices are open from 7.30am to noon and 1.45pm to 6.30pm, and Saturdays untill 11am. The telephone system is fully automatic.

SHOPPING

Department stores are generally open from 8am to 4pm, except on Saturdays when they close at 4 or 5pm.

In the index of street names, those printed in red are where the principal shops are found.

TIPPING

In hotels, restaurants and cafés the service charge is generally included in the prices.

SPEED LIMITS

The speed limit on motorways is 120 km/h - 74 mph, on other roads 80 km/h - 50 mph, and in built up areas 50 km/h - 31 mph.

SEAT BELTS

The wearing of seat belts is compulsory in all Swiss cantons.

BASLE (BASEL) 4000 Switzerland 66 ⑩, 216 ④ – pop. 180 463 – alt. 273 – ☎ Basle and environs from France 19-41-61, from Switzerland 061.

See : Cathedral (Münster)★★ : ≤★ CY – Zoological Garden★★★ AZ – The Port (Hafen)☼★, Exposition★ CX – Fish Market Fountain★ (Fischmarktbrunnen) BY – Old Streets★ BY – Oberer Rheinweg ≤★ CY – Museums : Fine Arts★★★ (Kunstmuseum) CY, Historical★ (Historisches Museum) CY, Ethnographic (Museum für Völkerkunde)★ CY **M1** – Haus zum Kirschgarten★ CZ, Antiquities (Antikenmuseum)★ CY – ☼★ from Bruderholz Water Tower 3,5 km by ⑥.

18 private ✆ 89 68 50 91 at Hagenthal-le-Bas (68-France).

✈ Basle-Mulhouse ✆ 57.31.11 at Basle (Switzerland) by Zollfreie Strasse 8 km and at Saint-Louis (68-France) ✆ 89 69 00 00.

ℹ Blumenrain 2 ✆ 22.50.50, Télex 63318 – Automobile Club Suisse, Birsigstr. 4 ✆ 23.39.33 – T.C.S., Petrihof, Steinentorstr. 13 ✆ 23.19.55.

Paris 551 ⑧ – Bern 95 ⑤ – Freiburg 71 ① – Lyon 387 ⑧ – Mulhouse 35 ⑧ – Strasbourg 145 ①.

Plan on following pages

Trois Rois, Blumenrain 8, ✉ 4001, ✆ 25.52.52, Telex 62937, ≤, 😀 – |♦| ▤ TV ☎ – 🏛 80. AE ⓓ E VISA. ✻ rest — BY a
st. : Rôtisserie des Rois **M** 85 ♁ - rest **Rhy-Deck M** a la carte approx. 50 ♁ – ☐ 12 – **90 rm** 150/355, 13 apartments 460/710.

Hilton M ⛵, Aeschengraben 31, ✉ 4002, ✆ 22.66.22, Telex 965555, 🏊 – |♦| ▤ TV ☎ ♿ 🚗 – 🏛 50-300. AE ⓓ E VISA. ✻ rest — CZ d
st. : M a la carte 60/80 ♁ – ☐ 9,50 – **217 rm** 125/250, 10 apartments.

Hôtel International M ⛵, Steinentorstrasse 25, ✉ 4001, ✆ 22.18.70, Telex 962370, 🏊 – |♦| ▤ TV ☎ 🚗 – 🏛 25-250. AE ⓓ E VISA. ✻ rest — BZ b
st. : Steinenpick M a la carte 30/65♁ - **Rôt. Charolaise M** a la carte 60/90 ♁ – **210 rm** ☐ 190/260, 5 apartments 250/500.

H. Basel M ⛵, Münzgasse 12, ✉ 4001, ✆ 25.24.23, Telex 64199, « Tasteful decor » – |♦| ▤ rest TV ☎. AE ⓓ E VISA — BY x
st. : M a la carte 40/58 ♁ – **72 rm** ☐ 105/225.

Euler, Centralbahnplatz 14, ✉ 4051 ✆ 23.45.00, Telex 962215 – |♦| ▤ TV ☎ 🚗 – 🏛 120. AE ⓓ E VISA. ✻ rest — BZ a
st. : M a la carte 60/95 ♁ – ☐ 10 – **53 rm** 130/265, 11 apartments 330/500.

✿ **Europe and rest. Quatre Saisons** M, Clarastrasse 43, ✉ 4058, ✆ 26.80.80, Telex 64103, 😀 – |♦| ▤ TV ☎ 🚗 – 🏛 180. AE ⓓ E VISA. ✻ rest — CX k
st. : M *(closed Sunday)* a la carte 75/95 ♁ – **170 rm** ☐ 102/190.

Schweizerhof, Centralbahnplatz 1, ✉ 4002, ✆ 22.28.33, Telex 962373 – |♦| ▤ TV ☎ P – 🏛 30-90. AE ⓓ E VISA — CZ n
st. : M a la carte approx. 65 ♁ – **75 rm** ☐ 100/180.

Victoria M, Centralbahnplatz 3, ✉ 4002, ✆ 22.55.66, Telex 62362 – |♦| ▤ rest TV ☎ – 🏛 25 – **115 rm.** — CZ n

Métropol M without rest, Elisabethenanlage 5 ✉ 4051 ✆ 22.77.21, Telex 962268 – |♦| TV ☎ – 🏛 120. AE ⓓ E VISA — CZ a
st. : 46 rm ☐ 93/137.

Alexander M, Riehenring 85, ✉ 4058, ✆ 26.70.00, Telex 63325 – |♦| TV ⛲wc ☎ 🚗. AE ⓓ E VISA — CX s
st. : M *(closed Sunday)* a la carte 35/55 ♁ – **64 rm** ☐ 60/150.

City, Henric Petri-Strasse 12, ✉ 4010, ✆ 23.78.11, Telex 962427 – |♦| ▤ 🛁wc ☎. AE ⓓ E VISA — CZ f
st. : M a la carte approx. 50 ♁ – **85 rm** ☐ 70/150.

Krafft am Rhein, Rheingasse 12, ✉ 4058, ✆ 26.88.77, Telex 64360, ≤, 😀 – |♦| 🛁wc ⛲wc ☎. AE ⓓ E VISA — CY z
st. : M a la carte approx. 55 ♁ – **52 rm** ☐ 52/140 – P 95/140.

Bernina without rest, Innere Margarethenstrasse 14, ✉ 4051, ✆ 23.73.00, Telex 963813 – |♦| TV 🛁wc ⛲wc ☎. AE ⓓ E VISA — BZ u
st. : 35 rm ☐ 65/200 – P 100/120.

Drachen, Aeschenvorstadt 24, ✉ 4010, ✆ 23.90.90, Telex 962346 – |♦| ▤ rm 🛁wc ⛲wc ☎ 🚗 – 🏛 40. AE ⓓ E VISA — CY w
st. : M a la carte 50/75 ♁ – **41 rm** ☐ 88/168 – P 120/150.

Muenchnerhof, Riehenring 75, ✉ 4058 ✆ 26.77.80, Telex 64476 – |♦| 🛁wc ⛲wc ☎. AE ⓓ E VISA – **st. : M** 10/30 ♁ – **40 rm** ☐ 70/180 – P 80/120. — CX u

Flügelrad, Küchengasse 20, ✉ 4051, ✆ 23.42.41 – ⛲wc — BZ v
st. : M *(closed Saturday dinner and Sunday)* a la carte approx. 40 ♁ – **30 rm** ☐ 40/130.

XXXX ✿✿ **Stucki,** Bruderholzallee 42, ✉ 4059, ✆ 35.82.22, « Terrace » – E VISA — by ⑥
closed 20 July-10 August, Sunday and Monday – **st. : M** 85/140
Spec. Homard grillé à la sauge, Rognon de veau rôti, Tarte fine chaude aux quetsches (15 July-15 October).

XX **La Marmite du Beaujolais,** Klybeckstrasse 15, ✉ 4057, ✆ 33.03.54, Modern decor – ▤. AE ⓓ E VISA — CX e
closed Saturday, Sunday and Bank Holidays – **st. : M** a la carte 40/60 ♁.

XX **Donati,** St-Johannsvorstadt 48, ✉ 4056, ✆ 57.09.19, Italian cuisine — BX p
closed July and Monday – **st. : M** 23/27 ♁.

X Taverne l'Escargot (basement of SBB Railway Station), Centralbahnstrasse 10, ✉ 4002, ✆ 22.53.33, Telex 62538 – ▤ — BZ

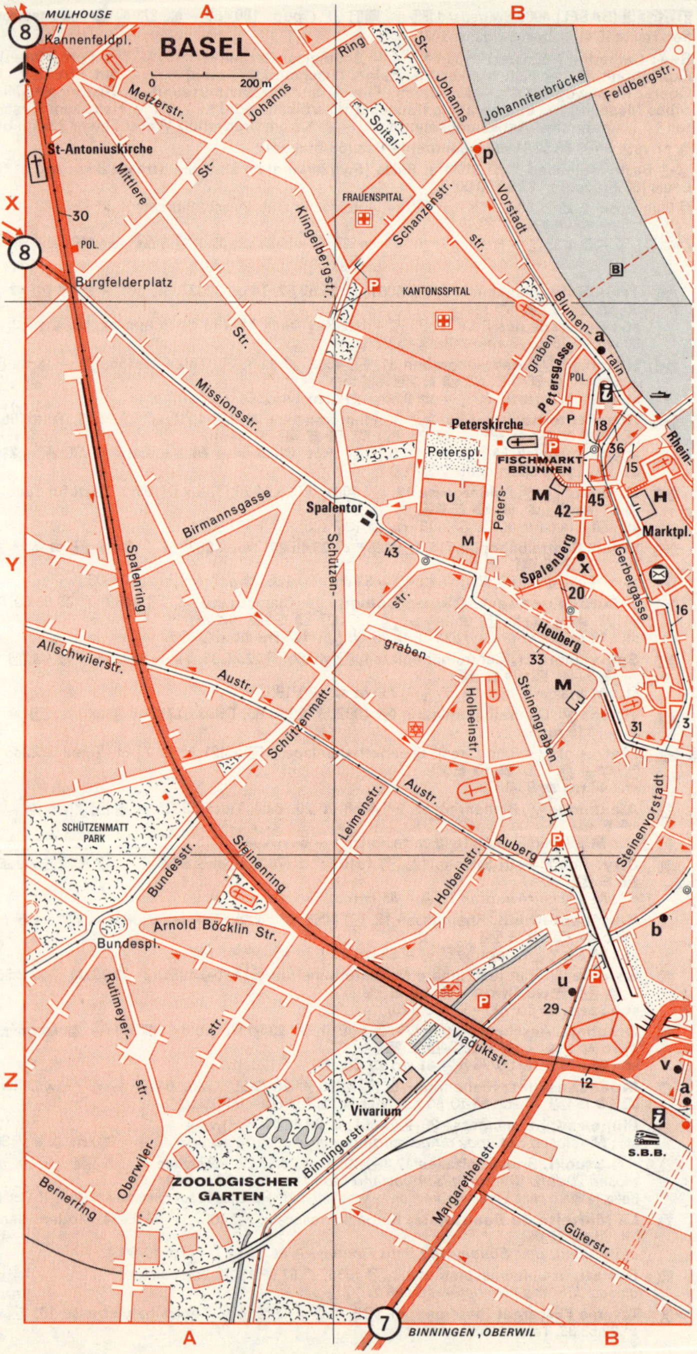

BASEL
0
200 m
MULHOUSE
A
B
X
Y
Z
8
Kannenfeldpl.
St-Antoniuskirche
30
POL.
Burgfelderplatz
Metzerstr.
Mittlere
St-
Johanns
Ring
Spital-
St-
Johanns
Vorstadt
Johanniterbrücke
Feldbergstr.
FRAUENSPITAL
Klingelbergstr.
Schanzenstr.
str.
KANTONSSPITAL
Str.
Missionsstr.
Blumen-
rain
graben
Petersgasse
POL.
18
36
15
Rhein-
Peterskirche
Peterspl.
FISCHMARKT-
BRUNNEN
M
42
45
H
Marktpl.
U
Spalentor
43
Schützen-
str.
M
Peters-
Spalenberg
X
20
Gerbergasse
16
Birmannsgasse
Spalenring
graben
Heuberg
33
M
Allschwilerstr.
Austr.
Schützenmatt-
Holbeinstr.
Steinengraben
31
3
Austr.
Leimenstr.
Auberg
Steinenvorstadt
SCHÜTZENMATT
PARK
Bundesstr.
Steinenring
Holbeinstr.
b
Arnold Böcklin Str.
Bundespl.
u
29
Rutimeyer-
str.
str.
Viaduktstr.
v
a
12
Vivarium
S.B.B.
Binningerstr.
Margarethenstr.
Oberwiler-
ZOOLOGISCHER
GARTEN
Bernerring
Güterstr.
7
BINNINGEN, OBERWIL

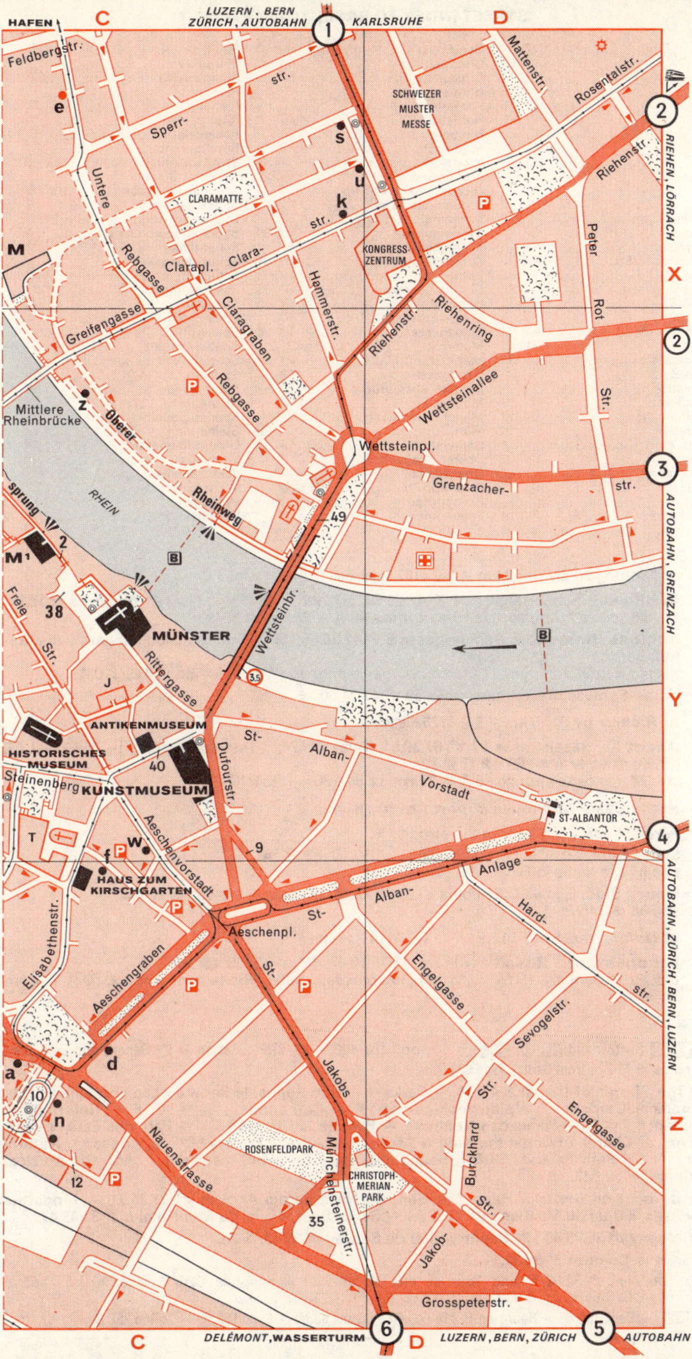
HAFEN
C
LUZERN, BERN
ZÜRICH, AUTOBAHN
KARLSRUHE
D
Feldbergstr.
Sperr-
str.
SCHWEIZER MUSTER MESSE
Mattenstr.
Rosentalstr.
RIEHEN, LÖRRACH
Riehenstr.
CLARAMATTE
Untere
Rebgasse
Clarapl.
Clara-
str.
KONGRESS-ZENTRUM
Hammerstr.
Peter
Rot
Str.
X
M
Greifengasse
Claragraben
Riehenstr.
Riehenring
Wettsteinallee
Mittlere Rheinbrücke
Oberer
Rebgasse
Rheinweg
RHEIN
Wettsteinpl.
Grenzacher-
str.
AUTOBAHN, GRENZACH
sprung
M¹
Freie
Str.
MÜNSTER
Wettsteinbr.
Rittergasse
Y
ANTIKENMUSEUM
HISTORISCHES MUSEUM
Steinenberg
KUNSTMUSEUM
Dufourstr.
St-
Alban-
Vorstadt
ST-ALBANTOR
Aeschenvorstadt
HAUS ZUM KIRSCHGARTEN
Anlage
Alban-
St-
Aeschenpl.
Hard-
str.
AUTOBAHN, ZÜRICH, BERN, LUZERN
Elisabethenstr.
Aeschengraben
St-
Engelgasse
Sevogelstr.
Jakobs
Str.
Z
Burckhard
Engelgasse
Nauenstrasse
ROSENFELDPARK
Münchensteinerstr.
CHRISTOPH-MERIAN-PARK
Str.
Jakob-
Grosspeterstr.
C
DELÉMONT, WASSERTURM
D
LUZERN, BERN, ZÜRICH
AUTOBAHN

STREET INDEX TO BASEL TOWN PLAN

Aeschenvorstadt .... CYZ
Barfüsserpl. .... BY 3
Centralbahnpl. .... CZ 10
Clarapl. CX
Eisengasse .... BY 15
Falknerstr. .... BY 16
Freie Str. .... CY
Gerbergasse .... BY
Greifengasse .... CY
Marktpl. .... BY
Steinenvorstadt .... BY

Aeschengraben .... CZ
Aeschenpl. .... CZ
Allschwilerstr. .... AY
Arnold Böcklin-Str. .... AZ
Auberg .... BYZ
Augustinergasse .... CY 2
Austr. .... ABY
Bernerring .... AZ
Birmannsgasse .... AY
Blumenrain .... BY
Brunngässlein .... CY 9
Bundespl. .... AZ
Bundesstr. .... AYZ
Burgfelderpl. .... AX
Centralbahnstr. .... CZ 12
Claragraben .... CY
Clarastr. CX
Dufourstr. .... CY
Elisabethenstr. .... CZ
Engelgasse .... DZ
Feldbergstr. .... BCX
Fischmarktpl. .... BY 18
Gemsberg .... BY 20
Grenzacherstr. .... DY
Grosspeterstr. .... DZ
Güterstr. .... BZ
Hammerstr. .... CXY
Hardstr. .... DZ
Heuberg .... BY
Holbeinstr. .... BYZ
Innere-
Margarethenstr. .... BZ 29
Jacob Burckhardt-Str. .... DZ
Johanniterbrücke .... BX
Kannenfeldpl. .... AX
Kannenfeldstr. .... AX 30
Klingelbergstr. .... AX
Kohlenberg .... BY 31
Leimenstr. .... BY
Leonhardsgraben .... BY 33
Lindenhofstr. .... CZ 35
Margarethenstr. .... BZ
Marktgasse .... BY 36
Mattenstr. .... DX
Metzerstr. .... AX
Missionsstr. .... AY
Mittlere-Rheinbrücke .... CY
Mittlere-Str. .... AXY
Münchensteinerstr. .... CZ
Münsterpl. .... CY 38
Nauenstr. .... CZ
Oberer-Rheinweg .... CY
Oberwilerstr. .... AZ
Peter Rot-Str. .... DXY
Petersgasse .... BY
Petersgraben .... BY
Peterspl. .... BY
Rebgasse .... CY
Rheinsprung .... BCY
Riehenring .... DY
Riehenstr. .... DY
Rittergasse .... CY
Rosentalstr. .... DX
Rutimeyerstr. .... AZ
St-Alban-Anlage .... CDZ
St-Alban-Graben .... CY 40
St-Alban-Vorstadt .... CDY
St-Jakobs-Str. .... CDZ
St-Johanns-Ring .... ABX
St-Johanns-Vorstadt .... BX
Schanzenstr. .... BX
Schneidergasse .... BY 42
Schützengraben .... ABY
Schützenmattstr. .... ABY
Sevogelstr. .... DZ
Spalenberg .... BY
Spalenring .... AY
Spalenvorstadt .... BY 43
Sperrstr. CX
Spitalstr. .... BX
Stadthausgasse .... BY 45
Steinenberg .... CY
Steinengraben .... BY
Steinenring .... AYZ
Untere-Rebgasse CX
Viaduktstr. .... BZ
Wettsteinallee .... DY
Wettsteinbrücke .... CY
Wettsteinpl. .... CDY
Wettsteinstr. .... CY 49

at Binningen by ⑦ : 2 km – ✉ **4102** Binningen :

Schlüssel, Schlüsselgasse 1 ✆ **47.25.66,** – 🛗 wc wc ☎ 🅿. AE ⓓ E VISA
st. : M *(closed Sunday)* a la carte approx. 45 – **32 rm** 50/90.

XXX **Schloss Binningen,** Schlossgasse 5 ✆ **47.20.55,** « 16C mansion, elegantly decorated, garden » – 🅿. AE E VISA
closed 6 to 21 July, 8 to 17 March, Sunday dinner and Monday – **st. : M** 80/110.

XXX Holee-Schloss, Hasenrainstrasse 59 ✆ **47.24.30,** ≤ – ▤.

at Riehen by ② : 5 km – ✉ **4125** Riehen :

Ascot Ⓜ, Baselstrasse 67 ✆ **67.39.51, Telex 62424,** « Tasteful decor » – 🛗 ▤ rest TV wc wc ☎. AE ⓓ E VISA
st. : M a la carte approx. 55 – **22 rm** 84/180 – P 134/168.

at the Basle-Mulhouse airport : by ⑧ : 8 km :

XX **Airport rest,** 5th floor in the airport, ≤.
Swiss Side, ✉ 4030 Bâle ✆ 57.32.32 – ▤. AE ⓓ E VISA
st. : M a la carte 45/60.
French Side, ✉ 68300 St-Louis ✆ 89 69 77 48 St-Louis – ▤. AE ⓓ E VISA
st. : M 45/145 FF.

at Hofstetten by ⑦ : 12,5 km – ✉ **4114** Hofstetten :

X **Landgasthof "Rössli"** with rm, ✆ **75.10.47,** – 🅿. AE ⓓ VISA
closed 10 January-15 February and Wednesday – **st. : M** a la carte approx. 50 – **7 rm** 30/60.

GENEVA Switzerland 74 ⑥, 217 ⑪ – pop. 157 406 – alt. 375 – Casino – Geneva and Environs : from France 19-41-22 ; from Switzerland 022.

See : The Shores of the lake ≤★★★ – Parks★★ : Mon Repos, la Perle du Lac and Villa Barton – Botanical Gardens★ : alpine rock-garden★★ – Cathedral★ : ✳★★ FY **F** – Reformation Monument★ FYZ **D** – Palais des Nations★ – Parc de la Grange★ GY – Parc des Eaux-Vives★ – Nave★ of Church of Christ the King – Museums : Art and History★★★ GZ, Ariana★★, Natural History★★ GZ, Petit Palais★ GZ **M1**, Baur Collection★ (in a 19C mansion) GZ **M2**, Old Musical Instruments★ GZ **M3**.

Exc. : by boat on the lake Rens. Cie Gén. de Nav., Jardin Anglais ✆ 21.25.21 – Mouettes genevoises, 8 quai du Mt-Blanc ✆ 32.29.44 – Swiss Boat, 4 quai du Mont-Blanc ✆ 32.47.47.

18 at Cologny ✆ 35.75.40 ; 18 Country Club du Bossey ✆ 50 43 75 25.

✈ Genève-Cointrin ✆ 99.31.11.

🅸 gare Cornavin ✆ 32.53.40 and Tour de l'Ile ✆ 28.72.33 Automobile Club Suisse, 10 bd Théâtre ✆ 28.07.66 - T.C. Suisse, 9 r. P.-Fatio ✆ 37.12.12.

Paris 513 ⑦ – Bern 154 ② – Bourg-en-B. 118 ⑦ – Lausanne 63 ② – Lyon 159 ⑦ – Torino 252 ⑥.

Plan on following pages

1° - *Right bank (Cornavin Railway Station - Les Quais - B.I.T.)*

Richemond, Brunswick garden, ✉ 1201, ✆ 31.14.00, Telex 22598, ←, – rest – 50. AE ① E VISA. ✂ rest FY u
st. : rest **Le Jardin M** a la carte 55/95 and see also **Le Gentilhomme** below – **68 rm** 180/450, 30 apartments.

Rhône M, quai Turrettini, ✉ 1201 ✆ 31.98.31, Telex 22213, ← – P – 25-150. AE ① E VISA. ✂ rest EY r
st. : M 37 (dinner a la carte) and see also Rôt. **Le Neptune** below – **290 rm** 170/450, bedrooms for no smokers, 29 apartments.

Noga Hilton M, 19 quai Mt-Blanc ✉ 1201, ✆ 31.98.11, Telex 289704, ← lake and Mt-Blanc, – – 450. AE ① E VISA GY y
st. : see rest. **Le Cygne** below - **La Grignotière M** a la carte approx. 55 - **Le Bistroquai M** a la carte approx. 30 – 17 – **300 rm** 250/400, 20 apartments.

Président M, 47 quai Wilson, ✉ 1211, ✆ 31.10.00, Telex 22780, ← lake – P – 25-80. AE ① E VISA. ✂ rest GX d
st. : M a la carte 65/130 **La Palmeraie M** a la carte approx 50 – 19 – **160 rm** 195/355, 30 apartments.

Les Bergues, 33 quai Bergues, ✉ 1201, ✆ 31.50.50, Telex 23383, ← – – 350. AE ① E VISA FY k
st. : Le Pavillon M a la carte approx. 60 and see also rest **Amphitryon** below – 17 – **117 rm** 245/420, 8 apartments.

Beau Rivage, 13 quai Mont-Blanc, ✉ 1201, ✆ 31.02.21, Telex 23362, ← lake – P – 30-200. AE ① E VISA FY d
st. : M see rest. **Le Chat Botté** below - **Le Quai 13 M** a la carte approx 55 – 15 – **115 rm** 150/370, 8 apartments.

Ramada Renaissance M, 19 r. Zurich, ✉ 1201, ✆ 31.02.41, Telex 289109 – – 150. AE ① E VISA. ✂ rest FX s
st. : La Toquade *(Closed July and August)* **M** a la carte 60/80 - **La Cortille M** 57/75 **café Ragueneau M** a la carte approx. 40 – 18 – **211 rm** 240/290, 8 apartments.

Paix, 11 quai Mont-Blanc, ✉ 1201, ✆ 32.61.50, Telex 22552, ← – – 80. AE ① E VISA. ✂ rest FY s
st. : M a la carte 70/95 – 14 – **91 rm** 145/340, 11 apartments.

Bristol M, 10 r. Mont-Blanc, ✉ 1201, ✆ 32 38 00, Telex 23739 – rest – 40-120. AE ① E VISA FY w
st. : M a la carte 60/90 – 14 – **100 rm** 190/325, 4 apartments 550.

P.L.M. Rotary M, 18 r. Cendrier, ✉ 1201, ✆ 31.52.00, Telex 289999 – rest. AE ① E VISA. ✂ rest FY t
st. : M 30/45 – 12 – **94 rm** 150/260.

Warwick-Méditerranée M, 14 r. Lausanne, ✉ 1201, ✆ 31.62.50, Telex 23630 – – 200. AE ① E VISA FY n
st. : M *(closed Saturday and Sunday)* a la carte 60/105 – **164 rm** 160/250, 4 apartments.

Angleterre, 17 quai Mt-Blanc, ✉ 1201, ✆ 32.81.80, Telex 22668, ← – rest. AE ① E VISA. ✂ GY t
st. : M a la carte 50/75 – **60 rm** 150/310, 7 apartments 350/650.

Cornavin without rest, 33 bd James-Fazy, ✉ 1211, ✆ 32.21.00, Telex 22853 – . AE ① E VISA EY t
st. : 125 rm 100/185.

Berne, 26 r. Berne, ✉ 1201, ✆ 31.60.00, Telex 22764 – – 30-100. AE ① E VISA. ✂ rest FY x
st. : M 25 – **92 rm** 128/171 – P 136/178.

Ambassador, 21 quai Bergues, ✉ 1201, ✆ 31.72.00, Telex 23231 – – 40. AE ① E VISA FY p
st. : M 36/50 – **92 rm** 88/224.

Amat-Carlton M, 22 r. Amat, ✉ 1202, ✆ 31.68.50, Telex 27595 – kitchenette rest FX a
123 rm.

Alba without rest, 19 r. Mt-Blanc, ✉ 1201, ✆ 32.56.00, Telex 23930 – wc. AE ① E VISA FY a
st. : 60 rm 135/185.

Cristal M without rest, 4 r. Pradier ✉ 1201 ✆ 31.34.00, Telex 289926 – wc wc. AE ① E VISA FY e
st. : 79 rm 120/180.

Savoy M, 8 pl. Cornavin ✉ 1201 ✆ 31.12.55, Telex 27951 – wc. AE ① E VISA EY y
st. : M *(closed Saturday dinner and Sunday)* a la carte 30/60 – **50 rm** 117/171 – P 101/128.

Suisse M without rest, 10 pl. Cornavin, ✉ 1201, ✆ 32.66.30, Telex 23868 – wc wc EY y
60 rm.

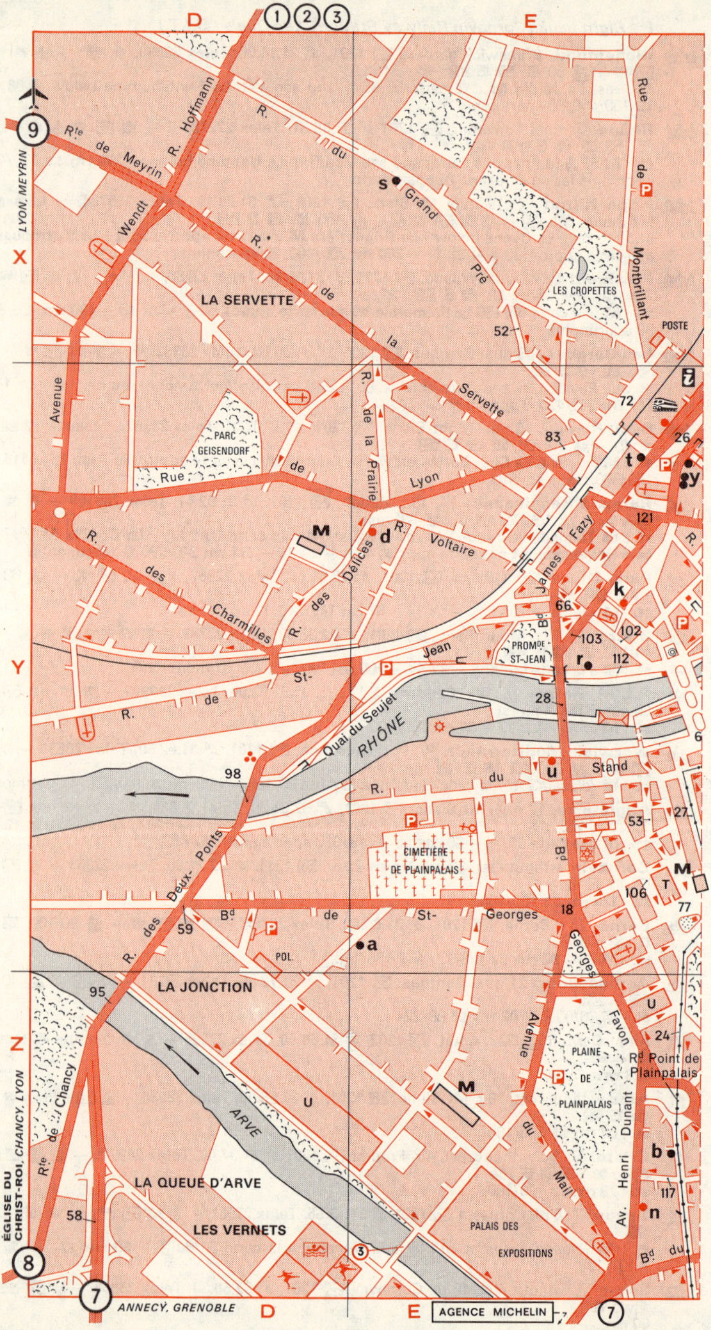
D
E
X
Y
Z
LA SERVETTE
PARC GEISENDORF
LES CROPETTES
POSTE
PROMDE ST-JEAN
RHÔNE
Quai du Seujet
CIMETIÈRE DE PLAINPALAIS
POL.
LA JONCTION
PLAINE DE PLAINPALAIS
LA QUEUE D'ARVE
LES VERNETS
ARVE
PALAIS DES EXPOSITIONS
R. Hoffmann
Rte de Meyrin
R. Wendt
R. du Grand Pré
R. de la Servette
Rue de Montbrillant
Avenue
Rue de Lyon
R. de la Prairie
R. Voltaire
R. des Délices
R. des Charmilles
Bd James Fazy
R. de St-Jean
Bd de St-Georges
R. du Stand
R. des Deux-Ponts
Bd Georges Favon
Rd Point de Plainpalais
Avenue du Mail
Av. Henri Dunant
Bd du
Rte de Chancy
LYON, MEYRIN
ÉGLISE DU CHRIST-ROI, CHANCY, LYON
ANNECY, GRENOBLE
AGENCE MICHELIN

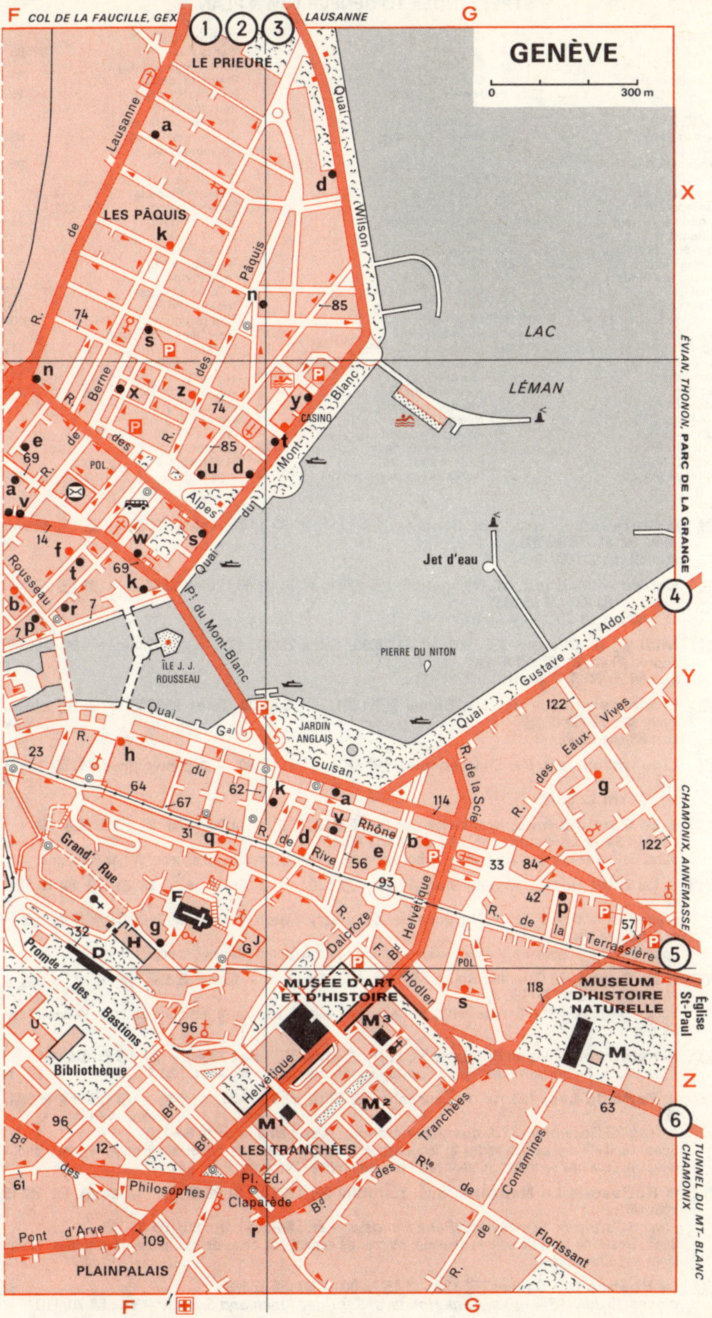
GENÈVE
0
300 m
COL DE LA FAUCILLE, GEX
LAUSANNE
LE PRIEURÉ
LES PÂQUIS
R. de Lausanne
Quai Wilson
Pâquis
R. de Berne
R. des Alpes
Quai du Mont-Blanc
CASINO
LAC
LÉMAN
Jet d'eau
ÉVIAN, THONON, PARC DE LA GRANGE
PIERRE DU NITON
ÎLE J. J. ROUSSEAU
Pt du Mont-Blanc
Quai Gal Guisan
JARDIN ANGLAIS
Quai Gustave Ador
R. du Rhône
R. de Rive
Grand' Rue
R. de la Scie
R. des Eaux-Vives
R. de la Terrassière
CHAMONIX, ANNEMASSE
Église St-Paul
MUSÉE D'ART ET D'HISTOIRE
MUSEUM D'HISTOIRE NATURELLE
Promde des Bastions
Bibliothèque
R. Dalcroze
F. Bd Helvétique
Bd Helvétique
Hodler
LES TRANCHÉES
Bd des Tranchées
Rte de Florissant
R. de Contamines
Bd des Philosophes
Pl. Ed. Claparède
Pont d'Arve
PLAINPALAIS
TUNNEL DU MT-BLANC CHAMONIX
POL.
CASINO
F
G
X
Y
Z

STREET INDEX TO GENEVE TOWN PLAN

Confédération (R.) .... FY 23
Marché (R. du) .... FY 64
Mont-Blanc (R. du) .... FY 69
Rhône (R. du) .... FGY
Rive (R. de) .... GY

Ador (Quai G.) .... GY
Alpes (R. des) .... FY
Bel-Air (Pl.) .... EY 6
Bergues (Q. des) .... FY 7
Berne (R. de) .... FY
Candolle (R. de) .... FZ 12
Chantepoulet (R.) .... FY 14
Charmilles (R. des) .... DY
Cirque (Pl. du) .... EY 18
Claparède (Pl. Ed.) .... FGZ
Conseil-Général (R.) .... EZ 24
Contamines (R. de) .... GZ
Cornavin (Pl. de) .... EY 26
Corraterie (R. de) .... EY 27
Coulouvrenière (Pt) .... EY 28
Croix-d'Or (R. de la) .... FY 31
Croix-Rouge (R.) .... FY 32
Délices (R. des) .... DEY
Deux-Ponts (R. des) .... DY
Dunant (Av. H.) .... EZ
Eaux-Vives (Pl.) .... GY 33
Eaux-Vives (R.) .... GY
Favon (Bd G.) .... EYZ
Fazy (Bd James) .... EY
Frontenex (Av. de) .... GY 42
Grand-Pré (R. du) .... DEX
Grand-Rue .... FY
Grottes (R. des) .... EX 52
Guisan (Q. Gén.) .... FGY
Helvétique (Bd) .... FGZ
Hodler (R. F.) .... GYZ
Hoffmann (R.) .... DX
Hollande (R. de) .... EY 53
Italie (R. d') .... GY 56
J.-Dalcroze (Bd) .... FGZ
Jargonnant (R. de) .... GY 57
Jeunes (Rte des) .... DZ 58
Jonction (Rd-Pt) .... DY 59
Lausanne (R. de) .... FX
Leschot (R.) .... FZ 61
Longemalle (Pl.) .... FY 62
Lyon (R. de) .... DEY
Mail (Av. du) .... EZ
Malagnou (Rte de) .... GZ 63
Mercier (Pl. Isaac) .... EY 66
Meyrin (Rte de) .... DX
Molard (Pl. du) .... FY 67
Mont-Blanc (Pt) .... FY
Mont-Blanc (Q.) .... FGY
Montbrillant (Pl.) .... EY 72
Montbrillant (R.) .... EX
Monthoux (R. de) .... FXY 74
Neuve (Pl.) .... EY 77
Pâquis (R. des) .... FXY
Pépinière (R. de la) .... EY 83
Philosophes (Bd) .... FZ
Pictet de Rochemont (Av.) .... GY 84
Plainpalais (Rd-Pt) .... EZ
Plantamour (R. Ph.) .... FGY 85
Pont d'Arve (Bd du) .... EFZ
Prairie (R. de la) .... EY
Rive (Rd-Pt de) .... GY 93
Rousseau (R.) .... EFY
St-Georges (Bd de) .... DEY
St-Georges (Pt de) .... DZ 95
St-Jean (R. de) .... DEY
St-Léger (R.) .... FZ 96
Scie (R. de la) .... GY
Servette (R. de la) .... DEY
Seujet (Quai du) .... DEY
Sous-Terre (Pt) .... DY 98
Stand (R. du) .... EY
Temple (R. du) .... EY 102
Terrassière (R.) .... GY
Terreaux-du-Temple (R. des) .... EY 103
Théâtre (Bd du) .... EY 106
Tour (Bd de la) .... FZ 109
Tranchées (Bd des) .... GZ
Turrettini (Q. Th.) .... EY 112
Versonnex (R.) .... GY 114
Vignier (R.) .... EZ 117
Villereuse (R. de) .... GZ 118
Voltaire (R.) .... EY
Wendt (Av.) .... DXY
Wilson (Quai) .... GX
22-Cantons (Pl.) .... EY 121
31-Décembre (R. du) .... GY 122

Astoria without rest, 6 pl. Cornavin, ✉ 1211, ☎ 32.10.25, Telex 22307 – lift TV bath wc shower wc ☎. AE ① E VISA — EY **y**
st. : 62 rm ⊐ 80/128.

Balzac without rest, pl. Navigation, ✉ 1201, ☎ 31.01.60, Telex 289430 – lift TV bath wc shower wc ☎ P. AE ① E VISA — FX **n**
st. : 40 rm ⊐ 75/148, 4 apartments 170.

Midi M, pl. Chevelu, ✉ 1201, ☎ 31.78.00, Telex 23482, terrace – lift kitchenette air-conditioned rest TV bath wc shower wc ☎. AE ① E VISA — FY **r**
st. : M 25/60 – **85 rm** ⊐ 128/163.

Moderne without rest, 1 r. Berne, ✉ 1201, ☎ 32.81.00, Telex 289738 – lift TV bath wc shower wc ☎. AE ① E VISA — FY **v**
st. : 55 rm ⊐ 48/115.

Lido without rest, 8 r. Chantepoulet, ✉ 1201, ☎ 31.55.30 – lift bath wc shower wc ☎. AE ① E VISA — FY **v**
st. : 31 rm ⊐ 55/95.

XXXXX ✿ **Le Gentilhomme,** Brunswick garden, ✉ 1201, ☎ 31.14.00 – air-conditioned. AE ① E VISA. no dogs
closed Saturday lunch – **st. : M** a la carte 95/130 — FY **u**
Spec. Ravioli de foie gras aux truffes, Turbot au beurre d'orange, Noisettes d'agneau. **Wines** Pinot gris.

XXXX ✿ **Le Chat Botté,** 13 quai Mont-Blanc, ✉ 1201, ☎ 31.65.32, ← – air-conditioned P. AE ① E VISA. no dogs — FY **d**
closed 22 March-6 April, 21 December-6 January, Saturday, Sunday and Bank Holidays – **st. : M** a la carte 80/110
Spec. Civet de langouste aux deux cépages, Tartare de bar à l'aneth.. **Wines** Dezaley, Dôle.

XXXX ✿ **Le Cygne,** 19 Quai Mt-Blanc ✉ 1201 ☎ 31.98.11, ← – AE ① E VISA. no dogs — GY **y**
st. : M a la carte 77/130
Spec. Salade de homard, Aiguillettes de canard en salmis, Bar cuit à la fumée de bois. **Wines** Pessy, Dardagny.

XXXX **Amphitryon,** 33 quai Bergues, ✉ 1201, ☎ 31.50.50, Telex 23383 – AE ① E VISA. no dogs
Closed 25 December-1 January, Sunday lunch and Saturday – **st. : M** 40/70. — FY **k**

XXX ✿ **Perle du Lac,** 128 rte de Lausanne ✉ 1202, ☎ 31.79.35, ←, terrace – P. AE ① E VISA. no dogs — by quai Wilson GX
closed 22 December-22 January and Monday – **st. : M** a la carte 80/120
Spec. Feuilleté d'asperges vertes et langoustines (season), Blanc de turbot aux lentilles et deux choux (season), Escalope de truite saumonnée à l'estragon. **Wines** Pinot-gris, Pinot-noir.

XXX ✿ **Rôtisserie Le Neptune,** quai Turrettini ✉ 1201 ☎ 31.98.31, terrace – air-conditioned P. AE ① E VISA. no dogs rest — EY **r**
closed Saturday, Sunday and Bank Holidays – **st. : M** a la carte 80/105
Spec. Tresse de filets de sole et saumon, Magret de canard aux baies de cassis, Flan aux truffes. **Wines** Pinot gris, Chardonnay.

XXX **Le Bouhec** 18 r. Délices ✉ 1203 ☎ 45.73.00 – AE ① E VISA — EY **d**
closed 15 July-16 August, Bank Holidays, Saturday lunch and Sunday – **st. : M** 70/110.

XXX Tsé Yang, 19 quai Mont-Blanc ✉ 1201 ☎ 32.50.81, ← – air-conditioned — GY **y**

XXX **Fin Bec,** 55 r. Berne, ✉ 1201, ✆ 32.29.19, – AE ⓓ E VISA FX **k**
closed 4 to 17 August, 22 December-4 January, Saturday lunch and Sunday – **st. : M** a la carte 55/80.

XXX **Aub. Mère Royaume,** 9 r. Corps-Saints, ✉ 1201, ✆ 32.70.08, **« Decorated in the old Genevan style »** – AE ⓓ E VISA EY **k**
closed mid July-mid August, Saturday lunch, Sunday and Bank Holidays – **st. : M** a la carte 55/80.

XX **Mövenpick-Cendrier,** 17 r. Cendrier, ✉ 1201, ✆ 32.50.30 – ▤. AE ⓓ E VISA FY **f**
st. : M a la carte 37/50.

XX **Buffet Cornavin,** 3 pl. Cornavin, ✉ 1201, ✆ 32.43.06 – AE ⓓ E VISA EY
st. : French rest. M a la carte 50/70 - **Buffet (1st class) M** a la carte approx. 60.

XX **Locanda Ticinese,** 13 r. Rousseau, ✉ 1201, ✆ 32.31.70, **Italian and Italo Swiss (Ticino), cuisine** – AE ⓓ E VISA FY **b**
closed 15 July-5 August, Saturday and Sunday – **st. : M** a la carte approx. 50.

X **Boeuf Rouge,** 17 r. A.-Vincent ✉ 1201, ✆ 32.75.37, **French (Lyons) cuisine** FY **z**
closed Saturday, Sunday and Bank Holidays – **st. : M** a la carte approx. 55.

2° - *to the N (Palais des Nations, Servette) :*

Intercontinental Ⓜ, 7 petit Saconnex, ✉ 1211, Genève 19 ✆ 34.60.91, Telex 23130, ≤, – ▤ TV ☎ Ⓟ – 25-270. AE ⓓ E VISA. rest by ①
st. : Les Continents (1st floor) *(closed Sunday lunch and Saturday)* **M** a la carte approx. 85 – 13 – **323 rm** 190/275, 32 apartments.

Grand Pré without rest, **35 r. Gd-Pré,** ✉ **1202, Genève 16** ✆ **33.91.50, Telex 23284** – TV wc wc ☎. AE ⓓ E VISA EX **s**
st. : 80 rm 105/200.

XXX Fu Lung, 30 av. G.-Motta ✉ 1202 ✆ 34.56.27 – Ⓟ by rue Hoffmann DX

3° - *Left bank (Commercial Centre) :*

Métropole Ⓜ, 34 quai Gén.-Guisan ✉ 1204 ✆ 21.13.44, Telex 421550, ≤, – ▤ rest TV ♿ – 80-200. AE ⓓ E VISA. rest GY **a**
st. : Le Grand Quai M 30/55 and see rest **L'Arlequin** below – **125 rm** 180/290, 5 apartements.

Armures Ⓜ, 1 r. Puits-Saint-Pierre ✉ 1204 ✆ 28.91.72, Telex 421129 – ▤ TV ☎ ♿. AE ⓓ E VISA FY **g**
st. : M a la carte approx. 55 – **24 rm** 165/260, 4 apartments 340.

L'Arbalète, 3 r. Tour-Maîtresse, ✉ 1204, ✆ 28.41.55, Telex 427293 – ▤ rm TV ☎ ♿ – 25. AE ⓓ E VISA GY **v**
st. : M a la carte approx. 50 – **32 rm** 190/270.

Century without rest, **24 av. Frontenex** ✉ **1207** ✆ **36.80.95, Telex 23223** – kitchenette TV ☎ Ⓟ – 35. AE ⓓ E VISA GY **p**
st. : 122 rm 137/245, 16 apartments 245/285.

Touring Balance, 13 pl. Longemalle, ✉ 1204, ✆ 28.71.22, Telex 427634 – TV wc wc ☎ – 40. AE ⓓ E VISA GY **k**
st. : M *(closed Saturday and Sunday)* 36/40 – **56 rm** 70/150 – P 134/176.

Lutetia Ⓜ without rest, **12 r. Carouge,** ✉ **1205,** ✆ **20.42.22, Telex 28845** – kitchenette wc EZ **b**
30 rm.

Le Grenil, 7 av. Ste-Clotilde, ✉ 1205, ✆ 28.30.55, Telex 429307 – wc – 220. AE ⓓ E VISA EY **a**
st. : M a la carte 35/60 – **50 rm** 43/85 – P 70/99.

XXXX ✿ **Parc des Eaux-Vives,** 82 quai Gustave-Ador, ✉ 1207, ✆ 35.41.40, **« Pleasant setting in extensive park, attractive view »,** – Ⓟ. AE ⓓ E VISA by ④
closed 1 January-15 February Saturday dinner and Monday – **st. : M** a la carte 70/120
Spec. Papillote de langoustines au Roquefort, Filet de St. Pierre au beurre de poivrons doux, Canard nantais rôti. **Wines** Dezaley, Yvorne.

XXXX ✿ **L'Arlequin,** 34 quai Gén.-Guisan ✉ 1204 ✆ 21.13.44 – ▤. AE ⓓ E VISA. GY **a**
closed Saturday and Sunday – **st. : M** 55/110
Spec. Terrine de bar aux langoustines, Cassolette de langouste au fumet d'estragon, Salade de pigeonneau et foie de canard. **Wines** Pinot gris, Pinot noir.

XXX **Olympe,** 1 r. Est ✉ 1207 ✆ 35.81.80 – AE ⓓ VISA GZ **s**
closed 1-24 August, 24 December-2 January, Saturday and Sunday – **st. : M** 52/110.

XXX **Via Veneto,** 10 r. Tour Maitresse ✉ 1204 ✆ 21.65.93 – ▤. AE ⓓ E VISA GY **d**
closed July-August, Saturday lunch and Sunday – **st. : M** 75/100.

XXX Mövenpick Fusterie, 40 r. Rhône ✉ 1204 ✆ 21.88.55 – ▤ FY **h**

XXX ✿ **La Coupole,** 116 r. Rhône ✉ 1204 ✆ 35.65.44 – ▤. E VISA GY **b**
closed 20 July-7 August and Sunday – **st. : M** a la carte 50/80 –
Spec. Pot-au-feu (September-June). **Wines** Tartegrin, Salvagnin.

XXX **Roberto,** 10 r. P.-Fatio, ✉ 1204, ✆ 21.80.33, **Italian cuisine** – ▤. AE E VISA GY **e**
closed Saturday dinner and Sunday – **st. : M** a la carte approx. 70.

XX ❀ **Béarn** (Goddard), 4 quai Poste, ✉ 1204, ✆ 21.00.28 – AE ◑ E VISA EY u
closed mid July-mid August, Saturday (except dinner from September-June) and Sunday – **st. : M** 90/115
Spec. Aumonière de grenouilles à la fricassée de homard (in Spring), Soufflé aux truffes fraîches (15 December-15 February), Bavarois d'écrevisses (in Summer). **Wines** Dardagny.

XX **Sénat,** 1 r. E.-Yung, ✉ 1205, ✆ 46.58.10, 佘 – AE ◑ E VISA FZ r
closed Sunday – **st. : M** 32/70 ₰.

XX **La Pescaille,** 15 av. H.-Dunant, ✉ 1205, ✆ 29.71.60 – ▤. AE ◑ E VISA EZ n
closed Saturday lunch and Sunday lunch – **st. : M** a la carte 85/120.

XX **Cavalieri,** 7 r. Cherbuliez, ✉ 1207, ✆ 35.09.56, Italian cuisine – ▤. AE ◑ E VISA GY g
closed July and Monday – **st. : M** a la carte 50/75 ₰.

XX **Laurent,** 13 r. Madeleine, ✉ 1204, ✆ 21.24.22 – AE ◑ E VISA FY q
closed July and Sunday – **st. : M** 43/75 ₰.

XX Parc Bertrand, 62 rte Florissant, ✉ 1206, ✆ 47.59.57, 佘 by rte Florissant GZ

Environs

by the Lakeside road, Route de Lausanne :

at Bellevue **by ③ : 6 km – ✉ 1293** Bellevue :

La Réserve M 🐎, 301 rte de Lausanne ✆ 74.17.41, Telex 23822, ←, 佘, « Lakeside and park setting, port with mooring facilities », ⛱, 🎾 – ▤ TV ☎ ♿ P – 🏛 80. AE ◑ E VISA. ✱ rest
st. : La Closerie **M** a la Carte 75/105 – **55 rm** ⊏ 250/360, 7 apartments.

XXX ❀ **Tsé Fung,** 301 rte de Lausanne ✆ 74.17.41, chinese cuisine – P. AE ◑ E VISA. ✱
st. : M a la carte 80/110
Spec. Langouste Setzcheran, Aileron de requin Impérial, Canard laqué pékinois.

at Genthod by ③ : 7 km – ✉ **1294** Genthod :

XX **Rest. du Château de Genthod,** 1 rte Rennex ✆ 74.19.72, 佘, 𝄐 – E VISA
closed 10-18 August, 20 December-10 January, Sunday and Monday – **st. : M** 40/70.

Towards Savoy via the Lakeside :

at Cologny by ④ : 3,5 km – ✉ **1223** Cologny :

XXX ❀ **Aub. du Lion d'or** (Large), au Village ✆ 36.44.32, 佘, « Overlooking the lake and Geneva, terrace » – P. AE ◑ E VISA
closed 20 December-20 January, Saturday and Sunday – **st. : M** a la carte 80/115
Spec. Millefeuille de saumon et galinette à l'oseille, Bouillabaisse (15 September-May), Aiguillettes de canard au miel et gingembre. **Wines** Lully, Yvorne.

X **Pavillon de Ruth,** 86 quai Cologny ✆ 52.14.38, ←, 佘 – AE E
1 March-20 December and closed Thursday – **st. : M** a la carte approx. 60 ₰.

at Vandoeuvres by ④ : 5,5 km – ✉ **1253** Vandoeuvres :

XX **Cheval Blanc,** ✆ 50.14.01, Italian cuisine – AE E VISA. ✱
closed 1 to 21 July, Christmas, 1 January, Sunday and Monday – **st. : M** a la carte 55/70.

at Vésenaz by ④ : 6 km by rte de Thonon – ✉ **1222** Vésenaz :

La Tourelle without rest, 26 rte Hermance ✆ 52.16.28, park – ⊟wc 🚿 ☎ P. AE ◑ E VISA. ✱
closed 16 December-16 February – **st. : 24 rm** ⊏ 75/130.

XXX **Chez Valentino,** 63 rte Thonon ✆ 52.14.40, 佘, Italian cuisine, 𝄐 – P. AE VISA. ✱
closed 1-20 August, 20 December-5 January, Tuesday lunch and Monday – **st. : M** a la carte 55/90 ₰.

by route de St-Julien :

at Carouge : 3 km by r. Carouge – ✉ **1227** Carouge :

XX **Olivier de Provence,** 13 r. J.-Dalphin ✆ 42.04.50, 佘 – AE ◑ E VISA
closed Sunday – **st. : M** 55/80.

X **Aub. Communale,** 39 r. Ancienne ✆ 42.22.88, 佘
closed Tuesday – **st. : M** a la carte 35/70 ₰.

at Troinex by ⑦ : 5 km – ✉ **1256** Troinex :

XXX ❀❀ **Vieux Moulin** (Bouilloux), 89 rte Drize ✆ 42.29.56, 佘 – P. AE E VISA
closed 1 to 15 April, 1 to 15 September, Sunday and Monday – **st. : M** (booking essential) 105 and a la carte
Spec. Blanquette de homard au vinaigre de safran (season), Volaille de Bresse pochée à la crème d'échalotes, Gâteau d'agneau aux aubergines (season). **Wines** Lully, Pinot.

XX **La Chaumière,** r. Fondelle ✆ 84.30.66, 佘, 𝄐 – P. AE ◑ E VISA
closed Sunday dinner and Monday – **st. : M** a la carte 55/95.

at Grand-Lancy by ⑦ : 3 km – ✉ **1212** Lancy :

XXX ❀ **Marignac** (Pelletier), 32 av. E.-Lance ✆ 94.04.24, park, 🍽 – ▤ **P**. AE ⓓ E VISA
closed 28 March-6 April, 22 December-11 January, Saturday lunch and Sunday – **st. : M** 90/115
Spec. Soupe au foie gras de canard et jus de truffe, Couscous de poissons de mer (Easter-End September), Canard de Barbarie aux pêches. **Wines** Côteau de Lully, Dardagny.

at Plan-les-Ouates by ⑦ : 5 km – ✉ **1228** Plan-les-Ouates :

Plan-les-Ouates without rest, 135 rte St-Julien ✆ 94.92.44 – 🛗 ⬚wc ☎. AE ⓓ E VISA
closed 23 December-6 January – **st. :** ☕ 6 – **24 rm** 35/90.

at Landecy by ⑦ : 7,5 km – ✉ **1257** Landecy :

XX **Au Fer à Cheval,** 37 rte Prieur ✆ 71.10.78, 🍽 – AE ⓓ E VISA
closed February, Wednesday lunch and Tuesday – **st. : M** 45/95.

by route de Chancy :

at Petit Lancy by ⑧ : 3 km – ✉ **1213** Petit Lancy :

❀ **Host. de la Vendée and rest. Pont Rouge,** 28 chemin Vendée ✆ 92.04.11, Telex 421304, 🍽 – 🛗 TV ☎ **P** – 🏛 80. AE ⓓ E VISA
closed 23 December-6 January – **st. : M** *(closed Easter, Saturday lunch and Sunday)* 68/90 🍷 – **30 rm** ☕ 86/200
Spec. Noix de St-Jacques en blanquette (October to March), Rognon et ris de veau, Pavé de chocolat. **Wines** Lully, Dardagny.

at Confignon by ⑧ : 6 km – ✉ **1232** Confignon :

XX Aub. de Confignon, 6 pl. Église ✆ 57.19.44, 🍽, 🌳.

at Cartigny by ⑧ *:* 12 km – ✉ **1236** Cartigny :

XX **L'Escapade,** 31 r. Trably ✆ 56.12.07, 🍽, 🌳 – **P**. AE ⓓ E VISA
closed, 20 December-30 January, Sunday and Monday – **st. : M** 60/100.

Towards the Jura :

at Cointrin by ⑨, route de Meyrin : 4 km – ✉ **1216** Cointrin :

Penta M, 75-77 av. L.-Casaï ✆ 98.47.00, Telex 27044 – 🛗 ▤ TV ☎ 🚗 **P** – 🏛 30-700. AE ⓓ E VISA. ✂ rest
st. : M 17/32 🍷 – ☕ 16 – **316 rm** 122/180, bedrooms for no smokers.

Hôtel 33, 82 av. L.-Casai ✆ 98.02.00, Telex 27991, 🍽 – 🛗 TV ⬚wc ☎ **P**. AE ⓓ E VISA
st. : M *(closed Sunday)* a la carte approx. 50 🍷 – **33 rm** ☕ 82/130.

at the airport of Cointrin by ⑨ : 4 km – ✉ **1215** Genève :

XX **Rôt. Plein Ciel,** ✆ 98.22.88, ← – ▤. AE ⓓ E VISA
st. : M a la carte 60/90.

ZÜRICH 8001 **427** ⑥ **216** ⑱ – pop. 356,800 - Alt. 441 m – ☎ 01.

See : The Quays★★ BYZ – Fraumünster cloisters★ (Alter Kreuzgang des Frauenmünsters) BZ D – View of the town from the Zürichhorn Gardens★ V – Church of SS. Felix and Regula★ U E – Church of Zürich-Altstetten★ U F – Zoological Gardens★ (Zoo Dolder) U K – Museums : Swiss National Museum★★★ (Schweizerisches Landesmuseum) BY – Fine Arts Museum★★ (Kunsthaus) CZ – Rietberg Museum★★ V M3.

✈ Kloten ✆ 812 71 11.

ℹ Offizielles Verkehrsbüro, Bahnhofplatz 15 ✉ 8023 ✆ 211 40 00, Telex 813 744 – A.C.S. Forchstrasse 95 ✉ 8032 ✆ 55 15 00 – T.C.S. Alfred-Escher-Strasse 38 ✉ 8002 ✆ 201 25 36.

Basel 84 ⑥ – Bern 125 ⑥ – Genève 278 ⑥ – Innsbruck 288 ② – Milan 304 ⑤.

Plans on following pages

On the right bank of river Limmat (University, Fine Arts Museum).

❀ **Dolder Grand Hotel and rest. La Rotonde** 🐎, Kurhausstr. 65, ✉ 8032, ✆ 251 62 31, Telex 816416, ← Zürich and lake, 🏊, 🏊, 🏌9, park, 🎾 – 🛗 ▤ rest TV ☎ 🚗 **P**. 🏛. AE E VISA. ✂ rest — V f
M a la carte 46/94 – **193 rm** ☕ 250/380.

Eden au Lac, Utoquai 45, ✉ 8023, ✆ 47 94 04, Telex 816339, ←, 🏊 – 🛗 ▤ TV ☎. 🏛. AE ⓓ E VISA. ✂ rest — V a
M a la carte 44/91 – **54 rm** ☕ 160/320 Bb.

Zurich M, Neumühlequai 42, ✉ 8001, ✆ 363 63 63, Telex 56809, ←, 🏊, 🏊 – 🛗 ▤ TV ☎ 🚗. 🏛. AE ⓓ E VISA. ✂ rest — U b
M a la carte 33,50/69 – **221 rm** ☕ 170/290.

International M, Am Marktplatz, ✉ 8050, ✆ 311.43.41, Telex 823251, ←, 🏊, 🏊 – 🛗 ▤ TV ☎. 🏛 — U s
350 rm.

Waldhaus Dolder M, Kurhausstr. 20, ✉ 8030, ☎ 251 93 60, Telex 816460, < Zürich and lake, park, – rest P. AE E VISA — V r
M a la carte 30/52,50 – 12 Bb – **100 rm** 150/300.

Zürich Continental H., Stampfenbachstr. 60, ✉ 8006, ☎ 363 33 63, Telex 55393 – — U a
134 rm.

Excelsior, Dufourstr. 24, ✉ 8008, ☎ 252 25 00, Telex 59295 – P. AE E VISA. rest — CZ f
M 25,50/58,50 – **40 rm** 130/230.

Europe, without rest., Dufourstr. 4, ✉ 8008, ☎ 47 10 30, Telex 54186 – — CZ e
42 rm.

Central M, Central 1, ✉ 8001, ☎ 251 55 55, Telex 54909, < – AE E VISA — BY z
M a la carte 34/58,50 – **99 rm** 180/300 Bb.

Bellerive au Lac, Utoquai 47, ✉ 8008, ☎ 251 70 10, Telex 816398, <, – AE E VISA — V a
M a la carte 32,50/63 – **57 rm** 120/220.

Opéra without rest., Dufourstr. 5, ✉ 8008, ☎ 251 90 90, Telex 814080 – wc wc. AE E VISA — CZ b
61 rm 95/200.

Zürcherhof, Zähringerstr. 21, ✉ 8025, ☎ 47 10 40, Telex 816490 – rest wc wc. AE E VISA — CY q
M *(closed Sunday)* a la carte 24,70/46 – **35 rm** 95/160 Bb.

Ambassador, Falkenstr. 6, ✉ 8008, ☎ 47 76 00, Telex 816508 – wc wc. AE E VISA — CZ a
M a la carte 31,50/49 – **45 rm** 110/200.

Ammann without rest., Kirchgasse 4, ✉ 8001, ☎ 252 72 40, Telex 56208 – wc wc. AE E VISA — BCZ n
21 rm 96/195 Bb.

Chesa Rustica, Limmatquai 70, ✉ 8001, ☎ 251 92 91, Telex 57380, < – wc wc. AE E VISA — BY r
closed 24 to 27 December – **M** a la carte 36/66 – **23 rm** 95/120 Bb.

Rütli M without rest., Zähringerstrasse 43, 8001, ☎ 251 54 26, Telex 816037 – wc — CY a
47 rm.

Helmhaus without rest., Schiffländeplatz 30, ✉ 8001, ☎ 251 88 10, Telex 816525 – wc wc. AE E VISA — BCZ s
25 rm 93/155.

XXX ✿ **Agnès Amberg,** Hottingerstr. 5, ✉ 8032, ☎ 251 26 26, tasteful installation – AE E VISA — CY d
closed Saturday lunch and Sunday – **M** a la carte 41/109
Spec. Galette de pommes de terre, saumon mariné maison et caviar Beluga, Ragoût de homard au Sauternes, Mignon de veau, sauce Beluga.

XX Haus Zum Rüden, Limmatquai 42, ✉ 8001, ☎ 47 95 90, former guildhall – — BY m

XX **Jacky's Stapferstube,** Culmannstr. 45, ✉ 8033, ☎ 361 37 48, Meat specialities – P. AE E VISA — U r
closed Sunday, Monday and 7 July-4 August – **M** a la carte 37/80.

XX **Kronenhalle,** Rämistrasse 4, ✉ 8001, ☎ 251 02 56, Zürich's atmosphere, paintings – . AE E VISA — CZ r
M a la carte 44,50/81,50.

XX **Casa Ferlin,** Stampfenbachstr. 38, ✉ 8006, ☎ 362 35 09, Italian rest. – . AE E VISA — BY u
closed Saturday lunch, Sunday and mid July-mid August – **M** a la carte 39/68.

XX **Bolognese,** Seegartenstr. 14, ✉ 8008, ☎ 252 37 37, Italian rest. — V u
closed Saturday, Sunday and 20 December-16 January – **M** a la carte 24/54.

On the left bank of river Limmat (Main railway station, Business centre).

Baur au Lac, Talstr. 1, ✉ 8022, ☎ 221 16 50, Telex 813567, «Lakeside setting, park » – P. AE. rest — BZ a
M a la carte 50/99 – **150 rm** 200/380.

Savoy Hotel Baur en Ville M, Poststr. 12, ✉ 8022, ☎ 211 53 60, Telex 812845 – AE E VISA. rest — BZ e
M 42/120 – **112 rm** 240/500.

Schweizerhof M, Bahnhofplatz 7, ✉ 8023, ☎ 211 86 40, Telex 813754 – AE E VISA — BY a
M *(closed Sunday)* a la carte 36/77,50 – **115 rm** 140/320.

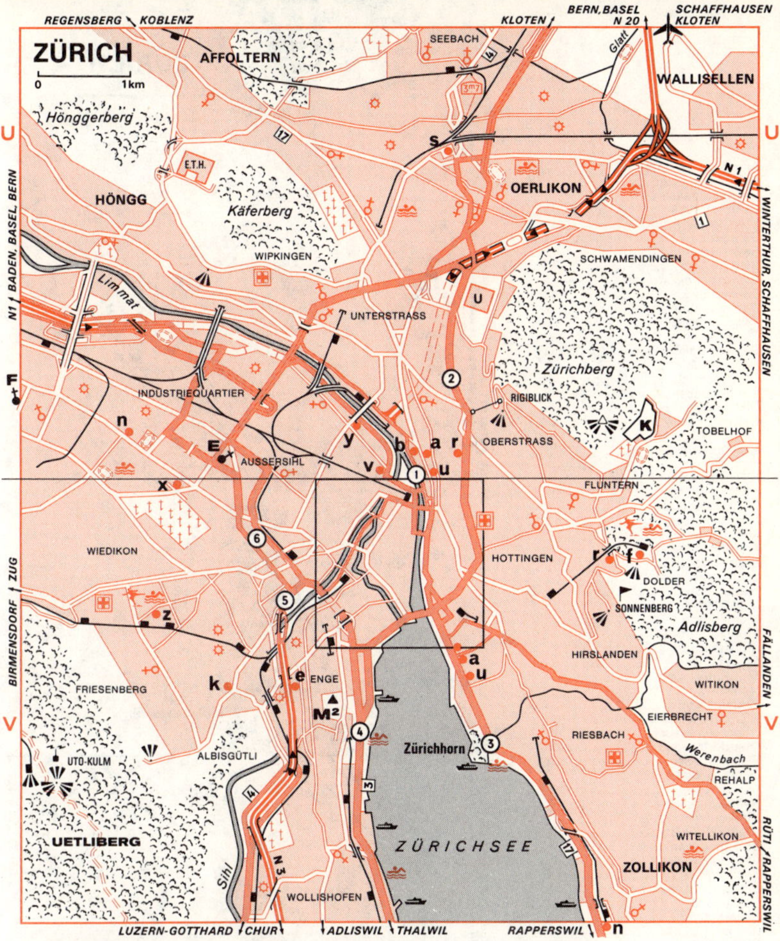

Zum Storchen, Weinplatz 2, ✉ 8022, ☎ 211 55 10, Telex 813354, €, ≪ Limmat-side setting » – . . rest — BY **u**
M a la carte 42,50/65 – **77 rm** 130/295.

Splügenschloss, Splügenstr. 2, ✉ 8002, ☎ 201 08 00, Telex 815553 – . . rest – **M** a la carte 31/58 – **55 rm** 140/280. — AZ **e**

St. Gotthard, Bahnhofstr. 87, ✉ 8023, ☎ 211 55 00, Telex 812420 – . **136 rm**. — BY **b**

Carlton Elite Bahnhofstr. 41, ✉ 8023, ☎ 211 65 60, Telex 812781 – rest . — BY **d**
M *(closed Sunday)* a la carte 35/61 – 12 Bb – **72 rm** 137/314.

Atlantis Sheraton M, Döltschiweg 234, ✉ 8055, ☎ 463 00 00, Telex 813338, , – . — V **z**
M Rotisserie – **Döltschi-Stube** a la carte 36/73 – **161 rm** 180/310 Bb.

Nova Park M, Badenerstr. 420, ✉ 8040, ☎ 491 22 22, Telex 822822, , – rest . rest — U **n**
M a la carte 26/51,50 – 9 – **363 rm** 127/160.

Glärnischhof, Claridenstr. 30, ✉ 8022, ☎ 202 47 47, Telex 815366 – rest . — BZ **k**
M La Rotisserie a la carte 35/64 – **70 rm** 120/220 Bb.

Glockenhof, Sihlstr. 31, ✉ 8001, ☎ 211 56 50, Telex 812466 – rest . – **M** a la carte 6,50/35 – **106 rm** 110/176 Bb — AY **e**

Bahnhofstrasse	BYZ	
Bellevueplatz	CZ	
Limmatquai	BYZ	
Löwenstrasse	ABY	
Paradeplatz	BZ	
Poststrasse	BZ	10
Rennweg	BY	13
Storchengasse	BY	19
Strehlgasse	BY	20
Uraniastrasse	ABY	
Alfred Escher-Strasse	AZ	
Augustinergasse	BY	2
Badenerstrasse	AY	
Bahnhofbrücke	BY	
Bahnhofplatz	BY	
Bahnhofquai	BY	
Bederstrasse	AZ	
Bleickerweg	AZ	
Brandschenkestrasse	AZ	
Bürkliplatz	BZ	
Dreikönigstrasse	AZ	
Falkenstrasse	CZ	
Freigutstrasse	AZ	
General Guisan-Quai	ABZ	
General Wille-Strasse	AZ	3
Genferstrasse	AZ	
Gessnerallee	AY	
Gessnerbrücke	AY	
Gloriastrasse	CY	
Gotthardstrasse	AZ	
Heimplatz	CY	
Hirschengraben	CYZ	
Hirschenplatz	BCY	
Hottingerstrasse	CZ	
Kasernenstrasse	AY	
Kirchgasse	CY	
Kreuzbühlstrasse	CZ	
Leonhardstrasse	CY	
Löwenplatz	BY	
Marktgasse	BY	5
Militärstrasse	AY	
Mühlegasse	BCY	
Münsterbrücke	CZ	
Münstergasse	BCY	
Münsterhof	BZ	
Museumstrasse	BY	6
Neumarkt	CY	7
Neumühlequai	BY	9
Niederdorfstrasse	BY	
Nüschelerstrasse	AY	
Oberdorfstrasse	CZ	
Pelikanstrasse	BY	
Quaibrücke	BZ	
Rämistrasse	CYZ	
Rathausbrücke	BY	12
Rindermarkt	CY	14
Rudolf Brun-Brücke	BY	
St-Annagasse	BY	
St-Jakobstrasse	AY	
Sechseläutenplatz	CZ	
Seefeldstrasse	CZ	
Seestrasse	AZ	15
Seilergraben	CY	
Selnaubrücke	AZ	
Selnaustrasse	AYZ	
Sihlbrücke	AY	
Sihlhölzlistrasse	AZ	
Sihlporte	AY	
Sihlstrasse	ABY	
Sonneggstrasse	CY	16
Stadelhoferplatz	CZ	
Stadthausquai	CZ	
Stampfenbachstrasse	BY	17
Stauffacherbrücke	AY	
Stauffacherplatz	AY	
Stauffacherquai	AYZ	
Stauffacherstrasse	AY	18
Stockerstrasse	AZ	
Talstrasse	ABYZ	
Theaterplatz	CZ	
Tunnelstrasse	AZ	
Universitätstrasse	CY	21
Usteristrasse	BY	23
Utoquai	CZ	
Waisenhausstrasse	BY	
Walchebrücke	BY	
Weinbergstrasse	CY	
Weinplatz	BY	
Werdmühlestrasse	BY	
Werdstrasse	AY	
Zeltweg	CZ	
Zeughausstrasse	AY	
Zwingliplatz	CY	

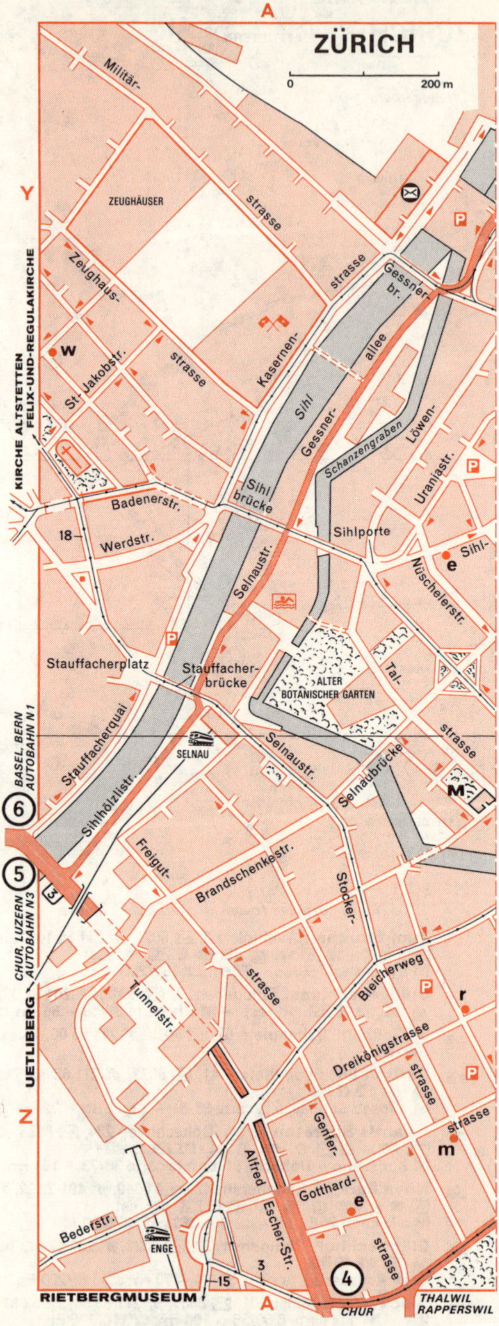

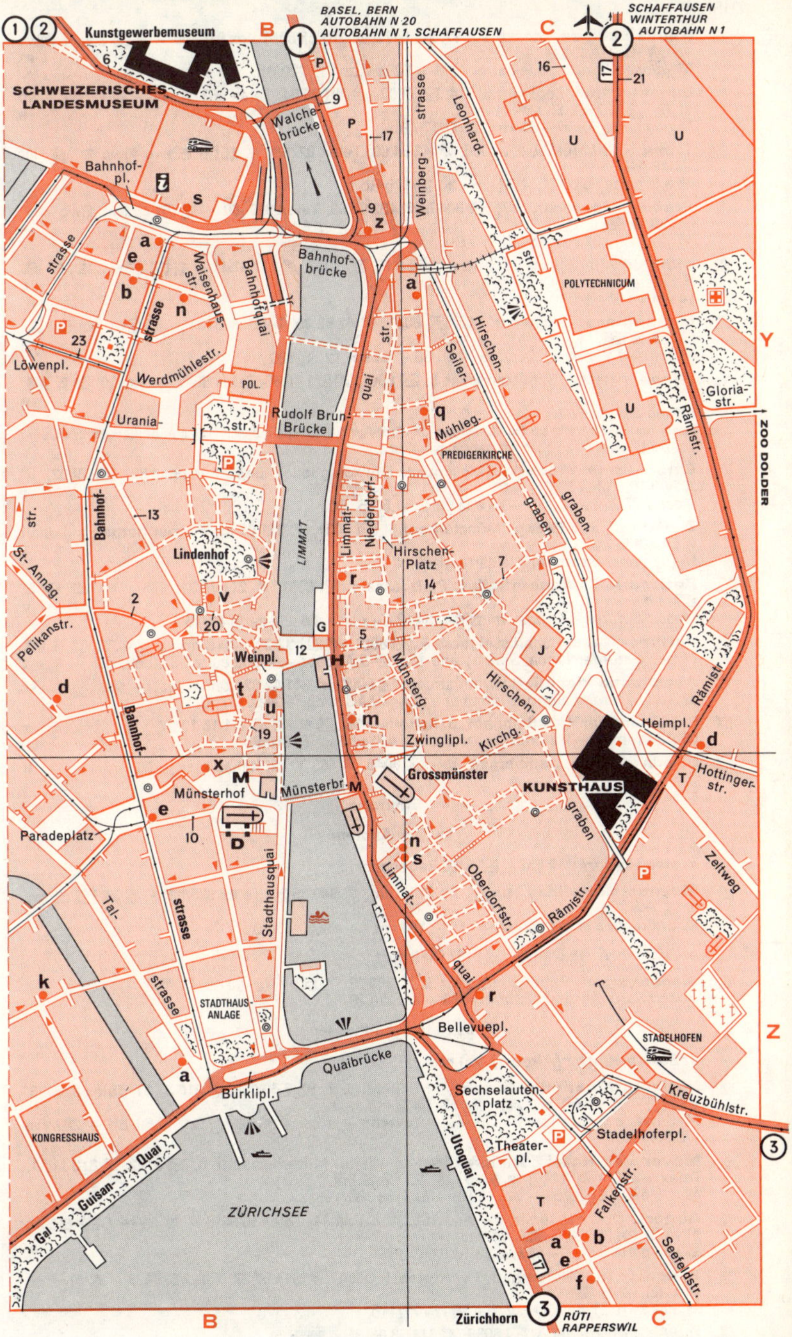
1 2 Kunstgewerbemuseum
B
1
BASEL, BERN
AUTOBAHN N 20
AUTOBAHN N 1, SCHAFFAUSEN
C
SCHAFFAUSEN
WINTERTHUR
AUTOBAHN N 1
2
SCHWEIZERISCHES
LANDESMUSEUM
Walchebrücke
Weinbergstrasse
Leonhard.
Bahnhof-pl.
Bahnhofbrücke
POLYTECHNICUM
Waisenhaus-str.
Bahnhofquai
Seiler-
Hirschen-
Löwenpl.
Werdmühlestr.
POL.
Gloria-str.
Urania-
Rudolf Brun Brücke
Mühleg.
PREDIGERKIRCHE
Rämistr.
ZOO DOLDER
Bahnhof-
LIMMAT
Limmatquai
Niederdorf-
Hirschen-Platz
graben
St-Annag.
Lindenhof
Pelikanstr.
Weinpl.
Münsterg.
Hirschen-
Heimpl.
Zwinglipl.
Kirchg.
Grossmünster
KUNSTHAUS
Hottinger-str.
Münsterhof
Münsterbr.
Paradeplatz
Zeltweg
Oberdorfstr.
Tal-
strasse
Stadthausquai
Rämistr.
STADTHAUS ANLAGE
Bellevuepl.
STADELHOFEN
Z
Y
Quaibrücke
Bürklipl.
Sechselautenplatz
Kreuzbühlstr.
Stadelhoferpl.
Theaterpl.
KONGRESSHAUS
Gal. Guisan-Quai
Utoquai
Falkenstr.
ZÜRICHSEE
Seefeldstr.
B
Zürichhorn
3
RÜTI
RAPPERSWIL
C

Neues Schloss, Stockerstr. 17, 8022, 201 65 50, Telex 815560 – wc wc. rest AZ m
M *(closed Sunday)* a la carte 31/71 – **58 rm** 155/220 Bb.

Engematthof, Engimattstr. 14, 8002, 201 25 04, Telex 56327 – wc wc V e
M a la carte 30/56 – **79 rm** 90/170 Bb.

Trümpy, Sihlquai 9, 8005, 42 54 00, Telex 822980 – wc wc U v
M a la carte 35,50/56 – **72 rm** 110/175 Bb.

Stoller, Badenerstr. 357, 8040, 492 65 00, Telex 822460 – wc wc V x
M 12/25 – **101 rm** 125/170 Bb.

Simplon without rest., Schützengasse 16, 8023, 211 61 11 – wc BY e
74 rm 95/165.

Limmathaus, Limmatstr. 118, 8031, 42 52 40, Telex 823161 – wc U y
M *(closed Sunday)* a la carte 10,50/36 – **58 rm** 58/120.

Rebe (Witschi), Schützengasse 5, 8001, 221 10 65, Telex 58477 – BY n
closed Sunday – **M** a la carte 63/112
Spec. Soufflé de truite du lac au cerfeuil (January-April), Poularde aux écrevisses et petits légumes (June-October), Tarte fine au chocolat, sabayon au Kirsch.

Baron de la Mouette (Mövenpick Dreikönighaus), Beethovenstr. 32, 8002, 202 09 10, Telex 59956 – AZ r
closed 21 June-21 July – **M** a la carte 41,50/56,50.

Zunfthaus zur Waag, Münsterhoof 8, 8001, 211 07 30, Former hatters guildhall – BZ x
M (booking essential) a la carte 41/63,50.

Rotisserie Lindenhofkeller, Pfalzgasse 4, 8001, 211 70 71 – BY v
closed Saturday, Sunday and 26 July-18 August – **M** a la carte 40/75.

Veltliner Keller, Schlüsselgasse 8, 8001, 221 32 28, « 14C house » – BY t
closed Saturday lunch, Sunday and 13 July-3 August – **M** a la carte 38,50/69,50.

Accademia Piccoli, Rotwandstr. 48, 8004, 241 42 02, Italian rest. – AY w
closed Saturday, Sunday lunch and July – **M** a la carte 34,50/67,50.

Restaurants im Hauptbahnhof, Bahnhoflatz 15, 8023, 211 15 10 BY s
M Au Premier – **Da Capo** Italian rest. – **Alfred-Escher Stube**.

Osteria da Primo, Uetlibergstr. 166, 8045, 463 30 22, Italian rest. – V k

Environs

by ① to Affoltern :

at Regensdorf : 12 km – **8105** Regensdorf :

Mövenpick Holiday Inn M, im Zentrum, 840 25 20, Telex 825888 – wc
M Grillroom a la carte 22,50/47,50 – **149 rm** 137,50/184 Bb.

at Dielsdorf : 15,5 km – **8157** Dielsdorf :

Bienengarten, Regensbergerstr. 9, 853 12 17 –
closed Saturday and October – **M** a la carte 29/64.

by ② to Schaffhausen :

at Zürich-Kloten (Airport) 10 km :

Hilton International Zürich M, Hohenbühlstr. 10, 8058, 810 31 31, Telex 825428, – rest
M Sutter's Grill a la carte 43/73 – **Taverne** a la carte 30/50 – 18,50 Bb – **287 rm** 173,50/268,50.

Mövenpick Hotel Zürich Airport M, Walter Mitterholzerstr. 8, 8152, 810 11 11, Telex 57979 –
M a la carte 21,20/50 – 15 Bb – **333 rm** 160/195.

Airport, Oberhauserstr. 30, 8152, 810 44 44, Telex 825416 – rest wc wc rest
M a la carte 32/52 – **48 rm** 120/160 Bb.

Welcome Inn, Holbergstr. 1 at Kloten, 8302, 814 07 27, Telex 825527 – wc
M a la carte 21/44,50 – 7 – **95 rm** 77/116.

Top Air, in Terminal A, 8058, 814 33 00, –.

by ③ North bank :

at Zollikon : 5 km – ✉ **8702** Zollikon :

XXX ❀ **Chez Max** (Kehl), **Seestr.** 53, ✆ 391 88 77 – AE ⓓ E VISA
closed Sunday, Monday and 8 to 28 July – **M** lunch a la carte 42/88, dinner 110/175
Spec. Tartare de homard à l'huile d'amandes, Raviole de faisan aux truffes blanches, Soufflé chaud à la Williamine.

XX **Wirtschaft zur Höhe,** Höhestr. 73, ✆ 391 59 59, ☂, – ⓟ. AE ⓓ E VISA
M *(closed Tuesday, last Monday of the month, 7 to 17 February and 13 July-5 August)* a la carte 33/62.

at Küsnacht : 6 km – ✉ **8700** Küsnacht :

Ermitage, Seestr. 80, ✆ 910 52 22, Telex 825707, ≤, ☂, « Attractive lakeside setting, terrace and garden » – |‡| wc ☎ ⓟ
M 35/90 – **25 rm** 80/190 Bb.

XXX ❀❀ **Petermann's Kunststube,** Seestr. 160, ✆ 910 07 15 – ⓟ.
closed lunch Saturday and Sunday, Monday, 22 July-10 August and 8 to 10 February – **M** a la carte 54/88
Spec. Cabri de la région au fumet de morilles (March-May), Truite du lac à la vapeur aux algues (March-June), Canard sauvage à la goutte de sang (15 september-15 November).

by ④ to Chur-South bank :

at Rüschlikon : 9 km – ✉ **8803** Rüschlikon :

Belvoir Ⓜ, Säumerstr. 37, ✆ 724 02 02, Telex 59447, ≤ lake, ☂ – |‡| rest TV wc wc ☎ ⓟ. AE ⓓ E VISA. rest
M a la carte 15,50/51 – **25 rm** 83/146.

at Gattikon : 13,5 km – ✉ **8136** Gattikon-Thalwil :

XX ❀ **Sihlhalde,** Sihlhaldenstr. 70, ✆ 720 09 27, ☂
closed Monday, Tuesday and 20 July-10 August – **M** a la carte 27/64
Spec. Saumon de Norvège en choucroute, Gibier (10 September-November).

at Wädenswil : 22 km – ✉ **8820** Wädenswil :

XX ❀ **Eichmühle** (Wannenwetsch), **Neugutstr.** 933, ✆ 780 34 44 – ⓟ. AE ⓓ VISA
closed Tuesday and 26 July-12 August – **M** a la carte 48/84
Spec. Soupe aux truffes de Périgord, Filet de rouget de roche au beurre blanc, Pigeonneau de Bresse en cocotte aux champignons des bois.

Town plans of Basle, Geneva and Zürich : with the permission from Federal directorate for cadastral surveys, 2 January 1986

United Kingdom

London
Birmingham
Edinburgh
Glasgow
Leeds
Liverpool
Manchester

PRACTICAL INFORMATION

LOCAL CURRENCY

Pound Sterling : £ 1 = 1.44 US $ (Jan. 86)

TOURIST INFORMATION

Tourist Information offices exist in each city included in the Guide. The telephone number and address is given in each text under ℹ.

FOREIGN EXCHANGE

Banks are open between 9.30am and 3pm on weekdays only. Most large hotels have exchange facilities, and Heathrow and Gatwick Airports have 24-hour banking facilities.

SHOPPING

In London : Oxford St./Regent St. (department stores, exclusive shops) Bond St. (exclusive shops, antiques)
Knightsbridge area (department stores, exclusive shops, boutiques)

For other towns see the index of street names : those printed in red are where the principal shops are found.

THEATRE BOOKINGS IN LONDON

Your hotel porter will be able to make your arrangements or direct you to Theatre Booking Agents.

In addition there is a kiosk in Leicester Square selling tickets for the same day's performances at half price plus booking fee. It is open 12-6.30pm.

CAR HIRE

The international car hire companies have branches in each major city. Your hotel porter will be able to give details and help you with your arrangements.

TIPPING

Many hotels and restaurants include a service charge but where this is not the case an amount equivalent to between 10 and 15 per cent of the bill is customary. Additionally doormen, baggage porters and cloakroom attendants are generally given a gratuity.

Taxi drivers are customarily tipped between 10 and 15 per cent of the amount shown on the meter in addition to the fare.

SPEED LIMITS

The maximum permitted speed on motorways and dual carriageways is 70 mph (113 km/h.) and 60 mph (97 km/h.) on other roads except where a lower speed limit is signposted.

SEAT BELTS

The wearing of seat belts in the United Kingdom is compulsory for drivers and front seat passengers.

ANIMALS

It is forbidden to bring domestic animals (dogs, cats...) into the United Kingdom.

LONDON

LONDON (Greater) **404** folds ㊷ to ㊹ – pop. 7 566 620 – ☎ 01.

✈ Heathrow, ✆ 759 4321, Telex 934892 – **Terminal** : Airbus (A1) from Victoria, Airbus (A2) from Paddington, Airbus (A3) from Euston – Underground (Piccadilly line) frequent service daily – Helicopter service to Gatwick Airport.

✈ Gatwick, ✆ 0293 (Crawley) 28822 and ✆ 01 (London) 668 4211, Telex 877725, by A 23 and M 23 – **Terminal** : Coach service from Victoria Coach Station (Flightline 777) – Railink (Gatwick Express) from Victoria (24 h service) – Helicopter service to Heathrow Airport.

✈ Stansted, at Bishop's Stortford, ✆ 0279 (Bishop's Stortford) 502380, Telex 81102, NE : 34 m. off M 11 and A 120.

BA Air Terminal : Victoria Station, ✆ 834 2323, p. 16 BX.

British Caledonian Airways, Victoria Air Terminal : Victoria Station, SW1, ✆ 834 9411, p. 16 BX.

🚗 Euston ✆ 387 8541 – King's Cross ✆ 837 4200 ext 4700 – Paddington ✆ 723 7000 ext 3148.

ℹ London Tourist Board, Head Office, 26 Grosvenor Gardens, SW1W 0DU, ✆ 730 3450, Telex 919 041.
National Tourist Information Centre, Victoria Station Forecourt, SW1, ✆ 730 3488.
British Tourist Authority, 64 St. James's St., SW1, ✆ 499 9325.
Telephone Information Service ✆ 730 0791 or Teletourist ✆ 246 8041 (English), 246 8043 (French), 246 8045 (German).

The maps in this section of the Guide are based upon the Ordnance Survey of Great Britain with the permission of the Controller of Her Majesty's Stationery Office. Crown Copyright reserved.

SIGHTS

HISTORIC BUILDINGS AND MONUMENTS

Palace of Westminster*** p. 9 NX – Tower of London*** p. 10 QU – Banqueting House** p. 9 NV – Buckingham Palace** p. 16 BV – Kensington Palace** p. 8 JV – Lincoln's Inn** p. 17 FV – London Bridge** p. 10 QV – Royal Hospital Chelsea** p. 15 FU – St. James's Palace** p. 13 EP – South Bank Arts Centre** p. 9 NV – The Temple** p. 5 NU – Tower Bridge** p. 10 QV – Albert Memorial* p. 14 CQ – Apsley House* p. 12 BP – George Inn*, Southwark p. 10 QV – Guildhall* p. 6 PT – Dr Johnson's House* p. 6 PTU A – Leighton House* p. 7 GX – The Monument* (☀*) p. 6 QU G – Royal Opera Arcade* p. 13 FGN – Staple Inn* p. 5 NT Y.

CHURCHES

The City Churches

St. Paul's Cathedral*** p. 6 PU – St. Bartholomew the Great** p. 6 PT **K** – St. Mary-at-Hill** p. 6 QU **B** – Temple Church** p. 5 NU – All Hallows-by-the-Tower (font cover**, brasses*) p. 6 QU **Y** – St. Bride* (steeple**) p. 6 PU **J** – St. Giles Cripplegate* p. 6 PT **N** – St. Helen Bishopsgate* (monuments**) p. 6 QTU **R** – St. James Garlickhythe (tower and spire*, sword rests*) p. 6 PU **R** – St. Margaret Lothbury* p. 6 QT **s** – St. Margaret Pattens (woodwork*) p. 6 QU **N** – St. Mary Abchurch* p. 6 QU **X** – St. Mary-le-Bow (tower and steeple**) p. 6 PU **G** – St. Michael Paternoster Royal (tower and spire*) p. 6 PU **D** – St. Olave* p. 6 QU **S**.

Other Churches

Westminster Abbey*** p. 9 MX – Southwark Cathedral** p. 10 QV – Queen's Chapel* p. 13 EP – St. Clement Danes* p. 17 FV – St. James's* p. 13 EM – St. Margaret's* p. 9 NX **A** – St. Martin in-the-Fields* p. 17 DX – St. Paul's* (Covent Garden) p. 17 DV – Westminster Roman Catholic Cathedral* p. 9 MX **B**.

STREETS – SQUARES – PARKS

The City*** p. 6 PU – Regent's Park*** (Terraces**, Zoo***) p. 4 KS – Bedford Square** p. 5 MT – Belgrave Square** p. 16 AV – Burlington Arcade** p. 13 DM – Hyde Park** p. 8 JU – The Mall** p. 13 FP – Picadilly** p. 13 EM – St. James's Park** p. 9 MV – Trafalgar Square** p. 17 DX – Whitehall** (Horse Guards*) p. 9 MV – Barbican* p. 6 PT – Bond Street* pp. 12-13 CK-DM – Charing Cross* p. 17 DX – Cheyne Walk* p. 8 JZ – Jermyn Street* p. 13 EN – Piccadilly Arcade* p. 13 DEN – Queen Anne's Gate* p. 9 MX – Regent Street* p. 13 EM – St. James's Square* p. 13 FN – St. James's Street* p. 13 EN – Shepherd Market* p. 12 CN – Strand* p. 17 DX – Victoria Embankment* p. 17 EX – Waterloo Place* p. 13 FN.

MUSEUMS

British Museum*** p. 5 MT – National Gallery*** p. 13 GM – Science Museum*** p. 14 CR – Tate Gallery*** p. 9 MY – Victoria and Albert Museum*** p. 15 DR – Courtauld Institute Galleries** p. 5 MT **M** – Museum of London** p. 6 PT **M** – National Portrait Gallery** p. 13 GM – Natural History Museum** p. 14 CS – Queen's Gallery** p. 16 BV – Wallace Collection** p. 12 AH – Imperial War Museum* p. 10 PX – London Transport Museum* p. 17 EV – Madame Tussaud's* p. 4 KT **M** – Sir John Soane's Museum* p. 5 NT **M** – Wellington Museum* p. 12 BP.

LONDON p. 7 LONDON p. 8 LONDON p. 9 LONDON p. 10

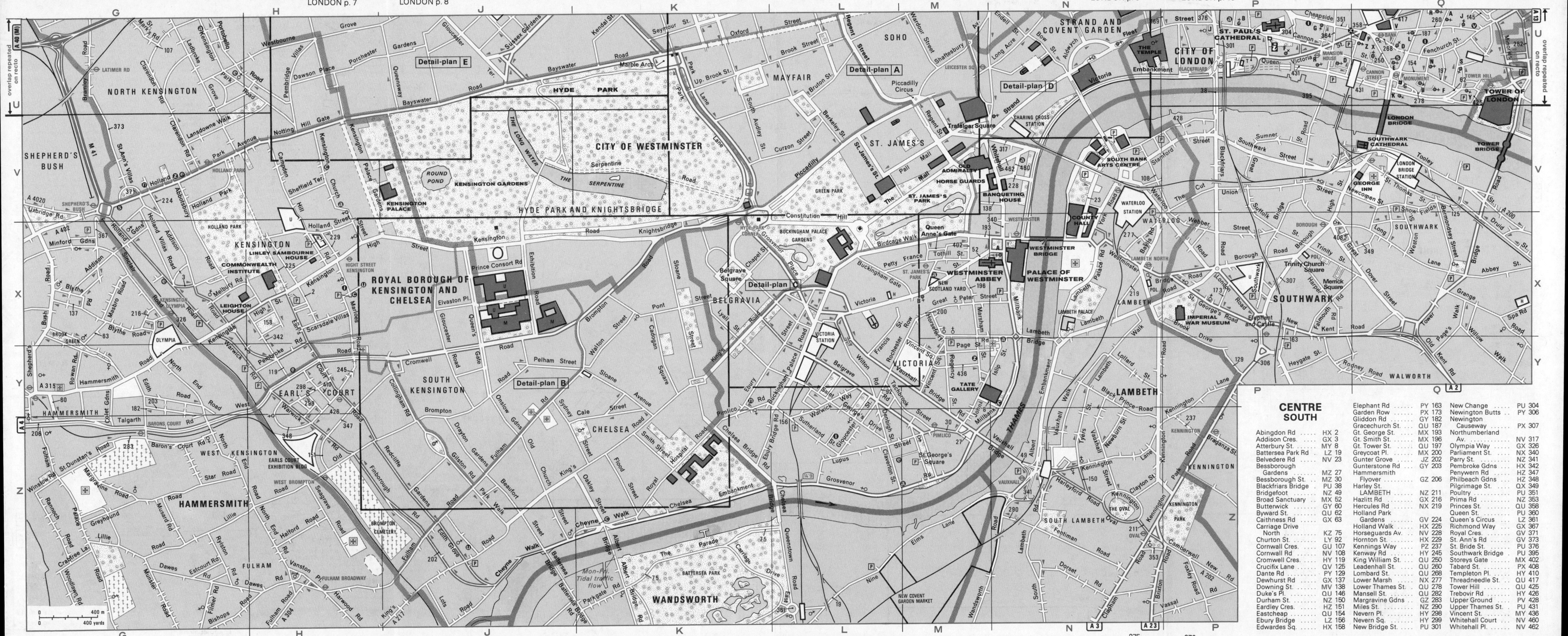

CENTRE SOUTH

373 374 375 376

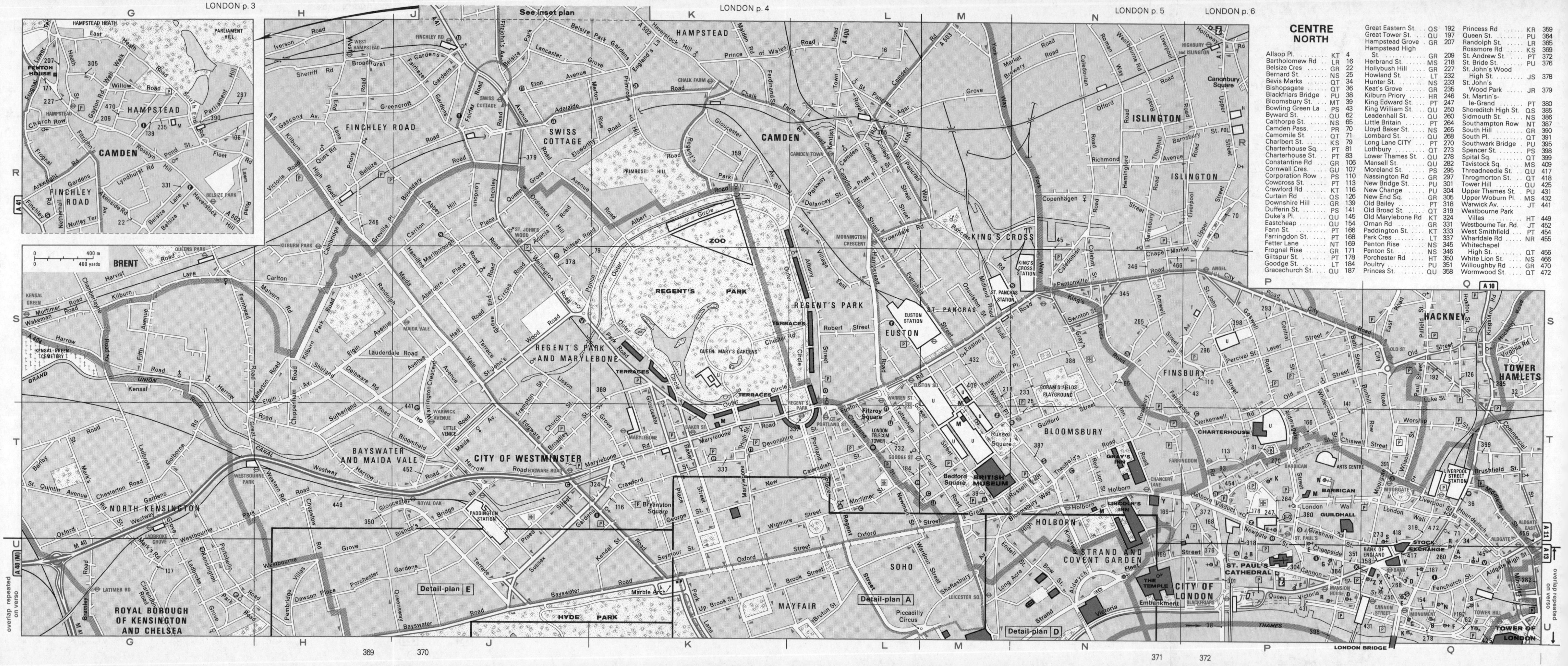

CENTRE NORTH

Allsop Pl.	KT	4
Bartholomew Rd	LR	16
Belsize Cres	GR	22
Bernard St.	NS	25
Bevis Marks	QT	34
Bishopsgate	QT	36
Blackfriars Bridge	PU	38
Bloomsbury St.	MT	39
Bowling Green La	PS	43
Byward St.	QU	62
Calthorpe St.	NS	65
Camden Pass.	PR	70
Camomile St.	QT	71
Charlbert St.	KS	79
Charterhouse Sq.	PT	81
Charterhouse St.	PT	83
Constantine Rd	GR	106
Cornwall Cres.	GU	107
Corporation Row	PS	110
Cowcross St.	PT	113
Crawford Rd	KT	116
Curtain Rd	QS	126
Downshire Hill	GR	139
Dufferin St.	PS	141
Duke's Pl.	QU	145
Eastcheap	QU	154
Fann St.	PT	166
Farringdon St.	PT	168
Fetter Lane	NT	169
Frognal Rise	GR	171
Giltspur St.	PT	178
Goodge St.	LT	184
Gracechurch St.	QU	187
Great Eastern St.	QS	192
Great Tower St.	QU	197
Hampstead Grove	GR	207
Hampstead High St.	GR	209
Herbrand St.	MS	218
Hollybush Hill	GR	227
Howland St.	LT	232
Hunter St.	NS	233
Keat's Grove	GR	235
Kilburn Priory	HR	246
King Edward St.	PT	247
King William St.	QU	250
Leadenhall St.	QU	260
Little Britain	PT	264
Lloyd Baker St.	NS	265
Lombard St.	QU	268
Long Lane CITY	PT	270
Lothbury	QT	273
Lower Thames St.	QU	278
Mansell St.	QU	282
Moreland St.	PS	295
Nassington Rd	GR	297
New Bridge St.	PU	301
New Change	PU	304
New End Sq.	GR	305
Old Bailey	PT	318
Old Broad St.	QT	319
Old Marylebone Rd	KT	324
Ornan Rd	GR	331
Paddington St.	KT	333
Park Cres	LT	337
Penton Rise	NS	345
Penton St.	NS	346
Porchester Rd	HT	350
Poultry	PU	351
Princes St.	QU	358
Princess Rd	KR	359
Queen St.	PU	364
Randolph St.	LR	365
Rossmore Rd	KS	369
St. Andrew St.	PT	372
St. Bride St.	PU	376
St. John's Wood High St.	JS	378
St. John's Wood Park	JR	379
St. Martin's-le-Grand	PT	380
Shoreditch High St.	QS	385
Sidmouth St.	NS	386
Southampton Row	NT	387
South Hill	GR	390
South Pl.	QT	391
Southwark Bridge	PU	395
Spencer St.	PS	398
Spital Sq.	QT	399
Tavistock Sq.	MS	409
Threadneedle St.	QU	417
Throgmorton St.	QT	418
Tower Hill	QU	425
Upper Thames St.	PU	431
Upper Woburn Pl.	MS	432
Warwick Av.	JT	441
Westbourne Park Villas	HT	449
Westbourne Ter. Rd.	JT	452
West Smithfield	PT	454
Wharfdale Rd	NR	455
Whitechapel High St.	QT	456
White Lion St.	NS	466
Willoughby Rd	GR	470
Wormwood St.	QT	472

■ ALPHABETICAL LIST OF AREAS INCLUDED

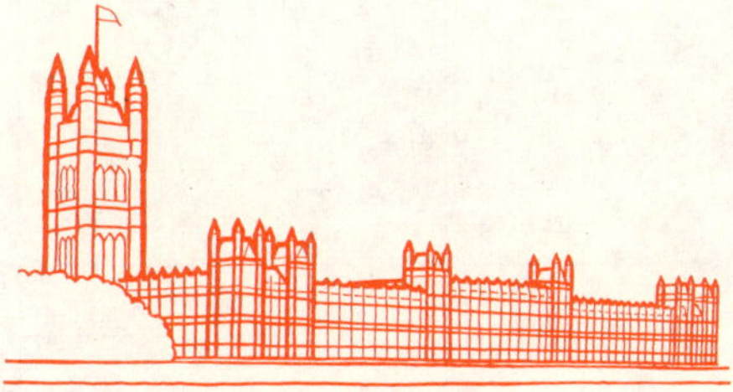

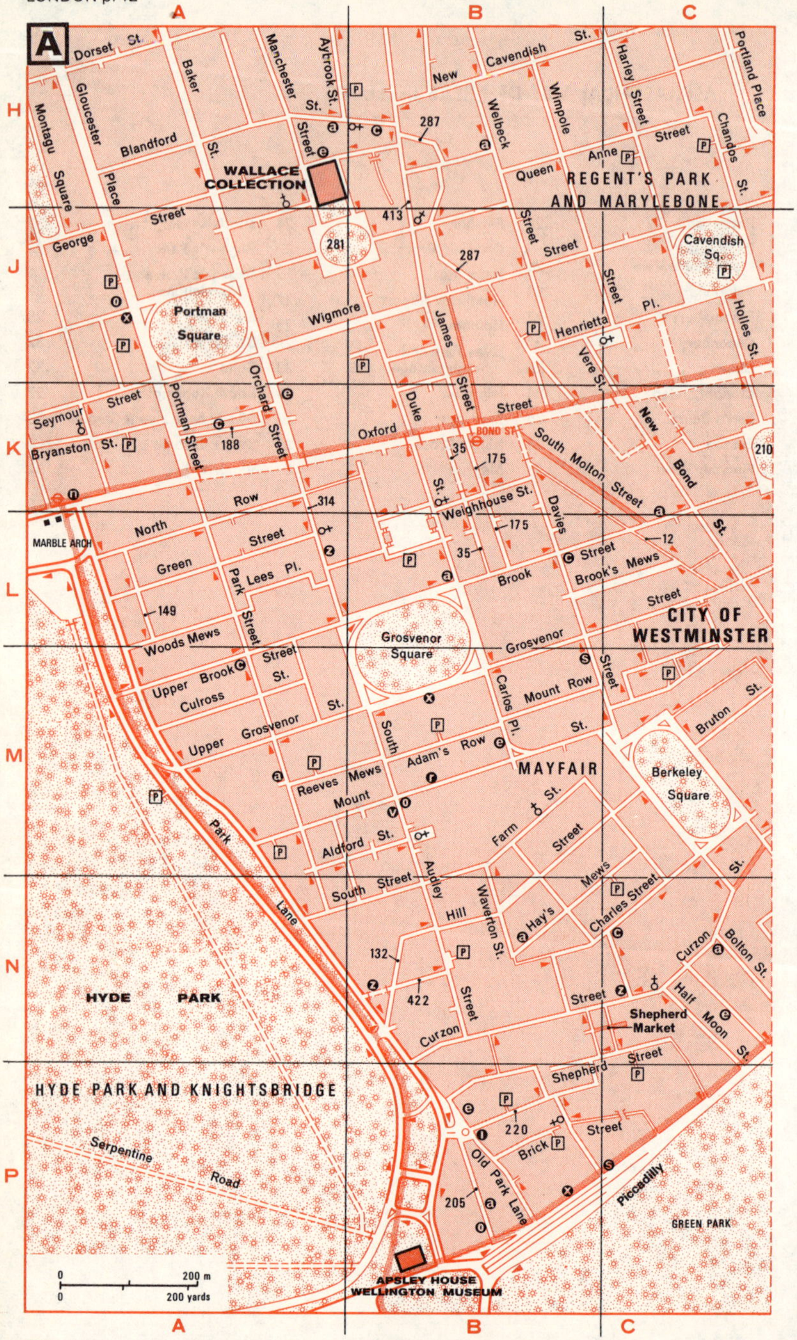
A
B
C
H
J
K
L
M
N
P
WALLACE COLLECTION
REGENT'S PARK AND MARYLEBONE
Cavendish Sq.
Portman Square
BOND ST.
MARBLE ARCH
Grosvenor Square
CITY OF WESTMINSTER
MAYFAIR
Berkeley Square
HYDE PARK
Shepherd Market
HYDE PARK AND KNIGHTSBRIDGE
Serpentine Road
Piccadilly
GREEN PARK
APSLEY HOUSE WELLINGTON MUSEUM
Dorset St.
Gloucester Place
Montagu Square
Baker St.
Manchester Street
Aytrook St.
Blandford Street
George Street
New Cavendish St.
Welbeck Street
Wimpole Street
Harley Street
Portland Place
Chandos St.
Queen Anne Street
Wigmore Street
James Street
Henrietta Pl.
Vere St.
Holles St.
Seymour Street
Bryanston St.
Portman Street
Orchard Street
Duke Street
Oxford Street
New Bond St.
South Molton Street
North Row
Green Street
Lees Pl.
Park Street
Weighhouse St.
Davies Street
Brook Street
Brook's Mews
Woods Mews
Upper Brook Street
Culross St.
Upper Grosvenor St.
Grosvenor Street
Carlos Pl.
Mount Row
Bruton St.
South St.
Adam's Row
Reeves Mews
Mount St.
Aldford St.
Farm Street
Park Lane
South Street
Audley Hill
Waverton St.
Hay's Mews
Charles Street
Curzon Street
Bolton St.
Half Moon St.
Shepherd Street
Brick Street
Old Park Lane
0 200 m
0 200 yards
287
413
281
188
35
175
314
12
149
210
132
422
220
205

Arlington Street	DN	6	Dunraven Street	AL	149	Manchester Square	AJ	281
Avery Row	CL	12	Gerrard Street	GL	174	Market Place	DJ	286
Bateman Street	FK	18	Gilbert Street	BL	175	Marylebone Lane	BJ	287
Berwick Street	FK	26	Glasshouse Street	EM	179	North Audley Street	AK	314
Binney Street	BL	35	Granville Place	AK	188	Old Burlington Street	DM	322
Carlton Gardens	FP	74	Great Castle Street	DJ	189	Old Compton Street	GK	323
Deanery Street	BN	132	Greek Street	GK	198	Panton Street	FM	336
Denman Street	FM	133	Hamilton Place	BP	205	Romilly Street	GL	368
Denmark Street	GJ	134	Hanover Square	CK	210	Thayer Street	BJ	413
Duke of York Street	EN	143	Hertford Street	BP	220	Tilney Street	BN	422
Duke Street ST. JAMES	EN	146	Leicester Square	GM	261	Warwick Street	EM	444

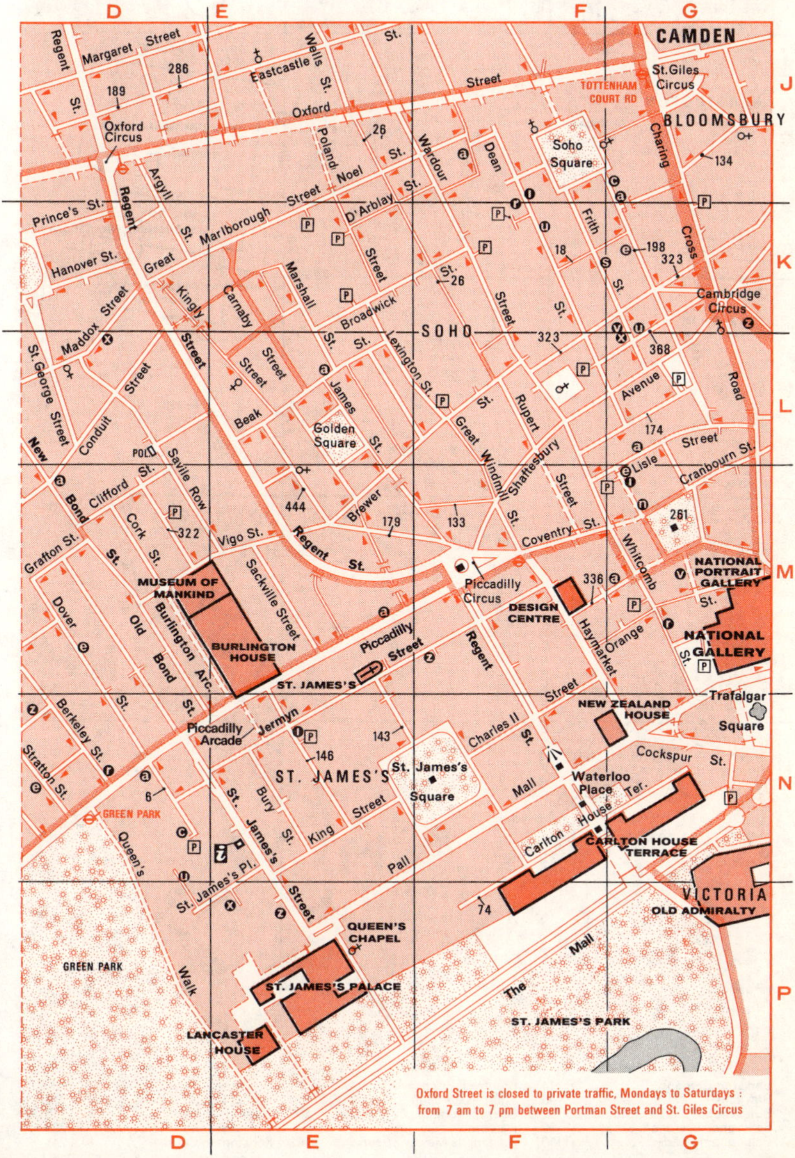

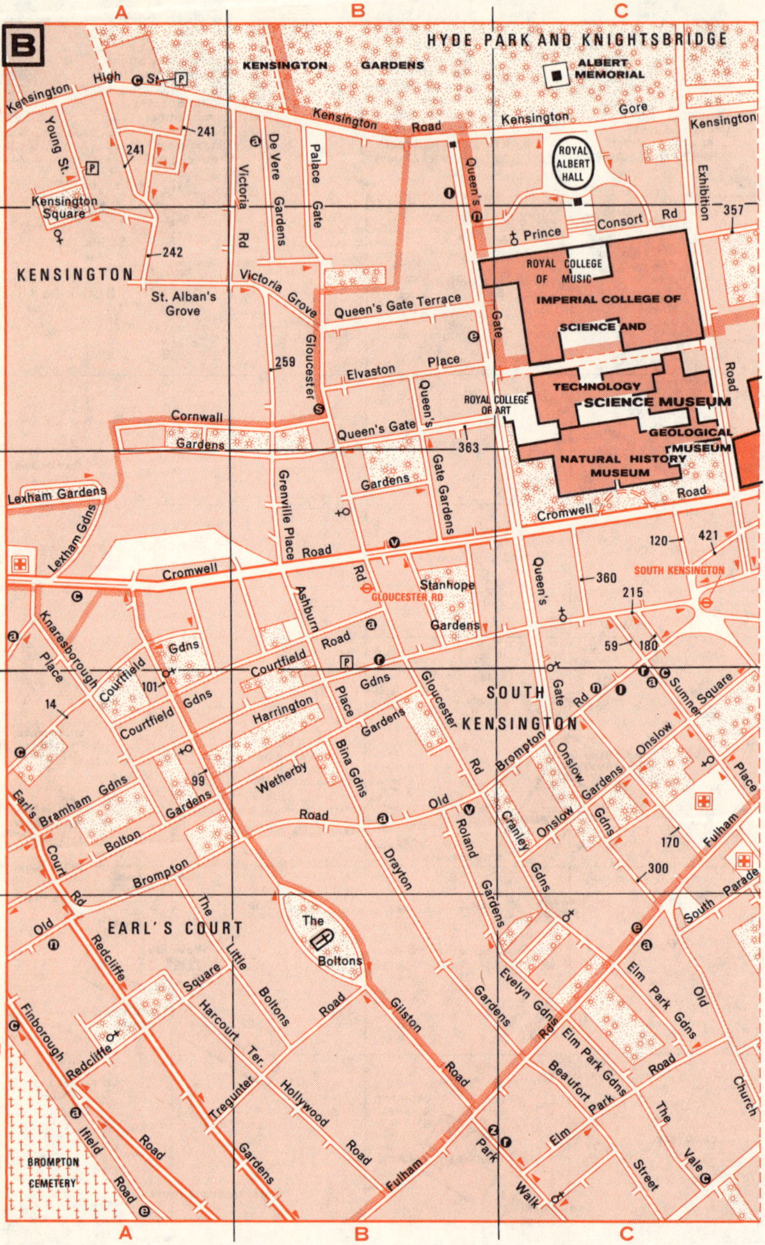
B
HYDE PARK AND KNIGHTSBRIDGE
KENSINGTON GARDENS
ALBERT MEMORIAL
Kensington High St.
Kensington Road
Kensington Gore
Kensington
ROYAL ALBERT HALL
Young St.
Kensington Square
KENSINGTON
St. Alban's Grove
Victoria Rd
De Vere Gardens
Palace Gate
Queen's Gate
Prince Consort Rd
Exhibition Road
ROYAL COLLEGE OF MUSIC
IMPERIAL COLLEGE OF SCIENCE AND TECHNOLOGY
SCIENCE MUSEUM
ROYAL COLLEGE OF ART
GEOLOGICAL MUSEUM
NATURAL HISTORY MUSEUM
Victoria Grove
Queen's Gate Terrace
Gloucester Road
Elvaston Place
Queen's Gate Place
Queen's Gate Gardens
Cornwall Gardens
Lexham Gardens
Lexham Gdns
Grenville Place
Cromwell Road
Stanhope Gardens
GLOUCESTER RD
SOUTH KENSINGTON
Ashburn Place
Courtfield Road
Courtfield Gdns
Knaresborough Place
Harrington Gdns
Gloucester Rd
SOUTH KENSINGTON
Sumner Place
Onslow Square
Onslow Gardens
Brompton Rd
Bina Gdns
Wetherby Gardens
Bramham Gdns
Earl's Court Rd
Bolton Gardens
Old Brompton Road
Roland Gardens
Cranley Gdns
Drayton Gardens
Fulham Road
South Parade
EARL'S COURT
The Little Boltons
The Boltons
Redcliffe Square
Redcliffe Gardens
Harcourt Ter.
Finborough Road
Tregunter Road
Hollywood Road
Gilston Road
Evelyn Gdns
Elm Park Gdns
Elm Park Road
Beaufort Street
Elm Park Gardens
The Vale
Old Church Street
Park Walk
Ifield Road
BROMPTON CEMETERY
241
242
259
363
357
120
421
360
215
59
180
101
14
99
170
300

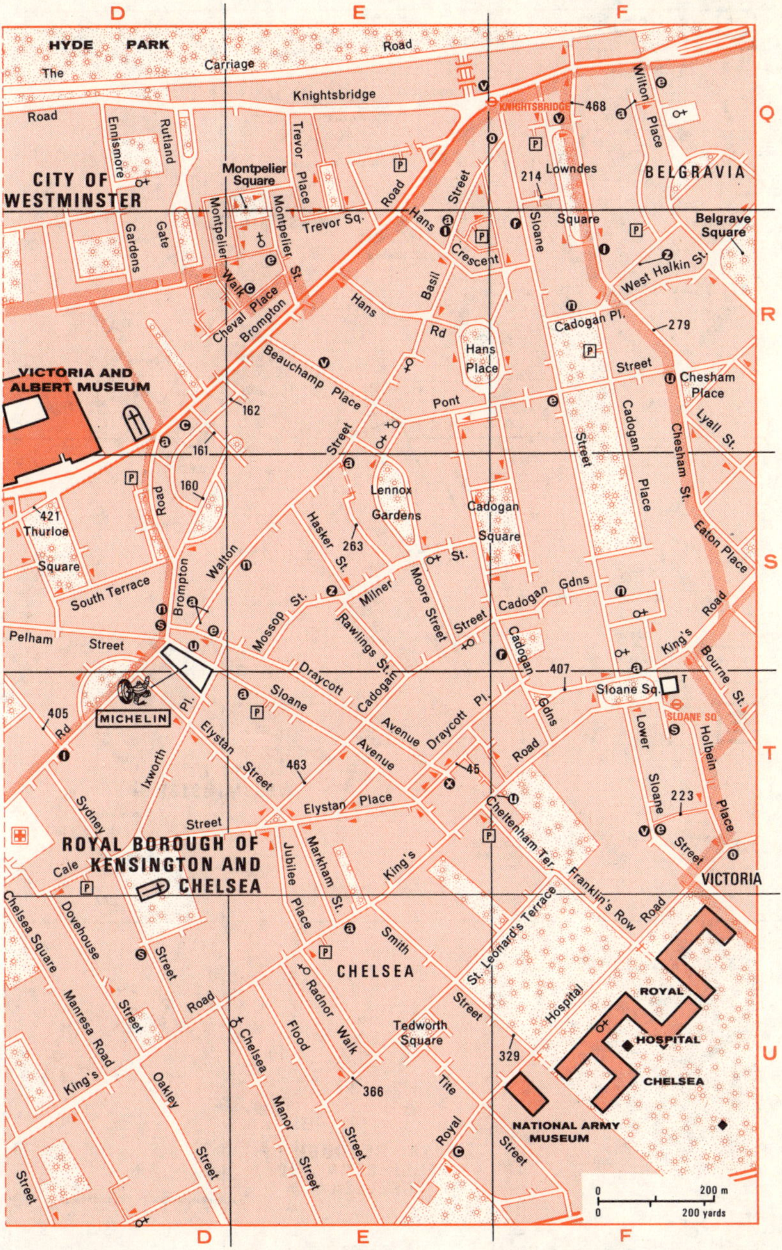

Kensington Court Place	AR	242	Ormonde Gate	FU	329	Sydney Place	DT	405
Launceston Place	BR	259	Prince's Gardens	CR	357	Symons Street	FT	407
Lennox Gardens Mews	ES	263	Queensberry Place	CS	360	Thurloe Place	CS	421
Lowndes Street	FR	279	Queen's Gate Place	BR	363	Whitehead's Grove	ET	463
Neville Terrace	CT	300	Redesdale Street	EU	366	William Street	FQ	468

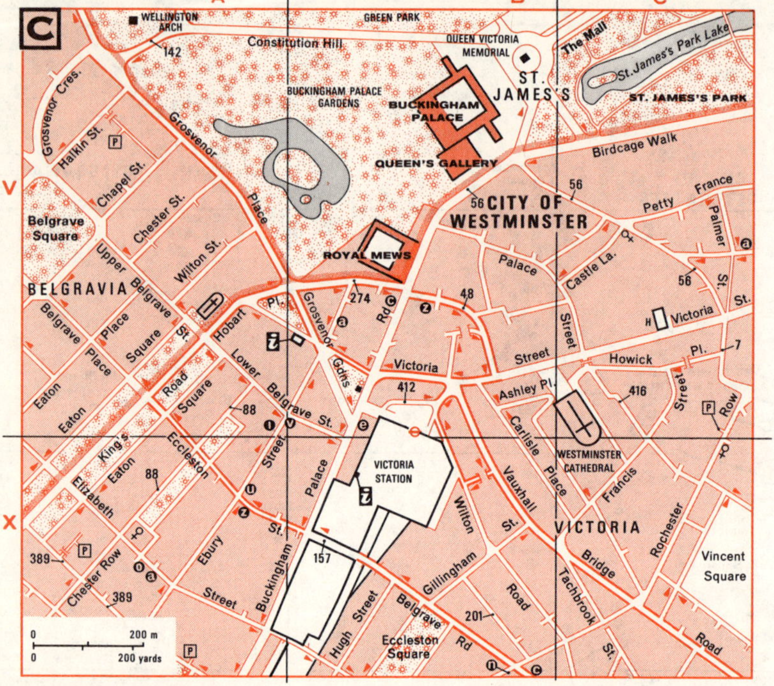
A
B
C
V
X
C
WELLINGTON ARCH
142
GREEN PARK
Constitution Hill
QUEEN VICTORIA MEMORIAL
The Mall
St. James's Park Lake
ST. JAMES'S
ST. JAMES'S PARK
BUCKINGHAM PALACE GARDENS
BUCKINGHAM PALACE
QUEEN'S GALLERY
Birdcage Walk
Grosvenor Cres.
Halkin St.
Chapel St.
Grosvenor Place
Belgrave Square
Chester St.
Wilton St.
Upper Belgrave St.
BELGRAVIA
ROYAL MEWS
56
CITY OF WESTMINSTER
Petty France
Palmer St.
Palace St.
Castle La.
274
48
Victoria St.
Belgrave Place
Eaton Place
Hobart Pl.
Grosvenor Gdns
Victoria
Street
Howick Pl.
7
Eaton Square
Lower Belgrave St.
412
Ashley Pl.
416
Row
88
King's Road
Eccleston
Eaton
Elizabeth St.
Street
Palace
VICTORIA STATION
Carlisle Place
WESTMINSTER CATHEDRAL
Francis
Vauxhall Bridge Road
Wilton Road
VICTORIA
Rochester
Vincent Square
389
Chester Row
Ebury Street
Buckingham Palace Road
157
Gillingham St.
Belgrave Rd
Hugh Street
Tachbrook St.
201
Eccleston Square
0 200 m
0 200 yards

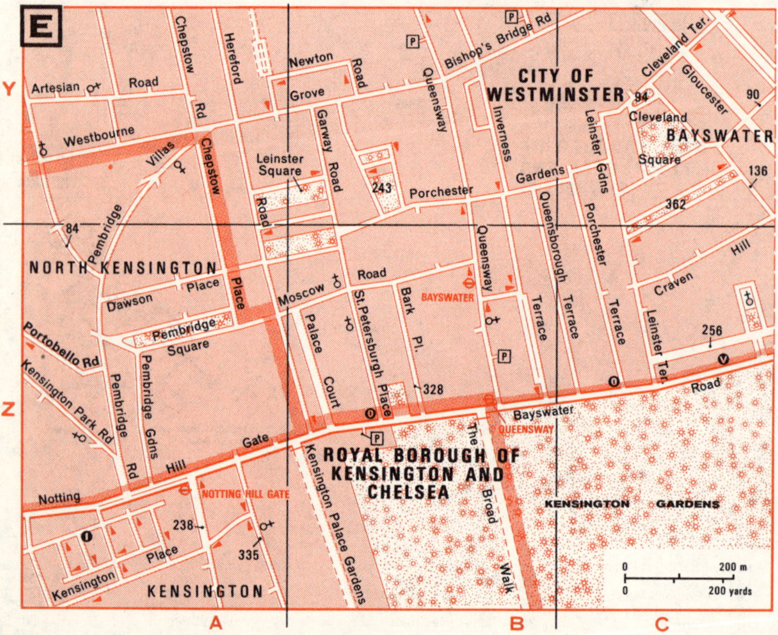
E
Y
Z
A
B
C
Chepstow Rd
Hereford Road
Newton Road
Bishop's Bridge Rd
Artesian Road
Grove
Queensway
CITY OF WESTMINSTER
Cleveland Ter.
Gloucester
90
94
Westbourne Grove
Villas
Chepstow Place
Leinster Square
Garway Road
Inverness Terrace
Leinster Gdns
Cleveland Square
BAYSWATER
243
Porchester Gardens
136
362
84
Pembridge Villas
NORTH KENSINGTON
Dawson Place
Moscow Road
St.Petersburgh Place
Bark Pl.
BAYSWATER
Queensborough Terrace
Porchester Terrace
Craven Hill
Leinster Ter.
256
Pembridge Square
Portobello Rd
Kensington Park Rd
Pembridge Rd
Pembridge Gdns
Palace Court
328
Bayswater Road
QUEENSWAY
Notting Hill Gate
NOTTING HILL GATE
Kensington Palace Gardens
ROYAL BOROUGH OF KENSINGTON AND CHELSEA
The Broad Walk
KENSINGTON GARDENS
238
335
Kensington Place
KENSINGTON
0 200 m
0 200 yards

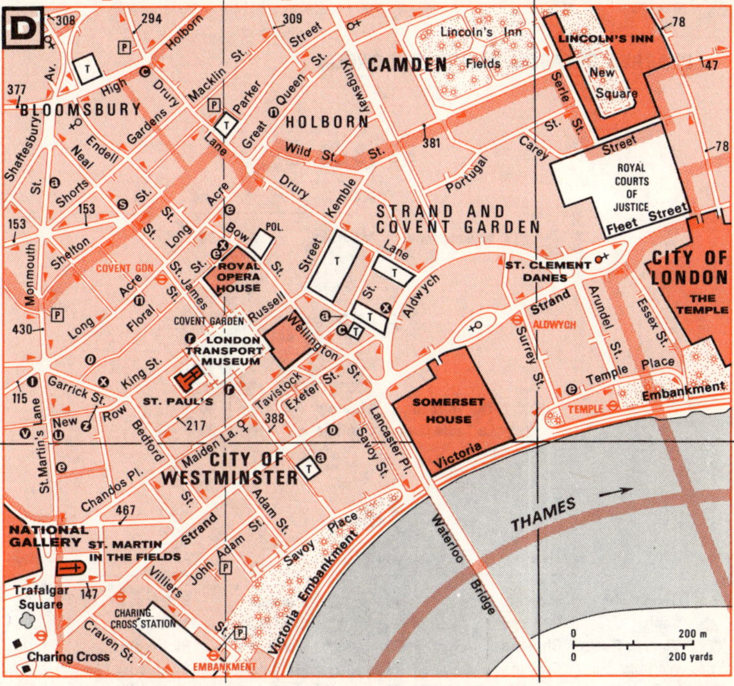
D
E
F
V
X
D
BLOOMSBURY
CAMDEN
HOLBORN
Lincoln's Inn Fields
LINCOLN'S INN
New Square
ROYAL COURTS OF JUSTICE
STRAND AND COVENT GARDEN
ST. CLEMENT DANES
CITY OF LONDON
THE TEMPLE
ROYAL OPERA HOUSE
COVENT GDN
COVENT GARDEN
LONDON TRANSPORT MUSEUM
ST. PAUL'S
SOMERSET HOUSE
ALDWYCH
TEMPLE
CITY OF WESTMINSTER
NATIONAL GALLERY
ST. MARTIN IN THE FIELDS
Trafalgar Square
CHARING CROSS STATION
Charing Cross
EMBANKMENT
THAMES
Victoria Embankment
Waterloo Bridge
Strand
Fleet Street
Kingsway
Aldwych
Shaftesbury Av.
High Holborn
Drury Lane
Long Acre
Garrick St.
King St.
Bedford St.
Chandos Pl.
Maiden La.
Tavistock St.
Exeter St.
Savoy St.
Lancaster Pl.
Savoy Place
Adam St.
John Adam St.
Villiers St.
Craven St.
St. Martin's Lane
New Row
Monmouth St.
Shelton St.
Shorts Gdns
Neal St.
Endell St.
Floral St.
Bow St.
Wellington St.
Russell St.
Kemble St.
Wild St.
Great Queen St.
Parker St.
Macklin St.
Drury Lane
Portugal St.
Carey St.
Serle St.
Arundel St.
Surrey St.
Essex St.
Temple Place
Embankment
POL.
0
200 m
200 yards
308
294
309
377
153
430
115
217
388
467
147
381
78
47

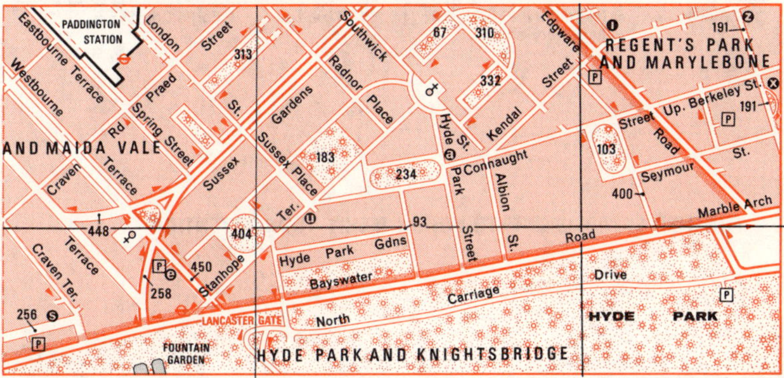
Y
Z
PADDINGTON STATION
REGENT'S PARK AND MARYLEBONE
AND MAIDA VALE
HYDE PARK AND KNIGHTSBRIDGE
HYDE PARK
LANCASTER GATE
FOUNTAIN GARDEN
London Street
Eastbourne Terrace
Westbourne Terrace
Praed St.
Spring Street
Sussex Gardens
Sussex Place
Southwick St.
Radnor Place
Hyde Park St.
Hyde Park Gdns
Connaught St.
Kendal St.
Albion Street
Edgware Road
Up. Berkeley St.
Seymour St.
Marble Arch
Bayswater Road
North Carriage Drive
Craven Rd
Craven Terrace
Craven Ter.
Stanhope Ter.
Sussex Ter.
67
310
313
332
191
183
234
103
400
93
448
404
450
258
256

D E F

STARRED ESTABLISHMENTS IN LONDON

✿✿✿

		Area	Page
XXXX	**Le Gavroche**	Mayfair	30

✿✿

		Area	Page
XXXXX	**The Terrace**	Mayfair	30
XXX	**La Tante Claire**	Chelsea	25

✿

		Area	Page
	Connaught	Mayfair	30
	Capital	Chelsea	25
XXXX	**Chelsea Room**	Chelsea	25
XXXX	**Waltons**	Chelsea	25
XXXX	**Le Soufflé**	Mayfair	30
XXX	**Rue St. Jacques**	Regent's Park and Marylebone	32
XX	**L'Arlequin**	Battersea	28
XX	**Chez Nico**	Battersea	28
XX	**Lichfield's**	Richmond	28
XX	**Ma Cuisine**	Chelsea	26
XX	**Le Mazarin**	Victoria	34
XX	**Tiger Lee**	Earl's Court	26

FURTHER ESTABLISHMENTS WHICH MERIT YOUR ATTENTION

M

XXX	**Martins**	Earl's Court	26
XXX	**Odins**	Regent's Park and Marylebone	32
XXX	**Suntory**	St. James's	32
XX	**Bagatelle**	Chelsea	26
XX	**Ken Lo's Memories of China**	Victoria	34
XX	**Lampwicks**	Battersea	28
XX	**Le Poulbot**	City	24
X	**Bubb's**	City	24

RESTAURANTS CLASSIFIED ACCORDING TO TYPE

BISTRO	WESTMINSTER (City of)			
	Victoria	X	**Bumbles**	p. 35
DANCING	WESTMINSTER (City of)			
	Mayfair	XXX	**Tiberio**	p. 31
	St. James	XXXXX	**Maxim's de Paris**	p. 32
SEAFOOD	CITY OF LONDON			
	City of London	XXX	**Wheeler's**	p. 24
	–	XX	**Bill Bentley's**	p. 24
	KENSINGTON & CHELSEA (Royal Borough of)			
	Chelsea	XX	**Poissonnerie de l'Avenue**	p. 26
	–	X	**Wheelers**	p. 26
	Earl's Court	XX	❁ **Tiger Lee**	p. 26
	WESTMINSTER (City of)			
	Mayfair	XXXX	**Scott's**	p. 30
	Strand & Covent Garden	XX	**Frère Jacques**	p. 34
	–	XX	**Sheekey's**	p. 33
	–	X	**Flounders**	p. 34
	–	X	**Grimes**	p. 34
CHINESE	CAMDEN			
	Bloomsbury	XX	**Mr. Kai**	p. 23
	Finchley Road	XX	**Green Cottage II**	p. 23
	KENSINGTON & CHELSEA (Royal Borough of)			
	Chelsea	XXX	**Zen**	p. 25
	–	XX	**Good Earth**	p. 26
	–	XX	**Good Earth**	p. 26
	Earl's Court	XX	❁ **Tiger Lee**	p. 26
	Kensington	XX	**Mama San**	p. 27
	South Kensington	XX	**Pun**	p. 28
	WESTMINSTER (City of)			
	Mayfair	XXX	**Princess Garden**	p. 31
	–	XX	**Ho-Ho**	p. 31
	–	XX	**Mr Kai**	p. 31
	Soho	XX	**Poons**	p. 33
	–	X	**Fung Shing**	p. 33
	–	X	**Gallery Rendezvous**	p. 33
	–	X	**Joy King Lau**	p. 33
	Strand & Covent Garden	X	**Happy Wok**	p. 34
	–	X	**Poons of Covent Garden**	p. 34
	Victoria	XX	**Ken Lo's Memories of China**	p. 34
ENGLISH	KENSINGTON & CHELSEA (Royal Borough of)			
	Chelsea	XX	**English Garden**	p. 25
	–	XX	**English House**	p. 26
	WESTMINSTER (City of)			
	Strand & Covent Garden	XXX	**Simpson's-in-the-Strand**	p. 33
	Victoria	XXX	**Lockets**	p. 34
	–	X	**Tate Gallery Rest.**	p. 35

INDIAN & PAKISTANI (continued)

WESTMINSTER (City of)			
Bayswater	XXX	**Bombay Palace**	p. 29
Belgravia	XX	**Salloos**	p. 29
Hyde Park & Knightsbridge	XXX	**Shezan**	p. 29
Regent's Park	XX	**Gaylord**	p. 32
Soho	XX	**Red Fort**	p. 33
Victoria	XXX	**Kundan**	p. 34

ITALIAN

CITY OF LONDON			
City of London	XXX	**City Tiberio**	p. 24
–	XX	**Villa Augusta**	p. 24
KENSINGTON & CHELSEA (Royal Borough of)			
Chelsea	XXX	**Mario**	p. 25
–	XX	**Eleven Park Walk**	p. 25
–	XX	**La Firezza**	p. 25
–	XX	**Meridiana**	p. 26
–	XX	**Ponte Nuovo**	p. 26
–	XX	**Toto**	p. 26
Kensington	XX	**La Paesana**	p. 27
WESTMINSTER (City of)			
Bayswater & Maida Vale	XX	**San Marino**	p. 29
–	XX	**Trat-West**	p. 29
Hyde Park & Knightsbridge	XX	**Montpeliano**	p. 29
Mayfair	XXX	**Tiberio**	p. 31
–	X	**Trattoria Fiori**	p. 31
Regent's Park & Marylebone	XX	**La Pavona**	p. 32
Soho	XXX	**Leonis Quo Vadis**	p. 32
–	XX	**Rugantino**	p. 33
–	XX	**Venezia**	p. 33
Strand & Covent Garden	X	**Laguna 50**	p. 34
Victoria	XXX	**Santini**	p. 34
–	XX	**Villa Claudius**	p. 34
–	X	**Fontana (La)**	p. 35
–	X	**Mimmo d'Ischia**	p. 35
–	X	**Villa Medici**	p. 35

JAPANESE

CITY OF LONDON			
City of London	X	**Ginnan**	p. 24
WESTMINSTER (City of)			
Mayfair	XX	**Miyama**	p. 31
–	XX	**One Two Three**	p. 31
–	XX	**Shogun**	p. 31
–	X	**Ikeda**	p. 31
St. James's	XXX	**Suntory**	p. 32
Strand & Covent Garden	XX	**Azami**	p. 34

KOREAN

WESTMINSTER (City of)			
Soho	XX	**Kaya**	p. 33

ORIENTAL

KENSINGTON & CHELSEA (Royal Borough of)			
South Kensington	XX	**Non-ya**	p. 28

THAI

WESTMINSTER (City of)			
Soho	X	**Chiang Mai**	p. 33

VIETNAMESE

WESTMINSTER (City of)			
Soho	X	**Saigon**	p. 33

LONDON AIRPORTS

Heathrow Middx. W : 17 m. by A 4, M 4– **Underground Piccadilly line direct** – 404 (42) – 01 – 759 4321, Telex 934892.

Sheraton Skyline, Bath Rd, Harlington, Hayes, UB3 5BP, 759 2535, Telex 934254, « Exotic indoor garden with » – AE VISA.
M 6.50/8.25 **t.** and a la carte 3.15 – 6.45 – **354 rm** 60.00/82.00 **s.**, **5 suites** 150.00/420.00 **s.**

Excelsior (T.H.F.), Bath Rd, West Drayton, UB7 0DU, 759 6611, Telex 24525, heated – AE VISA
M 9.25 **st.** and a la carte 2.70 – 6.50 – **609 rm** 57.00/62.50 **st.**

Heathrow Penta, Bath Rd, Hounslow, TW6 2AQ, 897 6363, Telex 934660, <, – AE VISA
M 10.25/11.00 **st.** and a la carte 4.75 – 6.75 – **670 rm** 62.10/78.20 **st.**, **9 suites** 97.75/207.00 **st.**

Holiday Inn, Stockley Rd, West Drayton, UB7 9NA, 0895 (West Drayton) 445555, Telex 934518, – AE VISA
M 9.75 **st.** and a la carte – 4.95 – **400 rm** 55.00/65.00 **st.**, **2 suites** 75.00/160.00 **st.**

Sheraton Heathrow, Colnbrook by-pass, West Drayton, UB7 0HJ, 759 2424, Telex 934331, – AE VISA.
M 5.90/7.50 **st.** and a la carte 3.00 – 5.50 – **405 rm** 49.50/58.50, **5 suites** 110.00/135.00.

Skyway (T.H.F.), 140 Bath Rd, Hayes, UB3 5AW, 759 6311, Telex 23935, heated – rest AE VISA
M 8.50 **st.** and a la carte 2.70 – 6.50 – **411 rm** 44.00/50.50 **st.**

Post House (T.H.F.), Sipson Rd, West Drayton, UB7 0JU, 759 2323, Telex 934280 – AE VISA
M 9.25 **st.** and a la carte 2.80 – 6.50 – **597 rm** 49.50/57.00 **st.**

Crest (Crest), Bath Rd, Longford, West Drayton, UB7 0EQ, 759 2400, Telex 934093 – AE VISA
M *(closed Sunday)* approx. 11.50 **st.** – 5.75 – **314 rm** 49.50/59.50 **st.** – SB (weekends only) 55.00 **st.**

Ariel (T.H.F.), Bath Rd, Hayes, UB3 5AJ, 759 2552, Telex 21777 – wc AE VISA
M 9.25 **st.** and a la carte 2.80 – 6.50 – **177 rm** 46.00/54.00 **st.**

Arlington, Shepiston Lane, Hayes, UB3 1LP, 573 6162 – wc wc AE VISA – **M** *(closed lunch Saturday and Sunday)* 8.00 **st.** and a la carte 3.15 – 4.00 – **80 rm** 32.50/45.00 **st.**

Gatwick West Sussex S : 28 m. by A 23 and M 23 –**Train from Victoria : Gatwick Express** 404 T 30 – West Sussex – 0293 Gatwick.
0293 (Crawley) 28822 and 01 (London) 668 4211.

Gatwick Hilton International, Gatwick Airport, RH6 0LL, 518080, Telex 877021, – AE VISA
M 25.00/30.00 **t.** and a la carte 4.50 – 6.00 – **333 rm** 65.00/80.00 **t.**, **13 suites** 135.00/225.00 **t.**

Gatwick Penta, Povey Cross Rd, Horley (Surrey), RH6 0BE, 785533, Telex 87440, – AE VISA – **M** 8.50/10.95 **st.** and a la carte 4.50 – 5.85 – **260 rm** 56.00/67.00 **st.**, **4 suites** 75.00/105.00 **st.**

Post House (T.H.F.), Povey Cross Rd, Horley (Surrey), RH6 0BA, 771621, Telex 877351, heated – AE VISA
M 10.50/10.75 **st.** and a la carte 2.70 – 6.00 – **148 rm** 46.00/57.00 **st.**

Gatwick Moat House (Q.M.H.), Longbridge Roundabout, Horley (Surrey), RH6 0AB, 785599, Telex 877138 – wc AE VISA
5.25 – **121 rm** 42.50/55.00 **st.**, **4 suites**.

CAMDEN Except where otherwise stated see pp. 3-6.

Bloomsbury – NW1/W1/WC1.

Russell (T.H.F.), Russell Sq., WC1B 5BE, 837 6470, Telex 24615 – AE VISA NT o
M (carving rest.) 9.25 **st.** and a la carte 2.70 – 6.50 – **316 rm** 49.50/61.50 **st.**

Grafton, 130 Tottenham Court Rd, W1P 9HP, 388 4131, Telex 297234 – rest AE VISA. LT n
M 10.75 **t.** and a la carte 3.50 – 6.50 – **171 rm** 59.90/78.90 **st.**

Kenilworth, 97 Great Russell St., WC1B 3LB, 637 3477 – AE VISA
M a la carte 10.25/14.75 **t.** 3.00 – 6.50 – **180 rm** 59.90/78.90 **st.**, **1 suite** 200.00/275.00 **st.** MT a

Bonnington, 92 Southampton Row, WC1B 4BH, 242 2828, Telex 261591 – wc AE VISA NT s
M (buffet lunch)/dinner 8.50 **t.** and a la carte 2.95 – **242 rm** 29.00/60.00 **t.** – SB (weekends only) 53.00/64.00 **t.**

XXX **White Tower,** 1 Percy St., W1P 0ET, ✆ 636 8141, Greek rest. – AE VISA
closed Saturday, Sunday, 3 weeks August, 1 week Christmas and Bank Holidays – **M** a la carte 11.10/22.75 **t.** 3.00. MT **u**

XXX **L'Etoile,** 30 Charlotte St., W1P 1HJ, ✆ 636 7189, French rest. – AE VISA LT **e**
closed Saturday, Sunday and Bank Holidays – **M** a la carte 14.85/27.35 **t.** 3.00.

XX **Neal Street,** 26 Neal St., WC2 9PH, ✆ 836 8368 – AE VISA p. 17 DV **s**
closed Saturday, Sunday and Christmas-New Year – **M** a la carte 16.30 **t.**

XX **Mr Kai,** 50 Woburn Pl., WC1 0JU, ✆ 580 1188, Chinese-Peking rest. – AE VISA MT **z**
closed Bank Holidays – **M** 15.00 **t.** and a la carte.

XX **Porte de la Cité,** 65 Theobalds Rd, WC1 8TA, ✆ 242 1154, French rest. – AE VISA NT **c**
closed Saturday, Sunday and Bank Holidays – **M** (lunch only) 14.50 **st.** 3.00.

XX Lal Qila, 117 Tottenham Court Rd, W1P 9HL, ✆ 387 4570, Indian rest. LT **u**

X **Mon Plaisir,** 21 Monmouth St., WC2H 9DD, ✆ 836 7243, French rest. p. 17 DV **a**
closed Saturday lunch, Sunday and Bank Holidays – **M** 7.50 **t.** (lunch) and a la carte 7.30/12.50 **t.** 3.30.

Euston – ✉ NW1.

Kennedy (Mt. Charlotte), 43 Cardington St., NW1 2LP, ✆ 387 4400, Telex 28250 – TV wc AE VISA LS **r**
M 8.50 **st.** and a la carte 3.50 – 3.25 – **320 rm** 45.00/57.00 **st.** – SB (weekends only) 63.00 **st.**

Finchley Road – ✉ NW1/NW3.

Charles Bernard, 5 Frognal, NW3 6AL, ✆ 794 0101, Telex 23560 – TV wc AE VISA GR **s**
M (bar lunch)/dinner a la carte 5.80/9.00 **st.** 2.80 – **57 rm** 39.10/55.20 **st.** – SB (weekends only) 41.00/61.00 **st.**

XX Green Cottage II, 122a Finchley Rd, NW3 5HT, ✆ 794 3833, Chinese Vegetarian rest. – JR **u**

X **Sheridans,** 351 West End Lane, NW6 1LT, ✆ 794 3234 – AE VISA
closed Saturday lunch, Monday and 23 December-1 January – **M** 7.50/12.75 **t.** 3.00.

Hampstead – ✉ NW3.

Ladbroke (Ladbroke), Primrose Hill Rd, NW3 3NA, ✆ 586 2233, Telex 22759 – TV KR **a**
84 rm.

Swiss Cottage, 4 Adamson Rd, NW3 3HP, ✆ 722 2281, Telex 297232, « Antique furniture collection » – TV wc wc AE VISA JR **n**
M 6.00/8.00 **t.** 2.00 – 4.50 – **65 rm** 33.00/67.00 **t.**, **4 suites** 67.00/80.00 **t.**

Post House (T.H.F.), 215 Haverstock Hill, NW3 4RB, ✆ 794 8121, Telex 262494 – TV wc AE VISA GR **r**
M 7.95 **st.** and a la carte 2.70 – 5.50 – **140 rm** 46.00/54.00 **st.**

XXX **Keats,** 3-4 Downshire Hill, NW3 1NR, ✆ 435 3544, French rest. – AE VISA GR **i**
closed Sunday – **M** (dinner only) 19.00 **st.** and a la carte 10.00.

Holborn – ✉ WC2.

Drury Lane Moat House (Q.M.H.), 10 Drury Lane, High Holborn, WC2B 5RE, ✆ 836 6666, Telex 8811395 – TV AE VISA p. 17 DV **c**
M 11.25 **st.** (lunch) and a la carte 12.15/16.20 **st.** 3.95 – 6.50 – **128 rm** 65.00/95.00 **st.** – SB (weekends only) 74.00 **st.**

XXX **L'Opera,** 32 Great Queen St., WC2B 5AA, ✆ 405 9020 – AE VISA p. 17 EV **n**
closed Saturday lunch and Sunday – **M** 11.45 **t.** and a la carte 12.50/15.15 **t.** 2.50.

King's Cross – ✉ N1.

Great Northern, N1 9AN, ✆ 837 5454 – TV wc AE VISA MNS **s**
closed Christmas – **M** (carving rest.) 8.50 **st.** 3.30 – **87 rm** 47.50/63.00 **st.**

Regent's Park – ✉ NW1.

White House (Rank), Albany St., NW1 3UP, ✆ 387 1200, Telex 24111 – rest TV AE VISA LS **o**
M a la carte 9.50/19.75 **t.** 2.75 – 6.00 – **580 rm** 56.00/79.00 **t.**, **18 suites** 100.00/280.00 **t.**

XX **Pratts,** Commercial Pl., Camden Lock, NW1 8AF, ✆ 485 9987, <, « Attractive setting at Camden Lock » – AE LR **a**
closed Saturday lunch, Sunday dinner, Monday, 25 to 26 December and 1 January – **M** a la carte 10.55/14.35 **t.** 4.00.

Swiss Cottage – ✉ NW3.

Holiday Inn, 128 King Henry's Rd, NW3 3ST, ℘ 722 7711, Telex 267396, – TV ☎ ♿ P. AE VISA JR a
M (buffet lunch) 12.50 (wine included) dinner/12.00 **t.** and a la carte – 6.60 – **291 rm** 78.00/101.20 **t.**, **4 suites** 182.00/225.00 **t.** – SB (weekends only) 87.00/95.00 **st.**

XX **Peter's,** 65 Fairfax Rd, NW6 4EE, ℘ 624 5804 – AE VISA JR i
closed Saturday lunch and Sunday dinner – **M** 8.95 **t.** (lunch) and a la carte 9.10/13.35 **t.** 2.50.

CITY OF LONDON Except where otherwise stated see p. 6.

St. Paul's Churchyard, EC4, ℘ 606 3030 ext 2456.

XXX **Wheeler's,** 33 Foster Lane, EC2V 6HD, ℘ 606 8254, Seafood – AE VISA PT o
closed Saturday, Sunday and Bank Holidays – **M** (lunch only) a la carte 11.25/26.75 **t.** 2.50.

XXX **City Tiberio,** 8-11 Lime St., EC3M 7AA, ℘ 623 3616, Italian rest. – . AE VISA
closed Saturday, Sunday and Bank Holidays – **M** (lunch only) a la carte 10.00/13.00 **t.** 2.75. QU i

XX **Le Poulbot** (basement), 45 Cheapside, EC2V 6AR, ℘ 236 4379, French rest. – . AE VISA PU i
closed Saturday, Sunday and Bank Holidays – **M** (lunch only) 24.50 **st.**

XX **Corney and Barrow,** 118 Moorgate, EC2M 6UR, ℘ 628 2898 – . AE VISA
closed Saturday and Sunday – **M** a la carte 13.45/18.45 **t.** 3.50. QT a

XX **Bill Bentley's,** Swedeland Court, 202-204 Bishopsgate, EC2M 4NR, ℘ 283 1763, Seafood – AE VISA QT e
closed Saturday, Sunday and Bank Holidays – **M** (lunch only) a la carte 13.60/20.45 **t.** 3.00.

XX **Shares,** 12-13 Lime St., EC3M 7AA, ℘ 623 1843 – AE VISA QU s
closed Saturday, Sunday and Bank Holidays – **M** (lunch only) 19.00 **t.**

XX **Villa Augusta,** Bucklersbury House, Queen Victoria St., EC4 9XX, ℘ 248 0095, Italian rest. – AE VISA PQU x
closed Saturday, Sunday and Bank Holidays – **M** (lunch only) a la carte approx. 13.50 **t.**

X **Bubb's,** 329 Central Market, Farringdon St., EC1A 9NB, ℘ 236 2435, French rest. PT a
closed Saturday, Sunday, August and Bank Holidays – **M** (booking essential) a la carte 13.20/14.60 **t.** 3.50.

X **La Bourse Plate,** 78 Leadenhall St., EC3A 3DN, ℘ 623 5159, French rest. – AE VISA QU v
closed Saturday and Sunday – **M** (lunch only) 15.00 **st.** 3.10.

X **La Bastille,** 116 Newgate St., EC1A 7AE, ℘ 600 1134, French rest. – AE VISA
closed dinner Monday and Friday, Saturday, Sunday, Christmas and Easter – **M** 13.95 **st.** (lunch) and a la carte 13.70/17.65 **st.** 3.00. PT z

X **Le Gamin,** 32 Old Bailey, EC4M 7HS, ℘ 236 7931, French rest. – AE VISA PU a
closed Saturday, Sunday and Bank Holidays – **M** (lunch only) 16.75 **st.**

X Ginnan, 5 Cathedral Pl., St. Paul's, EC4M 7EA, ℘ 236 4120, Japanese rest. PT e

ISLINGTON pp. 3-6.

Canonbury – ✉ N1.

X **Anna's Place,** 90 Mildmay Park, N1, ℘ 249 9379
closed Sunday, Monday, 1 week at Easter, August and 1 week at Christmas – **M** (booking essential) 12.00/16.00 **st.** and a la carte.

Finsbury – ✉ WC1/EC1.

London Ryan (Mt. Charlotte), Gwynne Pl., King Cross Rd, WC1X 9QN, ℘ 278 2480, Telex 27728 – rest TV wc ☎ P. AE VISA. NS a
M (bar lunch)/dinner 8.50 **t.** and a la carte 3.25 – 5.00 – **211 rm** 40.50/72.50.

XX **Café St. Pierre,** 29 Clerkenwell Green (1st floor), EC1, ℘ 251 6606 – AE VISA
closed lunch Sunday Easter-September and Saturday, Sunday dinner, 25 December-1 January and Bank Holidays – **M** 12.50 **t.** (dinner) and a la carte 15.40/19.00 **t.** 2.40. PT c

Islington – ✉ N1.

XX **Frederick's,** Camden Passage, N1 8EG, ℘ 359 2888, « Conservatory and walled garden » – . AE VISA PR a
closed Sunday, 25 December, 1 January and Bank Holidays – **M** a la carte 12.00/15.95 **t.** 3.10.

XX **Varnom's,** 2 Greenman St., N1 8SB, ℘ 359 6707 – . AE VISA
closed Saturday lunch, Sunday dinner and Monday – **M** 8.95/12.95 **t.** and a la carte 3.00.

KENSINGTON and CHELSEA (Royal Borough of).

Chelsea – SW1/SW3/SW10 – Except where otherwise stated see pp. 14 and 15.

Hyatt Carlton Tower, 2 Cadogan Pl., SW1X 9PY, 235 5411, Telex 21944, – . AE VISA. FR **n**
M (see **Chelsea Room** below) – **Rib Room** 18.50 **t.** (lunch) and a la carte 21.50/29.50 **t.** 5.00 – **217 rm** 126.00/166.00 **t.**, **30 suites** 220.00/1250.00 **s.**

Sheraton Park Tower, 101 Knightsbridge, SW1X 7RN, 235 8050, Telex 917222 – . AE VISA. FQ **v**
M 10.75 **st.** (lunch) and a la carte 16.85/29.00 **st.** – 7.00 – **295 rm** 115.00/125.00 **s.**, **22 suites** 260.00/515.00 **s.**

Capital, 22-24 Basil St., SW3 1AT, 589 5171, Telex 919042 – . AE VISA. ER **a**
M 14.50/16.50 **st.** and a la carte 20.50/27.50 **st.** 5.00 – 7.50 – **60 rm** 95.00/110.00 **st.**
Spec. Salade de pêcheurs tiède au Xérès, Suprême de canard au miel et au citron, Escalope de loup de mer Viennoise.

Basil Street, 8 Basil St., SW3 1AH, 581 3311, Telex 28379 – . AE VISA FQ **o**
M 9.25 **st.** (lunch) and a la carte 12.25/17.00 **st.** 3.50 – 5.90 – **95 rm** 33.00/78.50 **st.**, **1 suite** 110.90 **st.**

Holiday Inn, 17-25 Sloane St., SW1X 9NU, 235 4377, Telex 919111, – . AE VISA. FR **r**
M a la carte 12.00/15.50 **st.** 4.20 – 5.80 – **198 rm** 81.65/94.30 **st.**, **4 suites** 224.25 **st.**

Cadogan Thistle (Thistle), 75 Sloane St., SW1X 9SG, 235 7141, Telex 267893 – . AE VISA. FR **e**
M a la carte 10.50/15.00 **t.** 3.65 – 6.25 – **68 rm** 60.00/110.00 **st.**, **5 suites** 130.00 **st.**

Royal Court (Norfolk Cap.), Sloane Sq., SW1W 8EG, 730 9191, Telex 296818 – rest . AE VISA. FST **a**
M a la carte 11.55/14.95 **t.** – 6.50 – **98 rm** 65.00/80.00 **st.**, **5 suites** 98.00/120.00 **st.** – SB (weekends only)(except summer) 76.50 **st.**

L'Hotel without rest., 28 Basil St., SW3 1AT, 589 6286, Telex 919042 – wc . AE. ER **i**
12 rm 70.00/85.00 **st.**

Wilbraham without rest., 1-5 Wilbraham Pl., Sloane St., SW1X 9AE, 730 8296 – wc wc . FS **n**
3.50 – **56 rm** 24.00/52.00.

Fenja without rest., 69 Cadogan Gdns, SW3 2RB, 589 1183 – wc . FS **r**
16 rm.

Willett without rest., 32 Sloane Gdns, Sloane Sq., SW1W 8DJ, 730 0634 – wc. FT **s**
17 rm 25.00/38.00 **t.**

XXXX **Chelsea Room** (at Hyatt Carlton Tower H.), 2 Cadogan Pl., SW1X 9PY, 235 5411 – . AE VISA. FR **n**
M 16.50 **t.** (lunch) and a la carte 21.50/28.50 **t.** 5.00
Spec. Pâté de crabe sauce rouille, Fricassée de turbot et homard aux concombres, Filet d'agneau à la crème d'ail et champignons.

XXXX **Waltons,** 121 Walton St., SW3 2HP, 584 0204 – . AE VISA DS **a**
closed Bank Holidays – **M** 12.65/20.15 **st.** and a la carte 5.00
Spec. 'Moneybag' of chicken and asparagus, Pan-fried rosettes of beef with wild mushrooms, Little apple turnover.

XXX **La Tante Claire,** 68 Royal Hospital Rd, SW3 2HP, 352 6045, French rest. – AE EU **c**
closed Saturday, Sunday, 10 days at Easter, 3 weeks August-September, 10 days at Christmas-New Year and Bank Holidays – **M** 18.00 **st.** (lunch) and a la carte 25.60/31.00 **st.**
Spec. Galette de foie gras à la laitue et brunoise de légumes, Rougets rôtis au cumin et tomate-gateau de foie, Pied de cochon farci aux morilles-pomme mousseline.

XXX **Zen,** Chelsea Cloisters, Sloane Av., SW3 3DW, 589 1781, Chinese rest. – . AE VISA ET **a**
closed 25 to 27 December – **M** a la carte 14.50/33.50 **t.**

XXX **Le Français,** 257-259 Fulham Rd, SW3 6HY, 352 4748, French rest. – AE VISA CU **a**
closed Sunday and 4 days at Christmas – **M** 15.00 **st.** 5.70.

XXX **Mario,** 260-262a Brompton Rd, SW3 2AS, 584 1724, Italian rest. – AE VISA DS **n**
closed Bank Holidays – **M** 8.50 **t.** (lunch) and a la carte 15.00/23.60 **t.**

XX **Daphne's,** 110-112 Draycott Av., SW3 3AE, 589 4257 – AE VISA DS **e**
closed Sunday and Bank Holidays – **M** (dinner only) a la carte 12.20/20.00 **t.** 3.25.

XX La Finezza, 62-64 Lower Sloane St., SW1, 730 8630, Italian rest. FT **v**

XX Eleven Park Walk, 11 Park Walk, SW10, 352 3449, Italian rest. CU **r**

XX **English Garden,** 10 Lincoln St., SW3 2TS, 584 7272, English rest. – . AE VISA ET **x**
closed 28 March and Christmas Day – **M** a la carte 14.25/19.75 **st.** 3.50.

XX **English House,** 3 Milner St., SW3 2QA, ✆ 584 3002, English rest. – AE VISA
closed 25 and 26 December – **M** 10.50/14.50 **st.** and a la carte 3.50. ES **z**

XX **Toto,** Walton House, Walton St., SW3 2JH, ✆ 589 0075, Italian rest. – AE VISA ES **a**
closed Christmas – **M** a la carte 16.50/21.50 **t.** 2.75.

XX Ponte Nuovo, 126 Fulham Rd, SW3, ✆ 370 6656, Italian rest. CU **e**

XX ❀ **Ma Cuisine,** 113 Walton St., SW3 2JY, ✆ 584 7585, French rest. – AE DS **a**
closed Saturday, Sunday, 10 days Easter, 14 July-14 August, 10 days Christmas and Bank Holidays – **M** a la carte 13.20/17.10 **t.** 4.25
Spec. Galette de lotte et St. jacques au pistou, Filet de porc aux épices, Mousse brûlée.

XX **Gavvers,** 61-63 Lower Sloane St., SW1W 8DH, ✆ 730 5983, French rest. – FT **e**
closed Sunday, 24 December-2 January and Bank Holidays – **M** (dinner only) 18.25 (wine included) **st.**

XX **Poissonnerie de l'Avenue,** 82 Sloane Av., SW3 3DZ, ✆ 589 2457, French rest., Seafood – AE VISA DS **u**
closed Sunday, 10 days at Christmas and Bank Holidays – **M** a la carte 13.50/17.50 **t.** 3.50.

XX **Ménage à Trois,** 15 Beauchamp Pl., SW3 1NQ, ✆ 589 4252 – AE VISA ER **v**
closed Sunday, 28 March, 25-26 December and Bank Holidays – **M** (booking essential) a la carte 10.40/26.25 **t.** 3.00.

XX **St. Quentin,** 243 Brompton Rd, SW3 2EP, ✆ 589 8005, French rest. – AE VISA
M 8.50/12.90 **t.** and a la carte 4.40. DR **a**

XX **Bagatelle,** 5 Langton St., SW10 0JL, ✆ 351 4185, French rest. – AE VISA
closed Sunday and Bank Holidays – **M** 11.00 **t.** (lunch) and a la carte 13.80/17.50 **t.** 2.90.
pp. 7-10 JZ **u**

XX **Pier 31,** 31 Cheyne Walk, SW3 5HG, ✆ 352 5006 – AE VISA pp. 7-10 KZ **c**
M 11.00 **st.** (lunch) and a la carte 12.60/17.00 **st.** 3.50.

XX **Bewick's,** 87-89 Walton St., SW3 3HP, ✆ 584 6711 – AE VISA ES **n**
closed 28 to 30 March and 24 December-1 January – **M** (dinner only) a la carte 16.45/20.50 **t.** 4.00.

XX **Meridiana,** 169 Fulham Rd, SW3 6SP, ✆ 589 8815, Italian rest. – AE VISA DT **i**
closed Monday Bank Holidays – **M** a la carte 16.80/23.20 **t.** 2.90.

XX **Good Earth,** 233 Brompton Rd, SW3 2EP, ✆ 584 3658, Chinese rest. – AE VISA
M a la carte 8.50/17.20 **t.** 2.40. DR **c**

XX **Good Earth,** 91 King's Rd, SW3, ✆ 352 9231, Chinese rest. – AE VISA EU **a**
closed 24 to 27 December – **M** a la carte 7.95/15.30 **t.**

X Dan's, 119 Sydney St., SW3 6NR, ✆ 352 2718 – AE VISA DU **s**
closed Saturday lunch, Saturday dinner October-May, Sunday and Bank Holidays.

X **Wheelers,** 33c King's Rd, SW3 4LX, ✆ 730 3023, Seafood – AE VISA FT **u**
M 12.75 **st.** (lunch) and a la carte 14.50/19.75 **t.** 2.50.

X Nayab, 9 Park Walk, SW10, ✆ 352 2137, Indian rest. BU **z**

X **Thierry's,** 342 King's Rd, SW3, ✆ 352 3365, French rest. – AE VISA CU **c**
closed Sunday, Easter, 18 to 31 August, Christmas and Bank Holidays – **M** 6.50 **t.** (restricted lunch) and a la carte 11.70/15.05 **t.** 2.75.

X **La Brasserie,** 272 Brompton Rd, SW3 2AW, ✆ 584 1668, French rest. – AE VISA
closed 25 and 26 December – **M** a la carte 10.20/12.50 **t.** 2.90. DS **s**

Earl's Court – ✉ SW5/SW10 – Except where otherwise stated see pp. 14 and 15.

Barkston, 34-44 Barkston Gdns, SW5 0EW, ✆ 373 7851, Telex 8953154 – wc AE VISA AT **c**
M (buffet lunch)/dinner 9.00 **st.** and a la carte – 5.00 – **80 rm** 38.00/50.00 **st.**

Hogarth, 27-35 Hogarth Rd, SW5 0QQ, ✆ 370 6831, Telex 8951994 – rest wc wc AE VISA AS **a**
M (bar lunch)/dinner a la carte 6.00/9.00 **st.** 3.00 – 3.50 – **85 rm** 30.00/48.00 **st.** – SB (weekends only)(November-February) 68.00/80.00 **st.**

Town House, 44-48 West Cromwell Rd, SW5 9QL, ✆ 373 4546, Telex 918554 – wc AE VISA pp. 7-10 HY **o**
M 8.25 **st.** and a la carte 2.25 – **40 rm** 21.00/50.00 **st.**

XXX **Martin's,** 88 Ifield Rd, SW10 9AD, ✆ 352 5641 – AE VISA AU **e**
closed Sunday and 24 to 31 December – **M** (dinner only) 19.50 **t.** 4.00.

XX ❀ **Tiger Lee,** 251 Old Brompton Rd, SW5 9HP, ✆ 370 2323, Chinese rest., Seafood – AE VISA AU **n**
closed Christmas Day – **M** (dinner only) a la carte 19.80/24.50 **t.**
Spec. Shredded crispy fillet of eel, Sunflower Pigeon, Prawn and beancurd wafer appetiser.

XX **L'Olivier,** 116 Finborough Rd, SW10, ✆ 370 4183 – AE VISA AU **c**
closed Monday lunch, Sunday and 2 weeks at Christmas – **M** 18.00 **t.** and a la carte.

XX **Brinkley's,** 47 Hollywood Rd, SW10 9HY, ✆ 351 1683 – AE VISA BU **a**
closed Sunday and Bank Holidays – **M** (dinner only) a la carte approx. 13.90 **t.**

Kensington – SW7/W8/W11/W14 – Except where otherwise stated see pp. 7-10.

Royal Garden (Rank), Kensington High St., W8 4PT, ✆ 937 8000, Telex 263151, < – AE VISA pp. 14 and 15 AQ c
M Royal Roof *(closed Sunday)* (Dancing) 14.00/20.00 **t.** and a la carte – 7.50 – **395 rm** 77.50/140.00 **st.**, **38 suites**.

Kensington Palace Thistle (Thistle), De Vere Gdns, W8 5RA, ✆ 937 8121, Telex 262422 – rest AE VISA pp. 14 and 15 BQ a
M 9.00/10.50 **t.** and a la carte 3.25 – 5.25 – **298 rm** 54.00/85.00 **t.**

Hilton International, 179-199 Holland Park Av., W11 4UL, ✆ 603 3355, Telex 919763 – AE VISA GV s
M 16.00 **st.** and a la carte 3.50 – 6.75 – **606 rm** 53.95/82.65.

London Tara (Best Western), Scarsdale Pl., W8 5SR, ✆ 937 7211, Telex 918834 – AE VISA HX u
M 8.50/10.00 **st.** and a la carte 3.40 – 5.60 – **831 rm** 49.00/60.00 **st.**

Kensington Close (T.H.F.), Wrights Lane, W8 5SP, ✆ 937 8170, Telex 23914, squash – AE VISA HX c
M (buffet lunch)/dinner 11.50 **st.** and a la carte 2.70 – 5.50 – **530 rm** 44.00/54.00 **st.**

La Ruelle, 14 Wright's Lane, W8 6TF, ✆ 937 8525, French rest. – AE VISA
closed Saturday, Sunday, Christmas, New Year and Bank Holidays – **M** 12.50 **st.** (lunch) and a la carte 15.20/26.60 **st.** 4.10. HX i

Le Crocodile, 38c Kensington Church St., W8, ✆ 938 2501, French rest. – AE VISA HV a
closed Saturday lunch, Sunday, first 2 weeks August and Bank Holidays – **M** 10.75/16.75 **t.** and a la carte 3.50.

Clarke's, 124 Kensington Church St., W8, ✆ 221 9225 – VISA HV c
closed Saturday lunch, Sunday, 2 weeks August-September and 1 week Christmas – **M** 11.50/17.00 **st.**

La Pomme d'Amour, 128 Holland Park Av., W11 4UE, ✆ 229 8532, French rest. – AE VISA GV e
closed Saturday lunch, Sunday and Bank Holidays – **M** 9.50 **t.** (lunch) and a la carte 9.00/15.60 **t.** 4.25.

La Résidence, 148 Holland Park Av., W11 4UE, ✆ 221 6090, French rest. – AE VISA GV z
closed Saturday lunch, Monday and Bank Holidays – **M** 8.60 (lunch) and a la carte 10.30/18.00 **t.** 2.75.

La Paesana, 30 Uxbridge St., W8 7TA, ✆ 229 4332, Italian rest. – AE VISA
closed Sunday, 28 to 30 March and 25 to 26 December – **M** a la carte 9.15/11.55 **t.** 2.30. pp. 16-17 AZ i

Mama San, 11 Russell Gdns, W14, ✆ 602 0312, Chinese rest. – AE VISA
closed Saturday lunch, 25 to 27 December and Bank Holidays – **M** 11.75/17.50 **t.** and a la carte 3.00. GX e

North Kensington – W2/W10/W11 – Except where otherwise stated see pp. 3-6.

Leith's, 92 Kensington Park Rd, W11 2PN, ✆ 229 4481 – AE VISA GU e
closed 25 to 26 August and 4 days at Christmas – **M** (dinner only) 28.50 **st.**

Chez Moi, 1 Addison Av., Holland Park, W11 4QS, ✆ 603 8267, French rest. – AE VISA pp. 7-10 GV n
closed Sunday, 2 weeks August, 2 weeks at Christmas and Bank Holidays – **M** (dinner only) a la carte 14.50/20.75 **t.** 3.50.

Monsieur Thompsons, 29 Kensington Park Rd, W11 2EU, ✆ 727 9957, French rest. – AE VISA GU a
closed Sunday, Christmas-New Year and Bank Holidays – **M** 10.00/13.00 **t.** and a la carte 3.00.

South Kensington – SW5/SW7/W8 – pp.14 and 15.

Gloucester (Rank), 4-18 Harrington Gdns, SW7 4LH, ✆ 373 6030, Telex 917505 – AE VISA BS r
M 12.75/18.75 **t.** and a la carte 5.25 – 7.00 – **531 rm** 86.50/112.00 **t.**, **12 suites** 220.00/525.00 **t.**

London International (Swallow), 147c Cromwell Rd, SW5 0TH, ✆ 370 4200, Telex 27260 – AS c
416 rm.

Gore (Best Western), 189 Queen's Gate, SW7 5EX, ✆ 584 6601, Telex 296244, « Attractive decor » – wc wc ✆ AE VISA BR n
M (coffee shop) a la carte 7.00/13.50 **t.** 2.75 – 5.50 – **56 rm** 45.00/60.00 **t.**

John Howard, 4 Queen's Gate, SW7 5EH, ✆ 581 3011, Telex 8813397 – wc wc ✆ AE VISA BQ i
M 20.00/35.00 **st.** and a la carte 6.00 – 6.50 – **44 rm** 65.00/95.00 **st.**, **1 suite** 130.00/190.00 **st.**

Vanderbilt, 76-86 Cromwell Rd, SW7 5BT, ☎ 589 2424, Telex 919867 – wc wc. VISA BS v
M 8.75/9.75 **t.** and a la carte 3.25 – 6.50 – **230 rm** 50.90/69.90 **st.**

Embassy House (Embassy), 31-33 Queen's Gate, SW7 5JA, ☎ 584 7222, Telex 8813387 – wc. VISA. BR e
M *(closed lunch Saturday and Sunday)* (restricted lunch) 6.00/10.00 **st.** 2.50 – **69 rm** 48.00/60.00 **st.**

Number Sixteen without rest., 15-17 Sumner Pl., SW7 3EG, ☎ 589 5232, Telex 266638, – wc wc. VISA. CT c
32 rm 31.00/75.00 **st.**

Alexander without rest., 9 Sumner Pl., SW7 3EE, ☎ 581 1591, Telex 917133, – wc wc. VISA. CT a
40 rm 40.00/75.00 **st.**

Bombay Brasserie, Courtfield Close, 140 Gloucester Rd, SW7 4QH, ☎ 370 4040, Indian rest. – VISA BS a
M (buffet lunch) 8.95/17.50 **t.** and a la carte 5.95.

Reads, 152 Old Brompton Rd, SW5 0BE, ☎ 373 2445 – VISA BT a
closed Sunday dinner, 2 weeks Christmas-New Year and Bank Holidays – **M** 12.50 **t.** (lunch) and a la carte 16.90/20.80 **t.**

Hilaire, 68 Old Brompton Rd, SW7, ☎ 584 8993 – VISA CT n
closed Saturday lunch, Sunday and Bank Holidays – **M** (booking essential) 12.50/21.50 **t.**

Non-Ya, 73 Old Brompton Rd, SW7 3JS, ☎ 584 4323, Oriental cuisine – CT i

Memories of India, 18 Gloucester Rd, SW7 4RB, ☎ 589 6450, Indian rest. BR s

Pun, 53 Old Brompton Rd, SW7, ☎ 225 1609, Chinese rest. – CST r

Chanterelle, 119 Old Brompton Rd, SW7 3RN, ☎ 373 5522 – VISA BT v
closed 4 days at Christmas – **M** 7.00/11.00 **t.** 3.35.

RICHMOND-UPON-THAMES

Richmond – Surrey.

18, 18 Richmond Park ☎ 876 3205 – Central Library, Little Green ☎ 940 9125.

Lichfield's, 13 Lichfield Terr., Sheen Rd, TW9 1DP, ☎ 940 5236 – .
closed Saturday lunch, Sunday, Monday, 26 May-1 June, first 2 weeks September and 1 week at Christmas – **M** (booking essential) 14.00 **st.** (lunch) and a la carte approx. 22.25 **st.** 3.50
Spec. Hot tart of foie gras and apples, Game (in season), Salmon with confit of onions (April-October).

WANDSWORTH

Battersea – SW8/SW11.

Chez Nico, 129 Queenstown Rd, SW8 3RH, ☎ 720 6960, French rest. – VISA
closed Saturday, Sunday, 4 days at Easter, 3 weeks July-August, 10 days at Christmas and Bank Holidays – **M** (booking essential) 19.50 **st.** (lunch) and a la carte 25.00/31.25 **st.** 4.75
Spec. Escalope de barbue en feuilleté garni crabe et gingembre au beurre blanc, Ris de veau rôti au lard avec sa sauce truffe, Mousse Légère d'oranges avec sa sauce au zeste.

Alonso's, 32 Queenstown Rd, SW8 3RX, ☎ 720 5986 – VISA
closed Saturday lunch, Sunday and Bank Holidays – **M** 8.15/13.75 **t.** and a la carte.

Lampwicks, 24 Queenstown Rd, SW8 3RX, ☎ 622 7800 – . VISA
closed Sunday, last 2 weeks August and Christmas – **M** 10.50/17.50 **t.** 3.50.

L'Arlequin, 123 Queenstown Rd, SW8, ☎ 622 0555, French rest. – . VISA
closed Saturday, Sunday, 3 weeks August and 2 weeks at Christmas – **M** 11.50 **st.** (lunch) and a la carte 23.20/27.50 **st.** 6.50
Spec. Persillé de ris de veau et homard, Rable de lièvre aux betteraves (October-February), Délice au cassis.

WESTMINSTER (City of)

Bayswater and Maida Vale – W2/W9 – Except where otherwise stated see pp. 16 and 17.

Royal Lancaster (Rank), Lancaster Terr., W2 2TY, ☎ 262 6737, Telex 24822, ← – rest . VISA. DZ e
M *(closed Saturday lunch and Sunday)* 11.50/14.95 **t.** and a la carte 4.75 – 7.00 – **418 rm** 85.00/125.00 **st.**, **27 suites** 250.00/815.00 **st.**

London Metropole, Edgware Rd, W2 1JU, ☎ 402 4141, Telex 23711, ← – . VISA. pp. 3-6 JT c
M (dinner only) a la carte approx. 18.00 **t.** – 7.25 – **586 rm** 58.50/75.00 **st.**, **9 suites.**

Hospitality Inn (Mt. Charlotte), 104 Bayswater Rd, W2 3HL, ☎ 262 4461, Telex 22667, ← – . VISA CZ o
M 6.50/9.50 **t.** and a la carte 3.50 – 6.25 – **175 rm** 52.50/85.00 **t.**, **1 suite** 140.00/180.00 **t.**

White's (Mt. Charlotte), Bayswater Rd, 90-92 Lancaster Gate, W2 3NR, ✆ 262 2711, Telex 24771 – wc ☎ P. AE VISA CZ v
M 17.00/19.00 **t.** and a la carte 4.00 – 5.75 – **61 rm** 55.00/115.00 **st.** – SB (weekends only) 85.00/100.00 **st.**

London Embassy (Embassy), 150 Bayswater Rd, W2 4RT, ✆ 229 1212, Telex 27727 – wc ☎ P. AE VISA BZ o
M (carving rest.) 9.50 **st.** and a la carte 2.75 – 5.00 – **192 rm** 54.00/76.00 **st.**, **1 suite** 95.00/105.00 **st.**

Colonnade, 2 Warrington Cres., W9 1ER, ✆ 286 1052, Telex 298930 – wc wc. AE VISA pp. 3-6 JT e
M (dinner only) 7.95 **t.** 2.50 – **53 rm** 28.50/49.50 **t.**

Mornington Lancaster (Best Western) without rest., 12 Lancaster Gate, W2 3LG, ✆ 262 7361, Telex 24281 – wc ☎. AE VISA DZ s
closed Christmas – 3.00 – **65 rm** 30.00/52.00 **st.**

XXX Bombay Palace, 50 Connaught St., Hyde Park Sq., W2, ✆ 723 8855, North Indian rest. EY a

XX **San Marino,** 26 Sussex Pl., W2 2TH, ✆ 723 8395, Italian rest. – AE VISA EY u
closed Sunday and Bank Holidays – **M** a la carte 12.30/15.00 **t.** 3.80.

XX Trat West, 143 Edgware Rd, W2 2HR, ✆ 723 8203, Italian rest. pp. 3-6 KT i

Belgravia – SW1 – Except where otherwise stated see pp. 14 and 15.

Berkeley, Wilton Pl., SW1X 7RL, ✆ 235 6000, Telex 919252, – ☎. AE VISA FQ e
M Restaurant *(closed Saturday)* a la carte approx. 21.00 **st.** – **Buttery** *(closed Sunday and August)* a la carte 16.50/20.75 **st.** – **160 rm, 26 suites.**

Lowndes Thistle (Thistle), 21 Lowndes St., SW1X 9ES, ✆ 235 6020, Telex 919065 – ☎. AE VISA FR i
M 13.75 **t.** and a la carte – 6.75 – **79 rm** 78.00/120.00 **st.**, **5 suites.**

Sheraton-Belgravia, 20 Chesham Pl., SW1X 8HQ, ✆ 235 6040, Telex 919020 – ☎. AE VISA FR u
M *(closed lunch Saturday and Bank Holidays)* 15.00 **t.** (lunch) and a la carte 12.25/16.25 **t.** 3.50 – 7.00 – **89 rm** 97.00/112.00, **7 suites** 170.00/200.00 **t.**

XX **Motcombs,** 26 Motcomb St., SW1X 8JU, ✆ 235 6382 – AE VISA FR z
closed Sunday, Easter, Christmas and Bank Holiday Mondays – **M** a la carte 11.25/14.50 **t.** 2.70.

XX **Salloos,** 62-64 Kinnerton St., SW1 8ER, ✆ 235 4444, Indian and Pakistani rest. – . AE VISA FQ a
closed Sunday and Bank Holidays – **M** a la carte 14.80/18.80 **t.** 2.50.

Hyde Park and Knightsbridge – SW1/SW7 – pp. 14 and 15.

Harrods, Knightsbridge, SW1 ✆ 730 3488.

Hyde Park (T.H.F.), 66 Knightsbridge, SW1Y 7LA, ✆ 235 2000, Telex 262057, ← – ☎. AE VISA EQ v
M *(closed Saturday)* 14.50/19.50 **st.** and a la carte 4.50 – 9.00 – **180 rm** 115.00/129.00 **st.**, **20 suites.**

XXX **Shezan,** 16-22 Cheval Pl., Montpelier St., SW7 1ES, ✆ 589 7918, Indian and Pakistani rest. – . AE VISA ER c
closed Sunday and Bank Holidays – **M** 14.00/16.00 **t.** and a la carte.

XX Montpeliano, 13 Montpelier St., SW7 1HQ, ✆ 589 0032, Italian rest. ER e

Mayfair – W1 – pp. 12 and 13.

Claridge's, Brook St., W1A 2JQ, ✆ 629 8860, Telex 21872 – ☎. AE VISA BL c
M a la carte 21.50/24.50 **st.** 3.30 – **Causerie** – 11.00 – **205 rm** 100.00/175.00 **st.**, **55 suites** 275.00/550.00 **st.**

Dorchester, Park Lane, W1A 2HJ, ✆ 629 8888, Telex 887704 – ☎. AE VISA BN z
M (see **The Terrace** below) – **Grill** 16.00 **t.** and a la carte – 9.50 – **280 rm** 105.00/160.00 **st.**, **66 suites** 250.00/500.00 **st.**

Grosvenor House (T.H.F.), Park Lane, W1A 3AA, ✆ 499 6363, Telex 24871, – ☎ P. AE VISA AM a
M (see **90 Park Lane** below) – 8.00 – **472 rm** 102.00/118.00 **st.**, **50 suites.**

Inn on the Park, Hamilton Pl., Park Lane, W1A 1AZ, ✆ 499 0888, Telex 22771 – ☎. AE VISA BP a
M Four Seasons 20.50/22.50 **st.** and a la carte 6.50 – **Lanes** 21.00 **st.** (lunch) and a la carte 20.50/22.50 **st.** 6.50 – 7.50 – **228 rm** 130.00/162.00 **s.**, **19 suites** 260.00/607.00 **s.**

New Piccadilly, Piccadilly, W1V 0BH, ✆ 734 8000, Telex 25795, , squash – ☎. AE VISA EM a
M 14.00/28.00 **st.** and a la carte 5.50 – 7.25 – **290 rm** 105.00/130.00 **st.**, **19 suites** 150.00/350.00 **st.**

❀ **Connaught,** 16 Carlos Pl., W1Y 6AL, ✆ 499 7070 – rest. BM **e**
M (booking essential) – **90 rm, 25 suites**
Spec. Pâté de turbot froid au homard, sauce pudeur, Rendez-vous du pêcheur, sauce légère au parfum d'Armorique, Salmis de canard strasbourgeoise en surprise.

Athenaeum (Rank), 116 Piccadilly, W1V 0BJ, ✆ 499 3464, Telex 261589 – rest. CP **s**
M 16.50 **st.** (lunch) and a la carte 19.05/24.45 **st.** 4.00 – 8.00 – **112 rm** 108.00/150.00 **st.**, **22 suites** 180.00/220.00 **st.** – SB (weekends only) 90.00/100.00 **st.**

Brown's (T.H.F.), 29-34 Albemarle St., W1A 4SW, ✆ 493 6020, Telex 28686 – DM **e**
M 22.00/23.00 **st.** and a la carte 4.25 – 8.00 – **125 rm** 88.00/113.00 **st.**, **5 suites**.

May Fair (Inter-Con.), Stratton St., W1A 2AN, ✆ 629 7777, Telex 262526 – DN **z**
M 15.00/18.00 **t.** and a la carte 5.50 – 8.10 – **327 rm** 90.00/125.00, **24 suites** 175.00/700.00.

Marriott, Duke St., Grosvenor Sq., W1A 4AW, ✆ 493 1232, Telex 268101 – BL **a**
M 17.50 **t.** and a la carte 4.50 – 8.00 – **229 rm** 115.00/140.00 **t.**, **18 suites** 230.00/805.00 **t.**

Inter-Continental (Inter-Con.), 1 Hamilton Pl., Hyde Park Corner, W1V 0QY, ✆ 409 3131, Telex 25853 – BP **o**
M (see also **Le Soufflé** below) 16.00/28.00 **t.** and a la carte 6.40 – 9.00 – **491 rm** 121.00/141.00, **15 suites** 220.00/810.00.

Britannia (Inter-Con.), Grosvenor Sq., W1A 3AN, ✆ 629 9400, Telex 23941 – BM **x**
M 15.50 **st.** and a la carte 4.50 – 9.00 – **356 rm** 88.00/160.00 **s.**, **12 suites** 200.00/1075.00 **s.**

Westbury (T.H.F.), New Bond St. (entrance on Conduit St.), W1A 4UH, ✆ 629 7755, Telex 24378 – DM **a**
M 12.25 **t.** (lunch) and a la carte 21.15/28.70 **t.** 5.50 – 8.00 – **240 rm** 85.00/99.00 **st.**, **15 suites**.

Londonderry, Park Lane, W1Y 8AP, ✆ 493 7292, Telex 263292 – BP **i**
M a la carte 22.00/29.00 **st.** 6.50 – 8.50 – **150 rm** 115.00/140.00 **s.**, **12 suites** 180.00/265.00 **s.**

Hilton International, 22 Park Lane, W1A 2HH, ✆ 493 8000, Telex 24873, ≤ London – BP **e**
M 18.90/25.00 **st.** and a la carte 6.50 – 8.50 – **501 rm** 125.00/145.00, **54 suites** 175.00/700.00.

Holiday Inn, 3 Berkeley St., W1X 6NE, ✆ 493 8282, Telex 24561 – DN **r**
M 11.00/12.00 **st.** and a la carte – 7.50 – **188 rm** 83.00/95.00 **st.**, **7 suites** 175.00/345.00 **st.**

Park Lane, Piccadilly, W1Y 8BX, ✆ 499 6321, Telex 21533 – BP **x**
M 13.50/15.50 **st.** and a la carte 5.50 – 7.50 – **323 rm** 89.95/120.00 **st.**, **54 suites** 130.00/350.00 **st.**

Chesterfield, 35 Charles St., W1X 8LX, ✆ 491 2622, Telex 269394 – CN **c**
closed 25 and 26 December – **M** 15.00/16.00 **t.** and a la carte 4.50 – 7.25 – **114 rm** 95.00/110.00 **st.**, **1 suite** 200.00 **st.**

XXXXX ❀❀ **The Terrace,** (at Dorchester H.), Park Lane, W1A 2HJ, ✆ 629 8888, Telex 887704, French rest. – BN **z**
closed Sunday – **M** (dinner only) 32.00 **st.** and a la carte 23.50/30.00 **st.**
Spec. Parfait de foies de volailles aux truffes, Sole de Douvres poelée aux poireaux et truffes, Rosette de boeuf pochée sabayon parfumé aux grains de moutarde.

XXXXX **Mirabelle,** 56 Curzon St., W1Y 8DL, ✆ 499 4636 – CN **a**
closed Sunday and Bank Holidays – **M** 13.50/30.00 **st.** and a la carte 7.50.

XXXXX **90 Park Lane** (T.H.F.), (at Grosvenor House H.), Park Lane, W1A 3AA, ✆ 409 1290, Telex 24871 – AM **a**
closed Saturday lunch, Sunday and Bank Holidays – **M** 17.50/39.00 **st.** and a la carte 6.25.

XXXX ❀❀❀ **Le Gavroche,** 43 Upper Brook St., W1P 1PS, ✆ 408 0881, French rest. – AM **c**
closed Saturday, Sunday, 24 December-2 January and Bank Holidays – **M** (booking essential) 19.50/30.00 **st.** and a la carte 4.90
Spec. Soufflé suissesse, Assiette du boucher, Sablé aux fraises.

XXXX ❀ **Le Soufflé** (at Inter-Continental H.), 1 Hamilton Pl., Hyde Park Corner, W1V 0QY, ✆ 409 3131, Telex 25853 – BP **o**
M 16.00/28.00 **t.** and a la carte 6.40
Spec. Les paupiettes de turbot aux langoustines, La salade de homard au foie gras, Les filets d'agneau au basilic.

XXXX **Scott's,** 20 Mount St., W1Y 6HE, ✆ 629 5248, Seafood – BM **r**
closed Sunday lunch and Bank Holidays – **M** a la carte 27.70/40.20 **t.** 3.25.

XXX **Princess Garden,** 8-10 North Audley St., W1Y 1WF, ☎ 493 3223, Chinese-Peking rest. – ▤. AE ⓓ VISA AL z
M 20.00/35.00 **t.** and a la carte 🍷 4.00.

XXX **Tiberio,** 22 Queen St., W1X 7PJ, ☎ 629 3561, Italian rest., Dancing – AE ⓓ VISA
closed Saturday lunch, Sunday and Bank Holidays – **M** a la carte 17.05/28.25 **t.** CN z

XX **Greenhouse,** 27a Hay's Mews, W1X 7RJ, ☎ 499 3331 – AE ⓓ VISA BN a
closed Saturday lunch, Sunday, 24 December-5 January and Bank Holidays – **M** a la carte 12.80/16.40 **t.** 🍷 2.65.

XX **Langan's Brasserie,** Stratton St., W1X 5FD, ☎ 491 8822 – AE ⓓ VISA DN e
closed Saturday lunch, Sunday and Bank Holidays – **M** (booking essential) a la carte 13.30/20.00 **t.** 🍷 4.50.

XX **Miyama,** 38 Clarges St., W1Y 7PJ, ☎ 499 2443, Japanese rest. – ▤. AE ⓓ VISA
closed Saturday lunch, Sunday, Christmas-New Year and Bank Holidays – **M** 7.00/24.00 **t.** and a la carte. CN e

XX Mr. Kai, 65 South Audley St., W1 5FD, ☎ 493 8988, Chinese-Peking rest. – ▤ BM v

XX Shogun (at Britannia H.), Adams Row, W1, ☎ 493 1255, Telex 8813271, Japanese rest. BM x

XX **Ho-Ho,** 29 Maddox St., W1, ☎ 493 1228, Chinese rest. – ▤. AE ⓓ VISA DL x
closed Sunday and Bank Holidays – **M** 8.00/13.00 **t.** and a la carte.

XX One Two Three, 27 Davies St., W1, ☎ 409 0750, Japanese rest. – ▤ BM s

X **Ikeda,** 30 Brook St., W1Y 1AG, ☎ 629 2730, Japanese rest. – ▤. AE ⓓ VISA CKL a
closed Sunday lunch, Saturday and Bank Holidays – **M** 10.00/25.00 **t.** and a la carte.

X **Trattoria Fiori,** 87-88 Mount St., W1Y 5HG, ☎ 499 1447, Italian rest. – AE ⓓ VISA
closed Sunday and Bank Holidays – **M** 15.80 **t.** and a la carte 🍷 2.80. BM o

Regent's Park and Marylebone – ✉ NW1/NW6/NW8/W1 – **Except where otherwise stated see pp. 12 and 13.**

ℹ Selfridges, Oxford St., W1 ☎ 730 3488.

Churchill, 30 Portman Sq., W1A 4ZX, ☎ 486 5800, Telex 264831 – |‡| ▤ TV ☎ ♿ Ⓟ. AE ⓓ VISA. AJ x
M a la carte 15.80/23.80 **t.** – ☕ 7.50 – **489 rm** 95.00/107.00, **39 suites** 175.00/420.00.

Portman Inter-Continental (Inter-Con.), 22 Portman Sq., W1H 9FL, ☎ 486 5844, Telex 261526 – |‡| ▤ TV ☎ ♿ Ⓟ. AE ⓓ VISA. AJ o
M 15.00 **t.** (lunch) and a la carte 26.00/34.00 **t.** 🍷 8.00 – ☕ 8.50 – **278 rm** 94.00/121.00, **8 suites** 275.00/350.00.

Montcalm, Great Cumberland Pl., W1A 2LF, ☎ 402 4288, Telex 28710 – |‡| ▤ TV ☎. pp. 16 and 17 FY x
116 rm.

Holiday Inn, 134 George St., W1H 6DN, ☎ 723 1277, Telex 27983, – |‡| ▤ TV ☎ ♿ Ⓟ. AE ⓓ VISA pp. 16 and 17 FY i
M 12.50 **t.** and a la carte 🍷 4.30 – ☕ 6.60 – **241 rm** 94.30/100.05 **st.**, **2 suites** 250.00/375.00 **st.**

Selfridge (Thistle), 400 Orchard St., W1H 0JS, ☎ 408 2080, Telex 22361 – |‡| ▤ TV ☎ ♿ Ⓟ. AE ⓓ VISA. AK e
M 12.50/14.50 **t.** and a la carte 🍷 3.95 – ☕ 7.00 – **298 rm** 85.00/106.00 **t.**

Ladbroke Westmoreland (Ladbroke), 18 Lodge Rd, NW8 7JT, ☎ 722 7722, Telex 23101 – |‡| ▤ TV ☎ Ⓟ. AE ⓓ VISA pp. 3-6 JS v
M (carving rest.) 12.50 **t.** and a la carte 🍷 4.00 – ☕ 7.00 – **347 rm** 69.00/95.00 **st.** – SB (weekends only) 73.00/80.00 **st.**

Clifton Ford, 47 Welbeck St., W1M 8DN, ☎ 486 6600, Telex 22569 – |‡| TV ☎. AE ⓓ VISA BH a
M a la carte 13.45/19.95 **st.** 🍷 3.95 – ☕ 6.75 – **220 rm** 65.00/97.00 **st.**, **2 suites.**

St. George's (T.H.F.), Langham Pl., W1N 8QS, ☎ 580 0111, Telex 27274, ≤ – |‡| TV ☎. AE ⓓ VISA pp. 3-6 LT a
M 13.50 **st.** and a la carte 🍷 2.75 – ☕ 6.50 – **85 rm** 64.50/82.00 **st.**, **3 suites.**

Cumberland (T.H.F.), Marble Arch, W1A 4RF, ☎ 262 1234, Telex 22215 – |‡| TV ☎ ♿. AE ⓓ VISA. AK n
M (carving rest.) 9.65 **st.** and a la carte 🍷 2.70 – ☕ 6.00 – **894 rm** 61.50/79.00 **st.**, **9 suites.**

Durrants, 26-32 George St., W1H 6BJ, ☎ 935 8131, Telex 894919 – |‡| TV ⇔wc ☎. AE ⓓ VISA. AH e
M a la carte 12.90/16.80 **t.** 🍷 3.25 – ☕ 5.00 – **102 rm** 29.00/60.00 **st.**, **3 suites** 150.00 **st.**

Savoy Court, Granville Pl., W1H 0EH, ☎ 408 0130, Telex 8955515 – |‡| TV ⇔wc ☎ ♿. AE ⓓ VISA. AK c
M 10.50 **t.** and a la carte – ☕ 6.00 – **97 rm** 55.90/79.90 **st.**

Bryanston Court, 56-60 Great Cumberland Pl., W1H 7FD, ☎ 262 3141, Group Telex 262076 – |‡| TV ⇔wc ⋔wc ☎. AE ⓓ VISA. pp. 16 and 17 FY z
M *(closed Saturday, Sunday and Bank Holidays)* 11.50 **t.** 🍷 2.50 – ☕ 4.00 – **53 rm** 39.00/52.00 **st.**

XXX **Odins,** 27 Devonshire St., W1N 1RS, ☏ 935 7296 – AE pp. 3-6 KT n
closed Saturday lunch, Sunday and Bank Holidays – **M** 13.00 **t.** (lunch) and a la carte 15.05/23.60 **t.** 3.25.

XXX ✿ **Rue St. Jacques,** 5 Charlotte St., W1P 1HD, ☏ 637 0222, French rest. – AE VISA pp. 3-6 MT c
closed Saturday lunch, Sunday, 25 to 28 December and Bank Holidays – **M** 15.00 **t.** (lunch) and a la carte 21.20/31.25 **t.**
Spec. Warm oysters with a very light vinaigrette, Sauteed scallops garnished with mussels, Cutlets of venison and piquant blackcurrant sauce.

XX **D'Artagnan,** 19 Blandford St., W1H 3AD, ☏ 935 1023, French rest. – AE VISA
closed Saturday lunch, Sunday and Bank Holidays – **M** 11.50/13.50 **t.** and a la carte. AH a

XX **Gaylord,** 79-81 Mortimer St., W1N 7TB, ☏ 580 3615, Indian and Pakistani rest. – AE VISA pp. 3-6 LT c
M 8.25 **t.** and a la carte 8.05/9.85 **t.** 3.60.

XX **La Pavona,** 5-7 Blandford St., W1H 3AF, ☏ 486 9696, Italian rest. – AE BH c
closed Saturday lunch, Sunday and Bank Holidays – **M** 8.25 **t.** (lunch) and a la carte 13.00/19.00 **t.** 3.00.

X **Le Muscadet,** 25 Paddington St., W1M 3RF, ☏ 935 2883, French rest. – VISA
closed Saturday lunch, Sunday, 3 weeks August, 2 weeks Christmas-New Year and Bank Holidays – **M** a la carte 8.15/9.90 **t.** 2.80. KT e

X L'Aventure, 3 Blenheim Terr., NW8 4JS, ☏ 624 6232, French rest. JR s

St. James's – ✉ W1/SW1/WC2 – pp. 12 and 13.

Ritz, Piccadilly, W1V 9DG, ☏ 493 8181, Telex 267200, « Elegant restaurant in Louis XV style » – TV AE VISA DN a
M 17.50/26.50 **st.** and a la carte 5.25 – 8.50 – **139 rm** 100.00/160.00 **st.**, **17 suites** 300.00/525.00 **st.**

Stafford, 16-18 St. James's Pl., SW1A 1NJ, ☏ 493 0111, Telex 28602 – TV AE DN u
M 15.00/17.50 **st.** and a la carte – 7.50 – **62 rm** 103.00/136.50 **st.**, **5 suites** 198.00/400.00 **st.**

Dukes, 35 St. James's Pl., SW1A 1NY, ☏ 491 4840, Telex 28283 – TV AE VISA EP x
M a la carte 22.00/27.00 **st.** – 7.50 – **51 rm** 90.00/140.00 **st.**, **14 suites** 190.00/400.00 **st.**

Cavendish (T.H.F.), Jermyn St., SW1Y 6JF, ☏ 930 2111, Telex 263187 – rest TV P AE VISA EN i
M (bar lunch Saturday) 12.95 **st.** (lunch) and a la carte 16.00/24.00 3.95 – 6.00 – **253 rm** 71.00/90.50 **st.**

Royal Trafalgar Thistle (Thistle), Whitcomb St., WC2H 7HG, ☏ 930 4477, Telex 298564 – rest TV wc AE VISA GM r
M a la carte 10.50/16.00 **t.** 3.65 – 5.95 – **108 rm** 52.00/78.00 **t.**

Pastoria, 3-6 St. Martin's St., WC2H 7HL, ☏ 930 8641, Telex 25538 – TV wc AE VISA GM v
closed January and February – **M** 12.50 **t.** 3.00 – 5.00 – **52 rm** 57.00/75.00 **st.**

XXXXX **Maxim's de Paris,** 32-34 Panton St., SW1, ☏ 839 4809, French rest., Dancing – AE VISA GM a
closed Saturday lunch, Sunday, Christmas and Bank Holidays – **M** 18.50 **t.** (lunch)and a la carte 19.20/28.20 **t.** 4.50.

XXXX **A L'Ecu de France,** 111 Jermyn St., SW1, ☏ 930 2837, French rest. – AE VISA
closed lunch Saturday and Sunday – **M** 15.00/22.00 **st.** and a la carte 5.50. FM z

XXX **Suntory,** 72-73 St. James's St., SW1A 1PH, ☏ 409 0201, Japanese rest. – AE VISA EP z
closed Sunday and Bank Holidays – **M** 20.00 and a la carte 12.30/23.40.

XX **Le Caprice,** Arlington House, Arlington St., SW1A 1RT, ☏ 629 2239 – AE VISA
closed lunch Saturday and Bank Holidays and 25 December-2 January – **M** a la carte 11.25/15.75 **t.** DN c

Soho – ✉ W1/WC2 – pp. 12 and 13.

XXX **Leonis Quo Vadis,** 26-29 Dean St., W1V 6LL, ☏ 437 9585, Italian rest. – AE VISA
closed lunch Saturday, Sunday and Bank Holidays – **M** a la carte 11.95/16.45 **t.** 2.95. FK u

XX **Au Jardin des Gourmets,** 5 Greek St., Soho Sq., W1V 5LA, ☏ 437 1816, French rest. – AE VISA GJ a
closed lunch Saturday and Bank Holidays, Sunday and 4 days at Christmas – **M** 20.00 **t.** and a la carte 11.65/19.40 **t.** 2.75.

XX **L'Escargot,** 48 Greek St., W1V 5LQ, ☏ 437 2679 – AE VISA GK e
closed Saturday lunch, Sunday, Christmas-New Year and Bank Holidays – **M** a la carte approx. 15.50 **t.**

XX **Gay Hussar,** 2 Greek St., W1V 6NB, ☏ 437 0973, Hungarian rest. – GJ c
closed Sunday and Bank Holidays – **M** 10.00 **t.** (lunch) and a la carte 13.00/17.50 **t.** 3.00.

XX **Red Fort,** 77 Dean St., W1V 5HA, ✆ 437 2525, Indian rest. – AE VISA FJK **r**
M 10.00/15.00 **t.**

XX **Chesa (Swiss Centre),** 2 New Coventry St., W1V 3HG, ✆ 734 1291 – ▤. AE VISA GM **n**
closed Christmas Day – **M** 14.50 **st.** and a la carte 11.40/18.20 **st.** 🍾 2.60.

XX **Venezia,** 21 Great Chapel St., W1V 3AQ, ✆ 437 6506, Italian rest. – AE VISA
closed Saturday lunch, Sunday and Bank Holidays – **M** a la carte 9.75/16.45 **t.** 🍾 2.40. FJ **a**

XX **Kaya,** 22-25 Dean St., W1, ✆ 437 6630, Korean rest. – ▤ FJ **i**
closed lunch Saturday and Sunday and Bank Holidays – **M** 6.00/17.00 **t.** and a la carte.

XX **Poons,** 4 Leicester St., WC2, ✆ 437 1528, Chinese rest. – ▤ GM **i**
closed Sunday and Christmas – **M** 8.50 **t.** 🍾 3.80.

XX **Rugantino,** 26 Romilly St., W1V 5TQ, ✆ 437 5302, Italian rest. – AE VISA GK **u**
closed Saturday lunch, Sunday and Bank Holidays – **M** 13.50 **st.** and a la carte 10.95/13.05 **t.** 🍾 2.25.

X **Frith's,** 14 Frith St., W1, ✆ 439 3370 – AE VISA FGK **s**
closed Saturday lunch and Sunday – **M** 15.00 **t.** 🍾 3.00.

X **Chiang Mai,** 48 Frith St., W1, ✆ 437 7444, Thai rest. – AE VISA GK **v**
M a la carte approx. 12.00 **t.** 🍾 2.60.

X **Gallery Rendezvous,** 53-55 Beak St., W1R 3DH, ✆ 734 0445, Chinese-Peking rest. – ▤. AE VISA EL **a**
M 15.00/30.00 **t.** and a la carte 🍾 2.60.

X **Fung Shing,** 15 Lisle St., WC2H 7BE, ✆ 437 1539, Chinese-Cantonese rest. – AE VISA GL **a**
M 10.00/15.00 **t.** and a la carte.

X **Joy King Lau,** 3 Leicester St., WC2H 7BL, ✆ 437 1132, Chinese rest. – AE GM **e**
M 9.00 **t.** and a la carte 🍾 2.00.

X **Saigon,** 45 Frith St., W1V 5TE, ✆ 437 7109, Vietnamese rest. – AE VISA GL **x**
closed Sunday and Bank Holidays – **M** 8.70 **t.** and a la carte.

Strand and Covent Garden – ✉ WC2 – p. 17.

Savoy, Strand, WC2R 0EU, ✆ 836 4343, Telex 24234 – TV ☎. AE VISA. EX **a**
M Grill *(closed Saturday lunch, Sunday, first 3 weeks August and Bank Holidays)* a la carte 15.75/30.25 **st.** 🍾 3.50 – **River** 16.50/25.00 **st.** and a la carte 🍾 3.30 – ☕ 8.25 – **200 rm** 110.00/135.00 **st.**, **48 suites**.

Howard, 12 Temple Pl., WC2R 2PR, ✆ 836 3555, Telex 268047 – ▤ TV ☎. AE VISA. FV **e**
141 rm, **2 suites**.

Waldorf (T.H.F.), Aldwych, WC2B 4DD, ✆ 836 2400, Telex 24574 – ▤ rest TV ☎. AE VISA EV **x**
M *(closed lunch Saturday and Sunday)* 10.50/15.00 **st.** and a la carte 🍾 4.00 – ☕ 6.00 – **310 rm** 63.50/81.50 **st.**

XXXX **Boulestin,** 1a Henrietta St., WC2E 8PS, ✆ 836 7061, French rest. – ▤. AE VISA
closed Saturday lunch, Sunday, last 3 weeks August and Bank Holidays – **M** 14.00 **t.** (lunch) and a la carte approx. 17.25 **t.** 🍾 5.00. EV **r**

XXX **Inigo Jones,** 14 Garrick St., WC2E 9BJ, ✆ 836 6456 – ▤. AE VISA DV **o**
closed Saturday lunch, Sunday and Bank Holidays – **M** 14.75 **t.** and a la carte 24.50/33.50 **t.** 🍾 6.10.

XXX **Simpson's-in-the-Strand,** 100 Strand, WC2R 0EW, ✆ 836 9112, English rest. – ▤. AE VISA EV **o**
closed Sunday, Easter, 25 and 26 December, 1 January and Bank Holidays – **M** a la carte 14.60/19.85 **st.** 🍾 2.90.

XXX **Thomas de Quincey's,** 36 Tavistock St., WC2E 7PB, ✆ 240 3972 – AE VISA
closed Saturday lunch, Sunday, last 3 weeks August and Bank Holidays – **M** 25.00/30.00 **st.** and a la carte 🍾 3.50. EV **c**

XX **Interlude de Tabaillau,** 7-8 Bow St., WC2, ✆ 379 6473, French rest. – ▤. AE VISA DEV **x**
closed Saturday lunch, Sunday, 1 week Easter, 3 weeks August, 1 week Christmas and Bank Holidays – **M** 18.50/23.00 (wine included) **st.**.

XX **Tourment d'Amour,** 19 New Row, WC2N 4LA, ✆ 240 5348, French rest. – AE VISA DV **z**
closed Saturday lunch, Sunday, 1 week Christmas and Bank Holidays – **M** 18.00 **t.** 🍾 4.40.

XX **Sheekey's,** 28-32 St. Martin's Court, WC2N 4AL, ✆ 240 2565, Seafood – ▤. AE VISA DV **v**
closed Sunday, 24 to 26 December, 1 January and Bank Holidays – **M** a la carte 12.95/15.65 **t.**

XX **Chez Solange,** 35 Cranbourn St., WC2H 7AD, ✆ 836 5886, French rest. – ▤. AE VISA DV **i**
closed Sunday – **M** 11.50 **t.** and a la carte 11.95/17.55 **t.** 🍾 2.95.

XX Azami, 13-15 West St., WC2H 9BL, ✆ 240 0634, Japanese rest. pp. 12 and 13 GK z

XX **Frère Jacques,** 38 Longacre, WC2, ✆ 836 7823, Seafood – ▤. AE VISA DV n
closed Sunday – **M** 10.00 **st.** and a la carte 12.55/16.10 **st.** 2.50.

X **Poons of Covent Garden,** 41 King St., WC2E 8JS, ✆ 240 1743, Chinese-Cantonese rest. – AE VISA DV r
closed Sunday and 24 to 27 December – **M** 7.50/14.00 **t.** and a la carte.

X **Cafe Pelican,** 45 St. Martins Lane, WC2N 4EJ, ✆ 379 0309, French rest., « Art deco » – ▤. AE VISA DX e
M 10.95 **t.** and a la carte 3.45.

X **Magnos Brasserie,** 65a Long Acre, WC2E 9JH, ✆ 836 6077, French rest. – AE VISA EV e
closed Saturday lunch, Sunday, 24 December-2 January and Bank Holidays – **M** 7.45 **st.** (dinner) and a la carte 12.05/16.65 **t.** 4.25.

X Laguna 50, 50 St. Martin's Lane, WC2N 4EA, ✆ 836 0960, Italian rest. DV u

X **Flounders,** 19 Tavistock St., WC2, ✆ 836 3925, Seafood – ▤. AE VISA EV a
closed Sunday and Bank Holidays – **M** a la carte 10.80/12.80 **t.** 3.15.

X **Happy Wok,** 52 Floral St., WC2, ✆ 836 3696, Chinese rest. – AE VISA DV e
closed Sunday – **M** 18.00 **t.** and a la carte.

X **Grimes,** 6 Garrick St., WC2R 9BH, ✆ 836 7008, Seafood – AE VISA DV x
closed Saturday lunch, Sunday and 24 to 27 December – **M** 9.00 **t.** (lunch) and a la carte 12.00/15.50 **t.** 2.50.

Victoria – ✉ SW1 – Except where otherwise stated see p. 16.

Goring, 15 Beeston Pl., Grosvenor Gdns, SW1W 0JW, ✆ 834 8211, Telex 919166 – ▤ TV ☎. AE VISA BV a
M 12.50/14.00 **t.** and a la carte 3.50 – 6.50 – **90 rm** 67.50/95.00 **st.**, **4 suites** 140.00 **st.**

Royal Horseguards Thistle (Thistle), 2 Whitehall Court, SW1A 2EX, ✆ 839 3400, Telex 917096 – ▤ rest TV ☎. AE VISA pp. 7-10 NV a
M 12.00 **t.** and a la carte 6.45 – 5.75 – **284 rm** 59.00/69.00 **t.**, **6 suites**.

Stakis St. Ermin's (Stakis), Caxton St., SW1H 0QW, ✆ 222 7888, Telex 917731 – ▤ rest TV ☎. AE VISA CV a
M (carving rest.) 25.00 **t.** and a la carte – 6.50 – **250 rm** 68.00/83.00 **t.**, **6 suites** approx. 150.00 **t.**

Royal Westminster Thistle (Thistle), 49 Buckingham Palace Rd, SW1W 0QT, ✆ 834 1821, Telex 916821 – TV ☎. AE VISA BV z
M 9.00/15.00 **t.** and a la carte 3.15 – 5.50 – **118 rm** 53.50/95.00 **t.**, **18 suites**.

Grosvenor, 101 Buckingham Palace Rd, SW1W 0SJ, ✆ 834 9494, Telex 916006 – ▤ rest TV wc. BV e
– **365 rm**.

Ebury Court, 26 Ebury St., SW1W 0LU, ✆ 730 8147 – wc. VISA AV i
M a la carte 7.10/11.90 **t.** 2.10 – **39 rm** 32.00/58.00 **t.**

Hamilton House, 60-64 Warwick Way, SW1V 1SA, ✆ 821 7113 – TV wc. VISA BX n
M (grill rest. only) (dinner only) a la carte approx. 4.10 **t.** 2.30 – **40 rm** 24.00/43.00 **t.** – SB (November-March) 42.00 **st.**

XXX Lockets, Marsham Court, Marsham St., SW1P 4JY, ✆ 834 9552, English rest. pp. 7-10 MY z

XXX **Kundan,** 3 Horseferry Rd, SW1P 2AN, ✆ 834 3434, Indian and Pakistani rest. – ▤. AE VISA pp. 7-10 NXY a
closed Sunday and Bank Holidays – **M** 10.00/15.00 5.00.

XXX Santini, 29 Ebury St., SW1W 0NZ, ✆ 730 4094, Italian rest. – ▤ ABV v

XX **Ken Lo's Memories of China,** 67-69 Ebury St., SW1W 0NZ, ✆ 730 7734, Chinese rest. – AE VISA AX u
closed Sunday and Bank Holidays – **M** 15.50/20.50 **t.** and a la carte.

XX ✿ **Le Mazarin,** 30 Winchester St., SW1, ✆ 828 3366, French rest. – ▤. AE pp. 7-10 LZ i
closed Sunday – **M** (dinner only) 22.50 **st.** 5.70
Spec. Fricassée de poulet au basilic, Filet de sole Mazarin, Tranchettes d'onglet poêlees aux échalotes.

XX Villa Claudius, 10a The Broadway, SW1, ✆ 222 3338, Italian rest. MX a

XX **The Restaurant,** Dolphin Square, Chichester St., SW1V 3LX, ✆ 828 3207, French rest., « Art deco » – AE VISA pp. 7-10 LZ e
closed Sunday and Bank Holidays – **M** 16.50 **t.** and a la carte 3.50.

XX **Pomegranates,** 94 Grosvenor Rd, SW1V 3LG, ✆ 828 6560 – AE VISA pp. 7-10 LMZ a
closed Saturday lunch, Sunday and Bank Holidays – **M** 15.90 **t.** (lunch) and a la carte 13.60/19.80 **t.** 3.50.

XX **Eatons,** 49 Elizabeth St., SW1W 9PP, ✆ 730 0074 – AE VISA AX a
closed Saturday, Sunday and Bank Holidays – **M** a la carte 10.15/14.00 **s.** 2.80.

XX **Ciboure,** 21 Eccleston St., SW1W 9LX, ✆ 730 2505, French rest. – AE VISA AX z
closed Saturday lunch, Sunday and Bank Holidays – **M** 17.00 **t.** (lunch) and a la carte 14.55/16.85 **s.** 2.95.

✗ **La Fontana,** 101 Pimlico Rd, SW1W 8PH, ✆ 730 6630, Italian rest. – AE VISA
closed Bank Holidays – **M** a la carte 10.90/15.60 **t.** 3.00. pp. 14 and 15 FT **o**

✗ La Poule au Pot, 231 Ebury St., SW1W 8UT, ✆ 730 7763, French rest. pp. 7-10 KY **n**

✗ **Mimmo d'Ischia,** 61 Elizabeth St., SW1W 9PP, ✆ 730 5406, Italian rest. – AE VISA AX **o**
closed Sunday, Easter, Christmas and Bank Holidays – **M** a la carte 12.65/17.75 **t.** 3.75.

✗ Tate Gallery Rest., Tate Gallery, Millbank, SW1P 4RG, ✆ 834 6754, English rest., « Rex Whistler murals » – pp. 7-10 NY **c**
M (lunch only).

✗ **Bumbles,** 16 Buckingham Palace Rd, SW1W 0QP, ✆ 828 2903, Bistro – AE VISA
closed Saturday lunch and Sunday – **M** 10.95 **t.** and a la carte 10.25/12.20 **t.** 2.15. BV **c**

✗ **Villa Medici,** 35 Belgrave Rd, SW1, ✆ 828 3613, Italian rest. – AE VISA BX **c**
closed Saturday lunch, Sunday and Bank Holidays – **M** a la carte 9.50/15.60 **t.** 2.50.

Bray-on-Thames Berks W : 34 m. by M 4 (junction 8-9) and A 308 – 404 R 29 – pop. 9 ,427 – ✉ ☎ 0628 Maidenhead

✗✗✗✗ ✿✿✿ **Waterside Inn,** Ferry Rd, SL6 2AT, ✆ 20691, Telex 8813079, <, French rest., « Thames-side setting », – **P**. AE VISA
closed Tuesday lunch, Sunday dinner 20 October-Easter, Monday, 26 December-February and Bank Holidays – **M** 20.00/33.00 **st.** and a la carte
Spec. Huitres tièdes en feuilleté au vinaigre de framboises (October-March), Caneton croisé challandais aux clous de girofle et au miel (October-March), Tarte citron et délice cassis.

Reading

at Shinfield Berks. W : 43 m. by M 4 (Junction 11) and B 3350 on A 327 403 404 Q 29 – ✉ ☎ 0734 Reading :

✗✗✗ ✿✿ **Chez Nico,** The Old Vicarage, Church Lane, RG2 9BY, ✆ 883783, French rest., – **P**. VISA
closed Monday lunch, Sunday, Easter, 3 weeks July-August and 10 days at Christmas – **M** 19.50/24.50 **st.** and a la carte
Spec. Foie gras frais, sa gelée au sauternes et sa petite salade, Tourte de cailles au fumet de truffes, Gratin de fruits rouges à la crème vanille.

Oxford

at Great Milton Oxon NW : 49 m. by M 40 (junction 7) and A 329 – 403 404 Q 28 – ✉ ☎ 084 46 Great Milton :

✗✗✗✗ ✿✿ **Le Manoir aux Quat'Saisons** with rm, Church Rd, OX9 7PD, ✆ 230, <, « 15C and 16C manor house », heated, , park, – TV wc ☎ **P**. VISA
closed 24 December-21 January – **M** *(closed Tuesday lunch, Sunday dinner and Monday)* 21.50/40.00 **st.** and a la carte 34.00/41.00 **st.** 7.05 – **10 rm** 100.00/180.00 **st.**, **1 suite** 210.00 **st.** – SB (weekdays only) (October-April) 140.00/180.00 **st.**
Spec. Sole soufflée à la brunoise de petits légumes et coquilles St Jacques, Assiette aux saveurs de mon terroir à l'essence de cèpes, Feuilleté tiède de poire rôtie au gingembre et citron vert..

In this Guide,
a symbol or a character, printed in red or black
does not have the same meaning.
Please read the explanatory pages carefully.

BIRMINGHAM West Midlands 403 404 O 26 – pop. 1 ,013,995 – ECD : Wednesday – ☎ 021.

See : Museum and Art Gallery★★ JZ **M1** – Museum of Science and Industry★ JY **M2** – Cathedral (stained glass windows★ 19C) KYZ **E**.

18 Cocks Moor Woods, Alcester Rd South, King's Heath ✆ 444 2062, S : 6 ½ m. by A 435 FX – 18 Edgbaston, Church Rd ✆ 454 1736, S : 1 m. FX – 18 Pype Hayes, Eachelhurst Rd, Walmley ✆ 361 1014, NE : 7 ½ m. – 9 Warley, Lightwoods Hill, ✆ 429 2440, W : 5 m.

✈ Birmingham Airport : ✆ 767 7153, E : 6 ½ m. by A 45.

2 City Arcade, ✆ 643 2514 – National Exhibition Centre ✆ 780 4141 – Birmingham Airport ✆ 767 7145.

London 122 – Bristol 91 – Liverpool 102 – Manchester 86 – Nottingham 50.

Plans on following pages

Albany (T.H.F.), Smallbrook, Queensway, B5 4EW, ✆ 643 8171, Telex 337031, <, , squash – TV ☎ . AE VISA JKZ **a**
M 8.25 **st.** and a la carte 2.70 – 5.50 – **254 rm** 47.50/57.00 **st.**, **8 suites**.

Plough and Harrow (Crest), 135 Hagley Rd, Edgbaston, B16 8LS, W : 1 ½ m. on A 456 ✆ 454 4111, Telex 338074, – TV ☎ **P**. AE VISA EX **a**
6.50 – **44 rm** 65.00/75.00 **st.**, **3 suites** – SB (weekends only) 92.00 **st.**

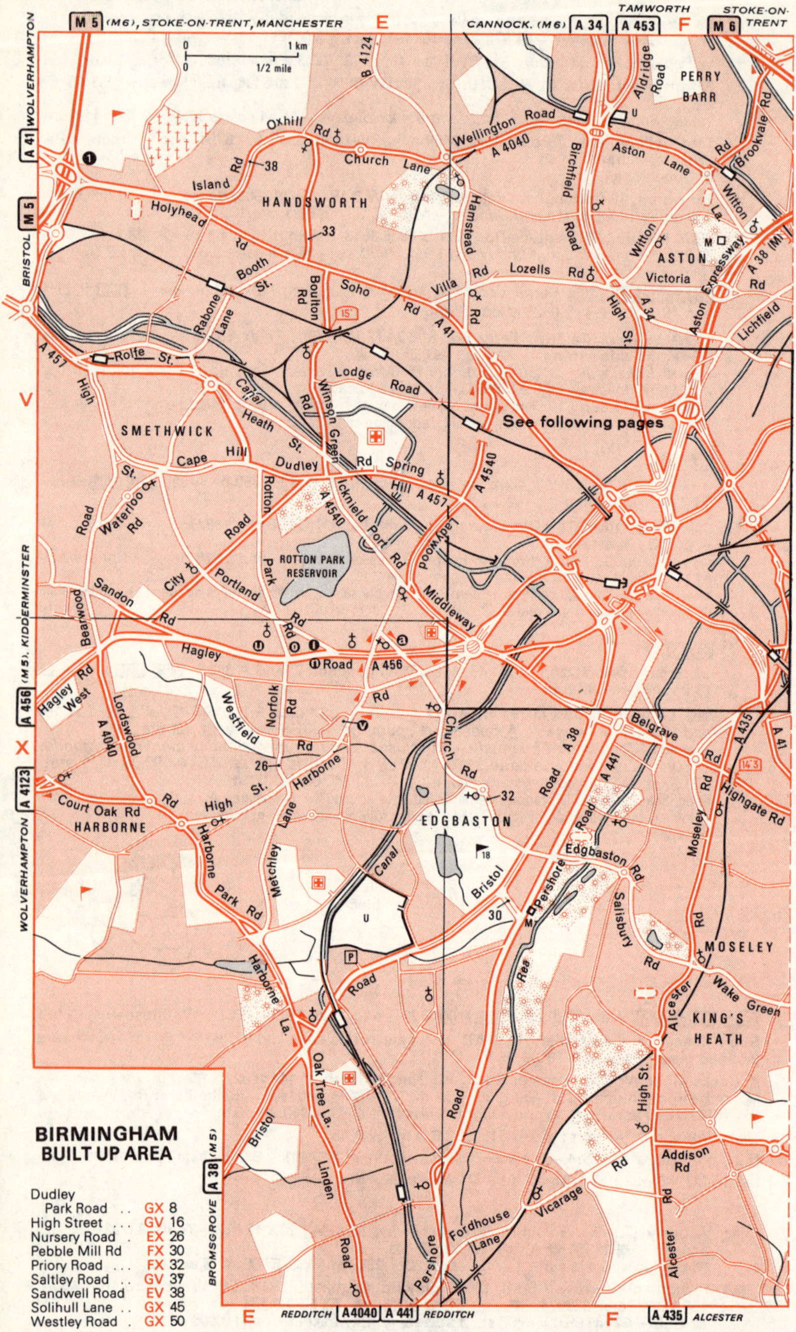

BIRMINGHAM BUILT UP AREA

Dudley Park Road ..	GX	8
High Street ...	GV	16
Nursery Road .	EX	26
Pebble Mill Rd	FX	30
Priory Road ...	FX	32
Saltley Road ..	GV	37
Sandwell Road	EV	38
Solihull Lane ..	GX	45
Westley Road .	GX	50

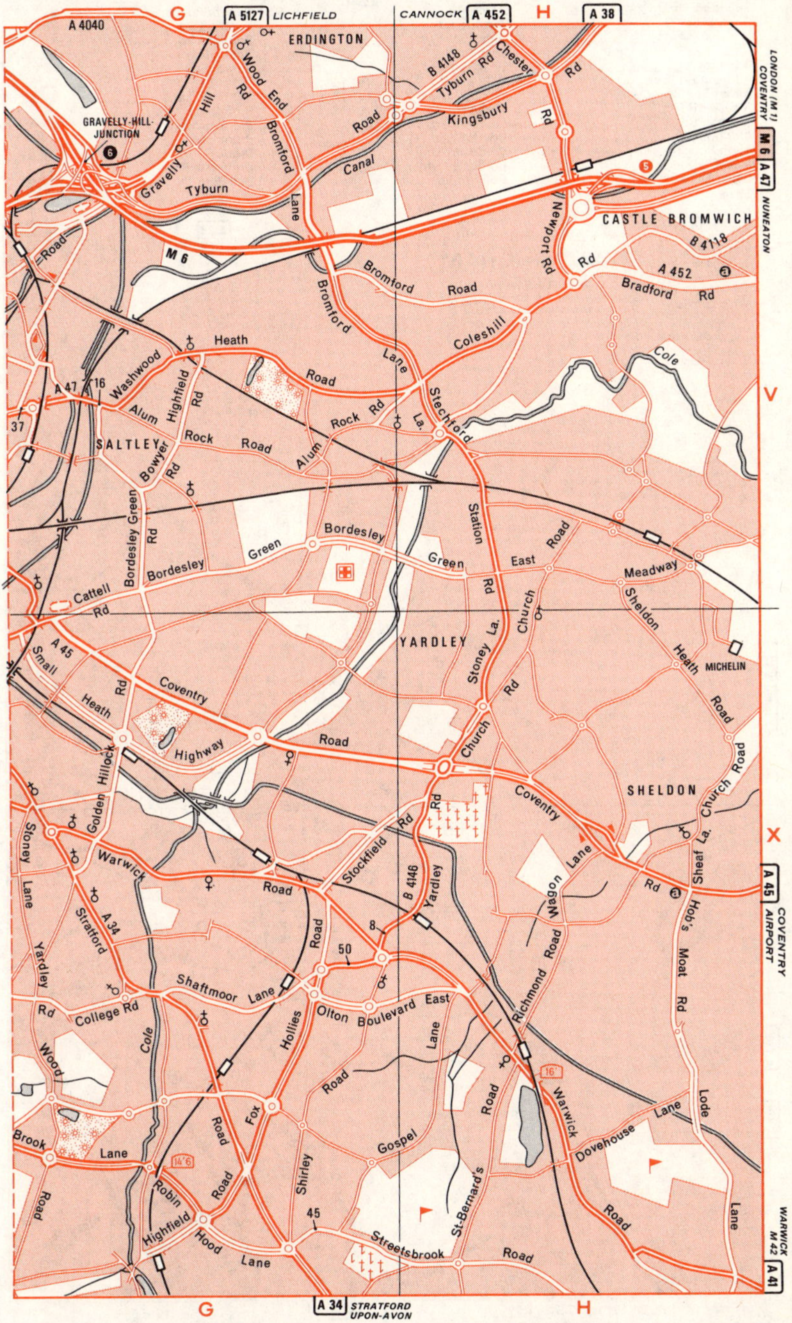
G
H
A 5127 LICHFIELD
CANNOCK A 452
A 38
A 4040
ERDINGTON
B 4148
Tyburn Rd
Chester
Rd
LONDON (M 1) COVENTRY
M 6
A 47
NUEATON
GRAVELLY-HILL-JUNCTION
Wood End Rd
Hill
Gravelly
Tyburn
Bromford Lane
Road
Kingsbury
Canal
Rd
CASTLE BROMWICH
Newport Rd
B 4118
A 452
Bradford Rd
Rd
M 6
Road
Bromford Road
Bromford Lane
Coleshill
Heath Road
Washwood
Highfield Rd
Cole
A 47
16
37
V
Alum Rock Road
SALTLEY
Bowyer Rd
Alum Rock Rd
La.
Stechford
Station Rd
Bordesley Green Rd
Bordesley Green
Bordesley Green
Green
East Road
Meadway
Cattell Rd
Sheldon Heath Road
YARDLEY
MICHELIN
A 45
Small Heath
Rd
Coventry
Highway
Road
Stoney La.
Church Rd
Church
SHELDON
Church Road
Coventry
X
Golden Hillock
Stoney Lane
Warwick Road
Stockfield Rd
Rd
B 4146
Yardley
Wagon Lane
Rd
Sheaf La.
Hob's Moat Rd
A 45 COVENTRY AIRPORT
A 34
Stratford
Road
50
8
Richmond Road
Yardley Rd
Shaftmoor Lane
College Rd
Olton Boulevard East
Hollies
Lane
Cole
Wood
Road
Road
Fox
Road
16'
Warwick
Dovehouse Lane
Lode Lane
Gospel
Brook Lane
Road
14'6
Robin
Highfield
Hood Lane
Road
Shirley
45
St-Bernard's
Streetsbrook Road
Road
WARWICK M 42
A 41
A 34 STRATFORD UPON-AVON

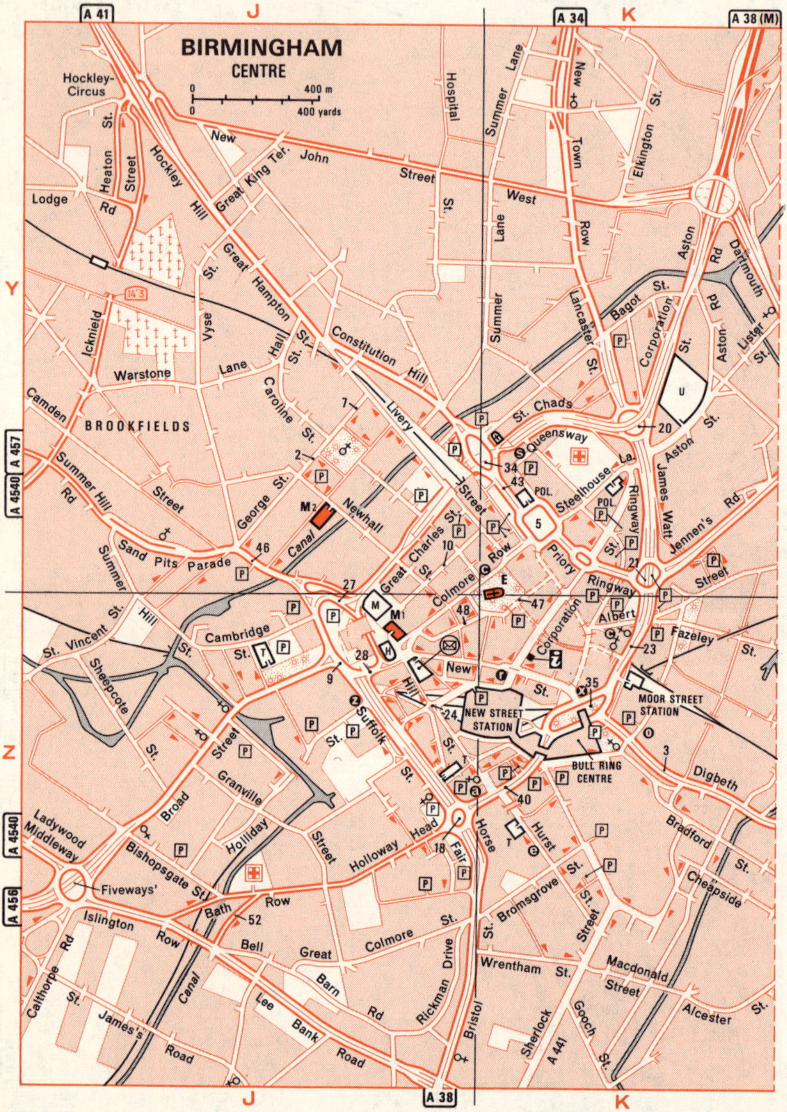

BIRMINGHAM
CENTRE
0 400 m
0 400 yards
A 41
J
A 34
K
A 38 (M)
Y
Z
A 457
A 4540
A 456
A 38
Hockley-Circus
New John Street West
Great King Ter.
Hockley Hill
Heaton St.
Street
Lodge Rd
Hospital St.
Summer Lane
New Town Row
Elkington St.
Aston Rd
Dartmouth
Great Hampton St.
Vyse St.
Icknield
Warstone Lane
Hall St.
Constitution Hill
Lancaster St.
Bagot St.
Corporation St.
Aston Rd
Lister St.
Camden
BROOKFIELDS
Caroline St.
Livery Street
St. Chads
Queensway
Aston St.
James Watt Ringway
Jennen's Rd
Summer Hill Rd
Street
George St.
Newhall
Canal
POL.
Steelhouse La.
Sand Pits Parade
Great Charles St.
Colmore Row
Priory Ringway
Street
Summer Hill St.
St. Vincent St.
Cambridge St.
Corporation St.
Albert St.
Fazeley St.
Sheepcote St.
New St.
Suffolk St.
NEW STREET STATION
MOOR STREET STATION
BULL RING CENTRE
Digbeth
Street
Granville
Broad St.
Holliday St.
Hill St.
Street
Holloway Head
Fair
Horse
Hurst St.
Bradford St.
Cheapside
Ladywood Middleway
Bishopsgate St.
Fiveways'
Bath Row
Islington Row
Bell
Great Colmore St.
Bromsgrove St.
Street
Calthorpe Rd
St. James's Road
Canal
Lee Bank Road
Barn Rd
Rickman Drive
Wrentham St.
Macdonald Street
Alcester St.
Bristol
Sherlock
A 441
Gooch St.

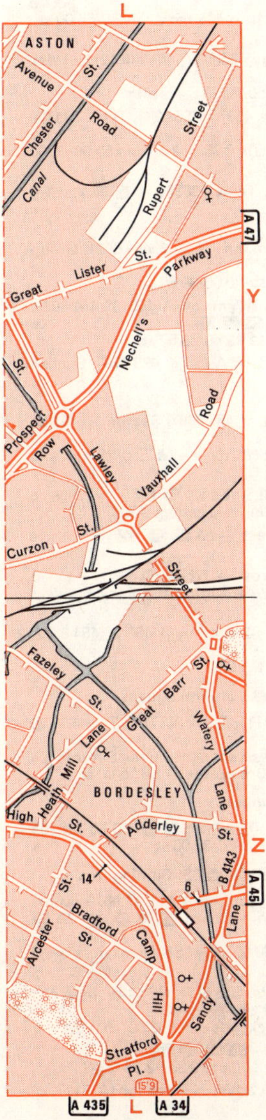

L
ASTON
Avenue
St.
Chester
Road
Street
Canal
Rupert
A 47
St.
Parkway
Lister
Great
Y
Nechell's
St.
Road
Prospect
Row
Lawley
Vauxhall
St.
Curzon
Street
Fazeley
St.
Barr
Great
St.
Watery
Lane
Mill
BORDESLEY
Lane
High
Heath
St.
Adderley
St.
Z
B 4143
A 45
14
6
St.
Bradford
St.
Camp
Alcester
Lane
Hill
Sandy
Stratford
Pl.
A 435
L
A 34

Holiday Inn, Central Sq., Holliday St., B1 1HH, 643 2766, Telex 337272, ≤, – TV. AE VISA. JZ z
M 8.95/9.45 **t.** and a la carte 3.00 – 5.25 – **304 rm** 45.00/55.00, **4 suites** 120.00/205.00.

Midland (Best Western), 128 New St., B2 4JT, 643 2601, Telex 338419 – rest TV. AE VISA. KZ r
M 12.50 **t.** and a la carte 2.75 – **107 rm** 27.50/66.00 **st.**, **1 suite** 71.50/104.50 **st.** – SB 44.00/63.80 **st.**

Strathallan Thistle (Thistle), 225 Hagley Rd, Edgbaston, B16 9RY, W : 2 m. on A 456 455 9777, Telex 336680 – TV. AE VISA EX i
M 6.95/10.50 **t.** and a la carte 2.50 – 5.50 – **164 rm** 43.50/70.00 **t.**, **4 suites** 85.00 **t.**

Grand (Q.M.H.), Colmore Row, B3 2DA, 236 7951, Telex 338174 – TV. AE VISA JKY c
closed 4 days at Christmas – **M** 8.50 **st.** and a la carte 3.10 – **145 rm** 44.50/55.00 **st.**, **3 suites** 95.00 **st.** – SB (weekends only) 52.00 **st.**

Royal Angus Thistle (Thistle), St Chad's, Queensway, B4 6HY, 236 4211, Telex 336889 – TV. AE VISA. KY s
M 9.00/11.00 **t.** and a la carte 2.75 – 5.25 – **139 rm** 43.50/70.00 **t.**, **1 suite.**

Apollo, Hagley Rd, Edgbaston, B16 9RA, W : 2 ¼ m. on A 456 455 0271, Telex 336759 – rest TV wc. AE VISA EX o
M 9.05/11.70 **st.** and a la carte 2.75 – 4.95 – **130 rm** 33.50/46.75 **s.**, **3 suites** 69.00/76.00 **s.** – SB (weekends only) 60.00 **st.**

Birmingham International, New St., B2 4RX, 643 2747, Telex 338331 – rest TV wc. KZ x
– **198 rm, 4 suites.**

Cobden, 166-174 Hagley Rd, Edgbaston, B16 9NZ, W : 2 m. on A 456 454 6621, Group Telex 339715, – TV wc wc. AE VISA EX n
closed Christmas – **M** 4.50/7.50 **st.** (unlicensed) – **210 rm** 20.00/39.50 **st.**

Norfolk, 257-267 Hagley Rd, Edgbaston, B16 9NA, W : 2 ¼ m. on A 456 454 8071, Group Telex 339715, – TV wc wc. AE VISA EX u
closed Christmas – **M** 4.50/7.50 **st.** (unlicensed) – **175 rm** 19.50/38.50 **st.**

Jonathans', 16-20 Wolverhampton Rd, B68 0LH, W : 4 m. by A 456 429 3757, English rest., « Victoriana », – AE VISA
closed Saturday lunch – **M** a la carte 10.70/21.10 **t.** 2.60.

Sloans, Chad Sq., off Harborne Rd., Edgbaston, B15 3TQ, 455 6697, Seafood – AE VISA EX v
closed Saturday lunch, Sunday, last 2 weeks July and Bank Holidays – **M** 7.50/21.00 **t.** and a la carte.

Rajdoot, 12-22 Albert St., B4 7UD, 643 8805, Indian rest. – AE VISA KZ c
closed lunch Sunday and Bank Holidays – **M** 4.50/10.00 **t.** and a la carte 2.70.

Dynasty, 93-103 Hurst St., B5 4TE, 622 1410, Chinese rest. – AE VISA KZ e
M 10.50 **t.** (dinner) and a la carte 2.60.

Lorenzo, 3 Park St., Digbeth, B5 5JD, 643 0541, Italian rest. – AE VISA KZ o
closed Saturday lunch, Monday dinner, Sunday, 3 weeks July-August and Bank Holidays – **M** a la carte 9.30/14.40 **t.** 3.10.

Pinocchio's, 8 Chad Sq., off Harborne Rd, B15 3TQ, W : 2 ¾ m. by A 456 454 8672, Italian rest. – AE VISA EX v
closed Sunday – **M** 5.75 **t.** (lunch) and a la carte 9.40/13.00 **t.** 2.50.

at Walmley NE : 6 m. by B 4148 – ✉ Sutton Coldfield – 021 Birmingham :

Penns Hall (Embassy), Penns Lane, B76 8LH, 351 3111, Telex 335789, – TV. AE VISA.
closed Bank Holidays – **M** *(closed Sunday dinner to non-residents)* (bar lunch Saturday) a la carte 13.25/18.50 **st.** 2.75 – 5.00 – **115 rm** 45.00/52.00, **5 suites** – SB 55.00 **st.**

at Castle Bromwich NE : 6 m. by A 47 – ✉ 021 Birmingham :

Bradford Arms Motel, Chester Rd, B36 0AG, 747 0227 – TV wc. AE VISA
closed 3 days at Christmas – **M** (grill rest. only) – **30 rm** 27.50/32.00 **st.** HV a

at Sutton Coldfield NE : 8 m. by A 38 – ✉ Sutton Coldfield – 021 Birmingham :

Belfry (De Vere), Lichfield Rd, Wishaw, B76 9PR, E : 3 m. on A 446 0675 (Curdworth) 70301, Telex 338848, ≤, park, squash – rest TV. AE VISA
M 7.95/9.95 **st.** and a la carte 3.50 – **168 rm** 53.50/80.00 **st.** – SB (weekends only) 73.00 **st.**

Moor Hall (Best Western), Moor Hall Drive, Four Oaks, B75 6LN, NE : 1 m. by A 453 308 3751, Telex 335127, – TV wc. AE VISA.
M 10.95/16.50 **st.** 2.75 – **50 rm** 40.00/48.00 **t.** – SB (weekends only) 48.00/55.00 **st.**

Le Bon Viveur, 65 Birmingham Rd, B72 1QF, 355 5836 – AE VISA
closed Saturday lunch, Sunday, Monday and August – **M** a la carte 9.95/13.95 **t.** 2.75.

La Gondola, Mere Green Precinct, 304 Lichfield Rd, B74 2UW, N : 2 m. on A 5127 308 6782, Italian rest..

at National Exhibition Centre E : 9 ½ m. on A 45 – ✉ ☎ 021 Birmingham :

Birmingham Metropole, Blackfirs Lane, Bickenhill, B40 1PP, ✆ 780 4242, Telex 336129, ←, squash – 🛗 ▤ TV ☎ ♿ P. 🏫. AE ⓞ VISA
M a la carte 10.70/22.50 **t.** 🌢 3.75 – ☕ 4.00 – **501 rm** 49.50/75.00 **st.**, **9 suites** 180.00/210.00 **st.**

Warwick, Blackfirs Lane, Bickenhill, B40 1PP, ✆ 780 4242, Telex 336129, squash – 🛗 ▤ TV ⛀wc ☎ P. AE ⓞ VISA
Exhibitions only – **M** (rest. see **Birmingham Metropole H.**) – ☕ 4.00 – **200 rm** 44.00/65.00 **st.**

Arden Motel, Coventry Rd, Bickenhill, B92 0EH, S : ½ m. on A 45 ✉ Solihull ✆ 067 55 (Hampton-in-Arden) 3221, Telex 337766 – 🛗 TV ⛀wc ☎ P. 🏫. AE ⓞ VISA
closed 3 days at Christmas – **M** 7.50/10.50 **t.** and a la carte 🌢 2.40 – ☕ 3.50 – **46 rm** 23.00/36.00 **st.** – SB (weekends only)(April-June) 45.50 **st.**

at Sheldon SE : 6 m. on A 45 – HX – ✉ ☎ 021 Birmingham :

Wheatsheaf (Golden Oak), 2225 Coventry Rd, B26 3EH, ✆ 743 2021 – ▤ rest TV ⛀wc ☎ P. 🏫. AE VISA. ✻ HX a
M 6.00/6.50 **t.** and a la carte 🌢 3.75 – **84 rm** ☕ 33.00/42.00 **st.**

at Birmingham Airport SE : 7 m. on A 45 – ✉ ☎ 021 Birmingham :

Excelsior (T.H.F.), Coventry Rd, Elmdon, B26 3QW, ✆ 743 8141, Telex 338005 – 🛗 TV P. 🏫. AE ⓞ VISA
M 6.55/10.50 **st.** and a la carte 🌢 4.00 – ☕ 5.50 – **141 rm** 39.00/48.50 **st.**

at West Bromwich NW : 6 m. on A 41 – ✉ West Bromwich – ☎ 021 Birmingham :

West Bromwich Moat House (Q.M.H.) Birmingham Rd, B70 6RS, SW : 1 m. by A 41 ✆ 553 6111, Telex 336232 – 🛗 ▤ rest TV ⛀wc ☎ P. 🏫. AE ⓞ VISA
M 8.75/9.25 **st.** and a la carte 🌢 3.60 – **179 rm** ☕ 40.50/53.50 **st.** – SB (weekends only) 40.00 **st.**

at Great Barr NW : 6 m. on A 34 – ✉ Great Barr – ☎ 021 Birmingham :

Post House (T.H.F), Chapel Lane, B43 7BG, ✆ 357 7444, Telex 338497, heated – TV ⛀wc ☎ P. 🏫. AE ⓞ VISA
M 6.50/23.00 **st.** and a la carte 🌢 2.70 – ☕ 5.50 – **204 rm** 38.00/45.00 **st.**

Barr, Pear Tree Drive, Newton Rd, B43 6HS, W : 1 m. by A 4041 ✆ 357 1141, Telex 336406, – TV ⛀wc ☎ P. 🏫. AE ⓞ VISA. ✻
closed 24 to 26 December – **M** 6.50/7.00 **st.** and a la carte 🌢 4.00 – **111 rm** ☕ 36.50/47.00 **st.** – SB (weekends only) 72.00 **st.**

EDINBURGH Midlothian (Lothian) 401 K 16 – pop. 408 ,822 – ☎ 031.

See : Site*** – International Festival*** (August) – Castle** (Site***, <**, ✻*** Great Hall : hammerbeam roof**, Palace block : Honours of Scotland***) DZ – Abbey and Palace of Holyroodhouse** (Plasterwork ceilings***) – Royal Mile** : Gladstone's Land* EYZ **A** St. Giles' Cathedral** (Crown Spire***) EZ Wax Museum* EZ **M1** Canongate Tolbooth* EY **B** – Victoria Street* EZ **84** – Royal Scottish Museum** EZ **M2** – New Town** : Charlotte Sq.*** CY **14** National Museum of Antiquities** EY **M3** The Georgian House* CY **D** National Portrait Museum* EY **M3** Dundas House* EY **E** – Princes Street and Gardens : National Gallery of Scotland** DY **M4** Scott Monument* EY **F** – Calton Hill EY : ✻ from Nelson Monument*** – Royal Botanic Gardens*** – Edinburgh Zoo** – Scottish Agricultural Museum* – Craigmillar Castle*.

Envir. : Rosslyn Chapel**, Apprentice Pillar***, S : 7 m. by A101 – 18 Silverknowes, Parkway, ✆ 336 3843, W : 4 m. – 18 Craigmillar Park, Observatory Rd ✆ 667 2837 – 18 Carrick Knowe, Glendevon Park ✆ 337 1096, W : 5 m.

✈ ✆ 333 1000, Telex 727615, W : 6 m. by A 8 – **Terminal** : Waverley Bridge.

🚗 ✆ 556 1100.

ℹ Waverley Market, 3 Princes St., ✆ 557 2727 – Edinburgh Airport ✆ 333 2167.

Glasgow 46 – Newcastle-upon-Tyne 105.

Plan on next page

Caledonian, Princes St., EH1 2AB, ✆ 225 2433, Telex 72179 – 🛗 TV ☎ P. 🏫. AE ⓞ VISA. ✻ CY n
M (rest. see **Pompadour** below) – ☕ 6.80 – **254 rm** 45.00/95.00 **st.**, **15 suites** – SB (weekends only) (October-April) 75.00 **st.**

Sheraton, 1 Festival Square, EH3 9SR, ✆ 229 9131, Telex 72398, – 🛗 ▤ TV ☎ ♿ P. 🏫 CDZ v
263 rm, 16 suites.

George (Forum), 19-21 George St., EH2 2PB, ✆ 225 1251, Telex 72570 – 🛗 ▤ rest TV ☎ ♿ P. 🏫. AE ⓞ VISA. ✻ DY z
M 9.75/12.00 **st.** and a la carte 🌢 3.75 – ☕ 7.40 – **195 rm** 55.00/99.00 **st.**, **2 suites** 132.00/242.00 **st.**

EDINBURGH

Castle Street	DY	
Frederick Street	DY	
George Street	DY	
Hanover Street	DY	
High Street	EYZ	37
Lawnmarket	EYZ	
Princes Street	DY	
St. James Centre	EY	
Waverley Market	EY	
Bernard Terrace	EZ	3
Bread Street	DZ	6
Bristo Place	EZ	7
Candlemaker Row	EZ	9
Castlehill	DZ	10
Chambers Street	EZ	12
Chapel Street	EZ	13
Charlotte Square	CY	14
Deanhaugh Street	CY	23
Douglas Gardens	CY	25
Drummond Street	EZ	27
Forrest Road	EZ	31
Gardner's Crescent	CZ	32
George IV Bridge	EZ	33
Grassmarket	DZ	35
Home Street	DZ	38
Hope Street	CY	39
Johnston Terrace	DZ	42
King's Bridge	DZ	44
King's Stables Road	DZ	45
Lawnmarket	EZ	46
Leith Street	EY	47
Leven Street	DZ	48
Lothian Street	EZ	51
Mound (The)	DY	55
North Bridge	EY	61
North St. Andrew Street	EY	66
Raeburn Place	CY	69
Randolph Crescent	CY	71
St. Andrew Square	EY	73
St. Mary's Street	EY	75
Shandwick Place	CYZ	77
South Charlotte Street	DY	78
South St. David Street	DEY	79
Spittal Street	DZ	83
Victoria Street	EZ	84
Waterloo Place	EY	87
Waverley Bridge	EY	89
West Maitland Street	CZ	92

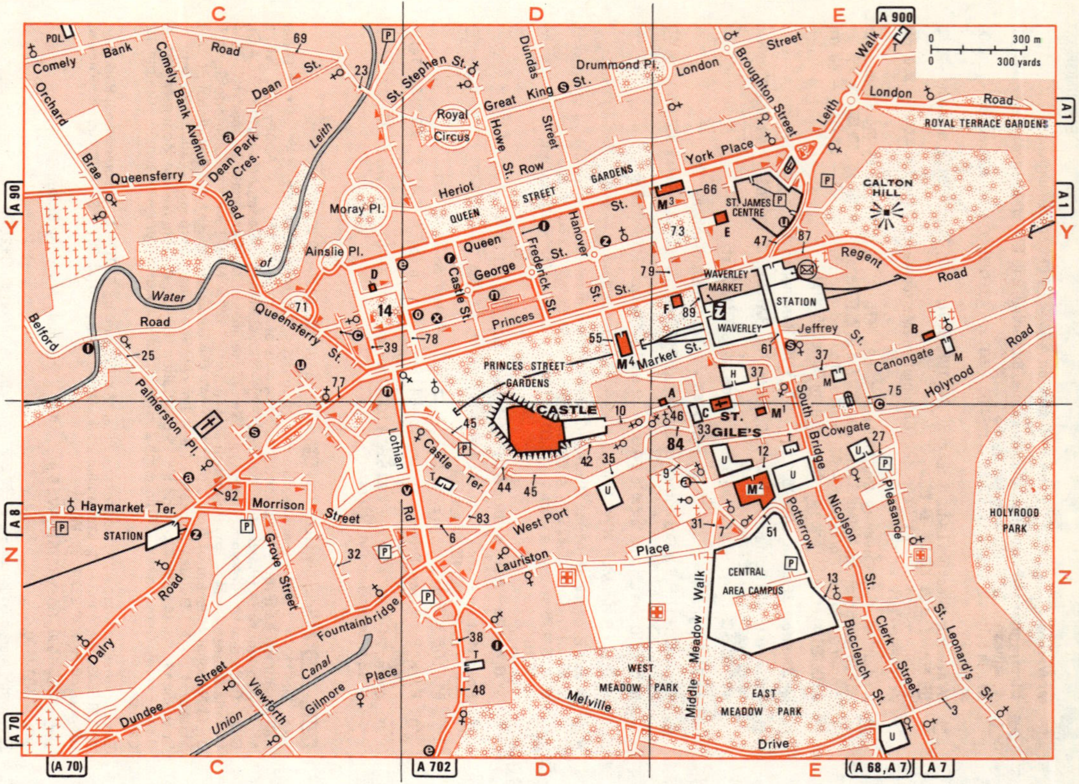

Carlton Highland, 1 North Bridge, EH5 1SD, ✆ 556 7277, Telex 727001, squash – rest – **110 rm, 4 suites.** EY **s**

Roxburghe (Best Western), 38 Charlotte Sq., EH2 4HG, ✆ 225 3921, Telex 727054 – – **76 rm, 2 suites.** DY **o**

Ladbroke Dragonara (Ladbroke), Bells Mills, 69 Belford Rd, EH4 3DG, ✆ 332 2545, Telex 727979 – AE VISA. CY **i**
M 9.50/11.50 **t.** and a la carte 3.40 – 6.25 – **146 rm** 60.00/95.00 **t.**, **3 suites** – SB (weekends only) 67.50 **st.**

Royal Scot (Swallow), 111 Glasgow Rd, EH12 8NF, W : 4 ½ m. on A 8 ✆ 334 9191, Telex 727197 – AE VISA
M (carving lunch)/dinner 10.25 **st.** and a la carte 3.40 – **251 rm** 50.00/62.00 **st.** – SB (weekends only) 55.00/60.00 **st.**

King James Thistle (Thistle), 1 Leith St., EH1 3SW, ✆ 556 0111, Telex 727200 – wc AE VISA EY **u**
M 8.50/9.50 **t.** and a la carte 3.00 – 4.75 – **147 rm** 42.00/80.00 **t.**, **5 suites** 95.00 **t.**

Crest (Crest), Queensferry Rd, EH4 3HL, NW : 2 m. on A 90 ✆ 332 2442, Telex 72541 – rest wc wc AE VISA.
M approx. 12.25 **st.** – 5.75 – **118 rm** 50.00/65.00 **st.**, **1 suite** – SB (weekends only) 67.00 **st.**

Post House (T.H.F.), Corstorphine Rd, EH12 6UA, W : 3 m. on A 8 ✆ 334 8221, Telex 727103, ≤ – wc AE VISA
M 7.50/10.45 **st.** and a la carte 2.70 – 5.50 – **207 rm** 46.00/56.00 **st.**, **1 suite.**

Howard, 32-36 Gt. King St., EH3 6QH, ✆ 557 3500, Telex 727887 – wc wc AE VISA DY **s**
M (bar lunch)/dinner 15.00 **t.** 3.75 – **25 rm** 40.00/70.00 **t.** – SB (weekends only) (November-March) 66.00 **st.**

Stakis Grosvenor (Stakis), Grosvenor St., EH12 5EF, ✆ 226 6001, Telex 72445 – wc wc AE VISA CZ **a**
M 5.95/7.95 **t.** and a la carte 3.25 – **130 rm** 51.00/70.00.

XXXX **Pompadour** (at Caledonian H.), Princes St., EH1 2AB, ✆ 225 2433, Telex 72179 – AE VISA CY **n**
closed lunch Saturday and Sunday – **M** 12.50/27.00 **st.** and a la carte 3.95.

XXX **Aye,** 80 Queen St., EH2 4NF, ✆ 226 5467, Japanese rest. – AE VISA CDY **e**
closed Sunday lunch and Monday – **M** 10.00/50.00 **t.** and a la carte.

XXX **Prestonfield House** with rm, Priestfield Rd, EH16 5UT, SE : 2 ½ m. off A 68 ✆ 667 3346, Telex 727396, ≤, « Elegant 17C mansion », park – AE VISA
M 10.00/14.00 **t.** and dinner a la carte 2.75 – **5 rm** 44.00/57.50 **t.**

XXX **Howtowdie,** 27a Stafford St., EH3 7BJ, ✆ 225 6291 – AE VISA CY **u**
closed Sunday, 25-26 December and 1 to 2 January – **M** 8.95/20.00 **st.** and a la carte 4.60.

XX **Cosmo,** 58a North Castle St., EH2 3LU, ✆ 226 6743, Italian rest. – VISA DY **r**
closed Saturday lunch, Sunday and Monday – **M** a la carte 9.70/15.80 **t.** 2.75.

XX **Raffaelli,** 10-11 Randolph Pl., EH3 7TA, ✆ 225 6060, Italian rest. – AE VISA CY **c**
closed Saturday, Sunday, Christmas Day and New Years Day – **M** a la carte 10.35/12.80 **t.** 2.30.

XX **L'Auberge,** 56 St. Mary's St., EH1 1SX, ✆ 556 5888, French rest. – AE VISA EYZ **c**
closed 25-26 December and 1 January – **M** 7.50 **t.** (lunch) and a la carte 10.55/15.45 **t.** 3.50.

X **Martins,** 70 Rose St., North Lane, EH2 3DX, behind pedestrian precinct ✆ 225 3106 – AE VISA DY **n**
closed Saturday lunch, Sunday, Monday, 2 weeks June and 25 December-6 January – **M** 8.50/16.50 **t.** 3.50.

X **Alp-Horn,** 167 Rose St., EH2 4LS, ✆ 225 4787, Swiss rest. – DY **x**
closed Sunday, Monday, first 3 weeks July and 2 weeks at Christmas – **M** 5.00/13.00 **t.** and a la carte 3.40.

X **Verandah,** 17 Dalry Rd, EH11 2BQ, ✆ 337 5828, Indian Rest. – AE VISA CZ **z**
M 7.55/9.95 **t.** and a la carte 2.95.

at Bonnyrigg S : 8 m. by A 7 on A 6094 – ✉ Bonnyrigg – 0875 Gorebridge :

Dalhousie Castle, EH19 3JB, SE : 1 ¼ m. on B 704 ✆ 20153, Telex 72380, ≤, « Converted 12C castle », park – AE VISA.
M a la carte 12.75/21.45 **t.** 3.25 – **24 rm** 38.00/98.00 **t.**

In addition to establishments indicated by
XXXXX ... X ,
many hotels possess
good class restaurants.

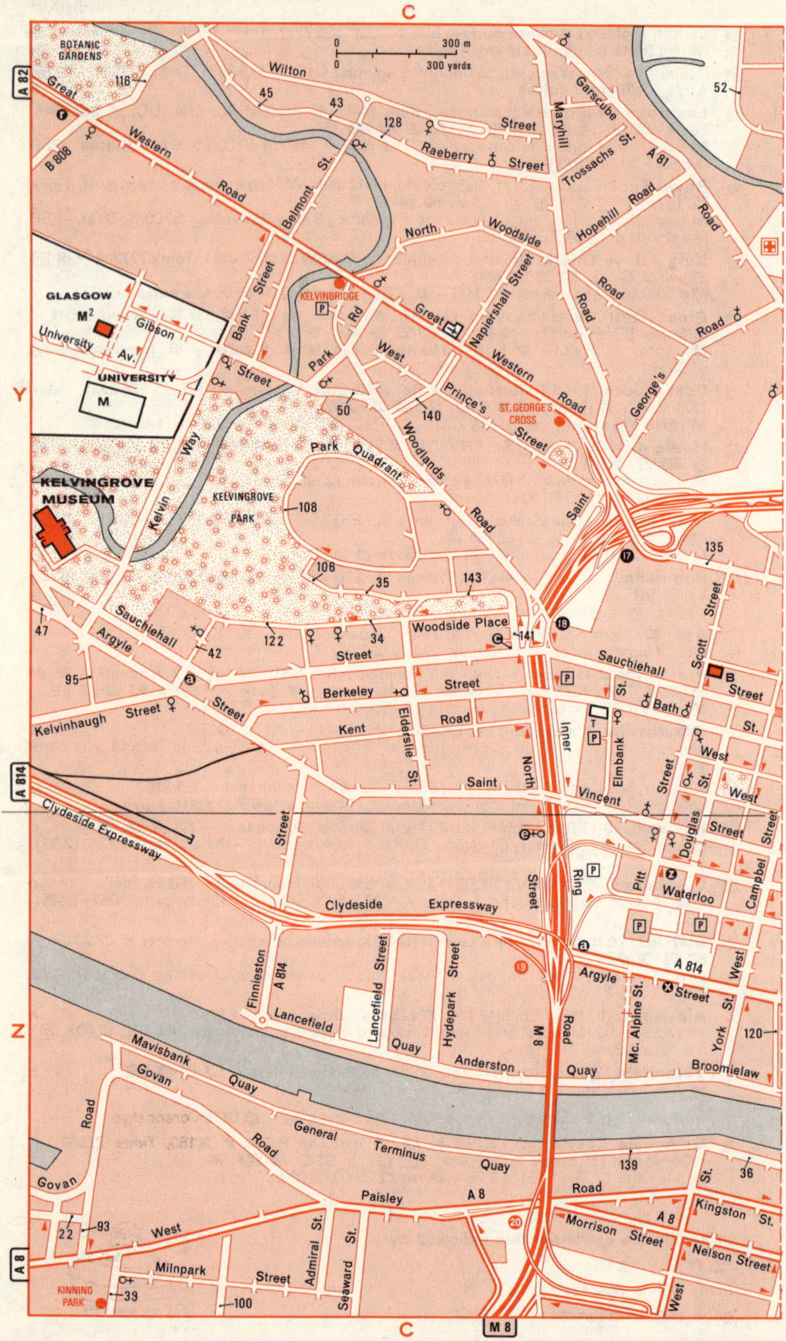
C
Y
Z
C
0 300 m
0 300 yards
BOTANIC GARDENS
A 82
B 808
Great Western Road
Wilton
Raeberry Street
Street
Maryhill
Garscube
Trossachs St.
A 81
Hopehill Road
Road
Belmont St.
North Woodside Road
Napiershall Street
Road
Road
GLASGOW
M2
UNIVERSITY
M
University Av.
Gibson
Bank Street
Street
KELVINBRIDGE
Park Rd
Great Western Road
West Prince's Street
ST. GEORGE'S CROSS
Saint George's
Park Quadrant
Woodlands Road
KELVINGROVE MUSEUM
KELVINGROVE PARK
Kelvin Way
Sauchiehall Street
Argyle Street
Woodside Place
Sauchiehall Street
Berkeley Street
Bath St.
Kelvinhaugh Street
Kent Road
Elderslie St.
Inner Ring Road
Elmbank St.
Scott Street
B
West St.
Saint Vincent
Street
North Street
Douglas Street
West Street
A 814
Clydeside Expressway
Clydeside Expressway
Pitt
Waterloo
Campbel
Finnieston A 814
Lancefield Street
Lancefield Quay
Hydepark Street
Argyle Street
A 814
Mc. Alpine St.
York St.
West St.
M 8
Anderston Quay
Broomielaw
Mavisbank Quay
Govan Road
General Terminus Quay
Govan Road
Paisley Road A 8
Paisley Road West
Kingston St.
Morrison Street A 8
Nelson Street
West St.
Milnpark Street
Admiral St.
Seaward St.
KINNING PARK
A 8
M 8
116
45
43
128
52
50
140
108
106
35
143
135
47
122
34
141
42
95
120
139
36
22
93
39
100
17
18
19
20

GLASGOW CENTRE

Brand Street	CZ	22
Bridegate	DZ	24
Bridge Street	DZ	25
Cambridge Street	DY	32
Claremont Gardens	CY	34
Claremont Terrace	CY	35
Clyde Place	CZ	36
Commerce Street	DZ	37
Cornwald Street	CZ	39
Derby Street	CY	42
Doune Gardens	CY	43
Doune Quadrant	CY	45
Dumbarton Road	CY	47
Eldon Street	CY	50
Ellesmere Street	CDY	52
Glasgow Bridge	DZ	60
Gordon Street	DZ	65
Jamaica Street	DZ	77
John Knox Street	DZ	80
Kyle Street	DY	86
Lorne Street	CZ	93
Lymburn Street	CY	95
Middlesex Street	CZ	100
Moir Street	DZ	102
Oxford Street	DZ	105
Park Gardens	CY	106
Park Terrace	CY	108
Queen Margaret Drive	CY	116
Robertson Street	CZ	120
Royal Terrace	CY	122
Stirling Road	DY	126
Stockwell Street	DZ	127
Striven Gardens	CY	128
Suspension Bridge	DZ	130
Victoria Bridge	DZ	132
West Graham St.	CY	135
Windmillcroft Quay	CZ	139
Woodlands Drive	CY	140
Woodside Crescent	CY	141
Woodside Terrace	CY	143

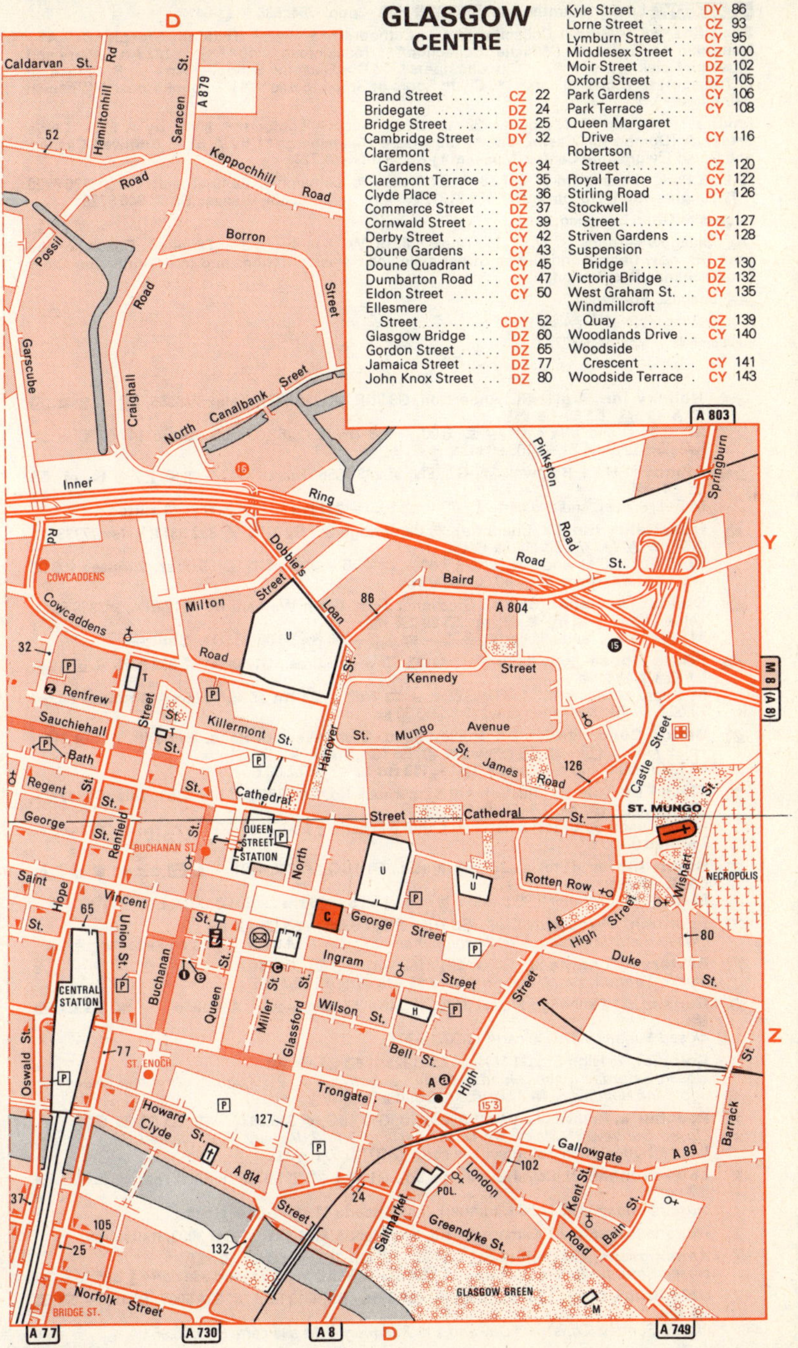

GLASGOW Lanark. (Strathclyde) 401 402 H 16 – pop. 754 ,586 – ☎ 041.

See : Site★★★ – Burrell Collection★★★ – Cathedral★★★ DYZ – Tolbooth Steeple★ DZ **A** – Hunterian Art Gallery★★ (Whistler Collection★★★ Mackintosh wing★★★) CY **M2** Art Gallery and Museum Kelvingrove★★ CY – City Chambers★ DZ **C** – Glasgow School of Art★ CY **B** – Museum of Transport★★ (Scottish cars★★★, Clyde Room of Ship Models★★★) – Pollok House★ (Spanish paintings★★).

Envir. : Trossachs★★★ N : by A 739 and A 81 – Loch Lomond★★ NW : by A 82 – Clyde Estuary★ (Dumbarton Castle, Site★, Hill House Helensburgh★) by A 82 – Bothwell Castle★ and David Livingstone Centre (Museum★) SE : 9 m. by A 724.

18 Linn Park, Simshill Rd ✆ 637 5871, S : 4 m. – 18 Lethamhill, Cumbernauld Rd ✆ 770 6220 – 9 Knightswood, Lincoln Av. ✆ 959 2131, W : 4 m. – 9 Ruchill, Brassey St. ✆ 946 9728.

Access to Oban by helicopter.

✈ Glasgow Airport : ✆ 887 1111, Telex 778219, W : 8 m. by M 8 – **Terminal :** Coach service from Glasgow Central and Queen Street main line Railway Stations and from Anderston Cross and Buchanan Bus Stations.

✈ see also Prestwick.

ℹ 35 St. Vincent Pl. ✆ 227 4880.

Edinburgh 46 – Manchester 221.

Plan on preceding pages

Holiday Inn, Argyle St., Anderston, G3 8RR, ✆ 226 5577, Telex 776355, – CZ **a**
M 12.95 **t.** and a la carte – 6.00 – **296 rm** 52.00/62.00 **s.**, **3 suites** 147.00 **s.** – SB (weekends only) 71.90/109.90 **st.**

Albany (T.H.F.), Bothwell St., G2 7EN, ✆ 248 2656, Telex 77440 – AE VISA CZ **z**
M 5.95/8.25 **st.** and a la carte 2.70 – 5.50 – **251 rm** 45.50/59.00 **st.**, **3 suites**.

Hospitality Inn (Mt. Charlotte), 36 Cambridge St., G2 3HN, ✆ 332 3311, Telex 777334 – TV AE VISA DY **z**
M 10.50/11.50 **st.** and a la carte 3.00 – 4.75 – **316 rm** 42.50/55.00 **st.**, **2 suites** 100.00 **st.** – SB (weekends only) 48.00/60.00 **st.**

Stakis Grosvenor (Stakis), Grosvenor Terr., Great Western Rd, G12 0TA, ✆ 339 8811, Telex 776247 – TV AE VISA CY **r**
M 8.50/15.00 **t.** and a la carte 3.75 – 4.75 – **96 rm** 55.00/80.00 **t.**, **2 suites**.

White House without rest., 11-13 Cleveden Cres., G12 0PA, ✆ 339 9375 – TV AE VISA
M (room service only) 11.60/13.60 **t.** – 5.60 – **32 rm** 45.45/65.55 **t.**, **13 suites** 84.55/92.00 **t.** – SB (weekends only) 49.65/60.30 **st.**

Stakis Pond (Stakis), 2-4 Shelley Road, Great Western Road, G12 0XP, ✆ 334 8161, Telex 776573, – TV wc AE VISA
M 7.00/9.00 **t.** and a la carte 3.50 – **133 rm** 42.00/52.00 **t.**

Tinto Firs Thistle (Thistle), 470 Kilmarnock Rd, G43 2BB, ✆ 637 2353, Telex 778329 – TV wc AE VISA
M (bar lunch Saturday) 6.00/11.00 **t.** and a la carte 3.60 – 5.25 – **25 rm** 42.00/54.00 **t.**, **2 suites** 60.00 **t.**

Stakis Ingram (Stakis), 201 Ingram St., G1 1DQ, ✆ 248 4401 – TV wc AE VISA DZ **c**
M (bar lunch)/dinner 9.95 **t.** and a la carte 3.25 – **90 rm** 35.00/60.00 **t.**

XXX **Fountain,** 2 Woodside Cres., G3 7UL, ✆ 332 6396 – AE VISA CY **c**
closed Saturday lunch, Monday dinner and Sunday – **M** 8.00/13.50 **t.** and a la carte 4.95.

XX **Buttery,** 652 Argyle St., G3, ✆ 221 8188 – AE VISA CZ **e**
closed Saturday lunch and Sunday – **M** a la carte 12.90/17.75 **t.**

XX **Rogano,** 11 Exchange Pl., G1 3AN, ✆ 248 4055, Seafood, « Art deco » – AE VISA DZ **i**
closed Sunday – **M** a la carte 11.90/15.30 **t.**

XX **Colonial,** 25 High St., G1 1LX, ✆ 552 1923 – AE VISA DZ **a**
closed Saturday lunch, Monday dinner, Sunday, 20 July-3 August, Christmas, New Year and Bank Holidays – **M** 4.50/16.00 **st.** and a la carte 3.20.

X **Poacher's,** Ruthven Lane, off Byres Rd, G12 9BG, ✆ 339 0932 – AE VISA
closed Sunday, 31 March, 25 December and 1 to 2 January – **M** *(closed Bank Holiday lunch)* (buffet lunch Saturday) a la carte 12.00/15.50 **t.** 3.00.

X **Le Provençal,** 21 Royal Exchange Sq., G1 3AJ, ✆ 221 0798, French rest. – AE VISA DZ **e**
closed Sunday – **M** 11.50 **t.** (dinner) and a la carte 11.75/15.65 **t.** 3.25.

X Trattoria Sorrento, 87 Kilmarnock Rd, Shawlands, G41 3YR, ✆ 649 3002, Italian rest..

X **Kensingtons,** 164 Darnley St., G41 2LL, ✆ 424 3662 – AE VISA
closed Saturday lunch, Sunday and Monday – **M** 6.00/13.50 **t.** and a la carte 2.65.

X **Ubiquitous Chip,** 12 Ashton Lane, off Byres Rd, G12 8SJ, ✆ 334 5007, Bistro – AE VISA
closed Sunday, Christmas Day and 1 to 2 January – **M** a la carte 5.90/16.95 **t.**

at Glasgow Airport Renfrew. (Strathclyde) W : 8 m. by M 8 – ✉ ☎ 041 Glasgow :

Excelsior (T.H.F.), Abbotsinch, PA3 2TR, ☎ 887 1212, Telex 777733 – TV ☎ ♿ P. AE VISA
M 8.95 **st.** and a la carte 3.00 – 6.00 – **290 rm** 46.00/58.00 **st.**, **7 suites**.

LEEDS West Yorks. 402 P 22 – pop. 445 ,242 – ECD : Wednesday – ☎ 0532.

See : St. John's Church★ 17C DZ **A**.

Envir. : Temple Newsam House★ 17C (interior★★) *AC*, E : 4 m. – Kirkstall Abbey★ (ruins 12C) *AC*, NW : 3 m.

18, 18 The Lady Dorothy Wood, The Lord Irwin, Temple Newsam Rd, Halton ☎ 645624, E : 3 m. – 18 Gotts Park, Armley Ridge Rd, ☎ 638232, W : 2 m. – 18 Horsforth, Layton Rise ☎ 586819, NW : 6 m. – 18 Middleton Park, Town St., Middleton ☎ 700449, S : 3 m..

Leeds and Bradford Airport : ☎ 0532 (Rawdon) 503431, NW : 8 m. by A 65 and A 658.

Central Library, Calverley St. ☎ 462454.

London 204 – Liverpool 75 – Manchester 43 – Newcastle-upon-Tyne 95 – Nottingham 74.

Plan on next page

Ladbroke Dragonara (Ladbroke), Neville St., LS1 4BX, ☎ 442000, Telex 557143 – TV ☎ ♿ P. DZ **r**
234 rm.

Queens (T.H.F.), City Sq., LS1 1PL, ☎ 431323, Telex 55161 – TV wc ☎. AE VISA DZ **a**
M 8.50/9.50 **st.** and a la carte 4.00 – 5.50 – **198 rm** 42.00/56.00 **st.**

Metropole (T.H.F.), King St., LS1 2HQ, ☎ 450841, Telex 557755 – TV wc ☎ P. AE VISA CZ **o**
M (carving rest.) 8.25 **st.** and a la carte 2.70 – 5.50 – **110 rm** 37.00/45.00 **st.**

Merrion, Merrion Centre, 17 Wade Lane, LS2 8NH, ☎ 439191, Telex 55459 – TV wc ☎ P. AE VISA. DZ **x**
M 7.50/9.50 **st.** and a la carte 3.25 – 5.25 – **120 rm** 44.00/57.00 **st.** – SB (weekends only) 57.00/62.00 **st.**

XXX Gardini's Terrazza, Minerva House, 16 Greek St., LS1 5RU, ☎ 432880, Italian rest. – CDZ **n**

XXX Mandalay, 8 Harrison St., LS1 6PA, ☎ 446453, Indian rest. – DZ **e**

XX **Embassy,** 333 Roundhay Rd, LS8 4HT, NE : 2 ½ m. by A 58 ☎ 490562 – P. AE VISA BY **v**
closed Sunday, 1 week January, 2 weeks August-September and Bank Holidays – **M** (dinner only) 11.20 **t.** and a la carte 2.75.

XX Shabab, 2 Eastgate, LS2 7JL, ☎ 468988, Indian rest. – DZ **v**

at Seacroft NE : 5 ½ m. at junction of A 64 and A 6120 – ✉ ☎ 0532 Leeds :

Stakis Windmill (Stakis), Ring Rd, LS14 5QP, ☎ 732323 – rest TV wc ☎ ♿ P. AE VISA
M (grill rest. only) 4.95/8.00 **t.** and a la carte – **40 rm** 42.00/50.00 **t.**

at Garforth E : 6 m. at Junction of A 63 and A 642 – ✉ ☎ 0532 Leeds :

Ladbroke (Ladbroke), Wakefield Rd, LS25 1LH, ☎ 866556, Telex 556324 – TV wc ☎ ♿ P. AE VISA
M *(closed Saturday lunch)* (carving rest.) 8.50/10.65 **t.** 3.70 – 5.50 – **142 rm** 42.00/56.00 **t.** – SB (weekends only) 39.50/57.00 **st.**

at Oulton SE : 6 ¼ m. at junction of A 639 and A 642 – ✉ ☎ 0532 Leeds :

Crest (Crest), The Grove, LS26 8EJ, ☎ 826201, Telex 557646 – TV wc ☎ ♿ P. AE VISA.
M approx 11.50 **st.** – 5.75 – **40 rm** 46.00/56.00 **st.** – SB (weekends only) 51.00 **st.**

at Horsforth NW : 5 m. by A 65 off A 6120 – ✉ ☎ 0532 Leeds :

XXX **Low Hall,** Calverley Lane, LS18 4EF, ☎ 588221, « Elizabethan manor », – P. VISA
closed Saturday lunch, Sunday, Monday, 25 to 30 December and Bank Holidays – **M** 7.95/15.00 **st.** and a la carte 2.85.

XX **Roman Garden,** Hall Lane, Hall Park, LS18 5JY, ☎ 587962, ←, Italian rest. – P. AE VISA
closed Saturday lunch, Sunday and Monday – **M** 11.25 **t.** (dinner) and a la carte 3.30.

at Bramhope NW : 8 m. on A 660 – ✉ ☎ 0532 Leeds :

Post House (T.H.F.), Otley Rd, LS16 9JJ, ☎ 842911, Telex 556367, ← – rest TV wc ☎ ♿ P. AE VISA
M 7.00 **st.** (lunch) and a la carte 9.40/16.15 **st.** 2.70 – 5.50 – **120 rm** 43.00/51.50 **st.**

Parkway (Embassy), Otley Rd, LS16 8AG, S : 2 m. on A 660 ☎ 672551, – TV wc ☎ P. AE VISA.
M *(closed Saturday lunch)* (Sunday residents only) 9.00 **st.** and a la carte 2.75 – 5.00 – **39 rm** 30.00/50.00 **st.** – SB (weekends only) 55.00 **st.**

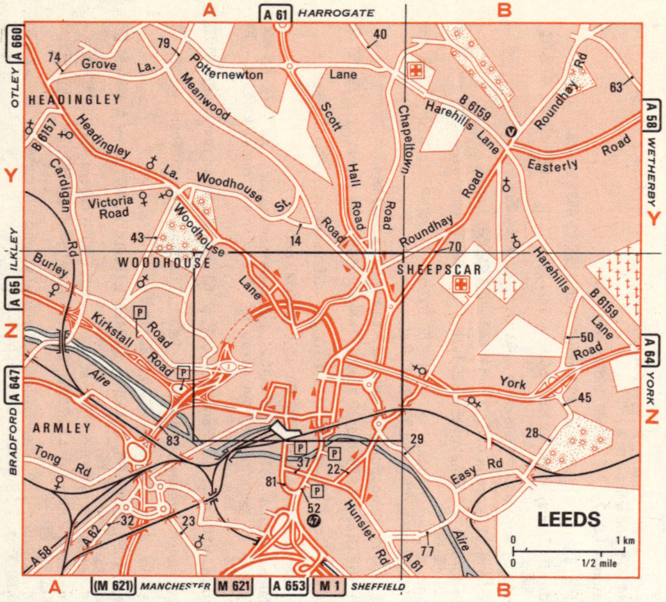

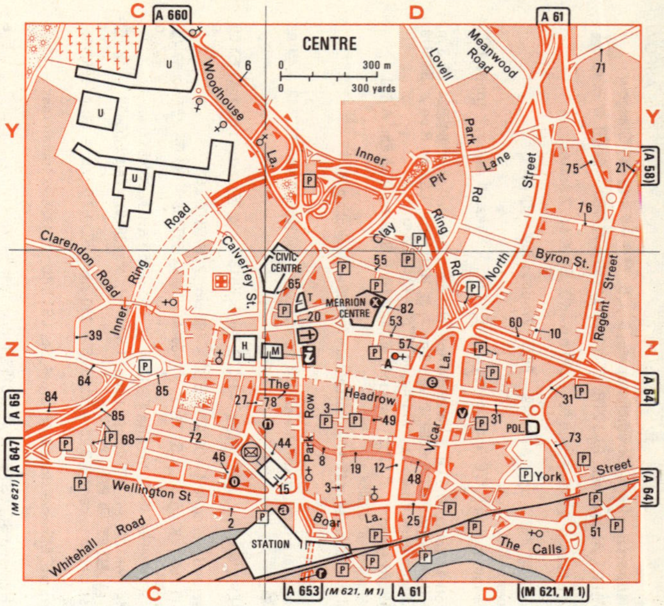

Street	Grid	No.
Albion Street	DZ	3
Bond Street	DZ	8
Briggate	DZ	12
Commercial Street	DZ	19
Headrow (The)	DZ	
Kirkgate	DZ	48
Lands Lane	DZ	49
Merrion Centre	DZ	
Aire Street	CZ	2
Blenheim Walk	CY	6
Bridge Street	DZ	10
Cambridge Road	AY	14
City Square	DZ	15
Cookridge Street	DZ	20
Cross Stamford Street	DY	21
Crown Point Road	AZ	22
Domestic Street	AZ	23
Duncan Street	DZ	25
East Parade	CDZ	27
East Park Parade	BZ	28
East Street	BZ	29
Eastgate	DZ	31
Gelderd Road	AZ	32
Great Wilson Street	AZ	37
Hanover Way	CZ	39
Harrogate Road	AY	40
Hyde Park Road	AY	43
Infirmary Street	DZ	44
Ivy Street	BZ	45
King Street	CZ	46
Lupton Avenue	BZ	50
Marsh Lane	DZ	51
Meadow Lane	AZ	52
Merrion Street	DZ	53
Merrion Way	DZ	55
New Briggate	DZ	57
New York Road	DZ	60
Oakwood Lane	BY	63
Park Lane	CZ	64
Portland Crescent	DZ	65
Queen Street	CZ	68
Roseville Road	BYZ	70
Roundhay Road	DY	71
St. Paul's Street	CZ	72
St. Peter's Street	DZ	73
Shaw Lane	AY	74
Sheepscar Street South	DY	75
Skinner Lane	DY	76
South Accommodation Road	BZ	77
South Parade	CDZ	78
Stainbeck Road	AY	79
Victoria Road	AZ	81
Wade Lane	DZ	82
Wellington Road	AZ	83
West Street	CZ	84
Westgate	CZ	85

at Liversedge SW : 9 m. on A 62 – ✉ Liversedge – ☎ 0924 Heckmondwike :

XX **Lillibet's** with rm, Ashfield House, 64 Leeds Rd, WF15 6HX, ☎ 404911, – TV ⊟wc ⋔wc ☎ P. AE VISA.
closed Sunday, 2 weeks July, 25 December-2 January and Bank Holidays – **M** (dinner only) 11.95 **t.** 3.50 – **7 rm** 25.00/45.00 **st.**

Ilkley West Yorks NW : 16 m. by A 660 on A 65 – 402 O 22 – pop. 13,060 – ☎ 0943.

XXX ✿✿ **Box Tree,** 35-37 Church St., LS29 9DR, ☎ 608484, « Ornate decor » – AE VISA
closed Sunday, Monday, 25-26 December and 1 January – **M** (dinner only) (booking essential) a la carte 16.35/19.75 **t.**
Spec. La salade de Pigeonneau fumé, vinaigrette a l'orange, Noisette d'agneau Edward VII, Timbale de fraises Box Tree..

LIVERPOOL Merseyside 402 403 L 23 – pop. 538,809 – ECD : Wednesday – ☎ 051.

See : Walker Art Gallery** CY **M1** – City of Liverpool Museums* CY **M2** – Anglican Cathedral* (1904) CZ **A** – Roman Catholic Cathedral* (1967) DZ **B**.

Envir. : Knowsley Safari Park** *AC*, NE : 8 m. by A 57 – Speke Hall* (16C) *AC*, SE : 7 m. by A 561.

Dunnings Bridge Rd, Bootle ☎ 928 1371 N : 5 m. by A 5036 – Allerton Park ☎ 428 1046,S : 5 m. by B 5180 – Childwall, Naylor's Rd, Gateacre ☎ 487 9982, E : 7 m. by B 5178.

Liverpool Airport : ☎ 494 0066, Telex 629323, SE : 6 m. by A 561 – **Terminal :** Pier Head.

to Ireland (Dublin) (B & I Line) 1 nightly (8 h 45 mn) – to Belfast (Belfast Car Ferries)1 daily (9 h).

to Birkenhead (Merseyside Transport) frequent services daily (7-8 mn) – to Wallasey (Merseyside Transport) frequent services daily (7-8 mn).

29 Lime St. ☎ 709 3631 and 8681.

London 219 – Birmingham 103 – Leeds 75 – Manchester 35.

Plan on following pages

Holiday Inn, Paradise St., L1 8JD, ☎ 709 0181, Telex 627270, – TV ☎ P. AE VISA CZ **n**
M 5.50/8.00 **t.** and a la carte 3.00 – **253 rm** 48.00/65.00 **t.**, **7 suites** 74.00/165.00 **st.** – SB (weekends only) 56.90/66.90 **st.**

Atlantic Tower Thistle (Thistle), 30 Chapel St., L3 9RE, ☎ 227 4444, Telex 627070, ← – TV ☎ P. AE VISA. CY **r**
M 7.45/9.50 **t.** and a la carte 2.85 – 5.50 – **226 rm** 45.00/70.00 **t.**, **10 suites** 85.00 **t.**

St. George's (T.H.F.), St. John's Precinct, Lime St., L1 1NQ, ☎ 709 7090, Telex 627630 – TV ☎ P. AE VISA CY **v**
M (carving rest.) 5.00/8.25 **st.** and a la carte 2.70 – 5.50 – **155 rm** 42.00/50.50 **st.**, **3 suites**.

Crest (Crest), Lord Nelson St., L3 5QB, ☎ 709 7050, Telex 627954 – TV ⊟wc ☎ P. AE VISA. CY **i**
M approx. 10.85 **st.** – 5.75 – **165 rm** 43.00/53.00 **st.**, **1 suite** – SB (weekends only) 55.00 **st.**

XXX Ristorante del Secolo, First Floor, 36-40 Stanley St., L2 6AL, ☎ 236 4004, Italian rest. CY **x**

XXX **Churchill's,** Churchill House, Tithebarn St., L2 2PB, ☎ 227 3877 – AE VISA CY **a**
closed Saturday lunch and Sunday – **M** 7.55/8.95 **t.** and a la carte.

XX **Jenny's Seafood,** Old Ropery, Fenwick St., L2 7NT, ☎ 236 0332, Seafood – AE VISA CZ **e**
closed Saturday lunch, Monday dinner, Sunday, 25 December-3 January and Bank Holidays – **M** 8.75 **t.** and a la carte 2.50.

at Bootle N : 5 m. by A 565 – ✉ ☎ 051 Liverpool :

Park, Park Lane West, L30 3SU, on A 5036 ☎ 525 7555, Telex 629772 – TV ⊟wc ⋔wc ☎ P. AE VISA
M 5.50 **st.** and a la carte 4.90 – **60 rm** 32.50/44.00 **st.**

at Blundellsands N : 6 ½ m. by A 565 – ✉ ☎ 051 Liverpool :

Blundellsands, The Serpentine, South, L23 6TN, ☎ 924 6515 – TV ⊟wc ☎ P. **44 rm**.

GREEN TOURIST GUIDES
Picturesque scenery, buildings
Attractive routes
Touring programmes
Plans of towns and buildings.

LIVERPOOL
CENTRE

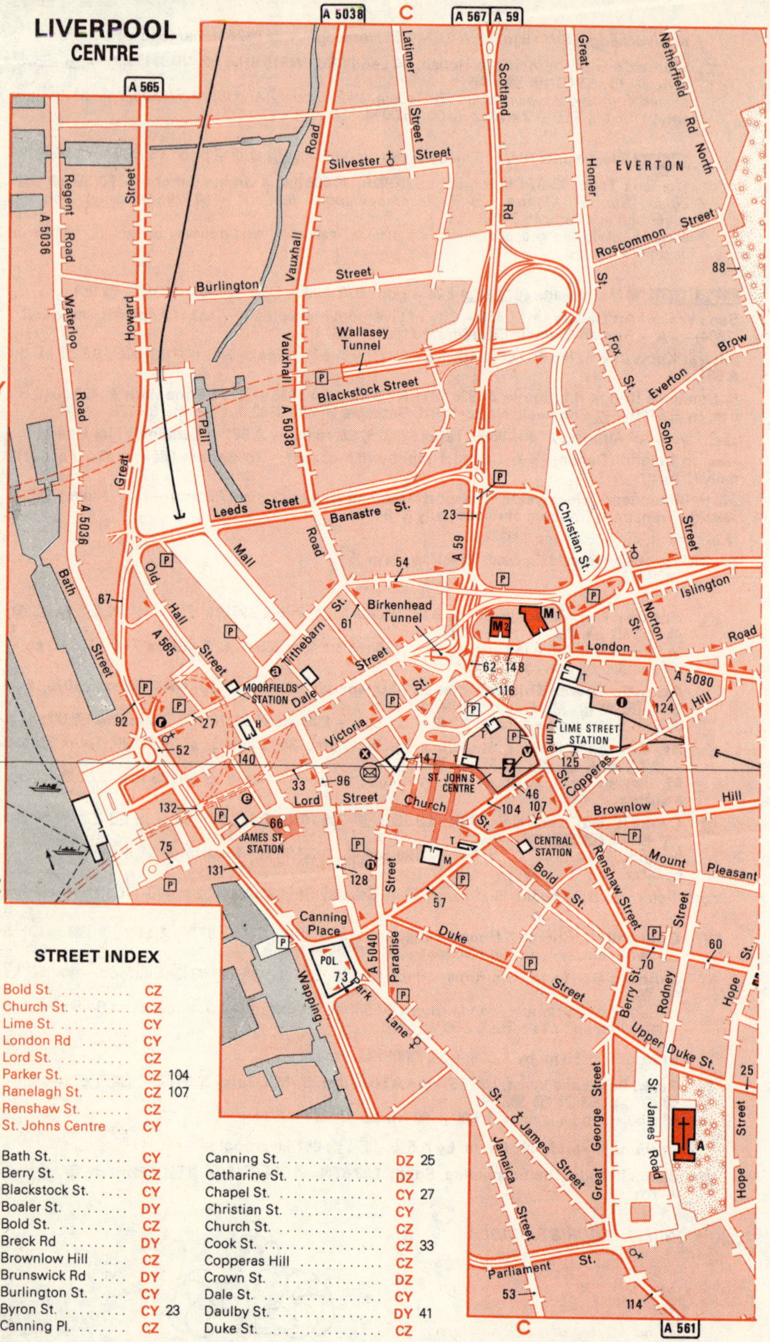

STREET INDEX

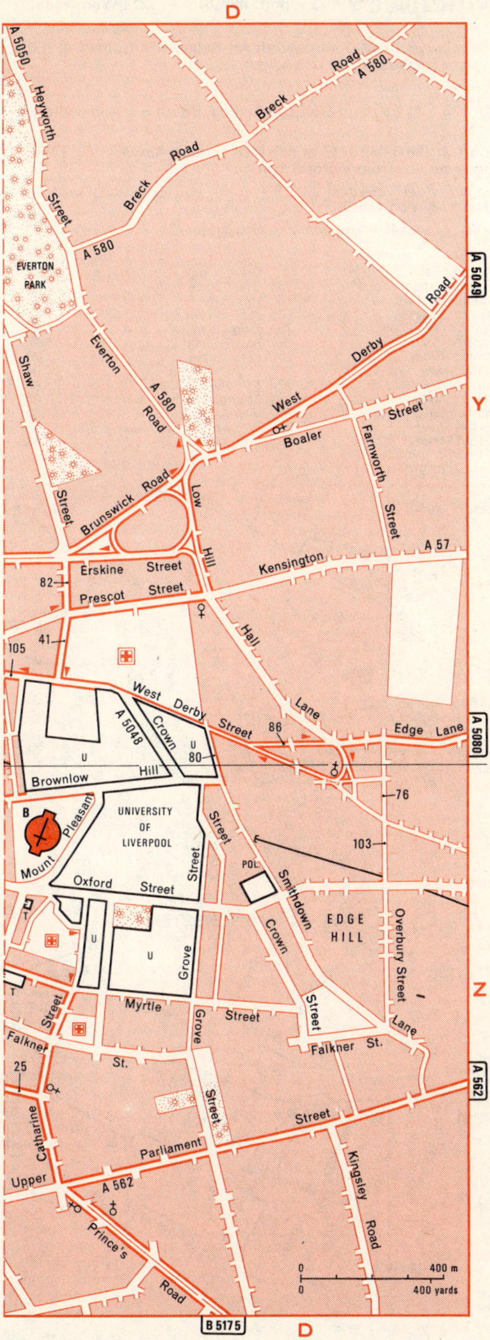
D
A 5050
Heyworth
Street
EVERTON
PARK
Breck
Road
A 580
Breck
Road
A 580
A 5049
Road
Derby
West
Everton
Road
A 580
Shaw
Street
Brunswick
Road
Boaler
Street
Farnworth
Street
Low
Hill
Y
A 57
Kensington
Erskine
Street
Prescot
Street
82
41
105
Hall
Lane
West
Derby
Street
86
Edge
Lane
A 5080
A 5048
Crown
U
80
U
Brownlow
Hill
76
B
Mount
Pleasant
UNIVERSITY
OF
LIVERPOOL
Street
Street
103
POL.
Oxford
Street
Smithdown
EDGE
HILL
Overbury
Street
U
U
Grove
Crown
Z
T
T
Myrtle
Street
Street
Street
Lane
Falkner
St.
Falkner
St.
Grove
25
A 562
Catharine
Street
Street
Parliament
Kingsley
Road
Upper
A 562
Prince's
Road
0
400 m
0
400 yards
B 5175
D

MANCHESTER Greater Manchester 402 403 404 N 23 – pop. 437,612 – ECD : Wednesday – ✆ 061.

See : Town Hall★ 19C DZ – City Art Gallery★ DZ **M** – Whitworth Art Gallery★ – Cathedral 15C (chancel★) DZ **B** – John Ryland's Library (manuscripts★) CZ **A**.

Envir. : Heaton Hall★ (18C) *AC*, N : 5 m.

Heaton Park, ✆ 798 0295, N : by A 576 – Fairfield Golf and Sailing, Booth Rd, Audenshaw, ✆ 370 1641, E : by A 635.

Manchester International Airport ✆ (061) 489 3717 or 489 2404 (British Airways) S : 10 m. by A 5103 and M 56 – **Terminal** : Coach service from Victoria Station.

Magnum House, Portland St., Piccadilly ✆ 247 3694 and 3712/3 – Town Hall Extension, Lloyd St. ✆ 236 1606/2035 – Manchester International Airport, Concourse and Arrivals Hall ✆ 437 5233/5262.

London 202 – Birmingham 86 – Glasgow 221 – Leeds 43 – Liverpool 35 – Nottingham 72.

MANCHESTER CENTRE

Deansgate .... CZ
Lower Mosley Street .... DZ
Market Place .... DZ
Market Street .... DZ
Mosley Street .... DZ
Princess Street .... DZ

Addington Street .... DZ 2
Albert Square .... CDZ 5
Aytoun Street .... DZ 8
Blackfriars Street .... CZ 13
Cannon Street .... DZ 15
Cateaton Street .... DZ 16
Cheetham Hill Road .... DZ 18
Chepstow Street .... DZ 19
Chorlton Street .... DZ 20
Church Street .... DZ 21
Dale Street .... DZ 27
Dawson Street .... CZ 28
Ducie Street .... DZ 33
Egerton Street .... CZ 36
Fairfield Street .... DZ 39
Great Bridgewater Street .... CZ 41
Great Ducie Street .... CZ 48
High Street .... DZ 51
John Dalton Street .... CZ 52
King Street .... DZ 53
Parker Street .... DZ 75
Peter Street .... CZ 76
St. Ann's Street .... CZ 84
St. Peter's Square .... DZ 87
Spring Gardens .... DZ 89
Viaduct Street .... CZ 92
Whitworth Street West .... CZ 95
Withy Grove .... DZ 97

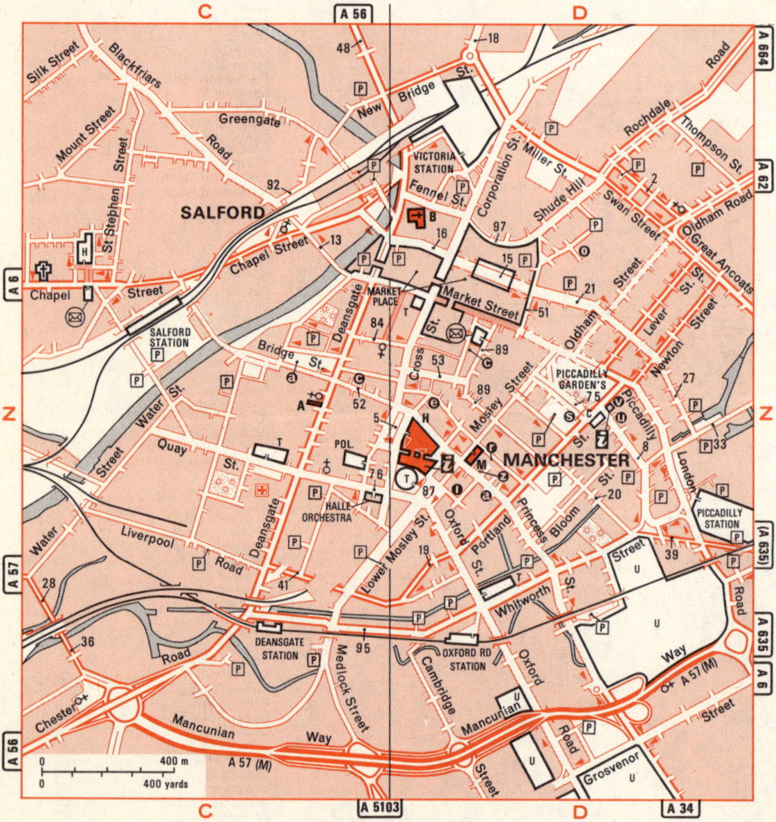

The names of main shopping streets are printed in red at the beginning of the list of streets.

Piccadilly (Embassy), Piccadilly Plaza, M60 1QR, ✆ 236 8414, Telex 668765, ≤ – 🛗 📺 ☎ Ⓟ. 🏃. AE VISA. DZ **s**
M 11.00 **st.** and a la carte 10.25/16.25 **st.** 3.50 – 5.75 – **250 rm** 55.00/77.00 **st.**, **9 suites** 90.00/160.00 **st.**

Portland Thistle (Thistle), Portland St., Piccadilly Gdns., M1 6DP, ✆ 228 3400, Telex 669157 – 🛗 📺 ☎. AE VISA DZ **v**
M 8.50/9.75 **t.** – 5.50 – **219 rm** 54.00/85.00 **t.**, **1 suite** 85.00 **t.**

Grand (T.H.F.), Aytoun St., M1 3DR, ✆ 236 9559, Telex 667580 – 🛗 📺. AE VISA
M (carving rest.) 9.25 **st.** and a la carte 2.70 – **140 rm** 48.50/59.00 **st.**, **3 suites**. DZ **u**

Hazeldean, 467 Bury New Rd, M7 0NX, ✆ 792 6667 – 📺 wc wc Ⓟ. AE VISA.
M *(closed dinner Friday to Sunday and Bank Holidays)* (bar lunch Monday to Saturday)/dinner a la carte 9.40/14.60 **t.** 3.20 – **21 rm** 22.80/43.00 **st.**

Terrazza, 14 Nicholas St., M1 4FE, ✆ 236 4033, Italian rest. DZ **r**

Isola Bella, 6a Booth St., M2 4AW, ✆ 236 6417, Italian rest. – AE VISA DZ **e**
closed Sunday and Bank Holidays – **M** a la carte 10.50/16.40 **st.** 3.00.

Gaylord, Amethyst House, Marriott's Court, Spring Gardens, M2 1EA, ✆ 832 6037, Indian rest. – AE VISA DZ **c**
M 7.45 **t.** and a la carte 3.50.

Leen Hong, 35 George St., M1 4HQ, ✆ 228 0926, Chinese rest. – AE DZ **z**
M a la carte 6.50/9.85 **st.**

Rajdoot, St. James' House, South King St., M2 6DW, ✆ 834 2176, Indian rest. CZ **c**

Truffles, 63 Bridge St., M3 6BQ, ✆ 832 9393 – AE VISA CZ **a**
closed Saturday lunch, Sunday, Monday, first 2 weeks August and Bank Holidays – **M** 9.95 **t.** (lunch) and a la carte 11.40/17.45 **t.** 3.50.

Market, 30 Edge St., M4 1HN, ✆ 834 3743, Bistro – AE DZ **o**
closed Sunday, Monday, 1 week spring, August and 1 week after Christmas – **M** (dinner only) a la carte 6.90/10.45 **t.** 2.50.

Mina, 63 George St., ✆ 228 2598, Japanese rest. – AE VISA DZ **i**
closed Sunday and 1 January – **M** 8.00/16.00 **t.** and a la carte.

Yang Sing, 34 Princess St., ✆ 236 2200, Chinese rest. – AE DZ **a**
M 2.30/7.75 **t.** and a la carte.

at Fallowfield S : 3 m. on B 5093 – ✉ 061 Manchester :

Willow Bank, 340 Wilmslow Rd, M14 6AF, ✆ 224 0461, Telex 668222 – 📺 wc Ⓟ. AE VISA
M *(closed lunch Sunday and Bank Holidays)* 4.00/7.00 **st.** and a la carte 3.00 – 4.00 – **123 rm** 20.00/35.00 **st.** – SB (weekends only) 42.00/54.00 **st.**

at Northenden S : 6 ½ m. by A 5103 and M 56 – ✉ 061 Manchester :

Post House (T.H.F.), Palatine Rd, M22 4FH, ✆ 998 7090, Telex 669248 – 🛗 📺 wc ♿ Ⓟ. AE VISA
M 6.95/9.25 **st.** and a la carte – 5.50 – **200 rm** 43.00/50.50 **st.**

at Manchester Airport S : 9 m. by A 5103 and M 56 – ✉ 061 Manchester :

Excelsior (T.H.F.), Ringway Rd, Wythenshawe, M22 5NS, ✆ 437 5811, Telex 668721, heated – 🛗 📺 ☎ ♿ Ⓟ. AE VISA
M *(closed Saturday lunch)* 6.45/7.95 **st.** and a la carte 2.70 – 5.50 – **304 rm** 49.00/58.00 **st.**, **4 suites**.

at Heald Green S : 10 m. by A 5103 and M 56 – ✉ 061 Manchester :

La Bonne Auberge, 224 Finney Lane, SK8 3QA, ✆ 437 5701 – Ⓟ. AE
closed Monday dinner, Sunday and Bank Holidays – **M** 8.00 **t.** (lunch) and a la carte 10.60/13.40 **t.**

CALENDAR OF TRADE FAIRS AND OTHER INTERNATIONAL EVENTS

AUSTRIA		
Vienna	Wiener Festwochen	9 May to 15 June
Salzburg	Salzburg Festival (Festspiele)	22 to 31 March 26 July to 31 August
BENELUX		
Amsterdam	Holland Festival	June
Bruges	Ascension Day Procession	Ascension
Brussels	Guild Procession (Oumegang)	first Thursday of July
DENMARK		
Copenhagen	Scandinavian Furniture Fair	7 to 11 May
	World Fishing 86	17 to 21 June
FRANCE		
Paris	Paris Fair	30 April to 11 May
	Motor Show	2 to 12 October
Cannes	International Film Festival	8 to 19 May
Lyons	Lyons Fair	5 to 14 April
Marseilles	Marseilles Fair	19 to 29 Sept
GERMANY		
Berlin	Berlin Fair (Grüne Woche)	24 Jan to 2 February
Frankfurt	International Fair	1 to 5 March 23 to 27 August
	Frankfurt Book Fair	1 to 6 October
Hanover	Hanover Fair	9 to 16 April
Munich	Beer Festival (Oktoberfest)	20 Sept to 5 Oct
IRELAND		
Dublin	Dublin Horse Show	5 to 9 August
ITALY		
Milan	Milan Fair	12 to 20 April
Palermo	Mediterranean Fair	24 May to 8 June
Turin	Automotor	23 April to 4 May
PORTUGAL		
Lisbon	International Fair	13 to 18 May
SPAIN		
Barcelona	International Fair	7 to 15 June
Valencia	International Fair	6 to 11 May
SWEDEN		
Stockholm	International Fashion Fair	18 to 21 Sept
	International Technical Fair	16 to 22 October
	Medicin 86, International Fair	3 to 5 December
Gothenburg	RO-RO, International Marine Transport Exhibition	13 to 15 May
SWITZERLAND		
Geneva	Motor Show	March 87
UNITED KINGDOM		
London	London International Boat Show	7 to 18 January 87
Birmingham	British Motor Show	15 to 26 October
Edinburgh	Arts Festival	11 to 31 August
Leeds	Harrogate International Toy Fair	10 to 15 Jan 87

EUROPEAN DIALLING CODES

INDICATIFS TÉLÉPHONIQUES EUROPÉENS

TELEFON-VORWAHLNUMMERN EUROPÄISCHER LÄNDER

ヨーロッパ内通話コード番号

(A)	Österreich, Autriche, Austria	43
(B)	Belgique, België, Belgium	32
(CH)	Schweiz, Suisse, Svizzera, Switzerland	41
(D)	Bundesrepublik Deutschland, RFA, West Germany	49
(DK)	Danmark, Danemark, Denmark	45
(E)	España, Espagne, Spain	34
(F)	France	33
(GB)	Great Britain, Grande-Bretagne	44
(GR)	Hellás, Grèce, Greece	30
(I)	Italia, Italie	39
(IRL)	Ireland, Irlande	353
(L)	Luxembourg	352
(MC)	Monaco	33
(N)	Norge, Norvège, Norway	47
(NL)	Nederland, Pays-Bas, Netherlands	31
(P)	Portugal	351
(S)	Sverige, Suède, Sweden	46
(SF)	Suomi, Finland	358
(YU)	Jugoslavija, Yougoslavie	38

Between certain neighbouring countries the dialling code may vary. Make enquiries.

Entre certains pays limitrophes, il existe des indicatifs spéciaux. S'informer.

Zwischen bestimmten benachbarten Ländern gibt es spezielle Vorwahlnummern. Informieren Sie sich.

いくつかの国境付近では、特別なコード番号が使われていますので、
お問い合わせ下さい。

SPEED

To determine the speed at which you are travelling :

Check the time you take to cover a kilometre at constant speed ; in the table below, you will find the corresponding speed in kilometres or miles per hour. (The figures have been rounded to the nearest m.p.h.).

VITESSE

Comment déterminer la vitesse à laquelle on roule :

Chronométrer le temps employé pour parcourir un kilomètre à vitesse constante ; lire ensuite dans le tableau ci-dessous, en face du temps relevé, la vitesse correspondante en kilomètres ou en miles par heure. (Cette vitesse est calculée avec une approximation pratiquement négligeable).

GESCHWINDIGKEIT

Wie man die Geschwindigkeit bestimmt, mit der man fährt :

Messen Sie genau die Zeit, die Sie brauchen, um einen Kilometer bei gleichbleibender Geschwindigkeit zurückzulegen. Auf der untenstehenden Tabelle können Sie dann Ihre Geschwindigkeit in Kilometern oder Meilen pro Stunde ablesen. (Diese Werte weisen eine nur geringfügige Ungenauigkeit auf).

速 度

走行中に速度を測定するには:

一定の速度で１キロメートル走り、かかった時間を調べます。下記の表で該当する時間に合わせて、キロメートル数又はマイル数がわかります（当速度は概算にすぎません）。

	km	miles		km	miles		km	miles
0mn18s	**200**	124	**0mn49s**	73	45	**1mn30s**	**40**	25
19	189	117	**50s**	72	44,5	33	39	24
20s	**180**	112	51	**70**	43,5	35	38	23,5
21	171	106	52	69	43	37	37	23
22	164	**102**	53	68	42	**40s**	36	22,5
23	157	97	54	67	41,5	43	35	21,5
24	**150**	93	55	66	41	46	34	21
25	144	89	56	64	**39,5**	**50s**	33	20,5
26	138	86	57	63	39	53	32	**20**
27	133	82	58	62	38,5	56	31	19
28	129	**80**	59	61	38	**2mn00**	**30**	18,5
29	124	77	**1mn00**	**60**	37	5	29	18
30s	**120**	74	1	59	36,5	10	28	17,5
31	116	72	2	58	36	15	27	16,5
32	113	70	3	57	35,5	20	26	16
33	109	68	4	56	34,5	24	25	15,5
34	106	66	6	55	34	**30s**	24	15
35	103	64	7	54	33,5	35	23	14,5
36	**100**	62	8	53	33	45	22	13,5
37	97	**60**	9	52	32	55	21	13
38	95	59	**10s**	51	31,5	**3mn00**	**20**	12,5
39	92	57	12	**50**	31	15	19	12
40s	**90**	56	14	49	30,5	20	18	11
41	88	55	15	48	**30**	**30s**	17	10,5
42	86	53	17	47	29	45	16	**10**
43	84	52	19	46	28,5	**4mn00**	15	9,5
44	82	51	**20s**	45	28	15	14	8,5
45	**80**	**50**	22	44	27,5	**30**	13	8
46	78	49	24	43	26,5	**5mn00**	12	7,5
47	77	48	26	42	26	30	11	7
48	75	46	28	41	25,5	**6mn00**	**10**	6